COMPANY
PROFILES
for Students

COMPANY PROFILES
for Students

Volume 3

Amanda Quick, Project Editor

GALE®

THOMSON

GALE

Detroit • New York • San Diego • San Francisco • Cleveland • New Haven, Conn. • Waterville, Maine • London • Munich

Company Profiles for Students

Project Editor
Amanda C. Quick

Editorial
Rebecca Marlow-Ferguson

Manufacturing
NeKita McKee

Imaging and Multimedia
Dean Dauphinais, Mary Grimes, Lezlie Light,
Dan Newell

Product Design
Michael Logusz

For permission to use material from this product, submit your request via Web at http://www.gale-edit.com/permissions, or you may download our Permissions Request form and submit your request by fax or mail to:

Permissions Department
The Gale Group, Inc.
27500 Drake Rd.
Farmington Hills, MI 48331-3535

Permissions Hotline:
248-699-8006 or 800-877-4253, ext. 8006
Fax: 248-699-8074 or 800-762-4058

Since this page cannot legibly accommodate all copyright notices, the acknowledgments constitute an extension of the copyright notice.

While every effort has been made to ensure the reliability of the information presented in this publication, The Gale Group, Inc. does not guarantee the accuracy of the data contained herein. The Gale Group, Inc. accepts no payment for listing; and inclusion in the publication of any organization, agency, institution, publication, service, or individual does not imply endorsement of the editors or publisher. Errors brought to the attention of the publisher and verified to the satisfaction of the publisher will be corrected in future editions.

ISBN 0-7876-2936-7 (Set)
ISBN 0-7876-2937-5 (Volume 1)
ISBN 0-7876-2938-3 (Volume 2)
ISBN 0-7876-4903-1 (Volume 3)
ISSN 1520-815X

Printed in the United States of America
10 9 8 7 6 5 4 3 2 1

Table of Contents

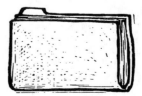

Advisors and Contributors

Advisory Board

A panel consisting of teachers and librarians on young adult economics, business, and history needs was consulted to help determine the contents of *Company Profiles for Students, Volume 3.*

The members of the board for this volume include:

Chris Erdman: Teacher, Skyview High School, Vancouver, Washington. Mr. Erdman served as one of the original advisors to *Company Profiles for Students.*

Bob Kirsch: Librarian, Lake Forest High School, Lake Forest, Illinois. Mr. Kirsch served as one of the original advisors to *Company Profiles for Students.*

Barbara Lakeberg Dridi: Educator; Founder and director, Concordia International Research, Philadelphia, Pennsylvania.

Contributors

The following writers contributed to the text of *Company Profiles for Students, Volume 3*:

Donald F. Amerman Jr.

Mark Berger

Kari Bethel

Gerald Brennan

Paul Greenland

Dan Harvey

Kathleen Mahoney

Carol Marshall

Hank Nuwer

Ruth Ann Prag Carter

Anna Marie Sheldon

Hilary White

Introduction

Company Profiles for Students (CPFS) has been designed specifically to meet the curricular needs of high school and undergraduate college students taking courses in economics, business, and history. Now in its third volume, *CPFS* provides information on both the current operations and performance of 151 contemporary public and private U.S.-based and significant foreign-owned companies, in addition to the historical events, people, and strategies that shaped them. This volume contains 127 new company profiles, and 27 profiles revised from their first publication. *CPFS* satisfies research assignments regarding a particular company's stock performance, new product lines, or comparisons of the management styles of companies in different industries. By focusing on the many different aspects of a company, which are typically studied in high schools and frequently omitted from standard business publications, *CPFS* meets the strong curricular need for business information written at the high school level. See Gale's *Business Leader Profiles for Students*, now in its second volume, for in-depth information on nearly 350 prominent individuals who have made significant contributions to business and industry.

An advisory panel of high school teachers and librarians reviewed a list of potential companies and, based on their knowledge and experience, helped select the companies to be covered. Each company and industry essay was then researched and compiled or updated by a professional writer.

How Each Entry Is Organized

Company Profiles for Students provides users with a single, comprehensive resource. Data was pulled together from annual reports, press releases, numerous print resources, and online databases to give users a one-stop reference source containing a wide variety of information. Each entry in *CPFS* focuses on one company. Each entry heading lists the name of the company, a variant name of the company if one applies, and the year the company was founded. In addition, each entry lists contact information, including address and phone number, as well as fax and toll free number, e-mail address, and URL when available. Essays cover some or all of the following topics:

- **Overview:** Provides a brief synopsis outlining the importance of the company, along with its market(s), broad strategies, competitors, etc.

- **Company Finances:** Gives textual information and, in many cases, graphical information illustrating revenues and stock prices over a period of time.

- **Analysts' Opinions:** Discusses various analyses of the company's market share, strategies, stock market position, etc.

- **History:** Gives historical information on the company's genesis and provides a description of inventions or trends that spurred the establishment of the company and of key events throughout the company's existence.

- **Strategy:** Provides an overview of past and current strategies.

- **Influences:** Covers successes or failures that impacted how the company has done business or has positioned itself.

- **Current Trends:** Explains the current influences on company strategy and how the company intends to proceed.

- **Products:** Provides a description of the company's current products and/or information about new products the company plans to introduce in the future.

- **Corporate Citizenship:** Outlines the company's policies and record in regard to the environment, human rights, affirmative action/diversity, etc.

- **Global Presence:** Explains which foreign markets the company has entered and any challenges it faces there. Includes information on the company's global market share, operations, etc.

- **Employment:** Provides information on corporate culture.

- **Sources of Information:** First, a **Bibliography** is provided that includes annotated citations for publicly accessible books, periodical articles, and online sources used to compile the entry. Second, a section titled **For an annual report** provides the Internet address, telephone, or address to locate the company's annual report. Third, a section titled **For additional industry research** contains primary Standard Industrial Codes (SICs) and descriptions that apply to the company.

Other Features

Company Profiles for Students includes 35 photos, as well as graphs illustrating revenue and stock prices. Most entries also include a chronology of key events in the company's history and, when appropriate, sidebars on prominent individuals and/or products associated with the companies. In addition, each entry includes a "Fast Facts" sidebar that includes all or some of the following elements:

- **Ownership:** Explains whether the company is a public or privately owned company and who it is owned by.

- **Ticker Symbol:** Provides the company's or the company owner's ticker symbol when applicable.

- **Officers:** Contains a list of up to four company officers, their titles, and their ages and salaries (if available).

- **Employees:** Gives the number of employees at the company.

- **Principal Subsidiary Companies:** Supplies a summary of significant corporate relationships.

- **Chief Competitors:** Provides a summary of the company's primary competitors.

An appendix of 35 industry profiles is also included, which give information regarding the industry as a whole. These entries contain all or some of the following topics:

- **Overview:** Provides an overview of the industry, including such aspects as key regulatory bodies affecting the industry.

- **History of the Industry:** Gives historical information on the industry's genesis and development, including major technological advances, historic events, scandals, major products, key legislation, and other factors that have shaped the industry.

- **Significant Events Affecting the Industry:** Explains important events that have affected and are currently affecting the industry, such as major advances and the impact of these on the industry.

- **New Trends Influencing the Industry:** Provides information on major advances and their impacts on the industry, including environmental issues if pertinent.

- **Key Competitors:** Covers background information, historical highlights, and current status of specific industry leaders.

- **Employment:** When available, contains information on the employment practices of the industry including data on salaries and benefits, type of worker/education preferred, positions available, and any other information about the industry's employment needs.

- **Global Presence:** Includes information on the leading countries in the world that have key companies in this industry or where this industry provides significant income to the country's economy.

- **Industry Projections:** Explains where the industry is heading in the future.

- **Bibliography:** Provides users with suggested further reading on the industry. These sources, also used to compile the essays, are publicly accessible materials such as magazines, general and academic periodicals, books, annual reports, government sources, and online databases.

Other features include a general business chronology of events specifically pertaining to companies; a glossary of economic and business terms found within the company and industry profiles, a directory of business web sites; and a general index that includes primary people, company names, and brand names.

Comments and Suggestions

Gale welcomes your comments and ideas pertaining to *Company Profiles for Students*. Readers who wish to suggest companies for inclusion in future volumes or are interested in further information about other Gale business products for students are encouraged to contact the editor:

Managing Editor, *Company Profiles for Students*
Gale Group, Inc.
27500 Drake Rd.
Farmington Hills, MI 48331-3535
Telephone: (248)677-4253
Toll-Free: (800)347-GALE
Fax: (248)699-8070
Email: BusinessProducts@gale.com

Chronology of Key Business Events

1865: The Civil war brings the value of Confederate paper money down and the value of Union Gold rises. The Confederate money remains worthless for another 13 years.

1866: The National Labor Congress convenes in Baltimore and forms the National Labor Union; Western Union Telegraph absorbs two small telegraph companies becoming the first great U.S. monopoly.

1867: Steel rail production begins in the United States, which had been using iron rails or imported steel; Milwaukee printer Christopher Sholes invents the typewriter; inventor Benjamin Tilghman devises a process for producing wood pulp for paper production.

1868: U.S. businesses resist government intervention by quoting the fourteenth amendment; Congress enacts a law restricting work days to 8 hours for government workers, but in the private sector, most laborers work 10 to 12 hour days.

1869: Wall Street crashes for the first time, ruining small speculators, as a small group of financiers try to corner the market on gold and close half the banks and businesses in New York in the process; the Noble Order of the Knights of Labor, a secret society, is founded following the death of the president of the National Labor Union; the Union Pacific and Central Pacific railroads meet in Promontory Point, Utah, completing the first transcontinental railroad.

1872: Congress enacts the first consumer protection law, making it illegal to use the mail for fraudulent purposes.

1873: A farmers' convention attacks monopolies, calling them "detrimental to the public prosperity," and urges an end to government subsidies to corporations and an end to tariff protection for industry; The Fourth Coinage Act is passed by Congress making gold the sole U.S. monetary standard and inadvertently making trade dollars legal tender in amounts up to $5.00.

1877: The Supreme Court sustains the state law of 1871 of state supervised grain elevators and lays the ground work for all regulation of U.S. businesses by government.

1878: Congress votes to reduce circulation of paper money, which has regained its value for the first time since 1865; shares in gas companies plummet as Thomas Edison works out methods for cheap production and transmission of electrical current, making it adaptable for household use.

1883: U.S. railroads adopt standard time with four time zones: Eastern, Central, Rocky Mountain, and Pacific; Thomas Edison pioneers the radio tube.

1886: Labor struggles for an eight-hour work day and better working conditions leads 610,000 workers to strike, the most ever in nineteenth-century America; a new American Federation of Labor (AF of L) is founded; the Supreme Court rules that only the federal government can regulate interstate railway rates.

1887: The Interstate Commerce Act is passed by Congress and orders railroads to keep their rates fair and reasonable.

1890: The Sherman Antitrust Act is passed by Congress to curb the power of U.S. monopolies; the McKinley Tariff Act is passed by Congress and increases the average U.S. import duty to its highest level ever; the United Mine Workers of America is founded as an affiliate of the AF of L.

1891: The first full-service advertising agency opens in New York, providing copy, art, production, and placement.

1893: Wall Street prices plummet and the market collapses, 600 banks close their doors, and more than 15,000 businesses fail as an economic depression hits the United States.

1894: The Wilson-Gorman Tariff Act reduces tariffs by 20 percent and includes an income tax on incomes over $4,000 a year.

1895: The Supreme Court fails to uphold the Sherman Antitrust Act by ruling that controlling the manufacturing process affects interstate commerce only indirectly and incidentally; The Supreme Court rules that the income tax provision of the Wilson-Gorman Tariff Act is unconstitutional; a gold rush to Canada's Klondike begins.

1897: The Dingley Tariff Act raises costs of living by increasing duties to an average of 57 percent; The influx of gold from the Klondike gold rush helps end the economic depression; after a 12-week strike, bituminous coal workers win an eight-hour day, semi-monthly pay, abolition of company stores that charge premium prices, and biennial conferences; The Supreme Court rules that railroads are subject to the Sherman Antitrust Act.

1899: Congress passes the Refuse Act giving the Army Corps of Engineers the power to prosecute polluters, providing fines of up to $2,500 for oil spills and other similar pollution, but the act is not enforced.

1901: Wall Street panics as brokerage houses sell off stock so they can raise funds to take over the Northern Pacific Railroad; the stock prices in the railroad fluctuate from a high of $1,000 per share to a low of $150 per share and the Northers Securities holding company ends up owning most of the country's railroads.

1902: United Mine Workers lead a strike of 147,000 anthracite coal workers that cripples the United States; President T. Roosevelt begins instituting antitrust proceedings against many U.S. corporations; Congress passes the National Reclamation Act, which gives the federal government the rights to build irrigation dams throughout the West and limits the size of individual land holdings receiving federal water to 160 acres.

1904: The Supreme Court rules that the Northern Securities trust formed in 1901 violates the Sherman Antitrust Act.

1905: The Industrial Workers of the World (IWW) joins U.S. workers and attacks the AF of L for supporting the capitalist system; a New York law limiting hours of work in the baking industry is considered unconstitutional by the Supreme Court; Upton Sinclair exposes the horrific working conditions in the meat-packing industry in his novel The Jungle.

1906: The Hepburn Act is passed, which extends jurisdiction of the Interstate Commerce Commission (ICC) and gives the ICC the power to fix railroad rates; Congress appoints $2.5 million and New York bankers loan hundreds of millions of dollars to San Francisco to rebuild the city after an earthquake and fire devastates the city; a Pure Food and Drug bill is passed by Congress to regulate producers and sellers of food.

1907: New York Stock Exchange prices drop sharply because of financial drains from rebuilding San Francisco, several railroad expansion programs, and the Russo-Japanese War of 1905, sparking an economic depression.

1908: The Supreme Court rules that discrimination against union labor in interstate commerce violates the fifth amendment.

1910: The Manns-Elkins Act amends the Interstate Commerce Act and regulates telephone, telegraph, and cable companies under ICC regulations.

1911: Yale political economic professor Irving Fisher proposes the theory that prices rise in proportion to the supply of money and the speed at which money circulates, and pioneers indexing the economy with price indexes, cost-of-living indexes, etc.; the first SAE handbook on automotive standardization is published by the Society of Automotive Engineers.

1912: The Shirley amendment to the Pure Food and Drug Law prohibits far-fetched claims of therapeutic effects; the Associated Advertising Clubs of America adopts a Truth in Advertising code.

1913: The U.S. Bureau of Labor Statistics computes its first monthly consumer price index to determine the fairness of wages; the Underwood-Simmons Tariff Act lowers import duties by an average of 30 percent, which hurts many U.S. manufacturers who fight for restoration of tariff protection; the Glass-Owen Currency Act establishes 12 Federal Reserve banks in 12 major cities and requires member banks to maintain cash reserves proportionate to their deposits with the Federal Reserve system; the Federal Reserve's board of governors determines the amount of cash in circulation, provides elasticity to the supply of currency, and can act to control inflation.

1914: The New York Stock Exchange closes as Montreal, Toronto, Madrid, London, and many other European exchanges close due to the escalation of war in Europe; the Clayton Antitrust Act strengthens the federal government's power against restraint of trade as outlawed by the Sherman Antitrust Act; A Federal Trade Commission is established to prevent unfair competition in U.S. industry.

1915: Delaware begins revising and liberalizing its corporation laws to attract corporations and soon becomes the national leader in chartering the largest corporations; IWW leader Joe Hill is executed.

1916: The Owen-Keating Act forbids shipment in interstate commerce of goods on which children under 14 have labored or on which children 14 to 16 worked more than eight hours a day; the Adamson Bill provides an eight hour work day on interstate railroads with time and a half for overtime; the U.S. railroad industry reaches its peak of 254,000 miles of track.

1917: President Wilson issues an embargo proclamation and places government control over exports of U.S. food, fuel, iron, steel, and war material.

1918: The Supreme Court rules that the Owen-Keating Act is unconstitutional and encroaches on a state's rights.

1919: Four million workers either strike or are locked out in one of the biggest years for labor unrest in U.S. history; World War I costs the United States nearly $22 billion and an additional $9 billion in loans to allied powers.

1921: Nearly 20,000 businesses fail and 3.5 million Americans are out of work; Boll weevils cut cotton production in Georgia and South Carolina in half.

1922: The Fordney-McCumber Tariff Act returns tariffs to higher levels and gives the president the power to raise or lower duties by 50 percent to equalize production costs; a six-month strike by coal miners to protest wage cuts cripples U.S. industries reliant on coal and leads to a period of chronic depression in the coal mining industry, whose operators resort to cutthroat competition to remain in business; the first paid radio commercial airs, setting the pattern for private control of radio airwaves.

1926: Scheduled airline service begins for the first time.

1929: The Dow Jones Industrial Average reaches 381.17 up from 88 in 1924, but it crashes on October 29; a record 16.4 million shares are traded, the Dow plummets 30.57 points, speculators that bought on margin are forced to sell, and almost $30 billion disappears, sending the United States into the worst economic depression in history.

1930: Stock prices regain some of their losses, but investors fearing a business depression continually lower prices; the Smoot-Hawley Tariff Bill raises tariffs to their highest level in history, and other countries raise their tariffs in response; a general world economic depression begins, U.S. unemployment reaches 4.5 million, and more than 1,300 banks close.

1931: The U.S. wheat crop breaks all records, driving down prices and leading to many farmers being forced off their farms as banks foreclose on their property.

1932: The average weekly wage falls from $28 to $17 in 1929; 21,000 businesses go bankrupt, 1,616 banks close, and industrial production drops to one-third

the 1929 level; the Dow Jones Industrial Average reaches its low point of 41.22; Congress enacts a Reconstruction Finance Corp. with the power to lend $1.8 billion to the states to finance industry and agriculture; Congress passes a Home Loan Act that will lend money to mortgage loan institutions to rescue banks being forced to close; unemployment reaches 17 million.

1933: The Emergency Banking Act gives the president control over banking transactions and foreign exchange and forbids exporting of gold; President F. Roosevelt declares a bank holiday and only authorizes banks to reopen after an examiner has determined them solvent; all private gold holdings are required to be turned over to federal reserves in exchange for coin or currency; the United States abandons the gold standard; the Glass-Steagall Act forbids banks to deal in stocks and bonds and insures bank deposits; a National Industrial Recovery Act provides for codes of fair competition in industry and collective bargaining with labor; the unemployment rate peaks at 24.9 percent.

1934: The Reciprocal Trade Agreement Act passed by Congress gives the president power to negotiate trade pacts without consent of the Senate; the new act replaces the high tariffs of the Smoot-Hawley Act, believed to have contributed to the worldwide depression; the nation's first general strike starts in San Francisco to show sympathy for a strike of 12,000 International Longshoremen's Association workers; the Securities and Exchange Commission (SEC) is created by Congress to limit bank credit for speculators and to police the securities industry.

1935: An Emergency Relief Appropriations Act is passed by Congress to provide work and employment by "providing useful projects"; the Federal Reserve System is reorganized and establishes an open market committee to buy and sell government securities held by the Federal Reserve and thus control the money supply; a Federal Deposit Insurance Corp. (FDIC) is developed with assistance from the banks; the Committee for Industrial Organization (CIO) is founded.

1936: The Robinson-Patman Act supplements the Clayton Antitrust Act by forbidding manufacturers to practice price discrimination.

1938: The Fair Labor Standards Act limits working hours in the first national attempt to set maximum hours and minimum wages; the Dow Jones average falls to 98.95 but regains to 158.41; the Civil Aeronautics Authority (CAA) is created to regulate the growing aviation industry; the Federal Trade Commission, through the Wheller-Lea Act, is given the power to regulate advertising of food, drugs, cosmetics, and therapeutic devices.

1940: The Export Control Act gives the president power to halt or slow export of materials vital to U.S. defense; exports of aviation gas outside the Western hemisphere, and export of scrap iron and steel to Japan is embargoed.

1942: President Roosevelt calls for production of 60,000 planes, 45,000 tanks, 20,000 anti-aircraft guns, and 6 million tons of merchant shipping; the federal budget of $59 billion has $52 billion marked for the war effort; an Emergency Price Control Act gives the Office of Price Administration the power to control prices; an order by the newly created Office of Economic Stabilization limits salaries to $25,000 per year.

1944: A United Nations Monetary and Financial Conference establishes the International Bank for Reconstruction, which formulates a system, used until 1973, whereby every participating nation keeps its currency within a few percentage points of an agreed dollar value; the first automatic, general-purpose computer, which takes 4 seconds to perform simple multiplication and 11 seconds to perform simple division, is completed at Harvard University.

1946: The worst work stoppage since 1919 idles 4.6 million workers with a loss of 116 million man-days; the Office of Economic Stabilization, shutdown after the World War II, is reinstated by President Truman to control inflation; ENIAC (electronic numerical integrator and computer) is the world's first electronic digital computer and is the first to use vacuum tubes instead of mechanical relays—its 18,000 vacuum tubes perform 4,500 additions per second.

1947: The Taft-Hartley Act restricts a labor union's power to strike, outlaws businesses that can only hire union workers, introduces an 80-day waiting period before a lockout or a strike can begin, and empowers the government to obtain injunctions if the strike is detriment to national safety; the General Agreement on Tariffs and Trade (GATT) lowers tariff barriers significantly and helps revitalize world trade; coal mines return to private ownership after being run by federal government for the last year.

1948: The cost-of-living index reaches a record high as does U.S. production, employment, and national income; President Truman orders the Army to operate the railroad to prevent a nationwide strike.

1950: The Celler-Kefauver Amendment to the Clayton Antitrust Act curbs mergers of U.S. business firms and stops companies from buying up stock in other companies; the Revenue Act increases income and corporation taxes; the Defense Production Act establishes a system of priorities for materials, provides for wage and price stabilization, and curbs installment buying.

1951: The Federal Reserve Board raises stock-purchase margin requirements to discourage credit expansion; the Wage Stabilization Board freezes salaries and wages.

1952: President Truman orders federal seizure of steel mills to avoid a nationwide strike, but the Supreme Court rules the seizure illegal and 600,000 CIO steel workers go on strike; the railroads once again return to private ownership after nearly two years of being run by the federal troops.

1954: The Dow Jones average finally passes its 1929 high of 381 and closes the year above 404.

1955: The AF of L and CIO merge into the AFL-CIO.

1957: Senator Kefauver investigates the effect on consumers of increasing mergers by auto and steel makers, bread bakers, and pharmaceutical firms.

1959: The Landrum-Griffin Act requires labor unions to file financial reports with the secretary of labor and includes a labor Bill of Rights; the federal government gains an injunction against striking steel workers, a decision upheld by the Supreme Court; supermarkets account for 11 percent of food stores, but 69 percent of all food store sales.

1960: In an effort to curb a rising deficit in the U.S. balance of payments, President Eisenhower orders a reduction of government spending abroad; Eisenhower warns against the military-industrial complex that maintains high levels of spending for defense.

1963: U.S. factory workers average more than $100 per week for the first time in history.

1966: There are a record 2,377 corporate mergers in the United States, up from 844 in 1960; Congress passes the Fair Packaging and Labeling Act, which calls for clear labeling of the net weight of every package and imposes controls over the confusing proliferation of package sizes, but food continues to be sold in packages that make it difficult for consumers to determine the price per pound they are paying; many airline companies suffer financial losses because of inability to fill seats on the new Boeing 747 jumbo jets.

1967: The United Auto Workers quits the AFL-CIO, charging a lack of leadership and organizing effort; the record numbers of corporate mergers in the United States continue to rise with 2,975 mergers taking place; a U.S. Federal Meat Inspection Act takes effect as the Pure Food and Drug act of 1906 is strengthened.

1968: Corporate mergers continue to rise as 4,462 take place; Congress passes a Consumer Credit Protection Law requiring banks and other lending institutions to disclose clearly the true annual rate of interest and other financing costs on loans.

1969: Unemployment hits its lowest point in 15 years, and the Dow Jones average rises above 1000 for the first time in history, but does not hold.

1970: The Dow Jones average bottoms out at 631 then jumps 32.04 points, the largest one day jump ever recorded; the Rail Passenger Service Act creates the

National Rail Passenger Corp. (Amtrak) to improve U.S. rail travel.

1971: President Nixon imposes a freeze on wages and prices, temporarily suspends conversion of dollars into gold, and asks Congress to impose a 10 percent surcharge to strengthen the dollar as the Vietnam War pushes inflation up; in response to Nixon's news, the Dow Jones average makes a record one-day jump of 32.93 points; the AFL-CIO announces it has no faith in Nixon's plan and refuses to cooperate with the wage freeze; U.S. imports top exports for the first time since 1888.

1972: The Dow Jones average loses at 1003.16, the first time it has ever closed above the 1000 mark; Soviet grain buyers begin buying U.S. soy and wheat and end up buying one quarter of the entire U.S. wheat crop.

1973: Speculative selling of U.S. dollars on foreign exchanges devalues the dollar, and Secretary of the Treasury George Schultz announces that the dollar will be devalued by up to 10 percent against major world currencies in an effort to make U.S. goods more competitive in foreign trade; President Nixon announces an embargo on exports of soybeans and cottonseeds, which lasts only five days; buyers bid up the prices of wheat as foreign buyers redouble their purchase of U.S. grain in case further embargoes are issued; Arab nations begin cutting back oil exports for political reasons.

1974: Economic recession hits the world following a hike in oil prices by major petroleum producers in the Middle East and a rising inflation rate; The Consumer Price Index rises a record 12.2 percent; the Dow Jones average bottoms out at 570.01.

1975: Investors fail to take advantage of the first opportunity since 1933 to buy gold, driving the price down by over $30 per ounce; Wall Street's fixed commission rate ends by order of the Securities and Exchange Commission, leading to lower rates, sometimes by as much as 90 percent, and forcing many brokers and dealers out of business.

1976: Federal Trade Commission figures show that the 450 largest companies control 70 percent of U.S. manufacturing assets and make 72 percent of the profits; the Energy Policy and Conservation Act sets gasoline mileage standards for cars, establishes petroleum reserves, and authorizes the president to develop contingency plans for future energy crises.

1977: Kohlberg Kravis Roberts pioneers the leveraged buy-out, using high-yield junk bonds to finance them; the Foreign Corrupt Practices Act provides for severe penalties, including up five years in jail and up to $1 million in fines, for any U.S. corporation that offers a bribe to a foreign government, political party official, or political candidate; the Semiconductor Industry Association is formed to lobby against government-subsidized Japanese efforts to dominate the semiconductor industry.

1978: President Carter announces a program of voluntary wage-price guidelines to curb the rising inflation; the Dow Jones Industrial Average sets another one day record by jumping up 35.4 points; the mandatory retirement age for workers is raised to 70.

1979: The Supreme Court rules that the valuation of warehouse items may not be reduced for tax purposes unless it is disposed of or sold at reduced prices; inflation continues to rise uncontrollably and balloons 13.3 percent for the year, the largest jump in 33 years; the Federal Reserve Board announces a 1 percent increase in the discount interest rate to curb inflation; Wall Street reacts drastically to the news, driving down the Dow Jones average by 26.48 points on the day of the announcement, starting a small recession; gold prices top $400 per ounce for the first time in history as world markets react to worries about inflation.

1980: Banks raise the prime loan rate, which fluctuates between a low of 12 percent to a peak of 21.5 percent; President Carter places a partial embargo on the export of grain to the Soviet Union in response to the Soviet Invasion of Afghanistan.

1982: Heavy tariffs are imposed on some steel imports that are foreign government subsidized to help struggling U.S. steel mills; unemployment reaches 10.8 percent, the highest since 1940, and the number of Americans living below the poverty line is the highest it's been in 17 years; fax machines gain popularity as the time per page goes from 6 minutes to 20 seconds, bringing phone bills down for faxing.

1984: Economic growth rises at 6.8 percent, the biggest in more than 30 years, and the inflation rate drops to 3.7 percent, the lowest in 17 years, but budget and trade deficits continue to rise to record levels.

1985: Corporate mergers and acquisitions continue to increase and 24 involve more than $1 billion each, with junk bonds used to finance most takeovers; world oil prices collapse, putting pressure on, and in some cases closing, many banks and savings institutions in energy sector states.

1986: Congress restructures the federal tax system raising taxes on businesses, which in turn raise prices; the Dow Jones average rises past 1900; the national debt rises above $2 trillion for the first time in history; Wall Street continues to suffer from insider trading scandals as Dennis B. Levine and Ivan F. Boesky are both found guilty of trading on non-public information.

1987: The Dow Jones average peaks at 2722.42, sets a one-day record rising 75.23 points, then plummets 508 points, or 22 percent, in one day—a bigger one-day drop than the October 1929 crash; the AFL-CIO allows the Brotherhood of Teamsters into the union.

1989: The Financial Institutions Rescue, Recovery and

Enforcement Act attempts to bail out the failed savings and loan institutions using tax dollars, but inadvertently jeopardizes commercial banks, and in the end fails in its purpose; the Dow Jones average drops 190.58 points in one day as junk bond financing of mergers and acquisitions shakes investors' confidence, but prices rebound the following week and Dow Jones closes the year at 2753.

1990: The record eight-year economic boom ends and the country goes into a recession; the Dow Jones peaks at 2999.75, then drops to a low of 2365.10; the Federal Reserve Board gives J.P. Morgan & Co. the power to underwrite stocks, the first time a bank has had that power since 1933.

1991: The Dow Jones Industrial Average closes above 3000 for the first time in history, but drops back down amid reports that the recession is not over.

1992: The national debt tops $4 trillion, rising $2 trillion in just six years.

1993: The North American Free Trade Agreement (NAFTA) phases out tariffs and other trade barriers between Canada, Mexico, and the United States, and the agreement is passed despite severe opposition from labor unions who claim it will take jobs into other countries; the Revenue Reconciliation Act seeks to reduce the national deficit by nearly $500 billion through budget cuts and modest tax increases.

1994: The General Agreement on Tariffs and Trade (GATT) is updated to extend patent protection and strengthen anti-dumping laws and sanctions, as well as new coverage for agriculture, textiles, services, and intellectual property rights.

1996: The Telecommunications Act of 1996 deregulates the telecommunications industry and allows any communications company to compete in any market against any other company.

1997: The Dow Jones begins unprecedented growth, growing nearly 1,500 points over five months to top 8000; the unemployment rate drops to 4.8 percent, the lowest figure since before the Great Depression.

1998: The Asian economic crisis begins to spread throughout the world with Japan, China, Russia, and eastern Europe suffering from severe depressions, which threaten to spread to outlying regions in Asia, western Europe, and North America; to keep the economy strong in the United States, the Federal Reserve drops the federal funds rate to 5.25 from 5.50 percent; Wall Street begins to see results of the crisis and, as of October, the Dow Jones average drops from a high of 9337 to a low of 7539, including a response to the federal funds cut with two one-day drops in a row of 237.9 points and 208.8 points; crude oil prices drop from $17.78 per barrel in 1997 to a low of $11.36, leading many oil companies to begin mass layoffs.

1999: Europe launches a new single currency called the Euro, good in all participating member countries of the European Union; the Dow Jones Industrial Average tops 10000 for the first time and peaks at 11035.31; e-commerce revenues climb 72 percent from the previous year to total $171.4 billion.

2000: Microsoft Corp. is found to be in violation of the Sherman Antitrust Act and sentenced to be broken into two separate companies; a multitude of dot-com companies begin to declare bankruptcy as investors begin pulling out of unprofitable ventures; the Dow Jones Industrial Average reaches a peak of 11497 before falling by nearly 20 percent as the North American economy weakens.

2001: America Online and Time Warner complete a $128 billion merger, the largest in media industry history, to form AOL Time Warner Inc.; a U.S. federal appeals court reverses the ruling that Microsoft must separate; when trading resumes after the September 11 terrorist attacks, the Dow Jones drops 684 points in a single day; Enron Corp., the largest energy conglomerate in the United States, declares bankruptcy.

2002: AOL Time Warner posts a quarterly loss of $54.2 billion, the largest quarterly loss in U.S. business history; Kmart Corp. declares bankruptcy; World-Com declares bankruptcy.

4Kids Entertainment Inc.

OVERVIEW

4Kids Entertainment is a vertically integrated children's entertainment company. A vertically integrated company owns and operates all the resources necessary to create a product from design to manufacture. In the case of 4Kids Entertainment, the company produces and distributes movies and television programs, develops and designs toys based on the characters in its properties, and sells merchandising rights for the characters to appear on products ranging from pajamas to notebooks to bedding. 4Kids Entertainment also engages in media buying and planning for other companies and develops Internet sites to enhance the marketing of its characters.

The company's structure consists of five wholly owned subsidiaries: 4Kids Entertainment Licensing Inc., 4Kids Entertainment International LTD., The Summit Media Group Inc., 4Kids Productions Inc., and 4Kids Websites Inc. All of the units are headquartered in the United States with the exception of 4Kids Entertainment International LTD., which is located in London.

COMPANY FINANCES

4Kids Entertainment Inc.'s financial history records modest gains for each year since its creation. In 1998 the company posted $2.7 million in net income on revenues of $14.8 million with a profit margin of 18 percent. Since then profits have steadily increased. In 1999 the company recorded a $23.6 million net income on $60.5 million in revenues, with a 39 percent profit margin. In 2000 and 2001, 4Kids Entertainment posted $38.8 million and $12.2 million in net income, on revenues of $88 million

FOUNDED: 1974 as American Leisure Industries Inc.

Contact Information:
HEADQUARTERS: 1414 Avenue of the Americas
  New York, NY 10019
PHONE: (212)758-7666
FAX: (212)980-0933
EMAIL: cwest@4kidsent.com
URL: http://www.4kidsent.com

FINANCES:

4Kids Entertainment Inc. Revenues, 1998-2001 (million dollars)

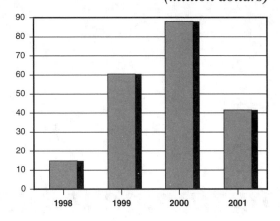

4Kids Entertainment Inc. 2001 Stock Prices (dollars)

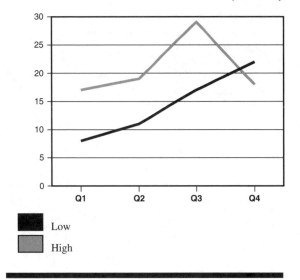

Low

High

and $41.5 million, respectively. In 2000 the company saw its highest profit margin ever, an astounding 44 percent.

ANALYSTS' OPINIONS

4Kids Entertainment Inc., is a publicly traded company but is largely ignored by Wall Street firms. It wasn't until the last quarter of 2000 that the first analyst, Dina Sternberg of Sidoti & Company provided the official coverage of the fledgling company. Her report on the future of 4Kids Entertainment Inc. was neutral.

Frustrated by the lack of respect his firm received from the investment community, chairman and CEO, Alfred Kahn, moved the stock from the NASDAQ exchange to the New York Stock Exchange in 2000. This was an attempt to raise the company's profile and garner positive attention. Industry insiders, however, are reluctant to invest time and resources following a company considered highly speculative.

More than 90 percent of the company's income to date has been derived from Pokemon sales, creating the impression that the company is a one-hit wonder. Kahn plans to silence his critics by using the Pokemon profits to diversify operations and build a more consistent stream of revenue. The fortunes of 4Kids Entertainment are still uncertain and stock analysts are reluctant to go on record with predictions.

HISTORY

American Leisure Industries Inc. was founded in 1974 as a licensing company specializing in children's products. Some of the earlier characters the company handled included: Gumby, ALF, Thundercats, and World Wrestling Federation celebrities. Alfred Kahn joined the company in 1988 as a highly regarded player in the field of children's marketing and licensing. His past experience included a stint as the EVP of marketing at Coleco Industries, where he was the mastermind behind the Cabbage Patch Kids phenomenon.

In 1993 Kahn directed acquisitions of television distribution and production, and media buying to complement the licensing business. Two new subsidiaries were created: The Summit Media Group and 4Kids Productions. Since then Kahn has managed the company's growth and earned a profit in 8 of the last 10 years. The number of employees has also doubled during the last decade.

In the late 1990s the company rose to prominence behind the strength of its Pokemon deal. 4Kids secured the exclusive rights to license the popular Japanese characters. The series' popularity soared, and merchandise flew off the store shelves.

STRATEGY

4Kids Entertainment intends to bolster its bottom line and gain credibility by diversifying revenue sources. Pokemon licensing accounted for 90 percent of all company revenues at the height of its popularity.

Criticized as a fad company, 4Kids does not want to rely on luck, or the fickle taste of 4-year-olds for its success. Prior to the tidal wave of licensed Pokemon goods, media buying accounted for 50 percent of the

Video of 4Kids Entertainment's animated Yu-Gi-Oh! captures attention during Licensing 2001 at New York's Javits Convention Center. (AP Photo/Richard Drew)

company's revenues. Kahn announced that he would like to use some of the Pokemon profits to invest in additional media buying companies. Along with the planned expansion of the media buying unit, the television production and distribution business will gain prominence in the organization. In a blockbuster deal signed in early 2002, 4Kids Entertainment secured the rights to provide a four-hour block of Saturday morning programming for the Fox Network. Kahn placed considerable resources into this deal, paying $100 million for the four-year agreement. He believed it is the final piece of a completely vertically integrated business plan. The agreement's cost was less expensive than buying a network

and provides the company with access to the most valuable block of children's television available. Of course, management acknowledged that it will continue to use its considerable expertise to identify the next white-hot trend in children's characters and licensing.

INFLUENCES

The popularity of video games and the Internet have guided the evolution of 4Kids Entertainment. As early as 1988 the company had signed an agreement to act as the

FAST FACTS:

About 4Kids Entertainment Inc.

Ownership: 4Kids Entertainment Inc. is a publicly traded company on the New York Stock Exchange.

Ticker Symbol: KDE

Officers: Alfred R. Kahn, Chmn., CEO and Dir., 54, 2000 base salary $395,000, bonus $7,560,729; Joseph P. Garrity, EVP, COO, CFO, and Director, 45, 2000 base salary $250,000, bonus $1,512,145; Norman Grossfield, Pres., 37, 2000 salary $250,000, bonus $786,113

Employees: 119

Principal Subsidiary Companies: 4Kids Entertainment Inc. operates five wholly owned subsidiaries: 4Kids Entertainment Licensing Inc., 4Kids Entertainment International Inc., The Summit Media Group Inc., 4Kids Productions Inc., and 4Kids Websites Inc.

Chief Competitors: 4Kids Entertainment is an entertainment and media company that develops properties and products for children. Its primary competitors are entertainment and media companies, including Walt Disney, Marvel, and Time Warner/America Online.

CHRONOLOGY:

Key Dates for 4Kids Entertainment Inc.

1974: Company launches under name of American Leisure Industries

1988: Signs agreement to license Nintendo characters

1992: Name changes to American Leisure Concepts

1999: Pokemon fever hits America, producing huge revenues for company

2001: Launches 4Kids Websites to enhance marketing capabilities

2002: Signs pact with Fox Kids to provide Saturday morning block of television for the network

value of Saturday morning programming, which was no longer the sole viewing day for perennial favorites.

CURRENT TRENDS

4Kids Entertainment has joined the growing ranks of entertainment companies leasing space on network television. In January 2002, the company entered into a bidding war with rival, DIC Entertainment, to provide programming for a four-hour block of Saturday morning time on the Fox Kids network. 4Kids paid a reported $100 million for a four-year contract. This dwarfs the arrangement made between the Discovery Channel and NBC for a three-hour Saturday morning programming block. The Discovery Channel only shelled out $58 million to air its wares on prime network time. ABC had already relinquished most of its programmable time to its sister network, The Disney Channel. Disney provides episodes of its popular original series to be aired on Saturday morning. CBS receives its supply of juvenile fare from Nickelodeon. The network's reluctance to continue producing such programming in house greatly enhances the role of the third party content provider.

licensing agent for Nintendo and its cast of characters. Some of its original properties included Donkey Kong, Super Mario Brothers, Zelda, and Gameboy. The success of these games, and the characters that populated them, was not lost on Kahn. Known for his keen eye for a breakout concept, he tracked the Japanese market. The advent of Internet technology increased the exposure of foreign characters to the American marketplace.

The creation of youth oriented television networks such as Nickelodeon, The Disney Channel, The Cartoon Network, ABC Family Channel, Fox, and the WB has also influenced the company's product development. Networks geared toward children and youth programming proved to be tough competition for traditional television networks. Unable to compete with these upstarts, the major networks began to abandon the development of children's programming. They looked for independent producers to supply them with products. In addition, the new networks offered cartoons and similar fare, all day and night. This greatly expanded the opportunities to place programming on television. It also diminished the

PRODUCTS

4Kids Entertainment offers products and services through five subsidiaries. 4Kids Licensing supplies domestic and international licensing rights to properties.

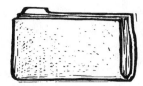

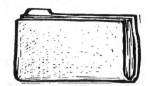

M-I-C-K-E-Y. . . . YU-GI-OH!

Times have changed in the field of animated characters. Once upon a time, the Disney Company had a monopoly on animated creatures, including one of the most famous, Mickey Mouse. Mickey Mouse, Donald Duck, Goofy, Pluto, and Minnie Mouse were some of the original animated characters that captured the imagination of American children. Flash forward and you'll see that the new crop of celluloid stars are a new breed of 'toon. YU-GI-OH! is poised to be the next breakout hit. Based on a comic book, show tells of the adventures of YUGI and his friends Joey, Tristan, and Tea. The gang uses magical powers to solve puzzles and battle mystical creatures. Scooby-Doo, where are you?

The property can be a product, a television show, or an individual character. The company acts as a third-party agent to sell the right to use the likeness of a character on a wide variety of items. The company receives a royalty fee and a share of the sales of the branded products. Its recently launched division, Technology 4Kids creates new concepts for toys and games using technology.

4Kids International is based in London and manages the use of properties in Europe and the United Kingdom. Summit Media offers media-buying marketing services to companies in youth oriented businesses such as toys and video game companies. 4Kids Productions creates programming for children in television, film or musical formats. The newest subsidiary is a Web site development company that designs sites to enhance the exposure of licensed characters, or create new opportunities.

In 2001 licensing accounted for 68 percent of total revenues. This figure represents a decline from the prior year when the figure climbed to 83 percent. Media buying and planning accounted for 10 percent of sales in 2001. This was an increase in business from past years when this sector derived only 4 or 5 percent of revenues. Television, film, home video, and music production accounted for 22 percent of revenues in 2001.

CORPORATE CITIZENSHIP

4 Kids Entertainment CEO, Alfred R. Kahn, was one of the recipients of the 2002 E-3 Awards (Emerald Entre-

FINDING WAYS TO STRETCH YOUR EDUCATION

NBA: Inside Stuff teaches peaceful conflict resolutions and global awareness. Phil Donahue promotes teenage learning with a show about strippers. These are actual claims made by television stations in response to the Children's Television Act passed by Congress in 1990. The Act requires all local television stations to provide educational programming for children 16 years and younger. The major networks are required to show at least three hours a week of educational viewing in compliance with a 1996 FCC ruling. What constitutes educational viewing? The rules do not specify and enforcement has been minimal. Fox's recent move to lease its Saturday morning slot to 4Kids Entertainment may bring this debate front and center once again. The animated fare offered by 4Kids is described as "animated programs designed to sell toys to kids." It is unclear how Fox intends to meet the requirements of the educational rules. Stay tooned!

preneurial and Excellence Award) presented by Emerald Asset Management. The award winners were chosen by a staff of investment analysts who used the following criteria: an entrepreneurial approach that maximizes human initiative, a demonstrated record of achievement, creating jobs and stimulating growth, and serving as a role model for ethical business practices. Norman Grossfield has also been recognized for the quality of his work. In 1996 he was presented with The Golden Rings, which is the highest award bestowed by the International Olympic Committee. Grossfield was singled out for his work with 4Kids Entertainment providing coverage of the 1996 Olympic Games in Atlanta.

GLOBAL PRESENCE

The company operates in the United States and in Europe. Its most notable successes have come as a result of importing Japanese characters and games to the United States. Personnel at 4Kids Entertainment have developed expertise in evaluating characters for crossover value. Nothing can be taken for granted when predicting the tastes of children, but the company has posted an impressive track record in this area.

EMPLOYMENT

4Kids Entertainment Inc. employs a workforce of approximately 120 full-time staffers. The licensing division, which accounts for the majority of the company's revenues, employs 75 people. Television and media production, and television and media distribution, each retain about 20 employees. The company offers little information on its personnel policies or recruiting practices. In early 2002 the company was not hiring new employees. The size of the workforce has increased from 42 members in 1992 to 120 in 2002, with the bulk of expansion occurring in the late 1990s.

SOURCES OF INFORMATION

Bibliography

"4Kids Entertainment's Animated Television Series YU-GI-OH! Will Expand to Six Days a Week on Kids' WB." *Business Wire*, 28 February 2002.

Adalian, Josef, and Paula Bernstein. "4KidsEntertainment Pocketing Fox Kids Ayem Block." *Daily Variety*, 21 January 2002.

James, Meg. "TV Networks Find Ways to Stretch Educational Rules." *Los Angeles Times*, 23 February 2002.

Keenan, Charles. "Life After Pokemon; 4Kids Entertainment Looks for the Next Big Thing." *Crain's New York Business*, 9 October 2000.

"Pokemon Battles to Boost Licensing." *Discount Store News*, 7 February 2000.

"Pokemon Powers Up." *Playthings*, February 2000.

"Retailers Pocketing Pokemon Sales." *Discount Store News*, 7 February 2000.

For an annual report:
on the Internet at: http://www.4kidsentertainment.com/investor/

For additional industry research:
Investigate companies by their Standard Industrial Classification Codes, also known as SICs. 4Kids Entertainment Inc.'s primary SIC is:

7812 Motion Picture and Video Production

Also investigate companies by their North American Industry Classification System codes, also known as NAICS codes. 4Kids Entertainment Inc.'s primary NAICS code is:

512110 Motion Picture and Video Production

7-Eleven, Inc.

OVERVIEW

7-Eleven Inc., formerly known as the Southland Corporation, operates the largest chain of convenience stores in the world. The company boasts nearly 21,000 stores operating in the United States, Canada, and 15 other countries around the world. Approximately 6,000 7-Eleven and other convenience stores are operated and franchised by 7-Eleven, Inc. in the United States and Canada alone, and together they serve about 6 million customers daily.

For 7-Eleven, the emphasis is on convenience, with stores and products designed to meet the needs of busy shoppers with fair prices and speedy transactions in a clean, safe, and friendly shopping environment. Among its best-known proprietary products are the Big Gulp fountain-style soft drinks, Slurpee beverages, Café Select fresh brewed coffee, and Big Bite hot dogs. In addition to its own branded products and other nationally known brands, each 7-Eleven outlet offers a variety of convenient services based on the individual needs of the neighborhood in which it is located. Such services include the sale of money orders, long distance phone cards, and lottery tickets in states where they are legal. Most stores also have photocopying equipment available to customers for a small fee, as well as automated teller machines.

Of the company's 5,300 stores in the United States, approximately 3,300 are operated by franchisees, while another 430 are operated by licensees. More than 15,000 7-Eleven and other convenience stores are operated by licensees and affiliates in the countries of Australia, Canada, China, Denmark, Japan, Malaysia, Mexico, Norway, the Philippines, Singapore, South Korea, Spain,

FOUNDED: 1927 as the Southland Corporation

Contact Information:

HEADQUARTERS: 2711 North Haskell Avenue
    Dallas, TX 75204
PHONE: (214)828-7011
FAX: (214)828-7848
EMAIL: invest@7-11.com
URL: http://www.7-eleven.com

FINANCES:

7-Eleven Inc.
Total Revenues, 1997-2000
(million dollars)

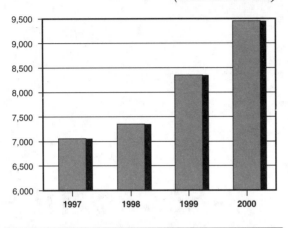

Sweden, Taiwan, Thailand, and Turkey, as well as the U.S. territories of Puerto Rico and Guam.

COMPANY FINANCES

Since 2000, 7-Eleven Inc. has shown a somewhat uneven pattern in profits. In 2001 the company posted a net profit of $83.8 million on revenues of nearly $9.8 billion. This was a decline of 22.6 percent from 7-Eleven's 2000 net profit of $108.3 million on sales of $9.35 billion. In 1999, the company posted net income of $83.1 million on revenues of about $8.3 billion. In the 52 weeks ended March 31, 2002, the company's stock traded between a low of $8.25 and a high of $14.00. The company's price/earnings ratio was 13.70.

The company's financial performance in 2001, announced January 31, 2002, narrowly beat Wall Street expectations. However, shortly after announcing its results for 2001, the company revealed its plan to close between 115 and 120 of its convenience stores. Company executives expressed the hope that the announced closures and other belt-tightening measures would add $.05 to $.10 per share to the bottom line for 2002.

ANALYSTS' OPINIONS

Although positively impressed by 7-Eleven's proprietary Retail Information System, most analysts following the company had turned neutral on the company by early spring of 2002. Analyst Mark Husson of Merrill Lynch in February 2002 said that the company's year-over-year decline in earnings was largely attributable to its heavy investments in systems and human resources. Merrill Lynch cut its long term rating for the company's stock from "buy" to "neutral." Husson observed: "While 7-Eleven is a valuable brand, it is unclear when its heavy investments will begin to generate positive (return on invested capital), and we believe management needs to still work out a strategy to translate these into strong earnings growth."

The company's announced intention to continue opening new outlets, as well as its strategies to attract more women shoppers, positively impressed Dennis Telzrow, a retail analyst with Hoak, Breedlove, Wesneski & Company. "The company is doing a lot of new things, and the strategies make sense," he said. "And they're opening new stores, which they didn't do for years." Those sentiments were echoed by Jonathan H. Ziegler, a retail analyst at Deutsche Bank in San Francisco. He said, "This company has the ability to innovate and bring new things to the market. They have quite a bit of proprietary product, and to me that's what retailing is all about."

HISTORY

The convenience store concept was pioneered in 1927 by the Southland Ice Company of Dallas, Texas. That year, one of Southland's visionary employees on the company's ice dock began selling such staples as bread, milk, and eggs in addition to blocks of ice on Sundays and evenings when grocery stores were ordinarily closed. Ice customers, pleased with this new convenience, embraced Southland's expanded product line, increasing sales substantially. Thus, convenience retailing was born.

Southland's first convenience outlets were called Tote'm stores, and several of them were even decorated with genuine native Alaskan totem poles. However, in 1946 the stores' names were changed to 7-Eleven to reflect the chain's new extended hours, operating from 7 a.m. to 11 p.m. each day, seven days a week. More than half a century later, Southland Corporation officially changed its corporate name to 7-Eleven, Inc. in 1999.

Since 1991 IYG Holding Company, a wholly owned subsidiary of Ito-Yokado Company, Ltd., and Seven-Eleven Japan Company, Ltd., has owned a majority interest in the in the chain. Under an area licensing agreement with 7-Eleven, Inc., Seven-Eleven Japan operates more than 8,400 7-Eleven outlets in Japan and Hawaii. As of early 2002, 7-Eleven Inc. operated, franchised, or licensed more than 22,500 stores worldwide and boasted 2001 revenue of nearly $9.8 billion.

STRATEGY

There are four key elements in 7-Eleven's corporate strategy for future growth: increasing same-store merchandise sales; expanding in existing markets; providing greater convenience to customers; and increasing the value of the company's licenses and expanding internationally.

In the area of increasing same-store merchandise sales, corporate merchandising experts work to develop and introduce new products. The company's Retail Information System allows franchisees and individual store managers to evaluate sales on individual products in their inventory, providing an opportunity to analyze sales trends and customer preferences as well as the many factors that affect each of these areas. Using the Retail Information System, store managers are better able to maintain optimal inventory levels and, most importantly, remove slow-selling products from their shelves. This ability to analyze product trends and pinpoint slow-moving products gives the corporate merchandising team the ability to work with franchisees and store managers to increase sales by custom-fitting the product mix to each individual store and its unique customer base.

7-Eleven's store development efforts are concentrated on its core urban and suburban markets, where the company feels there exists a great deal of potential for significant expansion. It announced plans to open 125 to 150 new stores by 2003 in such existing markets. The rationale for tapping the potential in existing markets focuses on the efficiencies that can be achieved by drawing on existing distribution centers, bakeries, and commissaries. Factors considered in the evaluation of potential sites for new stores include demographics, ease of access, population density, traffic volume, visibility, and overall economic activity immediately surrounding the site.

Because it is the granddaddy of convenience retailing, it comes as no surprise that an important element in 7-Eleven's strategy for future growth is to look for new ways in which to provide greater convenience to its customers. The company has been developing and testing its proprietary V.com kiosk program. Eventually, self-service V.com kiosks will be located in many of the chain's outlets, offering check cashing, money orders, money transfer, and traditional ATM services. V.com developers hope that in the future, 7-Eleven customers will also be able to use the service to purchase tickets to major entertainment and sporting events and even pay bills electronically. Most importantly, the company believes these new and innovative services should fuel growth by attracting new customers to its stores.

The last element of the corporate growth strategy focuses on international expansion and attempts to increase the value of licenses. The company feels that it can offer prospective licensees a more attractive financial opportunity through its continuing expansion and broadening of the corporate infrastructure, all of which will strengthen the value of the 7-Eleven brand. Long-range corporate

FAST FACTS:
About 7-Eleven, Inc.

Ownership: 7-Eleven, Inc. is a publicly owned company traded on the New York Stock Exchange.

Ticker Symbol: SE

Officers: James W. Keyes, Pres. and CEO, 46, 2000 base salary $437,500

Employees: 33,300

Principal Subsidiary Companies: 7-Eleven, Inc. owns a number of subsidiaries worldwide, most of which operate varying sizes and numbers of outlets in regional markets. Its domestic subsidiaries include 7-Eleven Beverage Company of Texas; 7-Eleven of Idaho, Inc.; 7-Eleven Sales Corporation of Texas; and 7-Eleven of Massachusetts, Inc. Outside the United States, subsidiaries include Phil-Seven Properties Corporation in the Philippines; Sao Paulo-Seven Comercial, S.A., in Brazil; 7-Eleven Mexico, S.A. de C.V.; and 7-Eleven Canada Inc.

Chief Competitors: The central business of the company is the operation, franchising, and licensing of convenience stores. Its principal competitors in the convenience store market are Kroger, which operates the Circle K chain, and ExxonMobil and Royal Dutch Shell, oil companies that each own an extensive chain of convenience stores operated in conjunction with their gasoline retailing stations.

plans envision moving into a number of countries where 7-Eleven, Inc. currently has no presence. Additionally, in late 2001 the company announced plans to look into the expansion of its licensing arrangement in China.

INFLUENCES

7-Eleven has been better able to cope with the inevitable ups and downs of the economy worldwide through the introduction of its Retail Information System, which allows store managers and the corporate merchandising team to closely monitor inventory and consumer buying trends. Additionally, the company has been well-positioned to face the challenge of sudden changes in consumer demand through its daily delivery system.

CHRONOLOGY:

Key Dates for 7-Eleven

1927: Southland Ice Company employee starts selling convenience items off ice dock

1946: Southland's Tote'm stores change name to 7-Eleven

1999: Southland Corporation changes name to 7-Eleven, Inc.

2001: 7-Eleven plans further expansion in China; Store of the Future opens in Plano, Texas

CURRENT TRENDS

7-Eleven has moved aggressively to add new products and services that meet its customers' needs and to increase the convenience of its stores. To facilitate these additions, the company has undertaken a fairly ambitious investment program to further broaden its infrastructure and technology.

Working in conjunction with systems specialists at Electronic Data Systems (EDS), 7-Eleven in December 2001 opened a "Store of the Future" in Plano, Texas, which is also the headquarters of EDS. The new store, a laboratory for possible future changes that, if successful, may migrate throughout the chain, is loaded with innovative new devices to simplify life for both employees and shoppers. Customers may place orders at a drive-up window. In the back room of the Plano store is an ice machine that automatically fills the store's dispensers without staff intervention. A similar back room device sees to it that the store's soft drink dispensers never run out of syrup. The outlet's 21-spout coffee bar is equipped with airtight dispensers that keep the coffee from burning. Of the company's experiment in Plano, Gary Rose, the company's senior vice president of operations, said, "Whether it's a new fresh sandwich, a better way to provide a great cup of coffee, or a fast way to pay for a purchase, we'll try it all in Plano."

PRODUCTS

Perhaps the one branded product with which 7-Eleven is most closely identified is its "Big Gulp" soft drink beverage. Around for years, the Big Gulp was so branded because of its oversized portions. The company added a new wrinkle to its Big Gulp marketing strategy by allowing customers to customize their Coke, Pepsi, and Dr. Pepper Big Gulps with a splash of cherry, vanilla, or lemon flavoring. The company merchandising team reports that vanilla-flavored Dr. Pepper Big Gulps have proved especially popular.

To meet the ever-changing needs of its customers, 7-Eleven also makes available the Big Gulp Car Cup, which is big enough to hold 32 ounces of the traveler's favorite soft drink and tailored to fit into the cup holder of most cars and trucks. For those who are "truly thirsty," the company markets the Super Big Gulp Cup, which holds 44 ounces of soft drink, and the X-treme Gulp Mug, an insulated mug that will keep 52 ounces of soft drink cold for up to six hours.

Another big seller in 7-Eleven's product lineup is the Slurpee, an icy refreshment that comes in a variety of flavors. Among the most recent flavors being marketed is Mountain Dew. In the Slurpee lineup are the regular Slurpee, the Slurpee Strata Cup, and the Super Slurpee Strata Cup.

Another of the company's popular frozen refreshments is the 7-Eleven Café Cooler Beverage, a creamy, coffee-flavored treat available in such flavors as mocha and French vanilla. Among its wide variety of hot coffee offerings, 7-Eleven's Premium Dark Mountain Roast Coffee, made from a blend of 100 percent Arabica beans, is one of the latest.

In the realm of cash and communications, popular 7-Eleven products and services include prepaid callings cards for both regular and wireless telephones, money orders, and automated teller machines. The company has also introduced V.com kiosks into 100 or so of its stores. These kiosks were developed to meet customers' needs for convenient financial services and are linked into the Internet. In addition to offering the services now available from conventional ATMs, the V.com kiosks offer money orders, money transfers, check cashing, and eventually will be expanded to include bill paying, deposit capability, and event ticketing.

In 2001 the sale of tobacco products accounted for 26.6 percent of total 7-Eleven merchandise sales in the United States and Canada, compared with 26.4 percent in 2000 and 25.8 percent in 1999. Non-alcoholic beverages made up the second biggest segment of total merchandise sales, accounting for 22.5 percent in 2001, unchanged from 2000 and down slightly from 22.9 percent in 1999. Beer and wine accounted for 11.1 percent of total merchandise sales, compared with 10.9 percent in 2000 and 10.8 percent in 1999. Outside of merchandise sales, gasoline sales (not available at all stores) in 2001 accounted for 28.2 percent of total net sales in the United States and Canada; this compared with 29 percent in 2000 and 24.7 percent in 1999.

CORPORATE CITIZENSHIP

In a purposeful effort to be a good neighbor in the thousands of communities the company serves, 7-Eleven, its stores, franchisees, employees, and customers help the less fortunate around them in a wide variety of ways. In 2000, more than $2.3 billion was distributed to charitable programs through in-store fundraising activities, contributions of cash and goods, and local involvement in the programs. Recipients of contributions in 2000 included programs addressing such issues as crime prevention, multicultural understanding, and literacy. Through Harvest, another 7-Eleven program, nearly 800,000 pounds of unsold fresh food items were donated to local food banks.

Also serving the widely diverse needs of the communities in which it operates are the Community Outreach Programs of 7-Eleven, Inc. In 1999 alone, the company provided more than $3 million in grants to grass roots literacy programs and organizations. Additionally, the company has provided support for disaster relief efforts through the American Red Cross, Salvation Army, and other charitable organizations. Such support came in the form of cash and product donations, services, and volunteers. 7-Eleven also works to promote voter awareness, registration, and participation through its partnerships with the National Association of Colored People, League of Women Voters, and League of United Latin American Citizens (LULAC). Partnered with LULAC's National Education Service Centers, the company sponsors the 7-Eleven/LULAC Youth Leadership Academies in California, Florida, Colorado, and Texas.

GLOBAL PRESENCE

With more than three-quarters of its stores outside the United States, 7-Eleven is a major presence in the international market. The chain is widely represented in Japan with 8,924 stores operated under license. The company has licensed stores in the following countries: Taiwan, 2,908; Thailand, 1,722; South Korea, 1,001; China, 516; Mexico, 328; Australia, 267; Malaysia, 189; Philippines, 161; Singapore, 156; Norway, 63; Sweden, 60; Denmark, 37; Spain, 15; Puerto Rico, 13; Turkey, 10; and Guam, 8.

In the fall of 2001, the company announced plans to expand the development and operation of 7-Eleven stores in China through licensing agreements. The bulk of the company's existing stores in China can be found in Hong Kong and the southern Chinese province of Guangdong. Discussions have been undertaken about entering into a licensing arrangement for at least one additional market area in China with Seven-Eleven Japan, the President Chain Store Corporation of Taiwan, and a local Chinese participant. Seven-Eleven Japan operates almost 9,000 7-Eleven stores in Japan. The President Chain Store is

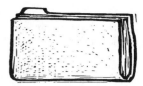

RIS CLOSELY MONITORS SALES

7-Eleven's proprietary Retail Information System (RIS) allows the company's corporate management, franchisees, and individual store managers to closely monitor sales information by item, thus providing them with the input they need to manage both their time and product mix most effectively. Under RIS, individual stores can be connected to vendors, the company's primary third party distributor, and their combined distribution centers for quick access to item-level information sharing and for ordering. The central feature of RIS is a point-of-sale touch screen system with scanning and integrated credit card authorization, all linked into a centralized price book.

Other features of the system include daily ordering for all product items; product category management and item-level sales analysis; integrated gasoline and "pay-at-the-pump" functionality; and the automation of such back office functions as payroll, sales and cash reporting, gasoline pricing, and inventory control.

During 2001, a number of enhancements were made to RIS, including debit card processing, lottery management, additional support for age verification on restricted sale items, and integration of money orders and check authorization into the POS registers.

7-Eleven's current licensee in Taiwan, where it operates more than 2,900 stores.

EMPLOYMENT

At the end of 2001, 7-Eleven, Inc. had on its payrolls more than 33,000 employees worldwide. In recognition of the important role its employees play in its financial success, the company designed a number of new training programs to be introduced in 2002 and subsequent years. Its new staffing model, according to the company's 2001 annual report, "will clearly define a store employee's career path and require mandatory certification of certain skills in order to be promoted." All employees will undergo computerized training in the company's stores, after which they will be tested and certified if they pass. The company's field consultants, each of whom provides support for a group of about eight stores, will be required to undergo a program to ensure that they not only are fully able to manage a store's operations but also able to train new employees in key aspects of those operations.

To further strengthen the company's hiring process, 7-Eleven has introduced new screening tools and new pay scales to improve recruitment and selection of both employees and franchisees. Also planned is an incentive program to grade employees on their execution of five of the company's business fundamentals and reward them according to how well they score. The five business fundamentals are product assortment, quality, service, cleanliness, and value.

SOURCES OF INFORMATION

Bibliography

7-Eleven 2000 Annual Report. Dallas, TX: 7-Eleven, Inc., 2001.

"7-Eleven, Inc." *Hoover's Online*, 2002. Available at http://www.hoovers.com.

7-Eleven, Inc. Home Page, 2002. Available at http://www.7-eleven.com.

"7-Eleven to Close Up to 120 Stores." *Associated Press*, 31 January 2002.

Halkias, Maria. "7-Eleven's Window to the Future: Convenience Store Chain Reinventing Itself in Plano." *Dallas Morning News*, 13 December 2001, 1D.

"Snapshot Report: 7-Eleven, Inc." *Multex Investor*. Available at http://www.marketguide.com.

For an annual report:
write: Investor Relations, 7-Eleven, Inc., 2711 N. Haskell Avenue, Dallas, TX 75204-2906

For additional industry research:
Investigate companies by their Standard Industrial Classification codes, also known as SICs. 7-Eleven's primary SICs are:

5411 Grocery Stores

6719 Holding Companies NEC

6794 Patent Owners and Lessors

Also investigate companies by their North American Industrial Classification System codes, also known as NAICS codes. 7-Eleven's primary NAICS codes are:

445120 Convenience Stores

447110 Gasoline Stations with Convenience Stores

533110 Lessors of Nonfinancial Intangible Assets

551112 Offices of Other Holding Companies

Abbott Laboratories

OVERVIEW

Founded in 1888, Abbott Laboratories is a global, diversified, healthcare company that discovers, develops, manufactures, and markets pharmaceutical, diagnostic, nutritional, and hospital healthcare products. Headquartered in Chicago, Illinois, it is one of the top healthcare product makers in the United States. Abbott employs 70,000 people worldwide, and it has 150 facilities and 60 manufacturing sites. The company focuses on advancing medical science and the practice of healthcare, and it has demonstrated expertise in the therapeutic areas of diabetes, pain management, respiratory infections, HIV/AIDS, men and women's health, and pediatrics. Its products are sold in 130 countries. Abbott has five business segments: Pharmaceutical Products, Diagnostic Products, Hospital Products, Ross Products, and International. Its Ross Products division makes such well-known nutritionals as Similac, an infant formula, and Ensure, an adult nutrition supplement. Pharmaceuticals and hospital products make up about one-half of the company's sales.

COMPANY FINANCES

In 2000 the company's sales and net earnings were $13.7 billion and $2.8 billion, respectively, with diluted earnings per share of $1.78. For the fiscal year ended December 31, 2001, sales rose 18 percent to $16.29 billion; net income fell 44 percent to $1.55 billion. The company's hospital and pharmaceutical segments have been receiving higher unit sales, which is reflected as higher revenues. Approximately $1.33 billion of its 2001 revenues went into research and development.

FOUNDED: 1888

Contact Information:

HEADQUARTERS: 100 Abbott Park Rd., Dept. 393-AP51
  Abbott Park, Illinois 60064-3537
PHONE: (847)937-1608
URL: http://www.abbott.com

FAST FACTS:
About Abbott Laboratories

Ownership: Abbott Laboratories is a publicly owned company. It is listed on the New York, Chicago, Pacific, London and Swiss Stock Exchanges and is traded on the Boston, Cincinnati, and Philadelphia exchanges.

Ticker Symbol: ABT

Officers: Miles D. White, Chmn. and CEO; Richard A. Gonzalez, Pres. and COO, Medical Products Group; Jeffrey M. Leiden, MD, PhD, Pres. and COO, Pharmaceutical Products Group; Christopher B. Begley, SVP, Hospital Products; William G. Dempsey, SVP, International Operations

Employees: 70,000

Principal Subsidiary Companies: Abbott Laboratories owns 50 percent of TAP Pharmaceutical Products Inc. Subsidiaries and affiliates include Abbott Laboratories MediSense Products, Knoll GmbH, and Vysis, Inc.

Chief Competitors: Abbott Laboratories' competitors include AstraZeneca; Aventis; Bristol Myers Squibb Co.; Eli Lilly and Company; Merck and Company, Inc.; Pfizer; and Roche.

ANALYSTS' OPINIONS

Abbott Laboratories boasts an impressive record of long-term financial performance and continuous growth. It is one of 25 companies to appear in all six annual editions of *The 100 Best Stocks to Own in America.* In 2001, the company ranked high on lists compiled by financial magazines and experts. It was number 166 in the performance rankings of the S&P 500, number 77 in *Business Week* magazine's "Global 1000," and ranked number 70 in *Forbes* magazine's "500 Top Companies." Abbott Laboratories was also named to the Deloitte and Touche "Fast 50 Companies" list. It has posted sales growth for 47 consecutive years, and it has showed dividend growth for 312 consecutive quarters since 1924.

Further, the company holds a first or second market position in the following business segments: adult nutritionals, anti-infectives, blood screening for infectious diseases, hematology diagnostics, immunodiagnostics, infant formulas/nutritionals, inhalation anesthetics, and vessel closure devices.

In 2001 analysts and observers believed that Abbott Laboratories' new AIDS drug, Kaletra, would give its pharmaceutical division an economic boost. They pointed to the fact that Abbott's Kaletra proved effective in more patients than Viracept, a drug produced by top competitor Pfizer. Analysts expected that Kalestra would improve Abbott's share of the $6.5 billion market for HIV and AIDS treatments and that it would generate $500 million in global sales in the early part of the twenty-first century. The news made investors happy, as they felt Kalestra would place a much-needed "block-buster" drug in Abbott's product portfolio.

HISTORY

Abbott Laboratories was founded in 1888 by Wallace Calvin Abbott, MD, a Chicago physician, who proved to be a pioneer in the science of pharmaceuticals by producing a new form of medicine called "dosimetric granules." These pills enabled a precisely measured amount of drug. Within two years, the demand for these granules became overwhelming, setting the stage for the continual growth the company would consistently demonstrate through the years.

In 1900 Dr. Abbott officially incorporated the company as the Abbott Alkaloidal Company, and in 1915 he changed the name to Abbott Laboratories. Product demand spurred Dr. Abbott to build a new manufacturing facility in 1920. The building served as the company headquarters for 40 years, and it remains Abbott Laboratories' primary manufacturing location today.

In 1931 the company established its first international affiliate in Montreal, Canada. Five years later, it introduced the anesthetic agent Pentothal, which was developed by Abbott scientists Drs. Ernest Volwiler and Donalee Tabern, who were later named to the U.S. Inventors Hall of Fame for their discovery. Ten years later, Abbott started commercial production of penicillin. In 1945 the company entered the field of radiopharmaceuticals, which are radioactive drugs used for diagnostic or therapeutic purposes.

Throughout the next two decades, Abbott Laboratories continued to be an innovator. In 1952 it introduced Erythrocin, an antibiotic used to fight gram-positive bacteria. In 1962 Abbott entered a joint venture with Dainippon Pharmaceutical Co., Ltd., of Osaka, Japan, to manufacture radiopharmaceuticals. This venture would become Dainabot, which would grow to become the company's largest operation outside the United States.

The company continued to grow during the 1960s, 1970s, and 1980s. In 1964 Abbott merged with M&R Dietetic Laboratories of Columbus, Ohio, the maker of Similac infant formula. M&R would eventually become

Abbott's Ross Products Division. Abbott formed its Diagnostics Division in 1973. That same year, it introduced the product Ensure, which would become the world's leading adult nutritional product. In 1977 Abbott entered into a joint venture with Takeda Chemical Industries, Ltd., which resulted in the formation of TAP Pharmaceuticals Inc., now known as TAP Holdings Inc. In 1980 Abbott acquired Sorenson Research of Salt Lake City, Utah.

As the company continued to grow, Abbott Laboratories' strong focus on research and development produced significant medical advancements. In 1985, the U.S. Food and Drug Administration (USFDA) gave the company clearance to market the world's first diagnostic test to detect AIDS. During the same period, TAP received approval to market Lupron, a new therapy for prostate cancer. Two years later, Abbott received USFDA approval for Hytrin (terazosin), a new cardiovascular drug used for treatment of hypertension. In Abbott's centennial year of 1988, the company introduced the IMx diagnostic instrument, which would become the world's leading immunoassay system and one of the Abbott's all-time best-selling new products.

In the 1990s, Abbott introduced Clarithromycin, a macrolide antibiotic that would become one of the world's leading respiratory antibiotics. Abbott also ventured into the hematology testing market when it acquired Sequoia-Turner Corp. As a result, it introduced several major products including Survanta (for treatment of neonatal respiratory distress syndrome), disease-specific medical nutritionals, and a second-generation diagnostic test for hepatitis C. The decade also saw Abbott launch AxSYM, a labor-saving diagnostic system for high-volume laboratories.

In 1995 Abbott scientists researched chemical interactions inside the brain in order to develop new therapies for neurological and psychiatric disorders. This resulted in the company's introduction of a new treatment for bipolar disorder. That same year, the company received expanded indications for Clarithromycin for both prevention and treatment of Mycobacterium avium complex, an infection common in AIDS patients; sought new drug applications for Norvir, to help combat AIDS, and tiagabine, to treat patients with epilepsy; and launched Abbott PRISM, the first fully automated, high-volume blood analyzer.

In 1996 Abbott scored another key acquisition when it bought MediSense, Inc., a company that produced blood glucose self-testing systems for diabetics. Also, it formed strategic alliances with Berlex Laboratories, Magnevist, and Ultravist, and SONUS Pharmaceuticals. The same year, Abbott's research into AIDS treatment resulted in Norvir being cleared for marketing around the world. Its HIV antigen assay for use in blood screening centers was cleared by the USFDA for the detection of the HIV-l antigen.

In 1997, on the nutritional front, the Ross Products division introduced an improved version of Similac,

CHRONOLOGY:

Key Dates for Abbott Laboratories

1888: Company is founded by Wallace Calvin Abbott, MD, in Chicago, Illinois

1915: Abbott Alkaloidal Company becomes Abbott Laboratories

1931: Abbott establishes its first international affiliate in Montreal, Canada

1936: Abbott scientists Ernest Volwiler and Donalee Tabern develop Pentothal

1962: Abbott enters a joint venture with Dainippon Pharmaceutical Co., Ltd. of Osaka, Japan

1964: Abbott merges with M&R Dietetic Laboratories, the maker of Similac infant formula

1973: Abbott introduces Ensure, which will become the world's leading adult nutritional product

1977: Abbott enters into a joint venture with Takeda Chemical Industries, Ltd. to form TAP Pharmaceuticals Inc.

1985: USFDA gives Abbott clearance to market the world's first AIDS diagnostic test

1996: Abbott acquires MediSense, Inc., a company that produced blood glucose self-testing systems for diabetics

1998: Miles D. White elected chief executive officer

1999: Abbott Laboratories acquires Perclose, Inc., the leading arterial closure device manufacturer

which featured a specialized blend of ingredients similar to breast milk, a new protein system, and an improved fat blend. That same year, four of Abbott's inventors were named 1997 National Inventors of the Year for developing protease inhibitors, a class of drugs for the treatment of HIV infection and AIDS.

As Abbott Laboratories forged ahead into the future, 1998 proved to be pivotal when Miles D. White elected chief executive officer. During the next two years, White would make several important acquisitions and agreements. (That was also the year that the USFDA granted marketing clearance for TriCor, a drug for patients with very high triglyceride levels.) In 1999, the year that White was elected chairman of the board, Abbott acquired Perclose, Inc., the leading arterial closure device manufacturer. Also, Abbott and Triangle Pharmaceuticals Inc. formed a worldwide alliance for six antiviral products.

Also in 1998, Abbott's Depakote became the most prescribed agent by psychiatrists for treating manic episodes associated with bipolar disorder. On the acquisitions and agreements front, Abbott and Boehringer Ingelheim of Germany agreed to co-market Boehringer Ingelheim's meloxicam in Latin America. Abbott acquired control of International Murex Technologies Corporation, a medical diagnostics company. The USFDA cleared the way for Abbott to market Zemplar, a treatment for secondary hyperparathyroidism associated with chronic renal failure, and Synagis, a monoclonal antibody for the prevention of serious lower respiratory tract disease caused by respiratory syncytial virus (RSV) in pediatric patients. Nutrition news included the launching of Similac Lactose Free, the Ensure Glucerna nutritional bar, and Ensure Glucerna OS beverage. The last two products were formulated for diabetics to help them better manage their blood glucose levels.

As the century drew to a close, Abbott's product portfolio continued growing. In 1999 Abbott received USFDA clearance for Depacon, for the temporary treatment of certain types of epilepsy, and for PREVACID, for treatment of ulcers. Also that year, Abbott expanded its hospital products area when it acquired the parenteral products business of Sanofi Pharmaceuticals, Inc.; this move gave Abbott worldwide rights to pre-filled, single-dose syringe technology with Sanofi's proprietary Carpuject drug delivery system. Also, Abbott received approval for Norvir soft-gelatin capsules and the right to market Precedex (dexmedetomidine hydrochloride injection), a sedative for the use in patients hospitalized in intensive care settings.

STRATEGY

Committing itself to innovation, Abbott strives to push the limits of pharmaceutical science and product development. Its corporate strategy focuses on developing highly integrated franchise areas, specifically in anti-infectives, anti-virals, neuroscience, urology, vascular medicine, and oncology. Utilizing both internal and external resources, and employing more than 5,000 international scientists, the company is committed to developing innovative healthcare technologies. To support the advancement of medical science, the company spends more than $1 billion each year toward research and development. The company's drug discovery efforts involve teams of specialized scientists working with advanced technologies including genomics, structural biology, combinational chemistry, and Structure Activity Relationships (SAR) by Nuclear Magnetic Resonance (NMR).

In the area of genomic research, Abbott scientist employ bioinformatics to analyze genetic data that leads to better understanding of the human genetic code. In the area of structural biology, Abbott researchers employ computer modeling to study the three-dimensional shape of molecules responsible for causing disease. In the area of combinational chemistry, Abbott scientists catalogue more than 250,000 compounds for analyzing. Abbott scientists have used SAR by NMR to identify inhibitors of a family of enzymes that affect cancer metastasis and arthritis.

In its anti-infective research, Abbott focuses on the development of potential new uses for existing antibiotics, as well as developing the next generation of anti-infectives designed to safely and effectively defeat emerging drug-resistant pathogens.

INFLUENCES

Abbott's continual growth and success, especially in the last two decades of the twentieth century, can be attributed to its focus on research and development and in its pursuit of strategic alliances and acquisitions. This approach has enabled the company to assume market leadership positions in the areas of AIDS/anti-viral drugs, anti-infectives, neuroscience, urology, and oncology.

Abbott's pharmaceutical business grew to nearly $9 billion in 2001, thanks to the development of core products such as Depakote, Flomax, and Kaletra, as well as through key business acquisitions. The company's medical products business, which includes its diagnostics, hospital products, and nutritionals businesses, reached more than $7 billion in sales.

Abbott's diagnostic division has become the recognized leader in the laboratory testing of body fluids, and the company has continually sought new ways to detect infectious diseases. Research areas focus on immunodiagnostics, hematology, blood glucose monitoring, and DNA testing. In the late 1990s, Abbott researchers discovered a new strain of the hepatitis E virus and developed the world's first test to screen for HIV.

Another major focus for the company has been preventive health care through nutrition, which became a major concern for the U.S. population in the later part of the twentieth century. In the area of nutritionals, Abbott managed to take a top market position by utilizing the largest research industrial research team in the industry (more than 500 scientists). The company has developed and improved upon well-known products such as Similac infant formula and the Ensure brand of adult nutritionals.

CURRENT TRENDS

Abbott Laboratories has adopted an approach of innovation for sustained performance that is taking the company into the fields of biotechnology and molecular medicine. By combining biotechnology and traditional drug development, Abbott feels that it is creating a new model for pharmaceutical development. This, the company believes, will yield discoveries that have the potential to transform the practice of health care.

Abbott also feels that the companies best able to build on discoveries to create and commercialize differentiated, breakthrough products will have the advantage in the marketplace. To this end, Abbott acquired Knoll and formed an alliance with Millennium Pharmaceuticals, Inc. The acquisition of Knoll brought new scientific talent into the company, as well as new research centers in the United States, Germany, and Japan. Through its alliance with Millennium Pharmaceuticals, Abbott increased its investment in its genomics capability and established a major research program focused on diabetes and obesity. This, the company believes, will result in genetically based drugs and diagnostics to treat obesity and metabolism-related illnesses.

Also, Abbott strengthened itself in the area of genomics research with the acquisition of Vysis, Inc., a leading genomic disease management company. This acquisition brings with it new and innovative technology that detects subtle changes in genes and chromosomes. This, Abbott believes, will lead to a more precise diagnosis and monitoring of diseases.

Abbott also intends to build upon past successes. Since the 1930s, Abbott Laboratories has led discovery in the anesthesia market, and it continues seeking ways to develop new products in that area. Its Ross Product Division is in the process of developing next generation "Nutriceuticals," specially formulated products to help manage disease and enable self-treatment of lifestyle and health concerns.

PRODUCTS

Abbott Laboratories is involved in four significant business areas: nutritional products, pharmaceutical products, diagnostic products, and hospital products.

Abbott's nutritional brands are produced by its Ross Products Division, which has made the company a leader in adult and pediatric nutritionals. The adult products are designed to promote, maintain, and restore physical health. The division's best-known products include the adult nutritional product Ensure, and Similac and Similac 2, leading infant formulas. Other products include Isomil, NeoSure, Ensure Plus, Ensure High Protein, Ensure Light, PediaSure, Pedialyte, and Pulmocare. Most of those products are sold under the recommendation of healthcare professionals. The division's consumer products include Fact Plus Select and Fact Plus Pro pregnancy tests; Selsun Blue dandruff shampoo; and Murine eye care and ear care products.

Abbott's pharmaceutical products include anti-infective, cardiovascular, neuroscience, hormonal, and anti-ulcer drugs. The division produces a large line of adult and pediatric pharmaceuticals sold primarily by prescription or recommendation of physicians. Principal products include Depakote, Clarithromycin, Omnicef, Synthroid, TriCor, and the anti-virals Kaletra and Norvir (protease inhibitors for the treatment of HIV infection). Other products include Meridia for the treatment of obesity, Mavik and Tarka for the treatment of hypertension, and Vicodin and Vicoprofen for the treatment of pain.

Abbott's diagnostic products include diagnostic systems and tests for blood banks, hospitals, commercial laboratories, alternate care testing sites, and consumers. Principal products include reagents used to perform immunoassay tests (including Architect, AxSYM, IMx, and Abbott Quantum); Abbott PRISM; screening and diagnostic tests for hepatitis B, HTLV-I/II, hepatitis B core, and hepatitis C; tests for the detection of HIV antibodies and antigens, as well as other infectious disease detection systems; and cancer monitoring tests, including tests for prostate-specific antigens.

Other diagnostic products include the Vysis product line of genomic-based tests, including the PathVysion HER-2 DNA probe kit and the UroVysion bladder cancer recurrence kit; the LCx amplified probe system and reagents; the Abbott TestPack and Determine systems for rapid diagnostic testing; a full line of hematology systems and reagents known as the Cell-Dyn series; the MediSense product line of blood glucose monitoring meters, test strips, data management software, and accessories for diabetics, including Precision Xtra, MediSense Optium, Sof-Tact, Precision Q.I.D., MediSense II, ExacTech and ExacTech RSG, TrueMeasure strip technology, Precision Link Direct, and Precision Sure-Dose insulin syringes.

Hospital products include a full line of anesthetics, injectable drugs, infection-control products, diagnostic imaging agents, IV solutions, advanced drug-delivery systems, and other medical specialty products for hospitals, clinical labs, and alternate health care sites around the world. Specific products are hospital injectables including Carpuject and FirstChoice generics; ADD-Vantage and Nutrimix drug and nutritional delivery systems; anesthetics, including Pentothal, Amidate, Ultane, Isoflurane, and Enflurane; Precedex for sedation; cardiovascular products, including Corlopam; Calcijex and Zemplar, injectable agents for treatment of bone disease in hemodialysis patients; and parenteral nutritionals such as Aminosyn and Liposyn.

CORPORATE CITIZENSHIP

Abbott Laboratories values and champions corporate social responsibility about as much as it does innovation and research and development. The company has

MODEST BEGINNINGS

Abbott Laboratories' first product, "dosimetric granules," produced in the late 1880s by company founder Wallace Calvin Abbott, MD, was made from the active part of medicines. These granules enabled drugs to be precisely measured, which revolutionized the industry.

established the Abbott Laboratories Fund, which contributes millions of dollars each year to health and human service organizations and sponsors programs that enhance science education, promote diversity, and provide access to healthcare for people in need. Through the fund, the company matches gifts employees make to hospitals, universities, secondary and elementary schools, and public broadcasting. The company also supports local communities through employee volunteerism and donations. Cash donations have helped support the United Way, the American Cancer Society, the American Heart Association, and other health and human service organizations.

Abbott also partners with health and human service organizations around the world, donating health care products to help alleviate human suffering. In recent years, Abbott has supported relief efforts for victims of the earthquakes in western Turkey, Taiwan, and Colombia; flooding in Venezuela; and the refugee crisis in Kosovo.

Abbott Laboratories also advocates environmental responsibility. It has developed ongoing partnerships with community organizations to provide education, opportunities for collaboration, and resources for environmental initiatives.

GLOBAL PRESENCE

Abbott's International segment produces a broad line of hospital, pharmaceutical, and adult and pediatric nutritional products marketed and primarily manufactured outside the United States. This segment also includes consumer products. While the largest part of Abbott Laboratories' sales are generated in the United States (63 percent), the company does 5 percent of its business in Japan, 4 percent in Germany, 3 percent in Italy, 3 percent in Canada, and approximately 20 percent in other countries.

Abbott has entered into joint business ventures with organizations around the world including Takeda Chemical Industries, Ltd. and Taisho Pharmaceutical Co., Ltd. (Japan), Antisoma plc (United Kingdom), Karo Bio AB (Sweden), and NeuroSearch A/S (Denmark).

EMPLOYMENT

Abbott Laboratories embraces a corporate culture that fosters workplace diversity, career encouragement, and a commitment to excellence and achievement, especially toward advancing science and the practice of healthcare. For its employees, it provides a full range of benefits in a nationally recognized package, as well as training and development opportunities across the entire company. (*Money* magazine has ranked the company's benefits package as one of the ten best in the United States.

Fortune magazine ranked Abbott Laboratories as one of the "Top 50 Companies for Minorities" for four consecutive years, while *Working Mother* magazine named it one of the "Best Companies for Working Mothers."

SOURCES OF INFORMATION

Bibliography
BioScorpio. "Abbott Laboratories," 1 April 2002. Available at http://www.bioscorpio.com/abbott_laboratories_inc.htm.

Chicagotribune.com. "Company Profile-Abbott Laboratories." *CareerBuilder*, 1 April 2001. Available at http://hire.chicagotribune.com.

Hoover's Online. "Abbott Laboratories," 28 March 2002. Available at http://www.hoovers.com.

NFIA. "Abbott Laboratories." *Company Profiles*, 2002. Available at http://www.nfia.com.

Spaulding, B.J. "Abbott Laboratories: Monkish No More." *Pharmacogenomic Medicine*, 31 August 1999. Available at http://www.biospace.com/articles/.

Yahoo! Finance. "Abbott Laboratories." *Yahoo Market Guide*, 28 March 2002. Available at http://biz.yahoo.com.

For an annual report:
on the Internet at: http://www.knoll-pharma.com/investor/annual_reports.html

For additional industry research:
Investigate companies by their Standard Industrial Classification Codes, also known as SICs. Abbott Laboratories' primary SICs are:

2099 Food Preparations, Not Elsewhere Classified

2834 Pharmaceutical Preparations

2844 Perfumes and Cosmetics

3841 Surgical And Medical Instruments

Also investigate companies by their North American Industry Classification System codes, also known as NAICS codes. Abbott Laboratories' primary NAICS codes are:

311423 Dried and Dehydrated Food Manufacturing

325412 Pharmaceutical Preparation Manufacturing

325620 Toilet Preparation Manufacturing

339112 Surgical and Medical Instrument Manufacturing

Airborne, Inc.

FOUNDED: 1968 as Airborne Freight Corp.

Contact Information:

HEADQUARTERS: 3101 Western Ave.
 Seattle, WA 98111
PHONE: (206)285-4600
FAX: (206)281-1444
TOLL FREE: (800)247-2676
URL: http://www.airborne.com

OVERVIEW

The third-largest airfreight express delivery operation in the United States, behind UPS and FedEx, Airborne, Inc. is a Fortune 500 company with more than $3 billion in annual sales. The firm's Airborne Express unit specializes in overnight deliveries to large corporations. Another subsidiary, ABX Air, oversees Airborne's fleet of 120 airplanes and 15,000 trucks, as well as the firm's Wilmington, Ohio-based package sorting terminal. Along with operating ten regional hubs in the United States, Airborne offers its shipping services at more than 300 facilities serving more than 200 countries.

COMPANY FINANCES

Sales at Airborne fell from $3.276 billion to $3.211 billion in 2001. The firm posted a $19.5 million loss that year. In fact, profits had steadily declined since 1998, when they reached their peak at $137.3 million. While Airborne did achieve meager sales gains in both 1999 and 2000, this modest growth paled in comparison to that realized by rivals such as FedEx, UPS, and Yellow, thanks to the booming North American economy. Airborne's stock performance reflected its struggles. After reaching a high of $42.88 per share in 1998, stock prices dropped consistently for the next three years. In 2001, stock ranged from a low of $7.00 per share to a high of $15.08 per share.

ANALYSTS' OPINIONS

Of concern to many analysts in the early 2000s was the fact that Airborne had not seen significant sales growth in the economic boom years of 1999 and 2000. Some pointed to this as an indication that Airborne had failed to identify the key growth markets in its industry, such as Internet-based logistics, which is essentially the use of Internet technology to coordinate all aspects of freight shipping, from ordering and pick-up to payment and delivery. While the firm had held a reputation as a leader in logistics for many years, some analysts believed that its adoption of Internet technology was too slow. In addition, many felt that the firm suffered from its failure to diversify its services to the extent its competitors had. With the express shipping services of rivals like UPS and FedEx growing faster than Airborne, the firm found itself losing market share in the late 1990s and early 2000s. To make matters worse, due to its lack of diversification, the firm did not have many other business segments on which to rely.

In late 2000, when Airborne reshuffled its management team and revealed plans to diversify into ground shipping services, the firm's outlook appeared to improve. Stock recommendations in 2001 and 2002 were mixed. Some analysts believed that the lower prices of Airborne stock would prove to be a bargain as Airborne was a company on the road to recovery; others were less certain that the move into ground shipping, where competition between the likes of UPS and FedEx was already fierce, would prove lucrative for the firm.

FAST FACTS:
About Airborne, Inc.

Ownership: Airborne, Inc. is a publicly owned company traded on the New York Stock Exchange.

Ticker Symbol: ABF

Officers: Robert S. Cline, Chmn., 64, 2001 base salary $675,000; Robert G. Brazier, VChmn., 64, 2001 base salary $575,000; Carl Donaway, Pres. and CEO, 50, 2001 base salary $500,000; Lanny H. Michael, EVP and CFO, 50, 2001 base salary $275,000

Employees: 32,000

Principal Subsidiary Companies: Airborne, Inc. is the parent company of three main subsidiaries: Airborne Express, Inc.; ABX Air, Inc.; and Sky Courier, Inc.

Chief Competitors: The two largest rivals of Airborne, Inc. are FedEx Corp. and United Parcel Service (UPS) Inc. The firm also competes with airlines like Delta and US Airways, trucking companies like American Freightways and Yellow Corp., and the U.S. Postal Service.

HISTORY

Airborne Freight Corp. was created in 1968 when Seattle, Washington-based Pacific Air Freight Inc., an air freight forwarder founded in 1947, merged with another freight forwarding firm, San Francisco, California-based Airborne. The young air freight company began to consider a move into express delivery, particularly the overnight delivery of letters and small parcels, in the late 1970s. To gain entrance into this market, Airborne acquired Midwest Air Charter and an airport in Wilmington, Ohio, in 1980. Airborne was able to make such purchases thanks to the late 1970s deregulation of the airline industry, which had removed restrictions on who could buy commercial airplanes and airports. Eventually, the firm focused the bulk of its efforts on express air-freight operations.

Initially, breaking into the express air delivery industry proved difficult due to the strength of industry giant Federal Express. Aggressive marketing campaigns that focused on the speed with which Airborne could make deliveries helped the firm eventually establish itself as a viable contender. Sales reached $630 million in 1987. By then, Airborne had become the third largest air freight

company in the United States, with a 12 percent share of the industry. (However, its sales continued to pale in comparison to the $8.6 billion in revenues achieved by UPS and the $3.2 billion in revenues secured by Federal Express.) Also that year, IBM Corp. awarded Airborne a three-year contract to handle all of its express air mail under 150 pounds in weight. Airborne purchased Sky Courier, a same day delivery service provider, in 1988. Shipments increased by 40 percent the following year, despite intense competition throughout the industry.

When FedEx began to target many of Airborne's corporate customers in 1991, Airborne responded by reducing its rates. Sales that year reached $1 billion for the first time. Airborne Logistics Services was created in 1993 to offer warehousing and distribution services to companies. Growth continued throughout the 1990s, fueled by things like the well-publicized UPS strike in 1997. That year, Airborne saw its stock prices triple. Record profits boosted Airborne into the ranks of the Fortune 500 in 1998. The following year, the U.S. Postal Service and Airborne jointly created Airborne@home as a delivery service for online merchants shipping products to customers' homes.

FINANCES:

Airborne, Inc.
Revenues, 1998-2001
(million dollars)

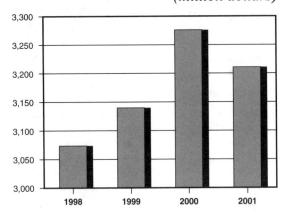

Airborne, Inc.
2001 Stock Prices
(dollars)

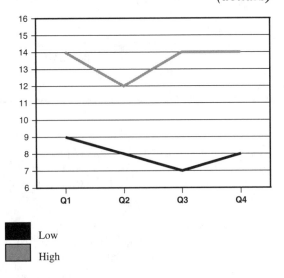

■ Low

▨ High

The firm's performance began a slow, steady decline in the late 1990s. A management shakeup in 2000 resulted in the promotion of Carl Donaway to the position of president. In an effort to boost its ability to compete with increasingly diversified firms like FedEx, Airborne launched ground service in 2001. The firm also upgraded its Web site. Sluggish demand and declining market share prompted the lay off of 640 workers, roughly 2.5 percent of Airborne's workforce, that year.

STRATEGY

When Airborne first entered the express air freight industry in the early 1980s, it faced competition from established giant Federal Express, as well as from a host of smaller rivals, such as Emery Air Freight and Purolator Courier Corp. To gain a foothold in the industry, Airborne launched an aggressive marketing strategy that included television advertisements. The ads were designed to not only showcase Airborne's delivery speed, but also to portray Federal Express as an impersonal corporate giant. The strategy proved successful, and Airborne saw its number of shipments, as well as its sales and profits, grow throughout the mid-1980s. Shipments grew from 5.7 million packages in 1982 to 35.0 million packages in 1987. By then, Airborne had secured 12 percent of the U.S. express air market.

Also important to Airborne's success in the 1980s was its strategy of focusing on offering speedy air freight services to corporate clients. By narrowing its focus to corporations, Airborne was able to tailor its services to meet the specific needs of corporate clients. For example, the firm offered modestly priced pickup on demand services, which meant that businesses could call Airborne to pick up a package whenever it was ready, rather that attempting to have a package ready for a prescheduled pickup. To win contracts, the firm also offered special discounts to certain firms. As a result, companies like IBM Corp. began to negotiate long-term delivery service contracts with Airborne. While this tight focus served the firm well throughout the remainder of the decade and into the early 1990s, by the late 1990s, it had become clear to management that a new strategy was needed. Several new managers were hired in 2000, and they began to work on turning around what was by then a struggling firm. Key elements of the firm's new strategy included launching ground shipping services and increasing its use of Internet technology, both of which happened in 2001. What impact these initiatives will have on the firm's performance remains to be seen.

INFLUENCES

Perhaps most influential in Airborne's decision to diversify into three- and four-day ground shipping was the fact that Airborne's express delivery service had actually started to grow more slowly than the express services of FedEx and UPS, both of which were focused on offering increasingly comprehensive delivery services. The firm's narrow focus had once allowed it to outperform rivals in the next-day and two-day delivery market segments; however, the lack of diversification had become a liability by the late 1990s. According to an August 2000 article in *Air Cargo World*, "The carrier's strict adherence to basic overnight and second-day service has helped keep costs down, a key factor as it seeks to come in below UPS on the rate scale. But the opera-

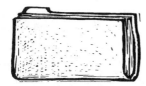

FLOWERS AT THE ROOT OF AIRBORNE

Airborne's main predecessor company, Airborne Freight of California, was founded in 1946 in San Francisco as the Airborne Flower Traffic Association of California. Its original purpose was to transport, via air, fresh flowers from the Hawaiian Islands to California for sale in the mainland states.

tional restrictions also keep Airborne in something of a straightjacket as it tries to respond to market conditions."

CURRENT TRENDS

The trend of intermodalism, whereby air freight services work in conjunction with trains, boats, and trucks to complete deliveries, became increasingly important to all types of fright companies, including Airborne, in the late 1990s. Using other modes of transportation to complete deliveries (typically via alliances with other shipping companies) has allowed Airborne, Inc. to expand internationally. For example, the firm uses ocean freight operations to complete many of its international deliveries. Like many other freight companies, Airborne also continues to focus on using Internet technology to improve internal operations and to extend a variety of services to its clients. In November 2001, Airborne added two online shipping systems to its Web site: ShipExchange, which allows small businesses and individuals to manage their shipping needs online; and CorporateExchange, which allows several individuals within a corporation to complete various shipping tasks, depending on their level of clearance.

PRODUCTS

While overnight and two-day services remain Airborne's largest revenue generators, the firm also offers same-day and next-flight-out services via its Sky Courier subsidiary. Airborne@Home offers business-to-resident delivery services. Logistics services include warehousing, distribution, time-specific distribution, and product retrieval. International services include customs clear-

CHRONOLOGY:
Key Dates for Airborne, Inc.

1968: Airborne of California and Pacific Air Freight merge to form Airborne Freight Corp.

1980: Airborne begins offering express air delivery services

1987: IBM Corp. awards Airborne a three-year contract to handle all of its express air mail under 150 pounds in weight

1988: Airborne purchases same day delivery service provider Sky Courier

1991: Sales reach $1 billion

1998: Airborne becomes a Fortune 500 company

2001: Airborne begins offering ground delivery services

ance and ocean freight. In addition, new three- and four-day ground delivery services were launched in April 2001.

GLOBAL PRESENCE

International expansion intensified at Airborne in the early 1990s. For example, Airborne and two Japanese firms, Mitsui and Panther Express, created Airborne Express Japan in 1990. Airborne maintained a 40 percent stake in its Japanese subsidiary. Within a few years, Airborne had become the fourth-largest Japanese air freight carrier. IBM merged its international operations with those of Airborne in 1993. The firm also began to make use of ocean freight carriers, a less expensive alternative for international shipping, in 1994; in fact, Airborne was the first express service to offer ocean shipping. By the mid-1990s, offices in Australia, New Zealand, and the United Kingdom were in operation. The firm also had forged alliances with established air freight carriers in Canada and Thailand. Airborne had extended its reach to nearly 90 percent of the major world markets. In 2001, international deliveries accounted for 11 percent of total sales, and more than 300 shipping facilities operated in roughly 200 countries.

SOURCES OF INFORMATION

Bibliography

"Airborne Freight Corp." *International Directory of Company Histories.* Detroit: Gale Group, 1992.

Airborne, Inc. Home Page, 2002. Available at http://www.airborne.com.

"Airborne Reports Fourth Quarter and Year-End 2000 Results." *PR Newswire*, 1 February 2001.

"Airborne Reports Fourth Quarter and Year-End 2001 Results." *PR Newswire*, 1 February 2002.

Gille, John. "Seattle-Based Airborne Notes Net Loss of $19.5 Million for 2001." *Fortune*, 2 February 2002. Available from http://www.fortune.com.

Page, Paul. "Getting Airborne." *Air Cargo World*, August 2000.

For an annual report:

on the Internet at: http://www.airborne.com

For additional industry research:

Investigate companies by their Standard Industrial Classification Codes, also known as SICs. Airborne, Inc.'s primary SICs are:

4213 Trucking, Except Local

4731 Arrangement of Transportation of Freight and Cargo

6719 Holding Companies, Not Elsewhere Classified

Also investigate companies by their North American Industry Classification System codes, also known as NAICS codes. Airborne, Inc.'s primary NAICS codes are:

488510 Freight Transportation Arrangement

492110 Couriers

551112 Offices of Other Holding Companies

Albertson's Inc.

FOUNDED: 1939

OVERVIEW

Albertson's Inc. is the second largest grocery store chain in the United States. With 2,549 stores in 36 states, the Boise, Idaho-based grocery chain posted revenues of $37.9 billion for fiscal year 2001, up from just 826 stores and $13 billion in revenues in 1996. The company's main operations are food and drugstore combination supermarkets with 1,977 of its stores housing a full-service pharmacy. Most stores range in size from 35,000 up to 107,000 square feet. More than one-half of the stores have added services such as full-service meat and fish counters, one-hour photo processing services, and floral departments. A smaller number of stores offer other amenities including coffee bars, in-store banks, and fuel centers. In 1999 Albertson's completed a merger with American Stores, adding 1,558 grocery stores and 750 stand-alone drug stores to the company under the banners of Jewel Osco, Acme Markets, Sav-on, and Osco Drug stores. Albertson's also operates no-frills discount warehouse stores under the names Max Foods and Super Saver, which specialize in discount meat and produce.

Contact Information:

HEADQUARTERS: 250 Parkcenter Blvd.
   Boise, ID 83726
PHONE: (208)395-6200
FAX: (208)395-6349
TOLL FREE: (888)746-7252
EMAIL: cs_online@albertsons.com
URL: http://www.albertsons.com

COMPANY FINANCES

In fiscal year 2001, Albertson's sales totaled $37.9 billion, up from $36.8 billion in fiscal 2000, representing an increase of 3.2 percent and $1.1 billion. However, Albertson's 1999 merger with American Stores, which immediately pushed revenue up from $14.7 billion in 1998 to $35.9 billion in 1999, cost the company $12 billion and a good portion of its market value, causing the company to miss sales and earnings estimates for several

FAST FACTS:
About Albertson's Inc.

Ownership: Albertson's is a publicly owned company traded on the New York Stock Exchange and the Pacific Stock Exchange.

Ticker Symbol: ABS

Officers: Lawrence R. Johnston, Chmn. and CEO, 52, 2001 salary $1,250,000; Peter L. Lynch, VP and COO, 49, 2000 salary $460,406, 2000 bonus $402,321; Felicia D. Thornton, EVP and CFO, 37, 2001 salary $540,000

Employees: 235,000

Principal Subsidiary Companies: When Albertson's purchased American Stores in 1999, it added several regional supermarket and drugstore chains to its organization, including Philadelphia-based Acme Markets and Chicago-based Jewel supermarkets, along with Osco Drug and Sav-On drugstores. The company also does business through its no-frills discount warehouse stores under the names Max Foods and Super Saver.

Chief Competitors: As the nation's second largest grocery store chain, Albertson's main competition comes other traditional grocery chains as well as discount supercenters. Some major competitors are Kroger, Safeway, and Wal-Mart.

years following the deal. Stocks were trading at slightly more than $33 a share in April 2002, compared to a high of $67.13 a share in December of 1998. Net earnings for fiscal 2001 totaled $795 million, up from $870 million in fiscal 2000. However, when adjusted to reflect the cost of restructuring, net earnings drop to $501 million, down from adjusted net earnings of $765 million in fiscal 2000. The significant decrease in actual earnings represents the major cost of restructuring caused by the American Stores acquisition.

ANALYSTS' OPINIONS

The retail grocery market is notorious for its low profit margins. Accordingly, analysts have generally viewed Albertson's purchase of American Stores as a significant risk. However, the move also positioned Albert-

son's for the most potential for gain, compared to its chief competitors Kroger and Safeway. Analysts differ in their opinions on the ability of Albertson's to complete its turnaround, regain its market value, and post consistent profits. Nonetheless, most saw the appointment of former General Electric executive Lawrence Johnston as Albertson's new chief executive officer in April 2001, as a step in the right direction. Johnston immediately announced the closure of 165 unprofitable stores, followed by the sale of 80 Osco pharmacies in the Northeast, signaling investors that the company is willing to take difficult steps to cut costs and focus on growing markets. Analysts continue to view Albertson's stock as a positive investment, likely to increase in value in the long term, but they warn that the company's future remains at the wait-and-see stage.

HISTORY

Albertson's was founded by Joe Albertson, who opened his first grocery store in Boise, Idaho, in 1939. Profits for the first year of operation were a respectable $9,000, but just two years later, Albertson had opened two more stores and sales topped $1 million. In 1945 Albertson incorporated his company as Albertson's Inc. and, by the end of the 1940s, six Albertson's stores were in operation in Idaho with annual sales nearing $3 million. Albertson had also opened the Stone Poultry Company, a poultry processing operation, and the Dutch Girl Ice Cream Plant in Boise, with the Dutch Girl becoming the company's trademark.

During the 1950s Albertson began expanding beyond the borders of Idaho, opening stores in Montana, Oregon, Utah, and Washington. Although Albertson experimented with a few department stores, he soon phased out these operations to focus on the grocery business. In the grocery stores, Albertson continued to push for innovation, and in 1951 the first store appeared with an in-house drug store. In 1957 Albertson's purchased Sugarhouse Drug of Salt Lake City, Utah, and began systematically incorporating pharmacies into its stores. The first frozen food distribution center opened in 1957, and a frozen food storage facility opened in Boise in 1958. In 1959 Albertson's introduced its own line of products under the brand name Janet Lee, named after the executive vice president's daughter. When the company went public in the same year, the funds generated from stock sales fueled increasing expansion.

In 1961 Albertson's expanded into Wyoming by acquiring three grocery stores in Casper, and the following year Albertson's opened its one-hundredth store. In 1964 operations expanded into California with the purchase of 14 supermarkets belonging to Los Angeles-based Greater All American Markets. In the same year, Albertson stepped down as chief executive, although he remained as chairman of the board. J. L. Berlin became the company's second chief executive. Two years later, Jonathan Scott, Albertson's son-in-law, who was already serving as the company's president, replaced Berlin as chief executive officer. Through the remainder of the 1960s, Albertson's continued to expand through acquisitions and construction of new stores. In 1965 the purchase of eight markets owned by Semrau and Sons, based in Oakland, California, gave the company a stronger foothold in California. In 1967 eight stores were acquired in Colorado from Furr's, Inc. The company was listed for the first time on the New York Stock Exchange in 1969, and by 1970 Albertson's operated 200 stores with sales exceeding $400 million.

In 1969 Scott signed a deal with L. S. Skaggs, Jr., the son of his father-in-law's former partner, to develop six combination food and drug superstores in Texas in conjunction with Skaggs Drugs Centers. The stores, jointly financed and managed by the partners, took the next step in the transformation of the grocery store into the supercenter. Whereas even large supermarkets of the day averaged 30,000 square feet, the Skaggs-Albertson's stores were as large as 55,000 square feet. Also, a new emphasis was placed on nonfood items; new departments such as cosmetics, perfumes, camera supplies, and electrical equipment were added. The first store opened in Texas in 1970. Along with the new venture into Texas, Albertson's paid close attention to its other stores, constantly remodeling, updating, and even rebuilding or closing outdated locations. Scott's plan was twofold: stay ahead of the industry in innovation, services, and convenience and increase sales of nonfood items, which returned a higher rate of profit than food goods. The strategy paid off. By 1974 sales topped $850 million and net earnings neared $9 million. The following year sales surpassed the $1 billion mark.

In 1974 Albertson's ran into trouble with the United States Justice Department, who contested Albertson's 1972 acquisition of Mountain States Wholesale of Idaho. The Justice Department argued that because Albertson's was already the largest grocery chain in the region, the addition of Mountain States, which controlled 43 percent of the market share, constituted a monopoly. Despite Albertson's objections that the suit was baseless, the settlement, reached in 1977, required Albertson's to divest of Mountain States and placed a five-year ban on any further grocery acquisitions in southern Idaho or eastern Oregon. The company also came under fire from the Federal Trade Commission in 1974, which found fault with Albertson's advertising practices. As a result, the company was ordered to issue rain checks for on-sale items no longer in stock.

Although Skaggs and Albertson's considered merging, the idea was eventually put aside and, in 1977, the partnership was amicably dissolved with the assets split equally. Albertson's created the subsidiary Southco to assume control of the stores. Throughout the 1970s, conventional stores were phased out and the company focused on larger combination stores. Acquisitions also

continued, including the purchase of 46 supermarkets in the Los Angeles area owned by Fisher Foods, Inc. As the economy went into recession at the end of the 1970s, Albertson's sought to cut overhead by converting several of its stores into mass-merchandise warehouses with a no-frills emphasis on nonfood items. The stores were profitable, but never replaced the mainstream supermarket venue. Still working to stay ahead of the industry, during the 1970s 87 percent of all Albertson's stores were either newly opened or completely remodeled. Also during the decade Albertson's opened its first full-line distribution facilities in Brea, California, and Salt Lake City in 1973 and 1976, respectively.

During the 1980s Albertson's focused on restructuring and building existing markets. In 1982 the company reorganized into four region operating groups: California, northwest, intermountain, and Southco. Two more distribution centers were built in Denver and Portland. To build business in existing markets, Albertson's launched a new advertising campaign that promoted "every day low costs." Rather than running ongoing special promotions and sales as was the norm in the industry, Albertson's advertised that they wouldn't advertise specials, and the money saved would be passed on to customers. The technique helped Albertson's break into the competitive Dallas market, one of the few new areas into which the company expanded in the 1980s.

In 1991 the company unveiled a five-year, $2.7 billion modernization and expansion plan through renovation, new construction, and a company-wide push toward automation. The next year Albertson's purchased 74 Jewel Osco combination food and drug stores owned by American Stores in Arkansas, Florida, Oklahoma, and Texas. By 1994 the company had become the nation's sixth largest grocery chain, with more than 500 stores in operation. In 1999 Albertson's merged with American Stores, which instantly jumped the company to the second place in the industry, behind Kroger. To gain the Federal Trade Commission's approval for the $12 billion deal, Albertson's sold 145 stores in areas where the markets overlapped. In 2000 Albertson's abandoned its regional organizational structure and turned over more control of operations to the division-level managers.

STRATEGY

Albertson's claims to provide convenience, quality, and variety under one roof. Its strategic focus includes finding solutions to customer needs, pharmacy service, online shopping, cost reduction, and increasing return on capital. To meet customers' needs, Albertson's uses the tag line "It's your store," suggesting that its stores are tailored to provide services and products desired by today's shoppers at value prices. In 2001 Albertson's launched a new customer service program, "Service First, Second to None." The program audits individual stores by a list of customer service criteria with rewards given

CHRONOLOGY:

Key Dates for Albertson's Inc.

1939: Joe Albertson, in partnership with L. S. Skaggs and Tom Cuthbert, opens the first Albertson's Food Center in Boise, Idaho

1945: Albertson dissolves the partnership and incorporates as Albertson's, Inc.

1959: Offers stock to the public to fund expansion; operating 62 stores in four states by 1960

1963: Opens its one-hundredth store

1969: Albertson's is listed on the New York Stock Exchange for the first time

1970: Operates more than 200 stores with sales in excess of $400 million

1975: Corporate sales exceed $1 billion

1985: Sales hit record high of $5 billion

1989: Has highest net earnings of any U.S. food chain, with 497 stores, 127 combination food and drug stores, 175 super stores, 167 supermarkets, and 38 warehouse stores operating in 17 states

1997: Net income surpasses $516 million, marking the twenty-eighth consecutive year of net income increase

2000: Launches $500 million common stock repurchase plan

2002: Operates more than 2,500 stores in 36 states

---

for achieving specific goals. New incentives for employees were also put in place. By building loyalty with its employees, which are considered the company's "best customers," Albertson's hopes to positively impact sales. The "Associate Advantage" program uses sweepstakes and shopping incentives to encourage employee purchases.

The company is also in the process of testing a new loyalty card program, based on a similar successful program operated by the Jewel stores for the last 10 years. Moving to improve the public's perception of its pricing, Albertson's has become diligent in tracking its pricing and promotions. Battling its trendy image for slightly higher prices, the company now claims that its prices are at parity or better than other grocery chains in 15 of the 20 largest markets. Increased emphasis has also been placed

on promotions, which has assisted in revising Albertson's image as a high-line chain. In another move to cut prices, in 2001 Albertson's began the process of restructuring its distribution system, which was previously operated as separate entities that sold to Albertson's stores for a profit. The reorganization will lower the cost of inventory to the individual stores, allowing them to increase their competitive edge in their market areas.

Although it continues to maintain a small number of traditional grocery stores, Albertson's strategy is to develop the food and drug combination store to create centers of convenience that provide a wide range of products along with high quality service. Particular emphasis is targeted for California, Arizona, and Nevada, where Albertson's hopes to capitalize on its distinct brands such as Sav-On, thus copying the success of the Jewel Osco units.

Within its stores, Albertson's is focusing on improving its perishable products, especially its fresh produce selection. Measures include improving temperature management in storage and in transit, improve procurement and quality assurance, and increased focus on displays and store presentation. Another in-store area of strategic importance is the increased sale of the company's private label products. Albertson's corporate brands make up 17 percent of units sold, which lags significantly behind Kroger's 31 percent. Albertson's sees this area as a key goal for the company to build both profits and customer loyalty.

INFLUENCES

Not only does Albertson's face stiff competition from its traditional rivals, Kroger and Safeway, the company also faces increasing pressure from a new breed of supercenter retailers. Wal-Mart has already made a strong impact in the grocery and drug store markets, and Target and Kmart are both making plans to significantly increase the number of food and drug combination stores operating under their respective banners. To keep up, Albertson's began to focus on its food and drug combination stores, which offer variety, convenience, and service. Additionally, the company is promising to maintain its growth by continuing to open new stores. In 2001, 145 new stores opened and 110 new stores are planned to open in 2002. Also 75 existing stores were remodeled in 2001, and Albertson's plans to step up its remodeling pace in the years to come.

CURRENT TRENDS

Pharmacies are considered a vital part of Albertson's products and services package. With more than 800 stand-alone drug stores under the banners of Sav-On and

Osco, Albertson's is slowly moving its stores out of shopping centers to corner locations where a drive-though window can assist pharmacy customers. Albertson's also centralized its pharmacy operations to better coordinate its health product services. The company is making plans to expand its fuel center program and is experimenting with nontraditional stores and locations. For example, Albertson's has expanded from the suburbs back into the inner city, building a store in a Chicago high-rise and another in San Francisco that will house 400 condominiums above the store.

Online shopping was introduced in 1999. Customers in 36 western Washington locations can shop at albertsons.com, with the option for delivery or in-store pick-up. Savon.com offers customers nationwide the ability to order prescriptions online. The site also provides a selection of 18,000 over-the-counter products along with health-related information.

PRODUCTS

After the merger with American Stores, Albertson's combined its store-brand products with American Stores products under a single label, Corporate Brand. Along with its store brand selection, the company developed new specialty labels, including Village Market meats, Timberwood wines, and Identity bath and beauty products. Quick Fixin' meal ideas were introduced in 1996 for customers in need of quick, nutritious, easy meal ideas. Weekly recipe ideas that can be made in 30 minutes or less are placed at the front of stores with all the ingredients located in one place. Albertson's product line also includes eight prepackaged heat-and-serve dinners.

CORPORATE CITIZENSHIP

Albertson's takes seriously its commitment both to the local communities in which it operates and the overall environment. To help reduce waste, the company began using plastic pallets in 1997 to ship products between distribution centers and stores. The pallets, which at 20 pounds weigh only one third of a traditional wooden pallet, help reduce fuel consumption, last up to 60 times longer, and are fully recyclable. For smaller stores and pharmacies, products are shipped in reusable plastic containers and returned to the distribution centers filled with recyclable goods from the stores. Albertson's has had a cardboard recycling policy in place since the late 1960s. In 2000 the company recycled 318,000 tons of cardboard as well as 34,000 tons of other resources. Other innovative strategies have been implemented to reduce waste. For example, in the past, ice cream was wasted at the Boise, Idaho, ice cream plant each time flavors were alternated as the two flavors became mixed. Now compatible flavors are produced back to back and

THE BEGINNINGS

In 1939 Joe Albertson quit his job as a district manager for Safeway Stores and opened the first Albertson's in Boise, Idaho. With the financial backing of L.S. Skaggs, whose family helped build the Safeway empire, and Skaggs' accountant, Tom Cuthbert, Albertson hoped to create the largest food store in the state. Indeed, the first store was 10,000 square feet, nearly eight times larger than the average grocery store of the day. Albertson also stocked his store with innovations, such as an in-store bakery, a magazine section, and ice cream parlor. Albertson's new superstore helped usher in the age of one-stop shopping.

the resulting mixtures are labeled as "Odds & Ends" and sold or donated locally. In 2000 Albertson's donated in excess of $48 million in cash and in-kind gifts to help meet community needs, including more than 20 million pounds of food.

EMPLOYMENT

Albertson's offers employment opportunities in numerous areas. At the corporate level, the information systems and technology department hires both experienced professionals and trainees, as does its store development and financial departments. Constantly growing with ambitious plans for store expansion or renovation, Albertson's hopes to attract or develop high quality personnel in the fields of accounting, architecture, engineering, construction, design, real estate, legal, economic research, and purchasing. Most management level positions are filled from current employees, and most employees join the Albertson's team at an entry-level position. Training programs and internships are available in the following areas: financial department, pharmacy, warehouse and distribution, and grocery management.

SOURCES OF INFORMATION

Bibliography
"Albertson's Announced Market Exits; *eNewswire,* 13 March 2002.

"Albertson's Reports Strong Quarterly Sales Results, Earnings Meet Wall Street Expectations and Company Guidance." Company News Release, 4 December 2001. Available at http://www .albertsons.com.

"Closing Division Offices." *PR Newswire,* 13 March 2002.

Duff, Mike. "'New Breed' Rivals Put Albertson's in a Bind." *DSN Retailing Today,* 6 August 2001.

Gentry, Connie Robbins. "Recession-Resistant." *Chain Store Age*, February 2002.

Gibbs, Lisa. "Supermarket Sweep." *Money,* January 2002.

Kepos, Paula, ed. *International Directory of Company Histories,* Vol. 7. Detroit: St. James Press, 1993.

Regent, Nancy, ed. *Hoover's Handbook of American Business.* Austin, TX: Hoover's Business Press, 2001.

For an annual report:

on the Internet at: http://www1.albertsons.com/corporate

For additional industry research:

Investigate companies by their Standard Industrial Classification Codes, also known as SICs. Albertson Inc.'s primary SICs are:

5411 Grocery Stores

5912 Drug Stores and Proprietary Stores

Also investigate companies by their North American Industry Classification System codes, also known as NAICS codes. Albertson Inc.'s primary NAICS codes are:

311520 Ice Cream and Frozen Dessert Manufacturing

445110 Supermarkets and Other Grocery (except Convenience) Stores

446110 Pharmacies and Drug Stores

Allstate Corporation

OVERVIEW

Coming in behind insurance giant State Farm, Allstate Corporation ranks as the second-largest U.S. home and auto insurance company, holding 13 percent of the market share. It also ranks number 17 as the largest life insurer and holds the largest market capitalization ($24 billion) of all personal line insurers in the nation. The company operates two main business segments: Allstate Personal Property and Casualty and Allstate Financial. Allstate Personal Property and Casualty provides private passenger auto and homeowners' insurance along with other specialty coverage to more than 14 million households, serviced by approximately 13,000 exclusive Allstate agents in the United States and Canada. Auto insurance accounts make up 70 percent of its insurance premiums revenue. Allstate Financial offers life and annuity products, such as whole life, traditional term, and variable life, as well as fixed and variable annuities, through Allstate Life, Deerbrook Insurance, and Glenbrook Life. As of September 20, 2001, Allstate's assets totaled $108.6 billion dollars and the company held $17.3 billion in equity.

COMPANY FINANCES

Allstate's net income for 2001 was $1.2 billion on revenues of $28.9 billion. These figures reflect a 47.6 percent decrease in net income and a less than one percent decrease in revenues compared to the previous year's net income of $2.2 billion on $29.1 in revenues. In turn, the $2.2 billion profit posted in 2000 was down from a net income of more than $2.7 billion in 1999. Shares of All-

FOUNDED: 1931

Contact Information:

HEADQUARTERS: 2775 Sanders Road
   Northbrook, IL 60062
PHONE: (847)402-5000
FAX: (847)402-2351
TOLL FREE: (800)547-3553
URL: http://www.allstate.com

FAST FACTS:

About Allstate Corporation

Ownership: Allstate is a publicly owned company traded on the New York Stock Exchange.

Ticker Symbol: ALL

Officers: Edward M. Liddy, Chmn., Pres., and CEO, 55, 2001 base salary $990,000, 2001 bonus $103,356; John L. Carl, VP and CFO, 53, 2001 base salary $473,200, 2001 bonus $265,687; Thomas J. Wilson II, Pres. Allstate Financial, 43, 2001 base salary $510,050, 2001 bonus $404,485; Richard I. Cohen, SVP and Pres. Allstate Property & Casualty, 56, 2001 base salary $540,000, 2001 bonus $206,464

Employees: 41,800

Principal Subsidiary Companies: Allstate Corporation serves as a holding company for its two main divisions: Allstate Personal Property and Casualty; and Allstate Financial. Its other interests include Allstate Bank, American Heritage Life Investment Corporation, Deerbrook Insurance Company, Encompass Insurance, and Sterling Collision Centers, Inc.

Chief Competitors: Allstate's primary competition for its auto and homeowner products comes from State Farm, which leads the industry. Increasingly tough competition is also coming from discount insurance companies, such as GEICO and Progressive. Allstate Financial competes with a variety of companies offering financial services, including MetLife, Mutual of Omaha, and Prudential.

state stock were trading at $33.70 per share at the end of 2001, down 23 percent from $43.56 per share at the end of 2000. Despite the recent losses, primarily due to increased claims and cost of repairs, property and liability premium revenues increased from $18.9 billion in 1997 to $22.6 billion in 2001. Similarly, Allstate Financial operations premiums and contracts totaled more than $2.2 billion in 2001, compared to $1.5 billion in 1997. However, within the same time period, the company's debt load increased from $1.7 billion to $3.9 billion.

ANALYSTS' OPINION

Although Allstate reacted quickly to its financially disappointing performance in 2001 by altering policies,

increasing premiums, and streamlining operations, most analysts believe that the repercussions from the poor year have not come to an end. The company's poor underlying trends, along with lower investment income available for 2002, put Allstate at risk for ongoing financial woes in the immediate future. Analysts are concerned about the deterioration of the profitability of homeowners' insurance due to the increasing number of claims filed and the severity of the damage incurred. Also Allstate's auto insurance business has suffered from increased losses, caused in part by lower gas prices and the trend toward travel by auto rather than air after the terrorist attacks of September 11, 2001. The result was an increase in miles driven, which in turn translated into more accidents and claims. Increased competition and a slow economy adversely affected Allstate Financial. Nonetheless, analysts tend to place significant weight on Allstate's name recognition, excellent claims management system, and its large customer base. Although the company has suffered setbacks, analysts contend that it takes time to turn a ship as big as Allstate, and positive results from changes already implemented should be realized in the foreseeable future.

HISTORY

Allstate was formed in 1931 as a unit of Sears, Roebuck & Company to sell auto insurance through the Sears catalog and by direct mail. During its first year of business, Allstate sold 4,217 policies, bringing in premiums of $118,323. A staff of 20 employees ran the operation, housed in the Sears headquarters in Chicago. Although the new company posted underwriting losses for the first two years, in 1933 active policies reached 22,000, and the company posted its first profit of $93,000.

Allstate came on the scene at a time when Sears was making the transition from catalog sales into the retail business. When Sears, which was previously only a catalog operation, began to open retail stores, Allstate expanded by opening sales offices within the Sears stores. Although the venture into traditional insurance marketing added the new expense of sales commissions, overhead was limited by the use of Sears' facilities. The business grew slowly but steadily during the Depression years, with premiums reaching $1.8 million in 1936. Over the next five years, premium revenues more than tripled to $6.8 million on 189,000 active policies. In 1941 only one quarter of all drivers owned auto insurance, but then the state of New York passed a law requiring auto insurance, and other states soon followed suit. The new legislation created new customers, which offset the loss of business due to the slow-down in auto production and sales during World War II.

During the 10 years following the end of World War II, Allstate grew dramatically. Spurred by the post-war economy, the company nearly doubled its size every two years. In 1945 revenues were $12 million; in 1955 that number swelled to $252 million. Allstate reacted to its rapid expansion by decentralizing its operations and instituting a three-tiered structure that stretched from the company's headquarters to its zone offices and ultimately to the regional offices. Some regional offices were further broken down into district service offices and local sales centers. Free-standing agencies joined Sears store offices as sales outlets.

In 1950 Allstate premiered its long-standing advertising campaign, "You're in Good Hands with Allstate." The slogan, coupled with the use of easy-to-understand policies complete with pictures, helped make Allstate a household name. In 1953 Allstate became a multinational corporation by opening its first Canadian office. The company also expanded its product line, introducing personal liability insurance in 1952 and residential fire insurance in 1954. In 1957 commercial fire, personal theft, and homeowners insurance were offered to customers, followed by personal health and commercial liability insurance in 1958. Boat, group life, and group health insurance followed in 1959. Also, in 1957 Allstate formed the subsidiary Allstate Life Insurance Company, which grew at an astronomical rate, bringing in $1 billion in life insurance revenues after just six years in business. In 1960 Allstate launched Allstate Enterprises, Inc., as the umbrella for a number of non-insurance based activities including a motor club, and finance businesses such as vehicle financing, mortgage banking, and mutual fund management.

Throughout the 1960s, Allstate continued to expand its product line, introducing workers compensation in 1964, surety bonds in 1966, ocean marine insurance in 1967, and a business package in 1968. Two new subsidiaries formed in 1964 to manage Allstate's Canadian interests: Allstate Insurance Company of Canada and Allstate Life Insurance Company of Canada. In 1966 the Judson B. Branch Research Center (later renamed the Allstate Research and Planning Center) opened in California, and the following year, company headquarters moved into spacious new offices in the Chicago suburb of Northbrook, Illinois. By 1970, Allstate employed some 6,500 insurance agents to sell Allstate products.

The 1970s brought continued growth and expansion. The 1972 acquisition of National First Corp. put Allstate in the mortgage banking business, and the acquisition of PMI Mortgage Insurance Co. the following year marked the company's entrance into the mortgage insurance business. In 1975 Allstate expanded globally, opening Seibu Allstate Life Insurance Company, Ltd., a joint venture in Japan with The Saison Group. In the same year Allstate bought Lippman & Moen, a group of Dutch insurers. Allstate also formed Tech-Cor,Inc., an auto-body research and reclamation business, in 1976. In 1978 the company established two wholly owned subsidiaries: Northbrook Property and Casualty Insurance Company and Allstate Reinsurance Company, Ltd., a London-based subsidiary of Allstate's international operations. A new commercial insurance division (later renamed Allstate Business Insurance) was also formed in the same year.

By 1980 Allstate was the sixth largest U.S. insurance group, posting a net income of $450 million on revenues of $6.2 billion and a maintaining a workforce of 12,500, the largest in the industry. In 1981 Allstate purchased Surety Life Insurance Company and Lincoln Benefit Life Company from the Dean Witter Reynolds group. The following year Allstate teamed with Dean Witter and Coldwell Banker to form the Sears Financial Network. In 1987 net income was $946 million. Facilitating the growth was the introduction of Allstate's Neighborhood Office Agent program, which placed more than 1,500 agents in more than 900 locations. A new, aggressive advertising campaign launched using the motto, "Leave It to the Good Hands People." The company's rapid growth finally caught up to earnings, and in 1990 the company posted a decreased net income, barely surpassing $700 million. Two years later, large premiums paid to cover damages caused by Hurricane Andrew left Allstate with a net loss of $825 million.

Rebounding from the loss, Allstate offered 20 percent of its stock to the public in 1993, generating $2.4 billion in capital. Revenues for the year jumped to $1.3 billion. However, in 1994 a major earthquake in California cost the company much of its profits as insurance claims surpassed $1 billion. In June of 1995 Sears decided to spin off Allstate and allow it to operate independently. Despite damage done by Hurricane Opal in 1995, Allstate posted a record $1.9 billion in income on $22.8 billion in revenues. Business continued to flourish for the next several years, as Allstate sold off some of its smaller interests to focus on its major business components.

By the late 1990s, new competition from discount insurance companies began to cut into Allstate's market, and automobile insurance rates dropped for the first time in a quarter of a century. Allstate responded by introducing Internet and telemarketing sales in 1999, which quickly sparked the ire of agents bypassed in the new process. Then, Allstate restructured its sales force so that agents were no longer Allstate employees, but instead independent contractors. The changes prompted a class action lawsuit filed by agents against the company.

STRATEGY

In 1950 Allstate launched its highly successful advertising campaign with the tag line, "You're in Good Hands with Allstate," which has remained a consistent theme for more than 50 years. In the 1980s the slogan "Leave it to the Good Hands People" built on the original campaign, producing an extraordinarily high level of name recognition for the company. In December 2001, Allstate added another twist to the original line. Using notable sports personalities, and advertising in such

CHRONOLOGY:

Key Dates for Allstate Corporation

1931: Allstate Insurance Company is founded by Sears, Roebuck and Co. Allstate offers auto insurance through the Sears catalog

1934: First sales office opens in a Sears store in Chicago

1945: Revenues top $12 million

1950: Launches "You're in Good Hands with Allstate" campaign

1953: Becomes international by opening first office in Canada

1957: Expands insurance offerings to include commercial fire, personal theft, and homeowners insurance along with life insurance through the establishment of Allstate Life Insurance Company

1975: Expands into Japan

1978: Becomes sixth largest U.S. insurance group with net income of $450 million on revenues of $6.2 billion

1985: Institutes the Neighborhood Office Agent program

1992: Damage from Hurricane Andrew causes Allstate to post a net loss of $825 million

1995: Sears spins off its 80 percent ownership for $9 billion and Allstate becomes 100 percent publicly owned

1998: Auto insurance rates drop nationwide for the first time in 25 years, and Allstate faces new competition from discount auto insurers such as Geico

2002: Allstate is the second-largest personal property-casualty insurer in the United States, providing insurance to more than 14 million American households

---

financial services: "Insure Today. Secure Tomorrow." Allstate also began experimenting with a targeted advertising strategy by supplementing its mass-market approach with direct mail campaigns aimed at specific groups.

INFLUENCES

Allstate's strategy to transform itself from a traditional personal property and liability company into a major player in the financial services industry is not without risk. Allstate has yet to prove that customers will be comfortable buying mutual funds from the same agent that provides their auto and homeowners' insurance. The company is also moving away from its long history of success in traditional insurance for a less certain future in the highly competitive financial arena. However, management feels that this is a necessary risk; given the pressure from shrinking profits in traditional insurance, despite a steady growth in premium revenues. State Farm has led the insurance industry toward rock-bottom prices that have cut profit margins to near zero. Discount insurance providers, such as GEICO and Progressive, have added to the downward trend in insurance pricing. Allstate has determined that the higher profit margins of financial services are worth the risk of entering the competitive field. Its chief rival, State Farm, is also making a move into mutual funds.

CURRENT TRENDS

Allstate's chief executive officer Edward Liddy set the company on a clear course for the future in 1998, announcing that Allstate was working to become a major player in the financial services industry. By 2002 Allstate was pushing its agents to obtain securities licenses and begin selling financial services, especially targeting its existing base of insurance customers. By 2002 almost half of Allstate's 13,000 agents held securities licenses. Allstate also increased its staff of exclusive financial agents by half to assist its entrance into the financial field. Allstate Bank began operating in October 2001 and offered products and services such as savings accounts, certificates of deposit, and insured money-market accounts. Additionally, Allstate began to use independent agents and brokers much more extensively. Four of every five new dollars earned by the financial service business during 2001 were generated by independent agents. Allstate is also pushing its own exclusive Allstate agents to sell financial products by increasing commissions for financial sales; lowering them for traditional insurance products; and, for the first time in company history, setting sales quotas.

To cut costs and improve customer service, Liddy also instituted the Good Hands Network, which com-

---

venues as *Sports Illustrated*, Allstate promoted its financial services with the line, "The right hands make all the difference." The goal of the new campaign was to transition the public's perception of Allstate from a protective insurance provider to a viable choice for proactive financial planning. A master of the tag line, Allstate has also developed a motto to tie together its insurance and

bined the Allstate agent force with allstate.com and 1-800-Allstate. By the end of 2001 the Good Hands Network extended to 30 states plus Washington DC and reached nearly 90 percent of the U.S. population. Allstate's entrance, albeit late, into Internet-based services and toll-free customer service was well received; in 2001 allstate.com recorded approximately 1 million hits every month and the toll-free help line answered 170,000 calls per week.

Allstate's restructuring has not been wholly endorsed by its force of agents. In 2000 Liddy fired all 6,200 agents as employees of the company and offered them positions as independent agent contracts. About 3,800 accepted the offer. Then Liddy cut an additional 4,000 jobs, representing approximately 10 percent of the company's workforce. As a result, dozens of former employees and the Equal Employment Opportunity Commission have threatened to file suit, claiming Allstate violated federal employment laws when it repositioned its agent workforce to independent contractor status and required them to sign waivers agreeing not to sue the company. Some of those agents who continued with Allstate in the new contractor role have expressed concerns regarding the company's demands that they sell financial products; an area in which they lack knowledge, skill, and training. Although the company is taking the problem seriously, Allstate describes the tension as a typical, yet temporary reaction to an aggressive change.

PRODUCTS

Allstate divides their product line into five segments: asset protection, family life protection, short-term financial objectives, asset management and accumulation, and wealth transfer. Asset protection products consist of Allstate's fundamental auto and homeowner insurance products. Within this product category, Allstate also places such specialty insurance as renter insurance, residential fire, boats, commercial package policies, and emergency roadside assistance. Family life protection products include life, long-term care, and disability insurance. Services provided under the umbrella of short-term financial objectives consist of banking products, such as checking, savings, and mortgages, as well as certificates of deposit and money market accounts. Asset management and accumulation refers to all products used for retirement fund management, such as fixed and variable life insurance and annuities, mutual funds, and individual retirement accounts. Wealth transfer services provide estate planning products such as life insurance and trust funds.

CORPORATE CITIZENSHIP

Allstate conducts its community service activities through the Allstate Foundation, an independent corpo-

CARD TALK TO ALLSTATE

During a bridge game on a Chicago commuter train in 1930, insurance broker Carl L. Odell suggested to his neighbor and morning card partner, Robert E. Wood, the idea of selling auto insurance by direct mail, thus cutting out the commission costs paid to agents and thereby greatly increasing profits. Wood, as the president and chief executive officer of Sears, Roebuck and Co., liked the idea and subsequently offered the idea to his board of directors. The result was the formation of the Allstate Insurance Company in April 1931, named after an automobile tire sold by Sears. Allstate offered auto insurance by direct mail and through the Sears catalog. The first claim settled was for $1.65 to replace a broken car door handle. By 2002 Allstate insured one of every eight cars on the road in the United States.

ration created in 1952 funded by Allstate Insurance. It acts as the service arm of Allstate to fulfill the company's three-point community mission: tolerance, inclusion, and diversity; safe and vital communities; and economic empowerment. During 2001 the Allstate Foundation contributed $7.1 million to nonprofit organizations. In the areas of tolerance, inclusion, and diversity, Allstate has focused its resources on teaching tolerance to youth, alleviating discrimination, and ending hate crimes through corporate sponsorship of mentoring, education, and community-building organizations such as the National Urban Council. In the spirit of creating safe and vital communities, Allstate offers support to organizations and programs such as the American Red Cross; Street SMART, a program sponsored by the Boys and Girls Club of America that teaches children to resist violence and gangs; and Allstate's Neighborhood Partnership Program, which promotes neighborhood development. To fulfill its third objective of economic empowerment, Allstate engages directly and indirectly in providing financial and insurance education and economic literacy training. The company also sponsors initiatives aimed at increasing women's roles in the business world.

GLOBAL PRESENCE

Allstate Canada, in operation for more than 45 years, offers auto and home insurance through its Canadian Allstate agents and via the Allstate Canadian Web site:

www.allstate.ca. The Canadian Allstate network employs 1,500 people, including 450 agents who serve 250 communities. Financial and saving products, as well as life, travel, and home security insurance, are also sold through partnerships with Clarica, Unum, Travel Underwriters, and Voxcom Security.

EMPLOYMENT

Allstate has consistently earned kudos for the diversity of its employee base. More than 60 percent of its workforce is made up of women. Even more impressive is the fact that nearly 40 percent of the company's professional staff is female. On February 13, 2002, the National Association for Female Executives recognized Allstate Corporation on their "Top 25" list of the nation's best companies for executive women. Noting Allstate's large number of female officials and managers, the organization also acknowledged Allstate for it programs that groom women for upper management positions, flexible work arrangements, and child-care benefits. Allstate has also received recognition from such publications as *Careers and the disABLED*, *Hispanic*, *Minority MBA*, and *Working Mother*.

SOURCES OF INFORMATION

Bibliography

Barr, Aaron. "Allstate Plays a Broader Hand." *Adweek*, 10 December 2001.

Daniels, Steve. "Allstate Puts Teeth into Revamp Plan." *Crain's Chicago Business*, 4 February 2002.

Gogoi, Pallavi. "Is Allstate in Good Hands?" *Business Week*, 21 May 2001.

Grant, Tina, ed. *International Directory of Company Histories*, Vol. 27. Detroit: St. James Press, 1999.

Regent, Nancy, ed. *Hoover's Handbook of American Business*. Austin, TX: Hoover's Business Press, 2001.

Roman, Monica. "Is Allstate Covered for This?" *Business Week*, 14 January 2002.

For an annual report:

on the Internet at: http://www.allstate.com/investor/annual _report/ **or** telephone: (800) 416-8803 **or** write: Allstate Insurance Company, Investor Relations, Northbrook, IL 60062

For additional industry research:

Investigate companies by their Standard Industrial Classification Codes, also known as SICs. Allstate Corporation's primary SICs are:

6311 Life Insurance

6331 Fire, Marine, and Casualty Insurance

6371 Pension, Health, and Welfare Funds

Also investigate companies by their North American Industry Classification System codes, also known as NAICS codes. Allstate Corporation's primary NAICS codes are:

524113 Direct Life Insurance Carriers

524126 Direct Property and Casualty Insurance Carriers

551112 Offices of Other Holding Companies

Amazon.com, Inc.

FOUNDED: 1995

Contact Information:

HEADQUARTERS: 1200 12th Ave. S, Suite 1200
   Seattle, WA 98144
PHONE: (206)266-1000
FAX: (206)266-1821
TOLL FREE: (800)201-7575
URL: http://www.amazon.com

OVERVIEW

When first launched in July 1995, Amazon.com set out to give book buyers a faster, easier, and more enjoyable way to do their shopping. The company's product line in its early years included recordings and videos as well as books. Although Amazon has widely expanded its product offerings in the years since it first went online, the company remains committed to its original goals of customer satisfaction and making the online shopping experience both educational and inspiring. Literally millions of products are now available from Amazon.com's Web sites. These include consumer electronics, toys, computer and video games, tools and other hardware, lawn and garden supplies, kitchen products, cameras, and computer software.

In addition to its broad selection of retail products, the company hosts on its Web site Amazon Marketplace, Auctions, and zShops, which provide a virtual marketplace where individuals and businesses can offer for sale virtually any product to Amazon's millions of customers. In addition to its U.S.-based Web site (http://www. amazon.com) the company operates four internationally-oriented sites: http://www.amazon.co.uk, based in the United Kingdom; http://www.amazon.de, based in Germany; http://www.amazon.fr, based in France; and http://www.amazon.co.jp, based in Japan.

COMPANY FINANCES

In the early years after it opened its virtual doors for business in 1995, Amazon.com focused on winning

FAST FACTS:

About Amazon.com, Inc.

Ownership: Amazon.com is a publicly owned company traded on the NASDAQ Stock Exchange.

Ticker Symbol: AMZN

Officers: Jefffrey P. Bezos, Chmn., Pres., and CEO, 38; Richard L. Dalzell, Sr., SVP and CIO, 44

Employees: 7,800

Principal Subsidiary Companies: As one of the most prominent online retailers, Amazon.com, Inc. has participated in the ownership and operation, frequently with partners, of several other online retail operations. Prominent among these are drugstore .com and Back to Basics Toys. Amazon also owned a substantial portion of HomeGrocer.com, which in September 2000 was acquired by Webvan, although Amazon reportedly retained a six percent share in the online grocery retailer.

Chief Competitors: Major competitors for Amazon's original product line of books, CDs, DVDs, and videos are Barnes & Noble and CDnow. Amazon's entry into the online auction market puts it head to head with such powerhouses in the Internet auction field as eBay.com and uBid.com.

Christmas selling season. Commenting on this "first," Diego Piacentini, senior vice president of Amazon.com International, said, "Clearly we are pleased, but the business has reached only one milestone. Now we have to make profits for the full year."

Although total revenue has steadily increased, net sales for Amazon's U.S. books, music, and DVD/video segment declined slightly in 2001, dropping to $1.69 billion from $1.70 billion the previous year. In 2000 sales for this segment had climbed nearly 30 percent over the $1.31 billion reported in 1999.

Far more promising was the 2001 performance of Amazon's U.S. electronics, tools, and kitchen segment, where net sales climbed 13 percent to $547 million from $484 million in 2000. Amazon's sales in this market segment didn't begin until the second half of 1999, when net sales totaled $151 million.

For Amazon's services segment, net sales in 2001 climbed 13 percent to $225 million from $198 million in 2000. The services segment didn't begin operations until late 1999, when net sales totaled only $13 million.

Amazon's fastest growing market segment in 2001 was international, which includes the retail sales of the company's foreign-based Web sites. Net sales for international total $661 million, an increase of 74 percent over $381 million in 2000. Net sales for the international segment totaled $168 million in 1999.

For the year ended December 31, 2001, the stock of Amazon.com traded in a range of $6.01 to $21.88, off sharply from 2000, when it traded in a range of $14.88 to $91.50. The sharp decline reflects the malaise that afflicted almost all dot-com stocks beginning in the latter half of 2000.

market share at the expense of fast profits, in the hope that wide customer recognition of the company's quality operations would eventually pay off in sound financial performance. More recently the company has turned its attention to profits. Despite the depressed economy of 2001, Amazon managed to sharply reduce its net loss from that recorded in the previous year. For 2001 the company reported a net loss of $567.3 million on revenue of $3.1 billion, against a 2000 net loss of $1.4 billion on revenue of nearly $2.8 billion. In 1999, Amazon posted a net loss of $720 million on revenue of slightly more than $1.6 billion.

What was truly remarkable about Amazon's performance in 2001 was its profit of $5.1 million in the fourth quarter. Not only was it the first such profit ever posted by the Internet's largest retailer, it was achieved in the downbeat economic climate at the time; a year earlier, the company had recorded a loss of $545 million in the fourth quarter. Helping tip the scales toward profitability was a decision by Amazon to cut book prices for the

ANALYSTS' OPINIONS

Some security analysts who follow the dot-com stocks were clearly underwhelmed by Amazon's $5.1 million profit in the fourth quarter of 2001. Holly Becker, an analyst with Lehman Brothers, Inc., expressed doubt that Amazon could duplicate its profit-making experience of the fourth quarter and suggested that the company's stock might be substantially overvalued. Also somewhat skeptical was Dan Gleiman, an analyst with McAdams Wright Ragen of Seattle. Gleiman observed: "It looks like volume-wise, they might be doing okay. But the understanding is that customers are buying lower-priced items, so they are going after value." According to a survey published in the Toronto Star in April 2002, ten of the 24 Wall Street analysts tracked by Bloomberg rate Amazon's stock a "buy," 12 say "hold," and only two rate it a "sell."

Although Lehman Brothers' Becker questioned the valuation of Amazon.com stock, suggesting that the

Workers at Amazon.com's Seattle distribution warehouse scramble to fill orders for the Christmas rush. (AP Photo/Barry Sweet)

company was too dependent on the sales of its international and services segments, which she said were "more risky and less valuable," she was not without praise for some aspects of the company's operation. In a March 2002 research report, she wrote that Amazon's performance in the fourth quarter of 2001 had put the company "out of the woods" as far as any risk of bankruptcy. She credited the company's turnaround to its decision in August 2001 to slash prices on all books priced over $20. As for Amazon's closely-watched cash position, Becker reported that the company had finished fourth quarter 2001 with nearly $1 billion in cash and marketable securities and predicted that its

operations for all of 2002 promise to generate positive cash flow.

HISTORY

Jeffrey P. Bezos, a Wall Street brainstormer who was convinced early on that the Internet would transform the world of retailing, left his job New York and headed west in the mid-1990s with a dream of opening an online bookstore. With wife MacKenzie, Bezos flew from New York to Fort Worth, Texas, where he bid goodbye to his

FINANCES:

*Amazon.com Inc.
Revenues, 1999-2001
(million dollars)*

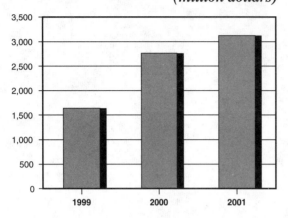

*Amazon.com Inc.
2001 Stock Prices
(dollars)*

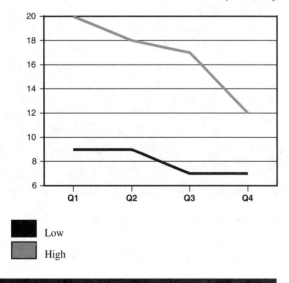

Shel Kaphan. By June 1995 the team had created a primitive test site on the Internet and invited friends and family members to test it out. Less than two months later, Amazon.com went live. In its first month online, the company sold books in all 50 states and more than 40 foreign countries. Bezos later told *Time*, "Within the first few days, I knew this was going to be huge. It was obvious we were on to something much bigger than we ever dared to hope."

After its phenomenally successful launch, it was almost inevitable that Amazon.com would become one of the forerunners of the new dot-com revolution. Despite repeated losses, the company expanded rapidly, broadening its product lineup and establishing a foreign presence with sites in France, Germany, Japan, and the United Kingdom.

The company has yet to post an annual profit, although a glimmer of hope appeared in late 2001 when Amazon.com reported its first-ever quarterly profit. Most remarkably, despite its sizeable losses over several years and its heavy debt load, the company has managed to survive in a hostile climate that has chewed up and spit out so many other once-promising Internet ventures.

STRATEGY

As defined in Amazon.com's 2001 Annual Report, the company's goal is "to offer the Earth's biggest selection and to be the Earth's most customer-centric company, where customers can find and discover anything they may want to buy online." To realize this goal, Amazon.com has developed three sales channels: online retail; marketplace and other; and third-party sellers.

The company's online retail sales channel includes its several Web sites, all of which offer a wide range of products, including Amazon's original core products (books, music, and videos) as well as consumer electronics, tools, hardware, kitchen products, and services. This network of Web sites includes, as stated, Amazon's four foreign-based online outlets in France, Germany, Japan, and the United Kingdom. The majority of the products Amazon sells through its online retail sales channel are purchased by Amazon from outside vendors and held in Amazon order fulfillment centers until orders are received. In some cases, the company's vendors are asked to fulfill the orders directly. Amazon indicates that it hopes to continue expanding the range of products available through this sales channel.

Amazon's marketplace and other sales channel, made up of Amazon Marketplace, Auctions, zShops, and certain of the company's other non-retail Web sites, provides a marketplace where individuals and other businesses can offer new and used products, many of which supplement Amazon's product offerings on its retail sales channel. Amazon Auctions allows buyers and sellers to do business in a simple auction format, while zShops pro-

parents and then drove to Seattle in a 1988 Chevrolet Blazer. As his wife drove northwestward, Bezos worked feverishly on a laptop computer to draft a business plan. His original name for the venture, "Cadabra," was soon abandoned in favor of Amazon.com.

In the Seattle suburb of Bellevue, Bezos and his wife rented a modest two-bedroom home, which quickly became the headquarters for Bezos' start-up venture. The home's garage was converted into an office, and Bezos brought in three Sun work stations on which to continue building his dream, closely aided by veteran programmer

vides both individuals and businesses with an opportunity to set up mini-shops online to offer popular items as well as products that otherwise might be hard to find.

With its third-party sellers channel, Amazon provides an array of e-commerce services and tools that allows other companies to market their goods and services. As of late 2001, Amazon had third-party seller arrangements with Circuit City Stores, Inc.; Toysrus.com, Inc.; Waterstones; Expedia, Inc.; the Borders Group; Hotwire; National Leisure Group, Inc.; Virgin Wines; Target Corporation; and other companies. Among the tools and services Amazon provides to its third-party sellers are technology infrastructure, a strong global brand recognition, Web merchandising, customer service, and global fulfillment.

INFLUENCES

Amazon.com has faced and will continue to face some very formidable challenges. Not the least of these is competition. The overall retail market for most of the products sold by Amazon is extremely competitive and even more intensely competitive online. Amazon.com has sought to answer this challenge by making the Amazon.com shopping experience as quick and trouble-free as possible for its customers, giving them an online shopping experience rewarding enough to ensure their return for future shopping trips. Another important element in Amazon's strategy has been the expansion of its network of alliance with third-party sellers and the addition of auction-type sales to its online marketplace.

CURRENT TRENDS

Growth through strategic alliances with third-party sellers would seem to be a promising way for Amazon.com to continue expanding its overall business. To that end, the company in 2001 introduced three new services to better serve its third-party sellers and also give Amazon's customers an even greater selection of products from which to choose. The new services for third-party sellers include the Merchant@amazon.com program, which allows outside companies to offer their products for sale in one of Amazon's online retail stores or in co-branded stores situated on the Amazon Web site. Customers may order products from these third-party sellers as well as products from Amazon itself with a single checkout transaction. Under this program, Amazon also offers to provide fulfillment-related services to third-party sellers.

Another service for Amazon's third-party sellers is the Merchant Program. Under this arrangement, third-party sellers can utilize Amazon technology and features at their own e-commerce Web site. The seller then pays Amazon fixed fees, sales commissions, and/or per-unit

CHRONOLOGY:
Key Dates for Amazon.com

1995: Amazon.com launches Web site

1996: Company launches Associate program

1997: Amazon.com goes public

1998: Company enters online music business

2001: Amazon.com posts first quarterly profit

activity fees for products sold through this arrangement. Amazon also offers fulfillment-related services to third-party sellers operating in the Merchant Program.

The final service for third-party sellers is Amazon's Syndicated Stores Program, under which the third-party seller's e-commerce Web site utilizes Amazon's services and tools and also offers Amazon's product selection. Under this program, Amazon is responsible for providing both customer and fulfillment services. Amazon is the seller of record for such transactions and remits a commission to the third-party seller.

PRODUCTS

Amazon's products cover a broad range of goods, beginning, of course, with its original core product group—books, music, and videos. To better showcase its e-book offerings, the company in 2000 opened an e-Books store, which features downloadable e-audiobooks from Audible, Inc. as well as e-books in Microsoft Reader format for PCs and laptops. Amazon.com also launched Bargain Music, Latin, and Box Set stores, and a Music Accessories store, which offers blank media and MP3 players. For videos and DVDs, the company opened more than 30 genre or franchise stores, covering such categories as Fitness, Bargain, Cult, and European Cinema.

The rest of Amazon's product offerings are grouped in its early-stage businesses and other segments. Within this segment, one of the biggest-and most promising-categories is other U.S. retail, which includes the electronics business, home improvements, and kitchen products. In 2000 the selection of products available to customers was further expanded with the launch of Amazon Marketplace and Amazon Outlet. Amazon Marketplace enables customers to buy and sell second-hand,

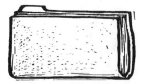

AMAZON.COM
POPULAR ABROAD

One of the fastest growing segments of Amazon .com's business is the international market. The company's international segment recorded net sales of $661 million in 2001, a stunning increase of 73 percent over the $381 million in sales posted in 2000. In 1991, sales of the International segment totaled $168 million. The company operates four Web sites in the international market. Each offers essentially the same shopping experience as offered by Amazon's flagship American site but is localized in terms of language, products, customer service, and fulfillment. The four international sites are based in France, Germany, Japan, and the United Kingdom.

The Japanese site, launched in November 2000, had attracted 800,000 visitors by March 2002, confounding skeptics who predicted an e-commerce scheme such as Amazon's wouldn't make it in Japan because of the consumer preference for shopping in large department stores. The company was predicting the Japanese site's sales would top $100 million in 2002. So well has Amazon done outside the United States that further expansion abroad is expected, although the company has been close-mouthed about which country might be next. Diego Piacentini, senior vice president of worldwide retail and marketing, said, "Our international expansion is not a matter of if but when."

rare, and collectible merchandise alongside Amazon's offering of the corresponding new product. Amazon Outlet offers year-round bargains on thousand of products from all segments of Amazon's product line.

Other important products in Amazon's lineup include its auction-format sales, including Amazon Auctions and Amazon zShops, and its other services offered through third-party sellers.

CORPORATE CITIZENSHIP

Amazon.com operates on an international scale and has long sought to make a positive contribution to the world. To help environmentally friendly sites on the occasion of Earth Day 2001, the company launched its honor system "Earth Day Every Day" section. The special section provided visitors links to participating sites,

all of which provided a variety of content for people interested in learning more about protecting the environment, recycling, and energy conservation. The program also provided a way in which visitors to participating sites could tip one dollar or more in exchange for the valuable content such sites provided.

Amazon also teamed in 2001 with the Red Hot Organization (RHO), the entertainment industry's leading organization devoted to fighting AIDS through popular culture. RHO provided content for Amazon's Free Music Downloads area. The downloads area also featured Amazon's "virtual tipping" technology that allows users to leave an online donation after listening to a free, full-length download. RHO provided 36 MP3 files from Red Hot's catalog of popular songs recorded during the previous decade.

GLOBAL PRESENCE

Amazon maintains a significant international presence through its four foreign-based Web sites: http://www.amazon.co.uk in the United Kingdom, http://www.amazon.de in Germany, http://www.amazon.fr in France, and http://www.amazon.co.jp in Japan. All of the company's foreign sites feature essentially the same technology and customer services that have made the domestic site so popular with customers.

EMPLOYMENT

As of December 31, 2001, Amazon.com employed about 7,800 full and part-time employees. The company also employs temporary personnel on a seasonal basis and independent contractors as needed. None of the company's employees are unionized. Amazon.com believes that the company's future success depends in large part on its continued ability to attract, hire, and retain qualified personnel.

SOURCES OF INFORMATION

Bibliography

Amazon.com 2000 Annual Report. Seattle: Amazon.com, Inc., 2001.

Amazon.com 2001 Annual Report. Seattle: Amazon.com, Inc., 2002.

Amazon.com Home Page, 2002. Available at http://www.amazon .com.

"Amazon.com, Inc." *Hoover's Online,* 2002. Available at http:// www.hoovers.com.

"Amazon Down 4 Percent after Lehman Analyst Questions Value." *Associated Press,* 27 March 2002.

"Amazon Profitable, But at What Price?" *Toronto Star*, 1 April 2002.

Cope, Nigel. "Amazon in Profit at Last after $3 Billion Losses." *Independent*, 23 January 2002.

Fishman, Charles. "Face Time with Jeff Bezos." *Fast Company*, 1 February 2001.

Hillis, Scott. "Santa Seen Delivering Amazon.com's First Profit." *Reuters Business Report*, 21 December 2001.

Quittner, Joshua. "Person of the Year/Jeff Bezos." *Time,* 27 December 1999.

For an annual report:

write: Amazon.com, Investor Relations, PO Box 81226, Seattle, WA 98108-1226

For additional industry research:

Investigate companies by their Standard Industrial Classification codes, also known as SICs. Amazon.com's primary SIC is:

5961 Catalog and Mail-Order Houses

Also investigate companies by their North American Industry Classification System codes, also known as NAICS codes. Amazon .com's primary NAICS code is:

454110 Electronic Shopping and Mail-Order Houses

AMC Entertainment Inc.

FOUNDED: 1920 as Durwood Theatres
VARIANT NAME: AMC Theatres

Contact Information:

HEADQUARTERS: 106 West 14th Street
   Kansas City, MO 64121-9615
PHONE: (816)221-4000
FAX: (816)480-4625
TOLL FREE: (877)AMC-4450
EMAIL: InvestorRelations@amctheatres.com
URL: http://www.amctheatres.com

OVERVIEW

AMC Entertainment Inc., the owner and developer of movie theatres and real estate, is one of the major forces and leaders in the theatrical exhibition industry. The company is also involved in selling and producing on-screen advertising for theatres. The organization made its greatest impact when it introduced the concept of the "megaplex" theatre in 1995. A megaplex is defined as a facility with 14 or more screens. Some AMC theatres have up to 24 screens.

At the end of fiscal year 2001, AMC operated 177 theatres with 2,836 screens in 21 states and the District of Columbia, Canada, France, Hong Kong, Japan, Portugal, Spain, and Sweden.

COMPANY FINANCES

For the fiscal year 2001, AMC had revenues of $1.3 billion. AMC's primary revenues are generated from box office admissions and concessions sales. For the fiscal year 2001, admissions accounted for 67 percent of its revenues, while concession sales accounted for 28 percent. The rest of AMC's revenues are generated by advertising, video games located in theatre lobbies, and the rental of theatre auditoriums. At the end of 2001, AMC had $596.5 million of debt, $57.7 million in capital and financing lease obligations, and $153.7 million in cash and equivalents.

ANALYSTS' OPINIONS

In the last part of the twentieth century and the early part of the twenty-first century, movie theatre companies experienced considerable financial pressure due to over-building and heavy debts. The biggest problem was too many screens, which created a situation where screen growth outpaced attendance. Since 1995, screen growth grew at an annual rate of 7.8 percent, while attendance grew only 3.8 percent. The situation created too much competition. Screen reduction appeared to be the only answer. AMC competitors like Loews Cineplex experienced significant financial trouble. The situation caused financial analysts to predict that AMC Entertainment could benefit from the financial troubles of other companies. However, AMC Entertainment was not unmarked by the situation. In 2001, it announced that it would be closing 300 of its older theatres due to increasing competition from other megaplexes.

HISTORY

AMC's beginnings go back to 1920 and a man named Edward Durwood. At the time, Durwood and his brothers were operating tent shows in the Midwest. Seeking a more settled lifestyle, Durwood acquired the lease to a motion-picture theatre in Kansas City, Missouri. Edward's son, Stanley H. Durwood, eventually came into the business and constantly brought new ideas into the company. He would help AMC Entertainment become the third-largest movie theatre company in the country.

A Harvard graduate, Stanley Durwood joined the company when it comprised a small chain of moviehouses and drive-in theatres after World War II. When he became president of Durwood Theatres in 1960 (as AMC was called back then), he started developing the concept of the multiple-screen theatre, which would become AMC's trademark. In 1963, using pre-existing theatre space, he developed the first-ever multiplex, which was a two-screen theatre with 700 seats, located in a Kansas City shopping center. In 1966, he introduced the first-ever four-plex and, three years later, he introduced the six-plex. At the time, the company had expanded beyond Kansas City and into Arizona, California, Nebraska, and Texas. Now owning 68 screens, the company was incorporated as American Multi-Cinema, Inc.

AMC established another milestone in 1987, when it opened the Century City multiplex in west Los Angeles. The site included the features that would become AMC signatures: large screens, free parking, and large, comfortable seats equipped with cup holders in the armrests. Similar multiplex centers soon followed in its wake, in places like the Universal Citywalk in Pasadena, California, and the Third Street Promenade in Santa Monica, California.

FAST FACTS:
About AMC Entertainment Inc.

Ownership: A charitable trust created after the death of former CEO Stanley Durwood owns 17 percent of AMC Entertainment but controls 66 percent of the voting power.

Ticker Symbol: AEN

Officers: Peter Brown, Chmn., Pres., and CEO, 62, 2000 base salary $970,000; Richard Fay, Pres., AMC Film Marketing, 51, 2000 base salary $430,000; Philip Singleton, EVP, Pres., and COO, 2000 base salary $651,000

Employees: 14,320

Principal Subsidiary Companies: AMC Entertainment Inc. (AMCE) is a holding company with principal subsidiaries that include American Multi-Cinema, Inc. (AMC); AMC Theatres of Canada (a division of AMC Entertainment International, Inc.); AMC Entertainment International, Inc.; National Cinema Network, Inc.; and AMC Realty, Inc. The company's North American theatrical exhibition business is conducted through AMC and AMC Theatres of Canada. The company develops theatres outside North America through AMC Entertainment International, Inc. and its subsidiaries. The company engages in advertising services through National Cinema Network, Inc. (NCN).

Chief Competitors: AMC's main competitors are other major theatre chains including Regal Cinemas, Inc.; Loews Cineplex Entertainment Corp.; Cinemark USA, Inc.; United Artists Theatre Company; Carmike Cinemas; National Amusements, Inc.; Edwards Theatres Circuit, Inc.; GC Companies, Inc.; and Hoyts Cinemas Corporation. However, significant competition comes from other forms of so-called "out of home" entertainment including concerts, amusement parks, and sports events. In recent years, the industry has been facing increasing competition from the home entertainment market, including cable and satellite television, pay-per-view, and home video technology (videotape and DVD).

FINANCES:

AMC Entertainment Inc.
Total Revenues, 1999-2001
(thousand dollars)

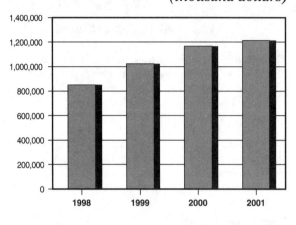

In May 1995, AMC opened its first megaplex. Located in Dallas, Texas, it was called the AMC Grand 24 and, as its name implied, it housed 24 screens. Megaplexes like the Grand were characterized not just for their number of screens—they came to be known for the comfort they provided, as they were a vast improvement over multiplex theatres, which were small, cramped, and often dirty. Also, multiplexes tended to be low-key as far as design was concerned. AMC adorned its megaplexes with a colorful array of neon lights and elaborate decorative touches. Most importantly, the viewing experience was vastly improved, as sound quality and picture quality were significantly upgraded via new technology. Not only were the floor designs larger, but so were the screens; reportedly, each screen cost as much as $1 million.

Customer comfort was also a major concern when AMC enlarged the scope of the movie theatre. The small, cramped seats of the multiplex were replaced with large chairs that featured retractable armrests and cupholders. These chairs were arranged in a tiered "stadium seating" structure that ensured that no one's view of the screen would be obstructed. This tiered seating arrangement was once common in the large "movie palaces" of the 1920s and 1930s.

In 1996, AMC opened the largest megaplex in the United States at the 200-store Ontario Mills Mall in Ontario, California. It boasted 30 screens and 5,700 seats. This theatre helped advanced the concept of the location-based entertainment complex, or the LBE, as it is known in the industry. The concept of LBE is designed to turn the megaplex into the attractive center of what is essentially a mall-sized entertainment theme park. In the

Ontario mall, the AMC megaplex is surrounded by a huge acarde, an IMAX theatre, Dreamworks, Sega, and indoor attractions like a zoo and rides.

It didn't take long for AMC's advancements to translate into financial success. By 1997, eight of North America's 20 top-grossing theatres bore the AMC trademark. Today, more than 60 percent of AMC Theatres are megaplexes that house at least 14 different movie screens.

STRATEGY

AMC's corporate strategy involves achieving continued success by focusing on business fundamentals, which includes maximizing revenues and managing overhead costs and capital expenditures. This aim is reflected in its strategic plan, which includes three stated elements: maximizing the performance of its existing operations by focusing on the fundamentals of its business; growing and improving its theatre portfolio through strategic acquisitions, selective new builds, and the continued disposition of older, underperforming theatres; and enhancing and extending its business and brands.

The most fundamental element of AMC's strategy is customer comfort and pleasure. From its very beginning, AMC has made designing the most pleasurable movie-going experience the main focus of its strategy. This simple strategy would seem to be a given for any organization intent on succeeding in the industry. However, inspired by the vision of its founder, Edward Durwood, AMC implements specific elements and innovations to achieve its aims. The company is always on the lookout for new opportunities that will enable it to enhance the movie-going experience.

INFLUENCES

AMC has been at the forefront of improving the public's night at the movies. Other companies have followed its lead, as AMC has initiated nearly every industry improvement, including theatre design, cupholder armrests, computerized box offices, automated projection booths, state-of-the-art presentations, and stadium-style seating. AMC also created the MovieWatcher club, the first frequent moviegoer reward program, which now has more than 2 million members. Essentially, AMC helped revolutionize the movie-going experience and the theatrical exhibition industry. In doing so, it became one of the most successful companies in the history of the industry.

Perhaps AMC's most influential innovation came in 1995, when it introduced the industry to the megaplex concept. With the construction and design of The Grand 24 in Dallas, it set an industry standard. Other theatres are upgrading their facilities to include stadium-style seating, and they endeavor to provide the top-of-the-line amenities that have become one of the hallmarks of AMC's style.

CURRENT TRENDS

The driving force behind all of the company's innovations has been improving the movie-going experience for the public. AMC desired to change the way the world watches movies, and it succeeded. It continues to seek innovations. In 2000, AMC announced that it would enter into a joint venture to create MovieTickets.com, an Internet ticket seller and source of movie information. The venture includes CBS, Famous Players, Hollywood.com, Marcus Theatres, and National Amusements.

Also, AMC plans to build an entertainment district in downtown Kansas City, Missouri, which will transform a decaying 12-block area into one of the Midwest's most exciting attractions. The $454 million project, to be known as the Power & Light District, will include a 30-screen AMC megaplex, restaurants, live concert and theatre venues, retail shops, and new office buildings and hotels.

Other stated future plans include enhancing and extending its brands and business. Examples of new products and marketing strategies include installation of digital projection technology and streamlining the delivery of in-theatre advertising.

PRODUCTS

Essentially, AMC's primary product is a movie-going experience that is enjoyable and comfortable. AMC says the key characteristics that differentiate them from the competition include its "modern theatre circuit," in which it seeks to continually upgrade the quality of its theatre circuit by adding new screens through new theatres and the acquisition and expansion of older theatres. From April 1995 through March 2001, it opened 90 new theatres with 1,902 screens and added 86 screens to existing theatres, acquired 4 theatres with 29 screens and closed or disposed of 146 theatres with 879 screens.

Another key characteristic is its megaplex theatre format, defined as a theatre with 14 or more screens. A component of the format is the provision of amenities that enhance the moviegoing experience, including stadium seating that provides unobstructed viewing, enhanced seat design, and state-of-the art technology. It also includes increasing of film choice and film starting times to accommodate the tastes and convenience of the public. In this fashion, AMC feels it has raised the standards expected by moviegoers.

CHRONOLOGY:
Key Dates for AMC Entertainment Inc.

1920: Company is founded by Edward Durwood in Kansas City, Missouri

1960: Stanley Durwood becomes president of Durwood Theatres and starts developing the concept of the multiple-screen theatre

1963: Durwood Theatres introduces the first multiplex theatre, in Kansas City

1966: Durwood Theatres introduces the first four-plex theatre

1969: Company expands into Arizona and California and incorporates as American Multi-Cinema Inc.

1987: AMC opens the Century City multiplex in west Los Angeles

1995: AMC opens its first megaplex, in Dallas, Texas

1996: AMC opens the largest megaplex in the United States, at the Ontario Mills Mall in Ontario, California

2000: AMC announces a joint venture to create MovieTickets.com

For its movies, AMC predominantly licenses first-run motion pictures from distributors. It licenses the entertainment on a film-by-film and theatre-by-theatre basis. When obtaining licenses, AMC considers several factors, including theatre location, competition, season of the year, and motion picture content.

AMC's theatres also provide appealing concession counters that provide quick service. Items include popcorn, soft drinks, candy, hot dogs, and other food products. One popular item is the "combo-meal," which offers a pre-selection of concession products. The company offers different varieties of concession item at different theatres based on preferences of geographic regions. AMC has developed the idea of strategic placement of concession stands to heighten their visibility and to reduce long lines.

AMC also applies strategic placement when selecting theatre locations. It endeavors to place its theatres in large urban and suburban markets, and in areas that include retail stores, restaurants and other activities that complement the movie-going experience. Approximately 74 percent of its U.S. screens are located in

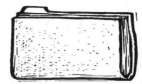

NEW YORK'S MOVIE MECCA

AMC Entertainment, the pioneer of the megaplex, helped take the concept to a new level. In 1999, AMC opened its Empire 25 in Manhattan. When the Loews Cineplex opened across the street with 13 theatres, it created the largest concentration of movie screens in New York City, with 38 screens and 8,100 seats.

areas that are among the 25 largest "designated market areas."

CORPORATE CITIZENSHIP

AMC provides resources and opportunities for customers, employees, and surrounding communities. On a national level, AMC helps raise money for non-profit organizations through events like special grand openings and in-theatre fund-raisers and through a children's reading program called "Read for the Stars." It also helps raise awareness and money for many local and regional non-profit organizations.

GLOBAL PRESENCE

Besides its U.S. locations, AMC has theatres in Canada, France, Hong Kong, Japan, Portugal, Spain, and Sweden. The international circuit currently includes a total of 128 screens in 7 theatres. AMC has implemented an international expansion program and plans on providing more theatres in overseas locations.

EMPLOYMENT

AMC offers a professional management training program. This program combines classroom style training with hands-on training in all aspects of theatre operations. For its employees, AMC provides a comprehensive benefits package that includes health, dental, vision, life insurance, and disability coverage. It also provides flexible spending accounts, a pension plan, a 401 (k) retirement plan, incentive programs, paid vacations, educational assistance programs, and complimentary passes. Jobs within the organization include theatre manager and staff positions including concessionist, usher, cashier, and projectionist.

SOURCES OF INFORMATION

Bibliography

Hoover's Online. "AMC Entertainment," 2002. Available at http://www.hoovers.com.

Industry Channel. "Industry Environment." *US Business Reporter*, 5 March 2001. Available at http://www.activemedia-guide.com/entertainment_industry.htm.

Mann, Jennifer. "Star 50 Profile: AMC Entertainment, Inc." *The Kansas City Star*, 14 May 2001. Avaiable at http://www.kcstar.com.

"MovieTickets.com Announces Agreement with Yahoo!," 2 October 2001. Available at http://www.investor.amctheatres.com.

Yahoo! Market Guide. "Profile-AMC Entertainment." *Yahoo Finance*, 28 March 2002. Available at http://biz.yahoo.com/p/a/aen.html.

For additional industry research:

Investigate companies by their Standard Industrial Classification Codes, also known as SICs. AMC Entertainment Inc.'s primary SICs are:

6719 Offices of Other Holding Companies

7832 Motion Picture Theaters, Except Drive-In

Also investigate companies by their North American Industry Classification System codes, also known as NAICS codes. AMC Entertainment Inc.'s primary NAICS codes are:

512131 Motion Picture Theaters, except Drive-In

551112 Offices of Other Holding Companies

American Airlines, Inc.

OVERVIEW

American Airlines, Inc. is the principal subsidiary of AMR Corporation (AMR). In 1982 stockholders voted to approve a plan of reorganization under which they formed a new holding company, AMR Corp., which became the parent company to American Airlines Inc. They took the name "AMR" from the airline's three-letter New York Stock Exchange symbol. American also operates American Eagle, a regional airline that connects passengers from smaller markets into American's hub system. AMR also has a computerized reservation subsidiary (owned cooperatively by American Airlines, Delta Air Lines, and Northwest Airlines) known as WORLDSPAN that connects some 20,000 travel agencies in almost 70 countries. In 2000 the corporation moved its even more complex SABRE reservation system, the world's largest privately owned real-time computer network in the world, into a separate holding company.

American Airlines' Passenger division is one of the largest scheduled passenger airlines in the world. American provides scheduled jet service to more than 160 destinations throughout North America, the Caribbean, Latin America, Europe, and the Pacific. American's cargo division is one of the largest scheduled air freight carriers in the world. It provides a full range of freight and mail services to shippers throughout the airline's system. In addition, through cooperative agreements with other carriers, it can transport shipments to any country in the world. On an average day, American Airlines flies nearly 4,000 flights.

FOUNDED: 1934 as American Airways, Inc.
EMPLOYEES: 128,215
VARIANT NAME: AMR Corporation

Contact Information:

HEADQUARTERS: 4333 Amon Carter Blvd.
 Fort Worth, TX 76155
PHONE: (817)963-1234
FAX: (817)967-9641
URL: http://www.aa.com
 http://www.amrcorp.com

FAST FACTS:

About American Airlines, Inc.

Ownership: AMR Corporation is a publicly owned company traded on the New York, Zurich, Basel, and Geneva Stock Exchanges. AMR stocks are also traded unlisted on the Midwest and the Pacific Stock Exchanges.

Ticker symbol: AMR

Officers: Donald J. Carty, 55, Chmn. and CEO; Gerald J. Arpey, 42, Pres. and COO, American Airlines, Inc., AMR Airline Group; Anne H. McNamara, 53, SVP and Gen. Counsel

Employees: 128,215

Principal Subsidiary Companies: AMR's selected subsidiaries and affiliates include American Airlines, Inc.; AMR Eagle, Inc.; AMR Investment Services, Inc.; and AMR Services Corp.

Chief Competitors: As a major airline, American Airlines' competitors include United Airlines, USAir, Continental Airlines, TWA, Delta, Southwest Airlines, Northwest Airlines, America West, and Air France.

HISTORY

Robertson Aircraft Corporation and about 85 other small airline companies were consolidated in 1929 and 1930 into the Aviation Corporation, which eventually formed American Airways, the immediate predecessor of today's American Airlines. In 1934 the company reorganized American Airways and became American Airlines, Inc. Not long after, American developed an air traffic control system that would later be used by all airlines and administered by the U.S. government. The company also introduced the first domestic scheduled U.S. freight service in 1944. The Douglas 7Aircraft Company and American took the initiative and debuted the first commercial flight with the Douglas DC-3 between Chicago and New York on June 25, 1936. American focused on the innovation and modernization of its fleet and acquired its first McDonnell Douglas MD-11 in 1991, which accommodated 251 passengers and made it possible for American to venture into international markets.

In 1989 AMR bought Eastern Air Lines' Latin American routes, the U.S.-London routes from TWA, and Continental's Seattle-Tokyo routes. In addition, the corporation obtained approval to fly to Manchester, England, from the Department of Transportation.

Following a decade of prosperity in the 1990s, AMR was one of numerous major airlines to see its bottom line drastically drop in the early 2000s. However, American also received much passenger approval in the 2000s by taking out at least two rows on every plane to provide greater comfort. In 2001 American expanded by purchasing the air fleet of Trans World Airlines, Inc. (TWA). TWA's 168 aircraft were repainted in American's colors.

COMPANY FINANCES

In 2002 AMR Corp. posted a first-quarter loss of $575 million, and officials saw no way the industry could recover to keep all of 2002 from being a disappointment to employees and shareholders. AMR Chairman and Chief Executive Officer Donald J. Carty pointed to slumping business ticket sales for the company's ongoing woes, according to the *Dallas Morning News*. Adding to the revenue losses are mounting costs for labor. The poor 2002 quarterly report comes on the heels of a horrific fourth quarter of 2001 when AMR self-reported losses of $798 million. Losses for 2001 were $1.8 billion. In contrast, just five years earlier, AMR Corp. was enjoying one of its most prosperous time periods. In 1997 AMR Corp. generated revenues of $18.5 billion, up 4.6 percent from $17.7 billion in 1996. Of that, the Airline Group (which consists of American Airlines, Inc., AMR Eagle, Inc., and American's Cargo Division) brought in combined revenues of $16.9 billion in 1997.

STRATEGY

American Airlines maximizes passenger traffic and revenue potential by channeling into or through its hubs, which serve as gateways for the airlines' route network. Through its hub-and-spoke system, American serves more markets with greater frequency than would be possible with the same number of aircraft in a point-to-point route system. American's largest hub is the Dallas/Fort Worth International Airport; additional hubs include Chicago, Miami, New York (Kennedy), and San Juan. American has begun construction of a new, $1-billion terminal at Kennedy that, by 2005, will considerably enhance American's ability to raise profits serving the competitive New York area. The company believes these hubs are well positioned as geographically favorable locations for continued growth, but as with other airlines, hubs have drawn governmental raised eyebrows regarding perceived higher rates in hub cities where carriers are presumed to have a size advantage. American Airlines has many cooperative-service relationships (sometimes called code shares) with selected airlines across the world. These airlines service many destinations worldwide that American does not serve itself. Through these relationships, American can offer service to destinations throughout the world. Although tickets show American Airlines' flight numbers, all or part of the journey might be on one of their cooperative partners.

Further efforts toward continued growth for the company include expanding foreign routes in areas such as Latin America, Asia, and Europe, as well as alliances with carriers such as British Airways. In addition, American put plans on hold to upgrade its air fleet in 2003, but the company plans to aggressively return to the building of its fleet in 2004 and beyond. This arrangement will allow the airline to move gradually toward a very high level of fleet commonality and provide for modest capacity growth in future years.

INFLUENCES

American Airlines, while struggling financially and caught in the general downfall of the airline industry during the 2000s, seems headed for recovery and seems no where close to the bankruptcy filings almost certain to be the fate of USAir and United Airlines, according to analysts. In addition to stable management under its chief executive officers, the company itself attributes its comparative success to several factors, including sensible pricing and favorable fuel prices. The company also gave a nod to its employees around the world, adding that it was their dedication and teamwork that gave American's customers the good service that keeps them coming back.

Compared to its competition, American has certain advantages. Its fleet is young (average aircraft age—eight years), efficient, and quiet. It has an immense domestic and international route structure, secured by efficient hubs. In addition, the company's AAdvantage frequent flyer program is the largest in the industry, and it has added members formerly with TWA, a flight acquired by American. American established this program to develop passenger loyalty by offering awards to travelers for their continued patronage. Aadvantage members earn mileage credits for flights on American and American Eagle.

CURRENT TRENDS

A key element of Americans' strategic growth plan took place in 1996, when the company began creation of a worldwide alliance between American and British Airways, introducing extensive code sharing across each other's networks and establishing full reciprocity between frequent flyer programs. Additionally, the carriers combined passenger and cargo activities between the United States and Europe and agreed to share the

CHRONOLOGY:
Key Dates for American Airlines, Inc.

1934: American Airways, Inc. reorganizes to form American Airlines, Inc.

1936: American uses Douglas DC-3 for first domestic flight between Chicago and New York

1944: The first domestic scheduled freight service is introduced

1953: An 80-passenger DC-7 makes the first scheduled non-stop transcontinental flight

1959: The first Boeing 707s enter into service for American

1968: President C.R. Smith leaves to join the Johnson Administration

1974: C.R. Smith returns to bring American out of its financial crisis

1981: AAdvantage Program is introduced

1989: Expands into Latin America, the United Kingdom, and Japan

1991: Purchases McDonnell Douglas MD-11, which carried 251 passengers

1994: Chemical Product Control Program is initiated

1998: First flight attendant class in which all attendants will be bi- or multi-lingual

2000: Sabre Holdings Corp. became a separate entity from its former parent company

2001: On September 11 at 8:45 a.m. EDT, terrorists crash American Airlines Flight 11 out of Boston into the north tower of the World Trade Center, causing a conflagration and later the disintegration of the building with large loss of life; American Airlines was cited for environmental awareness actions by the State of California EPA's 2001 Governor's Environmental and Economic Leadership Awards Program

resulting profits on these services. This alliance positioned American to compete in thousands of new markets and made them competitive with global alliances of other major U.S. carriers.

Due to competition, fares secured by customers in advance have remained substantially low in the past 15

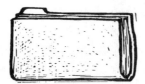

PREPARATION FOR CRISIS

A horrific reality of business as usual for American Airlines in the modern era has been the transference of information to the general public, United States government, and to families of victims following an airline crash, hijacking, or attempted hijacking. In 2001 managing director of strategic communications for American Airlines August Whitcomb was called upon to handle breaking a crisis of previously unfathomable consequence. On September 11, 2001, two American Airlines jets, flights 11 and 77, were commandeered by hijackers and ultimately destroyed with large loss of life. Whitcomb and his crisis team consulted American Airlines' crisis manual, but the extraordinary loss of human life and worldwide focus on the crisis forced the team to improvise, according to the *Albuquerque Tribune*. "The first thing the company's crisis plan said was to disseminate information: how many people were on the flight, where it was going, where it was from," reported the *Tribune*, but as the team prepared to do so, the FBI ordered all information halted. The company normally would fly key crisis management personnel and executives to the crash scenes, but the nation's planes were grounded for fear of additional terrorists perhaps boarding planes elsewhere. The company then chose to put a human face on the tragedy, making CEO Don Carty (since retired) the spokesperson for the airline on all major TV networks. "He could explain what we were going through," Whitcomb told the *Tribune*. "The first two hours of any crisis determine whether you win or lose [and] whether [the public] forgive[s] you," he said. "It's how you respond that allows people to embrace you and come back to you." American Airlines, quite evidently, performed well under pressure that day and has been given immense public support and empathy. The main lesson Whitcomb had to impart to others, he said, at a meeting of other public relations professionals attended by the *Tribune* is this: "You need to be ready."

years, but airlines generally reap larger profits from last-minute purchases, mainly from the business sector. To fill seats on weekend flights, or flights suffering reduced capacity due to the generally flat economy or fears after September 11, 2001, American promotes reduced or one-time favorable fares via the Internet. Participants in its NetsAAvers program register through Americans' Web site to receive a weekly e-mail message outlining reduced fare offerings.

PRODUCTS

To focus on air safety, American equips planes in its fleet with early warning devices called Enhanced Ground Proximity Warning Systems. The new system provides flight crews with a map-like display of nearby terrain on all sides of the aircraft. Existing ground proximity systems, by contrast, can only read terrain that is directly below the aircraft. On the other hand, American Airlines has taken a vigorous stand against security checks that its executives deem are either not-productive against terrorism or outright intrusive and causing fliers to find alternative means of travel or to stay home. " I don't think great security comes from strip-searching Aunt Molly in Iowa," Donald J. Carty told the *Dallas Morning News*. He also objected to overly vigorous pilot searches prior to flights.

CORPORATE CITIZENSHIP

Environmental awareness is promoted throughout the company. In the late 1990s, the company was committed to developing and carrying out business practices that help safeguard the earth's environment. They started the in-flight recycling program that recycles more than 336,000 pounds of aluminum annually. Since October 1999, AMR has followed a ten-point code of corporate environmental conduct, known as the Ceres Principles, assuring commitment to energy conservation, reduction and disposal of wastes, and management commitment, according to a company statement.

GLOBAL PRESENCE

American provides service to and from cities in various other countries, across the Atlantic and the Pacific, and also between the United States and the Caribbean, and Central and South America. International travel normally contributes about 30 percent of American's annual revenues. However, with a stagnant economy, plus traveler fears following the outbreak of hostilities involving such countries as Afghanistan, Israel, Palestine, Pakistan, and India, international travel was significantly and adversely affected. For example, in March 2002, International traffic for the month was down 18.1 percent for American Airlines, while international capacity was down 19.6 percent.

American is the dominant U.S. carrier to Latin America, serving 27 nations in the Caribbean, Mexico, Central America, and South America, and the number two U.S. carrier to Europe. Current American code share alliances include South African Airways, British Midland Airways, Gulf Air, Quantas Airways, Canadian Airlines, Singapore Airlines, LOT Polish Airlines, China Airlines, El Al Israel Airlines, and TACA Group. The TACA group is composed of TACA International Airlines of El Salvador and its affiliate partners-AVIATECA of Guatemala, COPA of Panama, LACSA of Costa Rica, NICA of Nicaragua, and TACA de Honduras. Current additional partners pending with the TACA Group of Central America carriers include LAPSA of Paraguay, BWIA, Transaero Airlines, EL AL, and Avianca.

EMPLOYMENT

The airline business is labor intensive. American has employees based in the Americas, Asia, the Caribbean, Europe, and the Middle East. After years of relative prosperity for the airline, American was forced to lay off more than 13,000 employees between the end of 2001 and February 2002. Some were recalled by May 2002.

On March 2, 1998, American Airlines began its first flight attendant training class in the company's history in which all the prospective U.S.-based attendants have either bilingual or multilingual skills. The first class included 52 new hires who were expected to begin work on flights in the spring. This group of flight attendants spoke Spanish, French, Japanese, German, Portugese, Italian, and Swedish; all also speak English and some speak additional languages.

SOURCES OF INFORMATION

Bibliography

"AMR/American Airlines: A Brief History." Dallas, TX: American Airlines, May 2002.

"AMR. . .A Global Company," 4 May 1998. Available at http://www.amrcorp.com/amr/global.htm.

"AMR, American Airlines Ratings Raised to Investment Grade by S&P." *Standard & Poor's CreditWire*, 16 June 1997. Available at http://wwwa.pcfn.com/sitelite/standard/investhelp.htm.

"AMR At A Glance," 12 June 1998. Available at http://www .amrcorp.com.

"AMR Corporation Corporate Facts." Dallas, TX: American Airlines, September 1996.

"AMR Corporation 2001 Annual Report." Dallas, TX: American Airlines, January 1997.

"AMR Corporate Communications," 4 May 1998. Available at http://www.amrcorp.com.

"AMR's Environmental Programs," 4 May 1998. Available at http://www.amrcorp.com/amr/environ.htm.

"Carty Gets Options, Less Pay, No Bonus." *The Houston Chronicle*, 23 April 2002.

Cronin, Mary. "The Travel Agents' Dilemma." *Fortune*, 11 May 1998. Available at http://www.pathfinder.com/fortune.

"Financial Results," 4 May 2002. Available at http://www .amrcorp.com/amr/investor/results.htm.

"Hundreds at American Airlines Take Voluntary Pay Cuts." *The New York Times,* 5 October 2001.

Jones, Kathryn. "How the CEOs of American, Continental, and Southwest Are Navigating the Uncertainty of the World Since 9-11." *Texas Monthly*, February 2002.

"Major Airlines' Shares Fall." *Newsday*, 5 June 2002.

Maxxon, Terry, and Terri Langford." American CEO criticizes Transportation Security Administration." *The Dallas Morning News*, 21 May 2002.

Merrion, Paul. "Flight Plans Diverge for Rivals." *Crain's Chicago Business*, 3 June 2002.

"Net Loss For Airlines In 2002 Climbs To $4 Billion." *Airline Financial News*, 6 May 2002.

"Newest AA Flight Attendant Class Is Speaking Your Language," 10 March 1998. Available at http://www.amrcorp.com.

For an annual report:

on the Internet at: http://www.amrcorp.com/air/investor/ investor.htm **or** write: AMR Corporation, Mail Drop 5651, PO Box 619616, Dallas/Ft. Worth Airport, TX 75261-9616

For additional industry research:

Investigate companies by their Standard Industrial Classification Codes, also known as SICs. American Airlines, Inc.'s primary SICs are:

4512 Air Transporation Scheduled

4513 Air Courier Services

Also investigate companies by their North American Industry Classification System codes, also known as NAICS codes. American Airlines, Inc.'s primary NAICS code is:

481110 Scheduled Air Transportation

AOL Time Warner Inc.

FOUNDED: 1989
EMPLOYEES: 89,300

Contact Information:

HEADQUARTERS: 75 Rockefeller Plz.
New York, NY 10019
PHONE: (212)484-8000
FAX: (212)956-2847
URL: http://www.aoltimewarner.com

OVERVIEW

AOL Time Warner stands as the largest entertainment and information company in the world. It was formed in 2001 after America Online Inc. bought Time Warner Inc. for $124 billion. Based in New York, the company has a hand in everything from marketing books, magazines, music, and videos through Time Inc., to the television production business. It also has interests in the Atlanta Braves professional baseball team and the Atlanta Hawks professional basketball team.

In 2002, AOL Time Warner has seen stock prices drastically fall following the merger of AOL and Time Warner. In addition, the company has been burdened by a heavy debt load. Company executives publicly apologized to shareholders at a 2002 meeting and promised to be better stewards of investor moneys. A large portion of the company's cash flow is from cable operations, an industry in flux, and AOL itself has seen its worth downgraded considerably in 2001 and 2002. Can AOL Time Warner reverse its decline? As of May 2002, the jury was still out as stockholders continue to unload shares, and many analysts pointed to AOL Time Warner as a textbook example of how a merger may not be the best financial situation for two giant companies.

Due to slumping AOL and cable operations, excessive stock options for executives, and the declining worth of AOL Time Warner stock, analysts have wondered aloud if and when a company turnaround is coming. Even after the economy eventually improves, most analysts were uncertain if the future looked bright for AOL Time Warner.

AOL Time Warner produces innumerable products. Its major industries are publishing books and magazines;

direct marketing, such as the Book-of-the-Month Club; music, including Warner Brothers and Atlantic; America Online services, and cable, with Time Warner Cable and networks CNN and HBO.

COMPANY FINANCES

The picture was bleak indeed in 2002, as AOL Time Warner shares in mid-year were worth around $17.80, a decline of 66 percent since the merger of AOL and Time Warner in 2002. Worse, the company posted a total loss of $54.2 billion for the first quarter of 2002 alone, raising the number of doubters who saw a reversal in the company's financial misfortunes before the end of 2003 or even 2004.

Another sign of weakness in 2001 was AOL Time Warner's ad revenue which slipped 3 percent to $8.49 billion for the year. The company has been plagued by a substantial debt load, much of which is due to sputtering cable operations and less-than-anticipated revenues by America Online.

AOL Time Warner, which traded shares of stock for $95.81 just before the merger of AOL and Time Warner, can only return to that heady time of success if it can shore up its sagging AOL Internet property, said CEO Richard Parsons at a stockholder meeting in 2002.

ANALYSTS' OPINIONS

Much of the controversy surrounding AOL Time Warner Inc. stems from the company's outstanding debt, the declining ad revenues of America Online, a generally poor economic outlook for cable enterprises in 2002, and the bold predictions of success by AOL prior to its merger with Time Warner. In 2002, Lehman Brothers analyst Holly Becker said that AOL earnings before interest, taxes, depreciation and amortization growth will stay stagnant or fall further through 2005 until the company can replace lost advertising revenues and jumpstart sagging operations, Becker said.

HISTORY

Rumors of a Time Warner and America Online merger were rampant in 1999, and these proved to have basis in fact in January 2000 when the two giants announced plans to merge. The announcement resulted in impressive gains to the value of AOL stock. Soon after, a Senate Judiciary Committee interviewed executives Steve Case of AOL and chairman Gerald Levin of Time Warner, grilling them to make sure cable broadband services would be available to Internet providers other than just America Online to prevent monopolistic business

FAST FACTS:
About AOL Time Warner Inc.

Ownership: AOL Time Warner is a publicly owned company traded on the New York Stock Exchange.

Ticker Symbol: AOL

Officers: Stephen (Steve) M. Case, Chmn. of the Board; Robert E. "Ted" Turner III, VChmn.; Richard D. Parsons, CEO; Robert W. Pittman, COO

Employees: 89,300

Principal Subsidiary Companies: AOL Time Warner, Inc. owns hundreds of companies. Included are AOL, Book-of-the-Month-Club; Cable News Network; Cartoon Network; Castle Rock Entertainment; Digital Services Development Group; HBO; Little, Brown (book publishers); New Line Cinema; Time, Inc. (magazine publishing); Time Life; Time Warner Cable; Time Warner Communications; Turner Broadcasting System; Warner Books; Warner Brothers; and Warner Music Group.

Chief Competitors: AOL Time Warner, Inc. competes against almost every company in the entertainment field: book publishers, cable systems, magazine publishers, movie and television production companies, pay cable stations, and record companies. Some competitors include Advance Publications, Cablevision Systems, Direct TV, Dow Jones, EMI Group, Forbes, MGM, Sony, TCI, Times Mirror, and Viacom.

practices. In spring of 2000, as the Federal Communications Commission (FCC) investigated details of the merger, the market in high-tech stocks plummeted, but shareholders in both Time and Time Warner approve the merger. Later, Ted Turner commented that he should have moved to purchase Time Warner in order to fire some executives whose vision and actions failed to meet his expectations. In January 2001, the FTC approved the merger. Soon afterward, the stock value of AOL Time Warner stock fell dramatically.

INFLUENCES

Like other conglomerates, AOL Time Warner's recent past and future has been enhanced and stymied by

CHRONOLOGY:

Key Dates for AOL Time Warner Inc.

1917: The Warner brothers—Jack, Albert, Harry, and Sam—begin making films

1923: Two reporters from the *Boston News* launch a weekly news magazine called *Time*; Warner Brothers is incorporated

1927: Warner Bros. releases the first talking film to reach a wide audience

1936: Time Inc. introduces a weekly picture magazine called *Life*

1949: A government antitrust suit makes Warner Bros. give up its theater chain

1952: Time-Life Broadcast subsidiary is founded

1954: Time diversifies its line by publishing *Sports Illustrated*

1966: Warner is sold to Seven Arts Productions

1971: Steven Ross buys Warner Bros. and renames it Warner Communications

1972: Due to production costs, Time ceases publication of *Life* magazine; a Time subsidiary launches Home Box Office

1986: Warner purchases Warner Amex Cable from American Express

1989: Warner Communications and Time Inc. merge to form Time Warner

1991: Time Warner goes public by issuing shares whose price was based on the number of shareholders who participated

1996: Time Warner purchases Turner Broadcasting

1998: TCI Cable and Time Warner sign an agreement for TCI to carry the WB network

2001: America Online and Time Warner merge to form AOL Time Warner

2002: AOL Time Warner stockholders express anger and disappointment over stock prices, which dropped considerably since merger, while company's six top executives earned millions of dollars in stock options from the merger

mergers and acquisitions. Time Warner CEO Gerald M. Levin launched the idea to distribute HBO in 1975 using satellites. The company continued to purchase cable companies as it saw opportunities for growth. After the company merged with Turner Broadcasting, a $7.6 billion investment, its cable business had become an expensive one to operate. In fact, the company sold a portion of the E! Entertainment Network and dumped its Interactive-TV Network in 1997. Previously held high hopes for the company's dominant presence in the information field vanished. High-tech costs to implement such cable systems ended up being more than the company was willing to invest after the merger with Turner. Turner himself predicted that no more than two rivals would monopolize the cable industry in the twenty-first century.

Time Warner demonstrated a defined strategy by merging with Turner Broadcasting. In doing so, Time Warner was able to acquire powerful assets like CNN, TNT, and New Line Cinema. However, while Time Warner was perceived to be a powerhouse in the areas of "old" media such as print and broadcast media, it was viewed as deficient in the "new" media areas as "media convergence" became the buzz phrase of 2000. In 2001, the corporate marriage of AOL and Time Warner was applauded by investors as the ultimate "blue skies" business merger. Instead, by 2002, it was clear those blue skies had caved in, as angry investors confronted AOL Time Warner execs at an annual shareholder meeting held in New York City.

CURRENT TRENDS

Feel very, very sorry for AOL Time Warner in the short term, say many analysts, but the company's many strengths in new and old media, plus its stable of solid executives in management positions, should dictate its eventual rebound. As analyst Tom Wolzien, of Sanford C. Bernstein predicted on CNBC's Business Center in 2002, AOL Time Warner has unlimited prospects for growth. With well over three million people spending 70 minutes a day with AOL Time Warner print, broadcast, or Internet media, the company eventually is going to see its advertising revenues expand, noted Wolzien.

PRODUCTS

AOL Time Warner, as the largest entertainment and information conglomerate in the world, has influence in the business of media and entertainment. Through Little, Brown, Time Life, Time Inc., and Warner Books, the company publishes books and magazines. It produces films for television and theatrical release under the studio brands of New Line Cinema, Warner Brothers, Turner Broadcasting, Castle Rock Entertainment, and HBO. The cable television news and entertainment industry is carried through Time Warner Cable, and other movie and cartoon networks. Countless other smaller companies operate, as well, under its banner. The America Online merger in 2001 gave the company unprecedented expansion possibilities in the areas of media convergence and online publishing.

In addition to its many media companies, Time Warner owns two professional sports teams, the Atlanta Braves baseball organization and the Atlanta Hawks basketball team. Both of these acquisitions came from the merger with Turner.

CORPORATE CITIZENSHIP

AOL Time Warner has been involved in and has encouraged its employees to participate in community services through the ECHO (Employees Caring and Helping Others) program. The company also annually honors employees who have volunteered their services with the Andrew Heiskell Community Service Award. Co-workers nominate employees for these awards, and AOL Time Warner issues each winner a cash reward. In 2002 AOL Time Warner Foundation provided a grant to the Museum of the City of New York for the archiving of September 11, 2001, video footage of the terrorist attack on New York and the Pentagon.

GLOBAL PRESENCE

With sales in the United States, Europe, the Pacific Rim, and other regions, AOL Time Warner Inc. has become a media and entertainment company dominant in the industry but plagued with debt service and the continued stalling of high tech stocks.

SOURCES OF INFORMATION

Bibliography

"AOL Time Warner Logs $54.2 billion Loss." *CNNMoney* 25 April 2002. Available at http://www.cnnmoney.com.

Howe, Peter J. " Insider Faces a Tough Time Steering AOL Time Warner Through Turbulent Times in the Net-Media Industry." *The Boston Globe,* 16 December 2001.

Kapadia, Reshma. "AOL Time Warner Stock Tumbles." *Toronto Star,* 21 February, 2002.

Picchi, Aimee. "AOL Time Warner CEO Says Revitalizing AOL a Top Goal." *Bloomberg News,* 16 May 2002.

Schifrin, Matthew. "The Mess at Time Warner." *Forbes,* 20 May 1996.

Shook, David. "Old Trumps New at AOL; Cyber-age Dynamo? Not Quite." *Business Week Online,* 15 May 2002.

"AOL Time Warner Inc." May 2002. Available at http://www.aoltimewarner.com.

"AOL Time Warner Inc." *Hoover's Online,* May 2002. Available at http://www.hoovers.com.

"Time Warner Selling E!" *Cable News Network, Inc.,* 16 December 1996.

"Tom Wolzien, of Sanford C. Bernstein, talks about the future of AOL Time Warner." *CNBC News Transcripts,* 18 March 2002.

For an annual report:

write: Investor Relations, Time Warner, Inc., 75 Rockefeller Plz., New York, NY 10019

For additional industry research:

Investigate companies by their Standard Industrial Classification Codes, also known as SICs. AOL Time Warner Inc.'s primary SICs are:

4841 Cable and Other Pay TV Services

5699 Miscellaneous Apparel and Accessories

6794 Patent Owners and Lessors

7812 Motion Picture and Video Production

7819 Services Allied to Motion Pictures

7822 Motion Picture and Tape Distribution

7832 Motion Picture Theaters

7922 Theatrical Producers and Services

Also investigate companies by their North American Industry Classification System codes, also known as NAICS codes. AOL Time Warner Inc.'s primary NAICS codes are:

511120 Periodical Publishers

512120 Motion Picture and Video Distribution

541990 All Other Professional, Scientific, and Technical Services

Apple Computer Inc.

FOUNDED: 1977

Contact Information:
HEADQUARTERS: 1 Infinite Loop
    Cupertino, CA 95014-2084
PHONE: (408)996-1010
FAX: (408)974-9974
TOLL FREE: (800)MY-APPLE
EMAIL: investor_relations@apple.com
URL: http://www.apple.com

OVERVIEW

Apple Computer Inc. is one of the world's leading computer companies. The company designs, builds, and markets computers, peripheral equipment, and software for homes, businesses, educational institutions, and the government. Apple also provides customers with multimedia and connectivity solutions. Apple was a pioneer in the field of personal computers with its easy-to-use, object-based Apple Macintosh—the bulk of Apple's net sales come from the sale of this line. This user-friendly computer interface "for the rest of us" has since spawned competitive imitations, namely Microsoft's Windows '95. In 1997 Apple began fighting back to recapture users lost to dominant IBM-compatible computers running the Windows operating system. By 2002 the company had returned to profitability under co-founder and CEO Steve Jobs, thanks to its Unix platform OSX operating system, the popular Titanium Powerbook G-4, and ultra-spaceage design of the flat screen iMac desktop models.

COMPANY FINANCES

Apple Computer returned to profitability in 2001 and 2002, shaking off an earlier slump when customers rejected its G-4 cube release. The company earned $40 million in the second quarter of 2002 on revenues of $1.5 billion. In the second quarter of 2001, Apple earned a comparable $43 million. Second quarter sales of 813,000 Macintosh computers in 2002 represented an 8 percent gain over second quarter 2001 shipments. The company's stock price in spring 2002 was $26.11 per share, down from around $28.00 in 1998. For the years 1993 through

1997, Apple stock had a five-year high of $65.25 per share, and $12.75 was its five-year low.

ANALYSTS' OPINIONS

Steve Jobs' return to Apple as CEO in the 1990s was applauded by some and criticized by others, but few could voice complaints in the 2000s as the company co-founder brought the company back to profitability. Many praise his pioneering work in taking object-oriented technology to the World Wide Web and see the creation of the OSX operating system as Apple's best selling point.

Analysts also gave kudos to Jobs and Apple for opening 27 walk-in Apple Computer super stores in the United States to augment its already strong Internet sales.

Apple's presence in the education markets and in the offices of graphics professionals has always been high, but by 2002 the company still found itself with only a 3 to 5 percent market share of the higher-growth corporate and consumer markets. Still, there was hope. "Apple now boasts operating margins of about 30 percent—triple or quadruple the average for the temporarily downtrodden PC biz," according to a 2002 article for *Business Week Online*. The article continued, "Apple's too-small market presence in the higher-growth corporate and consumer markets reflects a new for significant speed and options to be incorporated in the next line of PowerMac models which seem like relatively old plugs in the Apple stable where flashy steeds such as iMacs and G-4 Titanium Powerbooks also reside."

Cited as positives for the company were its strong position in the education and desktop publishing markets where *Mac Addict* graphics designers rule, as well as Apple's significant progress in reducing staff and operating costs. This, and its improved financial position in 2002 (including healthy cash flow of $4.3 billion in 2002), helped improve Apple's outlook for the remainder of the 2000s, although analysts warned that the company could falter if a significant new product bombs the way the G-4 desktop cube once did.

HISTORY

Steve Jobs and Stephen Wozniak, two college dropouts, built the first Apple computer in Jobs' garage in 1976. This microcomputer, the Apple I, was a bare-bones creation with no monitor, casing, or keyboard. These were later added, as were software and ports for third-party peripherals. On January 3, 1977, Apple Computer Inc. was incorporated. In 1980 with the sale of more than 130,000 Apple IIs and $117 million under its belt, the company went public at $22 per share. After a 1981 plane crash, Wozniak returned briefly but ultimately left the company, reappearing on the scene many years later

FAST FACTS:
About Apple Computer Inc.

Ownership: Apple is a publicly owned company traded on NASDAQ, the Tokyo Stock Exchange (under symbol AAPLE), and the Frankfurt Stock Exchange (symbol APCD).

Ticker Symbol AAPL

Officers: Steven P. Jobs, CEO and Co-founder, 46; Fred D. Anderson, CFO, 57, 2001 salary $657,039; Timothy D. Cook, EVP of Worldwide Sales and Operations, 41, 2001 salary $452,219, 2001 bonus $500,000; Nancy R. Heinen, SVP, Gen. Counsel, and Sec., 45

Employees: 9,603

Chief Competitors: Apple Computer's main competitors in the electronic computer industry include Hewlett-Packard, Dell, Gateway, Intel, and IBM. Networking and software competitors include Microsoft, Novell, and Sun Microsystems.

---

in 2002 with his new company offering wireless technology innovations.

In 1984 Apple revolutionized microcomputing with the introduction of its Macintosh (Mac) personal computer. Unlike other computers on the market, the Mac interface allowed users to forgo the ubiquitous text commands, instead opting for a system whereby the user would control operations by clicking and dragging on-screen "icons."

According to some accounts, Jobs originally opposed the Mac and only embraced it (dismissing its very proponents and taking the credit himself) after the dismal market failure of his Lisa system. After a volatile power struggle within the company, Apple's board of directors voted unanimously to replace Jobs with former PepsiCo executive, John Sculley. Soon thereafter, Apple entered the desktop publishing market with the Mac Plus and LaserWriter printer. In 1987 Apple founded a software company, later named Claris, then replaced by File-Maker.

The rise of archnemesis Microsoft took larger and larger bites out of Apple's market share, and the company soon had to contend with a comparable opponent with a similar product. Complicating matters was the fact that Apple would not license its software to other computer manufacturers, a move that did not improve the company's marketability. Widespread competition in the PC market often made IBM clones more economical, with software widely available. In 1994 the company released its Power Mac computer, though sales did not live up to expectations. In 1995 the company was forced to shut down its online service, eWorld. In 1996 Apple brought in a new CEO, Gilbert Amelio.

Widely regarded as the force behind the successful turnaround at National Semiconductor, Amelio immediately announced major changes at Apple. He divided the company into seven divisions, each responsible for its own success or failure. Nonetheless, under this new organizational structure, divisions were more accountable to top management, which would have tighter control over the company's actions. Soon thereafter, Amelio announced the purchase of Jobs' company, NeXT software. Jobs would return to Apple as a consultant and soon, in a display of fireworks, Amelio was out and Jobs was in as CEO. Under Jobs, Apple introduced its Unix platform OSX operating system and marketed such products as the unsuccessful G-4 cube and the highly popular, stylized G-4 Titanium Powerbooks, iMacs and iPod digital players to take the once-foundering company back to respectability and profitability in 2001 and 2002.

STRATEGY

Analysts generally agree that the challenge facing Apple and its highly visible CEO Steve Jobs in the 2000s is a strong need for the continued improvement of the Mac OSX operating system and the addition of the iPhoto application. What's needed is a strong counterpunch to Microsoft's lawsuit-weakened midsection that can see Apple Computer taking a sweeter market share of the corporate and consumer sales market as it already has in its self-claimed 25 percent market share of the educational sales market. Apple has failed to deliver software for business with anywhere the regularity of the software coming out for Windows-based PCs, begrudgingly putting the popular Microsoft Office on its Apple products.

Apple's primary strategy during the late 1990s was to maintain and augment its market share in the personal computer industry while developing and expanding similar endeavors such as personal interactive products, client/server systems, online services, and the licensing of its Macintosh operating system. The company's original strategy of not licensing the operating system to other developers, or authorizing the production of Mac clones, came back to haunt it.

In 1994 the company made an about face, licensing three companies to produce Macintosh clones and, in turn, lost some of its market share. That same year, it released its Power Mac, a much faster computer running on a PowerPC microchip, which allowed users to use

software for several different platforms, including Windows. In order to spark the creation of more Mac-compatible software, Apple licensed the rights to its operating system (Mac OS) to IBM and Motorola in 1996. In 1997 then-interim CEO Steve Jobs announced the company was pursuing an alliance with Microsoft to offer a Mac version of Microsoft Office.

In 1997, in the interest of long-term viability, the company embarked on a major reorganization and draconian cost-cutting measures, including the layoffs of several thousand employees (almost a third of the company). It also brought Steve Jobs back as interim (and soon-to-be permanent) CEO, replacing Gil Amelio and resulting in yet another strategy shift for Apple Computer. These and other moves resulted in Apple's first profitable quarter in years (first quarter 1998). Jobs streamlined the organization, squelched Mac cloning, bear-hugged old nemesis Microsoft, forged a foothold in network computers costing less than $1,000, and (taking a cue from Dell Computer) started selling built-to-order systems over the Internet. Apple generates sales through catalogs, through regional retailers, and nationally through CompUSA.

In May 1998, Jobs announced that Apple was pursuing a new strategy focused on regaining market share in software development—developers who deserted the Macintosh operating system in favor of Windows during the mid- to late 1990s. Toward this goal, Jobs was scrapping the company's Rhapsody operating system except as a transition vehicle to the new Mac OSX (OS "10"). Rhapsody would have allowed the Mac's operating system to run software for chips made by Intel, IBM, and Motorola as well as Apple, but would have required software developers to rewrite old Macintosh code from scratch. The new system, OSX, would have features such as hardware memory protection, more efficient multitasking, and faster networking. It also would not require programmers to rewrite old code from scratch. Jobs' strategy was supported by Microsoft, Adobe, and Macromedia executives, who were happy to be able to write applications that worked on both the old and new Mac systems. In the wake of Jobs' announcement, Apple's stock price rose to $39.9, the highest it reached in a year.

INFLUENCES

Apple's comfortable advantage was eclipsed in the late 1980s when Microsoft released its Windows operating system. The Windows graphical interface was in many ways similar to the look and feel of the Macintosh—so similar that Apple decided to sue, albeit unsuccessfully. In the mid-1990s, with Windows running on more affordable IBM clones, Apple's earnings began to fall. The company's problems included shrinking revenues, defecting executives, market-stealing clone sales, and troubled products, such as its discontinued Newton handheld computers. However, Apple owners remain the industry's most loyal repurchasers. And Macintosh computers still had a niche in educational institutions and design shops. Designers specializing in Web page design and graphic arts especially liked the Mac systems, making the company a major Internet products provider.

CURRENT TRENDS

While third-party software designed for Windows abounded, Macintosh-compatible software was much harder to come by. In 2002 Apple Computer was offering a few more items than it had in the past, but not enough to draw standing ovations from analysts. In Java server applications for the Internet, Apple offered powerful WebObjects 5.1. The OSX operating system was upgraded to OSX.1, which benefits those using popular digital peripherals such as DV camcorders, MP3 players, and digital cameras, but another upgrade is sorely needed to satisfy the *Mac Addict* graphics designers and art directors who have remained loyal to the company through some mighty thin years. If there is one area that Jobs has failed, say analysts, it is in bringing software designers into the fold to remedy the great lack of Macintosh-compatible software products. The 1990s saw a boom in the commercialization of the Internet. Customers by the millions were joining the online market, an area in which Apple hoped to shine. One of the company's major efforts to do so was the forming of its WebObjects Consulting Group, which was formed around WebObjects, Apple's leading Web application development platform. The consulting group provides in-depth consulting for businesses on strategic web-based solutions for database publishing, digital asset management, and e-commerce.

PRODUCTS

New products offered at Apple include the 10-gigabyte hard drive iPod capable of holding some 2000 songs, the smart and sleek iMac line, and the immensely popular (especially with students) G-4 Powerbooks. In March 2002 Apple Computer took the sheet off Bluetooth wireless-data standard, a low-bandwidth, open-specification solution that runs off the OSX operating system to wirelessly connect (cable-absent) computers and printers and/or personal digital assistants. According to Apple, "Bluetooth also enables short-range wireless voice and data connectivity between desktop and laptop computers, personal digital assistants (PDAs), mobile phones, printers, scanners, digital cameras and even home appliances." The first iMac, a Macintosh computer designed for consumers, came out in 1998. "Reception from the Macintosh community and computer industry as a whole to the iMac has been reminiscent of the rollout of the first Macintosh in 1984, which also featured a break-

CHRONOLOGY:
Key Dates for Apple Computer Inc.

1976: Steven (Steve) Jobs and Stephen Wozniak build the first Apple computer in Jobs' Santa Clara Valley, California, garage

1977: Apple Computer Inc. is incorporated

1980: Apple Inc. goes public at $22 per share

1984: Introduces the Macintosh personal computer

1985: Jobs leaves Apple and creates a new computer company, NeXT Incorporated

1988: Apple reorganizes into four operating divisions and the company brings suits against Microsoft and Hewlett-Packard for copyright infringement of its operating system

1991: PowerBook notebook is introduced, gaining 21 percent market share in less than six months

1992: Most of its lawsuit against Microsoft and Hewlett-Packard is dismissed

1994: The Power Mac is released

1996: Apple brings in new CEO Gilbert Amelio

1997: NeXT is purchased, bringing Jobs back to Apple as a consultant and interim CEO; Apple's board ousts Amelio in July, and Jobs surprises industry by agreeing to release Mac version of Microsoft Office

1998: Apple dumps its Claris division and puts the operation into a new Apple unit called FileMaker; Jobs announces release of popular G-3 Powerbook laptop and iMac desktop model with attractive design

1999: Apple Computer Inc. releases Mac OSX Server operating system for its Unix strength in a Macintosh environment for the Web

2000: Jobs transitions from interim head to formally take over as CEO; Apple releases cube G-4, which proves to be a huge company loss for the year

2002: Apple puts releases a digital music player called the iPod and gives iMac a facelift with flat-panel display; the company posts second straight year of profitability with a $40 million posting in the second quarter of 2002

EVEN MAC ADDICTS DEMAND APPLE AGAIN "THINK DIFFERENT"

"Macworld 2001 will live in infamy—for completely and totally wasting the biggest billboard and bus-stop shelter ad campaign New York has ever seen," wrote Lukas Hauser for *Wired News,* expressing the general opinion that Apple Computer advertising hasn't had a winner since the late 1990s. Instead, Apple Computer seems to have placed all its marketing eggs in promoting its high profile Apple Stores, popping up in America at something-less-than-Taco Bell-like numbers of about twenty a year. The best Apple has done in the 2000s was its March 2001 TV commercial to promote Mac custom CD burning, which featured the likes of musical artists Barry White, George Clinton, Liz Phair, Steve Harwell (Smashmouth), De La Soul, Lil' Kim, Ziggy Marley, Chuck Berry, Dwight Yoakam, Exene Cervenka, and Deep Dish.

Way back in September 28, 1997, Apple Computer, Inc. introduced its first major ad campaign in a decade. The "Think Different" campaign uses photographs of major figures in recent history, along with the simple line, "Think Different." Each person is someone who was considered a "rebel," "misfit," or pioneer. They did things differently and wound up changing the world. Although none of the people in the pictures are identified, they are symbols for change.

The campaign honors creative geniuses who have touched the lives of many people through the things they have done. Figures past and present include astronaut Neil Armstrong, fighter Muhammad Ali, inventor Thomas Edison, singer-activist Joan Baez, physics' genius Albert Einstein, singers John Lennon and his singer-wife Yoko Ono, pilot Amelia Earhart, comedians Lucille Ball and Desi Arnaz, activist Rosa Parks, and Muppets creator Jim Henson. Although many advertising campaigns today use celebrities to promote their products, Apple is using celebrity figures in a way that honors their spirits and accomplishments.

Apple Computer, Inc.'s Steve Jobs said, "Think Different celebrates the soul of the Apple brand—that creative people with passion can change the world for the better," and with people like Mahatma Ghandi and Pablo Picasso in ads for Apple, who can argue with that?

through design for its time," said Andy Gore of *Macworld* magazine. The popular G-4 desktop models and G-4 Titanium Powerbooks being sold in the 2000s are more powerful, greatly evolved products developed back in 1997-1998 that included Apple's G3 Powerbooks and the Power Macintosh G3.

CORPORATE CITIZENSHIP

Apple is an active corporate citizen. In 2002 Apple remained an important contributor to the Computer Learning Project, an enterprise that helps schools earn credits to purchase state-of-the-art hardware and software for schools. Since the early 1980s, the company has donated computer products to schools and nonprofit groups. Its grants have provided for the collaboration of K-12 schools with schools of education to strengthen teacher training. Volunteer organizations are using donated Apple products to serve their communities. At its key sites around the world, the company has established Community Affairs teams to ensure a proactive community presence. In June 1998, Apple pledged up to $1 million in network software and training to Los Angeles County schools through the county Office of Education's Technology Learning program.

GLOBAL PRESENCE

With headquarters in Cupertino, California, Apple has manufacturing facilities in Singapore and Ireland. It also has distribution facilities in the United States, Canada, Australia, Europe, Singapore, and Japan. The company has business, education, government, scientific, and consumer entertainment customers in more than 140 countries. In 2002 Apple's main revenue sales were in North and South America, followed by Europe, Middle East, Africa, and then Japan. In terms of geography, Apple's three selling territories are known as Apple Americas, Apple Europe, and Apple Pacific. In May 2002, Apple offered the Worldwide Developer Conference at the San Jose, California, Convention Center in an attempt to spur global interest in the OSX operating system.

EMPLOYMENT

In 2001 and 2002, Apple cut a small number of employees, but for the most part kept its labor force intact at a time when the rest of Silicon Valley computer hardware and software companies were faced with wholesale layoffs in view of a stagnant economy. Apple Computer was back to 10,176 employees in 2001 after declining sales led to mass employee cuts in the late 1990s. In 1996, the company laid off 1,800 workers. In 1997 the company began more major layoffs—this time more than 2,000 of its remaining 11,000 full-time employees. The layoffs were a crucial part of Apple's plan to slash operating expenses by 20 percent. The company refocused, however, and in 1998, under returning CEO Steve Jobs, was hiring employees to fill positions needed to pursue Apple's new technical goals, satisfy customer needs, and identify new markets. In the first half of 1998, the company hired more than 600 new employees and employed 9,049 people worldwide.

As part of its corporate culture, Apple considers the work environment critical. The corporate workspace is open, and informal meeting areas are located throughout offices for meetings or just relaxing with colleagues. Some offices are even furnished with pool tables, ping pong tables, and basketball and volleyball courts. At Apple's headquarters, a coffee shop, fitness center, company store, and bookstore are all available onsite. For offices that do not have fitness facilities, reimbursement for fitness memberships is available as a benefit to employees. Other benefits offered by Apple include bonus programs, stock purchase plans, and 401(k) plans. The company also provides health benefits, profit sharing, tuition reimbursement, and substantial discounts on Apple computer equipment.

SOURCES OF INFORMATION

Bibliography

"11-Year Financial History." Cupertino, CA: Apple Computer Inc., 1998.

"Apple at-a-Glance." Cupertino, CA: Apple Computer Inc., 1997. Available at http://product.info.apple.com.

"Apple Computer, Inc." *Hoover's Online*, 2002. Available at http://www.hoover.com.

"Apple Extends WebObjects Consulting Group to Design and Publishing Market." Cupertino, CA: Apple Computer Inc., 17 March 1998.

"Apple Pledges Up to $1 Million in Network Software and Training to Los Angeles County Schools." Apple Computer Inc. Press Release, 3 June 1998. Available at http://www.apple.com/pr/library/1998/.

"Apple Worldwide Community Affairs: A Letter from Gilbert Amelio." Apple Computer Inc., 1997. Available at http://www2.apple.com/communityaffairs.

Gruman, Galen. "Apple's Make-or-Break Decision Time," 20 March 1997.

"Hewlett-Packard: Bid Approved." *The Washington Post*, 18 April 2002.

"Late Push by Apple Saves Quarter." *The San Francisco Chronicle*, 18 April 2002.

"Mac Faithful Like the New Apple iMac: It's Just Right." *Macworld*, 10 June 1998. Available at http://macworld.zdnet.com.

Markoff, John. "Rhapsody's Out, OSX In, in Shift of Gear at Apple." *The New York Times*, 12 May 1998.

"Report Suggests Ailing Apple Will Eliminate 40% of Work Force." *Dow Jones & Company, Inc.*, 24 February 1997.

Rupley, Sebastian. "Apple's NeXt OS: Steve Jobs Makes an Apple Comeback." *PC Magazine*, 18 February 1997.

Salkever, Alex. "Finally, a Chance for Apple to Flourish." *Business Week Online*, 23 January 2002.

Salkever, Alex, and Jay Mehta. "Why OSX May Be a Growth Factor." *Business Week Online*, 23 January 2002.

Sanford, Glen. "A History of Apple," 1997. Available at http://www.apple-history.pair.com.

For an annual report:

on the Internet at: http://www.apple.com/investor/annualreports.html **or** telephone: (408)974-3123 **or** write: Apple Investor Relations, 1 Infinite Loop, MS 301-4IR, Cupertino, CA 95014

For additional industry research:

Investigate companies by their Standard Industrial Classification Codes, also known as SICs. Apple Computer Inc.'s primary SICs are:

3571 Electronic Computers

5045 Computers, Peripherals and Software

7372 Prepackaged Software

7379 Computer Related Services, NEC

Also investigate companies by their North American Industry Classification codes, also known as NAICS codes. Apple Computer Inc.'s primary NAICS codes are:

334111 Electronic Computer Manufacturing

334119 Other Computer Peripheral Equipment Manufacturing

511210 Software Publishers

Archer Daniels Midland Co.

FOUNDED: 1923
VARIANT NAME: ADM

Contact Information:

HEADQUARTERS: 4666 Faries Pkwy.
   Decatur, IL 62525
PHONE: (217)424-5200
FAX: (217)424-6196
URL: http://www.admworld.com

OVERVIEW

With more than $20 billion in sales and 300 facilities in operation across the globe, Archer Daniels Midland, or ADM, is one of the world's largest processors of agricultural commodities, such as soybeans, corn, and wheat. The firm, which refers to itself the "Supermarket to the World," sells its products to three main industries: food, beverage, and chemical. International sales account for 35 percent of total revenues.

COMPANY FINANCES

Sales at ADM jumped from $12.8 billion in 2000 to $20.1 billion in 2001. Profits rose from $300 million to $383 million after the same time period. This growth followed two years of declining sales, which were caused at least in part by a well-publicized price fixing scandal that resulted in a jail term for three ADM executives. However, while sales had reached a record high in 2001, profits were less than half of the $795.9 million earned by ADM in 1995. Stock prices in 2001 ranged from a low of $7.80 per share to a high of $15.22 per share. They had peaked in 1998 at a high of $20.22 and a low of $15.19.

ANALYSTS' OPINIONS

ADM struggled with a public relations disaster related to its price fixing conviction in the late 1990s. As a result, stock prices dropped, and many analysts were cautious about the firm's outlook. However, by 2001, despite posting profits that remained well below their mid-1990s level, some industry experts began to look favorably upon the firm. Profits improved in both 2000 and 2001 due to various cost-cutting measures launched in 1999 by new CEO Allen Andreas. As stated in a September 2001 issue of *Forbes*, "Prudential Securities analyst John McMillan thinks the best is yet to come for Archer Daniels. Signs that the strong dollar is weakening and China's admission into the World Trade Organization should catalyze the company's export sales. Also, high energy costs have enhanced growth prospects for. . .ethanol. Archer Daniels controls half the market." Increased demand of soybean meal appeared to bode well for ADM as well. In addition, many observers believed that the firm's healthy cash reserves would allow it to make acquisitions in emerging growth markets, where demand for agricultural commodities was strong. One area of concern expressed by some analysts was the firm's heavy reliance on the agricultural commodities market, which tended to fluctuate in terms of both demand and price.

HISTORY

When the Minneapolis, Minnesota-based Archer-Daniels Linseed Co., founded in 1902, merged with Midland Linseed in 1923, Archer Daniels Midland was born. The firm initially focused on processing flaxseed for the manufacture of linseed oil. Early growth came from acquisitions of oilseed processing companies throughout the Midwest. In 1930, the firm diversified into flour milling with the purchase of Commander-Larabee Co., a leading U.S. flour miller.

By the mid-1940s, ADM was able to process 36.6 million bushels of flaxseed per day, compared to a processing capacity of 20.0 million bushels per day in 1929. Grain storage capacity increased from 7.5 million to 50.4 million bushels per day during the same period. Additionally, wheat flour capacity had reached 30 million bushels per day. By supplying a growing number of basic ingredients to a broad spectrum of industries (such as food, beverages, paint, gasoline, paper, cosmetics, pharmaceuticals, rubber, and ceramics) the firm had grown into an agricultural commodities leader. Profits in 1949 reached $12 million on sales of $277 million. ADM was the largest processor of linseed and soybean oil in the United States, as well as the fourth-largest flour miller. To increase profit margins, the firm began processing its products more fully, rather than selling them in a raw or semi-finished state.

To move into international markets, ADM began seeking alliances with established oilseed processors in places like Peru, Mexico, the Netherlands, and Belgium in the 1950s. Instability in commodities prices in the 1960s undercut the firm's performance. Profits fell from

FAST FACTS:
About Archer Daniels Midland Co.

Ownership: Archer Daniels Midland Co. is a publicly owned company traded on the New York Stock Exchange. Roughly 8 percent of the firm's stock remains in the hands of the Andreas family, who has managed ADM since the late 1960s.

Ticker: ADM

Officers: Dwayne O. Andreas, Chmn. Emeritus, 83; G. Allen Andreas, Chmn. and CEO, 58, 2001 base salary $2.39 million; Paul B. Mulhollem, Pres., 52; Martin L. Andreas, SVP and Dir. of Mktg., 62

Employees: 32,000

Principal Subsidiary Companies: Archer Daniels Midland Co. has subsidiaries in North America, Europe, South America, and Asia.

Chief Competitors: Competitors to Archer Daniels Midland Co. include soybean processor and exporter Bunge Ltd., grain processor and exporter Cargill, and other firms involved in the corn, soybean, and wheat industries.

$75 million in 1963 to $60 million in 1964 and to $50 million in 1965. Dwayne O. Andreas joined ADM's management team in 1966. He advocated a more narrow focus on soybean processing, a move that paid off when textured vegetable protein (TVP) became more widely accepted and when soybean oil became the most used cooking oil. In 1967, ADM bought Fleischmann Malting Co. Three years later, it purchased Corn Sweeteners, Inc., a producer of high fructose syrups, glutens, oil, and caramel color.

TVP plants were constructed in Europe and South America during the 1970s. Dwayne Andreas began to fill several management positions with other members of his family. In fact, three Andreas family members were placed in charge of specific divisions. Profits reached $117 million in 1973 as the firm increased its domestic soybean production to 1.3 billion bushels per day. Growth continued into the early 1980s when ADM bought grain merchandiser Growmark and oil and peanut producer Columbian Peanut Co. Acquisitions in the early 1990s included Canada's Ogilvie Mills.

ADM diversified into consumer food products for the first time in the early 1990s by introducing the Har-

FINANCES:
Archer Daniels Midland Co.
Revenues, 1998-2001
(million dollars)

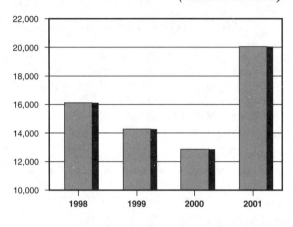

CHRONOLOGY
Key Dates for Archer Daniels Midland Co.

1923: Archer Daniels Linseed Co. and Midland Linseed Products Co. merge to form Archer Daniels Midland Co.

1930: ADM scientists are able to extract lecithin from soybean oil

1966: Dwayne O. Andreas joins ADM's management team

1996: ADM pleads guilty to price fixing charges; punitive fines of $100 million are the largest in corporate criminal antitrust history

1999: Allen Andreas takes over as CEO

vest Burger, a soy-based, meatless "hamburger," with less fat and cholesterol and fewer calories than a traditional burger. (ADM sold the Harvest Burger brand to Worthington Foods in 1998.) Public scandal rocked the firm in 1995 when the U.S. Federal Bureau of Investigation (FBI) began investigating claims by ADM executive Mark Whitacre that ADM was guilty of lysine price fixing. ADM pled guilty the following year and was fined $100 million, setting a record for the highest fine ever paid in criminal antitrust litigation. Eventually, two ADM executives and Whitacre himself received prison sentences for their involvement. Coupled with declining prices for agricultural commodities, these problems contributed to a drop in profits from $403.6 million in 1998 to $266.0 million in 1999. The European Commission found ADM guilty of lysine price fixing in 2000, fining the firm another $45 million. In fact, price fixing litigation continued to plague ADM into the early 2000s.

Growth continued despite the scandal. Acquisitions in 1997 included the cocoa operations of W.R. Grace; Moorman Manufacturing, a soybean processor serving the animal feed industry; and a 43 percent stake in United Grain Growers of Canada. Allen Andreas took over as CEO in 1999. Farmland Industries agreed to allow a unit of ADM to handle its grain processing in 2001. That same year, Japan-based Kao Corp. and ADM began working together to produce diacylglycerol oil, known for its ability to help control body fat, for sale in the United States, Europe, and Oceania. The product had been selling as an alternative to traditional vegetable oil in the Japanese market since 1999.

STRATEGY

Since its inception, Archer Daniels Midland has focused on two complementary business strategies: intensive research and development efforts—designed to foster innovative methods of production and uses for agricultural products—and highly efficient production. ADM began to explore methods to modify the chemical structure of linseed oil in the mid-1920s; this effort marked the firm's first research and development program. Although research and development budgets were not a regular occurrence for companies in the 1930s, ADM earmarked 70 percent of its earnings for development efforts.

When Dwayne Andreas took over in the late 1960s, he modified the company's strategy to focus on innovation with a single product: soybeans. Maintaining ADM's tradition of devising low-cost means of production, Andreas promoted the development of a soy product that was roughly 50 percent protein, much less expensive to manufacture than a product that was 100 percent protein. Demand for ADM's products surged as textured vegetable protein (TVP) became commonplace in foodstuffs and soybean oil became the leading cooking oil in use. Because Andreas had focused on devising a low-cost method of production, ADM was able to maintain a healthy profit margin on soybeans.

Cost cutting and product innovation remained the firm's focus well into the late 1990s. To reduce ADM's reliance on the unstable agricultural commodities market, Allen Andreas, who took over in 1999, began to increase the firm's focus on nutritional products, which accounted for 10 percent of sales in 2001. These soy- and corn-based "nutraceutical" food ingredients offered certain health benefits, which ADM intended to market heavily. Andreas planned to increase these products to 25 percent of company sales by 2006.

INFLUENCES

Early successes with innovative developments prompted ADM to devote more of its resources to research and development than was commonplace at the time. For example, in the 1930s, ADM discovered how to extract lecithin, an emulsifier commonly used in the food and confectionery industries, from soybean oil. This knowledge lowered the price of lecithin tenfold. Other new processes devised by ADM included the use of flax straw fibers, considered a waste product at that time, in the manufacture of flax papers. Roughly 40 percent of sales growth during the 1940s was attributable to new products and processes, according to ADM. Successes like these fueled ADM's focus on research and development well into the early 2000s.

CURRENT TRENDS

Health products, such as meatless products using TVP, flaxseed oil, and vitamin E—all products manufactured by ADM—grew in popularity throughout the late 1990s and early 2000s. Environmental concerns prompted U.S. President George W. Bush and his administration to support the use of ethanol, another ADM product, in gasoline. ADM plans to take advantage of these trends by increasing its production of both ethanol and nutritional products.

PRODUCTS

Soy and other oilseed products, such as vegetable oil and TVP, account for roughly 75 percent of revenues. Corn-based products include ethanol and high fructose corn syrup, as well as a variety of other sugars. Wheat products include flour and bulgar. ADM also processes cocoa butter and powder. Early in the twenty-first century, ADM unveiled a new line of food ingredients, dubbed "nutraceuticals," which offered various health benefits. The firm, partnering with Japan's Kao Corp., also announced plans to make and sell diacylglycerol oil, which helps control body fat.

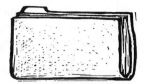

ADM SEES ETHANOL MARKET INCREASE

In 1994, the U.S. Environmental Protection Agency decreed that ethanol, one of ADM's key corn-based products, be combined with at least 10 percent of all gas purchased in the United States. To lobby for government support of ethanol, the Andreas family had made sizable donations to both Republican and Democratic parties in the 1992 election.

CORPORATE CITIZENSHIP

ADM's management described the development of soy protein as a humanitarian effort, as well as a business venture, because soy was less expensive than other forms of protein, and it lasted much longer than conventional proteins like meat or milk; these characteristics made it easier to use in third-world countries battling hunger and starvation problems. The firm also promoted various environmental causes, such as no-till farming, a process that lowers soil erosion, as well as the use of ethanol as an environmentally friendly fuel additive. (Ethanol was also a major source of company profits.)

In April 2001 the firm introduced a new leaf-shaped corporate logo with the caption, "The Nature of What's to Come." According to the firm's CEO, "Archer Daniels Midland is at the forefront of developing new products based on natural, renewable resources. 'The Nature of What's to Come' is more than just an advertising campaign—it's a promise to our customers, shareholders, and the world."

GLOBAL PRESENCE

International operations account for 35 percent of ADM's sales. Via a multitude of subsidiaries, the firm operates in Canada, Germany, Turkey, the Netherlands, the United Kingdom, Mexico, Bolivia, and Luxembourg. The firm's decision to open grain processing units in North America to handle increased demand from Asia proved premature in the late-1990s, particularly when the Asian economy fell into a recession. By 2001, however, the market had recovered and ADM began to see increased demand from Asia. In fact, overcapacity in many developed markets such as the United States and Western Europe prompted ADM to increase its focus on emerging markets like Asia, as well as Eastern Europe and South America, for future growth. In 2001, ADM held a 5 percent share of the Asian oilseed market.

SOURCES OF INFORMATION

Bibliography

"Archer Daniels Midland Co." *International Directory of Company Histories.* Detroit: Gale Research, 1994.

Archer Daniels Midland Homepage, 2002. Available at http://www.admworld.com.

Burke, Monte. "Streetwalker." *Forbes,* 17 September 2001.

DeGuzman, Doris. "ADM Eyes Key Markets for Global Expansion." *Chemical Market Reporter,* 10 December 2001.

Einhorn, Cheryl. "A Grain of Hope: After 10 Terrible Years, ADM Poised for a Comeback." *Barron's,* 16 October 2000.

Forster, Julie. "A Different Kind of Andreas at ADM." *BusinessWeek Online,* 9 July 2001. Available at http://www.businessweek.com.

For an annual report:

on the Internet at: http://www.admworld.com/investor/pdf/adm_annual_report_2001.pdf

For additional industry research:

Investigate companies by their Standard Industrial Classification Codes, also known as SICs. Archer Daniels Midland's primary SICs are:

2041 Flour and Other Grain Mill Products

2046 Wet Corn Milling

2048 Prepared Feed and Feed Ingredients, Not Elsewhere Classified

2066 Chocolate and Cocoa

2074 Cottonseed Oil Mills

2076 Vegetable Oil Mills

Also investigate companies by their North American Industry Classification Codes, also known as NAICS codes. Archer Daniels Midland's primary NAICS codes are:

311119 Other Animal Food Manufacturing

311211 Flour Milling

311221 Wet Corn Milling

311225 Fats and Oils Refining and Blending

Arthur Andersen LLP

OVERVIEW

Until June 2002, Arthur Andersen was a global firm providing economic and financial consulting services; business consulting services; tax and business advisory services; and audit and business advisory services. Unless its court conviction is overturned on appeal, its audit practice was almost certainly slated to be dissolved in 2002. Almost all divisions of the company experienced mass client defections. The company's audit business was effectively ended in June 2002 as a result of a guilty verdict in a jury trial that found the company had obstructed justice in another case, according to the Andersen Web site. Arthur Andersen serves the market through a fully integrated organization comprising separate practice entities organized under the laws of the country in which they are based.

COMPANY FINANCES

Global revenues for Arthur Andersen looked so bright at the start of 2001, and the company's 11.2 percent growth and $1.4 billion consulting profits were the stuff of corporate dreams. Total revenues in 2000 were $8.4 million from all sources. But the fat dream turned into the darkest of nightmares as Anderson failed to distance itself from unethical attempts to hide losses in annual reports at fast-failing Enron and, worse, shredded important documents related to its Enron consultancy.

FOUNDED: 1913
VARIANT NAME: Andersen Worldwide

Contact Information:
HEADQUARTERS: 33 W. Monroe St.
    Chicago, IL 60603
PHONE: (312)931-1826
EMAIL: firmwide@arthurandersen.com
URL: http://www.arthurandersen.com

FAST FACTS:

About Arthur Andersen

Ownership: Arthur Andersen is a privately owned company.

Officers: Aldo Cardoso, Acting CEO, Andersen Worldwide

Employees: 59,000

Principal Subsidiary Companies: Arthur Andersen, along with Arthur Andersen Knowledge Enterprises and Andersen Consulting (a vision threatened with extinction in June 2002, according to published reports quoting Andersen executives), is a division of Andersen Worldwide. Arthur Andersen Franchise Services and Cross Roads Savings and Loan Association are two other subsidiaries.

Chief Competitors: Arthur Andersen is part of one of the largest financial services and consulting companies in the world. As such, its primary competitors are: Ernst and Young, KPMG, PricewaterhouseCoopers, and Booz Allen and Hamilton.

HISTORY

Arthur Edward Andersen, the founder and guiding force behind Andersen Worldwide, was born in Plano, Illinois. Young Andersen displayed a propensity for mathematics, and upon graduation from high school he worked in the office of a comptroller while attending classes at the University of Illinois. In 1908 he received a degree as a certified public accountant (CPA) becoming the youngest CPA in Illinois at 23.

Andersen served as senior accountant for Price Waterhouse from 1907 to 1911. Afterwards, Andersen worked as comptroller for a year before being appointed chairperson of Northwestern University's accounting department. In 1913, Andersen decided to establish his own accounting firm, and at 28 he founded the public accounting firm of Andersen DeLany and Company in Chicago.

Following Congress' establishment of Federal Income Tax and the Federal Reserve in 1913, the demand for accounting services increased dramatically. This resulted in rapid growth for Andersen's small firm. One of Andersen's first clients was Schlitz Brewing. The list expanded rapidly to include International Telephone and Telegraph, Colgate-Palmolive, Parker Pen, and Briggs and Stratton, among many others. The company's primary business, however, consisted of numerous utility companies throughout the Midwest, including Cincinnati Gas and Electric Company, Detroit Natural Gas Company, Milwaukee Gas Light Company, and Kansas City Power and Light Company.

Fifty percent of Andersen's revenues during the 1920s were derived from work generated by utility companies. Andersen's firm was becoming labeled as a "utility firm" in accounting circles. In 1917 Andersen was awarded an honorary B.B.A from Northwestern University. In 1918, when DeLany left the partnership, the firm became known as Arthur Andersen and Company.

The company grew rapidly with many employees becoming licensed as accountants and auditors in many states. Six offices were opened nationwide. Those in New York (1921), Kansas City (1923), and Los Angeles (1926) were the company's main offices. Already serving as an auditor for many industrial corporations, Arthur Andersen began providing financial and industrial investigation services. About 400 people were employed with the company in 1928, and by 1940 that figure had increased to 700. The firm opened more offices in Boston and Houston in 1937 and Atlanta and Minneapolis in 1940.

During World War II, Andersen reached the pinnacle of his success. His numerous writings on accounting related subjects prompted a growing admiration and respect for him in financial, industrial, and academic circles. Andersen served as president of the board of trustees at Northwestern University and as a faculty member in accounting at the school. During this time Andersen groomed his associate, Leonard Spacek, for the company's leadership position. Spacek joined Arthur Andersen and Company in 1928 and was named partner in 1940. After Arthur Andersen died in 1947, Spacek took over the company, remaining committed to the regimented management style of the founder.

By the time Spacek retired in 1973, Arthur Andersen and Company had opened 18 new offices in the United States and more than 25 offices in countries throughout the world. The company had a staff of more than 12,000, and revenues increased from $6.5 to more than $51 million between 1947 and 1973. Arthur Andersen had grown into one of the world's preeminent accounting firms, featuring a profitable consulting service that helped large corporations install and use computer systems in the 1950s, and it branched out into production control, cost accounting, and operations research during the 1960s. In the 1970s, the company became involved in a host of consulting activities, including systems integration services, strategic services, developing software application products, and providing a variety of other technological services.

Harvey Kapnick succeeded Spacek, and under him the consulting division expanded and developed rapidly. By 1979, the consulting division's fees represented 20

CHRONOLOGY:

Key Dates for Arthur Andersen

1913: Arthur Andersen establishes his own accounting firm at the age of 28 called Andersen DeLany and Company

1918: DeLany leaves the partnership and the firm becomes Arthur Andersen and Company

1938: Arthur Andersen is offered the presidency of the New York Stock Exchange, which he declined

1947: Andersen dies and Leonard Spacek takes over the company

1950: Begins a consulting service, which helped corporations install and use their first computer systems

1960: Adds production control, cost accounting, and operations research services

1970: Begins involvement in technological services such as systems integration and software application

1984: Arthur Andersen & Co. is forced to pay settlements totaling $65 million within two months

1988: More than 40 percent of revenues come from consulting fees, making the company the largest consulting firm in the world

1989: Lawrence Weinbach becomes president and revenues nearly double within four years

1992: The firm is sued by the government's Resolution Trust Corporation for negligence in its audit of a failed financial institution

1998: Andersen considers scuttling Enron Corp. as client after discovering how Enron hid debt through complex partnerships to improve bottom line; Andersen keeps Enron to avoid losing a potential $100 million annual fee-paying client

2001: In Houston offices, document shredding takes place with regard to Enron and similar documents, and it is done without knowledge of many key Andersen employees; Arthur Andersen announced that it was planning a name change in coming months to "Andersen" for simplicity's sake

2002: The company's future was damaged, perhaps beyond repair, after the U.S. Justice Department indicted Andersen in March; another client of Arthur Andersen, Worldcom, was caught overstating profits, hiding losses, and omitting line cost information in annual reports; Andersen auditors deny involvement or impropriety in their work for Worldcom in a company statement; Arthur Andersen appealed its conviction, claiming the jury was given flawed instructions; the guilty verdict brought back by a jury against Arthur Andersen means the end of the company's audit practice—the company conceded even before a judicial motion of conviction was filed

---

percent of Andersen's total revenues. Kapnick was succeeded by Duane Kullberg (who originally joined the company in 1954 as an auditor), whose first years at Andersen were wrought with problems. Nevertheless, the company on the surface continued to thrive, but the audit business was under pressure to accede to client wishes that the company founders never would have tolerated. By 1988, 40 percent of the company's total revenues were generated from consulting fees, making Arthur Andersen the largest consulting firm in the world. Around this time, tension between the auditors of the firm and the consultants was brewing, centering on discrepancies in payscale (auditors were paid more than the consultants) and disagreement over the control of consulting operations. Tensions increased, consultants left the company, and lawsuits were filed. The company was in one of its most confused stages.

In an effort to end the internal discord, Arthur Anderson was restructured into an auditing and tax firm known as Arthur Andersen, and a subsidiary consulting firm was formed called Andersen Consulting. Each became a separate entity with its own management structure responsible only to the parent company, Andersen Worldwide.

Lawrence Weinbach, a graduate of the Wharton Business School, replaced Kullberg in 1989. Known for his diplomacy, Weinbach tried to smooth out the hard feelings between the two divisions of Arthur Andersen. Under his leadership the company's revenues skyrocketed from under $3.0 billion in 1988 to $5.6 billion in 1992. This increase, nearly 50 percent, was generated by the company's increase in consulting activities. During the years 1988-1992, Andersen Consulting's revenues grew by 89 percent while Arthur Andersen's revenues grew by 38 percent. In 1997, Weinback retired from Andersen Worldwide, and W. Robert Grafton was named acting CEO. Andersen Consulting, though still a part of parent company Andersen

Worldwide, was in negotiation to break off from the firm.

Over the years, too cozy relationships formed between Andersen and its consulting clients, in some cases leading to laxness on the part of the company's auditing arm, according to the *Bloomberg News*. Andersen clearly was gravitating toward the Enron scandal for many years, and company management needed to more carefully train its partners to make ethical judgments when dealing with difficult, high-pressure clients. According to media reports, no Andersen cash-cow client was bigger than Enron, paying $52 million a year for audit and consulting fees. Nonetheless, Andersen should have been forewarned since Enron had enduring previous accounting scandals going back to an oil trading the late 1980s, according to the *Bloomberg News*. By 2001, some Andersen executives clearly had become overwrought by some of the dealings their company had experienced with Enron. According to the *Bloomberg News*, Enron auditors were concerned about indications that Enron was hiding losses from Enron shareholders, but instead of disconnecting from Enron, the accounting firm, foolishly in retrospect, continued its auditing and consulting work in expectation of even higher payments—more than $100 million annually perhaps—to come in future years.

Later that year, Andersen received correspondence from a highly placed Enron employee indicating that highly questionable practices—later called fraudulent by a U.S. congressional inquiry—were being tolerated by key Andersen officials. (Andersen continues to defend itself in June 2002.) Instead of taking hard internal action, the U.S. Justice Department maintained that some Andersen employees actually shredded and documents and tried, unsuccessfully, to destroy electronic mail documents. In March 2002, the Justice Department indicted Anderson for obstructing attempts by the Justice Department looking into earnings restatements by Enron, according to *Bloomberg News*. Some important Andersen officials were then fired, but it was too late to stop judicial proceedings, and these officials fingered higher-ups at Andersen for allegedly ordering or encouraging the destruction of documents. Andersen top officials argued that the company itself should not be found to blame for the actions of a few and argued that if all facts were known, the company should not be held responsible for Enron wrongdoings. The Justice Department indictment, unparalleled in the history of auditing, made it clear that the shredding and accounting improprieties were part of a bigger picture of malfeasance, a big picture that Andersen officials continued to emphatically deny in statements posted on the company Web site in June of 2002. (The conviction was in appeal at this writing, and there was no way of knowing by this writer whether the appeal would be denied or sustained.) Andersen officials maintained that Enron officials withheld key information from Andersen auditors.

In 2002, high-profile corporate clients by the hundreds—some who had been with Andersen for 20 years or more—severed relations with Arthur Andersen for such reasons as fear of being tainted by association, repugnance over the company's admissions, and, most often cited, a sense that its past association with Enron and considerable downsizing mean that it cannot pay attention to the present pressing needs of its once-vast clientele. Many of the companies such as Stagecoach, a transportation company in the United Kingdom, switched their business to PricewaterhouseCoopers. According to Hoover's Online, "Andersen's demise as a major force in accounting is all but certain; the firm had already been hemorrhaging clients and will cease auditing publicly owned companies after being found guilty of obstructing justice in relation to former auditing client Enron."

In the 2000s, the Enron (see Enron listing in this volume for particulars) and Andersen scandal was reminiscent of Teapot Dome and other business scandals that rocked the United States in the early twentieth century. If any good can come out of the scandal, it is that the entire global accounting industry heard the loudest possible wakeup call. One pervasive practice practiced by Andersen and other prominent accounting firms that has led to ethical breeches is that of selling audit services for an unprofessional lowered fee in expectation of earning millions in consulting fees. Doing so often gives the client the upper hand dealing with accounting firms doing the auditing and may allow unethical client practices to go unchecked and unreported to the Securities and Exchange Commission. In effect, in some situations, the client gets the accounting firm into a compromised position. Wayne Shaw, an accounting professor at Southern Methodist University in Dallas, told *Bloomberg News* that a compromised accounting firm lacks the integrity to hold a high-paying client accountable. "The standards aren't demanding enough to provide sufficient information to investors," Shaw informed the *Bloomberg News*. "We've set up a system where creativity is rewarded. I'm not sure you want an auditor to be creative."

STRATEGY

In June 2002, the company's strategy to save the once-respected accounting giant came down to a legal appeal on one hand and attempts to save whatever portions of the company that had not yet been tainted by the court's jury conviction in 2002.

GLOBAL PRESENCE

Arthur Andersen had been a highly respected and successful global organization, with 390 worldwide offices in the early 2000s. In 2002, it remained to be seen if the company could maintain any sort of global presence, though as employees jumped ship to competitors and clients left by the dozens, it was eminently clear that Andersen's international reputation was in tatters unless it could show, by winning an appeal, that its conviction was the result of improper instructions to a jury. Andersen also maintained that its attorneys had not been able to offer all evidence in defense of its practices. If it is successful with its appeal, no doubt the company will slowly, painfully attempt to pick up its pieces and go on, or it will sell what remains of value to rival firms. In June of 2002, at this writing, the company's global future is quite unclear, as is evident by the large number of Andersen employees finding employment at rival accounting firms, and by the large number of once-loyal Andersen accounting clients that have fired the company and taken their business elsewhere in spite of vociferous denunciations of the judicial verdict by Andersen executives.

EMPLOYMENT

The 7,000 employees let go by Andersen were the tip of the iceberg, and most of these were guiltless of any company wrongdoing. Thousands more opted to accept similar positions at rival companies such as Ernst & Young and PricewaterhouseCoopers.

SOURCES OF INFORMATION

Bibliography

Andersen Home Page, June 2002. Available at http://www.arthurandersen.com.

"Arthur Andersen Announces New Accounting Reference Series." Arthur Andersen News Releases, 21 May 1998.

Ward, David. "Andersen's Enron Lapses Followed Faulty Audits of Other Firms." *Bloomberg News,* 24 April 2002.

Wayne, Rich. "Arthur Andersen Loses Clients." *Bloomberg News,* 15 June 2002.

For additional industry research:

Investigate companies by their Standard Industrial Classification Codes, also known as SICs. Arthur Andersen's primary SICs are:

8721 Accounting Auditing and Book Keeping Services

8742 Management Consulting Services

Also investigate companies by their North American Industry Classification System codes, also known as NAICS codes. Arthur Andersen's primary NAICS codes are:

541211 Offices of Certified Public Accountants

541611 Administrative Management and General Management Consulting Services

AT&T

FOUNDED: 1899

VARIANT NAME: American Telephone and Telegraph
Corporation

Contact Information:

HEADQUARTERS: 32 Avenue of the Americas
New York, NY 10013-2412
PHONE: (212)387-5400
FAX: (908)221-2528
TOLL FREE: (800)348-8288
EMAIL: att@equiserve.com
URL: http://www.att.com

OVERVIEW

AT&T is a communications company offering long-distance telephone service, voice, data and video communications, cable television and Internet communications services. In 1996 the company divided itself into three separate operations: AT&T Corp. (telecommunications), NCR Corporation (computers), and Lucent Technologies Inc. (network products). The two latter divisions were then sold. With increased long-distance competition during the 1990s, AT&T was forced to focus on retaining its market share in that core business area.

In 2000 the company restructured and created a family of four new companies: AT&T Wireless, AT&T Broadband, AT&T Business and AT&T Consumer. The following year, each of the separate companies began trading as public stock and tracking stock, and AT&T Wireless completed its spin-off, and became an entirely separate entity.

Other services offered by AT&T Corporation include WorldNet, an Internet-access provider; local phone services; and the AT&T Universal Card, a credit card. The company also provides cable television and wireless phone service in more than 100 cities in the United States. DIRECTTV, a television satellite system, is among the newest of AT&T's innovations.

COMPANY FINANCES

As reported by the company, AT&T's total 2001 revenues were $52.6 billion, a decrease of 5.4 percent from 2000 revenues of $55.5 billion. However, the AT&T Wireless spin-off and separation accounted for some of the revenues decrease. Of 2001 revenues, $28 billion was generated by the company's business markets division; $15.1 billion was generated by its consumer markets division; and $9.8 billion was generated by AT&T broadband services.

AT&T Wireless, whose sales after July 2001, were not included in AT$T's revenues, were $12.5 billion in 2001, a 25-percent increase over 2000 revenues of $9.4 billion. AT&T stock was valued at around $15.88 per share in early 2002. The company's 52-week high was $23.75, and its 52-week low was $14.18 per share. The company's earnings per share (EPS) in 2001 were -$1.36.

ANALYSTS' OPINIONS

Analysts tend to view long-distance service as a mature market in the United States, as well as a market characterized by increasing competition due to more cost-focused consumers. Some experts say AT&T's lack of swift reaction to this change accounted for some of the company's problems. For example, while companies such as Sprint offered flat rates for long-distance service early on, AT&T remained at the high end of the price scale. Eventually, the company offered a $.15-per-minute flat rate to compete with the lower prices of smaller companies. AT&T was also struck hard in 1996 by companies that purchased long-distance service in bulk and then resold to consumers and businesses at less expensive rates.

AT&T admitted to being caught off-guard by smaller companies offering fierce competition. This oversight caused AT&T's long-distance services to underperform. Analysts had expected AT&T CEO C. Michael Armstrong, who was named chairman in 1997, to help the struggling corporation recover. In late 2001, analysts questioned whether the remaining three AT&T companies would flourish after the complete spin-off of AT&T Wireless, the fastest-growing of the four AT&T companies. By 2002, it was apparent AT&T had still been slow to react to an increasingly more tech-savvy consumer.

Perhaps most vulnerable was the broadband company. In July 2001, Comcast Corp. made a $55 billion bid for AT&T's cable company. By December, the two companies had worked out a merger, which valued AT&T Broadband at $72 billion. The merger formed a new company, AT&T Comcast Corporation.

A continuing threat to AT&T is the rise of the Internet, offering fax capabilities, phone calls, live radio programs, and video conferencing—areas in which AT&T hoped to provide services. Many analysts view AT&T's launch of WorldNet as a successful answer to the challenge posed by the Internet in these areas. In fact, analysts say fewer than 50,000 people currently make phone

FAST FACTS:
About AT&T Corporation

Ownership: AT&T is a publicly owned company traded on the New York Stock Exchange as well as the Boston, Midwest, Pacific, and Philadelphia Exchanges in the United States. AT&T stock is also traded in Brussels, Geneva, London, and Paris.

Ticker symbol: T

Officers: C. Michael Armstrong, Chmn. and CEO, 62, $3,275,891; David W. Dorman, Pres., 46; Charles H. Noski, VChmn. and CEO, 48, $1,555,031; John D. Zeglis, Chmn. AT&T Wireless, 53, $3,098,976

Employees: 166,000

Principal Subsidiary Companies: The company's subsidiaries include WorldNet, AT&T Digital PCS, AT&T Broadband, AT&T Wireless, AT&T Business, and AT&T Consumer.

Chief Competitors: As a major telecommunications provider, AT&T's chief competitors include Ameritech, Bell Atlantic, BellSouth, Cable & Wireless, GTE, and MCI. Competitors in related industries in which AT&T also participates include AirTouch, America Online, IBM, NETCOM, PSINet, and WorldCom.

calls using the Internet, giving telecommunications companies like AT&T an edge in the market.

A technological advantage that some analysts believe may be beneficial to the company was AT&T's plan to implement "Project Angel." The project would give customers the option to choose their local telephone provider, which may be attractive enough to successfully launch such a program. Once in place, this technology could also offer consumers the capability to hook computers up at high speeds for minimal costs. Some analysts believed this technology was AT&T's competitive edge, although many kinks have not yet been ironed out.

From 1988 to 1996, analysts criticized CEO Robert Allen's strategies. During his years of service, the company spent $20 billion on purchases of businesses and $19 billion in redesign efforts. Since January of 1996, AT&T's stock has dropped 20 percent. Despite all of this, many analysts at the time agreed that AT&T remained financially strong. AT&T was the number one performing stock on the Dow-Jones index for the third quarter of the 1997 fiscal year. The company brought in more than $8.0 billion in annual cash flow. Its assets totaled $56.0 billion and outstanding debt totaled $8.5 billion. Today, many view AT&T's financial standing, coupled with its strong name-recognition, as its strongest asset for competitive survival.

Armstrong was also criticized for slow-moving initiatives. According to *Business Week*, the Telecom Act of 1996 laid the groundwork for the Baby Bells to get into long distance, which doomed AT&T. Armstrong cut prices and costs in AT&T's long-distance business, and then pumped $100 billion into the broadband arm of AT&T. Critics claimed he moved too slowly, and when the time the long distance business had collapsed, the local phone and Internet initiatives were not yet fully developed. AT&T had already lost customers and faced dissatisfied shareholders.

HISTORY

Alexander Graham Bell's invention of the telephone in 1876 led to the development of Bell Telephone (1877) and England Telephone (1878), which were later combined to create National Bell Telephone in 1879. After fighting off competitor patents from others, such as Western Union, in 1882 National Bell acquired Western Electric, the leading electrical equipment manufacturer in the United States at the time. After Bell's telephone patent expired in the 1890s, competing phone companies emerged. The company changed its name to American Telephone & Telegraph (AT&T) and moved from Boston to New York in 1899.

As a result of the company's acquisition of Western Union in 1909, AT&T controlled two markets: communications and electrical equipment manufacturing. Under President Woodrow Wilson, AT&T was forced to sell Western Union and refrain from purchasing other independent phone companies without approval. AT&T was also forced to provide access to its networks to other companies. In other words, the government was forcing AT&T to give up its standing as a monopoly (when one supplier controls one-third of a local or national market) This allowed competitors, such as MCI, to obtain access to AT&T's networks, which created instant long-distance competition.

A lawsuit initiated by the government caused AT&T to sell seven Bell companies in 1984. AT&T was allowed to keep its long-distance services and Western Electric. Many jobs were cut in order for AT&T Corp. to remain competitive in such a rapidly growing industry. AT&T bought the electronic mail service division of Western Union in 1990. AT&T Corp. ranked seventh in the world's computer makers after it bought Teradata and NCR in 1991 (sold along with Lucent in 1996); the company also bought McCaw Cellular in 1995.

STRATEGY

AT&T was organized into divisions and businesses addressing its specific markets. These divisions were: the Consumer Markets Division (CMD), Business Markets Division (BMD), AT&T Solutions (professional services), AT&T Wireless Service, AT&T Local Services Division, and AT&T Universal Card Services (UCS). These are bolstered by two other organizations—Network and Computing Services and AT&T Labs—that provide the company's divisions and businesses with a competitive advantage in serving their customers.

As a result of AT&T's declining core business—long-distance service—the company revised its corporate strategy for the 1990s. AT&T's new focus was geared toward communications solutions for large and small customers. Included among these solutions were long-distance, wireless, satellite TV, and credit card services. Local calling services emerged as well, along with a push to expand digital wireless networks.

An emphasis on international growth and outsourcing arose during the late 1990s as well. Refining their strategy in 1997, the AT&T Board of Directors announced its intent to sell two of the company's profitable but non-strategic businesses: AT&T Universal Card Services and the Customer Care unit (formerly known as American Transtech) of AT&T Solutions. Another part of the company's new strategy was its plan to cut costs by eliminating up to 17,000 positions by the year 1999.

INFLUENCES

AT&T's primary source of revenue was from its long-distance service. An industry leader, the company ventured into other business areas including computers, wireless services, credit cards, and satellite TV. However, an unfortunate combination of increased competition and AT&T's disregard for smaller telephone companies caused AT&T's long-distance service to suffer.

AT&T's venture into the computer industry in the 1980s failed. Purchasing NCR Corporation, AT&T hoped to breathe life back into its computer operations. After the company suffered losses totaling $10.1 billion, including several startup companies in the wireless and software sector, which were stifled shortly after their unveiling, AT&T decided to sell NCR. Even the company's Universal Card began to suffer due to enormous default rates. AT&T was forced to sell NCR and Lucent Technologies in order to focus on long-distance service and its increasing competition; therefore, AT&T Corp. was the only remaining segment of the previous three AT&T divisions.

Due to increasing cost-consciousness on the part of long-distance customers, new strategies were essential for AT&T to remain competitive. Operating at the high

CHRONOLOGY:

Key Dates for AT&T Corporation

1899: Founded as American Telephone & Telegraph

1909: Acquires Western Union

1913: AT&T agrees to the Kingsbury Commitment in which it will 1) buy no more independent phone companies without government approval; 2) sell Western Union; and 3) allow independent phone companies to use its networks

1925: Bell Labs is formed

1949: The Justice Department sues AT&T to try to force them to sell Western Electric

1956: A settlement in the Justice Dept. case allows AT&T to keep Western Electric but forbids them to enter any other unregulated markets

1968: FCC takes away AT&T's telephone equipment monopoly

1969: Allows other companies such as MCI to connect to their phone network

1984: The U.S. government forces AT&T to sell seven Bell companies

1990: Buys the electronic mail service division of Western Union

1991: Acquires Teradata and NCR Corp.

1995: Purchases McCaw Cellular

1996: Company is divided into three separate operations: AT&T Corp., NCR Corporation, and Lucent Technologies

1997: Forms a partnership with Bell Atlantic Corp. and Nynex Corp. to provide customers with lower rates

1998: Acquires Teleport Communications Group (TGG), the largest alternate provider of local telecommunications service in the United States

1999: Completes a 3-for-2 stock split, issuing one additional share of common stock for each two shares owned

2000: Announces restructuring plan to create a famiily of four new AT&T companies: AT&T Wireless, AT&T Broadband, AT&T Business and AT&T Comsumer; each would be independent, publicly-held and traded businisses

2001: Closes a $10-billion global bond offering, the second largest issuance by an American Corporation

2002: Announces an agreement to merge with Comcast in a $72-billion transaction to be completed by the end of 2002

---

end of the pricing scale in this market was no longer a practical move for AT&T, a company struggling to maintain its position as the long-distance leader of the nation. AT&T's challenge was to maintain market share while growing new services like WorldNet, the Internet access service launched in the late 1990s.

CURRENT TRENDS

WorldNet was one service among many in AT&T's latest strategy called "bundling," according to Catherine Arnst in *Business Week*. The company placed high expectations on its recognizable name to sell "bundles" or packages of products including local and long-distance calling, wireless service, and Internet access. AT&T's goal was to become a convenient one-stop communications services company. Since 1994, the company has been implementing this strategy by acquiring companies like McCaw Cellular. AT&T also seized opportunities in video with its 2.5 percent interest in Hughes Electronics

Corp.'s DirectTV, a satellite service being marketed to AT&T customers. AT&T's WorldNet service also ranked as the second largest Internet-access server.

While in 2002, the Internet and wireless communications were still considered new markets, they were expected to have a tremendous impact on trends within the communications industry. In 2002, AT&T launched its "M-Life" wireless messaging features. Although wireless messaging in 2001 was not widely used, with about 2 percent of Americans owning devices that can access mobile data, it was predicted that by 2007, 59 percent would own such devices.

PRODUCTS

AT&T runs the world's largest communications network and is the leading provider of long-distance and wireless services. The company also offers online services and cable television and, in the late 1990s, it began to deliver local telephone service.

"Project Angel" was among AT&T's newer developments in the late 1990s. More a "technology" than a product, the company introduced its plans for this new service in the mid-1990s. AT&T planned to use radio technology to deliver local telephone service and high-velocity Internet access without requiring a new wire to be connected to the customer's house. An 18-inch square box was designed to attach to the side of a house or small business, the box would be connected to the existing wire. When a call is made, a signal inside the box triggers an antenna nearby, which connects to AT&T's network. The intended result was wireless communication for local calling, an increasingly popular market as local telephone markets have been allowing customers choices in local service providers.

CORPORATE CITIZENSHIP

In 2000, AT&T donated more than $52 million and more than $20 milllion in products and services to non-profit organizations in 10 countries. Through the AT&T Foundation, AT&T awards grants to benefit programs in Education, Arts and Culture, and Civic and Community Service. In the area of education, AT&T has traditionally invested in pre-college and higher education programs with emphasis on math and science, both of which are important to the company's business. They place increasing importance on the use of technology and its role in the enhancement of teaching and learning. In late 1995, AT&T announced a five-year commitment totaling $150 million for its new program, the AT&T Learning Network. Designed to get the nation's schools onto the "Information Superhighway," the program represents AT&T's largest commitment to education thus far.

In 2000 AT&T gave $250,000 to each of the five universities participating in the AT&T Education Alliance. The grants were used to develop programs to meet future workforce requirements in the information technology industry.

AT&T also promotes arts and culture around the world by supporting arts programs. The company supports such initiatives by bringing artists and innovative work together with wide audiences. The Arts & Culture program awards between 150 and 200 grants every year. AT&T's efforts in the area of community service are directed toward enhancing life in the communities in which AT&T employees and customers live and work. The company does this by developing programs that address the needs of specific communities through communications and information technology and by encouraging employees to participate in public service.

GLOBAL PRESENCE

AT&T provides long-distance service to every country and territory in the world and direct-dial service is available to more than 270 countries. International growth is of increasing importance to AT&T. Current growth areas include China, where a China-United States cable network was slated for completion in 1998. China Telecom and AT&T are among the 10 carriers who signed agreements to construct the first fiber optic undersea telecommunications cable linking the two countries. With technology able to transmit voice, data, and images at eight times today's established capability, more than 1 million calls could be placed at the same time.

A similar undersea cable was planned to connect the United States and the United Kingdom, providing complete service by 1998. And yet another was developed to connect the United States, Germany, and the United Kingdom by 1998.

AT&T Corporation provides products and services worldwide. However, most of the company's sales are generated in the United States—90 percent of AT&T's total sales. International sales accounted for the remaining 10 percent. In 1997 AT&T announced plans to invest up to $9 billion in order to expand its network to new markets, including local phone and Internet services.

EMPLOYMENT

AT&T bills itself as a "demanding and dynamic organization that requires a commitment to community, environment, people, and most importantly, Our Common Bond." The company seeks people who thrive on challenges, are self-confident, and seek immediate responsibility. It also values previous exposure to international or multicultural environments.

AT&T offers competitive benefits that can be tailored to the needs of individual employees. The company also has a comprehensive corporate education program, providing in-house training courses to help employees improve technical and managerial skills. It also offers tuition reimbursement for those wishing to pursue advanced degrees. AT&T adheres to its policy of equal opportunity for employees, placing value on diversity.

SOURCES OF INFORMATION

Bibliography

Arnst, Catherine, and Amy Barrett. "AT&T?" *Business Week*, 10 March 1997.

Arnst, Catherine, and Peter Coy. "AT&T: Will the Bad News Ever End?" *Business Week*, 7 October 1996.

"AT&T Building the Network of the Future Today." *PRNewswire*, 17 March 1997.

"AT&T Corp." *Hoover's Online*. 30 June 2001. Available at http://www.hoovers.com.

"AT&T to Build First China-U.S. Undersea Cable." *Business Wire*, 30 March 1997.

"AT&T to Build World's Most Powerful Undersea Network." *Business Wire*, 24 March 1997.

Coy, Peter. "Can AT&T Keep Learning to Love the Net?" *Business Week*, 7 October 1996.

Elstrom, Peter. "How the Turnaround CEO Failed to Deliver." *Business Week*, 23 July 2001.

Fillion, Roger. "AT&T, Baby Bells Offer Plan to Cut Phone Rates." *Reuters*, 4 April 1997.

Nee, Eric. "10 Tech Trends to Bet On." *Fortune*, 19 March 2001.

Ziegler, Bart. "AT&T Cut Allen's Bonus in '96 Due to Company's Performance." *The Wall Street Journal*, 2 April 1997.

For an annual report:

on the Internet at: http://www.att.com/ir/investorinfo.html **or** telephone: (800)972-0784 **or** write: AT&T Investor Relations, Rm. 3349A2, 295 N. Maple Ave., Basking Ridge, NJ 07920

For additional industry research:

Investigate companies by their Standard Industrial Classification Codes, also known as SICs. AT&T's primary SICs are:

4813 Telephone Communications, Except Radio Telephone

4841 Cable And Other Pay Television Services

7389 Services-Business Services, NEC

Also investigate companies by their North American Industrial Classification System codes, also known as NAICS codes. AT&T's primary NAICS codes are:

334111 Electronic Computer Manufacturing

334210 Telephone Apparatus Manufacturing

513220 Cable and Other Program Distribution

513310 Wired Telecommunications Carriers

522298 All Other Non-Depository Credit Intermediation

522320 Financial Transactions Processing, Reserve, and Clearing House Activities

AutoZone Inc.

FOUNDED: 1979 as Auto Shack

Contact Information:

HEADQUARTERS: 123 S. Front St.
Memphis, TN 38103
PHONE: (901)495-7185
FAX: (901)495-8316
EMAIL: info@autozone.com
URL: http://www.autozone.com

OVERVIEW

A Fortune 500 company with annual sales nearing the $5 billion mark, AutoZone Inc. is the largest retailer of automobile and light truck parts in the United States.

COMPANY FINANCES

After reaching $1 billion in the early 1990s, sales at AutoZone grew steadily into the early 2000s. In 2001, the firm posted record revenues of $4.8 billion. Profits also climbed consistently throughout the 1990s, reaching their peak of $367.6 million in 2000. Although profits declined to $175.5 million in 2001, AutoZone's stock reached an all-time high of $49.20 per share; the low that year was $21.00 per share. Profits in the first quarter of 2002 grew 65 percent.

ANALYSTS' OPINIONS

The Standard & Poor's 500 listed AutoZone stock as the second best performer of 2001; shares had increased in value by 180 percent that year. According to a December 2001 article in *CBS.MarketWatch.com*, AutoZone's success was due, at least in part, to the sluggish North American economy of the early 2000s. "AutoZone is among the handful of companies that actually stand to benefit from a weak economy, with the theory being that drivers tend to hold on to and fix up their cars rather than replace them, plus they tend to find it cheaper to drive than fly to some destinations."

Along with the favorable market conditions created by a sluggish economy, many analysts pointed to the firm's decision to slow its new store openings to instead focus on the development of existing stores as a key reason for increased profits in 2002. Marketing efforts spearheaded by new CEO Steve Odland were also credited for boosting AutoZone's performance.

FAST FACTS:
About AutoZone Inc.

Ownership: AutoZone Inc. is a publicly owned company traded on the New York Stock Exchange.

Ticker Symbol: AZO

Officers: Steve Odland, Chmn., Pres., and CEO, 43; Michael G. Archbold, SVP and CFO, 41; Bruce G. Clark, SVP and CIO; Anthony D. Rose, SVP Advertising

Employees: 44,600

Principal Subsidiary Companies: AutoZone Inc. owns and operates 3,000 retail stores across the United States, as well as 21 stores in Mexico.

Chief Competitors: AutoZone Inc. competes with other auto parts retailers, such as Pep-Boys and Genuine Parts. Additional rivals include larger superstore chains, like Wal-Mart, that operate extensive auto parts departments.

HISTORY

In 1979, Joseph R. Hyde III opened a store called Auto Shack in Forrest City, Arkansas, to offer inexpensive auto parts to the general public. He organized his new venture as a division of Malone & Hyde, Inc., a family-owned business. Within a year, Hyde had opened seven more stores in Arkansas and Tennessee, as well as a warehouse in Memphis. The chain continued to grow quickly with the addition of another 23 stores in 1980. By then, Auto Shack stores existed in a total of seven states. The Memphis warehouse was expanded in 1982 to accommodate the rapid expansion. Two years later, Auto Shack stores in operation totaled 200 and spanned 13 states. Hyde sold a majority stake in Auto Shack to investment banker Kohlberg Kravis Roberts & Co. (KKR). Another 68 units opened in 1985.

In 1986, the firm created a lifetime warranty program for 42,000 of the parts it sold. To keep pace with growing demand, Auto Shack constructed a warehouse in South Carolina. The firm also created an electronic catalog to help its employees find parts for specific car makes and models more quickly. In 1987, Hyde sold all portions of the family business except its fastest-growing division: Auto Shack. Operating as an independent business for the first time, Auto Shack changed its company name, and the name of its stores, to AutoZone. The following year, AutoZone developed its own auto parts brand, Duralast. Sales exceeded $500 million in 1989. By then, AutoZone had become the third-largest U.S. retailer of auto parts. Its 500th store opened in Hobbs, New Mexico, that year.

The firm listed its shares publicly for the firm time in April of 1991. KKR kept a 68 percent share of AutoZone, while AutoZone managers retained another 16 percent, and former managers held on to 6 percent. Roughly 10 percent was left for other investors. Net income grew 89 percent that year to $44 million on sales of $818 million. In 1992, sales exceeded $1 billion for the first time. The firm's efforts, in 1994, to acquire 25 stores owned by Nationwise Automotive Inc. were thwarted by a higher bid from Western Auto Supply, a division of Sears, Roebuck & Co. Despite this setback, AutoZone continued to look for expansion opportunities. Nearly 1,000 stores spanned 25 states by 1995. New product releases that same year included Duralast batteries, which eventually became the top selling automotive batteries in the United States.

AutoZone diversified in 1996 with the $56.8 million purchase of Alldata Corp., a developer of software that offers diagnosis and repair information regarding various automotive problems. The firm also broadened its customer base from individual consumers to include businesses like automotive service stations. The following year, John Adams took over as CEO and president, marking the first time ever AutoZone was headed by someone other than a member of the Hyde family. Intense growth in 1998 included the acquisition of two automotive parts chains, Auto Palace and Chief Auto Parts Inc., as well as the purchase of 100 units from Pep-Boys. These newly acquired units, 800 in total, were transformed into AutoZone stores. The firm also expanded internationally for the first time, opening a store in Nuevo Lardeo, Mexico.

Six more new stores were opened in Mexico in 1999. That year, the Fortune 500 added AutoZone to its ranks. The heavy debt load AutoZone incurred from its rapid growth in 1998 resulted in a decreased profit margin (5.9 percent compared to a high of 7.7 percent in the mid-1990s). Stock prices began to decline, leaving the firm somewhat vulnerable to takeover. When ESL Investments, which purchased its initial stake in AutoZone in 1997, upped its share to 16.27 percent, it became the largest shareholder of AutoZone. As a result, AutoZone's

FINANCES:

AutoZone Inc.
Revenues, 1998-2001
(million dollars)

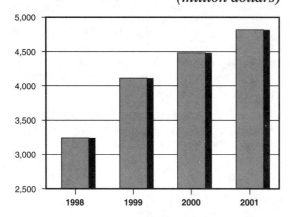

AutoZone Inc.
2001 Stock Prices
(dollars)

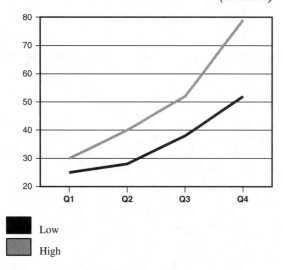

■ Low

▨ High

board of directors put in place a "poison pill," which safeguarded company from takeover by automatically weakening the stake of any shareholder who acquired more than 15 percent of the firm.

STRATEGY

When Hyde launched AutoZone, he focused on offering low prices and high quality customer service, business principals that remain at the core of the firm's

strategy. Throughout the 1980s and 1990s, developments in technology were used in an effort to continually improve customer service. For example, AutoZone began making use of an electronic catalog in the late 1980s to help employees more quickly and accurately determine which parts were needed for specific vehicles. Eventually, customer warranty information was added to this database. A satellite system, put in place in 1994, allowed employees from one store to set aside merchandise at a nearby stores to ensure that customers could purchase the parts they needed even if they were out of stock at a certain store. The launch of Autozone.com in 1996 allowed AutoZone to sell to its parts online to both individual consumers and to the new business clients it began targeting that year.

The strategy of rapid growth via acquisition also served the company well. Throughout the 1980s and 1990s, AutoZone purchased large automotive parts chains, quite often converting them into AutoZone stores to build upon AutoZone name recognition. Acquiring existing stores was not only often cheaper than building brand new ones, but it also allowed AutoZone access to a base of existing customers. This expansion strategy was changed, however, in the early 2000s, as AutoZone began to focus more closely on developing its existing stores. After closing 35 underperforming stores in 2001, CEO Steve Odland upped performance standards for the roughly 3,000 remaining stores. These efforts to boost profitability also included the launch of a marketing campaign centering on the firm's new tag line: "Get in the Zone: AutoZone." The reason for these changes, according to AutoZone, was the desire to increase its rate of return for investors to 15 percent.

PRODUCTS

AutoZone sells car and light truck parts such as carburetors, batteries, alternators, spark plugs, struts, lights, and filters. Vehicle maintenance products include antifreeze; oil; brake, power steering, and transmission fluids; paint; tools; and windshield wipers. The firm also sells accessories such as vehicle sound systems. AutoZone began to add more accessory products, such as sunglasses and decorator floor mats and seat coverings, to its stores in 2001.

CORPORATE CITIZENSHIP

AutoZone supports a variety of non-profit causes—including literacy tutoring, job training, community enrichment, and human services programs—in the communities in which it operates. The AutoZone Matching Gift Program also allows employees to request that AutoZone match their charitable contributions to various causes.

AUTOZONE FOUNDER LEARNS TRICK OF THE TRADE FROM WAL-MART

AutoZone founder Joseph Hyde sat on the board of directors for Wal-Mart for several years prior to opening his first auto parts store. Hyde modeled his initial corporate strategy, which focused on low prices and high quality customer service, after that of Wal-Mart.

GLOBAL PRESENCE

While the majority of AutoZone's stores are located in the United States, the firm does also operate 21 units in Mexico. Because drivers in Mexico tend to own older cars, which are more likely to need replacement parts than the new cars favored by many drivers in the United States, AutoZone plans to increase Mexican operations rapidly over the next several years.

EMPLOYMENT

AutoZone employees are known as AutoZoners. To foster high-quality customer service, AutoZone recognizes employees who "go the extra mile" for customers with the Extra Miler Award.

SOURCES OF INFORMATION

Bibliography

"AutoZone Inc." *Notable Corporate Chronologies.* Farmington Hills, MI: Gale Research, 1999.

AutoZone Inc. Home Page, 2002. Available at http://www.auto-zone.com.

CHRONOLOGY:
Key Dates for AutoZone Inc.

1979: AutoZone is founded as Auto Shack by Joseph R. Hyde III

1986: AutoZone begins offering a lifetime warranty on thousands of its parts

1989: Sales exceed $500 million and the 500th store opens

1991: AutoZone conducts its initial public offering

1997: John Adams becomes CEO and President (the first time a non-family member heads the company)

1999: AutoZone is added to the Fortune 500

2001: Steve Odland succeeds Adams as chairman and CEO

"AutoZone Profit Zooms 65 Percent." *CBS.MarketWatch.com*, 5 December 2001. Available at http://www.marketwatch.com.

Bechard, Theresa. "Store Focus, Marketing Helping AutoZone See Higher Profits." *Memphis Business Journal*, 28 September 2001, 34.

Farzad, Roben. "Pass Me That Spark-Plug Wrench, Clem." *SmartMoney.com*, 7 December 2001. Available at http://biz.yahoo.com/smart.

For an annual report:
on the Internet at: http://media.corporate-ir.net/media_files/NYS/AZO/reports/2001ar/annual.html

For additional industry research:
Investigate companies by their Standard Industrial Classification codes, also known as SICs. Autozone Inc.'s primary SIC is:

5531 Auto and Home Supply Stores

Also investigate companies by their North American Industry Classification System codes, also known as NAICS codes. Autozone Inc.'s primary NAICS code is:

441310 Automotive Parts and Accessories Stores

Bally Total Fitness Holding Corporation

FOUNDED: 1996

Contact Information:

HEADQUARTERS: 8700 W. Bryn Mawr Ave.
    Chicago, IL 60631
PHONE: (773)380-3000
FAX: (773)693-2982
EMAIL: mmessing@mww.com
URL: http://www.ballyfitness.com

OVERVIEW

Bally Total Fitness Holding Corporation is a commercial operator of fitness centers in North America. As of 2001, the company operated approximately 400 fitness centers in 28 states and Canada operating under the Bally, Crunch Fitness, Pinnacle Fitness and Gorilla Sports names, among others. Bally has locations in each of the top 25 metropolitan markets in the United States, where it is the only national commercial operator of fitness centers.

For its four million members, its facilities offer features such as exercise equipment, pools, aerobic programs, running tracks, and racquet courts. In many of its centers, it also provides personal trainers and sports medicine services. Bally also markets a line of private label nutritional products and sells health-related products through retail stores in about 120 of its clubs.

The company's business organization includes a back office infrastructure that allows it to efficiently support ongoing relationships with members.

Product and services business accounts for nearly 15 percent of Bally total revenues, which were about $750 million in 2000.

COMPANY FINANCES

In recent years, Bally has been posting strong numbers and showing steady and healthy gains. In 2001, the company recorded a net income of $72.4 million, an increase of 11 percent over the previous year. Operating income for 2001 was $64.5 million compared to $57.9

million in 2000. Net revenue for 2000 was $1,007.1 million compared to $861.1 million in 1999, an increase of $146 million or 17 percent. Operating income for 2000 was $126.4 million compared to $93.3 million in 1999. Net revenue for 1998 was $744.3 million in 1998, an increase of $116.8 million. Net revenue for 1997 was $661 million and $639 million for 1996.

ANALYSTS' OPINIONS

In 2001, Hayley Kissel, director of Merrill Lynch's Global Securities Research and Economics Division, commented that Bally Total Fitness was the only profitable U.S. publicly traded company in the Leisure Goods & Services sector. She pointed out that this resulted from the company's financial discipline and superior economic model. Another element, she said, was Bally's membership structure, which provides more visibility in revenue growth. Specifically, Bally's characteristic three-year membership plan results in a lower attrition rate.

HISTORY

Life truly began for the Bally Total Fitness Corporation in 1996. In its earlier incarnation, it was merely an unsuccessful subsidiary of the Bally Entertainment Corporation, which had been previously called Bally Manufacturing Corporation and was best known, perhaps, as a producer of pinball and video arcade games. The fitness subsidiary limped along until 1996, when it became a spinoff as a result of the merger of Bally Entertainment and Hilton Hotels Corporation. Bally Entertainment would go on to score big in the casino business. The subsidiary, on its own, would go on to become a robust organization, thanks in large part to Lee S. Hillman, whose name is pretty much synonymous with the new Bally Fitness.

Hillman joined Bally Total Fitness in 1991, when it was still part of Bally Entertainment Corporation. When he came on board, the subsidiary was struggling, as it suffered an increasingly severe cash flow problem and was facing almost inevitable bankruptcy. Hillman, its CFO at the time, would engineer the industry's most striking turnaround.

Bally started to shape up for real when Hillman was named CEO in 1996, the year the fitness subsidiary became a merger outcast and took on a life of its own. Once Hillman assumed the helm, he implemented a three-point strategy that changed the company's fortunes. This strategy included increasing the company's offerings. Starting in 1997, Bally offered a private label line of Bally branded nutritional products to its members. In 1998, the company entered joint venture agreements that enabled it to offer sports medicine services, including

FINANCES:
Bally Total Fitness Holding Corp. Net Revenues, 1997-2000 (million dollars)

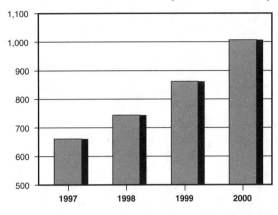

rehabilitative, chiropractic and massage therapy, in about 100 of its centers.

During 2000, the company opened approximately 120 retail stores. This brought the total number of retail outlets in its centers to approximately 340. In 2002, Bally purchased the fitness company Crunch in a deal worth $90 million.

STRATEGY

Bally states it has three current primary strategic objectives: improving the operating margins of its fitness center membership operations, its core business; increasing the number of fitness centers based on a more profitable fitness center prototype; and introducing new products and services to members. To meet these objectives, the company developed and implemented specific strategic initiatives.

The first initiative involves improving core business operations by growing and improving the quality of revenues while leveraging the largely fixed cost structure of its business. To accomplish this, it increased emphasis on the sale of higher margin all-club memberships, which are typically financed, unlike the sale of lower margin single-club memberships, and it significantly increased the monthly charge to new members for dues. Also, Bally continued focusing on maintaining higher down payments on financed membership plans and securing installment payments electronically, which resulted in a 14 percent growth in average down payments from 1997 to 2000. Emphasis on the sale of all-

FAST FACTS:

About Bally Total Fitness Holding Corporation

Ownership: Bally Total Fitness Holding Corporation is a publicly owned company traded on the New York Stock Exchange.

Ticker Symbol: BFT

Officers: Lee Hillman, Chmn. and CEO, 45, 2000 salary $1,100,000; John Dwyer, CFO, EVP, and Treasurer, 48, $1,100,000; Paul Toback, COO, 37, $1,200,000; William Fanelli, Sr., VP Finance, 38; Cary Gaan, SVP, Gen. Counsel, and Sec., 55, $429,000

Employees: 12,500

Principal Subsidiary Companies: Bally Total Fitness Holding Corporation operates fitness centers under its flagship Bally Total Fitness brand name as well as under the Crunch Fitness, Sports Clubs of Canada, Gorilla Sports, and Pinnacle Fitness brands. The majority of Bally's 400 fitness centers use the Bally Total Fitness service mark.

Chief Competitors: Bally's main competitors include other organizations that operate fitness centers, such as Gold's Gym, the YMCA, and 24 Hour Fitness. As Bally has also branched out into the areas of nutritional products and exercise equipment in recent years, it faces other competition from companies such as Weider and General Nutrition Centers (GNC).

club memberships contributed to a 39 percent increase in the weighted-average price of memberships sold from 1997 to 2000.

The second initiative involved developing new facilities. It achieved facility expansion in three ways. In late 1997, the company started upgrading and expanding existing facilities and exercise equipment beyond normal maintenance requirements. In 1998, Bally initiated a plan to increase new facility openings of its more profitable new fitness center prototype. Seven of these facilities were opened during 1998, 22 were opened in 1999 and 14 in 2000. Also, it set about acquiring existing fitness center operations at attractive prices. That led to the purchase of the fitness centers that had operated under the names of The Sports Clubs of Canada, Pinnacle Fitness, and Gorilla Sports.

The third initiative involves adding products and services. The additions, the company pointed out, did not require significant capital investment. Revenues from products and services grew eleven-fold since 1997, to $111 million in 2000.

INFLUENCES

The appointment of Lee Hillman proved pivotal in the survival of the faltering fitness enterprise. His three-point strategy was responsible for making the company profitable. The first goal of Hillman's strategy was to alleviate the company's cash problems. When he accomplished that, he designed a "store model" that could be replicated through the chain to increase profitability. Finally, he added new products and services to the basic offerings that increased membership value to existing and potential customers. This also added additional revenue streams to the company.

By 1999, Bally was in the black. In recent years, the company's market capitalization has increased from $40 million to well over $500 million. Stock prices rose from $4.00 to more than $20.00 a share. The chain grew to include 400 centers across North America, a figure that represents 31 percent of all commercial fitness center members in the United States. Hillman attributed the success to his focus on customer service. Beyond his three core strategies, Hillman placed strong emphasis on this aspect. Bally, he was determined, would provide members with a wide range of fitness services that would be attractive to a broad population. As a result, Bally Fitness became more than just a gym.

Thanks to Hillman's vision, the company's new fitness center prototype achieves efficiency by focusing on fitness services its members use most frequently. It also started attracting new customers through expansion of existing clubs and the creation of new centers. During 2000, Bally invested $108.4 million in property and equipment, including approximately $74 million related to new fitness centers, and major upgrades and expansions including new equipment in existing centers. The company invested $4.8 million to purchase land and buildings for new clubs and existing leaseholds. In addition, it acquired 17 clubs with a net cash investment of $4.1 million.

Also, Bally clustered its fitness centers in major metropolitan areas in order to achieve marketing and operating efficiencies. Over 86 percent of its fitness centers are located in markets in which the company has five or more facilities, with its largest concentrations in the New York City, Los Angeles, Chicago, Baltimore/Washington D.C., Dallas, Houston, Detroit, San Francisco, Toronto, Portland, Seattle, Philadelphia, and Miami areas.

CURRENT TRENDS

In 2001, Bally reduced its debt by nearly $30 million. Despite a difficult economy, it was able to increase revenues and exceed cash flow expectations as well as improve its sales processes and services for its members. Because of its improved centers and added services, Bally found that its existing members were staying with the company longer and were using the centers for longer periods of time, which increased sales of products and services such as such as drinks, group training and nutritional supplements.

Beyond 2002, Bally is looking to increase its business opportunities. It has entered into co-marketing agreements with Pepsi Cola Company, Eastman Kodak, Novartis Consumer Health, Inc., Sunkist Growers, Household International, Procter & Gamble, Sprint, Time Warner, and MBNA America and Sports Display, Inc. These companies want to work with Bally to reach its members, who they feel represent a potential target market.

The company is also focusing on increased acquisitions. It felt that acquiring Crunch Fitness in a $90 million deal would clear the way for other acquisitions beyond 2002.

In 2001, Bally announced plans to publish its own magazine, with the first issue of the proposed lifestyle health and fitness quarterly slated to be produced in spring 2002. It was looking to not only distribute the magazine to its members but to possibly extend sales to newsstands if the interest was there. The company sees the magazine as a revenue generator and a brand builder.

PRODUCTS

Bally Total Fitness Holding Corporation's primary product is, of course, its fitness centers. The company offers members affordable membership programs. The centers feature a selection of cardiovascular, conditioning, and strength equipment; extensive aerobic and other group fitness training programs; and pools, racquet courts, or other athletic facilities.

Cardiovascular equipment includes treadmills, elliptical trainers, stairclimbers, and exercise bikes. Weight training equipment includes a wide variety of plate-loaded equipment, weight machines, and a complete line of free weights ranging in size for beginners to advanced strength trainers. Group exercise areas have specially designed floors to reduce the impact to bone and joints.

Many centers also provide sports medicine services, including rehabilitative, chiropractic and massage therapy, and the company offers financial services to selected members by giving them the opportunity to transfer the balance of their financed membership fee to a pre-approved Visa account.

CHRONOLOGY:

Key Dates For Bally Total Fitness Holding Corporation

1996: Bally Total Fitness Holding Company is created when Bally Entertainment merges with Hilton Hotels

1996: Lee S. Hillman is named CEO

1997: Bally introduces a line of nutritional products

1998: Bally begins offering sports medicine services at its fitness centers

1999: The Bally chain grows to include 400 fitness centers

2000 Bally Total Fitness records total revenues of $750 million

2001: Bally acquires the Sports Club of Canada chain

2002: Bally purchases the fitness company Crunch in a deal worth $90 million

Bally Total Fitness also sells a licensed line of portable fitness equipment distributed by Sports & Leisure Technology Corporation of Yonkers, New York. The 70-item line is sold in national retail chains in the United States and Canada including Foot Locker, Champs, Lady Foot Locker, Zeller's, Modell's, Ames, Fingerhut, and Service Merchandise, as well as in the Amway and Avon catalogs.

Bally's nutritional products include meal-replacement powders, supplements such as vitamins and creatine, weight loss products, high protein bars, and ready-to-drink meal replacement shakes.

CORPORATE CITIZENSHIP

Bally Total Fitness Holding Corporation has created a "Stronger Communities" program that donates used exercise equipment to groups such as inner city schools, park districts, and police athletic leagues. As part of the program, which was started in 1997, Bally reconditions equipment that has been retired from its centers. Rather than turn the equipment back to the manufacturers in exchange for cash, Bally has decided to spend money on refurbishing the equipment. Since the program's inception, Bally has donated more than $10 million worth of

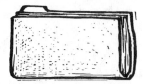

HEALTHY ECONOMY MEANS HEALTHY FITNESS CLUBS

According to health club industry sources, the vitality of the fitness club industry is strongly reflected by the health of the U.S. economy. The better off the economy, the better shape fitness clubs are in. Since 1982, it has been shown that the number of U.S. health clubs has tended to rise and fall with the nation's gross domestic product. The reason? When times are bad, consumers generally cut out health club memberships. In the past, this has resulted in hundreds of health clubs going out of business.

fitness equipment, apparel, and memberships. Also as part of the program, Bally provides members of its Personal Training Team to train and educate those who will be using the equipment.

Bally Total Fitness also supports the Challenged Athletes Foundation, a non-profit organization dedicated to building self-esteem and the desire to succeed in people with physical disabilities through competitive athletics.

GLOBAL PRESENCE

When Bally acquired the Sports Club of Canada chain in 2001, with its 10 upscale commercial fitness centers, it increased its total number of fitness centers in the Toronto area to thirteen. These centers are run by the Sports Club's experienced management team, which will spearhead Bally's intended expansion into other areas of Canada.

EMPLOYMENT

Bally Total Fitness Holding Corporation employs 12,500 people in its 400 centers. When recruiting new employees, Bally seeks candidates with previous business experience and fluency in more than one language. The company offers both flexible full-time and part-time work schedules. Positions include sales personnel, service managers, certified personal trainers, receptionists, child care staff, group fitness instructors, equipment mechanics, and janitorial. Bally provides a drug-free workplace and is an equal opportunity employer.

Bally offers a minority internship program for minority undergraduate or graduate students majoring in exercise physiology. The 12-week intensive internship opens doors into the fitness industry and possible future employment with Bally Total Fitness.

SOURCES OF INFORMATION

Bibliography

"Bally Total Fitness Holding Company," *Hoover's Online*, 8 April 2001. Available at http://www.hoovers.com.

"Company Details—Bally Total Fitness Holding Company," 8 April 2001. Available at http://www.forbes.com.

"Lee S. Hillman, W'77: Flexing His Muscles in the Fitness Business." *Wharton Alumni Magazine*, Spring 1999. Available at http://www.wharton.upenn.edu.

Markey, Patrick. "Bally Eyes More Acquisitions." *Reuters*, 15 January 2002.

"Profile—Bally Total Fitness." Yahoo! Finance, 8 April 2001. Available at http://biz.yahoo.com/p/b/bft.html.

Steele, Jeffrey. "Bally Total Fitness Shapes Up." *Chicago GSB Class Notes*, 2001. Available at http://gsbwww.uchicago.edu/news.

For an annual report:
on the Internet at: http://biz.yahoo.com/e/010309/bft.html

For additional industry research:
Investigate companies by their Standard Industrial Classification codes, also known as SICs. Bally's primary SIC codes are:

7991 Physical Fitness Facilities

7997 Membership

Also investigate companies by their North American Industry Classification System codes, also known as NAICS codes. Bally's NAICS codes are:

551112 Offices of Other Holding Companies

713940 Fitness and Recreational Sports Centers

Bank of America Corporation

FOUNDED: 1874

OVERVIEW

Formed from the 1998 merger of NationsBank Corp. and BankAmerica Corp., Bank of America operates as the third largest bank in the nation and is the first coast-to-coast banking operation in the United States. With more than 4,400 retail consumer banking locations and 13,000 ATMs, the company is ranked number one in terms of deposit market share in many key markets. Bank of America has four main business segments: consumer and commercial banking, asset management, global corporate and investment banking, and equity investments. Through these segments, the firm provides financial products, services, and solutions to customers in 48 states and 38 countries across the globe.

The consumer banking arm maintains more than 27 million customer relationships and handles three billion customer transactions each year—116 interactions per second. The company's commercial banking segment, which also includes its real estate and business credit businesses, serves entrepreneurs, multinational firms, real estate developers, and home construction companies, as well as non-profit firms and municipalities.

Bank of America's asset management unit serves 2.3 million affluent households and operates the firm's Private Bank, the largest private bank in the United States in terms of clients.

The global corporate and investment banking segment provides various banking services including capital-raising services and equity and debt sales and trading. It serves 76 percent of the Fortune Global 500 companies and 94 percent of the Fortune 500 companies in the United States.

Contact Information:
HEADQUARTERS: Bank of America Corporate Center
   Charlotte, NC 28255
PHONE: (888)279-3457
FAX: (704)386-6699
TOLL FREE: (800)299-2265
URL: http://www.bankofamerica.com

Bank of America's corporate center, right, is located in downtown Charlotte, North Carolina. (AP Photo/Chuck Burton)

The equity investments unit is a diversified portfolio of investments in companies during various stages of their life cycle, from startup to buyout.

Having grown by major merger and acquisition activity through the 1990s, Bank of America's strategy relies heavily on acquisition integration and organic growth, strong client relationships, and brand development. During 2001 the company launched its Six Sigma quality and productivity program, enabling its employees to analyze business procedures, identify problems, increase efficiency, and reduce error rates.

COMPANY FINANCES

During 2001 Bank of America secured revenues of $34.98 billion, up from $33.25 billion in 2000. Total assets fell to $621.76 billion, down from $642.19 billion in 2000. The firm's earnings per share have fluctuated over the past three years, growing from $4.48 in 1999 to $4.52 in 2000, and then falling to $4.18 in 2001.

The consumer and commercial banking segment secured earnings or net income of $4.8 billion, an increase of 6.4 percent over 2000. This segment also posted revenues of $21.4 billion, making up the largest portion of company revenues. The global corporate and investment banking segment's earnings climbed by 6.8 percent in 2001 to reach $1.9 billion on revenues of $9.2 billion. Bank of America's two other segments, asset management and equity investments, experienced declines in earnings and revenues during 2001. The asset management group posted earnings of $521 million, a decline of 11.5 percent, while equity investment recorded a loss of $94 million. Revenues for the two segments were $2.7 billion and $32 million, respectively.

ANALYSTS' OPINIONS

Bank of America believes that investor confidence in the firm stems from its balance sheet management and its goal to secure 10 percent annual earnings per share growth. During 2001 the company's stock increased in value by 37 percent, while many of its competitors experienced an average decline of 5 percent. At the start of 2002, Bank of America continued to outperform its peers. According to Datek Online Brokerage Services LLC, the company stood in a favorable position due to its broad product line and its geographical reach, and its departure from auto leasing as well as sub-prime real estate lending. Standard & Poor's anticipated the stock to maintain its growth and suggested the stock would continue to outperform as Bank of America continued to focus on its earnings strategy.

HISTORY

Bank of America was formed from the merger of NationsBank Corp. and BankAmerica Corp. Both companies dated back to the 1800s and had grown through a series of mergers and acquisitions before teaming up in 1998. Nationsbank was created in 1991 by the merger of the North Carolina National Bank Corporation (NCNB) and the C&S/Sovran Corp.

NCNB's roots go back to the Commercial National Bank, formed by several citizens of Charlotte, North Carolina. This bank spent most of its early history merging with other North Carolina-based financial institutions and eventually formed NCNB in 1960. The company continued to grow through acquisition, and by the end of the 1970s, it had become the state's largest bank. NCNB forged ahead amidst fierce competition and expanded into Florida in 1981, Georgia in 1985, South Carolina and Virginia in 1986, and Maryland in 1987. In 1989, the bank acquired full ownership of First Republic Bank in Texas. By that time, NCNB had earned a reputation for industry firsts, including opening a branch in London, operating a full service securities company, and listing on the Tokyo Exchange.

C&S/Sovran dates back to the 1860s in Richmond, Virginia. Sovran's predecessors served the likes of Confederate Army commander Robert E. Lee and eventually became known as Virginia National Bankshares and First and Merchants. These two firms merged in 1984 to create Sovran Financial Corporation. At the time, it was the largest banking merger in Virginia's state history. In 1986 Sovran merged with D.C. National Bancorp of Maryland. The following year, it teamed up with Commerce Union, a financial firm based in Tennessee. The predecessor to C&S, Citizens Bank of Savannah, Georgia, began operations in 1887. In 1906 it merged with Southern Bank to form Citizens and Southern Bank, the largest bank in Georgia. In 1928 the bank expanded into South Carolina, but sold its operations in 1940 when federal regulations prohibited banks from owning branches in more than one state. In 1986, however, Citizens and Southern repurchased its former South Carolina holding, by then known as the C&S Bank of South Carolina. C&S merged with Sovran in 1990.

During this time period, the banking industry was caught up in a wave of consolidation. NCNB, led by Hugh L. McColl, Jr., began to eye C&S/Sovran as a takeover target while the newly merged company suffered from a recession in the Southeast, along with loan losses. McColl, known for his aggressive acquisition style, negotiated the deal and in early 1992, NCNB merged with C&S/Sovran to form NationsBank, one of the top three banks in the United States. The bank continued its expansion strategy throughout the 1990s before teaming up with BankAmerica in 1998.

BankAmerica's history began in 1904 with the creation of the Bank of Italy in California. Founded by Italian immigrant Amadeo Peter Giannini, the Bank of Italy made a name for itself by lending money to average citizens, a practice unheard of at the time. The bank first began expansion in 1909, when a branch in San Jose, California, was purchased. The firm continued to grow throughout the 1920s and, in 1927, operations were consolidated into the Bank of America of California. By 1936 the institution was the fourth-largest bank in the United States with assets of $2.1 billion.

The company continued to grow through the postwar years. It became known for several innovations including computerized record keeping, student loans, and

FAST FACTS:
About Bank of America Corporation

Ownership: Bank of America Corporation is a public company traded on the New York, London, Pacific, and Tokyo Stock Exchanges.

Ticker Symbol BAC

Officers: Kenneth D. Lewis, Chmn., Pres., and CEO, 55; James H. Hance, Jr., VChmn. and CFO, 57, 2000 base salary $1 million; Amy Woods Brinkley, Chief Risk Officer, 46; Edward J. Brown, III, Pres., Global Corporate and Investment Banking, 53, 2000 base salary $700,000; Richard M. DeMartini, Pres., Asset Management, 49; Barbara J. Desoer, Pres., Consumer Products, 49; R. Eugene Taylor, Pres., Consumer and Commercial Banking, 54

Employees: 142,670

Principal Subsidiary Companies: Bank of America has banking and non-banking subsidiaries throughout the United States and in 38 countries. Subsidiary companies include credit card processor BA Merchant Services Inc. and Banc of America Securities LLC, an investment bank.

Chief Competitors: Bank of America competes with other banks, thrifts, credit unions, and various non-banking financial institutions. Its primary competitors include Citigroup, Inc.; J.P. Morgan Chase & Co.; and Wachovia Corporation.

---

the predecessor to the Visa credit card, BankAmericard. In 1968 BankAmerica was formed as holding company.

Inundated with bad loans, BankAmerica spent most of the 1980s restructuring and cutting costs. By 1990 the bank had recovered and posted revenues of $1 billion for the first time. Along with the rest of the industry, BankAmerica began merger activity and spent nearly the entire decade focused on growth and new product development.

The $62 billion deal between Nationsbank and BankAmerica in 1998 created the first coast-to-coast banking firm in the United States with assets of $572 billion. Adopting the name Bank of America, the newly merged company was run by McColl. He spent the next few years intent on integrating the two companies with each other, as well as with previous acquisitions. During 2000 Bank of America restructured, cut jobs, and streamlined

CHRONOLOGY:

Key Dates for Bank of America Corp.

1874: The Commercial National Bank is formed

1887: The Citizens Bank of Savannah, Georgia, opens its doors

1904: The Bank of Italy begins operation in California

1906: Citizens and Southern Bank (C&S) is created from the merger of Citizens and Southern Bank

1960: The North Carolina National Bank (NCNB) is formed

1968: BankAmerica Corp. is created to act as a holding company

1984: Virginia National Bankshares and First and Merchants merge to form Sovran Financial Corp.

1990: C&S and Sovran merge

1991: NationsBank Corp. is formed from the merger of NCNB and C&S/Sovran

1992: BankAmerica and Security Pacific Corp. merge

1998: NationsBank and BankAmerica merge and adopt the name Bank of America

operations. McColl retired in April 2001 and left Kenneth D. Lewis to take the helm. Under new leadership, Bank of America adopted a new strategy that focused on brand development, client relations, and organic growth.

STRATEGY

Bank of America's strategy throughout most of the 1900s relied heavily on acquisition activity. Interstate banking laws allowed for increased expansion in the 1980s and 1990s, and consolidation began to sweep through the industry, forcing the predecessors of Bank of America to join forces in order to remain competitive. After the deal, Bank of America's strategy shifted as integration became necessary. To compete as a new entity, the firm began to focus on brand development. As part of this strategy, Bank of America became a corporate partner of the 2002 Olympic Winter Games, running humorous ads during the games on television. Another

new company strategy included attracting, retaining, and deepening customer relationships by growing the number of households served, building relationship net income, increasing market share of deposits and investments, building multicultural growth, and improving customer satisfaction. The firm also began a Six Sigma quality and productivity program that was expected to result in cost savings that could be reinvested in high-growth opportunities.

INFLUENCES

Bank of America's strategy is influenced by its historical past of acquisition and consolidation as well as its desire to be a leader in the banking industry. Once focused solely on growth and expansion, the firm now looks to organic growth as key to its future development. After the 1998 merger, Bank of America was stymied by integration problems that led to lower revenue growth, net income, and earnings. Credit problems and bad loans played a part in the losses and forced the firm to reduce its minimally profitable corporate loans as well as boost deposits. The firm also began to streamline operations. When Kenneth Lewis was named chairman in 2001, his number one goal became making Bank of America one of the world's most admired companies. The company's strategies are now heavily influenced by this priority.

CURRENT TRENDS

One trend affecting Bank of America is the increased use of risk management strategies. Intense competition in the banking industry, along with an increased level of credit risk (a phenomenon showcased by Enron Corp.'s bankruptcy), prompted banks like Bank of America to adopt various risk management strategies. In fact, Bank of America restructured the four elements of its corporate planning process (strategic planning, financial planning, risk planning, and associate planning) to incorporate risk planning, including credit analysis, as well as market and operational analysis, into each element of the process. Management believes that a strong focus on risk planning will improve the consistency of company earnings.

PRODUCTS

Bank of America's Consumer Banking segment provides traditional banking services, including savings, checking, electronic bill payment, and online banking, to individuals. Bank of America's online customer base grew to 2.9 million in 2001. Its electronic payment service, with more than 3.5 million electronic payments made each month, allows customers to make credit card, mortgage, or loan payments electronically rather than by mail. The firm's commercial banking unit provides services including treasury and trade, credit and leasing, capital markets, and investment banking. The asset management group offers its private bank clients various fee-based products that enable them to access several money managers. Introduced in 2001, these products are part of the company's strategic investment portfolio package that allows clients to review various investment opportunities through the Banc of America Capital Management Multi-Strategy Hedge Fund. The company also began offering a 529 college investment plan that allows investors to save college funds free of federal taxes. Bank of America's Global Corporate and Investment Banking segment provides capital-raising solutions, merger and acquisition advisory services, equity and debt underwriting and trading, traditional services, cash management, foreign exchange, and payment services.

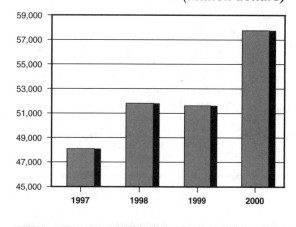

FINANCES:
Bank of America Revenues, 1997-2000 (million dollars)

CORPORATE CITIZENSHIP

Bank of America says it is committed to being a leader in making economic development and environmental protection work hand in hand. As part of its Environmental Commitment program, the company has made changes to its internal operations, developed associate programs that foster environmental care, and also developed environmental awareness in the communities in which it operates. Bank of America has won several awards for its environmental efforts, including the Spirit of the Land Award, related to its paper recycling efforts during the 2002 Olympic Games; the National Wildlife Federation National Conservation Achievement Award; and the President's Environment and Conservation Challenge Award Citation. Bank of America is also active in community development endeavors. The company has a 10-year goal to invest $350 billion in community development lending.

GLOBAL PRESENCE

The company's global activities are part of its global corporate and investment banking and equity investments segments. International operations are grouped into three regions: Asia, Europe, and Latin America. Because of turbulent and changing economic times, Bank of America limits its exposure in each region and constantly monitors the economic situation of the countries in which it operates. For example, dur-

ing 2001, Argentina began to experience an economic crisis. The firm's risk management procedures called for Bank of America to reduce its credit exposure to that country. During 2001 Bank of America reduced its exposure in high-risk countries to $21.9 billion, a decrease of $8.4 billion from 2000 figures.

EMPLOYMENT

Since 1998 executive recruiting has played a large role in Bank of America's employment strategy. The company looks to attract talent from various industries, including manufacturing, shipping, and consumer products, in order to tap into a wide array of knowledge and skills that will enable the company to reach its strategic goals. To retain its employees, the company offers a host of benefits that range from bonus awards to child care centers to adoption reimbursement. The company also offers healthcare, insurance plans, flex time, telecommuting, counseling, tuition reimbursement, and paid volunteer time. Within the company, a Diversity Advisory Council and a Diversity Network promote personal and professional development. The firm's commitment to its employees and diversity has been recognized by the NAACP. The company has also been ranked one of the "50 Best Companies in America for Asians, Blacks, and Hispanics" by *Fortune* magazine and one of the "10 Best Companies for Working Mothers" by *Working Mother* magazine.

FINANCING MOVIES

Bank of America has helped to finance thousands of movies from the very beginning of Hollywood's history. Included are the classic movies *Snow White and the Seven Dwarfs*, *It's a Wonderful Life*, *Lawrence of Arabia*, *Dances With Wolves*, and *Gone With the Wind*. The company also played a role in financing the Ryan Aircraft Company, the builders of the *Spirit of St. Louis* airplane that was used by Charles Lindbergh on the first solo flight across the Atlantic.

SOURCES OF INFORMATION

Bibliography

Bank of America Home Page, 2002. Available at http://www.bankofamerica.com

Boraks, David. "B of A Chief's Bonus Jumped 246 Percent in '01." *American Banker*, 26 March 2002.

————. "B of A Standing Pat." *American Banker*, 1 February 2002.

Stewart, Thomas A. "Where the Money Is." *Fortune*, 3 September 2001.

"Streetwalker." *Fortune*, 1 October 2001.

For an annual report:
write: Bank of America Corporate Affairs, 100 North Tryon Street, 18th Floor, NC1-007-18-01, Charlotte, NC, 28255

For additional industry research:
Investigate companies by their Standard Industrial Classification codes, also known as SICs. Bank of America's primary SICs are:

6021 National Commercial Banks

6712 Offices of Bank Holding Companies

Also investigate companies by their North American Industry Classification codes, also known as NAICS codes. Bank of America's primary NAICS codes are:

551111 Offices of Bank Holding Companies

522110 Commercial Banking

Bayer AG

OVERVIEW

Bayer AG is a globally diversified chemicals company with more than 350 individual companies in its portfolio. The parent company operates four major divisions: healthcare, crop science, polymers, and chemicals. The health care segment consists of five business groups: pharmaceuticals, biological products, consumer care, diagnostics, and animal health. The pharmaceutical business group researches, develops, manufactures, and markets prescription drugs. The consumer care business group researches, develops, manufactures, and markets nonprescription, over-the-counter products as well as pest control products. The diagnostics group provides diagnostic tools to assist in identifying diseases in their early stages of development. Bayer's crop science business group focuses on crop protection. The polymers division consists of five business groups: plastics, rubber, polyurethanes, coatings and colorants, and fibers. The chemical division's business groups include basic and fine chemicals and specialty products, as well as subsidiaries Haarmann & Reimer, H.C. Stark, and Wolff Walsrode.

COMPANY FINANCES

In 2001 Bayer Group posted a net profit of 965 million euro on net sales of 30.3 billion euro, down from a net profit of 1.8 billion euro on 31.0 billion euro in sales in 2000. (The average exchange rate in 2001 for 1 euro was $0.90.) Earnings per share also dropped significantly from 2.49 euro per share in 2000 to 1.32 euro per share in 2001. The 2001 year-end stock price was 35.80 euro

FOUNDED: 1863

Contact Information:

HEADQUARTERS: 51368 Bayerwerk, Bldg. W-1
    Leverkusen, Germany
PHONE: 49-214-305-8992
FAX: 49-214-307-1985
URL: http://www.bayer.com

Bayer AG, manufacturer of the anti-cholesterol drug Baycol, has its world headquarters in Leverkusen, Germany. (AP Photo/Hermann J. Knippertz)

per share, down from £55.87 at the end of 2000, and the company's market capitalization fell from 26.1 billion euro to 15 billion euro. During the year, Bayer took significant hits in three of its four divisions. The operating results for health care and polymers fell 71 percent, and chemicals dropped 49 percent. The biggest hits came in health care's pharmaceuticals division, which posted an operating result of £51 million in 2001 compared to £1.2 billion in 2000, and polymers, which posted an operating result of 284 million euro in 2001 compared to 988 million euro in 2000. Bright spots for the company included health care's consumer care and diagnostic divisions, which jumped in operating revenue from £177 million in 2000 to £341 million in 2001, and the agricultural division, which reported operating results of £625 for 2001, up from £584 in 2000.

Bayer's financial difficulties in 2001 were due to several factors. In August of 2001 Bayer was forced to withdraw its new cholesterol drug Baycol/Lipobay after reports of 52 patient deaths, and the company experienced production problems with its product Kogenate, used to treat hemophilia. The following month terrorist attacks in the United States significantly depressed the stock market. Several significant acquisitions also factored into Bayer's year-end statement, including the purchase in 2000 of Sybron Chemicals Inc. for 206 million euro and the polyols business of Lyondell Chemical Company for 202 million euro. However, despite the significant decrease in net income, net sales for the entire Bayer Group fell by 2.2 percent. To compensate shareholders for the lackluster year in 2001, Bayer announced that it would distribute to investors the net income of parent company Bayer AG, totaling 657 million euro and equaling a dividend of 0.90 euro per share.

ANALYSTS' OPINIONS

In light of an announcement in late 2001 that Bayer would restructure into a holding company format, with each of its four divisions becoming legally separate entities, analysts remain mildly optimistic regarding the future value of Bayer stock. Although the company will incur some restructuring costs, analysts are hopeful that the reorganization will lead to more radical changes. Also encouraging to analysts was a series of announcements by Bayer that it would be selling off numerous nonessential businesses. However, analysts agree that Bayer is moving slower than necessary to shed itself of its less profitable ventures and focus on its high margin segments such as pharmaceuticals. They question the wisdom of Bayer management's firm commitment to the benefits of being both a chemical and a pharmaceutical company. Thus, the reorganization of the company is viewed as a positive step, but it will require more extensive changes to garner the enthusiasm of the analysts.

HISTORY

Bayer AG was formed by Friedrich Bayer in Wuppertal, Germany in 1863 to produce synthetic magenta dye. Two years later, production facilities opened in Elberfield, followed by additional manufacturing operations in Leverkusen in 1891, Uerdingen in 1907, and Dormagen in 1913. The first significant discovery by Bayer scientists was made in 1892 when they discovered the first synthetic pesticide, naming it Antinonin. In 1899, Bayer chemist Felix Hoffman discovered aspirin, prompting Bayer to dedicate more resources to pharmaceuticals. In 1908 the basic compound for sulfa drugs was created synthetically in Bayer laboratories. The primary purpose of the compound was for use as a reddish orange dye; however, Bayer researchers quickly discovered that it could be used effectively as a drug against pneumonia, a major health threat at the turn of the century. Despite its obvious benefits to health care, Bayer refused to release the formula. Eventually French chemists reproduced the drug in their own work and introduced it to the market.

During World War I Bayer joined the German war effort by manufacturing mustard gas and explosives. Bayer scientists' development of the first synthetic rubber also added to military efforts. Bayer also actively sought to keep drugs and anesthetics out of the hands of Allied forces. As a result, in 1917 the United States government, under the Trading with the Enemy Act, confiscated all Bayer assets in the United States. The following year Sterling Winthrop Inc., a New York-based company, purchased the rights to the Bayer name and products for $3.3 million.

In 1921 Bayer chemists made another discovery, finding that a certain dye compound could cure African sleeping sickness, a bacterially based infection that made parts of Africa dangerous, if not impossible, to live in. Bayer, understanding the pharmaceutical importance of the discovery, also understood its political implications. The formula, known as Germanin, was offered to the British, who had significant colonial interests in Africa, in exchange for African territories. When the British declined, Bayer refused to release the drug.

In 1925 Bayer president Carl Duisberg and Carl Bosch of BASF AG orchestrated a mega-merger of all Germany's major chemical companies into a single, giant enterprise. Interessen Gemeinschaft Farbenwerke, known as I.G. Faben, effectively eliminated all competition in the chemical industry. It was the largest conglomeration in Europe and the fourth largest in the world. Along with dominating and controlling the market, I.G. Faben also maintained a strong political agenda. Fearing leftist workers' movements that might threaten its stronghold on the industry, I.G. Faben lavished financial support on right-wing politicians and groups, including the Nazi party.

Although Bosch stepped down as head of I.G. Faben in 1935 in protest of the company's growing involvement

FAST FACTS:
About Bayer AG

Ownership: Bayer AG is a publicly owned company traded on the Frankfurt and New York Stock Exchanges.

Ticker Symbol: BAYZY

Officers: Werner Wenning, CEO, 56; Attila Molnar, Pres., 54; Klaus Kuehn, CFO

Employees: 119,500

Principal Subsidiary Companies: Bayer AG is an international corporation with 350 companies in countries around the world, including Agfa-Gevaert N.V., Bayer Corporation, and Bayer Faser GmbH.

Chief Competitors: Bayer faces competition on many fronts in the fields of pharmaceuticals, crop production, polymers, and chemicals. Important competitors include ATOFINA, BASF AG, and Novartis.

with the Nazis, the company continued its support of the conservative movement, still under the guise of avoiding a workers' revolt. The company reaped vast financial rewards for its loyalty to Hitler. In 1942 profits reached 800 million marks, more than the company's entire worth when it was formed in 1925, and control of chemical companies in countries invaded by Germany was handed over to I.G. Faben. The chemical giant also took advantage of the abundance of slave labor for its manufacturing by building plants near Maidanek and Auschwitz. Because operations were placed outside the cities and often camouflaged, unlike many industries located in German cities, I.G. Faben was able to avoid significant destruction of its facilities from Allied bombings.

Although the physical structures remained for I.G. Faben, in 1947 the entire board of directors was sentenced to up to four years in prison for war crimes and Allied forces took over control of the company. In 1952 Allied control ended when the conglomerate was dissolved into three separate entities: Bayer AG, BASF, and Hoechst. For the next few years Bayer attempted to get back into the normal routine of doing business by updating and modernizing operations and focusing on advancements in insecticides, fibers, and plastics. In 1954 Bayer joined Monsanto to form U.S.-based Mobay. By the late 1950s the company had rebounded sufficiently

CHRONOLOGY:

Key Dates for Bayer AG

1863: Friedrich Bayer founds Bayer AG in Wuppertal, Germany to produce a synthetic magenta dye

1899: Bayer chemist Felix Hoffman discovers aspirin

1918: Sterling Winthrop Inc. of New York purchases right to use Bayer's name and products in the United States for $5.3 million

1935: Bayer AG supports Nazi party as a means of avoiding a workers' revolution

1947: All members of the board of directors are sentenced to up to four years in prison at the Nuremberg trials for their support of Hitler

1957: Bayer makes advances in insecticides, fibers, and raw and plastic finished materials

1962: Increases number of chemical laboratories, with operations in eight countries, making products mostly for farming and drugs

1969: During the 1960s U.S. production grew 350 percent and all other operations increased by 700 percent

1978: Purchases U.S.-based Miles Laboratories, makers of Alka-Seltzer and Flintstones and One-A-Day vitamins

1990: Becomes world leader in production of synthetic rubber after acquiring Polysar of Nova Corp. in Canada, Belgium and France

1991: The entire Bayer operation posts annual sales of $28 billion

1993: Bayer's first genetically engineered drug, Kogenate, a blood-clotting compound used to treat hemophiliacs, reaches the market

2000: Bayer becomes the largest supplier of polyurethane raw materials after purchasing the polyols business of Lyondell Chemical Co. for $2.45 billion

to begin to expand internationally, moving into eight countries, including India and Pakistan. Operations were also increased in the United States to avoid high import tariffs of Bayer products. By the end of the 1960s, domestic business had increased by 350 percent and overseas operations had jumped 700 percent during the decade.

During the 1970s Bayer continued to expand and diversify its operations, especially in the United States. In 1977 the company purchased Cutter Laboratories and Metzeler, a German rubber company, and was forced by a U.S. antitrust ruling to buy out Monsanto's share of Mobay. In 1978 Bayer acquired Miles Laboratories, makers of such brands as Alka-Seltzer and Flintstones children's vitamins. During the 1980s and 1990s, Bayer was negatively affected by an unstable market and economy in Western Europe and ongoing political instability in Eastern Europe. As a result, Bayer made significant efforts to reduce overhead and cut costs. Between 1991 and 1995 $1.6 billion was slashed from the budget through staff reductions of nearly 2,000 and abandoning unprofitable subsidiaries.

In 1986 Bayer paid $25 million to Sterling Drugs, who had made Bayer aspirin a household name, to regain partial use of the Bayer name in the United States. The rights to the name had been lost during World War I. When Eastman Kodak sold Sterling Drugs to British firm SmithKline Beecham PLC in 1994, within a few weeks SmithKline Beecham sold Sterling's North American interests to Bayer for $1 billion. Thus, Bayer regained full rights to its name and products in the United States. Sterling's strong over-the-counter drug business also made Bayer one of the top five nonprescription drug manufacturers in the world.

During the 1990s, Bayer introduced several new important drugs. Kogenate, a treatment for hemophilia, engineered in 1993, became the company's first genetically engineered product. The antibiotic Cipro produced $1.3 billion in sales by 1995. Bayer's ownership of the drug became headline news in 2001 when it became the antibiotic of choice after numerous anthrax attacks were delievered by mail in the United States.

STRATEGY

On January 24, 2002, Bayer AG's stocks began trading on the New York Stock Exchange. In so doing, Bayer gained direct access to the U.S. capital market, making it easier for U.S. investors to purchase Bayer shares and for Bayer's U.S. subsidiaries to initiate stock ownership programs for employees. Bayer also announced its intentions to reorganize as a management holding company with four legally independent operating units: Health Care, Crop Science, Polymers, and Chemicals, along with three service companies. The new structure, scheduled to be in place by January 2003, will allow Bayer to seek out strategic partnerships, which the company is actively pursuing for its HealthCare and Chemical divisions.

Other priority strategies addressed by Bayer included accelerated portfolio management. Namely, Bayer is looking closely at its long list of companies to see which are profitable and which are not. Having spent over 13 billion euro from 1997 to 2001 on new acquisitions, Bayer is determined to divest other areas of its business segments that are not performing well. Bayer projected at the end of 2001 that additional cost-containment and efficiency-improving projects already underway would shave off as much as 1.8 billion euro in expenditures by 2005. Cost-cutting measures include dissolving 4,000 employee positions worldwide, and due to the Lipobay/Baycol withdrawal, the pharmaceutical division was slated to lose 1,250 jobs.

INFLUENCES

In the recent past, Bayer has been negatively influenced by the overall world economy. Economic recession swept through the United States, moving around the globe and eventually finding its way to Japan, Southeast Asia, Canada, Mexico, and Western Europe. Pharmaceuticals, one division only slightly affected by the economic downturn, was rocked by the company's decision to take Lipobay/Baycol, one of its most profitable products, off the market. Crop protection products were impacted by languishing demand and strong price competition. Both the polymers and chemicals divisions were significantly affected by the world economy as automotive, construction, and electronics cut back on production and reduced inventories.

According to former Bayer chief executive officer Dr. Manfred Schneider, Bayer's decision to restructure was based on two factors. Positively, Bayer's acquisition of Aventis Crop Science for 7.25 billion euro promised to push its agricultural business to the top of the industry. Negatively, the withdrawal of Lipobay/Baycol forced the company to reexamine the relations between its chemical and pharmaceutical segments. Dividing the company into independent entities will allow each segment to pursue growth and increase value at its own pace. Thus, the Crop Science division, poised for tremendous growth, will be freer from the giant corporate beast of the parent company, thus enabling it to make quicker, more radical movements in the market.

CURRENT TRENDS

In 2002 Bayer announced that it was actively seeking partners for its healthcare and chemicals units. The company set specific criteria for the ideal partners; particularly, Bayer wants to remain in charge of any new relationships, and strong U.S. ties would be a definite advantage. Clearly, Bayer has placed its future with healthcare and crop sciences units because it believes that these segments, with combined annual sales totaling 18 billion euro, possess the greatest growth potential. However, Bayer is not quick to dismiss its polymer business,

which generated 11 billion euro in sales in 2001, although stiff competition and a saturated market arena are expected to contain any significant growth in this segment. A new partnership in the foreseeable future for its chemical division offers a potential 4 billion euro in sales. Unlike other chemical companies that have stripped operations, Bayer's polymer and chemical divisions are strongholds in their own right, and the company has no plans to divest of its interest in these fields.

PRODUCTS

Bayer companies produce an incredibly vast array of products. Within the health care division, Bayer produces pharmaceuticals that treat cardiovascular, respiratory, and infectious diseases, metabolic and immune disorders, and diseases of the central nervous system. Best-selling products include Ciprobay/Cipro, Adalat, Aspirin, Glucometer Elite, Baygon, ADVIA Centaur System, and Kogenate. Well-known over-the-counter brand names include Bayer Aspirin, Alka-Seltzer, and One-A-Day vitamins. The crop protection group researches and develops products that control crop diseases, pests, and weeds, such as fungicides and insecticides, and the animal health group focuses on the research, development, manufacture, and marketing of veterinary medicines and vaccines, as well as grooming and hygiene products such as Advantage flea control. Crop protection and animal health product brands include Confidor/Gaucho/Admire/Provado, Folicur/Raxil, Advantage, Baytril, FLINT, and Sencor.

The plastics group markets a wide range of products for use in automotive and electrical engineering, business machines and electronic appliances, housing and construction, and medical equipment, as well as sports equipment. The rubber group's product line provides synthetic rubber and rubber chemicals to the rubber and tire industry. Bayer's polyurethane group provides polyurethane raw materials and serves as a resource for processing polyurethane systems and products. The coatings and colorants group produces coatings, adhesives, sealants, and pigments for construction industries.

The chemicals segment plays a vital role in the foundational development of active ingredients in Bayer's pharmaceuticals, crop protection, and animal health products. Chemicals also play an important role as building blocks in the development of plastics, coatings, and pigments. The specialty group provides services to the paper and leather industries, including dyes, tanning materials, and processing chemicals, as well as other specialty chemicals needed for industrial use. The subsidiary Haarmann & Reimer manufactures fragrances, flavors, and cosmetic ingredients, and H.C. Stark operates in the field of metallic and ceramic powders, which it markets to the metal, optics, electronics, and advanced ceramic industries.

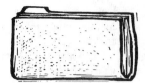

CIPRO

When numerous people in the United States began contracting anthrax through the mail during the fall of 2001, soon after the terrorist attacks in New York and Washington, D.C., Cipro, a synthetically produced antibiotic developed and marketed by Bayer, became the drug of choice for anthrax patients. Although Cipro is not the only drug that can be effective in fighting anthrax, it made headlines and was widely discussed by the media.

Cipro is a bestseller for Bayer, generating $1 billion in U.S. sales alone. Fearing future widespread anthrax attacks, the U.S. government contracted with Bayer to supply up to 300 million tablets at the cost of 95 cents a pill, reduced from the regular government discounted price of $1.77 per tablet. Bayer also donated 4 million Cipro tablets to be provided to frontline workers in New York and Washington, D. C., as well as U.S. Postal employees. Bayer, which holds exclusive rights to the drug until the patent expires in 2003, received short-term negative exposure in the press when it refused to release the patent early and for selling the drug to the U.S. government at a price that would still earn the company a profit on the deal.

CORPORATE CITIZENSHIP

With such an extended global presence, Bayer is faced with multiple issues in acting as good citizens. An annual report on sustainable development outlines Bayer's commitment to society and the environment. Bayer contends that it works hard to produce environmentally friendly products with the most benefits possible. The company also supports the United Nations' Global Compact initiative, designed to achieve sustainable development as well as ensure human rights and improve working conditions around the world. Bayer has also voluntarily stopped production of chemicals proven to be harmful, such as polychlorinated biphenyls, or PCBs. Bayer affirms the goals of responsibility beyond compliance, seeking the ideal product, voluntary withdrawal of products later found to be harmful, and the use of a six-prong eco-check that weighs the pros and cons of a product based on health, economy, public value, technology, life cycle, and environment. Bayer also supports hundreds of social, economic, educational and community-based programs at its sites around the world.

GLOBAL PRESENCE

Bayer's network of research, manufacturing, and marketing operations extend to nearly every country in the world, and global operations are managed from the company's headquarters in Leverkusen, Germany. The majority of its administration and marketing operations are located in Europe, but also extend across the map, including offices in Japan, Thailand, Russia, India, Zimbabwe, South Africa, Chile, Costa Rica, Cuba, and Canada. Manufacturing operations are also spread worldwide, including New Zealand, South Africa, the United States, Argentina, and Ghana, as well as multiple locations in Europe. Research is conducted in Germany, Japan, Sweden, Denmark, and the United States.

During 2001 Bayer sales totaled 13 billion euro in Europe, 9.8 billion euro in North America, 3.8 billion euro in Asia and the Pacific, and 2.3 billion euro in Latin America, Africa, and the Middle East.

EMPLOYMENT

Bayer employs some 112,000 around the world, with 65,200 in Europe, 23,200 in North America, 12,600 in Asia and the Pacific, and 11,000 in Latin America, Africa, and the Middle East. To create and sustain a creative and motivated workforce, Bayer commits more than 100 million euro each year to vocational training and continuing education for its employees. Bayer is also introducing new educational methods, such as Web-based training and e-learning. In 2001, the company launched the Bayer Academy to coordinate and support employee-learning opportunities. Other innovative approaches to staff competence and satisfaction include international development programs for young managers, flexible working hours, and using an Internet-based job rotation program that allows shuffling of Bayer specialists around the world to permanent or temporary assignments.

SOURCES OF INFORMATION

Bibliography

Andrews, Edmund L. "Bayer Forecasts Better Results." *The New York Times*, 14 March 2002.

"Bayer AG." *Chemical Week*, 20 March 2002.

"Bayer Suffers Major Slump." *Chemist & Druggist*, 23 March 2002.

"Bayer's Helge Wehmeier to Retire." *Chemical Market Reporter*, 11 March 2002.

Cage, Sam. "Bayer Deepens Cutbacks as Earnings Slide." *The Wall Street Journal*, 27 March 2002.

Capell, Kerry. "Can Bayer Cure its Own Headache?" *Business Week*, 28 January 2002.

Grant, Tina, ed. *International Directory of Company Histories.* Vol. 13. Detroit: St. James Press, 1996.

Hunter, David. "Bayer Lists its Shares on the NYSE; Targets Growth in Drug Intermediates." *Chemical Week*, 30 January 2002.

———. "Bayer's Journey." *Chemical Week*, 6 February 2002.

Uniworld Business Publications, Inc. *Directory of Foreign Firms Operating in the United States.*, New York: Author, 2000.

For an annual report:

on the Internet at: http://www.investor.bayer.com/index_en.cfm

For additional industry research:

Investigate companies by their Standard Industrial Classification Codes, also known as SICs. Bayer AG's primary SICs are:

2819 Industrial Inorganic Chemicals, Not Elsewhere Classified

2821 Plastics Materials Synthetic Resins

2822 Synthetic Rubber

2833 Medical Chemicals & Botanical Products

2834 Pharmaceutical Preparations

2865 Cyclic Organic Crudes Dies & Pigments

2879 Pesticides & Agricultural Chemicals, Not Elsewhere Classified

2899 Chemicals & Chemical Preparations, Not Elsewhere Classified

6719 Holding Companies, Not Elsewhere Classified

8731 Commercial Physical & Biological Research

Also investigate companies by their North American Industry Classification System Codes, also known as NAICS codes. Bayer AG's primary NAICS codes are:

325412 Pharmaceutical Preparation Manufacturing

325510 Paint and Coating Manufacturing

551112 Offices of Other Holding Companies

BET Holdings Inc.

FOUNDED: 1980

Contact Information:
HEADQUARTERS: One BET Plaza, 1900 W Street NE
    Washington, DC 20018-1211
PHONE: (202)608-2000
FAX: (202)608-2595
URL: http://www.bet.com

OVERVIEW

BET Holdings Inc. is a entertainment and media company that specializes in programming for African Americans. Its entertainment division operates the Black Entertainment Network (BET), an advertiser-funded basic cable television network with more than 60 million subscribers, which accounts for more than 90 percent of the company's revenues. BET also offers the digital cable channels BET Gospel, BET on Jazz, and BET Hip-Hop. The company's media division operates BET Pictures, Arabesque Books, and BET International. BET also owns a majority stake in BET.com.

BET was founded in 1980 by Robert L. Johnson, who continues to serve as the chief executive officer as he has done since the company's inception. Although the company went public briefly in the 1990s, for the majority of its history, BET has been a privately owned company, with Johnson holding a controlling interest. In 2001 Johnson and co-owner Liberty Media sold BET to media conglomerate Viacom for a deal worth $3 billion in stock options and debt takeover. As a part of the settlement, Johnson signed a 5-year contract to remain as the company's executive leader.

COMPANY FINANCES

The latest financial figures available are from fiscal 1997, ending July 31, 1997, the last year that BET was an independent, publicly owned company before being taken private by Johnson and Liberty Media and sold to Viacom as a wholly owned private subsidiary. In 1997 BET reported a net income of $23.8 million on revenues of $154.2 million. Of that total $80.6 million was generated from advertising sales, $69.3 million from subscriber fees, and $4.4 million from other sources. Of advertising dollars earned, $51.7 million came from national spot advertising, $21.2 from infomercials, and the remainder from direct response advertising (30- or 60-second spots for merchandise not sold in stores).

HISTORY

BET television is the brain child of Robert L. Johnson, who was working as a lobbyist for the National Cable Television Association in 1979 when he approach Dr. John C. Malone, head of cable giant Tele-Communications Inc. (TCI) with the idea of introducing a cable channel that specifically targeted African Americans. Malone liked Johnson's proposal and provided him with a half million dollars to start BET Cable Network, with Johnson serving as the new company's president, chief executive officer, and director. In 1980, having secured agreements with cable providers Warner, ATC, and TCI, BET went on the air. Anheuser Busch, Coca-Cola, and Sears were among the channel's first advertisers.

BET began operations by broadcasting two hours of music per week to 3.8 million viewer in 350 market areas. By 1984, bolstered by investment from Taft Broadcasting and Time's HBO, programming increased to 24 hours a day, 7 days a week with more than 6 million subscribers. The network continued to grow at a rapid pace. Three years later, in 1987, subscriber numbers had more than doubled to 15 million, and the company posted a $1 million net income on $10.7 million in revenues. The following year revenues grew to $15.1 million, and net income tripled to $3.2 million. By 1990, BET, which opened a $12 million production facility in Washington, D.C. in 1989, was posting a net income of more than $6 million on revenues that neared $36 million.

In 1991 BET went public and reestablished itself as BET Holdings Inc. It is the first company ever traded on the New York Stock Exchange with a majority of the ownership in the hands of African Americans. In August 1991, through its newly formed wholly owned subsidiary Paige Publications Inc., BET began to publish *Young Sisters and Brothers*, a national lifestyle magazine for black American teenagers and young adults, which it published until the magazine was discontinued in September 1996. In December 1991 BET purchased 44 percent of Emerge Colorado Inc., giving BET a controlling interest in the company, which published *Emerge*, an issue-driven magazine that provided a black perspective on news with commentary and analysis. Four years later BET purchased entire ownership of the magazine and, in 2001, BET ceased publication of the magazine. In 1992 the company was rocked by scandal when the chief financial officer and comptroller were terminated from their positions for allegedly embezzling nearly $700,000. Also, the Cable and Television Consumer Protection and

FAST FACTS:
About BET Holdings Inc.

Ownership: BET Holdings Inc. is a wholly owned private subsidiary of Viacom Inc.

Officers: Robert L. Johnson, Chmn. and CEO; Debra L. Lee, Pres. and COO; Robert Ambrosini, CFO

Employees: 565

Principal Subsidiary Companies: BET Holdings includes cable channel Black Entertainment Television (BET) and digital cable channels BET Gospel, BET Jazz, and BET Hip-Hop. The holding company also includes BET Pictures, Arabesque Books, and BET International, as well as owning a majority stake in the Web site, BET.com.

Chief Competitors: As a part of the Viacom media empire, BET competes on a broad level with other major media companies, including Time Warner and ABC. Other individual networks that compete directly with BET include the WB, which offers some programming targeted toward African Americans, as well as smaller cable channels Major Broadcasting Cable Network (MBC) and New Urban Entertainment (NUE-TV).

Competition Act of 1992 went into effect, threatening to hamper BET's growth. Nonetheless, the cable channel continued to do well, with net income reaching $11.7 million on $61.7 million in sales.

In 1993 BET Direct was launched. The channel used infomercials and direct marketing commercials to sell merchandise targeted to appeal to BET's subscribers. In 1996 BET Direct began to market Color Code skin products, an exclusive BET offering sold at drug stores and retail outlets. However, the venture quickly provided unsuccessful, and the company abandoned the product line in September 1997. In the same year, BET acquired an 80 percent interest in Avalon Pictures Inc., which provided the company with a national satellite pay-per-view channel. In January 1997, the Company opened the BET SoundStage restaurant, an entertainment-themed restaurant targeted to African-American customers, at Disney's Pleasure Island in Orlando, Florida. BET was also awarded the NEA Award for the Advancement of Learning through Broadcasting for its original half-hour children's program "Story Porch," which featured celebrities telling stories. Partnering with Encore Media Corp. in

CHRONOLOGY:

Key Dates for BET Holdings Inc.

1979: BET debuts its television network with two hours of music programming per week, reaching 3.8 million cable subscribers in 350 markets

1984: BET begins broadcasting twenty-four hours a day, seven days a week

1987: Sales approach $7 million; viewer numbers surpass 15 million

1991: BET becomes the first black-owned company to be listed on the New York Stock Exchange

1996: Joins Encore Media Corp. to create BET Movies/Starz!3, a premium cable movie channel catering to African Americans

1998: BET returns to private ownership, with founder Robert L. Johnson holding 64 percent of the stock and Liberty Media Group holding 36 percent; renamed BET Holdings II Inc.

2000: Goes online with bet.com, offering African Americans information and resources in such areas as news, music, finances, lifestyles, food, health, and career

2001: Cable giant Viacom buys BET for $3 billion; name changed to BET Holdings Inc.

1996, BET began broadcast of a premium film cable channel, BET Movies/Starz!3.

In 1998 Johnson, disappointed with BET's performance on the stock market, joined with Liberty Media Group to reclaim private ownership of the company, with Johnson holding a 64 percent interest and Liberty holding the balance. The company was reorganized as BET Holdings II Inc. However, the arrangement was relatively short-lived. In 2000 Johnson announced the sale of his company to media giant Viacom, which also owns MTV, VH-1, CBS, Nickelodeon, and Showtime, for $3 billion. The deal, completed in January 2001, translated into $2.4 billion in Viacom stock options for Johnson, who accepted a five-year contract with Viacom to remain at the helm of the company he founded.

STRATEGY

Viacom's strategy to squeeze the most from its new acquisition will be to grow subscriber numbers and increase advertising rates. Whereas in 2001 MTV averaged $8,000 for a 30-second advertisement, for the same amount of ad time, BET averaged $1,500. Viacom will increase BET's customer base by packaging it with other cable channels in its arsenal. Viacom will also start pushing BET advertising to its customers who regularly advertise on its other networks.

INFLUENCES

From its inception, BET has undergone some identity confusion between viewers and BET corporate management. As a black-owned media company, many hoped that BET would be a new, fresh voice for the African-American community. Yet BET's consistent programming of rap music videos, old sitcoms that employed typical black stereotypes, comedy showcases, and infomercials has disappointed those who hoped that a network that was not under the control of whites would offer more. However, considering BET's target audience, the network may be right on the mark. According to a BET survey of African Americans in 2001, 55 percent of blacks between the ages of 30 and 44 believe that rap and hip hop culture have a predominantly negative influence on young blacks; however, only 28 percent of blacks between the ages of 18 and 29 agreed that hip hop and rap were negative factors.

BET also came under fire from many in the African-American community, including Rev. Jesse Jackson and NAACP President Kweisi Mfume, for "selling out" to Viacom. Johnson has defended the sale, noting that the new relationship will offer BET new opportunities and resources for programming and distribution. Thus, criticism of its new ownership may go unnoticed by senior BET executives as long as the media company remains at the top of its industry as it has done for more than 20 years. However, BET may soon be facing serious competition for the first time. Major Broadcasting Cable Network (MBC) and New Urban Entertainment (NUE-TV) are upstart cable networks aimed to the African-American population. Although the two networks combined tally only 7 million subscribers, compared to BET's more than 60 million, both boast strong, seasoned executive leadership and have secured distribution deals with industry giants Time Warner, Fox, and Comcast. Johnson has voiced little concern to this point regarding the new networks, noting that significant success depends wholly on garnering a large investment from a major corporation, a feat the networks have yet to accomplish.

CURRENT TRENDS

Despite BET's network presence can be found in more than 60 million American homes via basic cable subscriptions, Nielsen ratings show that BET's prime time programming earns only 1 percent of the African-American viewing audience. Thus, on any given evening, only 350,000 black Americans are tuning in to BET. Yet Viacom and BET executives need not be concerned, considering BET consistently posts profits and garners the interest of advertisers looking for access to a large audience at a smaller price tag. Within its cable niche, BET is king of the hill.

Although BET will continue to build its programming around its core categories of music videos, reruns of syndicated shows, and movies, the network has increased its offerings of original programming. *How I'm Living* features interviews, tours through the homes, and in depth looks into the lives of African-American celebrities, and *Oh, Drama* is a women's daytime talk show. *NYLA* provides entertainment news, and *The Way We Do It,* hosted by Rick Smiley, airs an hour-long variety show on Saturday evenings. New programming includes *BET Nightly News, BET Tonight,* and *Lead Story.*

As a new member of the Viacom family, BET may also have new access to negotiate with Paramount Pictures and Showtime, both Viacom divisions, to show reruns of their movies. The network will also be gradually experimenting with original productions. In 2001 its film division announced that it had begun production on a new film, *A Huey P. Newton Story,* developed in association with the Public Broadcasting System and directed by noted black filmmaker Spike Lee.

PRODUCTS

Although the BET Network, which generates more than 90 percent of revenues, is the company's foundational product, BET Holdings has an array of smaller interests, such as digital cable channels BET Gospel, BET on Jazz, and BET Hip-Hop. BET has also experimented with film production, book publishing, a BET line of apparel, financial services (including a bank card in partnership with Chevy Chase Bank of Maryland) and BET restaurants. BET.com, launched in 2000, in partnership with Liberty Digital, News Corporation, USA Networks, and Microsoft, has become a prime choice of African Americans surfing the Web.

SOURCES OF INFORMATION

Bibliography

Hubbard, Lee. "BET: Fear of a Black Boycott." *Africana.com,* 10 December 2001. Available at http://www.Africana.com.

McKissack, Fred. "BET: The King of Black Mediocrity." *The Progressive,* January 2001.

Miller, Robert G. "Robert L. Johnson: A Business Titan Redefining Black Entrepreneurial Success." *Black Collegian,* October 2000.

BET'S VIEWER CHOICE AWARDS

In 2002 BET announced its plans to host the Second Annual BET Viewer Choice Awards, which allows BET viewers to vote via the BET Web site for their favorite actors, athletes, artists/groups, music videos, movies, and songs. Individual artist categories include female hip hop, male hip hop, male R&B, female R&B, gospel, best group, and best new artist. The 2002 leading nominees for best music video were Bow Wow, "Take Ya Home"; Aaliyah, "Rock the Boat"; B2K, "Uh Huh"; and Alicia Keys, "Fallen." At the event held during the summer of 2002, Muhammad Ali was presented with BET's Humanitarian Award, and the rock group Earth, Wind, and Fire was honored with a Lifetime Achievement Award.

Murphy, Kathleen. "BET Aims to Extend its Brand." *Internet World,* 1 November 2000.

"Tavis Smiley's Dismissal by BET Outrages Blacks Across the Nation." *Jet,* 16 April 2001.

Smith, Max. "Viacom Buys BET." *Africana.com,* 29 November 2001. Available at http://www.Africana.com.

Williams, Christopher. "A Canny BET." *Barrons,* 7 May 2001.

Woellert, Lorraine. "BET's Robert Johnson: A $390 Million Gamble on Synergy." *Business Week Online,* 21 August 1998. Available at http://www.businessweek.com.

For additional industry research:

Investigate companies by their Standard Industrial Classification Codes, also known as SICs. BET Holdings Inc.'s primary SICs are:

2731 Book Publishing & Printing

4833 Television Broadcasting

4841 Cable & Other Pay Television Services

7812 Motion Picture, Video Tape Production

Also investigate companies by their North American Industry Classification System codes, also known as NAICS codes. BET Holdings Inc.'s primary NAICS codes are:

511120 Periodical Publishers

513220 Cable and Other Program Distribution

551112 Offices of Other Holding Companies

Billabong International Ltd.

FOUNDED: 1973

Contact Information:

HEADQUARTERS: 1 Billabong Place
    Burleigh Heads, Queensland 4220 Australia
PHONE: +61 75 5899899
FAX: +61 75 5899800
URL: http://www.billabongcorporate.com

OVERVIEW

One of the leading manufacturers of surfing, skating, and snowboarding apparel and accessories, Billabong International Ltd. sells its branded merchandise at sporting shops throughout Australia, Europe, Japan, South America, and North America. The firm also operates its own retail outlets. In Australia, Billabong is the top brand of surfing apparel. To advertise its wares, the firm sponsors well-known athletes. It also hosts the Billabong Pro surfing competition series that takes place in South Africa, Spain, and Australia.

COMPANY FINANCES

Sales for Billabong International Ltd. exceeded expectations by 15 percent in 2001, reaching A$380.2 million (US$197.4 million), compared to A$226.8 million (US$121.1 million) in 2000. The firm's profits of A$42.1 million (US$21.5 million) were 12.6 percent higher than forecasts. Combined sales from Australia and Asia grew 127 percent to reach A$118.8 million, or 31 percent of total revenues. European sales grew 50 percent to reach A$82.1 million, or 21 percent of total revenues. In North America, sales grew 50 percent to reach A$179.3 million, or 41 percent of total revenues.

ANALYSTS' OPINIONS

Despite Billabong's solid financial performance, some investors began to express concern about the

FAST FACTS:

About Billabong International Ltd.

Ownership: Billabong International Ltd. is a publicly owned company traded on the Australian Stock Exchange.

Ticker Symbol: BBG

Officers: Matthew Perrin, CEO, 29; Shayne Palfreyman, CFO; Paul Naude, Gen. Mgr., North America; Derek O'Neill, Gen. Mgr., Europe; Dougall Walker, Gen. Mgr., Australia

Employees: 575

Principal Subsidiary Companies: Billabong International Ltd. operates subsidiaries in the United States, Europe, Australia/New Zealand, and Japan.

Chief Competitors: Competitors to Billabong include Burton Snowboards, Quiksilver, and other makers of clothing and accessories for surfers, skaters, and snowboarders.

---

firm's growth potential in North America, it largest market, due to the weakening economy in 2000 and 2001. In fact, the firm's reliance on the North American market prompted some investors to abandon its stock in early 2002. According to a February 2002 *Australasian Business Intelligence Report*, "One of 2001's greatest stock market successes, Billabong, was dumped by investors on 28 February 2002. The shares slumped 5.3 percent, even though the surfwear clothing group announced a 40 percent jump in profit to A$29 million for the December 2001 half." Billabong argued that investor concerns were unfounded, pointing out that its North American sales grew by 17 percent in the 6 months prior to the drop in stock prices. Other concerns included the trendiness of clothing for sports like surfing. The firm's target market (youths ranging in age from 14 to 24) was known for being fickle. Stock in early 2002 hovered around A$9 per share, still much higher than its price of A$4.70 per share in early 2001.

CHRONOLOGY:

Key Dates for Billabong International Ltd.

1973: Gordon Merchant founds Billabong

1998: Billabong creates its U.S. subsidiary

2000: Billabong completes its IPO

2001: A Japanese subsidiary is established

2002: Retail stores open in the United States for the first time

---

its products in other countries, such as the United States and Japan, via licensing agreements forged in the early 1980s.

Billabong International gave up its license to sell Billabong merchandise in the United States (a license it had held for 15 years) in 1998. As a result, Billabong U.S.A. was established as a wholly owned subsidiary. Paul Naude, a former professional surfer, was hired to head the new unit, which eventually accounted for 50 percent of Billabong's total revenues.

Matthew Perrin took over as CEO of Billabong International in 1999. The firm completed its initial public offering (IPO) in August 2000. Roughly 60 percent of Billabong's shares were made available to the public at $1.33 per share, while management held on to the remaining 40 percent. The capital generated from the IPO was used to increase expansion into Asia and South America. Later that year, Billabong released a new line of junior's swimwear, believing that the junior's market was relatively undeveloped.

In 2001 Billabong acquired Element, a skateboarding apparel and accessories brand made by U.S.-based Giant International. Because it had already been successfully established, Billabong planned to preserve the Element brand name. The firm also acquired sunglasses and snow goggles brand Von Zipper, which had been created in 1999. Having operated retail shops of its own in Australia, Europe, Japan, and South Africa for several years, Billabong opened three U.S. stores, all located in California, in 2002.

HISTORY

Billabong was founded in Queensland, Australia, by surfer Gordon Merchant in 1973. The firm began selling

STRATEGY

Limiting distribution had been a strategy employed by Billabong since its inception. Rather than selling its

---

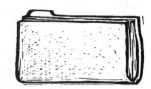

FINANCES:

Billabong International Ltd.
Revenues, 1997-2001
(million dollars)

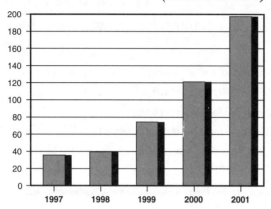

SURF'S UP FOR BILLABONG EMPLOYEES

According to CEO Matthew Perrin, the Billabong employees who work in Broadbeach, which is near the well-known surfing beach along Gold Coast of Queensland, Australia, come in to work late if surfing conditions are good. Employees are allowed to take this liberty as long as they follow company rules and are able to complete their work.

merchandise at sporting goods stores of all kinds, Billabong limited its distribution to specialty shops, wanting to create the perception that its products were somewhat exclusive. To tie its name even more closely to surfing and boarding sports, Billabong sponsored both famous and soon-to-be famous athletes.

In the early 2000s, Billabong began to rely more heavily on creating wholly owned subsidiaries to market its brand across the world. According to Billabong executive Paul Naude, as quoted in the August 2000 issue of *WWD*, "Up until two years ago, Billabong had numerous licensees around the world, but in the last couple of years, our focus has been on becoming a truly global brand. We are moving much more to wholly owned subsidiaries and taking control of key markets and secondary markets and setting ourselves up to maximize the brand's potential in those areas." In 2001, as part of this branding strategy, the firm created a subsidiary in Japan, where it had been selling its products via a licensing agreement for nearly two decades. Existing distributors in Italy and Belgium were placed under more direct control of Billabong as well. The firm also stepped up its marketing efforts, pushing the Billabong brand in surfing publications, both print and online, as well as in the Microsoft Xbox Transworld surfing game. In addition, Billabong lengthened an existing sponsorship agreement with Mark Occhilupo, a world-renowned surfer.

sales for Billabong. Snowboarding solidified its reputation as a viable sporting event when it made its debut as an Olympic event in the 2002 Winter Games. In fact, according to an American Sports Data Superstudy of Sports Participation, surfing, snowboarding, and skateboarding all saw participation levels jump by a minimum of 25 percent in 2001. As these once "underground" sports evolved into more mainstream activities, they were considered increasingly viable industries as well. As a result, firms like Billabong continued working to position themselves as top selling brands.

PRODUCTS

Billabong sells t-shirts, shorts, pants, jeans, wet suits, jumpers, bags, swimwear, and accessories to roughly 3,000 specialty surfing and boarding shops worldwide. More than 2,200 product lines are sold by Billabong in Australia; more than 1,300 lines are in North America; and more than 1,200 lines are in Europe.

GLOBAL PRESENCE

Billabong products are sold in more than 60 countries. While licensed distributors handle the sale of Billabong products in some countries, Billabong has gained more control over its international distribution by increasing its number of wholly owned subsidiaries.

CURRENT TRENDS

Surfing and extreme sports like snowboarding continued to grow in popularity in the early 2002s, boosting

EMPLOYMENT

Billabong's employees tend to be young, athletic individuals interested in surfing and boarding sports. In fact, some of Billabong's executives are former professional surfers. Billabong's founder, a surfer himself, was known for wearing shorts to work. Accordingly, the corporate culture at the firm is rather relaxed.

SOURCES OF INFORMATION

Bibliography

Bermudez, Andrea. "Billabong to Open U.S. Retail Stores." *Daily News Record*, 17 September 2001.

"Billabong Dumped." *Australasian Business Intelligence*, 1 March 2002.

Billabong International Ltd. Home Page, 2002. Available at http://www.billabongcorporate.com.

Ellis, Kristi. "Billabong Int'l Files for IPO." *WWD*, 7 August 2000.

Rennie, Philip. "Meet the Chairman of the Surfboard." *Business Review Weekly*, 1 December 2000.

For an annual report:

on the Internet at: http://www.billabongcorporate.com/reports/annualreports.cfm

For additional industry research:

Investigate companies by their Standard Industrial Classification Codes, also known as SICs. Billabong International Ltd.'s primary SICs are:

2389 Apparel and Accessories Not Elsewhere Classified

5941 Sporting Good Stores and Bicycle Shops

Also investigate companies by their North American Industry Classification Codes, also known as NAICS codes. Billabong International Ltd.'s primary NAICS codes are:

315999 Other Apparel Accessories and Other Apparel Manufacturing

451110 Sporting Goods Stores

Boston Market Corp.

FOUNDED: 1985

Contact Information:

HEADQUARTERS: 14103 Denver West Pkwy.
    Golden, CO 80401-4086
PHONE: (303)278-9500
FAX: (303)216-5339
URL: http://www.bostonmarket.com

OVERVIEW

Boston Market Corporation is a wholly owned subsidiary of the McDonald's Corporation and operates almost 700 company owned restaurants in 28 states. Boston Market specializes in providing homestyle meals in a take out format. The entree selections include chicken, turkey, ham, and meatloaf. Side dishes are available to suit every taste and salads, breads, and desserts are also top choices. Supplying home meal replacements is the primary objective of the revitalized chain. It also offers a convenient lunch time menu. Boston Market foods can be purchased frozen at your local grocery store. The H.J. Heinz company manufactures this line of foods. A catering division was added in 2001.

COMPANY FINANCES

Boston Market filed for bankruptcy protection in October 1998 and did not file annual financial reports after that date. The company had accrued $900 million in debt at the time of its bankruptcy. In 2000 McDonald's Corporation acquired the company, operating it as a subsidiary venture. Prior to filing Chapter 11, the company posted a $223.9 million dollar net loss on $261.1 million in revenues in 1997.

ANALYSTS' OPINIONS

Boston Market is no longer publicly traded, and analysts do not provide research or coverage specific to

FAST FACTS:

About Boston Market Corporation

Ownership: Boston Market Corporation is a privately held subsidiary of the McDonald's Corporation.

Officers: Michael D. Andres, Pres. and CEO

Employees: 15,000

Chief Competitors: Boston Market is a restaurant chain that offers home-cooked food in a fast-food setting. Its primary competitors are restaurants such as Burger King, Subway, Wendy's, Jack in the Box, Blimpie, and The Wall Street Deli.

Boston Market and its stock price. Analysts did not react strongly to McDonald's purchase of the Boston Market chain. The acquisition may have been too small in the scope of McDonald's operations to be viewed as significant. One analyst noted that the move constituted a risk for the hamburger empire—if it decided to resurrect the chicken franchises. Many observers believed that McDonald's saw the deal as a cheap land grab and a way to snap up choice store locations at a bargain price and convert them to McDonald's.

HISTORY

Boston Market Corporation, originally known as Boston Chicken, was founded in 1985. The initial business concept was based on the premise that the public would buy hot, home style meals that could be purchased and carried out for dinner. The company enjoyed phenomenal success with its initial venture and soon attracted the attention of the business community. The founding partners sold the company to one of its executives after only three years. This would be the first of numerous management changes at the top of the Boston Chicken food chain.

Executives relocated the corporate headquarters and outlined ambitious plans to make Boston Chicken a national restaurant chain. The company went public in 1993 and posted impressive numbers in the IPO (initial public offering) market. The stock opened at $10 per share and closed at $24.45, which represented a 145 percent gain on the day.

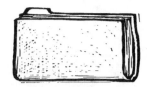

THE BEST BIRD IN BOSTON?

That would be former Celtic, Larry Bird. Bird agreed to act as spokesman for the Boston Chicken brand frozen entrees. These entrees are manufactured by H.J. Heinz as part of a licensing agreement with Boston Market. The company believes Bird is just the right guy to represent its homestyle meals.

In 1994 the company reinvented itself and switched its name to Boston Market to reflect a wider array of menu items. There were then 534 stores operating in 23 distinct markets. Restaurants offered the traditional chicken meals along with ham, turkey, meatloaf and a variety of hot and cold side dishes, salads, and desserts. Lunch and breakfast items were also developed in an attempt to promote the chain as an all-day establishment. A vast network of franchises sprung up across the country and it appeared there was no stopping the "Chicken" as it was nicknamed by Wall Street analysts.

In 1996 Boston Market moved forward with a plan to feature lunch entrees, introducing its Boston Carver line of sandwiches. This decision placed the company in competition with traditional fast food restaurants for the lunch dollars. In order to be successful Boston Market offered coupons, discounts, and promotions to entice customers into the stores. The strategy seemed to work, so the company increased advertising and discounted dinner items in the same manner. By the end of 1996, the company was operating two unique businesses from within the same storefronts. During the daytime hours, fast food, sandwich items were sold. At night the premise switched to the home style take out meals. This resulted in two separate and costly marketing campaigns.

The old adage, "Don't count your chickens before they've hatched," was never more applicable. Uncontrolled growth and a poorly devised marketing scheme derailed plans for a fast food empire. The excessive use of coupons had hurt the bottom line and the mixed message media campaign had destroyed the brand identity. By 1997 the company was struggling to maintain business and attract new customers. In a last ditch attempt to save the core business, management restructured the organization and bought back the now extensive collection of franchises. Mounting debts and decreased revenues proved insurmountable and in 1998 the company was forced to file for Chapter 11 Bankruptcy.

CHRONOLOGY:

Key Dates for Boston Market Corporation

1985: Boston Chicken was founded in Newton, Massachusetts

1992: Company bought by Blockbuster Inc. executives and relocated to Chicago

1993: Boston Chicken goes public

1994: Company name changed to Boston Market and moved to Colorado

1996: Entered the lunch business with Boston Carver sandwiches

1997: Company began restructuring and buying back franchises

1998: Filed Chapter 11 Bankruptcy

2000: McDonald's purchases company

2001: Launches catering business

Boston Market collapsed rapidly and with little warning. The company which had traded at a high of $41.50 in 1995, dropped to a dismal $0.75 a share in October of 1998, and faced delisting from the NASDAQ exchange. It was not until after the filing that investors and shareholders began to sort through the figures for the facts. Neither were encouraging. The company had been the victim of uncontrolled growth, creative financing, and poor management. A large number of franchises had been created before there was a clear market demand for the product. One analyst later likened it to the "Field of Dreams" strategy—build it and they will come. In addition, the company had funded the expansion itself with debt and equity offerings. It had then given this money to "area developers" to operate franchises. When the franchises failed, they were unable to pay back the company. The top-level management had no experience in the food industry. Scott Beck and Saad Hadhir, two former Blockbuster Entertainment executives, had assumed control of Boston Market and led it to bankruptcy. Beck and Hadhir abandoned the company before it reached bankruptcy proceedings, leaving newly appointed CEO J. Michael Jenkins to face angry investors and shareholders. Ultimately many parties contributed to the unraveling of the once promising company. Management, of course, was held accountable, but many financial analysts were also called to task for not identifying the problems with the balance sheet at Boston Market.

Boston Market is poised to make a comeback in the new century. Purchased by McDonald's in 2000, observers thought the deal was merely a real estate transaction to secure prime sites for future McDonald's, Chipotle Grills, or Donato's (two new themed eateries owned by the corporate giant). Several years later it appears that there may be a second chance for the "Chicken." Revived by the expertise and experience of the team from the Golden Arches, Boston Market is establishing a new identity in the dog-eat-chicken world of the food service industry.

STRATEGY

Boston Market's future survival strategy will be determined by its new owner, McDonald's. Once believed that McDonald's would simply close all Boston Market outfits and utilize the locations for its existing franchises, this does not appear to be the plan. McDonald's stated that it would decide the fate of each unit on a case by case basis. In January 2002 Boston Market was working on new initiatives designed to reestablish its customer base. The company is testing menu items in its Milwaukee franchises. A grilled chicken menu is in the works for dinner and the stores' interiors have been redecorated to facilitate in-store dining. Boston Market will also once again attempt to enter the lunch market.

INFLUENCES

The company's 1998 bankruptcy was a clear signal that certain programs were not advisable. The huge failure of the lunch time service ultimately proved to be the undoing of the company. By entering the lunch market the company cannibalized its own dinner customers. Frequent discount coupons for lunch items cut deeply into revenues and resulted in losses. As the company prepares to once again enter the lunch hour competition, it will not repeat its mistakes. Low fat and vegetarian items have been test marketed with promising results. There are no current plans to follow McDonald's lead and enter the breakfast market. The company did make an earlier attempt to break into this category in the mid-1990s with the purchase of a 52 percent stake in Einstein/Noah's Bagels. This proved to be an ill-conceived notion and only added to the company's substantial debt.

CURRENT TRENDS

The company has opened a catering division to provide meals for holiday dinners, picnics, tailgate celebrations and other informal gatherings. The offerings include sandwich platters, box lunches, dessert platters, and buffet-style meals with entrees and side dishes. This program is an extension of the family take-home meal designed to serve larger family gatherings.

PRODUCTS

Boston Market provides convenient hot meals for busy customers. Entrees include chicken, turkey, ham, and meatloaf. Side dishes include potatoes, corn, vegetables, soup, and salads. Sandwiches are available for lunchtime and are made fresh each day. Frozen entrees are available under the Boston Market name in local grocery stores throughout the nation. All of the food items available in the restaurants are available for delivery to catered events. Lunch sales account for 40 percent of sales with the remaining 60 percent coming from dinner meals.

GLOBAL PRESENCE

Boston Market operates in the United States. In December 1999 Jack Greenberg, Chairman and CEO of McDonald's, was questioned about the planned acquisition of Boston Market. On the subject of international expansion for the chain, he replied, "Given their problems today, it is a little too early to speculate about it, but we will see how the brand does. I think it has got something. . .it is a viable brand. We know they have good people because they have turned this business around. . .Will it ever be big enough to excite me? I hope so, but I don't know yet." The company announced in 2002 plans to open the first Boston Market in Sydney, Australia. McDonald's regards Boston Market as a potential growth vehicle and may expand next in Hong Kong.

CORPORATE CITIZENSHIP

Boston Market has a history of supporting charitable causes. In the past the company has asked its customers which organizations should receive the company's dollars. Boston Market's survey of customers indicated that breast cancer was an important issue with many of the patrons. In response Boston Market handed out informational flyers discussing breast cancer screening, donated money to the National Breast Cancer Hotline, and handed out coupons for $20 off the cost of mammograms.

In Boston the company participated in a community gardening program, Boston Market Gardens of Giving. The program taught children to garden and the food products were donated to local homeless shelters. The

SPUDS IN CYBERSPACE

Boston Market was the subject of an unfortunate Internet rumor concerning the integrity of its potato-making process. A post on an Internet message board claimed that the company did not use fresh potatoes for its mashed potatoes, but instead used powdered instant mashed potatoes. A concerned shareholder called the company for an explanation. He asked for and received a tour of the Boston Market kitchen where he witnessed the making of the mashed potatoes. The findings? The mashed potato side dishes are made fresh from real potatoes!

gardens included herbs, salsa, vegetables, and roots for soup making.

EMPLOYMENT

Boston Market has a comprehensive employee training program that goes beyond the usual opportunities afforded by the fast food industry. Once hired, employees receive extensive training to assist them in performing their duties. The first tier of training focuses on the technical requirements of operating the machinery, cooking appliances, computers, and cash registers. Successful candidates advance to managerial training and learn how to schedule shifts, order food and maintain operations. Interpersonal communication training is also provided as staff progress in their careers and assume supervisory roles. Boston Market encourages employees to attend skills training classes and set personal and employment goals.

SOURCES OF INFORMATION

Bibliography

Alexander, Devon. "Boston Market Fights Breast Cancer With Coupons." *Potentials in Marketing*, August 1997.

Allen, Robin Lee. "Boston Chicken Saga: Example of Biting Off More than the Operation Could Chew." *Nation's Restaurant News*, 19 October 1998.

"Boston Chicken Takes Up Gardening." *Nation's Restaurant News*, 25 September 1995.

Harper, Roseanne. "Boston Market to Redo Lunch." *Supermarket News*, 14 January 2002.

McDonald's to Launch Boston Market in Australia, Plans Brand Growth." *Nation's Restaurant News*, 18 June 2001.

Papiernik, Richard L. "Boston Chicken: Tough Year Ahead." *Nation's Restaurant News*, 1 June 1998.

———. "Boston Chicken Simmers in a Stew that's Boiling Over." *Nation's Restaurant News*,12 October 1998.

———. "Did Somebody Say McRescue? McD to Buy Boston Market." *Nation's Restaurant News*, 13 December 1999.

———. "Investors Show a Lack of Concern for McD's Boston Chicken Buyout." *Nation's Restaurant News*, 7 February 2000.

Schwartz, Nelson D. "The Boston Chicken Problem." *Fortune*, 7 July 1997.

Wilkerson, Jerry. "Sometimes More is Less: The Boston Chicken Decline." *Nation's Restaurant News*, 9 November 1998.

For additional industry research:

Investigate companies by their Standard Industrial Classification Codes, also known as SICs. Boston Market Corporation's primary SIC is:

5812 Eating Places

Also investigate companies by their North American Industry Classification System codes, also known as NAICS codes. Boston Market Corporation's primary NAICS code is:

722110 Full-Service Restaurants

BP p.l.c.

OVERVIEW

BP p.l.c. is a petrochemical company that engages in exploration and production, gas and power, refining and marketing, and chemicals. The company generates nearly 2 million barrels of crude oil and 8 billion cubic feet of natural gas daily. BP is the third-largest company in the world in terms of oil and gas reserves, and it trades or sells some 5.5 million barrels of refined products daily. BP is also the second-largest marketer of gasoline in the United States, with more than 17,000 gas stations around the country and nearly 12,000 service stations outside of North America in approximately 100 countries.

The company's petrochemicals division is the third largest in the world and boasts strong marketing positions throughout North America, Europe, and East Asia. The petrochemicals are used to produce plastics, polyester, and fibers and resins for use in bottles and containers.

COMPANY FINANCES

BP's revenues in 2001 were $174.2 billion, up from $148 billion the previous year and from $83.6 billion in 1999. However, gross profits rose only negligibly from 2000 to 2001, from $25.3 billion, to $25.6 billion, and operating income fell from $18 billion in 2000 to $16.7 billion in 2001.

The dividend rose to $.22 per share for 2001, up from $.20 per share in 2000. BP achieved a 5.5 percent production increase, despite a general economic slowdown that adversely affected trading. Further impacting

FOUNDED: 1909

VARIANT NAME: British Petroleum

Contact Information:

HEADQUARTERS: Britannic House, 1 Finsbury Circus
    London, EC2M 7BA United Kingdom
PHONE: +44-20-7496-4000
URL: http://www.bp.com

FAST FACTS:

About BP p.l.c.

Ownership: BP p.l.c., formerly BP Amoco, is a publicly owned company traded on the New York Stock Exchange.

Ticker Symbol: BP

Officers: Peter D. Sutherland, Co-Chmn., 54; John G. Buchanan, CFO and Dir., 57, 2001 salary $933,000, 2001 bonus $691,000; Judith C. Haratty, Sec., 57; Chris S. Gibson-Smith, Exec. Dir. of Policies and Technology, 55; Richard L. Olver, Chief Exec. of Exploration and Production, 54

Employees: 110,150

the demand for fuel was the shut-down of U.S. air travel at the beginning of the third quarter. Profit margins were poor during 2001 as oil companies competed during a time of decreased demand and unusually high inventories, especially in the U.S. market.

Prices were down in the oil sector by 15 percent throughout 2000. The chemicals sector in 2001 also operated at margins below the previous year. Further impacting BP's financial outlook in 2001 were an unpredictable stock market, developments that were delayed, and missed deadlines on maintenance projects.

ANALYSTS' OPINIONS

The oil refinery industry remains a volatile and worse-than-average business risk, according to Standard & Poor's, which stated that because of severe competition among participants, deep cyclicality, capital intensity, and unusually poor and unpredictable earnings, profitability is difficult to predict industry-wide. The high cost of constructing and operating refineries has nearly halted new refinery construction for three decades, and there have been no new U.S. refineries built since the early 1970s. Like BP, most oil companies have expanded by way of acquisition, rather than by constructing new facilities.

Oil companies such as BP, which have plentiful retail operations/gas stations, experience somewhat more stable sales because, although gasoline may experience swings in profit margins, items such as fast food, soft drinks, and cigarettes are traditionally high-profit items.

HISTORY

BP p.l.c. has survived a long history of volatile market and economic conditions. The company, first named Anglo-Persian, started in 1908 by wealthy and adventurous William Knox D'Arcy, has been impacted by fierce competition, global political conflicts, and market conditions for nearly 100 years. It has weathered the changing economic climate by becoming diversified early in the company's development. In fewer than 10 years, the company had started exploration and research in Iran, Canada, South America, Africa, Papua, and Europe. The company was the first to find commercial hydrocarbons gas fields off the British coast, as well as the first to make a major oil discovery in Alaska.

Early diversification helped BP, then named Anglo-Iranian Oil Co., through its first major political crisis, when Iran in 1951 nationalized all of its assets, and for three years oil exploration and exploitation halted.

The 1970s produced several crises, beginning with the 1973 oil price shock, which for the first time in 20 years created a decreased demand for oil. Again in 1978, when Iran was in the throes of a revolutionary war, BP was hard-hit by the war's impact.

It was the upheavals in the 1970s that more than any other events shaped BP's practices on diversification. BP broadened its activities and global reach to avoid being impacted too heavily by any one event worldwide. In the mid-1970s, the company became involved in animal feed, animal breeding, and consumer foods. The foods division purchased Purina Mills in 1986, and BP Nutrition became one of the world's largest feed millers.

During the same period, BP entered the minerals industry. By the close of the 1970s, BP had acquired chemical companies, Union Carbide and Monsanto. By 1980, the company successfully executed the largest takeover bid in the London stock market's history and bought Selection Trust, a British mining finance house.

The 1980s brought expansion by way of mergers and acquisitions. In 1987, BP purchased Standard Oil and made a bid for Britoil, a UK-based oil company. The Britoil acquisition was completed the following year. A decade later, the company acquired Amoco and Arco, creating the world's third-largest oil company.

STRATEGY

BP's strategy for the last decade has been one of expansion and mergers. By creating a larger global presence, the company has secured a spot among the world's largest oil producers. The larger scale of the company has afforded BP more credibility among global governments, and more stability, which are essential when a company seeks to expand in new markets. The additional size and stability may help BP expand in areas such as

CHRONOLOGY:

Key Dates for BP p.l.c.

1901: William Knox D'Arcy obtains concession from the Shah of Persia (now known as Iran) to explore for and exploit the oil resources of the country

1905: D'Arcy seeks financial assistance from the Burmah Oil company for continued exploration in Persia

1908: D'Arcy's engineer, George Reynolds, finally strikes oil in Masjid-i-Suleiman in southwest Persia-the first discovery in the Middle East

1909: The Anglo-Persian Oil Company was formed; Burmah Oil Company owned nearly all—97 percent—of the new company's stock; the remaining shares were owned by Lord Strathcona, the new company's first chairman

1910: Charles Greenway becomes managing director

1914: Greenway succeeds Strathcona as chairman; In order to avoid being dominated by Royal Dutch-Shell, Greenway appeals to the British government for financial assistance; the company and the government sign an agreement, shortly before the outbreak of World War I, in which the government pumped 2 million pounds of new capital into the company in exchange for a majority shareholding

1926: Anglo-Persian begins marketing its products in Iran and Iraq; before this move, the company had developed new marketing techniques, including curbside gas pumps, which replaced two-gallon tins for gasoline distribution

1921: The company establishes a new refinery in South Wales

1924: Anglo-Persian build refinery in Grangemouth, Scotland, and at Laverton, Australia

1927: Greenway retires; before his departure from the company, he had established global presence, and had built Anglo-Persian into one of the world's largest oil companies

1935: Anglo-Persian changes its name to the Anglo-Iranian Oil Company

1947: Newly involved in the petrochemicals industry, Anglo-Iranian entered into an agreement with the Distillers Company, which resulted in the formation of a joint company, British Hydrocarbon Chemicals

1951: Anglo-Iranian's operations come to a halt as the Iranian government nationalized the company's assets; the legislation created an international crisis, as the assets were at the time Britain's greatest single overseas investment

1954: Iranian oil industry activity resumes after intense negotiations resulted in an agreement between a consortium of oil companies and the Iranian government

1954: Anglo-Iranian changes its name to British Petroleum; the company begins marketing BP Visco-Static, Europe's first multigrade oil

1965: BP is the first company to discover hydrocarbons offshore in British waters

1969: BP discovers, after a decade of exploration, a major Alaskan oil field at Prudhoe Bay on the North Slope; with the find, BP owned the largest American oil field and sought a U.S. refining and marketing company to handle the processing; BP signed an agreement with Standard Oil Company

1970: BP discovers the Forties Field, the first commercial oil find in the United Kingdom

1973: The first of two major gas price explosions in the 1970s has dramatic effects on BP, and oil demand fell for the first time in 20 years

1978: The Iranian political crisis causes the second gasoline price explosion in one decade; BP acquires European assets from Union Carbide and Monsanto

1979: Nigeria and Kuwait nationalize their assets and scale back shipments overseas, creating a negative impact on supply to BP

1987: BP acquires Standard Oil; the British government sold its remaining 31.5 percent of BP holdings

1988: The company acquires UK-based oil company, Britoil

1998: BP and Amoco unite their global operations through a merger, the largest-ever industrial merger

1999: BP acquires Amoco and Arco

2000: BP acquires Burmah Castrol

China and Iran, although the Amoco and Arco mergers increased its American holdings and the sanctions imposed on U.S. companies doing business in Iran.

Following BP's acquisition of Arco and Amoco, the company shifted gears and worked toward maximizing efficiency and reducing redundancy. The company invested in upgrading its existing facilities in order to maximize efficiency in production. BP also cut some 700 jobs in 2001 in order to streamline efficiency.

CURRENT TRENDS

Several economic, political, and industry trends affect BP. Among them are deregulation, consolidation, fragmentation, and volatile prices and margins.

Deregulation has opened markets and sectors, which were previously closed, to competition. The utility industry, and BP's natural gas market, is particularly affected by this trend. Although in 2000 BP's gas market fared well thanks to adverse weather conditions and short supply in the United States, by 2001 prices had returned to normal levels. In 2000 the natural gas prices peaked at about $10/mcf, and the following year, they fell to $2.50/mcf. However, in 2001, unusually cold weather in Europe helped to keep the prices relatively stable.

Consolidation and mergers were the trend for the oil industry through the 1990s, creating a handful of mega-companies. The industry as a whole became more focused but, with fewer mid-sized companies, competition became even more intense than it had been. The heavy competition dramatically impacted price and profit margins for the remaining large players.

PRODUCTS

BP is the third-largest petroleum and petrochemicals holding company. It engages in exploration and production of crude oil and natural gas; refining, marketing, supply, and transportation; and gas power and solar power generation.

BP operates nearly 17,000 service stations in the United States and nearly 12,000 outside the United States. Castrol is BP's automotive and specialty/industrial lubricants brand. The company's newest outlets include fast food, and BP has established a partnership with McDonald's restaurants in the United States, Safeway and Sonae in Europe, and Iseya Kosan in Japan. At a growing number of retail outlets with food shops, more than one-half of revenues are from non-gasoline product sales.

BP owns 25,700 miles of pipeline, the most in the United States, and a 40-tanker fleet of vessels. The company is one of the largest aviation fuel companies, with more than 900 ports at 1,400 airports.

BP's products also include acetic acid; acrylonitrile; aromatics; purified terephthalic acid (PTA); alpha-olefins; purified isophthalic acid (PIA); and polypropylene, polyethylene, and oxygenated solvents. BP is the world's largest producer of PTA, which is used to produce polyester, fibers, and resins.

CORPORATE CITIZENSHIP

In December 2000, BP established an employee matching fund in order to support employee charitable giving in the community. In 2001 employees contributed more than $10 million to charities and donated more than 56,000 hours in service. BP added another $8.1 million to the employees' contributions.

GLOBAL PRESENCE

While in the early 2000s BP focused mainly on streamlining production, the company also was planning a few strategic acquisitions in Russia and Europe. In 1997 BP had purchased Russia's Sidanco for $571 million. Although the Russian company produced at first disappointing results, by 2002 it had regained its main assets, and BP was ready to take on a separate project and build in the Kovytka field in east Siberia.

BP also prepared in 2002 to expand its German gasoline retailing activities and purchase the German chain, Eon Aral. The purchase would give BP the leading market share, with Shell a close second.

BP was, in the early 2000s, focusing on expansion in Asia, particularly in China. Europe was also becoming an increasingly strong market. In 2001 the number of BP sites in Europe had grown to about 10,000, or about 15 percent saturation. BP estimated that the stores attracted some 1.6 million new customers daily in 2001.

BP operates in 100 countries around the world and produces in 23. The company's largest activities included three pipelines: the Trans Alaska Pipeline System (of which BP owns 50 percent), the Forties Pipeline System in the U.K. sector of the North Sea (BP owns 100 percent), and the Central Area Transmission System pipeline (BP owns 29.5 percent) in the U.K. sector of the North Sea.

EMPLOYMENT

BP p.l.c. says that its work environment is based upon mutual trust, respect, inclusion, and diversity. With more than 100,000 employees in more than 100 countries, the company offers promotion to internal candidates first before recruiting from outside the company. More than 80 percent of BP's new employees have between three to six years of professional experience prior to hire.

SOURCES OF INFORMATION

Bibliography

Baudouin, Nicolas. "Adverse Market Conditions Prevail for European Commodity Chemicals." *Standard & Poor's*, 28 November 2001.

"BP Hit as Margins Fall to 10-year Low." *Financial Times*, 4 April 2002.

Buchan, David. "BP: Pumped Up and Still Rising." *Financial Times*, 20 January 2002.

"Business Description: BP p.l.c." *Market Guide*, 1 April 2002.

Thieroff, John. "Many Factors Affect U.S. Oil Refining and Marketing Companies' Credit Ratings." *Standard & Poor's*, 13 June 2001.

For an annual report:

on the Internet at: http://www.bp.com

For additional industry research:

Investigate companies by their Standard Industrial Classification Codes, also known as SICs. BP p.l.c.'s primary SICs are:

2911 Petroleum Refining

5172 Petroleum Products, Not Elsewhere Classified

5541 Gasoline Service Stations

Also investigate companies by their North American Industry Classification System codes, also known as NAICS codes. BP p.l.c.'s primary NAICS codes are:

324110 Petroleum Refineries

422720 Petroleum and Petroleum Products (except Bulk Stations and Terminals) Wholesalers

447110 Gasoline Stations with Convenience Stores

British Airways Plc

FOUNDED: 1923

Contact Information:

HEADQUARTERS: Waterside HBA3, PO Box 365
  Harmondsworth, UB7 OGB Great Britain
PHONE: +44-20-8562-4444
FAX: +44-20-8759-4314
TOLL FREE: (800)545-7644
EMAIL: bafeedback@agency.com
URL: http://www.britishairways.com

OVERVIEW

British Airways Plc (BA), based at Heathrow Airport in London, is the world's largest international air carrier. BA carries approximately 36 million passengers each year with a global network spanning more than 250 destinations and 97 countries. The company was originally a government-run operation until 1987 when BA completed its initial public offering. After going public, BA posted impressive numbers, with stock prices topping $100 a share on the New York Stock Exchange during 1997 and 1998 before falling to $35.00 in 2002. Economic recession, combined with other uncontrollable factors such as an increase in fuel prices, the country's hand-and-foot disease crisis, and the terrorist attacks of September 11, 2001, have disrupted the airline's bottom line numbers. Burdened by a large debt load, BA has been looking to cut costs, improve customer services, and streamline operations to remain one of the world's leading airline service providers.

COMPANY FINANCES

For the year ending March 31, 1997, British Airways posted a profit before taxes of 640 million on revenues of £8.36 billion. Over the next three years, profits slid downward, and for the year ending March 31, 2000, the airline showed a profit before taxes of only £5 million, resulting in a net loss of £21 million, on revenues of £8.94 billion. The following year the company rebounded to post a profit before taxes of £150 million on £9.28 billion in sales. However, BA was struck with economic problems again for the year ending March 31, 2002, with income before taxes falling to reflect a loss of £200 million.

The majority of British Airway's revenues come from passenger ticketing. In 2001 of the £9.28 billion total sales, £7.8 billion was a result of passenger ticket sales. Cargo and mail services generated £579 million, and other services, including aircraft maintenance services and special holiday packages, accounted for £846 million.

ANALYSTS' OPINIONS

Analysts have expressed concern regarding British Airways' long-term success and tend to favor the airline's European peers Lufthansa, Air France, and KLM as better investments. BA has good reasons for its recent financial woes. The foot-and-mouth disease outbreak in Great Britain first stymied the economy, followed by a general slowdown in the global economy, and the airline's problems climaxed after the terrorist attacks of September 11, 2001. However, BA is not alone; the International Air Transport Association estimated that the airline industry lost approximately $17 billion last year. Although analysts can forgive BA short-term misfortunes, they show concern over the airline's large debt, its inefficient hub at Heathrow, continuing losses in its short haul network, and increasingly strong competition from discount, no-frills airlines. Given the difficult market, analysts are skeptical that BA will be set for any quick or remarkable recoveries in the near future.

HISTORY

In 1923, in response to stiff competition from foreign airlines that had forced all British-owned airline operations to suspend service, the British Parliament commissioned the Civil Air Transport Subsidies Committee to create a single British air carrier company from all existing operations. As a result, on March 31, 1924, Daimler Airway, British Marine Air Navigation, Instone Air Line, and Handley Page joined together to become Imperial Air Transport. As the airline industry grew, Imperial worked to connect the many points of the British Empire, with most of its revenues being generated by mail delivery services. Destinations included Calcutta, Cairo, Singapore, Brisbane, and Cape Town. By 1936 nearly all territories under British control were linked by Imperial flights.

Although Imperial was the leader in overseas air service, it was facing increasing competition from an aggressive new company, BA, which had been established in 1935 by the merger of three smaller airlines. Imperial decided the best strategy for survival in the European market was cooperation. Accordingly, in

FAST FACTS:
About British Airways Plc

Ownership: British Airways is a publicly owned corporation that trades on multiple exchanges around the world, including the London, Munich, XETRA, OTC, and New York Stock Exchanges.

Ticker Symbol: BAB

Officers: Lord Marshall, 67, Chmn; Rod Eddington, 51, CEO; Derek Stevens, 62, CFO

Employees: 62,175

Principal Subsidiary Companies: British Airways' wholly owned subsidiaries include, most importantly, British Airways Ltd., as well as CityFlyer Express Ltd., British Airways Holidays Ltd., British Airways Cargo, and Deutsche BA Luftfahrtgesellschaft GmbH. The company also holds partial equity in numerous ventures including The London Eye Company Ltd., Concorde International Travel Pty Ltd., and Qantas Airways Ltd.

Chief Competitors: British Airways' wholly owned subsidiaries include, most importantly, British Airways Ltd., as well as CityFlyer Express Ltd., British Airways Holidays Ltd., British Airways Cargo, and Deutsche BA Luftfahrtgesellschaft GmbH. The company also holds partial equity in numerous ventures including The London Eye Company Ltd., Concorde International Travel Pty Ltd., and Qantas Airways Ltd.

November 1937 Parliament was presented with a proposal to nationalize and merge Imperial and BA. The merger was completed on November 24, 1939, with the two companies reorganized as the British Overseas Airways Corp. (BOAC).

During World War II, the government took control of all British airlines. After the war ended, BOAC handed over all European destinations were assigned to British European Airways. Likewise all South American destinations were assigned to British South American Airways, a newly formed state-owned company; however, a series of equipment failures prompted BOAC to resume control of the South American network in 1949. During the remainder of the 1940s, BOAC spent large amounts of capital to upgrade its fleet, adding newer, faster airplanes. Purchases included Lockheed Constellations,

CHRONOLOGY:

Key Dates for British Airways

1923: British Parliament orders the formation of a single British international air carrier; Imperial Air Transport is founded the next year

1935: Start-up carrier BA offers increasing competition to Imperial

1939: BA is nationalized and merged with Imperial as British Overseas Airways Corporation (BOAC)

1951: BOAC's debt reaches £32 million due to recapitalization expenses

1961: Debt climbs to £64 million, caused by a decline in passengers; government finances company to prevent bankruptcy

1974: Out of debt and financially stable, company is reorganized and renamed BA (BA)

1983: More than 50 BA executives fired in a management shake-up

1987: BA becomes a publicly owned company, selling 720 million stock shares for £1 billion

1997: Reports fiscal year profit before taxes of £640 million

2000: BA considers merging with KLM Royal Dutch Airlines but decides to pull out of negotiations

2001: Reports a fiscal year profit before taxes of £5 million

---

Boeing 377 Stratocruisers, and Canadair Argonauts, as well as Handley Page Hermes and de Havilland's DH Comet 1, the world's first jetliner.

Despite increased passenger numbers, the rapid expansion of the company's fleet pushed its debt to £32 million. In January 1954 a Comet airliner crashed into the Mediterranean, followed by a second Comet crash just days after the investigation closed on the first accident. As a result, the Comet was declared unfit to fly and taken out of BOAC's schedule. With the Comet, the airliner's longest-range aircraft, out of commission, BOAC was forced to suspend all travel routes to South America. Eventually the mechanical problem with the Comet was discovered and resolved. Nonetheless, when the aircraft was reintroduced in 1958 as the DH Comet 4, its time had passed, and BOAC sold the fleet along with an

outdated fleet of prop-engine DC-7s for a loss of £51 million.

BOAC's financial outlook did not improve in the 1960s. Although cargo tonnage had increased steadily, there was a sharp unexplained decline in passenger purchases. Like many companies within the airline industry, BOAC took a loss for 1961, increasing the company's debt to £64 million. The government stepped in to protect BOAC from bankruptcy and ordered a drastic reorganization of the BOAC. As a result, money-losing services were scraped, equipment purchases were reconfigured, and debt payments were rescheduled. The restructuring was successful, and BOAC posted record profits from 1966 to 1972, at which time it had completely repaid its debt to the government. In 1974 BOAC underwent further restructuring by merging with British European Airways to create BA. The financial recovery experienced during the 1970s was topped off with the addition of the first supersonic Concorde, which flew at speeds up to 1,350 miles per hour, cutting the normal 7-hour London-New York flight in half.

During the early 1980s, BA began to prepare to become a privately owned company. A concerted push was made to improve customer service, for which the airline had a notoriously poor reputation. Once again cost-cutting measures were employed, and between 1980 and 1983 the workforce was reduced from 60,000 to 38,000. Over fifty executives were terminated, and a professional marketing group was commissioned to give the company's public image a makeover. Despite opposition from competitors, BA became a limited public company in 1985, with the government retaining all control of the stock. The initial public offering completed in 1987 resulted in 720.2 million shares being sold for £1 billion. In the same year, BA acquired British Caledonian, known as Bcal, one of its major competitors. With the addition of the Bcal fleet and routes, BA became one of the largest airliners in the world.

During the late 1980s and into the 1990s, British Airways attempted with limited success to expand its international operations. In 1988 the company formed an alliance with United Airlines to shuffle customers between the two airlines. However, when United purchased rights three years later to access London's Heathrow from struggling Pan Am and TWA, the partnership ended and United became BA' direct competitor. In 1991 the airline entered into an agreement with Aeroflot, a Russian company, to develop a new airline called Air Russia, but the venture never came to fruition. The next year BA looked to the large U.S. markets. Its attempt to purchase 44 percent of USAir was blocked by the U.S. government after the major U.S. carriers lobbied strongly against the deal.

British Airways did manage to purchase 49.9 percent of TAT European Airlines, a leading French airline, and 25 percent of Qantas, Australia-based airline. With these deals complete, BA placed on the table a revised offer for a portion of USAir, and this time received governmental approval. These acquisitions strengthened BA global presence, but negatively affected the organization's financial standing. In 1993 Qantas posted a lost of $271 million, and in 1994 TAT and USAir lost $60 million and $350 million, respectively. Despite the poor performance of its alliances, BA continued to post positive numbers. The late 1990s brought increased competition, establishing a tougher business environment for BA, and in 1997 the company sold off its interest in USAir. During 2000 the company considered merging with KLM Airlines, but backed out before the deal was completed.

STRATEGY

In 2002 BA conducted a Future Size and Shape review in order to determine the best solutions to the challenges facing the airline. The goal will be to create a simpler, leaner airline that is more focused on its core profitable routes. To quickly reduce overhead, the airline announced that it would cut 13,000 jobs by 2004. In another move to cut costs, BA has drastically reduced its plans for its terminal at Gatwick by abandoning plans to turn Gatwick into a second major hub for the airline. Instead, longhaul operations are scheduled for reduction from 43 to 25 by suspending unprofitable routes and moving others key routes to Heathrow. Gatwick will remain important to BA' shorthaul business. With more traffic moved to Heathrow, the airline will push the British government for improvements in the infrastructure of the airline industry so that its already inadequate terminal situation may in the future be alleviated.

In an attempt to reclaim the business of leisure travelers who were buying tickets from the no-frills airlines, on April 5, 2002, British Airways announced newly restructured fare plans that included domestic return fares starting as low as £69 and did away with the Saturday night stay restrictions. The airline also hopes to entice business and leisure travelers by providing quality products and services that are unmatched by its competitors. New offerings provided under the label of Air Travel For the 21st Century include refurbished First Class, the Club World flat bed, the improved Club Europe and World Traveller services, and the introduction of a new class, World Traveller Plus. Terminal facilities and lounges have also been upgraded and modernized to provide comfort and convenience to British Airway customers. To move to the forefront of technology, the airline has begun to offer innovative customer service options such as flight information and passenger check-up via mobile Internet. Discounts are offered to customers who book their flights at BA's Web site.

INFLUENCES

As a global company BA is continually affected—sometimes positively, sometimes negatively—by the world economy. Such uncontrollable variables as fuel prices and the strength or weakness of regional economies directly impact the profitability of the airline. Just as the airline was looking toward a recovery of the British economy after the outbreak of foot-and-mouth disease, which had resulted in a reduction in both passenger and cargo revenue, the terrorist attacks of September 11, 2001, weakened the global economy, sending the entire airline industry into a downward spin.

To encourage people to return to flying and to compete with the growing success of discount airlines, BA cut prices on numerous flights. However, this means that even if passenger numbers grow, as is expected to eventually occur, BA will be making less profit per passenger, thus requiring even greater increases in filled seats to make ends meet. Thus, BA is also continuing to look for ways to streamline operations and lower overhead.

CURRENT TRENDS

With a keen eye on cost reduction, BA announced the results of an in-house study "Future Size and Shape" in February 2001. The plan calls for the elimination of unprofitable segments of business operations by reducing capacity, eliminating unnecessary complexity, and reduction in the workforce, all of which is to be accomplished without affecting the quality of customer service.

To better position itself in the marketplace, BA has made a number of divestitures and acquisitions. The airline sold off its French subsidiary Air Liberté and its interest in Hogg Robinson. BA also sold GO, a low-fare regional airline. In its place, BA acquired British Regional Airlines Group, which it merged with its wholly owned regionally based Brymon Airways. CityFlyer Express was purchased and integrated into the mainline operations at BA's Gatwick terminal.

PRODUCTS

As of March 2002, BA had 360 aircraft in its fleet, including 7 Concordes (currently out of service for safety modifications), 56 Boeing 747-400s, 45 Boeing 777s, 44 Turbo Props, 33 Airbus A19s, and 21 Boeing 737-400s. This reflects an increase of 22 aircraft from the previous year, which is primarily due to the acquisition of British Regional Air Lines with 12 Jetstream 41, 13 British Aerospace ATP, 21 Embraer RJ145 and 5 British Aerospace 146 in service at year end. Aircraft removed from BA's service include 13 Boeing 737-300, which resulted from the sale of GO. Other changes are the consequence of regular operational procedures that introduces new aircraft and grounds outdated aircraft.

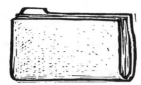

FROM "BLOODY AWFUL" TO "BEST AROUND"

In a major effort to overhaul its reputation for high-end ticket prices and low-end customer services and comforts, British Airways invested £600 million to upgrade and improve its product offerings. After conducting an extensive market research project to find out what passengers wanted from an airline, BA instituted numerous innovative changes in its products that were developed to maximize comfort and design. The most cutting-edge addition was the "lounge in the sky," which offers business class travelers a completely flat bed for resting during long flights. With the addition of the world traveler plus cabin, which provides more space, leg room, facilities, and double carry-on baggage allowance, BA became the first airline to offer four distinct cabins: first class, club world, world traveler, and world traveler plus. As a result of its investment in customer satisfaction and service, BA can proudly claim to have shed its old acronym's side-meaning of "bloody awful" to boast that it offers the "best around."

CORPORATE CITIZENSHIP

BA's Sustainable Business Unit provides the airline with input on environmental and social concerns as well as economic impact of business decisions. The Sustain Business Unit creates community and environmental policy through provision of support and advice, as well as monitoring, measuring, and reporting on the airline's performance in the areas of social and environmental responsibility.

As a corporation BA sponsors numerous ongoing charities as well as responding to special emergency needs. The company's Change of Good fundraising efforts have raised more than £12.5 million to help UNICEF. For the year ending March 31, 2001, BA provided £782,000 in direct funding to charities and community projects. However, accounting for in-kind goods and services donations, that total jumps to £6.4 million. BA focuses specific efforts in the areas of youth development, heritage and tourism, and the environment. Specific environmental concerns include noise, fuel efficiency and emissions, waste, water use, climate change, and congestion in the air.

GLOBAL PRESENCE

Of total ticket sales, business conducted within Great Britain accounted for £4.63 billion in revenues; continental Europe, £1.42 billion; the Americas, £1.75 billion; Africa, the Middle East, and the Indian subcontinent, £783 million; and the Far East and Australasia, £696 million. Strongest growth was seen in Africa, the Middle East, and the Indian subcontinent, which showed an increase of revenues by area of destination of nearly 7 percent.

Forming alliance has also been a trend in BA's global strategy. The **one**world alliance, founded in February of 1999 with BA as one of its founding members, is an international consortium of eight full members, including airline powerhouse American Airlines, and 23 affiliate member airlines. The goal of **one**world is to coordinate routes, scheduling, and ticketing to provide advantages to all airlines that are involved in the consortium. Benefits include reciprocal reward and recognition programs, common lounge access, smoother transfers, and increased customer support. BA has also worked to establish a unique relationship with American Airlines outside the realm of **one**world, but the future of the two superpower airline's interact has yet to be played out.

EMPLOYMENT

British Airways offers career opportunities in the areas of customer contact (terminal and in air), commercial sales and marketing, e-business and information technology, technical and operations, and corporate positions such as public relations, finance, legal, and human resources. Training resources, such as computer-based interactive learning centers, library facilities, reference materials, audio- and video-based learning, and numerous leadership and teambuilding programs are used for career enhancement. BA looks for candidates who possess the skills required for the position as well as initiative and good communication and teambuilding skills. For senior positions, proven leadership is an important factor also.

SOURCES OF INFORMATION

Bibliography

"BA Cuts Staffing Costs During Turbulent Times." *Personnel Today*, 16 April 2002.

"BA Vows to Regain Lost Sales." *Travel Trade Gazette UK & Ireland*, 22 April 2002.

"British Airways Introduces New Products." *Africa News Service*, 18 April 2002.

"British Airways Offers New Deals to Compete with Low-cost Airlines." *Airline Industry Information*, 4 April 2002.

"British Airways to Cancel 12 Routes and Cut Staff." *Airline Industry Information*, 25 April 2002.

"British Airways to Cut 5,800 More Jobs." *Air Transport World*, March 2002.

Burke, W. Warner. "Plane Talk about Change: How Lord Colin Marshall Transformed British Airways Into a Customer-Service Powerhouse." In *Business Climate Shifts: Profiles of Change Makers*. Boston: Butterworth Heinemann, 2000.

"Cowen on...British Airways." *Campaign*, 18 January 2002.

"Taking." *Airline Business*, 1 May 2002.

"UK Company: British Airways Shrinking to Grow." *Financial Times*, 20 May 2002.

Vowler, Julia. "Can BA Slash £45 million from its IT Budget and Keep on Flying?" *Computer Weekly*, 14 March 2002.

For an annual report:

on the Internet at: http://www.britishairways.com

For additional industry research:

Investigate companies by their Standard Industrial Classification Codes, also known as SICs. British Airways Plc's primary SICs are:

4512 Air Transportation Scheduled

4513 Air Courier Services

4522 Air Transportation Nonscheduled

4581 Airports Fields & Terminal Services

4731 Arrangement Transport Freight & Cargo

Also investigate companies by their North American Industry Classification System codes, also known as NAICS codes. British Airways Plc's primary NAICS code is:

481110 Scheduled Air Transportation

British Broadcasting Corporation

FOUNDED: 1922
VARIANT NAME: BBC

Contact Information:

HEADQUARTERS: Broadcasting House, Portland Place
    London, W1A 1AA United Kingdom
PHONE: +44-20-7580-4468
FAX: +44-20-7765-1181
URL: http://www.bbc.co.uk

OVERVIEW

Founded in 1922 as the British Broadcasting Company and reorganized as the British Broadcasting Corporation under a royal charter in 1927, the BBC is the largest public media company in the world. The BBC Group consists of two noncommercial entities, BBC Home Services and BBC World Service, and several commercial companies, including BBC Worldwide Limited, BBC Resources Limited, and BBC Technology Holdings Limited. BBC's Home and World segments are divided into eight programming and broadcasting divisions: news; television; radio and music; new media; nations and regions; drama, entertainment, and children; factual and learning; and sports. BBC Worldwide is the BBC's commercial media business. As a for-profit entity, Worldwide operates separately from nonprofit segments of the company. Its purpose is to create and market the commercial value of BBC programs and services by selling programs to overseas broadcasters and operating commercial channels in joint ventures with others, along with publishing magazines, books, videos, and CDs. Resources Limited provides facilities and program resources to both the BBC and the commercial media market. Technology Holdings was formed in 2000 to bring together more than 900 BBC employees in the fields of desk-top support, Web-hosting, and networking.

Over the years of its existence, the BBC has expanded its home media services to include two popular programming television stations, BBC One and BBC Two, as well as specialized channels, BBC Choice, BBC News 24, BBC Knowledge, and BBC Parliament, and five radio stations. The two television stations garnered 38 percent of the United Kingdom viewing audience during 2001, and BBC radio accounted for more than 50 percent of radio listening time. Through its commercial subsidiary BBC Worldwide Limited, BBC programming, including news and popular entertainment such as *Weakest Link* and children's shows *Teletubbies* and *Bob the Builder,* is broadcast around the world. Governed by a 12-person board of governors, the majority of operating revenue comes from a licensing fee charged for the BBC's services.

COMPANY FINANCES

The total income for 2001 for the entire BBC Group was £3.85 billion, up from £3.71 billion in 2000. Homes Services accounted for £2.73 billion of 2001 revenues, with £2.37 billion of that amount being generated from licensing fees. This represents an increase over 2000 income of £2.67 billion. World Service posted an income of £204 million in 2001, up from £192 million in 2000. The majority of World Service's income is provided by a Grant-in-Aid distributed by the Foreign and Commonwealth Office, which totaled £181 million in 2001. Other income included over £15 million in subscription fees. The BBC's commercial mainstay, Worldwide, accounted for £587 million of 2001 income, with all other commercial entities bringing in £325 million.

ANALYSTS' OPINIONS

As a private company, the BBC does not trade its stocks on the open market. Analysts' opinions focus on the future of the BBC as a not-for-profit organization in the midst of the expansion of commercial television. There is significant debate whether the BBC should retain its royal charter in the future, and under its current charter just how far the BBC can step into commercial arena. Commercial television companies, especially the BBC's chief competitor in the United Kingdom ITV1, continuously raise concerns that the BBC has overstepped its boundaries and in so doing causes significant hardship on the for-profit television industry. According to some analysts, if privatized, the BBC could garner up to £7 billion. However, the BBC has no intentions of quietly giving up its preferred status. In 2002 the organization was continuing to expand its operations and programming and lobbying for governmental permission to launch a digital channel geared toward popular programming, a move the commercial television industry vehemently opposes.

HISTORY

The British Broadcasting Corporation (BBC) was founded on October 18, 1922 as the British Broadcast-

FAST FACTS:
About British Broadcasting Corporation

Ownership: British Broadcasting Corporation is a privately owned international and multinational company.

Officers: Greg Dyke, Dir.-Gen., 54; Gavyn Davies, Chmn.

Employees: 24,000

Principal Subsidiary Companies: British Broadcasting Corporation has numerous for-profit subsidiaries, including BBC Enterprises Ltd., BBC World Service Television Ltd., BBC Subscription Television Ltd., BBC Investments Ltd., and Opion and Broadcasting Research Ltd.

Chief Competitors: BBC's main competitor is ITV1, which garnered 29 percent of the viewing audience in 2001, compared to the BBC's major network, BBC One, which claimed 27 percent. Other competitors include Channel Four and Channel Five. The BBC also faces increasing competition from an influx of satellite and cable stations.

ing Company Ltd. through the joint efforts of Britain's leading radio manufacturers, such as Marconi Company, and the General Post Office. The companies decided to work together to provide a national radio service without allowing any one particular manufacturer to monopolize the emerging broadcast industry. Beginning with an initial share value of £100,000, the BBC sustained itself financially by collecting all the Post Office license fees of 10 shillings, equal to 75 cents, and by receiving royalties on the sales of all radio transmitters sold by member companies. BBC licenses became available on November 1, 1922, and by the end of the year, 35,744 licenses had been sold.

Broadcasting began on the BBC on November 14, 1922, when Arthur Burrows, the BBC's first director of programs, anchored two news bulletins from Marconi House in London. Operations spread rapidly, with radio stations opening in Manchester and Birmingham the very next day. By the end of November, BBC radio offered five hours of daily programming. Within a year, the number of radio stations had grown to 10, and the number of BBC employees jumped from just 4 in December 1922 to 177 in December 1923. Programming was expanded under the direction of the BBC's first general manager,

33-year-old John C. Reith. Reith added opera and theater programming along with live sports commentary and daily weather forecasts to the daily news broadcasts. Listeners were kept abreast of the BBC's expanding programming through the company's publication, *Radio Times,* which served as a programming guide but also included commentaries, articles, and additional information.

Throughout the remainder of the 1920s, the BBC continued to grow in strength and importance. By the end of 1923 an experimental broadcast had reached the shores of the United States, and Radiola Paris transmitted programming to southern England. When a general strike was called in May 1926, newspaper distribution was temporarily suspended, and the BBC became the sole means for public dissemination of information. The BBC responded by increasing daily news spots to five. Although the government restricted the BBC from interviewing strikers, the company did retain editorial independence in reporting on strike developments.

On January 1, 1927, the British Broadcasting Company Ltd. was reorganized under a royal charter as the British Broadcasting Corporation and the new motto became "And nation shall speak peace unto nation." The charter guaranteed that the BBC was not "a creature of Parliament and connected with political activity," thus was required to remain free from all partisanship and political favoritism. Reith was appointed director-general and, although the postmaster general continued to collect licensing fees, a five-member board of governors was created to oversee policy and administration.

During the early 1930s, the BBC issued up to 1,000 licenses every day, and by 1935 an estimated 95 percent of the population received at least one BBC program on their home radios. In 1938 the BBC introduced broadcasts in foreign languages, launching an Arabic service from Bush House in London in January, followed by Portuguese and Spanish programming two months later. During World War II, BBC radio was broadcast in occupied territories and its foreign language programming became increasingly important. Domestically, the BBC aired on a single wavelength, called the Home Service, which was used to boost morale. In 1940 another program offered was aimed at the military troops and featured many popular U.S. entertainers.

The BBC, under the leadership of its director of television Gerald Cock, began experimenting with television broadcasting in the early 1930s. In 1936 Cock supervised the first transmission of high-definition black-and-white television programming, the first in the world. High costs limited the initial viewing audience to approximately 20,000 even though the programming was considered exceptional for the time. The BBC was taken off the air from 1939 to 1952 during the course of World War II.

Despite fuel shortages during the late 1940s that temporarily interrupted television broadcasting, the postWar economy spurred the growth of the BBC. By 1950,

employees numbered 12,000, and a new television station was opened at Lime Grove in London. During the early 1950s the Labour Party was ousted from power by the Conservative Party, which held free market enterprise in high esteem. As a result, the Television Act of 1954 broke the BBC's monopoly on television. Within a year the Independent Television Authority (ITA), the country's first commercial television, hit the airwaves to compete with the BBC.

In April of 1964 the BBC introduced a second channel, BBC Two, which offered specialized and minority programming. Three years later the BBC Two became the first European station to provide regular broadcasts in color, with color broadcasts appearing on BBC One by 1969. As BBC television continued to expand so did BBC radio. In 1967 the BBC put its fourth radio station on the air. Called Radio 1, the station was devoted to popular music. The other stations subsequently became known as Radio 2, 3, and 4. In 1990 the BBC introduced Radio 5.

During the 1970s the BBC came under public scrutiny from many who believed its programming had deteriorated in quality. The company was also coming under increasing financial pressure, caused in part by increased competition from commercial television. In 1975 the financial situation came to light when revenues failed to meet expenditures for the first time. Although some advocated strongly for the introduction of commercials to the BBC to help its financial stability, ultimately a government report on the issue in 1986 rejected commercialization in favor of loosening rules that governed the manner in which the BBC could raise funds. Consequently, the BBC created a fully owned subsidiary, the BBC Subscription Television Ltd., which offered subscription-based broadcasting. In April 1991 the BBC added the BBC World Service Television Ltd. in Europe. Six months later, the service was extended into Asia.

During the 1990s the BBC continued to be hounded by financial dilemmas and increasingly serious competition from satellite and cable television. In 1994 all international and commercial BBC units were consolidated into BBC Worldwide, which consisted of BBC World Service and BBC Worldwide Ltd., which in turn consisted of BBC Publishing, BBC Worldwide Television, and BBC Worldwide Learning. Continuing to expand into new arenas and markets, in 1999 the BBC launched BBC Knowledge and in 2000 formed a partnership with a New York-based bank Veronis Suhler to create a publishing-based consumer media company in the United States. The BBC's current royal charter expires in 2006.

STRATEGY

The Board of Governors set 12 strategic objectives for the fiscal year 2001. According to their report, seven objectives were fulfilled and five objectives were partially fulfilled. Among the goals achieved were: develop creativity, citizenship, and learning in the digital age; provide effective sports coverage at an affordable cost; increase the percentage of the licensing fees dedicated to programming from 75 percent to 85 percent; make substantial progress in interactive and online services; increase financial efficiency and develop more effective commercial activities; improve openness and accountability to all stakeholders; and create an environment at BBC that inspires greater collaboration and creativity.

The BBC is posed to move into the digital age, but its progress has been slowed due to a sluggish response time for governmental approval to launch new services, a fact the BBC attributes to strong pressure by commercial interests to rein in the BBC. Traditionally a producer of highbrow programming, the BBC has significantly increased its programming of popular dramas and comedies, much to the chagrin of BBC diehards, who see the move as a degradation of programming, and commercial television executives, who see the BBC cutting sharply into their market share of entertainment television.

INFLUENCES

Until 1954 the BBC completely monopolized television and radio in the United Kingdom. However, once competition was introduced, the BBC moved into the unique position of a not-for-profit entity that competes head on with commercial media companies. Despite the increased competition, the BBC reaches 94 percent of the United Kingdom's population on a weekly basis. However, the influx of satellite and cable television options leave open the question of how long the license-based organization can remain solvent.

CURRENT TRENDS

In its 2001 Annual Report, the BBC announced the completion of an overhaul of its organization. Through its One BBC project, the company restructured its business segments into 53 units, down from its previous 190 units. By dismantling large divisions and focusing on streamlining non-program activities, the BBC planned to save £166 million in overhead by 2004. Savings will be transferred to increased spending in programming with the goal of upping the programming budget by more than £450 million by 2003.

Although viewership of BBC One, the corporation's dominant television station, fell during 2001, the number of viewers increased for BBC Two. BBC One claimed 26.8 percent of the audience and BBC Two took 11 percent of the market share. Among the commercial stations, ITV1 held 28.9 percent; Channel 4, 10.3 percent; Channel 5, 5.7 percent; and all others, 17.3 percent.

CHRONOLOGY:
Key Dates for the British Broadcasting Corporation

1922: The British Broadcasting Co. Ltd. (BBC) is founded by a coalition of radio manufacturers to provide national radio service to Britain

1927: Reorganizes as the British Broadcasting Corporation under a royal charter that guarantees it is free from political ties

1936: Creates the world's first high definition black-and-white television transmission

1939: For security reasons, all television broadcasts are prohibited from airing during the duration of World War II

1946: Begins broadcasting again with coverage of the British victory parade

1954: Parliament passes the Television Act of 1954, breaking the BBC's monopoly on television broadcasting

1955: First experimental color television transmission is introduced and programming time grows to 50 hours a week

1964: Creates second television channel, BBC Two

1967: BBC Two becomes the first European television station to broadcast regularly in color

1987: Creates BBC Subscription Television Ltd. as a commercial subsidiary

1992: BBC programming is aired in more than 100 countries and BBC World Services provides radio news broadcasts in 38 languages

1998: Introduces digital radio and television broadcasting

2000: Joins New York bank Veronis Suhler to establish a publishing and media company in the United States

PRODUCTS

BBC television offers a wide range of programming in news, sports, education, entertainment, and children's shows. Between 2000 and 2001, programs receiving the highest number of viewers on BBC One included the hit drama series *EastEnders* (18 million viewers) and *One*

OFF THE AIR

BBC television was completely removed from the air in 1939 as Britain entered World War II. The transmitting tower served as a clear location signal for enemy bombing runs, thus for national security reasons, all television broadcasts ceased through the remainder of the war. Service reopened in 1946 with 100,000 viewers around London watching the victory parade celebrating the end of World War II. BBC television increased in popularity by broadcasting such high-profile events as the coronation of Elizabeth II in Westminster Abbey on June 2, 1953, and made television history again in 2002 by televising her funeral.

Foot in the Grave (12.84 million viewers), as well as the Euro 2000 soccer finals (Romania vs. England; 14.56 million viewers) and the game show *The Weakest Link* (11.4 million viewers). On BBC Two the most popular programs included *The Weakest Link Celebrity Special* (6.59 million viewers) and the regular showing of *The Weakest Link* (5.54 million viewers), *Have I Got News for You* (5.77 million viewers), and the U.S.-produced animated series *The Simpsons* (5.41 million viewers).

The BBC radio stations offer programming targeting different audiences. Radio One airs popular music and artists for the 15- to 24-year-old demographic. Radio Two network provides topical discussion and documentary programs along with music and live concert performance. It targets listeners from 35 to 54 years old. Radio Three focuses its programming on classical music, but it has recently added new genres to the mix, such as reggae and jazz. Radio Four's foundational programs are built on news, investigative reporting, and special interests from food to farming to comedy. Radio Five, called Radio Five Live, functions as the BBC's outlet for sporting event broadcasts.

The BBC's nations and regions division provides programming tailored to specific geographical segments of the United Kingdom with news and information targeted to Wales, Northern Ireland, and Scotland. In addition to providing television programming both inside and outside the United Kingdom, BBC Worldwide publishes several magazines, such as well-established and highly profitable *Radio Times* and the new publication *BBC History Magazine.* Worldwide also publishes books and spoken word tapes. In yet another venue, the BBC provides news, sports, and entertainment information, and services

via its Web site, which has shown a significant increase in hits. In March 2001, total page impressions for the month reached 337.4 million.

CORPORATE CITIZENSHIP

In June 2000 the BBC Board of Governors approved the corporation first formal environmental policy that addresses five key areas of environmental impact: waste, utilities, transport, supply chain, and property. The BBC's main objective in waste reduction is the proper disposal of video and audio tapes. To this end, the corporation initiated aluminum film cans recycling. To save energy and water utilities, the BBC made modifications to its air condition systems by placing units on timers in several offices. The transportation impact of the corporation's employees is reduced by using shuttle buses between its London locations. Measures to reduce procurement of goods include an in-house stationery catalogue that saves thousands of reams of paper normally used for print versions.

GLOBAL PRESENCE

The commercial entities BBC World and BBC News 24 provide programming around the world, with BBC World reaching 178 million homes worldwide. BBC Worldwide Limited markets numerous programs that have proven successful in the United Kingdom and overseas in the United States, including *The Weakest Link, Teletubbies,* and *Bob the Builder.* As an international channel provider, Worldwide reaches 365 million homes worldwide. BBC World Service transmits FM radio broadcasts in 43 languages in 120 capitals around the world, reaching 153 million listeners each week.

EMPLOYMENT

The BBC divides its employee base of 24,000 into five divisions: business support, specialist/technical, journalism, technology, and program-making. Business support positions range from sales, marketing, and advertising to financial services and clerical jobs. The journalism division is made up of broadcasters, editors, and others that work directly with reporting and producing the news. Specialist and technical personnel fill production roles such as camera, lights, sound, makeup, and editing. The technology division includes information technology and broadcast engineering functions. Producers, directors, and others directly involved in the production of BBC services make up the program-making department.

The BBC wishes to attract creative and talented people that represent all segments of the population that the organization serves. The majority of the positions are in London, and with more than 10,000 applications every year, the competition for jobs is fierce. To assist in finding quality employees, the BBC operates several programs, including the BBC Talent Initiative, geared to find actors, comedians, writers, and program-makers. The BBC also provides a mentoring program that allows students to learn more about the BBC and includes a two-week work assignment. Trainee programs, traditional course education, and online learning are also available.

SOURCES OF INFORMATION

Bibliography

Bashford, Suzy. "BBC Four Reveals 'Sophisticated' Identity." *Marketing*, (London). 28 February 2002.

"Britain: The Perils of Popularity: the BBC." *The Economist*, 12 January 2002.

Cox, David. "For a Proper Public Service, Try Murdoch." *New Statesman*, 25 February 2002.

Garrahan, Matthew and Ashling O'Connor. "ITV and BBC to Step Up Digital Coalition Talks." *The Financial Times*, 25 March 2002.

Grant, Tina, and Jay P. Pederson, eds. *International Directory of Company Histories* Vol. 21. Detroit: St. James Press, 1998.

Hargreaves, Ian. "In Conversation with Greg Dyke." *The Financial Times*, 2 April 2002.

Marquis, Simon. "Privatisation Could be the Key to Unravelling BBC's Dual Identity." *Marketing* (London), 28 March 2002.

Riding, Alan. "What Price Success for a Newly Popular BBC?" *New York Times*, 3 February 2002.

Rogers, Daniel. "Advertisers Claim BBC Three Victory." *Marketing*, (London), 14 March 2002.

———. "BBC Three: The Battle Goes On." *Marketing*, (London), 21 March 2002.

For additional industry research:

Investigate companies by their Standard Industrial Classification Codes, also known as SICs. British Broadcasting Corporation's primary SICs are:

4832 Radio Broadcasting

4833 Television Broadcasting

Also investigate companies by their North American Industry Classification System Codes, also known as NAICS codes. British Broadcasting Corporation's primary NAICS codes are:

513112 Radio Stations

513120 Television Broadcasting

Cargill Inc.

FOUNDED: 1867

Contact Information:
HEADQUARTERS: PO Box 9300
    Minneapolis, MN 55440-9300
PHONE: (952)742-7575
FAX: (952)742-7393
URL: http://www.cargill.com

OVERVIEW

The largest privately owned corporation in the United States, Cargill operates a myriad of businesses related to the international marketing, processing, and distribution of agricultural, food, industrial, and financial products and services. With approximately 90,000 employees located in 57 countries, Cargill participates in its foundational business of commodities trading. Other business ventures include commodities transportation; supplier of feed, seed, fertilizer, and other agricultural products; processor of food ingredient, such as corn syrup and flour, and name brand meat and poultry products; industrial supplier of goods such as steel, salt, and polymers; and financial and technical services. Originally known as a commodities trader, by the mid-1990s, Cargill had successfully diversified its interests, with an increasing focus on products and services related to the food and ingredient industry by providing solutions in supply chain management and food applications, as well as health and nutrition.

COMPANY FINANCES

As a privately owned corporation, Cargill is not required to disclose financial information to the public. Traditionally, Cargill releases very limited financial performance figures. Annual sales for fiscal year ending May 31, 2001, totaled $49.4 billion, compared to $47.6 billion, $45.7 billion, and $51.4 billion in 2000, 1999, and 1998, respectively. Net income for fiscal year 2001 was $358 million, compared to $480 million, $597 million, and $468 million in 2000, 1999, and 1998, respectively. More than 25 percent of total revenues for fiscal year 2001 were generated by international business units. For the third quarter ending February 28, 2002, Cargill reported $161 million in earnings, up from $99 million reported for the same period of the previous year. During the first three quarters of fiscal 2002, Cargill showed a net income of $683 million, a 53 percent increase over the $445 million posted for the first nine months of the previous fiscal year.

HISTORY

William Wallace Cargill opened his first flat grain house in Conover, Iowa, in 1865. Following the expansion of the railroad, the company grew rapidly in the post-Civil War years. Upon Cargill's death in 1909, his son-in-law, John McMillan, took over control and ran the company until 1936. During his years at the helm, he established Cargill as a leader in the industry. Although he was conservative in his investment strategy, he made several bold moves to put the company at the head of the pack. When East Coast grain brokers moved into the Midwest, MacMillan took Cargill operations into New York. With operations firmly in place in Iowa, Minnesota, and North Dakota, and quickly spreading East, MacMillan also instituted an international export department, opening foreign offices in Canada, Italy, and Argentina. In 1930 the company's name was changed to Cargill Inc.

In 1936 MacMillan's son, John Jr., became Cargill's president. Under the younger MacMillan's aggressive leadership, the company continued to expand both nationally and internationally at a rapid pace. MacMillan also entered into the shipbuilding business after he failed to convince other builders to construct his newly designed improved barge. By the beginning of World War II, 60 percent of revenues were being generated by foreign operations. As a result, the onset of the war devastated the company. Although the shipbuilding division filled government contracts, the grain business was seriously hurt when it was cut off from its international markets. Cargill responded by aggressively diversifying its interests, moving into the fields of vegetable oil and animal feed. By the end of the 1940s, the company owned animal-feed producer Nutrena and had greatly increased its interest in soybean processing and high-fructose corn syrup as well as safflower and sunflower oils.

During the 1950 Cargill's international profits exploded. Its newly established Swiss subsidiary Tradax developed into a major power in the European market, and Cargill's 13-million-bushel grain elevator in Quebec gave the company a distinct market advantage during the long winter months. Cargill also instituted the profitable policy of backhauling. For example, a barge carrying grain to Quebec would return loaded with coal, and a barge shipping to New Orleans would return loaded with salt. Additionally, Cargill's animal feed and corn syrup divisions were producing their own substantive profits.

FAST FACTS:
About Cargill Inc.

Ownership: Cargill Inc. is a privately owned corporation.

Officers: Warren Staley, Chmn. and CEO; Gregory R. Page, Pres. and COO; Robert L. Lumpkins, VP and CFO

Employees: 90,000

Principal Subsidiary Companies: Cargill maintains an extremely large portfolio of businesses around the world.

Chief Competitors: Cargill's competitors include ADM, Bunge Limited, and Corn Products International.

When the Soviet Union purchased 20 million tons of wheat from the United States in 1972, Cargill provided 1 million tons at a loss to the company. However, the famous grain sale that reopened trade relations between the United States and the Soviet Union combined with a drought created increased demand and decreased supply, thus driving up the prices. As a result, Cargill's revenues soared, growing from $2.2 billion in 1971 to $28.5 billion in 1981.

The 1980s brought new challenges to the now mammoth-sized company. Although the entire company remained financially stable, the grain merchandising division suffered from a 1980 U.S. embargo on grain sales to the Soviet Union. As a result, throughout the decade sales fell short of target numbers. Company leadership was another growing concern. MacMillan and other senior executives were nearing retirement with no obvious leaders waiting in line. To ensure the future health of the company, MacMillan ordered an extensive overhaul of the company in 1990. Organizational and management structures were revamped to spur new ideas and new growth opportunities. In 1991 employees were given the opportunity to purchase Cargill stock, and for the first time in its long history Cargill, ceased to be owned only by the Cargills and MacMillans.

In an attempt to protect itself from the volatility of the grain market, during the 1990s Cargill began extend its operations to process its commodities into name-brand products. The company became involved in meatpacking as well as consumer-sale ready chicken and turkeys.

Even running at full capacity, Cargill's salt mine in Cleveland, Ohio, can't meet demands for road salt. (AP Photo/Tony Dejak)

Another area of growth that provided highly profitable was the expansion of the financial markets division. In the mid-1990s Cargill's financial services accounted for more than a quarter of the company's earnings. Diversification did not mean that Cargill abandoned its grain operations, which also continued to grow. During the late 1990s, the company opened, acquired, or expanded grain and fertilizer businesses in the United States, South Africa, South America, and Asia. At the turn of the century, Cargill had become the largest privately owned corporation in the United States.

STRATEGY

Since the early 1990s, Cargill has been shifting its business focus away from commodities trading toward diversification of its portfolio of businesses. At the turn of the twenty-first century, the company made a bold commitment to venture on a distinctly different path by committing itself to becoming a premier provider of solutions and products to food and agricultural customers. Traditionally known as a secretive company with a vast worldwide network that maintained a diligent eye on fluctuating prices in commodities around the globe, Cargill is set to give its company an image makeover, to become more dynamic and approachable in relationship to its customers and to the public. Along with a new logo and advertising campaign, Cargill expects to achieve its

transformation by engaging its employees, satisfying its customers, enriching the communities it serves, and maintaining profitable growth.

Utilizing the theme "Cargill. Nourishing Potential," Cargill launched a new advertising campaign in January of 2002. One print ad featured a small girl holding a book as she stands alone in the middle of a vast library. The text reads: "We are born into a world of unlimited possibilities. Every one of us has the potential to do great things. All we require is the proper nourishment of mind and body. Cargill believes strongly in the role of food in human advancement. Because the better we are fed, the more we hunger to achieve." By humanizing its giant-corporation image, Cargill is moving away from focusing on results and productivity as exemplified by its previous advertising tag line: It's not just what we do. It's how we do it." Rather than emphasizing what the company does, the advertisements show what the company enables; if people are well-fed, they are better able to achieve their full potential.

INFLUENCES

With a global presence in 57 countries and more than 25 percent of revenues being generated outside of the United States, Cargill is affected by a host of economic, political, and social factors. For example, the company's beef processing business was negatively impacted by a slowdown in the U.S. economy during 2001 as well as a weak export market demand for beef and beef byproducts. Also, the politically unsettled situation in Argentina, leading to economic and social upheaval, impacted Cargill, which has had a significant presence in the country for more than 55 years. Cargill's well-diversified product offerings, as well as the size and diversity of its customer base, allow the company to withstand economic problems in individual business segments.

CURRENT TRENDS

Cargill has seen significant growth in its food and ingredient business in both the North American and European markets. Animal nutrition; the egg, poultry, and pork processing business segments; and grain and oilseed exports have all provided positive profit results. Taking a proactive stance toward its customers, Cargill is pushing to discern and met its customer's needs. From the farm to the table, the company is striving to push beyond simply supplying products to providing service and solutions to its customers.

Cargill's acquisition in 2001 of the Paris-based Cerestar, a worldwide leader in starch and starch derivatives, displays Cargill's advancement in the food application industry. In another new venture, Cargill is teaming with Hormel Foods Corp. to produce and market branded, case-ready fresh beef and pork items under Hormel's label. This new "Always Tender" line of products combines Cargill's access to high-quality meat and Hormel's processing, distribution, and marketing experience.

In Cargill's crop businesses, the company advances the use of biotechnology to enhance crop production. Genetically enhanced grains, which have sparked controversy, are accepted by Cargill's grain elevators, oilseed-processing plants, and corn wet mills. During 2001 Cargill announced the development of a biodegradable polymer made from corn, called polylactic acid (PLA). Named "Technology of the Year" by the U.S. Department of Energy, PLA could replace traditional nonbiodegradable plastics for such uses as carpet materials, disposable cups, and product packaging. The product, which takes 45 to 60 days to break down under the heat and pressure of a landfill, could reduce the demand for 8 billion tons of plastics annually and cut carbon dioxide admissions by 10 million tons by 2020.

PRODUCTS

Cargill's wide array of products and services can be segmented into four broad categories: agricultural supplier, industrial producer, commodities trader, and financial and technical services provider. Cargill is a leader in

CHRONOLOGY:
Key Dates for Cargill Inc.

1865: Brothers William and Sam Cargill form W. W. Cargill and Brother in Lime Springs, Iowa, opening a grain flat house and a lumberyard; moves to Austin, Minnesota, the following year

1890: James Cargill, another brother, joins company; renamed Cargill Elevator Company and offices moved to Minneapolis

1895: William Cargill's daughter marries John Hugh MacMillan, who later forces out Cargill and gains control of the company

1936: Accused of trying to corner the corn market and refusing a request to sell its corn supplies, Cargill's membership is revoked by the Board of Trade

1945: Cargill purchases Nutrena, an animal feed producer

1960: Opens a 13-million-bushel elevator in Quebec

1972: Cargill sells 1 million tons of grain to Russia as part of a 20-million-ton sale made by the United States

1981: Sales reach $28.5 billion, up from $2.2 billion in 1971

1990: Company undergoes major restructuring

1991: Employee stock purchase option ends long history of total ownership by Cargill and MacMillan families

1995: Revenues reach $671 million on record sales of $51 billion

2000: Announces plans to build state-of-the-art facility in Blair, Nebraska, that will use dextrose derived from corn to make polymers for fibers and plastic packaging

the field of agricultural product development and supply, offering a wide variety of feed, fertilizers, and other agricultural supplies. Along with livestock feed and pet food, other agricultural products and services include agricultural salt products used as a livestock feed supplement; the production, marketing, storage, and transportation of fertilizer products; cattle feedlot operations; consultation, management, and technical assistance services in all aspects of agricultural and agribusiness development,

FINANCES:

Cargill, Incorporated
Sales, 1998-2001
(million dollars)

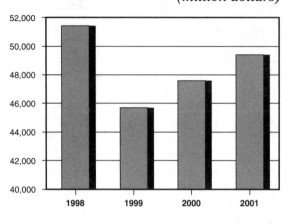

THE CARGILLS AND THE MACMILLANS

In Cargill's early existence, its founder, William Wallace Cargill, made the company a family affair, forming partnerships with his brothers Samuel and James. With Sam he created W. W. Cargill and Brother, and James ran businesses in North Dakota and Minnesota with partner John D. MacMillan until he and MacMillan sold out to William in 1882. Six years later James joined his two brothers to form Cargill Brothers. Headquarters were moved to Minneapolis, Minnesota, in 1890, and the name was changed to Cargill Elevator Company. In 1895 Cargill's daughter married John Hugh MacMillan and, later, his son William S. Cargill also married into the MacMillan family. When Cargill died in 1909, his son-in-law took over the company and forced the younger Cargill out of the company. The ensuing battle, which lasted a decade, resulted in a long-standing feud between the two families, with MacMillan eventually retaining control of the company. The MacMillan family continues to hold the majority of the company, with the Cargill family owning a minority interest.

natural resource management, and rural development; development of new agricultural products; corn wet milling operation, which produces and markets sweeteners and food and industrial starches; flouring wet milling operations, which supply wholesale, retail, and export markets; malting plants; cereal mills; cocoa and cocoa product processing; oranges, apples, and peanut processing; soybean, sunflower seed, rapeseed, corn, palm, and cottonseed processing for meal and oil; and beef, pork, and poultry processing.

Cargill's industrial business units provide goods and services that include small, efficient steel mills that produce merchant grade and special bar quality rounds, wire rods, reinforcing bars, seamless pipes, and flat-rolled steel; custom steel cutting services; concrete reinforcing wire, chain link fencing, wire mesh, and industrial wire production; industrial grade starches used in paper production; ethanol processing for use in reformulated gasoline; industrial and retail supplier of rock, as well as solar- and process-evaporated salt; phosphate mining and manufacturing of phosphate fertilizers; and industrial oils and lubricant processing for use in paints, inks, lubricants, pharmaceuticals, and specialty chemicals.

Cargill has a long-standing tradition as an important leader in the commodities market. Cargill purchases harvested grains and oilseeds directly from farmers, which are stored until ready to be shipped in bulk around the globe. The corporations maintains an impressive network of trading offices in the United States, Latin America, Europe, Africa, Asia, and the Pacific Rim. Cargill also trades cocoa and cocoa products, cotton, rice, palm and coconut oil, raw and processed sugar, tallow, crude and

refined petroleum products, natural gas, and electricity, iron and finished steels. To transport its products, Cargill uses a group of trucks, barges, railroad cars, and ships, which are either company-owned or operated under lease agreements.

As a provider of financial and technical services, Cargill relies on its long history and vast experience in risk management and investing. The Financial Markets group provides services to Cargill and its subsidiaries with a full spectrum of financial products and services, including money markets, value investing, and trade and structured finance.

CORPORATE CITIZENSHIP

In 2001 Cargill received the Points of Light Foundation's Award for Excellence in Corporate Community Service, which recognized Cargill's contributions and commitment to developing effective volunteer programs for its employees to serve in the community where they work. Cargill's corporate environment, health, and safety goals include zero deaths or major injuries due to work-related accidents; lowered disability frequency; and zero fires, explosions, or release of harmful materials. Each year Cargill honors individual businesses within the corporation with the President's Award for excellence in the areas of the environment and health and safety.

GLOBAL PRESENCE

Cargill operates in 59 countries around the world. For example, Cargill opened its first business in Argentina in 1947 and is now one of the largest agribusinesses in the country, with more than 30 locations, more than 1,800 employees, and total investments of $325 million. In Brazil, plants, warehouses, offices, port terminals, and farms total more than 120, located in 18 Brazilian states. Kenya is the home of Cargill's tea processing, packing, and exporting activities, where 6 percent of the world's traded tea is handled each year. Cargill entered Mexico during the 1920s and now has operational investments valued at $184 million.

EMPLOYMENT

With approximately 90,000 employees, Cargill offers a wide range of career paths with opportunities in advanced and entry-level positions. Although most positions are available in the United States, Cargill also offers numerous opportunities at it European facilities. The company's Web site has detailed job listings.

SOURCES OF INFORMATION

Bibliography

"Cargill 3Q Earnings Rise 63%." *FWN Select*, 16 April 2002.

"Cargill Adopts New Brand Logo." *Feedstuffs*, 25 February 2002.

"Cargill and Hormel to Establish Joint Venture." *The New York Times*, 30 April 2002.

"Cargill Inc." *The Wall Street Journal*, 17 April 2002.

"Cargill Launches New Brand Strategy." *Agri Marketing*, April 2002.

Cottrill, Ken. "Spread the Word: Cargill Creates Supply-Chain Management Center for 'Internal Outsourcing,' External Revenue Stream." *Traffic World*, 25 February 2002.

Fahey, Jonathan. "Shucking Petroleum." *Forbes*, 26 November 2001.

"Food Move Pays Off for Cargill." *Eurofood*, 31 January 2002.

"Plastic as High as an Elephant's Eye." *Business Week*, 9 July 2001.

Smith, Rod. "Cargill Cites Broad, Global Base of Businesses." *Feedstuffs*, 22 April 2002.

"U.S. Consumers Get a Sweet New Option." *PR Newswire*, 29 May 2002.

For additional industry research:

Investigate companies by their Standard Industrial Classification Codes, also known as SICs. Cargill's primary SICs are:

2013 Sausages & Other Prepared Meat Product

2015 Poultry Slaughtering & Processing

2041 Flour And Other Grain Mill Products

2044 Rice Milling

2046 Wet Corn Milling

2074 Cottonseed Oil Mills

2076 Vegetable Oil Mills

3312 Blast Furnaces And Steel Mills

3441 Fabricated Structural Metal

6221 Commodity Contracts Brokers & Dealers

Also investigate companies by their North American Industry Classification System Codes, also known as NAICS codes. Cargill's primary NAICS codes are:

311211 Flour Milling

311212 Rice Milling

311221 Wet Corn Milling

311225 Fats and Oils Refining and Blending

311612 Meat Processed from Carcasses

311615 Poultry Processing

331111 Iron and Steel Mills

332312 Fabricated Structural Metal Manufacturing

Carver Bancorp Inc.

FOUNDED: 1948

Contact Information:
HEADQUARTERS: 75 W. 125th St.
New York, NY 10027-4512
FAX: (212)426-6159
PHONE: (212)876-4747
URL: http://www.carverbank.com

OVERVIEW

The largest minority-owned financial institution in the United States, Carver Bancorp Inc. offers traditional banking services to African Americans and other minority groups via its five Carver Federal Savings Bank branches in New York City. The firm struggled to maintain profitability throughout the 1990s and underwent a series of management changes. It also successfully defended itself against various takeover attempts. Financial troubles continued into the early 2000s.

COMPANY FINANCES

Sales for Carver Bancorp grew 4.3 percent to $31.2 million in 2001. Although the firm posted a loss of $400,000 that year, its financial status was actually more solid than in the previous two years. In 2000 Carver had lost $1.1 million, and in 1999 it had lost $4.5 million. Assets for Carver grew from $420.1 million in 2000 to $424.5 million in 2001; despite two consecutive years of growth, assets remained lower than their peak of $437.5 million in 1998. After reaching a high of $17.50 per share in late 1997, stock prices fell to $8.50 per share in 1998 and to $7.30 per share in late 2000.

ANALYSTS' OPINIONS

The 1990s proved to be a tumultuous time for Carver Bancorp Inc. as it fended off takeover attempts and experienced a series of management shakeups. Losses

FINANCES:

Carver Bancorp Inc.
Net Incomes, 1997-2001
(million dollars)

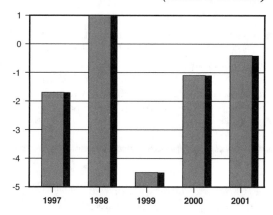

FAST FACTS:

About Carver Bancorp Inc.

Ownership: Carver Bancorp Inc. is a publicly owned company traded on the American Stock Exchange.

Ticker Symbol: CNY

Officers: Frederick O. Terrell, Chmn.; Deborah C. Wright, Pres., CEO, and Dir.; William C. Gray, SVP and CFO

Principal Subsidiary Companies: Carver Bancorp Inc. is the holding company for Carver Federal Savings Bank, which operates five branches in New York City.

Chief Competitors: Competitors to Carver Bancorp include banking industry giants such as Bank of New York, Citigroup, and J.P. Morgan Chase, all three of which have started to compete directly with Carver by targeting minority populations such as African Americans.

---

mounted, stock prices plummeted, and industry analysts began to wonder just how long the firm could function independently. Of major concern to analysts was the increased competition for minority business coming from the industry's largest players. As stated in a January 2000 issue of *Crain's New York Business*, competition was no longer "just from other ethnic-focused banks, but from big guys like Chase and Bank One, which see this as an expanding market. . . .The whole notion of whether an ethnically focused bank can work is in question." Despite its struggles, Carver remained first on *Black Enterprise*'s list of banks and on its Black Stock Index in the early 2000s.

HISTORY

Carver was created in 1949 as a savings and loan bank serving African Americans living in Harlem and the rest of New York City. The bank was named after African-American inventor George Washington Carver. Like most other banks serving minority groups, Carver focused mainly on securities, rather than loans. Its services were limited to savings and checking accounts and other standard banking functions. As a result, when the Community Reinvestment Act was passed in 1977 and traditional banks began to target poor neighborhoods, Carver found itself struggling to compete with the broad ranger of services offered by the larger banking firms. The firm established its first automated teller machine (ATM) in 1989.

To raise money for expansion, the bank conducted an initial public offering (IPO) in 1994. By then, seven branches were in operation throughout New York. Stock

prices began to fall shortly after the IPO, and the threat of takeover became imminent. As a result, Carver hired Thomas L. Clark, Jr. as CEO, charging him with the task of keeping Carver independent, despite shareholder demands that the board make the decision to sell the bank. A buyout offer from investment banker Joseph Curry was turned down by Carver's board in 1996. Under Clark's guidance, Carver began to increase its number of loans. The firm also launched a loan program backed by the Small Business Administration, established some mortgage lending offices, and recruited a marketing executive to identify and pursue new institutional clients, such as African-American churches, as well as more traditional customers. Recognizing that mortgage loans were more lucrative than the securities upon which Carver had traditionally relied, Clark also led Carver's purchase of roughly $150 million worth of existing mortgages from Countrywide Home Loans and Chase Manhattan Bank.

When Carver posted a $5.7 million quarterly loss in December of 1998, the board decided to replace him. Deborah C. Wright was hired as his successor in January of the following year. Within two years, Wright had replaced each of the firm's senior executives, as well as nearly 50 percent of its workforce. Boston Bank of Commerce, which owned 7 percent of Carver, made two unsolicited bids, the last one totaling $29.78 million, for Carver in April 1999. Carver's board rejected the offer,

CHRONOLOGY:

Key Dates for Carver Bancorp Inc.

1948: Carver Bancorp Inc. is established in Harlem

1989: Carver begins offering ATM services

1994: The firm completes its IPO

1995: Thomas L. Clark, Jr. is hired as CEO

1999: Deborah C. Wright takes over as CEO

2000: Carver begins a first-time home buyers mortgage program

and a bitter battle among the company's shareholders ensued.

In 2000, Carver secured a $2.5 million loan from Morgan Stanley Dean Witter & Co. and Provender Capital Group. The firm planned to use the money to broaden its product base with new online and telephone-based banking services, as well as a debit card. In 2001 Carver sold the two of its seven branches that served middle-class neighborhoods and began looking to open new units in inner city neighborhoods. Chief financial officer James Boyle, hired in early 2000 to help restore Carver to profitability, resigned in June 2001. William C. Gray succeeded Boyle in January 2002.

STRATEGY

In an effort to boost profits, Carver began issuing a growing number of loans—including car loans, consumer loans, and credit cards—in the mid-1990s. As a result, by early 1997 the bank's loan-asset ratio had increased to 47 percent, compared to 17 percent in 1993; this ratio grew to 55 percent in 1998. However, the firm's focus on consumer lending, a strategic decision prompted by shareholder demands for improved profitability, proved disastrous. Carver did not have a staff experienced in these types of consumer lending, which caused a variety of problems for the firm. According to *Crain's New York Business*, Carver's "stock plunged in 1998 as an expansion into consumer lending, including auto loans and credit cards, increased costs and produced a high percentage of defaults. The bad loans resulted in a $7.8 million charge in fiscal 1999, ended March 31, and the resignation of its CEO." Negative press continued when

TRUE COMMITMENT

The location of Carver Bancorp Inc.'s headquarters, on Harlem's well-known 125th St., is a reflection of the bank's commitment to serving inner city neighborhoods. Although Carver's headquarters burned down in 1992, the firm chose to rebuild in Harlem, which remains one of the more poverty-stricken neighborhoods in New York City.

one Carver executive was arrested and charged with defrauding the bank. Although Carver's stock did recover somewhat in later months, it failed to return to its $17.50 per share high of late 1997. Despite these problems, Carver continued with its strategy of increasing its loan-asset ratio, which grew to 67 percent in 2001. That year, loans originated by Carver rose to $30.5 million, compared to $4.6 million in 2000. Helping to improve the firm's performance in the early 2000s was its establishment and enforcement of stricter rules regarding delinquent loans.

Carver launched a major print and radio advertising campaign in late 2000. The campaign centered around the firm's new slogan, "Profit from the Partnership," and focused on two new products: a nine-month certificate of deposit (CD) and a first-time home buyers mortgage program. Carver sought to attract new clients wishing to "declare financial independence." The campaign also allowed Carver to showcase its 50-year anniversary, a milestone for a minority-focused bank.

INFLUENCES

A major cause of Carver's financial troubles in the 1980s and 1990s was its structure as a traditional minority bank. Like other minority banks, Carver's headquarters building was located in a major metropolitan area, which meant operating costs were much higher than those of banks operating from less pricey areas. In addition, Carver's banking activities were limited to offering standard savings and checking accounts and investments in money market funds and securities, neither of which produced high returns. For most banks, the interest paid on loans proves to be a major source of profits. Because Carver's loan-asset ratio (the percentage of assets attributable to loans), was a mere 17 percent in 1993, Carver struggled to generate enough revenue to cover expenses.

This prompted the firm's decision to increase its loan offerings in the mid-1990s.

PRODUCTS

Carver offers traditional checking and savings accounts; a range of investment vehicles, such as CDs and Individual Retirement Accounts (IRAs); money market accounts; mortgage loans; auto loans; consumer loans; and business loans. Online banking services and a debit card are scheduled for launch in mid-2002.

CORPORATE CITIZENSHIP

Via the Carver Federal Scholarship Fund, Carver Bancorp Inc. offers annual college tuition scholarships, worth up to $3000, to its customers and their family members.

SOURCES OF INFORMATION

Bibliography

Agosta, Veronica. "At Carver, the CEO Has Control; Now Comes the Hardest Part." *American Banker*, 30 October 2000.

Carver Bancorp Inc. Home Page, 2002. Available at http://www.carverbank.com.

Gandel, Stephen. "2 Minority Focused Banks Put Money on NY Expansion." *Crain's New York Business*, 17 January 2000.

Oestricher, Dwight. "Carver's in for a Fight." *Black Enterprise*, January 1999.

Smith, Eric L. "Financial News: A Deal to Bank On." *Black Enterprise*, May 1998.

Sullivan, Joanna. "Carver, Slowly Reviving, Doesn't Lack for Critics." *American Banker*, 19 May 1997.

Whiteman, Louis. "Carver Rejects Sweetened Bid from Persistent Boston Suitor." *American Banker*, 21 April 1999.

For additional industry research:

Investigate companies by their Standard Industrial Classification codes, also known as SICs. Carver Bancorp Inc.'s primary SICs are:

6035 Savings Institutions Federal Chartered

6712 Bank Holding Companies

Also investigate companies by their North American Industry Classification System codes, also known as NAICS codes. Carver Bancorp Inc.'s primary NAICS codes are:

522120 Savings Institutions

551111 Offices of Bank Holding Companies

Chanel S.A.

FOUNDED: 1910

Contact Information:

HEADQUARTERS: 135, Avenue Charles de Gaulle
   Neuilly-sur-Seine Cedex, 92521 France
PHONE: 33-1-46-43-4000
FAX: 33-1-47-47-6034
URL: http://www.chanel.com

OVERVIEW

Based in France, Chanel S.A. is a fashion design firm known for innovations such as the "little black dress," tweed suits, and two-tone pumps. Along with clothing and shoes, Chanel also sells cosmetics and fragrance lines at its 100 boutiques across the globe. One of the firm's most famous products is the Chanel No. 5 fragrance. Efforts in the late 1990s and early 2000s to target younger women and men helped revitalize the Chanel name.

COMPANY FINANCES

Despite its status as one of the top ten cosmetics makers in the world, Chanel held only 1.2 percent of the global cosmetics market in 2000, compared to the 16.8 percent held by leader L'Oreal SA. Chanel's cosmetics sales that year totaled $413.3 million. The firm was also the world's seventh-largest maker of fragrances, with sales of $570.4 million and a market share of 2.8 percent in that sector in 2000.

HISTORY

Chanel has at its roots the creation of a millinery (hat shop), in Paris, France, by Coco Chanel in 1910. The new shop, called Chanel Modes, began to attract attention when well-known French actresses began wearing Chanel hats. In 1913, Chanel expanded with a clothing boutique in Deauville. Two years later, Chanel opened a

FAST FACTS:
About Chanel S.A.

Ownership: Chanel S.A. is private company owned by the Wertheimer family.

Officers: Alain Wertheimer, Chmn.; Francoise Montenay, CEO and Pres.; Arie Kopelman, Pres. and COO, Chanel Inc.

Principal Subsidiary Companies: Chanel S.A. operates U.S.-based Chanel Inc., as well as other subsidiaries around the world.

Chief Competitors: Competitors to Chanel S.A.'s products include fashion and beauty brands such as Gucci, Prada, L'Oreal SA, and LVMH.

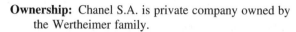

fashion house in Biarritz. *Harper's Bazaar* featured a Chanel dress design for the first time in 1916.

The Chanel No. 5 fragrance was released in 1921. Three years later, Chanel began to sell jewelry and beauty products, along with perfume and clothing. *Vogue* referred to Chanel's "little black dress," unveiled in 1926, as the "new uniform of the modern woman." The first Chanel tweed suits made their debut in 1928. By then, Chanel's simple clothing designs, in many cases modeled after men's clothing, had become accepted as a more casual option for women than the traditional fashion of the time. Chanel's designs also helped make the use of fabrics like chamois more commonplace. An accessories department was added to the fashion house the following year. Roughly 4,000 employees worked for Chanel by 1935.

Chanel shut down in 1939 when France entered World War II. The firm reopened again in 1954, after Coco Chanel, at the age of 74, returned to France from Switzerland. Her suits and simple black dresses became some of the most well-known designs in the fashion industry. In the mid-1950s, Chanel's quilted purse with the shoulder strap became an industry standard. Coco Chanel was named the most influential designer of the twentieth century at the Fashion Oscar awards in Dallas, Texas, in 1957. After her death in 1971, the firm struggled to find someone to fill the shoes of its legendary designer. Chanel began to distribute its accessories on a worldwide basis in the late 1970s. The firm moved into Korea in 1979, opening a shop in the well-to-do city of Pusan. Chanel's widower, Arie Kopelman, was hired by Alain Wertheimer (whose family owned Chanel by then)

DESPITE A 15-YEAR HIATUS, CHANEL MAKES A COMEBACK

When World War II arrived in France in 1939, Coco Chanel decided to shutter operations. After the war ended in 1945, Chanel was exiled to Switzerland when her affair with a Nazi soldier during the War was discovered by French authorities. Chanel lived in Switzerland until 1954. Despite the scandal, she was able to reopen a successful business upon her return.

to take the reins of Chanel Inc., the firm's new U.S. subsidiary, in 1985. Two years later, Chanel diversified into watches for the first time.

The Egoiste fragrance for men was released in the early 1990s. In 1993 Chanel added fine jewelry to its product lineup when it unveiled a new collection of jewelry and watches in Paris. The firm released the Allure fragrance in 1996. Chanel and famous French hairdresser Frederic Fekkai created a joint venture in 1997; the Frederic Fekkai Beaute began selling hair care products and fragrances in New York that year. Chanel forged its first licensing agreement ever in 1999, allowing eyeglasses giant Luxottica to distribute Chanel sunglasses. The deal increased the number of places selling Chanel eyewear from 200 Chanel boutiques to roughly 5,000 retail outlets. The reason for Chanel's reticence in licensing its brand to other retailers had been its desire to maintain an image of exclusivity for its products.

Boutiques featuring handbags and shoes made their debut in Paris in 1999. Two years later, Chanel opened similar shops in the United States. Plans for a 3,000-square-foot fine jewelry shop on Madison Avenue in New York City were also launched by Chanel Inc. in 2001. That year, Macys.com began to sell Chanel, Estee Lauder, and Clinique beauty products via its Web site.

STRATEGY

Chanel faced heightened competition in both Europe and North America from a growing number of luxury clothing and accessory lines, such as Christian Dior, Fendi, Gucci, Louis Vitton, and Prada in the 1990s. In the cosmetics sector, firms like Bobby Brown and MAC began to steal market share. Designer Karl

CHRONOLOGY:
Key Dates for Chanel S.A.

1910: Coco Chanel opens her first boutique

1921: Chanel releases the Chanel No. 5 fragrance

1979: Coco Chanel dies

1985: Chanel Inc. is founded in the United States

1999: The firm allows Luxottica to sell Chanel sunglasses

2001: Macys.com begins selling Chanel beauty products

Lagerfeld, who had been hired in 1983, began to focus on marketing the Chanel brand to a younger, more hip market. Lagerfeld added separates to the firm's traditional line of suits and expanded its handbag and shoe offerings to include less expensive options. A new skin care line, dubbed Precision, made its debut in mid-1999. In North America, Kopelman made the decision to pour more dollars into advertising, particularly for the 26 new skin care products. In fact, Chanel Inc. spent roughly $20 million on the Precision launch and upped its fashion and beauty marketing budgets by at least 20 percent. This strategy also included the upgrading of several Chanel boutiques in the United States and Asia to appeal to younger shoppers. Chanel's "plan to put a fresh focus on its brand around the world," paid off, according to an August 2000 issue of *WWD*: "Chanel is enjoying a resurgence worldwide with its glamorous, ladylike styles."

PRODUCTS

Chanel sells suits, dresses, separates, an extensive line of skin care products, hair care products, sunglasses, handbags, shoes, and other fashion accessories. A line of men's and women's fragrances includes Allure, Egoiste, Chanel No. 5 and Coco Mademoiselle, launched in 2001. Subsidiary Eres manufactures beachwear and lingerie in France.

A FASHION REVOLUTION

Coco Chanel began to design her own clothes because she was unable to afford the expensive clothes that were in fashion early in the twentieth century. At first, she made clothes simply for herself and her friends. She modeled her early designs after the clothing worn by men during different sporting events, such as horse racing. The fabric and styles she chose for her early clothing lines revolutionized European fashion in the 1920s.

SOURCES OF INFORMATION

Bibliography
Aktar, Alev. "At Chanel: Catching Arie's Act." *WWD*, 29 June 2000.

Chanel S.A. Home Page, 2002. Available at http://www.chanel.com.

Daswani, Kavita. "Chanel's Asian Extravaganza." *WWD*, 24 August 2000.

Raper, Sarah. "Chanel Signs Its First Licensing Agreement." *WWD*, 10 May 1999.

Sauer, Pamela. "A Makeover of Global Proportions." *Chemical Market Reporter*, 3 December 2001.

Wilson, Marc. "New Gem on Madison; Chanel Melds 5 Stores for Mega Jewel Box." *WWD*, 2 May 2001.

For additional industry research:
Investigate companies by their Standard Industrial Classification codes, also known as SICs. Chanel S.A.'s primary SICs are:

2331 Women's, Misses' & Juniors' Blouses and Shirts

2339 Women's, Misses' & Juniors' Outerwear, Not Elsewhere Classified

2844 Perfumes & Cosmetics

Also investigate companies by their North American Industry Classification System codes, also known as NAICS codes. Chanel S.A.'s primary NAICS codes are:

315232 Women's and Girl's Cut & Sewn Blouse & Shirt Manufacturers

315234 Women's and Girl's Cut & Sewn Suit, Coat, Tailored Jacket, and Skirt Manufacturers

325620 Toilet Preparation Manufacturing

ChevronTexaco Corporation

FOUNDED: 1926

OVERVIEW

Incorporated in 1926 as Standard Oil Company of California, the company adopted the name Chevron Corporation in 1984 and became ChevronTexaco in 2001 after acquiring Texaco Corporation.

ChevronTexaco Corporation, a global energy company, is the number two integrated oil company, behind ExxonMobil. With a presence in 180 countries, its operations include oil, chemical and natural gas businesses. It has reserves of 11.5 billion barrels of oil, produces 2.7 million barrels of oil a day, its global refining capacity is more than 2.2 million barrels a day, and it operates more than 25,000 service stations internationally. Its brands include Chevron, Texaco, and Caltex.

The company's activities include oil and gas exploration and production, refining, marketing and transportation, chemicals manufacturing and sales, and power generation. ChevronTexaco businesses also include a chemical venture, Chevron Phillips Chemicals Co., an interest in Dynegy, Inc., and equity interests in 47 global power projects.

Contact Information:
HEADQUARTERS: 575 Market St.
    San Francisco, CA 94105
PHONE: (415)894-7700
FAX: (415)894-0583
URL: http://www.chevrontexaco.com

COMPANY FINANCES

In 2001, ChevronTexaco revenues were $106.25 billion and net income was $3.93 billion. Before Chevron's merger with Texaco, its revenues were $50.6 million in 2000 and $35.4 million in 1999, and its net income was $5.1 million in 2000 and $2 million in 1999. For Texaco, revenues were $51 million in 2000 and $34.6 million in 1999. Net income was $2.5 million in 2000 and

FAST FACTS:

About ChevronTexaco Corporation

Ownership: ChevronTexaco Corporation is a publicly owned company traded on the New York, Chicago, Pacific, London, and Swiss Stock Exchanges.

Ticker Symbol: CVX

Officers: David O'Reilly, Chmn. and CEO, 54; Glenn Tilton, VChmn., 53; Darald Callahan, EVP Power, Chemicals, and Technology; John Watson, VP and CFO; Harvey Hinman, VP and General Counsel; Raymond Wilcox, Corporate VP and Pres. North America Exploration and Production; George Kirkland, Corporate VP and Pres. ChevronTexaco Overseas Petroleum, Inc.

Employees: 55,763

Principal Subsidiary Companies: ChevronTexaco's principal subsidiaries include two operating companies, International Upstream and North American Upstream, as well as Chevron Phillips Chemicals Co.

Chief Competitors: ChevronTexaco's primary competitors are Amoco Corporation, ExxonMobil Corporation, British Petroleum, Marathon Oil Co., Shell Oil Co., Arco, Phillips Petroleum Co., Dow Chemical, Pennzoil, and Union Carbide.

$35.6 million in 1999. Net income was $2.5 million in 2000 and $1.1 million in 1999.

ANALYSTS' OPINIONS

Analysts observing the merger of Chevron and Texaco as it unfolded during 1999-2001 had long felt that the move was both logical and inevitable in light of other significant mergers that had taken place in the industry in the late 1990s. Additionally, Chevron and Texaco had a relationship that spanned 60 years. The two companies had been the original partners in Aramco, and back in 1936, they entered into a joint venture to form Caltex. Because the two companies had a partnership history, analysts felt the merger would strengthen the new arrangement, as it would most likely help the integration process move more rapidly and ultimately save money. Analysts also felt that the new partnership would help

Chevron and Texaco's business interests in the Middle East, mainly because the two companies would not be working against each other as competitors.

HISTORY

Chevron's beginning goes back to 1879 with the discovery of oil in Pico Canyon near Los Angeles. As a result, the Pacific Oil Company was formed. Two decades later, in 1901, the roots of the Texaco Company were being planted in Beaumont, Texas. This future global corporation had very modest beginnings as a fledging company: it was headquartered in three rooms of a corrugated iron building. As each company grew in size through the years, they helped transform the oil business into an international, high-tech industry.

Chevron would prove to be significantly influential. In 1938, when it was still known as Standard Oil Co. of California, it made a huge oil discovery in Saudia Arabia, which eventually led to the discovery of 52 oil fields and changed the course of history throughout the world. After World War II, the company began a major effort to market Arabian crude oil, which was probably the single most important factor in establishing Chevron as a major multinational company. The company acquired thousands of service stations and terminals on America's East Coast and part ownership of many more throughout Europe, East Africa, and Asia.

Throughout the 20th century, the two companies would partner in business ventures. Finally, in September 2001, the Federal Trade Commission (FTC) allowed the $45 billion merger of Chevron Corp. and Texaco, Inc. The merger was officially completed and announced the following month. Under the terms of an FTC order, Chevron/Texaco was required to divest all of Texaco's interests in two joint ventures, Equilon Enterprises, LLC and Motiva Enterprises, LLC. Texaco was required to divest assets including its one-third interest in the Discovery natural gas pipeline system in the Gulf of Mexico; its interest in the Enterprise fractionating plant in Mont Belvieu, Texas; and its general aviation businesses in 14 states. In the merger agreement, Chevron agreed to acquire all of the outstanding common stock of Texaco in exchange for stock in Chevron.

Also under the terms of the agreement, ChevronTexaco would be headquartered in San Francisco until the second half of 2002, when its headquarters would move to San Ramon, California.

STRATEGY

Since 1989, Chevron has instituted cost-cutting initiatives in the upstream (exploration and production) and downstream (refining and marketing) businesses of the company, and these have had good results. In the 1990s, Chevron's strategy focused on improving financial performance through a list of components: building a committed team to accomplish the corporate mission; accelerating exploration and production growth in international areas; accelerating total growth in the Caspian region, where the countries are in a period of rapid economic growth; generating cash from North American exploration and production operations while maintaining value through sustained production levels; achieving top financial performance in U.S. refining and marketing; continuing to improve competitive financial performance in chemicals while developing and implementing attractive opportunities for growth; being selective in other businesses; and focusing on reducing costs across all activities. Chevron was guided through this strategy by Kenneth Derr, the former CEO who envisioned the plan.

ChevronTexaco's new strategy, developed as a result of the merger, in part builds upon the Derr strategy and has its foundation in a document titled "The ChevronTexaco Way," which establishes the company goals and vision. The document puts forth five "pillars." Essentially, the core of the strategy can be found in the "third pillar," which involves performance or the achievement of sustained world-class performance in four key areas: operational excellence, cost reductions through innovation and technology, investments, and the development of new business opportunities.

In 2001, ChevronTexaco set a goal of reaching 2.5 to 3 percent annual production growth over a five-year period. The company said that international exploration and production would remain the primary drivers for growth. Exploration led to the development of new projects in Latin America, western Africa, the Caspian region and Asia. Also, the company developed 30 upstream projects that include the gas-to-liquid plant and the Agbami field in Nigeria, the Benguela and Belize fields in Angola, and the Doba oil fields in southern Chad. ChevronTexaco planned a major expansion of its project in Kazakhstan that is expected to result in gross oil production of 700,000 barrels a day. In addition, it expected gross liquid production to double to 230,000 barrels a day by 2004 at its Karachaganak gas condensate field.

ChevronTexaco also looked to new technology to help increase growth. In 2002, the company invested approximately $275 million in emerging technologies and significant upgrades of information technology systems. Also, ChevronTexaco has been collaborating with General Motors Corporation to bring gasoline-fed fuel cell vehicles to the market sooner.

In areas of research, the company is seeking ways to develop high performance, environmentally friendly fuels through a partnership with Sasol, a leader in gas-to-liquids technology.

CHRONOLOGY:
Key Dates for ChevronTexaco Corporation

1926: Incorporates as Standard Oil

1938: Makes a large oil discovery in Saudi Arabia

1940: Discovers the Abquaic Field, which has produced more than 7.5 billion barrels of oil

1951: Safaniya, the world's largest offshore field, is discovered

1957: California Shipping Co. is formed

1965: Chevron Shipping Co. is formed

1969: The first very large crude oil carrier, the S.S. John A. McCone, begins service

1976: Chevron switches its tankers from steam to diesel power

1984: Changes name to Chevron Corporation

1991: Institutes condensed work week program

1993: Enters into joint venture with Kazakhstan

1998: Donates to American Red Cross Disaster Relief Fund to help flood victims

2001: Chevron acquires Texaco and becomes ChevronTexaco

INFLUENCES

First and foremost, the oil industry is strongly influenced by government regulation and environmental issues. When an oil spill occurs or the natural habitat is threatened, there is a negative impact on the industry at large. This negative impact will prohibit growth for the industry and as a result affect earnings across the board. To cut down on such risks, Chevron and other oil companies are forming partnerships. These partnerships also offer the companies operational and financial advantages. As a result of this trend, oil companies do not feel threatened by competitors because they are viewed as potential new partners. In 1998 Chevron developed a corporate mergers and acquisitions group specifically for this purpose. This resulted in the Chevron-Texaco merger of 2001. The aim of the merger was for the two companies to establish a joint venture of their global marine and industrial fuels and marine lubricant businesses, which operate in more than 100 countries worldwide.

FINANCES:

ChevronTexaco Corp.
Net Incomes, 2000-2001
(million dollars)

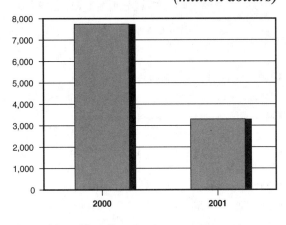

operates six major U.S. refineries and sells petroleum products, primarily gasoline; Global Lubricants, which markets motor oils and other types of lubricants; and Global Aviation, which oversees the marketing of general aviation fuels.

Chevron Products, based in San Ramon, California, has six refineries and 7,900 retail outlets, serving customers in 29 states in the West, Southwest and South. Its major refineries are located in Pascagoula, Mississippi and in Richmond and El Segundo in California. They produce large volumes of gasoline and diesel fuels. Chevron Products' retail network sells the company's patented gasoline additive Techron and offers self-serve pumps that employ FastPay technology, computerized point-of-sale terminals, and a satellite communication network.

The ChevronTexaco Base Oils division produces base oil products for lubricant manufacturers and distributors. Its base oils are high-quality blend stocks used in many products including passenger car motor oils, heavy duty motor oils, industrial engine oils, tractor hydraulic fluids, transmission fluids, gear oils, and greases, among others.

CURRENT TRENDS

During the three years it was involved in proposing, developing and finalizing the merger, ChevronTexaco still managed to score some impressive achievements that will impact the company's future direction. In 2001, it replaced 127 percent of the oil and gas it produced. It was the ninth straight year that Chevron managed to add more reserves than it produced.

Also, it started new oil and gas operations in the deepwater Gulf of Mexico, and began production at the Hamaca oil field in Venezuela and the Malampaya gas project in the Philippines. ChevronTexaco expected that collectively, the projects would result in more than 80,000 net oil-equivalent barrels a day in 2002. It also started up operations of the Caspian Pipeline, connecting the Tengiz oil field to the Russian port city of Novorossiysk.

In 2002, ChevronTexaco implemented a $9.4 billion capital and exploratory program focused on high-impact, long-term exploration and production growth projects. The cost was lower than combined expenditures in 2001.

PRODUCTS

ChevronTexaco is a leading producer and seller of refined products, including motor and diesel gasoline, lubricants, and aviation fuel. It has 8,340 retail outlets in the United States. Products bearing the Chevron brand are sold in North America by ChevronTexaco business units including: Chevron Products Company, which

CORPORATE CITIZENSHIP

As stated in "The ChevronTexaco Way," the company supports human rights by endorsing The Global Sullivan Principles, a code of corporate conduct drawn up in 1999. "The ChevronTexaco Way" also sets forth a very pro-environmental stance that is concerned with reducing greenhouse gas emissions, increasing energy efficiency, investing in research and development directed toward protecting the environment, and supporting sound corporate policies that protect the environment.

GLOBAL PRESENCE

ChevronTexaco is a truly global organization with numerous business units located throughout the world. Its refining and marketing activities are conducted in North America, Latin America, Europe, Asia, the Middle East and Africa. The company produces oil and gas in the Middle East, Africa, and North America. Its facilities are located in countries like Kazakhstan, Indonesia, Angola, Nigeria and Brazil. Its operating companies, International Upstream and North American Upstream, have business units throughout the world. International Upstream operates in China, Asia, Europe, Indonesia, Latin America, Middle East, North Africa, Nigeria, Southern Africa and Thailand. North American Upstream has business units in Canada, the Gulf of Mexico, the San Joaquin Valley and Alaska, among other locations.

EMPLOYMENT

ChevronTexaco has 55,763 employees working throughout the world. The company seeks recent college graduates looking to launch their careers as well as experienced professionals, and offers competitive salaries with comprehensive benefits. It also values diversity in the workplace and provides opportunities for advancement within the company.

SOURCES OF INFORMATION

Bibliography

Bole, Kirsten. "Chevron Inks $2B Agreement." *San Francisco Business Times*, 15 July 1996.

"Chevron and Texaco Intend to Form Joint Venture of Marine Lubricant Businesses." *PR Newswire*, 30 March 1998.

Chevron Corporation Annual Report. San Francisco, CA: Chevron Corporation, 1997.

Chevron Corporation. *The Corporate Directory of U.S. Public Companies.* San Mateo, CA: Walker's, 1998.

Chevron Home Page, 1 May 1998. Available at http://www .chevron.com.

"Chevron Launches M&A Unit." *The Oil Daily*, 3 February 1998.

"Chevron Set to Sack 200 Researchers." *San Francisco Business Times*, 5 August 1996.

"FTC Consent Agreement Allows the Merger of Chevron Corp. and Texaco, Inc., Preserves Market Competition." Federal Trade Commission, 7 September 2001. Available at: http://www.ftc .gov/opa/2001/09/chevtex.htm.

McAuliffe, Don. "Chevron's Nationwide ATM Network will be Satellite-Linked." *Knight-Rider/Tribune Business News*, 24 October 1997.

Mellow, Craig. "Big Oil's Pipe Dream." *Fortune*, 2 March 1998.

Morgan Stanley, Dean Witter. *Company Report*, 3 December 1997.

"Petroleum (integrated) Industry." *The Value Line Investment Survey*, 27 March 1998.

For an annual report:

on the Internet at: http://www.chevron.com **or** write: Chevron-Texaco Corporation's Comptroller's Dept., 575 Market St., Rm. 3519, San Francisco, CA 94105-2856

For additional industry research:

Investigate companies by their Standard Industrial Classification Codes, also known as SICs. ChevronTexaco Corporation's primary SICs are:

1311 Crude Petroleum and Natural Gas

1381 Drilling Oil and Gas Wells

1382 Oil and Gas Exploration Services

1389 Oil and Gas Field Services

2911 Petroleum Refining

2992 Petroleum Lubricating Oil and Grease Manufacturing

4412 Deep Sea Freight Transporation

4612 Pipeline Transportation of Crude Oil

4619 Other Pipelines Transportation, NEC

4923 Natural Gas Transmission and Distribution

5169 Other Chemical and Allied Products Wholesale

5171 Petroleum Bulk Stations and Terminals

Also investigate companies by their North American Industry Classification System Codes, also known as NAICS codes. ChevronTexaco Corporation's primary NAICS codes are:

324110 Petroleum Refineries

324191 Petroleum Lubricating Oil and Grease Manufacturing

325110 Petrochemical Manufacturing

483110 Deep Sea, Coastal and Great Lakes Water Transporta-tion

Cisco Systems Inc.

FOUNDED: 1984

Contact Information:

HEADQUARTERS: 170 W. Tasman Dr.
    San Jose, CA 95134-1706
PHONE: (408)526-4000
FAX: (408)526-4100
EMAIL: investor-relations@cisco.com
URL: http://www.cisco.com

OVERVIEW

Cisco Systems Inc. is the worldwide leader in the production, marketing, and sale of networking hardware, software, and support services. With Internet Protocol (IP) networking solutions as the company's flagship product, Cisco provides networking solutions for the Internet as well as a wide range of corporate, educational, and government networks around the world. Its extensive product line offers an array of solutions for transporting data, voice, and video to connect computers in a network or connect networks to each other. Whether a customer wants to move data quickly and securely between two computers in the same office building or between two computer networks at opposite ends of the globe, Cisco can provide the necessary hardware devices, software technology, and support services to made it possible.

Since 1984, when Cisco engineers first developed the groundbreaking IP technology, the basic language for communicating over the Internet or across networks, Cisco has continued to offer new advancements in networking technology, including advanced routing and switching, data, voice, and video over IP, optical networking, wireless, storage networking, security, broadband, and content networking.

COMPANY FINANCES

In fiscal 2000, ending July 31, 2000, the company reported a record-breaking net income of $2.7 billion on sales totaling $18.9 billion, but then the demise of the dot-com industry caught up to Cisco. Consequently, for fiscal year 2001 Cisco posted a net loss of $1.0 billion on revenues of $22.3 billion. The losses primarily stemmed from the accumulation of $2.2 billion of excessive inventory after demand for its routers and switches declined. The problems materialized in the third quarter of fiscal 2001 when the company posted a loss of $2.7 billion. During the fourth quarter, Cisco returned a profit of $7 million, less than 1 percent of its fourth quarter profit the previous year.

Cisco began a slow and tentative rebound in fiscal 2002, reporting revenues of $4.8 billion in both the second and third quarters resulting in net incomes of $660 million and $729 million, respectively. These totals reflect an improvement over the first quarter of fiscal 2002 results of a net loss of $268 million on revenues of $4.4 billion.

ANALYSTS' OPINIONS

Despite its fall from spectacular growth to a net loss in 2001, most analysts remain cautiously interested in Cisco's stock possibilities, who consider the company's excellent balance sheet along with its large market share as significant advances working in Cisco's favor. The majority of analysts have taken a "wait and see" approach as they remain uncertain about the timing and magnitude of the recovery of the Internet-based economy as well as the outlook for corporate spending. Cisco's mix of business with both service providers and the enterprise sector is considered a positive, and given the overall trends in the economy, Cisco's flat to slightly increasing revenues over the first three quarters of fiscal 2002 are considered encouraging.

HISTORY

Leonard Bosack was the manager of Stanford University's computer science laboratory in 1984 when he devised a way to connect his computer network to the computers in the graduate school of business, which were under the management of his wife Sandra Lerner. After unsuccessful attempts to sell the new technology to existing computer companies, in December 1984 Bosack and Lerner quit their positions at Stanford to form Cisco Systems, co-founded with partners Greg Setz, Bill Westfield, and Kirk Lougheed. The company struggled early to stay afloat. Bosack and Lerner used credit cards, mortgaged their house, and Lerner retained a second job to provide the family with a steady income.

Cisco's foundational product was the multiprotocol router, the Transmission Control Protocol/Internet Protocol (TCP/IP). The router is a hardware device that uses added software to automatically send data over the most effective route as it moves between networks. The multiprotocol feature allows dissimilar network systems to

FAST FACTS:
About Cisco Systems Inc.

Ownership: Cisco Systems Inc. is a publicly owned company traded on the NASDAQ Stock Exchange.

Ticker Symbol: CSCO

Officers: John T. Chambers, 52, Pres. and CEO, 2001 base salary $268,131; Larry R. Carter, 58, SVP Finance and Administration and CFO, 2001 base salary $424,212; Richard J. Justice, SVP World Field Operations, 2001 base salary $384,462; James Richardson, SVP and Chief Marketing Officer, 2001 base salary $383,108; Michelangelo Volpi, SVP Internet Switching and Services, 2001 base salary $380,346

Employees: 38,000

Principal Subsidiary Companies: Cisco operates numerous subsidiaries. Recent additions to the company's arsenal include Navarro Networks Inc. and Hammerhead Networks Inc., both acquired in May 2002, and Allegro Systems Inc. and AuroraNetics Inc., both acquired in 2001. Among the 24 companies acquired during 2000 are ExiO Communications Inc., Radiata Inc., Active Voice Corporation, CAIS Software Solutions, Vovida Networks Inc., IPCell Technologies Inc., PixStream Inc., IPMobile Inc., and NuSpeed Internet Systems Inc.

Chief Competitors: Among the many companies that vie for a place in the high-tech marketplace, Cisco's competitors include Juniper, Lucent, Nortel Networks, Siemens AG, Ericsson, and Alcatel.

communicate, for example, allowing a Windows-based computer to transmit and receive data from an Apple MacIntosh system, bridging difference in hardware and operating systems.

In 1985 Stanford filed suit against Cisco for $11 million in licensing fees, claiming entitlement because Bosack developed the new technology as a Stanford employee, using Stanford facilities. The following year the suit was settled when Stanford agreed to accept $150,000 and free routers. Cisco's first multiprotocol router went on the market in 1986. By the end of fiscal 1986, ending July of 1987, revenues totaled more than $1.5 million. At the time, the company still employed only eight people.

CHRONOLOGY:

Key Dates for Cisco Systems Inc.

1984: Leonard Bosack and Sandra Lerner leave Stanford University to form Cisco Systems

1986: Begins marketing the first multiprotocol router, the Transmission Control Protocol/Internet Protocol (TCP/IP)

1988: Bosack and Lerner give up control of Cisco to venture capitalist Donald T. Valentine

1990: Bosack and Lerner leave the company and divest themselves of all interests

1992: Rated by *Forbes* as the second fastest growing company in the United States; sales reach $339.6 million

1994: Cisco controls 57 percent of the world market for multiple protocol interconnectivity and communications solutions; net sales reach $1.24 billion

1998: Set record for shortest period of time to reach $100 billion market capitalization, doing it in less then 9 years and breaking Microsoft's previous record of 11 years

2000: Net income reaches $2.7 billion on record sales of $18.9 billion

2001: Excessive inventory and a decline in the economy leads the company to post a net loss for the fiscal year of slightly more than $1 billion.

2002: High tech industry begins to stabilize, and Cisco returns to profitability

At the end of fiscal 1989, less than four years since its formation, Cisco reported revenues of $13.90 million on sales of $69.7 million. Employee numbers had grown the 254. In the years preceding the Internet revolution, Cisco marketed its products to universities, governmental agencies, and scientific research centers, all of which tended to use internal network systems and could benefit from advanced routing hardware. Soon Cisco began targeting sales to large corporations, especially those with numerous locations using diverse systems, allowing the companies to link national, regional, and local offices. When the Internet appeared on the scene, Cisco was well prepared to take advantage of a greatly expanded market for its products. The company completed its initial public offering in 1990.

As the leading provider of Internetworking routers, in the early 1990s Cisco became one of the fastest growing companies in the United States. From fiscal 1991 to fiscal 1992, net income nearly doubled from $43.2 million to $84.4 million on revenues of $183.2 million and $339.6 million, respectively. Although Cisco worked to continuously update and improve its routers, in 1992 the introduction of asynchronous transfer mode (ATM) technology, which could manage data without a router, became a serious threat to Cisco's future. Cisco responded by working with others in the industry to set regulations and standards and installed ATM protocol support to its routers.

During the 1990s Cisco aggressively sought expansion opportunities in international markets. Operations were undertaken in Japan, Australia, and Hong Kong. By the end of fiscal 1994, more than 40 percent of the company's revenues were being generated by overseas sales. Whereas in the United States, the majority of sales were made directly to the consumer, in its international markets, Cisco did the bulk of its business with distributors. Both within the United States and abroad, telecommunications companies became important customers for Cisco. The company marketed it software technology to Bell South, Bell Atlantic, Pacific Bell, MCI International, and British Telecom, as well as Alcatel of France, Siemens AG of Germany, and Olivetti of Italy.

Cisco then began growing its operations through a string of acquisitions. In 1993 Cisco purchased Crescendo Communications for $100 million, followed by the purchase of Kalpana Inc. and Newport Systems Solutions in 1994 and Grand Junction Networks in 1996. These acquisitions offered Cisco the opportunity to position itself for the eventual market transition from routers to the newer technology of ATM and LAN. By 1997 Cisco was the supplier for 80 percent of the Internet routers in the world.

In 1998 the company set the record for shortest time to achieve $100 billion market capitalization after going public, a feat Cisco completed in just eight and a half years, which broke the 11-year record previously set by Microsoft. As competition increased as new Internetworking companies emerged, Cisco continued its growth, making two of its largest purchases by acquiring Cerent Corp, a manufacturer of fiber optic equipment, in 1999 for $7.3 billion and ArrowPoint Communications Inc. in 2000 for a $5.7 billion stock swap.

STRATEGY

Responding to the sudden shift in the computer networking industry, which has proved to be volatile, Cisco first enacted stop-gap measures to get through the worst of the industry crisis. In the face of an abysmal of $2.7 billion during the third quarter of fiscal 2001, Cisco announced a plan to restructure, which called for the elimination of 6,000 regular employee positions across the board. The company also consolidated its operations, cut operating costs, and reorganized to focus on its core moneymaking business segments. To eliminate product overlap and increase resource and innovation sharing, Cisco regrouped it engineering organization so that its customers can be offered consistent product goods and services that address all the needs of their integrated networks. Previously Cisco approached customers based on business categories; the reorganization restructured the engineering department into technology groups, each serving all business segments. As a result, Cisco began pushing their ability to deliver a seamless "Network of Networks."

INFLUENCES

Cisco operates in an industry marked by rapid and dramatic changes in trends. Just as the explosion in the Internet and networking demands rocketed, Cisco's annual revenues from $6.5 billion in fiscal 1997 to $22.3 billion in fiscal 2001. When slews of Internet-based companies went broke and the high-tech industry fell into a slump, Cisco's net income suddenly became a net loss of more than $1 billion. As a result of the fluctuating market demand, Cisco must manage its inventory carefully. If unable to supply its customers with products due to an inventory shortage, Cisco hurts its business. On the other hand, if caught in a slowdown with too much inventory on hand, the company gets hit with problems such as those experienced in fiscal 2001.

Other factors that influence Cisco's balance sheet include price fluctuations within the industry, the exchange rate of the dollar, the introduction of new technology that either bolsters sales or renders existing products obsolete, and the overall health of the economy. Because Cisco does the majority of its business with corporations, rather than service providers, a prolonged economic downturn could influence companies to cut back on information technology products and services, especially high-end products. Also important to Cisco's overall business is telecommunications providers; thus, changes in trends within specific industries may have a direct impact on Cisco's outlook.

CURRENT TRENDS

Cisco is looking to the future by focusing on new technology and new market opportunities. Taking calculated risks, despite its recent financial difficulties, Cisco hopes to tap into new "tornado" market opportunities set into rapid growth movement by the introduction of specific innovative products and capabilities. On Cisco's list of such potentially valuable market areas are voice over IP (VoIP), content networking, wireless Inter-

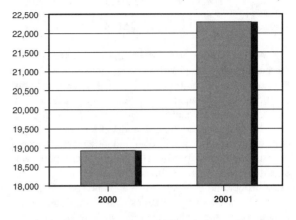

FINANCES:
Cisco Systems Inc.
Net Sales, 2000-2001
(million dollars)

net, storage networking, metro optical networking, security, and virtual private networks. Cisco will push the edge of the envelope to find ways for networking to become not just an advantage for its customers, but a necessity that reduces costs and improves productivity. Specifically, Cisco will move to strengthen its product portfolio, through in-house activities as well as acquisitions, in the areas of storage, security, and VoIP. Continued diversification of its customer base will also prove vital for the company to withstand downturns in specific industry sectors.

PRODUCTS

Cisco's bread-and-butter line product is its offering of routing devices. Routers allow information to travel between networks, taking the most direct route as well as traveling securely. Cisco provides a range of routers to serve the needs of large corporations who require a complete infrastructure for global operations or small businesses that may need to network with a single office. Switching technology devices, which have taken over routers as Cisco's major revenue producer, are used both in local-area networks and wide-area networks. Switching devices create temporary high-speed paths between network segments as needed. As with its routers, Cisco offers a diverse line of switching solutions that provide a range of flexibility, cost, and bandwidth that can be tailored to the needs of both large and small operations. Cisco uses the same technologies as employed by the rest of the industry, such as Ethernet, gigabit Ethernet, token ring, and asynchronous transfer mode (ATM).

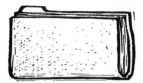

TOO MANY COOKS IN THE KITCHEN

Although sales were strong, the rapid expansion of the business caused a cash shortage, and in 1988 Cisco's husband-and-wife co-founders Leonard Bosack and Sandra Lerner were forced to enter into an agreement with venture capitalist Donald T. Valentine of Sequoia Capital. The deal required Bosack and Lerner to turn over a controlling interest in Cisco to Valentine, who became the company's chairperson. He then hired computer veteran John Morgridge as the company's new chief executive officer and president. As Valentine and Morgridge took over the company, relations with Bosack and Lerner deteriorated. Bosack assumed the position of chief scientist and Lerner was placed in charge of customer service, but neither was happy with the new arrangements. When Cisco completed its initial public offering in February 1990, the couple began selling their stock. In August 1990 the friction climaxed when Morgridge fired Lerner, and Bosack then quit. Divesting their remaining interest in the company for $200 million, they gave much of the profits to charity.

Cisco also provides access solutions for customers, including students, telecommuters, and mobile workers, who need remote access to the Internet or other networks. Its product line includes asynchronous and integrated services digital network (ISDN), remote-access routers, dial-up access servers, digital subscriber line (DSL) technologies, and cable universal broadband routers. Customer support services make up an increasing important part of Cisco's overall business. Online and telephone assistance, technical consultation, and solutions for streamlining operations using technology are provided as part of the customer services segment.

Along with its core products, Cisco also offers a variety of other standard and cutting-edge goods and services, such as Internet services, network management software, optical networking, and voice, video, and integrated data networking.

CORPORATE CITIZENSHIP

Partnering with the United Nations and the United States Agency for International Development, Cisco has created the Cisco Networking Academy Program, which teaches students to design, build, and maintain computer networks. The academies number more than 8,000 and are found in more than 130 countries, including locations in twenty-four of the world's forty-five least-developed countries. As a corporation, Cisco encourages its employees to contribute to the communities in which they work. Employees, who have contributed more than $3 million to the company's global food drive, also support such projects as the Habitat for Humanity and Netaid.org.

GLOBAL PRESENCE

Cisco's corporate headquarters is located in San Jose, California, which also serves as the company's regional headquarters for the Americas. Other regional headquarters are located in Amsterdam, The Netherlands, serving Europe, and Singapore, serving the Asia Pacific. Local offices are maintained in over 50 countries worldwide. For fiscal year 2001, net sales for the Americas totaled $15.1 billion; for Europe, the Middle East, and Africa, $6.3 billion; for Asia Pacific, $2.4 billion; and for Japan, $1.5 billion.

EMPLOYMENT

Cisco looks to attract employees committed to innovation who have an entrepreneurial spirit and are bold enough to take calculated business risks. To reward those who excel in these areas, Cisco maintains three employee recognition programs: the Distinguished Engineer Award, the Cisco Fellow Award, and the Pioneer Technology Award.

SOURCES OF INFORMATION

Bibliography

"Cisco Systems Inc." *Multex Investor*, 2002. Available at http://www.multex.com.

Galarza, Pablo. "Cisco Slayer." *Money*, April 2002.

"John Chambers: Cisco Rides Again." *Business Week*, 20 May 2002.

Lamb, Robin. "Excess Inventory Still Squeezing Cisco." *Ebn*, 13 August 2001.

Long, Timothy. "Content Networking." *Computer Reseller News*, 8 April 2002.

Sheng, Ellen. "DJ US Stocks Seen Higher on Surprising Cisco Sys Results." *FWN Select*, 10 May 2002.

Stires, David. "The Tech Wasteland." *Fortune*, 27 May 2002.

For an annual report:
on the Internet at: http://www.cisco.com

For additional industry research:
Investigate companies by their Standard Industrial Classification Codes, also known as SICs. Cisco Systems Inc.'s primary SICs are:

3577 Computer Peripheral Equipment, Not Elsewhere Classified

3661 Telephone And Telegraph Apparatus

7371 Computer Programming Services

7372 Prepackaged Software

Also investigate companies by their North American Industry Classification System codes, also known as NAICS codes. Cisco Systems Inc.'s primary NAICS codes are:

334119 Other Computer Peripheral Equipment Manufacturing

334210 Telephone Apparatus Manufacturing

511210 Software Publishers

541511 Custom Computer Programming Services

Clear Channel Communications, Inc.

FOUNDED: 1972

Contact Information:
HEADQUARTERS: 200 E. Basse Road
   San Antonio, TX 78209
PHONE: (210)822-2828
FAX: (210)822-2299
URL: http://www.clearchannel.com

OVERVIEW

With nearly $8 billion in annual sales, Clear Channel Communications is the largest radio station owner and operator in the United States. Along with approximately 1,200 U.S. radio stations, which accounts for roughly 11 percent of all radio programming, Clear Channel also owns portions of nearly 250 stations throughout the world. Broadcasting operations, including the operation of several television stations, account for roughly 45 percent of revenues. Outdoor advertising on things like billboards and mass transit vehicles brings in another 32 percent, while live entertainment promotion and production garners 17 percent.

COMPANY FINANCES

Clear Channel Communications Inc.'s sales nearly doubled from $697 million in 1997 to $1.35 billion in 1998. In 1999, sales doubled again, reaching $2.67 billion. They doubled for a third time in 2000, reaching $5.34 billion. Attributable to this rapid growth was a series of large outdoor media and radio station acquisitions Clear Channel completed between 1997 and 2000. Earnings for Clear Channel proved to be a bit less consistent during this time period, falling from $63.6 million in 1997 to $54.0 million in 1998, rebounding to $72.5 million in 1999, and surging to $248.8 million in 2000. However, the firm posted a $1.14 billion loss in 2001 due mainly to weak economic conditions in North America, which prompted many firms to rein in their advertising budgets. Stock prices, which had reached a high of $95.50 per share in 2000, tumbled to a low of $35.20

per share in 2001 due to the loss. In early 2002, stock prices recovered to roughly $50.00 per share.

ANALYSTS' OPINIONS

Clear Channel Communications stock proved to be one of the strongest performers of the 1990s, according to most industry analysts, as stock prices grew nearly 9,000 percent during the decade. The firm's move into live entertainment promotion via the purchase of SFX Entertainment in 2000 drew some criticism from analysts who believed that the firm would be better served by focusing on its core radio operations. When recessionary economic conditions in the North American economy in 2001 caused companies of all kinds to slash their advertising budgets, Clear Channel's stock prices plunged. However, many analysts continued to recommend Clear Channel stock due to the firm's likelihood of recovery when economic conditions improved. According to a July 2001 issue of *Barron's*, "America's largest radio operator should be an early beneficiary of any recovery in ad spending."

HISTORY

In 1972, at the age of 36, investment banker L. Lowry Mays acquired KEEZ, a floundering San Antonio, Texas based FM radio station, with the financial backing of car dealer B. J. McCombs and a $175,000 bank loan. Mays and McCombs changed the station's format to country music. In an effort to increase advertising sales, the partners boosted the station's promotions budget and increased its sales force. Within a year, KEEZ was operating profitably, and Mays decided to begin acquiring additional radio stations, folding them into the company he named San Antonio Broadcasting. In 1975 Mays ended his career as an investment banker after deciding to focus his efforts on managing radio stations. He also changed the name of San Antonio Broadcasting to Clear Channel Communications.

In 1984 the Federal Communications Commission (FCC) began deregulating the broadcasting industry, allowing a single company to own as many as 12 AM stations, 12 FM stations, and 12 television stations. Prior to deregulation, companies were limited to seven properties in each category. As a result, Clear Channel Communications, Inc. completed its initial public offering, planning to use the $7.5 million it raised to fund further expansion. By 1987 the firm had increased its radio station holdings to 16. However, in the late 1980s, Mays decided to refrain from making further radio station purchases because he believed the prices had become too high. Instead, the firm turned its attention to television stations for the first time, creating Clear Channel Television in 1988. Within four years, Clear Channel owned

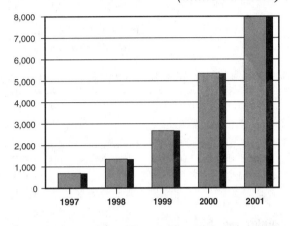

FINANCES:
Clear Channel Communications Inc. Revenues, 1997-2001 (million dollars)

seven radio stations, most of which were affiliates of the Fox TV network, which had started to emerge as the fourth major television network in the United States. As Fox became more successful, so did the television holdings of Clear Channel. In 1991, to reduce the debt it had accrued from making its many acquisitions, Clear Channel conducted a second stock offering, raising $25 million. By then, with 18 radio stations and 6 television stations, Clear Channel was pulling in profits in excess of $1 million on sales of nearly $75 million.

Mays' decision to refrain from purchasing radio stations in the late 1980s paid off early in the next decade. Companies that had paid high prices for radio stations during the late 1980s found themselves struggling with heavy debt loads when economic conditions weakened in the early 1990s. Many firms began to sell those stations at much lower prices. After securing $150 million in credit from a consortium of nine banks, Clear Channel began to add new radio stations to its holdings. By mid-1993 the firm had used $110 million to acquire 31 radio stations, along with 7 television stations. As a result, Clear Channel found itself among the ranks of U.S. broadcasting industry leaders.

The firm expanded internationally for the first time in 1995, when it acquired a 50 percent stake in the Australian Radio Network. With profits of $32 million on sales of $244 million that year, the firm found itself well positioned for growth when the Telecommunications Act of 1996 deregulated the broadcasting industry further. Within four months of the Act's passage, Clear Channel had spent $581 million to acquire more radio and television stations. By October 1996, Clear Channel had boosted its holdings to 121 radio stations and 11

FAST FACTS:

About Clear Channel Communications, Inc.

Ownership: Clear Channel Communications, Inc. is a publicly owned company traded on the New York Stock Exchange.

Ticker Symbol: CCU

Officers: L. Lowry Mays, Chmn. and CEO, 65, 2001 base salary $1,000,000; Mark Mays, Pres., COO, and Dir., 37, 2001 base salary $657,500; Randall T. Mays, EVP, CFO, and Dir., 35, 2001 base salary $655,000

Employees: 35,700

Principal Subsidiary Companies: Clear Channel Communications, Inc. operates subsidiaries in North America, Europe, South America, Australia, and Asia. Based in New York City, the firm's Clear Channel Entertainment unit is the leading live entertainment production company in the world. Another New York-based subsidiary, Katz Media Group, sells television and radio advertising. Clear Channel Communications also own a 26 percent share of Hispanic Broadcasting Corp., the largest Spanish language broadcasting company in the United States.

Chief Competitors: Competitors to Clear Channel Communications, Inc. include Infinity Broadcasting, Cox Radio, Citadel Communications, Cumulus Media, ABC Radio, Westwood One, and other media companies involved in radio and television broadcasting, live entertainment promotion, and billboard advertising.

television stations, and as a result, it had become the second-largest radio group in the country behind Westinghouse/CBS.

The following year Clear Channel Communications, Inc. diversified into outdoor advertising with the purchase of Eller Media Co. With more than 50,000 display boards in 15 major metropolitan markets, Eller Media was the leading U.S. billboard operator. Clear Channel also acquired Universal Outdoor, Inc., gaining another 88,000 display boards. Moving into a major metropolitan broadcasting market for the first time, Clear Channel purchased a 32 percent stake in Spanish-language broadcaster Heftel Broadcasting Corp. These acquisitions

boosted sales to $1.35 billion in 1998, compared to $697 million the previous year.

Growth via acquisition continued in 1999 when Clear Channel Communications, Inc. paid $4 billion for rival radio station owner and operator Jacor Communications. In 2000 the firm spent $23.8 billion for another major competitor, AMFM, Inc., which operated 441 radio stations and posted sales of $2 billion in 1999. Along with positioning Clear Channel as the largest radio station owner in the United States, the purchase expanded Clear Channel's reach to 110 million people across 187 markets. Also in 2000 the firm diversified into live events promotion and production for the first time by purchasing SFX Entertainment. SFX changed its name to Clear Channel Entertainment in 2001. That year, Clear Channel agreed to purchase Ackerley Group, a media company with radio, television, and outdoor advertising holdings. The firm also restructured its operations into eight regional units, each headed by a senior vice president.

STRATEGY

Since he founded Clear Channel Communications, Inc. in the 1970s, founder Lowry Mays has been focused on how to turn struggling radio stations into money-making ventures. Boosting advertising dollars became his top goal, and this strategy served the firm well in its early years. Although he did make some programming and format changes to the stations he acquired, Mays' key concern was the relationship he developed with advertisers. Throughout the late 1970s and 1980s, Clear Channel acquired struggling stations in mid-sized markets such as Memphis, Tennessee, New Orleans, and Louisiana. Before making a purchase, Mays analyzed the cost and potential growth of each station to ensure that the likely return on investment met his bottom line criteria. Following a similar strategy with each station he acquired, Mays typically doubled sales forces and increased marketing activities in an effort to lure new advertisers.

Clear Channel continued to employ this strategy in the 1990s. According to a January 1997 issue of *Forbes*, "Essentially Mays makes money by buying weak stations and building them up with heavy promotions and value-added deals for advertisers." The firm's discipline in limiting its acquisitions to those available at bargain prices, as well as its success in boosting the financial performance of struggling stations, helped push stock prices from $1.81 per share in 1990 to nearly $40.00 per share in 1996.

In the late 1990s, Clear Channel diversified into outdoor advertising for the first time. This allowed the firm to offer combined radio and billboard advertising packages to companies looking for less expensive alternatives to television advertisements. These packages

CHRONOLOGY:

Key Dates for Clear Channel Communications, Inc.

1972: L. Lowry Mays acquires his first radio station

1984: Clear Channel completes its IPO

1997: The firm diversifies into outdoor advertising with the purchase of Eller Media Co.

1999: Clear Channel acquires Jacor Communications

2000: In its largest acquisition ever, Clear Channel acquires AMFM, Inc.

proved successful, helping to boost Clear Channel's sales and earnings as well as its stock prices, which reached a high of $95.50 per share in 2000. By then, the firm's reach had grown to roughly 96 million listeners per week.

INFLUENCES

Because of the successful strategy employed by Mays, Clear Channel Communications, Inc. found itself well positioned to take advantage of the Telecommunications Act of 1996, which loosened both local and national radio ownership restrictions. Minimal debt and a healthy cash flow allowed Clear Channel to launch an aggressive expansion campaign in 1996 that eventually positioned the firm in the number one spot among U.S. radio station owners.

PRODUCTS

Clear Channel sells radio, television, and outdoor advertising such as billboard, mass transit, and furniture displays in mid-sized markets across the United States as well as in Australia, Asia, Europe, and South America.

GLOBAL PRESENCE

Clear Channel Communications, Inc.'s first international move, a $70 million deal to buy 12 Australian radio

CLEAR CHANNEL'S CREATIVE SALES TACTICS

To convince a car dealer in Tulsa, Oklahoma, to advertise on Clear Channel's radio stations there, Clear Channel Communications, Inc. agreed to promote the car dealership for an entire weekend via broadcasts from the dealership's site. Clear Channel charged nothing up front for the advertising. Instead, the firm requested a payment of $150.00 for each car sold that was in excess of the total number of cars sold the prior weekend. After selling 200 more cars that weekend than the weekend before, the dealership began to advertise regularly on Clear Channel's radio stations.

stations, took place in 1995. The firm's decision to expand internationally was largely due to the restrictions on radio and television station ownership still in place in the United States at the time. In fact, the lack of restrictions on foreign ownership in Australia allowed Clear Channel to become the second largest operator of radio stations there.

Although ownership restrictions were eased in the United States in 1996, Clear Channel continued to expand international operations. For example, the firm purchased a variety of outdoor advertising firms in Europe and Latin America in the late 1990s and early 2000s. In addition, Clear Channel Entertainment, the live performance promotions and production arm of the firm, bought two of the top concert promoters in Italy in 2001. By then, the firm's international radio operations included a 32 percent stake in Golden Rose, a group of radio stations based in the United Kingdom; a 33 percent stake in New Zealand Radio Network; a 26 percent stake in Hispanic Broadcasting Corp.; a 50 percent stake in Radio 1, a group of radio stations based in Norway; and a 50 percent stake in Radio Bonton, an FM radio station in the Czech Republic. Its international outdoor advertising operations included a 50 percent stake in Adshel Street Furniture, which operates in Australia and New Zealand; a 50 percent stake in Buspak, a transit display firm based in Hong Kong; a 51 percent stake in Jolly Pubblicita, based in Italy; and a 50 percent stake in Sirocco International, based in France.

SOURCES OF INFORMATION

Bibliography

Bachman, Katy. "Clear Channel No. 1 Group in Radio, BIA Reports." *MEDIAWEEK*, 19 March 2001.

Clear Channel Communications, Inc. Home Page, 2002. Available at http://www.clearchannel.com.

"Clear Channel Communications, Inc." *International Directory of Company Histories*. Detroit: Gale Group, 1997.

Defotis, Dimitra. "Radio Daze: Clear Channel Looks Cheap Versus Its Peers." *Barron's*, 30 July 2001.

Newcomb, Peter. "Tamales? Cars? Coke?" *Forbes*, 27 January 1997.

Norton, Leslie P. "Fading Signal? After Nine Years of Stunning Growth, Clear Channel May Be Facing Static." *Barron's*, 6 March 2000.

Pomerantz, Dorothy. "Free the Airwaves." *Forbes*, 15 April 2002.

Pully, Brett. "Clear Channel Boom Box." *Forbes*, 10 January 2000.

Trigoboff, Dan. "Clearheadedly Restructuring." *Broadcasting & Cable*, 3 September 2001.

For an annual report:

on the Internet at: http://www.clearchannel.com/Files/CC_AR_01.pdf.

For additional industry research:

Investigate companies by their Standard Industrial Classification codes, also known as SICs. Clear Channel Communications, Inc.'s primary SICs are:

4823 Radio Broadcasting

4833 Television Broadcasting

6719 Holding Companies (not elsewhere classified)

7312 Outdoor Advertising Services

Also investigate companies by their North American Industry Classification System codes, also known as NAICS codes. Clear Channel Communications, Inc.'s primary NAICS codes are:

339950 Sign Manufacturing

513112 Radio Stations

513120 Television Broadcasting

541850 Display Advertising

541870 Advertising Material Distribution Services

551112 Offices of Other Holding Companies

Coach Inc.

FOUNDED: 1941

OVERVIEW

Coach Inc. is a specialty retailer that designs, manufactures, and markets quality leather goods and accessories. The company originated in New York in 1941 as a family run artisan and craft studio. For decades the company was regarded as a manufacturer of classic, practical pocketbooks and wallets. Its reputation for solid but uninteresting products allowed the company to operate for many years with little publicity or notice. Ultimately the company's traditional image began to take on a negative connotation, and Coach products were described as dated or old-fashioned. In 1985 the company was purchased by Sara Lee as part of its retail division. It wasn't a natural fit amongst the cheesecakes and cookies, but the new management resuscitated the failing company. In recent years Coach has emerged as a strong presence in the fashion world with cutting edge new designs, expanded product lines, and state of the art marketing and distribution channels. In recognition of the company's new found clout, Sara Lee spun it off in 2001 to operate as a publicly owned fashion and leather retailer.

Contact Information:
HEADQUARTERS: 516 West 34th St., Floor 5
   New York, NY 10001-1394
PHONE: (212)594-1850
FAX: (212)594-1682
URL: http://www.coach.com

COMPANY FINANCES

Coach posted revenues of $616.1 million and a net income of $64.0 million in 2001. These figures represent a continuation of the company's growing profitability. In 2000 the company recorded a net income of $38.6 million on $548.9 million in revenues, up from $16.7 million in income on $507.8 million in revenues in 1999. Equally impressive is the company's profit margin, which has grown from 3.8 percent in 1999 to 7 percent

FINANCES:

Coach Inc.
Revenues, 1998-2001
(million dollars)

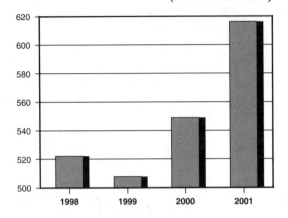

Coach Inc.
2001 Stock Prices
(dollars)

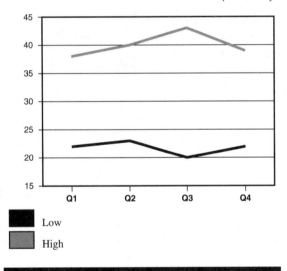

- ■ Low
- ▉ High

in 2000 and 10.4 percent in 2001. Although Coach is a traditionally American name, it has expanded its international customer base to include 18 countries. Japanese consumers generated 20 percent of Coach's $616 million in revenues for the year 2001.

ANALYSTS' OPINIONS

After experiencing several years of losses from 1997 to 1999, Coach polished its dusty image and ana-

lysts are hailing it as a shining star in the competitive fashion world. During the 2001 holiday season, sales of Coach products soared without benefit of deep discounts and in the midst of a recession. Lehman Brothers analyst, Robert Drbul, said the public considers Coach products "must-have items." He expected revenues from Japanese expansion to bolster sales figures even further. The company has done exceptionally well since its separation from Sara Lee. Drbul went on to observe, "The brand has a tremendous amount of momentum." He predicted even stronger stock prices in 2002 and 2003. Other analysts agree with this assessment. David Lamer of Ferris, Baker Watts expected sales to be fueled by the eager Japanese market where the growth potential is huge. Eric Beder of Ladenburg Thalman & Co. was also enthusiastic about the company's prospects, saying, "Coach has been right on the money in terms of fashions. It turned out people wanted to pamper themselves with affordable luxury items like a Coach bag for $300 and a lot of utility."

HISTORY

Coach Inc. has been in existence since 1941, yet there is little information recorded on the history or evolution of the company. According to published reports, the origins of the company can be traced to a loft in Manhattan where a small group of artisans crafted leather goods. It is described as a family-run shop known for high quality products crafted by generation after generation of family members.

In 1985 Coach was purchased by the Sara Lee Corporation, but little creative movement occurred for more than a decade. Everything changed under the leadership of Lew Frankfurt. It was evident by 1996 that Coach was no longer the name brand of choice for the fashion conscious. Hip European designers such as Gucci and Prada were no longer making products reserved for the rich and famous. When the elite fashion labels began designing stylish accessories at affordable prices, Coach's loyal customer base began to disappear. The classic, simple designs were considered antiquated, and this image did not appeal to consumers, particularly women, of any age. Frankfort illustrated this point by noting that women were still willing to carry the sturdy high-quality Coach wallets, but they would be tucked inside a trendy shoulder bag from Prada. Coach products were no longer a sign of status with American women.

Frankfort made plans to update the company's offerings and engineer an image makeover. In December 1996 Frankfort scored a coup when he lured designer Reed Krakoff to Coach. Krakoff was about to move to Italy to pursue a career in fashion design when Frankfort wooed him into accepting a position at Coach as its first executive creative director. Krakoff brought more than just design expertise to the firm. He brought an entirely new,

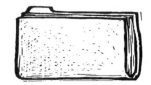

FAST FACTS:

About Coach Inc.

Ownership Coach Inc. is a publicly traded company on the New York Stock Exchange.

Ticker Symbol COH

Officers Lew Frankfort, Chmn. and CEO, 55, 2001 base salary $500,000; Keith Monda, EVP and COO, 55, 2001 base salary $410,000; Reed Krakoff, Exec. Creative Dir., 37, 2001 base salary $450,000

Employees 2,700

Chief Competitors Coach Inc. is a specialty retailer that designs and manufactures high quality leather goods and accessories. Its competitors range from the ultra chic fashion houses Gucci and Prada to the traditional craftsmen of Samsonite and Wilsons The Leather Experts.

A COACH WITH WHEELS

Coach, the upscale leather products company, has joined forces with luxury car manufacturer, Lexus to create the ultimate ride. The partnership originated in 1996 when Coach first offered its design services to the car dealer. In spring 2002 the latest joint venture will hit the streets. The Lexus RX 300 will sport perforated leather trimmed seats and Coach-embossed headrests. The floor mats will also be crafted from Coach leather. The special Coach Edition car will come in Burnished Gold, Crystal White, and Graphite Gray. The price tag for this special edition interior only starts at $2,830. Customers who select this option will receive a black Coach Hamptons Bag and a Coach Signature Demi-Pouch handbag to hold what money they have left after purchasing of the car.

---

modern sensibility to the brand and was a veteran of Polo Ralph Lauren and Tommy Hilfiger. He was on board at Hilfiger when it successfully re-invented itself as a diversified design label offering housewares, linens, accessories, and women's clothing in addition to its youthful sportswear.

During his first several years, Krakoff studied the Coach archive of products and styles and learned more about the brand. Armed with a solid knowledge of the company's tradition, he began the process or modernizing the product lines. Profits for the company were down in the late 1990s, but Krakoff and Frankfurt were working behind the scenes to re-engineer the company's image. Coach stores were updated to present a sleek, modern look. Collections were redesigned using mixed materials instead of all leather products. Production time for collections was shortened, allowing new merchandise to arrive in stores more frequently. When the new millennium arrived, Coach was moving forward with the times.

STRATEGY

The traditional Coach products and core collections were updated and ready for the next century. Krakoff and Frankfurt wanted to go one step further and transform Coach into a lifestyle brand. In order to do this, Coach

needed to move beyond the familiar territory of handbags and briefcases. Every type of product was considered fair game for inclusion in this new initiative.

Despite the focus on new product development, the management did not lose sight of the opportunities to introduce existing products to new markets. Japan was a huge untapped market and its consumers were in love with the Coach brand. Plans for a Japanese flagship store were approved and expansion was underway.

INFLUENCES

After years of operating independently, Coach Inc. was forced to take a look at the world and its competitors. Although Kenneth Cole and Dooney Bourke were viewed as traditional rivals for the Coach customer, it was the fashion houses that caught the eye of management. Gucci, Prada, Ralph Lauren, and Tommy Hilfiger influenced the direction of the company. Gucci and Prada showed that it was possible to produce stylish, classy accessories at affordable prices. Leather was optional. Lauren and Hilfiger each managed to expand a small niche in the market and establish a branded line of goods. These were the firms and the individuals that influenced the evolution of Coach.

CURRENT TRENDS

Coach is diversifying its product lines through licensing agreements and strategic partnerships.

CHRONOLOGY:

Key Dates for Coach Inc.

1941: Manhattan Leather Goods founded in a New York city loft

1962: First handbag designed after a paper shopping bag

1973: Introduction of the Duffle Sac

1979: Lew Frankfort joins Coach Inc.

1980: Coach publishes first catalog

1981: Opens first NYC flagship store on Madison Avenue

1985: Coach is acquired by Sara Lee Corp.

1997: Reed Krakoff joins Coach as first executive creative director

1998: First mixed material bags produced

1999: Coach launches Web site

2000: Coach becomes a publicly traded company

2001: Coach Signature collection is introduced

Carolee Design Inc. is developing a jewelry collection featuring leather and silver items. Movado Group is responsible for crafting a line of Coach watches. Footwear will be designed by Jimlar and manufactured in Italy from fine leather. Shoes will coordinate with Coach bags. A leather furniture collection is available from Baker Knapp & Tubbs. All of these new ventures are part of the "lifestyle" brand that Coach hopes to establish.

PRODUCTS

Coach makes fine leather products. Handbags, purses, and wallets are the original offerings of the company and still account for a substantial amount of revenues. Handbags generated 57 percent of net sales in 2001. Women's accessories, wallets, and belts accounted for 12 percent of sales, while men's accessories were 8 percent. Business cases and computer bags, duffel bags and travel accessories combined posted 10 percent. Other small items such as gloves, scarves, and leather folios accounted for the remaining profits. The next several

GOING TO THE DOGS

This isn't Coach's new merchandising strategy, but it could be. In an effort to attract younger, hipper customers, Coach has fashioned a collection of trendy items. The junior executives in training may not be ready to plunk down $500 for an expensive bag, but $150 for a pair of leather-trimmed sunglasses is fine. Leather headbands, cellphone cases, and key rings are also popular items for the young and wealthy. For those who still live at home and need to walk the family dog, leather dog jackets are available for $108, and collars are a mere $48. All items come adorned with the Coach signature "C" embossed on the side. Even Fido can cruise the neighborhood in style, though there is no word on the creation of a line of leashes. Perhaps they are not considered luxury items since they are mandatory in most states.

years will reveal the acceptance of the newly created lifestyles division and its offerings.

CORPORATE CITIZENSHIP

The company is always ready to help with a good cause. The investor relations department receives frequent requests for donations for use in fundraisers, auctions, and raffles. Coach has a history of generously giving back to the communities in which it operates and welcomes the chance to participate in events and lend the Coach name in support of worthwhile causes.

GLOBAL PRESENCE

Coach is an American tradition, but the products are known around the world. International business accounted for 16 percent of sales in 2001. Coach distributes its products in 18 countries including Japan, Korea, Hong Kong, Singapore, and Australia. The Japanese market is the most lucrative, and Coach places most of its international promotional efforts in this area. It will open a flagship store in Japan and expects it to do tremendous business. Coach also relies on international partners to supply materials for use in the manufacture of products. Additionally, the company operates a product development team headquartered in Florence, Italy, which works with a design team in New York. The company requires all vendors around the world to operate in compliance with Coach's standards of integrity.

EMPLOYMENT

Coach Inc. has 2,700 employees in locations around the world. Positions range from sales associate and retail store manager to leather workers and designers. The company has design professionals headquartered in Florence, Italy, to be close to the heart of the fashion industry. Coach encourages creativity and integrity in all employees and considers each employee to be an extension of the Coach brand name.

SOURCES OF INFORMATION

Bibliography

Curan, Catherine. "Coach Carries the Trendy Set." *Crain's New York Business*, 11 March 2002.

———. "Reed Krakoff-President, Executive Creative Director Coach." *Crain's New York Business*, 28 January 2002.

Hessen, Wendy. "Reed Krakoff. . .Transforms Company into a Must-Have American Icon."*Women's Wear Daily*, 5 June 2001.

Karimzadeh, Marc. "Coach Inc. Expanding into Jewelry." *Women's Wear Daily,* 26 June 2001.

Lenetz, Dana. "Coach Class." *Footwear News*, 26 November 2001.

"Lexus Introduces Two Special Model Editions." *Motor Trend News*, 7 April 2002.

McGrath, Courtney. "Coach Connects." *Kiplinger's Personal Finance Magazine*, April 2002

Weitzman, Jennifer. "Coach Bullish after Strong Quarter," *Women's Wear Daily*, 24 January 2002.

———. "Strong Sales Buoy Coach Net." *Women's Wear Daily,* 10 January 2002.

For an annual report:
on the Internet at: http://www.coach.com

For additional industry research:
Investigate companies by their Standard Industrial Classification Codes, also known as SICs. Coach Inc.'s primary SIC is:

2389 Apparel & Accessories

Also investigate companies by their North American Industry Classification Codes, also known as NAICS codes. Coach Inc.'s primary NAICS code is:

315999 Other Apparel & Accessories Manufacturing

ConAgra Foods, Inc.

FOUNDED: 1919 as Nebraska Consolidated Mills

Contact Information:

HEADQUARTERS: 1 ConAgra Drive
    Omaha, NE 68102-5001
PHONE: (402)595-4000
FAX: (402)595-4702
URL: http://www.conagra.com

OVERVIEW

ConAgra Foods, Inc., headquartered in Omaha, Nebraska, is a foodservice manufacturer and retail food supplier. It ranks as the top food service manufacturer (meat and poultry, French fries, and dough-based products) in the United States. It is ranked second as a food company (behind Kraft Foods), and a frozen foods company (behind Nestle USA) and in meat and poultry sales, behind IBP, Inc. Its annual sales reach approximately $27 billion.

The general public knows ConAgra best through its numerous and well known brand names that include Banquet, Chef Boyardee, Healthy Choice, and Van Camp's. Indeed, consumers are likely to see ConAgra products wherever they turn. In supermarkets, the products are found on the shelves, in the dairy case, the frozen food section, at the deli, and in the fresh and prepared meat case. Products can also be found at restaurants and hotels, convenience stores, and vending and snacking areas.

ConAgra Foods has been called a brand "powerhouse," as it boasts more than 80 brands. These include 25 food brands that record annual retail sales exceeding $100 million. One brand, Healthy Choice, has retail sales of about $1.5 billion dollars.

The company's major business subdivisions include agricultural products, packaged foods, and refrigerated foods. The agricultural business segment processes and distributes ingredients for food and beverage products and meat and poultry production. Also, the segment distributes crop protection chemicals, fertilizers, seeds, and information systems at wholesale and retail levels.

The packaged food segment produces shelf-stable foods, frozen foods, dairy case products, and foodservice products for retail, foodservice, and specialty markets. Shelf-stable products include tomato products, pasta products, cooking oils, popcorn, soup, puddings, meat snacks, canned beans, canned pasta, tuna, canned chili, cocoa mixes, and peanut butter. Frozen food products include dinners, pizzas, entrees, snacks, ice cream, and seafood. Dairy products include tablespreads, cheeses, egg alternatives, and dessert toppings. Foodservice products include potato products, ethnic food products, hand-held dough-based products, specialty meats, and other products primarily for foodservice markets.

The refrigerated foods segment produces and markets fresh and branded processed meats, beef and pork products, chicken and turkey products, and meat alternative products for retail, foodservice, institutional, and specialty markets. The processed meat products include hot dogs, bacon, ham, sausages, cold cuts, turkey products, and kosher products. Fresh meat products include beef, pork, and lamb. The poultry businesses include chicken and turkey products. Meat alternative products include soy-based items like meatless hot dogs and patties.

COMPANY FINANCES

In 2000, ConAgra Foods Inc.'s agricultural products segment reported fiscal year sales of $5.2 billion. The packaged foods segment had sales of $7.7 billion. The refrigerated foods segment had sales of $12.5 billion.

For fiscal 2001, overall sales grew 7 percent to reach $27.2 billion, while operating profit reached $1.9 billion. ConAgra reported that it had a tough first half of the year, but it bounced back in the second. During the fourth quarter, sales for the company's food businesses (packaged and refrigerated) grew 5 percent to $5.5 billion. Total food business operating profit declined to $372.0 million, versus $415.0 million in fiscal 2000. For all of 2001, food business sales grew 7 percent to $21.9 billion, and food business operating profit stayed the same at $1.6 billion.

Fourth quarter sales for the packaged food segment showed a 17 percent increase ($2.3 billion), while operating profit was $276.0 million compared to $294.0 million in the fourth quarter of 2000. For the full fiscal year, the segment's sales grew 14 percent to $8.7 billion and operating profit grew 5 percent to $1.1 billion.

For the same quarter, refrigerated foods sales went down by 2 percent to $3.3 billion, and operating profit decreased to $97.0 million (down from $121 million in the fourth quarter 2000). For the full year, sales rose 3 percent to $13.2 billion, and operating profit declined to $438.0 million from $491.0 million in 2000.

Fourth quarter sales for the agricultural products segment increased 4 percent to $899 million. Operating profit was $33 million, compared to $47 million in the fourth quarter of fiscal 2000. For the full fiscal year, agricultural products sales rose 5 percent to $5.3 billion and

FAST FACTS:
About ConAgra Foods, Inc.

Ownership: ConAgra Foods, Inc. is a publicly owned company traded on the New York Stock Exchange.

Ticker Symbol: CAG

Officers: Bruce Rohde, Chmn., Pres., CEO, 52, 2001 Salary $982,000; James O'Donnell, CFO, VP, Sec., 53, 2001 salary $466,000; Owen Johnson, EVP, Human Resources and Administration, 55, 2001 salary $415,000; Dwight Goslee, EVP, Operations Control and Development, 51, 2001 salary $133,000; Kenneth Gerhardt, SVP, CIO, 51, 2001 salary $373,000

Employees: 90,000

Principal Subsidiary Companies: ConAgra Foods Inc. is subdivided into three major business segments, including agricultural products, packaged foods, and refrigerated foods. These segments are further subdivided into various companies. The companies include more than 500 subsidiaries, many with well-known names such as Butterball Turkey, Bumble Bee Seafoods, Hunt Foods, and Swift & Company.

Chief Competitors: ConAgra Foods operates in the consumer/non-cyclical sector of the food processing industry. Its main competitors include Cargill, Kraft Foods, and Nestle USA.

operating profit totaled $281 million, down slightly from the 2000 operating profit of $283 million.

In 2002, for the 39 weeks ended February 24, 2002, revenues rose 3 percent to $21.22 billion. Net income rose 6 percent to $592.8 million.

ANALYSTS' OPINIONS

Some analysts have a bit of trouble reading ConAgra Foods, Inc. for several reasons. For one thing, the company has employed a complex trading strategy. In recent years, using cash earnings rather than reported earnings, ConAgra traded 34 percent below the price-cash flow ratios of the food industry group. Also, ConAgra is viewed by some as a complex company that has a "commodity-like image" because two-thirds of its sales are

CHRONOLOGY:

Key Dates for ConAgra Foods, Inc.

1919: Nebraska Consolidated Mills, which will become ConAgra Foods, Inc., is founded in Grand Island, Nebraska

1922: Nebraska Consolidated Mills moved to Omaha, Nebraska, the future headquarters of ConAgra Foods, Inc.

1971: Nebraska Consolidated Mills changes its name to ConAgra

1980: ConAgra begins a long series of acquisitions when it purchases Banquet Foods from RCA

1998: Bruce Rohde is appointed CEO of ConAgra

1999: ConAgra begins "Operation Overdrive," a major organizational restructuring program

1999: ConAgra integrates its five beef subsidiaries and begins operating them under one name, ConAgra Beef Co.

2000: ConAgra buys International Home Foods for $2.9 billion; ConAgra changes its name to ConAgra Foods, Inc. to reflect its changing business focus

2001: ConAgra Foods, Inc. acquires the David & Sons sunflower seeds and snack business from Nestle USA, Inc.

---

derived from activities such as meatpacking, poultry production, and agriproducts. For ConAgra Foods, low margins typical in those businesses result in an overall margin well below those of other food industry leaders. And because the company has three significant business segments, sometimes it's hard to determine exactly where the profits are really coming from.

However, Shields and Company of New York feels that ConAgra Foods, Inc. is a strong, well-managed food company that is "under-recognized" by the market. In 2000, it rated ConAgra a "strong buy." It based this rating on its increased confidence in ConAgra's ability to maintain its long-established record of double-digit earnings growth. "With annual sales of $27 billion, ConAgra is the nation's second largest food company, deriving 36 percent of sales and 63 percent of profits from Packaged Foods, 45 percent and 22 percent from Refrigerated Foods, and 19 percent and 15 percent from Agricultural

Products," Shields reported in October 2000. "The company has an unusually strong position in the growing foodservice market, which accounts for 37 percent of revenues, and where it is the industry's number one supplier."

HISTORY

It all started back 1919. The company that would become ConAgra Foods Inc. began when four flourmills in Grand Island, Nebraska, consolidated and incorporated as Nebraska Consolidated Mills. Three years later, the new company moved to Omaha, the city where ConAgra Foods, Inc. is now based.

For the next 50 years, Nebraska Consolidated Mills operated primarily as a commodity producer and food industry supplier. But that would start to change in the second half of the twentieth century, when it would move into other areas and enterprises. The company's evolving nature was reflected in its name change to ConAgra in 1971.

ConAgra really started becoming the company it is known as today in the 1980s and 1990s when it made a long series of acquisitions in a period when conglomerates were breaking apart. The process began in 1980, when ConAgra bought Banquet Foods from RCA. By 2000 the company would amass 33 brands that would turn an impressive $100 million in sales.

In 1998 ConAgra named Bruce Rohde as its chief executive officer. The appointment would prove crucial, as Rohde strengthened ConAgra's overall performance and enhanced the company's potential. Rohde implemented cost reduction steps, and he placed more emphasis on product development and marketing. He also focused on acquisitions and divestitures. The results of his actions had a significantly positive impact. By the end of the decade, ConAgra's profit margins would be at record highs. As the company moved into the twenty-first century, it appeared that these margins would continue rising.

In 1999 ConAgra integrated its five beef subsidiaries and began operating them under one name, Congra Beef Co. In August 2000, ConAgra made one of its most significant acquisitions when it bought International Home Foods for $2.9 billion. It was the company's largest acquisition in its history, and it would increase the sales of its packaged foods segment by 30 percent. The company scored another major acquisition that same year when it purchased Bumble Bee, a tuna company.

In September 2000, ConAgra renamed itself ConAgra Foods, Inc., to underscore its new emphasis on its increasing role as a foodservice manufacturer. As part of this image makeover, Rohde placed advertisements in the *Wall Street Journal*, the national financial newspaper. With the ads, he wanted the country to see that ConAgra Foods was a major food company, and not just an agricultural ingredients supplier. Rohde wanted nothing less than for ConAgra Foods, Inc. to become America's favorite food company.

In December 2001, the company acquired the David & Sons sunflower seeds and snack business from Nestle USA, Inc., a subsidiary of Swiss-based Nestle S.A., one of its major competitors.

STRATEGY

Management has implemented a strategic plan designed to result, over a long term, in single-digit sales growth, expanding profit margins, double-digit growth in operating profits, and an increasing return on investment. The plan has five key strategies including channelization, controlling capital, "cleaning house," margin and mix, and targeted acquisitions.

Channelization involves focusing on the specific needs of each class of customers, including general consumers, supermarkets, club stores, and convenience stores in the retail sector, and restaurant chains and broadline distributors in foodservice. Controlling capital involves establishing tight controls over capital expenditures to provide more funds for acquisitions and other purposes. The "cleaning house" strategy is part of ConAgra Foods Inc.'s intent to strengthen the company and increase its profitability by divesting unproductive assets and businesses that no longer fit in with its long-term plans. The margin and mix strategy involves the company's "Operation Overdrive," a major restructuring program that began in 1999 and has resulted in significant cost reductions and expanded margins. Through its targeted acquisitions strategy, ConAgra Foods intends to continue its active acquisition programs, which has resulted in tremendous gains for the company, including diversity of product, increased sales, and rising cash flow.

INFLUENCES

When ConAgra wanted to become known as a major food company, it found it has some obvious catching up to do with food industry competitors. The company was able to achieve this rather rapidly, thanks to a massive organizational restructuring that includes divestiture of businesses like barges, wool, and pet supplies last year, as well as reorganizing its remaining business into three lines: retail foods, foodservice supply, and agricultural products.

The appointment of Bruce Rohde as CEO had no small impact on the company's successful navigation of its new direction. Possessing a track record of initiating change, Rohde helped ConAgra Foods become the largest U.S. foodservice manufacturer and the second largest retail food supplier. One of the things Rohde did

was step up ConAgra Foods' acquisition efforts. Under his watch, the company scored some pivotal business acquisitions, including International Home Foods. It amassed important brand names like Chef Boyardee, Bumble Bee, Pam, and Gulden's, and it reinforced some of its brands through line extensions that included new products such as gravy, stuffing, broth (for the Butterball brand name), and a casserole mix (for the Banquet brand name).

CURRENT TRENDS

Moving into 2001, ConAgra continued making acquisitions, the most high-profile element of its strategic plan. It also started forming strategic alliances. However, the company doesn't absorb other companies and branded names indiscriminately, nor does it choose partners randomly.

For instance, in 2001, ConAgra joined forces with Wolfgank Puck to manufacture, market, and distribute gourmet foods such as frozen entrees, pizzas, and side dishes under the Wolfgang Puck name. According to reports, ConAgra entered into the agreement to capitalize on a growing trend: American consumers are cooking less, eating out more, and relying more and more on gourmet meals that are easy to prepare. Faced with a shrinking market for vegetables, meats, and other farm products that need to be prepared, ConAgra aggressively went after high-margin gourmet products, which Rohde sees as a gold mine, and for good reason. In 2001, consumers were spending about $1 billion a day on food eaten away from home (according to the National Restaurant Association), and prepared foods remain one of the few growth segments in the industry.

PRODUCTS

ConAgra has perhaps the largest number of leading brand names in the food industry. Thirty of its brands have sales in excess of $100 million a year, including Healthy Choice, with sales of more than $1 billion. Its three major business segments include packaged foods, refrigerated foods, and agricultural products.

Its packaged foods segment includes many well-known brand names. Its major shelf-stable brands include Hunt's, Healthy Choice, Chef Boyardee, Wesson, Orville Redenbacher's, Peter Pan, Van Camp's, Gulden's, Swiss Miss, Bumble Bee, and La Choy. Major frozen food brands include Banquet, Marie Callender's, Kid Cuisine, and Wolfgang Puck. Major dairy brands include Parkay, Blue Bonnet, Fleischmann's, Egg Beaters, and County Line. Foodservice major brands include Lamb Weston, Fernando's, Casa de Oro, Holly Ridge, Rosarita, and Zoll. Major brands from its refrigerated foods segment

GOING TO BAT FOR CONAGRA

In August 2000 baseball superstar Sammy Sosa joined the ConAgra Foods team. The outfielder was turned into a pitcher; that is, his role was designated to be a "pitchman" for ConAgra's popular Hunt's Snack Pack and Orville Redenbacher's Gourmet Popping Corn brands. He was also slated to go to bat for ConAgra's Feeding Children Better program.

include Armour, Butterball, Cook's, Country Pride, Healthy Choice, Brown 'N Serve, National Deli, and Swift Premium.

ConAgra's agricultural products segment distributes crop protection chemicals, fertilizers, seeds, and information systems at wholesale and retail levels. Major agricultural brands include Clean Crop, ACA, Savage, Shotgun, Saber, Signature, and Loveland Industries.

The company also is a leading supplier of both hamburger patties and frozen French fries to McDonald's, Burger King, Wendy's, and other fast food chains. Other customers include Pizza Hut, Taco Bell, Arby's, Popeyes, Jack in the Box, Applebee's, and Aramark. In addition, it is the top supplier to just about all of the major foodservice distributors including SYSCO, U.S. Foodservice, PYA/Monarch, Alliance, and Performance Food Group.

CORPORATE CITIZENSHIP

ConAgra Foods, Inc. commits itself to improving the quality of life in communities across America. It does this through leadership partnerships and financial contributions. Specifically, its activities are focused on two major national initiatives: Feeding Children Better, a multi-million-dollar, multi-year commitment to helping end child hunger in the United States; and a national program aimed at educating consumers about home food safety.

The company has also implemented an environmental program that includes four key initiatives: water and energy conservation, prevention of air pollution, waste reduction and recycling, and land management protection and enhancement. In 2000 the company's pro-

gram saved 448.3 million gallons of water, reduced landfill waste by nearly 14.0 million pounds, cut electrical use by 35.7 million kilowatts, and cut natural gas use by 86.8 million square cubic feet.

GLOBAL PRESENCE

ConAgra Foods has principal operations in about 25 countries and more than 200 operating groups and plants around the globe. It has foreign offices located in Hong Kong, Korea, Mexico, Taiwan, and Tokyo.

EMPLOYMENT

ConAgra Foods employs more than 90,000 people worldwide, and it provides a strong employee support system that includes a flexible benefits package and a family-friendly working environment. Employees are offered a menu of benefits that best suit their individual or family needs. Plans include 401(k) with company match; PPO, HMO, or POS health coverage; and dental and vision coverage.

In striving to create an environment that encourages creativity and innovation, the company has installed an online internal job posting process, promotional and rotational career opportunities, and recognition and reward programs. It also offers encourages advancement through educational reimbursement programs, memberships in professional and industry associations, conference and seminar attendance, and through programs offered at its Learning Center in Omaha, Nebraska.

SOURCES OF INFORMATION

Bibliography

Business 2.0.com. "ConAgra Foods, Inc." 1 April 2002. Available at http://www.business2.com.

CBS MarketWatch. "Profile: ConAgra Foods, Inc." 2002. Available at http://cbs.marketwatch.com.

Cohen, Debra. "ConAgra Mulls the Fate of Laggard Units—Analysts," 26 December 2001. Available at http://www.google.com/fdc/ads.

Cummins, Robert J. "Investment Highlights: ConAgra Foods, Inc." *Shields & Company*, 17 October 2000. Available at http://www.shieldsandco.com.

Hoover's Online. "ConAgra Foods, Inc.," 1 April 2002. Available at http://www.hoovers.com.

Independent Sector. "ConAgra Foods and America's Second Harvest." *Mission and Market*, 2002. Available at http://www.independentsector.org/mission_market/conagra.htm.

Yahoo! Finance. "ConAgra Foods, Inc." *Yahoo Market Guide*, 28 March 2002. Available at http://biz.yahoo.com/p/c/cag.html.

For additional industry research:

Investigate companies by their Standard Industrial Classification Codes, also known as SICs. ConAgra Foods, Inc.'s primary SICs are:

2011 Meat Packing Plants

2013 Sausages and Other Prepared Meat Products

2015 Poultry Slaughtering and Processing

2022 Natural, Processed, and Imitation Cheese

2038 Frozen Specialties, Not Elsewhere Classified

2041 Flour and Other Grain Mill Products

2048 Prepared Feeds and Feed Ingredients for Animals and Fowls, Except Dogs and Cats

2875 Fertilizers, Mixing Only

2879 Pesticides and Agricultural Chemicals, Not Elsewhere Classified

6211 Security Brokers, Dealers, and Flotation Companies

Also investigate companies by their North American Industry Classification System Codes, also known as NAICS codes. ConAgra Foods, Inc.'s primary NAICS codes are:

311119 Other Animal Food Manufacturing

311211 Flour Milling

311412 Frozen Specialty Food Manufacturing

311513 Cheese Manufacturing

311611 Animal (except Poultry) Slaughtering

311612 Meat Processed from Carcasses

311615 Poultry Processing

325314 Fertilizer (Mixing Only) Manufacturing

325320 Pesticide and Other Agricultural Chemical Manufacturing

523120 Securities Brokerage

Costco Wholesale Corporation

FOUNDED: 1983

Contact Information:
HEADQUARTERS: PO Box 34331
Issaquah, WA 98027
PHONE: (425)313-8100
FAX: (425)313-6430
TOLL FREE: (800)774-2678
URL: http://www.costco.com

OVERVIEW

Costco Wholesale Corporation operates a chain of 386 no-frills membership warehouse stores that carry name-brand merchandise at substantially discounted prices. Costco stores are geared to meet the needs of small- and medium-sized businesses. Individual memberships are also available to those who belong to a qualifying organization. More than 22 million households hold Costco memberships, accounting for more than 39 million cardholders. As of February 2002, Costco operated 386 locations. Of that total, 285 stores were located in 36 United States and Puerto Rico. International locations include Canada, Mexico, the United Kingdom, Taiwan, Korea, and Japan.

Three types of membership are offered, and membership is required to shop at a Costco warehouse. Business members pay annual fee of $45, which includes a spouse card. Up to six additional cards may be purchased by a business member for $35 each for partners or associates in the business. Gold Star membership is for individuals not associated with a business. Individual members pay a $45 annual fee, which includes a free spouse membership. The Executive membership plan provides the regular benefits of shopping at Costco, as well as allowing executive members to purchase a range of discounted consumer services such as auto and homeowner's insurance and long-distance telephone service. Additional discounted business services are also made available, including health insurance, payroll processing, and merchant credit card processing. Executive membership costs $100 annually. The largest membership group is Gold Star, with 14.0 million members, followed by Business, with 4.4 million members. Executive accounts and add-on members accounted for 1.3 million and 3.6 million memberships, respectively.

COMPANY FINANCES

For fiscal year 2001, net sales totaled $34.14 billion. Adding memberships fees of $66 million, the total income for 2001 was $34.8 billion, reflecting an increase of $2.6 billion over fiscal year 2000 total revenues of $32.16 billion. Despite the increase in net sales, net income dropped from $631 million in 2000 to $602 million, due primarily to increased operating expenses. Earnings per share also fell, from $1.35 per share in 2000 to $1.29 per share in 2001. Although Costco's value decreased slightly during 2001, the company grew significantly in the last 10 years. In 1992 net income totaled $242.0 million on total revenues of $14.1 billion, and stock earnings were $0.49 a share; therefore, in the 10 years prior to fiscal 2001, Costco more than doubled its total annual revenues as well as its earnings per share. Of total revenues from fiscal 2001, operations in the United States accounted for $28.6 billion, Canadian operations accounted for $4.7 billion, and all other international operations accounted for $1.5 billion. During the second quarter of fiscal 2002, net sales increased 13 percent compared to the same time period of the previous year. Stocks traded at the beginning of March 2002 for $39 a share, nearly in the middle of the 52-week high of $46 and low of $29.

ANALYSTS' OPINIONS

Based on increased positive performance in the first two quarters of fiscal year 2002, analysts mark Costco stock at under $40 as a strong buy. Analysts viewed the downgrading in Costco stock as more indicative of the overall downturn in the retail industry and, in general, the economy. Positive signs identified by analysts included a 13 percent increase in net sales during the second quarter of fiscal 2002, the approaching end of a promotional 2 percent rebate offered to Executive members, an overall membership renewal rating of 85 percent, and Costco's plans for continued aggressive growth in square footage. The major negative factors affecting Costco included increased expenses from new openings, rising utility prices, and an increase in wages paid to employees. Most analysts believe that Costco holds promise for both short- and long-term growth, and stock prices are estimated to increase to between $50 and $60 a share.

HISTORY

The journey toward the entity now known as Costco Wholesale Corporation began in 1954 when Sol Price

FAST FACTS:
About Costco Wholesale Corporation

Ownership: Costco is a publicly owned company traded on the NASDAQ Stock Exchange.

Ticker Symbol: COST

Officers: James D. Sinegal, 65, Pres. and CEO, 2001 salary $350,000; Jeffrey H. Brotman, 59, Chmn., 2001 base salary $350,000; Richard D. DiCerchio, 58, SEVP, 2001 salary $429,423; Richard A. Galanti, 45, EVP and CFO, 2001 base salary $429,423

Employees: 92,500

Principal Subsidiary Companies: Costco, whose business market is primarily the Eastern and Western United States and Canada, has a subsidiary that operates in Japan and does business in Mexico, South Korea, Taiwan, and the United Kingdom through joint ventures. Costco Wholesale Industries, a division of the company, operates manufacturing businesses such as special food packaging, optical laboratories, and meat processing.

Chief Competitors: Costco competes against a wide range of the retailers in the consumer market in various products groups, including Wal-Mart, Kmart, Service Merchandise, Home Depot, and Dollar General.

created Fedmart, a discount department store for all government employees willing to pay the $2 annual membership fee. The members-only warehouse concept caught on quickly, and within 20 years, Price was operating 45 stores that produced more than $300 million in annual sales. Price's involvement with Fedmart ended in 1975 when he sold the company to Hugo Mann after losing leadership control. The company dissolved seven years later.

Price then set his sights on small businesses. Partnering with his son, Robert, along with Rick Libenson and Giles Bateman, Price started Price Club. Using $800,000 of his own money along with $1 million contributed by California businesses and $500,000 added by former Fedmart employees, Price opened the first Price Club in San Diego in 1976. Price's vision was to offer a small selection of products to businesses at steeply discounted prices, usually no more than 10 percent above

Japanese shoppers experience the no-nonsense American approach to shopping at a Costco outlet in Chiba, east of Tokyo. (AP Photo/ Atsushi Tsukada)

invoice. By targeting small businesses, Price hoped to supplement profits with membership fees. He also wanted to attract financially stable customers, which would reduce costs associated with bad checks and shoplifting.

After the first year of operation, Price Club posted a net loss of $750,000 on sales of $16 million. As a result the company moved to expand its membership by including government, utility, and hospital employees, along with credit union members. Additional stock was sold, primarily to friends, to keep the company afloat another year. By 1978 Price Club had rebounded from its rocky start and was able to expand its operations by opening a second store in Phoenix, Arizona. In the same year, Price helped his other son, Laurence, establish a tire-mounting and battery installation business adjacent to a Price Club store. The shop leased space from Price Club and serviced tires and batteries sold by Price Club.

By 1980 Price Club was operating four stores in California and Arizona and was generating $150 million in annual sales. In the same year, the company went public. In 1984 Price Club expanded to the East Coast, opening two stores in Virginia, followed by a store opening in Maryland in 1986. During this time, Price Club also moved into New Mexico and expanded into Canada, in a joint venture with Canadian retailer Steinberg, with a store opening in Montreal. Because Price Club insisted on owning the land on which it built its warehouses, the company created the subsidiary, TPCR Corporation, to

handle its land management and development. Through TPCR, Price Club worked with developers to bring in other retailers to Price Club property sites. Increased competition was offset by increased traffic flow and the rent paid by retailers to Price Club. By 1985 profits had grown to $45 million on sales of $1.9 billion.

In 1986 Price Club purchased A.M. Lewis, a grocery distributor serving Southern California and Arizona. In 1988 it opened two Price Club Furnishings outlets, which served as home and office furnishings stores based on the Price Club warehouse concept. In 1990, Price bought out Steinberg's share of the Montreal store and expansion continued in numerous markets including California, Colorado, and British Columbia. In 1992 Price Club partnered with Controladora Comericail Mexicana to open a store in Mexico City, with a second store opening in the following year. Conditions such as steep land prices, traffic congestion, and increased competition resulted in the closing of two stores on the East Coast in 1992.

Increasingly strong competition from new warehouse membership clubs, such as the Wal-Mart spinoff, Sam's Club, and Kmart's PACE membership club, were challenging Price Club's hold on the warehouse market. Price Club was also facing stiff competition on the West Coast from Costco Wholesale. Costco was formed by James D. Sinegal, a former executive of both Fedmart and Price Club, and Jeffrey H. Brotman, an oil exploration company executive. Basing their stores closely on the Price

Club concept, Sinegal and Brotman opened the first Costco in Seattle, Washington, in 1983. Costco went public two years later, expanded into Canada, and became the first warehouse retailer to add fresh foods such as produce, bakery products, and meat. Just five years after its start up, Costco's annual sales reached $2 billion.

As competition increased, Price Club began to experience problems. In 1986 Sol Price was sued by his son, Laurence, for attempting to buy out the tire-service business, then valued at $5 million. The furniture store concept failed, and expansion was slowed by the heavy cost of purchasing land and building warehouse. Other companies pursued less costly and more aggressive expansion programs and, by 1987, Price Club had been passed by both Costco and Sam's. Although both sales and earnings had grown steadily each year, in 1988 Sol Price resigned as head of the company, and was replaced by Robert Price. In 1992 earnings dropped for the first time since 1980.

By 1993 Sam's Clubs were dominating the industry, with nearly half of the market. With Price Club's market value continuing to drop and Costco in fear of being taken over by Sam's, the two companies entered merger negotiations. The result was the creation of Price-Costco Inc., with Sinegal serving as chief executive officer and Robert Price serving as chairman of the board. Price shareholders retained a 48 percent interest in the new company, and Costco shareholders took a 52 percent interest. From the start, the merger did not develop smoothly. Numerous ongoing conflicts arose between Sinegal and Price; continued declining sales only spurred the dissention. In 1994 Price took the commercial real estate operations and several other international assets, all totaled about 10 percent of the PriceCostco's worth, and spun off as Price Enterprises.

Upon Price's departure, Sinegal focused on expansion and international development. In 1997 the company's name was changed to Costco Companies. Online sales were launched in 1998, and by 1999 warehouses had opened in South Korea, England, and Japan. Also in 1999 the company underwent yet another name change, becoming Costco Wholesale Corporation.

STRATEGY

From its first store opening until the present, Costco's basis strategy has remained unchanged: cut costs at every corner in order to provide customers with discounted prices. The stores sell an array of goods, from five-pound bags of rice to televisions and jewelry. Selection within product types is limited, thus reducing the costs of excessive inventory. Every measure is taken to reduce overhead and keep costs low. The warehouse stores are built on cheap industrial land and are void of decoration, products are stocked in bulk on the warehouse floor, sales help is kept to a bare minimum, and

CHRONOLOGY:

Key Dates for Costco Wholesale Corporation

1983: The first Costco warehouse opens in Seattle, Washington

1985: Costco becomes a publicly held company

1991: Completes public stock offering of 3.45 million shares, generating $200 million for expansion and debt reduction

1993: Merges with The Price Company to form Price/Costco Inc.

1997: Spins off most non-warehouse assets to Price Enterprises, Inc. and changes name to Costco Companies Inc.

1998: Begins online sales and operates internationally in Canada, England, South Korea, and Japan

1999: Re-incorporates and changes name to Costco Wholesale Corporation

2001: Generates $73 million in e-commerce sales

2002: Net sales for the first half of fiscal year 2002 top $17.5 billion

there is no advertising budget, except to announce a new store opening.

Rapid expansion has also been become an increasingly important aspect of Costco's overall strategy. In fiscal 2001 the company spent nearly $1.5 billion to upgrade and expand its operations. Of that total, almost $1 billion was used to open new warehouses or relocate existing stores, and $150 million was spent on remodeling efforts. Another $200 million was used to expand Costco's support facilities. In all, Costco opened 39 new warehouses in fiscal 2001, of which 26 were located in new markets. Notably, seven stores began operations in Texas, with positive early results. Along with increasing the number of warehouses, Costco has also increased the average size of its operations from 135,000 square feet to 148,000 square feet.

INFLUENCES

The major factor influencing Costco is the state of the economy. Retailers are prone to be significantly

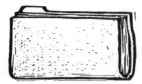

MORE THAN A WAREHOUSE

Costco doesn't just sell bulk candy and discounted housewares; the company offers its members a range of services beyond what is stocked on the warehouse floor. For small businesses that want to accept credit cards, Costco will handle the administration and paperwork. Small businesses can also apply for small business loans, set up a checking account, or set up a retirement account. Companies can even purchase background music through Costco. Special services for individuals include discounted auto sales, auto financing, home and auto insurance, travel packages, long-distance service, and check-printing services. Costco also coordinates special rates for real estate services, financial planning, and mortgage services.

---

impacted by any downturn in the economy as consumers cut back on spending, especially on nonessential items. However, despite the recession of the early 2000s, Costco remained on track for significant growth. The company committed to look beyond the recession and be prepared for a re-energized marketplace; however, if economic hard times last longer than Costco anticipates, the estimated annual earnings growth of 15 percent may be difficult to achieve. On the other hand, if the recession ends quickly, Costco will be ahead of many of its competitors who have cut back on expansion efforts due to the slow economy. Another factor influencing the future of Costco is the efforts of its competitors. Sam's Clubs have already infiltrated a large share of the market, both Target and Kmart have plans for aggressive expansion into the wholesale business, and grocery chains such as Kroger and Albertson's are trying hard to attract customers to their supercenters.

CURRENT TRENDS

Rapid expansion plans called for Costco to nearly double in size by 2005. With 32 new stores opening and 7 relocations in 2001, Costco planned to open another 35 to 40 each year for several years. With a presence in 35 states, most new stores will be located in existing markets, as the company has no plans to expand into sparsely populated areas such as North Dakota or Wyoming.

Recently entered market areas include Missouri, Minnesota, Ohio, North Carolina, South Carolina, and Tennessee. Because new stores cover more square footage, sales are expected to grow faster than actual store count. Focus on ancillary services has also increased. Nearly 85 percent of Costco warehouses include pharmacies, optical centers, and one-hour photo centers, and the company's goal is to provide these services at all locations. Costco fueling centers are also considered an area of potentially large growth. In 2001, 150 Costco locations included a gas station, and plans called for adding increasing numbers of fuel services to both new and existing warehouses. Another area of significant growth for Costco is online sales. E-commerce sales reached $73 million in fiscal 2001 and were expected to top $100 million by the end of fiscal 2002.

Never before accepting credit cards in order to avoid the administrative costs, in 2001 Costco introduced a partnership with American Express that provided customers with membership to both Costco and American Express in one card. By the end of fiscal 2001, nearly 1.9 million Costco members held the co-branded cards. The Special Order Kiosk program, also introduced in 2001, allows members to special-order certain "big-ticket" items, such as Kohler and Grohe bathroom fixtures, Sealy mattresses, brand name tires, and furniture. In 2002 Costco announced the introduction of a new cash card program. The card can be used for gifts or for returned items.

PRODUCTS

Products categories include groceries, candy, appliances, television and media, automotive supplies, toys, hardware, sporting goods, jewelry and watches, cameras, books, housewares, apparel, health and beauty aids, tobacco, furniture, office supplies, and office equipment. Costco carries national and regional name brand products, including recent contracts with merchandisers Titleist, Levi, Thomasville, Elizabeth Arden, and Sony computers. Costco also carries a line of private label products under the name Kirkland Signature. The Kirkland Signature line includes juice, cookies, coffee, tires, housewares, luggage, appliances, clothing, and detergent. New private label products recently added included baby formula and frozen foods. In 2001 the Kirkland Signature brand of olive oil accounted for 15 percent of sales in the United States. With wine sales of more than $500 million, Costco is the largest wine retailer in the nation; additionally, more than 50,000 carats of diamonds passed into the hands of Costco customers in 2001.

CORPORATE CITIZENSHIP

Costco supports a wide range of national and regional philanthropic endeavors. For example, after the terrorist attacks of September 11, 2001, Costco responded quickly by donating vital supplies to more than a dozen help organizations, including fire and police departments, the Red Cross, the Salvation Army, and Staten Island Relief. The corporation donated $1 million directly to the New York Trade Center Relief Fund and collected donations at its warehouses from members and employees, which totaled more than $3 million. Another $100,000 was donated by the company to the families of those lost at the Pentagon.

GLOBAL PRESENCE

Canada is Costco's largest international market, with 60 stores. Eleven stores operated in the United Kingdom, and 20 stores operated in Mexico. Other international locations include Taiwan (three stores), Korea (five stores), and Japan (two stores). Costco operations have been particularly productive in Canada, Mexico, and the United Kingdom. Growth has been slower in the Asian markets, which can be attributed to several factors. First, the Asian economy has experienced a significant downturn from which it has not fully recovered. Second, the region has a strong tradition of established retail shopping. As a result, Costco has had more difficulty lining up distributors and enticing customers. Finally, in most parts of Asia, households are very small and storage space is limited; therefore, Costco has found it necessary to reduce the size of its bulk items to accommodate smaller purchase amounts.

EMPLOYMENT

Costco seeks ambitious, highly motivated individuals who enjoy the fast-paced environment of the retail industry. Most Costco employees begin their careers at a warehouse, where they learn the details of the Costco business. Careers are also available at the home and regional offices, which employ individuals in the fields of accounting, marketing, buying, graphic arts, journal-

ism, information systems, human resources, and law. Costco rewards its best employees with promotions, with 85 percent of management positions filled from within the organization. Costco offers its employees exciting opportunities, personal and career growth, a friendly and supportive work environment, stability, excellent benefits, and a workplace focused on ethical, legal behavior. *ComputerWorld* named Costco information systems division one of America's best places to work in information technology in 1999, and *Washington CEO* chose Costco as one of the top three companies to work for in the state of Washington.

SOURCES OF INFORMATION

Bibliography

"Clubbed Club." *Business Week*, 18 March 2002.

"Costco Earnings: Financials." *Drug Store News*, 19 December 2001.

"Costco Wholesale Corporation." *Hoover's Company Profiles*, 2002. Available at http://www.hoovers.com.

"Costco Wholesale Corporation: Financials." *Drug Store News*, 6 March 2002.

"Costco Wholesale Corporation Reports Second Quarter and Year-to-date Operating Results for Fiscal 2002 and February Sales Results." *Business Wire*, 5 March 2002.

Desjardins, Doug. "Costco Charts Growth Plan for FY 2002." *DSN Retailing Today*, 11 February 2002.

Grant, Tina, ed. *International Directory of Company Histories*, Vol. 14. Detroit: St. James Press, 1996.

For additional industry research:

Investigate companies by their Standard Industrial Classification Codes, also known as SICs. Costco Wholesale Corporation's primary SIC is:

5331 Variety Stores

Also investigate companies by their North American Industry Classification System codes, also known as NAICS codes. Costco Wholesale Corporation's primary NAICS code is:

452990 All Other General Merchandise Stores

CSX Corporation

FOUNDED: 1980

Contact Information:

HEADQUARTERS: 901 East Cary Street
    Richmond, VA 23219-4031
PHONE: (804)782-1400
URL: http://www.csx.com

OVERVIEW

CSX Corp. operates a 22,700-mile rail system spanning 23 eastern, southeastern, and midwestern U.S. states and the Canadian provinces of Ontario and Quebec. Rail services account for roughly three-fourths of revenues. Via 33 units throughout North America, CSX Intermodal offers hauling services that make use of various modes of transportation including trains, trucks, and ocean vessels. These intermodal services bring in 14 percent of sales. CSX Lines, which contributes 8 percent of sales, operates a fleet of 16 vessels that offer domestic container shipping services to and from the United States and Guam, Puerto Rico, Alaska, and Hawaii. International operations include terminals in Australia, Asia, the Caribbean, and Europe. Non-transportation assets include CSX Real Property and the Greenbrier, a resort based in West Virginia.

COMPANY FINANCES

Revenues for CSX fell to $8.11 billion in 2001 compared to $8.19 billion the previous year. Earnings fell from $565 million to $293 million over the same time period, causing the firm's profit margin to drop from 6.9 percent to 3.6 percent. CSX's performance had been strongest in the mid-1990s. Along with sales in excess of $10 billion, CSX posted profits of $855 million in 1996. That year, the firm's profit margin peaked at 8.1 percent, as did earnings per share, which reached $3.96; its stock reached a high of $62.44 per share and a low of $41.25 per share. In comparison, stock prices in 2001 ranged from a high of $41.30 to a low of $24.81, and earnings per share totaled $1.38.

FINANCES:

CSX Corp.
Revenues, 1997-2001
(million dollars)

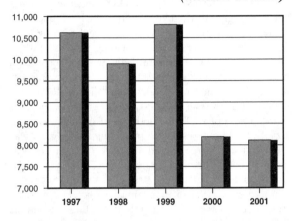

ANALYSTS' OPINIONS

Many analysts were critical of CSX's decision in 1999 to jointly acquire Conrail with rival Norfolk Southern. Two years later, this acquisition continued to undermine the outlook for CSX despite an overall upturn in the railroad industry prompted by natural gas shortages that boosted demand for coal shipments. According to a May 2001 issue of *Business Week*, "East Coast rails are still mired in problems related to the dismemberment of Conrail, which Norfolk Southern and CSX Corp. purchased in 1999. Standard & Poor's thinks these two major railroads overpaid for Conrail assets and will not realized positive contributions for several more years." However, CSX management attributed strong earnings in the fourth quarter of 2001 to reduced costs, which the firm was able to achieve by making better use of its Conrail assets. "Having single-line through service allowed us to eliminate several handoffs, which saved us several days and makes our product more reliable," stated a CSX executive in a January 2002 issue of *Traffic World*.

HISTORY

In 1973 the Baltimore & Ohio Railroad (BOR) combined with the Chesapeake & Ohio Railroad (COR) under the control of a holding company called The Chessie System. The BOR had been created in 1827 to offer a rail and canal system between the Eastern Seaboard and the industrial centers around the Great

FAST FACTS:
About CSX Corporation

Ownership: CSX Corp. is a publicly owned company traded on the New York Stock Exchange.

Ticker Symbol: CSX

Officers: John W. Snow, Chmn., Pres., and CEO; Paul R. Goodwin, VChmn. and CFO; Jessie R. Mohorovic, VP Corporate Communications; James A. Searle, Jr., VP Administration

Employees: 39,011

Principal Subsidiary Companies: CSX operates CSX Transportation, Inc., a leading U.S. railroad company serving the United States and Canada. Other subsidiaries include CSX Intermodal, Inc.; CSX World Terminals, LLC; and CSX Lines, LLC.

Chief Competitors: Competitors to CSX include other railway companies such as Burlington Northern Santa Fe and Canadian National Railway, as well as air and ground shipping companies like FedEx and J.B. Hunt.

Lakes. The COR had been taken over by J.P. Morgan in 1878 after the company suffered losses and neared bankruptcy following the Civil War. In 1980 The Chessie System, Inc. merged with Seaboard Coast Line Industries (SCL), which dated back to the 1830s, to create CSX Corp. Prime F. Osborn became chairman of the new company, while Hays T. Watkins was named president. Two years later, Watkins also took over the chairman position when Osborn retired.

Watkins diversified CSX with a series of acquisitions beginning with the 1983 purchase of Texas Gas Resources. CSX purchased AMR Commercial Lines, Inc. in 1984 and Sea-Land Corp. in 1986. CSX also entered into the leisure and lodging industry with the acquisition of Rockresorts, Inc. By 1988, however, CSX was forced to sell off many of its recent acquisitions in a corporate restructuring program developed in response to complaints about company performance. In 1989 John W. Snow replaced Watkins as president and CEO, and he immediately began divesting subsidiaries in an effort to refocus the company on its core operations.

In October 1996 Conrail accepted a $8.4 billion acquisition bid by CSX. Along with boosting CSX's sales to $14 billion, the merger would have allowed

CHRONOLOGY:

Key Dates for CSX Corp.

1980: Chessie System Inc. and Seaboard Coast Line Industries merge to form CSX Corp.

1984: U.S. authorities allow CSX to operate American Commercial Lines, reversing regulations that prevented railroads from owning steamship or barge lines

1986: CSX pays $800 million for Sea-Land Corp., the largest U.S. ocean container shipping company

1987: CSX creates its CSX Intermodal subsidiary

1996: CSX bids $8.4 billion for Conrail

1999: Norfolk Southern and CSX jointly acquire Conrail

CSX to offer barge, container shipping, rail, and intermodal services in more than 80 countries. It would also have secured for CSX control of 70 percent of the eastern U.S. railroad market. Management estimated economies of scale would produce $730 million in savings for CSX. The deal also appealed to Conrail, which needed to find a merger partner to reduce costs, increase services, and offer more competitive prices to consumers. However, rival Norfolk Southern, recognizing that it would become a minor player in the East if Conrail and CSX merged, fought the proposal with a higher bid of its own. As a result, Conrail's board eventually voted against the CSX takeover. By June 1998 a three-way deal had been forged. CSX acquired 40 percent of Conrail's assets while Norfolk received the remaining 58 percent when the deal was finalized on June 1, 1999.

In 1999 CSX separated Sea-Land into three distinct units: CSX World Terminals, CSX Lines, and an international container shipping unit that was purchased by Denmark-based A.P. Moller for $800 million. The firm spent the second half of the year folding its new Conrail assets into existing operations, and the integration process proved problematic. Service problems with Conrail assets persisted into 2000, which prompted CSX to restructure its rail operations management team. That year, TNT Post Group paid $650 million for CTI Logistx, a transportation logistics company that CSX had acquired in the early 1990s, and CSX used the cash to whittle down its substantial debt. In 2001 CSX created Transflo

Corp. to handle the transfer of freight between railcars, truck, and ships.

STRATEGY

Shortly after its inception, CSX began to pursue a strategy of growth via diversification. In 1983, under the leadership of Hays T. Watkins, CSX paid $1 billion for Texas Gas Resources Corp., a leading U.S. natural gas pipeline operation with significant gas and petroleum reserves. As a result of the deal, CSX also gained access to the American Commercial Lines, Inc. (ACL) subsidiary of Texas Gas, which was a large barge operator at the time. For CSX, the addition of oil and gas to its sizable coal holdings was a major undertaking, as was the addition of barge operations. In fact, the diversification into barge shipping was an unprecedented move for a railroad. However, in July 1984 U.S. authorities granted permission to CSX to maintain and operate American Commercial Lines, reversing longstanding regulations that prevented railroads from owning steamship or barge lines. Three years later, CSX gained approval for its $800 million-acquisition of Sea-Land Corp., the largest U.S. ocean container shipping company. At the time, Watkins' strategy of structuring CSX as an intermodal operation able to serve national and international markets was somewhat controversial; however, diversification efforts continued.

In 1986 CSX moved into resort operations with the purchase of Rockresorts, Inc. from Laurance Rockefeller. That year, it also bought a 30 percent stake in natural gas pipeline builder Yukon Pacific Corp. CSX created its CSX Intermodal, Inc. subsidiary, the first full-service intermodal company to serve more than one continent, in 1987. Despite the firm's pioneering efforts in intermodal services, which proved to be a profitable market for many transportation firms in the 1990s, Watkins' diversification strategy left CSX struggling to integrate many of its new assets. Weak profits and low stock prices plagued CSX in the late 1980s. As a result, the firm's directors appointed John W. Snow as president and CEO in 1989. Watkins remained chairman until 1991, when Snow assumed that post as well.

Between 1988 and 1990, CSX returned its focus to railway operations with the goal of increasing profits. The majority of the firm's oil and gas holdings were divested, as were most resort properties. To lower labor costs, CSX began to reduce its crew size. CSX also boosted earnings per share by using the capital from the sale of its various holdings to repurchase roughly 40 percent of its outstanding common stock. Snow's efforts paid off during the 1990s, as sales grew from $8.21 billion in 1990 to $10.54 billion in 1996, when earnings peaked that year at $855 million.

Snow decided the firm was once again ready to begin making acquisitions, although the focus this time would be on strengthening core transportation operations. For example, the purchase of Valley Line in 1992 boosted the barge capacity of American Commercial Lines by more than 33 percent. ACL acquired the marine assets of Conti-Carriers & Terminals, Inc. in 1996, increasing its fleet size to 3,700 barges and 137 towboats. That year, CSX also began what would become a three-year effort to acquire Conrail. When the three-way deal with Norfolk Southern was completed in 1999, CSX hired Conrail executive Ronald J. Conway to oversee its rail operations. Once again, the integration of new assets proved to be problematic for CSX. On-time performance fell from roughly 80 percent in the mid-1990s to 50 percent. In April 2000, Conway was dismissed by CSX, and Snow added the management of CSX's rail operations to his CEO and chairman duties.

Along with making service improvements a top priority, Snow spearheaded a marketing and sales campaign designed to win freight transportation business back from trucking companies. In 2001 roughly $100 million in new business was attributed to this effort. Working in CSX's favor was the increase in fuel prices across North America, which placed trucking companies at a disadvantage to railroads throughout 2001.

CURRENT TRENDS

Logistics management, the coordination of shipments from sender to receiver, became an increasingly lucrative area for transportation companies throughout the 1990s. Hoping to capitalize on this trend, CSX acquired Customized Transportation, Inc. (CTI) in 1993. One of the largest logistics companies serving the automotive industry, CTI offered not only distribution services but also warehousing and assembly services for just-in-time delivery. This meant that products such as cars and car parts were stored by CTI and assembled and shipped only as needed. CTI later added service in Europe and South America to its existing U.S. operations and, in 1996, began to service new industries, including electronics, retail, and chemicals. Despite the growing popularity of logistics management services in the late 1990s and early 2000s, CSX sold CTI for $650 million in 2000 to help pay down its debt.

PRODUCTS

CSX Transportation offers rail transportation and distribution services throughout the eastern half of the United States and two Canadian provinces. CSX Intermodal offers multi-carrier transportation services at 33 terminals throughout North America. Ocean liner services between the continental United States and Alaska, Hawaii, Guam, and Puerto Rico are provided by CSX Lines, which operates a fleet of 16 vessels. CSX World

CSX CHALLENGED ON SAFETY RECORD

In September 1997, a jury serving on a case related to a CSX chemical car fire 10 years prior ordered CSX to pay damages of $3.37 billion, including $2.5 billion in punitive damages, to the plaintiff. However, two months later, the Louisiana Supreme Court overturned the ruling and sent it back to a lower court for adjustment. At roughly the same time, the Federal Railroad Administration (FRA) released a report that was critical of safety procedures at CSX. The FRA had launched an investigation of CSX in 1996 after two CSX trains collided, killing one employee and injuring another. Also that year, a CSX freight train and an Amtrak passenger train had collided in Maryland, leaving 16 people dead. Safety violations discovered during the investigation resulted in a $750,000 fine.

Terminals operates terminal facilities in Asia, Australia, Europe, and the Caribbean. Through its 34 percent stake in American Commercial Lines, CSX also offers marine container shipping services.

GLOBAL PRESENCE

Although the majority of CSX's operations are domestic, the firm does operate terminal facilities in Hong Kong, China, Australia, Europe, Russia, and the Dominican Republic.

SOURCES OF INFORMATION

Bibliography

"CSX Corp." *International Directory of Company Histories.* Detroit: Gale Group, 1998.

CSX Corp. Home Page, 2002. Available at http://www.csx.com.

Gallagher, John. "Freight Conversion: CSX Grabs $100 Million in New Business for System in 2001, Most From the Highways." *Traffic World*, 28 January 2002.

Stephens, Bill. "CSX Still Struggling; Snow Re-Assumes Reins." *Trains Magazine*, July 2000.

Stice, Richard. "Railroads: Picking Up Steam." *Business Week*, 31 May 2001.

For an annual report:

on the Internet at: http://www.csx.com/aboutus/financial/annual-report/2001/2001annualreport.pdf.

For additional industry research:

Investigate companies by their Standard Industrial Classification Codes, also known as SICs. CSX's primary SICs are:

4011 Railroads, Line-haul Operating

4491 Marine Cargo Handling

4922 Natural Gas Transmission

6719 Holding Companies, Not Elsewhere Classified

Also investigate companies by their North American Industry Classification Codes, also known as NAICS codes. CSX's primary NAICS codes are:

333924 Industrial Truck, Tractor, Trailer and Stacker Machinery

336211 Motor Vehicle Body Manufacturing

336510 Railroad Rolling Stock Manufacturing

336611 Ship Building and Repairing

482111 Line-Haul Railroads

483211 Inland Water Freight Transportation

484121 General Freight Trucking, Long Distance, Truckload

CVS Corporation

FOUNDED: 1892

OVERVIEW

CVS is the leading U.S. retail drugstore chain based on sales. The company operates nearly 4,200 retail and specialty pharmacy stores in 33 states and the District of Columbia. CVS filled more than 309 million prescriptions in 2001 and had a leading market share in 35 of the top 100 U.S. drugstore markets, a feat unrivaled by its competitors.

CVS has two main business segments: retail pharmacy and pharmacy benefit management. The retail pharmacy unit includes the operations of CVS retail outlets, as well as the online business of CVS.com. The company's PBM division is among the top ten full service PBMs in the United States and offers managed care drug programs that serve 12 million customers.

Contact Information:
HEADQUARTERS: One CVS Drive
   Woonsocket, RI 02895
PHONE: (401)765-1500
FAX: (401)766-2917
URL: http://www.cvs.com

COMPANY FINANCES

CVS secures most of its sales from its pharmacy operations, which accounted for 66 percent, or $14.8 billion, of total net sales in 2001. This figure has grown steadily over the past several years, up from 59 percent in 1999, and 63 percent in 2000. The remainder of the firm's sales stem from front store operations, which include things like film processing. Sales from this segment reached $7.4 billion in 2001, an increase of 3.9 percent over the previous year. Total revenues for CVS reached $22.2 billion in 2001, compared to $20 billion in 2000.

While net income grew dramatically from $396 million in 1998 to $746 million in 2000, it fell during 2001

FINANCES:

CVS Corp.
Revenues, 1998-2001
(million dollars)

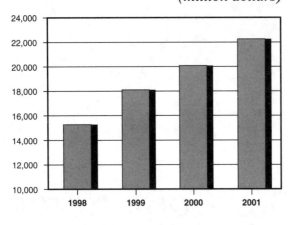

to $413 million. Stock prices ranged from a high of $63.75 per share in 2001 to a low of $22.89 per share. Earnings per share fell from $1.83 in 2000 to $1.00 in 2001.

ANALYSTS' OPINION

The aging American population, the increasing popularity of managed care, and the continual development of new drugs all point toward future growth in the U.S. pharmacy industry. In fact, pharmaceutical consulting firm IMS Health Inc. predicts that pharmacy industry sales will grow from $140 billion to almost $280 billion by 2005. As the leading pharmacy prescription dispenser, CVS believes it is well positioned to capture significant market share as demand for its pharmacy services increases.

However, CVS battled a slowing economy during 2001 that caused sluggish sales in its front store operations. The company also suffered from a pharmacist shortage, which forced some stores to shorten pharmacy hours. Increased competition, higher payroll costs related to attracting new pharmacists, and extended advertising budgets weakened company earnings. As a result, CVS began to restructure certain operations in 2002, and it set an aggressive expansion program in motion to capture new market share. While analysts at Standard & Poor's applauded the firm's strategy, they rated CVS stock a hold and did not expect to see growth until the company reported improvement in both its pharmacy and front store sales.

HISTORY

CVS dates back to 1892, when Frank Melville formed Melville Corp. and acquired three shoe stores with the hopes of developing a chain. His dream became a reality in 1922, when he and his son teamed up with J. Franklin McElwain to establish the Thom McAn Shoe Corp. Within ten years, sales had reached $26 million and the company was operating nearly 480 shoe stores under a variety of brand names.

During the next several decades, the company achieved several milestones including going public, producing its 100 millionth pair of shoes, and acquiring the Miles Shoes chain. In 1968 the company branched out into the apparel industry by opening a Chess King clothing store and purchasing the Foxwood chain, which was later renamed Foxmoor. One year later, Melville purchased the CVS chain.

CVS was created in 1963, when Stanley and Sid Goldstein, along with partner Ralph Hoagland, opened the first Consumer Value Store (CVS) in Lowell, Massachusetts. By 1969 the trio had 40 stores in operation and wished to expand further. Melville expanded CVS's operations throughout the 1970s via several purchases. In 1972 the Clinton Drug and Discount was acquired and, in 1977, Mack Drug was also purchased. By the early 1980s, CVS operated more than 400 stores. Sales reached $1 billion for the first time in 1985. The chain also continued to add pharmacies to its stores, a strategy that had started in the 1970s.

In the mid-1990s, Melville decided to focus on its successful drugstore chain; as a result, the firm began selling off other holdings, including Marshall's Inc., Kay-Bee Toys and Hobby Shops Inc., Linens 'n Things, and the footwear businesses. During this time, the company officially changed its name from Melville Corp. to CVS Corp. to reflect its new focus.

Along with the 1990 purchase of the Peoples Drugstore chain, CVS made several other acquisitions during the 1990s to secure its leading position in the industry. The 1997 purchase of Revco D.S. Inc. added 2,600 stores in 17 states. CVS then bought the Michigan-based Arbor Drugs Inc. chain, increasing its store count to 4,100. In the late 1990s, CVS gained an online presence when it acquired pharmacy Web site Soma.com, which was eventually renamed CVS.com.

STRATEGY

Melville Corp.'s strategy throughout most of the 1900s included expanding into various retail operations through acquisition. The strategy shifted, however, when the company made a commitment to focus solely on its drugstore operations in the 1990s. To realize its mission of becoming a leader in the pharmacy and drugstore

FAST FACTS:

About CVS Corp.

Ownership: CVS Corp. is a publicly owned company traded on the New York Stock Exchange.

Ticker Symbol: CVS

Officers: Thomas M. Ryan, Chmn., Pres., and CEO, 49, 2001 base salary $993,750; David B. Rickard, EVP, CFO, and CAO, 54, 2001 base salary $595,000; Larry J. Merlo, EVP Stores, 45, 2001 base salary $495,000

Employees: 107,000

Principal Subsidiary Companies: CVS Corp. has subsidiary companies and retail locations in 33 states and the District of Columbia. Along with its drugstores, the company operates PharmaCare Management Services Inc., a pharmacy benefits manager (PBM).

Chief Competitors: CVS competes with retail drugstore chains, supermarkets, discount merchandisers, convenience stores, mail order prescription providers, and Internet pharmacies. Its primary rivals include Rite Aid, Wal-Mart, and Walgreen.

CHRONOLOGY:

Key Dates for CVS Corp.

1892: Frank Melville purchases three shoe stores

1922: Thom McAn Shoe Corp. is established

1963: The first CVS store opens

1969: Melville acquires the CVS chain

1990: The Peoples Drug Stores chain is purchased

1996: Melville changes the company's name to CVS Corp. to reflect the firm's new focus on its drug store operations

1997: Revco D.S. Inc. is acquired

1998: CVS purchases Arbor Drugs Inc.

1999: Soma.com is acquired and renamed CVS.com

As part of its customer relations strategy, CVS launched the ExtraCare card program in early 2001. Customers who signed up for the program received special coupons, healthcare information, and a $1 rebate for every $25 spent with the card. By mid-2002 ExtraCare cards were used by 25 million customers in 50 percent of store transactions.

industry, CVS began acquiring large chains that had a strong presence in markets that CVS had yet to infiltrate. For example, the Revco purchase catapulted CVS into a leading position in the Northeast, Mid-Atlantic, Midwest, and Southeast markets. In addition, the Arbor Drugs purchase gave CVS a foothold in Michigan for the first time.

In order to maintain its industry dominance, CVS developed several strategies during the early years of the new millennium. Attracting pharmacists became a priority as the company struggled to keep its growing number of pharmacies staffed. By offering attractive benefits and state-of-the-art technology, the company was able to hire 2,000 pharmacists during 2001. Nearly 60 percent came from competition. Another strategy included penetrating the fastest growing drugstore markets in the United States: Chicago, Illinois; Florida; Las Vegas, Nevada; and Houston and Fort Worth, Texas. During 2001, CVS opened 43 stores in these markets. The company also planned to open new stores in existing markets and relocate poorly performing stores to new locations.

INFLUENCES

CVS Corp.'s operations have been influenced by past success with acquisitions and entering new markets. During the mid-1990s, growth in the pharmacy industry prompted Melville to sell off its various retail operations in order to focus on the CVS drugstore and in-store pharmacies business. The company's growth had historically been via acquisition, a strategy that continued after the company adopted the CVS name. During the mid-to-late 1990s, the drugstore industry went through a period of consolidation. Putting its past experience with expansion to good use, CVS grew in size by purchasing smaller chains, which gave it access to many new markets and the necessary market share to become a leader in the industry. Its success with entering new markets has also influenced the company's long-term strategy. While large acquisitions have tapered off, the firm's goals include establishing new stores in emerging markets.

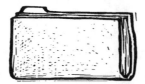

HELPING HANDS

The CVS corporate mission is to help people live longer, healthier, happier lives. The company put this statement into action after the terrorist attacks that occurred on September 11, 2001. The company converted its store on Fulton Street in lower Manhattan into an emergency medical staging area in order to help victims. At its store inside of the Pentagon, CVS provided food, water, and medicine to emergency personnel. In Somerset, Pennsylvania, where United Airlines Flight 93 crashed, CVS workers gave food and water to emergency crews at the site. Through CVS-sponsored events and an employee and customer fundraising effort, CVS was also able to make a substantial donation to the American Red Cross Disaster Relief Fund.

CURRENT TRENDS

CVS was forced to deal with several negative trends—including a slowing North American economy during 2000 and 2001, fierce competition, and a pharmacist shortage—in the early 2000s. To combat weakening sales, the company implemented a plan in 2001 to shut more than 200 poorly performing stores, a distribution center, and a mail order facility. To ward off competition, the company also began to spend heavily on advertising and developed new customer incentive programs. CVS also implemented an aggressive pharmacist recruitment program to staff its in-store pharmacies.

Another trend affecting CVS is the growing popularity of pharmacy benefit management that can offer specialty pharmacy services. During 2001 the company announced that it was integrating ProCare, its specialty pharmacy business that provides drug therapies for serious conditions (including organ transplants, HIV, or cancer) with PharmaCare Management Services Inc. By combining the businesses, CVS believes it will better serve its clients—managed care organizations, self-insured employers, and third party administrators—by enabling them to offer more comprehensive pharmaceutical care.

PRODUCTS

Along with prescription drugs, CVS stores offer a wide variety of merchandise. The firm's main product categories include health, cosmetics, skin care, hair care, photo, and seasonal merchandise. The company also sells bath and body products, along with shampoo and hair care products under the private label Essence of Beauty. Overall, the company's private label products accounted for 12 percent of front store business during 2001.

To bolster the sale of its beauty products, as well as cater to female shoppers, the company developed a new beauty care concept entitled Beauty at the Door. As part of the program, CVS stores revamped their floor plans to position beauty departments at the very front of the store, a high traffic area. The company also placed Healthy Women store kiosks, which provided information on female health and wellness issues, in the beauty department.

CORPORATE CITIZENSHIP

CVS Corp.'s corporate mission is to help people live longer, healthier, happier lives. As part of this mission, the company has partnerships with the American Diabetes Association, the American Heart Association, Easter Seals, and the United Way to educate people on the prevention of and cures for diseases. CVS also promotes the Reach Out and Read program, a pediatric literacy program. The company supports public schools in local communities and also raises money for charities by hosting the CVS Charity Golf Classic.

EMPLOYMENT

Because of the strong emphasis on its pharmacy operations, CVS has an aggressive recruitment program in place to attract pharmacists to the company. New hires are attracted to CVS for the following reasons: the firm's pharmacy operations are at its core, unlike most of its competitors; it invests heavily in pharmacy technology to create a user-friendly work environment; and it created the Excellence in Pharmacy Innovation and Care (EPIC) project that develops new technology and sets workplace standards.

SOURCES OF INFORMATION

Bibliography
"CVS Bigger and Better After Meteoric Rise." *Chain Drug Review*, 10 December 2001.

"CVS Corp." *DSN Retailing Today*, 7 January 2002.

CVS Corp. Home Page, 2002. Available at http://www.cvs.com.

"CVS Hones Women's Health Effort." *Chain Drug Review*, 4 March 2002.

Eder, Rob. "CVS Has New Look With Beauty at the Door."*Drug Store News*, 22 October 2001.

"Premium PL Line a Success at CVS." *Chain Drug Review*, 18 March 2002.

For an annual report:

write: Nancy R. Christal, Vice President of Investor Relations, CVS Corp., 670 White Plains Rd., Suite 210, Scarsdale, NY 10583

For additional industry research:

Investigate companies by their Standard Classification Codes, also known as SICs. CVS Corp.'s primary SICs are:

5912 Drug Stores and Proprietary Stores

5961 Mail Order Houses

6719 Holding Companies, Not Elsewhere Classified

Also investigate companies by their North American Industrial Classification System Codes, also known as NAICS codes. CVS Corp.'s primary NAICS codes are:

446110 Pharmacies and Drug Stores

454110 Electronic Shopping and Mail Order Houses

551112 Offices of Other Holding Companies

DaimlerChrysler Corporation

FOUNDED: 1925

Contact Information:
HEADQUARTERS: 1000 Chrysler Dr.
   Auburn Hills, MI 48326-2766
PHONE: (248)576-5741
FAX: (248)576-4742
TOLL FREE: (800)CHRYSLER
URL: http://www.chryslercorp.com

OVERVIEW

Chrysler Motors Corporation in 1998 announced an imminent merger with Daimler-Benz, which resulted in the creation of DaimlerChrysler, a new German company with headquarters in Germany and the United States. Both companies have very distinct product lines and compete in different markets for different customers (except in the sport utility vehicle category). DaimlerChrysler, in the 2000s, has started expanding into global markets where only one of the former companies may have previously been competing. The largest proposed industrial merger in history—valued roughly at $92 billion—combined two giant companies with similar corporate cultures to create a single entity capable of becoming one of the world's leading designers and producers of cars and trucks. DaimlerChrysler is an automotive and transportation giant that lists its passenger car brands as Maybach, Mercedes-Benz, Chrysler, Jeep, Dodge, and smart. Commercial vehicles are produced under the Mercedes-Benz, Freightliner, Sterling, Western Star, Setra, Thomas Built Buses, Orion, and American LaFrance brands. In addition, in 2000 the company formed an alliance with Mitsubishi Motors and owns 37 percent of that company. In May 2002 DaimlerChrysler and Mitsubishi Motors Corporation expanded their alliance to include the Hyundai Motor Company to establish a joint venture company called Global Engine Alliance to design and construct in-line four cylinder gasoline engines. The engines will be used by Chrysler Group, Mitsubishi Motors, and Hyundai Motor Company.

COMPANY FINANCES

Following slumping sales in 2000 and 2001, DaimlerChrysler announced that some signs of rebounding occurred in 2002 in spite of the 2001 total operating loss of $1.9 billion thanks to poor management decisions and the ongoing customer reluctance to buy in the United States, Japan, Argentina, and Europe, among other markets. The Chrysler Group, following a large loss and massive employee layoffs in the United States in the first quarter of 2001, posted an adjusted operating profit of $111 million for the first quarter of 2002. That, largely stemming from the sale of 1.1 million cars the first quarter, coupled with strong international sales of smart and Mercedes Benz brand lines, gave DaimlerChrysler an operating profit excluding one-time effects of $0.9 billion for the first quarter of 2002. Unless the global economy sputters again, or if a threatened strike among German autoworkers does occur, the company cautiously saw itself returning to modest profitability by 2002's end or 2003. But small profits were not good enough, or so says the battle cry of DaimlerChrysler shareholders at the April 2001 annual meeting in Berlin, a nearly 13-hour marathon, which was less like a stockholder meeting and more like a rowdy soccer match as up to 10,000 shouting angry holders of stock expressed anger, disappointment, or frustration—and some hecklers even cried out for the removal of Jurgen E. Schrempp, CEO and chairman of the board of management since 1995. Schrempp is also under fire from Mercedes Benz aficionados who say the quality of the Mercedes has gone downhill. Shareholders uniformly blasted the ambitious global mergers and alliances that had increased DaimlerChrysler's size but yanked all profits out of the pockets of shareholders. Payouts for stockholders in 2001 amounted to about half what the stock was worth at one point in 1999 before the yoking of Daimler-Benz and Chrysler, and shareholders learned that 1999 profits could not possibly be attained before 2005, if then. In short, either DaimlerChrysler achieves stunning financial turnaround by 2002 or Schrempp may find himself in the same jobless situation that many Chrysler execs found themselves following the Daimler-Benz and Chrysler merger—thanks to Schrempp's aggressive purging of those who disagreed with the merger. In articles in the *Washington Post* and other newspapers, a pattern has emerged with Chrysler from the 2,700 employees who lost their job building buses and trucks for Chrysler's Freightliner subsidiary or the tens of thousands connected to Chrysler whose long-term loyalty was rewarded with little-notice firings: many people are angry and many say the company gave them false hopes and assurances.

ANALYSTS' OPINIONS

Business writer Michael Craig poked fun at DaimlerChrysler top dog Jurgen Schrempp's ruthless decision-

FAST FACTS:
About DaimlerChrysler Corporation

Ownership: DaimlerChrysler is a publicly held company traded on the New York Stock Exchange.

Ticker Symbol: DCX

Officers: Jurgen E. Schrempp, Chmn. of the Board of Management and CEO, 57; Dieter Zetsche, Chrysler Group, Pres. and CEO, 49

Employees: 372,000

Principal Subsidiary Companies: DaimlerChrysler Corporation oversees many subsidiaries. Some of the most well-known are Mercedes-Benz, Chrysler, Dodge, Jeep, Sterling, Freightliner, American La-France, Setra, Plymouth, Powertrain, Setra, Evobus, Lenkungen GmbHn, DaimlerChrysler Aerospace (Dasa), Adtranz, and Alle Server.

Chief Competitors: DaimlerChrysler's top competitors include General Motors, Ford Motor Company, Toyota, Volkswagen, Nissan, Fiat, Honda, Kia, Hyundai, and Mazda.

making following the financial problems of the early 2000s that accompanied the marriage of Daimler-Benz with Chrysler to form DaimlerChrysler. Schrempp "told Chrysler it would be a merger of equals, then scared off or dismissed all the executives responsible for the renegade culture that originally motivated Daimler to make the deal," wrote Craig. But Rod Lache, analyst with Deutsche Bank in New York, wasn't joking when he told the *Detroit News* that the turnaround DaimlerChrysler's Schrempp has likely overoptimistically hoped for is in jeopardy because of pricing pressures. "A lot of the assumptions the company made are going to be difficult to achieve."

HISTORY

In 1925 the Chrysler Corporation was incorporated by Walter Percy Chrysler. Chrysler was a former vice president of General Motors who had resigned over policy differences and had gone on to restore the Maxwell Motor Corporation to solvency. He designed Maxwell's first Chrysler automobile and exhibited it in 1924 in the lobby of the Hotel Commodore in New York City, since

CHRONOLOGY:

Key Dates for DaimlerChrysler Corporation

1925: Walter Percy Chrysler, a former GM vice-president, incorporates the Chrysler Corporation

1928: Dodge becomes a division of Chrysler

1942: Production of cars comes to a halt as Chrysler concentrates on war machine production

1957: Chrysler's space division is formed and Chrysler becomes the main contractor for the Saturn booster rocket

1963: Chrysler revolutionizes the industry with a 5-year, 50,000-mile powertrain warranty

1974: Chrysler continues manufacturing gas guzzlers through the Arab oil embargo; losses totaled $52 million

1978: Lee Iacocca becomes the head of Chrysler

1980: Iacocca secures a federal loan worth $1.2 billion to keep Chrysler alive

1983: Chrysler pays off loan seven years ahead of schedule

1984: The company boasts record earnings of $2.4 billion

1987: Chrysler takes over the American Motors Corporation, getting the prized Jeep line along with it

1992: Cab-Forward Design, for greater stability and handling, debuts

1998: Chrysler accepts merger offer with Daimler-Benz

2001: DaimlerChrysler losses approached $2 billion, and all remaining Chrysler top-ranking execs are replaced by execs from Germany

2002: The company, remaining under fire from shareholders, vows turnaround but analysts are unsure if it can be done fast enough to preserve Chrysler brand name

a vehicle not yet in production could not be displayed at the New York Auto Show. The car was a major success—the company sold 32,000 vehicles at a profit of $4 million before the year's end.

Following the success of his first car, Chrysler designed four more automobiles—the 50, 60, 70, and Imperial 80—named for their maximum speeds, which surpassed the 35-mph top speed of the Ford Model T. By 1927 the Chrysler Corporation had firmly established itself with sales of 192,000 cars, becoming the fifth largest company in the industry.

Chrysler realized the need to build his own plants in order to exploit his firm's manufacturing capabilities. Dillon Read of the New York banking firm of Dillon Read and Company had bought the Dodge Corporation of Detroit from the widows of the Dodge Brothers and reached an agreement with Walter Chrysler. In 1928 the Dodge Corporation became a division of the Chrysler Corporation, and the size of the company increased five-fold.

The manufacture of Chrysler, Plymouth, and Dodge cars was suspended during World War II while Chrysler converted to war production. Chrysler's wartime service earned it a special Army-Navy award for reliability and prompt delivery. Some of its main war products included the B-29 bomber engines and anti-aircraft guns and tanks.

The company began experiencing three significant problems in the immediate postwar period: a loss of the initial enthusiasm and drive that had helped its constant innovation and experimentation in the early days; an exhaustion of engineering breakthroughs; and changes in American tastes and the increased demand for sleeker, less traditional models of cars. In addition, Chrysler, confident of its reputation and war record as a patriotic company, did not focus on marketing to the American public, which was then a crucial, fast-emerging trend in the auto industry.

L.L. Colbert, a lawyer, became the president of Chrysler in 1950 and hired McKinsey and Company, a management consulting firm, to put Chrysler sales back on track. The result was three reforms: development of international markets, centralized management, and a redefined engineering department. Colbert's reforms did not significantly improve Chrysler's competitiveness though.

Lynn Townsend was hired to be the new corporate head in 1952. He consolidated the Plymouth and Chrysler car divisions, closed some unproductive plants, reduced the workforce, installed an IBM computer system to replace 700 clerical staff workers, and enhanced sales by providing the best warranty in the industry. Within five years Lynn Townsend had revitalized the corporation. A Space division was formed that became the prime contractor for the Saturn booster rocket. By the end of the 1960s Chrysler had plants in 18 different countries.

Before the end of the 1960s, the domestic market was undergoing major changes—inflation was taking a toll, imports of foreign vehicles had increased, and crude oil prices had risen steadily. Chrysler, intent on fighting domestic competition, lost pace in the rapidly changing market and did not produce enough of its popular compact cars to meet consumer demand. In addition, with an overstock of larger vehicles, Chrysler reported a $4-million loss in 1969 in sharp contrast to its profit of $122 million the previous year.

John J. Ricardo succeeded Townsend as president and immediately began cutting expenses by reducing salaries, workforce, and the budget, and he experimented with the marketing of foreign cars. However, Chrysler blindly still failed to read the public mood. The company continued manufacturing large gas-guzzling cars even during the 1973-1974 Arab oil embargo in a market already dominated by Cadillacs and Lincolns. In 1974 losses totaled $52 million, and the following year's deficit was five times that amount. The company experienced a brief respite in 1976-1977, but that lasted all too short a time.

In 1978 Chrysler reported a loss of $205 million, causing great concern among the company's financiers. Chrysler saved itself from bankruptcy through highly charged negotiations with the federal government, which guaranteed loans up to $1.5 billion on the condition that Chrysler raise $2.0 billion on its own. Under the leadership of Lee Iacocca, an ex-Ford executive with a flair for marketing, intense self-promotion, media aggrandizement, and public relations, Chrysler recovered in spite of plant closures, layoffs, and a company-wide restructuring worth $577 million. The dedication and hard work of Chrysler's employees played a key part in the resurgence of the corporation, but Iacocca hogged all headlines to take much of the credit for the turnaround. Nonetheless, Iacocca's brash, never-say-die attitude might have just been enough to give the American people enough confidence in Chrysler products to bring the company back from the edge of oblivion (a fate many analysts wrongly had forecast).

The 1980s brought exciting changes to the corporate structure, as well as to the product lines. General Dynamics bought Chrysler Defense, and the loans that the government had guaranteed were paid back seven years early. The K-car debuted in the 1981 model year, and minivans, a category Chrysler pioneered, were introduced in 1983. A merger with American Motors put the Jeep and Eagle brands in dealers' showrooms. The sleek and speedy Dodge Viper concept car excited crowds at the North American Auto Show in 1989 and revived interest in Chrysler's products.

In 1992 Chrysler introduced the concept of Cab-Forward design. This concept made the wheels appear to be pushed forward, back, and out, creating greater stability and enlarging the passenger compartment. The 1990s saw the reporting of record net earnings for multiple quarters and the dedication of the world headquarters building in Auburn Hills, the European headquarters in Brussels, and the Chrysler Japan office in Tokyo.

Chrysler's reputation in the mid-to-late 1990s was earned for daring designs and its vaunted seven-year or 100,000-mile powertrain warranty. The Chrysler Cirrus had a sleek look in spite of its affordability when introduced in 1995, and the Sebring convertible combined the look and feel of a sports car with the roomy back seat of a sedan. In 1999, for its seventy-fifth anniversary year, Chrysler brought a protype to the 1999 Detroit Auto Show—a Chrysler PT ("Personal Transportation") Cruiser that appeared in dealer showrooms nationwide in 2001. Loaded with space saving gimmicks like a foldout bench to stuff in extra passengers, and combining a futuristic design with that of its historic 1934 Airstream and Airflow models, PT Cruiser was the last head-turner car devised by Chrysler engineers before the merger with Daimler-Benz.

In 1998 Chrysler linked its fortunes with the oldest car manufacturer in the world, Daimler-Benz of Germany, accepting the latter's merger offer. The company's automotive heritage goes back to the 1870s when inventor and machinist Karl Benz perfected a two-stroke engine. The Daimler connection goes back to 1885 and Gottlieb Daimler's motorcycle with a four-stroke, single-cylinder engine. In 1886 Benz and Daimler had parallel successes. Benz was awarded a German patent for the first motor car, and Daimler found a way to insert an advanced engine into a carriage to make it a horseless carriage. Independently successful for decades in spite of Germany's vanquishing in World War I, Daimler Motoren Gesellschaft and Benz & Cie merged into Mercedes Benz in 1924, the "Mercedes" name being a pseudonym for well-known rally racer and Daimler salesman Emil Jellinek. The company's best-known car in Europe was its 1929 classic Stuttgart; the car had six cylinders and a 38 horsepower engine. In the 1930s the company became synonymous with great German engineering feats based on the superlative design and performance of the 500 K and the 540 K models. Daimler-Benz's pre-World War II glory days became days of shame as the company used Jews, Gypsies and others regarded as undesirable by Hitler's Third Reich to work as forced labor in the company's automobile factories. Beginning in 1983, the company offered apologies, psychological counseling, and eventually, reparations to the victims. It also supports the Holocaust Memorial in Detroit and European memorials to those who suffered because of actions by then company executives.

In the late 1990s, at the time of the merger, the Mercedes Benz name was synonymous with automotive quality and customer comfort and status. Daimler-Benz executives, however, perceived a need to appeal to other niche markets and to position itself more strongly in international markets. Daimler-Benz CEO Jurgen Schrempp predicted that DaimlerChrysler Aktiengesellschaft would soon be the leading global automaker. But in 2001 and 2002, with Chrysler sales sagging horrifically, Daimler-Chrysler found itself mired in fifth place among car manufacturers. The company's losses in 2001 approached $2 billion, and Schrempp fired whatever Chrysler top-ranking execs hadn't left on their own. Many rank-and-file employees at Chrysler continue to vilify Robert J.

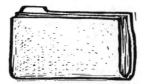

CHRYSLER: SPEED, POWER, AND STATUS

If you're an affluent American, but you consider yourself a bit of a risktaker and a lover of fast, sleek, differently designed cars, you just may be one of the millions who have chosen a Chrysler product for your chosen vehicle. Whether it is the big and powerful Imperial of the 1970s, or the Dodge Viper of 2000, or tomorrow's car of the future, the speedy two-seater Crossfire, DaimlerChrysler has as many cars in its stable termed "classics" by car fanciers as any American manufacturer. When Chrysler merged with Daimler-Benz, many predicted great stylistic improvements for the European status favorite, the Mercedes, but instead that car has been derided and dismissed by the same fanciers in the 2000s. Having come back from more falls than Rocky Balboa in the "Rocky" movies, DaimlerChrysler now has to succeed without a bailout from the U.S. government, or else the German management, in order to preserve its Mercedes Benz line, may be forced, reluctantly, to scuttle the Chrysler division.

(Bob) Eaton, chairman of the board and CEO for Chrysler in 1998, who walked away from Chrysler with millions in his pockets after agreeing to merge. In 2001 Schrempp put another German executive, Dieter Zetsche, in charge of Chrysler's third attempt to avoid closing. In 2002 signs of small recovery were apparent, but few analysts were completely confident in Chrysler.

STRATEGY

DaimlerChrysler's immediate strategy is to somehow affect a "turnaround" to make Chrysler products profitable once again. To that end, company executives in recent years have created a document that lists the best properties and characteristics of Chrysler and Mercedes Benz each, in order to market each vehicle properly.

INFLUENCES

In the 1930s Chrysler's farsightedness helped the company survive the Great Depression far better than others in the industry that folded then or soon there-

after. Chrysler realized the dangers associated with rapid growth and the importance of maintaining flexibility in his vehicle models and designs. Although he had to pay more for car parts than other companies, he discontinued his policy of manufacturing as many parts as possible for his cars. On more than one occasion, Chrysler did not keep pace with the rapidly changing industry, particularly in marketing and converting from big cars to compacts, and suffered massive losses. Restructuring the organization, its processes, and strategies maneuvered the company to a favorable position in the industry by the time of merger in the late 1990s. But in the 2000s, unstable management, thin sales of radical new brands such as the PT Cruiser, and worker dissatisfaction with management helped spawn Chrysler's current crisis.

CURRENT TRENDS

DaimlerChrysler has been working to reduce the amount of time it takes for a vehicle to get from concept to market and has provided a benchmark for others in the industry. The company has a program in place for its suppliers to submit ideas for saving costs that resulted in identified savings of more than $1.2 billion in one recent years. In 2004, Chrysler campaigns will stress the best of each partner as it markets "American design and German engineering."

PRODUCTS

The Chrysler Corporation was known for many of its historical vehicles, which include the Imperial, New Yorker, Valiant, Barracuda, PT Crusier, the Viper, and now the now highly touted Crossfire. In 2004 DaimlerChrysler hopes to win back market share with two new streamlined models, the Pacifica, a six-passenger sport wagon with a splashy front grille and lights that should go head-to-head with Subaru's outdoor wagons; and the Crossfire, a two seat sports coupe with a 3.2-liter 90-degree V-6, 18-valve SOHC engine available with a six-speed manual or five-speed automatic transmission.

CORPORATE CITIZENSHIP

DaimlerChrysler in Germany has employers that make up 14 orchestras and miscellaneous music groups that play to raise funds for the World Childhood Foundation, founded by Queen Silvia of Sweden in 1999. With the aid of DaimlerChrysler and other corporations, its aim is to rescue children from lives of violence and deprivation.

GLOBAL PRESENCE

DaimlerChrysler's new slogan reflects its global expansion: "Innovation, Global Presence and Attitude, Leadership, Responsibility, Openness, Agility, Quickness and Excellence." DaimlerChrysler has taken a strong stand to build its presence in Asia, particularly as the market for subcompact cars expands. To this end, the company has acquired a 37.3 percent stake in Japan-based Mitsubishi Motors Corporation, profitable in 2002 for the first time in three years. DaimlerChrysler is affiliated with 11 factories in Asia. DaimlerChrysler's main plants are in Germany and the United States.

EMPLOYMENT

The company is down to around 372,000 employees in 2002, following massive layoffs between 1999 and 2002, according to the Knight Ridder newspaper chain. In 2000 the company employed 428,000 persons. Employees who were let go complain bitterly that they had been led to expect a merger but received nothing less than a corporate takeover by Daimler-Benz.

SOURCES OF INFORMATION

Bibliography

Chrysler Home Page, 14 May 2002. Available at http://www.chrysler.com.

Craig, Michael. "How to Be a Wealthy Failure." *Business 2.0*, 11 June 2001. Available at http://www.Business2.com.

"DaimlerChrysler Group with Improved Earnings in the First Quarter of 2002." *PR Newswire*, 25 April 2002.

DaimlerChrysler Home Page, 14 May 2002. Available at http://www.daimlerchrysler.com.

Harnischfeger, Uta. "DaimlerChrysler Tries to Calm Investors' Nerves." *Financial Times (London)*, 12 April 2001.

Mason, Anthony. "DaimlerChrysler Merger Sours." *CBS News Transcripts*, 7 January 2001.

Muller, Joan. "Can This Man Save Chrysler?" *Business Week*, 14 May 2001.

Rubin, Daniel. " Both German, American Shareholders Unhappy with DaimlerChrysler." *Knight Ridder/Tribune News Service*, 10 April 2001.

Schmid, John. "DaimlerChrysler Upbeat Despite Chrysler Group Loss." *The International Herald Tribune*, 12 April 2002.

Swoboda, Frank. "A Model Comeback? Chrysler, in 3rd Crisis in 3 Decades, Hopes to Be Profitable by End of 2003, but It Won't Be Easy." *Washington Post*, 13 May 2001.

Tierney, Christine N. "Small Shareholders Give the Slumping Giant's CEO a Piece of Their Mind. The Big Question Now: When Will Institutional Investors Chime In." *Businessweekonline*, 16 April 2001. Available at http://www. Businessweekonline .com.

For an annual report:

on the Internet at: http://www.investor-rel.com/chrysler **or** write: Investor Relations, Chrysler Motors Corp., 1000 Chrysler Dr., Auburn Hills, MI 48326-2766

For additional industry research:

Investigate companies by their Standard Industrial Classification Codes, also known as SICs. DaimlerChrysler Corporation's primary SICs are:

3679 Electronic Components, NEC

3711 Motor Vehicles and Car Bodies

3714 Motor Vehicles Parts and Accessories

6159 Miscellaneous Business Credit Institutions

6399 Insurance Carriers

Also investigate companies by their North American Industry Classification System codes, also known as NAICS codes. DaimlerChrysler Corporation's primary NAICS codes are:

327211 Flat Glass Manufacturing

333924 Industrial Truck, Tractor, Trailer and Stacker Machinery Manufacturing

336111 Automobile Manufacturing

336211 Motor Vehicle Body Manufacturing

336399 All Other Motor Vehicle Parts Manufacturing

522298 All Other Non-Depository Credit Intermediation

Dell Computer Corporation

FOUNDED: 1984

Contact Information:

HEADQUARTERS: 1 Dell Way
   Round Rock, TX 78682-2222
PHONE: (512)338-4400
FAX: (512)728-3653
TOLL FREE: (800)289-3355
URL: http://www.dell.com

OVERVIEW

Dell Computer Corporation is the world's leading direct seller of computer systems. The company's direct marketing practice allows it to offer its products at lower prices than retailers or value-added resellers. The company sells computers assembled to order. The company sells predominantly to corporate accounts, but its 2001 home computer sales grew by 38 percent over the previous year. In the fourth quarter of 2001, home computer sales were particularly strong, up 56 percent from the third quarter. The increase coincided with the company's "Dude, you're gettin' a Dell" television advertising campaign.

Dell has expanded rapidly, and sometimes it appeared the company could not control its own growth. After establishing itself as a leader in the direct marketing sector, Dell attempted to move into retail stores with an expanded product line but was unsuccessful. Refocusing on its core strategy and hiring experienced managers helped put Dell back on the right track. In mid-1998 Dell's stock reached a high of $114.25 per share; in 1990 it could have been purchased for $0.23 per share.

Michael Dell founded the company in his dorm room as a freshman at the University of Texas. He bought excess components from companies; built and sold computers; and offered over-the-telephone support. He realized that customers wanted low-priced computers that offered the most current technologies and came with a good service plan. To save consumers money, Dell sells and ships directly to the customer. Dell also builds its computers to order, eliminating the need for customers to buy more than they need.

The emergence of the Internet allowed customers to place orders online. Internet sales reached $6 million per day by mid-1998. The direct sales strategy worked to Dell's advantage, as more tech savvy consumers began to shop online and custom order their computers. Two years later in 2000, online sales had topped $50 million per day and 840 million page requests per quarter. The company also used the Internet to boost sales overseas by offering Web sites targeted to 82 country sites in 21 languages.

COMPANY FINANCES

Dell's sales for fiscal year 2001 were $31.9 billion, up 26.2 percent from 2000 sales. Net income rose 42.8 percent, to $1.2 billion in 2001. In 2001 Dell's Web site generated $50 million per day in sales. As the company grew, its stock also grew in value. From 1990 to May 1998 the stock price went from $0.23 per share to $68.00, an increase of 29,600 percent. For a 52-week period in 1997-98, the company's stock reached a high of $114.00; with a low of $35.00. Dell does not pay dividends to shareholders, preferring to reinvest in the company. The stock has split a number of times—July 25, 1997; March 6, 1998; September 4, 1998; and March 5, 1999—and shareholders were awarded additional shares.

ANALYSTS' OPINIONS

Corporate leaders, investors, analysts, and industry watchers track Dell Computer Corporation. The company pioneered the concept of direct marketing in the computer industry. Whether or not the company continues to lead the industry will be determined in time. Some analysts praise the company and its simple yet radical idea of direct marketing. As one analyst said, "Who wouldn't want to sell directly to the customer?"

With computer and technology companies reporting less than expected sales and revenues in 2000 and 2001, analysts are waiting to see how Dell will respond to new market conditions. By mid-2001 almost every personal computer (PC) manufacturer, except Dell, had realized a drop in sales and market share. Dell is expected to remain a leader, as other PC makers try to emulate Dell's approach.

HISTORY

Michael Dell was a freshman at University of Texas when he began selling computer components from his dorm room. He opted to pursue a career in business rather than continue with another three years of colleage as a pre-med student. He went into business for himself as a reseller of IBM PCs. At that time dealers were forced to

FAST FACTS:
About Dell Computer Corporation

Ownership: Dell Computer is a publicly held company trading on the NASDAQ Stock Exchange. Michael Dell owns slightly more than 12 percent of the company.

Ticker Symbol: DELL

Officers: Michael S. Dell, Chmn. and CEO, 36, $2,560,770; Kevin B. Rollins, President and CEO, 48, $1,847,385; James T. Vanderslice, PhD., Vice Chmn. of the Board, 60, $1,900,722; Joseph A. Marengi, SVP and Gen. Mgr., 47, $923,701; Morton L. Topfer, Dir., 64, $872,500

Employees: 40,000

Principal Subsidiary Companies: Dell has 75 subsidiaries worldwide.

Chief Competitors: Dell competes with other computer companies, both direct marketing and retail. Some primary competitors include Hewlett-Packard, Gateway, and IBM.

make huge purchases from IBM, which was not practical for a single salesman. He offered to take IBM's excess stock and sell it for them. His discounts of 10 to 15 percent represented a healthy markdown. Soon the burgeoning market for personal computers transformed Dell's dorm space into more office than living quarters, and he dropped out of college to devote his time to making IBM clones.

Dell was no ordinary company and Michael Dell was no ordinary entrepreneur. Dell Computer Corporation was not the first time Michael had reinvented a way to sell a product. When he was 12, Michael held an auction to sell stamps; it netted him $1,000. As a senior in high school, he sold newspapers, making $18,000. His secret was the old business adage: know your customer. Since new residents and newlyweds were the most likely subscribers, Michael researched marriage licenses and real estate transfers to solicit customers. At college Michael decided he could give computer owners better service via telephone than the original store sales people could. His experiences taught him that customers often knew more about computers than the people selling them. Eventually, Michael formulated his goal: to compete head-to-head with IBM.

CHRONOLOGY:

Key Dates for Dell Computer Corporation

1984: Michael Dell drops out of the University of Texas to found Dell Computers

1988: Dell goes public, opens a London office, and forms a Canadian subsidiary

1990: Subsidiaries in Italy and France are set up; Dell ranks number one in J.D. Powers & Associates' first survey of PC-customer satisfaction

1993: Digital Equipment Corporation surpasses Dell to become the biggest computer mail order company

1998: Dell and Gateway, Inc. are announced as the only PC companies to turn a profit

1999: Dell opens manufacturing facility in Eldorado Do Sul, Brazil, to serve Latin America

2000: Company's daily sales via Internet reach $50 million

2001: Dell ranks No. 1 in global market share

Dell, the man and the company, were pioneers in direct marketing of computer system. Despite management problems in the mid-1980s, the fledgling company plodded on. The name, Dell Computers, was not affixed to the operation until about 1987, when staff was added to sell to government and corporate accounts. A year later the company went public with a $34.2 million initial public offering.

The company's growth was rapid—going from $546 million in fiscal 1991 to $2 billion in 1993. In 1993 the inexperience of top management, especially Dell himself, became an obvious problem. With sales of about $3 billion in 1993, the company still posted a loss of nearly $36 million. Of greater concern was the fact that Dell lost ground to rival computer makers Packard Bell and Gateway and fell from fifth to sixth place in the market. The stock began to fall as well. In January 1993 it was worth $49 per share, by July it hit a low of $16 per share.

The biggest problem facing Dell in 1993 was the inability to track profit and loss by product type. The company had no idea which products were bringing in money and which were losing money. Experienced managers and high-level executives were retained to put the company back on track. The company returned to its core

products and customers, and was rewarded with soaring sales, income, and stock prices.

STRATEGY

Dell's strategy is simple: the customer deserves the best product, at the best price, with the best service. Not only that, the customer deserves the product he wants. Dell computers are made to order so customers get exactly what they want, which is a stark contrast to many retail computer stores, where customers end up buying more computer than they need. Since Dell knows what the customer wants, it can more accurately predict future needs and develop products based on those needs. Dell also offers superior customer service, providing on-site service for its computers for one year and offering extended warranties.

Dell runs its procurement, manufacturing, and distribution processes in the most efficient manner possible. By selling direct and making computers to order, Dell reduces its inventory and the risk of the parts becoming obsolete. The company only keeps about 8 days of inventory on hand, versus the industry average of 8 to 12 weeks. This strategy allows Dell to be one of the first companies to capitalize when prices fall at the wholesale level. Unlike retailers, Dell doesn't need a network of wholesalers and distribution centers. It can sell at lower prices because there are no middlemen, no need to carry a high inventory, and no need to spend time and money competing for shelf space in retail stores. Dell maintains good working relationships with the top technology companies. Obtaining input from these companies allows Dell to design computers using the best technology available. Dell spent $204 million on research and development in 1998, up from $126 million in 1997.

INFLUENCES

After making a tremendous start, the company faltered in the early 1990s. Direct selling worked well, and Dell decided to offer retail units to capture more sales. Customers didn't respond, however, and Dell withdrew from the retail market. Dell aggressively expanded its product line but had little success in new markets. Michael Dell learned from the experience and refocused his efforts on streamlining operations. He also hired more experienced executives to help run the company. By 1994 the company returned to its core strategy of quickly delivering the best technology to suit the needs of its customers at a low price with excellent service.

CURRENT TRENDS

Dell started the trend for direct sale, made-to-order computers. While the industry averaged a growth rate of

-12 percent for shipped units in 2001, Dell's growth rate was 11 percent. While the industry tried to catch the wave Dell created, it was busy engineering the next business model. This includes reducing the shelf life of inventory, offering even better customer service, tapping into Internet markets, and turning first time customers into repeat customers.

Dell jumped on the Internet bandwagon with enthusiasm. A natural extension of direct sales, the Internet offers customers a place to look at Dell products and offerings at their leisure. In 1997 sales from the Internet site topped $1 million per day; a year later daily sales reached $6 million. In 2001 sales had reached $50 million per day. In addition, Dell is using the Internet to increase international sales; the company has designed more than 82 country-specific Web sites.

To keep customers coming back, Dell offers a lease program on some of its computers. This program has proved popular among customers concerned with the costs associated with replacing rapidly obsolete technology. The program also appeals to customers who do not want to invest a large sum of money at once. Monthly payments of under $65 represent an affordable risk. Operating much like a car-easing program, the Dell Personal Lease program lasts from 2 to 3 years, has no up-front costs, and allows the customer to buy the computer at the end of the lease. The final price is 15 percent of the computer's original price after a three-year lease or 22 percent after a two-year lease. Gateway, Dell's direct-selling competitor, has gone one step further. Gateway's program offers free Internet access during the lease term and allows the customer to trade the omputer in after two years for a newer one.

PRODUCTS

Dell offers two models of desktop computers: the OptiPlex and Dimension. The OptiPlex is suited for larger companies and institutions requiring network capabilities. It also allows for remote manageability and control. The Dimension line is tailored to meet the needs of small businesses and individuals. This line includes models with cutting edge technology, as well as basic, low cost units. Dell also sells two lines of notebook computers. The Latitude serves business customers and has networking capabilities, and the Inspiron, introduced in late 1997, is for users needing the latest in technology and multimedia capabilities.

During 1998 the company expanded its product lines to include high-performance workstations, forming a special business unit to take care of this new market. The Workstation products run the Microsoft Windows operating software and are for businesses seeking advanced technology to run sophisticated programs. The Workstations are for those who work in industries such as computer-aided design and software development.

Dell also offers network servers, software, and accessories. The company will install off-the-shelf software, such as Microsoft Office or a company's own, specifically designed software. Dell has many different service and support options customized to the customer's needs.

CORPORATE CITIZENSHIP

Dell believes in investing in the community, especially its home base of Austin, Texas. The Dell Foundation, through cash and non-cash donations, partners with non-profit organizations, especially those dealing with children. The company provides corporate sponsorship of various programs in the community. Dell also encourages charitable donations and the volunteer efforts of its employees. In addition to charitable efforts, Dell tries to maintain a positive economic impact in communities and to be an environmentally aware company.

GLOBAL PRESENCE

Approximately 30 percent of Dell's sales are derived outside the United States. The company's products are sold in more than 170 countries, covering three geographic regions. The Americas include the United States, Canada, and Latin America. The European region covers European countries, as well as areas in the Middle East and Africa. The Asia-Pacific-Japan region includes the Far East, Japan, Australia, and New Zealand.

In addition to its manufacturing facility in Austin, Texas, Dell has facilities in Limerick, Ireland, and Penang, Malaysia. By the end of 1998, Dell had opened a second plant in Limerick and one in Xiamen, China. In 1999 Dell opened a manufacturing facility in Brazil. In all, Dell has 39 subsidiaries in 33 countries. In 1998 the company held a 10 percent share of the worldwide market. However, the company anticipated increasing to a 20 percent share. In 2001 Dell's market position was second in Europe, fifth in Japan, and had grown by 37 percent in the Middle East.

EMPLOYMENT

Dell invites technology professionals to "Make your mark at Dell." Offering the opportunity to work at a revolutionary company with plenty of potential for growth, Dell also links the company's success directly to each employee. Dell offers its employees stock options, profit-sharing, and incentive programs.

SOURCES OF INFORMATION

Bibliography

Corcoran, Elizabeth. "The Direct Approach." *Washington Post*, 1 July 1998.

"Dell Computer Corporation 10-K Form," April 2002. Available at http://www.sec.gov.

"Dell Computer Corporation." *Hoover's Guide to Computer Companies.* Austin, TX: The Reference Press, 2001.

The Dell Computer Home Page, 30 March 2001. Available at http://www.dell.com.

"Dell Internet, Overseas Sales Up." *Reuters* , 17 July 1998.

Durhahm-Vichr, Deborah. "Computers: Let the Price Wars Begin." *E-commerce Times*, 2 May 2002.

Einstein, David. "Dell, Gateway Use Payment Plans to Attract Buyers." *San Francisco Chronicle*, 10 July 1998.

Jacob, Rahul. "The Resurrection of Michael Dell." *Fortune,* 18 September 1995.

Kirkpatrick, David. "No Big Deal Why Michael Dell Isn't Afraid of the New Compaq." *Fortune*, 2 March 1998.

McGraw, Dan. "The Kid Bytes Back." *U.S. News & World Report*, 12 December 1994.

Serwer, Andy. "Michael Dell Rocks." *Fortune*, 11 May 1998.

"Why Compaq Envies Dell: The Leading Maker Alters Course." *Fortune*, 17 February 1997.

For an annual report:

on the Internet at: http://www.dell.com **or** write: Investor Relations, Dell Computer Corp., 2214 W. Braker Ln., Austin, TX 78758

For additional industry research:

Investigate companies by their Standard Industrial Classification Codes, also known as SICs. Dell Computer Corporation's primary SICs are:

7371 Computer Programming Services

7372 Prepackaged Software

7373 Computer Integrated Systems Design

7376 Computer Facilities Management

7378 Computer Maintenance & Repair

7379 Computer Related Services, NEC

Also investigate companies by their North American Industrial Classification System codes, also known as NAICS codes. Dell Computer Corporation's primary NAICS codes are:

334111 Electronic Computer Manufacturing

334119 Other Computer Peripheral Equipment Manufacturing

454110 Electronic Shopping and Mail-Order Houses

511210 Software Publishers

Delphi Corp.

FOUNDED: 1998

OVERVIEW

With net sales for 2001 of $26.1 billion, Delphi Automotive Systems Corp. is a worldwide leading supplier of vehicle electronics, transportation components, integrated systems, and modules. With a broad range of products and expertise in systems integration, Delphi can provide vehicle manufacturers with comprehensive, system-based solutions in an array of vehicle component lines. Delphi's products are marketed within three product sectors: electronics and mobile communications, which includes automotive electronics and audio and communications systems; safety, thermal, and electrical architecture, including safety, thermal, and power and signal distribution components; and dynamics and propulsion, which includes energy and engine management, as well as chassis and steering products.

Along with providing components to vehicle manufacturers, Delphi also sells its products to the aftermarket (i.e., for needs arising after the automobiles have been manufactured and sold). In the aftermarket business segment, Delphi focuses on electronic and electrically enhanced replacement parts such as fuel pumps, oxygen sensors and injectors, batteries, and clutches. New offerings may also include satellite digital audio receivers, rear seat entertainment systems, and MP-3 music playback products. Delphi also provides comprehensive service and solution to the component and equipment installer.

After the automotive production and sales slowed during the first years of the 2000s, Delphi began increasingly to pursue customers outside the vehicle manufacturing industry. The company hopes find ways to apply its expertise in automotive technology to

Contact Information:
HEADQUARTERS: 5725 Delphi Dr.
   Troy, MI 48098-2815
PHONE: (248)813-2000
FAX: (248)813-2670
URL: http://www.delphiauto.com

FAST FACTS:

About Delphi Corp.

Ownership: Delphi is a publicly owned company that trades on the New York Stock Exchange.

Ticker Symbol: DPH

Officers: J.T. Battenberg III, 58, Chmn., Pres., and CEO, 2001 base pay $1.45 million; Donald L. Runkle, 56, EVP, 2001 base pay $800,000; Alan Dawes, 48, EVP and CFO, 2001 base pay $700,000; Rodney O'Neal, 48, EVP, 2001 base pay $600,000; David B. Wohleen, 51, EVP, 2001 base pay $550,000

Employees: 195,000

Principal Subsidiary Companies: Delphi operates a number of subsidiary businesses, including Delphi Diesel Systems, Delphi Energy and Chassis Systems, and Delphi Technologies Inc.

Chief Competitors: Delphi's primary competitors include Johnson Controls, Robert Bosch, and Visteon.

increase it presence in a wide range of business markets including medical, computer, telecommunications, military, aerospace, home appliances, agriculture, and construction.

In February 1999 Delphi, previously a private, wholly owned subsidiary of General Motors, completed its initial public offering. In May 1999 General Motors sold its remaining interest to the public. Although the majority of Delphi's business is generated by it previous parent company, both General Motor and Delphi have begun to expand its automotive component business to include new providers and new customers, respectively.

COMPANY FINANCES

For 2001 Delphi posted a net loss of $370 million on net sales of $26.1 billion, compared to a net profit of $1.1 billion on net sales of $29.1 billion in 2000. The totals for 2000 reflect a slight decrease over the net income and net revenues posted for 1999. The negative balance for 2001 resulted in a loss of $0.61 per adjusted basic share of Delphi stock, compared to earnings per

adjusted basic share of $1.94 and $1.99 in 2000 and 1999, respectively.

The dynamics and propulsion product sector was the largest generator of revenue during 2001 with sales totaling $12.6 billion, down from $14.2 billion in 2000. Of 2001's total, General Motors and its affiliates accounted for $8.8 billion. Safety, thermal, and electrical architecture was the second-largest revenue producer, posting sales of $9 billion in 2001, down $1 billion from 2000. Of 2001's total, General Motors and its affiliated accounted for $5.6 billion. Electronics and mobile communication posted revenues of $4.8 billion for 2001, down from $5.3 billion in 2000. Of 2001's total, General Motors and its affiliates accounted for $3.2 billion.

Of the $26.1 billion in total sales for 2001, $16.4 billion in goods and services were sold in the United States and Canada and $3.9 billion in Mexico, making the entire North American market valued at $20.3 billion. Europe accounted for $4.8 billion in sales and South America accounted for $412,000, with the remaining $600,000 provided by the rest of the world. North American sales totals were down nearly $3.4 billion from 2000, and European sales were up nearly $350,000.

Year-on-year net sales for the first quarter of 2002 improved to $6.7 billion, up from $6.5 billion the previous year. Although still not showing a profit, net losses for the quarter were down to $51 million, compared to $429 million during the same period of 2001. The increases over 2000's figures are reflected in improved sales in all three of Delphi's major product sectors.

ANALYSTS' OPINIONS

With 67 percent of Delphi's sales going to General Motors in 2001, analysts tend to tie Delphi's fate with that of its largest customer. Although General Motors showed an 11.4 percent increase in its North American production, the auto giant's overall revenue growth was only 2.7 percent due to a 20 percent decline in European production. Delphi's increased revenues for the first quarter of 2002 reflect its limited benefit from General Motor's increased production schedule. Analysts predict a positive performance in the short term; however, the auto industry's propensity to be volatile limits the accuracy of any long-range predictions.

Because Delphi's strategy link to General Motors is not expected to generate significant growth, analysts look to the outcome of Delphi's restructuring as a means to reduce excess capacity and drive earnings. Generally analysts see Delphi's move to fix, close, or sell unprofitable and barely profitable businesses and cutting costs via closures, consolidations, and layouts, as positive steps, but warn that situation is complicated by its largely union workforce that must approve changes in labor contracts, which slows the restructuring process.

Some analysts view the mobile multimedia product segment as a weakness in Delphi's product offerings. Expected to be a growth driver, mobile multimedia reported a 28 percent decline in sales for the fourth quarter of 2001, followed by a 23 percent decrease in sales during the first quarter of 2002.

HISTORY

Delphi traces its earliest history back to the New Departure Bell Company of Bristol, Connecticut, which manufactured the first ringing doorbell device in 1888. In 1897 the company introduced the first bicycle coaster brake. In 1906 Delphi delved into the new automobile industry by working on improvements and advancement in automobile lighting components, and two years later the company began manufacturing high-quality wooden automobile bodies. In the same year, Delphi started manufacturing and marketing spark plugs under the name Champion Ignition Corp., which has since become a long-standing industry leader in the field.

In 1912 Delphi engineer Charles F. (Boss) Kettering invented the first self-starting engine. The advanced motor, which eliminated the need to hand crank the engine manually, was first introduced on Cadillacs. During the next decades Delphi continued to develop innovative advancements in the automobile industry, including the development of the first instrument-panel installation of car radios in 1936, followed three years later by the first multi-button mechanical radio tuner. In 1951 Delphi developed power steering, and in 1974 introduced rack and pinion steering. In 1954 the company began to market an air conditioning system with all major components located under the car's hood, a technology that has continued to advance so that currently nine of every ten automobiles in North America are built equipped with air conditioning. Delphi made another revolutionary advancement when it introduced the first inflatable airbag restraint system in 1973.

Delphi was incorporated in 1998 as Delphi Automotive Systems Corp., having changed its name from Automotive Component Group in 1995, as a wholly owned subsidiary of General Motors Corporation. In February of 1999 Delphi completed its initial public offering and began trading its shares to the public. In May of 1999 the company's spin off from General Motors was completed when General Motors divested itself of all remaining Delphi stocks. The company's name was changed to Delphi Corp. in March of 2002 to denote the organization's growing independence from General Motors and its diversification into non-automotive industries, such as home appliances and fiber optics telecommunications components.

CHRONOLOGY:

Key Dates for Delphi Corp.

1906: Delphi begins marketing spark plugs under the name Champion Spark Plugs

1912: Delphi engineer Charles F. (Boss) Kettering invents the first self-starting engine

1936: Installs first instrument-panel car radio

1939: Develops first multi-button mechanical radio tuner

1951: Introduces first power steering system

1954: Begins marketing first under-the-hood automobile air conditioning system

1973: Develops first inflatable airbag safety system

1999: Company is spun off from General Motors as a publicly owned independent corporation

2002: Changes name from Delphi Automotive Systems Corp. to Delphi Corp. to reflect an increased interest in non-automotive business segments

STRATEGY

Delphi's strategy plan is fourfold: diversification of its customer base; strengthening its global presence; accelerating into higher-end, higher-profit margin product lines; and resolving non-strategic business lines. Uncertain of when the automotive industry will rebound and hit with a net loss for 2001, Delphi announced on March 29, 2001, that it would begin to realize its strategic goals by undergoing global restructuring designed to reduce structural costs, improve the earning potential of its core businesses, and streamline operations. The restructuring plans called for Delphi to sell, close, or consolidate nine manufacturing plants, reduce its worldwide workforce at 40 other facilities, and sell underperforming and noncore product segments. During 2001 the company divested or closed 17 product lines as it moves away from low-end, mostly mechanically based products to high-end, high-tech electronically based products. During 2001 approximately the workforce was reduced by more than 10,000 people. Additional job cuts of more than 6,000 employees, announced in April 2002, are scheduled through 2003.

INNOVATIVE TECHNOLOGIES

FOREWARN Collision Warning System provides the driver with forward, side, and rear detection systems that help monitor the road using infrared, ultrasonic, vision, and global positioning sensors. FOREWARN alerts drivers to possible hazards within its detection zone. FOREWARN can also be integrated into a car's cruise control to detect vehicles in front of the driver and make necessary adjustments to speed via throttle control and braking to maintain a preset distance between cars.

E-STEER is an innovative, fully electric, power steering system that is highly efficient. It eliminates the need for the power steering pump, hoses, and hydraulic fluid, as well as the belt and pulley on the engine. E-STEER provides high performance, improved fuel economy, acceleration, and safety, and it is environmentally friendly.

COMMUNIPORT systems address the growing market demand for mobile communications, entertainment, and information as part of the driving experience. COMMUNIPORT systems offer high-tech innovations such as global positioning satellite receivers, in-car integrated navigation, MP-3 playback, Satellite Digital Audio Receiver Service, and portable rear seat entertainment systems with DVD and multiple game system capabilities.

Under the corporate banner of "Driving Tomorrow's Technology," Delphi intends to remain focused on advancing high tech innovations that apply to both the automotive and non-automotive sectors. At the end of 2001, the company had approximately 350 new products, in various stages of production, with plans to introduce them during the next three years. To put its put its money where its mouth is, Delphi maintains an annual budget of $1.7 billion for engineering, research, and development. During 2001 Delphi engineers earned more than 600 patents worldwide.

INFLUENCES

Delphi's business is significantly dependent on trends in automotive sales as its revenues relate directly to the automobile production schedules of its automotive customers, most importantly General Motors. Production rates, in turn, depend on factors such as general economic conditions, consumer spending, and customer preference. In an industry that tends to cyclical, the year 2001 proved exceptionally challenging. Automobile production in North America was erratic and much lower in volume than the previous year. Although production stabilized during the second half of the year, the events of September 11, 2001, further eroded consumer confidence in an already depressed market. Vehicle manufacturers responded with unique incentives such as zero percent interest rates, which increased demand, but dealer primarily sold stock on hand, and so Delphi did not benefit from the strategy. As a result, Delphi's revenues for the year declined, and the company posted a net loss. Continuing uncertainties regarding the economy as well as the return of regular pricing by the automobile industry may continue to adversely affect Delphi's sales.

CURRENT TRENDS

Delphi has identified seven market trends. First, consumers are increasingly demanding greater electronic and technological content in the vehicles they purchase. Customers want better vehicle performance, functionality, and convenience at an affordable price. Improvements in technology are also driven by the introduction of more stringent regulatory standards for automotive emissions and safety. Second, there is an increasing interest in manufacturing vehicles that can be sold in a variety of world markets that meet regional and cultural expectations of a specific area's population. Automotive suppliers, including Delphi, must adapt to the industry's move toward automobile production in which a car is designed in a single location, but produced and marketed in many different geographic locations. Namely, Delphi expects to make move to improve its global capabilities as a supplier.

Third, more and more vehicle manufacturers are outsourcing entire systems and modules as a means to streamline and simplify design and assembly processes thereby reducing their costs. Consequently, Delphi expects to increase its sales of sophisticated pre-assembled systems. Fourth, ongoing consolidation within the automotive parts industry has impacted customer and supplier relationships as suppliers work to provide vehicle manufacturers with single-point sourcing of integrated systems in an increasing global market.

Fifth, Delphi has recognized increased pressure from its customers to respond more quickly to customer preferences, advancing technology, and changing regulations by shortening the time from research and design to finished product. Also automobile manufacturers wish to adjust to the trends in vehicle preferences rapidly, shifting production of vehicle types as the market demands, from light trucks to sport utilities vehicles to passenger cars. Sixth, the growth of e-business has required Delphi to adopt Internet-based strategies that offer tools to facilitate customers' needs and improve supply chain efficiency. Finally, since 2001 Delphi has been making a concentrated effort to increase its sales outside the automotive industry. The company envisions the adaptation of its vehicle components and systems to numerous fields that also require high-tech parts and services, such as consumer appliances, medical, construction, aerospace, and telecommunications.

PRODUCTS

Within the electronics and mobile communication business segment, Delphi offers automotive electronics products, including audio systems, security systems, and powertrain and engine control modules. The company's safety, thermal, and electrical architecture business unit provides such products as powertrain cooling systems, climate control systems, and safety airbag system as well as a range of connective wiring, switch, and electrical components. Delphi's dynamic and propulsion product segment produces engine management systems for both gasoline and diesel engines and major electronic chassis controls related to brakes, steering, and suspension. The company's aftermarket segment offerings include consumer and vehicle electronics and innovative diagnostic and service equipment.

CORPORATE CITIZENSHIP

Delphi's corporate citizenship focuses on education, community relations, and volunteering. It carries out its commitment to education through its For Inspiration and Recognition of Science and Technology (FIRST) program, which provides opportunities for students compete with Delphi engineers serving as FIRST coaches to student teams or as FIRST judges. As part of its drive to better community relations Delphi participates in a number of community programs, such as Habitat for Humanity and special housing projects in Mexico. Employee volunteering is encouraged and supported at Delphi. For example, following the events of September 11, 2001, Delphi employees responded with monetary collections and blood drives.

GLOBAL PRESENCE

Delphi's world headquarters in based in Troy, Michigan, along with regional offices in Tokyo and San Paulo, Brazil. In all, Delphi operates more than 300 manufacturing, engineering, and customer service and sales facilities in 42 countries around the world. As a part of its restructuring plan, Delphi has reduced or eliminated some of its international operations. By the end of 2001, Delphi had closed, sold, or consolidated manufacturing plants in Ande, France; Betim, Brazil; Casoli, Italy; Robertsdale, Alabama; Saginaw, Michigan; Fort Defiance, Arizona; Piracicaba, Brazil; and Bochum, Germany. Another plant located in Southampton, United Kingdom, was closed in the first quarter of 2002.

EMPLOYMENT

At the heart of Delphi's workforce is its roster of 16,000 engineers, scientists, and technicians who introduced 126 new products during 2001 and have 350 more in different stages of development. Of Delphi's approximately 195,000 employees, 36,000 are salaried and 159,000 are hourly. Of the hourly employees, 93 percent, or 147,000 people, are represented by one of fifty-six unions. Approximately 47,500 U.S. employees are represented by a union, with three-quarters of that total aligned with the United Automobile Workers. In Mexico two unions represent nearly 60,000 hourly workers, and in Europe 38 unions represent more than 32,000 people.

SOURCES OF INFORMATION

Bibliography

"Delphi Injects $60m into Parts Production." *Professional Engineering*, 16 January 2002.

"Delphi Launches Wireless Diagnostic System." *Motor Age*, May 2002.

"Delphi Shortens Its Name to Reflect Its New Markets." *The New York Times*, 16 March 2002.

"Delphi to Cut 6,100 More Jobs." *United Press International*, 17 April 2002.

Freeman, Sholnn. "Delphi Posts Narrower Loss as Rival Dana's Loss Widens." *Wall Street Journal*, 18 April 2002.

"Relationship is Linchpin of Lean Manufacturing." *Automotive News*, 27 May 2002.

Sherefkin, Robert. "Suppliers Drop 'Automotive'; Auto Firm by Any Other Name May Lure Investors." *Automotive News*, 1 April 2002.

Willoughby, Jack. "Revving Up." *Barrons*, 22 April 2002.

For an annual report:
on the Internet at: http://www.delphiauto.com

For additional industry research:
Investigate companies by their Standard Industrial Classification Codes, also known as SICs. Delphi Corp.'s primary SICs are:

3714 Motor Vehicle Parts And Accessories

Also investigate companies by their North American Industry Classification System codes, also known as NAICS codes. Delphi Corp.'s primary NAICS codes are:

336399 All Other Motor Vehicle Parts Manufacturing

Delta Air Lines, Inc.

FOUNDED: 1924

Contact Information:
HEADQUARTERS: Hartsfield Atlanta International Airport,
PO Box 20706
  Atlanta, GA 30320-6001
PHONE: (404)715-1400
FAX: (404)715-2600
URL: http://www.delta-air.com

OVERVIEW

Suffering from financial loss in 2001 and much of 2002, executives of Delta Air Lines, Inc. rallied the company to again become profitable as it had been from 1996 through 2000. Cutting costs is among the priorities at Delta in an effort to remain competitive with the low-budget airlines, whose popularity is rising, and in 2002, encouraging customers to purchase tickets at the Delta.com Web site, Delta drastically cut commissions to travel agencies. Delta Air Lines, Inc. has operations in 201 U.S. cities in 45 states and in 50 cities in 32 international countries.

COMPANY FINANCES

Delta stated that for the first quarter of 2002, the airline operated with a loss of $ 397 million. For the 2001 full year, the company posted a serious loss of $1 billion, although the company's executives assured shareholders they saw a way back to profitability by the end of 2002 or sometime in 2003, barring unforeseen problems similar to the September 11, 2001, terrorist attacks using aircraft as instruments of attack.

ANALYSTS' OPINIONS

Many analysts agree that Delta Air Lines, Inc.'s assurances that it plans to return to profitability in the early 2000s are largely merited. In the mid-1990s, the company faced a similar financial period of uncertainly as it aggressively jettisoned its lavish in-flight services. In 2002, the company aggressively marketed its business travel to that lucrative market sector and also offered lower fares and special deals on its Delta.com Web site to lasso profits heretofore going to travel agencies. "He's effectively been able to position Delta as the lowest cost of the three majors," said Bill Mastoris, managing director of research at BNY Capital Markets Inc., in a Bloomberg News interview. "He is going to more conservatively manage the balance sheet, and that means something to investors." John Buckingham, a fund manager at Al Frank Asset Management Inc. told Bloomberg News he concurred with that analysis. "Delta is in far better shape" than some of its competitors, said Buckingham, adding that DAL is "a survivor if we do get a big shakeout in the industry."

HISTORY

Founded in Macon, Georgia, in 1924, Huff-Daland Dusters (renamed Delta Air Service in 1928) was established as a crop-dusting service to treat boll weevils that were overrunning cotton fields. The company began offering passenger flights in 1929 from Dallas to Jackson, Mississippi. Delta contracted with the United States Postal Service in 1934 to fly from Fort Worth to Charleston, South Carolina, using Atlanta as a hub. The company relocated to Atlanta in 1941.

Over the years, Delta Air Lines, Inc. added flight destinations to include Cincinnati, New Orleans, Chicago, and Miami. When the company bought Southern Airlines in 1952, other destinations included cities in the South, the Midwest, Texas, and the Caribbean. Almost instantaneously the company has become the fifth largest airline in the United States. International service increased when the company bought Northeast Airlines in 1972 and offered service to New England, Canada, and London.

In 1983 the company reported its first financial loss due to a poor economy. Having become profitable once again by 1985, Delta purchased Western Air Lines, and also used its profits to begin flights to Asia in 1987. International flights accounted for 11 percent of Delta's passenger revenues by 1989, and during this time the company made deals with Swissair and Singapore Airlines. Delta also conducted a joint venture with TWA (replaced by American Airlines) and Northwest to create WORLDSPAN, a computer service that managed reservations. Delta owned a 40 percent share of WORLDSPAN in 2002.

Delta witnessed a financial setback in 1990 as a result of fuel and labor increases coupled with reduced fare rates. Delta followed this disappointment with the purchase of gates, planes, and three Canadian routes from Eastern. The company also purchased Pan Am's New

FAST FACTS:
About Delta Air Lines, Inc.

Ownership: Delta Air Lines, Inc. is a publicly owned company traded on the New York Stock Exchange.

Ticker symbol: DAL

Officers: Frederick W. Reid, Pres. and COO, 51, $1.4 million; M. Michele Burns, EVP and CFO, 44, $735,000; Leo F. Mullin, Chmn. and CEO, 59, $2.2 million

Employees: 76,273

Principal Subsidiary Companies: Delta Air Lines, Inc.'s chief subsidiaries include Delta Express, the Delta Shuttle, the Delta Connection, and Delta's Worldwide Partners.

Chief Competitors: Competition among airlines is strong. Delta competes with many major airlines on its principal routes as well as with regional, national, and all-cargo carriers. Some primary competitors include Continental Airlines, USAir, United, Alaska Air, and British Airways.

York-Boston shuttle, European routes, and a Frankfurt hub. These purchases made the company the largest airline in the world based on the cities it served and its fruitfulness.

Once again the company began to see financial difficulties due to price wars and a weak economy, and by 1992, Delta was forced to evaluate cost-cutting possibilities. The company reduced planes and short-distance routes. In 1995 the company decided to cease its flights to Bangkok, Hong Kong, and Taipei, since they had not been financially rewarding. In the mid to late 1990s, DAL hoped to take away some of the strategic advantage of no-frills carriers by cutting back on its more expensive customer perks such as lavish in-flight meal service. Delta's advantage in the marketplace in the 2000s as it strives for a return to profitability is that it has avoided the catastrophic battles with union workers that have assailed such air carriers as United and USAir. Delta, largely nonunion save for the pilots' union, pays wages that are competitive for the most part with air carriers that are union workers, but it has been able to deny costly wage increases to flight attendants and airport workers in 2002 at a time of crisis for the airline, thus holding down costs.

CHRONOLOGY:

Key Dates for Delta Air Lines, Inc.

1924: Huff-Deland Dusters is established as a crop dusting service

1928: Renames company to Delta Air Service

1929: Begins offering passenger flights from Dallas, Texas, to Jackson, Mississippi

1941: Delta relocates to Atlanta, Georgia

1953: Merges with Chicago and Southern Airlines

1967: Delta Air Lines becomes the company name after a merger with Delaware Airlines

1972: Northeast Airlines is purchased

1982: Delta forms two computerized marketing subsidiaries to coordinate and sell tickets on Delta flights

1991: Purchases a package of assets from Pan Am, giving Delta a hub in Frankfurt, Germany, as well as dozens of European routes

2000: Announced creation of SkyTeam, a global alliance, partnering Delta with AeroMexico, Air France and Korean Air

2001: Delta posts first loss in six years

2002: Chautauqua Airlines and Delta form a partnership

STRATEGY

CEO Leo F. Mullin in 2002 stressed to the trade publication *Aviation Week & Space Technology* that the company anticipated continued success in international, vacationer and leisure and regional Delta markets, but that the company was vigorously courting the lucrative corporate travel market that shrunk disastrously after the September 11, 2001 terrorist attacks using aircraft. M. Michele Burns, EVP and CFO, told *Aviation Week & Space Technology* that Delta's strategy was to pay strict attention to "capacity discipline, cost containment and cash preservation."

INFLUENCES

Changes in the industry begun in the early 1990s have escalated in the 2000s and eventually will see leg-islative debate in the U.S, Congress over the issue of mandatory arbitration for workers in spite of union objections. Although many of Delta's rank and file workers are non-union, a battle with the Air Line Pilots' Association in 2001 nearly shut down the airline and helped make the airline unprofitable for the year. The rising popularity of low-cost, low-fare airlines has continued to force Delta to make continual cutbacks in order to stay competitive. Customers clearly tend to choose lower costs over amenities as the top consideration when purchasing a ticket.

The airline industry, most analysts agree, is a mature one in the United States and abroad. The European market has been one of increasing demand, especially since competing airlines have begun service improvements. Also a major strength for Delta has been its Delta Connection strength as a server of regional markets. Beginning in 2002, Chautauqua Airlines starts service as the fifth such regional carrier in the DAL system.

CORPORATE CITIZENSHIP

Delta Air Lines, Inc.'s community involvement has revolved primarily around youth, investment in minority education, and cultural affairs. The company supports numerous charities targeting childhood diseases. Its four main charities include the American Red Cross, CARE, Children's Miracle Network and the Juvenile Diabetes Foundation. At the community level, Delta has become a major supporter of Habitat for Humanity. Delta also allows frequent traveler mile contributions to be used to aid the Make-A-Wish-Foundation and Make-A-Wish Foundation International.

GLOBAL PRESENCE

In 2002 Delta Air Lines announced that it now serves more passengers worldwide than any competitor, through its large worldwide route system. In 2001, some104 million passengers chose Delta, more than any other competitor. Delta and its partners boast that they operate 6,400 daily flights to more than 450 cities in 98 countries.

EMPLOYMENT

The company has a successful contract in place with its union airline pilots in 2002, but it has vigorously resisted attempts by its flight attendants, ground crews, and other personnel to unionize. Delta maintains that its executives' salaries are below their peers' at other airlines, so they have developed an Incentive Compensation plan (pay for performance) aligned that with the company's strategic objectives. In addition, safety, customer satisfaction, and on-time performance are continually stressed. Although it has not endured quite the paralyzing labor situation that competitors United and USAir have struggled with in the 2000s, Delta nonetheless has announced it favors some sort of mandatory arbitration to reduce the specter of strikes that invariably cause travelers to book with alternate airlines.

SOURCES OF INFORMATION

Bibliography

"Airlines Paving Way For 'Binding Arbitration' Law." *Airline Financial News,* 29 April 2002.

"Delta Air Lines, Inc." *Hoover's Online,* 15 June 2002. Available at http://www.hoovers.com.

Delta Air Lines, Inc. Home Page, 17 June 2002. Available at http://www.delta-air.com.

Marek, Lynne. "Delta's Mullin Cuts Costs and Copes with Low Fares." *Bloomberg News,* 17 April 2002.

"Phillips, Edward H. From Big Losses to a Small Profit, Airlines Report Rocky Quarter." *Aviation Week & Space Technology,* 22 April 2002.

For an annual report:

on the Internet at: http://www.delta.com/inside/investors/annual_reports/2001_annual/pages/financials/note11.html

For additional industry research:

Investigate companies by their Standard Industrial Classification Codes, also known as SICs. Delta's primary SIC is:

4512 Air Transportation Scheduled

Also investigate companies by their North American Industry Classification System codes, also known as NAICS codes. Delta's primary NAICS code is:

481110 Scheduled Air Transportation

Deutsche Lufthansa AG

FOUNDED: 1926

Contact Information:

HEADQUARTERS: Von-Gablenz-Str 2-6
   Cologne 21, D-50679 Germany
PHONE: +49-69-696-0
FAX: +49-69-696-6818
URL: http://www.lufthansa.com

OVERVIEW

Deutsche Lufthansa is an international airline company that operates in six business areas: passenger business; logistics; maintenance, repair, and overhaul; catering; leisure travel; and information technology services. Along with providing passenger and cargo flight services, Lufthansa offers customers a range of solutions and services across the spectrum of the air transport industry, from aircraft maintenance and overhaul to airline catering.

COMPANY FINANCES

In 2001 Lufthansa posted a net loss of 633.2 million euro on revenues of 16.69 billion euro, compared to a net income of 689 million euro on revenues of 15.2 billion euro in 2000. Of total sales for 2001, 12.25 billion euro were generated by traffic revenues, which break down as follows: passenger, 9.86 billion euro; freight, 2.27 billion euro; and mail, 122.3 million euro. Other activities provided 4.44 billion euro during 2001 as follows: maintenance, 1.49 billion euro; catering services, 1.48 billion euro; convenient meal solutions, 366.8 million euro; travel commissions, 182.5 euro; IT services, 292.7 million euro; ground services 314.3 euro; and other services, 309 million euro.

Although revenues were up in 2001 over 2000's totals, operating expenses increased disproportionately. The company also took a major blow in its loss/profit from ordinary activities, posting a net loss of 744.7 million euro in 2001, compared to a net profit of 1.22 billion euro in 2000. In 2000 Lufthansa recorded earnings per share of 1.81 euro, but in 2001 the company posted a loss per share of 1.66 euro. As a result of its poor financial showing in 2001, Lufthansa did not pay its shareholders a dividend for the year, breaking a seven-year trend in dividend payments. Also, the company's overall debt grew substantially from 1.47 billion euro in 2000 to 3.81 billion euro in 2001.

ANALYSTS' OPINIONS

Despite its disappointing performance for 2001, analysts remain confident that Lufthansa is a solid investment. In fact, many analysts have pegged the airline company's low stock prices as an attractive buy. Many of Lufthansa's recent financial problems were caused by external factors, namely, a downturn in the world economy, a 29 percent increase in fuel costs, a 17 percent increase in staff costs, a significant increase in insurance costs, and the devastating effect the terrorist attacks of September 11, 2001, which affect the entire airline industry. Analysts expect air traffic to eventually return to its previous pace; the only question is when the turnaround will take place.

Lufthansa's competitive positioning and strong balance sheet should allow the airline to weather the storm and is positioned to quickly benefit when air travel rates pick up again. Although stock prices are expected to remain volatile in the short-term, most analysts see Lufthansa as having a competitive advantage over its competitors in the long-term. The investment risk lies primarily in the uncertainty regarding the depth and duration of the slowdown in air travel with the possibility of further political or terrorist activity that would further deter customers from boarding airplanes.

HISTORY

Deutsche Lufthansa has it roots in several early German airlines. In 1917 Deutsche Luft-Reederi, the first German airline, was created and made its first flight in 1919. In 1923 Deutscher Aero Lloyd was founded and grew to become a major German airline. Deutscher Aero Lloyd dominated the German airways along with Junkers Luftverkehr AG, founded in 1924 by Junkers Flugzeugwerke, an airplane manufacturer. Two years later, on January 6, 1926, Deutscher Aero Lloyd, Junkers Luftverkehr, and all other smaller German airlines merged to form Deutsche Luft Hansa AG.

In 1934 the airline changed its name to Deutsche Lufthansa AG, and on February 3, 1934, a Lufthansa airliner made the world's first transatlantic flight. Beginning in Berlin, the trip, which took five days and included four stops, ended in Rio de Janeiro, Brazil. Later in the year the company began the first regular transatlantic

FAST FACTS:
About Deutsche Lufthansa AG

Ownership: Deutsche Lufthansa AG is a publicly held corporation that is traded on multiple international stock exchanges and traded in the United States as pink sheet stocks.

Ticker Symbol: DLAKY.PK

Officers: Jürgen Weber, Chair of Executive Board, 61; Wolfgang Mayrhuber, Deputy Chair of the Executive Board, Passenger Business Division; Stefan Lauer, Chief Executive Human Resources and Labour Director, 47; Dr. Karl-Ludwig Kley, CFO, 51

Employees: 87,975

Principal Subsidiary Companies: Deutsche Lufthansa AG's major business units are Lufthansa German Airline, Lufthansa Cargo, Lufthansa Technik AG, LSG Sky Chef, Thomas Cook AG, and Luthansa Systems Group GmbH.

Chief Competitors: Deutsche Lufthansa AG competes with other major air carriers including Air France, KLM, and British Airways. The company also is experiencing increasing competition from discount carriers, including easyJet and Ryanair.

mail route between Berlin and Buenos Aires, Argentina. On September 28, 1934, the airline logged its one-millionth passenger. Before the end of the year, the Nazi Party took over control of Lufthansa. Despite the onset of World War II, Lufthansa's profits continued to rise and, by 1939, the airline controlled 7.5 percent of the world market and was the largest airline in Europe.

During the war years, Lufthansa was run by the German Luftwaffe, the Nazi air force. Many employees were drafted into service to aid the war cause. Despite the efforts of Dr. Klaus Bonhoefer, the head of the airline's legal department who was later executed for his involvement in a plot to kill Hitler, Lufthansa remained firmly in the hands of the military. When the war ended, the terms of occupation set out by the Allied forces in West Germany and the Soviet Union in East German did not allow for a German airline. Luftag, the first post-war airline was allowed to form in 1953 in West German, but no Germans were allowed to pilot the planes until 1956. In 1954 the name Luftag was changed back to Lufthansa AG.

CHRONOLOGY:

Key Dates for Deutsche Lufthansa AG

1926: All major German airlines combine to form Deutsche Luft Hansa AG

1934: Name is changed to Deutsche Lufthansa AG; Nazi Party gains control of the airline

1941: All Deutsche Lufthansa AG aircraft come under direct control of the German air force; planes are modified for war purposes

1945: World War II ends; under terms of Allied occupation of Germany, airline operations are prohibited

1951: Luftag becomes the first post-war airline, but German pilots are not allowed to fly the planes

1954: Name is changed back to Deutsche Lufthansa AG

1964: Lufthansa carries its ten-millionth passenger

1972: Terrorism peaks with 92 bomb threats, 23 hijacking threats, and 2 actual hijackings

1980: Lufthansa carries its twenty-millionth passenger

1990: Germany's reunification allows Lufthansa to fly into Berlin for the first time in 45 years

1997: Government ownership of Lufthansa ends; Lufthansa becomes a publicly held company

2001: Lufthansa suffers significant profit losses due to economic recession, a pilot strike, and a drastic reduction in passenger numbers following the terrorist attacks of September 11

As control of the occupied country gradually was returned to Germans, Lufthansa upgraded its fleet and expanded its routes. By 1964 the airline had served ten million passengers. For the first time, in 1965 Lufthansa carried more than one million passengers in one year, making it the sixth largest international airline. The following year profits exceeded DM1 billion. In 1971 Lufthansa introduced Boeing 737s and 747s jetliners into its fleet, and by the ended of the year, its older propeller-driven aircraft, MacDonnell Douglas DC-10s, were completely phased out of operation.

During the 1970s the German airlines, including Lufthansa, were plagued by terrorist threats and attempts. In 1972 alone there were ninety-two bomb threats, twenty-three hijacking threats, and two actual hijackings.

This caused Lufthansa to institute improvements in airport security, notoriously lax at German airports. In 1973 German air traffic controllers conducted a slowdown of flights for a seven-month stretch to protest their working conditions. As a result, Lufthansa posted a significant net loss for the year. However, the following year the airline rebounded to post a net income of DM69 million.

During the 1980s the German government began preparing Lufthansa for privatization. By 1985 the government owned approximately 82 percent and private investors owned the remaining 18 percent. In 1990, with the reunification of East and West Germany, Lufthansa flies into Berlin for the first time in 45 years. The 1990s brought financial difficulties to the airline. Although it produced the fifth largest annual revenue of all airlines, Lufthansa posted a loss in 1991 of DM436 million, followed by losses in 1992 and 1993. However, the money generated by privatization bolstered the company's numbers, and in 1994 the airline returned to profitability.

In preparation for total privatization, Lufthansa reorganized in 1994 by dividing its freight, technical, and systems operations into legally separate entities. In October of 1997 the privatization of the airline was complete when the German government sold its remaining 37.5 percent of stocks to the public for $2.4 billion. During the late 1990s and into the early 2000s, Lufthansa made numerous acquisitions and alliances to increase it passenger and cargo business sectors.

STRATEGY

Lufthansa first recognized troubles toward the end of 2000, when the economy began to show signs of slowing. During the spring of 2001, the airline became mired in labor despites and strikes, causing the company to downgrade its projected earnings target of 1 billon euro to 700 million euro. However, with the terrorist attacks of September 11, 2001, the entire picture changed. It soon became clear that the global implications for the airline industry would be significant yet unpredictable with no clear signs of when a recovery of both the economy and, specifically, the airline business would occur. As a result, Lufthansa moved from a strategy of profit growth to a strategy of survival.

Luckily the airline had initiated a cost-cutting program in the fall of 2000, which was well in place before September 11. The "D-Check" program, launched in the spring of 2001, sought to find ways to boost efficiency and prepared the organization to withstand slowdowns in the economy. Lufthansa anticipated that its newly optimize business processes would result in an additional 1 billion euro in cash flow by 2004. Although Lufthansa's plans were thwarted by the collapse in air travel demand, it benefited from its strategic preparedness that enabled the company to quickly respond to the crisis. Specifically, Lufthansa's reaction included grounding forty-five aircraft (forty-three passenger and two cargo), putting a freeze on hiring and investment spending, and canceling or postponing planned projects.

INFLUENCES

When the aerospace industry in the United States came to a grinding halt in the fall of 2001, Lufthansa first felt the impact in its catering business segment, which services numerous U.S. airlines. The company was in the process of integrating Sky Chefs with its existing catering service LSG. When U.S. carriers enacted rigorous cost-cutting measures, including reducing or eliminating in-flight services, LSG Sky Chefs was seriously affected and its market value impaired. Another business segment that felt a significant impact was Lufthansa's cargo services, which traditionally the first segment to feel the impact of a slowdown in the economy and the first to pick up again when the economy rebounds. As the economy fell into recession, the demand for air transport services dried up. The passenger business segment was also negatively impacted by the sharp decline in air travel.

A wage dispute with its unionized pilots in the spring of 2001 led to a three-day strike that resulted in wholesale flight cancellations. Lost profits due to the strike were compounded an eventual labor agreement that resulted in staff cost increases of approximately 800 million euro on the year. Despite cost cutting measures, Lufthansa incurred significant revenue losses that resulted in a net loss for the year.

CURRENT TRENDS

Expecting the eventual recovery of air travel, Lufthansa is continuing to prepare for the future. In December 2001, the company placed an order for fifteen new Airbus 380 superjumbo jets to be delivered in 2007. By spring of 2002 other strategic plans were being reactivated, including an extension of online distribution channels via the Internet travel portal Opodo, the planned introduction of in-flight Internet access, and the increased use of digital technologies for business processes such as purchases and internal organization. With a stable, but not stagnant, portfolio, Lufthansa hopes to weather the storm and be prepared to enjoy the benefits of better days ahead.

PRODUCTS

Lufthansa Passenger Business, which functions as Lufthansa German Airlines, and its Logistics Business, which functions as Lufthansa Cargo AG, operated a combined fleet of 345 aircraft as of December 31, 2001. Of these, 135 are Airbus models A300, A310, A319, A320, A321, A340, and A380. The company's Boeing jets include 73 737s, 45 747s, and 14 MD 11-F models. Other aircraft in the fleet are 49 Canadair Regional Jets, 18 Avro RJ85s, and 11 Fokker 50s. Planned additions to the fleet between 2002 and 2015 include 14 Airbus A340s, 15 Airbus A380s, 15 Canadair Regional Jets, and 60 Fairchild Dornier 728JETs. Specialized delivery services offered by Lufthansa Cargo include time-definite, temperate-controlled delivery for temperate-sensitive goods and live animals.

Lufthansa's Maintenance, Repair, and Overhaul services operate as Lufthansa Technik AG. Upgrading cabins to provide in-flight Internet access is this division's high profile project. Catering services are provided by LSG Sky Chef, which serves over 260 airlines and maintains 200 catering centers in 45 countries. The acquisition in April of 2001 of the British leisure travel firm Thomas Cook Holdings UK greatly expanded Lufthansa's presence in the leisure travel market. Lufthansa Systems Group is the company's IT business unit. It serves as a systems integrator and provides such services as customer loyalty programs, enterprise resource planning, and customer relationship management.

CORPORATE CITIZENSHIP

In 2001 Lufthansa was awarded the Environmental Prize awarded by the German Committee for the Promotion of Environmentally Aware Management for its longstanding commitment to environmental protection. The company's key environmental objectives are reducing noise pollution, reducing fuel emissions, and increasing fuel efficiency. Between 1991 and 2001 Lufthansa cut fuel consumption by more than 23 percent and is working on advanced technology to determine direct path routing to save on fuel consumption. To protect endangered species and wildlife, Lufthansa does not carry birds captured in the wild, primates, or any animals transported for commercial use. Lufthansa also supports numerous environmental and climatic research studies to determine the impact of air traffic.

GLOBAL PRESENCE

Lufthansa provides passenger and cargo services throughout the world. During 2001 Lufthansa aircraft transported 36.3 million European passengers. In the North Atlantic region, the airline flies to 18 different locations, including the addition of stops in Denver and Phoenix in 2001. Passenger numbers for the North Atlantic region totaled 4.5 million, down 3 percent from 2000. South American destinations included the addition of a Munich-San Paulo route as well as the discontinuation of flights to Lima, Rio de Janeiro, and Bogota. Although

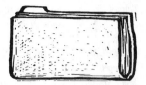

GOING FIRST CLASS

Lufthansa offers its first class passengers preferential treatment. On the ground, first class passengers can access Lufthansa's lounges, which provide exclusive access to refreshing drinks, newspapers and magazines, a business center, television, and restrooms—as well as expedited check-in services and Lufthansa's limousine service. Once in the air, first class travelers enjoy Lufthansa's finest treatment. The first class cabin is designed to provide opportunities for rest, work, and entertainment. Designed to increase privacy and allow plenty of room for comfort, first class seats easily fold out flat into six-foot, six-inch bed. Adjustable screens provide passengers with the opportunity to create privacy or be accessible to the cabin and converse with other passengers. If business is on the agenda, first class passengers can work uninterrupted by plugging into laptop connections available at every seat, with promises that in-flight Internet access will soon be available. Lufthansa's preferred customers also enjoy personal in-seat television monitors and video players with access to a video library for their entertainment.

capacity was expanded by 3 percent to the Middle East, after September 11, bookings fell sharply. Demand for flights to Africa were down for most of 2001, but rose noticeable after September 11, resulting in the addition of a Munich-Johannesburg route. Prior to the terrorist attacks, Lufthansa's Asian routes were the best utilized, with the greatest increase in passenger numbers and the best capacity-to-filled-seat ratio.

EMPLOYMENT

During 2001 nearly 88,000 men and women were employed by Lufthansa. Although this represents a 26.5 percent increase in workforce, much of the increase was due to the incorporation of operations into the Lufthansa group. The addition of Sky Chef alone accounted for an increase of almost 13,000 employees. Of its employee base, 36 percent were located outside Germany. Of its 32,600 international workers, 21,200 were located in the

United States, primarily in association with LSG Sky Chef. Women accounted for 43 percent of the total workforce and 66 percent of the Passenger Business crews. Lufthansa maintains an extensive training program for its recruits as well as ongoing educational opportunities through its Lufthansa Corporate College, launched in 2001.

SOURCES OF INFORMATION

Bibliography

Andrews, Edmund L. "Germany: Lufthansa's Income is Down." *The New York Times*, 13 March 2002.

"Carrier Sees Growth Beyond Lean Years." *Australasian Business Intelligence*, 12 March 2002.

"Day of the Discounters." *Business Week*, 11 February 2002.

"Hailey, Roger. "Lufthansa Considers No-frills Subsidiary." *Air Transport World*, March 2002.

Lazo, Shirley A. "Turbulence Grounds a Payout: Lufthansa Aims to Emerge Stronger After 'Crisis.'" *Barron's*, 18 March 2002.

"Lufthansa: 2001 Earnings Results." *Air Transport World*, April 2002.

"Lufthansa Incurs Loss After 13 Years." *United Press International*, 13 March 2002.

"Lufthansa Operating Profits Climb." *Country ViewsWire*, 17 May 2002.

"Lufthansa Ordered Not to Lower Fares." *Airline Industry Information*, 20 February 2002.

"Lufthansa Posts $565 Million Loss." *The Wall Street Journal*, 24 April 2002.

Michaels, Daniel. "Passenger Drop Pushes Lufthansa into Red." *The Wall Street Journal*, 13 March 2002.

Pilling, Mark. "Lufthansa Business Jet Crosses Atlantic." *Airline Business*, 1 June 2002.

"Results: 2001 Not a Good Year of Lufthansa." *Flight International*, 30 April 2002.

For an annual report:
on the Internet at: http://www.lufthansa.com

For additional industry research:
Investigate companies by their Standard Industrial Classification Codes, also known as SICs. Deutsche Lufthansa AG's primary SIC is:

4512 Air Transportation Scheduled

Also investigate companies by their North American Industry Classification System codes, also known as NAICS codes. Deutsche Lufthansa AG's primary NAICS code is:

481110 Scheduled Air Transportation

Dow Chemical Company

OVERVIEW

With its February 2001 acquisition of Union Carbide Corporation, Dow Chemical Company became the second largest chemical company in the United States, second only to E.I. du Pont de Nemours and Company, which is popularly known as simply DuPont. With ample justification, Dow describes itself as "a leading science and technology company that provides innovative chemical, plastic, and agricultural products and services to many essential consumer markets." Dow serves customers in more than 170 countries worldwide in a wide range of markets, including home and personal care, food, transportation, health and medicine, and building and construction. At more than 200 manufacturing sites in 38 countries, the company supplies more than 3,200 products spread across its 6 major market segments: performance plastics, performance chemicals, agricultural products, plastics, chemicals, and hydrocarbons and energy.

Dow products in the performance plastics category are used in a wide range of applications, including automotive interiors and exteriors, roofing, telecommunications cables, carpeting, food and beverage containers, and sports and recreation equipment. Performance chemical products include building materials, paintings, coatings, inks, adhesives, lubricants, personal care products, water purification products, and agricultural and pharmaceutical products. Dow's agricultural products include seeds, herbicides, pesticides, and fungicides. Products in the plastics category include housewares, industrial films and foams, oil tanks and road equipment, toys, playground equipment, recreational products, and wire and cable. Dow's products in the chemicals segment include

FOUNDED: 1897

Contact Information:
HEADQUARTERS: 2030 Dow Center
   Midland, MI 48674
PHONE: (989)636-1000
FAX: (989)636-1830
TOLL FREE: (800)422-8193
URL: http://www.dow.com

FINANCES:

Dow Chemical Co.
Net Sales, 1998-2001
(million dollars)

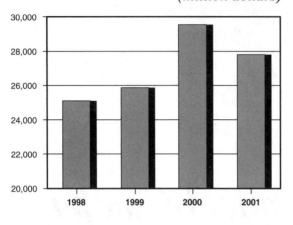

Despite Dow's disappointing financial performance in 2001, a number of analysts voiced confidence that the company was likely to turn things around dramatically, given a more upbeat economic climate worldwide. Michael Judd, chemical industry analyst at Merrill Lynch, predicted that things would start looking up for Dow in 2002 after its disappointing performance in the fourth quarter of 2001, which Judd believed would be the bottom for the chemical profits slump. "We anticipate that a typical spring seasonal demand pick-up could end the current cycle of inventory destocking," Judd said. His views on the inventory situation were echoed by Morgan Stanley analyst Leslie Ravitz, who said of Dow's dismal fourth quarter: "The key point is, this is the bottom. . .because inventory liquidation will have ended. Operating rates and production numbers will be going up."

Judd predicted that Dow's diversification would help the company to stage a major recovery in earnings even before an improvement is seen in global demand for ethylene, one of Dow's major products. He predicted that the company's chlor alkali and polystyrene businesses would probably rebound first, helping the company to resume its winning ways. In Judd's view, the outlook for Dow is extremely bright. He estimated that the company's earnings per share could well peak above $7 in 2005. Other analysts seem even more bullish about Dow's prospects, suggesting that Judd's optimistic prediction may prove to be conservative.

Analysts are divided in their views about the lingering effect of Dow's exposure to asbestos lawsuits. Union Carbide, which Dow acquired in February 2001, mined asbestos until 1985. The mineral, once widely used in insulation applications, has been linked to cancer and lung disease. In January 2002 Dow settled a Texas-based asbestos lawsuit. The Wall Street Journal estimated that Dow's overall liability for such asbestos-related litigation ranges between $140 and $150 million. While Andrew Cash, an analyst with US Warburg, lowered his rating of Dow to "hold" because of uncertainty about the company's liability in this area, Morningstar analyst Dan Quinn suggested that "over the long term, we believe its asbestos liability is largely immaterial."

alumina, household cleaners, inks, food and beverage containers, personal care products, and snow and ice control products. Applications for products in its hydrocarbons and energy category include polymer and chemical production and power generation.

Business conditions throughout the chemical industry in 2001 were as bad as they've been in decades. For Dow, this translated into a very disappointing earnings performance. The company's revenue for the year declined 6 percent to a total of $27.8 billion from $29.5 billion in 2000. For 2001 Dow reported a net loss of $385 million, down sharply from a net profit of nearly $1.7 billion in 2000. The company's stock traded in a range of $23.66 to $39.67 for the year.

Looking at the performance of individual market segments for 2001, the best performing sectors by far were performance plastics with net sales of $7.3 billion and plastics with net sales of nearly $6.5 billion. Performance chemicals sales totaled nearly $5.1 billion while chemicals and agricultural products posted sales of $3.6 billion and $2.6 billion, respectively. Hydrocarbons and energy sales totaled $2.5 billion, with sales of $276.0 million credited to "unallocated" and "other."

Geographically, the United States accounted for slightly more than $11.7 billion of Dow's total sales in 2001. Europe followed with nearly $8.9 billion in sales. Sales for the rest of the world totaled nearly $7.2 billion.

Incorporated in 1897 with Albert E. Convers as its president, the Dow Chemical Company was essentially the brainchild of Herbert Dow, who in about 1890 came up with a revolutionary scheme for the extraction of bromide, an ingredient in bleach, from brine. His original plan was to extract the mineral from the vast subterranean reservoirs of brine left from prehistoric times when Lake Michigan had been an inland sea. Dow used an electric current to separate bromide and other chemicals from the

brine. His attempts to market the bromide and bleaching agents abroad ran into stiff opposition from German and British bromide producers and bleach makers who slashed their prices in an attempt to run this new rival out of business. Dow refused to back down, sustaining substantial losses just to continue the fight.

In the wake of World War I, the U.S. Congress passed import tariffs to protect the American chemical industry from foreign competition. By 1920 Dow Chemical was selling $4 million-a-year worth of bulk chemicals like salt, chlorine, calcium chloride, and aspirin. A decade later, annual sales had climbed to $15 million.

The company weathered the Great Depression well through the expansion of its product line to include iodine, ethylene, and materials that could be used to flush out oil from the ground. As the country's only magnesium producer, Dow's fortunes soared during World War II when the demand for the chemical skyrocketed. In addition to magnesium, Dow also produced styrene and butadiene for synthetic rubber. The company's expansion continued in the postwar years, fueled to a large degree by the company's involvement in plastics production.

Continuing to reach into untapped markets and constantly expanding its product mix, Dow Chemical prospered through the latter half of the twentieth century and, in 2001, acquired Union Carbide Corporation, making Dow the country's second largest chemical company.

STRATEGY

Dow's corporate strategy is keyed to three main elements: people, innovation, and value. The company recognizes that its people are its lifeblood, and to maximize its employees' role in driving business success, Dow is renewing its efforts to build leadership and accountability at all levels. To that end, the company is taking steps to ensure that all its employees are united in purpose and equipped with the tools they need to achieve success.

At Dow the preoccupation with innovation is not so much about the discovery of a new technology or molecule but rather in the company's desire "to find a better way." Dow tries to bring this corporate passion for innovation into virtually every corner of its business. In the company's view, "Innovation comes from applying science and technology to solve problems for our customers, our communities, and the world."

As to value, the third key element in Dow's strategy, the focus is on the creation of long-term value for the company's shareholders as well as its customers, employees, and the communities in which it operates. Dow seeks to do this by balancing economic, environmental, and social responsibilities.

FAST FACTS:
About Dow Chemical Company

Ownership: Dow Chemical Company is a publicly owned company traded on the Amsterdam, Berlin, Brussels, Chicago, Dusseldorf, Frankfurt, Hamburg, Hanover, London, New York, Pacific, Paris, Switzerland, and Tokyo Stock Exchanges.

Ticker Symbol: DOW

Officers: William S. Stavropoulos, Chmn, 62, 2000 base salary $1,278,333; Michael D. Parker, Pres. and CEO, 55, 2000 base salary $960,000; Anthony J. Carbone, VChmn., 61, 2000 base salary $691,368

Employees: 52,600

Principal Subsidiary Companies: Dow Chemical is a widely diversified company with scores of subsidiaries and joint venture enterprises. Three of its most important subsidiary or joint venture operations are Cargill Dow, LLC; Dow Agro Sciences, LLC; and Dow Corning Corporation.

Chief Competitors: As a major player in the production of chemicals, plastics, and agricultural chemicals, Dow faces intense competition on a worldwide scale. Its major competitors include DuPont, the largest chemical company in the United States, and German chemical giants BASF AG and Bayer AG.

Some more specific elements of Dow's strategy include capturing synergies created through the integration of Union Carbide into the company, accelerating its Six Sigma program of cost reduction, pursuing a business-by-business approach, and recognizing and exploiting new value growth opportunities.

INFLUENCES

Rarely has Dow been as profoundly challenged as it was during 2001. With worldwide chemical demand in a deep slump, the company was forced to focus on cost reduction to minimize its losses. Throughout the difficulties of 2001, Dow concentrated on four key financial objectives: generating a return on equity of 20 percent or more; returning 3 percent above the company's cost of capital; earning its cost of capital at the trough; and growing earnings per share by 10 percent each year.

CHRONOLOGY:
Key Dates for Dow Chemical Company

1897: Dow Chemical Company is founded

1900: Midland Chemical merges into Dow

1913: Dow shifts focus from bleach to chlorine

1918: Dow adopts diamond trademark

1925: Dow wins patent for new calcium chloride flake

1935: Dow enters the plastics business

1942: Dow Chemical of Canada is founded

1948: Plastics reach 20 percent of sales

1952: Asahi-Dow, Ltd. is first overseas subsidiary

1964: Annual sales top $1 billion

1970: Complete line of products for automotive applications introduced

1986: Dow ranks as world's largest thermoplastics producer

1995: Sales reach record $20.2 billion

1996: Dow enters PET, polypropylene businesses

2001: Dow acquires Union Carbide

CURRENT TRENDS

Although some improvement can be expected in chemical industry demand worldwide, Dow anticipates that it will be some time before the market for chemicals returns to anything approaching normalcy. The company hopes to counter the softness in the basic chemical market by looking further afield for opportunities outside the conventional confines of the chemical business. The emphasis at Dow will be on innovation, which the company feels is essential to ensure its continued success. This innovation will permeate all corners of Dow's operations, including new product research and the search for advances in technology and e-business that will allow the company to better serve its customers.

PRODUCTS

Dow Chemical produces a broad range of chemicals, plastics, and agricultural products. The company's

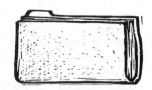

SIX SIGMA WORKS FOR DOW

Six Sigma, a set of quality management tools, didn't originate with Dow but has quickly become a guiding strategy for the chemical giant since its implementation in the latter half of 1999. And Dow is not the only major American corporation to embrace Six Sigma as a way to keep customers happy and cut costs at the same time. Originated in Arizona, the Six Sigma strategy focuses on the elimination of problems by rethinking tasks and streamlining processes. Six Sigma is a statistical term that means keeping defects to 3.4 per million products. Michael D. Parker, Dow's president and CEO, reported that the company had ramped up its Six Sigma efforts in 2001, "intensifying our focus on cost reduction." He added that at the end of 2001, Dow was halfway toward its Six Sigma goal of creating $1.5 billion in cumulative earnings before interest and taxes by the end of 2003.

performance plastics segment is subdivided into seven product areas: Dow automotive, engineering plastics, epoxy products and intermediates, fabricated products, polyurethanes and polyurethane systems, technology licensing and catalysts, and wire and cable compounds. Dow's performance chemicals market segment also has seven principal product categories: custom and fine chemicals, emulsion polymers, industrial chemicals, oxide derivatives, specialty polymers, UCAR emulsion systems, and water soluble polymers.

For the agricultural products market segment, virtually all of the company's products are produced by Dow's subsidiary, Dow Agro Sciences, LLC. Some of its better known products include Clincher herbicide, Dithane fungicide, Dursban and Lorsban insecticides, FirstRate herbicide, Fortress fungicide, Garlon, Glyphomax, Grandstand, Lontrel, and Mustang herbicides, Mycogen seeds, Sentricon insecticide, Telone soil fumigant, and Tracer Naturalyte insect control.

Dow's plastics market segment is subdivided into three main product categories: polyethylene, polypropylene, and polystyrene. The key product categories in the company's chemicals market segment are core chemicals and ethylene oxide/ethylene glycol. Some of the better-known products of Dow's hydrocarbons and energy market segment include benzene, butadiene, butylene, cumene, ethylene, propylene, and styrene. This segment also is involved in the generation of power.

CORPORATE CITIZENSHIP

Fiercely dedicated to the principles of sustainable development, Dow Chemical believes that as a good corporate citizen, it must balance economic prosperity with corporate social responsibility and environmental stewardship. The company publicly reports its progress against measurable standards and remains committed to an environmental health and safety "Vision of Zero," no accidents, no injuries, and no degradation of the environment. The company's efforts in this area have not gone unnoticed. It has won the Responsible Care Leadership Award of the American Chemistry Council and has attained a top ranking in the Dow Jones Sustainability Group Index.

In the communities in which the company operates, Dow seeks to ensure the safety of its operations, earn the trust of its neighbors, and take a leadership role in meeting local needs. Communications between Dow executives and community leaders are facilitated by Community Advisory Panels, which have been established at all of the company's major facilities.

Dow takes considerable pride in its efforts to help take care of the communities in which it operates, as well as supporting its global neighbors. Beginning in 1961 the company has invested considerable sums of money and a great deal of time in projects to purify drinking water from the ocean.

GLOBAL PRESENCE

More than half of Dow Chemical's sales are in markets outside the United States. The company operates more than 200 manufacturing facilities in 38 countries around the world.

EMPLOYMENT

As of December 31, 2001, Dow's employees worldwide numbered more than 52,600. Fully aware that its people are among its greatest assets, the company has taken steps to guarantee that its employees are well equipped to handle the responsibilities they've been given. The company has introduced a Web-based training system called learn@dow.now, offering employees an online option for continuing education with a flexibility that can be found only in electronic training. Dow employees in 2001 completed more than 315,000 courses under this new system.

SOURCES OF INFORMATION

Bibliography

"Analyst Highlights Dow Chemical's New Products." *The Wall Street Transcript*. Available at http://www.twst.com.

"Dow Chemical Company." *Hoover's Online*, 2002. Available at http://www.hoovers.com.

Dow Chemical Company 2001 Annual Report. Midland, MI: Dow Chemical Company, 2002.

"Dow Chemical Falls on Analyst Cut, Asbestos Liability Concerns." *Business Today*. Available at http://www.businesstoday.com.

"Dow Chemical Co. History." *Gale Business Resources*. Available at http://galenet.galegroup.com/servlet/GBR.

Dow Chemical Company Home Page, 2002. Available at http://www.dow.com.

"Dow Chemical to Miss 4th-Quarter Earnings Target." *Reuters Business Report*, 3 January 2002.

"Morningstar.com Stock Analyst Notes: 01/10/02." *Yahoo! Finance*. Available at http://biz.yahoo.com.

"Snapshot Report: Dow Chemical Company." *Multex Investor*. Available at http://www.marketguide.com.

For an annual report:

on the Internet at: http://www.dow.com/financial/reports/index.htm **or** write: Dow Chemical, EquiServe Trust Co., N.A., PO Box 43016, Providence, RI 02940-3016

For additional industry research:

Investigate companies by their Standard Industrial Classification Codes, also known as SICs. Dow Chemical Company's primary SICs are:

2800 Chemicals and Allied Products

2810 Industrial Inorganic Chemicals

2812 Alkalis and Chlorine

2819 Industrial Inorganic Chemicals NEC

2820 Plastics Materials and Synthetics

2821 Plastics Materials and Resins

2830 Drugs

2840 Soap, Cleaners, and Toilet Goods

2841 Soap and Other Detergents

2842 Polishes and Sanitations Goods

2869 Industrial Organic Chemicals NEC

2891 Adhesives and Sealants

2899 Chemical Preparations NEC

3000 Rubber and Miscellaneous Plastics Products

3083 Laminated Plastics Plate and Sheet

3084 Plastics Pipe

3086 Plastics Foam Products

Also investigate companies by their North American Industry Classification System, also known as NAICS codes. Dow Chemical Company's primary NAICS codes are:

325188 All Other Basic Inorganic Chemical Manufacturing

325199 All Other Basic Organic Chemical Manufacturing

325211 Plastics Material and Resin Manufacturing

325611 Soap and Other Detergent Manufacturing

325612 Polish and Other Sanitation Goods Manufacturing

Duke Energy Corporation

OVERVIEW

Duke Energy Corporation is an integrated energy service provider that offers physical delivery and management of both electricity and natural gas throughout the United States, as well as Europe, Latin America, and Australia. The company is divided into seven business segments: Franchised Electric, Natural Gas Transmission, Field Services, North American Wholesale Energy (NAWE), International Energy, Other Energy Services, and Duke Ventures. Duke conducts business in a range of energy-related activities, including buying and selling energy and commodities; managing energy, commodity risk, and energy consumption; and building and operating energy transmission networks and facilities.

With a net income in fiscal 2001 of almost $1.9 billion on revenues of $59.5 billion, Duke Energy ranked 14th on the Fortune 500 list in 2002, up from 17th in 2001 and 67th in 2000. The jump in ranking is a result of the $9 billion acquisition of PanEnergy, which transformed Duke Energy from a regional supplier of electricity into an international full-service energy company. Duke energy made another mega-acquisition in 2002 when it purchased Canadian-based Westcoast Energy for $8.5 billion. The deal added 6,900 miles of natural gas transmission pipeline, increasing Duke's overall total to 18,900 miles. The Westcoast addition also increased storage capacity by 141 billion cubic feet, bringing Duke's total to 241 billion cubic feet.

COMPANY FINANCES

Duke Energy posted a net income of $1.89 billion on $59.5 billion in revenues in fiscal 2001, reflecting a

FOUNDED: 1904 as the Southern Power Company

Contact Information:
HEADQUARTERS: PO Box 1244
    Charlotte, NC 28202-1803
PHONE: (704)594-6200
FAX: (704)382-3814
URL: http://www.dukeenergy.com

FINANCES:

Duke Energy Corporation Operating Revenues, 1999-2001 (million dollars)

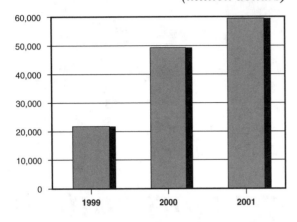

Duke Energy Corporation 2001 Stock Prices (dollars)

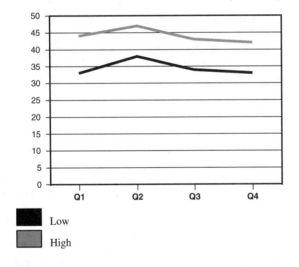

■ Low
▧ High

21 percent increase in total sales from the previous year in which the company had $49.3 billion in revenues resulting in a net income for fiscal 2000 of $1.78 billion. Net income more than doubled and total revenues jumped over 350 percent since 1997 when the corporation reported $902 million in income on $16.3 billion in sales. In fiscal 2001, earnings per share from ongoing operations increased a record 26 percent over the year. Stock prices were down over 10 percent from the previous year, but the decrease must be viewed in light of an overall industry average drop of 24 percent.

In earnings before interest or taxes (EBIT), the Franchised Electric segment rankest highest among the company's division with an EBIT result of $1.63 billion in 2001, down from $1.82 billion in 2000 with the loss being attributed primarily to milder weather and the economic downturn that reduced the amount of industrial business. Benefiting from an exceptionally volatile market in the natural gas industry, NAWE rocketed from an EBIT of $434 million in 2000 to over $1.35 billion in 2001. Natural Gas Transmission posted an EBIT of $608 million; Field Services, $336 million; International Energy, $286 million; and Duke Ventures, $183 million. The Other Energy Services segment posted a EBIT loss of $13 million, an improvement over a $59 million loss in 2000.

ANALYSTS' OPINIONS

Impressed by its excellent combination of low-risk, high-quality electric and natural gas businesses, most analysts view Duke Energy as one of the premier integrated energy corporations in the world. Sources of earnings are very diversified so the corporation does not rely upon a single business to achieve growth. Other positive aspects noted by analysts are Duke's strong balance sheet, which provides income for expansion, and Duke's lack of financial trading with Enron, which shielded it from the fallout of that firm's bankruptcy filing in 2001. Despite a less-than-expected gain in the fourth quarter of 2001, analysts stand by Duke Energy as a solid stock option. Nonetheless, after the report of flat earnings was released, Duke Energy's stock prices fell slightly, but began rebounding by April of 2002. General consensus among analysts is that investors should take advantage of the depressed stock price, until the price per share hits $40. After that point, risks to the overall energy industry, such as mild weather and economic recession, begin to factor in more heavily.

HISTORY

Duke Power, later to become Duke Energy Corporation, had its start in the late 1800s with tobacco tycoon James B. Duke. By 1938 Duke's tobacco company controlled 38 percent of U.S. cigarette sales. The following year a merger with several other leading cigarette companies created The American Tobacco Company, making Duke one of the wealthiest and well-known figures in the United States. Duke used his wealth to expand into numerous business ventures, including textile industries. He understood the potential electricity had to revolutionize industry, and as early as the 1890s began purchasing river property to later develop into hydroelectric sources. In 1905 he stepped firmly into the power business when he joined W. Gill Wylie, founder of Catawba Power Company, to form Southern Power Company

(SPC). With the help of Wylie's chief engineer, William S. Lee, Duke and Wylie made plans to bring electricity to the Piedmont.

By 1907 SPC was operating two hydroelectric plants in South Carolina, the India Hook Shoals and the Great Falls Hydro Station. In April of 1909 SPC began construction of the Rocky Creek Hydro Station. In the same year, the company built the nation's first 100,000-volt power line to connect its network of generators. In 1910 Duke replaced Wylie as the president of SPC and created the Mill-Power Supply Company to manufacture and sell the equipment needed to convert the textile industry from steam power to electricity. Already heavily invested in the textile industry, Duke poured money into bringing more textile shops to the area. By offering financial support to any textile mill that would purchase power from SPC, Duke was able to entice a large number of new manufacturers to the Piedmont area, making it one of the centers of the U.S. textile industry. By the mid-1920s, Duke was providing power to over 300 textile mills which accounted for one-sixth of all U.S. garment-producing machines.

In 1911 the U.S. Supreme Court broke up Duke's tobacco monopoly, ordering him to divest much of his tobacco assets. Because Duke had already turned his attention to the power business, the loss of his tobacco assets had little impact on his wealth. In 1913 he established the Southern Public Utilities Company to acquire utility companies, and in 1917 he formed the Waterlee Electric Company as a holding company for SPC. In 1924 Waterlee was reorganized and renamed the Duke Power Company. During this time, Duke Power began pursuing residential customers. As electrical appliances became more popular, Duke's residential base of customers increased to become a vital part of its overall operations.

Wylie died in 1923, and Duke's death followed in 1925. Lee took over leadership of the company. He pushed for increased production of steam generators, which soon usurped the company's hydroelectric production. The first steam-driven power plant went on line on October 26, 1926. The following year Duke Power absorbed SPC and Great Falls Power Company. By 1935 Duke Power had also taken over the Southern Power Utilities Company, bringing all operations under one governing body for the first time. The Great Depression produced difficult years for Duke Power. Wylie died in 1934, no new construction was undertaken until 1938, and full-fledged growth did not return to the company until after the end of World War II.

Following the war, Duke Power's business gained vitality, as did the national economy. In 1949 the company committed $20 million to expand its operations and develop modern, state-of-the-art, steam-driven power plants. The first results of this investment were realized in 1952 when two new plants opened. Dan River and Plant Lee increased Duke Power's capacity by 320,000 kilowatts. In 1956 Duke Power took a step toward nuclear power production by joining three other area utility com-

FAST FACTS:

About Duke Energy Corporation

Ownership: Duke Energy Corporation is a publicly held company that trades on the New York Stock Exchange.

Ticker Symbol: DUK

Officers: Richard B. Priory, Chmn., Pres., and CEO, 54, 2000 salary $954,164, 2000 bonus $1,908,328; H.J. Padewer, Pres. Energy Services, 2000 salary $500,004, 2000 bonus $750,006; William A. Coley, Pres. Duke Power, 57, 2000 salary $450,000, 2000 bonus $585,000; F.J. Fowler, Group Pres. Energy Transmission, 2000 salary $450,000, 2000 bonus $585,000

Employees: 23,000

Principal Subsidiary Companies: Duke Energy is an energy service provider that operates 11 subsidiaries and 439 branch locations. Subsidiary ventures include Westcoast Energy Inc.; Duke Energy Field Services; Duke/Fluor Daniel; and DukeNet Communications, LLC.

Chief Competitors: Duke Energy competes with other energy service providers including AED, Mirant, and Reliant Energy.

panies to form the Carolinas-Virginia Nuclear Power Association. The association worked together to create an experimental nuclear generator prototype. Duke Power, which began trading shares on the New York Stock Exchange in 1961, opened its first nuclear power station at Parr Shoals, South Carolina, in 1962. The following year, its last hydroelectric plant opened at Cowans Ford, South Carolina.

By the late 1960s, Duke Power was making plans to convert all of its thermal plants to nuclear power. To that end, the company received a license from the Atomic Energy Commission to begin construction on a full-scale nuclear plant. The Oconee Nuclear Station Unit One opened in 1973. However, the oil embargo by the Organization of Petroleum Exporting Countries (OPEC) sent the economy into a downward spiral, just as Duke Power was gearing up for massive expansion. The company was further disrupted when its subsidiary Eastover Mining came under fire for its operation of four coal mines in Kentucky. Workers lodged numerous charges against the

Kayakers paddling the Elkhorn Slough pass near Duke Energy's 1,090-megawatt Moss Landing Plant on Monterey Bay, California. (AP Photo/Richard Green)

company, including claims that Duke Power was anti-union, provided poor worker housing, and added to pollution. Eventually the suit was settled and Duke Power sold off Eastover Mining. Duke Power was helped out in 1974 by the approval of a rate hike that kept the company afloat through the energy crisis.

By the mid 1970s, nuclear power made up over 30 percent of Duke Power's energy capacity. However, plans for a full-scale conversion to nuclear-based power were being questioned. The nuclear meltdown at Three Mile Island nuclear plant in Pennsylvania in 1979 fueled opposition against nuclear power, and Duke Power backed off its production of nuclear plants. Although most plants already under construction were completed, plans for six additional plants were cancelled by 1985, with no new construction beginning after the early 1980s. McGuire Nuclear Station Unit One went on line in 1981 and Catawba Nuclear Station Unit One followed in 1985. Although Duke Power did not abandon its interest in or commitment to nuclear power, renewed focus was given to its hydroelectric and steam operations.

By 1990 Duke Power was the seventh largest public utility operating in the United States. In 1994 revenues reached $4.5 billion. In the same year, the company's employee base was reduced by more than 1,500 people, followed by another cut of 900 employees in 1995. In 1996 Duke Power faced the uncertain future of energy deregulation with a bold move. Company president William H. Grigg approached Houston-based

PanEnergy, the nation's third largest natural gas company, with a merger offer. The deal, completed in June of 1997 and worth $7.7 billion, created Duke Energy Corporation, the nation's largest gas-electric utility company. Under the leadership of Richard B. Priory, the newly named chief executive officer and chairman of the board, Duke Energy continued to expand through acquisitions, albeit on a smaller scale. In 2000 Duke Energy teamed with several power companies to launch an independent, Internet-based business-to-business electric transmission exchange that could coordinate transmission capacities through a single gateway. In the same year Duke Energy also joined Carolina Power & Light, and SCANA Corporation to create an independent regional transmission organization, known as GridSouth, that coordinates the operation and planning for the transmission systems of the three companies.

STRATEGY

The five pillars of Duke Energy's overall strategy are operational excellence, the overlay of energy transmission and production, portfolio diversity, strategic acquisitions and divestitures, and consistent financial strength. First, Duke Energy aims to provide quality services and goods within a fiscally responsible organization. Second, by combining the production and marketing of natural gas and electricity with its transmission, Duke Energy can participate in its customer's energy systems from start to finish. Third, Duke Energy's diversity protects the company from a downturn in any one segment. However, the company has diversified selectively. Unlike other energy companies that expanded heavily in non energy-related businesses, Duke Energy has remained focused on diversifying within the industry itself. Fourth, Duke Energy combines its natural gas and power assets with trading and marketing. Basically, Duke Energy participates in the market by buying and selling its own entities, working hard to buy low and sell high. Finally, the company continually looks for ways to develop a positive income result while engaging in the least amount of risk possible to the overall financial base of the corporation. By so doing, the company earnings-per-share growth remains modest, but the company retains ongoing financial stability in return.

INFLUENCES

Duke Energy, as well as the entire energy industry, faced numerous challenges in 2001. California underwent a major energy crisis, Enron folded in the midst of accounting scandals, energy prices were pushed down, milder weather around the nation decreased energy consumption as much as 20 percent, and the aftermath of the terrorist attacks on New York and the Pentagon shook the entire economy, pushing it into a full recession. Duke Energy is continually susceptible to fluctuations in the wholesale price of electricity, the price of natural gas, and the weather. One risk management tool Duke Energy uses to protect itself from sudden swings in prices is called hedging, meaning the company sells long-term contracts for energy production and transmission that lock the spread between cost of production and sale price.

CURRENT TRENDS

Based on the prediction that even in economically difficult times, U.S. energy consumption will continue to increase at least 1 to 2 percent annually, Duke Energy has continued to expand its energy capabilities. Since 1997 the company has vastly increased the size of its natural gas pipelines, capacity for storage of natural gas, production of natural gas liquids, and increased its transportation network. Energy production operations have also expanded, with 6 new facilities going on line in 2001, 11 more in 2002, and 5 more planned to go on line in 2003. Duke Energy is also creating its presence on the Web. Through its interest in InterContinental Exchange, the corporation provides an online exchange for buyers and seller of power and natural gas.

Within the Franchised Electric segment, growth is expected to be moderate, resulting primarily from an

CHRONOLOGY:
Key Dates for Duke Energy Corporation

1905: Tobacco merchant James B. Duke joins with Dr. W. Gill Wylie, founder of Catawba Power Co., to form Southern Power Company (SPC)

1911: The U.S. Supreme Court rules that Duke's tobacco operation is a monopoly and orders him to divest himself of many of his tobacco-related assets

1924: Duke changes the name of SPC's holding company, Waterlee Electric Co., to Duke Power Company, and establishes a $40 endowment for Trinity College, later renamed Duke University

1961: Duke Power Co. stock is traded on the New York Stock Exchange for the first time

1962: Duke opens its first nuclear facility, the Parr Shoals plant in South Carolina

1975: The Oconee Nuclear Station Unit One, in operation since 1973, wins an award from the American Society of Civil Engineering

1979: The Meltdown at the Three Mile Island nuclear plant in Pennsylvania discourages plans for further nuclear plant development, but plans continue to open operations already under construction

1991: Oconee Unit One is the first U.S. nuclear station to produce 100 billion kilowatt hours of electricity

1994: Revenues reach $4.5 billion

1997: Duke Power and PanEnergy Corp complete $7.7 billion merger to create Duke Energy Corporation

2001: Joins Progress Energy and SCANA to form a regional transmission organization

increase in residential and general services sectors but offset somewhat by the ongoing decline in the textile industries. Natural Gas Transmission is set to grow through careful acquisitions and increased services. Field Services, which also already expanded substantially, will be grown through additional investments in natural gas gathering and processing services. As part of the company's overall strategy, NAWE and International Energy segments are set to achieve new growth through strategic acquisitions and divestitures, along with improvement and expansion of existing services and facilities. Energy Services is working to expand its customer base, and Duke Ventures is set

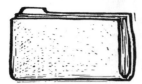

DUKE UNIVERSITY

Lifelong Methodists, the Dukes had long practiced financial stewardship. James B. Duke's father, Washington Duke, supported Methodist-affiliated Trinity College's move from Fayette, North Carolina, to Durham. In 1924 James B. Duke set up a $600,000 endowment fund for Trinity on the sole condition that the school be renamed Duke University. Trinity agreed, and Duke University was born. A statue of James B. Duke, holding a cigar, stands in the center of campus in his honor.

Several long-standing folk legends exist regarding Duke's contribution to Trinity. The most frequently told story is that Duke, who had significant assets in New Jersey, first offered his money to Princeton University on the same condition—change the name to Duke. Princeton refused so Duke turned to Trinity. In addition, stories circulate that the bell tower of Duke University's new majestic chapel was built to be slightly taller than Princeton's, perhaps as a dig at the school that refused Duke's offer.

---

to focus on its interests in real estate, telecommunications, and capital financing for its business units.

PRODUCTS

Franchised Electric generates, transmits, sells, and distributes electricity in central and western North Carolina and western South Carolina, primarily through the subsidiaries Duke Power and Nantahala Power and Light. The Natural Gas Transmission division provides natural gas transportation and storage to customers primarily in the Mid-Atlantic, New England, and the southeastern states. The main subsidiary for this business segment is Duke Energy Gas Transmission Corporation. Field Services gathers, processes, transports, markets, and stores natural gas and produces, transports, markets, and stores natural gas liquids, operating primarily through Duke Energy Field Services. NAWE, which conducts most of its business in the United States, develops, operates, and manages merchant generation facilities. NAWE is also involved in commodity sales and services related to natural gas and electricity. The main subsidiaries within the NAWE segment include Duke Energy North America LLC, Duke Energy Trading and Marketing LLC, and Duke Energy Merchants Holdings LLC.

Duke Energy International conducts international electric and natural gas operations, and Energy Services covers ancillary products and services, such as engineering, construction, consulting, and integrated energy solutions. The main subsidiaries within the division are Duke Engineering and Services Inc. and Duke/Fluor Daniel Inc., a joint partnership with Flour Enterprises Inc. Duke Ventures is the catch-all division for a diverse array of financial services and investments, including Crescent Resources LLC, DukeNet Communications LLC, and Duke Capital Partners LLC.

CORPORATE CITIZENSHIP

As a large energy corporation, Duke Energy purports to take a proactive stance on environmental issues including the impact of its operations on greenhouse gas emissions. By engaging in voluntary actions to create the cleanest, most environmentally sound energy systems, Duke Energy makes serious attempts to reduce its contribution to changes in the global climate. For its efforts, Duke Energy has received multiple recognitions, which included the 2001 Distinguished Service Award from the American Fisheries Society Southern Division, the Outstanding Stewardship of America's Rivers award from the National Hydropower Association, and a Building With Trees award (Crescent Resources) from the National Arbor Day Foundation. The company combines its environmental concern with its values regarding cultural sensitivity, economic development, resource conservation, and facilitating quality of life improvement. To that end, Duke Energy contributes to and participates in myriad social, economic, and youth projects and initiatives.

GLOBAL PRESENCE

Duke Energy's targeted areas for international service and growth are Europe, Latin America, and the Asia-Pacific region. European operations are located in London, with additional facilities in Milan and The Hague. Latin American markets include Argentina, Bolivia, Brazil, Ecuador, El Salvador, and Peru, as well as a new operation opening in Guatemala in 2002. Australia functions as the headquarters for the Asia-Pacific area, supplying energy products and services in Australia and extending into the region. In the middle east, Duke Energy holds an interest in the National Methanol Company in Saudi Arabia.

EMPLOYMENT

Duke Energy actively recruits talented new employees. Recruiting events are held at colleges, universities, and technical schools for candidates with master's, bachelor's, and two-year or technical degrees for a wide variety of positions requiring diverse skills and education. Graduate-level degreed candidates are targeted for Duke Energy's business operations as well as opportunities to pursue specific fields of study. Candidates with an undergraduate degree are eligible for positions in areas such as electrical, civil, mechanical, nuclear, petroleum and environmental engineering; accounting and finance; marketing-related positions; information technology; and risk management. Opportunities are also available for candidates with a two-year, technical degree or military equivalent in the areas of electronics, instrumentation, mechanics, nuclear technology, radiology, environmental sciences, chemistry, information systems, communications, and other fields.

SOURCES OF INFORMATION

Bibliography

"Duke Energy Corporation." *Hoover's Company Profiles*, 2002. Available at http://www.hoovers.com.

Fisher, Daniel. "Trading Places." *Forbes Magazine*, 21 January 2001.

Foust, Dean, and Christopher Palmeri. "Against the Flow at Duke Energy: CEO Priory is Making an Integrated Utility Pay Off Big." *Business Week*, 5 November 2001.

Grant, Tina, ed. *International Directory of Company Histories.* Vol. 27. Detroit: St. James Press, 1999.

"Loss is Projected Due to Sale of DukeSolutions Division." *The Wall Street Journal*, 1 April 2002.

Schwartz, Nelson D. "The Un-Enron: Duke Energy Used to Hate Explaining Why It Wasn't More Like Its Houston Rival. Not Anymore." *Fortune Magazine*, 15 April 2002.

Smith, Rebecca. "Duke Energy's Profit Slides 21% Reflecting Slack Demand, Charge." *The Wall Street Journal*, 18 January 2002.

For an annual report:

on the Internet at: http://www.dukeenergy.com

For additional industry research:

Investigate companies by their Standard Industrial Classification Codes, also known as SICs. Duke Energy Corporation's primary SICs are:

1311 Crude Petroleum And Natural Gas

1321 Natural Gas Liquids

1381 Drilling Oil & Gas Wells

1382 Oil & Gas Field Exploration Services

4911 Electric Services

4923 Gas Transmission And Distribution

4925 Gas Production &/or Distribution, Not Elsewhere Classified

4932 Gas And Other Services Combined

6719 Holding Companies, Not Elsewhere Classified

Also investigate companies by their North American Industry Classification System Codes, also known as NAICS codes. Duke Energy Corporation's primary NAICS codes are:

221122 Electric Power Generation, Transmission and Distribution

221210 Natural Gas Distribution

eBay Inc.

FOUNDED: 1995

Contact Information:

HEADQUARTERS: 2145 Hamilton Ave.
   San Jose, CA 95125
PHONE: (408)558-7400
FAX: (408)558-7401
EMAIL: investor_relations@eBay.com
URL: http://www.eBay.com

OVERVIEW

eBay is the world's first and largest person-to-person online auction Web site. The company boasts the largest number of traders online and is the Web's most popular shopping site, consisting of a community of 42.4 million registered users made up of individuals and businesses that form the largest online marketplace in the world. The online auction site consists of more than 8,000 categories of goods and services that range from antiques, jewelry, electronic equipment, furniture, sporting goods, tickets, and collectibles to used automobiles and boats.

eBay facilitates trade locally, nationally, and internationally, featuring a variety of international sites, specialty sites, and categories and services that provide users with the tools to trading efficiently online in auction-style and fixed-price formats. eBay's major feature and services include Billpoint, a service that facilitates credit card payments between buyers and sellers; Half.com, a fixed-price trading site of previously owned mass-market goods; eBay International, with country specific sites in Austria, Canada, France, Germany, Ireland, Italy, Korea, New Zealand, Switzerland, and the United Kingdom; eBay Motors, the Internet's largest auction-style marketplace for buying and selling all things automotive; eBay Stores, allowing sellers to create customized shopping destinations to merchandise their items on eBay and allow buyers a convenient way to access sellers' products; Buy it Now, a feature allowing buyers to buy an item at a specified price without waiting for the end of an auction; eBay Professional Services, which serves the small business community by providing a way on eBay to find professionals and freelancers in a variety of areas from web design to writing and technical support; eBay

Local Trading, with 60 local markets in the United States to aid in the sale of difficult-to-ship items; eBay Premier, which presents fine art, antiques, fine wine, and rare collectibles from leading auction houses and dealers worldwide; and eBay Live Auctions, offering live, real-time auctions on items at the world's leading auction houses. All these features and services further the company's mission to "develop a global online trading platform that will help practically anyone trade practically anything on earth."

COMPANY FINANCES

In 2001 eBay transacted more than $9 billion in annualized gross merchandise sales, which is the value of all goods traded on eBay that year. More than $1 billion of that total is estimated to come from the less than two-year-old automobile category alone. Sales for 2001 totaled $748.8 million, with a one-year sales growth of 73.6 percent. Net income for 2001 was $90.4 million, up 87.2 percent over the previous year.

The company has shown consistent and impressive financial growth since its inception, with a 160 percent increase in net revenues from 1998 to 1999, a 92 percent increase in net revenues from 1999 to 2000, and a 73 percent increase in net revenues from 2000 to 2001. eBay Inc.'s stock ranged from a low of $29.25 to a high of $72.74 over a 52-week period. eBay's price-earnings ratio is a very high 143, based on 2001 estimated results, but lowers to approximately 80, based on 2002 results. Financial goals for the company are to reach $3 billion in revenues and $1 billion in operating profits by the year 2005, which would mean more than tripling the number of registered buyers and sellers to 150 million.

ANALYSTS' OPINIONS

eBay will tell any potential investor that they have established themselves as the world's largest and most popular online marketplace by pioneering online personal trading and that they have shown consistent profits since their inception in 1995 and subsequent incorporation in 1996. Several analysts agree with eBay's assessment and consider it a desirable stock. RBC Capital Markets reported in 2002 that as a result of eBay's alliance with Priceline.com and Sotheby's, along with continued expansion of eBay Motors, eBay maintained their Sector Perform-Above Average rating. CIBC World Markets Corp. reiterated its buy rating on eBay in 2002, as well. Robertson Stephens reported in January 2002 that eBay's impressive fourth quarter 2001 results suggest that business at the online trader remains strong and combines desirable growth initiatives consistent with prior expectations, therefore warranting a Buy rating on eBay stock. As one of the sole survivors of the dot-com downturn,

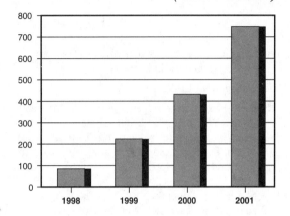

FINANCES:

eBay, Inc.
Net Sales, 1998-2001
(million dollars)

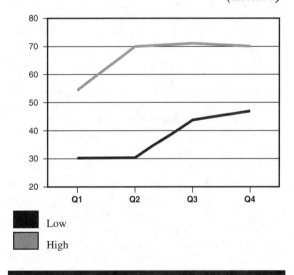

eBay, Inc.
2001 Stock Prices
(dollars)

■ Low
▨ High

eBay's low overhead, continued financial performance, and growth into new markets makes its stock one of the few attractive technology buys in 2001 and early 2002.

HISTORY

eBay founder Pierre Omidyar was considering an Internet venture when he realized collectors needed a central location to get together to trade and chat about their hobbies. In 1995 he launched an online person-to-

FAST FACTS:

About eBay Inc.

Ownership: eBay Inc. is a publicly owned company traded on the NASDAQ Stock Exchange.

Ticker Symbol: EBAY

Officers: Pierre M. Omidyar, Chmn., 34; Margaret C. (Meg) Whitman, Pres. and CEO, 45, 2000 base salary $210,000; Rajiv Dutta, CFO, 40; Maynard G. Webb, Jr., Pres., eBay Technologies, 46, 2000 base salary $450,000; Jeffrey D. Jordan, SVP and Gen. Mgr., U.S. Business, 43, 2000 base salary $290,000; Matthew J. Bannick, SVP, International, 37, 2000 base salary $207,250; Michael R. Jacobson, VP, Legal Affairs, Gen. Counsel and Sec., 47, 2000 base salary $190,000

Employees: 1,927

Principal Subsidiary Companies: eBay owns and operates Half.com, which provides an alternative, fixed-price format for trading a variety of goods, including books, recorded music, movies (VHS, DVD), and video games. Through the 65 percent owned subsidiary Billpoint Inc., eBay also facilitates online trading transactions by providing buyers and sellers with the necessary tools to conduct person-to-person credit card and electronic check payments on the Internet. eBay also owns the traditional auction house Butterfields Auctioneers and leading collector car auction company Kruse International.

Chief Competitors: Though the clear leader in the field of online auction providers, eBay's top competitors are the Internet companies Amazon.com, which operates its own online auctions; uBid, another online auctioneer; Buy.com; and Yahoo! shopping. eBay potentially competes with a number of companies depending on the category of products it sells, as well as those serving broad ranges of goods. These broad-based competitors include Wal-Mart, Target, K-Mart, Sears, Macy's, Sam's Club, Costco, and JCPenney. Subsidiary Billpoint competes with PayPal and Bidpay.

person trading Web site called Auction Web, later renamed eBay. The basic, black-and-white Web site was free to use and, largely though word of mouth, the business was quickly catching on. In 1996 the business grew to the point where Omidyar quit his day job that year to devote himself fully to eBay.

The site was easy to use: seller and buyers coming together trading a wide variety of items, including antiques and collectibles. Omidyar settled on the auction format as a way of creating an efficient market—rather than setting prices for items, bidders could determine the true value of an item simply by bidding the price up. Users suggested charging small fees for selling an item to keep people from putting up things with little value. The fee system also served to make the company profitable. In February 1996 the company began charging the seller a placement fee, starting at $.25, and also a percentage of the item's closing price. The auction process is as follows: after registering, sellers put up an item for auction for a specific length of time, from 3 to 14 days, and set a minimum bid or reserve price, if applicable. Bidders put in the maximum that they are willing to pay for the item, and eBay automatically bids on their behalf until their maximum has been reached. If bidders are outbid, they are notified by eBay and can enter a new, higher maximum if desired. At the end of a successful transaction, the seller and buyer are sent each other's e-mail addresses through eBay and they contact each other to arrange for payment and shipping of the item. After a transaction is complete, appropriate feedback is left by the buyer and seller for each other remarking on the transaction. Omidyar's idea of developing a feedback system was one of the keys in building trust among buyers and sellers and weeding out any dishonest users.

The company was incorporated in May 1996. eBay's staff at the time consisted of Omidyar and Chris Agarpao, a part-time employee who is still with the company. Omidyar, who still was running the business out of his home, brought on Jeff Skoll to serve as vice president of strategic planning and analysis in 1996, and who formulated the company's first business plan. The company moved from Omidyar's home to Skoll's and a temporary office in Sunnyvale before settling into their San Jose home where the company is still headquartered. One year later, the amount of e-mail the three employees were getting was unmanageable, and Omidyar quickly brought in a customer support staff of about 12 people. In mid-1997 the company had almost 800,000 auctions a day. By late 1997, more than 3 million items had been sold with $94.0 million in transactions and $5.7 million in sales.

Skoll and Omidyar knew the company needed more direction than they could provide, and so approached the venture capital firm Benchmark Capital, located in Menlo Park. Benchmark invested $5 million in eBay, and they immediately began searching for a CEO who could provide the needed leadership. They found Meg Whitman, who started with the company in 1998. Whitman had previously been the general manager of the preschool division at Hasbro Inc. Whitman was skeptical about leaving the toy giant to join the small upstart, but she was convinced after a meeting with Omidyar when she started realizing the company's potential. When the company went public in September 1998, the initial public offering price was $18 and climbed to $47.38 by the end of the first day of trading. Omidyar left the daily business operations to Whitman to pursue outside interests, including philanthropy.

Under Whitman, eBay saw considerable growth in 1999. The company acquired the traditional offline auction houses Butterfields Auctioneers—providing fine art, antiques, and collectibles—and Kruse International—providing collector cars—and began a fixed-price shopping site called Half.com. The company also acquired a 65 percent stake in Billpoint, which now enabled individual users and small businesses to accept credit card and electronic check payments online. In 2000 eBay launched both eBay Real Estate, for real estate and real estate-related services, and the highly successful eBay Motors, for used automobiles and automotive items.

In 2001 eBay boasted more than 8,000 categories of items with 34 million registered users. The company has country-specific sites in Austria, Australia, Canada, France, Germany, Ireland, Italy, Korea, New Zealand, Switzerland, and the United Kingdom. eBay continued its expansion into new markets in 2001 with its purchase of iBazar S.A., Europe's largest online trading platform. In 2002 the company also teamed with Priceline.com for new travel service on eBay and with Sotheby's fine art auction house to develop its high-end auction presence.

STRATEGY

eBay's corporate strategy is to leverage its position as the leading community-commerce model in the world and the Internet's most popular commerce platform. The company's vision, as stated in their annual report, is to "help practically anyone buy or sell practically anything in the world;" this vision is supported by five key elements. To broaden the eBay trading platform, eBay pursues growth within product categories; with new product categories, including eBay Motors and eBay Real Estate; through local and international geographic expansion; through acquisitions; and with new pricing formats such as Buy it Now. To foster eBay community affinity, the company will continue to instill a sense of community with tools such as About Me pages and eBay's trust and safety initiatives. To enhance features and functionality, eBay aims to provide continuous enhancements and updates to the Web site's features and functionality to ensure improvement in the trading experience. To expand value-added services, the company provides a number of services, including photo hosting and payment facilitation. To continue to develop U.S. and international markets, eBay will continue to strive to provide a truly global trading environment with the addition of regional and international sites through expansion and acquisition.

CHRONOLOGY:
Key Dates for eBay Inc.

1995: eBay is founded by Pierre Omidyar

1996: eBay is incorporated in California

1997: Approximately 3 millions items were sold on eBay with net revenues of $5.7 million

1998: eBay Inc. goes public on the NASDAQ Exchange

1998: Meg Whitman named president and CEO of eBay

1999: eBay acquires Billpoint, Inc. enabling users to accept credit cards as payment for online auctions; Acquires Butterfields Auctioneers; eBay goes online in the United Kingdom and Canada

2000: eBay Motors is launched creating the Internet's largest auction-style Web site for buying and selling used cars

2001: eBay has 34 million registered users and 8,000 categories

2002: eBay acquires NeoCom Technology Co. in Taiwan and a 33 percent stake in the Chinese auction site EachNet; eBay partners with Priceline.com and Sotheby's

INFLUENCES

eBay is constantly improving its site with ever-expanding merchandise categories and sub-categories and new bidding policies, like the popular "Buy it Now" feature that enables bidders to buy an item for a set price without waiting for the auction to end. The addition of eBay Motors, an automobile category, was another major success for the company. Over the years they have added chat rooms and bulletin boards to help users connect with each other and talk about their hobbies, interests, or what they're looking to buy next. According to Media Metrix's September 2000 results, people spend more time on eBay than any other Web site. eBay's forte has been listening to its millions of users and using their suggestions for changes and upgrades to the site.

Challenges that eBay has faced include frequent outages during its early years online, due to a burgeoning

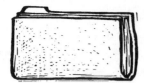

PEZ SPARKS AN ONLINE AUCTION REVOLUTION

During a casual dinner conversation with his girlfriend, Pierre Omidyar learned that she was having trouble trying to find and trade with other Pez collectors and thought it would be a great idea to be able to do that online. Omidyar realized that collectors needed a central location to get together to trade and chat about their hobbies. Still a full-time employee elsewhere, Omidyar launched an online person-to-person trading Web site on Labor Day 1995. Originally called Auction Web, he later renamed it eBay for "electronic Bay" in honor of his San Francisco Bay-area home. The basic, black-and-white Web site was free to use and Omidyar didn't even draw at salary at the time, viewing the early venture as a hobby. Largely though word of mouth, the business was quickly catching on and, by 1996, his Internet service provider, Best Internet, told him that he would need to upgrade his $30 a month system due to heavy traffic. Omidyar quit his day job that year to devote himself to eBay's burgeoning business.

community of users and ever-expanding list of products and services listed for auction. This prompted the company to upgrade its technology and seek solutions for its future growth. A feature called Automatic Checkout (added in 2001) had many users complaining that it was confusing for buyers and sellers, and the auction giant listened, making it an optional feature. The site was built by listening to users and continues to evolve to meet the users' needs.

CURRENT TRENDS

The company continues to focus on growth through the introduction of new categories, through existing product categories, through worldwide expansion, and through new pricing formats including fixed price sales. The acquisition of the fixed price Web site Half.com and the Buy it Now feature on eBay indicate a trend towards an alternative to the auction format on eBay. New categories such as the highly successful eBay Motors and eBay Real Estate have spurred the company to continue growth in similar areas, partnering with Priceline.com in early 2002 with the intention of launching eBay Travel.

Growing its high-end auction presence, eBay teamed with fine art auction house Sotheby's Holdings Inc. in 2002 to launch a new site in the summer of that year, Sothebys.com, with the intention of selling fine art, jewelry, and antiques. eBay also continues its expansion into foreign markets, as well as defining regional markets within the United States.

PRODUCTS

eBay's major services and features include Half.com, Billpoint, eBay International, eBay Motors, eBay Stores, Buy it Now, eBay Professional Services, eBay Local Trading, eBay Premier, and eBay Live Auctions. Proposed new services include eBay Travel and Sotheby's.com. These services and features are marketed by the company to attract both buyers and sellers to the Web site. eBay began marketing these services initially by word of mouth and by sponsorship or distribution relationships with highly frequented Web sites. The company later began more sophisticated marketing strategies, including buying online advertisements and marketing activities in other mass media, including radio; national, broadcast, and local television; trade shows and related events; and print media, including ads in category-specific publications. eBay also benefits from the publicity it has generated as a high-profile Internet company and its relationship with America Online (AOL) as the online service provider's preferred provider of online trading services.

CORPORATE CITIZENSHIP

The eBay Foundation was established in 1998 with the goal of supporting "organizations that provide hope, tools, and direction to assist people in reaching their full potential through the creative application of technology," as stated on the company's Web site. Since its inception, the foundation has made grants of more than $2.5 million to more than 75 nonprofit organizations. Additionally, eBay also began a Charity Auction program, enabling nonprofit organizations to raise money through auctions on the Web site, which have totaled $4.7 million since the program's inception. The company's Auction for America, launched after the attacks of September 11, 2001, enabled some 100,000 users raise $10 million for victims and families affected by those events. These initiatives are consistent with the principles of community and exchange of information that eBay was founded on.

GLOBAL PRESENCE

eBay has country-specific sites in Austria, Australia, Canada, France, Germany, Ireland, Italy, Korea, New

Zealand, Switzerland, and the United Kingdom. eBay continued its expansion into foreign markets in 2001 with its purchase of iBazar S.A., Europe's largest online trading platform.

eBay was forced to cease operations in Japan in March 2002, two years after establishing a site there, due to Yahoo Japan Corp.'s dominance in that market, low numbers traded on the site, and tactical errors by eBay. One such error was eBay's reasoning that the Japan site would mimic the growth of the U.S. site; thus, the company emphasized the used collectibles categories on the site while failing to anticipate that the Japanese users were interested in new goods. Undeterred, eBay also announced in March 2002 that it acquired the Internet auction company NeoCom Technology Co. in Taiwan. In its continuing efforts to expand into the Asian market, eBay also acquired a 33 percent stake in the Chinese auction site EachNet, the largest online trading community in China, which boasts 3.5 million registered users.

EMPLOYMENT

eBay had 1,927 full-time employees as of March 1, 2001. Due to its technical nature, the company is dependent on the performance of its key technical personnel and senior officers and seeks to find and retain such personnel. eBay does not have long-term employment agreements with any key personnel. The company's land-based auction business is especially dependent on specialists due to the relationships they have with established sellers who consign property for auction sales. The company has experienced some turnover of these personnel, whose continued losses could result in loss of future business. eBay's success also depends on attracting and retaining highly skilled technical, marketing, and customer support personnel in the San Francisco Bay Area, where competition for these individuals is intense and fluctuations in stock price could adversely affect employment.

SOURCES OF INFORMATION

Bibliography

"Company Overview." eBay Inc., 2002. Available from http://pages.eBay.com/community/abouteBay/overview.

"eBay, Conceding Missteps, Will Close Its Site in Japan. *The Wall Street Journal*, 27 February 2002.

"eBay Foundation." eBay Inc., 2002. Available at http://pages.eBay.com/community/abouteBay/foundation.

"eBay's 'Auction for America' Comes to An End." eBay Inc., 2002. Available at http://eBay.client.shareholder.com/news.

"eBay Inc." Gale Group, 2002. Available at http://www.galenet.galegroup.com.

"eBay Inc." Hoover's Online, 2002. Available at http://www.hoovers.com.

"eBay and Priceline.com to Share Travel Sales." *The New York Times*, 2 February 2002.

"eBay's Secret Ingredient." *Business 2.0.*, March 2002. Available at http://www.business2.com.

"Online EBay Expands to China." *Associated Press*, 18 March 2002.

"Sotheby's, eBay Team Up to Sell Fine Art Online—Auction Competitors Hope Joint Venture Will Heal Past Weaknesses of Both." *The Wall Street Journal*, 31 January 2002.

Wong, May. "Online Auction Powerhouse eBay Expands to China." *Associated Press*, 18 March 2002.

For an annual report:

on the Internet at: http://www.shareholder.com/eBay/annual.cfm **or** write: eBay Inc., 2145 Hamilton Ave., San Jose, CA 95125

For additional industry research:

Investigate companies by their Standard Industrial Classification Codes, also known as SICs. eBay Inc.'s primary SICs are:

7375 Information Retrieval Service

7389 Business Services, Not Elsewhere Classified

Also investigate companies by their North American Industry Classification System codes, also known as NAICS codes. eBay Inc.'s primary NAICS codes are:

453998 All Other Miscellaneous Store Retailers (except Tobacco Stores)

514191 On-Line Information Services

Eco-Challenge Lifestyles Inc.

FOUNDED: 1992

Contact Information:
HEADQUARTERS: 9899 Santa Monica Blvd.
   Beverly Hills, CA 90212-1672
PHONE: (310)553-8855
URL: http://www.ecochallenge.com

OVERVIEW

Eco-Challenge Lifestyles Inc. was founded in 1992 by British entrepreneur Mark Burnett. Burnett, a life long sportsman and competitor, wanted to introduce adventure racing to a global audience. The businessman in Burnett saw an opportunity to transform his passion for outdoor adventures into a profitable venture. Three years after founding the company, he produced his first televised Eco-Challenge race. The grueling event features co-ed teams of four people who travel across the wilderness from checkpoint to checkpoint. The course usually covers several hundred miles of diverse terrain. Contestants often compete with little or no sleep, with the goal to be the first complete team to arrive at the final destination. The company stages the event annually.

The company expanded into the reality TV genre with the launches of *Survivor* and *Combat Missions.* The former debuted in the summer of 2000 and features a group of contestants stranded on an island or deposited in the middle of a wilderness area. Contestants are known as "tribe members" who attend tribal council and cast votes to banish individuals from the tribe. The object of the game is to be the last person eliminated; the winner receives a million dollar paycheck.

Since its inception in the early 1990s, the company has also launched several smaller ancillary businesses. The Eco-Challenge Travel agency helps outdoor enthusiasts plan non-competitive, non-televised adventure excursions. The Eco-Challenge Lifestyles Web site provides current information on adventure racing and upcoming events of interest.

COMPANY FINANCES

Eco-Challenge Lifestyles does not publicly report profits, but it is widely accepted that Mark Burnett has made a fortune from the success of his *Survivor* series. The Eco-Challenge Expedition undoubtedly generated revenue for the company, but Burnett struck gold in the summer of 2000 when *Survivor* took the country by storm. Consider these figures: in August 2000 advertisers paid an incredible $600,000 for a 30-second spot during the two hour finale of the original *Survivor*. The price of an ad was $100,000 when the show first premiered three months earlier in May. The advertising rates for *Survivor 2* began at $300,000 in 2001. NBC has paid Burnett $50 million for the rights to his new show, which will attempt to send the winning contestant into space. Ten years after launching his own business, Burnett's fortunes are literally out of this world.

ANALYSTS' OPINIONS

In the case of Eco-Challenge Lifestyles Inc., the most important analysts aren't on Wall Street; they're in Hollywood and they're network programming analysts. A privately held company, it does not rely upon the good will and good ratings of investors. Instead this company focuses on Nielsen ratings and good buzz. *Survivor* has been the cash cow for the company since it premiered in the summer of 2000 and achieved instant hit status. The idea of low cost reality programming with the ability to attract huge viewing audiences was very appealing to network executives. Each network scrambled to develop the next hit. A new genre in television programming was created. The television schedule quickly filled with clones of the hit show, or poor substitutes depending on your perspective. Programs were cast with characters willing to participate in the most outrageous situations on *Temptation Island*, *Big Brother*, and *Who Wants to Marry a Multi-Millionaire*. Scandals erupted over the behavior or past behavior of cast members. In late 2001 the public appeared to be disenchanted with the format, and many of the shows were dropped from the airwaves. *Survivor* remained strong and demonstrated its potential to endure in 2002 as its ratings climbed. It is unlikely that the genre will dominate the network schedules as was once predicted, but if Mark Burnett should survive.

HISTORY

The history of Eco-Challenge Lifestyles Inc. begins with the life history of J. Mark Burnett. Burnett is a British citizen with a wide range of interests. His career includes time in the military as a member of the British Army Parachute Regiment where he earned distinguished service medals for participation in active combat. His

FAST FACTS:
About Eco-Challenge Lifestyles Inc.

Ownership: Eco-Challenge Lifestyles Inc. is a privately owned company.

Officers: J. Mark Burnett, 41, Founder and Exec. Producer

Employees: 10

Chief Competitors: Eco-Challenge Lifestyles Inc. occupies a unique niche as sports event and entertainment company. The competitive landscape of extreme sports and reality programming is constantly changing as different players enter and leave the field. Ultimately, in order to be successful, the company and its programs compete for television viewers, ratings, and sponsorship and advertising dollars. Burnett's wildly popular television series *Survivor* competes directly with long time sitcom favorite *Friends* for network ratings.

own survival skills are impressive. He is a certified SCUBA diver and Level A skydiver. In addition, his training includes a white water course and an Advanced Wilderness First Aid certification. His interests led him to the extreme sport of adventure racing.

The concept of adventure racing can be traced to French journalist, Gerard Fusil, who pioneered the event in 1989. The premier event in the sport is the Raid Gauloises, a 250-mile gauntlet staged annually for a prize of $40,000. The sport captured the imagination of native New Zealanders who were attracted to the rugged and demanding nature of the sport. A country filled with harsh and challenging terrain, New Zealand offered the perfect venue for great contests. Expedition racing gained popularity and the attention of Mark Burnett. After observing the success of the events held in New Zealand and throughout the world, he decided to introduce the discipline to North America.

After completing market research, Burnett developed a philosophy that evolved into a business plan. In a 1998 interview with Web site Mountain.com, Burnett is quoted as saying that "he learned that smart business in the '90s and beyond was about. . .health and fitness, ecology and growth—personal growth through unconventional experiences." From this he created the Eco-Challenge Lifestyles Inc. company. The goal of the company was to promote outdoor adventure and

CHRONOLOGY:

Key Dates for Eco-Challenge Lifestyles Inc.

1992: Eco-Challenge Lifestyles Inc. founded by Mark Burnett

1995: First Eco-Challenge race is held in Southern Utah with 50 teams competing

1996: Two races are staged in New England and British Colombia; Eco-Challenge Lifestyles is nominated for an Emmy Award; Burnett signs a multi-year pact with the Discovery Channel

2000: *Survivor* premieres during the summer re-run season and beats the competition handily

2001: Military reality game show *Combat Missions* makes it debut on USA cable network to lukewarm reviews; Burnett faces a lawsuit from disgruntled contestant who claims that the results of *Survivor* were fixed

2002: Plans underway for a reunion of champions *Survivor* series

environmental stewardship. Burnett's personal goals were also incorporated into the plan: "I had two goals in mind when I founded Eco-Challenge," Burnett told Mountain.com, "one was obviously very commercial. It's for profit business and I hope to make excellent returns on my investment. Number two, I'd hoped to have a really good time making that money."

In 1995 Burnett staged his first North American competition. Before the race began, Burnett experienced his first challenge. Utah, the host state for the event, questioned the environmental impact of the competition on the land. A local group, the Southern Wilderness Alliance protested the path of the course, which strayed through land that contained archaeological sites and supported wildlife habitats. The Utah Bureau of Land Management allowed the race to proceed, but required Burnett to post an $80,000 bond against damages. The inaugural Eco-Challenge race began on April 25, 1995, and it concluded when the Hewlett-Packard team crossed the finish line of the 370-mile course, seven days and sixteen hours later. Collectively 50 teams competed in the event. Forty of the teams were from the United States, and ten international squads made the trek. The event was filmed and edited for both MTV and NBC. A

90-minute special documenting the race aired on network television.

There are no clear financial records to show whether or not Burnett was able to make money on the event, but it is very likely he did. Despite the problems with the state government, it is estimated that television and corporate sponsorships netted the company about $1.5 million. Burnett was encouraged by the initial success he enjoyed and wiser from the initial difficulties he faced. Armed with lessons learned in Utah, Eco-Challenge Lifestyles decided to head east. In 1996 the company staged two more challenges: New England Eco-Challenge and British Colombia Eco-Challenge. The New England version was filmed in cooperation with ESPN and its *Extreme Games* series. The British Colombia expedition marked a partnership with the Discovery Channel.

STRATEGY

Eco-Challenge Lifestyles Inc. continues to operate as a privately owned company founded by Mark Burnett. No formal business plan or company filings exist to detail past or future plans. The direction of the company is largely determined by the personality of Burnett. He is a motivated businessman and a very savvy marketer. Several smaller businesses have been created as a result of the Eco-Challenge. In a move to expand the company and increase visibility, Burnett decided to award franchises for the Eco-Challenge Expedition races. In 2000 the first Eco-Challenge Lifestyles franchise was awarded to a national non-profit organization. The Tragedy Assistance Program for Survivors (TAPS), a group that provides assistance to families who have lost loved ones in service to the Armed Forces, produced the Armed Forces Eco-Challenge in Alaska. After the selection of TAPS for the first franchise, Burnett issued the following statement: "The Eco-Challenge brand has been developed carefully and steadily over the last eight years. Therefore we took careful consideration when nominating TAPS as our first franchise. TAPS was chosen because they have the important ingredients to maintain the Eco-Challenge integrity, a passion for adventure, good business acumen, and a positive social message. We will provide them with our experience in order to put on a very successful and safe Eco-Challenge."

Burnett has also announced plans to develop several new programming options. In addition to *Survivor* and *Combat Missions*, a space travel adventure show is planned for NBC. A drama tentatively titled *Langley* will chronicle life at the famed CIA training center. It appears that the company will attempt to create new programming while maintaining the quality of existing properties through innovative new twists and rule changes. Evidence suggested that this strategy is working well for the company.

INFLUENCES

In many ways the Eco-Challenge Lifestyles company is a leader in a unique field. Others have been influenced by its prosperity. Despite the hybrid quality of its programming, its roots can be traced to other genres. The Eco-Challenge Expedition races can be classified as sporting events, albeit extreme. This new discipline of adventure and sport emerged from the extreme sport movement, popular with young people worldwide. The popularity of these competitions continues to grow, evidenced by the inclusion of several events in the 2002 Winter Olympic Games in Salt Lake City.

While many people refer to *Survivor* as reality television, Burnett would characterize it as a game show. The tradition of game shows is evident in the evolution of the *Survivor* series. Most notably, the show is regulated by the same rules and regulations that apply to typical daytime game shows—it is not permissible to tamper with the results or provide any of the contestants with an unfair advantage. Beyond the policies and restrictions governing the rules of play, Burnett has borrowed certain concepts from other thriving franchises. Taking a cue from longtime favorite, *Jeopardy*, a tournament of *Survivor* Champions contest was announced in April 2002. This installment will reunite past winners from the first four or five series, along with a collection of notable fan favorites. Burnett is also exploring the possibility of attempting another game show stunt, a celebrity edition. It may be difficult to replicate the success of *Celebrity Millionaire* or *Celebrity Jeopardy*. Many highly paid actors and sports figures welcome the opportunity to showcase their intellectual abilities and earn money for a favorite charity with an appearance on a favorite game show. However, spending two months in the wilderness under constant surveillance may shine the spotlight a bit too brightly on even the biggest stars.

CURRENT TRENDS

Mark Burnett uses his company to create trends, not follow them. He delights in keeping the viewing public guessing about what may happen next. It is unlikely that he will abandon the lucrative franchises he has developed. The awarding of the Eco-Challenge franchise hints that he might be willing to share leadership in some of the more established ventures. Burnett's use of corporate sponsorships continues to grow, and it is reasonable to assume this will continue.

PRODUCTS

Eco-Challenge Lifestyles Inc. produces extreme sporting and entertainment events. The annual Eco-Challenge races bring together contestants from around the

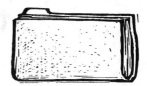

LOST IN SPACE

The next challenge produced by Mark Burnett and company will send a lucky contestant into space. In 2000 NBC and Burnett announced a joint venture to produce a reality game show tentatively titled, *Destination Mir*. A dozen American contestants will travel to Russia to train at the Star City training center. The contestants will endure 10 weeks of physical and psychological testing as they are eliminated from contention one by one. The final contestant wins the right to travel to the Mir Space station courtesy of a program operated by MirCorp of the Netherlands. General Electric, the parent company of NBC, has agreed to pay $40 million dollars to cover the costs of the production and flight into space. General Electric is also a contractor for the space program.

world to compete for cash prizes. Co-ed teams of four or five members must complete a series of physically demanding challenges and travel from point A to point B using their wits and survival skills. This event is televised and aired over several nights each year. The company also produces several outdoor-themed reality game shows.

CORPORATE CITIZENSHIP

One of the tenets of Eco-Challenge Lifestyles is environmental awareness. Each event is planned with great attention given to the preservation of wildlife and natural habitats of the region. In addition Mark Burnett organizes a volunteer activity to improve each site that is used by the show. Trees were planted in Australia; a dumpsite in Utah and a river in British Colombia were both cleaned of pollutants. Also, broadcasts of the television versions of the Eco races often feature public service announcements concerning various environmental issues.

GLOBAL PRESENCE

Spanning the globe, Eco-Challenge Lifestyles Inc. is a youth-oriented Wide World of Sports. Productions feature locations and contestants from around the world. Global participation in the Eco-Challenge races continues to grow with teams from more than 27 countries reg-

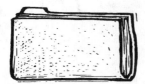

DESSERT ISLAND

The *Survivor* cast members are forced to forage for natural food most of the time, but every so often a challenge might yield a treat. During the fourth installment of the popular reality show, the tribe members were treated to Snickers Bars by producer Mark Burnett. It was no accident that this confection was the dessert of choice. Snickers and the *Survivor* series have entered into a promotional agreement. Snickers commercials feature clips from the series with captions such as "Going to be somewhere for a while?" In return the Snickers Bar received product placement in the highly rated show. Network executives might have something to say about this practice. A 30-second spot on the coveted show can cost upwards of $300,000, which goes to the network. By prominently featuring the candy bar during the broadcast, the production company collects the fee and removes the network from the equation. Who's laughing now?

istering for events. There are no geographic guidelines for placing the shows, and countries do not bid or apply to host events as they do for the Olympics. The company approaches the local authorities to secure government permission to hold an event. In early 2002, Mark Burnett received permission to hold a future *Survivor* competition in Thailand.

EMPLOYMENT

The company has only a small number of permanent full-time employees. Crew and production workers are hired on a contract basis for each event. *Survivor* host, Jeff Probst is perhaps the most visible employee of the company. Jeff is an experienced game show host, doing double duty as the host of Rock and Roll Jeopardy for VH1. The contestants for each show are not employees, but the recruitment and selection process is probably more stringent than for an actual job.

SOURCES OF INFORMATION

Bibliography

Active.com. "Survivor Producer Mark Burnett Interview," 19 March 2001. Available at http://www.theactivenetwork.com.

Dugard, Martin. "Adventure: Feel the Burn! Treasure the Earth! Be on TV!" OutsideMag.com, December 1995. Available at http://www.outsidemag.com.

Eco-Challenge-The Expedition Race, Press Release. "Eco-Challenge Announces the Armed Forces Eco-Challenge the First World Qualifier," 17 August 2000.

Environment News Service. "Eco-Challenge Winners: America's Team Salomon Eco-Internet," 31 August 2000. Available at http://www.ens-news.com.

Keith, Alexander L. "And the Winner of 'Survivor' is. . .CBS." *USA Today*, 24 August 2000.

Kennedy, Alice. "Meet the Man Behind the Show." *The John Hopkins News-Letter*, 26 April 2001. Available at http://www.jhu.edu.

Levin, Gary. "Mark Burnett: Father of 'Survivor' Craze." *USA Today*, 28 December 2000.

Mountainzone.com. "Eco Challenge '98 Mark Burnett Interview," 12 December 1999. Available at http://www.mountainzone.com.

———. "Eco Challenge '99," 12 December 1999. Available at http://www.mountainzone.com.

Reynolds, Gretchen. "Master of the Ego Challenge." *National Geographic Adventure*, July/August 2000.

For additional industry research:

Investigate companies by their Standard Industrial Classification Codes, also known as SICs. Eco-Challenge Lifestyles Inc.'s primary SIC is:

7812 Motion Picture and Video Tape Production

Also investigate companies by their North American Industry Classification System codes, also known as NAICS codes. Eco-Challenge Lifestyles Inc.'s primary NAICS code is:

512110 Motion Picture and Video Production

eGames Inc.

FOUNDED: 1992

OVERVIEW

eGames develops and markets entertainment software targeted to home personal computer users. The entire stock of the company's games are marketed under the trademark of Family Friendly, reflecting that fact that every product sold by eGames is rated E for Everyone by the Entertainment Software Ratings Board, meaning that they are nonviolent and appropriate for all ages. Software titles are promoted as full-featured, value-priced, and easy-to-use. The majority of titles are entertainment-based, although the company also offers a limited number of home office and productivity software products.

During fiscal year 2001, ending June 30, 2001, Walgreen Company, Infogrames Inc., and Rite Aid Corporation accounted for 20 percent, 17 percent, and 10 percent of sales, respectively. During the previous fiscal year, Infogrames Inc. and Navarre Corporation accounted for 22 percent and 13 percent of sales, respectively. eGames also markets its software titles via its Web sites, egames.com and outerbounds.com.

COMPANY FINANCES

For fiscal year 2001, ending June 30, 2001, eGames posted a net loss of $5.93 million on revenues of $7.17 million, compared to a net income of approximately $252,600 on revenues of $10.79 million for fiscal year 2000, representing a decrease of $3.62 million in revenues and $6.18 million in net income. The decline in sales was primarily caused by a decrease of $4.88 million in net sales to distributors who sell to software retailers, as well

Contact Information:
HEADQUARTERS: 2000 Cabot Blvd., Suite 110
    Langhorne, PA 19047-1833
PHONE: (215)750-6606
FAX: (215)750-3722
URL: http://www.egames.com

FAST FACTS:

About eGames Inc.

Ownership: eGames is a publicly owned company that trades its stock on the OTC Bulletin Board.

Ticker Symbol: EGAM.OB

Officers: Gerald W. Klein, 53, Pres. and CEO, 2001 base salary $176,086; William C. Acheson, 51, VP, Product Development, 2001 base salary $165,961; Lawrence Fanelle, 49, VP, Operations, 2001 base salary $123,012; Richard Siporin, VP, Sales, 41, 2001 base salary $150,825

Employees: 19

Chief Competitors: Based on product and price similarities, Electronic Arts, Havas, Activision, Infogrames, Inc., Hasbro Interactive, Mattel Media, Cosmi, Take-Two Interactive, Microsoft, and Interplay are eGames' most significant competitors.

Excluding the impact of this agreement, eGames would have reported for the first nine months of fiscal 2002 net sales of $5.82 million, representing a year-over-year decrease of $612,000, and a net loss of $113,000, representing a year-over-year net loss decrease of $2.38 million. During the first three quarters of fiscal 2002, eGames successfully reduced its operating expenses by more than $2.4 million, or 48 percent.

Until April 1, 2001, eGames traded on the NASDAQ SmallCap Market; however, the company was delisted after its price per share fell below $1.00 for 30 consecutive days of trading, after which eGames began trading on the Over-the-Counter (OTC) Bulletin Board. Because the company's stock trades at less than $5.00 per share and its net tangible assets are less than $2 million, it is subject to restrictive trading under the rules of the Securities Exchange Act of 1934. A broker may not recommend purchase of so-called penny stocks to other than established clients with significant assets without written permission from the purchaser prior to the transaction. During fiscal 2000, stock prices peaked during the first quarter at $3.813 per share before falling to $0.500 per share during the fourth quarter. In fiscal 2001, prices in the first quarter topped out at $1.875 per share but fell to $0.100 during the fourth quarter. On June 11, 2001, eGames stocks sold for $0.27 a share; on April 12, 2002, prices reached a low of $0.03 a share.

as direct sales to such retailers. Of that total, eGames reported an estimated loss of $2.91 million due to a retailers' trend toward reducing their value-priced software selections, with the remaining loss sustained due to increased value-priced software competition from major software distributors, which eroded eGames' hold on its niche market. Net sales of $1.13 million to food and drug retailers only partially offset the losses incurred in the retail market. International sales also declined by $98,000.

Compounding the disparity between profit/loss and revenues was an increase in cost of sales by $1.73 million, from $4.28 million in fiscal 2000 to $6.01 million in fiscal 2001, representing a 40 percent increase. The increase in cost of sales is attributed primarily to a provision to absorb $1.27 million in costs for obsolete inventory. Other factors driving up cost of sales include processing costs for product returns totaling $324,000 and freight costs totaling $206,000.

For the first three quarters of fiscal 2002, ending March 31, eGames reported a net income of $1.01 million on net sales totaling $7.93 million, compared to a net loss of $768,000 on revenues of $6.43 million during the same period of the previous year. Income and revenues totals were significantly impacted by an agreement reached between eGames and one of its retailers in February of 2002, which made final all sales of previously shipped software and eliminated return privileges.

ANALYSTS' OPINIONS

By its own assessment after the close of fiscal 2001, eGames was uncertain that a return to profitability would be possible during fiscal 2002 given the ongoing sluggish economy as well as the significant increase in competition from larger competitors with greater ability to engage in development, distribution, and marketing activities. In fact, eGames management warned its 123 shareholders that the company was holding on by a thread. After defaulting on a $2 million line of credit from Fleet Bank during 2001, the bank shut off the company's access to the credit, causing a cash flow crisis.

On November 2, 2001, eGames and Fleet reached an agreement that allowed eGames to repay the bank on an amortizing term loan over the course of 22 months. In return, Fleet agreed not to exercise its default agreement as long as eGames remains in compliance with the new agreement as outlined in a turnaround plan that stipulated that eGames achieve certain earnings benchmarks and periodically disclose financial performance to Fleet. If eGames defaults, Fleet may liquidate the company at the expense of shareholder investments. Because eGames no longer has access to credit, operational costs must be funded via ongoing business. With a $5.93 million loss in fiscal 2001 and a net loss, albeit much smaller, for the first three quarters of fiscal 2002, eGames' future is not yet secure. If the company cannot generate sufficient revenues to sustain operations and if the company cannot secure additional credit due to its previous default and debt load, the viability of the company may be jeopardized.

HISTORY

eGames, previously known as RomTech Inc., was incorporated in July of 1992. Between 1992 and 1997, the company experienced significant annual losses. Fiscal year 1998 was the first time that eGames turned a profit, reporting a net income of 1.253 million, followed by positive performances in both fiscal years 1999 and 2000, with earnings totaling $463,000 and $253,000, respectively. In August of 1998 eGames acquired Software Partners Publishing and Distribution Ltd., a distributor of consumer entertainment and home office applications based in the United Kingdom. On March 31, 1999, Software Partners was renamed eGames Europe Ltd. On May 11, 2001, eGames sold eGames Europe to Greenstreet Software Limited.

STRATEGY

Using the tag line "eGames—Where the 'e' is for Everybody!" eGames intends to be a leading publisher of high quality, low-priced interactive consumer entertainment software. To accomplish this, the company's strategic plan includes: building on brand name recognition of its Family Friendly products; ongoing development of high quality, top selling titles within existing brands; development of new brand lines; creating strong ties with retail and distribution partners; providing a comprehensive portfolio of software titles within the company's consumer entertainment market segment that is attractive to retail and distribution customers for its sales and profit potential; and maintaining and improving a productive Internet presence and comprehensive Web site.

The eGames model for conducting its business successfully is based on two factors: brand recognition and value pricing. eGames functions on the assumption that the under-$15 retail segment of the software entertainment industry will be the fastest growing for the foreseeable future. By using marketplace sales data eGames is able to identify products that are the hottest sellers on the market and respond by developing its own titles or obtaining rights to externally developed titles, focusing in particular on sustainable product life that appeal to a broad age range and both genders. Because the software entertainment market is in constant flux, reacting to consumer preference and technological advancements, eGames strives to correctly identify products that will retain the attention of customers and then reacts by quickly and efficiency putting similar Family Friendly titles on the shelves, packaged and priced to encourage impulse buying. Although eGames provides technical

CHRONOLOGY:
Key Dates for eGames Inc.

1992: eGames incorporates

1995: Completes initial public offering of common stock; begins trading on NASDAQ SmallCap Market

1998: Posts first annual net profit of $1.253 million

2001: eGames is de-listed from Nasdaq; begins trading on the Over-the-Counter (OTC) Bulletin Board; posts a net loss for the fiscal year in excess of $5 million

2002: Stock prices fall to $0.03 a share

support for all its products, its software is designed to provide easy installation and use.

Another important factor in eGames' strategic plan is to develop a widespread network of retail and Internet distribution. The goal is to offer retailers multiple methods to contract for eGames products. During fiscal year 2001, direct sales to retailers made up over 50 percent of revenues; however, due to costs associated with direct-to-store shipments, eGames will focus more on sales to wholesale distributors such as Infogrames Inc., United American Video, and Triad Distributors Inc. eGames ultimate distribution goal is to place its software titles in front of as many consumers as possible.

eGames' Internet presence, which provides such features as technical support, game demos and previews, free games, and opportunities to buy software titles via download or traditional package purchase, complements the company's distribution system. The foundation of eGames' Internet strategy is the eGames browser, which was introduced in 1998 to provide a standard, user-friendly interface to present eGames products to consumers on their personal computers.

Building customer loyalty by providing a brand name that reflects consistent quality is important. Because the stores are inundated with rapidly changing titles from a myriad of companies, eGames believes that strong name recognition is a necessary advantage because consumers will repeatedly return to a brand name that has previously provided a high rate of satisfaction. eGames' difficulty remains in its financial troubles, which have not provided sufficient cash to invest in any significant marketing strategy. Nonetheless, eGames

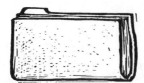

EGAMES ONLINE

At its Web site, eGames hosts a free arcade of online games for its patrons. Games are available in nine different categories: arcade, board, card (including 14 versions of solitaire), casino, kids, puzzles, sports, strategy, and trivia. Want to buy a game? Download or order one of eGames' top ten best-sellers: Blast Thru, Bowling Mania, Crazy Puzzle, Mahjongg Empire, Mahjongg Master 3, Mahjongg Master, Mini Golf Master, RaJongg-The Curseof RA, Solitaire Master 2, or Speedy Eggbert.

management understands the importance of successfully marketing the software title with attractive packaging and product promotion.

INFLUENCES

eGames offers its products to retailers under either sell-in or sell-through terms. Sell-in business means that the retailer purchases the product directly from eGames; sell-through means that eGames only realizes its profit after the end-user makes a purchase in the retail store. An ongoing and unpredictable problem for eGames has been product returns from retailers. If a sell-in retailer returns unsold software in bulk, eGames could owe the retailer a substantial refund. Although sell-through returns have not yet appeared as revenue, often by the time software is returned, the titles may have been rendered obsolete by new software advancements or changing trends in consumer preference. Although eGames may not be contractually obligated to accept the returns, the company's need to retain distribution channels may result in flexibility that impacts eGames negatively.

Because the entertainment software market is highly competitive and changes rapidly, eGames is increasingly fighting for shelf space. Retailers have a limited amount of room to display software, and they place on their shelves what is expected to sell. Because large, well-known software developers and distributors are entering the value-priced software market, eGames must struggle to compete with already-established high levels of brand recognition and much bigger promotion and marketing resources. The increased availability of low-priced software provides retailers with an advantage in negotiating the purchase of software titles due to limited shelf space, leading to ongoing price erosion.

CURRENT TRENDS

The consumer entertainment software market is expected to be valued at more than $37 billion worldwide by 2003, up from $16 billion four years earlier. According to eGames, approximately 145 million people in the United States alone confirm that they play computer games. As prices of computers and software decline and computer technology advances, eGames expects the entertainment software market to continue on its growth path.

During eGames' profitable years, large software companies produced primarily higher-end titles, leaving the below-$15 market to eGames. However, since major software developers have enters the low-end software business, eGames has found itself as a battling much larger competitors for both shelf space and customers. As competition grows fierce, retailers are empowered to require significant promotional funding commitments when contracting to display entertainment software titles on their shelves. As a result, larger competitors with greater financial resources are better able to provide these required marketing tools, thereby reducing space left available for smaller developers such as eGames. Unable to provide required promotional spending, eGames was forced to decrease its presence particularly in office superstore retail outlets.

eGames' decision to turn to food and drug retailers in 2001 as an alternative to traditional software retailers did create positive results. Often based on short-term promotional events that resulted in poorer than expected sell-through totals, eGames found itself burdened with a large inventory of returns from its food and drug customers. Because the products were returned late, their shelf life had expired and eGames was forced to scrap them, at a cost of more than $1.27 million. Still eGames and other independent software developers continue to pursue new avenue for distribution, including publishing companies.

PRODUCTS

eGames provides several lines of brand name software titles, including eGames Series, Galaxy of Games, Game Master Series, Galaxy of Home Office Help, and Outerbounds Games. The eGames Series usually sells at a retail price of less than $15. Game Master Series titles are sold at retail for $14.99, but the titles' attractive boxed packaging provides the products with a higher-end appearance. Outerbound Games usually retail between $9.99 and $14.99. Other software product lines are usually packaged in a jeweled CD case and sell for a retail price of $9.99.

GLOBAL PRESENCE

After selling off its wholly owned subsidiary eGames Europe in 2001, eGames began conducting its international sales via licensing agreements whereby eGames is paid a royalty fee based on product sales.

SOURCES OF INFORMATION

Bibliography

"eGames Announces Fiscal 2002 Third Quarter Financial Results and Other Events." *PR Newswire*, 19 April 2002.

"eGames Inc." *Hoovers Online*, 2002. Available at http://www .hoovers.com.

"eGames Inc." *Multex.com*, 2002. Available at http://www .multex.com.

"eGames Inc. Introduces a New Line of Value Priced Software for the Mainstream-Gaming Market-OuterBounds Games." *Market News Publishing*, 15 August 2001.

"eGames Inc. Stock Moves to the OTC Bulletin Board." *Market News Publishing*, 8 June 2001.

Key, Peter. "Not All's Been Fun and eGames Seeks Change." *Philadelphia Business Journal*, 18 January 2002.

For additional industry research:

Investigate companies by their Standard Industrial Classification Codes, also known as SICs. eGames Inc.'s primary SIC is:

7372 Prepackaged Software

Also investigate companies by their North American Industry Classification System codes, also known as NAICS codes. eGames Inc.'s primary NAICS code is:

511210 Software Publishers

Electronic Data Systems Corp.

FOUNDED: 1962

Contact Information:

HEADQUARTERS: 5400 Legacy Dr.
   Plano, TX 75024-3199
PHONE: (972)604-6000
FAX: (972)605-2643
TOLL FREE: (800)474-2323
EMAIL: info@eds.com
URL: http://www.eds.com

OVERVIEW

Electronic Data Services is the leading provider of information technology (IT) services in the United States. Prior to April of 2002, EDS organized its business operations into five segments: Information Solutions, Business Process Management (BPM), E Solutions, A.T. Kearney, and Product Lifecycle Management (PLM) Solutions. Each business unit works in conjunction with eight Global Industry Groups: Communications, Energy, Financial, Government, Health Care, Manufacturing, Retail, and Transportation.

Information Solutions, the company's largest business unit, encompassed all activity related to traditional IT outsourcing. Businesses contract with EDS to provide such services as network and systems operations, data management, application development and maintenance, desktop management and field services, Internet hosting, and Web site management. BPM deliveries outsourcing services for business processes or functions that provides clients with seamless operations in the delivery, performance, quality, and cost thereby improving the clients' customers' satisfaction. E Solutions, the company's global solutions consulting business unit, provides innovative solutions for a wide variety of clients in the areas of enterprise consulting, digital enablement, and digital value chain. E Solutions provides expertise along the entire continuum of e-commerce to allow clients to benefit from the trends in the high tech economy.

In April of 2002, EDS organized these three business units into two: Operations Solutions and Solutions Consulting. Operation Solutions will provide the company's traditional IT outsourcing operations services along with its business process outsourcing, and Solutions Consulting will combine E Solution services with applications services.

A.T. Kerney, an EDS subsidiary since 1995, offers high-value management consulting services that include strategy and organization, operations and technology solutions, executive search services. Working in conjunction with other EDS business units, A.T. Kerney provides services to clients in an array of business segments, including automotive, consumer products and retail, communications, media and entertainment, financial institutions, health care and pharmaceuticals, aerospace and defense, and utilities. PLM Solutions, formed in 2001 from the merger of two recently acquired companies, provides integrated software and services to support the entire lifecycle of a product. Services focus on digital product design, simulation, manufacturing, and collaboration, which allow clients to reduce cost, increase innovation, and decrease the time from product concept to market delivery.

COMPANY FINANCES

In 2001 EDS posted a net income of $1.36 billion on revenues of $21.5 billion, compared to a net income of $1.14 billion on revenues of $19.2 billion in 2000. Of total revenues for 2001, Information Solutions accounted for $16.2 billion, BPM accounted for $3.0 billion, E Solutions accounted for $1.2 billion A.T. Kearney accounted for $1.2 billion, and PLM Solutions accounted for $738 million. Sales to General Motors totaled 14 percent of all revenues, compared to 18 percent and 19 percent of revenues in 2000 and 1999, respectively. Fifty-seven percent of revenues ($12.36 billion) were generated within the United States, and 16 percent ($3.36 billion) of sales were generated in the United Kingdom. The remaining 27 percent ($5.82 billion) of revenues were made in sales around the world. Compared to 2000, these totals reflect an increase in business in the United States and the United Kingdom of 1 percent and 4 percent, respectively, and a decrease in other worldwide sales of 3 percent. EDS' long term debt increased from $2.59 billion in 2000 to $4.54 billion at the end of 2001.

ANALYSTS' OPINIONS

Analysts express mixed opinions regarding EDS. After the company reported double-digit growth for the tenth consecutive quarter in the first quarter of 2002, analysts acknowledged that EDS was effectively increasing its contract bookings and outsourcing business. Other positives include the company's diversity in product offering, customer base, and geographical presence. However, analysts express concern regarding the declining contributions of General Motors, down year-over-year 10 percent, and a weak performance by A.T. Kerney,

FAST FACTS:
About Electronic Data Systems Corp.

Ownership: Electronic Data Systems Corp. is a publicly owned company that trades on the New York and the London Stock Exchanges.

Ticker Symbol: EDS

Officers: Richard H. Brown, 54, Chmn. and CEO, 2001 base salary $1.5 million, 2001 bonus $7 million; Paul J. Chiapparone, 62, EVP, 2001 base salary $600,000, 2001 bonus $1.5 million; James E. Daley, 60, EVP and CFO, 2001 base salary $585,000, 2001 bonus $1.5 million; Troy W. Todd, EVP, 2001 base salary $465,000, 2001 bonus $1.2 million

Employees: 143,000

Principal Subsidiary Companies: EDS has businesses operating in numerous countries to provide services to customers outside of the United States. A.T. Kearney is a wholly owned subsidiary belonging to EDS.

Chief Competitors: The IT services industry is highly fragmented and very competitive. Among EDS' competitors are IBM, Perot Communications Systems, Cap Gemini Earnest & Young, Accenture, and Computer Science Corp.

down year-over-year 8 percent. Some analysts also have questioned EDS' realignment from five business units into four, noting that the move would change financial reports so that previous results would not compare side-by-side with the new structure, thus making it possible to hide changes in growth rates. Other concerns expressed included the increasing level of competition within the IT industry, decreasing growth rate, 23 percent year-over-year decline in stock prices, and the resignation of three top executives in the first quarter of 2002.

HISTORY

EDS was founded by H. Ross Perot and incorporated in 1962. Perot, at the time a salesman for IBM, suggested that the company provide electronic data processing management services along with its computer sales. Basically, IBM would sell high tech equipment and then provide trained professional to operate it. When

CHRONOLOGY:

Key Dates for Electronic Data Systems Corp.

1962: H. Ross Perot forms Electronic Data Systems Corp. (EDS)

1965: Medicare and Medicaid legislation open opportunity for EDS to organize claims processing systems

1971: Stocks jump from $16.50 a share to $160 a share before fall to $66 during the month of April

1973: Stock prices hit a low of $15 per share

1978: Two EDS employees are jailed and later released in Iran

1984: General Motors purchases EDS for $2.8 billion

1986: General Motors buys all remaining interest in EDS owned by Perot

1988: *Fortune* names EDS the leading company in diversified services

1989: EDS opens 153,000 square-foot Information Management Center in Plano, Texas

1995: EDS purchases A.T. Kearney

1996: General Motors spins off EDS, which again becomes a publicly owned company

1999: EDS undergoes restructuring, including job cuts

2002: EDS reorganizes five business units into four to focus on technology outsourcing services

---

IBM rejected Perot's proposal, he left the company to form EDS.

Perot began his business by renting time on an IBM 7070 computer at Southwestern Life Insurance in Dallas, Texas. Paying wholesale prices, Perot turned a profit by reselling the time to Collins Radio at retail price. In 1963 Perot landed a data processing contract with Mercantile Security Life and a commercial facilities management contract with Frito Lay. Uncommon at the time, EDS offered long-term contracts of up to five years at a fixed price to install a system and provide trained EDS staff to operate it, which are gradually withdrawn as in-house employees learn the system.

During the 1960s EDS began providing outsourcing services to Medicare and Medicaid claims processing

systems, which by 1968 accounted for a quarter of EDS' sales. In the same year the company entered another important market when it landed its first account with a financial institution, Dallas Bank. Later, EDS would become the worldwide leader in data processes services within the banking industry. During the late 1960s Perot took his company public and began organizing regional data centers.

The early 1970s provided EDS a roller coaster ride of success and failures. In the spring of 1971 EDS stocks were trading at $16.50 per share but suddenly soared to $160 a share before falling to $66 a share. By 1973 the company's stock prices had fallen to a record low of $15.00 a share. Nonetheless, the company continued to grow, posting revenues of over $100 million in 1974. In 1976 EDS landed its first international clients: King Abulaziz University in Saudi Arabia and the government of Iran, which agreed to a three-year contract valued at $41 million for computer services and training. However, Perot voided the contract with Iran in 1978 after the Iranian government failed to make payments for six months. When Perot ordered his employees to leave the country, two EDS workers were arrested but later released by a mob. Also during the late 1970s EDS began to extend its reach into new markets, including hospitals, small banks, small businesses, and the federal government.

In 1982 the U.S. Army signed a ten-year contract worth $656 million with EDS to computerize the Army's administrative system, now known as Army Standard Information Management Systems. Two years later General Motors purchased EDS, previously a publicly held corporation, for $2.8 billion, a record amount for a computer services firm. The automobile manufacturer wanted to use EDS to cut its $6 billion yearly expenditure for its data processing operations. Perot assumed a seat on the General Motors board of directors. In 1986 General Motors acquired Perot's remaining interest in EDS for $700 million, ending Perot's affiliation with EDS and General Motors. During the latter half of the 1980s the company underwent massive expansion, moving into the United Kingdom, China, Canada, Mexico, Brazil, Venezuela, Australia, New Zealand, France, Japan, and Germany. By 1988 EDS was operating in 27 countries. Although sales had tripled by 1985, after just one full year under General Motors' ownership, net income fell by over 5 percent. In 1986 employee numbers reached 40,000, nearly three times more than two years ago. Business markets were also expanded to include telecommunications and factory automation and expanded international markets in automobile manufacturing, electronics, and banks.

EDS underwent several significant changes in 1989, including the opening of its new 153,000 square-foot Information Management Center in Plano, Texas, which with over 7,000 employees served as command central for over 20 domestic and international information processing centers. In the same year EDS launched its ongoing JASON project, a program that offers children nationwide the opportunity to explore science and nature live via "telepresence." In May of 1989 EDS joined Hitachi to form Hitachi Data Systems Corp. to market Hitachi computer products. The following month EDS combined its communications network with General Motors' network to create the largest privately owned digital telecommunications system.

By 1992 EDS had expanded its customer base so that General Motor accounted for only 41 percent of the company's $8.5 billion in annual revenues. In 1994 a merger with Sprint was considered by ultimately rejected by EDS. The following year EDS purchased consulting firm A.T. Kearney for $628 million, merging EDS' 1,600 consultants with A.T. Kearney's 1,900 to create one of the largest consulting operations in the world. On June 10, 1996 General Motors spun off EDS, which becomes a publicly held company trading on the New York Stock Exchange.

The late 1990s proved challenging for EDS. The company's stock prices floundered and new major contract signings were scarce, leading to major cost cutting measures and restructuring. Over 13,000 employees were released, and 48 business units were reorganized into just four. As a result of the changes, the company responded by entering the 2000s with $42 billion of contract-signings, including a $7 billion deal with the U.S. Navy and Marine Corp. to build and maintain its computer networks.

STRATEGY

When Dick Brown joined EDS as the chief executive officer in January of 1999, he came in with the reputation for overhauling companies. By 2002, Brown had laid off one-third of the sales force and cut annual costs by $2 billion. At the same time, EDS successfully landed $89 billion in multiyear contracts. Yet start up of new contracts cause a drain on cash flow so even though revenues were growing, net income increases were not proportional. To maintain across-the-board positive numbers, EDS must continue to secure new contract as it continues to carry out its commitments to its current customers.

To keep EDS growing, the company plans to build new partnership and acquire new business interests. On July 2, 2001, EDS purchased the airline infrastructure outsourcing business and internal IT operational assets of Sabre Holdings Corporation for $676 million, providing EDS with airline outsourcing contracts with American Airlines, US Airways, and other major airline industry clients. The day following the acquisition of Sabre, EDS purchased a controlling interest in Systematics AG, a German IT service organization, for cash and stock worth $533 million, doubling EDS' presence in German.

On August 31, 2002, EDS acquired all outstanding shares of Structural Dynamics Research Corp. for $840 million, followed by the acquisition of the publicly held shares of Unigraphics Solutions Inc. for $174 million. The two new additions were combined to form PLM Solutions, the manufacturing industry's only single source for complete service in product lifecycle management.

INFLUENCES

With General Motors' revenues remaining flat, sales to General Motors have steadily decreased as the automobile manufacturer curbs discretionary spending. Both General Motors and EDS' other clients have been negatively affected by a stagnant economy and foreign currency fluctuations during 2001, especially in the value of the dollar against the euro and the British pound. With over 40 percent of its revenues being generated by its international businesses, EDS is directly impacted by downturns in the world economy and changes in the exchange rate in multiple currencies.

CURRENT TRENDS

Although the terrorist attacks of September 11, 2001, devastated the economy and paralyzed consumer spending, the tragic events opened the door to a unique opportunity for EDS: an increasing demand for computer security. Since September 11, security-related inquiries rose 150 percent at EDS. With over one thousand experts in data encryption, computer forensics, and disaster planning and recovery on the payroll, EDS is positioned to respond to the increasing willingness of corporations to shell out big bucks to back up their systems and protect against cyberterrorism.

PRODUCTS

The Operation Solutions business unit offers services such as centralized systems management, including Web site hosting and data warehousing; distributed systems management, which provides end-to-end services in planning, deployment, and operation of a client's computer network; communication management, which defines, develops, and manages consistent voice, video, data, and other global communication services; financial process management, which includes credit card processing, ATM processing, mortgage and consumer loan processing, and other document management services; and administrative process management, which provides end-to-end services in a wide range of business processes including medical claims administration, electronic traffic enforcement, and alarm tracking.

UNPLUGGED AND ON WHEELS

EDS, which promotes a creative and fun working environment, opened a new office facility in Troy, Michigan, in early 2002. The entire office has no private offices, and the conference room walls are made of glass. All of the furniture is on wheels, and all the computer equipment is wireless, creating unending possibilities for office arrangements. Everything from desks, chairs, filing cabinets, and black metal screens that serve as office dividers is moveable. There's a table filled with Legos, Play-Doh, and a sorcerer's cap; close by is a basketball net. During meetings in the conference rooms, employees write notes with a marker on the glass walls, and when the crowd get too big, all the furniture is pushed back to create a mini-auditorium. Not all EDS offices offer such flexibility and creative planning, but the office in Troy shows proof that the company values creativity, freedom to be innovative, and the ability break down traditional barriers.

Solution Consulting services include application services, offering application development and management; and enterprise consulting, which provides consulting services in technology, engineering and manufacturing. EDS' subsidiary A.T. Kearney provides strategy and organization consulting, operations consulting, technology consulting, and executive search services. The PLM Solutions business unit provides digital product development, collaborative product data management, and support services in systems integration.

CORPORATE CITIZENSHIP

EDS' JASON Project, debuted in 1989, is its longest standing contribution to education. The project offers hundreds of thousands of school children the opportunity to explore distant places and nature via telepresence. EDS also operates an Educational Outreach program that offers employees the opportunity to volunteer at schools as teachers, coaches, and mentors. EDS Technology Grants provide schoolteachers with funds to purchase computer equipment. Global Volunteer Day, held every October, gives thousands of EDS employees opportunities to contribute to their local communities. The EDS

Foundation exists to provide funds to bridge the gap between wealthy and poor communities to work toward equal access to the digital technology available.

GLOBAL PRESENCE

Approximately 43 percent of EDS' 2001 revenues were generated outside the United States. EDS does business in more than 60 countries.

EMPLOYMENT

EDS boasts of a work atmosphere of team spirit, freedom, and fun that fuels visionary thinking and innovative ideas. Career opportunities include the fields of systems engineering, technical delivery, customer business service, operations, communications, marketing, and sales.

SOURCES OF INFORMATION

Bibliography

Bills, Steve. "EDS Follows Two Downgrades With $1B Package of Deals." *American Banker,* 1 April 2002.

"EDS on Enron Path?" *Investment Dealers' Digest,* 22 April 2002.

"EDS Promotes Three Senior Executives, Realigns Business Units for Growth." EDS Company Press Release, 5 April 2002. Available at http://www.eds.com.

"E.D.S. Reorganizes to Focus on Technology Consulting." *The New York Times,* 6 April 2002.

"EDS Tests a Remedy for Enronitis." *Business Week Online,* 19 February 2002. Available at http://www.businessweek.com.

"Electronic Data Systems Corp.: Leading Companies Reap Savings 13 Times Greater Than Investment; In eProcurement, According to A.T. Kearney Study." *Market News Publishing,* 6 May 2002.

"Electronic Data Systems Corp.: Procurement Solutions Tops $20 Billion in Total Negotiated Spend; Has Saved Clients More Than $3 Billion." *Market News Publishing,* 17 May 2002.

Gaither, Chris. "E.D.S. Cites Lag in Orders for Decline in Earnings." *The New York Times,* 23 April 2002.

"Meet the 'Completely Different EDS.'" *Business Week,* 18 December 2000.

Spagat, Elliot. "EDS Says Profit Fell 21%, Revenue Will Fall Short." *The Wall Street Journal,* 23 April 2002.

Spagat, Elliot. "Electronic Data's Management Shake-up Realigns Five Business Units into Four." *The Wall Street Journal,* 8 April 2002.

Weinberg, Neil. "Scare Tactics." *Forbes,* 4 March 2002.

For an annual report:

on the Internet at: http://www.eds.com

For additional industry research:

Investigate companies by their Standard Industrial Classification Codes, also known as SICs. Electronic Data Systems Corp.'s primary SICs are:

6719 Holding Companies, Not Elsewhere Classified

7372 Prepackaged Software

7373 Computer Integrated Systems Design

7374 Data Processing Services

7376 Computer Facilities Management Service

Also investigate companies by their North American Industry Classification System codes, also known as NAICS codes. Electronic Data Systems Corp.'s primary NAICS codes are:

511210 Software Publishers

514210 Data Processing Services

541512 Computer Systems Design Services

541513 Computer Facilities Management Services

Eli Lilly and Company

FOUNDED: 1876

Contact Information:

HEADQUARTERS: Lilly Corporate Center
    Indianapolis, Indiana 46285
PHONE: (317)276-2000
FAX: (317)277-6579
TOLL FREE: (800)545-5979
URL: http://www.lilly.com

OVERVIEW

Headquartered in Indianapolis, Indiana, and incorporated in 1901, Eli Lilly and Company is probably best known for introducing the world to Prozac, a pharmaceutical treatment for clinical depression. However, the organization boasts a large portfolio of products. Eli Lilly and Company is a global, research-based company that discovers, develops, manufactures, and sells products in a large business segment called Pharmaceutical Products. It stresses innovation in its laboratories located around the world. Through its research division, Lilly Research Laboratories, the company discovers, develops, and evaluates therapies and products to help diagnose, prevent, and treat human diseases. The company also manufactures and sells animal health products. All of Lilly's products are sold in approximately 160 countries.

COMPANY FINANCES

In 2001, Eli Lilly's net sales rose 6 percent to $11.54 billion, but its net income fell 8 percent to $2.81 billion. Company earnings were significantly affected by higher research and development expenses and $311.9 million in acquired in-process R&D and asset impairment charges. A substantial portion of its revenues came from increased sales of the products Zyprexa, Evista, Gemzar, Humalog and Actos.

ANALYSTS' OPINIONS

Among the new drugs that Eli Lilly has produced in the last five years, observers speculate that the company could have at least 15 potential "megasellers" including its already established best-sellers. Analysts and investors expressed concerns about Lilly's Prozac problem. In 2001, a, a U.S. Court of Appeals ruled that Lilly would have to cede its Prozac patent in 12 months, rather than in late 2003, as Lilly had hoped. The decision caused the company's stock to drop by almost a third in one day (to $75 a share), which erased a whopping $36.8 billion in equity. A month later, the stock bottomed out at $66. But because of the new products Eli Lilly researchers have been developing, analysts are expecting that annual earnings should increase by 17 percent as profits begin to show in the beginning of 2003. This will put Eli Lilly's profits back up in the double-digit figures. Lilly was expected to only show a 4 percent profit in 2001. As a result, shares of Lilly stock rose to $76. Observers feel that Lilly's prospects look positive.

HISTORY

Before he founded Eli Lilly and Company in Indianapolis, Indiana in 1876, Colonel Eli Lilly had already tried to launch several unsuccessful business ventures. When he started his pharmaceutical company, he found the right formula. From the outset, his goals were to make pharmaceutical products of the highest possible quality, develop only medicines that would be prescribed by physicians, and to base his products on the best scientific knowledge. A veteran of the American Civil War, Colonel Lilly was 38 years old at the time. He was motivated by a frustration with the inadequate medicines then available. From the start, the business flourished, a testimony to Colonel Lilly's continual quality improvement. The company would soon develop an excellent reputation. Consumers not only respected the quality of the products; they respected the quality of the man as well. Colonel Lilly was seen as a generous man with community spirit.

In 1886, Lilly implemented a novel pharmaceutical research program when he hired a chemist, Ernest Eberhard, who would perform as a full-time scientist to test the quality of products. Eberhard was one of the first graduates of a new pharmacy program at Purdue University. The move would prove significant, as it helped establish what would become a company tradition: dedication to quality and the discovery and development of new and better pharmaceuticals.

Later, Colonel Lilly would bring his family into the business. His two grandsons, Eli Lilly and Josiah K. Lilly Jr., both served as president of the company, forging their own management styles that contributed to the organization's ongoing success. The grandsons were instrumental in helping to establish company policies that regarded employees as its most valuable asset—a philosophy that many U.S. corporations would not adopt until well into the twentieth century.

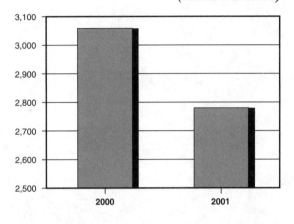

FINANCES:
Eli Lilly and Company
Net Incomes, 2000-2001
(million dollars)

From these roots the company grew to become a world leader in pharmaceutical-based, integrated health care. Into the next century, the company's history was marked by innovation and achievement. In the 1920s, Lilly's researchers worked with Frederick Banting and Charles Best of the University of Toronto to isolate and purify insulin to treat diabetes. At the time, diabetes was a fatal disease. In 1923, Lilly provided a treatment option where none had existed before when it introduced Iletin, the world's first commercially available insulin product. During the same period, the company started a research program to find a treatment for pernicious anemia. This resulted in the introduction of a liver-extract product that became standard therapy for the disorder. The researchers who developed the product received a Nobel Prize for their efforts.

Developments continued as the century progressed. In the 1940s, Lilly was one of the first companies to develop a way to mass-produce penicillin. In the 1950s, it introduced vancomycin, an antibiotic that treats patients suffering from serious hospital infections associated with resistant bacteria. The company also introduced erythromycin, an antibiotic that proved vital to patients allergic to penicillin.

During the next decade, Lilly launched a line of oral and injectable antibiotics in a new class called cephalosporins. It also introduced two anti-cancer drugs, vincristine and vinblastine. In the 1970s, it launched Ceclor, which would become the world's best-selling oral antibiotic, and Dobutrex, a cardiovascular product.

In the 1980s, Lilly engineered a breakthrough in diabetes treatment when it developed Humulin, insulin that

Nicole Johnson, Miss America 1999, performs blood tests during a national diabetes action campaign sponsored by Eli Lilly and Co. (AP Photo/Eli Lilly and Co., Peter Barreras)

was identical to that produced by the human body. Introduced in 1982, it was the world's first human-healthcare product created with recombinant DNA technology. Lilly later used the same technology when it developed Humatrope, a therapy for growth hormone deficiency in children. In 1988, it produced perhaps its best known product when it developed Prozac, the first drug of its kind to treat clinical depression.

Eli Lilly continued to innovate as the century drew to a close. In the 1990s, Lilly introduced Gemzar, a drug to treat pancreatic and non-small-cell lung cancer; ReoPro, a cardiovascular drug that prevents blood clots following certain heart procedures; Zyprexa, an antipsychotic drug used to treat schizophrenia; Humalog, a highly improved insulin product; and Evista, the first of a new class of drugs used for the prevention and treatment of postmenopausal osteoporosis. In 1999, working with Takeda Chemical Industries, Ltd., Lilly successfully introduced the oral anti-diabetes agent Actos.

Toward the end of the twentieth century, the appointment of Sidney Taurel would have a great impact on the organization. Taurel became chief executive officer in July 1998 and chairman of the board of directors in 1999. Taurel had been president and chief operating officer since February 1996 and a member of the Lilly board of directors since July 1991. He is chairman of the company's policy committee and senior management forum.

STRATEGY

Beginning with Colonel Lilly's initial vision, the strategy of Eli Lilly and Company has been to apply the latest research and encourage scientific collaboration toward the development of new product. This tact fostered innovation, led to the company's continually growing portfolio of products, and contributed greatly to its success. The company also strived to identify and understand the world's most pressing medical needs. Research has been its focal point, as the company has established major research and development facilities in nine countries and conducts clinical trials for its drugs in more than 30 countries.

Lilly also attributes a great deal of its success to the development and adherence to a core set of values, which include respecting people (both its customers and its employees, as well as its business associates and communities) and maintaining integrity in all elements of its enterprises. It has dedicated itself to the pursuit of excellence, and it seeks ways to continually improve its business and, thus, its products. Along the way the company developed a two-fold purpose: to save lives and to cut overall healthcare costs.

Those purposes are integrated into its specific strategic initiatives. To help save lives, Eli Lilly uses new technology as a driving force in the discovery of new drugs. Believing that the latest technologies provide the key to understanding, treatment, and cure of diseases, the company seeks out and applies advances such as genomics, combinatorial chemistry, molecular biology, and informatics. To help cut healthcare costs, and thus make its products more available to the people who need them most, it employs access and cost-containment measures.

As part of its future direction, Eli Lilly will continue exploring strategic partnerships with academic research institutions and biotechnology firms. This, the company feels, enables it to apply new technologies in the production of new and better drugs.

INFLUENCES

Eli Lilly and Company's stated goal is to become the industry's "partner of choice." To this end, it has committed itself to establishing relationships with third parties to supplement and enhance its internal capabilities, and it aggressively seeks to establish strategic alliances toward the development and marketing of new products. The intent is to create mutually beneficial relationships for both Lilly and its partners.

So far, the company has become involved in more than 140 research and development collaborations with leading companies and universities. Collaboration has been a company hallmark since the 1920s when it partnered with the University of Toronto to introduce insulin to the market.

One recent significant collaboration involved Takeda Pharmaceuticals of America that resulted, in 1999, in the successful launching of Takeda's oral anti-diabetes agent Actos, a therapy for the treatment of Type II diabetes. Current collaborations include a partnership with Vertex Pharmaceuticals. Working with this company, Eli Lilly is seeking a treatment for chronic infection caused by the hepatitis C virus, a potentially deadly disease. Eli Lilly is also collaborating with Ribozyme Pharmaceuticals, Inc., to pursue treatments for hepatitis C. Together with Stanford University, Eli Lilly has formed the Lilly/Stanford Program for Excellence in Hepatitis Research, which brings together the world's leading experts in the area of hepatitis research.

Eli Lilly continues to encourage pharmaceutical and biotechnology organizations to contact the company for possible collaborations that could lead to potential products or new research technologies. This approach is in keeping with the company's philosophy of "research without walls," which means that it seeks out the latest in science and technology from external and internal sources.

CURRENT TRENDS

When Sidney Taurel took over as CEO of Eli Lilly and Company in 1998, he immediately sought to increase

FAST FACTS:
About Eli Lilly and Company

Ownership: Eli Lilly and Company is a publicly owned company traded on the New York, London, and Canadian Stock Exchanges.

Ticker Symbol: LLY

Officers: Sidney Taurel, Chmn, CEO, and Pres., 62, 2000 salary $6,100,000; Charles Golden, CFO, EVP, Dir., 54, 2000 salary $2,400,000; August Watanabe, MD, EVP Science & Technology, 59, 2000 salary $2,400,000; John Lechleiter, EVP Pharmaceutical Products and Corporate Development, 47; Gerhard Mayr, EVP Pharmaceutical Operations, 54, 2000 salary $2,200,000

Employees: 35,000

Principal Subsidiary Companies: Lilly has subdivisions and facilities in 18 countries. Its research division, Lilly Research Laboratories, is responsible for the discovery, development, and clinical evaluation of pharmaceutical products. Research and development locations in the United States include four sites in Indiana and a subdivision in North Carolina, as well as international facilities in eight countries. Also, the company markets animal health care products through its division called Elanco Animal Health. Division facilities are located in North America, Europe, the Middle East, Africa, the Asia-Pacific area and Latin America.

Chief Competitors: Eli Lilly's major competitors include companies in the healthcare sector and drug manufacturing industry. Some of its primary competitors include Abbott Laboratories, AstraZeneca, Aventis, Bayer, Johnson & Johnson, Merck & Co., Inc., Novartis, Pfizer Inc., and Wyeth.

the company's new drug development by increasing the research and development budget by 30 percent (or $2.2 billion). As part of this plan, he hired 700 scientists in the span of one year. Further, he told the company's researchers not to pursue the development of any drug that would seem likely to create less than $500 million in annual sales. This strategy resulted in the creation of numerous new and highly marketable drugs.

Research and development has always been an integral part of the company's success. Colonel Lilly him-

CHRONOLOGY:

Key Dates for Eli Lilly & Company

1876: Eli Lilly and Company is founded in Indianapolis, Indiana by Colonel Eli Lilly

1886: Lilly implements a first-ever pharmaceutical research program

1923: Lilly introduces the world's first commercially available insulin product

1982: Lilly introduces Humulin, insulin that is identical to that produced by the human body

1988: Lilly introduces Prozac, the first drug of its kind

1998: Sidney Taurel becomes CEO

1999: Lilly collaborateswith Takeda Chemical Industries, Ltd., to produce the oral antidiabetes agent Actos

self once described research as "the heart of the business, the soul of the enterprise." The company has held to that stance in the twentieth century and its sees no reason to alter this line of thinking in the twenty first century. Today, the company is recognized as one of the industry leaders in research and development. Its all-important research division, Lilly Research Laboratories, includes more 6,000 employees working in a variety of scientific disciplines, and the company invests substantial sums of money into research. In 1999, it spent approximately $1.8 billion in the development of new medicines. In 2000, it increased that figure to $2 billion.

PRODUCTS

Eli Lilly and Company's main products are pharmaceuticals designed to treat patients and reduce total health care costs. Specifically, through its pharmaceuticals, the company strives to eliminate the need for surgery and hospitalization, and to slow, reverse, or prevent disease. The company focuses research in the areas of neuroscience, endocrinology, infectious diseases, oncology, and cardiovascular diseases. In recent years, it has introduced new and successful drugs to treat cancer, schizophrenia, osteoporosis, diabetes, and cardiovascular complications.

Eli Lilly's neuroscience products include the well-known Prozac, a treatment for clinical depression;

Zyprexa, for treatment of schizophrenia and acute bipolar mania; Darvon, a line of analgesic products; Permax, a treatment for Parkinson's disease; and Sarafem, for the treatment of pre-menstrual dysphoric disorder. Endocrine products include Humulin, human insulin produced through recombinant DNA technology; Humalog, an injectable human insulin analog of recombinant DNA origin; Iletin, animal-source insulin; Actos, an oral agent for Type II diabetes; Evista, for the prevention and treatment of osteoporosis in post-menopausal women; and Humatrope, a human growth hormone produced by recombinant DNA technology. Products to treat infectious disease include the oral antibiotics: Ceclor, Dynabac, Keflex, Keftab and Lorabid. They also include the injectable antibiotics: Vancocin HCl, Nebcin, Tazidime, Kefurox and Kefzol. Cardiovascular products include ReoPro, an antibody product for use as an adjunct to percutaneous coronary intervention; Dobutrex, an agent for cardiac decompensation and Cynt, for treatment of hypertension. Oncology products include Gemzar, for treatment of pancreatic cancer and non-small-cell lung cancer; Oncovin, for treatment of acute leukemia and advanced cancers; Velban, used in a variety of cancers; Eldisine, for treatment of acute childhood leukemia, and Axid, an antiulcer agent.

Eli Lilly produces animal health products through its division called Elanco Animal Health. The products are marketed primarily to cattle, poultry, and swine producers, and are sold throughout the world. The current product line focuses on four therapeutic classes including: antibacterials, parasiticides, anticoccidials, and productivity enhancers. Products include Tylan, an antibiotic used to control certain diseases in cattle, swine, and poultry, and to improve feed efficiency and growth, and Rumensin, a cattle feed additive that improves feed efficiency and growth. The portfolio also includes Coban, Monteban, and Maxiban, which are anticoccidial agents for use in poultry. Other products include Apralan, an antibiotic used to control enteric infections in calves and swine; Micotil and Pulmotil, antibiotics used to treat respiratory disease in cattle and swine; Surmax, a performance-enhancer for swine and poultry, and Paylean, a leanness and performance enhancer for swine.

CORPORATE CITIZENSHIP

Eli Lilly takes a strong pro-environmental stance. It has adopted environmental quality indicators that include, among many others, organic solvent emissions as a percent of usage, water and energy usage, global warming emissions and acidification potential emissions (CO_2 and SO_2), and waste generation. It also tracks the number and amount of fines imposed by government agencies for environmental deviations, and the number of complaints from the public registered for environmental concerns.

As part of its community service initiatives, the company has established the Eli Lilly and Company Foundation, a non-profit corporation made possible by the profits of Eli Lilly and Company. It is the major source of the company's support for non-profit organizations. For its employees it has set up community involvement opportunities including the "Now for the Future Program," an educational program that seeks volunteers to acts as tutor/mentors for young people ages 10 to 17; and a crisis and suicide intervention service, that uses volunteer clinical associates to staff a 24-hour telephone hotline.

GLOBAL PRESENCE

Eli Lilly has research and development facilities in Australia, Belgium, Canada, England, Germany, Japan, Singapore, Spain, and the United States. It conducts clinical research in approximately 70 countries around the world. Manufacturing facilities are located in Australia, Brazil, China, Egypt, England, France, Germany, Ireland, Italy, Japan, Korea, Mexico, Pakistan, Puerto Rico, Spain, Taiwan, and the United States. It operates 14 administrative, research and development, and manufacturing plants in the United States and Puerto Rico.

EMPLOYMENT

Eli Lilly and Company has often been recognized as one of the top employers in the United States. For three years (1999-2001), it was selected by *Forbes* magazine as one of the country's "100 Best Companies to Work For." In making the selection, the magazine cited the company's many employee benefits, including a stock-option grant program and on-site child-care centers. Lilly also provides its employees with career path development. Eli Lilly actively encourages employees to enhance their skills, look for learning opportunities, and explore career opportunities within the company.

SOURCES OF INFORMATION

Bibliography

Arndt, Michael. "Eli Lilly: Life After Prozac." *Business Week Online*, 23 July 2001. Available at http://www.businessweek.com.

HEALTHY HERBS

Eli Lilly and company has come a long way from its modest beginning to human insulin production, recombinant DNA technology, and human growth hormones. The company's very first products, produced by Colonel Lilly himself, were herbal preparations extracted from Bear's Foot, Black Haw, Cramp Bark, Hardhack, Life Root, Skullcap, Sea Wrack, Squaw Vine, Wahoo, and Wormseed.

BioSpace.com. "Eli Lilly and Company New from the Biospace Beat" *Biospace News*, 2002. Available at http://www.biospace.com.

Hamilton, Joan. "Interneuron is Listening to Prozac." *Signals Magazine*, 19 January 1998. Available at http://www.signalsmag.com.

Lilly.com. "Lilly Makes Magazine List Again as Top Employer in the United States." *Lilly Newsroom*, 23 January 2002. Available at http://newsroom.lilly.com/news/story.

Petersen, Lynn, Betsy Porter, and Jitesh Tank. "A Day in the Life: Eli Lilly." *TheMSJ.com*, 1 April 2002. Available at http://www.themsj.com.

Yahoo! Finance. "Eli Lilly & Company." *Yahoo Market Guide*, 28 March 2002. Available at http://biz.yahoo.com.

For an annual report:
on the Internet at: http://www.lilly.com/about/investor.

For additional industry research:
Investigate companies by their Standard Industrial Classification Codes, also known as SICs. Eli Lilly and Company's primary SIC is:

2834 Pharmaceutical Preparations

Also investigate companies by their North American Industrial Classification System codes, also known as NAICS codes. Eli Lilly and Company's primary NAICS code is:

325412 Pharmaceutical Preparation Manufacturing

Enron Corp.

FOUNDED: 1930

Contact Information:

HEADQUARTERS: PO Box 1188, Suite 4712
    Houston, TX 77251-1188
PHONE: (713)853-6161
FAX: (713)853-3129
URL: http://www.enron.com

OVERVIEW

Enron Corp.'s foundational business is in the production, transportation, and distribution of electricity and natural gas resources. When the U.S. government deregulated the sale of natural gas and electricity during the 1990s, Enron built an empire within the energy industry, at one point holding one-fourth of all U.S. natural gas business, and recorded impressive financial gains by trading in energy futures. When questions arose regarding Enron's accounting methods, the company suffered a stunning and rapid demise amid allegations of criminal and ethical misconduct. Enron filed for bankruptcy on December 3, 2001. More than 90 lawsuits have been filed against Enron, and the company continues to work through the complicated process of bankruptcy proceedings. Federal investigations into the conduct of both Enron and its outside accounting firm, Arthur Andersen, are ongoing and may be open for years. Criminal charges were filed against Arthur Andersen for obstruction of justice caused by the destruction of documents. It is unclear whether Enron or any of its executives will eventually be indicted on criminal charges.

COMPANY FINANCES

According to Enron's 2000 annual report, the last to be filed prior to filing for bankruptcy, the company posted a net income of $979 million on revenues of $100.8 billion. However, on November 8, 2001, in the midst of a scandal making daily headlines, Enron made the unusual move to restate its profits for years 1997 through 2000, in effect acknowledging that its previous

numbers were inappropriately inflated due to accounting procedures that moved assets and debts on and off Enron's books. The restated figures reported net income as $880 million rather than the previously stated $979 million. Other changes included a revised accounting of debt and equity, which reflected an increase in debt of $628 million and a decrease in equity of $754 million.

At the core of Enron's downfall was the use of complicated accounting methods to hide losses and inflate income. To keep stock prices high, the company raised investment against its own assets and maintained an appearance of a highly successful company. Enron removed losses from its books by placing certain money-losing assets with so-called independent partnerships. Conversely, Enron posted as profits money that it received from these partnerships, even if those profits reflected projects or assets that did not actually exist.

Using such complex accounting tools that were beyond the comprehension of the average investor, Enron convinced Wall Street it was riding high. In actuality, by the end of 2000 Enron was becoming increasing dependent on smoke-and-mirrors accounting to show its impressive profits. For the purposes of accountability, legitimate partnerships must necessarily be independent from Enron. However, Enron was doing hundreds of millions of dollars worth of business with "special purpose entities," which were funded by Enron stocks and under the direct control of Enron executives, who personally made millions of dollars through these transactions, yet resulted in little benefit to shareholders.

After investing heavily in broadband trading and making several unprofitable major international deals, Enron's ability to cover its losses with profits from its partnerships became problematic. Stock prices began to decline through the first three quarters of 2001. In August of 2001, Enron's chief financial officer abruptly resigned, citing personal reasons, but the move was enough to spook Wall Street, and investors, including numerous high-level Enron executives, began unloading stock. Amidst ongoing discoveries regarding Enron's accounting practices through Andersen, Enron essentially collapsed. On November 28, 2001, after being given junk-bond status by major credit raters, meaning investment was considered to be a massive risk, Enron stocks dropped below $1 per share. On December 2, 2001, Enron filed for bankruptcy, the then-largest filing in the history of the United States.

ANALYSTS' OPINIONS

In retrospect, analysts acknowledge that a close look at Enron's books left provided more questions than answers. Enron successfully bluffed most of Wall Street into thinking that the books made sense, and considering its positive growth, which was benefiting traders as well as investors, Wall Street had little reason to question

FAST FACTS:
About Enron Corp.

Ownership: Enron is a publicly owned company that trades on the Over-the-Counter Bulletin Board.

Ticker Symbol: ENRNQ

Officers: Stephen Cooper, Interim CEO and Chief Restructuring Officer; Mark Frevert, 46, VChmn.; Raymond Bowen, Jr., 41, CFO and EVP

Employees: 20,600

Principal Subsidiary Companies: Enron has retained some of its business units, but as it undergoes restructuring or liquidation due to its bankruptcy filing, its corporate structure remains uncertain.

Chief Competitors: Duke Energy has emerged as the leader of the energy industry in wake of Enron's absence. Having scaled down in size dramatically, Enron also now competes with smaller utility providers, including Dynergy and Reliant Energy.

Enron's accounting. Not only was Enron's collapse the largest ever, it was also unbelievably rapid. In just over three months, the company went from being a multibillion-dollar corporation to bankruptcy. The fact that analysts failed to recognize or turned a blind eye to the discrepancies in Enron's numbers has been the topic of considerable conversation.

HISTORY

Enron has its origins in the Northern Natural Gas Company, established in Omaha, Nebraska, in 1930 by North American Light & Power Company, United Light & Railways Company, and Lone Star Gas Corporation. Forming just months after the stock market crash in 1929, Northern actually found the ensuing Depression beneficial. First, the low cost of natural gas provided the new company with an instant customer base. Second, widespread unemployment drove down wages; thus, Northern had access to inexpensive labor to build its pipeline. As a result, Northern had doubled its system capacity by 1932.

The Natural Gas Act of 1938 created the Federal Power Commission, which began regulating the natural

CHRONOLOGY:

Key Dates for Enron Corp.

1985: InterNorth purchases Houston Natural Gas Company, creating Enron Corp.

1994: Federal government approves the deregulation of natural gas and electricity

2000: Enron reports revenues in excess of $100 billion; stock prices reach all-time high of $90

2001: Stock prices fall to $50 in March; CFO Jeffrey Skilling resigns in August; Sherron Watkins sends memo to CEO Kenneth Lay warning of serious accounting problems; in October, Enron's accounting firm, Arthur Andersen, shreds documents related to Enron; Enron reports first quarter loss of $618 million; stock price plummets; the Securities and Exchange Commission opens investigation; in November, Enron admits inflating profits and restates figures for 2000; stock prices fall below $1; Enron files for bankruptcy in December

2002: Numerous congressional and federal investigations ensue; more than 90 lawsuits are lodged against Enron; the Arthur Andersen firm is charged with criminal behavior for destroying documents

gas industry. In 1941 United Light & Railways sold its 35 percent share of Northern to the public, the following year Lone Star Gas distributed its 30 percent holding among its stockholders, and in 1947 North American Light & Power sold its shares to underwriters who then sold the stock to the public. In the same year Northern was listed on the New York Stock Exchange.

During the next four decades, Northern made numerous acquisitions, expanding its network of operations in the generation, transportation, and distribution of natural gas, electricity, and other energy-related products. In 1980 it changed its name to InterNorth Inc. In 1985 InterNorth made it largest acquisition in a $2.26-billion bid purchase Houston Natural Gas Corporation. The merger between the two companies created the largest natural gas pipeline system in the United States. In 1986 HNG/InterNorth took on the name Enron Corp. with its headquarters in Houston. Kenneth Lay, previously chairman of HNG, was named as chairman of Enron. Under Lay's leadership, Enron sold off

non-vital business assets that were deemed incongruent with Enron's goal of becoming a prime player in the energy industry.

Enron posted revenues of $16.3 billion in 1985, but a decline in natural gas prices led to a corresponding decline in revenues over the next four years. Nonetheless, Enron continued to expand both its domestic and international operations, and by 1990 held a market share of 18 percent, putting the company in a prime position to benefit from the deregulation of the natural gas and electricity in 1994. Prior to deregulation, utility companies generated and supplied power to customers who had no choice in provider or say in price. After deregulation, utility companies were allowed to sell energy to outside sources that then sold it to customers, who could choose their provider. Deregulation increased competition but also caused significant fluctuations in price. Enron cashed in on the fear of price fluctuations by trading in energy futures, that is, by buying tomorrow's electricity and natural gas at a fixed price today.

By 2001 the company had expanded its commodities trading internationally to include paper and pulp, credit, shipping, steel, crude oil, coal, plastics, metals, emissions allowances, bandwidth, and weather derivatives. For example, Enron would sell a future supply of natural gas to an industrial user who would rather pay a fixed price than worry about upward fluxes in price due to exceptionally cold weather. At the same time, Enron would also ensure a fixed price for the supplier, who would be harmed by low demand caused by unseasonably warm weather. Basically, Enron earned money by taking on the risk of price fluctuations.

When the strategy proved successful, Enron began shifting more of its attention to trading rather than its physical asset. Eventually some 90 percent of Enron's revenues were being generated through trading. One of the first to trade over the Internet, the value of products bought and sold online totaled an incredible $880 billion in just two years. Stock prices reached an all-time high of $90 during the summer with annual revenues for the year totaling $100 billion. Murmurs of concern within both Enron and Arthur Andersen went largely unnoticed or ignored.

During the early months of 2001 Enron's stock showed the first signs of trouble under pressure from the demise of the dot-com industry and instability in energy costs. When questions over accounting procedures surfaced in the fall of 2001, Enron's empire came crashing down. By the end of the year, both Enron and its accounting firm Arthur Andersen were under investigation by the federal government, and stock prices had fall to less than $1 per share. On December 2, 2001, Enron filed for bankruptcy. In the aftermath of the company's collapse and allegations that Andersen purposefully destroyed documents, Enron has been attempting to restructure. It has sold off many of its interests around the world, including its energy trading unit, to refocus on its core business of energy production, transportation, and distribution.

STRATEGY

Since filing for bankruptcy on December 2, 2001, Enron has been working to reorganize itself into a viable, albeit smaller, new company by refocusing on its core business of supplying, generating, transporting, and selling energy. With all top executive leadership replaced and an entirely new board of directors, Enron has devised a strategy to restructure itself into a profitable entity. In May 2002 Enron filed a proposed business plan for life-after-bankruptcy for the company. Enron has suggested the formation of a new entity, OpCo Energy Company, which would retain a specific asset-based portfolio separate from the items considered under the bankruptcy filing. OpCo would build on Enron's energy infrastructure of businesses focused on the transportation, distribution, generation and production of natural gas and electricity with an expected income before interest and taxes of $1.3 billion.

Enron's rationale is that its collapse had very little to do with its physical assets, namely its power generation and supply units, and was almost solely a result of its commodity trading business. If the company's positive assets remain lumped in with its debt obligations, it will severely hamper these business units' attempt to compete in the open market and value will decrease. To avoid the deterioration of value, Enron argues, these assets should be removed from the equation and allowed to form a viable new entity, namely OpCo. Enron agrees that all other assets held by the company should be liquidated to satisfy creditors, although predict creditor recovery has been estimated as low as 20 percent. Such a plan would remove a majority of risk from the new entity and maximize its value.

Enron does not want to reorganize as the old Enron under the chapter 11 bankruptcy filing because to do so reduces value and allows for long on-going litigation and claims reconciliation that would be contested for years to come. Also, under the cloud of bankruptcy status, Enron would not have access to the capital investments necessary to sustain business in a competitive marketplace. Enron has also argued against liquidation of all assets because the nature of such sales results in bids lower than actual value, thereby reducing recovery totals to creditors.

Under Enron's proposed plan, OpCo's organizational structure would include: transportation services, power distribution, generation and production, finance and administration, and corporate communications. By separating its reputation from Enron and achieving an investment credit rating, Enron proposes that OpCo's formation would prove most beneficial to investors and

WHISTLEBLOWER

Sherron Watkins, a former vice-president of corporate development at Enron, testified before the House Energy and Commerce Committee that she had sent a seven-page memo to Enron's chief executive officer (CEO), Kenneth Lay, expressing deep concern over Enron's use of Special Purpose Entities and the company's improprieties in accounting. Watkins pointed the finger of blame at the company's former president and one-time CEO Jeffrey Skilling and former chief financial officer Andrew Fastow. Although testifying that she believed Lay had been "duped" by Skilling and Fastow, Watkins was critical of Lay's failure to respond aggressively after she warned him that the company was in serious trouble and that Skilling's sudden resignation would trigger inquiries that would scandalize the company. In the memo, subsequently released to the press, Watkins wrote: "I am incredibly nervous that we will implode in a wave of accounting scandals." Skilling has denied his involvement in any misconduct. Lay, who exercised his fifth amendment right not to incriminate himself, refused to answer the Congress committee's questions.

creditors alike. Despite its plans for the future, creditors wishing to cut their losses may likely push for the liquidation of all Enron's assets.

CURRENT TRENDS

In the fallout out after Enron's scandalous demise, new federal regulations are likely to be enacted to ensure full disclosure and tightened accountability in financial reporting. The situation has also focused acute attention on corporate accountability across the board, including the board of directors, outside auditors, corporate executives, bankers, regulators, and Wall Street analysts.

PRODUCTS

Enron continues to operate a number of businesses, including natural-gas pipelines and utilities. It has divested itself from numerous assets and plans to reemerge as a much smaller company.

GLOBAL PRESENCE

Enron built its first overseas power plant in Teesside, England, in 1991. During the 1990s Enron aggressive pursued international investments, eventually building power plants all over the globe, including such places as Italy, Turkey, Argentina, China, India, Brazil, Guatemala, Bolivia, Columbia, the Dominican Republic, Poland, and the Philippines. By 1997 international projects were generating one fourth of all revenues. Enron made a major commitment to the construction of a massive power plant in India, the largest foreign investment in the country, but when its only customer in the venture pulled in 2001, Enron took a significant loss from the project.

EMPLOYMENT

During its restructuring, Enron is not accepting applications. Due to its bankruptcy status, thousands of employees, particularly those located in the Houston home office, have lost their jobs. A class action suit is being brought against Enron by employees whose pensions were rendered worthless when Enron went under. In particular, at issue is Enron's decision in October 2001 to prohibit its employees from selling their stock shares in an attempt to avert share price collapse. Because a majority of employee pension funds were tied up in Enron stocks, a large number of long-time employees lost significant amounts of money. On the other hand Enron's top executives were selling in mass quantities when the stock was at its peak, cashing in more than $1 billion.

SOURCES OF INFORMATION

Bibliography

Berger, Eric, Mary Flood, Laura Goldberg, Julie Mason, and Patty Reinert. "The Fall of Enron." *Houston Chronicle,* 24 February 2002.

Byrne, John A., Louis Lavelle, Nanette Byrnes, Marcia Vickers, and Amy Borrus. "How to Fix Corporate Governance." *Business Week,* 6 May 2002.

"Complete Enron Coverage." *Forbes.* Available at http://www.forbes.com.

Dobbs, Lou. "The Impact of Money." *Money,* May 2002.

Elkind, Peter, and Bethany McLean. "Is There Anything Enron Didn't Do?" *Fortune,* 29 April 2002.

"Enron and the Mule." *Power Engineering,* May 2002.

"Enron Files Voluntary Petitions for Chapter 11 Reorganization." Enron Corp. Press Release, 2 December 2001. Available at http://www.enron.com.

"Enron Investigation." British Broadcasting Corp., 9 June 2002. Available at http://www.news.bbc.co.

"Enron Presents Process to Creditors' Committee for Separating Power, Pipeline Company from Bankruptcy." Enron Corp. Press Release, 3 May 2002. Available at http://www.enron.com.

"Enron Probe." *The Washington Post.* Available at http://www.washingtonpost.com.

McLean, Bethany. "Why Enron Went Bust." *Fortune,* 24 December 2001.

Meyer, Dick. "Enron: Too Serious for a Scandal." CBS News, 17 January 2002. Available at http://www.cbsnews.com.

For additional industry research:

Investigate companies by their Standard Industrial Classification Codes, also known as SICs. Enron's primary SICs are:

1311 Crude Petroleum And Natural Gas

4932 Gas And Other Services Combined

6719 Holding Companies, Not Elsewhere Classified

Also investigate companies by their North American Industry Classification System codes, also known as NAICS codes. Enron's primary NAICS codes are:

211111 Crude Petroleum and Natural Gas Extraction

221210 Natural Gas Distribution

Essence Communications, Inc.

OVERVIEW

Essence Communications publishes *Essence*, one of the leading general interest magazines targeting African American women. The monthly publication boasts a circulation of more than 1 million and a readership of 7.6 million, nearly one-third of which is male. In addition, the company operates a mail order business through which it sells books, art, and apparel. Other activities include the Essence Awards, a prime-time televised network special which honors African American entertainers, athletes, government officials, community activists, and other noteworthy individuals, and the Essence Musical Festival, an annual three-day celebration of African American culture that features artists such as Stevie Wonder and Luther Vandross.

COMPANY FINANCES

Sales for Essence Communications grew steadily throughout the 1990s. After reaching $77 million in 1994, sales grew to $92.8 million in 1996, and to $104.8 million in 1997. In 2000, Essence posted sales of $145 million , a 17.5 percent increase over the previous year. Despite falling advertising revenues for most magazine publishers, largely the result of a North American economic recession, Essence saw its advertising pages grow 5 percent in the first half of 2001.

ANALYSTS' OPINIONS

The reason for Essence Communications' strong performance in the first half of 2001, despite weakening

FOUNDED: 1969

Contact Information:

HEADQUARTERS: 1500 Broadway
    New York, NY 10036
PHONE: (212)642-0600
FAX: (212)921-5173
URL: http://www.essence.com

FINANCES:

Essence Communications Inc. Revenues, 1994-2000 (million dollars)

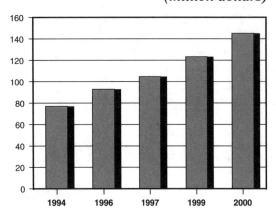

market conditions, had to do with its target market, according to some analysts. In a September 2001 issue of *Crain's New York Business*, columnist Valerie Block explained, "During the heady days of the advertising boom, one of the biggest changes in the landscape was the ascension of ethnic media. Buoyed by the growing number and wealth of their constituents, ethnic media outlets, especially those catering to African Americans and Latinos, began to catch up to their mainstream rivals." When the advertising boom began to fizzle in late 2000, many ethnic publishers continued to see their advertising dollars increase. According to Block, the reason for this is multifaceted, but it has a lot to do with the fact that "advertisers, finding traditional markets tapped, are looking to the minority media to help them attract new customers." In addition, some analysts believed that working in the Essence Communications' favor was the fact that it had not embraced online advertising and publishing to the extent more mainstream publishers had; as a result, when the dot-com market crumbled along with the economy, minority focused firms like Essence Communications simply weren't hit as hard as those who had come to rely more heavily on the Internet.

HISTORY

After attending an African American entrepreneurship conference, bank manager Edward Lewis and insurance salesperson Clarence O. Smith—along with graphics designer Cecil Hollingsworth, advertising salesperson Jonathon Blount, and photographer and writer Gordon Parks—created Hollingsworth Group in 1969.

The new firm began working on the development of the first general interest magazine targeting African American women. To launch operations, the partners used their own savings and asked friends and family members for loans. Freedom National Bank, based in New York City, was the first organization to fund the new company, offering $13,000 in startup capital. In addition, a consortium of banks and venture capitalists willing to invest in a minority venture loaned Hollingsworth Group $130,000. Eventually, the new firm secured $1.87 million in loans from Equitable Life Assurance Society of the United States and other investors.

The first issue of *Essence* was published in 1970. The magazine's pages numbered roughly 100, 13 of which contained advertising. At a price of 60 cents each, Hollingsworth Group sold nearly 50,000 copies of the new publication. In 1971, Marcia Ann Gillespie took over as editor-in-chief, a role she would retain for nine years, despite various shifts in the firm's management. Hollingsworth Group was renamed Essence Communications early in the decade, following a management restructuring that left Lewis serving as both chairperson and publisher and Smith acting as president. In 1977, Hollingsworth, Parks, and Blount filed suit against Essence Communications in an effort to gain control of the firm; after three years of legal wrangling, Essence neared bankruptcy, and the trio dropped their suit. However, legal fees had cost nearly $2 million, and as a result, the firm was unable to pay off its startup loans until the mid-1980s.

Throughout the 1970s, *Essence* covered general interest topics such as beauty, fashion, food, child rearing, and health. A fiction section included original works by African American writers like Maya Angelou, Toni Morrison, and Alice Walker. The magazine also addressed more controversial topics at the time, such as women's careers and political scandals. Circulation grew to 450,000 in 1975. The number of pages containing advertising grew from a total of 455 in 1974 to 884 in 1979. It was this increase in advertising revenues that allowed the magazine to achieve profitability in 1976. The firm itself turned its first profit in 1980 on sales of $14 million.

Susan L. Taylor took over as editor-in-chief in 1981. She expanded the magazine's target market to include African American males. Along with a new yearly issue devoted to men, *Essence* also launched a "Say, Brother" column, written by various African American men, in each issue. Sales grew to more than $20 million by the mid-1980s. The firm began publishing a mail-order catalog in conjunction with Hanover House Inc., and it also started to license the Essence name for products such as hosiery, eyeglasses, and lingerie. In 1983, Taylor began producing and hosting a television show that evolved into the first African American talk show to achieve national syndication in the United States. Two years later, Essence Communications acquired a stake in a New York-based television broadcaster. Eventually, a new subsidiary,

Essence Television Productions Inc., began to handle the firm's television production operations. The firm purchased a portion of Amistad Press, another black-owned publishing house, in 1987.

Essence Communications added to its holdings in 1992 with the purchase of *Income Opportunities*, a magazine targeting aspiring entrepreneurs. Estee Lauder began advertising in *Essence* in 1993. Monthly circulation reached 1 million the following year. It was during the early 1990s, that the Essence Television Productions Inc. subsidiary began producing the annual Essence Awards program. Essence Communications expanded its target market to include Hispanic women with the launch of *Latina* magazine in 1995. In conjunction with Golden Books, Essence Communications also began to develop children's books written by African American authors and illustrated by African American artists. To celebrate its 25th anniversary, the firm hosted the first annual Essence Musical Festival, which featured performances by the likes of Bill Cosby, Aretha Franklin, and Boyz II Men. More than 150,000 people attended the event, which garnered national press coverage.

Essence redesigned its look in 1997, increasing its existing content, adding new content, and boosting the number of advertisements on its pages. The magazine also raised its price from $2.50 to $2.75. In January of 2000, Monique Greenwood took over as editor-in-chief. She instituted another redesign of the magazine, adding special sections, such as bridal guides, to various issues of *Essence*. In November, Time Inc. acquired a 49 percent stake in Essence Communications. By then, Essence Communications had sold *Latina* and refocused solely on the African American market.

STRATEGY

To attract more advertisers in the early 1990s, Essence Communications put in place a market research strategy designed to bolster the firm's insistence that advertisements targeting minority groups were a good investment for various businesses. To this end, the firm created focus groups of *Essence* readers who completed extensive surveys about what types of products and services they purchased. The firm also began hosting various events, such as free mall tours which provided attendees with free samples of products from various advertisers, as well as seminars on topics such as fitness, spirituality, and beauty.

Efforts to attract new advertisers continued into the early 2000s. New editor-in-chief Monique Greenwood decided to increase fashion and beauty coverage, hoping to attract apparel and cosmetics makers. The strategy paid off when Estee Lauder upped its advertising with the magazine; firms like L'Oreal and Jaguar began to purchase adds as well. In 2000, Time Inc. acquired 49 percent of Essence Communications. According to a January 2002

FAST FACTS:
About Essence Communications Inc.

Ownership: Essence Communications Inc. is a privately held company. Time Inc. owns a 49 percent stake in the firm.

Officers: Edward Lewis, Chmn., CEO, and Publisher; Clarence Smith, Pres.; Barbara Britton, Dir. of Advertising

Employees: 178

Principal Subsidiary Companies: Essence Communications operates offices in Atlanta, Georgia; Chicago, Illinois; Detroit, Michigan; Los Angeles, California; and New York City.

Chief Competitors: Major rivals of Essence Communications include Johnson Publishing, publisher of *Ebony* and *Jet*, Vanguarde Media Inc., and other publishers of minority focused magazines.

issue of *Mediaweek*, Essence Communications planned to "reap the benefits of its new partner's consumer-marketing muscle and ad-sales savvy." In early 2002, the firm also began to make use of the subscription fulfillment and distribution services in place at Time Inc.

PRODUCTS

Along with its flagship product, *Essence* magazine, Essence Communications also sells art reproductions, books, hosiery, and apparel for African American women. Most non-magazine sales take place via the firm's mail-order catalog.

EMPLOYMENT

The work environment at Essence Communications is casual and boisterous, according to *Folio: the Magazine for Magazine Management*. The firm does face issues of high turnover because it can't offer pay comparable to what some larger publishing companies offer. Benefits include healthcare coverage, profit sharing, management bonuses, and paid vacations. Hours are fairly unpredictable as no fixed schedule is in place.

CHRONOLOGY:

Key Dates for Essence Communications, Inc.

1969: Hollingsworth Group is founded

1970: The first issue of *Essence* is published

1981: Susan L. Taylor takes over as editor-in-chief of *Essence*

1984: Essence begins licensing its name for various products

1994: Monthly circulation exceeds 1 million for the first time. Essence begins producing the Essence Awards

1995: Essence hosts the first Essence Music Festival in New Orleans, Louisiana

2000: Time Inc. acquires 49 percent of Essence Communications

MINORITY ADVERTISING GROWS AFTER RACISM IS EXPOSED

Minority media firms like Essence Communications began to see their advertising revenues grow in the late 1990s after the racist advertising tactics of Katz Media Group were made public. An internal Katz Media memo discouraged salespersons from placing advertisements with minority media outlets, explaining that advertisers wanted "prospects, not suspects." This revelation validated the complaints of many minority media firms, who had insisted for years that national advertisers avoided advertising their products with minority publications, radio stations, etc. due to racist beliefs about the populations those media outlets targeted. According to Valerie Block, writing in *Crain's New York Business*, the incident "embarrassed national advertisers, which were forced to face deep-seated prejudices and pony up with advertising buys."

SOURCES OF INFORMATION

Bibliography

Block, Valerie. "Advertising Darlings: Amid Slump, Ethnic Media Continues Climb." *Crain's New York Business*, 3 September 2001.

"Corporate Culture: Essence Communications Inc." *Folio: the Magazine for Magazine Management*, 1 December 2001.

"Essence Communications, Inc." *International Directory of Company Histories.* Detroit: Gale Research, 1998.

Essence Communications Inc. Home Page, 2002. Available at http://www.essence.com.

Granatstein, Lisa. "All in Good Time." *Mediaweek*, 7 January 2002.

Lefevre, Lori. "Essence Plans to Branch Out." *Mediaweek*, 16 October 2000.

For additional industry research:

Investigate companies by their Standard Industrial Classification Codes, also known as SICs. Essence Communications' primary SIC is:

2721 Periodicals Publishing & Printing

Also investigate companies by their North American Industrial Classification System codes, also known as NAICS codes. Essence Communications' primary NAICS code is:

511120 Periodical Publishers

E*TRADE Group Inc.

OVERVIEW

Considered a pioneer in online trading, E*TRADE Group Inc. operates as a leading online brokerage as well as a diversified financial services firm with nearly 3.5 million active brokerage accounts. Through the E*TRADE Financial brand name, the company offers its retail customers banking, lending, planning, and advice services. In the United States, the firm offers corporate services such as employee stock plan administration and market-making services to brokerage firms. E*TRADE also offers securities brokerage products to its global customers, mainly in Europe, Asia, and South Africa. Strategic moves in the early 2000s include diversifying financial product and service offerings and continuing global expansion. The company has also cut costs and restructured various operations to combat falling revenues in its online trading business.

As part of its restructuring, the firm streamlined its financial services businesses into four main segments in 2001. Through its Domestic Retail Brokerage unit, which includes subsidiary E*TRADE Securities, the firm offers fully-automated stock, option, fixed income, and mutual fund order processing. It provides these services 24 hours a day, seven days a week through the Internet, automated telephone service, direct modem access, Internet-enabled wireless devices, live telephone support, and through the E*TRADE Financial Centers. E*TRADE's Banking segment is the largest Internet bank in the United States with 490,913 accounts at the end of 2001. The Bank offers a wide variety of consumer banking products and services. E*TRADE Access Inc., the firm's ATM network, and E*TRADE Mortgage Corp., a mortgage banking subsidiary, are operated as part of the Banking segment.

Contact Information:
HEADQUARTERS: 4500 Bohannon Dr.
    Menlo Park, CA 94025
PHONE: (650)331-6000
FAX: (650)331-6804
URL: http://www.etrade.com

FINANCES:
E*TRADE Group Revenues, 1997-2000 (million dollars)

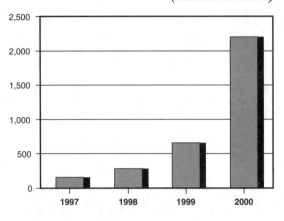

As an Internet-based company, E*TRADE has also seen its stock price rise and fall dramatically. Its low in 1999 hit $2.50 per share, while its high reached $72.25. In 2000, the firm's stock price ranged from $13.13 to $40 per share. It continued to fluctuate throughout 2001 and was trading between $8 and $9 per share in early 2002.

ANALYSTS' OPINIONS

E*TRADE has experienced a varying degree of success. Its stock price soared during 1999, but fell off dramatically in 2000 as the Internet industry became volatile. The firm's dependence on its online trading business hurt profits, and most analysts applaud the company's new strategy of acquisition and expansion into different financial services. Standard & Poor's believes that the firm's cost cutting measures, its emergence in new lines of business, and an improving economy should result in higher revenues and profits in the early 2000s. A November 2001 *Value Line Investment Survey* suggested that E*TRADE stock remained better suited to high risk investors due the instability in the Internet industry.

The company's third business segment, Global and Institutional, is comprised of E*TRADE Institutional and E*TRADE Technologies Corp. and its international affiliates. The focus of this unit is to develop and launch an electronic trading platform for institutional investors. The company also provides U.S. equities to its customers in foreign countries in real-time via the Internet. All other emerging E*TRADE businesses fall into the Wealth Management and Other segment. This division includes its mutual fund operations, and subsidiaries E*TRADE Business Solutions Group Inc., E*TRADE Advisory Services, and Electronic Investing Corp. (eInvesting). This unit also provides services related to corporate stock option programs, college savings plans, electronic advice, and money management.

HISTORY

In just 20 years, E*TRADE has grown from a $15,000 startup to a diversified financial services firm serving more than 3,000,000 households. Its roots date back to 1982, when William Porter established TradePlus to provide electronic brokerage services to stockbrokers. That year, the new company partnered with C.D. Anderson & Co. to develop a computerized order entry system. The system went online in July 1983, when the first online trade was completed.

For the remainder of the 1980s, the company marketed its services to discount brokers. Porter, however, was not satisfied and continued to develop new business plans. He had long been wary of paying high broker fees and set out to create a low-cost online trading venue for individual investors like himself. In 1992, he launched E*TRADE Securities Inc. as one of the first electronic discount brokerage service firms that offered flat rate fees and free information online through America Online and Compuserve. By 1993 revenues had reached $2 million.

COMPANY FINANCES

Most of E*TRADE's sales stem from its U.S. domestic retail brokerage operations. Over the past several years, E*TRADE's revenues have increased dramatically, growing from $285 million in 1998, to $662.3 million in 1999, to $2.2 billion in 2000. During 2001, however, E*TRADE's sales fell 7 percent to $2.0 billion. Net income has fluctuated since 1997, when the firm posted a gain of $13.9 million. In 1998 and 1999, E*TRADE reported losses. Net income bounced back to $19.2 million in 2000, but the firm reported a loss of $241.5 million in 2001, due in part to restructuring charges.

In 1994 the company adopted the E*TRADE Group name. Revenues continued to climb to $11 million, making it the fastest-growing private firm in the United States. In 1996, Christos Cotsakos was named president and CEO of the company. That year, E*TRADE went public and launched its own site, etrade.com. Revenues jumped to $52 million, and the firm experienced a dramatic increase in trading volume. The system crashed in May of that year due to the increased volume, and

E*TRADE paid out over $1.7 million to compensate its customers for the downtime. Initial problems like these proved short-lived, and E*TRADE entered a period of dramatic growth as the popularity of the Internet grew at breakneck speed. The company began to forge partnerships with the likes of Yahoo! and America Online to promote its online trading services. In 1997, E*TRADE handled the initial public offering (IPO) of Sportline USA Inc. The firm also began its global expansion, focusing on Australia, Canada, Germany, Israel, and Japan.

Towards the end of the 1990s and into the new millennium, E*TRADE began to expand its offerings and also made key acquisitions. It purchased TIR Holdings Ltd., a firm dealing with multiple currencies. In 1999, revenues increased by over 132 percent to $662.3 million. During 2000, the firm acquired Telebanc Financial Corp., Versus Technologies, Card Capture Services Inc., and Electronic Investing Corp. That year, the company launched E*TRADE Bank, an online bank offering a variety of services to consumers.

During 2001 E*TRADE continued to diversify its products and services due in part to the fallout in the dotcom industry. Having relied heavily on its online trading revenues, the firm looked for new opportunities to stabilize its earnings. It moved from the NASDAQ to the New York Stock Exchange that year and continued making acquisitions, including online mortgage originator LoansDirect (renamed E*TRADE Mortgage), PrivateAccounts Inc. (renamed E*TRADE Advisory Services), and online brokerage firm Web Street Inc. The purchase of Dempsey & Company LLC, a market-making services firm, enabled E*TRADE to handle all aspects of equity trading.

FAST FACTS:
*About E*TRADE Group Inc.*

Ownership: E*TRADE is a public company traded on the New York Stock Exchange.

Ticker Symbol: ET

Officers: Christos M. Cotsakos, Chmn. and CEO, 52, 2001 base salary $575,000; Jerry Gramaglia, Pres. and Chief Customer Operations Officer, 45, 2001 base salary $339,904; Leonard C. Purkis, CFO and CAO, 52; Amy J. Erret, Chief Asset Gathering Officer, 42

Employees: 3,495

Principal Subsidiary Companies: E*TRADE and its subsidiary companies operate in North America, Latin America, the Asia Pacific region, Europe, Africa, and the Middle East. Its major subsidiary companies are E*TRADE Securities Inc., TIR Ltd. Holdings, E*TRADE Financial Corp., and E*TRADE Bank.

Chief Competitors: As a diversified financial services holding company, E*TRADE competes with firms that provide investing, investment planning and advice, banking, and lending services to retail, corporate, and institutional clients. Major rivals include Ameritrade Holding Co., The Charles Schwab Corp., and TD Waterhouse Group Inc.

STRATEGY

During E*TRADE's short history, its strategy has focused on growth via the use of cutting edge technology. When the hype surrounding dot-com startups began to die in 2000, however, E*TRADE was forced to retool its products and services to decrease its dependency on online trading revenues. By 2002, the firm's strategy included seeking out opportunities to promote product and revenue diversification. E*TRADE launched several new tools on its Web site; expanded through acquisition into a wide variety of financial services including banking, lending, and investment planning and advice; and opened E*TRADE Financial Centers in New York, Boston, Beverly Hills, Denver, and San Francisco. The firm also developed a global homepage in 2001 and continued to utilize its technology platforms to enable international clients to trade U.S. stocks in real-time. As part of its strategy to promote its new offerings, the company launched the E*TRADE Financial brand in February

2002 to reflect its commitment to offering diversified financial services to its customers.

CURRENT TRENDS

One trend that greatly influenced E*TRADE's product development strategy was a growing demand for "one-stop shopping" financial services. According to an October 2001 *Forbes* article, "consumers are drowning in seven to ten financial relationships apiece: a bank around the corner, a mortgage lender across the country, a credit card issuer in Delaware and so on. Few investors can see the whole pie." To solve this problem, E*TRADE worked to diversify its services, as well as the ways in which its customers could access those services. In fact, E*TRADE's mission—to enable its customers to have access to their financial information

CHRONOLOGY:
*Key Dates for E*TRADE*

THE FIRST ONLINE TRADE

1982: William Porter establishes TradePlus

1983: The system goes online

1992: E*TRADE Securities begins to offer online investing services

1994: The company adopts the name E*TRADE Group

1996: Christos Cotsakos is named president and CEO; the firm goes public

2000: E*TRADE Bank is established

A doctor in Michigan placed the first online trade in July 1983, using early E*TRADE technology developed by inventor and physicist William Porter. With just $15,000 in capital, Porter created TradePlus, the predecessor to E*TRADE, to provide online quotes and trading services to brokerage firms. Shortly afterwards, Porter recognized the opportunity to create a company that would provide online trading services to individuals and save them hundreds of dollars in broker fees. Porter's dream turned into a reality as the proliferation of home computers and the increasing popularity of the Internet helped transform E*TRADE into a leading online financial services firm.

anytime, anywhere, and on any device-was related directly to this trend.

PRODUCTS

E*TRADE offers its investment clients automated order placement and execution of market and limit equity orders, streaming quotes and advanced trading platforms, personalized portfolio tracking, charting and quote applications, access to mutual funds, bond trading, money management, IRA and college saving plan products, real-time market commentary, quotes, news, and professional research reports. The firm's banking services include money market and savings accounts, checking accounts, funds transfer, electronic bill payment, and ATM access. Its lending services provide clients access to mortgages and mortgage refinancing and home equity loans. The company also provides a variety of investment planning and advice services.

To market its various products and launch its new brand, E*TRADE Financial, the firm began offering its services through financial centers in several large cities and also in "financial zones" that it opened in 18 Target stores in six states during 2001. Known for its aggressive advertising campaigns, the firm continued to market its products heavily via television and newspaper, despite a drop in advertising by most dot-com firms. In fact, the company paid $10 million in advertising fees during the Super Bowl in 2002. It sponsored the half-time show, ran commercials, and offered cushions emblazoned with the E*TRADE logo to fans.

CORPORATE CITIZENSHIP

E*TRADE established the E*SPIRIT Giving Program to provide financial and business resources to nonprofit organizations in local communities. The program offers grants to help fund organizations that share E*TRADE's vision. The grants support organizations and programs that promote education related to the Internet.

GLOBAL PRESENCE

The company's global activity is part of its Global and Institutional business segment. Through its international subsidiaries, E*TRADE offers foreign investors online retail brokerage services and also provides services to institutional investors. By 1998, the company had clients in Australia, Canada, Germany, Israel, and Japan. The company continued its international expansion during 2001 by launching branded retail brokerage Web sites in Hong Kong, Israel, and Germany. The firm also developed a Web-based platform that provided global institutional clients online trading and administrative services. The company's global strategy includes promoting cross-border trading, promoting its financial products to foreign investors, and enabling foreign retail investors affordable access to U.S. equities in real-time via online avenues.

SOURCES OF INFORMATION

Bibliography

Bills, Steve. "4 Q Earnings: New Mix Paid Off in 2001." *American Banker*, 16 January 2002.

Carey, Theresa W. "Wild Wide on the Web." *Barron's*, 18 March 2002.

*E*TRADE Home Page*, 2002. Available at http://www.etrade.com.

Helyar, John. "At E*TRADE, Growing Up Is Hard to Do." *Fortune*, 18 March 2002.

"Internet Investment Survey." *The Value Line Investment Survey*, 30 November 2001.

Weinberg, Neil. "After the Bubble." *Forbes*, 1 October 2001.

For an annual report:

write: E*TRADE Group, 4500 Bohannon Dr., Menlo Park, CA 94025

For additional industry research:

Investigate companies by their Standard Industrial Classification Codes, also known as SICs. E*TRADE's primary SIC is:

6211 Security Brokers, Dealers, and Flotation Companies

Also investigate companies by their North American Industrial Classification System codes, also known as NAICS codes. E*TRADE's primary NAICS codes are:

523110 Investment Banking and Securities Dealing

523120 Securities Brokerage

Expedia Inc.

FOUNDED: 1996

Contact Information:

HEADQUARTERS: 13810 SE Eastgate Way, Suite 400
    Bellevue, WA 98005
PHONE: (425)564-7200
FAX: (425)564-7240
URL: http://www.expedia.com

OVERVIEW

In the highly competitive travel industry, Expedia operates as a leading provider of branded online travel services for both leisure and small business customers. Through its Web site, the company offers travel and reservation services; real-time access to schedules; and pricing and availability information for over 450 airlines, 65,000 lodging properties, and for all of the major car rental firms.

By 1999, over 1.2 million customers had utilized Expedia's services and had booked nearly $1 billion in airline tickets, and hotel and car reservations. The company also was the most visited travel site according to Jupiter Media Metrix, securing 3.3 million unique visitors each month. In 2001, the company reported gross bookings of $2.9 billion.

Expedia acts as both an agent and a merchant. As an agent, the company forwards the customers' reservations to the travel supplier, who then pays a commission to Expedia. The supplier determines the retail price that is paid by the consumer. As a merchant, Expedia purchases inventories of hotel rooms, airline seats, car rentals, and destination services from suppliers at negotiated rates. The company then sells this inventory to its customers at its own price.

COMPANY FINANCES

Expedia's revenue from agency operations was $24.7 million in 1999, $59.5 million in 2000, and $123 million in 2001. Its merchant business secured $10.9 million in 2000 and $64.5 million in 2001. Overall sales for 2001 reached $222 million, an increase of 64.7 percent over the previous year.

By 2001, the company had yet to post a positive net income, with losses ranging from $19.6 million in 1999, to $118.3 million in 2000, and $78.1 million in 2001. The company did report its first net profit of $5.2 million for the quarter ending in December 2001. During 2001, Expedia's stock price ranged from a low of $7.75 per share to a high of $47.70 per share. As part of its financial strategy, Expedia is increasing its merchant business, which produce larger gross profits per transaction than agency operations.

ANALYSTS' OPINIONS

The online travel industry recovered quickly from both the economic slowdown that began in 2000, as well as the events of September 11, 2001. A money manager at Baron Capital claimed in an April 2002 *Business Week* article that "the speed with which those businesses bounced back surprised even the people most bullish about the sector." Expedia not only successfully weathered the downturn; it was actually able to increase its market share and become the leading online travel company based on customers, revenues, and market capitalization.

The travel industry remained highly competitive during 2002, and large online travel firms including Expedia and competitor Travelocity fared well despite price wars. In fact, according to Web measurement firm, Score Networks Inc., many U.S. online travel sites recorded their highest monthly sales and site traffic in January 2002. Jupiter Media Metrix predicted that the online travel industry would grow to $50 billion by 2005, up from $31 billion projected in 2002. Despite the positive industry outlook and Expedia's market leadership, Expedia's stock, considered Internet-related, was deemed high risk by Standard & Poor's (S&P) In fact, S&P listed the stock as a hold and predicted that it would not see significant growth during 2002.

HISTORY

In October of 1996, Microsoft Corp. launched an online travel service. Revenues from this operation reached $2.7 million in 1997 and grew to $13.8 million in 1998. The company was incorporated as Expedia Inc. in August 1999. Three months later, Microsoft sold 18 percent of the company through an initial public offering.

Expedia grew in popularity and evolved quickly into a premier online travel site. During 2000, the company expanded with the purchases of Travelscape.com Inc. and VacationSpot.com Inc. The acquisitions gave the firm an

FINANCES:
Expedia Inc.
Revenues, 1998-2001
(million dollars)

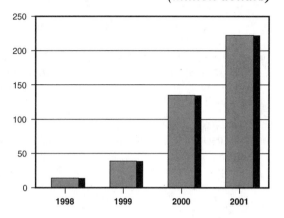

Expedia Inc.
2001 Stock Prices

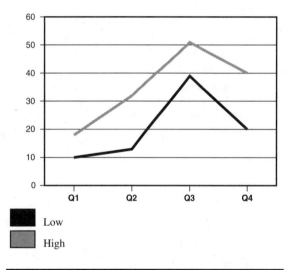

edge in both travel planning services and lodging selection. That year, revenues climbed to $134.9 million.

By 2001, the firm was operating travel Web sites for consumers in Canada, Germany, and the United Kingdom. It also began operating a private label travel Web site under the Worldwide Technology Enterprises (WWTE) name. In a partnership with SNCF, a state-owned railways group in France, Expedia began providing travel planning services on the Voyages-scnf.com Web site.

Expedia continued growing in 2002 with the purchase of Classic Custom Vacations Inc., a luxury vacation

FAST FACTS:
About Expedia Inc.

Ownership: Expedia is a public company traded on the NASDAQ Stock Exchange. USA Networks Inc. owns approximately 65 percent of the company's outstanding shares.

Ticker Symbol: EXPE

Officers: Richard N. Barton, Dir., Pres., and CEO; Gregory S. Stanger, SVP, CFO, and Dir.; Byron D. Bishop, SVP Transportation and Core Technologies; Erik C. Balchford, SVP Marketing and Programming; Kathleen K. Dellpain, SVP Human Resources

Employees: 896

Principal Subsidiary Companies: Expedia and its subsidiaries operate travel Web sites in the United States, Canada, Germany, and the United Kingdom. Two of the company's subsidiaries, Travelscape .com Inc. and VacationSpot.com Inc., offer travel planning services in the aforementioned countries and in France, Italy, and the Netherlands.

Chief Competitors: As the leading online travel service provider, Expedia competes with both online and traditional travel agencies and travel consortiums including Orbitz and Hotwire. Its primary competitors are Travelocity, Lowestfare.com, and American Express.

packages provider. In February of that year, USA Networks purchased a controlling interest in Expedia from Microsoft. While competition in the online travel industry remained intense, Expedia's management felt the company was well positioned for future success.

STRATEGY

Expedia's early strategy included developing new technology that would allow online travel shoppers to access information quickly and with ease. As part of this strategy, the company launched the Expert Searching and Pricing (ESP) platform in January 2001. This technology granted Expedia customers a range of travel options, including enhanced flight search options and build-your-own vacation package capabilities.

CHRONOLOGY:
Key Dates for Expedia Inc.

1996: Microsoft creates an online travel service

1998: Early revenue grows to $13.8 million

1999: The company incorporates as Expedia Inc. and goes public

2000: Travelscape.com Inc. and VacationSpot.com Inc. are acquired

2002: USA Networks purchases a controlling interest in Expedia

Developing new technology continues to be at the forefront of the company's strategy, along with increasing brand awareness, converting shoppers to buyers, expanding product offerings in order to cross sell, and expanding globally. Driving these initiatives is the company's long-term goal to be the largest and most profitable provider of travel planning services in the world.

The company has formed strategic partnerships with the likes of MSN, Excite, and Amazon.com in an effort to build brand recognition. To entice shoppers, Expedia negotiates with suppliers to obtain competitive pricing and attractive travel options. To build its product offerings, the company has increased its destination offerings and add-on travel items to include in-destination tours, event and theme park tickets, ground transportation options, and parking and travel insurance. The firm's global strategy includes utilizing its technology platform to emerge in large, international markets.

CURRENT TRENDS

One trend directly affecting Expedia is the expanding consumer interest in online travel planning. The industry is expected to continue growing, and Expedia plans to fully exploit its leadership position by focusing on its merchant business operations. By acting as a merchant—rather than an agent—Expedia can offer its customers lower pricing. The company hopes these lower prices will entice the increasing number of Internet travel shoppers to use the Expedia Web site.

PRODUCTS

The Expedia Web site offers a host of travel services including airfare, hotel, rental car, vacation packages, cruise packages, and theme park tickets. In 2001, using its ESP platform, the company launched Expedia Vacations, a service that enables a customer to combine air and hotel bookings to create their own custom travel packages. The firm also began offering Expedia Bargain Fares (EBFs). These fares, negotiated rates with nearly 20 different airlines, are 10 to 60 percent below published rates. The EBF program allows consumers to see the price and date, but airlines and flight times are not disclosed until after the customer makes the purchase.

GLOBAL PRESENCE

Expedia's international operations accounted for $9.8 million in revenues during 2001. The company offers direct-to-consumer travel planning services to its international customers through its Web sites and telephone call centers. The company's global strategy is to increase the popularity of online travel planning in foreign countries and to build the Expedia brand name internationally by entering new markets. By 2002, the company had operations in the United Kingdom, Germany, Canada, France, the Netherlands, and Italy.

EMPLOYMENT

In 2002, the company employed nearly 900 workers. Expedia believes that its ability to attract and retain qualified and friendly employees is critical to its future success. The firm utilizes equity-based compensation programs to reward and motivate its employees.

SOURCES OF INFORMATION

Bibliography

Expedia Home Page, 2002. Available at http://www.expedia.com

WORK HARD.
PLAY HARD.

Expedia describes its work environment as vibrant, energetic, and dynamic, and prides itself on its friendly and down-to-earth management staff. As a survivor of the dot-com fallout, Expedia works hard at fostering a team spirit throughout all facets of company operations, whether it be its cutting edge technology development department or its employee soccer team.

"Expedia's Magic Act." *Travel Weekly*, 18 March 2002.

Michels, Jennifer. "Expedia's Future." *Travel Agent*, 4 March 2002.

Oser, Kris. "Survivor Tale." *Direct*, 1 November 2001.

Zellner, Wendy. "Online Travel Takes Wing." *Business Week*, 1 April 2002.

For an annual report

write: Expedia Inc., 13810 SE Eastgate Way, Suite 400, Bellevue, WA 98005

For additional industry research:

Investigate companies by their Standard Industrial Classification Codes, also known as SICs. Expedia Inc.'s primary SICs are:

4724 Travel Agencies

4729 Arrangement of Passenger Transport, NEC

Also investigate companies by their North American Industry Classification System codes, also known as NAICS codes. Expedia Inc.'s primary NAICS codes are:

561510 Travel Agencies

561599 All Other Travel Arrangement and Reservation Services

ExxonMobil Corporation

FOUNDED: 1882

VARIANT NAME: Formerly Exxon Corporation and
previously named Standard Oil of New Jersey

Contact Information:

HEADQUARTERS: 5959 Las Colinas Blvd.
  Irving, TX 75039-2298
PHONE: (972)444-1000
FAX: (972)444-1882
URL: http://www.exxon.com

Exxon stands as the number two company in the United States after Wal-Mart, according to Fortune 500, but the Global 500 ranks it number one. After the merger with Mobil in 1999, the company became the number one oil and gas producer in the world, eclipsing the giant British Petroleum. The company owns more than 40,000 gas stations in 118 countries and does business in nearly 200 countries. It has dozens of refineries with a total capacity of 6 million barrels a day, and it is involved in selling and producing petrochemicals, and mining coal and other minerals.

The 1989 Exxon *Valdez* oil tanker spill in Prince William Sound, Alaska, tarnished the company's reputation for years and brought financial headaches after a punitive damages fine of $5 billion was levied. Recovering from that disaster, the company has been looking to expand its power generation business in China. It also has been putting massive funds into its refining and retail businesses in the Asia/Pacific region by expanding operations in Japan, Malaysia, Singapore, and Thailand. Many of the areas where ExxonMobil elects to do business are in volatile areas of the world where rebel insurrections, government coups, and even widespread killings are commonalities.

In a powerful 2001 speech given to an audience of international business leaders, Renè Dahan, director and EVP, presented a sober analysis of what it is like for a company to seek profits in global hotspots such as the once infamous killing fields of Chad: "Business has had a hand in improving the condition of local people, and we have repeatedly seen an improvement in condition go hand in hand with a reduction in the resort to violence.

We have helped the situation, in my view, by staying away from a highly political role, by avoiding religious bias, by guarding against moral arrogance, and by treating people fairly and equally. We have been particularly effective in those places where we could use our leverage to promote better national policies. We have been successful also through our determination not to compromise our key values. We have achieved progress where we have been willing to take a leadership role. We have seen conflict deterred by good corporate citizenship and a recognized value to the nation from our operations. We have found that partnership with other international parties, including the World Bank, has been of significant benefit. When we are successful in our business, it provides a clear demonstration to everyone of the benefits that arise from a focus on economic efficiency and the application of advanced technology. And it also tells people in troubled societies that progress is possible, perhaps only possible, where individual differences are tolerated and the skills of all are used."

COMPANY FINANCES

After years of profit, the company endured some short-term sputtering in the new century, particularly after air and auto travelers stayed home in droves following the September 11, 2001, terrorist attacks. In late April 2002, ExxonMobil disclosed that its first quarter 2002 earnings of $2.15 billion had fallen $730 million from final quarter 2001 earnings of $2.88 billion, well below the $2.9 billion recorded the first quarter of 2001. ExxonMobil calculated that it would return to normal profits and better refining margins before the end of 2002 as the U.S. economy, in particular, steadily climbed toward recovery.

Hampering global recovery was the complete collapse of the economic system and devaluation of the peso in Argentina in 2001 and 2002. Also hurting Exxon and other large oil companies was the month-long end of oil exports from Iraq as Saddam Hussein protested the Israeli invasion of Palestinian territory in the West Bank. Consequently, in May 2002, ExxonMobil stock was valued at $36 a share.

ANALYSTS' OPINIONS

Analyst John Hervey of Donaldson, Lufkin, & Jenrette summed up the value of ExxonMobil stock, "The company offers one of the best and most consistent return records in the oil industry." Much of the controversy surrounding the ExxonMobil Corporation has not been its financial condition, but rather its handling of the Exxon *Valdez* oil spill. The March 24, 1989, mishap resulted in a $5-billion fine from the courts, which eventually was ruled too high by an appeals court, leading to specula-

FAST FACTS:
About ExxonMobil Corporation

Ownership: ExxonMobil Corporation is a publicly owned company traded on the New York Stock Exchange.

Ticker Symbol: XON

Officers: Lee R. Raymond, Chmn., Pres., and CEO, 64, 2001 salary $2,850,000, 2001 bonus $2,700,000, stock options $16,400,000; Renè; Dahan, Dir. and EVP, 60, $4,500,000; Harry J. Longwell, EVP and Operations Mgr., Production Dept., 60, $4,500,000

Employees 99,600

Principal Subsidiary Companies: ExxonMobil's chief subsidiaries include Natuna gas field (50 percent ownership); ExxonMobil China Inc.; ExxonMobil Coal and Minerals Company; ExxonMobil Company International; ExxonMobil Company U.S.A.; ExxonMobil Computing Services Company; ExxonMobil Exploration Company; ExxonMobil Production Research Company; ExxonMobil Research and Engineering Company; ExxonMobil Upstream Technical Computing Company; Exxon Mobil Upstream Development Company; ExxonMobil Ventures, Inc. (CIS); ExxonMobil Chemical Company; Imperial Oil Limited; and SeaRiver Maritime Financial Holdings.

Chief Competitors: Some of ExxonMobil's primary competitors are Amerada Hess; Ashland; ARCO; British Petroleum; Broken Hill; Caltex Petroleum; Chevron; Dow Chemical; Eastman Chemical; Elf Aquitaine; FINA; Huntsman; Imperial Oil; Koch; Norsk Hydro; Occidental; PDVSA; PEMEX; Pennzoil; Petrobras; Phillips Petroleum; Royal Dutch/Shell; Sun; Texaco; Tosco; Total and Union Carbide.

tion in the news media that the fine might be reduced to less than $1.65 billion. The National Transportation Safety Board found that the cause of the spill was neglect of the third mate to appropriately manipulate the ship due to extreme exhaustion and his heavy workload. The cause most people recall was the intoxication of the master on board, placed in charge of an oil-loaded vessel. By January 2002, although ExxonMobil had yet to pay punitive damages, it had substantially recovered many customers

CHRONOLOGY:

Key Dates for ExxonMobil Corporation

1882: Incorporates as the Standard Oil Company of New Jersey

1899: Standard Oil (New Jersey) becomes the sole holding company for all Standard Oil interests

1911: The Supreme Court orders Standard Oil (New Jersey) to separate from its subsidiaries

1919: Standard (Jersey) purchases 50 percent of Humble Oil & Refining, the biggest of Standard's suppliers

1926: Standard (Jersey) introduces the Esso brand name

1931: The Socony-Vacuum Corporation, with roots tracing back to the Standard Oil breakup, merge. Their emblem is the winged horse Pegasus, used in the 1800s as a logo by Standard Oil

1948: Purchases 30 percent ownership of Arabian American Oil Company

1954: Purchases a 7 percent interest of Iranian production, making Standard (New Jersey) the largest oil company in the world

1959: The "Put a Tiger in Your Tank" slogan begins this year as the brainstorm of a Chicago advertising writer for a northern Illinois Esso ad campaign. Subsequently, the Esso and Exxon tiger become one of the world's best-known trademark animals

1972: Exxon Corporation becomes the official name of the company

1989: The Exxon *Valdez* crashes off the coast of Alaska spilling 260,000 barrels of crude oil

1994: The company opens the first of its "On the Run" convenience stores

1996: Exxon announces a huge oil discovery in the Gulf of Mexico

1998: Exxon and Mobil merge. All but one of the merged companies' executives (Lucio A. Noto) come from Exxon, and Noto retires a few years after the merger

2001: ExxonMobil pays a $225,000 fine for a pipeline blast in Texas that killed a police officer

2002: ExxonMobil is rated the top company in America on the Global 500 list and number two on the Fortune 500 list, making it as powerful a corporate entity as its predecessor Standard Oil had been

lost after the *Valdez* incident, although some diehard activists have vowed to maintain a lifelong boycott. With BP and ConocoPhillips continuing to increase in size, few analysts expect ExxonMobil to remain complacent as its rivals kick and claw for market share.

Throughout the rest of the twenty-first century, therefore, consolidations are increasingly likely for such energy giants, noted oil and gas analyst John Thieroff of Standard and Poor's in a January 2002 issue of *Physicians Financial News*. Indeed, ExxonMobil already has acquired enough resources and wealth to a degree that Ida M. Tarbell, the early twentieth-century muckraker whose journalistic exposé of Standard Oil led to its forced dismantling by the government, could never have foreseen.

HISTORY

After forming the Standard Oil company in 1870, John D. Rockefeller created the Standard Oil Trust, which enabled the firm to establish new, independent companies in various states by dissolving existing Standard Oil associates. The Supreme Court, however, ordered these companies to be split into 34 entities since the Trust owned 90 percent of the petroleum industry. One of the split companies was New Jersey's Standard Oil (Jersey Standard). When Walter Teagle was president of Jersey Standard in 1917, he quietly bought half of Humble Oil of Texas and moved operations into South America. The company also participated in the Red Line Agreement in 1928, which designated most Middle East oil to selected companies. Other overseas ventures included the 1948 purchase of a 30 percent ownership in Arabian American Oil Company along with a 7 percent interest of Iranian production purchased in 1954. These two moves deemed Jersey Standard the biggest oil company in the world. When oil companies still using the Standard Oil name protested Jersey Standard's use of the name Esso, the company became Exxon in 1972. This change cost the company $100 million.

Other financial difficulties hit Exxon after the oil crisis of the 1970s, which quickly reduced its oil reserves. Exxon was hit hard again in 1989 when the *Valdez* oil tanker spilled 11 million gallons of oil into Alaskan waters. Shoveling out billions of dollars in cleanup costs, the company was called "reckless" by a federal jury in Alaska, but punitive damages were reduced late in 2001, minimizing loss to the company financially but little helping its reputation.

The 1990s were characterized mostly by expansion for the Exxon Corporation. The Natuna gas field was developed after Exxon and Pertamina, the Indonesia state oil company, agreed to terms, but civil revolt in Indonesia during the 2000s has made the country's oil fields a dangerous place to work. The company also agreed to a $15-billion development of three oil and natural gas fields near Sakhalin Island in Russia, and was able to entertain further expansion plans after it announced a large oil discovery in the Gulf of Mexico in 1996. In the 1990s the corporation elected to attempt the laying of a pipeline and exploration of oil fields in the midst of upheaval caused by rebels in the African nation of Chad. By the 2000s, the company could point with pride to the progress it had made, as well as quantify specific areas where residents of that nation had benefited from prosperity.

The most notable story in recent years has been Exxon's merger with Mobil, a business decision that certainly will predate other such mergers on the part of ExxonMobil, as well as its worldwide competitors such as BP. The difficult job of bringing a company back from the *Valdez* travesty, as well as the challenge of combining employees and resources with the giant Mobil, was generally handled quite well by Lee R. Raymond (chairman, president, and CEO). But Raymond, in 1998, strongly vowed to retire at 65, and so the best chairs on the corporate deck almost definitely will be reshuffled in a corporation whose top directors have most visibly been male.

STRATEGY

ExxonMobil's chairman, Lee Raymond, refers to the company's strategy in *Forbes* as "the relentless pursuit of efficiency." Reducing operating costs and focusing on return on capital have been core strategies for the company, as has been earning profits for the company and shareholders. ExxonMobil's exploration and production businesses have revolved around the following strategies as well: to make existing oil and gas production sites as profitable as possible, to invest only in projects that produce returns, and to profit from strengthening natural gas markets. Furthermore, in 2001, Renè Dahan, director and EVP, revealed yet another facet of company policy and strategy in a speech he delivered in Denver about the company's willingness and capacity to accept risks. "It is a sometimes forgotten, or possibly ignored, truth that if a company fails to respect the priorities and the values and the market focus that make it successful, then it will fail not only in its primary mission, it will also be unable to assist in other areas as well," he said. "When it comes to the role that my company or any company can play in addressing conflict, it will be recognized by all here that conflict and instability threaten not only the safety and well-being of nations but also the basic success of our business operations. Most companies, faced with an extremely difficult business environment, often choose to stay away rather than assume the risks inherent in latent or active conflicts. But while we all dislike instability and risk, we must remember that the ability of any company to deal successfully with these difficult conditions, and the risks they bring, can be a determining condition for its success. Good companies are not just risk takers; they must be good risk managers. They identify

and analyze risks and develop plans to deal with those risks if and when they materialize. This is part of our everyday job."

ExxonMobil's refining and marketing businesses have had strategies of their own. One ingredient has been the expansion in profitable, growing markets, like Asia-Pacific, civil war-torn Africa, Eastern Europe, and Latin America. A second strategy involved the company's restrictions on refining investments in markets that do not produce high growth. A third element has been the company's constant efforts to lower operating expenses and to refine production. ExxonMobil Corporation also has aimed to remain focused on research investment activities. Its merger with Mobil has shown that it is capable of making hard decisions about the futures of workers in the company it takes over, making cuts if those employees are deemed expendable.

INFLUENCES

Exxon appealed the $5 billion-fine assessed against it for the *Valdez* oil spill, and the company stored away that amount in case the appeal was lost, but in 2001 it became apparent following a court ruling that the amount of judgment was going to be billions less than at first thought. Additionally, falling oil prices and the reluctance of people to travel after September 2001 because of perceived dangers from terrorist attacks may cause ExxonMobil to cut its prices, which eventually should result in lower profits. Energy demand is decreasing, partially because of the unusually mild winters, while at the same time, oil supplies are increasing. Exxon estimates that crude oil use in Asia is going to increase dramatically, perhaps to exceed the combined use of crude oil in the United States and Europe; as a result, the company is pursuing expansion efforts in the Asian market, including the opening of a $2-billion petrochemical facility in Singapore.

CURRENT TRENDS

Formerly, Exxon stayed away from large investments in liquefied natural gas (LNG). Beginning in the late 1990s and throughout the 2000s, however, the company began pursuing LNG projects in Yemen and Indonesia. It also developed natural gas fields in Russia. Still recovering from a marred reputation after the *Valdez* disaster, the company launched a request to be allowed back into the same Alaskan waters it polluted in 1989, Prince William Sound. The ship, now renamed the SeaRiver Mediterranean, was prohibited from entering the waters after the spill by the Oil Pollution Act. The company's motivation for such a request stemmed from the fact that it was losing money operating the ship in

Europe and Egypt, where less expensive ships are readily available.

Another strategic move by ExxonMobil Corporation has been the introduction of its Tiger Express and On the Run retail stores. The stores offer customers a one-stop, so-called "multi-task" gas station shopping experience. Employees wear khaki pants and specially designed polo shirts. Other conveniences include a Taco Bell Express drive-through window, a Check Express check-cashing service, a service that allows customers to pay at the pumps, indoor bathroom facilities, diaper changing tables in men's and women's restrooms, and recorded music playing at the pumps and inside the store.

PRODUCTS

ExxonMobil's primary products are oil and gas, however, its chemical division also manufactures and sells plastics, synthetic rubbers, performance fluids, plasticizers, basic chemical building blocks, and lubricant and fuel additives.

CORPORATE CITIZENSHIP

ExxonMobil Corporation has launched several efforts in aiding the community and its environment. One such effort has been the financial contributions aimed at preventing the tiger, the company's symbol, from becoming extinct. It planned to donate approximately $5 million to support breeding efforts and zoo information displays and tiger projects in Siberia and Sumatra. Controversy surrounding Exxon's efforts has stemmed from accusations that the company has not addressed the real threats facing the extinction of tigers: poaching, illegal trade in tiger parts, and annihilation of the animals' prey by hunters. Some have said the company has no plans to enter anti-poaching efforts since such activities have been touchy in Asia, a large, fast-emerging market for ExxonMobil. Critics have said that without attention to the real dangers, the company's contributions will be of little value and that the tiger's disappearance from Western India, for example, is all but inevitable in the twenty-first century.

Other efforts to incorporate community involvement have included the company's efforts in education. Through the ExxonMobil Education Foundation, in 2002 alone it offered $16.1 million in grants to more than 800 institutions of higher learning. Under the Foundation's Educational Matching Gift Program, all employees' donations are then matched by ExxonMobil 3-to-1.

ExxonMobil has also provided assistance in the Ambassador Franklin Williams Scholarship Program from the Stevens Institute of Technology. Exxon gave

$1.5 million in grants within an eight-year period to award scholarships for minority students.

ExxonMobil has preserved the charitable interests formerly the main province of Mobil. One of these is the Genesis Fund of Boston, Massachusetts, which assists children born with physical and mental defects, and another is Paul Newman's Hole in the Wall Gang charities that assist children with life-threatening illnesses.

GLOBAL PRESENCE

ExxonMobil does business in nearly 200 countries. Exxon China Inc. is headquartered in Beijing. Activities there include exploration, refining, and marketing. Chemical and electric power businesses have been established there as well. ExxonMobil's Coal and Minerals Company is located in Colombia, the United States, and Australia. Also accountable for electrical generation capabilities in Hong Kong, the company conducts business in power generation and coal and mineral exploration. Europe, offshore Malaysia, and Australia serve as oil and gas production cites for ExxonMobil. One subsidiary, Exxon Ventures Inc., manages exploration and production activities in the former Soviet Union. The company runs offices in Baku, Azerbaijan; Almaty, Kazakstan; and Moscow, Yuzhno-Sakhalinsk, and Arkhangelsk, Russia. Another subsidiary, Imperial Oil Limited, stands as a leading member of the Canadian petroleum business. It has been Canada's largest crude oil producer and the biggest refiner and marketer of petroleum products.

EMPLOYMENT

Statistics show that ExxonMobil Corporation makes efforts to hire, retain, and promote minorities and women, although the very highest positions in the company following consolidation with Mobil were all male. In 2002 Lee Raymond stressed the importance of never overlooking any possible source of human talent, as well as the need for finding the best native people possible already living in the countries where ExxonMobil establishes or builds a business presence.

Two of the company's important philanthropies are the United Negro College Fund and the Hispanic Scholarship Fund. It also supports the efforts of the Society of Women Engineers to encourage female entry into the profession. ExxonMobil allies itself with the National Action Council for Minorities in Engineering (NACME), the Texas Alliance for Minorities in Engineering (TAME), and the National Society of Black Engineers. ExxonMobil also participates in university internship programs.

SOURCES OF INFORMATION

Bibliography

Armstrong, James. "Low Voltage for Energy Stocks." *Physicians Financial News*, 15 January 2002.

Clarke, Jim. "Exxon to Appeal $5 Billion Oil Spill Judgment." *San Diego Daily*, 13 February 1997.

Dupree, Jr., Thomas H. "Federal Court's Exxon Ruling Sets Punitive Damage Precedent." *Washington Legal Foundation*, 22 February 2002.

Exxon Corporation Home Page, 13 May 2002. Available at http://www.exxon.com.

The ExxonMobil Corporation Home Page, 13 May 2002. Available at http://www.exxonmobil.com.

"ExxonMobil Corp." *The Regulatory News Service*, 23 April 2002.

Galvin, Kevin. "Exxon Wants Exxon *Valdez* Allowed Back in Prince William Sound." *San Diego Daily*, 16 January 1997.

Kennett, Jim. "ExxonMobil Fined $225,000 in Texas Pipeline Blast." *Bloomberg News*, 6 November 2001.

Koenig, David. "Exxon Is Upbeat on Future; It Says Demand for Energy Will Revive As World Economy Recovers." *The Hamilton (Canada)Spectator*, 11 March 2002.

Mack, Toni. "The Tiger Is on the Prowl." *Forbes*, 21 April 1997.

Teitelbaum, Richard. "Giants of the Fortune 5 Hundred: Exxon: Pumping up Profits for Years." *Fortune*, 28 April 1997.

For an annual report:

on the Internet at: http://www.exxon.com

For additional industry research:

Investigate companies by their Standard Industrial Classification Codes, also known as SICs. ExxonMobil Corporation's primary SICs are:

1311 Crude Petroleum and Natural Gas

1382 Oil and Gas Exploration Services

2911 Petroleum Refining

5172 Petroleum Products, Not Elsewhere Classified

5541 Gasoline Service Stations

Also investigate companies by their North American Industry Classification System codes, also known as NAICS codes. ExxonMobil Corporation's primary NAICS codes are:

324110 Petroleum Refineries

422720 Petroleum and Petroleum Products (except Bulk Stations and Terminals) Wholesalers

447110 Gasoline Stations with Convenience Stores

Federated Department Stores Inc.

FOUNDED: 1929

Contact Information:

HEADQUARTERS: 7 W. Seventh St.
   Cincinnati, OH 45202
PHONE: (513)579-7000
FAX: (513)579-7555
TOLL FREE: (800)261-5385
URL: http://www.federated-fds.com

OVERVIEW

One of the largest department store retailers in the United States, Federated operates more than 450 stores in 34 states, Guam, and Puerto Rico. In 2001 the firm's largest division, Macy's East, operated 115 stores in the eastern U.S. and Puerto Rico and brought in roughly $5 billion in revenues. The 138 stores operated by Macy's West spanned the western half of the nation, as well as Guam; sales for that division totaled $4.1 billion. Rich's/Lazarus/Goldsmith's generated sales of more than $2 billion and operated 76 stores, 44 of which were Lazarus units, 26 of which were Rich's units, and six of which were Goldsmith's units. The firm's 26 Bloomingdale's stores, scattered throughout the United States, garnered another $1.6 billion in revenues. The Florida-based Burdines chain operated 55 stores and secured sales of nearly $1.4 billion. Federated's smallest division, the Bon Marche, operated 47 stores in the northwestern United States and posted sales of $967 million. In addition to its retail outlets, Federated is also sells merchandise via its macys.com Web site and its Bloomingdale's By Mail catalog business.

COMPANY FINANCES

Total revenues for Federated fell from $18.4 billion in 2000 to $15.6 billion in 2001. Losses of $184 million in 2000 grew to $276 million in 2001. The firm's last profitable year had been 1999, when earnings reached $795 million on sales of $17.7 billion, resulting in a profit margin of 4.5 percent. Earnings per share that year had been $3.62.

In 2000, feminine accessories, such as intimate apparel, shoes, and cosmetics, accounted for 30 percent of Federated's revenues. Women's apparel secured 26 percent; men's and children's apparel and accessories, 23 percent; and home and miscellaneous merchandise, 21 percent.

ANALYSTS' OPINIONS

Despite falling sales and mounting losses in 2001, many analysts continued to look favorably on Federated's outlook for 2002. A significant portion of the firm's losses in 2001 were related to shuttered operations, such as Fingerhut and Stern's. According to ABN AMRO analyst Christine Kilton-Augustine, as quoted in a February 2002 issue of *WWD*, Federated "has the most potential among the traditional department store group for margin expansion." When Federated predicted in early 2002 that its earnings per share would rebound to $3.30 that year, stock prices rose 6.8 percent to $41.66 per share.

FINANCES:
Federated Department Stores, Inc.
Revenues, 1999-2001
(million dollars)

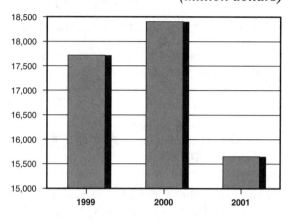

HISTORY

Federated Department Stores was created in 1929 to act as a holding company for three family-owned departments stores: Brooklyn, New York-based Abraham & Straus, founded in 1865; Columbus, Ohio-based F&R Lazarus & Co., founded in 1851; and Cincinnati, Ohio-based Shillito's, founded in 1830. Federated acquired the Bloomingdale's chain in 1930. Sales that year, the firm's first full year of operations, reached $112 million.

In 1939, Federated's chairman, Fred Lazarus, convinced U.S. President Franklin D. Roosevelt to move the Thanksgiving holiday from the last Thursday of November to the fourth Thursday of November, a change with lengthened the Christmas shopping season. The following year, the firm began to extend credit to its customers. In the mid-1940s, Shillito's became the first U.S. store to offer credit to African Americans, as well as the first to employ African American salespeople and executives. Federated acquired Burdines of Miami in 1956.

Growth continued in 1959 with purchase of two department stores, Rike's and Goldsmith's. Sales exceeded $1 billion for the first time in 1964. Four years later, Abraham & Straus created Black Retail Action Group to offer financial assistance to minority-owned businesses and African American students studying retailing. By the mid-1970s, Federated operated more than 240 stores, and revenues have exceeded $3 billion. The firm added Rich's, the largest department store in Atlanta, to its holdings.

In 1984, Federated consolidated its Shillito's, Rikes, and Lazarus operations into a new subsidiary operating

under the Lazarus name. Federated acquired William H. Block, a department store chain based in Indiana, in 1987. The following year, Campeau Corp. acquired Federated and merged it with Allied Stores Corp., the department store giant Campeau had acquired in 1984. Campeau moved Allied's New York headquarters to Federated's home base in Cincinnati. In 1990, Campeau restructured Federated and Allied as subsidiaries of Federated Stores, Inc., a new holding company operating under Campeau. However, Federated Stores found itself struggling with the $8 billion in debt Campeau had taken on to complete the takeovers of Allied and Federated. As a result, Federated and Allied file for Chapter 11 bankruptcy protection. New management launched a consolidation program that included merging all Florida operations into the Burdines division. In 1992, Federated Department Stores, Inc. emerged from bankruptcy with 220 department stores in 26 states and roughly $7 billion in annual revenues. The firm also began to list its stock on the New York Stock Exchange.

The mid-1990s marked a period of growth for Federated. In 1994, the firm acquired R.H. Macy & Co., becoming the largest U.S. department store operator. The following year, Federated paid $575 million in stock for Los Angeles, California-based Broadway Stores Inc. Federated was named to the Standard and Poor's 500 stock index shortly thereafter. Bloomingdale's moved into California for the first time in 1996, creating four new stores there. Federated began to remodel many of its flagship stores, including the New York City Macy's store, in 1998. Federated paid $1.7 billion for mail order giant Fingerhut Cos. in 1999. Early in 2002, as part of its plan to refocus on its core department store opera-

FAST FACTS:

About Federated Department Stores Inc.

Ownership: Federated Department Stores Inc. is a public company traded on the New York Stock Exchange.

Ticker Symbol: FD

Officers: James M. Zimmerman, Chmn. and CEO; Terry J. Lundgren, Pres. and COO; Karen M. Houget, SVP and CFO

Employees: 115,000

Principal Subsidiary Companies: Federated operates seven subsidiary chains: Bloomingdale's, The Bon Marche, Burdines, Goldsmith's, Lazarus, Macy's, and Rich's.

Chief Competitors: Major rivals of Federated include Dillard's, Saks Inc., and other large department store chains.

tions, the firm announced its intent to either sell or liquidate Fingerhut. In addition, Federated shuttered its Macy's By Mail operations, and stopped selling products via its Bloomingdales.com Web site. (However, Macy.com remained operational, as did Bloomingdale's By Mail.) The firm also eliminated its Stern's division, a unit that had been acquired by Allied in the early 1950s, and transformed most Stern's stores into Bloomingdale's or Macy's units.

STRATEGY

A key marketing strategy for Federated has been, for many decades, the development of major special events, such as the Macy's Thanksgiving Day Parade, the lighting of Rich's Great Tree, and the Holiday Star at the Bon Marche. However, as department stores lost ground to discounters in the 1990s, firms like Federated were forced to adopt new strategic initiatives designed to lure customers back into their stores. To this end, some Federated stores added services like supervised play areas for children. Believing that customers were somewhat overwhelmed by the amount of merchandise offered in a typical department stores, Federated also began to alter its format by opening smaller stores with a more limited

selection of goods in 2000. For example, Federated opened a new Macy's in West Palm Beach, Florida, that was less than half the size of a traditional Macy's store. A new Bon Marche store in Helena, Montana, offered only one level of merchandise, one entrance and exit, and one checkout area. These smaller stores were not only designed to appeal to traditional Federated customers; they also allowed the firm to expand its reach into smaller markets.

Federated also began to increase its focus on developing its private brands. The firm started developing national advertising campaigns for various private label clothing and kitchenware lines. As a result, the Bloomingdale's division saw its private brand sales grow from 11.5 percent of revenues to 15 percent of revenues between 1999 and 2001. Along with promoting existing private brands like clothing line I.N.C., Federated also developed new brands, such as Greendog, a children's line of apparel and accessories created in 2000.

CURRENT TRENDS

Federated was quick to embrace the trend of online retailing in the mid-1990s. In 1996, the firm went online with the launch of macys.com. Two years later, Federated began actually selling its products via the Internet. Because the firm already operated the Bloomingdale's By Mail catalog, it was familiar with direct sales to customers and the shift to electronic commerce was fairly smooth. In 1999, Federated acquired a 20 percent stake in WeddingChannel.com, and the two firms began to integrate their print and online bridal registries. That year, the firm created a new subsidiary, Federated Stores Direct, to oversee all direct-to-customer operations, including both catalog and online sales.

PRODUCTS

Federated's various chains sell women's, men's and children's apparel and accessories, outerwear, shoes, cosmetics, jewelry, gifts, kitchenware, and home furnishings. The firm's private labels include Alfani men's clothing; I.N.C., Jennifer Moore, Style & Co., and Charter Club women's clothing; Greendog children's wear; and Tools of the Trade kitchenware. Federated stores also carry leading national brands such as Ralph Lauren and Tommy Hilfiger.

CORPORATE CITIZENSHIP

In 1980, Federated invested $15 million of its earnings to establish a charitable foundation. By 2002, the Federated Department Stores Foundation was donating

Federated Department Stores' officials are joined by New York Stock Exchange Chairman Richard Grasso for the 25th annual Macy's fourth of July fireworks display, which marked the opening of trading on July 3, 2001. (AP Photo/Richard Drew)

CHRONOLOGY:

Key Dates for Federated Department Stores Inc.

1929: Federated Department Stores is created

1956: Federated acquires Burdines

1964: Sales exceed $1 billion for the first time

1976: Federated acquires Rich's

1988: Campeau Corp. acquires Federated and merges it with Allied

1990: Federated files for bankruptcy

1992: Federated emerges from bankruptcy

1994: Federated acquires Macy's

1999: Federated acquires Fingerhut

2002: Federated announces its intent to liquidate or sell Fingerhut

nearly $13 million annually to various charities, such as United Way, Susan G. Komen Foundation, and the Pediatric Aids Foundation. The firm also sponsors things like the Florida Teacher of the Year award and the Brookline, Massachusetts-based Kids Clothes Club. In addition, Federated operates Partners in Time, a program designed to encourage employee volunteerism.

GLOBAL PRESENCE

In 2000, Federated opened its first store outside the United States when it created a Macy's unit in San Juan, Puerto Rico. Federated sells its private label merchandise—including clothing brands such as I.N.C., Alfani, Charter Club, Style & Co., Jennifer Moore, and Greendog-to retailers in Japan, Australia, Chile, and Peru.

EMPLOYMENT

Developing a positive corporate culture is a pivotal part of Federated's corporate strategy. According

to a March 2002 issue of *Training,* "In 1998, CEO Jim Zimmerman thought something more was needed to maintain a competitive advantage. He turned to the company's training department to find ways to attract the top talent, reduce employee turnover, and improve customers' shopping experiences. The department's early assessment highlighted what they always believed: The keys to improved retention, increased performance, and customer satisfaction are a top training environment and a positive work atmosphere." As a result, Federated decided to launch a Leadership Institute for its store managers and company executives in 1999. The intensive four-day training program—which explained the corporate culture Federated wanted to adopt and offered strategies on how to achieve it—was named an American Retail Excellence Best Practice by the National Retail Federation in 2000.

To bolster its recruitment efforts, Federated also operates Retailology.com. a site that details various career paths entry-level employees can take, as well as the training opportunities Federated will provide for them. Targeting college students, Retailology.com allows users to apply for the college internships offered by Federated, as well as for various full-time executive trainee positions with the company.

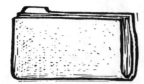

ONE OF THE WORLD'S LARGEST MARKETING EVENTS

The first Macy's Thanksgiving Day Parade in New York City drew a crowd of 10,000 people in 1924. By the early 2000s, the parade was attracting more than two million onlookers, as well as million of television viewers. According to Federated, the parade is the largest yearly spectator event in the United States.

SOURCES OF INFORMATION

Bibliography
Clark, Evan, and David Moin. "Federated Expands Sale of Private Labels." *Daily News Record*, 13 August 2001.

Clark, Evan, and Vicki M. Young. "Federated Reports Net Loss of $447 M." *WWD*, 27 February 2002.

Cuneo, Alice Z. "Macy's Goes West with Brand Effort." *Advertising Age*, 12 March 2001.

Federated Department Stores Inc. Home Page, 2002. Available at http://www.federated-fds.com.

Hobson, Katherine. "Miracle on 34th Street." *U.S. News & World Report*, 26 November 2001.

Schettler, Joel. "Federated Department Stores, Inc." *Training*, March 2002.

For an annualreport:
on the Internet at: http://www.federated-fds.com/annual_report/2000/annual00.pdf

For additional industry research:
Investigate companies by their Standard Industrial Classification Codes, also known as SICs. Federated Department Stores' primary SICs are:

5311 Department Stores

5961 Mail Order Houses

6719 Holding Companies, Not Elsewhere Classified

Also investigate companies by their North American Industrial Classification System codes, also known as NAICS codes. Federated Department Stores' primary NAICS codes are:

452110 Department Stores

454110 Electronic Shopping and Mail Order Houses

551112 Offices of Other Holding Companies

Fleetwood Enterprises, Inc.

OVERVIEW

Based in California, Fleetwood Enterprises, Inc. is the largest maker of recreational vehicles, including motor homes, folding trailers, and travel trailers, in the United States. The Fortune 500 company is also the second largest maker of manufactured homes. Along with selling its products via 190 retail outlets, Fleetwood also uses roughly 2,600 independent dealers. Manufactured homes account for 56 percent of revenues while motor homes bring in 23 percent, travel trailers 16 percent, and folding trailers 4 percent.

COMPANY FINANCES

After three consecutive years of growth, sales in 2001 fell to $2.5 billion compared to nearly $3.8 billion the previous year. Net income fell from $108.5 million in 1998 to $107.1 million in 1999, and to $83.4 million in 2000. In 2001 Fleetwood posted a net loss of $283.9 million. Earnings per share dropped from $3.01 in 1998, to $2.94 in 1999, and to $2.41 in 2000. In 2001 losses per share totaled $8.67. Stock prices, which peaked in 1998 at a high of $48 per share, had fallen to a high of $16 per share by 2001.

ANALYSTS' OPINIONS

Despite a 35 percent drop in housing sales and a 37 percent drop in RV sales in 2001, due in large part to the North American economic recession, some analysts

FOUNDED: 1950 as Coach Specialties Co.

Contact Information:

HEADQUARTERS: 3125 Myers Street
    Riverside, CA 92503-5527
PHONE: (909)351-3500
FAX: (909)351-3500
URL: http://www.fleetwood.com

FINANCES:

Fleetwood Enterprises Inc. Revenues, 1997-2001 (million dollars)

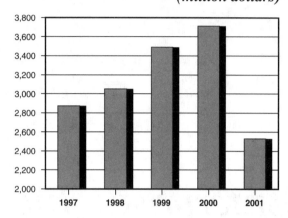

Fleetwood Enterprises Inc. 2001 Stock Prices (dollars)

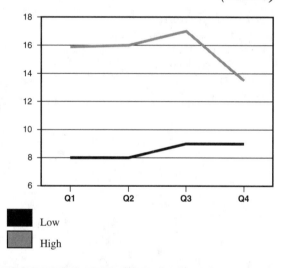

believed that Fleetwood stock was worth a second look. The firm's drastic cost cutting measures, which included the elimination of one-third of its workforce and the shuttering of 13 plants, was predicted to boost performance in early 2002. However, when Fleetwood's performance worsened during the first three months of 2002, Standard & Poor's downgraded its stock from "hold" to "sell." Some analysts criticized the firm for weak product development, as well as for failing to build strong relationships with dealers.

HISTORY

Fleetwood was established in 1950 as Coach Specialties Co. by John C. Crean. Initially, the new California-based firm sold window blinds for travel trailers. Early in the decade, Crean built his own personal travel trailer, and one of his window blind customers who happened to be a trailer dealer asked Crean to assemble trailer units for him during the busy summer months. When the summer travel trailer season ended, Crean began building mobile homes instead of trailers. Increased demand for inexpensive housing in southern California boosted sales of mobile homes, which typically cost one-third the price of traditional homes in the 1950s. By 1954 operations had grown to encompass three production plants. Three years later, Coach Specialties changed its name to Fleetwood Enterprises, Inc.

In 1964 Fleetwood diversified into recreational vehicles (RVs) with the purchase of Terry Coach Industries, Inc. and Terry Coach Manufacturing, Inc. The RV market was booming, thanks to the growing number of U.S. residents who had made traveling a hobby. Low gasoline prices also contributed to the industry's growth. Eventually, Fleetwood created a line of fifth-wheel travel trailers designed to be towed behind larger pickup trucks. The firm completed its initial public offering in 1965. Fleetwood continued to expand with the purchases of Pace-Arrow, Inc., a motor home manufacturer, and Avion Coach Corp., manufacturer of luxury class trailers.

Although the 1970s proved to be lucrative years for Fleetwood, the industry had begun to slow by the end of the decade. Soaring gasoline prices, public fears about a recession, and rising interest rates all contributed to a sales slowdown. Because nearly 66 percent of Fleetwood's products were reliant upon gasoline, fuel shortages (which prompted rationing in some states) battered the RV market. RV retailers began to shutter operations and many manufacturers saw their orders slow to a trickle. To stay afloat Fleetwood found itself having to slash both production and staffing. In 1980 Fleetwood shut down nine of its production factories: three travel trailer plants, three motor home facilities, and three manufactured housing plants.

Early in the 1980s, Fleetwood restructured its housing operations along regional lines. As the recession eased, RV sales began to recover. In fact, the firm achieved $1 billion in RV sales in 1989. However, this growth was not without problems. In 1985 the U.S. Department of Housing and Urban Development (HUD) began investigating Fleetwood for potential safety defects in 4,000 mobile homes manufactured in the early 1980s. The investigation resulted in a U.S. Justice Department complaint filed against Fleetwood in 1988. The Justice Department sought civil penalties in excess of $20 million, alleging the existence of standards violations in manufactured homes produced by Fleetwood. The following year, Fleetwood, HUD, and the Justice Department reached a settlement.

The firm's legal woes didn't end there, however. A class action lawsuit filed in Delaware in 1985 alleged that Fleetwood, among other manufactured housing makers, had charged excessive prices and finance fees to veterans by sending false certifications to the Veterans Administration. In 1990 two Fleetwood subsidiaries pled guilty to six counts of filing false certifications. As a result, Fleetwood paid $650,000 in fines.

Fleetwood diversified into financing in 1986 with the creation of Fleetwood Credit Corp. By the early 1990s, Fleetwood Credit had lending operations in California, Oregon, Indiana, Massachusetts, Georgia, New Jersey, and Texas. Growth continued with the purchase of the folding trailer assets of Coleman Co., which held a 30 percent share of the U.S. folding trailer market. The firm also introduced a line of less expensive trailer models.

In 1996 Fleetwood sold its credit arm to Associates First Capital Corp. for $156.6 million. The firm created 49 Fleetwood Home Centers, retail centers selling Fleetwood homes, in 1997. That year, Fleetwood also established a joint venture with Bloomfield Hills, Michigan-based Pulte Corp. to create a nationwide network of retail centers selling manufactured homes as well as home financing and insurance. Recessionary economic conditions undercut sales in 2000, prompting the firm to lay off 800 workers and shutter five plants. Another 13 plants were closed in 2001 as Fleetwood reduced one-third of its workforce.

STRATEGY

Forced to reexamine its structure during the recession of the late 1970s, Fleetwood drafted a management policy that divided its housing operations along regional lines. This strategic shift was designed to help the firm react more quickly to market trends. Housing design and development operations were divided into five units: West Coast, Central, Southeast, Mid-Atlantic, and Florida. Each plant facility operated autonomously and management decisions were made locally.

Strategic efforts during the mid-1990s centered around refocusing on domestic RV and manufactured housing operations. For example, Fleetwood divested Fleetwood Credit, which it had created in 1986, to Associates First Capital Corporation for $156.6 million in 1996. The firm also sold off real estate holdings and its German RV unit. Later in the decade, Fleetwood began to add retail operations to its holdings. Retail units acquired included HomeUSA, Better Homes, Central Homes, Jasper Homes, Classic City Homes, America's Best Homes, Viking Homes, JR's Mobile Homes, and D&D Homes. However, this strategy undermined the firm's performance in the early 2000s, when retail sales of manufactured homes plunged as interest rates rose and the economy deteriorated. In an effort to boost lagging RV sales, Fleetwood launched a "Rediscover America"

FAST FACTS:
About Fleetwood Enterprises, Inc.

Ownership: Fleetwood Enterprises, Inc. is a public company traded on the New York Stock Exchange.

Ticker Symbol: FLE

Officers: Thomas B. Pitcher, Interim Chmn., 62; David S. Engelman, Interim Pres., CEO, and Dir., 63; Boyd R. Plowman, EVP Finance and CFO, 57; Charles A. Wilkinson, EVP Operations, 60; Forrest Theobald, SVP, Gen. Counsel, and Sec., 59

Employees: 14,000

Principal Subsidiary Companies: Fleetwood Enterprises, Inc. operates roughly 60 manufacturing plants and 190 retail outlets across the United States and Canada.

Chief Competitors: Fleetwood Enterprises competes with Champion Enterprises, Pioneer Housing, and other makers of manufactured homes, as well as with recreational vehicle manufacturers such as Winnebago.

advertising campaign that offered rebates of up to $15,000 to customers who purchased an RV in January 2002.

INFLUENCES

Fleetwood's decision to refocus on its core manufactured housing and RV operations in the mid-1990s was partially the result of failed efforts to diversify into new markets. For example, hoping to move into traditional home development, Fleetwood had paid $6.3 million for 75 acres of land in southern California in the early 1990s. These plans failed to materialize, however, and the firm sold the land in 1996 for a mere $2.8 million, the lower price reflecting a sharp downturn in the California real estate market. This divestment underscored Fleetwood's need to refocus on its core domestic manufactured housing and RV units, both of which were losing market share to fierce rivals. After peaking at 21.6 percent in 1994, the firm's share of the manufactured housing market had declined to 20.1 percent in 1995. It fell further to 18.5 percent in 1996. Fleetwood's main competitor was the Auburn Hills, Michigan-based

CHRONOLOGY:
Key Dates for Fleetwood Enterprises, Inc.

1950: Fleetwood is established as Coach Specialties Co.

1957: Coach Specialties Co. changes its name to Fleetwood Enterprises, Inc.

1989: Fleetwood achieves $1 billion in RV sales

1986: The firm creates Fleetwood Credit Corp.

1996: Associates First Capital Corp. buys Fleetwood Credit Corp.

2001: Fleetwood lays off one-third of its workforce

Champion Enterprises, Inc. By undercutting Fleetwood's prices, Champion had secured a 16.5 percent share of the manufactured home market by 1996. Similarly, Fleetwood's share of the motor home market, the most lucrative sector of the RV industry, dropped from 34 percent in 1992 to 27.5 percent in 1996. Although Winnebago held only a 16.7 percent share, it had gained ground on Fleetwood by adding popular "slide-out" features to increase space to its motor homes long before Fleetwood made this addition in 1996.

PRODUCTS

Fleetwood sells manufactured homes up to 2,340 square feet in size. Motor home brands include American Dream, American Eagle, American Heritage, Jamboree, Expedition, Bounder, Flair, Pace Arrow, Southwind, Tioga, Storm, and Discovery. Travel trailer brands include Avion, Prowler, Terry, Wilderness, Mallard, Savanna, and Westport. The folding trailer business markets its products under the Coleman name.

GLOBAL PRESENCE

In September 1992 Fleetwood purchased an 80 percent stake in Niesmann & Bischoff, a Koblenz, Germany-based manufacturer of luxury Clou Liner and Clou Trend motor homes. The deal marked Fleetwood's first overseas venture. However, a sluggish German economy resulted in slow sales despite Fleetwood's efforts to introduce less expensive models. In May 1996 Fleetwood sold its stake in Niesmann & Bischoff.

FLEETWOOD USES INTERNET FOR PRODUCT LAUNCH

Rather than using a trade or retail show, Fleetwood decided to introduce its new all-terrain camper, dubbed the Outfitter ATC, via its Web site in 2002. The vehicle launch was the firm's first to take place solely on the Internet.

SOURCES OF INFORMATION

Bibliography

"Fleetwood Enterprises, Inc." *International Directory of Company Histories*. Detroit: Gale Group, 1997.

Fleetwood Enterprises, Inc. Home Page, 2002. Available at http://www.fleetwood.com.

"Fleetwood Lowered to Sell." *Business Week*, 1 March 2001. Available at http://wwwbusinessweek.com.

Kurowski, Jeff. "New Fleetwood Management Faces Job of Fixing a Giant." *RV Business*, January 2002.

For an annual report:
on the Internet at: http://199.230.26.96/fle/annrep/fleetwood_ar/default.htm

For additional industry research:
Investigate companies by their Standard Industrial Classification Codes, also known as SICs. Fleetwood Enterprises' primary SIC codes are:

2451 Mobile Homes

3716 Motor Homes

3792 Travel Trailers and Campers

6141 Personal Credit Institutions

Also investigate companies by their North American Industry Classification System Codes, also known as NAICS codes. Fleetwood Enterprises' primary NAICS codes are:

321991 Manufactured Home Manufacturing

336213 Motor Home Manufacturing

336214 Travel Trailer and Camper Manufacturing

522291 Consumer Lending

FMR Corp.

FOUNDED: 1946

OVERVIEW

FMR Corp. is the holding company for Fidelity Investments, one of the world's largest providers of financial services, with $862.6 billion in managed assets as of April 30, 2002. Fidelity offers 323 mutual funds to its 17 million corporate and individual customers. Not until the early 2000s was Fidelity Magellan Fund usurped by the Vanguard 500 Index Fund as the largest mutual fund in the United States. Along with mutual fund management and related investment services, Fidelity also offers trust services through Fidelity Personal Trust Company, created in 2000. Non-financial assets include a 54 percent stake in COLT Telecom Group as well as various real estate and transportation holdings.

Contact Information:
HEADQUARTERS: 82 Devonshire Street
   Boston, MA 02109
PHONE: (617)563-7000
TOLL FREE: (800)343-3548
URL: http://www.fidelity.com

COMPANY FINANCES

Revenues for Fidelity Investments grew steadily throughout the 1990s, reaching $11.096 billion in 2000, compared to $1.474 billion in 1991 and $5.047 billion in 1996. Net income grew from $89.0 million in 1991 to $423.1 million in 1996 and $1 billion in 1999. That year, the firm's profit margin reached 11.4 percent.

The North American economic downturn that began in 2000 and continued through 2001 undercut the performance of all large mutual fund groups, including Fidelity Investments. In fact, the mutual fund manager saw its total return on investment plunge to −12.1 percent in 2001. One bright spot for FMR Corp. was its Fidelity Capital unit, which posted revenues of $1.162 billion in 2001, nearly 43 percent higher than 2000 revenues of $815 million.

FINANCES:

FMR Corp.
Revenues, 1996-2000
(million dollars)

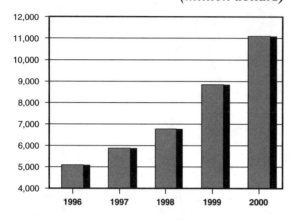

ANALYSTS' OPINIONS

In the early 2000s, many financial industry analysts began to question the viability of large diversified fund companies like Fidelity. Recessionary economic conditions precipitated a prolonged depression of the stock market. As a result, profits for investment firms tumbled, prompting some to raise their fees and minimum investment requirements. According to a December 2001 article in *Business Week*, "The be-everything-to-everybody business model of giants such as Fidelity Investments, Dreyfus, Putnam Investments, and T. Rowe Price is showing serious chinks." Fidelity executive Richard A. Spillane, Jr. defended the business model, however, asserting that a large, diversified asset base "improves your odds of delivering the performance" and "allows us to have a 500-person equity staff spread all over the globe."

HISTORY

In 1930 investment counsel Anderson & Cromwell, a money management firm based in Boston, Massachusetts, created the Fidelity Fund. In 1938, the Fidelity Fund began to operate its own office and Anderson & Cromwell (by then named Cromwell & Cabot) began to charge fees for its investment recommendations. The first management fees introduced in 1933 were based on fund performance. However, officers and directors received no payment from the Fund prior to 1938.

In 1945 while it was still being managed by Cromwell & Cabot, Edward C. Johnson, II, a Harvard Law School graduate, left as in-house legal counsel for Incorporated Investors, one of Boston's first open-end mutual funds, and was elected to take over the Fidelity Fund as President and Director. Johnson came from a wealthy Boston family and acted as trustee on the Johnson family's investments. As President and Director of Fidelity Fund, Johnson was able to condense his family's trust funds and experiment with picking stocks. What proved to be a knack for selecting successful stocks not only helped Johnson boost his family's assets, it also fueled Fidelity Fund's rapid growth. The fund's assets reached $10 million in 1945.

In 1946 the Fidelity Management and Research Company was formed by Edward C. Johnson, II, to serve as investment adviser to Fidelity Fund, replacing Cromwell & Cabot and with Mr. Johnson managing the fund himself. Today Fidelity Management and Research Company is a subsidiary of FMR Corp.

For the next several years, Johnson concentrated on expanding Fidelity's product offerings. In 1947 Fidelity introduced the Fidelity Puritan Fund, the first income-oriented mutual fund to invest primarily in common stocks. Between 1947 and 1957, the assets managed by Fidelity grew from $15 million to $265 million.

In 1957 Johnson's son, Edward C. (Ned) Johnson, III, joined Fidelity as a research analyst. In 1958 he managed the Trend Fund, one of two new growth funds - the other was the Capital Fund - Fidelity began offering that year. The Trend and Capital Funds became two of the investment industry's first funds to be aggressively managed for performance and proved to be the firm's highest performing funds throughout the 1960s. They were merged into the Trend Fund in 1979.

Fidelity's assets grew from $500 million in 1960 to $2.3 billion in 1965. Among key developments that took place during this time, Fidelity launched the International Fund in 1963, managed by Ned Johnson. It was renamed the Fidelity Magellan Fund in 1965. In 1964, the firm began offering investment services for corporate pension plans; and in 1969, Fidelity Service Company was incorporated, making Fidelity one of the first mutual fund companies to bring servicing of shareholder accounts in-house.

In 1972 Edward C. Johnson, II, was named Director and Ned Johnson was named President of FMR Corp., which was to act as a holding company for Fidelity Investments. Ned then spearheaded a diversification program aimed at broadening Fidelity's financial services portfolio. In 1973, he began moving all shareholder servicing in-house, eliminating outside servicing and giving Fidelity more control and direct contact with customers.

The remainder of the 1970s was a time of high interest rates and sub-par returns on equity investments, and Fidelity focused its efforts on offering different and better service. In 1973, in the midst of a terrible bear market, Congress added an option to put tax sheltered 403(b) retirement account money directly into mutual funds.

Fidelity was one of the first mutual fund companies to offer 403(b) accounts to not-for-profit institutions. In 1974, Fidelity introduced the Fidelity Daily Income Trust (FDIT), which was the first money market fund to offer check-writing services. Because shareholders could get money out easily, they readily put it in, and assets grew to more than $500 million in the first seven months of the fund's existence. When the stock market started to improve, many of these assets were moved into stock funds.

The year 1974 also saw Fidelity begin to sell mutual fund shares directly to the public through direct response advertising and a toll-free telephone number. Starting with one WATS line and a few newspaper ads, Fidelity found calls were soon coming in so quickly that it added eight more lines and hourglass egg timers to remind telephone representatives to take waiting calls. Direct phone mutual fund sales were so successful that in 1978, Fidelity installed a computerized telephone system to manage its growing telephone traffic, provide a high level of service to customers and minimize customer waiting. In 1979 Fidelity introduced Fidelity Information Phone, the first voice-activated computer response system for the general public, providing price and yield quotes on a 24-hour basis. The system responded to questions about prices and yields with a human voice for the ease and convenience of customers and freed telephone representatives to handle inquiries more complicated than fund quotes.

In 1976 Fidelity offered the first open-ended municipal bond fund sold without a sales charge. The Fidelity Municipal Bond Fund offered investors a way to invest in public entities around the country, receive interest tax free, and invest without having to pay a sales charge.

When the Securities and Exchange Commission in 1978 abolished fixed-rate brokerage commissions, Fidelity became the first major financial services institution to offer discount brokerage in the United States. Ned Johnson decided that since many investors bought Fidelity funds because they didn't need the advice of a broker, these same investors might also be interested in making their own decisions about individual securities, so he created Fidelity Brokerage Services, Inc. and opened several branch offices to support consolidation of an individual's stock, bond and mutual fund investments in one account. In 1979 Fidelity removed its 81/2 percent sales charges on almost all its funds and began selling its funds directly to the public with no sales charges (no load) or a low load of two to three percent. Also in 1979, because of Fidelity's success in selling its funds directly, many brokers wanted a way to sell Fidelity products, and the Fidelity Investments Institutional Services Company, Inc. was created to provide brokers with a line of Fidelity products to sell on a commission basis and also to provide advice of a third party to investors who wanted it.

The 1980s saw much growth for Fidelity, highlighted perhaps by the considerable attention it gained

FAST FACTS:
About FMR Corp.

Ownership: FMR Corp. is a private company with voting common stock owned by the Johnson family and employees. Abigail Johnson, granddaughter of founder Edward C. Johnson, II, owns a 25 percent share of the company.

Officers: Edward C. (Ned) Johnson, III, Chmn. and CEO; Robert L. Reynolds, VChmn.; James C. Curvey, VChmn., Dir., and COO; Stephen P. Jonas, EVP and CFO

Employees: 31,000

Principal Subsidiary Companies: FMR Corp. is the holding company for Fidelity Investments, the largest mutual fund company in the United States. Subsidiaries of FMR Corp. include Fidelity Brokerage Company, Fidelity Employer Services Company, Fidelity Investments Institutional Services Company and Fidelity Strategic Initiatives. Fidelity International Limited is a separate holding company established for all of Fidelity's international investment operations.

Chief Competitors: Fidelity Investments competes with other traditional mutual fund managers such as Vanguard Group, Putnam Investments, T. Rowe Price, and Charles Schwab, as well as newer online investment firms such as E*TRADE.

from the stellar performance of its Fidelity Magellan Fund. Managed by Peter Lynch since 1977, Magellan became the best performing mutual fund in the United States. In fact, it consistently posted higher percentage gains than Standard & Poor's 500 Stock Index, the standard of the industry. Between March 1984 and March 1989, it realized an average annual gain of 21.07 percent compared to the 17.48 percent average annual gain posted by S & P's 500 Index.

1980 also saw Fidelity introduce the country's first tax-exempt money market fund and, later, state-specific municipal bond and money market funds, enabling Fidelity investors to place portions of their assets in more conservative investments while receiving the tax benefits of owning municipal securities. Then in July 1981, Fidelity launched a group of "Select" portfolios, the first industry-specific mutual funds sold as a group to allow investors to switch back and forth between sectors at

CHRONOLOGY:

Key Dates for FMR Corp. and Fidelity Investments

1930: The Fidelity Fund is created

1946: Edward C. Johnson, II, creates Fidelity Management & Research Company to manage the Fidelity Fund

1963: International Fund (later renamed Fidelity Magellan Fund) launched, managed by Edward D. Johnson, III

1969: Fidelity Service Company is incorporated, making Fidelity one of the first mutual fund companies to service shareholder accounts in-house

1972: FMR Corp. is created to act as a holding company for Fidelity's operations

1974: Fidelity creates the first money market fund to offer check writing and begins to sell mutual fund shares directly to the public

1978: Fidelity becomes first major financial services institution to offer discount brokerage in the U.S.

1979: Fidelity begins serving institutional investors

1980: Fidelity introduces nation's first tax-exempt money market fund

1983: Fidelity becomes first mutual fund company to offer an asset management account

1984: Fidelity one of first financial services companies to offer computerized trading

1987: Fidelity creates umbrella company for startup ventures, a life insurance company, and Canadian mutual fund subsidiary

1989: Fidelity makes funds from other companies available to Fidelity customers

1992: Fidelity software gives its customers direct access to financial markets through their personal computers

1995: First industry Home Page on World Wide Web created by Fidelity

1997: Fidelity becomes first discount broker to offer initial public offerings and third-party investment research

1998: Fidelity announces a new college savings plan and brings wireless access to information and trading to its customers

2000: Fidelity Personal Trust Company offers trust services

2001: Fidelity teams with OnStar to offer industry's first in-vehicle investment services

---

relatively low cost. Included were Select Health Care Portfolio, Select Technology Portfolio, Select Energy Portfolio, and Select Precious Metals and Minerals Portfolio, which was later merged into the Select Gold Portfolio. Fidelity became the first financial services company to offer investors a family of sector-specific funds.

In mid-1981, the 30-year fixed mortgage rate stood at 16.63 percent, the annual inflation rate was more than eight percent and the Dow Jones Industrial Average was at 948. In December 1981, Fidelity launched Select Financial Services Portfolio and Select Utilities Growth Portfolio, offering investors who were less risk averse and who wanted further ways of diversifying their portfolios a method of doing so by investing in certain industries and the companies in them. The Select line was later expanded to 41 portfolios. These portfolios also became a vehicle for training Fidelity analysts. Fidelity Management Trust Company was also established in 1981 to serve both large institutions and individuals, managing employee benefit assets for large corporations and holding individual IRA account assets in custody.

1983 saw Fidelity begin the first use of interactive automated telephone service technology. This allowed its customers, with greater ease and efficiency, to obtain price and yield quotes as well as check their account balances; and later, to make exchanges. Winning an award from the Smithsonian Institution for innovative use of technology in finance, it was further evidence of Fidelity's commitment to technology that would enable it to do a better job for its customers. Fidelity also developed and established a technology systems backup in Dallas, designed to take over if service disruptions in other technology areas occurred. Six other sites were added later. And Fidelity became the first mutual fund company to offer an asset management account through its Fidelity Ultra Service Account (USA), providing a way for customers to manage their investments and other holdings with Fidelity through one account, with check writing and other features.

In 1984, Fidelity Investor's Express (FIX) enabled customers to place orders through their personal computers and Fidelity became one of the first financial services to offer computerized trading. FIX later became Fidelity Online Express (FOX) in 1992, winning a Most

Valuable Product Award from *PC Magazine*. In 1986, Fidelity created the industry's first 24-hour-a-day access to telephone representatives and became the first company in the industry to provide hourly pricing of mutual funds in its Select portfolios, enabling its customers to buy and sell shares in their portfolios based on current prices.

Fidelity's growth wasn't trouble-free, however. After the stock market crash of October 1987, its assets fell by nearly $5 billion and it was forced to trim its work force from 8,100 to 5,600 people. The late 1980s also marked a period of increased diversification for Fidelity. Ned Johnson believed that Fidelity should be developing new businesses - some not related to its core business - to teach new competencies and how to thrive through down market cycles. To this end, in 1987, Fidelity Capital was created to oversee businesses as diverse as real estate, telecommunications, retailing, publishing and transportation; Fidelity Investments Life Insurance Company was created to develop and market its own insurance products as well as those of other high-quality insurers, becoming the nation's leading writer of variable income annuities by 2001; and subsidiary Fidelity Investments Canada, Limited was launched to provide Canadian investors strong-performing mutual funds through Canadian broker/dealers.

In 1989, Fidelity became one of the first mutual fund companies to create a separate business unit, Fidelity Institutional Retirement Services Company (FIRSCo) to provide corporations with investment management, education and record keeping services for 401(k) plans which it recognized were about to explode in popularity. By the end of its first year of operation, FIRSCo had 200 employees serving 200 plan sponsors and their 200,000 participants who had $14.2 billion in assets. In response to the 1987 stock market crash and nervous investors turning to fixed-income markets, Fidelity also launched its Spartan Funds in 1989, selling a new line of money market and bond funds directly to the public and offering lower costs to investors who could meet higher minimums and thus obtain higher yields. 1989 also saw Fidelity launch FundsNetwork, a "mutual fund supermarket" enabling Fidelity's retail customers to access funds from Fidelity and dozens of other fund companies through their brokerage accounts. By 2001, Fidelity had expanded the program to include retirement accounts and its program has become the largest in the industry.

Fidelity's expansion and diversification in the 1990s was equally impressive. In 1991, it created business units to focus on retirement savings plans for small companies and for employees in the not-for-profit sector. Its Emerging Corporate Market Fund was organized to provide 401(k) services to companies with up to 1,000 employees and Fidelity Investments Tax-Exempt Services Company was formed to focus on 403(b) and 401(a) retirement savings plans for tax-exempt organizations and the public sector.

FIDELITY'S EARLY LEADERSHIP

Fidelity Investments founder Edward C. Johnson, II, spent a large portion of his life watching the stock market. In fact, he kept a daily stock market diary for more than 50 years in an effort to chronicle different trends and deepen his understanding of stock investments.

Fidelity has a long history of corporate giving and in 1992 it created the Fidelity Charitable Gift Fund as a model of the best practices for handling donor-advised funds, which was sanctioned by the IRS and emulated by many other organizations, including community foundations that offer donor-advised funds. This fund has become the nation's largest grant-maker and second largest public charity. Also in 1992, Fidelity launched Fidelity Online Express, a software package giving customers direct access to the financial markets through their personal computers, which evolved from Fidelity Investor's Express of 1984; it introduced *Stages*, a first-of-its-kind monthly magazine for 401(k) plan participants, containing articles on retirement planning, investing, the economy, general savings ideas and other subjects of interest to plan participants, which was lauded by both plan sponsors and participants; and it entered the telecommunications arena in 1992 when it established City of London Telecommunications (COLT) Group.

Although the Fidelity Magellan Fund continued to rank among the top ten mutual funds in the early 1990s, other funds, many created by Fidelity Investments, began to outperform Magellan. For example, the Fidelity Select Health Fund, a biotech fund, emerged as the top performer and Magellan fell to the number three spot. Another Fidelity fund, Fidelity Destiny I, also made the top ten during that period. Also, as the stock market began to boom in the mid-1990s, several fund managers left Fidelity to take positions with public investment firms that were able to offer stock options as part of their compensation packages. In 1997, Fidelity turned to outside fund managers for the first time when it contracted the management of its index funds to Bankers Trust.

In 1995, Fidelity created the first financial services industry Home Page on the World Wide Web, which was immediately welcomed by rapidly-growing numbers of Internet users. At that time, the Fidelity Web site included information on Fidelity's mutual funds and brokerage services, investor tools and information about Fidelity events and seminars around the country. Also, Fidelity Employer Services Company was created to provide employers the option of using Fidelity for benefits services beyond traditional defined contribution 401(k) plans. Later it expanded to include payroll and human resources functions. In 1996, Fidelity launched NetBenefits to provide 401(k) access and transactions over the Internet. After its first year of operation, NetBenefits was awarded a Microsoft Example of Excellence Award and went on to become a platform for several other future Fidelity innovations. 1997 also saw Fidelity create PortfolioPlanner, an online management tool for 401(k) plan sponsors providing model portfolio recommendations customized to their retirement plan options, and Plan Sponsor Webstation, an online tool for benefits administrators to use in managing their company retirement plans.

In 1998, Fidelity announced a new college savings plan, the UNIQUE College Investing Plan, and other plans that took advantage of the Taxpayer Relief Act of 1997 to provide qualified state tuition savings programs. It also offered its customers wireless access to information and trading through its new InstantBroker, which enabled customers to manage their investments from almost any location, using a pager, email, fax, or personal data assistant, and other enhancements subsequently announced.

Fidelity introduced the country's first 401(k) plan for small business sold and serviced over the Internet in 1999. Developed to help meet the retirement needs of small businesses, Fidelity's e401k offers employers all the features of a full service 401(k) plan online: plan administration by the employer, record-keeping reports, personalized communication, education, retirement planning tools and ongoing account monitoring and management. It also launched Powerstreet, a Web-based brokerage platform offering enhanced trading, research and personalization. In this complete retooling of its discount brokerage, Fidelity uses the Internet as the platform for Powerstreet through which individual investors can take advantage of a broad range of trading and cash management features including buying and selling stocks, bonds, options and more than 4,400 mutual funds from Fidelity and other well-known fund companies; access exclusive Lehman Brothers research; receive personalized news and information; and access IPOs, margin borrowing, unlimited check writing and other features. Fidelity also opened its state-of-the-art Fidelity Center for Applied Technology in 1999 to seek technology solutions that focus on wireless technology and database products designed to make it even easier for customers to use Fidelity's products and services.

In 2000, the Fidelity Electronic Payroll system for small businesses was introduced. Designed to meet the evolving technology needs of the small business market, Internet-based Fidelity Electronic Payroll followed Fidelity's successful introduction of its e401k in 1999;

but while it includes Fidelity's existing Web-based Fidelity Plan Sponsor Webstation and Fidelity NetBenefits, in use by Fidelity's 7,000 clients and seven million participants, Electronic Payroll is part of a broader range of outsourcing services that includes defined contributions, defined benefits and health and welfare. Also in 2000, Fidelity offered trust services through Fidelity Personal Trust Company.

The following year, in 2001, the Frank Russell Company and Fidelity Institutional BrokerageGroup announced a strategic alliance designed to help Register Investment Advisors and correspondent broker/dealers meet the sophisticated investing needs of their affluent clients through a separately managed accounts program. Fidelity also formed an alliance with OnStar, a wholly owned subsidiary of General Motors Corporation, enabling OnStar subscribers, including many of Fidelity's 7.3 million 401(k) customers, to monitor, manage and trade in their Fidelity personal investing accounts via OnStar's hands-free, voice-enabled Virtual Advisor. Fidelity also unveiled the Fidelity Compensation Planner, its latest compensation planning service addition to Fidelity's Web-based HR/payroll tool set called Fidelity eWorkplace, a suite of integrated employee and manager self-service tools to facilitate issues resolution, making informed decisions, and the processing of HR and payroll changes through a single Web interface. Fidelity Compensation Planner allows for employee compensation data and recommendations to be submitted and approved online, greatly reducing the time associated with traditional labor-intensive paper or spreadsheet-based planning cycles. 2001 also saw Fidelity enhance its PortfolioPlanner into the first available tool to integrate data from investors' multiple accounts, then analyze up to ten financial goals and help investors develop investment strategies to meet them.

STRATEGY

Taking calculated risks is a strategy Fidelity has embraced throughout its history. In the early 1970s, Fidelity decided to diversify into a broad range of financial services. Fidelity became the first money market fund manager to offer check writing in 1974. Rather than relying on traditional brokerage distribution channels, in 1974 Fidelity began to market its funds directly to the public via print advertising and direct mail. In 1976, Fidelity once again acted as an industry pioneer when it launched the first open-end, no-load municipal bond fund. Three years later, Fidelity became the first major financial institution to offer discount brokerage services.

The risks the firm took with Magellan also proved worthwhile. Rather than placing 200 or so companies into its portfolio, as was typically done with an equity fund like Magellan, Fidelity put more than 1,000 companies into Magellan. The firm also marketed the fund aggressively. As a result, Magellan grew from $22 million in assets in 1977 to $12 billion in assets in 1990. Believing that its advertising efforts, which included targeting the general public, had paid off with Magellan, the firm increased its advertising budget to $28 million per year in the early 1990s. In fact, Fidelity spent more on advertising than any other mutual fund manager.

Internal operations were also structured differently than most other mutual fund companies. In the 1980s, CEO Ned Johnson had put in place a management style modeled after many Japanese businesses. The company became more self-sufficient by doing things like handling its own back-office account processing rather than relying upon an outside bank for that service. Eventually, Fidelity was able to sell its expertise in these areas to other investment firms.

In the early 1990s, Fidelity used its extensive technological capabilities to offer clients help with everything from retirement planning to saving for a college education. Many of Fidelity's premium services, which had once been designed to serve the firm's wealthiest customers, were offered to all six million of its clients.

CURRENT TRENDS

Fidelity began to invest a signification portion of its budget in technology in the 1960s, long before technology became a buzz word among other banking and investment firms. The firm's goal was to become technologically self-reliant. Consequently, Fidelity kept abreast of the data processing and telecommunications developments that revolutionized the financial industry in the 1980s and 1990s. In fact, by the early 1990s, Fidelity had earmarked more than $150 million a year for technology-related efforts.

Fidelity was a leader among the financial firms that began to transform themselves into technology-based customer service centers offering a wide range of financial services . For example, Fidelity installed an interactive, automated telephone system in 1983. Fidelity Investors Express, a service that permitted customers to conduct stock trades via personal computers, was offered in 1984. Fidelity also designed software that allowed its staff to access information such as margin calculations and options analysis for customers on demand. In the early 1990s, Fidelity began to operate Investor Liquidity Network, an electronic stock trading system that matched the buy and sell orders of outside institutional investors with the orders of Fidelity fund operators.

Fidelity was also quick to embrace Internet technology. In 1999, it teamed up with Charles Schwab, Donaldson, Lufkin & Jenrette, and Spear, Leeds & Kellogg to create a network that allowed investors to trade NASDAQ stocks on the Internet. That year, popular Internet gateway Lycos worked with Fidelity, to create Power-

street, an online brokerage run by Fidelity allowing investors to customize their Web experiences. The firm also announced the nationwide availability of its Instant-Broker service to investors via the Palm VII organizer, the first integrated wireless hand-held computing product.

PRODUCTS

Fidelity Investments under holding company FMR Corp. offers a wide range of financial planning products and services to individual and institutional investors, such as mutual funds, annuities, life insurance, retirement planning, college tuition planning, and discount brokerage. Fidelity Capital invests private equity on behalf of Fidelity Investments using a variety of investment approaches but primarily focuses on majority-owned operating businesses in various industries including insurance, transportation, hospitality, and human resources. Fidelity Employer Services Company provides corporations and tax-exempt organizations with defined contribution retirement plans and other benefits outsourcing services. Fidelity Brokerage Company provides a full range of investment products and services to individual mutual fund and brokerage customers. Fidelity Investments Institutional Services Company, Inc. distributes Fidelity products, programs and services through a variety of financial institutions, including banks, insurance companies and broker/dealers.

CORPORATE CITIZENSHIP

To promote volunteerism among its employees, Fidelity operates an Intranet site that helps employees locate volunteer activities in their communities. The firm also operates a workplace giving program that makes it convenient for employees to make donations to their favorite non-profit organizations. Activities to promote literacy include sponsoring book fairs for Reading is Fundamental.

GLOBAL PRESENCE

In 1969, Fidelity International was founded in Bermuda to manage and administer Fidelity's offshore funds. In 1979, Fidelity International Limited (FIL) was established as a separate, independent holding company for all Fidelity's international investment operations. FIL is a privately owned company, separate from FMR Corp., with its headquarters in Bermuda. FIL provides investment management services to individual and institutional investors outside the United States. Its products and services include equity, fixed income and money funds as well as institutional portfolio management.

SOURCES OF INFORMATION

Bibliography

Der Hovanesian, Mara. "The Mutual Fund Mess." *Business Week*, 17 December 2001. Available at http://www.businessweek.com.

Dickey, Sam. "Financial Firms Confront the Challenge of Keeping Brokers in the Loop." *InformationWeek*, 11 September 2000.

Egan, Jack. "The $13 Billion Honey Pot." *Forbes*, 15 May 2000.

"Fidelity Unit Revenue Rises 30 Percent." *The Boston Herald*, 1 March 2002.

"FMR Corp." *International Directory of Company Histories*. Detroit: Gale Research, 1992.

FMR Corp. Home Page, 2002. Available at http://www.fidelity.com.

For additional company research:

Investigate companies by their Standard Industrial Classification Codes, also known as SIC codes. FMR Corp.'s primary SICs are:

6211 Security Brokers and Dealers

6282 Investment Advice

6719 Holding Companies, Not Elsewhere Classified

Also investigate companies by their North American Industry Classification System Codes, also known as NAICS codes. FMR Corp.'s primary NAICS codes are:

523120 Securities Brokerage

523930 Investment Advice

551112 Offices of Other Holding Companies

Ford Motor Company

OVERVIEW

One of the "big three" car companies in the United States, Ford has a rich history and heritage. Ford has been responsible for some of the largest contributions to the U.S. economy and its growth. Aside from its status as a car company, Ford also had considerable stakes in the financial services area. The company manufactures car parts and accessories in various divisions such as the Body and Assembly Operations, Casting Division, Climate Control Operations, Glass Division, Parts and Services Division, Plastics Products Division, and Transmission and Chassis Operations.

As late as 1997, Ford had impressive sales of $153.6 billion; it also ranked second on the Fortune 500 list of the largest U.S. industrial corporations based on sales, and it was the leading exporter of cars and trucks from the United States and Canada. But by 2002, company executives admitted that the company somehow had lost sight of its mission and goals with disastrous consequences. Somehow the company would find a way to return to years of profitability and to take itself from a $2 billion loss in 2001 to be again profitable by 2005, William Clay (Bill) Ford Jr., the company's newest CEO, promised stockholders. To help right the company, in 2002 he persuaded the retired and highly respected Allan Gilmour to return as chief financial officer. The company also showed it was serious about cutting losses when it not only unloaded several plants and cut loose 35,000 workers, but also axed such well-known but lately unprofitable models as the Lincoln Continental, Mercury Cougar and Ford Escort, replacing them with models aimed at younger buyers with expendable cash.

FOUNDED: 1903

Contact Information:

HEADQUARTERS: The American Rd.
   Dearborn, MI 48121
PHONE: (313)322-3000
FAX: (313)323-2959
TOLL FREE: 800) 392-3673; (800) 232-5952 (TDD for the Hearing Impaired)
URL: http://www.ford.com

FAST FACTS:

About Ford Motor Company

Ownership: The Ford Motor Company is a publicly held company traded on the New York Stock Exchange.

Ticker symbol: F

Officers: William Clay (Bill) Ford Jr., CEO, 45; Carl Reichardt, VChmn., 69; Allan Gilmour, CFO, 67

Employees: 345,000

Principal Subsidiary Companies: Ford Motor Company has many subsidiaries—some of the better known are Ford Motor Credit Co., Hertz Corp., Lincoln Mercury Division, and Jaguar Ltd.

Chief Competitors: As a major automobile manufacturer, Ford's competitors include DaimlerChrysler, General Motors, Toyota, Honda, BMW, Mitsubishi, Nissan, Hyundai, Kia, and Volkswagen.

COMPANY FINANCES

As late as 1997, Ford's worldwide net income was $6.9 billion, a 56 percent increase from 1996. All that market share was soon gone, however, as were those in charge of the company as it declined. By 2001 Ford stock had dropped like a fallen chassis—some 33 percent from 2000. Burdened with heavy debt service, the company suffered Standard & Poor's "BBB+" rating—lowest since another dismal sales period in 1984. Among other disasters, four-door Ford Explorers equipped with Firestone tires were shown to have a problematic safety record with regard to rollovers, and even worse, the Insurance Institute for Highway Safety told the *St. Petersburg Times* in 2001 that 231 deaths occur in every 1-million two-door, two-wheel-drive Explorer Scouts. No turnaround was in sight by the first quarter of 2002 as Ford posted a disappointing loss of $800 million. While General Motors and Chrysler were showing small signs of recovery in 2002, Ford just couldn't seem to buy a better idea to reverse its ghastly tailspin. "We absolutely must make money on everything we sell," Bill Ford told the Bloomberg News. "We just have to hit a lot of singles and hope they turn into home runs." In 2002 Bill Ford literally stepped to the plate, filming a series of commercials that emphasized Ford tradition and his family's insistence on giving good value to car owners. Analysts warned that putting CEOs on television was risky business, capable of winning viewers hearts as Wendy's Dave Thomas did before his death, or performing miserably.

ANALYSTS' OPINIONS

Ford executives in the 2000s seem to delight in giving their critics the ammunition required to shoot them. In 2000 Ford announced that it was going to develop a gas-saving SUV, but by 2002, analysts pointed out that Ford SUVs were delivering way below the 23 mpg performances the company had promised. In 2002 chairman Bill Ford admitted that the company's goals had not been met, but that technology was on the way for an environmentally friendlier Ford SUV. Nonetheless, analysts expressed far higher expectations for the company's forthcoming (2003) gasoline-electric Escape HEV—marketed to hip, environmentally conscious buyers—and engineered to deliver 40 mpg in combined city/highway road performance. Can the company extricate itself from the reef where it has run aground? Michael Bruynesteyn, a Prudential Securities Inc. analyst, told the *Bloomberg News* that it can. "I believe Ford can improve its earnings by cutting costs and getting more flexible, but this isn't something that happens over-night," says Bruynesteyn. "It will take years." Many analysts are predicting that Ford will need to sell assets such as Hertz, the rental car company, to get operating capital and to shrink killing debt service.

HISTORY

Born July 30, 1863, on a farm near Dearborn, Michigan, Henry Ford made his first rudimentary car, the *Quadricycle*, in a shed behind his home. Ford formed one company that folded, and for a time his main interest was racing cars, including one driven by Barney Oldfield that set a then-speed record. With $28,000 and a lot of faith and courage, Henry Ford and 12 associates incorporated the Ford Motor Company in 1903 in Lansing, Michigan. Between 1903 and 1908, Henry Ford and his engineers used the first 19 letters of the alphabet to designate their creations, although many of these cars were experimental and never reached the public. Ironically, Ford had very little school learning and was only marginally literate.

The first production Ford car, the *Model A*, was sold a month after its incorporation to a Chicago dentist named Pfennig. By this time, the company's bank balance had dwindled to $223.65. During the next five years, Henry Ford graduated from being chief engineer to president, acquired a majority of the stock, and directed a development and production program that began in a converted wagon factory. In the first 15 months, 1,700 Model A cars chugged out of the old wagon factory.

CHRONOLOGY:

1903: Henry Ford establishes the Ford Motor Company

1908: Ford introduces the Model T

1909: Henry Ford applies his assembly line concept to Model T production

1918: Henry Ford retires, naming his son, Edsel Ford, as president

1919: Edsel and Henry Ford buy out the other stockholders and incorporate

1922: Acquires the Lincoln Motor Company

1937: Ford produces its 25-millionth automobile

1943: Edsel Ford dies

1945: Henry Ford II is named president

1949: Henry Ford I dies

1956: Ford Motor Company goes public

1958: The Ford Edsel debuts with a prominent grille and flops horribly

1962: The Mustang debuts and sells 500,000 in 18 months

1979: Henry Ford II relinquishes his position to Philip Caldwell

1986: Ford's income passes General Motors' for the first time since 1924

1993: Ford products are five of the top eight best-selling vehicles in the United States

1999: All Ford sport utility vehicles are manufactured as low-emission vehicles

2000: With adverse publicity from deaths from SUV rollovers, and severe management problems, Ford stock value begins to plunge

2001: Company begins extensive shakeup at the top with Bill Ford taking control of the company, restoring Ford to management by a descendent of the founder; numerous other executives are replaced and 35,000 employees were scheduled for layoffs; Bill Ford makes it clear that members of the Ford family are going to have a huge say in company policy as he names cousin Elena Ford, granddaughter of Henry Ford II, group manager of the Lincoln Mercury division

2002: Struggling Ford axes 22,000 employees in attempt to turnaround struggling company; 13,000 more employees will lose jobs eventually; Ford announced that it is ending some of its best-known but lately poorest-selling models: the Ford Escort sedan, Mercury Cougar, Mercury Villager, and Lincoln Continental

2003: Ford celebrates its centennial year

By the year 1913, Ford had embarked on establishing the world's first moving automobile assembly line production operation (it was fully operational by 1917) and began sales operations in Argentina, China, Indonesia, Siam (now called Thailand), and Brazil. By 1915 Ford had built 1 million cars, and by 1922 that number had reached 10 million. Ford production reached 20 million, and the company built its first V-8 automobile in 1931. A new line, Mercury, was introduced in 1938, and the Lincoln Continental was introduced the same year. However, at the start of WWII, Ford was forced to halt civilian production and shift to total military production. By the time the WWII ended, Henry Ford died at the age of 83, in 1947. However, his mental health had been destroyed by a stroke many years before his end came, and at the end, suffering hallucinations and allowing thugs to beat union organizers, he was removed from control before he could destroy his own company with bad management.

Henry Ford II, the oldest grandson of Henry Ford assumed presidency of the company in 1945. As he drove the first post-war car off the assembly line, Henry Ford II made plans to reorganize and decentralize the company. At the time, Ford Motor Company was losing several million dollars a month, in large part because the obdurate Henry Ford had lost touch with the car-buying public, and the company was in a critical condition to resume its pre-position as a major force in the now fiercely competitive auto industry.

Henry Ford II turned out to be the ideal individual to tackle the job of leading the family business to becoming a modern, publicly owned corporation. His genius was in his ability to find talented people such as Lee Iacocca and Robert McNamara, and put them into leadership positions. Those hired by Henry Ford II brought quantitative analysis and the science of modern management to the company, something that had been absolutely lacking under Ford who, the last 30 years of his life, had turned into an autocratic, uncompromising, bully.

In 1956 the Ford Motor Company took a major step and went public. In the largest stock issue of all time, 10,200,000 shares of the Ford Motor Company were put

---

up for sale and 250,000 investors rushed to pay $657 million for 20 percent of what, until then, had been a family business. In 1958 Ford announced its entry into the heavy and extra-heavy truck market (it had entered the light truck market in 1917), and by 1959, Ford had produced 50 million vehicles.

STRATEGY

Ford started as a domestic company and capitalized on domestic demand. However, this did not detract from the company's focus on globalization. Henry Ford's policy was to become a contributing citizen in every country where Ford sold cars. His slogan was, "Build them where you sell them." In the same vein, Ford believed in equal employment opportunity throughout his company. However, unable or unwilling to accept change, Henry Ford's reluctance to upgrade the Model T, and to add improvements desired by customers, allowed Chevrolet and other brands to outdistance Ford models in the late 1920s and 1930s.

Henry Ford II, by many accounts a wise and prudent company head, continued his grandfather's equal employment policies, predating federal civil rights legislation. In the late 1970s, when American workers were criticized for producing poor quality, Henry Ford II said, "there is no such thing as a bad employee, only bad managers." Company leadership accepted responsibility, and Ford was the first American auto company to make quality "Ford's number one operating priority."

Ford continued to believe in improving quality via its employees, as opposed to the rest of the industry, which was moving on to the use of high-tech robots. "Teamwork" became the norm from in-plant participatory groups to a new way of developing cars based on cross-functional teams. The idea was to bring in representatives from all engineering and management specialties together into each vehicle development team, then give them the authority to make as many decisions as possible. The first team effort was on a bold new car—the Taurus—off the assembly line in 1986. The immensely successful effort encouraged management to give the teams more authority and independence. "Have you driven a Ford—lately?" became the advertising battle cry of the 1980s for the company.

In efforts to increase profitability, Ford continued restructuring its business and reducing process costs. The company discontinued low-volume, low-profit vehicles such as the Aerostar, Aspire, and Probe; sold its heavy truck operations; reduced excess car capacity; and added capacity for its best-selling light trucks. In 1997 Ford announced financial goals for its automotive business, including targeting a return on sales of 4 percent in North America; in Europe, they hoped to break even; in South America, the company sought reduction in losses compared with 1996. Overall, Ford hoped to reduce total costs

by $1 billion and reduce capital spending. The company was able to exceed all of those goals, as stated in its 1997 Annual Report.

All that success was gone and forgotten in just five years. By 2002 the company's latest strategy was clearly to survive first and then to find ways to prosper. The company used the approaching centennial to remind American automobile buyers that Henry Ford, from the early 1900s to the 1920s, was regarded as an American inventive genius, and that the Ford automobile was inextricably linked to America's past. In addition to advertising campaigns that were a mixture of history and sentiment, the company reaffirmed its commitment to providing quality and value. Dead last in new-owner satisfaction in 2001, according to J.D. Power & Associates' annual poll, Ford Motor Company improved greatly in 2002 under new management, which aggressively worked to meet concerns of new car buyers. The result has been that Ford customer satisfaction in 2002 increased dramatically, according to the latest Power & Associates ranking, although the company still was well behind frontrunner Toyota.

For all the hype on television and Internet ads about Ford's American traditions, the company clearly was becoming, or had already become, a truly international maker of cars. Bumper stickers on Ford automobiles in the company's manufacturing plants in Ohio and Michigan still urge readers to "Buy American," but the Ford products Americans now bought increasingly were becoming about as American as chopsticks and curry. The company long has owned a one-third interest in the Japanese car corporation Mazda, and production plans for the Taurus are to incorporate some of the Mazda features buyers seem to prefer, according to *Forbes* magazine. With Ford brands such as the Focus almost 100 percent a European-featured car, it likely is only a matter of time before wholly-American engineered cars such as the Mustang, Crown Victoria, and Lincoln Town Car either succumb to European influences and market preferences or go out of production.

INFLUENCES

Since its beginning, world events have shaped Ford Motor Company and played a role in the company's prominence and growth. Also important was the influence of Henry Ford in the pre- 1930s period, and the influence of his oldest grandson, Henry Ford II in the post-World War II war period. The success of the Ford Motor Company post-World War II was in the fact that Ford grew and adapted to the changing times, while at the same time anticipating industry events and setting trends and milestones of its own.

In the 1960s, for instance, Ford leaders anticipated a weakening of trade barriers and moved to regional trading way ahead of the pack. Ford of Europe was established in 1967, some 20 years ahead of the European Economic Community's arrival. Similarly, Ford established the North American Automotive Operations (NAAO) consolidating the United States, Canada, and Mexico in 1972, more than a decade ahead of the North American Free Trade Agreement (NAFTA).

CURRENT TRENDS

In 1994, with the consolidation of Ford's North American and European operations, Ford 2000 was initiated. The Ford 2000 commitment was to bring the entire Ford global organization into a single operation by the year 2000. Ford 2000 created a single global management team to allow the company to eliminate duplication, initiate best practices, use common components and designs for the advantage of scale, and allocate resources to wherever they are needed to best serve market needs.

Ford expected to save billions with the Ford 2000 initiative, but Ford's profit margins fell 60 percent during the 1994-1996 phase because of tough competition, a failure to standardize enough parts, and design flaws in vehicles such as the Explorer. With heavy competition from foreign and other domestic auto makers in the mid-1990s, Ford went through a difficult period trying to remain profitable. New product introductions and aggressive marketing were results of this effort. In February 1997, Ford announced its decision to quit the heavy truck business after launching the much-publicized HN80 model introduced in fall 1996; this move reflected the importance that Ford executives placed in a company-wide strategic review. "Industry analysts said that Ford's decision to drop out of the heavy truck business recognizes it wouldn't easily have caught the market leaders," according to the *Knight Ridder/Tribune Business News*.

In another move expected to improve performance, Ford moved its Lincoln-Mercury headquarters to Irvine, California, in 1998. Ford hoped that southern California's "innovative, trend-setting culture and strong automotive market will foster development of unique vehicles and creative new looks for both brands." But by 2002, as the Lincoln Continental and several Mercury models were discontinued, it became clear that Ford needed to find ways to sell the Lincoln and Mercury brands to the buying public or these two would join Oldsmobile in oblivion.

PRODUCTS

Ford has always been a trend setter with its new products. In 1904, Henry Ford, a major racing car enthusiast and early builder, set the first speed record with his "999" race car traveling 91.37 miles per hour on frozen Lake St. Clair, near Detroit, Michigan. Ford introduced

the first V-8 engine. In the fall of 1954, the Thunderbird, an American classic, joined the Ford car family as a 1955 two-seater sports car. The original Thunderbird was offered with a 160-horsepower V-8 engine with a three-speed manual transmission and had a new and unique feature—a convertible canvas roof for fair and sunny weather and a detachable plastic hardtop for foul weather. In 2002 the redesigned Thunderbird went back to some of the design features that had made the car so treasured in the 1950s.

Ford changed the direction of the American auto industry forever on April 17, 1964, when it unveiled the *Mustang* at the World's Fair in New York. The Ford Mustang, a personal favorite of Lee Iacocca, caused a sensation that confirmed the theories of Ford product planners who thought a car with a youthful touch would appeal to baby boomers ready to purchase their first car. Dealers were swamped with 22,000 orders the car's first day.

In 1980 Ford introduced the 1981 Escort in its first attempt at a world car, but by 2002, that model's defects and dwindling sales had caused the company to halt production. CDW27 was Ford's genuine global car. Named "Mondeo" in Europe, Taiwan, and the Middle East, slightly modified versions went on sale in North America with the names Ford Contour and Mercury Mystique. Ford's CDW27 became a new way of thinking about product development for the Ford Motor Company. It proved that true globalization was possible and that customer focused teams were the way of the competitive future. Runaway successes during the 1990s included the company's sports utility vehicles, save for serious safety defects, and the F-series pick-ups. The F-series pick-ups outsold any other car in the world during the 1980s and 1990s. In the late 1990s and early 2000s, Ford sold cars under the brands Ford, Lincoln, Mercury, Aston Martin, and Jaguar, but it also held a third interest in Japanese Mazda.

CORPORATE CITIZENSHIP

Ford announced that beginning with 1999 model year cars, all of its sport utility vehicles (SUVs) would be low-emission vehicles, as clean as new cars, but that promise backfired as it was unable to deliver on that promise even as late as 2002. Ford was the first large company in the world to commit globally to ISO 14001 certification, the international environmental management system standard covering all of a factory's environmental efforts, such as energy use, water treatment, waste disposal, and air quality. In the United Kingdom, Ford's Bridgend Engine Plant just began operating the largest solar power installation at any manufacturing site in Europe. Over a 30-year period, its solar panels were expected to reduce the amount of carbon dioxide emitted at the plant by more than 4,000 tons. In 2002 Ford began its campaign to match

CAN HISTORY REPEAT ITSELF?

In 1945, Henry Ford II, with the government's blessing, left the Armed Forces to take on the unenviable job of trying to rejuvenate the company his famous namesake father had run into the ground and which had produced vehicles for the war effort much of the 1940s. In the 2000s, with the Ford Motor Company unwillingly seeming to be following Oldsmobile into industry extinction, the task of rebuilding faltering Ford is in the hands of William (Bill) Ford—a youthful, perhaps hyperactive man in his early forties with a love of the martial arts, fly fishing, and the environment. His takeover of the company was tantamount to a coup, as he replaced nearly the entire upper tier of company management with his own players. He raised eyebrows by appointing a cousin to head the Mercury brand and by convincing Allan Gilmour, a retired onetime Ford exec nicknamed the "Whiz Kid," to return as chief financial officer.

Just as his famous ancestor Henry Ford had craved the center stage, so too has Bill Ford thrust himself into international recognition seemingly overnight as his face graced Ford's 2002 print and broadcast advertisements. While proud of his family's history, Ford, according to the *Bloomberg News*, doesn't take the family name so seriously that he cannot make small jokes about it. Well educated, holder of an undergraduate degree in history from Princeton University and a graduate degree in business from Massachusetts Institute of Technology, he has always had the image of a strong environmentalist until 2002 when he very visibly fought attempts by activists and politicians to put fuel economy regulations into law, according to the *Bloomberg News*. In 2002 Bill Ford shows every indication of being as ruthless as old Henry Ford himself, cutting lose Ford executives with decades of service who offer either an opposition or threat. The idealism of his youth, manifested in pro-environmental action and statements, has been thrown alongside the road as he's come to realize Ford Motor Company is in too precarious a position in the 2000s to become a poster company for Audubon and other environmental groups. Old Henry Ford, ultimately, became nearly the ruin of his own company and was ousted by his own family. Most analysts say that Bill Ford has until about 2005 to stand and deliver the turnabout in company fortunes he has promised, or he will have the same fate.

Honda and other forward-looking manufacturers in the production of energy-saving hybrid cars.

GLOBAL PRESENCE

While Ford was growing domestically, parallel growth was occurring as part of a foreign expansion program that began in 1904, a year after the company was formed. On August 17, 1904, Ford Motor Company of Canada was formed in the small town of Walkerville, Ontario. From this small beginning grew a large overseas organization of manufacturing plants, assembly plants, parts depots, and dealers. In 2002, Ford was represented in some 200 countries and territories around the world.

Markets Ford targeted during in the twenty-first century included Asia, where the company saw great long-term growth opportunities despite the area's economic turmoil. They aimed for 10 percent market share by 2007. Also as part of its Asian expansion, Ford began manufacturing the Ford Transit in Belarus, China, Malaysia, and Vietnam. The company was also expanding manufacturing opportunities and investing in areas like central and eastern Europe and South America.

EMPLOYMENT

Ford values diversity in its employees and states that "Our global workforce is a competitive strength." The company believes that diversity in its workforce helps it better understand and serve customers. Once hired, the company strives to educate and develop its employees. The company's overall goal was for each employee to receive at least 40 hours of training each year.

SOURCES OF INFORMATION

Bibliography

Evanoff, Ted. "Ford to Exit Heavy Truck Business." *Knight-Ridder/Tribune Business News*, 20 February 1997.

Fitzgerald, Alison. "Toyota Tops Quality Poll; General Motors, Ford Rise." *Bloomberg News*, 30 May 2002.

"Ford Motor Company." *Hoovers Online*, 2002. Available at http://www.hoovers.com.

Ford Motor Company Annual Report 2001. Ford Motor Company, 2001.

Ford Motor Company Web Site, 3 June 2002. Available at http://www.ford.com.

"Improving Automotive Operations Drive Ford to Record First Quarter Earnings of $1.7 Billion, Up 15%." Ford Motor Company Press Release, 16 April 1998.

International Directory of Company Histories. Vol. 11. Detroit, MI: St. James Press, 1995.

Koenig, Bill. "Ford Paid Former CEO Nasser $17.9 million in 2001." *Bloomberg News*, 9 April 2002.

————. "Ford CEO Cuts Workers, Shuts Plants to Staunch Losses." *Bloomberg News*, 17 January 2002.

Kumar, Anita. " Ford Leaves 2-door SUV Unchanged." *St. Petersburg Times*, 29 July 2001.

Lippert, John. " Ford Leaves 2-door SUV Unchanged." *Bloomberg News*, 31 May 2002.

Row, Christopher, and Tim Burt. " New Finance Chief Signals Further Ford Restructuring." *Financial Times (London)*, 21 May 2002.

Taylor, Alex. "The Gentlemen at Ford Are Kicking Butt." *Fortune*, 22 June 1998.

Turrettini, John. " Bye-Bye, American Car." *Forbes*, 27 May 2002.

For an annual report:

write: Ford Motor Company, Shareholder Relations, The American Road, PO Box 1899, Dearborn, MI 48121-1899

For additional industry research:

Investigate companies by their Standard Industrial Classification Codes, also known as SICs. Ford Motor Company's primary SICs are:

3711 Motor Vehicles and Car Bodies

3714 Motor Vehicle Parts and Accessories

6035 Savings Institutions, Federal Chartered

6141 Personal Credit Institutions

6159 Miscellaneous Business Credit Institutions

6331 Fire, Marine, and Casualty Insurance

7515 Passenger Car Leasing

Also investigate companies by their North American Industry Classification System codes, also known as NAICS codes. Ford Motor Company's primary NAICS codes are:

327211 Flat Glass Manufacturing

333924 Industrial Truck, Tractor, Trailer and Stacker Machinery Manufacturing

336111 Automobile Manufacturing

336211 Motor Vehicle Body Manufacturing

336399 All Other Motor Vehicle Parts Manufacturing

522298 All Other Non-Depository Credit Intermediation

Fox Broadcasting Company

FOUNDED: 1986

Contact Information:
HEADQUARTERS: 10201 W. Pico Blvd.
   Los Angeles, CA 90035
PHONE: (310)269-1000
EMAIL: askfox@foxinc.com
URL: http://www.foxworld.com

OVERVIEW

In 1986, Keith Rupert Murdoch launched Fox Broadcasting Company, the first new television network in the United States since 1948. Within a decade, what started as an apparently risky broadcasting endeavor became a network capable of reaching almost 96 percent of U.S. homes through 20 stations and more than 176 affiliates. By 1996 Fox was the top-ranked television group in the United States, with 34.8 percent of market coverage, and the collection of U.S. broadcasting networks that used to be called "The Big Three" came to be known as "The Big Four": ABC, CBS, NBC, and Fox. During the "sweeps" of early 1998, for the first time ever, Fox Broadcasting rose from its fourth place position capturing 12.2 million prime time viewers and dislodging ABC from its third place spot with 11.7 million viewers.

COMPANY FINANCES

Financial information about a company like Fox Broadcasting—a subsidiary of a subsidiary (Fox, Inc.) of a giant corporation (News Corporation, Limited)—is very difficult to obtain. Consider that News Corp. is one of the largest media empires in the world, and along with owning Fox Broadcasting Company, it owns newspapers (the *New York Post*, four major British newspapers, dozens of Australian newspapers) *TV Guide*, a movie company (Twentieth Century Fox), a book publisher (HarperCollins), a 40 percent stake in a U.K. satellite pay-TV service (British Sky Broadcasting), a majority interest in STAR television, an Asian satellite TV network, an airline, the Los Angeles Dodgers, and a sheep farm. It's not surprising that details of Fox Broadcasting's financial costs and contributions are largely buried or entirely obscured in the enormous network of numbers and facts that make up News Corporation's financial statements.

Nonetheless, some details can be gleaned from Fox Entertainment Group's annual reports. The Corporation's three reportable television segments include television stations, a television broadcast network, and other television businesses. These segments get most of their revenues by selling advertising time. For the most part, that time is sold to national advertisers by the Fox Broadcasting Company and to national "spot" and local advertisers by the Company's group of 23 owned-and-operated television broadcast stations in their respective markets.

Revenue from television stations was $1.55 million in 2001, $1.63 million in 2000, and $1.5 million in 1999. For the television broadcast network, revenues were $1.8 million in 2001, $1.75 million in 2000, and $1.74 million in 1999. Revenues for other television businesses were $91 million in 2001, $97 million in 2000, and $118 million in 1999. Operating income for television stations in 2001 was $286 million, compared to $128 million in 2000 and $355 million in 1999. For the television broadcast network, 2001 operating income was $65 million, compared to $29 million in 2000 and $32 million in 1999. For other television businesses, operating income was $8 million in 2001, $11 million in 2000, and $3 million in 1999.

ANALYSTS' OPINIONS

When Fox Broadcasting began delivering programming in 1986, many were skeptical about its chances of success. Brandon Tartikoff, president of NBC Entertainment, called Fox the "coat-hanger network," referring to the fairly weak UHF TV stations Fox had collected. ABC programming master Fred Silverman referred to Fox as "The Mickey Mouse network," and added that "Fox will fail."

Famously, Fox didn't fail. For the first time, Fox bumped one of "The Big Three," ABC, for the spot of third-ranked network in the sweeps of early 1998. Sweeps are considered important for broadcasters because networks use ratings to determine advertising charges. But some, like Christopher Dixon, analyst at Paine Webber, think that network broadcasters are fighting the wrong battle. "Whether or not these broadcasters are number one or number three is a little like shuffling deck chairs on the Titanic," Dixon said. Then he added, "To me, the most interesting thing is the shift between broadcast networks as a whole and the cable industry."

Still, it's a long way from *Herman's Head*, the notoriously bad Fox original comedy series that debuted in 1991, to *Malcom in the Middle*, the original comedy series that made its debut in 2000 to overwhelming critical acclaim. But in the television industry, it's the voice

FINANCES:

Fox Entertainment Group Inc. Operating Incomes, 1997-2001 (million dollars)

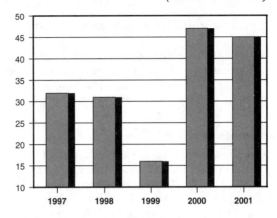

of the viewer that counts most. In 2001, Fox Broadcasting Company, in the most competitive season of its relatively short history, finished a close second in network ratings (behind NBC) in the key demographic of adults 18 to 49. The previous year, it finished third. In addition, in 2001, Fox was ranked first among young adults, teens and male viewers.

HISTORY

Soon after buying the 20th Century Fox film studio in 1985 and six U.S. Metromedia television stations in 1986, Rupert Murdoch announced his decision to launch the Fox Broadcasting Company. In a landscape dominated by broadcast giants CBS, NBC, and ABC, Murdoch wanted Fox to become truly competitive, the country's fourth broadcast television network. Many, including the other three networks, were skeptical about Fox's chances of succeeding. Some, like then ABC Entertainment president Brandon Stoddard, felt the television market was already too saturated for another network. "There probably is a two-network economy as it stands, so I don't know if" a fourth network "can be economically feasible," Stoddard said at the time.

On October 9, 1986, Fox broadcasted its first program, the premiere of *The Late Show With Joan Rivers*, with guests Elton John, Cher, Pee Wee Herman, and David Lee Roth. By mid-1987, Joan Rivers had left the show, which was then hosted by several guest hosts before being hosted by Arsenio Hall. Then Fox abandoned the late night slot to begin concentrating on prime time programming.

FAST FACTS:

About Fox Broadcasting Company

Ownership: Fox Broadcasting is a subsidiary of Fox Entertainment Group, Inc., which is itself a subsidiary of News Corporation Limited, a publicly owned multinational corporation traded on the New York Stock Exchange.

Ticker Symbol: NWS

Officers: K. Rupert Murdoch, Chmn. and CEO News Corporation, Ltd., 67; Chase Carey, COO and EVP Fox, Inc., 44; Peter Chernin, Pres. and COO Fox Entertainment Group, Inc.; David F. DeVoe, SVP and CFO Fox Entertainment Group, Inc., Inc.

Employees: 500

Principal Subsidiary Companies: Fox Broadcasting's subsidiaries include Fox Television Network, Fox Kids, and Fox Sports units.

Chief Competitors Fox Broadcasting Co. has as its main competitors the three other major television networks: National Broadcasting Company, Inc. (NBC), the top-ranked television network in the late 1990s, owned by industrial giant General Electric Company; CBS Corporation, formerly Westinghouse Electric, the second-ranked network toward the end of the twentieth century; and Capital Cities/ABC, Inc., subsidiary of entertainment and media behemoth Walt Disney Corporation.

In early April 1987, Fox offered its first full night of prime time shows that included an outrageous (and, to many, also hilarious) dysfunctional family, the Bundys, in a show Fox called *Married . . . With Children.* The show became a subject of controversy when a Michigan woman campaigned to have it removed from the air, but the free publicity helped bring the show national attention. By July of 1987, Fox added a second full night of prime-time shows.

More controversial than other networks, Fox attracted an audience with a collection of popular shows, including *21 Jump Street, The Tracey Ullman Show, America's Most Wanted*, and, in 1990, *The Simpsons.* Also in 1990,the Academy of Television Arts and Sciences voted to give Fox a three-year contract to broadcast the Emmy Awards, breaking with the show's traditional rotation between the three networks. In an

effort to expand its share of the youth market, Fox also launched the Fox Children's Network in 1990. The partnership with affiliate stations provided younger viewers with both animated and live-action programming. By 1997, the renamed Fox Kids Network enjoyed its fourth year as the top-rated children's program on broadcast television.

By June of 1993, Fox was offering an entire week's worth of prime-time programming. In May of the following year, the network took a serious step toward achieving a significant presence in major cities throughout the United States: it bought a minority stake in New World Communications Group, Inc. and then switched most of the company's stations from CBS to Fox. It was unquestionably the largest affiliation switch in the history of television broadcasting. As a result, in many of the areas in which Fox had been broadcasting on a UHF signal, the network could now transmit on a stronger VHF platform, providing a better channel position and the ability to reach a larger audience.

Two years later, in July of 1996, Rupert Murdoch acquired the remaining 80 percent of New World Communications Group, Inc. for $2.5 billion. With 22 owned-and-operated television stations, the Fox Television Station Group became the single largest group of television stations in the United States, reaching 10 of the 11 largest markets and at least 35 percent of the nation's television audience.

For the 1998-1999 TV season, Fox was number one among teenagers with two successful new series, *Ally McBeal* and *King of the Hill*, which complemented a strong Fox lineup that included perennial favorites *The Simpsons* and *The X-Files*.

By 2001 Fox Television Stations owned and operated 23 full power stations and Fox Broadcasting had 197 affiliated stations. During a typical week, Fox provided affiliates with 15 hours of prime time programming, one hour of late-night programming on Saturday and one hour of Sunday morning news programming.

The year 2001 proved especially strong. Fox finished a close second in the key demographic of adults 18-49 and the 40 Emmy nominations it earned were the most in its history. In addition, four of its new series turned out to be hits: *Malcolm in the Middle, Titus, Boston Public*, and *Dark Angel.*

STRATEGY

From its early days, Fox showed it would not be like the other networks. When it launched its first night of prime time television on April 5, 1987, Fox did not offer traditional family television. Instead, its first night of prime time programming marked the debut of *Married . . .With Children* and *The Tracey Ullman Show.* Instead of representing a conventional, wholesome household,

Married. . .With Children introduced viewers to an uncouth, dysfunctional family called the Bundys. The show would go on to win several Emmy Awards and would become the longest-running situation comedy on American television. That same night, *The Tracey Ullman Show* debuted, introducing the brash young comedienne and an animated segment called "The Simpsons." With its teen cop series *21 Jump Street*, the network demonstrated it wasn't afraid to take on serious life issues such as drugs, prostitution, and child abuse, and it perhaps gained some respect for the public service spots that ended most of its *21 Jump Street* shows. This aggressive approach to television programming paid off. By mid-1987, 113 affiliates joined the network and Fox attracted some major advertisers like Bristol-Myers, General Foods, and Johnson & Johnson.

In 1990, the network expanded its blunt, irreverent take on American home life with its debut of *The Simpsons*. Spun off from *The Tracey Ullman Show*, *The Simpsons* became the first Fox show to beat out its competition on the other networks. In the fall of 1990, Fox moved its animated sitcom to a Thursday night slot to take on NBC's top-rated comedy, *The Cosby Show*. While *The Simpsons* didn't beat out *The Cosby Show* in ratings, it did hurt NBC's ratings and helped establish Fox's image as a major force, especially with the youth market. Fox has become a main vehicle for advertisers wishing to reach the 18 to 34 age group. Many of its shows were youth-targeted or youth-oriented, like *The Simpsons*, *Beverly Hills 90210*, *The X-Files*, *Mad-TV*, and *Melrose Place*.

In the late 1990s and 2000, Fox found itself in the position of having to refurbish its strong primetime lineup after its two hugely successful primetime soaps, *Beverly Hills 90210* and *Melrose Place*, came to the end of their successful runs. Fox opted to develop quality programs and innovative comedies, an approach that resulted in two of its biggest hits, *Malcolm in the Middle* and *Titus*, shows that were as respected by television critics as they were enjoyed by the viewing audience. A mid-season replacement, *Malcolm in the Middle* was the second highest rated premiere in Fox history and soon became one of its most popular series. Its success had the effect of bolstering the viewership for the rest of the Fox Sunday night lineup, which included *King of the Hill* and *Futurarama*. *Titus* had the same effect on another Monday night Fox comedy, *That '70s Show*.

INFLUENCES

Since the early 1980s when only about 25 percent of U.S. homes subscribed to cable services, the cable television industry experienced incredible growth. By the late 1980s, the percentage of U.S. homes with cable services more than doubled. By 1997, cable reached 70 percent or about 65 million U.S. homes. To compete with

CHRONOLOGY:
Key Dates for Fox Broadcasting Company

1985: Rupert Murdoch purchases the 20th Century Fox film studio and announces his plans for a television network

1986: Fox broadcasts its first program, *The Late Show With Joan Rivers*

1987: Fox offers its first full night of prime time shows

1990: The Academy of Television Arts and Sciences gives Fox a three-year contract to broadcast the Emmy Awards and *The Simpsons* debuts

1993: Fox is offering a full week of prime time programming

1994: Murdoch purchases New World Communications Group, Inc. and switches most of the company's stations from CBS to Fox

1996: Fox Television Station Group becomes the single largest group of television stations in the United States

1998: In a company restructuring, the Fox Entertainment Group, Inc. is created

1999: Fox finishes the 1998-1999 TV season a close second to NBC in the key male-ages-18-to-49 segment

2000: News Corporation Chairman and CEO Rupert Murdoch offers free prime time airtime on the Fox network to the two major U.S. presidential candidates

2001: Fox garners 40 Emmy nominations, the most in its history

the expanding reach of cable television, some thought network broadcasters needed to increase sports coverage, particularly of high profile events like National Football League events and the Olympics. Indeed, when CBS covered the Nagano Winter Olympics in 1998, it dominated the Nielsen Media Research ratings. For Fox, an increase in major sports broadcasting came in 1993, when, to the shock of the industry, it succeeded in luring the National Football League from CBS. For almost $1.6 billion, the network bought four years of broadcast rights. The following year, Fox Sports signed a five-year contract with

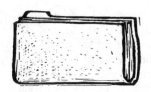

AY, CARAMBA!

He's an underachiever and "proud of it," as he (and thousands of T-shirts) will tell you. He gets himself into a lot of trouble and is a perpetual prankster. Once he filled the school groundkeeper's shack with creamed corn to get back at him for taking his skateboard. Another time he cut off the head of the statue of the town founder. You can often find this little good-for-nothing after school writing one of several admonishments on the blackboard: "I will not belch the national anthem; I will not call my teacher 'hot cakes;' the principal's toupee is not a Frisbee; spitwads are not free speech; I will not bury the new kid." Prank phone calls to the local watering hole are one of his bad habits: "Is Oliver there? Oliver Clothesoff?" If you make an issue of his less-than-perfect behavior, he'll tell you, "Don't have a cow, man!" or perhaps "Eat my shorts!" His father, a rather slow-witted chap, is often driven to choking the boy because of his misbehavior. This 1990s Dennis the Menace was once tried for killing his principal and once made the unfortunate miscalculation of selling his soul for five dollars.

Lisa, the little brat's sister and the brain of the family (but then, considering the family, that's not saying much), believes she has an explanation for her brother's delinquent deeds: "That little hell-raiser is the spawn of every shrieking commercial, every brain-rotting soda pop, every teacher who cares less about young minds than about cashing their big, fat paychecks." But, as *Time*

magazine points out, "The kid knows right from wrong. He just likes wrong better."

Despite of all his misdeeds and bratty behavior (or maybe because of them), *TV Guide* named him one of the 50 greatest TV stars of all time, and *Time* named him one of the twentieth century's most influential artists and entertainers, putting him next to Picasso, T. S. Eliot, James Joyce, Frank Sinatra, and the Beatles.

By this time you've probably figured out that the above-mentioned scalawag is none other than Bart Simpson, the impish star of Fox's hit animated series of the 1990s, *The Simpsons*, a cartoon tale about a dysfunctional family living in a dysfunctional town in a dysfunctional universe. Bart became the cultural icon of 1990s. He was the role model of slackers everywhere ("I will not fake my way through life," he was once forced to write on the blackboard). He was also a big boost to Fox, helping propel it to full-fledged network status. *The Simpsons* became the longest-running prime time cartoon in history and also won several Emmys. Eventually it became no longer cool to shout "Cowabunga, man!" or "Ay, caramba!" and Bart's popularity gave way to the likes of Beavis and Butthead and the foul-mouthed tykes of *South Park*, but one suspects that the little yellow rascal from Springfield will outlast them all.

the National Hockey League, and in 1996 it began a five-year deal with Major League Baseball.

Fox also began making inroads into cable when, in October 1996, the Fox News Channel began cable broadcasting with its News Channel. Unfortunately for the company, its earlier distribution plans with Time Warner, Inc. fell through a month earlier when the media monolith backed out of plans for Fox distribution on its New York City cable services. Time Warner was then in the process of merging with Turner Broadcasting, whose Cable News Network (CNN) was a direct competitor to Fox News. CNN was to be carried on Time Warner's cable along with the new 24-hour news station, MSNBC. This meant a loss of more than 1 million homes for Fox and it quickly filed a federal anti-trust lawsuit against Time Warner, requesting the court block the merger of Time Warner and Turner Broadcasting and award Fox $1 billion in damages. In spite of the unexpected reduction in distribution, that year, Fox News Channel was ranked twelfth among the top cable channels.

CURRENT TRENDS

By 1999, Fox Broadcasting Company was out in front of all the major networks in terms of audience growth and advertising gains. That year, the advertisers, realizing that Fox attracted a large following among a very attractive demographic market, spent a record $1.3 billion toward the fall primetime season. For Fox, this created a 14 per cent increase in upfront ad revenues, the largest percentage increase of all four networks. It was also the fourth straight year that Fox demonstrated double-digit growth.

Advertisers were also impressed by the quality and success of Fox's new prime time fare. Fox was forced to rebuild its lineup after its era of prime time soaps came to and end. The company responded by producing its best programs yet. As a result, Fox experienced the fastest viewership growth rate among all of the top networks.

PRODUCTS

In addition to news, sports, and children's programming, Fox in its relatively short history has offered some of the most successful shows on television. For instance, Fox's 1997 lineup included tremendously popular shows like *Ally McBeal* and *The X-Files*. Other top-rated prime time Fox programs have included *America's Most Wanted*, *COPS*, *Beverly Hills 90210*, and *Melrose Place*.

Some of Fox's more controversial programs include specials like "When Stunts Go Bad" and "Breaking the Magician's Code: Magic's Biggest Secrets Revealed." When Fox planned to air its third show revealing magicians' secrets on May 5, 1998, a coalition of over 1,000 magicians from the Society of American Magicians, the International Brotherhood of Magicians, and elsewhere, filed legal action, urged a viewer boycott, and organized free magic shows at public venues around the country at the time of the broadcast. The coalition denounced the program's host, who was dubbed "the Masked Magician" because he wore a costume concealing his face while he exposed secrets behind magic tricks. According to the magicians, the Fox specials threatened the careers of some magicians. They claimed that since the specials started airing in November 1997, some magicians have lost jobs and some have had to give up elaborate illusions that cost them a tremendous amount of time and money to learn. Magician Andre Cole went to court in Los Angeles in late April 1998 to try to obtain a temporary restraining order to keep Fox from exposing the secret behind his patented "Table of Death" illusion. Cole's request was denied. Veteran magician Chuck Jones said, "This has not affected me personally, but I worry about the amateur magicians who spend $1,000 or so on one prop, and then it's exposed on these specials. Now they can't use it anymore."

SOURCES OF INFORMATION

Bibliography

Braxton, Greg. "Magicians Wish Fox Special Would Vanish." *Los Angeles Times*, 1 May 1998.

Business Rankings Annual. Detroit, MI: Gale Research, 1998.

Fox Broadcasting Home Page, 1 June 1998. Available at http://www.foxworld.com.

"Fox Sweeps ABC Aside." CNNfn, 6 March 1998.

Fox Tenth Anniversary: A Decade of Revolutionizing Television. New York: Fox Broadcasting Co., 31 March 1997. Available at http://www.foxworld.com/presroom.htm#tenth.

Frank, Allan Dodds. "TV Titans Square Off." CNNfn, 9 October 1996. Available at http://www.cnnfn.com.

Lazich, Robert S., ed. *Market Share Reporter-1998*, Detroit, MI: Gale Research, 1997.

"Miller Brewing Teams With Fox in Groundbreaking Agreement." *Business Wire*, 28 August 1997.

"The News Corporation Limited." Hoover's Online, 1 June 1998. Available at http://www.hoovers.com.

Paeth, Greg. "Fox in the Penthouse After 10 Years, the ëCoat-Hanger Network' Is Sitting Pretty." *Rocky Mountain News*, 5 April 997.

Schwartz, Shelly. "ABC Shelves Ellen." CNNfn, 24 April 1998.

"S&P Description: News Corp., Inc." *Standard & Poor's*, 7 April 1998.

Wian, Casey. "Murdoch Enters New World." CNNfn, 17 July 1996.

Yahoo! Finance. "Fox Entertainment Group." CNNfn, 17 April 2002. Available at: http://biz.yahoo.com/p/f/fox.html

For an annual report:
on the Internet at: http://www.newscorp.com/feg/FEGannual_reports.html.

For additional industry research:
Investigate companies by their Standard Industrial Classification Codes, also known as SICs. Fox Broadcasting Company's primary SICs are:

4833 Television Broadcasting

4841 Cable Networks and Other Program Distribution

Also investigate companies by their North American Industry Classification System Codes, also known as NAICS codes. Fox Broadcasting Company's primary NAICS codes are:

513120 Television Broadcasting

513210 Cable Networks

513220 Cable and Other Program Distribution

FUBU

FOUNDED: 1992
VARIANT NAME: "For Us, By Us"

Contact Information:

HEADQUARTERS: 350 Fifth Avenue, Suite 6617
   New York, New York 10018
PHONE: (212)273-3300
FAX: (212)273-3333
EMAIL: info@fubu.com
URL: http://www.fubu.com

OVERVIEW

FUBU, an acronym for "For Us, By Us," is the name of the hugely successful "urban" sportswear business started in 1992 by a former waiter working in the basement of his mother's Queens, New York, home. The slogan reflects founder Daymond John's aim to create a line of clothing designed for African-Americans by African-Americans.

From its humble beginning, FUBU and Raymond soon moved to fashionable Fifth Avenue in Manhattan, occupying a suite in the Empire State Building with partners Alexander Martin, Carl Brown, and Keith Perrin. The company now has 15 of its own domestic and international outlets, and its label is sold in more than 5,000 stores across the world including Macy's, Foot Locker, Nordstrom, and Champs.

For many mention of the FUBU apparel line conjures images of rap stars, the hip-hop culture and, most importantly, baggy clothing. But the company soon acquired a much broader appeal, which led to phenomenal financial success and significant expansion.

Expansion included increased product offerings as well as an extended global reach. Its line grew to include men's, women's, and children's wear, footwear, and accessories such as watches, caps, and bags. In addition the company recently expanded into Asia, established 20 international franchised stores, and sold products internationally in Japan, Germany, France, England, and Australia. Expansion also included ventures into areas outside the clothing business. The company's FB Entertainment division is involved with recording artists. Its online retail site, Y2G.com, also targets lifestyle issues especially relevant to Latino and African-American visitors.

COMPANY FINANCES

FUBU is a privately owned company, and founder Daymond John has said it will never go public. For that reason, specifics about its finances are hard to come by. However, reports from various sources indicate the company has demonstrated impressive financial success over the course of a few short years. In 1998 it was reported that FUBU made more than $350 million in total sales in more than 5,000 stores worldwide. This included an annual sales volume of $200 million from its menswear business alone and $150 million from its licenses. It has been estimated that its annual revenues are close to $1 billion.

ANALYSTS' OPINIONS

For several years FUBU has been considered one of the "hottest" urban clothing lines in the industry. Success of that magnitude requires a broad base appeal and, in the beginning, FUBU had to overcome a perception that it was a racially exclusive label. This was due, in large part, to its slogan, "For Us, By Us," which many mistook as a hostile stance that reflected a reverse racism. This, however, was not the case. Founder John always intended the slogan as a statement of pride and empowerment. The negative notions were quickly dispelled and the FUBU line soon garnered a very broad appeal, meaning that its clothing was wildly popular with white kids in North America as well as young consumers internationally.

Not only did FUBU gain acceptance with consumers on a multi-cultural, global scale, it earned the recognition and respect among peers and observers of the fashion industry as well as the business world in general. In 1999 the company partners received the NAACP Entrepreneurs of the Year Award, while the company received a Citation of Honor from the Office of the President, Borough of Queens, City of New York. That same year, FUBU won an Outstanding Business Achievement Award as part of the New York African-American Business Awards, an Essence Award, and a Congressional Achievement Award for Entrepreneurship. The following year, FUBU collected a Black Alumni of Pratt Creative Spirit Award and the "Best Fashion Designer Label" award from the Online Hip Hop Awards. In 2001 FUBU received its second straight Hip Hop award, as well as a Source Foundation-Hip Hop Cares Award and a Salute to Urban Professionals in Business award from *NV* magazine.

HISTORY

FUBU was founded in 1992, its creation sparked by founder Daymond John's inability to find himself a decent hat. That circumstance compelled him to create

Tyson Beckford, left, FUBU CEO Daymond John, center, and LL Cool J. pose at a New York party introducing Platinum FUBU, a clothing line for men. (AP Photo/FUBU, Johnny Nunez)

his own tie-top hats in the basement of his mother's home in Queens, New York.

After John realized he could actually make some decent money selling his hats (he picked up $800 in one day selling them on the street), he took a $100,000 mortgage on the home, presumably with his mother's blessing, and turned part of the house into a factory. John then created ideas for coats and shirts and learned the necessary sewing skills from his mother. He also took on some partners from the neighborhood: J. Alexander Martin, who would become company vice president, and co-founders Keith Perrin and Carl Brown. They came up with the FUBU name and slogan and called themselves the "FUBU Team."

John learned how to create an apparel collection through a friend who was attending the Fashion Institute for Merchandising. The knowledge gained gave him insight on the technicalities for producing a complete collection. This allowed him to expand his collection to include bulk tee shirts, rugby shirts, hockey jerseys, and baseball hats, all of which displayed the FUBU logo.

At first, the partners encountered difficulty when they tried to sell their goods through the traditional means. To overcome the obstacles, they managed to get some celebrities and hip-hop artists to help promote their line. FUBU's first big break was convincing L.L. Cool

FAST FACTS:

About FUBU

Ownership: FUBU is a privately owned company. Its partners include founder Daymond John, Alexander Martin, Carl Brown, and Keith Perrin.

Officers: Daymond John, Pres. and CEO, 31; J. Alexander Martin, VP; Leslie Short, Pres. of Public Relations; Theresa Wang, CFO

Employees: 1,075

Principal Subsidiary Companies: FUBU includes 15 domestic and international outlets. Company divisions include Y2G.com, an Internet enterprise, and FB Entertainment, a record label.

Chief Competitors: The company operates in the apparel and clothing industry, where its top competitors include NIKE, Phat, and Tommy Hilfiger.

a distinctive void in the fashion industry. Even though young African-American consumers spend a great deal of money on clothes, there were no young African-American designers. By creating FUBU, John filled this void, to his company's benefit. It also helped that John knew LL Cool J. The effect this friendship had on the company's success cannot be underestimated. The rapper's celebrity status provided the company with a great deal of exposure and street validity. John also sought advice from acquaintances who worked with textiles and in the fashion industry, gaining insight from their experience. These relationships taught him a great deal about distribution, shipping, financing, and product timing.

John also established a special rapport with consumers, adopting a mindset of a potential FUBU customer. He ensured the partners' image would mirror FUBU consumers. The partners decided to wear the same clothes the customers wore and go after the same "look," which provided a strong identification factor. In addition the company continues to keep its ear to ground, still dealing with customers on a one-on-one basis to obtain valuable feedback about products and marketing strategies. This approach is what differentiated FUBU from other companies that catered to the young urban market, including Tommy Hilfiger, Naughty Gear, Phat Farm, Pure Playaz, UB Tuff, and Wu-Wear.

J. to become a company spokesperson. Cool J was also from the neighborhood, so it was relatively easy for John to convince him to wear the clothes.

Some more big breaks soon followed. In 1995, after FUBU made an impressive showing at a trade show in Las Vegas, the Samsung America company decided to become an investor, and it distributed FUBU shirts and bubble jackets in boutiques like Dr. Jay's and Casual Male on the East Coast. A year later FUBU became the only African-American-owned designer company to have its own display window in Macy's in New York City. In 1999 FUBU scored a coup when it signed an apparel deal with the National Basketball Association (NBA).

STRATEGY

Going into the business, John employed the kind of tactics all entrepreneurs should embrace when starting a small enterprise. First, he determined to himself that his product would actually be viable. This he did by giving it exposure at fashion shows, expos, and even by selling it on the street and from door-to-door. Then he developed a business plan, which included seeking backing from small-loan business outlets and by advertising in business newspapers.

John also recognized and then seized existing opportunities. Most important, perhaps, was his recognition of

INFLUENCES

To John, exposure was, and is, of paramount importance to success, especially for companies that markets similar products and caters to a youthful demographic. To ensure maximum exposure, he ventured into marketing areas that other companies catering to the same niche hadn't tried. FUBU, according to John, was the first clothing manufacturer to use music videos to market its products. By convincing music stars like L.L. Cool J to wear the FUBU label in their videos, the company essentially received a free endorsement. FUBU's own commercials have the look and feel of a music video, and they have appeared in heavy rotation on cable channels like Black Entertainment Television (BET) and MTV.

In addition, FUBU built upon its relationship with L.L. Cool J to increase its base of celebrity endorsement. Famous personalities such as Hype Williams, Billy Woodruff, Mariah Carey, Mary J. Blige, Boys II Men, Fugees, and Will Smith would become both friends and supporters. FUBU also sought out, and received, patronage from athletes in the National Football League (NFL) and the NBA.

CURRENT TRENDS

In recent years of FUBU's relatively short history, the company has gone from the street, into upscale stores, and into international outlets. FUBU now concentrates on the area of e-commerce to maximize its exposure and profits. John feels that the World Wide Web will become an integral part of his business, as it will enable FUBU to reach customers on a global scale. But e-commerce can be a tricky and risky area, as John well knows, especially for companies that sell clothing products. For one thing, retailers don't like manufacturers who sell products directly to consumers over the Internet, as FUBU has started to do at its own Web site. Additionally, Internet shopping does not seem to be the kind of shopping experience that the FUBU demographic seeks and enjoys. For targets of the FUBU market, shopping is a hands-on experience. They tend to like to see clothing up close, to be able to touch the product and try it on. Shopping, for them, is a "hanging out" activity. Despite these concerns, John forges ahead with his e-commerce activity, waiting and watching to see how it will play out. Still, he is going against the grain. Companies such as Nautica, Tommy Hilfiger, and Levi Strauss either take a conservative approach to e-commerce or they don't sell products online at all.

The FUBU Web site isn't John's only Internet enterprise. Company products are also sold at Y2G.com, a minority-oriented site that FUBU launched in 2000. More than just an online shopping outlet, Y2G is intended as a lifestyle portal, as it offers a broad range of content ranging from rap concert reviews, profiles of colleges, insurance information, career advice, and financial strategies.

FUBU has also branched out into the music business. This is in keeping with John's stated aim to ultimately transform FUBU into a corporate conglomerate involved in media and sports as well as fashion. In 2001 FUBU launched its own record label with the release of a hip-hop and R&B compilation titled "The Good Life." Artists featured include Nate Dogg, Ludacris, Dawn Robinson, L.L. Cool J, and Keith Murray. This first release was available in both music and clothing stores.

In the meantime, John is determined to increase the FUBU demographic and dispel any lingering perceptions that the company is only an "urban" clothing manufacturer.

PRODUCTS

FUBU's product line for men includes shirts, jackets, tee shirts, hooded sweatshirts, athletic shoes, formal wear including suits and tuxedos, and accessories including watches and athletic bags. Products for boys include sportswear and athletic shoes. Products for women including apparel items such as pants, shirts, intimate wear, halter tops, sweatshirts, sweaters, dress jackets, and full-length down jackets. Women's shoes include dressy boots, sandals, and athletic shoes. Accessories include bags and watches.

CHRONOLOGY:
Key Dates for FUBU

1992: Daymond John starts FUBU in the basement of his mother's home

1993: John take a $100,000 mortgage on his mother's home to build the business and takes on three partners

1995: Samsung America invests in FUBU

1996: FUBU products are showcased in a Macy's display window in New York City

1997: John establishes the charitable FUBU Foundation

1999 FUBU reports overall sales of $350 million; FUBU signs an apparel deal with the NBA

2000: FUBU launches the Y2G.com Web site

2001: FUBU branches out into the music business

FUBU's Home Collection includes a bath collection that offer towels, shower curtains, and soap dishes.

GLOBAL PRESENCE

In less than 10 years, FUBU managed to garner global recognition. According to the company, it serves cities "all over the world. In the international fashion arena, FUBU distributes product in Australia, France, Germany, Asia, and Japan."

CORPORATE CITIZENSHIP

The company established the charitable FUBU Foundation in 1997. According to the company, it donates approximately $1 million a year to the foundation. In 2001 the foundation donated to a New York radio station's fund to benefit families of the September 11 terrorist attack victims. FUBU also contributes to several community-based organizations such as Camp Cool J, and it provides academic scholarships for students interested in attending college.

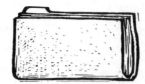

FROM MINIMUM WAGE TO MILLIONS

Before going into the business full-time with FUBU, Daymond John was a waiter at Red Lobster. Alexander Martin was in the U.S. Navy, serving during the Persian Gulf War. Keith Perrin was an apartment supervisor. Carl Brown worked on a loading dock. Looks like they made good career choices.

EMPLOYMENT

John reports that approximately 75 people work directly under him, while the company's affiliates, licensees, and stores employ about 1,000 people.

SOURCES OF INFORMATION

Bibliography

CNN.com. "Black History Month 2002." *Business-FUBU*, February 2002. Available at http://www.cnn.com/SPECIALS/2002/black.history.

CrosstownArts.com. "FUBU on the Rise." *Sets Web*, 1998. Available at http://www.crosstownarts.com.

"FUBU Industry Info." *Hoover's Online*, 2 May 2002. Available at http://www.hoovers.com.

HollisNY.com. "FUBU Born in Hollis, New York," 30 January 2001. Available at http://www.hollisny.com/fubu.htm.

"Ludacris, Nass, India.Arie to Appear on FUBU CD," 10 August 2001. Available at http://www.mtv.com.

"Start Me Up-Online Chats: Daymond John." *Smart Money Magazine*, 2002. Available at http://www.smartmoney.com.

Stein, Joel. "Getting Giggly with a Hoodie." *Time.com*, 19 January 1998.

Tate, Janine. "Black is Beautiful-and in Style." *The Southern Digest Online*, 5 April 2002. Available at http://www.southerndigest.com.

Walentas, David. "NY99: The New York Awards." *NewYork-Metro.com*, 1999.

Warner, Bernhard. "FUBU Sells 'Cool' Online-and Hats, Too." *The Industry Standard*, 8 May 2000. Available at http://www.thestandard.com.

Williams, Geoff. "Keeping Your Cool." *Business Startups*, 2002. Available at http://www.entrepreneur.com.

For additional industry research:

Investigate companies by their Standard Industrial Classification Codes, also known as SICs. FUBU's primary SICs are:

2321 Mens & Boys Shirts Except Work Shirts

5611 Men's & Boys' Clothing & Furnishings

Also investigate companies by their North American Industry Classification System codes, also known as NAICS codes. FUBU's primary NAICS code is:

315223 Men's and Boys' Cut and Sew Shirt (except Work Shirt) Manufacturing

General Dynamics Corporation

OVERVIEW

General Dynamics, the leading supplier of sophisticated defense systems in the United States, was formed in 1952 as a successor to the Electric Boat Company. The company's primary businesses are information and communications technology, land and amphibious combat systems, naval and commercial shipbuilding, and business aviation. Operations are conducted in four main business groups: Information Systems and Technology, Combat Systems, Marine Systems, and Aerospace. Information Systems specializes in data acquisition and processing, advanced electronics, and battlespace information networks and management systems. Combat Systems designs and manufactures land and amphibious combat machines and systems, such as armored vehicles, turrets, munitions, and gun systems. The Marine System division designs and builds submarines, battle ships, auxiliary ships, and large commercial ships. Aerospace, a division added in 1999 after the acquisition of Gulfstream Aerospace, specializes in the design and manufacturing of mid-size, large, and ultra-long range airplanes.

General Dynamic's most important customer is the U.S. military, which accounts for 59 percent of the company's business. Domestic commercial accounts total 30 percent of the company's revenues, and international defense and commercial customers bring in 11 percent of business, producing 5 percent and 6 percent, respectively. Headquartered in Falls Church, Virginia, General Dynamics employs approximately 52,000 people in the United States, Canada, Mexico, and the United Kingdom.

FOUNDED: 1952

Contact Information:

HEADQUARTERS: 3190 Fairview Park Drive
   Falls Church, VA 22042-4523
PHONE: (703)876-3000
FAX: (703)876-3125
TOLL FREE: (800)758-5804
URL: http://www.generaldynamics.com

FINANCES:

*General Dynamics Corporation
Net Sales, 1997-2001
(million dollars)*

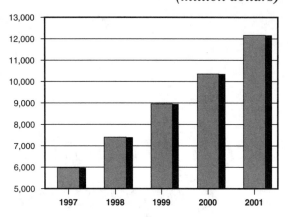

*General Dynamics Corporation
2001 Stock Prices
(dollars)*

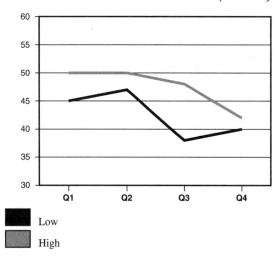

■ Low
■ High

COMPANY FINANCES

General Dynamics' net sales totaled $12.2 billion in 2001, an increase of 17 percent over the $10.4 billion posted in 2000. Removing sales gained through acquisitions during the year, the company's net sales increased over 7 percent, with growth realized in all four main business segments. Information Systems and Technology grew its total sales from $2.4 billion in 2000 to $2.8 billion in 2001 primarily through increased business from acquisitions. Combat Systems' good organic growth,

along with two key acquisitions during 2001, pushed total sales to $2.2 billion in 2001, up from $1.3 billion in 2000. Marine Systems increased total revenues by nearly $2 million, posting $3.6 billion in sales in 2001 compared to $3.4 billion in 2000. The Aerospace division pushed sales up from $3.0 billion in 2000 to $3.3 billion in 2001, primarily through acquisitions.

General Dynamics' total revenues for 2001 resulted in a net income of $943 million, up from $901 million in 2000. The company's cash balance increased from $177 million at year-end 2000 to $442 at year-end 2001. However, during the same time period company debt jumped from $336 million to $1.5 billion due primarily to significant investments in acquisitions during the year. Nonetheless, General Dynamics' debt load is 24 percent, well below the industry average of 45 percent. Stock prices opened January of 1999 at $59.75 per share; January of 2000 at $52.17; January of 2001 at $78.19; and January of 2002 at $79.50. By April of 2002, stock prices reached $94.15 per share. Because the company most often operates under long-term contracts, backlog amounts are significant. In 2001 total backlog amounted to $25.8 billion, of which $19.4 billion was already funded.

ANALYSTS' OPINIONS

Because General Dynamics' sales come predominately from the U.S. government and its agencies, funding for the company's products and services is generally linked to trends in U.S. and international defense spending. Prior to the terrorist attacks on New York and the Pentagon on September 11, 2001, the outlook for the defense industry was lackluster at best. However, when the markets reopened on September 17, defense sector stocks did not plunge in price, as did much of the market, instead posting a 15 to 20 percent gain. Although aggressive analysts predict that U.S. defense spending may increase as much as 30 percent or more by 2003, most analysts caution that the positive impact on the defense industry, although apparent, may not be as substantial if military efforts are directed at counter terrorism rather than traditional war machinery. However, because General Dynamics produces expendable goods, such as ammunition and bombs, as well as providing tactical-communications systems, analysts consider it safe to assume that it will experience growth, at least for the short- and medium-term future.

HISTORY

General Dynamics Corporation has its roots in the Electric Boat Company, founded by John Holland in 1899. Holland, an Irish-American inventor, was commissioned by a group of Irish nationalists to develop a submarine capable of sinking British naval ships. Although his plans to help the Irish nationalists were thwarted when his activities drew the attention of New York law enforcement officials, he continued to work on developing a viable submarine. Garnering some financial support from investors, Holland formed the Electric Boat Company, but he was unsuccessful in marketing his prototype. Eventually Isaac Leopold Rice, a wealthy businessman, agreed to provide substantial financial support to Electric Boat for an interest in the company. Consequently, Holland relinquished control of his company and gave up his patent rights to Rice, who in turn was able to negotiate sales to the U.S. Navy or several other foreign countries. By 1904 Holland was making $90 a week as chief engineer while his company, now firmly under Rice's control, was selling submarines for $300,000 each.

In 1905 Electric Boat came under government scrutiny for unscrupulously selling submarines to both Japan and Russia while the two countries were at war with each other. By 1914 the British Navy was purchasing submarines from Electric Boat, placing the submarine squarely in the arena of new, necessary war machinery. In the same year Holland resigned, frustrated over his lack of involvement and, as an Irishman, angered over the sales made to the British. He died within the year; Rice died the following year.

Under new chief engineer Lawrence Spear, the Holland submarine was redesigned for increased speed and added such features such as a periscope, conning tower, and torpedo tubes. With Henry Carse replacing Rice as the head of the company, Electric Boat made several acquisitions, including Electro Dynamics, Elco Motor Yacht, and New London Ship & Engine of Groton, Connecticut. Carse also renamed the company Submarine Boat Company. At the beginning of World War I, Carse moved away from building submarines to focus on the manufacturing of disposable cargo vessels. However, it was soon clear that the demand for submarines was greater. Carse moved to retool the company's operations, but by the time full production of submarines was achieved, the war had ended. The situation left the company on the verge of financial ruin. Carse once again reorganized, took back the name Electric Boat, and focused on the production of surface ships.

In the years following World War I, Electric Boat came under public scrutiny again when a congressional investigation concluded that the company had acted unethically by benefiting from sales to unscrupulous governments. Electric Boat countered that the sharp decline in orders from the U.S. Navy had forced the company to do business with less-than-ethical foreign governments in order to stay financially stable. The advent of World War II brought new life into the company. Government orders for submarines and patrol/torpedo, known as PT boats, skyrocketed. Operations at Groton and the New Jersey Elco plant swung into full force. The demand for labor necessitated the hiring of women to serve as welders and riveters. However, the prosperity lasted only

FAST FACTS:

About General Dynamics Corporation

Ownership: General Dynamics is a publicly held company traded on the New York, Chicago, and Pacific Stock Exchanges.

Ticker Symbol: GD

Officers: Nicholas D. Chabraja, Chmn. and CEO, 58, 2000 salary $950,000, 2000 bonus $1,750,000; W. William Boisture, Jr., EVP, 56, 2000 salary $400,000, 2000 bonus $450,000; Gordon R. England, EVP, 2000 salary $440,000, 2000 bonus $460,000; Michael J. Mancuso, SVP and CFO, 2000 salary $400,000, 2000 bonus $450,000

Employees: 49,000

Principal Subsidiary Companies: General Dynamics' operations world wide compete within one of four main business segments: Aerospace, Combat Systems, Information Systems and Technology, and Marine Systems. Larger units include: Bath Iron Works Corp. and the Electric Boat Corp.

Chief Competitors: General Dynamic Corporation's competitors include Boeing, ITT Industries, Lockheed Martin, Newport News Shipbuilding, Raytheon, and United Defense Industries.

as long as the war, and at its end in 1945, only 4,000 of the company's 13,000 employees were retained on its payrolls, and the stock price dropped quickly from $30 to $10 a share.

Needing to diversify, Electric Boat purchased Canadair from the Canadian government in 1945 for $22 million. As the Korean War approached Canadair filled increased orders for aircraft, such as T-33 trainers, F-86 Sabres, and DC-6s. Although Electric Boat was rather stagnant, proceeds from Canadair allowed the company to diversify once again, this time by acquiring Convair, which manufactured civilian and military airplanes. Convair subsequently became a leader in the development of nuclear-powered vessels. Although the idea for a nuclear-power aircraft was eventually abandoned as impractical, Convair was successful in launching its first nuclear submarine, the *Nautilus*, in 1955.

On February 21, 1952, Electric Boat and its entities were reorganized. General Dynamics was formed as the holding company for Electric Boat, Canadair, and

CHRONOLOGY:

Key Dates for General Dynamics Corporation

1899: John Holland forms the Electric Boat Company to develop a submarine prototype, but loses control of his company to electronics magnate Isaac Rice

1904: Electric Boat comes under fire for selling submarines to Japan and Russia, who were at war with each other

1914: The Holland submarine is redesigned, making it faster and adding a periscope and torpedo tubes for the first time

1918: Facing bankruptcy, emphasis is shifted to surface ships in order to meet U.S. Navy demands

1945: Stock drops from $30 to $10 and workforce falls from 13,000 to 400 after demand for submarines declines sharply at the close of World War II

1952: After diversifying its production by acquiring two subsidiaries, Convair and Canadair, General Dynamics is formed as a parent company for Convair, Canadair, and Electric Boat

1955: Launches its first nuclear-powered submarine, the *Nautilus*

1960: Wins government bid to build F-111 to replace the aging fleet of B-52 bombers

1963: Quincy shipbuilding works is purchased for $5 million from Bethlehem Steel

1971: Wins government award to manufacture a new submarine, the *668,* or *Los Angeles*, class

1977: Electric Boat is accused of poor workmanship and cost overruns of as much as $89 million per submarine on 18 of its *Los Angeles* vessels

1978: The F-16 fighter jet becomes a major product for the company

1982: Chrysler battle tank division, renamed Land Systems, is purchased to build M-1 battle tanks

1990: In the wake of the end of the Cold War after the collapse of the Soviet Union, General Dynamics suffers a loss of $578 for the year

1992: Labor force is reduced by 25% and $1.7 billion of assets were put up for sale

1993: Company reorganizes by limiting focus to nuclear submarines and armored vehicles, and workforce is dropped to 30,500, down from 86,000 three years earlier

1999: Net income rebounds to $880 million on revenues of almost $9 billion

2001: Employee base rebounds to 52,000 worldwide and revenues surpass $12 billion

---

Convair. The company took a major blow in 1954 when Convair was unable to introduce its new jetliner due to contractual obligations imposed on it by TWA and its major shareholder, Howard Hughes. While competitors Douglas and Boeing were launching their DC-8 and 707 passenger jets, Convair was caught trying to fulfill numerous design changes required by Hughes. As a result, General Dynamics' passenger jetliner program cost the company a $425 million loss. Financially weakened by the ordeal, in 1959 General Dynamics agreed to merge with Material Services Corporation, owned by Henry Crown, a Chicago-based construction materials magnate, who then claimed a 20 percent share of the company.

During the 1960s General Dynamics won the bid to produce a new F-111 aircraft for the U.S. military, despite the fact that many believed the Boeing design was superior. After design changes requested by the Air Force and Navy were implemented, the originally flawed design was virtually unable to get off the ground and nowhere

close to replacing the battle-tested B-52. The project was exorbitantly expensive, and congressional members sharply criticized the whole venture as a study of gross mismanagement, organizational incompetence, and an incredible waste of funding.

In 1971 the Electric Boat division and its chief competitor, Newport News Shipbuilding, were awarded government contracts to manufacture the new *668,* or *Los Angeles*, class submarine. The government also announced plans for a new fighter jet. Careful to avoid the problems encountered with the F-111, General Dynamic's F-16 model was awarded the contract and completed on schedule. However, the Defense Department chose to purchase McDonnell Douglas' independently produced F-15 Eagle, which rivaled the F-16 design and was cheaper. The government compensated General Dynamics by recommending the F-16 to its allies. In 1976 Canadair was repurchased by the Canadian government for $38 million.

An artist's rendering of the DD-21 next-generation destroyer. (AP Photo/General Dynamics)

Controversy stung General Dynamics again in 1977 when Admiral Rickover publicly denounced Electric Boat for its poor workmanship on 18 *Los Angeles* submarines. He was also angered by cost overruns totaling as much as $38 million per vessel, which the government was contractually obligated to absorb. The Defense Department threatened to withhold payment and Electric Boat countered by threatening to suspend production of the submarines. In the end, Electric Boat won a suit against the Defense Department. The situation lead to an overhaul of the management of Electric Boat.

In 1981 General Dynamics purchased the battle tank division of Chrysler for $336 million, renamed it as the Land Systems unit, and won a government contract to manufacture the new M-1 tank. The prototype received significant criticism for design flaws, such as exhaust heat that prohibited ground troops from seeking cover under fire; its tendency to breakdown; its excessive need for fuel; and an inadequately sized ammunitions bay. The tank's strong points included speeds of up to 50 miles per hour and a computer-guided aiming system that allowed accurate gunfire while traveling over rough terrain.

In 1982 General Dynamics executives were called to testify before a congressional hearing on matters related to alleged overcharging of the government by the company. Former company executive, Takis Veliotis, fled the country after coming under indictment for illegal business practices. In the midst of the investigation General Dynamics was awarded a new government con-

tract, including the production of the Ohio class Trident submarine. Eventually the investigation was dropped. Throughout the 1980s and early 1990s, General Dynamics continued both to sell off certain assets and acquire new ones. Its main source of business continued to be the federal government.

During the 1990s, as the federal budget for defense spending decreased, General Dynamics looked for ways to cut costs. Between 1991 and 1993 the company's work force dropped from 86,000 to 30,500. It sold its Texas aircraft operations to Lockheed Martin for $1.5 billion in 1992 and purchased National Steel and Shipbuilding Company for $415 million in 1998. A 1999 bid to takeover Newport News Shipbuilding was blocked by the government. Instead, General Dynamics acquired GTE Government Systems Corporation for $1.05 billion and Gulfstream Aerospace Corporation for $4.8 billion. By the end of the 1990s, General Dynamics was showing signs of increased financial health, posting net profits of $880 million on revenues of nearly $9 billion in 1999.

STRATEGY

During the 1990s as defense spending was reduced, General Dynamics took significant steps to trim its operating expenses, cutting its workforce by nearly one third and selling off numerous businesses. By the time the cutbacks were complete, the company retained only Electric

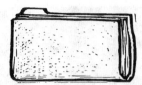

THE DEMISE OF THE A-12 PROJECT

In 1991 the U.S. Navy cancelled General Dynamics' contract to build the A-12 fighter jet because the project was so far behind schedule and over budget. As a result of the termination for default, the Navy demanded that General Dynamics and McDonnell Douglas, the other contractor for the project, repay $1.35 billion in payments already made. In turn, the two companies filed a challenge to the termination for default. In 1995 the U.S. Court of Federal Claims ruled in favor of the contractors with its decision that the termination for default was not supported and ruled the action as a termination of convenience. In the final decision in 1998 the court ordered the Navy to pay $1.2 billion plus interest.

The Navy appealed the decision, and in 1999 the Court of Appeals sent the case back to the Court of Federal Claims to further investigate whether the Navy's termination of the contract was justified. On August 31, 2001 the Court ruled that the contractors had failed to meet a reasonable schedule as was set out by the contract; therefore, the Court overturned the earlier ruling and upheld the termination by default. On November 30, 2001 General Dynamics filed an appeal. If the ruling is upheld, the contractors could be required to repay the Navy approximately $2.4 billion ($1.35 billion plus interest), of which General Dynamics would pay $1.2 billion.

Boat and Land Systems. However, as the outlook improved, the company quickly and substantially retooled its business with 21 acquisitions between 1997 and 2001. Most of the purchases were closely linked with General Dynamics' core businesses. Then, in 1997 it took the bold step of buying aircraft manufacturer Gulfstream for $4.5 billion, making its first substantial move outside the defense sector. With its backlog soaring from $6 billion to $30 in 2001, General Dynamics has its production schedule packed for several years to come. Sales have returned to pre-1990 figures, but the additional benefit of a market capitalization of $17 billion, up from just $1 billion in 1990.

INFLUENCES

The defense industry, including General Dynamics, was adversely affected by decreases in U.S. military spending following the end of the Cold War in the early 1990s. Since the terrorist attacks of September 11, 2001, the tide has turned back in General Dynamics favor. President Bush submitted a request to Congress for $328 billion for defense spending in fiscal year 2002, an 11 percent increase. The president's 2003 proposal calls for an increase of $68.7 billion in military spending. Approximately one of every three dollars budgeted for the military ends up in the hands of defense contractors. Accordingly, General Dynamics expects growth rates proportional to budget increase. The company's commercial activities, based primarily on the development and production of commercial aircraft depends generally on the state of the economy and specifically on the state of the airline industry. Although the airlines were substantially weakened in the wake of the terrorist attacks, as the economy rebounds, General Dynamics anticipates continued productivity from its aerospace unit.

CURRENT TRENDS

General Dynamics has targeted all segment of its business for substantial growth. In 2001 the number of U.S. Navy's fleet of ships was at its lowest level since the early 1930s, but now the Marine division of the company plans to benefit from increased shipbuilding contracts as the Navy attempts to regain its numbers under the Bush Administration. The Combat Systems division was awarded a contract to build the U.S. Marine Corps' Advanced Amphibious Assault Vehicle, a $4 billion project that allows marines to move from sea to land. The Aerospace division earned a contract from the U.S. Air Force in 2002 to build as many as 20, C37-A Gulfstream V and Gulfstream V-SPs to fly demanding military missions. The contract has a potential value of $1.6 billion. Finally, as military technology moves along the cutting edge, the Information Systems and Technology division is poised to lead the way. It is the company's fastest growing division and an increasing force in sales production.

PRODUCTS

The Aerospace group, a worldwide leader in design, development, manufacture, and marketing of mid-sized and intercontinental jet aircraft, is comprised of Gulfstream Aerospace and General Dynamics Aviation Services. Gulfstream has produced over 1,200 aircraft since 1958. Its diverse product line includes the ultra-long range Gulfstream V, the Gulfstream 200, the Gulfstream 100, and the Gulfstream V-SP. General Dynamics Aviation Services provides services in the areas of airframes, avionics, engine repair, and aircraft refurbishment.

Combat Systems engages in land and amphibious combat system development, production, and support. Its product line includes a full range of armored vehicles, light-wheeled reconnaissance vehicles, guns and ammunition handling systems, turret systems, and reactive armor and ordinance. Its business units are comprised of Armament Systems, Eagle Enterprise Inc., Land Systems (maker of the M-1 tank), Ordnance and Tactical Systems, and Santa Barbara Sistemas.

The Information Systems and Technology segment provides services in the area of information management and communications. Its two functionaries are Advanced Communication Systems, C4 Systems, Division Systems, Network Systems, and United Kingdom Limited.

Marine Systems operates a broad range of integration, design, engineering, and production services in naval shipbuilding and is the U.S. Navy's leading supplier of combat vessels, including nuclear submarines, surface combatants, and auxiliary ships. It businesses consist of American Overseas Marine, Bath Iron Works, Electric Boat, and NASSCO.

Major product lines for General Dynamics include the Virginia-class nuclear-powered attack submarine, Arleigh Burke-class Aegis destroyer, Abrams M1A2 digitized main battle tank, munitions and gun systems, advanced fiber-optics, high-security communication systems, and the Gulfstream IV-SP and Gulfstream V jets. The following are in production or testing stages: DD21 land attack destroyer, the U.S. Marine Corp Advanced Amphibious Assault Vehicle, and the next-generation of communication systems.

CORPORATE CITIZENSHIP

A variety of federal, state, local, and foreign environmental laws and regulations affect General Dynamics' operations related to the discharge, treatment, storage, and disposal of certain substances and wastes. The company systematically budgets for expenses related to ensuring ongoing assessment and compliance with all environmental laws.

GLOBAL PRESENCE

General Dynamics operates businesses outside the United States in the United Kingdom, Canada, and Spain. Sales in 2001 generated by these international locations totaled 3 percent of General Dynamics' consolidated sales and 1 percent of operating earnings. General Dynamic sales to international customers in 2001 added up to $1.2 billion, representing approximately 10 percent of the company's overall revenues. International defense sales were directly through defense contracts with U.S. allies, and international commercial sales were primarily related to the export of business aircraft.

EMPLOYMENT

General Dynamics employs approximately 52,000 individuals. Of that total, 32 percent are covered by collective bargaining agreements through various unions, including the International Association of Machinists and Aerospace Workers, the Marine Draftsmen's Association, and the United Auto Workers Union. The majority of positions are located within the United States, with limited international opportunities. Individual business units within the corporate structure are responsible for recruiting and hiring their own employees.

SOURCES OF INFORMATION

Bibliography

"Airforce to Buy Up to 20 Gulfstream Jets." *AP Newswire*, 13 March 2002.

Buursma, Ben, and Brian Edwards. "Defense Stocks Offer Some Security; New Budget Will Help Sector in the Long Term." *Chicago Tribune*, 26 February 2002.

Creswell, Julie, and Julie Schlosser, and Jessica Sung. "Armed and Dangerous: Defense Stocks Look Like Safe Havens But Will Leave Investors Shell Shocked."*Fortune*, 13 March 2002.

deJong, Andrea L., ed. *Ward's Business Directory of U.S. Private and Public Companies.* Vol. 1. Detroit: Gale Group, 1999.

"General Dynamics." *Hoover's Company Profiles.* Available at http://www.hoovers.com.

Kepos, Paula, ed.*International Directory of Company Histories.* Vol. 10. Detroit: St. James Press, 1995.

Pae, Peter, "Defense Stocks Still Posting Solid Gains." *Los Angeles Times*, 11 April 2002.

Squeo, Anne Marie. "The Contrarian: An Industry Outsider Cuts Against the Grain At General Dynamics—Chabraja Avoids Satellites, Glitzy Missile Defense, Focuses on Tanks, Ships—A Rainy-Night Test of Mettle."*The Wall Street Journal*, 13 March 2002.

———. "Spending for Defense: A Special Report. Ready for Battle: After a Decade of Hard Times, Military Contractors are Leaner, More Focused—And Eager to Grab a Piece of the Coming Spending Boom." *The Wall Street Journal*, 28 March 2002.

For an annual report:
on the Internet at: http://www.generaldynamics.com.

For additional industry research:
Investigate companies by their Standard Industrial Classification Codes, also known as SICs. General Dynamic Corporation's primary SICs are:

3599 Industrial Machinery, Not Elsewhere Classified

3679 Electronic Components, Not Elsewhere Classified

3731 Ship Building And Repairing

3732 Boat Building And Repairing

3795 Tanks And Tank Components

3812 Search Navigation & Aeronautical Systems

Also investigate companies by their North American Industry Classification System Codes, also known as NAICS codes. General Dynamic Corporation's primary NAICS codes are:

333319 Other Commercial and Service Industry Machinery Manufacturing

334419 Other Electronic Component Manufacturing

334511 Search, Detection, Navigation, Guidance, Aeronautical, and Nautical System and Instrument Manufacturing

336611 Ship Building and Repairing

336612 Boat Building

336992 Military Armored Vehicle, Tank, and Tank Component Manufacturing

General Electric Company

OVERVIEW

General Electric (GE) is the fifth-largest and most valuable company in the United States. It is a global conglomerate with business interests in manufacturing, technological services, financial services, network and cable television, and household appliances, and had 2001 revenues of $125.9 billion. The company's financial-services unit, GE Capital Services, has accounted for nearly half of the corporation's total revenue. GE also owns the National Broadcasting Company (NBC), which includes cable networks CNBC and MSNBC, and profits and ratings alike have soared under the company's control. NBC serves more than 220 affiliated stations throughout the United States, as well as 13 VHF and UHF stations. In 2001, NBCi, an Internet portal company was merged into NBC.

COMPANY FINANCES

Revenues for 2001 were $125.9 billion. International sales accounted for $50.0 billion of the total—about 40 percent. Net earnings were $14.1 billion, for a result of $1.41 per share. In 2001 the quarterly dividend was $.18 per share. This dividend has been paid every quarter since 1899, and has increased annually since 1975. Between 1994 and 1998, the company has bought back $17 billion worth of its stock. The most recent stock split was in April 2000 (3 for 1). GE's market capitalization (the total value of all its stock) is the highest in the world, at more than $399.07 billion (March 2002). The company was predicting 17 percent growth through 2002, despite an economic slowdown, which cut revenues by 3 percent

FOUNDED: 1892

VARIANT NAME: GE

Contact Information:

HEADQUARTERS: 3135 Easton Tpke.
  Fairfield, CT 06431-0001
PHONE: (203)373-2211
FAX: (203)373-3131
URL: http://www.ge.com

FAST FACTS:

About General Electric Company

Ownership: General Electric is a publicly owned company, traded on the New York, Boston, and London Stock Exchanges.

Ticker Symbol: GE

Officers: Jeffrey R. Immelt, Chmn. and CEO, $6,387,954; Dennis D. Dammerman, VChmn. and Chmn. GE Capital Services; Gary L. Rogers, VChmn. and Exec. Officer, $3,321,634; Robert C. Wright, VP, Chmn., and Executive Officer, $5,782,849

Employees: 310,000

Principal Subsidiary Companies: General Electric's subsidiaries include CFM International Inc.; GE Aircraft Engines; GE Appliances; GE Equity; GE ERC; GE Financial Assurance Holdings Inc.; GE Global eXchange Services; GE Industrial Products and Systems; GE Interlogix Inc.; GE Lighting; GE Medical Systems; GE Medical Systems Lunar; GE OEC Medical Systems Inc.GE Plastics; GE Power Systems; GE Supply; GE Transportation Systems; General Electric Capital Corporation; Heller Financial; and National Broadcasting Company Inc.

Chief Competitors: Some of General Electric's competitors include Allstate, Caterpillar, Cooper Industries, Electrolux, Krupp, General Motors, GTE, Hitachi, ITT Industries, Maytag, Merrill Lynch, Mitsubishi, Polaroid, Philips Electronics, Raytheon, Rockwell International, Rolls-Royce, State Farm, Time Warner, Walt Disney, Westinghouse, and Whirlpool.

in 2001. Further, GE targeted double-digit growth through 2003. GE Capital and its continued strong growth was credited for offsetting falloff sales of GE Power Systems gas turbines.

ANALYSTS' OPINIONS

GE has received high praise from many analysts for its conviction that resources should go mainly to business units that dominate their respective markets. The company has been a front-runner in every industry where

it is involved. As investment manager Steve Leeb stated in *Business Week,* "One very impressive thing about GE is that it's hard to find any fundamental benchmark on which it doesn't excel." CEO Jack Welch retired in the year 2000. Welch is considered to be one of the most effective CEOs in the world. Under his guidance, GE grew into one of the world's most powerful corporations. Much of the company's success can be attributed to his management style. "This guy's legacy will be to create more shareholder value on the face of the planet than ever—forever," said Nicholas P. Heymann, of Prudential Securities, in *Business Week.*

GE's new CEO as of September 2001, Jeff Immelt, has faced the challenge of taking the reigns of the valuable company during a time when the slowed economy has hit GE along with most companies. In the six months following Welch's retirement, GE lost some 18 percent of its value. During the same time period, the S&P 500 dropped only 6 percent. Goldman Sachs analyst Martin Sankey estimated in early 2002 GE's price/earning ratio is the lowest it's been in five years relative the S&P 500, and was on par with the index, down from the 35-50 percent premium it had recently held.

HISTORY

General Electric was established in 1892 after a merger between the Edison General Electric Company and the Thomson-Houston Electric Company. Thomas Edison was one of the company's first directors. GE's emphasis on research resulted in the development of innovative products such as elevators, light bulbs, toasters, and other household appliances. These products fueled the company's growth during the early 1900s. Diversification continued to increase GE's profit margins throughout the years.

Throughout its history, GE was involved with various ventures. In the 1920s GE, along with Westinghouse, became part of a radio broadcasting venture. In the 1950s, GE became involved with the computer industry but sold that part of the business to Honeywell in 1970. The 1980s were a period of reconstruction for the company.

Jack Welch was named the company's CEO in 1981. Over the next 10 years, GE sold off many of its business interests in order to focus primarily on high-return offerings, such as financial services, medical systems, and aircraft engines. The company acquired NBC in 1986, and entered the lighting industry as a manufacturer and supplier in the early 1990s.

STRATEGY

GE's enormous success is due primarily to its strict adherence to former CEO Jack Welch's doctrine of stick-

CHRONOLOGY:

Key Dates for General Electric Company

1892: Edison General Electric Company merges with Thomson Houston Electric Company to form General Electric Company

1901: GE manufactures a high speed turbine for greater electricity production

1905: GE moves into the realm of household appliances

1918: Pacific Electric Heating Company, Hughes Electric Heating Company, and GE merge

1919: At the request of the government, GE creates Radio Corporation of America (RCA) to develop radio technology

1924: Antitrust action is brought against the company causing GE to leave the utilities business

1932: Irving Langmuir, who developed the electron tube for GE, receives the Nobel Prize

1939: GE develops a new mode of radio transmission called Frequency Modulation (FM)

1945: The United States' first turboprop airplane engine is developed by GE

1955: GE develops the reactor for the *Seawolf*, the world's first nuclear-powered vessel

1961: Twenty-nine companies, including GE, are indicted by the federal government for price fixing on electrical equipment

1976: GE pays $2.2 billion for Utah International, the largest corporate purchase at the time

1986: GE purchases RCA and its NBC subsidiary

1997: GE becomes the first company in the world to exceed a market value of $200 million

1998: Employers Reinsurance Corporation introduces HERCULES, a comprehensive package of property, professional, liability, and other insurance coverage to meet the needs of hospitals and other healthcare institutions

1999: GE e-business concludes its year with more than $2 billion in electronic sales

2000: GE Research and Development Center celebrates its 100th anniversary

2001: The European Commission blocks a GE takeover of Honeywell, claiming it violated antitrust laws; the U.S. Justice Department had approved the deal

2002: GE Medical Systems Information Technologies announced that it completed the acquisition of the MedicaLogic business, a developer of electronic medical records for outpatient care, for $35.25 million in cash

---

ing with proven business winners. Welch believed that resources should not be wasted on businesses that are not leaders in the global market. "Don't play with businesses that can't win," he says. "Businesses that are number 3, number 5 in their market—Christ couldn't fix those businesses. They're going to lose anyway." The company's corporate decisions have consistently displayed a Darwinian outlook.

When Welch's successor took charge after his retirement in 2001, analysts speculated whether new CEO Jeffrey Immelt's strategies would work in a troubled global economy.

Early in his tenure, Immelt announced GE would expand through acquisitions and further explore cost savings. In December 2001, GE purchased electronic security company Interlogix for $777 million and Immelt announced that the company was considering acquisitions in the industrial businesses.

INFLUENCES

By the early 1980s, GE's emphasis on expansion and industrial diversity had created a mammoth organization with multiple levels of bureaucratic management. The company's corporate direction shifted dramatically in 1981, when Jack Welch became CEO. Within the next 10 years, GE dropped business units that had totaled a quarter of the company's sales in 1980. By 1988 the company's restructuring efforts had resulted in the downsizing of 100,000 employees. Management responsibilities had been redefined, resulting in more efficient business practices. The corporate-reengineering efforts paid huge dividends for the company. Profits grew from $1.65 billion in 1981 to $7.28 billion in 1996. By 1997, analysts acknowledged GE as one of the most profitable companies in the world. Market value grew from $12 to $280 billion under Welch.

GE aggressively moved into the investment banking field in 1987 with the purchase of Kidder, Peabody. This acquisition became a business unit of financial services division, GE Capital. The brokerage unit was ultimately a losing investment, and in 1993 a false-profit scandal came to light. In the wake of the turmoil, Michael Carpenter was terminated as Kidder's chair, and the company was sold to Paine Webber in 1994. Analysts criticized GE for its aggressive purchase of the investment banking company due to its limited experience in the industry.

The purchase of NBC in 1986 proved to be a more successful experience for GE. Jack Welch named Robert Wright, a lawyer by trade, with no prior television or entertainment experience, the network's CEO. Welch's decision met with widespread criticism from industry experts at first, but Wright has since silenced his critics by applying GE's business philosophy to network television. Under his guidance, NBC has broadened its business interests into the cable industry with CNBC, as well as into the global television marketplace. NBC experienced four consecutive years of record profits from 1993 to 1997, and, aided by such hit shows as *ER* and *Seinfeld,* consistently dominated the primetime television ratings by the mid-1990s.

GE was faced with several controversies in early 1997. The company had to pay Fonar Corporation almost $100 million as a result of a court order for violating the latter's MRI scanner patents. Furthermore, Dow Chemical sued GE in 1997, claiming that GE had marked, recruited, and hired former Dow workers who had knowledge of Dow's trade secrets. GE was also faced with the possibility of its first labor strike since 1969 when Jack Welch and Edward Fire, the president of the International Union of Electronic Workers (IUE), became involved in an intense war of words over the job security of union workers.

CURRENT TRENDS

Never content with its past successes, GE has continually reinvented itself in order to stay ahead of its competition. "We've just got to be faster," says Welch. "We come to work every day on the razor's edge of a competitive battle." An emphasis on product quality and statistical process control was introduced as a company-wide goal in 1997. GE adopted "Six Sigma," a quality-assurance methodology developed by Motorola Inc., to focus on "defining, measuring, analyzing, improving, and controlling" each process that takes place in the company. Trained GE employees called "Black Belts" and "Master Black Belts" oversee personnel's training in this philosophy. Says Welch of the concept in *Forbes,* "This is not about sloganeering or bureaucracy or filling out forms. It finally gives us a route to get to the control function, the hardest thing to do in a corporation." Welch pro-

jected the program's benefits to GE in 1998 to be worth $750 million.

After Welch's retirement in 2001, 45-year-old Jeffrey Immelt took reigns of GE as CEO. Within weeks, the company was hard-hit due to insurance claims associated with the Sept. 11, 2001, terrorist attacks on the United States. Insurance holdings were adversely affected by approximately $575 million related to the attacks. Further, the country was already in the throes of economic recession, and GE's turbine shipments and appliance shipments were expected to drastically decline. Earlier the same year, the company's bid for Honeywell was halted by the European Commission, which claimed anti-trust violations. Immelt remained optimistic, predicting 17 percent growth in 2002 and continued double-digit growth through 2003.

GE firmly believed it could not rely solely on its manufactured products. The concept that enormous revenue could be obtained by supplying services linked to GE's core businesses, such as assisting clients' business operations in a consulting capacity, was established as the company's ethos. Everything from running airline-engine service shops; to giving management-training classes to clients were considered vital keys to GE's future success. The company planned to share its extensive business experiences and lessons learned, as a service to its customers. Industry experts praised this approach. "This is the next big wave in American industry," reengineering expert Michael Hammer said in *Business Week.* "The product you sell is only one component of your business."

PRODUCTS

General Electric is involved in a broad array of industries. It builds everything from the most mundane lightbulbs to the most sophisticated power systems to hi-tech plastics. Each unit operates on a grand scale. The GE Aircraft Engines division, for example, is the world's largest builder of jet engines for military and commercial planes. Its GE90 engines, for example, power Boeing's 777 aircraft. In a joint venture with French manufacturer Snecma, GE fills engine orders for many major airlines. GE Appliances make familiar household equipment like the GE SmartWater faucet system. Also through this division, it continues to perfect its designs of items such as dishwashers, ovens, and clothes dryers.

GE Capital comprises 27 separate business, which operate all over the world. They include the Penske Truck Leasing company, various specialty insurance entities, and a financial services company in Ireland called Woodchester. The division has enjoyed more than 20 years of increased profits. It attributes its success to its "three-pronged strategic focus": globalization, a commitment to providing value-added services, and adherence to the Six Sigma principles of quality control.

GE Equity is the private equity arm of GE and is a subsidiary of GE Capital. GE Equity was formed in 1995 as part of GE Capital. With five business unites and 120 investment professionals, it offers deal structures, which include the use of preferred stock, convertible debt, subordinated debt and common stock. GE Equity boasts a portfolio of more than 150 companies throughout the United States, Latin America, Asia and Europe.

NBC is a leader in television broadcasting. Its programming, from evening news to prime-time situation comedies, which included the perennially popular *Seinfeld* in the 1990s, to political talk shows, consistently scores high in the ratings.

CORPORATE CITIZENSHIP

GE has long been active in community involvement, primarily through an entity called Elfun (derived from "Electrical Funds"), which the company established in 1928 to provide a vehicle whereby GE employees could fund charitable activities. The organization has expanded its outreach over the years to include volunteer work in the communities where GE is present, and in assisting in educational activities for underprivileged youth. Elfun's membership grew to 40,000 active and retired GE employees in 2001, with 90 local affiliates in 10 countries. In 2000 Elfun members logged 1.3 million hours in volunteer hours. Accomplishments included 800 community service projects worldwide, the construction of 100 playgrounds, mentor programs at 150 schools and 25 food programs.

In 1992 GE was given The National Science Foundation's first National Corporate Achievement Award, in observance of its support for minority students, educators, and professionals in science and mathematics. GE received the President's Volunteer Action Award in 1994, and in 1995, it was recognized with the Council for Aid to Education's Leaders for Change Corporate Award in recognition of its College Bound program. In 1996 the company and its employees donated more than $75 million to charitable organizations all around the world.

In 1998, The National Society of Black Engineers awarded GE the first Golden Torch Award for corporate community service. Additionally, Elfun employees contribute more than $90 million annually to support the arts, education and environment.

GLOBAL PRESENCE

GE's presence worldwide is unmistakable, with nearly every person around the world being exposed to at GE products and services. GE's revenues generated

outside the United States were $50 billion in 2001, or 40 percent of total revenue. GE employees more than 300,000 people in 100 countries.

Most investment analysts have agreed that the Asian market promised the most potential for growth in the 1990s and early 2000s, but GE revenues from the Pacific Basin decreased 19 percent, from $12,921 billion in 2000 to $11,447 billion in 2001.

General Electric began a large-scale investment in Europe. Between 1989 and 1997, the company invested more than $10 billion in European industrial plants and companies. GE's investment gamble yielded profits of $1.41 billion in 1996, as compared to its Asian profits of $585 million. Revenues in Europe also slipped in the early 2000s, from $24,144 billion in 2000 to $23,878 in 2001. While part of the decrease was caused by economic recession in parts of Europe, a poor exchange rate was also a contributor. "Investing in Europe today requires guts," London business school professor Sumantra Ghoshal said in *Fortune.* GE viewed the late 1990s Asian financial crisis as an opportunity to position itself for the new millennium. The strategy worked, and revenue from Pacific Basin soared between 1999 and 2000, growing from $7,879 billion to $12,921 billion.

A focus on expansion has prompted the company to target such markets as India and China. According to analyst Nicholas P. Heymann, in *Business Week,* "GE is now well positioned to outmaneuver its less flexible and more entrenched global competitors." Markets for GE products outside of the United States have included Asia, Europe, Mexico, and South America.

GE's brand name has not wielded the same clout in Europe as it has in the United States. Its European household-appliance business returned disappointing profit margins throughout the 1990s. GE has experienced its greatest success on the continent with GE Capital Services Europe, however. The European branch of the company's financial services group accounted for almost 13 percent of GE Capital Services' net income in 1996.

EMPLOYMENT

GE offers college students hundreds of internships and co-op programs each year that allow students to explore job opportunities with the company, In addition, recent graduates can begin a career with the company in two ways—Leadership Development Programs offer intensive programs in which participants undergo technical training, and Direct Hires, in which GE businesses hire graduates in positions and into business-specific leadership programs. Career opportunities can be explored at the company's Web site and resumes can be sent online.

THE WIZARD OF MENLO PARK

It's safe to say that without Thomas Alva Edison, there would have been no GE. True, Edison was with the company for only two years, but the Edison General Electric Company was GE's predecessor, and it was Edison's inventions and discoveries that paved the way for GE's success.

Edison got his start at inventing and experimentation when he built his first laboratory at age 10. By age 16 he had invented a transmitter and receiver for the automatic telegraph—enabling him to sleep and send messages at the same time (his boss was not too appreciative.) In 1869, Edison invented the Edison Universal Stock Printer and sold the rights for $40,000 (he was only hoping for $4,000). With that money Edison, started a business to build stock tickers and telegraphs, and he also used it to help him continue his experiments.

In 1876 Edison built his laboratory in Menlo Park, New Jersey. There 60 employees worked on 40 projects at a time. Out of the Menlo Park factory came the phonograph, the Edison dynamo, and the invention that Edison is most remembered for, a practical incandescent lamp. It took Edison more than $40,000 and more than 1,200 experiments before he succeeded at producing an effec-

tive light in 1879. In 1882, Edison set up the first light-power station, helping to illuminate part of New York City.

In 1887 Edison moved to a larger factory in West Orange, New Jersey. Out of that factory came an electrical storage battery, the motion picture camera, and silent and sound movies. In all, Edison was issued 1,093 patents for his inventions—more than anyone else in history. Edison applied for as many as 400 patents in a year. For 65 consecutive years, from 1868 to 1933, Edison had a least one patent issued to him in every year.

Edison attributed his success to hard work and perseverance. He is famous for saying, "Invention is 99 percent perspiration and 1 percent inspiration." He often worked up to 112 hours a week. He saw his failures as learning experiences. The story goes that Edison failed 10,000 times in his experiments to develop a storage battery. But of it he said, "Why, I have not failed. I've just found 10,000 ways that won't work." Edison kept on going where others might have given up. Because of his tenacity, he changed the world and lit the way for scientists working for companies like GE, enabling them to take up where he left off. In 1931, when Edison died, electric lights were dimmed for one minute across all the United States—a fitting tribute to the man who helped to transform the century.

SOURCES OF INFORMATION

Bibliography

Bernstein, Aaron. "High Tension at General Electric." *Business Week*, 24 March 1997.

Byrne, John A. "How Jack Welch Runs GE." *Business Week*, 8 June 1998.

Company profile, General Electric. *Market Guide*, 26 March 2002. Available at http://www.multex.com.

Conlin, Michelle. "For GE's Jack Welch, Cost-Cutting Isn't an Event, It's a Process." *Forbes*, 26 January 1998.

"Dow Chemical Sues GE over Plastics Secrets." *Reuters*, 1 April 1997. Available at http.pathfinder.com.

"Exxon and General Electric Top Forbes List." *Reuters*, 7 April 1997. Available at http.pathfinder.com.

"GE Posts Profits for Quarter, Year." *Fox News*, 16 January 1997.

"General Electric." *Hoover's Online*, 23 Sept 2001. Available at http://www.hoovers.com.

General Electric Company 1997 Annual Report. Fairfield, CT: General Electric Company, 1997.

General Electric's Home Page. April, 2002. Available at http://www.ge.com.

Greenwald, John. "Jack in the Box." *Time*, 3 October 1994.

Gunther, Marc. "How GE Made NBC No. 1." *Fortune*, 3 February 1997.

Hill, Andrew. "GE new-style accounts gain broad approval." *Financial Times*, 10 March 2002.

———. "GE pins expansion plans on acquisitions." *Financial Times*, 19 December 2001.

Koenig, Peter. "If Europe's Dead, Why Is GE Investing Billions There?"*Fortune*, 9 September 1996.

Marcial, Gene. "You Can't Go Wrong with GE." *Business Week*, 22 July 1996.

McClean, Bethany. "GE may have a power problem," *Fortune*, 4 Feb. 2002.

Morris, Betsy. "Roberto Goizueta and Jack Welch: The Wealth Builders." *Fortune*, 5 February 1996.

Smart, Tim. "GE's Efficiency Doctor Is In." *Business Week*, 28 October 1996.

Roberti, Mark. "General Electric: Welch isn't perfect." *The Industry Standard*, 2 July 2001.

Roberts, Dan. "GE chief faces questions from the skeptics." *Financial Times*, 3 Feb. 2002.

Smart, Tim. "GE's Welch: Fighting like Hell to Be No. 1." *Business Week*, (international edition), 8 July 1996.

Smart, Tim. "Jack Welch's Encore." *Business Week*, 28 October 1996.

Smart, Tim. "Who Will Fill Jack's Shoes?" *Business Week*, 28 October 1996.

Swoboda, Frank. "Talking Management with Chairman Welch." *Washington Post*, 23 March 1997.

For an annual report:
telephone: (203) 373-2211

For additional industry research:
Investigate companies by their Standard Industrial Classification Codes, also known as SICs. General Electric's primary SICs are:

3621 Motors & Generators

3639 Household Appliances, NEC

3724 Aircraft Engines & Engine Parts

4911 Electric Services

Also investigate companies by their North American Industry Classification System codes, also known as NAICS codes. General Electric's primary NAICS codes are:

221122 Electric Power Generation, Transmission and Distribution

334517 Irradiation Apparatus Manufacturing

335121 Residential Electric Lighting Fixture Manufacturing

335122 Commercial, Industrial, and Institutional Electric Lighting Fixture Manufacturing

335228 Other Major Household Appliance Manufacturing

335999 All Other Miscellaneous Electrical Equipment and Component Manufacturing

General Motors Corporation

FOUNDED: 1897
VARIANT NAME: GM

Contact Information:

HEADQUARTERS: 300 Renaissance Center
   Detroit, MI 48265-3000
PHONE: (313)556-5000
FAX: (313)874-2760
URL: http://www.gm.com

OVERVIEW

General Motors Corporation is the largest U.S. industrial corporation and the world's leading manufacturer of cars and trucks. GM designs, manufactures, and markets one out of every three cars and trucks produced in the United States. Its nameplates include Chevrolet, Pontiac, GMC, Oldsmobile, Buick, Cadillac, and Saturn. Overseas, the company is involved in the manufacturing and marketing of Opel, Vauxhall, Holden, Isuzu, Saab, Chevrolet, GMC, and Cadillac vehicles. Although the major portion of its business is derived from the automotive industry, GM has substantial interests in telecommunications and space, aerospace and defense, consumer and automotive electronics, financial and insurance services, locomotives, automotive systems, and heavy-duty transmissions.

COMPANY FINANCES

Since 1992, GM's financial picture has brightened considerably. When John Smith took over as CEO that year, GM owed its pension fund $22 billion; its core North American operations were losing money; and its net liquidity, or cash minus debt, was negative $2 billion. In 1997, according to Daniel Howes in a November 1997 *Detroit News* article, "North American operations are driving the corporation's profitability—though overall, profit margins are still shy of Smith's 5 percent goal—the pension fund is fully funded, and the cash hoard stands at $14.6 billion."

At the end of 1997, GM had a swelling cash flow of $13.9 billion and said that it is committed to returning value to its stockholders. GM announced a third stock repurchase program for $4 billion; following a $2.5 billion repurchase program started in August 1997. The repurchase programs reduced GM's outstanding shares by 20 percent. *The Value Line Investment Survey* reasoned that GM management decided on a stock repurchasing program (rather than increasing the dividend) because dividends are taxed twice, at both corporate and personal levels. In addition, GM's dividend yield is already well above the market average. A March 1998 *Fortune* magazine article explained GM's rationale in funneling money directly to shareholders; pointing out that by reducing its outstanding shares and boosting its stock price it increased earnings per share. This made the company a more attractive option for investors.

In 1997 GM had sales of $166 billion, compared with sales of $158 billion in 1996, and its net income rose 34 percent to a record $6.70 billion from $4.96 billion in 1996. GM stock ranged from a low of $52 to a high of $72 in 1997. The annual dividend for 1997 was $2.00 per share, and GM's price-earnings ratio was 9.5 in May 1998. In addition, earnings per share in 1997 were $8.62.

GM's earnings per share held fairly steady through 1999, shares earned $8.70. In 2000, earnings dropped off and GM stock earned only $6.80 per share. The following year was worse, when GM stocks earned only $1.78 per share in 2001. GMA's total net sales and revenues were $177.3 billion in 2001, $184.6 billion in 2000, and $176.6 billion in 1999. The decrease from 2000 to 2001 was largely credited to lower wholesale volumes in 2001 and unfavorable net prices in North America and Europe. In 2001, GM had cut the prices of its vehicles, particularly in the last quarter, in an effort to boost sales during the economic recession and fall-out after September 11, 2001. During 2001, GM sold in Europe far more smaller, less-profitable vehicles than it did the previous year, however, the loss was offset somewhat by the increase in truck and larger vehicle sales in North America.

Hughes Network Systems also saw falling sales during 2001, and revenues decreased from $8.7 billion in 2000 to $8.3 billion in 2001, due to a decrease in shipments of DIRECTV receiving equipment. In 2000, DIRECTV sales had skyrocketed from $7.6 billion in 1999 due to customers purchasing newly-available high-power DIRECTV service and equipment that year.

GMAC had an increase in adjusted income in 2001, growing from $1.5 billion in 1999 to $1.6 billion in 2000, to $1.8 billion in 2001, although total financing revenue fell from $15.5 billion in 2000 to $15.1 billion in 2001. The increase in adjusted income was due mostly to lower market interest rates and increased asset levels.

ANALYSTS' OPINIONS

In 2000 General Motors enjoyed the best earnings year in the history of the company. However, in 2001,

FAST FACTS:
About General Motors Corporation

Ownership: General Motors is a publicly owned company traded on the New York Stock Exchange.

Ticker symbol: GM

Officers: John F. Smith Jr., Chmn., 63, salary $3,293,797; G. Richard Wagoner Jr., Pres. and CEO, 49, salary $2,338,000; John M. Devine, EVP and CFO, 57; Robert A. Lutz, Vice Chmn. Product Development and Chmn. of GM North America, 70

Employees: 365,000

Principal Subsidiary Companies: General Motors has more than 160 subsidiaries, joint ventures, and affiliates. Its major subsidiaries include Delphi Automotive Systems, General Motors Acceptance Corporation, Hughes Electronics Corporation, General Motors Electro-Motive Division, and Allison Transmission.

Chief Competitors: General Motor's principal competitors in passenger cars and trucks in the United States and Canada include Ford Motor Company; DaimlerChrysler Corporation; Toyota Corporation; Nissan Motor Corporation Ltd.; Honda Motor Company Ltd.; Mazda Motor Corporation; Mitsubishi Motors Corporation; Fuji Heavy Industries Ltd. (Subaru); Volkswagen A.G.; Hyundai Motor Company, Ltd.; Bayerische, Motoren Werke A.G. (BMW); and Volvo AB.

worldwide sales fell as most economies experienced a recession. Despite a slight rebound in the first quarter of 2002, some analysts believed automotive sales would stabilize and decrease later that year. Credit Suisse First Boston's, Wendy Beale Needham, predicted a rise in interest rates by the end of 2002, which would soften the automotive industry's sales as mortgage refinancing activities slowed. Needham believed, however, that GM's purchase of Daewoo, which was completed 2002, would help GM's financial position. "GM's belief is that 65 percent of the growth auto sales in the next 10 years will occur in eight emerging markets. Korea is one of those markets, so they would like to have a presence there," she said.

CHRONOLOGY:

Key Dates for General Motors Corporation

1903: General Motors is formed by the joining of the Oldsmobile and Buick companies

1909: Cadillac and Oakland (later renamed Pontiac) join GM

1912: Cadillac cars introduce the electric self-starter replacing the hand crank

1918: Chevrolet joins GM

1924: Assembles first GM vehicle abroad in Denmark

1938: Introduces the column mounted gearshift, setting the industry standard

1940: Produces its 25 millionth automobile

1948: Introduces the first torque-converter automatic transmission available in passenger cars

1950: Introduces the Chevrolet Corvette

1961: Introduces the first V-6 for an American passenger car

1969: GM manufactures the guidance systems for the Apollo 11 spacecraft

1974: First company to offer air bags in production vehicles

1987: Wins the inaugural solar car race with its Sunracer

1995: First company to install daytime running lights as standard equipment

1996: Introduces the first electric car for consumers, the EV1

1997: General Motors and Hughes complete the spin-off of the Hughes defense electronics business

1998: GM North America shuts down vehicle production for nearly two months after UAW workers at two plants in Flint, Mich., go on strike

1999: GM creates a business, eGM, to bring together of GM's and OnStar's electronic commerce and Internet marketing initiatives

2000: General Motors announces a plan to allow holders of GM $1-2/3 commonstock to exchange up to $8 billion of GM $1-2/3 stock for GM Class H stock

2001: General Motors cuts back it European salaried workforce by 10 percent, or 1,500 jobs, as part of a restructuring of money-losing operations there

2002: General Motors announces recall of 1.9 million Chevrolet Cavalier, Pontiac Sunfire, Buick Skylark, Pontiac Grand Am, and Oldsmobile Achieva cars; the recall was the result of a potential electrical current flow through the ignition switch that could cause a fire in the steering column

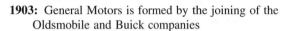

HISTORY

Though General Motors was formed in 1908, its history can be traced to 1892 when R.E. Olds founded the Olds Motor Vehicle Company to manufacture horseless carriages, according to the *International Directory of Company Histories*. Within a couple of years, Olds managed to convert this factory into the first American factory in Detroit devoted exclusively to the production of automobiles.

At the turn of the century, an engineer named David Buick founded the Buick Motor Company in Detroit. At the same time, Henry Leland founded the Cadillac Automobile Company, also located in Detroit. All three companies were setting their own milestones and performing well. However, in 1903, at a time of market instability, these three companies were forced to form a consortium, and General Motors was thus formed. William Durant, a

self-made millionaire, son of a Michigan governor, and a director of the Buick Motor Company, brought together Oldsmobile and Buick, and in 1909, Cadillac and Oakland (later renamed Pontiac) joined the union. Even though this merger drew very little attention, immediate positive financial results were seen.

In 1911, a central staff of specialists was put together to monitor and coordinate the activities in GM's different units and factories, and a testing laboratory was set up to serve as additional protection against costly factory mistakes. The research and development system adopted by GM became one of the largest and most complex in private industry. Additionally, Chevrolet became part of GM in 1918. By 1920 more than 30 companies had been acquired, including Ewing, Marquette, Welch, Scripps-Booth, Sheridan, Elmore, and Rapid and Reliance trucks.

During World War I, General Motors turned to wartime production. Ninety percent of GM's truck production between 1917 and 1919 was for the war effort. Cadillac supplied Army staff cars and V-8 engines, while Buick built airplane motors, tanks, trucks, ambulances, and automotive parts.

The Great Depression created suffering for GM. The company emerged, however, with a new and aggressive management, and coordinated policy control, which replaced the undirected efforts of prior years. Alfred Sloan Jr., who had converted a $50,000 investment into assets of $3.5 million in 24 years, joined the corporate management of GM. Sloan helped guide GM through the Depression and built a new management policy that was adopted by many other businesses. By 1941, GM accounted for 44 percent of total U.S. automotive sales, compared to 12 percent in 1921. During World War II, GM's factories were retooled in preparation for war, and between 1940 and 1945, GM produced defense materials valued at an estimated $12 billion.

The 1950s were marked by automotive sales records, innovations in styling, and new engineering discoveries. By 1950, all models built in the United States were available with an automatic gear-box. Between 1951 and 1955, the five divisions of GM— Buick, Chevrolet, Pontiac, Oldsmobile, and Cadillac— started offering a new V-8 engine, power steering, brakes, the first air-conditioning systems, and front seat safety belts. The entire look of the car, from the windows to the interior, was redesigned. Overall car sales in the 1950s were good, with growing American families creating a demand for a second family car. However, small European cars were gaining popularity, and American car companies were gradually losing market share to their foreign competitors. In 1957 despite a recession, the United States imported more cars than it exported. In 1959 GM's market share slipped to 42 percent of the year's new car sales.

The 1960 Detroit riots forced GM management to recognize urban poverty. Many minority workers were hired, as a result of the expansionist policies of Presidents Kennedy and Johnson. This move helped GM prosper and diversify. GM's interests included home appliances, insurance, locomotives, electronics, ball bearings, banking, and financing. By the late 1960s, GM's returns on investments increased from 16.5 percent to 25.8 percent. The 1970s were marked by heavy expenditures because GM had ignored the importance of pollution control for so long. The oil embargo sent sales of GM's luxury gas-guzzlers plummeting, but the company's compact and sub-compact cars gained a 40 percent market share by 1974.

Between 1985 and 1992, GM reported declines in earnings. An accounting change in 1987 provided a respite and created an increase in earnings. Since the early 1980s, GM had spent more than $60 billion redesigning many of its cars and the plants that built them. GM also made two expensive purchases in the 1980s: Hughes Aircraft and Electronic Data Systems

(EDS). The EDS purchase provided GM with better, more centralized communications and backup systems, as well as a vital profit center. In 1987 for the first time in 60 years, Ford's profits exceeded those of GM.

From 1990 to 1992 GM suffered losses totaling $30 billion. Manufacturing costs that exceeded those of its competitors because of high labor costs, overcapacity, complicated production procedures, and competition from 25 companies all contributed to these losses. GM's market share fell from 50 to 35 percent. In 1992, Jack Smith Jr. became CEO of GM, and in 1993, he simplified North American operations, cut the corporate staff, pared product offerings, and divested GM's parts operations. He also negotiated with the United Auto Workers; closed more than 24 plants by 1996; and pledged $3.9 billion in jobless benefits, raising blue-collar payroll costs more than 16 percent over three years.

In the early 1990s, GM entered the van, truck, and sports utility vehicle markets. Saturn Corp. was launched at this time, and the weak dollar caused the price of imported cars to increase much faster than domestic prices. All of this helped GM to recapture market share from Japanese manufacturers. In 1993, GM recorded a net income of $2.47 billion on sales of $138.22 billion. Increased 1994 sales totaled $154.95 billion, and 1995 sales were $168.83 billion with profit margins of 3.5 and 4.5 percent, respectively.

On June 7, 1996, GM announced the spin off of EDS. EDS entered into a 10-year agreement with GM to be its principal provider of information technology services.

STRATEGY

When GM chairman Jack Smith began his tenure, he introduced a series of "strategy boards" for each sector and region of the company, as well as a "global strategy board" for the company overall. "Each board draws together top executives in manufacturing, finance, purchasing, or various regions, among others, in an effort to manage business together—not as separate fiefdoms," said Daniel Howes in a November 1997 *Detroit News* article. According to Howes, these strategy boards have had a tremendous impact on GM as they have served to foster debate, evaluate data, and generally bring consensus.

The "strategy boards" are but one element in GM's ongoing restructuring efforts since 1992. Among the most significant has been the restructuring of the parts operations sector, which was renamed Delphi Automotive Systems. Thirty-three operations that were either unnecessary and expensive were sold, or closed, which created profitable independent suppliers. Delphi also opened 104 parts facilities worldwide, with only one in the United States.

In 1994, GM combined all its stamping plants in North America, each with its own set of processes, controls, and management style, into a single Metal Fabricating Division. The following year, according to Howes, "GM appointed a series of ëvehicle line executives' responsible for all facets of car and truck programs. Insiders say the change has dramatically improved the way cars and trucks are developed by injecting accountability into a once-confused web of overlapping responsibilities. The result has been fewer launch glitches and improved quality."

Another one of GM's restructuring moves has been what the company calls the "Hughes Transactions." This was a strategic restructuring of GM's Hughes Electronics subsidiary and included the spin-off and merger of Hughes' defense unit with Raytheon Company. In 1997, GM sold the defense end of this business to Raytheon for nearly $10 billion. At the same time, Delco Electronics, the automotive subsidiary of Hughes, was transferred from Hughes to Delphi Automotive Systems.

According to General Motors' 1997 annual report, the corporation concentrated on four business priorities: "run common, think lean and run fast, compete globally, and grow the business." For GM, getting "common" involves its processes, parts, and vehicle platforms worldwide. It is an effort that redirects the company's old strategy of independent, stand-alone companies to one of eliminating duplication, confusion, and waste. Global car platforms allow different varieties of the same car to be built in many different countries and marketed globally.

"Thinking lean" translates into cost reductions by streamlining its vehicle development process, for example. In 1997 GM spent $4 billion on a study of cost competitiveness. "Running fast" refers to the need to make changes in a timely fashion—from the construction of new plants to the launch of new models. Competing on a global basis is a strategic priority, as GM is undergoing the largest international production capacity expansion in the company's history. GM's strategy is to build cars and trucks in the location where it wants to sell them. Finally, GM would like to reestablish itself as a growth company, and it spent $21 billion in the United States between 1997 and 2000 investing in emerging markets.

One of the eight emerging markets GM identified was Korea, and the company expected to complete its purchase of Korea-based Daewoo in the first half of 2002. Daewoo was financially indebted at the time of the sale, GM agreed to purchase the company for $1.2 billion and absorb up to $17 billion in debts, a figure higher than GM originally anticipated.

Negotiations for the purchase Daewoo took longer than expected partly due to financial hurdles GM had not foreseen, but also due to labor issues. Daewoo management had assured its labor force there would be no layoffs after the takeover, although GM had laid off more than 3,500 of its own workers in the United States in 2001.

INFLUENCES

In 1997 several strikes by local unions, including two long work stoppages in the United States, influenced GM's market share. Another factor is the seasonal nature of the automotive business. During a changeover to a new model year, sales are affected by the disruption in car production. Strong competition in the already crowded sport-utility market was also a factor in 1997. Finally, due to the weakened currencies in Japan and Germany in 1997, these car manufacturers took advantage of the cost savings in these countries and increased their sales volume. The launch of several new vehicles— including the Saab in Europe—and the higher associated costs led to increased operating costs for GM.

Although car automotive sales remained strong through 2000 and 2001, with GM capturing about 28 percent of the total market share in the United States, and 15 percent worldwide both years, sales dropped dramatically during the third quarter of 2001. General Motors led the industry pack in offering incentives to new car buyers, including zero percent interest and dramatically increased rebates. Automotive industry analysts had predicted a 10 percent decline in automobile sales during 2001, however, the incentives which were offered industry-wide created better than expected results, and sales fell only 3 percent.

Although GM was able to keep cars rolling off the lots during the latter part of 2001, the incentives cut deeply into profits. By mid-2002, profits were on the rise again, and GM expected $1.20 a share increase in the first quarter, and $3.50 a share increase in the second.

CURRENT TRENDS

One trend in the automotive industry that has had particular significance for GM is the growing consumer demand for trucks. Truck sales were up 10.8 percent in April 1998 from the previous year. It was the sixth straight month of year-over-year truck sales increases. Truck sales that month were the highest ever for one manufacturer in the history of the industry.

Truck sales remained strong through 2001, but in 1999 and 2000, the car-truck sales ratio for GM was about 50-50. In 2001, GM trucks again outsold cars, with 2.4 million car sales and 2.75 million truck sales in North America. However, GM Asia Pacific's truck sales were much stronger than its car sales between 1999 and 2001. In 1999, GMAP sold 259,000 trucks to 162,000 cars. In 2000 the mix was 175,000 cars to 283,000 trucks and in 2001 sales were 202,000 cars to 258,000 trucks.

PRODUCTS

General Motors divides its business into seven global operating groups and major subsidiaries. General Motors North American Operations (GM-NAO) makes Chevrolet, Pontiac, GMC, Oldsmobile, Buick, Cadillac, and Saturn cars and trucks. In 1997, GM-NAO introduced a record 14 new models. In 1998 GM introduced six new cars and light trucks in North America.

General Motors' subsidiaries produce various products that are important to the company. GM's Delphi Automotive systems is a diverse supplier of automotive systems and components. Delphi's products and services include chassis, interiors, lighting, electronics, power and signal distribution, energy and engine management, steering and thermal systems. In August 1998, GM announced plans to establish Delphi as an independent company so that it could focus on its core business of building cars and trucks. General Motors International Operations (GMIO) makes cars outside of North America, including Opel, Vauxhall, Holden, Isuzu, Saab, Chevrolet, GMC, and Cadillac. General Motors Acceptance Corporation (GMAC) provides a broad range of financial services, including consumer vehicle financing, car and truck extended service contracts, residential and commercial mortgage services, and vehicle and home-owners insurance.

Hughes Electronics Corporation, another subsidiary, designs, manufactures, and markets advanced technology electronic systems, products and services for the telecommunications and space, automotive electronics, and aerospace and defense sectors. Hughes is the largest producer of commercial communications satellites in the world and the leader in distribution networks for cable television and private business networks worldwide. In the telecommunications and space segment, Hughes' products include satellite design and construction and DIRECTV, a direct broadcast satellite television system that had 2.3 million household subscribers in 1996. In 1997, it attracted 1.0 million new U.S. subscribers and was launched in Japan. Hughes' automotive electronics products include air bag electronics, anti-lock brake modules, remote keyless entry, audio systems, climate controls, ignition electronics, pressure sensors, and spark controls. In its aerospace and defense segment, Hughes makes missile systems, radar and communication systems, air defense, training and simulation systems, and guidance and control systems.

General Motors Locomotive Group designs, manufactures, and markets diesel-electric locomotives, medium-speed diesel engines, locomotive components, power generation units, locomotive maintenance services, and light-armored vehicles. Finally, Allison Transmission is the world's largest designer and producer of heavy-duty automatic transmissions.

CORPORATE CITIZENSHIP

General Motors contributes millions of dollars to a variety of charitable organizations all over the world. GM employees and retirees nationwide volunteer their time and talent by collecting food and clothing, aiding victims of violence and sexual assault, working at homeless shelters, mentoring at-risk students, and sponsoring youth programs and other activities.

The GM Foundation was founded in 1976 to guide the company's philanthropic efforts. In 2001 alone, the GM Foundation donated $47.4 million to a variety of activities and organizations in the areas of education, health and human services, arts and culture, civic and community, public policy, and environment and energy.

In addition to the GM Foundation, partnerships with community organizations are an important element in GM's philanthropic efforts. GM has had a 50-year commitment to the United Way and is the largest U.S. corporate contributor to this organization.

In 1978 GM formed the GM Cancer Foundation to recognize and reward scientists who have significantly contributed to the treatment and prevention of cancer. GM presents three awards annually: the Charles F. Kettering Prize for the most outstanding recent contribution to the diagnosis or treatment of cancer; the Charles S. Mott Prize for the most outstanding recent contribution related to the causes or ultimate prevention of cancer; and the Alfred P. Sloan Jr. Prize for the most outstanding recent basis science contribution to cancer research. Each prize consists of a gold medal and $100,000.

GLOBAL PRESENCE

General Motors is the largest U.S. exporter of cars and trucks and has manufacturing, assembly, or component operations in 50 countries. GM has a global presence in more than 190 countries. About one-third of GM's sales are generated outside North America, and the company hopes to draw half of its annual revenues that way by 2006. Major markets for exports are Latin America and the Middle East, but exports to the Asia-Pacific region are increasing.

General Motors International Operations, based in Zurich, Switzerland, operates 34 manufacturing and assembly facilities outside of North America. Its 44 sales and marketing operations are located on five continents. GM's international operations are organized into General Motors Europe, Latin America, Africa, Middle East Operations, and Asia-Pacific Operations.

GM would like to dominate the emerging consumer markets in eastern Europe and Russia. GM is also opening plants in Russia, Argentina, China, India, Indonesia, and Thailand. In Russia, Chevrolet Blazers, Cavaliers, and Transports are on the road. The company will invest $2.5 billion in expanding its Asian manufacturing operations and continues to expand in India, with GM, Delphi, Hughes Electronics, GMAC, and GM's Locomotive Group. Under GM chairman Jack Smith, "GM has launched the largest manufacturing expansion in company history—all outside the United States," according to a November 1997 *Detroit News* article.

EMPLOYMENT

General Motors is one of the largest employers in the world. In addition, GM also offers a Global Intern Program and a Global Cooperative Education Program. The intern program offers college students on-the-job experience through temporary full-time positions during college and university summer break periods. College students work throughout the year in GM's co-op program, with work sessions arranged to accommodate class schedules.

General Motors offers its employees one of the most comprehensive benefits programs in the country. GM benefits include a choice of health care plans, life and disability insurance, a savings-stock purchase program, retirement program, product discounts, and paid holidays and vacations.

SOURCES OF INFORMATION

Bibliography

"Auto sales pace likely to cool, analyst says."*Detroit Free Press*, 11 April 2002.

Blumenstein, Rebecca. "GM Doubles Net on Strong Factory Sales." *The Wall Street Journal*, 27 January 1998.

Bowe, Christopher. "GM pins hopes on cost savings." *Financial Times*, 19 March 2002.

Chappell, Lindsay. "Chevy topples Ford as sales leader." *Forbes*, 1 March 2002.

Flint, Jerry. "Bye-bye Oldsmobile, Hello Scion." *Forbes*, 11 March 2002.

General Motors 2001 Annual Report. Available at: http://www .gm.com.

"General Motors Corporation." *Hoover's Handbook of American Business 1998.* Austin, TX: The Reference Press, 1997.

"General Motors Corporation." *Moody's Handbook of Common Stocks.* New York: Moody's Investor's Service, Inc., 1997.

"General Motors." *Standard & Poor's Stock Reports.* New York: Standard & Poor's, 1998.

Howes, Daniel. "GM Now Running Leaner, Faster." *Detroit News*, 2 November 1997.

Morris, Thomas V. *If Aristotle Ran General Motors: The New Soul of Business.*, New York: Henry Holt and Co., 1997.

Paul, Anthony. "Indonesia: Life Under the Volcano." *Fortune*, 13 April 1998.

Shnayerson, Michael. *The Car That Could: The Inside Story of GM's Revolutionary Electric Vehicle.* New York: Random House, 1996.

Taylor, Alex, III. "The Big Three's Dilemma." *Fortune*. 16 March 1998.

Tenreiro, Michael. "General Motors." *The Value Line Investment Survey*, 13 March 1998.

For an annual report:
telephone: (800)331-9922

For additional industry research:
Investigate companies by their Standard Industrial Classification Codes, also known as SICs. General Motors' primary SICs are:

3711 Motor Vehicles and Car Bodies

3714 Motor Vehicles Parts and Accessories

6159 Miscellaneous Business Credit Institutions

Also investigate companies by their North American Industrial Classification System codes, also known as NAICS codes. General Motor's primary NAICS codes are:

327211 Flat Glass Manufacturing

333924 Industrial Truck, Tractor, Trailer and Stacker Machinery Manufacturing

336111 Automobile Manufacturing

336211 Motor Vehicle Body Manufacturing

336399 All Other Motor Vehicle Parts Manufacturing

522298 All Other Non-Depository Credit Intermediation

Gymboree Corporation

OVERVIEW

The Gymboree Corporation is a multi-national company that provides products and services designed primarily for children. The Gymboree Corporation operates in two distinct sectors, each with a focus on children. One division offers interactive play programs for parents and children. The other is a vertically integrated operation that designs, manufactures, and sells children's clothing and accessories in retail outlets. The initial business concept created a parent-child music and play program that promoted fitness activities. As the classes grew in popularity, the company offered franchise licenses to increase its visibility. Management developed retail stores as a natural progression of the company's goal to promote a healthy and fit lifestyle for children. The store's product lines include children's clothing, accessories, and videotapes.

The corporate structure is comprised of five divisions operating in four countries. The retail clothing sector accounts for the majority of operations and includes: The Gymboree Corp. (U.S. retail), Gymboree Inc. (Canada retail), Gymboree U.K., Ltd. (U.K. retail) and Gymboree of Ireland (Ireland retail). These divisions focus on producing high quality apparel and accessories for children. Products include sweaters, pants, overalls, dresses, socks, hats, underwear, and shoes. The launch of the online retail store, www.gymboree.com, provides a global presence for the company. The Gymboree Play & Music Programs offer interactive classes for infants, toddlers, and preschool age children. Approximately 420 corporate operated or franchised centers are located in 17 different countries.

FOUNDED: 1976

Contact Information:

HEADQUARTERS: 700 Airport Blvd., Suite 200
   Burlingame, CA 94010
PHONE: (650)579-0600
FAX: (650)696-2920
EMAIL: investor_relations@gymboree.com
URL: http://www.gymboree.com

FINANCES:

Gymboree Corporation Revenues, 2000-2002 (million dollars)

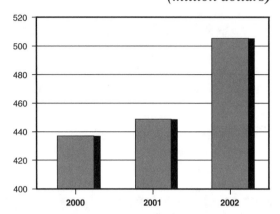

Gymboree Corporation 2001 Stock Prices (dollars)

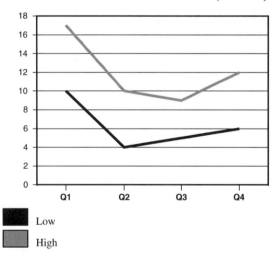

Low

High

COMPANY FINANCES

Gymboree earned a profit in the first quarter of 2002 after struggling with two years of losses. Revenues for the fiscal year ending in January of 2002 were roughly $505 million—an increase from $448 million in 2001 and $437 million in 2000. The stock price doubled in the final six months of 2001. Thomson Financial/First Call forecasts that profits will triple in the year 2003.

ANALYSTS' OPINIONS

The improved financial performance of Gymboree in 2001 caught the attention of Wall Street analysts. In April 2002 a Piper Jaffray analyst, Jeff Klinefelter, recommended Gymboree as a retail stock to own. He said, "Gymboree has been struggling for several years to regain traction with consumers and differentiation within the mall. Today, the new management team has demonstrated that they can deliver a product that is different and appealing to the consumer. The brand remains vibrant and has been bucking competitive trends and winning." Russell Jones, retail analyst for Cap Gemini Ernst & Young, offered his insight on Gymboree during a broadcast of "CNN Money Morning." He noted that the company had made improvements in its stores and increased efficiency, but it was not clear whether or not the company had actually developed a marketing and brand strategy that would attract new customers.

HISTORY

In 1976 Joan Barnes searched for an interactive class featuring fitness activities for her four-year-old daughter. She was unable to find one that she liked and concluded that other parents were equally frustrated with the lack of options. Her instincts were right on target. She created her own class and rented space at a local youth center in San Mateo, California. The launch of Gymboree was a huge success. Expansion began in earnest in 1979 when the first franchises were awarded. In 1984 Gymboree ventured into the global market, overseeing the start up of foreign franchises. By 1987 more than 50,000 children attended Gymboree classes. Barnes' small project had grown into the largest parent-child program in the country for children ages three months to four years. Three hundred and fifty centers operated nationwide and revenues exceeded $10 million.

Backed by U.S. Venture Partners, the same group that had financed the play centers, the company received an additional $300,000 in 1986 to enter the retail arena. Retail stores were considered a logical extension of the play programs. Designed to resemble gymnasiums, the stores featured play equipment, hardwood floors, bleachers and kiosks that played videotapes of actual Gymboree classes. The stores were all company owned and stocked with merchandise produced in house. The products included clothing for infants and children, toys, and videos. Sixty percent of each store's inventory was dedicated to apparel and the remaining 40 percent was comprised of toys and other accessories.

The company capitalized on its reputation as a child-friendly organization. Management drew upon the experiences and knowledge gained from parents in the play programs to differentiate itself from its competitors. The original strategy sent a simple message to the public:

Gymboree understands the needs of children and families. To illustrate this point, the company introduced a new sizing scheme for its outfits. Rather than using the traditional system, which labeled garments to match a child's age (six weeks, three months, 9 months or one year), outfits were designated as small, medium, or large. The appeal of this innovation was not in the labeling of the garments, but in their design. Each item was constructed so that it could be easily altered without sewing a stitch; this was accomplished by design features incorporated into the construction of the garments. Expandable waist bands and rolled cuffs for the ankles and wrists made it possible to adjust the pieces as the child grew larger. Size was not the only element of design used to maximize the life span of each item. Outfits were crafted in unisex styles and colors ensuring that they could be worn by future siblings regardless of gender.

By 1989 there were 32 retail stores operating, but they were not performing up to investor expectations, and the company brought in outside help. Nancy Pedot joined the Gymboree team as a general merchandise manager with nearly a decade of experience at Mervyn's department stores. She surveyed the situation and decided that the product lines were not appealing or distinctive. A design team was hired, and Gymboree began creating its own designs. Pedot shifted the emphasis from the unisex sweat suit style outfits to a line of colorful, durable play clothes. The line still favored the basic approach to children's dress but with a little more style and versatility in the designs, fabric, and stitching. Sales skyrocketed and Gymboree was back on track.

In 1990, in the midst of this period of revenues growth and expansion, Joan Barnes left the company she had founded nearly fifteen years earlier. The company achieved brand recognition in the market and continued to make great strides despite the loss of its leader. By 1993 the number of retail stores had grown from 32 to 170. Encouraged by its prosperity, Gymboree elevated Pedot to the position of president and decided to go public. On March 31, 1993, the stock made its debut on the NASDAQ Stock Exchange. The initial public offering (IPO) consisted of 2.1 million shares that opened at an impressive $20 per share, well above the $13 to $15 predicted by analysts. At the end of its first day as a publicly owned company, the stock price had risen a phenomenal 60 percent and closed at $31.50.

Pedot assumed the role of Chief Operating Officer in 1993 and began to evaluate the play center division. While the retail side of the business was posting consistently positive results, the play programs, which had once been the cornerstone of the company, were failing. In 1993 there were a total of 800 centers offering Gymboree play and music programs. The company owned slightly more than half of the centers, and the remainder were franchised units. In January 1994 Pedot made the decision to halt expansion and discontinue openings of any new play centers until the financial profile of this sector improved. The centers accounted for only 5 percent of

FAST FACTS:
About Gymboree Corporation

Ownership: Gymboree Corporation is a publicly traded company on the NASDAQ Stock Exchange.

Ticker Symbol: GYMB

Officers: Stuart G. Moldaw, Chmn.; Lisa M. Harper, Vice Chmn. and CEO, 41; Myles McCormick, CFO

Employees: 7,200

Principal Subsidiary Companies: Gymboree Corporation sold its subsidiary venture, Zutopia, to Wet Seal Inc. in 1999.

Chief Competitors: Gymboree Corporation's major competitors include OshKosh B'Gosh, The Gap, The Children's Place, and Toys "R" Us.

Gymboree's total revenues and were not strategic to the long term success of the organization.

During its first several years as a public company, Gymboree posted impressive earnings figures, and the stock price rose for almost eight consecutive quarters. In 1995 the company experienced its first setback. Merchandise sales in the retail stores slumped. The decline was attributed to a miscalculation in the clothing design and poor color choices for new clothing lines. The vertically integrated structure of the company introduced by Pedot added to the firm's inability to contain the losses. (A vertically integrated corporation controls every aspect of operations from product design to sales.) Since Gymboree designs, manufactures, and sells its own products, it must absorb the expense of a mistake in any phase of operations. Unlike other companies in the clothing industry that can attempt to return inventory to the original vendor to minimize losses, Gymboree was forced to keep the merchandise in its stores. Entire product lines were subject to huge price markdowns to clear the shelves. The problems were corrected, and the company returned to profitability the following year.

In 1996 Gymboree launched its first mail order catalog. The marketing plan proposed a series of catalogs that would be issued on a quarterly basis. Catalog sales were weak, and the mail order division was closed after only a few years. This experience did not dampen the overall plans for expansion. Pedot left the company, and Gary White assumed the role of CEO. In 1999 Gymboree launched a second chain of retail clothing stores, Zutopia,

CHRONOLOGY

Key Dates for The Gymboree Corporation

1976: Gymboree Play & Music Programs founded by Joan Barnes in San Mateo, California

1979: First U.S. franchises were opened

1984: First international franchises opened in Canada

1986: Gymboree entered the retail industry opening children's clothing stores

1990: Gymboree founder Joan Barnes leaves the company

1993: The company becomes a publicly traded corporation in a successful IPO

1996: Gymboree publishes mail order catalog

1999: The company launches chain of Zutopia clothing stores for older children

2001: Zutopia is sold to Wet Seal Inc.

2002: Lisa Harper is named CEO

---

targeted at older children. The international markets continued to be an attractive growth opportunity as well. By the year 2000, the company had lost its focus and sales began to falter. Gary White and Melanie Cox, two high level officers, left the company. The company also cancelled plans to relocate to a pricey office park in the San Francisco area.

In early 2000 Lisa Harper joined the struggling firm as a general merchandiser. She overhauled the clothing lines, which had become too trendy and hip for small children. She brought back the notion of mix and match outfits that had been lost, dubbing the concept "Match-matics." Harper's idea took off along with the stock price. Harper continued to make improvements in operations and was named CEO in 2002.

STRATEGY

Gymboree has developed a multi-faceted strategy for managing operations of its retail stores. The highlights of this plan include: production of high quality apparel, a recognizable brand name, integrated operations, exclusive distribution of merchandise, and superior customer service. Early in the company's history,

management realized the importance of maximizing the life span of children's clothes. Designing and manufacturing durable, timeless, and fashionable pieces were identified as critical elements in the process. By integrating operations, the company is able to maintain control over every aspect of manufacture and presentation of its products. This assures high quality control and improved brand name image. Perhaps the most important element in the Gymboree strategy is its commitment to customer service. In the fast paced world of children's retailing, an organization that is not responsive to the changing needs of its customer base may never recover its position in the market.

INFLUENCES

In an attempt to attract new customers, Gymboree implemented a new merchandising strategy in 1999. Instead of manufacturing and displaying coordinated play sets and outfits, a mix and match model was adopted. Coordinated items were no longer presented together in a cluster. Departments were organized and identified by category: girls' sweaters, boys' pants, dresses, or accessories. In theory this would increase sales of certain items that might not have been purchased by customers who did not wish to buy an entire outfit. Ideally, shoppers who wanted an entire ensemble would move from department to department and match coordinates, while others might just pick up a sweater. The plan did not achieve the desired results and was deemed a failure. The company suffered serious financial losses and returned to its initial concept of coordinated outfits.

CURRENT TRENDS

Although Gymboree reinstated its historical marketing strategy in regard to its design and selection of merchandise, it did recognize the value of updating the company image. A nation-wide store renovation plan was launched with a scheduled completion date of 2002. The signage and store fronts will undergo a facelift as part of this plan. The traditional front that features wooden children's blocks and arches will be replaced with a sleeker more modern look, and the signage will reflect the updated design. As part of a brand name recognition program, packaging, tags, and labels will all be altered to feature the new lettering and logo.

PRODUCTS

Gymboree Corporation operates infant and children's clothing stores and play centers. The play centers offer interactive fitness programs for infants and children from newborn to four years. Classes are designed for different developmental stages in a toddler's life. GymBabies caters to infants under six months old and focuses on sensory activities. GymCrawlers helps develop stability and coordination for babies aged 6 to 12 months. GymWalkers, GymRunners, GymExplorers, and GymKids teach motor skills, socialization, and coordination in a non-competitive environment.

Gymboree retail stores sell attractive, quality children's clothing and accessories. Clothes are designed to be comfortable and stylish without being trendy. The timelessness of design allows the pieces to be shared and handed down to younger siblings or friends. Coordinated outfits include pants, shorts, sweaters, shirts, dresses, stockings, hats, and shoes. Clothes are premiered by collections, which rotate on a seasonal basis, and contain separates that can be mixed and matched.

CORPORATE CITIZENSHIP

Gymboree is all about children. The company mission statement says, "The heart of our business is the celebration of childhood. Our aim is to enrich the lives of children with quality products and services and to learn and grow with them." The company contributes to children's charities whenever possible. One of the more colorful outings is the annual "Cincinnati Flying Pig Marathon." Gymboree sponsors family and children's activities in conjunction with the event, including a "Diaper Dash" for children less than one year of age. The length of the race has been shortened from the traditional 26 miles to a challenging 18 feet. Participants are allowed to walk or crawl, on Gymboree mats, to the finish line.

GLOBAL PRESENCE

Gymboree's corporate headquarters are located in Burlingame, California, and Leicester, England. The company owns 29 Play and Music Program Centers in the state of California. The remaining 410 centers are located across the United States and throughout the world. Program centers are located in Australia, Canada, France, Korea, Mexico, Taiwan, and other regions. The company operates more than 500 Gymboree stores in the United States, Canada, the Republic of Ireland, and the United Kingdom. Clothing is shipped to the retail outlets from distribution centers in Dixon, California, and Shannon, Ireland.

Most of Gymboree's products are manufactured outside of the United States. The company contracts with more than 200 independent vendors who are located in China, Indonesia, Thailand, Taiwan, Mexico, and South and Central America. Global accountability

TRUTH IN ADVERTISING

The Gymboree Corporation takes pride in its commitment to bettering the lives of children and families. As a result of a 1999 lawsuit that charged Gymboree (and a host of other companies) with human and civil rights violations in its overseas factories, the company has secured the services of an independent monitoring firm. Verite, a nonprofit organization that offers research in regard to global sourcing issues, has been retained to provide its services to vendors supplying goods to the Gymboree Corporation. Although Gymboree had processes in place to review plant operations, the company stated, "While we are comfortable with the processes we had in place, we are pleased to support the greater safeguards embodied in this agreement." The company has been applauded by human rights organizations for setting a standard of responsibility.

is important to the management of Gymboree, and they require vendors to be in compliance with local laws. In addition, they forbid the use of child or forced labor by any vendor, even if it is permitted by local law. Despite these efforts Gymboree was one of the retailers named in the 1999 Saipan lawsuits alleging human rights violations against factory workers. The company denied these claims, but they settled the lawsuit by agreeing to a system of third party monitoring in its manufacturing facilities.

EMPLOYMENT

Gymboree was founded by a mother, and employment at the company places great emphasis on the importance of family. This is evidenced by the benefits package offered to employees: parental leave, adoption assistance, pager programs for expectant parents, and team member discounts at stores and play centers. Two perks you don't see very often at large corporations are also included: snack time and recess! Gymboree isn't only for parents. The company values diversity and works to create a team atmosphere in all of its locations. Employees are encouraged to learn and grow as team members. Educational assistance programs are available for continuing education, and staff members are encouraged to contribute new ideas and concepts.

SOURCES OF INFORMATION

Bibliography

Carlsen, Clifford. "Gymboree Heads Abroad." *San Francisco Business Times*, 17 May 1996.

Eng, Sherri. "Market Share of California's Gymboree Rises on Merchandising Strategy." *San Jose Mercury News*, 14 February 1994.

"Gymboree Is More than Just Child's Play." *Chain Store Age Executive with Shopping Center Age"*, November 1987.

MacIntosh, Jeanne. "Firms Go Public." *Children's Business*, May 1993.

Rhine, Jon. "Gymboree Pulls Plug on Relocation to East Bay." *San Francisco Business Times*, 17 March 2000.

Rieger, Nancy. "Enter the Public Domain; IPOs Raise Capital for Kids' Firms Willing to be Tested by Wall St.'s Quarterly Exams." *Children's Business*, December 1994.

For an annual report:

on the Internet at: http:\\www.gymboree.com/our_company

For additional industry research:

Investigate companies by their Standard Industrial Classification Codes, also known as SICs. Gymboree Corporation's primary SICs are:

5641 Childrens' & Infants' Wear Stores

6794 Patent Owners & Lessors

Also investigate companies by their North American Industry Classification System Codes, also known as NAICS codes. Gymboree Corporation's primary NAICS codes are:

448130 Children's & Infants' Clothing Stores

533110 Owners and Lessors of Other Non-Financial Assets

Hertz Corporation

FOUNDED: 1924

OVERVIEW

Recognized as a worldwide leader in rental and leasing services and products, Hertz Corporation is an indirect wholly owned subsidiary of Ford Motor Company with approximately 7,000 businesses located throughout the United States and in more than 140 other countries. Hertz is comprised of two major business segments: rental and leasing of cars and light trucks, and rental of industrial and construction equipment. Profitable every year since it first became publicly owned in 1952, Hertz posted revenues of $4.9 billion in 2001.

Within its car rental sector, the company's 349 airport locations accounted for approximately 87 percent of profits in the United States in 2001. Suburban locations offer a variety of services, including customer pick up and delivery, insurance replacement, car dealer loaner programs, and local use rental services for commercial and leisure purposes. Referrals from automobile dealers and insurance companies for customers in need of temporary vehicle replacement due to an accident or repairs generate a significant portion of suburban location rentals.

Hertz's Equipment Rental Corporation, the company's subsidiary that operates in industrial and construction equipment, rents a wide variety of heavy equipment. The business is also one of the largest sellers of used heavy industrial and construction equipment in the United States. Branches are usually located in industrial or commercial zones and are built to emphasize efficiency, safety, and environmental compliance. Hertz's other minor business segments are claims management and insurance. Hertz Claim Management Corporation administers services such as investigating, evaluating, and

Contact Information:
HEADQUARTERS: 225 Brae Blvd.
   Park Ridge, NJ 07656
PHONE: (201)307-2000
FAX: (201)307-2644
URL: http://www.hertz.com

FAST FACTS:

About Hertz Corporation

Ownership: Hertz Corporation is wholly owned indirect subsidiary of Ford Motor Company.

Officers: Frank A. Olson, 68, Chmn., 1999 salary $1,000,000, 1999 bonus $1,003,000; Craig R. Koch, 54, CEO and Pres., 1999 salary $600,000, 1999 bonus $496,000; Joseph Nothwang, EVP, 1999 salary $310,000, 1999 bonus $250,000; Paul J. Siracusa, EVP and CFO, 1999 salary $296,000, 1999 bonus $212,000; Brian J. Kennedy, EVP Marketing and Sales, 2000 salary $281,000, 1999 bonus $183,000

Employees: 31,300

Principal Subsidiary Companies: Hertz Corporation's principal subsidiaries are Hertz Equipment Rental Corporation, Hertz International Ltd., and Hertz Claim Management Corporation.

Chief Competitors: Enterprise Rent-A-Car is Hertz Corporation's toughest competitor. Other major competitors include Alamo Rent-A-Car, Budget Group, Dollar Thrifty Automotive Group, and United Rentals.

handling a variety of claims, including bodily injury, property damage, and third-party claims. Hertz also maintains its own insurance operations to self-insure against general public liability and property damage.

COMPANY FINANCES

In 2001 Hertz generated $4.9 billion in revenues, down from $5.1 billion in 2000. In 2001 Hertz's car rental generated $3.8 million, industrial and construction equipment rental accounted for $1 billion, and $88 million came from other interests. Car rental revenues, although up from $3.3 billion in 1997, were down from $4.0 billion in 2000. Conversely, industrial rentals more than doubled since 1997, from $444 million to $1 billion in 2001, up from $970 million in 2000. Whereas total revenues decreased in 2001, total expenses increased from $4.5 billion to $4.9 billion, leaving the company with an income before taxes of $2.7 million, down from $581 million in 2000. After a tax credit for deferred taxes, total net income

for 2001 was $23.3 million, a decline of 93.5 percent from the previous year's net income total of $328 million.

ANALYSTS' OPINIONS

As of December 31, 2001, the entirety of Hertz's common stock was owned by Ford FSG Inc., a wholly owned subsidiary of Ford Motor Company, making Hertz a private, indirect subsidiary of Ford Motor Company. Consequently, Hertz's stock is no longer traded on the open market.

HISTORY

In 1918 22-year-old car salesman, Walter L. Jacobs, founded a car rental agency in Chicago with a dozen Ford Model Ts. By 1923 Jacobs' fleet of cars had grown to 600, and his company, DriveUrSelf, was producing nearly $1 million in annual revenues. In the same year Jacobs sold his business to John Hertz, who headed Yellow Cab and Yellow Truck. Jacobs remained as chief operating officer. By 1925 the company was operating coast to coast. Two years later Hertz sold the company, by then renamed to Hertz DriveUrSelf, along with Yellow Truck, to General Motors Corporation. In 1932 the first Hertz airport location opened at Midway Airport in Chicago. General Motors held the company, which it renamed GM Hertz Drive-Ur-Self, until 1953 at which time Hertz again acquired the company through his car and truck rental company, Omnibus Corporation.

In 1954 Omnibus changed its name to The Hertz Corporation and completed an initial public offering of stock, trading on the New York Stock Exchange. In the same year Hertz purchased Metropolitan Distributors, a New York-based truck leasing operation, for $6.75 million in cash. Metropolitan's 4,000 trucks brought Hertz's total fleet to 12,900 cars and 15,500 trucks. In 1959 Hertz introduced an innovative centralized billing system, the first such system in the car rental industry. Jacobs, credited for much of the company's success, was named chief executive officer of the new organization.

During the 1960s the travel industry expanded quickly as did Hertz. Although increased business also resulted in increased competition, Hertz remained number-one in the industry. In 1962 the company rolled out the industry's first travel agent booking system, and in 1965 the subsidiary Hertz Equipment Rental was founded to provide construction equipment rentals and leasing. Two years later the company was sold to Radio Corporation of America (RCA), becoming a wholly owned subsidiary, but continued to operate as a separate entity with its own management and board of directors.

In 1970 Hertz opened the Hertz Worldwide Reservation and Data Center in Oklahoma City, Oklahoma, offering a centralized reservation system, and in 1978 began its nationwide road service assistance program, another first in the industry. In 1984 Hertz began offering customers optional computerized driving directions. The following year RCA sold the company to United Airlines, which hoped to combine the rental company with its interests in hotels and travel agencies to create a premiere one-stop travel service. However, United Airlines was restructured in 1987 after a hostile takeover of the company. As part of the reorganization, all non-airline investments, including Hertz, were sold. In December 1987 Park Ridge Corporation, an investor group comprised of Ford Motor Company and Hertz executives, created for the sole purpose of purchasing Hertz, bought the company for $1.3 billion. Ford maintained an 80 percent interest, and Hertz's executives held the remaining 20 percent.

Approximately 50 percent of Hertz's fleet of passenger cars and light trucks were purchased from Ford. As an owner of Hertz, Ford sought to guarantee its continued majority market share of Hertz's business. Although the profit margin on sales to rental companies is traditionally low, if nothing else Ford could stop other car companies such as Chrysler from taking the dominant position with Hertz. In 1988 Ford reduced its interest in the company to 49 percent by selling shares to Volvo North America. In the same year Hertz was scandalized after pleading guilty to overcharging more than 100,000 insurance companies and others for repairs to damaged Hertz cars. The suit claimed that Hertz had charged insurance companies for repairs never made and had also secured repairs at wholesale prices, but charged insurance companies the full retail amount. In voluntary compliance with the ruling, Hertz paid $13.7 million in restitution and $6.35 million in fines, the largest fine ever imposed at that time in a criminal consumer fraud case, and fired 20 employees.

Despite its legal troubles Hertz continued to lead the industry. By 1993 the company operated in more than 90 U.S. and European markets, with 4,800 rental locations and a fleet of approximately 420,000 cars and trucks. During 1993 and 1994 Ford conducted a series of transactions that repositioned Hertz as a wholly owned subsidiary of the company. Three years later, on April 30, 1997, Hertz went public, selling nearly 61 percent of its Class A Common Stock, representing a 19 percent economic interest in the company. Stocks traded on the New York Stock Exchange until March 9, 2001, at which time Ford FSG, a wholly owned subsidiary of Ford Motor Company, purchased the 19 percent of outstanding Class A stocks for $35.50 per share, totaling approximately $735 million. Thus, Hertz once again became a wholly owned subsidiary of Ford.

STRATEGY

Car rentals, which accounts for two-thirds of Hertz's revenues, are provided under a wide variety of plans. Cars

CHRONOLOGY:
Key Dates for Hertz Corporation

1918: Walter L. Jacobs opens an automobile rental business in Chicago with a fleet of 12 Model T Fords

1923: Revenues reach $1 million and Jacobs sells company to John Hertz who renames the company Hertz DriveUrSelf System

1932: The first rent-a-car location opens at Chicago's Midway Airport

1954: Company is renamed the Hertz Corporation and is listed on the New York Stock Exchange for the first time

1967: Hertz Corporation is sold to RCA Corporation and becomes a wholly owned subsidiary

1978: Hertz offers nationwide roadside assistance for its customers, an innovative first in the industry

1985: United Airlines, who had purchased Hertz in 1983, sells 80 percent of the company to Ford Motor Co. and 20 percent to a group of Hertz executives

1988: Hertz is found guilty of overcharging thousands of customers for auto damage repairs and ordered to pay a fine of $6.85 million and $13.5 million in restitution fees

1993: Operates more than 90 U.S. and European branches, with more than 4,800 around the world and a fleet of approximately 420,000 vehicles

1994: Hertz drops O.J. Simpson, the company's spokesperson for the previous 19 years, after he is put on trial for murder

1997: Hertz begins service in the Republic of Yemen, its ninth Middle Eastern market

2001: Ford buys remaining shares to become sole owner of Hertz, which leads the industry with a dominant 30 percent of the airport car rental market

can be rented on a daily, weekend, weekly, or monthly basis with the options of an unlimited or limited mileage rate, or on a time rate plus mileage charge. Rates vary according to competitive and cost factors associated with individual markets. Almost always, the customer is responsible for gasoline used during the rental period.

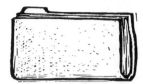

ADVERTISING ANGUISH

For 19 years retired professional football player O.J. Simpson was the official spokesperson for Hertz. During a long-standing television advertising campaign, Simpson could be seen leaping over luggage and other obstacles on a fun, albeit harried, dash through an airport to catch a flight. Simpson also regularly played golf at Hertz-sponsored events. But the happy relationship between Hertz and its spokesperson came to a crashing halt in 1994 when Simpson was arrested for the murder of his ex-wife and another man. Caught on national television was the live footage of Simpson driving a Hertz-owned white Ford Bronco trying to make a slow escape with police in pursuit. Hertz, who immediately dropped the former athlete as the company's public relations representative, refrained from airing commercials during Simpson's national televised murder trial. Due to the embarrassing situation caused by Simpson, Hertz no longer uses professional athletes to endorse the company.

The Hertz strategy for success is based on its extensive worldwide ownership of its operations, which contributes significantly to a consistently high quality of service, strict cost control, fleet utilization and maintenance, competitive pricing, and the ability to offer one-way rentals. At the end of 2001, Hertz owned 95 percent of all cars used in its fleet. On occasion, Hertz enters franchise agreements to provide rental services; however, such situations are usually limited to international locations where Hertz works with local rental businesses.

INFLUENCES

The recent decrease in revenues can be attributed to two interrelated factors: a slowdown in the economy and the impact the terrorist attacks of September 11, 2001, had on the travel industry. Both factors led to a decrease in car rental volume and pricing, resulting in a 50 percent reduction in Hertz's business. Because the vast majority of Hertz's car rental business is generated by its airport locations, when air travel fell off sharply in the wake of September 11, Hertz was significantly impacted. Other factors that influenced Hertz were higher 2001 model vehicle costs and lower proceeds received from selling off used vehicles. Even

before the terrorist attacks, Hertz was battling these economic factors. Revenues for the third quarter of 2001 were $25.5 million, compared to $54.2 million during the same period in 2000. During the fourth quarter, the company was hit hard, posting a loss of $57.5 million. In general, Hertz's business is continually influenced by a number of factors, including advertising costs, currency exchange rates, labor agreements, and new and used car pricing as well as fluctuating trends in the travel industry most often affected by changes in gasoline prices.

CURRENT TRENDS

Although revenues for 2002 were expected to top 2001 levels, Hertz expected results to remain significantly lower than historical levels. The most important seasons for Hertz's business are spring and summer when business and leisure travel increases, whereas winter months are usually marked by a decrease in travel. Available fleet and staff are increased during peak seasons and decreased during the off-season. However, numerous operating expenses remain fixed, such as rent, insurance, and administrative costs. Hertz is attempting to reduce the impact of seasonality by providing incentives for leisure and business travel during off-months.

In 2001 Hertz introduced the Prestige Collection, which offers luxury vehicle choices to its fleets in certain markets. Automobiles in the collection consist of makes and models from Premier Automotive Group, an enterprise of Ford, including Jaguar, Land Rover, Lincoln, and Volvo. The company planned to extend the program, both in the United States as well as Europe and Australia, through 2003. In an ongoing effort to cut costs, Hertz sold off Hertz Technologies due to trends in the telecommunications market that negated the economic benefits of operating the company. Instead Hertz invested in 2Roam Inc., which provides software services that allow customers to make, review, or update rental reservations from a variety of mobile devices.

Hertz continually looks for new ways to add customer convenience and value to their products and services. For example, in 1987 the company introduced Hertz Instant Return. Upon returning the rental car, customers are met in the return lot by a Hertz agent who processes the return on site with a portable computer and printer. A receipt is often ready before the customer has unloaded the truck. In 1989 Hertz's premium, expedited car rental service #1 Club Gold was launched, and by the end of 1996 approximately 7,500 cars in Hertz's fleet were equipped with the NeverLost onboard navigation system. In 1996 Hertz launched its Web site, which offers rate quotes, reservations, confirmation, and cancellation services.

PRODUCTS

Hertz markets a wide variety of automobiles and services. Makes and models of cars for daily rental are current year or previous year models. More than 50 percent of the cars in Hertz's fleet are manufactured by Ford. In addition to car rentals, Hertz provides ancillary products and services, such as Hertz premium program packed as #1 Gold Club; the Rent It Here—Leave It There program; supplemental equipment including child car seats and ski racks; loss or collision damage waivers; liability and personal effects insurance, NeverLost navigational system, and gasoline payment options. Hertz Equipment Rental offers its customers a broad range of equipment in the categories of earthmoving, material handling, aerial and electrical, air compressors, pumps, compaction, and construction-related trucks.

CORPORATE CITIZENSHIP

Hertz is subject to a number of legal and regulatory requirements related to the environment. Particularly, Hertz owns approximately 400 underground tanks and 1,600 aboveground tanks that store petroleum products. In 2001 Hertz spent $1.4 million to register, upgrade, and replace tanks to comply with regulations. The company is also monitored for the disposal of waste materials such as used oil, vehicle wash, and waste water.

GLOBAL PRESENCE

At the end of 2001, Hertz International Ltd., a subsidiary of Hertz Corporation, operated in more than 140 foreign countries and jurisdictions. Although most of its international operations are company-owned, a higher percent of branches are conducted through licensees. International locations that produced the greatest revenues in 2001 were France, Germany, Italy, the United Kingdom, Canada, Australia, Spain, the Netherlands and Switzerland. Operations are also conducted in Brazil, Puerto Rico, St. Thomas, New Zealand, Belgium, and Luxembourg. Hertz has also moved into Japan and China through associations with local companies. Almost all services offered in the United States are also offered at its international locations.

EMPLOYMENT

Approximately 30,000 individuals are employed by Hertz around the world. Some 6,200 U.S. employees are covered by terms of employment as enacted under labor contracts with 152 different local unions, most commonly related to the International Brotherhood of Teamsters and the International Association of Machinists. Hertz offers its employees a wide range of benefits such as group life insurance, health insurance, pension plans, and an income savings plan.

SOURCES OF INFORMATION

Bibliography

Barker, Robert. "Hijacking Hertz Shareholders." *Business Week*, 16 October 2000.

Flowers, Grant. "Hertz Debuts 'Prestige Collection.'" *Travel Weekly*, 18 June 2001.

"Ford Motor Launches Offer to Buy Hertz Shrs at $35.50." *Futures World News*, 17 May 2001.

Halliday, Jean. "Surge in One-Way Car Rentals Prompts Shift in Ad Message." *Advertising Age*, 24 September 2001.

"The Hertz Corporation." *Hoover's Company Profiles*, 2002. Available at http://www.hoovers.com.

Hutzler, Charles. "Hertz and Avis Make Inroads into China with Joint Ventures." *The Asian Wall Street Journal Weekly*, 18 March 2002.

Kepos, Paula, ed. *International Directory of Company Histories.* Vol. 9. Detroit: St. James Press, 1994.

Sawyers, Arlena. "Hertz Courts Upscale Vehicle Renters." *Automotive News*, 20 August 2001.

Stringer, Kortney. "Hertz, Others Quietly Raise Rates for Cars; Ford Unit Leads Bid to Lift Rental Revenue as Drop in Travel Fails to Let Up." *The Wall Street Journal*, 12 December 2001.

For additional industry research:

Investigate companies by their Standard Industrial Classification Codes, also known as SICs. Hertz Corporation's primary SICs are:

7514 Passenger Car Rental

7359 Equipment Rental & Leasing, Not Elsewhere Classified

Also investigate companies by their North American Industry Classification System codes, also known as NAICS codes. Hertz Corporation's primary NAICS codes are:

532111 Passenger Cars Rental

532310 Consumer Electronics and Appliances Rental

Hewlett-Packard Company

FOUNDED: 1939
VARIANT NAME: HP

Contact Information:

HEADQUARTERS: 3000 Hanover St.
   Palo Alto, CA 94304-1185
PHONE: (650)857-1501
FAX: (650)857- 5518
TOLL FREE: (800) 752-0900
EMAIL: news_dept@hp.com
URL: http://www.hp.com

OVERVIEW

Hewlett-Packard Company (HP) primarily designs, manufactures, and services electronic products and systems for computation, analysis, and measurement. HP offers more than 25,000 products and maintains manufacturing plants, research-and-development centers, warehouses, and administration facilities in more than 120 countries. Sales of computers and related products and services account for approximately 70 percent of the company's revenue. With 2001 net sales revenues of $45.2 billion, Hewlett-Packard moved from the nation's third to second-largest computer company, following the 2002 merger with Compaq Computer. Before the merger the company in 2002 was number 19 on the Fortune 500 list of the largest U.S. corporations and a leader in most of the markets in which it competes. It should remain in that position or improve slightly since Compaq before the merger was number 21 on the *Fortune* 500 rankings in 2002. These markets include servers, workstations, personal computers (including portables), computer peripherals, network equipment, and handheld calculators. Other products include electric test and measurement equipment, analytical instruments, and medical equipment. HP has become one of the largest diversified companies in the world, generating more than 55 percent of its business outside the United States. The merger gives the company additional opportunities for revenues in Africa, Latin America and Singapore thanks to Compaq's solid business foundation in those areas of the globe.

COMPANY FINANCES

Most of Hewlett-Packard's income comes from its broad range of computer products and peripherals, accounting for more than $35 billion of HP's total 1997 revenues. The company is the world's revenue leader for RISC and UNIX-based computers and the second largest supplier of workstations for engineering and business applications. Net revenue from the United States rose 12 percent in 1997, while international revenue grew 11 percent and accounted for 56 percent of total revenues. The company boasted a comfortable 1997 operating profit of 10.1 percent and net profit of 7.3 percent, with a return on assets of 9.8 percent. Strong earnings growth contributed to an increase of $1.6 billion in net cash, enabling the Board of Directors to add $1.0 billion to the authorization for repurchase of the company's common stock. During a 52-week period from 1997 to 1998, HP's stock reached a high of $82.00 (and a low of $50.00). Despite losses in early 1998, Hewlett Packard remained in excellent financial condition enabling it to easily continue investing in future growth. Nonetheless, the new HP in 2002 was far weaker than arch-rival IBM in total net income for HP and Compaq the last four quarters—HP's $1.1 billion to IBM's $8.4 billion.

Hewlett-Packard's world headquarters, located in Palo Alto, California. Hewlett-Packard

ANALYSTS' OPINIONS

Second only to IBM among the world's manufacturers of computer equipment and related technologies, Hewlett-Packard's history of consistently strong performance has always appealed to investors and analysts. The company itself remained confident in 1998 that it had the product offerings and resources needed for continuing success, though it warned that future revenue and margin trends could not be safely predicted. Indeed, that unpredictability caused investors to flee HP in the spring of 1998 after the company announced weaker than expected profits in the first quarter. No fewer than six firms and many analysts who had formerly been "bullish" on Hewlett-Packard slashed estimates on HP. HP blamed the drop in earnings on weakness in the Asian market and severe competition in the PC market. Also contributing to the decline was increasing erosion of HP's leading share in the workstation market caused by competitor Dell Computer. Analysts noted that, unlike IBM, Hewlett Packard did not have a major services business to fall back on when times were tough in the hardware market. New HP initiatives in the Internet arena also helped boost confidence in the early 2000s. That confidence seemed for many analysts all too absent following the HP and Compaq merger in 2002. Not only did the "new" HP experience subpar Moody's Investors Service and Standard and Poor's credit ratings in 2002, but Tony Sacconaghi, a computer hardware analyst with Sanford Bernstein investment house expressed doubts about the newly merged giant's ability to go head-to-head against

superpowers Dell, IBM, and Sun Microsystems, according to business writer Matt Beer.

HISTORY

Stanford University electrical engineers William Hewlett and David Packard began their joint venture in 1938 out of a Palo Alto garage with $538.00. They began working on their first product, a resistance-capacity audio oscillator, used for testing sound equipment. Their first order for eight oscillators was from Walt Disney Studios, who used them in the making of the film "Fantasia." Today that same garage is officially designated as a State Historical Landmark and recognized both as HP's birthplace and a Silicon Valley milestone.

Founded as a test-and-measurement company, HP's products quickly gained acceptance from engineers and scientists. When war broke out at the end of 1941, U.S. government orders poured in and the fledgling company expanded rapidly, building the first of its own buildings in 1942. Hewlett and Packard, still a little dazed by their sudden success, had the 10,000-square foot office/laboratory/factory designed so that it could be converted into a grocery store if the electronics business failed. In 1942 HP developed a line of microwave test signal generators and by the end of the war the

FAST FACTS:

About Hewlett-Packard Company

Ownership: Hewlett-Packard is a publicly held company traded on the New York Stock Exchange.

Ticker symbol: HPQ

Officers: Carleton (Carly) Fiorina, Chmn. and CEO, 47; Michael D. Capellas, Pres., 48, 2001 salary $1.6 million

Employees: 135,000

Principal Subsidiary Companies: Hewlett-Packard (HP) has subsidiary companies and facilities in 162 countries and claims to offer its services to one billion customers. Some of these include: Apollo Systems Div., CSTO Div., Four Pi Systems Corp., Hewlett-Packard Co. International Div., Hewlett-Packard Co. Microwave Technology, Hewlett-Packard Co. Optoelectronics Div., Hewlett-Packard Co. Personal Computer, Hewlett-Packard Co. Scientific Instruments, and Hewlett-Packard Co. Video Communications Div.

Chief Competitors: Hewlett-Packard's principal rival is IBM, the world's number one computer maker. HP's presence in the high-end workstation market also puts it in direct competition with companies such as Sun Microsystems, Inc.; Silicon Graphics. Its PC business pits it against leading PC manufacturers such as Dell Computer, but in 2002 it merged with another competitor, Compaq Computer. HP is also a leading player in the printer market where it competes against companies such as Canon, Epson, Lexmark, and Xerox.

company was the acknowledged leader in the field. The company was incorporated in 1947.

The 1950s was a time of growth and maturation for Hewlett-Packard. The company had grown tremendously in the decade since World War II began, from 3 employees in 1941 to 215 in 1951. Revenues had soared from $34,000 in 1941 to $5.5 million in 1951. In 1957 the company made its first public stock offering, and in 1958 it made its first acquisition, purchasing the F.L. Moseley company of Pasadena, California. By this time, HP was earning in excess of $30 million and employed nearly 1,800 people.

In 1959 HP ventured overseas for the first time, establishing a sales office in Geneva, Switzerland, and a manufacturing plant in Boeblingen, West Germany. A few years later, the German plant introduced a non-invasive fetal heart monitor and pioneered flexible working hours, an idea soon adopted at HP manufacturing facilities worldwide. The company continued its expansion overseas in 1963 forming a joint venture company, Yokogawa Hewlett-Packard in Tokyo, Japan. By 1965 the company's revenues had quintupled again, climbing to $165 million, and more than 9,000 people around the world worked for Hewlett-Packard.

For some U.S. companies, the 1970s was an unprofitable time of oil shocks and increasingly agile international competition, but for Hewlett-Packard it was a time of continued innovation and rapid growth. In 1972 HP introduced the world's first scientific hand-held calculator and branched into business computing with the HP 3000 minicomputer. In 1973 the company introduced the industry's first commercial distributed data processing system and, in 1974, it developed the first minicomputer based on dynamic random access semiconductors (DRAMS). This period was also marked by a significant growth in earnings and employment, with revenues cracking the $1-billion mark well before the end of the decade and computer sales accounting for half the company's revenues. The 1970s also saw the long reign of Bill Hewlett and Dave Packard come to an end as they handed over responsibility for management of day-to-day operations to John Young.

As with the economic problems of the 1970s, the bitter recession of the early 1980s left Hewlett-Packard virtually unscathed. Between 1980 and 1985, sales more than doubled from $3.0 to $6.5 billion and the number of employees rose from 57,000 to 85,000. The company launched a dazzling array of new products during this time, including its first personal computer, the HP-85, and its most successful product ever, the HP LaserJet printer. In 1984, HP also pioneered inkjet technology with the introduction of the HP Thinkjet printer. In the late 1990s and 2000s, the company's inkjet and laser printers remained among the most popular and technologically sophisticated in the world, as well as a constant product customers continually needed to purchase.

The early 1980s also saw HP make its first foray into the world of network computing when its U.K. subsidiary, HP Limited, developed an electronic mail system that was the first of its kind based on minicomputers. At about the same time, HP launched its most massive and expensive R&D effort ever, a five-year program to develop computer systems based on innovative RISC (Reduced Instruction Set Computing) architecture. The new line of computer systems was launched in 1986 and formed the basis for the powerful workstations, which by the end of the decade had transformed the world of computing.

By 1990 HP's revenues had doubled again from 1985's $6.5 to $13.2 billion and the company had moved into the top 50 in the Fortune 500. Though 1992 and 1993 saw growth briefly slow down to a less frantic 10 percent or so a year, by 1994 the company had still managed to double its 1990 earnings, taking in $25 billion. During this time HP concentrated on marrying its technologies of measurement, computing, and communication and developed new applications for its computer technology in analytical and medical instrumentation. New products included: the 11-ounce HP 95LX palmtop PC, weighing 11 ounces, which combined Lotus 1-2-3 software with advanced calculation features and data-communication capabilities; the HP SONOS 1500 echocardiograph system for real-time, non-invasive cardiac analysis using ultrasound waves; and a color scanner that allowed computers to read photographs and other visual images.

By the late 1990s Hewlett-Packard ranked as the second largest supplier of information technology in the world. From printers and scanners to desktop PCs and workstations, Hewlett-Packard was a dominant force in the world computing market and, in 1998 a study conducted by New York-based CMP Media named Hewlett-Packard the most recognized brand in the U.S. technology market, even finishing ahead of the ubiquitous Microsoft. Perhaps the company's only weakness was that its main strength lay in hardware, making it slow to take advantage of the many opportunities presented by the explosive growth of the Internet from the mid-1990s on. By 1997 the company was moving to correct this deficiency, however, acquiring VeriFone, the industry leader in electronic-payment systems and beginning development of its "Web Quality of Service" line of technologies, which were designed to prevent system overloads and allow businesses to prioritize transactions during peak usage periods. HP also began developing its own version of Java, a popular and versatile programming system originally developed by Sun Microsystems and widely used on the Internet. HP's plan was to focus on implementing this technology in printers and other devices, allowing them to link into and use a computer's interface to do such things as notify the systems administrator that the toner cartridge was running out, or even query a database and initiate an order for a replacement cartridge.

These moves put Hewlett-Packard in a position to play a more important role in the burgeoning Information Age. As CEO Lew Platt explained in his 1997 Letter to Shareholders, "Software has been one of HP's least visible businesses, but it is vitally important to our future." Thus, a second component of HP's new strategy was to form partnerships with electronic commerce software companies to offer what the company referred to in one press release as a "full-production Internet-commerce environment." Some analysts suggested the moves could give HP a leg up on its major competitor, IBM, in the electronic commerce field, a market expected to grow enormously by the end of the decade.

CHRONOLOGY:
Key Dates for Hewlett-Packard Company

1938: Stanford University electrical engineers William Hewlett and David Packard begin work on first product in a tiny garage; the first is an electronic instrument used to test sound equipment, the resistance-capacity audio oscillator (HP 200A), and the company said Walt Disney purchased these to use to assist with the sound track of the movie "Fantasia"

1939: Hewlett and Packard formalize venture as a partnership, deciding which name came first in company name by a coin toss

1942: Builds first of its own buildings

1947: Company is incorporated

1957: Makes first public stock offering

1958: Purchases F.L. Moseley company

1959: Establishes offices and plants overseas

1963: Forms joint venture company, Yokogawa Hewlett-Packard in Tokyo, Japan

1972: Introduces first scientific hand-held calculator

1973: Introduces industry's first commercial distributed data processing system

1974: Develops first minicomputer based on dynamic random access semiconductors (DRAMS)

1986: Introduces new family of Spectrum computer systems

1989: Pays $500 million for Apollo Computer

1994: Doubles 1990 earnings, taking in $25 billion

1998: CMP Media study names Hewlett-Packard the most recognized brand in the U.S. technology market

2002: Director Walter Hewlett tries to block the merger of HP with Compaq; before the issue is settled, Hewlett and Carleton (Carly) Fiorina, HP Chairman, engage in an angry mud-slinging duel in the press; Hewlett is unable to halt the Compaq merger, which he claimed would be ruinous for HP; the successful merger brings together two companies with combined revenues the last four quarters of $87.4 billion; Hewlett-Packard merges with Compaq Computer for $19 billion in stock, and Compaq name is absorbed, though for a time at least its products and inventory will be sold with the Compaq name attached

STRATEGY

Hewlett-Packard's growth has been generated by a strong commitment to research and development in electronics and computer technology combined with a decentralized organization that gives business units considerable decision-making authority. That growth has been accomplished by providing a continuous flow of new products and services to markets they currently serve, and by expanding into new areas. Reflecting the company's continued investments in new technologies, expenditures for research and development accounted for 7.2 percent of total expenditures in 1997, increasing by 14 percent to $3.1 billion, compared with $2.8 billion in 1996. Future increases in research and development expenditures are anticipated in order to maintain the company's competitive position and ensure a steady flow of innovative, high-quality products. In 2002, the new HP will have total r and d dollars comparable to the moneys both intended to spend separately in 2002—roughly $4 billion.

Hewlett-Packard strives to promote industry standards that recognize customer preferences for open systems in which different vendors' products can work together. Collaboration with other companies and technology alliances allow HP to expand into markets it might otherwise be unable to penetrate. For example, HP and Sybase, Inc. teamed up in a joint venture to develop Intel's up-coming 64-bit processor, the IA-64 (Intel Architecture-64-bit). HP and Intel jointly developed the original architecture, but in 2002, HP admitted again and again that it needed serious improvements in its Intel-related products. The company often bases its product innovations on such standards and seeks to make technology innovations into industry standards through licensing to other companies.

Like other large companies, HP flexes its financial muscle when necessary to strengthen its dominant position within the market. In acquiring Compaq in 2002, company executives belie they have accomplished a shrewd move by capturing a significant share of the electronic commerce market formerly held by Compaq. As Zona Research senior analyst, Vernon Keenan, told *Wired News* about an earlier merger with another competitor, such strategy is typical of HP's approach of "going after a competitor that's plowed the market initially." In fact, capitalizing on the innovations of others has always been a key part of HP's strategy. The company built its dominance of the printer market on a printer engine developed by the Japanese company, Canon, and was later sued—first by Apple Computer for copyright infringement and then by Xerox for patent infringement. Similarly, HP's decision to develop its own version of the Java programming system standardized by Sun Microsystems enabled it to gain a foothold in previously inaccessible markets.

INFLUENCES

In 1981 HP's computer peripherals group manager Richard Hackborn learned that Japan's Canon was working on a prototype of a small, cheap desktop printer that produced letter-quality type and could be sold for $3,000 retail. HP's only printer at that time was a $100,000 model sold with the company's minicomputers. HP started developing a new line of printers for consumers, using Canon's new engine. HP was confident that they could develop a cheaper, better product than the Japanese, exploiting HP's brand name and making up on volume whatever profits it had to share with Canon. HP had no experience selling to a broad consumer market. However, Richard Hackborn built up, over 15 years, a printer division that in the late 1990s brought in one-third of HP's revenues and 40 percent of its profits. In 2002 the company's printer revenues continued to be the mainstay of company profits.

Similarly, HP's purchase of Apollo Computer in 1989 leapfrogged it into the number two spot in the market for computer workstations, a field experiencing significant growth in the early 1990s. The company entered the PC field even later, but once again its immense resources allowed it to quickly catch up. In 1992 HP was the sixth leading supplier of personal computers, by 1996 it was the third largest. But while HP was gaining ground in the PC field, it was slow to make its products relevant to the Internet. Competitors like IBM and Sun Microsystems had gotten in on the ground floor and by 1997 had a significant lead in this area. HP responded by forming a partnership with Cisco Systems to develop new Internet business tools and by developing its own variant of the Java programming system originally developed by Sun. Likewise, in 2002, its $18.69-billion stock purchase of Compaq was designed to again leapfrog the company into competitive areas where heretofore it was lagging such as Compaq's handheld iPAQ, Armada laptop and ProLiant IA-32 server, according to business writer Nathan Cochrane.

CURRENT TRENDS

Hewlett-Packard is currently spending millions to develop new products such as printers that can produce photo-quality images from screens, and palm-size sensors that can transmit soil content data from the ground to farmers' PCs. On October 14, 1997, HP and Intel revealed the first details of their jointly defined Explicitly Parallel Instruction Computing (EPIC) technology and IA-64 (Intel Architecture 64-bit). The new technology was expected to offer breakthrough performance for the next-generation of 64-bit high-end workstation and servers. The company also announced a joint strategy with Microsoft to increase the productivity and simplify integration of enterprise computing technology while reducing costs. In another move, HP expanded its share of the computer printer market with new products such as the mopier (makes multiple original prints) and the HP Network ScanJet 5. The company estimated that even a gain as small as 1 percent could significantly increase its printer sales.

But it was in the Internet arena that the company hoped to make its biggest gains. By 1998 the Internet had become the fastest growing segment of the information technology market and all the major companies were scrambling to stake out a piece of the action. The emerging global network and a host of new specialized "information appliances" were revolutionizing the way people gathered and share information. HP believed it had the expertise to help create and manage these data highways, pointing to its expertise in both instrumentation and computing as a key advantage. The company's biggest step in this direction came with its alliance with Cisco Systems, Inc. early in 1997. The two companies agreed to a broad technology-development, Internet solutions, and customer-support alliance that would integrate computing, networking, and network management to supply complete, fully secure Internet-ready networked computing solutions.

Although the company continued to maintain its growth in 1998, earnings for the second quarter of fiscal 1998 were down slightly from the previous year, provoking many investors to sell their shares and pushing down the value of HP's stock. The company blamed the decrease in profitability on lower prices for computers and printers and on economic weakness in Asia.

In 2002, the company's merger with Compaq was regarded as well masterminded by HP, but nonetheless many retailers expressed strong fears that their inventory might contain a number of products headed toward the discontinued scrap pile, according to Business Wire magazine.

PRODUCTS

HP's first products were electronic measuring instruments used primarily by engineers and scientists. Later the company extended its range of measurement instruments to serve the areas of medicine and chemical analysis. The eventual move into the computer field was a logical progression based on the need to help its customers collect and manipulate large quantities of measurement data. By the late 1990s, though still a leader in instrumentation, HP was best known for its broad line of computer and computer-based products, including associated software, peripherals, support, and services. In 1998 HP was the world's leading supplier of RISC systems and UNIX system-based computers and the world's second largest supplier of powerful workstations for engineering and business applications. It was also one of the fastest-growing personal computer companies in the world. HP's merger with Compaq more than doubled its

available inventory of PC, laptop and handheld equipment, but as of May 2002 it was unclear which products would be showcased and which discontinued.

HP is also the world's leading supplier of printers. Products such as the HP LaserJet 4000 printers deliver high-resolution 1,200 dots-per-inch print performance at full engine speed and incorporate new technology that allows them to exchange information with printers, scanners, and other devices directly without a PC. The company also has a popular DeskJet inkjet printer, the 722C that features exclusive new color and photo enhancement technologies that enable it to produce photo-quality images more quickly. Other HP "hardcopy" products include DesignJet large-format printers, ScanJet scanners, OfficeJet all-in-ones, and CopyJet color printer-copiers.

The 2002 merger with Compaq not so coincidentally allows Hewlett Packard to strongly position itself in areas where it was formally weak such as handheld devices, server infrastructure softwarvoice control and voice-recognition software. While some analysts were skeptical and predicted a corporate disaster ahead similar to the yoking of AOL and Time Warner, other observers expressed belief that the merger might help the so-called "new" HP aggressively fight IBM for market share in the information technology (IT) industry.

CORPORATE CITIZENSHIP

In 1939, the year the company was founded with $538 and no revenues or profits, its ledger showed a $5 gift to the community. Co-founders Bill Hewlett and Dave Packard began a tradition of community involvement with a modest gift to a local charity in Palo Alto, California. Today HP is recognized as a leading giver among corporations in the United States. HP donates HP equipment, mostly for educational programs. In 1996 the company donated $72 million towards its philanthropy efforts and about 80 percent or $57 million of this amount went to education.

The company, recognized in the past for its philanthropy by the National Society of Fund Raising Executives who awarded it the Outstanding Corporation Award, contributed more than $54 million in resources worldwide to philanthropies in 2001. It also launched the Diversity in Education Initiative, a program aimed at encouraging females and minorities to consider technical careers, and to help improve the teaching of math and science in schools and colleges. During the 2000s, HP was widely praised for its innovative Digital Village Program, an attempt to introduce underserved populations to "social and economic opportunities of the digital age," according to an HP spokeperson in 2002.

Hewlett-Packard's environmental philanthropy focuses on many areas of concern, and the company continues to support environmental efforts throughout the world. In Europe HP contributes to a coalition of educational institutions, and government and environmental researchers working to improve the quality of water in several European rivers. This includes the Rhine Basin Program, to which HP Europe has donated more than $5 million. But HP does more than just donate money to environmental programs. It is a leading supplier of measurement and computation systems used for environmental monitoring and strives to develop products that minimize impact on the environment and on human health and safety. Most HP products are designed so that they can be taken apart and recycled. The company also offers customers in several countries a no-cost recycling program for HP LaserJet toner cartridges. Each month, HP recycles or reuses approximately 3 million pounds of material from old products at its product-recovery centers in Grenoble, France, and Roseville, California.

By the 2000s HP's products was able to announce that its products are made without the use of many toxic chemicals or ozone-threatening compounds, including carbon tetrachloride, HBFCs, chlorofluorocarbons, halons, trichloroethane, and methyl bromide. The company also has instituted steps to use fire extinguishers and air conditioning units that are less threatening to the ozone layer.

In 2001, the U.S. branch of Green Cross International, an environmental awareness group, awarded HP CEO Carly Fiorina its top environmental leadership award.

GLOBAL PRESENCE

Sales outside the United States make up more than half the company's revenue. Approximately two-thirds of HP's international orders prior to the Compaq merger were derived from Europe, with most of the balance coming from Japan, other countries in Asia Pacific, Latin America, and Canada. In addition, part of the company's product and components manufacturing, along with key suppliers, are outside the United States. HP is one of the top 10 U.S. exporters. The 2002 merger with Compaq tremendously strengthened HP's presence in Latin America and Singapore, among other international bases.

HP continues to keep an aggressive corporate presence in China. Space TV Systems, Inc. chose HP's MediaStream Broadcast Server as its on-air remedy for the world's first global direct-to-home satellite service that will feature Chinese programming. In 2002 HP established a Shanghai software research and development outpost with plans to expand to a 2,000-employee center by 2007.

HP's heavy dependence on international markets hurt the company in early 1998 as the Asian economy struggled in the wake of a region-wide economic collapse. Sales of medical instrumentation and test mea-

surement systems fell and the company found itself posting earnings well short of expectations. After HP merged with Compaq in 2002, the expanded company boasted four main Asian business sectors: the Enterprise Systems Group, HP Services, the Imaging & Printing Group, and the Personal Systems Group.

EMPLOYMENT

Hewlett-Packard believes strongly in the principles of equal opportunity and affirmative action for all employees and promotes an informal, non-authoritarian working atmosphere. In fact, HP won the prestigious Catalyst Award, an annual national prize that recognizes organizations for their programs to advance the careers of female professionals. The company also adheres to the belief that it is the employees who make the company's success possible and rewards them for their efforts with regular cash profit sharing and stock-purchase programs. Employees are eligible for profit sharing as soon as they have worked for the company for six months. In May 1998, HP distributed $210 million to more than 118,000 employees throughout the world. In 2000, as profits stalled worldwide and Hewlett Packard began serious negotiations with Compaq, no bonuses were paid rank-and-file employees. Although second quarter 2002 performance was still iffy, particularly in Europe and other international markets, the company nonetheless paid employees a substantial bonus in May 2002.

SOURCES OF INFORMATION

Bibliography
Antonelli, Cesca. "HP CEO Fiorina Must Boost Revenue, Investors Say." *Bloomberg News,* 14 May 2002.

Beer, Matt. ": Venerable HP Begins Life Anew with Compaq in Fold." *Agence France Presse,* 6 May 2002.

Brennan, Peter J. "HP to Keep Compaq Name on Corporate PCs." *Bloomberg News,* 7 May 2002.

Cochrane, Nathan. "New HP Cuts To The Chase." *The Age (Melbourne),* 14 May 2002.

"Compaq Keynote at Planet PDA Offers Insiders' View of HP Mega-Merger; Director in iPAQ Unit to Discuss Implications at Industry Trade Show Next Week." *Business Wire,* 10 May 2002.

Hewlett-Packard 1976 Annual Report. Palo Alto, CA: Hewlett Packard Company, January 1977.

Hewlett-Packard 2001 Annual Report. Palo Alto, CA: Hewlett Packard Company, 2001.

"Hewlett-Packard Company." *Hoover's Online,* 20 May 2002. Available at http://www.hoovers.com.

The Hewlett Packard Home Page, 20 May 2002. Available at http://www.hp.com.

"HP Awards $210 Million in Profit Sharing to Employees." *Business Wire,* 28 May 1998.

"HP Breaks the Bad News." *Wired News,* 15 May 1998. Available at http://www.wired.com/news/.

"HP Buys Out Korean Partner." *Wired News,* 27 May 1998. Available at http://www.wired.com/news/.

"HP Jumps Into Java War." *Wired News,* 20 May 1998. Available at http://www.wired.com/news/.

"HP Reports Second Quarter Results." *Business Wire,* 14 May 2002.

"HP LaserJet 5Si Mopier Wins Best New Product Award at FOSE; HP Also Ranked No. 1 in Federal Government Survey on Competitiveness and Past Performance." *MarketGuide,* 8 April 1997.

"HP Takes Internet Plunge." *Reuters,* 11 May 1998.

Kolesnikov, Sonia. "Day 1 for new HP in Asia." *United Press International,* 8 May 2002.

Williams, Martyn "How HP - Compaq Stacks Up." *IDG News Service,* 5 September 2001. Available at http://www.itworld.com

For an annual report:

on the Internet at: http://www.hp.com **or** write: Hewlett-Packard Company, 3000 Hanover St., Palo Alto, CA 94304

For additional industry research:

Investigate companies by their Standard Industrial Classification Codes, also known as SICs. Hewlett-Packard's primary SICs are:

3571 Electronic Computers

3572 Computer Storage Devices

3575 Computer Terminals

3577 Computer Peripheral Equipment, NEC

3578 Calculating & Accounting Equipment

7378 Computer Maintenance & Repair

Also investigate companies by their North American Industry Classification System codes, also known as NAICS codes. Hewlett-Packard's primary NAICS codes are:

334111 Electronic Computer Manufacturing

334119 Other Computer Peripheral Equipment Manufacturing

454110 Electronic Shopping and Mail-Order Houses

511210 Software Publishers

Hispanic Broadcasting Corporation

FOUNDED: 1949
VARIANT NAME: HBC

Contact Information:

HEADQUARTERS: 3102 Oak Lawn, Suite 215
   Dallas, TX 75219
PHONE: (214)525-7700
FAX: (214)525-7750
EMAIL: info@hbcca.com
URL: http://www.hispanicbroadcasting.com

OVERVIEW

Hispanic Broadcasting Corporation (HBC) is the largest Spanish-language radio broadcasting company in the United States. As of 2001, it owned or programmed 52 radio stations in 13 markets (Los Angeles, New York City, Miami, San Francisco/San Jose, Chicago, Houston, San Antonio, Dallas/Fort Worth, McAllen/Brownsville/ Harlingen, San Diego, Phoenix, El Paso and Las Vegas). Also, HBC stations are located in 12 of the top 15 Hispanic markets in the United States.

The company generates a large portion of its sales in Los Angeles with stations KLVE, KSCA, and KTNQ. HBC's stations also include Miami's WAMR and New York City's WCAA. The stations offer a variety of program formats including contemporary, full service, news and talk, Tejano, and tropical.

The company has always been a family affair. It was started in 1949 by McHenry Tichenor. Later, his son, McHenry Tichenor, II ran the business. In 2002, McHenry Tichenor, Jr. was the CEO.

According to the company, approximately 8.4 million Hispanics listen to its radio stations every week. In addition to its affiliated stations, it owns and operates the HBC Radio Network, the largest Spanish-language radio broadcast network in the United States in terms of audience delivery, and a network of Hispanic community-focused bilingual Web sites found at www.Netmio.com.

For its advertisers, HBC provides the Hispanic Marketing Group, a specialized division that helps retailers, manufacturers, brokers, and distributors achieve and exceed sales goals by developing unique programs that target the Hispanic market. The Hispanic Marketing

Group networks with over 30 merchandising units around the country to assemble resources and ideas that have been successfully executed in other markets. It also works with human resource directors and company managers to develop specific, targeted ways to recruit qualified job applicants in tight labor markets.

COMPANY FINANCES

In 2001, HBC's revenues rose 1.4 percent to $240.8 million. Net income fell 25 percent to $31 million. According to the company, results reflected revenues from stations acquired or reformatted, offset by increased promotion and operating expenses. Broadcast cash flow decreased 12.4 percent to $89.8 million. Net income totaled $31.0 million or $0.28 per share compared to $41.5 million or $0.38 per share for 2000. Net income for 1999 was $34,176 million, up from $26,884 in 1998.

In 2000, HBC's net revenues increased by $39.7 million or 20.1 percent to $237.6 million. This was up from $197.9 million in 1999. The 1999 revenues demonstrated an increase of $33.8 million or 20.6 percent over 1998, when revenues were $164.1 million for the same period in 1998.

ANALYSTS' OPINIONS

In March 2002, HBC's stock price hit a 52-week high of $32. In April 2002 UBS Warburg, a leading global investment banking and securities firm, rated the company "high," as it expected advertisers would keep shifting their dollars toward Spanish-language media outlets throughout the year. At the same time, the MSN Money Web site, employing its Stockscouter analytical tool, expected HBC to significantly outperform the market the rest of the year.

HISTORY

The beginnings of the Hispanic Broadcasting Company go back to 1949, when McHenry Tichenor, a Texas broadcast pioneer and son of a Texas broadcaster, applied for and received a license for KGBS-AM. Realizing that the large Hispanic population was largely ignored by South Texas radio, Tichenor experimented with a half English and half Spanish format. That same year, he bought a second station, KGBT, with a powerful signal that covered much of Mexico. At nights, the station would broadcast in Spanish.

Over the course of the next several decades, Tichenor acquired more stations and named his company Tichenor Media System (TMS). In 1962, encouraged by the success of the nighttime programs, Tichenor switched

FINANCES:
Hispanic Broadcasting Corp. Net Revenues, 1998-2001 (million dollars)

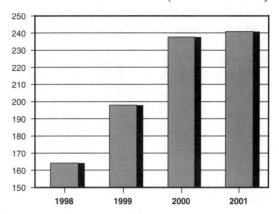

the format of his flagship KGBT to full time Spanish programming. In 1967, McHenry Tichenor, II took over as head of TMS.

As the Tichenor "broadcasting empire" continued to grow, TMS would make a great number of acquisitions in the ensuing decades. In 1975, Tichenor made a significant purchase when he bought radio station KCOR is San Antonio, the first-ever all-Spanish programming station.

In 1982, McHenry T. Tichenor, Jr. became president of TMS when he was only 26 years old. He decided to focus the company's growth on the Spanish market and proceeded to buy more stations including AM-FM sister stations KBNA in El Paso and, in 1986, WOJO in Chicago, which was the company's most expensive purchase at the time.

The empire continued to grow in the 1990s when Tichenor Media System bought half interests in stations in New York and Miami. In 1994, the company purchased 49 percent interest in Viva America Media Group, a Florida Partnership with two stations serving the Miami market.

In 1996, TMS began a merger with Heftel Broadcasting Company, which was founded in 1974 by Cecil Heftel. A year later, the merger was complete, and in 1998, the HBC Radio Network was created. In 1999, the merged companies officially become the Hispanic Broadcasting Corporation.

STRATEGY

According to its mission statement, the strategy of the Hispanic Broadcasting Corporation is to acquire or

FAST FACTS:

About Hispanic Broadcasting Corporation

Ownership: Hispanic Broadcasting Corporation is a publicly owned company traded on the New York Stock Exchange. Clear Channel Communications, another radio company, owns 26 percent while the family of chairman and CEO McHenry Tichenor, Jr. owns 17 percent.

Ticker Symbol: HSP

Officers: McHenry Tichenor, Jr., Chmn., Pres., and CEO, 45, 2001 salary $883,000; Jeffrey Hinson, CFO, VP, and Treas., 46, 2001 salary $525,000; Gary Stone, COO and SVP, 49; Jack Hobbs, Sr., VP New Business Development, Network Sales; Jorge Plasencia, VP Corporate Communications and Marketing

Employees: 1,108

Principal Subsidiary Companies: Through its subsidiaries, Hispanic Broadcasting Corporation owns and operates 52 Spanish-language broadcast radio stations. The company also owns and operates HBC Radio Network and HBCi, which operates the Company's radio station Internet Web sites. Its Hispanic Marketing Group division helps advertisers target markets.

Chief Competitors: Hispanic Broadcasting Corporation's biggest competitors include other radio syndicate organizations, especially Infinity Broadcasting, as well as other Hispanic radio organizations, including Radio Unica and Spanish Broadcasting.

develop additional Spanish language radio stations in the leading Hispanic markets. Also, HBC frequently evaluates strategic opportunities, both within and outside its existing line of business, concerned with serving the Hispanic market.

Above all, HBC, a quality-driven organization, is committed to being the premier marketing company dedicated to serving the major United States Hispanic markets. To accomplish this, it tries to provide superior service to audiences, advertisers, and communities.

On the Internet, company subsidiary HBCi, a network of Web sites, implements the Internet strategies of the parent company. HBCi, LLC is an online media company dedicated to serving Hispanics. Like its parent company, HBCi strives to enrich the quality of life for the community it serves and to provide advertisers with a dynamic platform to promote their goods and services. In building a Web network (www.netmio.com), HBC focused on developing culturally relevant content and communities, and it established strategic partnerships with vertical Web portals with interests that were compatible with the interests of its audience. In this way, HBC intends to provide partners with significant traffic to their own sites.

HBC developed HBCi to extend its radio stations' brand to an audience it was not reaching before. HBCi provides for the parent company synergies with its other operations. This includes creating a network of radio station Web sites, webcasting of audio content, building a database of its audience, and providing research tools, Overall, HBCi provides a worldwide platform and additional content appealing to a broader range of users. At the same time, HBCi Web properties benefit from the promotions that the radio stations provide. They also benefit from HBC's awareness of the tastes of the local Hispanic audiences.

INFLUENCES

HBC's acquisition strategy has led to increasing profit. The power of its strategy was evident following the attack on the World Trade Center on September 11, 2001, when broadcasters experienced a weak advertising market. HBC still managed to deliver a respectable revenue performance. National and network demands were stronger than expected, which offset the lower political revenues as well as the reduced event revenues due to the cancellation or postponement of events during the quarter.

About the company's results, president and CEO McHenry Tichenor, Jr. said, "The combination of a weak advertising environment and the events of September 11th made the year 2001 especially challenging. Nevertheless, during the course of the year, we vigorously defended and improved our competitive position, took advantage of our strong financial condition to strategically expand our coverage of both existing and new markets, and made important investments in station facilities and in our sales and marketing efforts." He added that he felt confident that steps taken in 2001 combined with the "fast-growing and increasingly important U.S. Hispanic market" would enable HBC to maintain its leadership position and result in market-leading growth in 2002. Those steps taken included increasing the promotion of its radio stations to improve the ratings and investing in on-air talent, programming research, additional sales and marketing personnel, staffing, and other costs associated with non-traditional revenue initiatives. Non-traditional revenues, the company explained, are revenues from the implementation of new business development techniques.

CURRENT TRENDS

As it headed into 2002, HBC anticipated revenue to increase by four to six percent. The company's optimism was fueled by three new "start-up" stations slated to begin operations in the second quarter of the year as well as two other start-ups that had been launched in 2001.

Besides acquiring new stations, HBC has, in recent years, pursued growth and increased profitability by entering into strategic alliances and partnerships. In late 2001, the company entered into a content-sharing agreement with MSNBC.com through its Netmio.com network of Web sites. In 2002, HBC and Katz Hispanic Media, a unit of the Katz Media Group, came together to form HBC Sales Integration, Inc., a marketing organization designed to better target media advertising money to Hispanic markets. The impetus behind the formation was the increasing buying power of Hispanic consumers. In 2001, Hispanics represented approximately 7 percent of total U.S. buying power; however, only about one percent of total U.S. advertising expenditures was directed toward the Hispanic market. The mission of the new marketing organization was to close that gap. It was believed that by entering into this alliance, HBC could attract more national spot advertising dollars over the coming years, as more advertisers created and deployed marketing plans aimed at the Hispanic audience.

PRODUCTS

HBC's primary product is its programming, which consists of regional Mexican programming, a tropical format, Tejano music, contemporary music, full-service format, news/talk and Spanish oldies. The on-air talent speaks in Spanish and English.

HBC's regional Mexican programming consists of various types of music originating from different regions of Mexico including Ranchera music, a traditional folkloric music commonly referred to as Mariachi music; Nortena music, which is representative of Northern Mexico and features an accordion to create a polka sound with a Mexican flavor; and Banda music, popular in California, which resembles marching band music with synthesizers. The tropical format consists of Salsa, Merengue and Cumbia music. Salsa is dance music combining Latin Caribbean rhythms with jazz, and it is popular with Hispanics living in New York, Miami and Chicago. Merengue music is dance music originating in the Dominican Republic. Tejano music originated in Texas and is based on Mexican themes. It is a combination of contemporary rock, Ranchera and country music. Contemporary music includes pop, Latin rock, and ballads,

CHRONOLOGY:

Key Dates for Hispanic Broadcasting Corporation

1949: McHenry Tichenor buys his first radio station

1962: Tichenor's flagship station goes to an all-Spanish format

1967: McHenry Tichenor, II takes over as president of the company, company now called TCM

1982: McHenry Tichenor, Jr. takes over as head of the company

1986: TCM buys WOJO in Chicago, its most expensive purchase to date

1994: TCM purchases 49 percent interest in Viva America Media Group

1996: TCM begins merger with the Heftel Broadcasting Company

1999: The merged companies are now called the Hispanic Broadcasting Corporation (HBC)

2001: HBC enters into a content-sharing agreement with MSNBC.com

2002: HBC and Katz Hispanic Media form HBC Sales Integration, Inc.

and is similar to English-speaking adult contemporary and contemporary hit radio stations. The full service format features all the traditional radio services including music, news, sports, traffic reports, special information programs, and weather. The news format includes local, national, and international reports and weather, business, traffic and sports. The talk format features commentary, analysis, discussion, interviews, call-in and information shows. The Spanish oldies format includes songs of all styles that were hits in Mexico in the 1960s and 1970s.

CORPORATE CITIZENSHIP

HBC through its stations frequently donates money toward humanitarian efforts and causes. In 2001, the company donated $50,000 toward a temporary program with the CFC Family Services to help Hispanics living in Houston who needed aid as a result of tropical storm Allison. In 2000, the company was involved in the Las

FROM JANITOR TO PRESIDENT

As is the case with most family businesses, when HBC President and CEO Max Tichenor, Jr. began working at the company his grandfather started, he started at the bottom. Of his early years, Tichenor jokes that he worked as a janitor. However, the more time he put in, the more responsibilities he assumed, and all at a youthful age. He recalls that during his seventh grade summer, he'd ride his bicycle to the KGBT station and sign the station on. Thirteen years later, when he was only 26, he became president of the company.

Vegas Community Blood Drive and the Las Vegas Community Service Activities. That same year, it donated funds to various educational and health organizations.

HBC stations have been cited for civic responsibility. In 2000, the company's KLVE 107.5FM, KSCA 101.9FM, and KTNQ 1020AM affiliates were awarded certificates of appreciation by the California Senate for their efforts in educating the Southern California Latino community about the importance of the Census 2000.

GLOBAL PRESENCE

All of HBC's radio stations are located within the United States, as are the 13 markets. HBC's mission is to service Hispanic communities in the United States.

EMPLOYMENT

Hispanic Broadcasting Corporation is always on the lookout for professionals to fill roles in all of its markets. Specifically, the company seeks individuals to fill positions in programming, operations, news, on-air work,

traffic, sales, engineering and administrative. For most positions, it is a requirement that the candidate be able to speak Spanish and write in Spanish, particularly with regard to individuals seeking work as an on-air personality or a station programmer. HBC offers competitive pay and benefits that include a retirement plan and stock options.

SOURCES OF INFORMATION

Bibliography

Forbes.com. "Company Details: Hispanic Broadcasting Corp.," 12 April 2002. Available at http://www.forbes.com/finance.

hbcifl.com. "Biography: McHenry Tichenor, Jr." April 2001. Available at http://www.hbcifl.com/x/Bio.htm.

Hoover's Online. "Hispanic Broadcasting Corp.," 12 April 2002. Available at http://www.hoovers.com/co/capsule/9/0,2163, 42149,00.html.

MSNBC.com. "MSNBC.com Enters into Agreement with Hispanic Broadcasting Corp. to Deliver Spanish Language Local Content," 1 October 2001. Available at http://www.msnbc.com.

Wentz, L. and J. Schnuer. "Hispanic Media Growth: Buffeted But Buoyant." Adage.com, 10 September 2001. Available at http://www.adage.com/hispanicawards2001/h_media.shtml.

Yahoo! Finance. "Profile-Hispanic Broadcasting Corp." Yahoo! Market Guide, 12 April 2002. Available at http://biz.yahoo .com/p/h/hsp.html.

For an annual report:
on the Internet at: http://biz.yahoo.com/e/010330/hsp.html

For additional industry research:
Investigate companies by their Standard Industrial Classification Codes, also known as SICs. Hispanic Broadcasting Corporation's primary SICs are:

4832 Radio Networks and Stations

7922 Radio Programs, Including Commercials, Producers Of

8748 Radio Consultants

Also investigate companies by their North American Industry Classification System Codes, also known as NAICS codes. Hispanic Broadcasting Corporation's primary NAICS codes are:

513111 Radio Broadcasting Syndicates, Networks, Services

513112 AM Radio Stations, Radio Broadcasting Stations, Radio Station Broadcasting Studios, FM Radio Stations

Hispanic Television Network Inc.

OVERVIEW

Hispanic Television Network (HTVN) produces and broadcasts television programs and content for the U.S. Spanish-speaking population. It is the smallest of three Spanish-speaking networks located in the United States. Whereas industry leaders Univision and Telemundo have successfully capitalized on the rapidly growing population of Latinos in the United States, HTVN has been heavily burdened by cash flow problems that have left it struggling to remain viable.

The company's first, and primary, network is a Spanish-language, Televisión Hispana, or HTVN, which produces and distributes television content and programming that targets Hispanic Americans of Mexican heritage. HTVN broadcasts news and news commentary, drama and comedy series, music videos, and children's programming 24 hours a day, seven days a week. HTVN owes and operates two Texas television stations, located in Beaumont and Eagle Pass. Its signal is available via six affiliate stations in the following locations: Springdale, Arkansas; Casa Grande, Arizona; San Diego, California; Wichita, Kansas; Reno, Nevada; and Charleston, South Carolina. HTVN is also distributed to the cable television market through contracts with Time Warner Cable, AT&T Broadband, and CNI Canal 40, which is based in Mexico City. Through its stations, affiliates, and cable contracts, HTVN is available in 130 U.S. cities.

HTVN's wholly owned subsidiary, American Independent Network (AIN), targets the general, English-speaking audience and is broadcast 24 hours a day, 7 days a week through 40 affiliate stations throughout the United States with a potential audience of 15 million households. AIN is managed by ParMedia LP, which receives 40

FOUNDED: 1999
VARIANT NAME: HTVN

Contact Information:

HEADQUARTERS: 6125 Airport Fwy, Suite 200
    Fort Worth, TX 76117
FAX: (817)222-9809
PHONE: (817)222-1234
URL: http://www.htvn.net
OFFICER: Steven Mortonson, 49, CFO

FAST FACTS:

About Hispanic Television Network Inc.

Ownership: Hispanic Television Network is a publicly owned company that trades on the Over-The-Counter Bulletin Board.

Ticker Symbol: HTVNE.OB

Officers: James Ryffel, 42, Chmn. and Interim CEO; Steven Mortonson, 49, CFO; Michael Fletcher, 45, COO

Employees: 44

Principal Subsidiary Companies: HTVN operates the HTVN network, Cubico.com Internet site, and American Independent Network. It also owns and operates two television stations in Texas.

Chief Competitors: HTVN is the third largest Spanish-language network, but lags far behind industry leaders, Telemundo and Univision.

percent of the network's net revenues for its services. HTVN also owns cubico.com, an interactive Internet site that targets young adult Latinos in the United States.

COMPANY FINANCES

As of September 30, 2001, HTVN had $5.59 million in net assets, down from $8.84 million as of December 31, 2000. Over the same period of time, net liabilities grew from $13.37 million to $16.69 million. The increase in liabilities is primarily attributed to an additional $1.94 million in accounts payable, $2.79 million in notes payable, and $1 million in accrued interest. For the first three quarters of 2001, ending September 30, HTVN reported a net loss of $18.94 million, compared to a net loss of $13.04 million for the same period of the previous year.

For the first nine months of 2001, total revenues were $1.4 million, representing a year-over-year increase from $396,000 from 2000. The nearly $6 million increase in net loss despite revenue growth of $1 million during the same period is explained by sharply higher costs in certain areas of expenditures. Although programming costs decreased by more than $1 million and salaries and wages declined by approximately $500,000, HTVN

experienced increases of $2.68 million in administrative costs, $1.54 million in professional services, and $4.74 million in interest payments, compounded by an additional $1.1 million loss from operations. Losses for operations were $11.01 million and $12.11 million for the first nine months of 2000 and 2001, respectively.

ANALYSTS' OPINIONS

During 2001 HTVN found itself in the midst of a serious financial crisis. HTVN spent a modest $25 to $30 million to launch its network operations, with expectations that it would engage in a secondary offering of stock. However, the economic downturn in the United States created a near lockdown on investing, which prevented the completion of the second stock offering, causing HTVN to be under funded.

As of November 15, 2001, the company had $2.9 million in accounts payable, most of which were past due. A number of vendors and suppliers began collection proceedings, several of which ended in judgments against HTVN for failure to pay. Matter became so dire that, in one case, a hearing was scheduled for January 15, 2002, to appoint a receiver to liquidate the company. Although the network was able to somehow dodge that fatal blow, with more money going out than coming in, HTVN executives have been in a constant scramble to keep the company afloat.

Along with its inability to pay its suppliers, HTVN defaulted on a credit facility of $7.3 million. While HTVN worked with the lender to find terms to extend or restructure the loan obligation, its failure to pay provided the lender with the legal right to liquidate the company's assets at any moment. In another narrow escape, HTVN was able to work out a revamped repayment schedule and averted bankruptcy.

HISTORY

HTVN was formed in 1999, when American Independent Network Inc. (AIN) and Hispano Television Ventures Inc. (HTV). AIN, a publicly owned company, was incorporated in Delaware on December 11, 1992. AIN is involved in the general market, family-oriented television network by providing programming and related services. HTV, a privately owned corporation that produced Spanish-language television programming, was incorporated in Texas on February 28, 1998. In September 1999 HTV purchased 11 million previously unissued shares of AIN common stocks for $500,000 in cash payment, which gave HTV ownership of approximately 60 percent of AIN's then outstanding common stocks. On December 15, 1999, HTV completed the integration of the two companies by merging into AIN, the surviving entity. As laid out by the merger agreement, AIN issued 70 million shares of common stock in exchange for all outstanding shares of HTV stock. Through this reverse acquisition, the emerging new corporation, renamed Hispanic Television Network Inc., underwent recapitalization.

On July 11, 2000, HTVN acquired full ownership of TeleVideo Inc. and MGB Entertainment Inc. The San Antonio-based companies produce English- and Spanish-language programming. On August 30, 2001, HTVN purchased all outstanding interest in Cubico.com Inc., an interactive Web site targeting young urban Latinos in the United States. Prior to the acquisition, HTVN had maintained a 48-percent interest in the Internet portal since 2000. Cubico.com offers free online services such as email, chat rooms, and message boards. Its main channels include Estilo, Music, Entertainment, El Campus, and Community.

Near the close of 2000, HTVN began to experience a critical shortage of operating funds due to ongoing significant operating losses and negative cash flow. Its financial problems stemmed from an inability to obtain funds from public markets, enter into a strategic partnership, or obtain credit financing. The fact that incoming revenues did not meet the level of outgoing expenses only served to exacerbate the situation. Throughout 2001 HTVN searched for a way out, namely, a strategic partner that could provide the company with a significant influx of cash. By the end of the second quarter of 2002, no such partnership had emerged, leaving the company continuing to scramble to keep creditors at bay and operations running.

STRATEGY

To remain a viable entity HTVN will be required to significantly increase revenues and decrease costs. At its inception, the corporate strategy was to grow the network through the purchase of television stations. As it became obvious that HTVN could not sustain this strategy, the company shifted its focus to growing its affiliate base and long-term contracts with cable operators. Although HTVN considers growth through acquisition an important strategy, the company's financial situation precludes any substantial purchases in the foreseeable future.

By increasing the number of affiliates and contracting with more cable providers, HTVN will expand its viewing audience. As the viewing audience grows, the company will be able to increase its advertising rates, thus boasting revenues at a disproportionally higher rate than its increased broadcast coverage. HTVN also decided to run limited amounts of paid programming that would become a direct source of revenues not yet tapped by the company.

CHRONOLOGY:
Key Dates for Hispanic Network Television Inc.

1992: American Independent Network (AIN) is incorporated as a publicly held company

1998: Privately owned Hispano Television Ventures (HTV) is formed

1999: AIN and HTV merge to form Hispanic Network Television Inc. (HTVN)

2000: HTVN begins to suffer cash flow shortages

2001: HTVN defaults on a $7.3 million loan and more than $2 million in accounts payable; company is de-listed from NASDAQ

2002: HTVN continues search for strategic partner to remain viable; stock prices fall to $0.01 per share

Expanding its presence on cable systems provides HTVN with a dual benefit. First, the increase in audience numbers allows for the increase in advertising revenues as airtime becomes more valuable. Second, HTVN receives subscriber fees from the cable companies. HTVN has secured ten-year contracts for cable and satellite distribution with Time Warner Cable; Satellite Services Inc., the program operations unit for AT&T Broadband, Cox Communications, Inc.; Liberty Spanish Group LLC a/k/a Canales ñ, the Spanish-language distributor for Comcast Cable; and Adelphia Cable, as well as a five-year contract with National Cable Television Coop. Because subscription fees are not paid until the end of the contract year, despite its numerous contracts, HTVN did not begin receiving any monetary benefit until well into 2002.

This expansion strategy should lead to increased revenues, but HTVN has dug a financial hole for itself that it will need help to get out of. Thus, the company continues to search for a strategic partnership that would provide an influx of approximately $10 million, which would place the network on firm footing again and provide the company an opportunity to become profitable in the foreseeable future. It appeared HTVN had found such a partner in February of 2001 when C-Networks agreed to provide a strategic investment in HTVN. To attract C-Networks' interest, several major founding shareholders returned a majority of their shares to the company, and HTVN allowed C-Networks' president and chief execu-

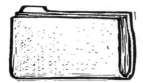

O PARTNER, WHERE ART THOU?

HTVN is in desperate need of forming a strategic partnership that would jumpstart the company back to profitability, but it has failed to find willing investors. Previously trading its common stock on the NASDAQ National Market, HTVN's stocks were de-listed in August 2001 due to the company's failure to retain a minimum of $4 million in net tangible assets and because its stock price fell below a minimum bid price of $1.00 for more than 30 consecutive trading days—both of which are requirements for maintaining a NASDAQ listing. On August 3, 2001, HTVN began trading on the Over-the-Counter Bulletin Board. In May 2002, stocks, which traded as high as $20 per share during 2001, were selling for slightly more than $0.01 per share.

tive officer, Emilio Goritti, to become a member of HTVN's board and chief executive officer. However, when C-Networks failed to fulfill its cash influx commitments, HTVN negated the deal and terminated Goritti. Spanish Network Partners showed interest in working with HTVN; however, for reasons undisclosed in February of 2002, after signing a letter of intent, HTVN and Spanish Network Partners terminated discussions.

While attempting to increase revenues and locate outside assistance, HTVN has undergone a dynamic cost-cutting campaign, reducing expenditures in almost every category, particularly in payroll and programming. Excluding debt and interest payments, these measures have reduced the monthly negative cash flow from $1.5 million to $300,000.

HTVN's primary source of revenues during the first three years of its operations were generated by sale of advertising airtime on its television stations. Advertising time is marketed to advertising agencies and independent advertisers, affiliate stations, and program owners. The rate for commercial airtime sold to advertising agencies and independent advertisers is based on the estimated size of the viewing audience. Because a larger audience can justify higher prices for advertising time, HTVN has committed to securing new affiliate relationships for AIN, which broadcasts in numerous smaller markets, in areas that are demographically favorable. The primary goal is to obtain as high a Nielsen rating as possible, thus justifying higher advertising rates.

HTVN benefits from relationships from affiliate stations by retaining a portion of advertising time as well as gaining access to the affiliates' viewing audience. Traditionally, affiliate stations work with networks under a standard fee agreement; however, by trading fee for commercial airtime, which HTVN then sells to outside advertisers, the network hopes to generate higher returns than would be obtains through a flat fee contract.

HTVN works with program owners by providing them with advertising time during the broadcast of their programs, which they sell to outsider advertisers for a profit. In return, HTVN obtains licensing rights to broadcast the programs, but does not receive any direct compensation.

Advertising categories include network advertising, national spot advertising, and local spot advertising. Network advertising is placed in slots that broadcast simultaneously across all of the network's markets. Every station, including affiliates, has a percentage of time dedicated to network advertising. National advertisers can purchase geographically specific "spot" advertising time. If a company wishes to target a particular demographic area or areas, those markets can be singled out and airtime sold. Local spot advertising is purchased by businesses that operate within a specific broadcast area. Basically, local companies advertising within their local markets.

PRODUCTS

HTVN provides a variety of programming that fills its continuous broadcast. For example, *Kolita*, which airs weekday mornings, is a children's program featuring games, contests, and music. *Bandazo* airs music videos during mornings and late-night time slots. Afternoon programming includes *Agua y chocolate*, a family drama centered around cooking show; *Explosivo Musical*, a music show with comedy skits and interviews; and *Mexico de mis amores*, a travel show featuring Mexican locations. *De Nueve A Diez*, which airs interviews with Latino entertainers, *Galeria*, an investigative series, and *Best of Las Nueve Y Sereno*, which provides Victor Trujillo's talk and entertainment program are among HTVN's prime time program offerings. HTVN also airs four movies daily, as well as a special concert and biographical series. News airs via *CNI Noticias*, and *Septimo Dia* provides live political discussion. AIN's programming is made up of movies, classic sit-coms, sports, and network specials.

SOURCES OF INFORMATION

Bibliography

"Canales to Distribute HTVN in More Than 130 U.S. Cities." *Business Wire*, 18 July 2001.

Chunovic, Louis. "Hispanic TV Network Faces Daunting Odds." *Electronic Media*, 14 January 2002.

Fox, Valerie, and Lisa Y. Taylor. "Hispanic Network Grows." *Dallas Business Journal*, 31 December 1999.

"Hispanic Television Network Acquires TeleVideo, Inc. and MGB Entertainment, Inc." *Business Wire*, 8 August 2000.

"Hispanic Television Network Begins Trading OTCBB Today." *PR Newswire*, 3 August 2001.

"Hispanic Television Network Receives Strategic Investment from C-Networks." *Business Wire*, 13 February 2001.

"Hispanic Television Network Takes Steps to Strengthen Balance Sheet." *Business Wire*, 19 December 2000.

"HTVN and Spanish Network Partners Terminate Funding Discussions." *PR Newswire*, 11 February 2002.

"HTVN and Time Warner Cable Sign Long Term Distribution Contract." *Business Wire*, 21 March 2001.

"HTVN Moving Ahead with Expansion Initiatives." *PR Newswire*, 11 September 2001.

"HTVN to Get Strategic Investment." *Dallas Business Journal*, 24 October 2001.

Nicholson, Gilbert. "Hispanic Television Net Seeking Funds." *Mediaweek*, 8 January 2001.

For additional industry research:

Investigate companies by their Standard Industrial Classification Codes, also known as SICs. Hispanic Television Network Inc.'s primary SICs are:

4833 Television Broadcasting

4841 Cable Networks and Other Program Distribution

Also investigate companies by their North American Industry Classification System codes, also known as NAICS codes. Hispanic Television Network Inc.'s primary NAICS codes are:

513120 Television Broadcasting

513210 Cable Networks

513220 Cable and Other Program Distribution

Hollywood Entertainment Corporation

FOUNDED: 1988
VARIANT NAME: Hollywood Video

Contact Information:

HEADQUARTERS: 9275 SW Peyton Lane
    Wilsonville, OR 97070
PHONE: (503)570-1600
FAX: (503)570-1680
EMAIL: info@hollywoodvideo.com
URL: http://www.hollywoodvideo.com

OVERVIEW

Founded in 1988, Hollywood Entertainment Corporation is today the second largest video retail chain in the world, trailing only Blockbuster in size. The company has grown from a single store in Portland, Oregon, into a chain of more than 1,800 retail outlets. The majority of the company's revenue is generated by the rental of motion pictures in both the DVD and VHS formats and video games. The remainder of the chain's sales are accounted for by the sale of new and used videos and video games. Unlike a number of its competitors Hollywood Entertainment has grown its chain mostly through organic growth rather than acquisitions. Nearly 95 percent of the company's superstores opened since 1995 were opened as new stores. The company projected it would open approximately 50 new stores during 2002 and would grow its store base by roughly 10 percent a year thereafter.

The video retail chain was founded by Mark Wattles in 1988 with the opening of the first Hollywood Video store in Portland, Oregon. Wattles and his wife personally ran the first store. The imminent death of the video rental business, rumors of which have abounded almost from the inception of the industry, are not causing Wattles to lose any sleep. He remains confident that the advance of technology will gradually lead to even greater profits rather than sound the death knell for the industry. "We can't be afraid of technology in this business," Wattles said. "I believe technology should be embraced."

COMPANY FINANCES

For 2001 Hollywood Entertainment posted a profit of $100.4 million on revenue of approximately $1.38 billion. This represented a major turnaround from the company's performance in 2000, which saw a net loss of $530 million on revenue of almost $1.3 billion. For 1999, the company reported a net loss of $51.3 million on revenue of nearly $1.1 billion. The company said its sharp improvement in 2001 financial results was largely attributable to improved operating performance in its existing store base, adjustments to the company's valuation allowance on its net deferred income tax asset, and the closure of its electronic commerce operations at Reel.com in June 2000.

Hollywood Entertainment's revenue increased by $83.3 million, or 6.4 percent, in 2001, primarily due to an increase of 6 percent in comparable store revenue. Another factor that favorably impacted the company's 2001 revenue was an increase of 62 in its weighted average number of stores. The company reported a sharp increase in rental gross margin as a percentage of rental revenue, which climbed in 2001 to 67.1 percent from 45.8 percent in 2000. This improvement was the result of changes the company had made in the final quarter of 2000 in estimates regarding rental inventory lives and residual values. In 2000 rental gross margin as a percentage of rental revenue had decreased to 45.8 percent from 68.8 percent in 1999.

Prospects for 2002 were looking very bright indeed in early spring of 2002. Interviewed in April 2002 on CNBC, Mark Wattles, chairman and CEO of Hollywood Entertainment, attributed the company's strength to a couple of factors. "Well, we've got two things going for our company right now." One, he said, was the company's new management team, brought in at the end of 2000. "I'm the founder of the company. I came back to the company at that time, brought a new COO, a new CFO as well. And then on top of that we're in a great industry with a lot of momentum right now." The company's stock, which had traded in a range of $1 to $18 a share over the previous 52 weeks, was at the top of its range in early April 2002.

Asked what was driving business, Wattles cited the phenomenal growth in popularity of DVDs, "which is the fastest growing entertainment technology in the history of the industry. That's benefiting us right now. And then we've got probably the most exciting thing of all since I have been in the industry, and that's the growth of games, which is just starting to kick in." Wattles also said that any thought of overtaking Blockbuster as number one in the business was, frankly, "a little unrealistic." He said, "The growth opportunity for us in the United States is probably about 3,000 stores, and we have about 1,800 today. Blockbuster has 5,000 stores, so I think they'll maintain that number one position."

FAST FACTS:
About Hollywood Entertainment Corporation

Ownership: Hollywood Entertainment is a publicly owned company traded on the NASDAQ market.

Ticker Symbol: HLYW

Officers: Mark J. Wattles, Chmn., Pres. and CEO, 41, 2001 base salary $945,814; Scott R. Schultze, EVP and COO, 47, 2001 base salary $365,794; Jim Marcum, EVP and CFO, 42

Employees: 22,600

Principal Subsidiary Companies: Hollywood Entertainment Corporation's only wholly-owned subsidiary during 2001 was Hollywood Management Co.

Chief Competitors: Competition within the video retail industry is very keen indeed. Hollywood Entertainment ranks second among U.S. video chains, trailing only Blockbuster, but its competition is not only limited to national video retail chains but also includes local and regional video retailers, mass marketers, mail order operations, supermarkets, pharmacies, convenience stores, bookstores, and even noncommercial sources, such as libraries. The principal competitive factors in the video retail market, according to Hollywood Entertainment's 2001 annual report, are price, title selection, rental period, the number of copies of popular titles available, store location and visibility, customer service and employee friendliness, and convenience of store access and parking.

ANALYSTS' OPINIONS

Most security analysts in the spring of 2002 were taking a decidedly bullish view toward the stock of Hollywood Entertainment and some of the other leaders in the video retail industry. As of early June 2002, all analyst recommendations for the company's stock were evenly split between Strong Buy and Buy. The company's stock, as well as that of some of its competitors, got a shot in the arm in the wake of the terrorist attacks on the World Trade Center and Pentagon on September 11, 2001. Stunned by the unprecedented attack on America, millions of frightened U.S. citizens looked for ways

CHRONOLOGY:

Key Dates for Hollywood Entertainment Corporation

1988: First Hollywood Video store opens in Portland, Oregon

1993: Hollywood Entertainment goes public

1995: Hollywood opens 122 new stores

1997: Hollywood opens 356 new stores aircraft.

1999: Hollywood's revenue tops $1-billion mark

2001: Founder Mark Wattles returns to lead company

to entertain themselves at home. This gave businesses favored by apprehensive couch potatoes a strong lift.

Frank Gretz, a technical analyst with Shields & Company, in late October 2001 told CNNfn interviewer Alan Chernoff: "I also like the stay-at-home theme like Blockbuster, Movie Gallery Inc., Hollywood Entertainment."

HISTORY

Mark Wattles, founder of Hollywood Entertainment Corporation, first got into the video retail industry in 1984 when he opened Downtown Video in Portland, Oregon. A couple of years later, Wattles decided that video rental kiosks in convenience stores were the wave of the future, so with a few partners, he opened Convenience Video. Only a year later, he decided that the industry's future lay in the video superstore, so he pulled out of Convenience Video. In June 1988 Wattles founded Hollywood Entertainment and four months later opened the fledgling company's first store in Portland. He took care to grow his company slowly and by year-end 1991, the company reported a net income of $281,000 on sales of $5.1 million. Only a year later, the chain had grown to a total of 15 stores, all in the Pacific Northwest, and the company's revenue had more than doubled to slightly more than $11 million. Even more surprisingly, Hollywood Entertainment's profit had soared to almost $1.2 million.

In 1993 Wattles decided to take the company public to raise capital for further expansion. In July 1993 the company's initial public offering on the NASDAQ national market netted $10.4 million. By year's end the chain's number of stores had climbed to a total of 25.

For the year as a whole, Hollywood posted a net income of $2.1 million on sales of $17.3 million. In early 1994 the company made a second equity offering to the public, netting $23.6 million, much of which was used to acquire the 33-store Video Central chain, headquartered in San Antonio, Texas. Another 11 stores were added to the Hollywood chain in May 1994 when the company acquired California-based Eastman Video. On the heels of the Eastman acquisition, the company picked up another 10 stores in California and Nevada with its acquisition of Video Park. Hollywood went back to the market again with a third equity offering in August 1994 that yielded $63.6 million, which was used to open 33 new "superstores." The company posted a profit of $8.1 million on sales of $73.3 million in 1994. By the end of 1994, the Hollywood Video chain had grown to a total of 113 stores in eight states.

Hollywood's acquisition spree continued in 1995. In the first quarter, the company acquired a 14-store Minnesota chain called Title Wave, shortly after which the company went back to the market with its fourth equity offering, this one netting $95.4 million. This new injection of funds was used to finance Hollywood's acquisition of a 42-store Midwest chain called Video Watch. At the same time the company was growing through acquisition, new superstores were being added. By the end of 1995, the chain had grown to a total of 305 outlets in 23 states. Net income for 1995 climbed to $11.8 million on revenue of $149.4 million, more than double its sales in the previous year.

As industry leader Blockbuster moved to diversify its product mix, adding magazines, books, and magazines to its offerings, Hollywood opted to remain focused on video rentals. In the middle of the 1990s, the video retail industry experienced something of a slowdown, but Hollywood bounced back quickly. The size of the chain grew dramatically in 1996, adding 250 new stores for a total of 551 outlets in 42 states. The company's profit hit $20.6 million on revenue of $302.3 million. Despite instability in the industry, Hollywood continued to grow its chain in 1997, adding 356 new stores for a total of 907 in 42 states. Sales for the year hit $550.5 million.

In April 1998, Hollywood opened its 1,000th store, an outlet in Mesquite, Texas. The chain also introduced five-day rentals in 1998. The following year saw a surge in the popularity of DVD rentals, and Hollywood moved to meet this new demand by sharply increasing its inventory of DVD titles. The chain's revenue continued to grow, topping the billion-dollar mark in 1999. In 2000 Hollywood's sales reached almost $1.3 billion, climbing in 2001 to $1.38 billion.

STRATEGY

Hollywood Entertainment, having resigned itself to being number two in the video retail industry, has crafted a business strategy designed to enhance its current position. The five key components of that strategy call for the company (1) to provide broad selection and superior service; (2) to provide excellent entertainment value; (3) to capitalize on DVDs; (4) to capitalize on new game platform rollouts; and (5) to pursue organic store growth.

To ensure that its outlets offer customers broad selection and superior service, the chain's superstores typically carry more than 7,000 movie titles on more than 16,000 VHS videos and DVDs, as well as a wide range of video games. To satisfy the demand for hit movies, each stores usually stocks 100 to 200 copies of such films. In terms of providing excellent entertainment value, Hollywood believes its pricing structure ($3.79 rental for hit films and $1.99 for catalog movies on VHS; $3.79 for all DVDs; and video games for $4.99 and $5.99) and rental terms offer consumers convenient entertainment and excellent value.

With rentals of DVDs expected to continue their climb in popularity, Hollywood expects to increase its stock of videos in this new format accordingly. With the proliferation of video game platforms, the company has expanded its operations in this area to provide video game enthusiasts with a marketplace where they can buy, sell, or trade new and used games. This business initiative provides for the establishment of "Game Crazy" stores within stores to capitalize on the skyrocketing demand for video games. Since the mid-1990s, nearly 95 percent of the outlets opened by the company have been new stores and not stores acquired from other video chains. Hollywood hopes to continue growing its chain in this fashion.

INFLUENCES

One of the most significant trends in the video retail industry of the early twenty-first century has been the surge in popularity of videos in the DVD format and video games. Hollywood has moved aggressively to capitalize on both these trends. The chain's overall inventory and selection of DVD titles has been sharply increased. To meet the frenzied demand for video games, the company introduced its "Game Crazy" store-within-a-store marketing concept. Such "Game Crazy" outlets, operating in nearly 70 of the chain's stores as of the end of 2001, will be expanded strategically throughout the chain in the years to come.

CURRENT TRENDS

Basic changes in the relationship between the major motion picture studios and video retailers have resulted in significant benefits to Hollywood Entertainment and other major players in the video retail industry. The move

from traditional "rental" pricing of new releases to a revenue sharing arrangement has increased the volume of newly released videos in Hollywood's outlets, aligned the economic interests of the studios more closely with those of video retailers because studios now share a portion of the rental revenue; and increased overall revenue because of the greater availability of videos in high demand.

Videos in the newer DVD format are generally acquired from the major studios on a "sell-through" basis, priced around $17 or $18 per video. However, by the spring of 2002 Hollywood Entertainment had struck revenue sharing agreements with two major studios, and it is hoped that this trend will continue.

PRODUCTS

Hollywood Entertainment's product lineup at its Hollywood Video stores consists of two major categories: products for rental and products for sale. The former category, which includes videos in both VHS and DVD formats and video games, accounted for roughly 83 percent of the company's revenue in 2001. The typical Hollywood Video superstore carries more than 7,000 movie titles on over 16,000 videocassettes and DVDs and approximately 550 video game titles. The movie rental inventory consists of new releases and so-called catalog movies, which are organized according to genre: Action, Comedy, Drama, Children, Musical, and so on. The company neither rents nor sells adult movies in any of its stores.

Generating the remaining 17 percent of the company's revenue in 2001 were sales of new and used movies in both VHS and DVD formats, video games, and concessions, including popcorn, soft drinks, and candy. Although capital constraints have limited the selection of new DVDs available for sale in Hollywood Video stores, the company has experienced a sharp increase in the sale of previously viewed movies in this format. Sales of video games (new and used) have increased significantly in stores that house a "Game Crazy" outlet—a store within a store that provides enthusiasts with a forum where they can buy, sell, and trade new and used games.

CORPORATE CITIZENSHIP

To fulfill its corporate responsibilities to the communities in which it operates, Hollywood Entertainment sponsors Spotlight on Education, Spotlight on Families, and Spotlight on Fundraising programs. The company's Spotlight on Education programs are composed of two main components: A Spotlight on Students and A Spotlight on Teachers. Under A Spotlight on Students, each participating K-12 school receives 100 Outstanding

COMPANY CUTS REEL.COM LOSSES

In the fall of 1998, Hollywood Entertainment paid about $97 million to acquire Reel.com, which had acquired a reputation as the premier online destination for film-related content and commerce. Between the date of its acquisition and mid-2000, the Reel.com Web site was a leader in e-commerce, offering a catalog of approximately 50,000 titles on videocassette and DVD. In addition to its sales of videos, Reel.com offered proprietary information about motion pictures, including plot synopses, ratings, critics' reviews, and links to star filmographies. Although Reel.com had grown to an annual run rate of about $80 million by June 2000, the operation was generating significant cash losses. When it became clear that Reel.com would be unable to access outside capital to fund its continued losses, Hollywood discontinued Reel.com's e-commerce business and merged it into Hollywood Entertainment Corporation. Although Reel.com continues to operate as a content-only Web site, Hollywood has closed down its corporate office and warehouse in Emeryville, California.

Achievement Awards that can be used by teachers and coaches to encourage and reward their students. Each award may be redeemed at any Hollywood Video outlet for a free rental of any New Release, DVD, or Film Library movie. A Spotlight on Teachers provides each participating school with 100 Educational Entertainment Coupons that can be distributed to faculty members who may redeem them for the free rental of any Hollywood Video Film Library title for use as an intructional aid in the classroom.

Under the company's Spotlight on Families program, participating local nonprofit organizations are each given five free rental certificates that can be used to reward volunteers, encourage donations, and brighten the lives of children and families in need. Nonprofit organizations interested in participating in a Spotlight on Families program may file an application online at Hollywood Entertainment's Web site. Under Hollywood Entertainment's Spotlight on Fundraising program, schools and nonprofit organizations may purchase Hollywood Video gift cards from local scrip organizations to raise monies. The gift cards can then be used to rent and/or purchase movies in both VHS and DVD formats and video games.

EMPLOYMENT

As of December 31, 2001, Hollywood Entertainment employed a workforce of 22,660 employees, the vast majority of whom (21,685) worked in the video retail chain's retail stores and zone offices. The remainder, slightly less than 1,000 in number, worked in the company's corporate administrative and warehousing operations.

SOURCES OF INFORMATION

Bibliography

"Business Summary: Hollywood Entertainment." *Multex Investor*, 2002. Available at http://www.marketguide.com.

Clifford, Lee. "Stay-at-Home Stocks: American Have Cut Back on Spending. But That Doesn't Mean They're Not Buying at All." *Fortune,* 12 November 2001, 197.

Haines, Mark. "Hollywood Entertainment-Chmn & CEO-Interview." *CNBC/Dow Jones Business Video,* 10 April 2002.

"Hollywood Entertainment Corp.—History." *Gale Business Resources*, 2002. Available at http://galenet.galegroup.com/servlet/GBR.

"Hollywood Entertainment Corporation." *Hoover's Online*, 2002. Available at http://www.hoovers.com.

Hollywood Entertainment Corporation 2001 Annual Report. Wilsonville, OR: Hollywood Entertainment Corporation, 2002.

Hollywood Entertainment Corporation Home Page, 2002. Available at http://www.hollywoodvideo.com.

For an annual report:
on the Internet at: http://www.hollywoodvideo.com

For additional industry research:
Investigate companies by their Standard Industrial Classification Codes, also known as SICs. Hollywood Entertainment Corporation's primary SIC is:

7841 Video Tape Rental

Also investigate companies by their North American Industry Classification System codes, also known as NAICS codes. Hollywood Entertainment Corporation's primary NAICS code is:

532230 Video Tape and Disc Rental

Honeywell International Inc.

OVERVIEW

Honeywell International Inc. is a widely diversified corporation that produces a wide range of products, most of which are used as components in other products manufactured by other companies. Honeywell's products and services include control technologies, automotive products, power generation systems, aerospace products and services, and chemicals, fibers, and other specialty materials. The company's product line is divided into four basic sectors: Aerospace Solutions, Automation and Control Solutions, Specialty Materials, and Transportation and Power Systems. Within Honeywell's aerospace section, leading products include aircraft landing systems; engines, systems, and services; federal manufacturing and technologies; and aerospace electronic systems. The company's automation and control sector offers control products, industry solutions, security and fire solutions, and related services. Among the products produced in Honeywell's specialty materials sector are nylon, polyester, polypropylene, fine chemicals, and coated products for use in manufacturing silicon chips, wafers, and circuit boards.

Headquartered in Morristown, New Jersey, Honeywell in late 1999 merged with AlliedSignal Inc. Under the terms of the merger agreement, it was decided that the new, larger company formed by the merger would operate under the Honeywell name. In addition to its chemical business, AlliedSignal also did a fair amount of business in the aerospace sector, producing satellite flight control systems and telemetry data and processing systems. More recently, plans for a merger between General Electric and Honeywell were abandoned in 2001 when European Union antitrust regulators blocked the

FOUNDED: 1906

Contact Information:
HEADQUARTERS: 101 Columbia Rd., PO Box 4000
    Morristown, NJ 07962-2497
PHONE: (973)455-2000
FAX: (973)455-4807
TOLL FREE: (800)707-4555
URL: http://www.honeywell.com

FAST FACTS:

About Honeywell International Inc.

Ownership: Honeywell International Inc. is a publicly owned company traded on the New York Stock Exchange.

Ticker Symbol: HON

Officers: Lawrence A. Bossidy, Chmn., 67, 2001 base salary $992,308; David M. Cote, Pres. and CEO, 49, 2002 base salary $1,500,000; Richard F. Wallman, SVP and CFO, 50, 2001 base salary $510,000

Employees: 115,000

Principal Subsidiary Companies: Honeywell owns a number of subsidiaries in North America and elsewhere around the world. Some of the company's major subsidiaries include ADEMCO Group, Honeywell Aerospace, and Honeywell International Specialty Materials. In addition to these subsidiaries, Honeywell has a number of foreign subsidiaries, each of which is responsible for operations in its geographical region. Such subsidiaries include Honeywell Asia Pacific Inc. in Hong Kong, Honeywell Ltd. in Canada, Honeywell Europe S.A., Tata Honeywell Ltd. in India, and GoldStar-Honeywell Company Ltd. in South Korea.

Chief Competitors: A widely diversified manufacturing and technology company, Honeywell International produces aerospace products and services, which account for roughly 40 percent of the company's annual revenue; automotive products; control technologies; power generation systems; and chemicals, fibers, and other materials. Some of its major competitors include Pratt & Whitney, Eaton Corporation, General Electric, Rolls-Royce plc, Boeing, Lockheed Martin, BASF AG, Bayer AG, and DuPont.

merger on grounds that its massive size would overpower its competition in the aerospace market.

COMPANY FINANCES

Honeywell's performance in 2001 was rather disappointing. The company reported a net loss of $99 million on revenue of $23.7 billion. This compared with a net profit in 2000 of almost $1.7 billion on sales of just over $25 billion. The company's net profit in 1999 totaled $1.5 billion on revenue of about $23.7 billion. Earnings per share Honeywell's net profit margin in 2000 was 6.6 percent, compared with 6.5 percent in 1999.

As of late May 2002, Honeywell's stock (HON on the New York Stock Exchange) in the previous 52 weeks had traded between a low of $22.15 and a high of $52.15. Thanks largely to the sale of the company's commercial vehicle braking systems, Honeywell's net earnings for the first quarter of 2002 were sharply higher. The company reported net income of $376 million on sales of $5.2 billion. However, lingering effects of the recent economic slowdown did not bode well for the remainder of 2002. Of the company's first quarter performance and the outlook for the rest of 2002, Honeywell Chairman Lawrence Bossidy said: "While we began to see signs of improvement in parts of the company in March, we are not experiencing robust economy recovery across the board." The company lowered its predictions for second quarter 2002 earnings, saying that sales and earnings in the company's ongoing businesses are not expected to bounce back quickly enough to sustain earlier predicted earnings levels. Despite the slowdown, Honeywell executives predicted that for 2002 as a whole they expected earnings to reach about $2.36 per share on revenue of $22.8 billion.

ANALYSTS' OPINIONS

Eli Lustgarten, an analyst with H.C. Wainwright & Co. in New York took a somewhat mixed view of Honeywell's financial performance in the first quarter of 2002. "The numbers were okay for the quarter," he said. "The main event was the reduced guidance on the second quarter."

Analysts were less sanguine about the effects on Honeywell of the collapse of its takeover by General Electric during the summer of 2001. The planned merger had already won the approval of antitrust regulators in the United States and Canada but was blocked in Europe. Paul Nisbet, an analyst at JSA Research Inc. in Newport, Rhode Island, said Honeywell would have to decide whether to seek another suitor or continue on its own. "It's sort of hard to find too many companies that can buy a $40 billion firm," he added. "On the other hand, if Honeywell opts to remain independent," said Nisbet, "it would take them awhile to get back on their feet." James Ayscue, an analyst with PNC Advisors in Philadelphia, said he anticipated a major restructuring and sharp cost cutting by Honeywell if it decided to remain independent. He said that he expected the company would proceed with divestitures of some of its under performing businesses, including its automotive consumer products, U.S. security monitoring, and friction materials businesses.

HISTORY

Honeywell's roots can be traced back to 1885, when inventor Albert Butz patented the furnace regulator and alarm. The following year he founded Butz Thermo-Electric Regulator Company in Minneapolis. Shortly thereafter inventor Butz came up with still another useful device that he called the "damper flapper." Not long after that, Butz's patents and his business were purchased by Consolidated Temperature Controlling Company, which in 1893 renamed itself Electric Heat Regulator Company. Three years later W.R. Sweatt, who by 1912 had changed his company's name to Minneapolis Heat Regulator Company (MHR) and expanded its product line, bought out Consolidated. The Honeywell name first entered the scene in 1906 when engineer Mark Honeywell founded Honeywell Heating Specialty Company in Wabash, Indiana. Honeywell's company specialized in the manufacture and sale of hot water heat generators.

Honeywell Heating Specialty Company and MHR merged in 1927 to form Minneapolis-Honeywell Regulator Company with W.R. Sweat of MHR serving as the new company's chairman and Mark Honeywell as its president. To bolster its share of the controls market, the company made a number of acquisitions, including the Brown Instrument Company, a major player in the field of industrial controls and gauges. The company also was quick to recognize the potential for sales of its products in overseas markets. At first it sold its products through a network of foreign distributors, but in 1934 it acquired Time-O-Stat Controls Corporation and launched an ambitious program of foreign expansion. The first office outside the United States was set up in Toronto, Canada, followed not long thereafter by the establishment of a European subsidiary, based in the Netherlands. This global expansion has continued throughout the company's history.

To adjust to changing times, Minneapolis-Honeywell Regulator made a number of important changes, moving to mass production and adding to its product line. In 1942 the company developed the electronic autopilot. Other products were added over the years. In 1963, the company's name was officially changed to Honeywell Inc. In 1970 Honeywell and General Electric merged their computer businesses to form Honeywell Information Systems. After the emergence of the personal computer in the 1980s, Honeywell joined with France's Compagnie des Machines Bull and NEC Corporation of Japan to form Honeywell Bull, although by 1991 Honeywell had completely withdrawn from this venture. Honeywell's market share in the aerospace industry was substantially increased in 1986 when the company purchased Sperry Aerospace. In 1999 Honeywell Inc. merged with AlliedSignal to form Honeywell International Inc. The merger broadened Honeywell's product line significantly, adding a wide range of chemicals and chemical-related products, and strengthened its aerospace business. In 2001, a planned takeover of Honeywell by

CHRONOLOGY:

Key Dates for Honeywell International Inc.

1906: Mark Honeywell forms Honeywell Heating Specialty Co. in Wabash, Indiana

1927: Honeywell Heating and Minneapolis Heat Regulator Co. merge to form Minneapolis-Honeywell Regulator Co.

1934: Minneapolis-Honeywell acquires Brown Instrument Co., a leader in industrial controls

1942: Minneapolis-Honeywell invents electronic autopilot

1955: Minneapolis-Honeywell enters computer business through joint venture with Raytheon

1963: Company name is changed to Honeywell Inc.

1970: Honeywell, GE merge computer businesses to form Honeywell Information Systems

1986: Honeywell purchases Sperry Aerospace

1999: Honeywell merges with AlliedSignal

2001: European Union blocks GE acquisition of Honeywell

General Electric was abandoned after antitrust regulators in the European Union declined to approve the takeover without substantial changes, acceptable to neither GE nor Honeywell. The plan for GE's acquisition had already won the approval of antitrust regulators in both the United States and Canada.

STRATEGY

In the wake of the collapse of its planned takeover by General Electric in the summer of 2001, Honeywell brought back former chairman Lawrence Bossidy to help put the company's financial house in order. Bossidy was to remain as chairman for only a year and was to be replaced on July 1, 2002, by David Cote, the former chairman, president, and CEO of TRW. Cote actually came on board at Honeywell in February 2002 as president and CEO. Together the two in late February 2002 discussed their expectations for the company's short-term future in a joint interview on cable channel CNBC with moderator Mark Haines. Bossidy expressed optimism that the U.S. economy "can improve in the second half for a number of reasons, one being low interest rates and low raw material costs, the first installment of the government's tax plan reduction, and a host of things that look favorable. And the consumer, who has been strong throughout the whole period, continues to be strong. So I'm now of the belief that in the second half we'll see some signs of recovery, and I'm delighted to be able to say that." For his part, Cote voiced the hope that Honeywell can achieve significant growth in the short-term future. Asked to clarify the type of growth he anticipated for Honeywell, Cote said: "Well, there are two aspects to growth. There's the organic side, the focus on your existing where you provide quality, delivery, value, and technology every day. And there are also acquisition possibilities. We have a strong balance sheet. We've got a lot of business that can be added to. And I think our growth prospects are very good."

Honeywell's strategy for 2002 focused on four major goals: (1) Focus relentlessly on satisfying customers; (2) Enlist every employee in the plan for growth; (3) Achieve productivity, earnings, and cash flow commitments by driving Six Sigma and Digitization; and (4) Create a great place to work through learning and innovation.

INFLUENCES

To cope with the effects of a sluggish economy and the downturn in the air transportation industry that followed the September 11, 2001, terrorist attacks on the World Trade Center and Pentagon, Honeywell embarked on an aggressive campaign of cost cutting in 2001. Nearly 16,000 employees were laid off. Former Chairman Lawrence Bossidy was brought back to help restructure Honeywell after European Union regulators shot down the plan for its takeover by General Electric. Bossidy's strategy focused on sharp cuts in company costs and improvements in productivity. He predicted that, together, cost cutting and productivity improvements would save Honeywell approximately $1.3 billion, an amount sufficient to offset the effects of the slowdown in aerospace and other of the company's businesses.

CURRENT TRENDS

One of the most widespread trends in business today is the move toward consolidation in an effort to achieve greater efficiencies of scale and reduce costs through the unification of overlapping operations. For Honeywell a bold move in this direction—namely its proposed takeover by General Electric—was blocked in the sum-

mer of 2001 when European Union antitrust regulators refused to approve the proposal without radical changes that neither GE nor Honeywell found acceptable. In the wake of this frustration, Honeywell appeared determined, at least for the short term, to go its own way.

David Cote, former chairman, CEO, and president of TRW Inc., came onboard at Honeywell as president and CEO in February 2002. He was to succeed Lawrence Bossidy as chairman on July 1, 2002. Interviewed by the *Arizona Republic* in late February 2002, Cote declared: "We will remain an independent company." He also indicated that the company, rather than seek out a possible suitor to take it over, will be shopping for possible acquisitions in the aerospace, chemicals, and industrial controls businesses. Although he declined to provide any specifics, Cote said, "We have a great balance sheet, and there are some good prices out there. Now is a great time to buy."

PRODUCTS

Operationally, Honeywell International is divided into four distinct product segments: Aerospace, Automation and Control Solutions, Specialty Materials, and Transportation and Power Systems. Major products of Honeywell's Aerospace segment include aircraft engines, auxiliary power units, avionics systems and related products, environmental control systems, landing systems, repair and overhaul services, spare parts, and support and services for space and communications facilities.

Honeywell's Automation and Control Solutions produces a broad range of products and services, including controls for heating, cooling, ventilation, humidification, industrial process automation, video surveillance, and access control equipment, as well as security/fire alarm and industrial safety systems and home automation systems. The segment's other products include advanced software applications for home/building control and industrial optimization and sensors, switches, control systems, and instruments for measuring pressure, air flow, temperature, and electrical current.

The company's Specialty Materials produces high-performance specialty materials such as nylon, polyester, polyethylene, fluorocarons, caprolactam, and other specialty and fine chemicals. The segment's brand-name products include Genetron refrigerants, Capron nylon resin, Anso carpet fiber, Spectra high-performance fiber, AstorLite wax additive, AccuGlass spin-on-glass series, and Lumilux luminescent pigments. Honeywell's Transportation and Power Systems division is the world's leading innovator of automotive turbochargers and also produces friction materials used by major brake manufacturers. Its brand-name products include Garrett turbochargers, Prestone antifreeze/coolant, Autolite platinum spark plugs, and FRAM automotive filters.

CORPORATE CITIZENSHIP

Honeywell has long recognized its commitment to the communities in which it operates worldwide. The company and its employees have made substantial financial contributions to worthy causes in those communities, but it is in the realm of volunteerism that Honeywell feels its greatest contribution to community improvement has been made. Thousands of the company's employees and retirees volunteer their time and services to nonprofit organizations each year. Theses volunteers act as mentors, serve on boards, and roll up their sleeves to take part in a wide variety of community service activities.

Honeywell in the mid-1990s established a partnership with Habitat for Humanity. Under this partnership, the company has supplied thousands of company employees as volunteers in Habitat projects, not to mention substantial financial and product donations. Close to 3,500 Honeywell volunteers have worked on Habitat projects in Arizona, Georgia, Illinois, Kentucky, Louisiana, Michigan, Minnesota, New Mexico, North Carolina, North Dakota, Texas, and West Virginia in the United States and in Australia, Canada, and Hungary outside this country. In addition, the company has donated more than 6,000 home security systems, 8,000 thermostats, and more than $1 million in cash.

GLOBAL PRESENCE

As its corporate name indicates, Honeywell is a truly international corporation. The company has manufacturing, sales, and research and development operations in Canada, Europe, Asia, and Latin America, in addition to which U.S. exports of Honeywell products represent a major contribution to the company's annual revenue. Honeywell's European sales accounted for nearly $4.3 billion in revenue in 2001, compared with slightly more than $4.3 billion the previous year. Other international sales accounted for approximately $2 billion in 2001 revenue, compared with $2.7 billion the previous year. All international sales accounted for just over 26 percent of Honeywell's total 2001 revenue of about $23.7 billion. This was down slightly from 2000, when foreign operations accounted for 28 percent of total revenue.

EMPLOYMENT

As of December 31, 2001, Honeywell International had a total of 115,000 employees worldwide. Approximately 79,000 of those employees were based in the United States. Of the company's U.S. employees, approximately 19 percent were unionized, represented by various national or local labor unions. At its corporate Web site, Honeywell explains its approach to employment in these words: "Hire extremely talented people,

SIX SIGMA *PLUS* PAYS DIVIDENDS

Scores of companies have managed to speed up improvements in their operations while at the same time sharply reducing costs and improving quality by implementing the Six Sigma strategy. Six Sigma focuses on the elimination of waste and the reduction of defects and variations in the manufacturing process. Long aware of the benefits Six Sigma can achieve, Honeywell has put into force its proprietary version of the strategy, calling it Six Sigma *Plus*. Developed through the merger of Honeywell with AlliedSignal, the strategy equips company employees with the tools and skills they need to create greater value for Honeywell's customers; improve its products, services, and processes; and grow the company by using the power of the Internet through e-commerce. One of Honeywell's Six Sigma *Plus* teams managed to meet a critical customer need by setting up the largest Internet auction site for used truck and automotive parts. Honeywell predicts that the site could generate more than $100 million in additional high-margin revenue for the company within five years. Another Six Sigma *Plus* team devised a system that uses the Internet to accelerate the retrieval of customer payments. Over a 14-month period, the system resulted in an improvement in cash flow worth $6 million.

nurture their growth, give them opportunities to make an impact, and promote heavily from within."

The company supports a comprehensive learning program for its employees, which ranges from 40 hours of mandatory, on-the-job experience to executive management courses at such prestigious schools as Harvard and Northwestern. Employees are also schooled in Six Sigma, Steven Covey's Seven Habits, team building, and other self-improvement programs at the company's on-site learning centers.

SOURCES OF INFORMATION

Bibliography

Barrett, Amy, and Diane Brady. "The Corporation: Strategies: At Honeywell, It's Larry the Knife." *Business Week*, 26 November 2001.

DeMarrais, Kevin G. "At Honeywell, Bad News Outweighs the Good." *The Record (Bergen County, NJ)*, 19 April 2002.

DeMarrais, Kevin G. "Merger Collapse Troubles Analysts." *The Record (Bergen County, NJ)*, 16 June 2001.

Haines, Mark, and David Faber. "Honeywell-Chmn. & Pres. & CEO Interview." *CNBC/Dow Jones Business Video*, 20 February 2002.

Honeywell 2001 Annual Report. Morristown, NJ: Honeywell International Inc., 2002.

"Honeywell International Inc." *Hoover's Online*, 2002. Available at http://www.hoovers.com.

Honeywell International Inc. Home Page, 2002. Available at http://www.honeywell.com.

Johnson, Linda A. "New Honeywell CEO to Get $3.4 Million." *AP Online*, 4 March 2002.

MacIntosh, Julie. "TRW CEO David Cote Resigns to Lead Honeywell." *Reuters Business Report*, 19 February 2002.

Mattern, Hal. "Honeywell's New Chief Focuses on Growth." *Arizona Republic*, 22 February 2002.

"Snapshot Report: Honeywell International." *Multex Investor*, 2002. Available at http://www.marketguide.com.

For an annual report:

on the Internet at: http://investor.honeywell.com/ireye/ir_site.html.

For additional industry research:

Investigate companies by their Standard Industrial Classification Codes, also known as SICs. Honeywell International Inc.'s primary SICs are:

3613 Switchgear and Switchboard Apparatus

3625 Relays and Industrial Controls

3812 Search and Navigation Equipment

3822 Environmental Controls

3823 Process Control Instruments

3826 Analytical Instruments

Also investigate companies by their North American Industrial Classification System codes, also known as NAICS codes. Honeywell International Inc.'s primary NAICS codes are:

334511 Search, Detection, Navigation, Guidance and Aeronautical Systems

334512 Automatic Environmental Control Manufacturing Stores

334513 Instruments for Measuring and Displaying Industrial Process Variables

Hyundai Corporation

OVERVIEW

Launched in 1976 as the trading arm of South Korea's Hyundai Group, Hyundai Corporation is undergoing some major changes as the South Korean government moves to sell some of Hyundai's ailing units to foreign investors. The principal divisions of Hyundai Corporation, before the current divestiture campaign began, were its Ship and Plant Division, Machinery Division, Steel Division, Chemical and Business Development Division, and e-Business Division.

The Ship Department of Hyundai's Ship and Plant Division has exported more than 1,000 vessels jointly with Hyundai Heavy Industries Inc. (HHI) and other Korean shipbuilders since 1973. The department acts as an organizer, coordinator, financier, and broker for Hyundai's ship-related businesses, including conversions, new buildings, repairs, sales and purchases, and financing for vessels of all sizes. To discharge these responsibilities, the department works closely with HHI, Hyundai Mipo Dockyard Company Ltd., and other South Korean shipyards, including Sambo Heavy Industries Company Ltd. Hyundai's stellar global reputation within the international shipbuilding industry is due in no small part to the efforts of this department. During 2000, exports overseen by the Ship Department broke down as follows: Cargo Vessels, 65 percent; Tankers, 27.9 percent; and Others, 7.1 percent. Geographically, 47.6 percent of Hyundai's 2000 ship exports went to Europe; 10.9 percent to Latin America; 9.7 percent to Africa; 8.9 percent to Asia; 8.5 percent to the Middle East; and 14.4 percent to other regions. The Plant Department provides services related to the marketing and development of projects to major Hyundai affiliates and other South Korean

FOUNDED: 1976

Contact Information:

HEADQUARTERS: 140-2, Kye-dong, Chongro-ku
    Seoul, 110-793 South Korea
PHONE: (822)746-1114
FAX: (822)741-2341
EMAIL: hyundaicorp@hyundaicorp.com
URL: http://www.hyundaicorp.com

Models pose in front of Hyundai sedans during a ceremony for the 2002 FIFA World Cup Korea/Japan games at Sangam World Cup Stadium in Seoul, Korea. (AP Photo/Yun Jai-hyoung)

industrial plant manufacturers. The Plant Department's exports in 2000 broke down as follows: Offshore Facilities, 46.8 percent; Power Plants, 24.1 percent; Oil and Gas Plants, 17.5 percent; and Others, 11.6 percent. Asia took 23.5 percent of the 2000 plant exports, with 20.1 percent going to the Middle East; 19.6 percent to West Africa; 17.2 percent to Europe; 13.7 percent to North America; and 5.9 percent to other regions.

Hyundai's Machinery Division supplies a wide variety of equipment, including industrial machinery, construction equipment, and electrical equipment, for use in major industrial sectors and markets. It is also responsible for the exportation of automobiles and automotive products made by Hyundai affiliates and other small and medium-sized South Korean manufacturers. The division also supplies general merchandise, new hides, and lamb pelts. In 2000 automobiles made up 91.4 percent of the Machinery Division's exports, followed by industrial machinery at 5.4 percent; electrical equipment at 1.5 percent; general merchandise at 1.1 percent; and other at 0.6 percent. North America took 46.1 percent of the division's exports, with 25.4 percent going to Europe; 8.3 percent to the Middle East; 7.4 percent to Asia; 7.1 percent to Latin America; and 5.7 percent to other regions. The corporation's Steel Division oversees the export of a wide variety of finished steel products made by Hyundai affiliates and other South Korean manufacturers. The Steel Division is also responsible for importing raw materials for the South Korean steel industry and fin-

ished steel products from outside the country. In 2000 steel products made up 76.3 percent of the division's exports, followed by metal products at 14.3 percent and others at 9.4 percent. The geographic breakdown of the Steel Division's exports is as follows: Asia, 68 percent; North America, 17.9 percent; Europe, 7.4 percent; Latin America, 3 percent; Middle East, 2.5 percent; and Others, 1.2 percent.

The Chemical Department of Hyundai's Chemical and Business Development Division handles trade in industrial chemicals, synthetic rubber, petrochemicals and petroleum, and plastic resins. In 2000, petrochemicals and petroleum made up 76.9 percent; plastic resins, 18.3 percent; industrial chemicals, 2.5 percent; and others, 2.3 percent. Asia took 86.6 percent of these chemical exports, followed by Europe at 3.8 percent; North American at 3.4 percent; Africa at 2.6 percent; and other regions, 3.6 percent. Other departments within this division are responsible for the development of new businesses in the following sectors: Natural Resource, Sports and Culture, and Wireless Internet and Mobile Commerce. Hyundai's e-Business Division, which was launched on January 1, 2000, is responsible for developing an Internet business strategy for Hyundai. Its ultimate goal is to develop a plan that will transform Hyundai into a "Global Digital Network Enterprise.

Hyundai's Korean name means "present time," and the watchword for the present time in South Korea is

change. Battered by a prolonged and profound economic downturn, South Korea's huge conglomerates known as "chaelbol" are under orders from the Seoul government to begin trimming down by selling off unprofitable operations. In the fall of 2001, Hyundai Heavy Industries (HHI) took steps to sever its relationship with Hyundai Corporation and Hyundai Securities.

COMPANY FINANCES

As a foreign-based public corporation traded exclusively on stock exchanges outside the United States, Hyyndai Corporation is not subject to the regulations of the U.S. Securities Exchange Commission in regard to deadlines for its financial reports. The company reported a net loss of $60.7 million on revenue of almost $32.4 billion in 2000. This compared with a profit of $20 million on sales of nearly $32.9 billion the previous year. Hyundai's profit in 1998 was $7 million on sales of about $28.4 billion.

HISTORY

The history of Hyundai Coporation is linked inextricably with that of Hyundai Group, for which it serves as trading arm. The Hyundai Business Group, established in 1947, grew rapidly in the years following World War II and the Korean War, its growth fosted by the ambitious reconstruction programs of the South Korean government. It was during this period that the South Korean economy came to be dominated by a relatively small number of huge conglomerates, knowns as "chaebols." The chaebols worked closely with the Seoul government to rebuild South Korea's shattered economy after the Korean War. In the process these conglomerates became a vital element in the nation's economic strategy and its efforts to beef up its industrial base.

The Hyundai Group grew up around the core of Hyundai Engineering & Construction Company, founded in 1947 by Chung Ju Yung. In 1958 the group expanded when it created Keumkang Company to produce construction materials. In 1964 the group added Danyang Cement plant, and in 1967 it set up the Hyundai Motor Company. By 1969, the group had set up a U.S. subsidiary, Hyundai America Inc., headquartered in Los Angeles. In the late 1960s and early 1970s Hyundai Group moved into still other sectors, including chemicals, petroleum, steel, and shipbuilding. Hyundai Corporation was formed in 1976 to serve as the trading arm for Hyundai Group. But the group was hardly through with its expansion. That same year, the conglomerate formed Hyundai Merchant Marine Company, Koryeo Industrial Development Company, and Hyundai Housing and

FAST FACTS:
About Hyundai Corporation

Ownership: Hyundai is a publicly owned company traded on the South Korean Stock Exchange.

Officers: Chun-jae Kwan, Pres. and CEO; Doo-seon Lee, SVP and CFO

Employees: 867

Principal Subsidiary Companies: Hyundai Corporation operates a number of subsidiaries, some of which are major operating divisions of the South Korean trading company, while others oversee the company's business in foreign countries. Hyundai's leading subsidiaries include Hyundai Engineering & Construction Ltd., Hyundai Heavy Industries, Hyundai Motor Company, Hyundai Merchant Marine Company Ltd., Korea Industries Development Company Ltd., Hynix Semiconductor Inc., Hyundai Petrochemical Company Ltd., Hyundai Corporation U.S.A., Hyundai Corporation Europe GmbH, Hyundai Corporation UK Ltd., Hyundai Japan Company Ltd., and Hyundai Australia Pty. Ltd.

Chief Competitors: Hyundai's principal competitors include rival South Korean trading companies, including LG International, Samsung, and SK Group.

Industrial Development Company. A year later, the group created Hyundai Precision and Industry Company to manufacture automotive and locomotive components, as well as containers.

Four years after the creation of Hyundai Corporation, the annual exports of Hyundai Group reached the $1 billion mark. A year later Hyundai's shipbuilding operation landed its biggest export order ever—a $400 million order for containerships from United Arab Shipping Company. The group began exporting steel in 1985. Hyundai Corporation in 1990 opened an office in Moscow, the first for a Korean company.

By 1995 less than 20 years after the founding of Hyundai Corporation, the group's annual exports had reached a level of $10 billion. Hyundai's exports continued to climb for the remainder of the decade, reaching an annual level of $15.6 billion in 1997 and $22.2 billion in 1999. The group's exports totaled $27.8

CHRONOLOGY:

Key Dates for Hyundai Corporation

1947: Hyundai Business Group is formed

1976: Hyundai Corporation is established as trading arm of Hyundai Group

1980: Annual exports handled by Hyundai Corp. reach $1 billion

1985: Export of steel products begins

2000: Annual exports reach $27.8 billion

billion in 2000, the last year for which figures were available.

STRATEGY

As Hyundai spins off some of the less profitable of its operations, the company is diligently exploring other sectors for possible acquisitions that show more promise. Hyundai Corporation's motto is "Creativity and Speed," and the company is counting on the innovative genius of its employees and its reputation for speedy-but carefully considered decisions-to steer it into new profitable businesses before the competition.

In early 2001, Hyundai Corporation signed a contract with the South Korean city of Nam-hae to become partners in the profitable business of operating Nam-hae's training camp for finalists playing in the 2002 World Cup. Under the terms of the agreement, Hyundai Corporation was given exclusive management rights for the Nam-hae sports park, the completion of which is scheduled in 2004. This is a new business for Hyundai, and it shows great promise. Not only will the company reap profits for attracting soccer players to the training camp in 2002, but it stands to benefit for a number of years thereafter under the terms of its management agreement with Nam-hae.

Another important element in Hyundai's short-term strategy involves the integration of its traditional marketing channels with its Internet-based sales operations to take full advantage of the growing potential offered by e-commerce. The company is also gearing up to maximize the benefits it will reap from the move toward the wireless Internet market, as more and more people worldwide seeks wireless access to the World Wide Web.

INFLUENCES

The South Korean government, recognizing that many of the country's general trading companies (GTCs), of which Hyundai Corporation is the largest, were being dragged down by unprofitable operations, ordered that the country's massive conglomerates, or "chaebols," begin selling off their ailing operating units. This has forced Hyundai to look to new sectors to increase its revenue. Hyundai Corporation, turning away from its heavy reliance on heavy industry, such as steel and chemicals, plans to focus much of its resources in coming years on such promising new businesses as e-commerce, e-projects, sports marketing, venture investment, and MRO (maintenance, repair, operations).

The Seoul government's economic reform campaign hit something of a snag in January 2002 when U.S. insurance giant American International Group (AIG) withdrew from a $838 million deal to take over South Korea's troubled financial companies. The government expressed confidence that it ultimately would find a buyer for Hyundai's ailing financial units, Hyundai Investment Trust and Securities, Hyundai Investment Trust and Management, and Hyundai Securities. For its part, the government said it had decided to terminate negotiations with AIG after the American company insisted on "unacceptable" terms. Reportedly AIG had demanded that the South Korean government guarantee compensation for any additional debt discovered after it completed its acquisition of the Hyundai units.

Despite the confident tone of government officials, outside observers expressed concerns that the aborted deal with AIG might erode foreign investor confidence and cause problems for the government's efforts to sell other ailing companies, including Hynix Semiconductor and Daewoo Motor. If the government is successful in selling off all of Hyundai's troubled operations, the once-giant conglomerate will be transformed into a mid-size business group centered on Hyundai Merchant Marine, Hyundai Elevator, Hyundai Asan, and some small subsidiaries.

CURRENT TRENDS

In terms of the short-term future for Hyundai, undoubtedly the most important trend in South Korea and worldwide has been the rapid growth of information technology, thanks in large part to the Internet. It is in this arena that Hyundai will concentrate much of its energies in the foreseeable future. The company is in the process of more closely integrating its existing marketing operations and those on its Web site. In an FAQ section on the company's Web site, Hyundai Corporation has this to say about how it plans to grow in the new millennium: "Hyundai Corp. will focus its resources on several highly profitable businesses, such as e-trading, e-project, MRO

(Maintenance, Repairs, Operations), sports marketing, and venture investment by using its enhanced global networks and knowledge-based management."

PRODUCTS

As the trading arm of the Hyundai Group, Hyundai Corporation produces no products as such but rather oversees the export of goods produced by Hyundai manufacturing units and other smaller South Korean manufacturers as well as the imports of raw materials and other products needed by the group's manufacturing units. The principal products exported by Hyundai Corporation include merchant ships, industrial plants, automobiles, industrial machinery, electrical equipment, steel products, petrochemicals and petroleum, plastic resins, and industrial chemicals.

GLOBAL PRESENCE

Hyundai Corporation exports to and imports from around the world. The company maintains a global network of 64 overseas branches, including eight subsidiaries responsible for regional operations. Hyundai operates branch offices on every continent except Antarctica.

HYUNDAI CORP. EXPANDS INTERMEDIARY TRADE

Although it lags well behind some of South Korea's other general trading companies (GTCs), Hyundai Corporation is beginning to increase its intermediary trading among third nations. The rapidly changing world trade climate, as well as Seoul's pressure on the GTCs to sell off their poorly performing subsidiaries, have prompted the South Korean trading companies to explore new forms of trade. Hyundai Corporation's involvement in third-nation trading, while still extremely small, is beginning to increase fairly dramatically. While it amounted to only 0.4 percent of total trade in 1998, such trade had increased to 1 percent of Hyundai's trade in 2000. This was roughly equivalent to $300 million in trade. A Hyundai spokesman said: "We are planning to compensate for the possible loss in income following the spinning off of the subsidiaries by strengthening the third-nation trading."

SOURCES OF INFORMATION

Bibliography

Hyundai Corporation Annual Report 2000. Seoul, South Korea: Hyundai Corporation, 2001.

"Hyundai Corp.—History." *Gale Business Resources*, 2002 Available at http://galenet.galegroup.com/servlet/GBR.

"Hyundai Corporation." *Hoover's Online*, 2002. Available at http://www.hoovers.com.

Hyundai Corporation Home Page, 2002. Available at http://www .hyundaicorp.com.

Lee, Jong-heon. "S. Korea Reform Drive Facing New Challenge." *United Press International*, 18 January 2002.

"Trade Firms Expand Intermediary Trade." *Korea Times*, 28 October 2000.

For an annual report:

on the Internet at: http://www.hyundaicorp.com/eng/investor/ annualreport.htm

For additional industry research:

Investigate companies by their Standard Industrial Classification Codes, also known as SICs. Hyundai Corporation's primary SICs are:

3679 Electronic Components, NEC

3711 Motor Vehicles and Car Bodies

5010 Motor Vehicles-Parts and Supplies

5013 Motor Vehicle Supplies and New Parts

Also investigate companies by their North American Industry Classification System codes, also known as NAICS codes. Hyundai Corporation's primary NAICS codes are:

327211 Flat Glass Manufacturing

333924 Industrial Truck, Tractor, Trailer and Stacker Machinery Manufacturing

336111 Automobile Manufacturing

336211 Motor Vehicle Body Manufacturing

336399 All Other Motor Vehicle Parts Manufacturing

522298 All Other Non-Depository Credit Intermediation

IBM

FOUNDED: 1910
VARIANT NAME: International Business Machines
Corporation

Contact Information:

HEADQUARTERS: One New Orchard Rd.
Armonk, NY 10504
PHONE: (914)499-1900
FAX: (914)765-6021
URL: http://www.ibm.com

OVERVIEW

IBM is the world's largest computer company, and throughout its history it has been a bulwark in the American economy. But in 2002, as IBM stock drop dramatically in June during a particularly horrendous economic time for computer hardware and software manufacturers, analysts were divided on whether "Big Blue" has seen its best days, or has merely run into a hurdle it will eventually clear. With clear indications that its sales expectations won't be met in 2002 and no real reason to trumpet a return to prosperity in 2003 or 2004, IBM management has prepared its shareholders and employees for widespread belt tightening, worker layoffs, and the peddling of its disk-drive operation to a rival company. In April 2002, IBM disclosed that it had endured its most dramatic earnings decline since 1993. Chief Financial Officer John Joyce projected a disappointing revenue prediction of $83 billion for 2002.

In addition to manufacturing hardware and software, IBM has diversified into the areas of Internet service and computer consulting. The company's struggles in 2002 were reminiscent of a similar crisis for IBM in the early 1990s that was met only after a major revamping, employee downsizing of 60,000 workers, and a reevaluation of the company's strong points and mission. Thousands—perhaps as many as 17,000 employees—will be axed by the end of 2002.

COMPANY FINANCES

From a financial standpoint, 2002 stands to be the worst year for IBM since 1993, and a crucial measure of the company's declining health was missing profit projections for the first quarter of 2002 by about $1 billion. The company also was badly hurt by a Wall Street Journal article in 2002 that blasted the company for being too fast-and-creative with earnings reports. Revenues for 2002 reached $ 88.4 billion with about half that coming from IBM's services. IBM jettisoned its most troubled hard disk drive division, unloading it to Hitachi for $2 billion.

ANALYSTS' OPINIONS

Analyst David Robertson of Allied Investment Advisors in Maryland told a Business Week reporter that IBM's short-term problems have not dampened his belief that the company eventually will find a way back to its traditional high profits. Analysts are divided as to whether or not IBM should sell off its poorly performing PC division; other analysts criticize poorer returns for shareholders because of slumping earnings in the semiconductor area.

HISTORY

In 1910 Charles Ranlett Flint started the earliest ancestor of IBM under the name Calculating-Tabulating-Recording, or CTR, by merging three firms: International Time Recording Co., Computing Scale Co. of America, and Tabulating Machine Co. The last was founded by an engineer, Herman Hollerith, who had invented a tabulating machine—an apparatus that sorted and counted punch cards. This machine was first sold to the U.S. Census Bureau, and later to businesses that needed to organize large amounts of data economically. In 1915 Thomas Watson was hired as CTR's general manager and, by 1920, had built CTR into the leader in tabulating design.

CTR changed its name to International Business Machines—or IBM—in 1924. By focusing on large, custom systems for businesses, the company found that it had fewer competitors than those that made smaller, mass-produced systems. The company leased its products, instead of selling them, and reported profits throughout the 1920s. Initially, IBM held onto its market and customers by making punch cards that only worked with its own machines. By 1932, this policy had led to a U.S. government antitrust suit filed against IBM. At the time, IBM controlled 85 percent of the U.S. market for tabulating, keypunch, and accounting equipment.

The New Deal programs of the Depression years expanded government bureaucracy, which led to a need for large calculators; IBM supplied this equipment. World War II bolstered IBM's sales as well, and increased public- and private-sector demand for tabulators helping to triple IBM's sales.

FAST FACTS:
About IBM

Ownership: IBM is a publicly held company traded on the New York Stock Exchange.

Ticker symbol: IBM

Officers: Louis V. Gerstner, Chmn., 60, 2002 base salary $12.6 million; Samuel Palmisano, 50, Pres. and CEO; John Joyce, 48, CFO, $2 million

Employees: 319,876

Chief Competitors: Some primary competitors include Acer Corp, AST Computer, Hewlett-Packard, Gateway 2000, and Microsoft.

In 1956 IBM took the lead in the computer business by introducing its 705 general-purpose business computer. Institutional customers appreciated the way IBM's computers utilized the equipment that they had already leased or bought. The recognizable blue-suited sales force was instrumental in placing IBM's computers into businesses. In 1961 IBM released the Stretch computer system, which used a magnetic memory core and transistors instead of the more primitive vacuum tube technology. With the capability of performing up to three quarters of a million additions per second, the Stretch was the most powerful computer on the market.

In 1970 IBM introduced the first "floppy" (5 1/4 inch) disks, which were made by forming thin wafers of silicon and then cutting them into chips, thus setting the stage for much smaller systems. IBM subsequently released a new system, the 370 family. It was faster and could do more simultaneous tasks than prior systems. In 1973, IBM doubled the storage space on floppy disks with the 3340 disk storage unit, which functioned like main memory but at a much lower cost.

In 1975 IBM attempted to release its first personal computer, the 5100, weighing 50 pounds and costing about $5,000. Sales were disappointing. Realizing that demand for personal computers was minimal at the time, IBM focused on building mainframes. It was not until 1980 that IBM tried again to crack the personal computer market. By then, many other companies were already making the machines, and IBM was not able to gain immediate control of the market. That same year, it rolled out the IBM 3687 Holographic Scanner, which was used with the IBM 3683 supermarket terminal to read bar

CHRONOLOGY:
Key Dates for IBM

1910: Charles Ranlett Flint starts the Calculating-Tabulating-Recording (CTR) firm

1924: CTR changes its name to International Business Machines or IBM

1932: A U.S. Government antitrust suit is filed against IBM

1956: IBM introduces its 705 general-purpose business computer

1961: The company releases the Stretch computer system

1970: The company introduces the first "floppy" disk

1975: IBM releases its first personal computer

1980: The 3687 Holographic scanner is released

1990: IBM researchers move individual atoms

1992: The Think Pad is introduced

1997: Deep Blue, an IBM Supercomputer, defeats the World Chess Champion

1998: IBM announces its "E-business Tools" line

2002: Longtime IBM CEO, President and chairman Louis V. Gerstner Jr. becomes chair only until December 31, 2002, when his retirement took effect; Samuel J. Palmisano becomes president and chief executive officer of IBM; IBM announced demonstrated self-diagnostic security protection against hackers with the Distributed Wireless Security Auditor (DWSA) that monitors wireless networks and report security problems to back-end servers instantly

codes. Throughout the 1990s, IBM continued to grow by producing many new systems and personal computers, and by providing various consulting services. It expanded its overseas operations and, in the late 1990s, continued to dominate the mainframe and computer-related service markets.

In 2001 and 2002, the faltering of IBM has been major news on the business pages of the nation's newspaper, although other companies such as Apple and Hewlett Packard also have been seeing plummeting stroke prices by June of 2002.

STRATEGY

In a 2002 New York Times interview, Louis V. Gerstner said that three specific strategies were "the fundamental underpinnings" for IBM in recent years. IBM built up its computer management services "that sold bundles of hardware, software, consulting and maintenance to manage business processes like manufacturing, purchasing or marketing." As a services unit, IBM Global Services began to , "look at technology through the eyes of the customer," he told the Times, not merely selling IBM products but working closely with the customer even if it meant sharing profits by using the products of Sun Microsystems, Microsoft and Oracle. "The customer would not accept a services company if all it did was flog I.B.M. products," he told the New York Times. Closely linked to the number one strategy, IBM decided its software would need to be made compatible with major competitive hardware, and vise versa with IBM hardware and competitor software. Third, and this strategy was adopted late but fully in 1995, was to gain mastery of the Internet and use its powerful computers, talented personnel and the best minds in technology to become competitive with what Gerstner termed the "ënetworked world' model of computing." Said Gerstner, "We were able to articulate a role for I.B.M. in the networked world that spoke of the value of all we did."

CEO Gerstner explained IBM's developing view of itself as a provider of solutions to the customer's needs, "Our ability to integrate is a unique advantage of this company. So we said: All right, now let's go build a strategy around integrating the technology into solutions for customers. That was the fundamental decision we made."

Aside from the company's strategy as a vendor, Gerstner once said in an annual company statement that IBM is "committed to maximizing shareholder value and to making productive use of our cash." IBM has made dozens of strategic acquisitions of companies, including Lotus Development Corp., the maker of the popular Lotus Notes messaging software.

INFLUENCES

Unquestionably, IBM is looking for leadership in 2002 to newly named CEO Samuel Palmisano. In an apparent gesture intended to motivate, Palmisano sent a message to all IBM employees to warn them that some cutbacks and layoffs would be inevitable as the company fought back in mid-2002 to stop losses and return to at least modest profitability by 2004.

CURRENT TRENDS

To restate an old cliché, much at IBM is broken, but the big question is whether management can do anything to fix the problem. Nearly the first thing new IBM CEO Samuel J. Palmisano did after taking his position in 2002 was sell off the troubled hard-disk drive business. The second was to save costs by announcing some immediate layoffs with thousands more to follow by the end of 2002. Analysts wondered how Palmisano would try to solve two additional pressing problems, plunging sales of personal computers and semiconductor chips, a part of the microelectronics group at IBM. Early indications have been that Palmisano believes both personal computers and chips are crucial to IBM's services component and overall company strategy for long-term success. The company has spent well over $5 billion on chip development since October 2000.

PRODUCTS

IBM makes leading computer hardware and software, and provides consulting services through its IBM Global Services unit. Hardware products include mainframes, servers, midrange, and desktop machines. Recent introductions are impressive though IBM emphasis seems to be more on marketing existing products in 2000s, note analysts.

Nonetheless, IBM has added clout in 2002 to its Web services group with an upgraded version of its Unix-based operating system called AIX version. The upgrade adds speed and versatility. The company also launched an upgrade of WebSphere Studio Application Developer for Linux and WebSphere Studio Site Developer, a business Web site building and maintenance package with wireless, portal and voice applications.

CORPORATE CITIZENSHIP

IBM is the largest corporate contributor in the world and is well known for matching the charitable gifts of its employees. The company has been extremely involved in philanthropic attempts to get computers into classrooms through its Reinventing Education program. Essentially, IBM works with school districts and worldwide governments to help raise student achievement and computer literacy. In addition, IBM employees long have been devoted to giving their time to school districts and to serve students through the IBM Mentor-Place.

In 2002, New York Governor George Pataki gave two IBM operations the state's Governor's Award for environmental awareness. Since 1971, IBM has embraced a global Environmental management system committed to protecting the environment worldwide. In 2000 IBM started its popular recycling program to charge a small fee ($29.95) to take used personal computers and find a match with charitable organizations that can use them.

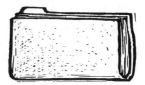

SECURITY: THE EYES MAY HAVE IT

One of the keys to jumpstarting a world economy that first came to a complete stop on September 11, 2001, and has yet to reach pre-September 11 levels of prosperity by mid-2002, is to assure business travelers that it is safe to assume traveling. The team of International Business Machines Corp. and Schiphol Group hopes its security check technology to scan irises in passenger eyes, already employed successfully at Amsterdam airport, will some day see wide use at airports worldwide. IBM hardware and software is used in the technology end of the scanning, while Schiphol provides the security and airport expertise. Essentially, a traveler's iris specs are put ahead of time into a computer system and each time that person gets to an airport, the iris identification system helps security personnel whether to admit or deny entry.

GLOBAL PRESENCE

IBM has a presence in more than 160 countries. It works with more than 1,000 businesses in central Europe and Russia alone, and is the leading vendor of personal computers in China. IBM's Global Campus Solution serves universities in the United States, Australia, Latin America, and Europe. Even in its research, IBM expands globally, with labs in Beijing working on Java, a programming language for use on the Internet. However, IBM rivals have done much better in China because Chinese businesses have shied away from multi-million dollar data management systems in favor of less expensive alternatives. IBM has positioned itself to serve not only international e-businesses, but also whole countries, according to Dr Michael Loh, Asia-Pacific leader of IBM Global Services Institute for Business Value.

EMPLOYMENT

IBM aims to be an employee-friendly institution. *Working Mother* magazine in 2001 found IBM to be in the top ten among all employers in providing a welcoming climate for females with children. IBM received Working Mother's number one ranking for childcare services in 2001. The company and its subsidiaries offer defined benefit and contribution plans to employees and a supplemental retirement plan to certain executives. Long considered a company with major security for employees, that image was shaken somewhat in 2002 as IBM began laying off the greatest number of employees it had turned loose since the early 1990s.

SOURCES OF INFORMATION

Bibliography

Cook, William J. "Interview with IBM CEO Louis Gerstner." *U.S. News Online,* 19 December 1997.

Foremski, Tom. "Palmisano Faces Tough Questions on IBM Plans." *Financial Times e,* 15 May 2002.

Hamid, Hamisah. "IBM Sees Online Deals between Markets." *Business Times,* 15 May 2002.

"IBM, Schiphol to Market Iris-Scan Security Check to Airports, Airlines." *AFX European Focus,* 25 April 2002.

"IBM." *Hoover's Online,* June 2002. Available at http://www .hoovers.com.

IBM Home Page, June 2002. Available at http://www.ibm.com.

Horvitz, Paul. " IBM's Gerstner Rides Services Profit." *Bloomberg News,* 16 October 2001.

Lohr, Steve. " He Loves to Win. At I.B.M., He Did.." *The New York Times,* 10 March 2002.

Martin, Jonathan. *International Directory of Company Histories.* Vol. 3. Detroit, MI: St. James Press, 1994.

Morgan Timothy Prickett." Palmisano Dodges IBM Layoffs, Revenue Growth Questions." *ComputerWire,* 16 May 2002.

"100 Best Companies for Working Mothers." *Working Woman Magazine,* June 2002. Available at http://www.workingwoman .com.

Tsao, Amy. "Can IBM Shake Its Big Blues." *Business Week Online,* 13 June 2002.

For an annual report:
on the Internet at: http://www.ibm.com **or** telephone: (800)426-3333

For additional industry research:
Investigate companies by their Standard Industrial Classification Codes, also known as SICs. IBM's primary SICs are:

3571 Electronic Computers

3572 Computer Storage

3575 Computer Terminals

3577 Computer Peripheral Equipment

7371 Computer Programming Services

7372 Prepackaged Software

7373 Computer Integrated Systems Design

7374 Data Processing and Preparation

7375 Information Retrieval Services

7377 Computer Rental and Leasing

7378 Computer Maintenance and Repair

7379 Computer Related Systems

Also investigate companies by their North American Industry Classification System codes, also known as NAICS codes. IBM's primary NAICS codes are:

334111 Electronic Computer Manufacturing

334119 Other Computer Peripheral Equipment Manufacturing

454110 Electronic Shopping and Mail-Order Houses

511210 Software Publishers

Imperial Sugar Company

OVERVIEW

Imperial Sugar is the largest processor and marketer of refined sugar in the United States. The company is also a leading distributor of sugar, sauces, seasonings, desserts, and drink mixes to the food services industry. Approximately 77 percent of the company's sales were in the sugar segment, and 23 percent were in the food service segment in 2001. Imperial Sugar also has a small market in beet sugar processing by-products, which are used as livestock feed, and beet seed. Brands include Imperial, Holly, Spreckels, Dixie Crystals, and Pioneer. Its subsidiaries include Wholesome Sweeteners L.L.C., Diamond Crystal Specialty Foods Inc., and Savannah Foods & Industries.

FOUNDED: 1905

Contact Information:

HEADQUARTERS: 1 Imperial Square, 8016 Highway 90-A
   Sugar Land, TX 77487-0009
PHONE: (281)491-9181
FAX: (281)490-9530
TOLL FREE: (800)727-8427
URL: http://www.imperialsugar.com

ANALYSTS' OPINIONS

Although Imperial Sugar drastically reduced its debts in 2001 while under bankruptcy protection, Standard & Poors remained somewhat pessimistic about a speedy recovery for the company and lowered its rating twice during 2001. Months after Imperial emerged from bankruptcy, it had an S&P rating of "D". The unfavorable rating was in part due to the volatile nature of commodities, according to S&P analysts. Five years in a row, favorable growing conditions eventually created a glut of sugar stockpiles, which kept prices low and the agribusiness industry depressed. Adding to the volatility of the sugar market, Mexico, and its potential for sugar trading in the United States under NAFTA, posed a threat to a highly governmentally protected American sugar market.

Founded in 1843, Imperial Sugar, located in Sugar Land, Texas, filed for bankruptcy protection in January, 2001, citing $250 million in debt. (AP Photo/David J. Phillip)

HISTORY

Imperial Sugar traces its roots back to a Texas sugar cane plantation in the early 1800s. The Samuel May Williams plantation in Sugar Land, Texas, began producing granulated sugar in 1843. The processing portion of the plantation became Imperial Sugar Company. Founded in 1905, and incorporated in 1924, Imperial Sugar remains one of the longest-surviving businesses in its home state of Texas. Imperial Sugar was a privately-

owned cane sugar refinery with just one facility for more than 80 years.

In 1988 the company acquired publicly-held Colorado-based Holly Sugar Corp., doubling the newly-named Imperial Holly Corp.'s size and adding beet sugar production to its business. In 1996 Imperial Holly bought California-based beet sugar company, Spreckels Sugar Company. The following year Imperial Holly acquired the then-largest sugar refiner in the country, Georgia-based Savannah Foods & Industries, which again doubled the company's size. Savannah Foods owned Michigan Sugar and Great Lakes Sugar, as well as Louisiana company Colonial Sugar Refinery, which expanded Imperial's nationwide scope further.

The company grew quickly again when it acquired healthcare and food service business, Diamond Crystal Specialty Foods, and Wholesome Sweeteners, which led the natural and organic foods industries, in 1998. The acquisition expanded Imperial's market in the industrial and food service markets. The Imperial acquisitions have made the company the first truly national sugar company in the United States. Imperial Holly changed its name in 1999 to Imperial Sugar Company, after the Diamond Crystal and Wholesome Sweeteners acquisitions.

Despite its longevity and growth, the company experienced financial difficulties. In 2001 the company made $1.55 billion in net sales, but had $322.8 million in net losses, and filed for bankruptcy in part to avert a default on $230 million of its total $600 million in debt. The filing was also designed to deal with longtime financial problems such as decreasing prices due to excess sugar supply, rising energy costs, and lower prices in the retail market, which accounts for nearly 80 percent of the company's sales. The company emerged from Chapter 11 bankruptcy protection in August 2001. During the bankruptcy period and extensive restructuring, Imperial Sugar sold its nutritional products business, which netted about 15 percent of its annually sales, and in December, 2001, the company sold King Packaging, its packaged disposable meal kits business, which made up 7.6 percent of its sales.

After Imperial emerged from bankruptcy, the company sold subsidiaries Michigan Sugar Company and Great Lakes Sugar Company to the Michigan Sugar Beet Growers Inc. growers' cooperative for $45 million. Michigan had been one of Imperial Sugar's leading producers of beet sugar and represented $162 million in net sales in 2001. The transaction was comprised of $29.0 million in cash, with the remaining $16.0 million to be financed by Imperial. The growers also assumed the $18.5 million in bond debt from Imperial Sugar. For nearly two years the cooperative tried to work out a deal with Imperial Sugar to buy four Michigan plants immediately before the bankruptcy filing, made a final offer of $75 million, but Imperial Sugar refused the offer.

When the company emerged from bankruptcy in August 2001, it moved forward in its restructuring plans,

FAST FACTS:

About Imperial Sugar Company

Ownership: Imperial Sugar is a publicly owned company traded on the OTC Bulletin Board.

Ticker Symbol: ISPU

Officers: Robert A. Peisner, Pres. and CEO, 53; Douglas W. Ehrenkranz, EVP, 44, 2001 base salary $315,000, bonus $212,625; William F. Schwer, EVP and General Counsel, 54, 2001 base salary $305,000, bonus $358,945; Mark Q. Huggins, CFO, 2001 base salary $295,086, bonus $323,125; William J. Smith, Managing Dir., 46, 2001 base salary $300,000, bonus $204,213

Employees: 3,250 year-round; 2,200 seasonal

Chief Competitors: Imperial Sugar's top competitors include: American Crystal Sugar, SYSCO, and Tate & Lyle.

---

and in October 2001, distributed 0.0062 shares of new common stock for every share previously held by shareholders. The company began trading under the symbol ISPU in September 2001 and began trading on the OTC Bulletin Board shares of the new common stock in March 2002, under the symbol ISPUZ.

INFLUENCES

The sugar growth and processing industry, including Imperial Sugar, is constantly affected by external influences, many of which are unpredictable. Abnormal weather patterns' affect on crop yields, sugarbeet quality, and energy costs pose a constant question mark for the sugar industry. While no one can argue with the weather, one influence that is debated regularly is the government regulation and subsidy of the sugar processing industry. Federal programs to support and stabilize the price of domestic crops have existed since 1934, and most recently, the Federal Agricultural Improvement and Reform Act of 1996, or the Farm Bill, has played an instrumental part in keeping the sugar processors afloat. The bill implemented a tariff rate quota that limits the amount of raw and refined sugar imported into the United States. Despite the federal protections under the Farm Bill, the sugar industry struggled through two consecu-

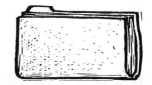

A BEET FOR ALL SEASONS

While sugar cane can be grown year-round in warm climates, and then harvested and stored for long periods of time, the sugar beet is highly perishable. It is grown in climates with short growing seasons. Unfortunately, the growing season for sugar beets doesn't match the season when the demand for sugar products is highest. Shipments of specialty products such as brown sugar and powdered sugar are highest in the fourth quarter, when holiday baking creates high demand. However, beet sugar factories operate for 120 to 180 days during the growing season in the northern United States.

Imperial Sugar can produce beet sugar nearly year-round because of its diverse manufacturing facilities located in nearly every climate region in the country, but production is most active in the summer months. The diversity of the regions also helps the increase efficiency and decrease costs of distribution. The diversity of the manufacturing locations serves yet another purpose. Adverse weather conditions are less a factor because they do not typically effect every growing region in the United States during a single season.

---

tive years in which sugar was plentiful. The government intervened in 2000, and purchased 132,000 short tons of refined sugar from Imperial. In the fall of the same year, the government gave growers 277,000 short tons of refined sugar in exchange for not harvesting 102,000 acres of already-planted sugarbeets.

Although the North American Free Trade Agreement (NAFTA) adopted in 1994, had the potential to adversely affect the sugar industry, it has had less influence on Imperial Sugar than the Farm Bill has because NAFTA limits the amount of sugar that can be imported to and exported from Mexico.

PRODUCTS

Imperial Sugar Company is known by several of its subsidiary names including Imperial Pure Cane Sugar, Savannah Foods & Industries Inc., Holly Sugar Company, Spreckels Sugar Company, and Pioneer Sugar. In addition to sugar products, Imperial Sugar produces molasses and syrups under its Savannah Molasses and Specialty group; glaze, fondant, icing, and free flowing brown or granulated sugars are produced by its Spreckles Specialty Sugars subsidiary.

EMPLOYMENT

Imperial Sugar employs approximately 3,250 year-round employees. Approximately 250 worked at the King Packaging factory, which the company sold in December 2001. Imperial also hires approximately 2,200 seasonal employees during the year. Imperial's Indianapolis and Perrysburg, Ohio, foodservice facilities operate under union contracts, and its Port Wentworth, Georgia, refinery employs non-union workers. The company entered into collective bargaining agreements with union representatives to discuss other sugar segment plants.

SOURCES OF INFORMATION

Bibliography

"Economic Difficulties Continue to Take a Toll on Global Agribusiness." *Standard & Poor's,*, 19 October 2001.

Gallagher, Sean. "Imperial Sugar Rebuilds on Web Services." *Baseline*, 18 March 2002.

"Imperial Sugar Company Sells Michigan Sugar Company to Michigan Sugar Beet Growers Inc." *Hoovers Online*, 13 February 2002.

"Imperial Sugar Files Chapter 11 Bankruptcy." *Food News*, January 2001.

"Sugar Industry Faces Big Test with Free Trade." *St. Petersburg Times*, 6 May 2001.

For an annual report:
on the Internet at: http:\\www.imperialsugar.com

For additional industry research:
Investigate companies by their Standard Industrial Classification codes, also known as SICs. Imperial Sugar Company's primary SICs are:

2062 Cane Sugar Refining

2063 Beet Sugar

Also investigate companies by their North American Industry Classification System codes, also known as NAICS codes. Imperial Sugar Company's primary NAICS codes are:

311312 Cane Sugar Refining

311313 Beet Sugar Manufacturing

Intel Corporation

OVERVIEW

Intel Corp. is a manufacturer of microprocessors, chipsets and motherboards, microprocessor peripherals, microcomputers and supercomputers, and semiconductors, including flash memory devices, best known for its "Intel Inside" advertising slogan designed to push its Pentium processors for personal computers. In June of 2002, Financial Times noted that good economic times for Intel, as the world's dominant power in chip production for PCs, communications equipment and mobile telephones, are crucial if the technology sector likewise is to prosper in coming years.

COMPANY FINANCES

Like all other giant chip makers, Intel, in early 2002, reported that the previous year's financial picture was the bleakest on record. To try to stop stock prices from sliding further, Intel curbed its production of chips. The good news was that Intel managed to check its downward slide by April 2002. Thanks to recovery shown by its microprocessor business, Intel reported a profit of $936 million for the first quarter of 2002. More good news for the quarter was that sales were up slightly for Intel, the posted $6.8 billion sales figure the highest in four quarters. The postings shored up confidence on Wall Street, and raised hopes that semiconductor sales would continue to show strong gains. However, at this writing in June of 2002, Intel shareholders were sorely disappointed when Merrill Lynch downgraded Intel stock, saying that the early hopes for semiconductor recovery earlier in the year were far too optimistic. By

FOUNDED: 1968

Contact Information:
HEADQUARTERS: 2200 Mission College Blvd.
Santa Clara, CA 95052-8119
PHONE: (408)765-8080
FAX: (408)765-9904
EMAIL: support@cs.intel.com
URL: http://www.intel.com

FAST FACTS:

About Intel Corporation

Ownership: Intel is a publicly held company, traded on NASDAQ.

Ticker Symbol: INTC

Officers: Craig R. Barrett, Director. and CEO, 62, $1.9 million; Andrew S. Grove, Chmn., 65, $1.8 million; Paul Otellini, Chmn., Pres., and COO, 51, $986,000

Employees: 83,400

Principal Subsidiary Companies: Intel's subsidiaries include American Communications Exchange Inc., Intel Corp. Military Special Products Div., Intel Corp. Personal Computer Enhancement Div., Intel Corp. Rio Rancho Div., Intel Corp. Supercomputer Systems Div., and Intel Products Group.

Chief Competitors: A maker of microprocessors, Intel's primary competitors include: Advanced Micro Devices (AMD), Cyrix, and Motorola.

June, it was clear that Intel's sixth straight quarter of disappointing revenues was a reality. However, rather than stew, Intel's management turned to its technology sector to help bail out the company, spending $7.3 billion on new plants capable of turning out far more chips at lower costs than its rival chip powers.

ANALYSTS' OPINIONS

Just as miners once looked to canaries in cages to warn them when gases had turned mines dangerous, so too do modern financial analysts study Intel's bottom line each quarter to anticipate if corporate spending is at safe or troubling levels. Analysts and investors alike are all too aware that as Intel goes, so goes all indications for the general health of corporate spending in other business sectors for the immediate future. Tom Foremski of the *Financial Times* noted how Wall Street keeps an anxious eye on Intel's global microchip sales revenues to see if information technology as a while might ascend from below-ground levels to higher altitudes. "As the leading supplier of chips for PCs, communications equipment and mobile telephones, Intel sits at the center of a complex global web of technology products," "It can quickly detect any movement in the

myriad supply chains and pick up the faintest signs of a turnaround," writes Foremski.

HISTORY

Intel Corporation was the creation of a couple of engineers who had left Fairchild Semiconductor in 1968 in an entrepreneurial desire to develop large scale integration technology for silicon-based chips. Robert Noyce had been the co-inventor of the integrated circuit while Gordon Moore was primarily responsible for the company's planning, and developed what is known as Moore's Law. He held that chip processing technologies tend to double every year-and-a-half.

"So far," stated a *Fortune* article, "Moore's law has been sustained by a regular cycle: Computer makers and software companies (especially Microsoft) develop new features and programs that require more power. Intel, meanwhile, creates brawny new chips to meet those new demands."

The founders were aided by Andy Grove who tended to the manufacturing end of the young business. Back then the calculator was beginning to be introduced in business applications, but computer punch cards were still standard practice in the computer technology industry.

Marcian "Ted" Hoff, an Intel engineer, invented the microprocessor, and is credited as the person responsible for the personal computer industry. In 1971 he introduced a device known as the 4004—a microprocessor consisting of 2,300 transistors located on a sliver of silicon. It was one-eighth of an inch wide by one-sixth of an inch long. It was seen as a breakthrough invention, used primarily for calculating.

The 8008 microprocessor, the first chip to be actively marketed, and the one that had been developed with the 4004, first appeared April 1972. This chip moved rudimentary computing from 4- to 8-bit processing. Though this changed the complexion of the industry, it was not until IBM decided in the 1980s to use the Intel 8086 and 8088 microprocessors to create a personal computer. It was about this time that Apple Computer was founded, and began using components from rival Motorola.

"IBM's decision to support the 8086 microprocessor, running an operating system called MS-DOS, resulted in a software company called Microsoft, founded by Bill Gates and Paul Allen." Eventually, these two companies would become the two most powerful firms in a marketplace that is now worth billions of dollars annually," recounted a *Computer Weekly* article commemorating the twenty-fifth anniversary of Hoff's invention.

"Since Intel's launch of the 4004, faster, smaller, and more complex microprocessor devices have been developed. Intel, Texas Instruments, Advanced Micro Devices (AMD), Digital Equipment, Cyrix, and many others have deluged the industry with tiny black microprocessor chips that have altered the courses of our lives," an article in *Computer Weekly* stated. "But Intel has dominated the market for microprocessor chips and looks likely to continue this for quite some time, unless companies such as AMD can break its monopolistic grip.

"The Motorola 68000 microprocessor family has been the single most significant threat to the dominance of Intel in the chip business. Apple's all-out adoption of the 68000 for use in its Macintosh computers forged a market with 12 million-plus loyal customers.

"But Intel saw off this competition, and has beaten off the challenge from firms such as AMD and Cyrix, which introduced Intel-compatible processors in an attempt to hijack Intel's market. During the early 1990s, thanks to a huge investment program in chip manufacturing plants, Intel was able to maintain its position as the only firm able to satisfy the burgeoning demand for PC chips."

Intel has had its problems even in the midst of its success. The company, in an attempt to protect its technology, was tangled in suits with rival chip makers, particularly AMD. In a 1992 arbitration, Intel was ruled against and AMD's claims regarding a technology exchange upheld. The company took a further hit in 1994 when, shortly after the introduction of the Pentium processor, a serious problem was found in the chip's calculation abilities, and the company's public relations suffered a direct hit. Other concerns surfaced, as well, including the chip's tendency to overheat the circuitry in existing computer systems that had been upgraded.

Intel was integral in the industry celebration of the microprocessor's "birthday" at Comdex, the international computer trade show. This included a museum containing artifacts that showed the microprocessor's history from the Intel 4004 and Busicom calculator to consumer products, such as the TRS-80 and Commodore PET, in addition to modern devices such as smoke detectors— microprocessors are embedded into these.

Grove took over as chief executive officer in January 1987. Since that time Intel's average annual return to investors has been 44 percent. Grove was named chairman May 21, 1997, replacing Moore. The move was seen as being symbolic, since Grove had effectively been running the company since his appointment as chief executive officer.

According to *Fortune,* "Even though he was one of the handful of employees who got the company up and running in 1968, Grove has never been considered a founder—a status reserved for Moore and Noyce. They have been celebrated as legends and visionaries, aided in their success by Andy Grove, the efficient manager. Now he must be considered their equal."

Time Magazine named Grove its "Man of the Year" in the last issue of 1997, featuring his accomplishments

CHRONOLOGY:
Key Dates for Intel Corporation

1968: Intel is founded

1971: An Intel engineer invents the microprocessor, the 4004 Microchip

1972: The 8008 microprocessor is Intel's first chip to be actively marketed

1981: IBM decides to put an Intel microprocessor into its first PC

1982: Intel creates the 286 chip with 134,000 transistors, the first chip to offer software compatibility with its predecessors

1985: The Intel386 is released with 275,000 transistors and 5 million instructions per second capacity

1993: The Pentium processor debuts with 3.1 million transistors and 90 million instrsuctions per second capacity

1994: A problem is found in the Pentium chip's calculation abilities

1997: The Pentium II is released with 7.5 million transistors

1998: Intel and Polaroid announce plans to produce a digital camera using Intel technology

2000: Pentium 4 processor-based PCs now can be used for absolutely the most sophisticated film and graphics chores

2001: Intel introduces the Itanium processor for high-end servers and workstations, used for such needs as e-business transactions, database creation, computer-aided engineering, and medical, scientific, and engineering functions

2002: Intel and other chip making giants reported that 2001 was the most disastrous year for unsold chips in the history of the industry

and vision in a cover story. Shortly afterward, Grove stepped down as president, allowing Craig Barrett to take over the role of CEO.

In 2002, Barrett continued to function as CEO, charged with the difficult job of revitalizing Intel in a time of economic lethargy—the worst year for Intel in its corporate history. In June 2002, Barrett addressed the need for the industry to pursue new growth opportunities while

THOSE WHO CAN—COMPUTE!

Intel Corporation announced in 2002 that in a little over one year, the company expects to train one million teachers from many of the world's nations through the Intel Teach to the Future program. In teaming up with Microsoft, the program hopes to enable teachers to more effectively apply computer technology to achieve better outcomes in the classroom. "Intel's goal is to provide educational programs, ideas and support that encourage innovation and learning, especially in the areas of science, math, and technology education," said Wendy Hawkins, Intel director of Education in an interview reprinted on the Intel Web site. "Our education initiatives help youth to develop skills needed to succeed in tomorrow's workplace."

lowering operating costs. "The focus during these difficult times should be the return the industry generates on its capital investments," Barrett said at the communications industry's Supercomm 2002 conference, reprinted on the Intel Internet home page. "To improve on this return, innovation must pervade all aspects of the industry from value-added services and software to the underlying communications infrastructure."

STRATEGY

Intel has been in the business of introducing cutting-edge technology and getting consumers to pay for the research and development (R&D) of the impressive speeds of its new chips. It is a cyclical process, which also necessitates more R&D of even faster, smaller products. The company does this to constantly renew the need and to keep its margins high. Perhaps Intel's best year profitwise was 1996, when it spent $5 billion on capital projects and R&D, and had record earnings that year—$5.2 billion in earnings on sales of $20.8 billion. This business model of Intel's has been compared to the automotive industry's "planned obsolescence." A new model means the old model is not good, or new, anymore, therefore the consumer feels compelled to purchase the newest, latest, greatest product. This strategy backfired in 2001 and 2002 as business corporations saw the global economy stagnate and limited spending for upgrades of technology, seriously affecting Intel revenues.

CURRENT TRENDS

The trends are pushed by more powerful applications, which in turn necessitate new microprocessors and other new generations of computer products. However, when corporate spending on technology drops drastically, as occurred in 2001 and 2002, Intel not only stops recording immense profits but also has to rethink its research budget and marketing strategy. Slowing of computer sales in the United States has made an impact on the market, and by 2001, not even new technologies and overseas sales keep Intel profits up at a point that makes shareholders and analysts happy.

PRODUCTS

Intel makes a wide range of computing products. These include video conferencing products, networking products, and a wide array of embedded devices. The mainstay of Intel's business is its microprocessors or chips. The most current of these is the Pentium line of microprocessors.

CORPORATE CITIZENSHIP

Intel donates generously to education in hopes of training students to be computer literate, critical thinkers, and skilled at interpreting and assimilating information. According to Intel, the Intel(r) Innovation in Education Program is a global program aimed at turning out superior students, particularly in science, math, engineering, and technology education.

GLOBAL PRESENCE

Intel Corporation in 2002 expressly targeted key Asian nations as critical to the overall technology industry's efforts to restore prosperity in slack economic times and to stretch the capabilities of the world to conduct commerce and exchange information. In June of 2002, on the Intel home page, CEO Craig Barrett called for a better-planned marriage of computing and communications to achieve global cooperation to get "computing devices [that] communicate" and "communications devices [that] compute. "Growth will depend on accelerated broadband development and finding better ways to manage digital media over the Internet," Barrett said in remarks captured at a technology conference. He said that countries such as Korea and Japan need to put broadband as their first priority to achieve as much as 100 megabits per second.

SOURCES OF INFORMATION

Bibliography

Detar, James. "Itanium Chip Could Put Sun On The Run Intel Rivalry Intensifies." *Investor's Business Daily,* 20 June 2002.

Dieterich, Robert. "Intel Plunge Shows No Tech Stock Is Safe." *Bloomberg News,* 10 June 2002.

Foremski, Tom. "Investors Look to Intel for Hint of Uplift." *Financial Times,* 6 June 2002.

Gaither, Chris. "Intel Meets Expectations For Earnings." *The New York Times,* 17 April 2002.

"Shares Tank on Intel Downgrade." *United Press International,* 6 June 2002.

For an annual report:

on the Internet at: http://www.intel.com **or** telephone: (800)298-0146

For additional industry research:

Investigate companies by their Standard Industrial Classification Codes, also known as SICs. Intel Corporation's primary SICs are:

3571 Electronic Computers

3577 Computer Peripheral Equipment, NEC

3674 Semiconductors and Related Devices

Also investigate companies by their North American Industry Classification System codes, also known as NAICS codes. Intel Corporation's primary NAICS codes are:

334111 Electronic Computer Manufacturing

334119 Other Computer Peripheral Equipment Manufacturing

334413 Semiconductor and Related Device Manufacturing

421430 Computer and Computer Peripheral Equipment and Software

International Flavors and Fragrances, Inc.

FOUNDED: 1909

Contact Information:

HEADQUARTERS: 521 W. 57th Street
  New York, NY 10019
PHONE: (212)765-5500
FAX: (212)708-7132
URL: http://www.iff.com

OVERVIEW

International Flavors and Fragrances (IFF) is a leading creator and manufacturer of flavor and fragrance products that are used by other manufacturers in a wide array of consumer products. IFF fragrances are sold mainly to makers of perfumes, cosmetics, toiletries, hair care products, deodorants, soaps, detergents, and air car products. Flavorings are sold mainly to producers of prepared foods, beverages, dairy foods, pharmaceuticals, and confectionery products.

COMPANY FINANCES

International Flavors and Fragrances, Inc.'s 2001 sales were $1.84 billion, a 26 percent increase over 2000 sales, which were $1.46 billion. Flavors accounted for $835.7 billion, up 40 percent from $597.7 billion in 2000. Fragrances made up $1.01 billion in sales, a 17 percent increase over $865.1 million in 2000. The weak European exchange rates in 2000 accounted for much of the increase in sales, which would have represented a 2 percent increase if exchange rates had been comparable (2000 sales would have been $1.88 billion). More than 70 percent of IFF sales are generated outside the United States.

In the first quarter of 2002, IFF shares were selling at $34.91 per share. The 52-week high price was $35.95 and the 52-week low was $20.75. The annual dividend for 2001 was $0.60. IFF's operating margin in 2001 was 10.18 percent and its gross margin was 42.32 percent. Its profit margin was 6.29 percent for the year.

In 2000, IFF acquired one-time competitor Bush Boake Allen (BBA) for $970 million.

ANALYSTS' OPINIONS

The consumer and personal care industries were soft performers in 2000 and 2001, due in part to a weakened economy in the United States and globally, and also due to increasing competition in the industry.

Industry conditions, as well as IFF's increased debt following the debt-financed merger with BBA, caused Standard and Poor's (S&P) to downgrade the company from an A rating to a BBB+. Although S&P predicted stable sales in IFF's markets, it noted that the challenging sales environment would not only require companies like IFF to continue to offer new products and stay on top of consumer demands but also the finished products produced by its customers would be required to compete in price. S&P stated that while consumers will always buy staple products during even the toughest economic conditions, shoppers often opt for cheaper brands and private label goods and that such a preference could adversely affect IFF's customers if they could not compete with low-cost goods.

HISTORY

International Flavors and Fragrances, Inc. traces its beginnings back to N.V. Polak and Schwarz's Essence-fabrieken, a Dutch company formed in 1889. In 1909 the company opened a site in the United States. In 1958 Polak and Schwarz merged with van Ameringen-Haebler, Inc., creating an instant global player in the flavors and fragrances industry.

STRATEGY

In 2000 IFF acquired Bush Boake Allen, Inc.(BBA), an international chemical company with $499 million in annual sales. The acquisition made IFF the largest flavors and fragrances company in the world, with annual sales just under $2 billion, and strengthened its global position, particularly in India, its product line, its customer base, and its management pool.

Only a month before the acquisition, IFF implemented a global reorganization plan in its Business Development and Operations divisions rather than separate the flavors and fragrances divisions. Business Development took on the driving of top-line growth, including strategy, consumer research, product development, global sales and marketing, and technical application. The Operations arm of IFF became responsible for the global supply chain, increasing productivity, manufac-

FAST FACTS:

About International Flavors and Fragrances, Inc.

Ownership: International Flavors and Fragrances, Inc. is a publicly owned company traded on the New York Stock Exchange.

Ticker Symbol: IFF

Officers: Richard A. Goldstein, Chmn. and CEO, 60, 2001 salary $943,750, 2001 bonus $374,693; Carol A. Lobbosco, EVP Global Business Development, 62, 2001 salary $537,500, 2001 bonus $540,000; Julian W. Boyden, EVP Integration, 57, 2001 salary $493,750, 2001 bonus $160,125; D. Wayne Howard, EVP Global Operations, 46, 2001 salary $393,750, 2001 bonus $128,100; Stephen A. Block, SVP, Gen. Counsel, and Sec., 57, 2001 salary $382,500, 2001 bonus $124,898

Employees: 5,929

Chief Competitors: International Flavors and Fragrances' top competitors include ICI, McCormick, and Sensient.

turing, customer service, quality control, logistics, and distribution. Under the restructuring, IFF estimated a $70-million cost savings, half of which would be realized in 2001 and the other half in 2002.

INFLUENCES

Increasing competition is a major influence on IFF's performance. The company estimates it has approximately 50 competitors in U.S. and global markets. Although many factors play a role in the company's standing, the creative skills and technological advances of each company are key. IFF's acquisition of BBA was primarily to strengthen its pool of technology, global locations, and technical and creative talent.

Another constant influence on IFF is government regulation. The company's products are subject to regulation by the Food and Drug Administration, the Agriculture Department, the Bureau of Alcohol, Tobacco and Firearms, the Environmental Protection Agency, the Occupational Safety and Health Administration, the Drug Enforcement Administration and state authorities. IFF's

CHRONOLOGY:

Key Dates for International Flavors and Fragrances, Inc.

1909: Polak and Schwarz, a thriving European aroma chemical business, opens a site in the United States

1917: A.L. van Ameringen comes from the Netherlands to the United States to work for Polak and Schwarz; Van Ameringen soon leaves the company to start his own essential oils import business in downtown Manhattan

1920: A.L. van Ameringen expands his business and begins manufacturing aromatic chemicals and flavors in a New Jersey plant

1929: Van Ameringen partners with Dr. William T. Haebler to acquire an aromatic chemical plant in New Jersey; the new company, van Ameringen-Haebler, Inc., thrives despite the economic depression in the United States

1952: Van Ameringen-Haebler establishes Aroma Chemical Plant and Aroma Chemical Research in Union Beach, New Jersey

1956: Haebler dies and van Ameringen resigns from the company as president but continues to serve as chairman of the board

1958: Polak and Schwarz and van Ameringen-Haebler merge; the new company is named International Flavors and Fragrances and is immediately a major supplier in the worldwide flavor and fragrance industry

1961: International Flavors and Fragrances (IFF) is incorporated and offers common stock to the public in October; the company's sales for the year are $36.4 million

1963: IFF introduces gas chromatography, a retention index system that becomes the industry standard

1964: IFF is listed on the NYSE; sales for the year are $52.2 million

1967: IFF opens a research and development center in Union Beach, New Jersey; the following year, the company opens the Monell Chemical Senses Center to research taste and smell

1981: Olfactory Research Fund becomes the Sense of Smell Institute

1982: IFF partners with Yale University's Psychophysiology Department to study the concept of aroma science—the effect of fragrance on human emotion

1985: IFF invents Living Flower technology, which captures a flower's aroma while it's at its peak. The technology creates major changes in perfume production technology industry-wide

1987: IFF develops techniques for identifying fragrance combinations that affect specific human emotions; they call the process Mood-Mapping

1994: The two-year renovation of IFF's New York world headquarters is completed; IFF wins "Food and Beverage marketing Innovation of the Year" award for its Living Flavor technology

2000: Richard A. Goldstein becomes chairman and CEO of IFF, following Eugene P. Grisanti; IFF introduces iPlots, a sensory and analytical tool that identifies sensory thresholds and intensity; sales are $1.9 billion

2001: IFF adds a hydroponic greenhouse in Union Beach, New Jersey, and forms a strategic alliance with AG Scent Communication Group; the two jointly develop flavor and fragrance technology and devices

foreign subsidiaries and operations are subject to similar agency regulation. In 2001, IFF spent more than $18 million in operating expenses and capital projects to comply with government regulations, particularly regulations addressing discharge of materials into the environment.

CURRENT TRENDS

Social trends have the greatest impact on demand for IFF products. Such factors as personal income,

employment of women, teenage population, leisure time, health awareness, and urbanization affect consumer tastes and tendency to purchase luxury items, hair care products, personal products, and personal fragrances.

The company's flavor markets are deeply impacted by similar influences and trends, which can affect demand for convenience foods, low-fat and low-cholesterol foods, soft drinks, and exotic or improved flavoring for foods.

IFF's perfumers and flavorists work in 38 laboratories in 27 countries. The company also maintains a research center in Union Beach, New Jersey. It spent $135 some million in 2001 on research and development activities to stay on top of trends and consumer tastes.

The company reported in its annual report for 2001 that it had never had a work stoppage or strike and that it considered its employee relations satisfactory.

PRODUCTS

IFF products are used by its customers to manufacture a wide variety of flavorings and fragrances. Fragrance products are used in soaps, detergents, cosmetic creams, lotions and powders, lipsticks, after-shave lotions, hair preparations, candles, air fresheners, cleaners, and perfumes and colognes. In 2001 fragrance products made up 55 percent of IFF sales. Flavor products are used in the food and beverage industries in soft drinks, candies, baked goods, desserts, prepared foods, dietary foods, dairy products, drink powders, pharmaceuticals, snack foods, and alcoholic beverages. In 2001 flavor products made up 45 percent of IFF sales.

IFF products are mainly compounds of ingredients. The combination in any one compound can be a major factor in consumer preference for one product over another. Most IFF products are produced exclusively for individual customers.

GLOBAL PRESENCE

IFF operates manufacturing and research sites throughout the world: in the United States, the Netherlands, the United Kingdom, Spain, Switzerland, Brazil, Germany, Mexico, India, China, Japan, and Australia.

The company's sales are largely generated outside the United States. Sales in the United States were $597.1 million in 2001. European sales accounted for $576.0 million in 2001. That same year, sales were $127.4 million, $256.5 million, and $286.2 million in Central Asia and the Middle East, Latin America, and the Asia Pacific, respectively. The area that grew the most between 2000 and 2001 was the Central Asia region, where sales jumped by 59 percent between 2000 and 2001.

EMPLOYMENT

IFF offers careers that promise "a great place to work: innovation, creativity, passion and excellence." The company frequently seeks scientists as well as sales and administrative personnel.

At year's end 2001, the company had 5,972 employees, 1,770 of which were employed in the United States.

SOURCES OF INFORMATION

Bibliography

Floreno, Anthony. "IFF Acquires Bush Boake Allen in $970 MM Cash-for-Stock Deal." *Chemical Market Reporter*, 2 October 2000.

Harris, Lori. "Credit Quality for U.S. Consumer Products Sector Continues to Decline."*Standard and Poor's*, 19 October 2001.

Harris, Lori. "More Pain in Store for Speculative-Grade Firms in U.S. Household Products/Personal Care Sector." *Standard & Poor's*, 28 February 2002.

"International Flavors & Fragrances, Inc.: Capsule." *Hoover's*, 1 April 2002.

"Significant Developments: International Flavors and Fragrances." *Market Guide*, 28 January 2002.

For an annual report:
on the Internet at: http://www.iff.com

Investigate companies by their Standard Industrial Classification Codes, also known as SIC codes. International Flavors and Fragrances, Inc.'s primary SICs are:

2068 Other Food Manufacturing

2087 Flavoring Extracts and Flavoring Syrups Not Elsewhere Classified

2099 Food Preparations Not Elsewhere Classified

2833 Medicinal Chemicals and Botanical Products

2834 Pharmaceutical Preparations

2844 Blending and Compounding Perfume Bases, Perfumes Manufacturing, Colognes Manufacturing

2899 Chemical Preparations Not Elsewhere Classified

Also investigate companies by their North American Industry Classification System Codes, also known as NAICS codes. International Flavors and Fragrances, Inc.'s primary NAICS codes are:

311930 Flavoring Syrup and Concentrate Manufacturing

311942 Spice and Extract Manufacturing

311999 All Other Miscellaneous Food Manufacturing

325410 Pharmaceutical and Medicine Manufacturing

325411 Medicinal and Botanical Manufacturing

325412 Pharmaceutical Preparation Manufacturing

325620 Blending and Compounding Perfume Bases, Perfumes Manufacturing, Colognes Manufacturing

iVillage Inc.

FOUNDED: 1995
VARIANT NAME: iVillage.com

Contact Information:

HEADQUARTERS: 500-512 Seventh Avenue
   New York, NY 10018
PHONE: (212)600-6000
FAX: (212)600-6100
URL: http://www.ivillage.com

OVERVIEW

iVillage Inc. is the leading site for women on the Internet. In 2001 it had nearly 6 million registered members and reached an estimated 9.4 percent of the total online population. By the beginning of 2001, it was getting about 214 million page views a month. iVillage convinced advertisers that it was able to reach a lucrative and elusive segment of Web surfers—women between the ages of 18 and 55. iVillage attracted them by means of a focused group of online communities centered around a variety of topics of interest to women, including birthing and child care, beauty, careers, and astrology.

iVillage is an e-business that maintains a virtual presence on the World Wide Web. Its Web site, iVillage.com, is organized around specific content areas: astrology, babies, beauty, books, diet and fitness, entertainment, food, games, health, home and garden, lamaze, money, news and issues, parenting, pets, pregnancy, relationships, relaxation, and work. iVillage and its channels are open to all members. Anyone can become a member by simply registering—there is no cost. iVillage members can also take part in chat rooms, use message boards, and receive an email account.

iVillage has expanded its offerings for women through the acquisition of companies with related content. Lamaze Publishing, for example, is a for-profit company that produces educational material about childbirth and infant care, in both English and Spanish, for maternity nurses and other healthcare professionals who are in regular direct contact with new parents. Similarly, iVillage's The Newborn Channel targets new mothers through satellite broadcasts in more than 1,000 U.S. hospitals. In a completely different vein, the Web site Astrology.com provides women with daily horoscopes and personalized forecasts related to family, relationships, money, and work. It has also put its own e-retailing system in place by which it produces and sells instantaneous individual digital astrological charts. Astrology.com is responsible for a significant portion of iVillage's total traffic. The company exploits the popularity of Astrology.com to draw visitors to other parts of the iVillage Web site.

iVillage has established important joint ventures with other companies. It has partnered with Unilever PLC, one of its major sponsors, to launch Substance.com, a beauty site that offers women tips, expert advice, and product recommendations on hair, nail and skin care, and cosmetics. Unilever distributes free samples of its products on the site, while iVillage built a community that Unilever can use for market research. iVillage's U.K. Web site was a joint venture with Tesco PLC, the U.K.'s largest food retailer that operates the world's largest grocery Web site.

COMPANY FINANCES

In the brief course of its existence, iVillage has experienced the euphoric peaks as well as the dismal depths of the Internet economy. After an astonishing initial public offering at the height of the e-boom in 1999, iVillage's share price plummeted by more than $90 until, by 2001, it had dropped below the $1 mark and was facing delisting by NASDAQ. A change in management halted the slide. Although as 2002 began iVillage had never reported a profitable year, it continued to inch closer to profitability. iVillage reported net revenues for fiscal 2000 of $76.35 million, a 108 percent increase over 1999. The company continued to be a losing venture nonetheless, posting a net loss for the year of $191.4 million, a 64 percent increase over the firm's 1999 loss. The 2000 loss translated to a loss of $6.45 per share.

iVillage showed relative improvement in the first three quarters of 2001. Revenues fell to $42 million from $57.7 million in the same period of 2000. However, the firm's net loss for those three periods was only $38.7 million, compared to a whopping $181.3 million in the first nine months of 2000, a 78 percent improvement. The improvement was reflected in iVillage's share price too, which rose from a meager $0.37 in March 2001 to $2.50 in early 2002.

By the beginning of 2001, more than 90 percent of iVillage's revenues were derived from advertising and sponsorships. One reason iVillage was able to survive the shakeout that came when the dotcom bubble burst in late 2000 was that, unlike other similar Internet businesses, few of iVillage's revenues came from traditional online banner advertising. Instead, it has relied on longer-term sponsorship deals with major companies. In 2000 about 23 percent of all iVillage's ad and sponsorship revenues came from its five largest advertisers. About 5 per-

FAST FACTS:
About iVillage Inc.

Ownership: iVillage is a publicly owned company traded on the NASDAQ National Market.

Ticker Symbol: IVIL

Officers: Douglas W. McCormick, Chmn. and CEO, 51, 2000 base salary $252,780; Nancy Evans, Co-Founder and Editor-in Chief, 50, 2000 base salary, $325,144; Steven A. Elkes, SVP, Sponsorship, 39, 2000 base salary $242,578

Employees: 309

Principal Subsidiary Companies: The company operates two Web sites: www.iVillage.com (U.S.) and www.iVillage.co.uk (U.K.). The latter is operated by iVillage UK Limited. iVillage's other subsidiaries include Astrology.com; Lamaze Publishing, a company that produces books, magazines, and other information about birthing and infant care; and The Newborn Channel, a satellite television network with instructional programming for new mothers that broadcasts into approximately 1,000 U.S. hospitals.

Chief Competitors: iVillage is a media company and competes with a variety of firms that include magazine and newspaper publishers, broadcast companies, and Web sites. Some of iVillage's competitors include Oxygen.com, condenet.com, CBS, NBC, America Online, Gruner & Jahr, Disney Publishing, and Children's Television Workshop.

cent of iVillage's sponsorship and advertising revenues were in the form of barter, or services traded for services.

ANALYSTS' OPINIONS

In 2000, most analysts remained extremely positive about iVillage's prospects despite its relatively bleak financial history. *BusinessWeek Online* called the late 2001 upturn in its share price a sign that Wall Street thinks iVillage will ultimately be a survivor. iVillage was seen as a leading and sustainable site for women on the World Wide Web. "iVillage has progressively grown its business by maintaining its focus on content that is relevant and specific to the needs of women. We believe

CHRONOLOGY:

Key Dates for iVillage Inc.

1995: iVillage Inc. is founded in New York, New York

1996: Parent Soup, the first iVillage site, debuts on AOL

1997: Life Soup, iVillage's first site specifically for women, goes online

1998: Total investments in iVillage reach $67 million

1999: iVillage's initial public offering raises more than $1 billion

2000: iVillage purchases KnowledgeWeb.com and renames it Astrology.com; iVillage and Unilever partner to form Substance.com; iVillage sells its iBaby ecommerce arm; Doug McCormack replaces iVillage founder, Candice Carpenter as CEO

2001: iVillage merges with Women.com to form the largest site for women on the Web; iVillage acquires control of Business Women's Network; iVillage reports the first profitable quarter in its history

that there is a compelling market opportunity for Web sites that are exclusively targeting women, driven both by their large numbers online and their importance to the economy, thus making this demographic group attractive to advertisers and merchants alike," observed a 2001 report by Bluestone Capital Partners. "We believe the company will capture a disproportionate amount of the advertising dollars that are expected to migrate from traditional media to the Internet." Positive signs included the site's steadily increasing membership, iVillage's above average "stickiness" (the length of time visitors spend at the site), and the respect it has garnered in both the Internet and bricks-and-mortar economies. Bluestone also noted that iVillage used its marketing budget more wisely than competitors, evidenced by a sharply declining rate of market costs to visitor ratio.

HISTORY

iVillage was the brain child of Candice Carpenter, seen by some as an overbearing manipulator, but by oth-

ers as a visionary genius. Carpenter received degrees from both Stanford and Harvard, and served as the president of TimeLife Video, before signing on as a consultant with America Online in 1995. At the time she admitted to knowing nothing about the nascent Internet, that she was even "technophobic," but was impressed by the online communities she found at AOL. Such communities were the future of the Internet, she realized. She took the idea and used it to create a branded media firm.

Carpenter, with Robert Levitan and Nancy Evans, the founder and editor of *Family Life* magazine, worked out the first business plan. It included three communities centered broadly on family, health, and careers. The name they chose, iVillage, was meant to suggest an intimate community; "i" as in "Internet" was the online prefix then in vogue. iVillage found investors rapidly. AOL was the most important—it was the first time it had given financial support to an independent company. After Parent Soup, iVillage's first channel, debuted in January 1996 other money flowed in, from the Tribune Company as well as from various venture capitalists.

iVillage was originally intended to support itself with advertising. In June 1996, however, it broadened its business plan to include e-tailing, launching the Parent Soup General Store. Ultimately it was iVillage's content that was responsible for attracting visitors to Parent Soup: directories of experts; articles of interest; forums and online chats on topics relevant to parents; advice on the most pressing problems, such as childhood illness, development, and nutrition; as well as interactive surveys and polls. Parent Soup was followed by About Work, the second community devoted to career and the workplace.

iVillage was not originally conceived as a site for women. However, it was soon evident that it was drawing a disproportionate number of female visitors. More significantly, it was attracting women who were well-educated, successful, and in the prime of their lives, a demographic group that most advertisers would kill to reach. At the time, it was being predicted that 34 million women were about to go online for the first time, and that by 2000 that number would grow fivefold. iVillage's prospects looked promising indeed.

By spring 1998, however, iVillage was still operating deeply in the red. It was able nonetheless to attract another $32.5 million in investments. The following March, at the height of the Internet craze, the firm launched a spectacular stock offering that, despite naysayers on Wall Street, succeeded beyond anyone's wildest hopes. Within a year, though, reality caught up with the company. Its shares plunged to less than $10 a share, and Douglas McCormick, the former CEO of the Lifetime cable TV network, was brought in to replace Candice Carpenter as president. McCormick's first move was to dramatically move the company out of e-tailing by selling off its iBaby arm that it had purchased less than a year before.

The shake-up continued in July 2000 when McCormick replaced Carpenter as iVillage's CEO. Carpenter's departure gave rise to speculation. Had she resigned or been fired? Some blamed her departure on her mercurial, often abrasive personality, which was said to have caused iVillage to have one of the highest rates of employee turnover in the online industry. Others said that iVillage's poor earnings record led to her downfall. There were also questions about Carpenter's handling of iVillage finances. Within a year she was gone completely, having left the iVillage board of directors as well.

Some observers questioned the wisdom of putting a man so visibly at the helm of the Internet's leading site for women, and McCormick was not able to turn the firm's fortunes around right away. A year after he was brought in, iVillage seemed to be in deep trouble—its stock had dropped under the dollar mark and was threatened with delisting by NASDAQ. Eventually he managed to steady the course. McCormick's most significant achievement was the February 2001 acquisition of Women.com, iVillage's leading online competitor. The company was expected to report its first profit sometime in 2002.

STRATEGY

Since iVillage abandoned e-tailing as a revenue source in 2000, it relied exclusively on advertising and corporate sponsorships for its revenues. An important element in the iVillage corporate strategy is not to rely on traditional advertising, for example the banner ads, a revenue source that has proven to be an Achilles heel for many e-businesses. Instead, iVillage seeks "sponsors" to whom it offers cost-effective access to one of the largest, most affluent group of women currently online. iVillage sponsors get far more than simply an advertising platform. iVillage offers a ready-made, interactive community where a company's new products can be introduced and evaluated, product and market research can be carried out, detailed product information can be disseminated, and highly targeted mass e-mailings can be generated. Given the nature of the Internet, sponsors are able to engage in *direct* communication with their customers via iVillage's online forums and chat rooms, a possibility that doesn't exist with most other advertising media. iVillage is able to provide unique access to a firm's core market group at costs that are lower in the long run than traditional advertising. iVillage sometimes develops individual pages on its Web site as tie-ins with its sponsors offerings. In general, iVillage's sponsorships have the added advantage of longer terms than advertising contracts, and they are frequently exclusive. Among the company's sponsors are Fuji Photo Film USA, Glaxo Wellcome, Johnson & Johnson, Kimberly-Clark, and Unilever.

INFLUENCES

The Internet stock crash of late 2000 proved to be an important turning point for iVillage Inc. Most importantly, by not going under, it proved that it had the support of its sponsors and backers. Immediately afterward it was able to absorb its biggest competitor, Women.com, and forge a major sponsorship agreement with that Web site's main backer, the Hearst Corporation. The result of those two deals was to make iVillage.com the undisputed leader in Internet sites for women, a fact that could only help it attract more revenues from manufacturers looking to reach the lucrative women's market.

CURRENT TRENDS

iVillage is going beyond traditional Internet models. It is no longer simply a group of online communities. It has given up all of its e-tailing businesses. Instead it is carving out a niche as a sort of online facilitator, a mediator between product manufacturers and their potential market. More and more, iVillage offers companies a combination of its reputation, its membership base, and its expertise in creating attractive and effective virtual realms. It creates designer Web sites that blur the distinction between "community" and "commerce." A prime example is the site Substance.com. On its surface, Substance.com is a site dedicated to beauty for women—skin care and hair care, along with product recommendations. However, the site is also a platform for iVillage's partner Unilever to market and evaluate new products.

PRODUCTS

In December 2000, iVillage entered an agreement with Hindustan Lever Ltd., a Unilever subsidiary, to launch a Web site targeted at women in India. iVillage will license its technology to Hindustan Lever, which will finance and operate the new site. iVillage will receive an annual royalty.

CORPORATE CITIZENSHIP

Through its subsidiary Lamaze Publishing, iVillage distributes free literature on pregnancy, childbirth, and parenting to maternity nurses and other healthcare professionals who deal directly with new parents. The cost of the materials is offset by advertisers interested in reaching young families.

GLOBAL PRESENCE

iVillage UK Limited, a foreign subsidiary of iVillage Inc. based in the United Kingdom, operates

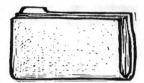

iVILLAGE'S SPECTACULAR IPO

In 1999 iVillage launched one of the most spectacular stock offerings in market history. iVillage's initial public offering (IPO) was made at the height of the craze for Internet stocks. However, because the company had never had a profitable quarter, many investors were still dubious about its chances. The day the stock debuted on the NASDAQ, shares were priced at $14. Incredibly, the opening bid was $95.88! Before the first day was over, the price had risen as high as $100. Based on this first day of trading, iVillage, a company that had never made a cent in profits, had a worth on Wall Street of about $2.22 billion.

---

www.iVillage.co.uk. The Web site is based on the original iVillage model, but it presents content specifically tailored for women in Great Britain and Ireland. The U.K. iVillage was a joint venture of iVillage and Tesco PLC, the operator of the largest grocery store chain in Britain. In exchange for its products and services being integrated into and prominently featured on the U.K. iVillage site, Tesco gives iVillage marketing support by means of in-store promotions, mailings, and exposure on Tesco's own Web sites. By 2001, iVillage's U.K. sister site had 25 U.K. advertisers and sponsors.

EMPLOYMENT

In early 2001, iVillage employed 309 full-time workers, nearly all of whom worked in the company's New York headquarters. Approximately 96 worked in sales and marketing; 85 in editorial and community; 53 in administration and customer service; and 75 in technology, operations, and support.

SOURCES OF INFORMATION

Bibliography

Brennan, Gerald E. "iVillage Inc." *International Directory of Company Histories.* Detroit: Gale Group, 2002.

"iVillage Inc." *Hoover's Company Profiles,* 2002. Available at http://www.hoovers.com.

iVillage Inc. Home Page, 2002. Available at http://www.iVillage.com.

For an annual report:

on the Internet at: http://www.iVillage.com/invest **or** write: iVillage Inc., 500-512 Seventh Avenue, New York, NY 10018

For additional industry research:

Investigate companies by their Standard Industrial Classification Codes, also known as SICs. iVillage Inc.'s primary SIC is:

7379 Computer Related Services, Not Elsewhere Classified

Also investigate companies by their North American Industry Classification System codes, also known as NAICS codes. iVillage Inc.'s primary NAICS code is:

541512 Computer Systems Design Services

Jenny Craig Inc.

FOUNDED: 1983

OVERVIEW

Jenny Craig Inc. (JCI) provides a comprehensive weight loss and weight management program through its Jenny Craig Weight Loss Centres. As of the end of January 2002, JCI operated 428 company-owned and 115 franchised centers in the United States and 115 company-owned and 38 franchised centers in Canada, Australia, and New Zealand. The center served approximately 74,000 U.S. customers and 23,000 international customers. The program combines weight loss counseling and motivation with a nutritionally balanced, low-calorie diet. The foundation of the company's business is Jenny's Cuisine, the food product line sold to clients as part of the overall weight loss program. Both men and women are customers of JCI; however the majority of participants are women who want to lose 30 pounds or more.

After experiencing robust growth through the 1980s and into the early 1990s, during which time the number of company-owned centers and franchises reached 643 and 138, respectively, the business began to decline during the late 1990s. In August 2001, JCI was removed from the New York Stock Exchange, after which the company began trading on the Over-The-Counter Bulletin Board (OCTBB). In February 2002 JCI announced its intentions to accept a buyout bid from ACI Capital, with the backing of DB Capital Partners, the private equity arm of Deutsche Bank. On January 28, 2002, cofounder Sid Craig stepped down as the company's chief executive officer. However, both Sid and Jenny Craig are part of the investment group that made the acquisition and remain as members of the board of directors.

Contact Information:

HEADQUARTERS: 11355 N. Torrey Pines Rd.
    La Jolla, CA 92037
PHONE: (858)812-7000
FAX: (858)812-2713
TOLL FREE: (800)597-5366
EMAIL: jennycraig@tpli.com
URL: http://www.jennycraig.com

FINANCES:

*Jenny Craig Inc.
Revenues, 1997-2001
(million dollars)*

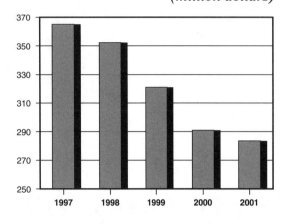

COMPANY FINANCES

For fiscal year 2001, ending June 30, Jenny Craig Inc. generated total revenues of $283.6 million, resulting in a net loss of $19.3 million. These figures compare negatively to those reported in fiscal 1997, at which time the company posted a net income of $8.3 million on revenues of $365.1 million. Net income fell to $2.1 million in fiscal 1998, and in 1999 the company posted its first net loss, totaling $2.8 million. In fiscal 2000 and 2001 the losses increased to $7.1 million and $19.3 million, respectively. After peaking at $33.88 a share in January of 1992, during the third quarter of 2001 stock prices hit a low of $1.01 per share before rebounding to $3.15 at the end of January of 2002. Upon the announcement of the proposed buyout by ACI Capital, trading increased and stock prices jumped to a 52-week high of $5.12. As part of the purchase agreement, stockholders received $5.30 per share, making the deal worth approximately $115 million. During the first two quarters of fiscal 2002, JCI regained some financial footing. For the six months ending December 31, 2001, JCI reported a net income of $23.6 million on total revenues of $142.9 million, compared to a net loss of $23.3 million on revenues of $127.1 million during the same time period of 2000.

ANALYSTS' OPINIONS

Analysts consider the acquisition of Jenny Craig Inc. by ACI Capital as a positive move for the company and viewed the appointment of Kent Kreh, former chief exec-

utive officer of Weight Watchers, as a good sign for hopes for the company's financial turn-around. Other positive signs include the company's low debt level and cash assets of $52 million. Nonetheless, analysts remain concerned that the diet market has changed so significantly in recent years that JCI will not be able to reclaim its original place in the industry.

HISTORY

Jenny Craig met her future husband, Sid Craig, when she joined Body Contours, a fitness center in New Orleans, Louisiana. Sid Craig was half-owner of Body Contours. When the couple married in 1979, Jenny became active in the business' development. By 1982 revenues reached $35 million. The Craigs sold Body Contours in 1983 and used the $3.5 million they received in the transaction to start Jenny Craig Inc. Temporarily barred by a noncompetition clause from doing business in the diet and fitness industry in the United States, the Craigs moved to Australia to open their fitness centers. Having established 69 weight loss centers in Australia generating some $50 million in gross income, in 1985 the Craigs returned to the United States and opened 13 centers in Los Angeles followed by six center openings in Chicago. By 1987 JCI was operating 46 U.S.-based centers and 114 international centers.

Having entered into business in the infancy of the diet industry, JCI grew at a tremendous pace during the late 1980s and early 1990s. The Craigs considered taking their company public in 1987, but weak market conditions caused them to reconsider. By 1991 the market had sufficiently rebounded for them to decide to go public. With the financial backing of a Wall Street investment bank that raised $100 million to support the initial public offering, JCI became a publicly owned company in October 1991. Issuing 3.5 million shares at $21 per share, the offering generated $73.5 million. After selling an additional 1.65 million shares, the Craigs retained a 59 percent share in their company.

By 1993 JCI was at its peak, operating 794 weight loss centers in the United States, Canada, Australia, and New Zealand. Revenues reached more than $490 million. However, the market was drying up quickly, and the tide seemed to be turning against JCI. In 1990 JCI was named in a class action lawsuit that claimed a link between the diet program and gallbladder problems. In addition, JCI was named in 11 personal injury cases. The suits were eventually settled even though the link between the diet and health problems was never proved. Nonetheless, the publicity prompted the Federal Trade Commission to investigate JCI's advertising practices. During the same period, dieting was receiving bad press from the medical community as it disclosed the dangers of "yo-yo" dieting, producing studies that suggested repeated cycles of losing and regaining weight can cause health problems.

Despite the market indicators, JCI continued to expand, opening 89 new centers and repurchasing 41 franchises in 1992, and adding 100 new centers and repurchasing 48 franchises in 1993. Some investors claimed the rapid expansion inflated sales figures, camouflaging the company's financial problems. Although total revenues increased by 6 percent in fiscal 1993 over fiscal 1992, individual company-owned weight loss centers revenues averaged 10 percent less than the previous year.

JCI reacted to the downturn in the market by revamping the program to include a wider variety of choices and more flexibility. Despite these efforts, membership continued to decline. The company was further affected by bad publicity in 1997 when the Federal Trade Commission charged JCI with false advertising and required the company to accompany its stories of success with a disclaimer that informed the public that the results reported were not typical.

The company's financial troubles continued to multiply, with net income turning into net loss in 1999. During the summer of 2000, the Craigs offered to purchase all outstanding stock for $3.75 per share, but then decided to withdraw the offer after deciding the weak market did not support the buyout. When the offer was removed, investors responded and stock prices fell. In early 2001 the New York Stock Exchange filed to remove JCI's listing unless the company could increase its market value from $32 million to $50 million. Unable to do so, JCI was delisted in August of 2002. Stocks were then traded on the OCTBB, and the Craigs considered selling the company. After financial consultants were hired to advise the company on the matter of a sale, JCI proceeded in shopping for a buyer. On January 28, 2002, the company announced its intentions to sell out to ACI Capital. Although not all shareholders agreed with the decision, the Craigs controlled 59 percent of the company and therefore could control the outcome. The deal was expected to be finalized in the second quarter of fiscal 2002.

FAST FACTS:
About Jenny Craig Inc.

Ownership: Jenny Craig Inc. is a private, wholly owned subsidiary of ACI Capital Company.

Officers: Kent Kreh, Chmn.; Patricia Larchet, 39, Pres. and COO, 2001 salary $422,000; Duayne Weinger, 52, VChmn., 2001 salary $398,000; James Kelly, 40, CFO and VP

Employees: 3,510

Principal Subsidiary Companies: Jenny Craig Inc.'s subsidiaries include Jenny Craig Weight Loss Centres Inc., Jenny Craig Australia Holdings Inc., Jenny Craig International Inc., Jenny Craig Weight Loss Centres (Canada) Company, Jenny Craig Management Inc., Jenny Craig Operations Inc., Jenny Craig Products Inc., and Jenny Craig (Canada) Holdings, LLC.

Chief Competitors: Jenny Craig's primary direct competition comes from Weight Watchers International, as well as regional and local weight loss enterprises. The company also competes against a wide range of weight loss alternatives, including self-administered weight loss plans; Internet-based programs; programs administered by doctors, nutritionists, and dietitians; and government and nonprofit organizations that may administer weight-loss drugs or other medications.

STRATEGY

Unlike many products, few celebrities want to endorse a product or service that requires them to admit a weight problem. During the 1990s, Weight Watchers scored a major coup by enlisting Sarah Ferguson, the Duchess of York, to become the company's spokeswoman. In an ill-fated move, JCI attempted to cash in on the notoriety of Monica Lewinsky, the White House intern at the center of the sex scandal surrounding President Clinton. When word got out in December 1999 that JCI had hired Lewinsky, investors reacted quickly and stock prices rose. However, as soon as the advertisements began appearing in January 2000, controversy was sparked immediately. The media picked up the story, giv-

ing JCI some much needed media exposure; unfortunately, the feedback from both the press and the public was less than positive. In fact, some JCI centers refused to run the ads in their areas, claiming that Lewinsky should not be held up as anyone's role model, and late night talk shows hosts such as Jay Leno and David Letterman had a heyday with the story. As quickly as stock prices had risen, they then dropped. By February the ads were removed from the air and the campaign abandoned. JCI subsequently dropped the advertising agency that developed the campaign.

Another strategic misstep took place during the 1990s when the weight-loss drug known as fen-phen was introduced on the market. At first JCI refused to advocate the drug, but under pressure from increased sales of competitors, added it to the program's regimen. Consequently, when the drug was withdrawn in 1997 after being deemed unsafe, JCI lost approximately $15 mil-

CHRONOLOGY:

Key Dates for Jenny Craig Inc.

1983: Sid and Jenny Craig form Jenny Craig, Inc.

1985: Operates 69 weight loss centers in Australia, 13 centers in Los Angeles, and 6 centers in Chicago

1987: Operations grow to 46 U.S. centers and an additional 114 locations in other countries

1991: Completes initial public offering, issuing 3.5 million shares at $21 per share

1993: Despite negative publicity generated by an ongoing investigation by the Federal Trade Commission into Jenny Craig's advertising practices, outlet total reaches 794 but stock drops to $6.25 per share

1999: Launches e-commerce on Web site and features former White House intern Monica Lewinsky in a controversial advertising campaign

2001: New York Stock Exchange suspends trading of Jenny Craig shares

2002: Jenny Craig agrees to sell out to ACI Capital in a public-to-private leveraged buyout; stockholders receive $5.30 per share

lion. The results of JCI's introduction of snack bars and beverages during the late 1990s was also unplanned. Intended as supplements to Jenny's Cuisines, clients began replacing menu items with the bars and beverages.

INFLUENCES

During JCI's peak years, cofounder Jenny Craig was the long-serving and well-received spokeswoman for her company, appearing in numerous television and print ads. But in 1995 a bizarre accident injured Craig's jaw and left her unable to speak for some time, prompting her to retire as spokeswoman. About the same time, the market was being inundated with new diet products and foods and nutritional supplements. Further, JCI's core group of customers, women of the baby boomer generation, were transitioning into latter life stages and were no longer as motivated to manage a strict diet regimen. Consequently during the late 1990s, JCI lost its identity in the public eye. The world of health, nutrition, and diet was chang-

ing and expanding rapidly. Prepackaged diet food products that listed nutritional values were not readily available in the 1980s when JCI launched its operations. Yet by the turn of the century, large sections of grocery store shelves and freezer space were dedicated to portion-controlled single serving menu items at a lesser cost than Jenny's Cuisine. Additionally, pharmacies stocked a variety of weight-loss pills, shakes, and bars, all of which posed competition to Jenny Craig Weight Loss Centres. Unlike the new line of products and Internet-based services, JCI must continue to maintain costly overhead expense such as property rentals and trained staff.

CURRENT TRENDS

JCI has reacted to the downturn in business by retaining its basic program structure, and providing additional services and broader choices to its clients. New programs include a vegetarian plan and a plan aimed at business travelers. During 2001 the company launched the Ultimate Choice program, which allows clients more flexibility in food choices. In the same year JCI began marketing a cookbook of healthy, easy-to-prepare recipes titled *30 Meals in 30 Minutes,* aimed at busy people with no time or desire to cook.

JCI has also upgraded its Web site to provide online menu planning. Clients can design and print customized menus. By making selections in advance, the customer can take advantage of more time available during the one-on-one sessions to discuss progress, results, and strategy for the upcoming week. The Web site also provides community support for its clients through email, message boards, and a 24-hour chat room. Jenny Craig Direct provides a new program for clients who do not have access to a JCI weight loss center or who prefer to participate from the privacy of home or office. The Direct program offers one-on-one consultation via telephone, and Jenny's Cuisine is delivered to the customer's door. Despite the changing market JCI plans to retain it holistic approach to weight loss and weight management and has no intentions of joining the trends toward quick fixes or pill-based dieting.

PRODUCTS

Jenny Craig Weight Loss Centres provide individual counseling to help customers identify and modify their eating habits. Jenny's Cuisine, the foundation of the diet and nutrition plan provided to participants, is manufactured under specific guidance of JCI dieticians. The food products are designed to provide portion- and calorie-controlled foods that are both nutritionally balanced and good flavored. All participants in a weight loss center are required to purchase meals. To participate in the program, customers pay a fixed service fee in addition

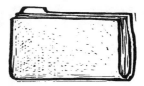

to the cost of the food. The Gold Program cost is $199. The Platinum Program, which includes such benefits as a Jenny Craig cookbook, program return privileges, and refund options if certain criteria are met, is priced at $295.

Upon enrollment of a customer, the center gathers information regarding the individual's height, weight, activity level, and overall health. Based on the information, a weight loss consultant then helps the participant establish a weight loss goal. With a goal in place, the customer begins the program by purchasing Jenny's Cuisine food products for the first week's meals. During the first half of the program, customers are advised to eat Jenny's Cuisine for every meal as well as fresh fruits, vegetables, and dairy products. One-on-one counseling is conducted weekly with a weight loss consultant; a participant's progress is monitored, meal plans are selected, and the customer leaves the center with another week's supply of Jenny's Cuisine. Eventually the participant's diet includes five days of Jenny's Cuisine and the customer is advised on meal plans and food selection for the remaining two days. Customers who remain active in the program continue weekly counseling and food purchases until the goal weight is achieved. On average, participants lose one to one and a half pounds per week and stay with the program for three to four months.

Jenny's Cuisine product line includes approximately 70 different items covering breakfast, lunch, dinner, and snack foods. The items are packaged as frozen meals, shelf-stable, and canned as well as snacks and dried foods. Meal items include blueberry waffles, French toast with berries, stuffed shells, baked turkey, pizza, chicken fajitas, teriyaki beefsteak, and chili con carne. Suppliers include Overhill Farms, Campbell's Soup Company, and International Home Foods.

GLOBAL PRESENCE

As of January 31, 2002, approximately 23,000 of JCI clients were located outside the United States, in Canada, Australia, and New Zealand. JCI, which originated in Australia in 1983, has more than 100 JCI weight loss centers, and New Zealand is home to 18 more centers.

CORPORATE CITIZENSHIP

JCI offers a wide variety of health and wellness information on the Jenny Craig Web site. A "Healthy Living" section provides advice and information on such topics as activity secrets, dining out dilemmas, grocery guide, eating right, portion control, relaxation, and finding your healthy weight. Personally, the Craigs have made numerous significant contributions to the community. They helped fund a health clinic in Mexico and once

THE BOSTON EIGHT

Jenny Craig Inc. made headlines of a different kind in 1995 when a group of men who became known as the "Boston Eight" brought a gender-discrimination suit against the company. The male employees of a Massachusetts Jenny Craig Centre filed suit in Massachusetts Superior Court for what they felt were condoned workplace practices that denigrated them because of their gender. In what came to be called a "reverse sexual harassment," the men claimed, among other complaints, that they were requested to shovel snow and were not invited for off-premise socializing with their mostly female co-workers.

funded the entire Australian Olympic team. A large donation to California State University at Fresno, Sid Craig's alma mater, resulted in the business school being named in his honor. In 1999, the Craigs donated nearly half of the funds needed to build the Jenny Craig Pavilion at the University of San Diego.

EMPLOYMENT

JCI typically employs individuals with training and experience in the fields of sales, customer service, and personal health. Jobs available include consultants, program directors, and center directors. Consultants work with clients, offering guidance and support during the weight loss program during weekly one-on-one counseling sessions as well as telephone contacts. Consultants are also responsible for meal selection and Jenny's Cuisine product sales. A program director works with customers to establish the most appropriate programs based on their individual needs. A center director manages the business aspects of the center, including sales, operations, customer service, and personnel. Career opportunities are also available at the company's headquarters in La Jolla, California, in a variety of fields including marketing, information technology, training, accounting, purchasing, distribution, and warehousing. JCI offers a basic employee benefit package that includes life, accidental death, and disability insurance, paid time off, and an employee assistance program. Optional benefits include comprehensive health insurance, supplemental life insurance, and a 401(k) savings plan with matching company contributions.

SOURCES OF INFORMATION

Bibliography

Cole, Benjamin Mark. "Diet Firm Deal Shines Light on Over-looked Small Caps." *Los Angeles Business Journal*, 4 February 2002.

Dickey, Fred. "Heavy Days at Jenny Craig The Diet Company Soared With Its Sensible Approach to Eating and Weight Control. Then the Market Changed—and the Company Didn't." *Los Angeles Times*, 11 June 2000.

Dillon, Nancy. "Jenny Craig Founders Pull Offer Off Table." *New York Daily News*, 15 August 2000.

Fong, Tony. "A Diet Change: Jenny Craig to Return to Private Ownership." *The San Diego Union-Tribune*, 29 January 2002.

Fugazy, Danielle. "Thin Stock Price Leads Jenny Private." *Buy-outs*, 18 February 2002.

Grant, Tina, ed. *International Directory of Company Histories*, Vol. 29. Detroit: St. James Press, 2000.

"Jenny Craig Redefines 'Fast Food' With Newest Collection of Recipes Designed for Busy People." *PR Newswire*, 14 August 2001.

Winter, Greg. "Jenny Craig Founders are Selling Chain in $115 Million Deal." *The New York Times*, 29 January 2002.

For an annual report:
on the Internet at: http://www.jennycraig.com

For additional industry research:
Investigate companies by their Standard Industrial Classification Codes, also known as SICs. Jenny Craig Inc.'s primary SICs are:

6794 Patent Owners And Lessors

7299 Miscellaneous Personal Services, Not Elsewhere Classified;

Also investigate companies by their North American Industry Classification System codes, also known as NAICS codes. Jenny Craig Inc.'s primary NAICS codes are:

533110 Owners and Lessors of Other Non-Financial Assets

812990 All Other Personal Services

Johnson Publishing Company Inc.

OVERVIEW

Johnson Publishing Company is the largest black-owned publishing company in the world. Its books and magazines target readers of color in North America, Africa, Europe, and the Caribbean and consciously strive to present a positive picture of black life and people. Johnson Publishing publishes the world's two leading black magazines; *EBONY*, the firm's flagship magazine, is the world's number one black magazine, while *Jet* is the world's largest black weekly. The firm's book publishing division has published works on history, cooking, black celebrities and other subjects. Johnson Publishing subsidiaries, Fashion Fair Cosmetics and Supreme Beauty Products, produce lines of women's makeup and hair-care products for women and men. As part of the EBONY Fashion Fair, the world's largest traveling fashion show, leading black male and female models visit over 200 cities a year. Johnson Publishing is fully owned and managed by founder John H. Johnson and his family.

COMPANY FINANCES

Johnson Publishing had sales of $400.4 million in 2000, an increase of about 3.5 percent over 1999. *EBONY* had a monthly circulation of 1.8 million in 2002, and *Jet*'s weekly circulation was more than one million. Johnson Publishing estimated, however, that some 13 million people the world over see each issue of *EBONY*, and more than 10 million see each issue of *Jet*. Approximately 90 percent of the two magazines' readers are black. Reportedly about 50 percent of all black Americans see a Johnson publication every month.

FOUNDED: 1942

Contact Information:
HEADQUARTERS: 820 S. Michigan Avenue
Chicago, IL 60605
PHONE: (312)222-9200
FAX: (312)222-0918
URL: http://www.ebony.com

FINANCES:

*Johnson Publishing Company
Net Sales, 1995-2001
(million dollars)*

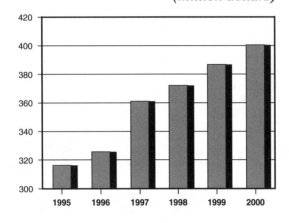

HISTORY

John H. Johnson, visionary founder of Johnson Publishing, has been described as the most successful black entrepreneur of the century. Born in Arkansas, his mother moved with him to Chicago as a child so he would be able to continue school past the eighth grade. Inspired by his mother's deep faith in him, Johnson applied himself vigorously to his studies and in the late 1930s won a scholarship to the University of Chicago. Johnson worried, however, that without a job he would not be able to accept the scholarship. By a stroke of good fortune, he met Harry H. Pace, the president of the Supreme Life Insurance Company, then the largest black-owned business in the northern United States. Pace took Johnson under his wing while he attended college part-time and made him his personal assistant at Supreme. The experience was a decisive one. It was Johnson's first exposure to a successful black business. "For the first time," he would later say, "I believed that success was possible for *me* in business." Twenty years later, in addition to his publishing firm, Johnson ended up owning Supreme Life Insurance.

One of John H. Johnson's jobs when he joined Supreme was compiling a monthly digest of articles about blacks and black affairs from the white press. It gave him the idea of publishing a monthly magazine for black readers comprised of such articles. In November 1942, with $500 in seed money, he launched *Negro Digest*. Supporting a periodical aimed at a black readership was difficult in the early days. Banks were unwilling to loan money to Johnson because he was black. He hoped to sell shares in the company, but was unable to

find investors. He came up with a variety of ideas to bring in cash. He offered lifetime subscriptions for $100. He set up a group of mail order companies that sold a wide variety of items, including wigs, vitamins, and hair care products. The mail order business provided income that supported the magazine while the magazine advertised the mail order companies. It was a business model that worked and Johnson continued to use mutually supporting companies into the twenty-first century.

Negro Digest eventually became *BLACK WORLD*. It continued publication until 1975 when it was discontinued due to low circulation. In 1945 Johnson established *EBONY*, the magazine that would make the company's fortune. A glossy magazine based on *Life*, then very popular among black readers, *EBONY* presented a mix of news and entertainment that was unprecedented. It featured subjects, writers, and editors, who were almost all black Americans. Within a year, Johnson got his first ad from a national company, Zenith Radio, and John H. Johnson knew his magazine would be a success. Years later when asked why he had succeeded where other black publishers had failed, John H. Johnson said a combination of factors had enabled him to succeed: he was in the right place at the right time, he had learned from the failures of others, and the black population in the United States at the end of World War II was ready for magazines produced with them in mind. In 1951, the same year he founded *Jet*, John H. Johnson was named one of the Ten Outstanding Young Men of the Year. Despite its successes, Johnson Publishing had to work hard, particularly in its early years, to find advertising dollars to support the magazines. For a long time white companies refused to consider advertising in Johnson's magazines. Only the persistence and the persuasiveness of John H. Johnson and his personally trained sales staff were able to break through the barriers to white advertising dollars.

Over the years Johnson Publishing introduced other magazines, including *EBONY Jr!*, *Black Stars*, *Tan*, and *EM*, all of which were eventually discontinued. However, the company continued to gain influence and respect. In 1972 John H. Johnson was awarded the Henry Johnson Fisher Award as Publisher of Year from the Magazine Publishers of America. In 1973, Johnson founded the Fashion Fair Cosmetics Company, in part to guarantee a source of advertising income. The company's revenues increased from about $30 million in 1972 to about $75 million in 1980 to nearly $250 million in 1990. In 1995 a South African edition of *EBONY* was launched; it was discontinued in 2000 when a large black middle class was slow to emerge in the country. Over the years Johnson Publishing has also been involved in television and radio broadcasting. EBONY/Jet was a long-time syndicated staple of black television in the 1980s and 1990s.

In 2002 the Johnson family remained the sole owner of the company. John H. Johnson, in his ninth decade, remained active as chairman and CEO. His daughter Linda Johnson Rice whom he had trained for over a decade, was poised to succeed him, and assume responsibility for the firm's daily operations. Johnson's wife, Eunice W. Johnson, continued to oversee the EBONY Fashion Fair.

STRATEGY

An essential strategy of the Johnson Publishing Company has been the development of businesses, which John H. Johnson calls "miniconglomerates," that create financial synergies. The most basic of these are his magazines and cosmetics firms, Fashion Fair Cosmetics and Supreme Beauty Products. Johnson considers his core business to be publishing. The cosmetics firms were established as a hedge against fluctuations in the advertising market, which provided most of *EBONY* and *Jet's* financial support. If outside advertising disappears, Fashion Fair and Supreme can provide a source of revenue.

A key policy of *EBONY* and other Johnson publications is to stress the positive side of black life. The firm is sometimes criticized for ignoring the unpleasant side of the black experience, but justifies its slant on the news by pointing to the overwhelmingly negative portrayal blacks customarily receive in the mainstream media. Johnson sees *EBONY* and *Jet* as counterweights to the way other media outlets portray blacks and black issues. In addition, he believes it is important to provide blacks with visible role models—the kind he had when he began working at the Supreme Life Insurance Company—to show them the things they want to achieve are possible. "We always play a positive role," John H. Johnson told the *Harvard Business Review,* "we are telling people what they can do rather than what they cannot do."

INFLUENCES

The fact that Johnson Publishing is black-owned and managed with a nearly exclusive black audience has naturally had a profound influence on the company. Bankers refused John H. Johnson loans to start his fledgling firm in the 1940s. Many white companies refused to advertise in Johnson publications in the 1940s, 1950s, and 1960s. In the early 1960s when John H. Johnson decided to move the company to a more modern structure in downtown Chicago, he ran up against the same walls of prejudice. He could not find a bank to finance the construction of a skyscraper. Johnson had to save his own money for ten years until he had enough for a smaller building. The firm moved into the new eleven-story headquarters in 1972. The company later boasted that it was the "the first building constructed in Chicago's loop by a black man since Jean Baptiste Pointe du Sable built his log cabin along the Chicago River in 1722."

FAST FACTS:
About Johnson Publishing Company Inc.

Ownership: Johnson Publishing is a privately owned company.

Officers: John H. Johnson, Publisher, Chmn., and CEO; Linda Johnson Rice, Pres. and COO; Eunice W. Johnson, Sec., Treas., and Dir. EBONY Fashion Fair

Employees: 2,614

Principal Subsidiary Companies: Johnson Publishing has offices in Chicago, New York City, Los Angeles and Washington, D.C. In addition to its magazine and book publishing ventures, the firm's subsidiaries, Fashion Fair Cosmetics and Supreme Beauty Products, offer a full line of beauty and hair care products for people of color.

Chief Competitors: Johnson Publishing competes with companies in both the publishing and cosmetics industries. Some primary competitors in the field of publishing include Time-Warner AOL, Essence Communications, Advance Publications, Forbes, Hearst, and Larry Flynt Publishing. Rivals in the cosmetics and perfume industry are L'Oreal, Revlon, and Mary Kay.

CURRENT TRENDS

From its birth until the onset of the twenty-first century, Johnson Publishing was under the direct leadership of its founder, John H. Johnson. When his daughter, Linda Johnson Rice, expressed an interest in working at the company, he developed a personal course of training for her, designed to groom her for the firm's leadership. In the late 1990s she assumed the positions of COO and President, and began to take over day-to-day management tasks. Rice was responsible for inaugurating the EBONY Web site and securing links to mail order firms such as Spiegel. Johnson Publishing will be influenced by the acumen of Linda Johnson Rice for many years to come.

PRODUCTS

John H. Johnson founded Fashion Fair Cosmetics after noticing that the models in the EBONY Fashion Fair

CHRONOLOGY:

Key Dates for Johnson Publishing Company Inc.

1942: Johnson Publishing is founded in Chicago, Illinois

1945: *EBONY* is founded

1946: *EBONY* gets its first advertising from a national company

1951: *Jet* is founded

1951: John H. Johnson is named an Outstanding Young Man of the Year

1972: John H. Johnson was awarded the Henry Johnson Fisher Award: Publisher of Year by the Magazine Publishers of America

1972: *EBONY Jr!* is founded

1973: Fashion Fair Cosmetics Company is founded

1975: *Black World* (formerly *Negro Digest*) is discontinued

1995: *EBONY South Africa* is founded

2000: *EBONY South Africa* is discontinued

had to mix their own makeup because the products sold by mainstream cosmetics companies weren't well matched to the skin tones of blacks. The company's subsidiary, Supreme Beauty Products, developed two lines of hair care products for blacks: Duke hair care for men, and Raveen for women. In 2002, Johnson's personal care items were sold in over 2500 stores worldwide. Johnson Publishing's Book Division published a number of books by black authors and on subjects of interest to blacks. Titles published in 2002 were *Forced Into Glory: Abraham Lincoln's White Dream* by Lerone Bennett Jr., the executive editor of *EBONY* and *Special Moments in African-American History 1955-1996: The Photographs of Moneta Sleet Jr.*

CORPORATE CITIZENSHIP

Johnson Publishing is a major contributor to national black causes, as well as various community groups, including YMCA, Urban League, NAACP and the United Negro College Fund. EBONY Fashion Fair, the largest

STARTING UP JOHNSON PUBLISHING

With the idea in mind for *Negro Digest*, a new magazine for and about blacks, 24-year-old John H. Johnson set out looking for backers. Because he was black, none of the banks Johnson approached would consider giving him a loan. As a last resort, he pawned his mother's furniture for $500. That was the seed that eventually grew into a multi-million dollar business. Insecure about what the future held, when Johnson started *Negro Digest* he did not resign, but took a leave of absence from the Supreme Life Insurance Company. This allowed him the option of returning to Supreme if things didn't work out with the magazine. Johnson didn't formally end the leave of absence until some 20 years later—when he *bought* Supreme himself.

traveling fashion show in the United States, visits some 200 cities every year to raise money for local causes. In 2001 the Fashion Fair donated over $2 million to charity.

GLOBAL PRESENCE

EBONY and *Jet* are distributed in the United States, Canada, nations in Africa, the United Kingdom, and in the Caribbean. Fashion Fair Cosmetics is one of the world's leading lines of makeup for people of color. It is sold in Canada, Africa, England, France, Switzerland, the Bahamas, Bermuda, and the Virgin Islands.

EMPLOYMENT

Johnson Publishing has grown from 245 employees in 1972 to more than 2,600 in 2002. In the best tradition of the family business—even one as large as Johnson Publishing—John H. Johnson makes it a point to personally take part in interviewing every potential employee for his Chicago headquarters. Johnson's employment policy is devised to provide a setting in which promising black business talent can rise above the glass ceiling imposed by white companies. Johnson strives to provide its employees with highly competitive salaries and benefits packages. In return, John H. Johnson demands their best work.

SOURCES OF INFORMATION

Bibliography

Berlau, John. "Ebony's John H. Johnson." *Investor's Business Daily*, 26 March 1998.

Black, Bob. "Cosmetics Firms Court Blacks." *Chicago Sun-Times*, 13 April 1994.

Cohen, Roger. "Black Media Giant's Fire Still Burns." *New York Times*, 19 November 1990.

Dingle, Derek T. "Doing Business John Johnson's Way." *Black Enterprise*, June 1987.

———. "Lessons From the Top." *Black Enterprise*, May 1999.

"EBONY Interview with John H. Johnson." *EBONY*, November 1985.

"'Failure is a word I don't accept': An Interview with John H. Johnson." *Harvard Business Review*, March-April 1976.

Gottschalk, Mary. "The Body is the Star of this Year's Ebony Fashion Fair."*Seattle Times*, 22 April 1992.

Higgins, Sean. "Publisher Soared Into History." *Investor's Business Daily*, 25 January 2002.

Johnson, John H. *Succeeding Against the Odds*, New York: Warner Books, 1989.

"Johnson Publishing Company, Inc." *Hoover's Company Profiles*, 2002. Available at http://www.hoovers.com.

Johnson Publishing Home Page, 2002. Available at http://www.ebony.com.

Martelli, Joan A. "Corporate Art Reflects Corporate Image." *Crain's Chicago Business*, 25 July 1988.

McCann, Herbert. "Jet Survives 50 Years by Sticking to Mission." *Associated Press*, 15 January 2002.

"Straight to the Top: John Johnson." *Inc.*, October 1993.

Whitaker, Charles. "The Most Successful of All." *N'DIGO*, March 1999.

For additional industry research:

Investigate companies by their Standard Industrial Classification Codes, also known as SICs. Johnson Publishing Company Inc.'s primary SIC is:

3721 Periodicals Publishing & Printing

Also investigate companies by their North American Industrial Classification System codes, also known as NAICS codes. Johnson Publishing Company Inc.'s primary NAICS code is:

511120 Periodical Publishers

Jostens, Inc.

FOUNDED: 1897

Contact Information:

HEADQUARTERS: 5501 Norman Center Dr.
  Minneapolis, MN 55437
PHONE: (952)830-3300
FAX: (952)830-3293
URL: http://www.jostens.com

OVERVIEW

Minneapolis, Minnesota-based Jostens, Inc. makes class rings for high school and college students. The firm also produces rings for sports championship teams such as the World Series, Super Bowl, and NHL Stanley Cup winners. Additional activities include yearbook production, school photography, and the manufacture of graduations caps and gowns.

COMPANY FINANCES

After four consecutive years of growth, revenues for Jostens reached $805 million in 2000. However, they had yet to return to their 1993 high of $914.8 million. Profits of $57.2 million in 1997 fell to $41.8 million in 1998. Although profits improved marginally to $43.2 million in 1999, the firm posted an $18.7 million loss in 2000. That year, an investment company called Investcorp took Jostens private. Jostens returned to profitability in 2001, posting earnings of $4.1 million.

ANALYSTS' OPINIONS

Many analysts believed Jostens was on the right track in the early 2000s. Shortly after the firm had decided to refocus on its core school-based operations, it had been taken private by Investcorp. As a private company, Jostens no longer needed to invest resources into efforts to boost its stock price, which had remained flat for years regardless of the firm's performance. According to Merrill Lynch Global Securities analyst George Chalhoub, as quoted in a May 2001 issue of *Minneapolis-St. Paul City Business*, "There's been a few bumps thus far as the jewelry hasn't met predictions during the last two quarters, but the company is now reorganizing and has the freedom to make the necessary changes. It's worked for them, and I would expect to see them grow." Other analysts, however, believe the school market for things like rings and yearbooks is nearing saturation.

HISTORY

Otto Josten founded a small jewelry and watch repair business in Owatonna, Minnesota, in 1897. Three years later, Josten began making emblems and awards for local schools. The young company started making class rings, which came in only one size and did not include gemstones, in 1906.

After several years of modest growth, Josten hired his first full-time salesperson, Daniel C. Gainey, in 1922. A former football coach and teacher, Gainey found he was also skilled in sales. During his first year, he sold $18,000 worth of rings. In 1923 Josten hired four additional part-time salespersons and focused his business, by then called Jostens Manufacturing Co., on ring making. Josten sold his watch making and repair assets in 1930, using the proceeds to build a ring manufacturing plant. By the mid-1930s, sales had exceeded $500,000. In addition, Gainey had taken over as chairman and CEO.

In an effort to lessen its reliance on ring sales, Jostens diversified into graduation announcements in 1946. Four years later, the firm launched the American Yearbook Co. Jostens bought Educational Supply Company, a school diploma maker, in 1958. The following year, Jostens completed its initial public offering. Growth via acquisitions helped boost sales to $26 million in 1962. The company listed its shares on the New York Stock Exchange in 1965. Acquisitions in the late 1960s included National School Studios, based in Winnipeg, Manitoba. By then the firm had positioned itself as the largest class ring and yearbook maker in the United States with sales of nearly $100 million.

The 1970s proved much more tumultuous for the firm. A power struggle that started in the late 1960s after Gainey retired left the firm without stable leadership for nearly four years. In 1972 H. William Lurton took over as CEO and began working to restore order to Jostens. Diversification beyond educational products, once thought to be essential to future growth, was soon halted. Lurton sold off a greeting cards manufacturer and a men's accessories business that had been acquired by previous management. Efforts to offer travel services via Jostens Travel, a unit created in 1972, were halted as well.

Declining high school enrollment began to concern Lurton in the early 1980s. Believing that investors would see this erosion of Jostens' core market as an

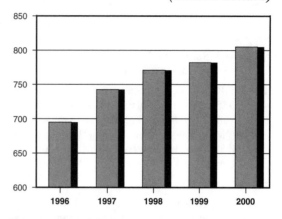

FINANCES:
Jostens, Inc.
Revenues, 1996-2000
(million dollars)

indication that the firm's outlook was in question, Lurton decided to organize a management buyout. The board of directors approved this plan in 1982. However, managers willing to invest money in such a buyout failed to materialize. Lurton then decided to ward off potential downturns in sales by targeting private schools for the first time. In fact, the firm actually began to purchase private schools. During 1983 and 1984, Jostens bought San Gabriel Colleges of California, Metridata Education Systems of Kentucky, and three vocational schools. The firm also diversified into educational software with the purchase of the Educational Systems Division of Borg-Warner Corp. Sales in 1985 grew to $400 million, and Jostens found itself listed as a Fortune 500 company for the first time. Prescription Learning Corporation (PLC), acquired in 1986, was consolidated with other educational software holdings in 1989 to form Jostens Learning Corp.

Jostens sold its proprietary schools, numbering 36 at the time, to CareerCom Corp. in 1987. By then, employees totaled 9,000, and the firm's independent sales staff had grown to 1,400. An average return on investment of 27 percent between 1983 and 1989 caught the attention of Wall Street analysts. *Fortune* magazine named Jostens one of the "Companies That Compete Best" in 1989. The following year, *Corporate Report Minnesota* named Lurton "Executive of the Year" and *Industry Week* named Lurton one of "America's Unsung Heroes."

Jostens diversified into award and recognition products in 1990 by acquiring both Gordon B. Miller & Co. and Lenox Awards. By 1992 Jostens Learning Corp. accounted for 20 percent of earnings. Because the edu-

FAST FACTS:
About Jostens, Inc.

Ownership: Since May 2000, Jostens, Inc. has operated as a private company owned by Investcorp.

Officers: Robert C. Buhrmaster, Chmn., Pres., and CEO, 54, 2001 base salary $561,808; John Feenan, SVP and CFO; Michael L. Bailey, Chmn., SVP, and Gen. Mgr. School Solutions, 45, 2001 base salary $260,385; Carl H. Blowers, SVP Manufacturing and Recognition, 61, 2001 base salary $308,617

Employees: 6,500

Chief Competitors: Competitors to Jostens include Commemorative Brands, Lifetouch, and Norwood Promotional Products.

CHRONOLOGY:
Key Dates for Jostens, Inc.

1897: Otto Josten founds a small jewelry and watch repair business in Owatonna, Minnesota

1906: Josten begins making class rings

1922: Josten hires Daniel C. Gainey as his first full-time salesperson

1946: The firm diversifies into graduation announcements

1959: Jostens completes its initial public offering

1972: H. William Lurton takes over as CEO

1985: The Fortune 500 adds Jostens to its ranks

1993: Robert C. Buhrmaster takes over as CEO

2000: Investcorp pays $950 million for Jostens

cational technology market was relatively untapped, many analysts believed that the firm was poised for continued success. In August of that year, Jostens acquired rival Wicat Systems and convinced Dell Computer Corp. to begin marketing a Jostens line of 386 and 486 personal computer systems. Instead of realizing the expected growth, however, Jostens posted a loss of $12.1 million in 1993. The downturn was due at least in part to educational budget cuts.

Robert C. Buhrmaster succeeded Lurton in 1993. He began to restore the firm's focus on its core class ring, yearbook, and recognition operations by reducing educational technology efforts. He eliminated layers of management and placed the firm's various divisions under more direct control of top executives. Losses persisted in 1994, prompting the firm to sell Jostens Learning Corp. to an investor group headed by Bain Capital, Inc. for $90 million the following year.

Restructuring continued into 1997, when the firm devised a new logo and increased marketing efforts. To reduce costs, Jostens moved a portion of its ring manufacturing operations to Mexico. That year, Jostens also bought Gold Lance, a retail class ring line, from Town & Country Corp. Investcorp paid $950 million for Jostens in 2000, taking the firm private. The following year, the firm began to divest its general awards and employee recognition operations. In addition, Jostens closed a distribution center in Memphis, Tennessee, and a manufacturing plant in Sherbrooke, Quebec.

STRATEGY

One of Jostens' key strategies throughout its growth and development in the twentieth century was direct sales. Although the firm first used its own salespersons to peddle class rings at nearby schools, rapid growth eventually prompted Jostens to develop a nationwide network of independent sales representatives. According to a May 1998 issue of *St. Paul Pioneer Press*, "Industry observers and Jostens' competitors attribute the company's market strength to making quality products, providing reliable service to students and parents, and hiring enterprising independent sales representatives who build long-term relationships with schools and gain access for in-school marketing."

Jostens tended to waver between strategies of growth via diversification and a return to core operations. In the late 1990s, as the firm once again narrowed its focus to school-based operations, it also began working on developing brand awareness. For example, Jostens developed a new corporate logo. In addition, the purchase of the Gold Lance class ring brand in 1997 was designed to push the Jostens brand into the retail class ring market, a segment traditionally dominated by retailing giants like J.C. Penney and Wal-Mart. Despite intense competition, Jostens' efforts to develop its brand awareness helped the company maintain a dominant share of the class ring market.

PRODUCTS

Along with class rings and athletic rings, Jostens sells graduation announcements, diplomas, caps and gowns, senior and prom portraits, student IDs, group and individual school pictures, and yearbooks.

CORPORATE CITIZENSHIP

The Jostens Foundation gives $500,000 annually to nonprofit community-based youth and education endeavors. The firm also matches a portion of the charitable donations made by employees, grants a number of post-secondary scholarships to family members of Jostens employees, and sponsors United Way fundraisers.

SOURCES OF INFORMATION

Bibliography

Carlson, Scott. "Running Rings Around Competition." *St. Paul Pioneer Press*, May 1998.

"Jostens, Inc." *International Directory of Company Histories.* Detroit: Gale Group, 1999.

Jostens, Inc. Home Page, 2002. Available at http://www.jostens .com.

"Jostens to Close Memphis and Canadian Operations." *Memphis Business Journal*, 23 March 2001.

Martyka, Jim. "Leveraged Buyouts Bring Flexibility." *Minneapolis-St. Paul City Business*, 4 May 2001.

For additional industry research:

Investigate companies by their Standard Industrial Classification Codes, also known as SICs. Jostens, Inc.'s primary SICs are:

3172 Personal Leather Goods, Not Elsewhere Classified

3911 Jewelry, Precious Metal

POWER STRUGGLE AT JOSTENS

Although Jostens CEO Daniel Gainey retired in the late 1960s, his position as a major shareholder allowed him to maintain a degree of control over Jostens. A power struggle ensued, and in a period of four years, the firm hired and fired three chairpersons as well as a president. In 1970 Gainey started secret negotiations to sell Jostens to Bristol-Myers. When the pending Bristol-Myers deal became public, several Jostens executives simply resigned, prompting Bristol-Myers to end negotiations with Jostens. A top Jostens salesperson, H. William Lurton, who was acting as Jostens' chief operating officer, remained. Lurton faced off against the CEO at the time, Richard Schall, who had been with Jostens for roughly 18 months. Lurton believed the outside management team Schall had put in place was having a negative impact on the corporate culture of Jostens and making strategic changes too quickly. He and several long-time Jostens executives demanded Schall's resignation, and eventually the board of directors agreed. Lurton was appointed CEO in February of 1972, a position he held for 21 years.

Also investigate companies by their North American Industry Classification System Codes, also known as NAICS codes. Jostens, Inc.'s primary NAICS codes are:

316993 Personal Leather Goods (except Women's Handbag and Purse) Manufacturing

339911 Jewelry (except Costume) Manufacturing

Kaiser Permanente

FOUNDED: 1945

Contact Information:

HEADQUARTERS: 1 Kaiser Plaza
   Oakland, CA 94612
PHONE: (510)271-5800
FAX: (510)271-6493
URL: http://www.kaiserpermanente.org

OVERVIEW

Kaiser Permanente is the largest not-for-profit health maintenance organization (HMO) in the United States. Headquartered in Oakland, California, the organization serves 8.2 million members in nine states and the District of Columbia. As an integrated health delivery system, Kaiser organizes and provides all aspects of members' medical care, including preventive care, hospitalization, medical treatment, and pharmacy services. Kaiser is comprised of three segments: Kaiser Foundation Health Plans, Inc.; Kaiser Foundation Hospitals; and the Permanente Medical Groups. The three groups cooperate under mutually exclusive contracts to provide one-stop health care services.

Kaiser Foundation Health Plans is a consortium of regionally based not-for-profit, public-benefit corporations that contract with groups and individuals to provide prepaid comprehensive medical and hospital care. Kaiser Foundation Health Plans works with Kaiser's Hospitals and Permanente Medical Groups to provide a full range of medical services. Kaiser Foundation Hospitals owns and operates hospitals in California, Oregon, and Hawaii, as well as numerous outpatient facilities in other states. The organization provides or coordinates hospital services for Kaiser members. Also providing services to members is Permanente Medical Groups, the second component of the Kaiser network. The Medical Groups segment consists of self-managed partnerships or professional corporations of physicians who assume the full responsibility for providing and coordinating all medical care for Kaiser members. Within the Kaiser network of services there are 29 medical centers, 42 medical offices, and 11,345 physicians.

Kaiser is divided into seven regions: California, Colorado, Georgia, Hawaii, Mid-Atlantic (Maryland, Virginia, and District of Columbia), Northwest (Washington and Oregon), and Ohio. A division of each of the three segments of service and care (Health Plans, Hospitals, and Physicians) operates within each region. Kaiser provides services in its Northwest region through a partnership with Group Health Cooperative based in Seattle, Washington. Most members are covered by Kaiser through their employers who may pay all or part of the monthly cost. Qualified individuals who do not have coverage may also become members through their employers.

COMPANY FINANCES

Kaiser Permanente posted a 78 percent increase in earnings during the fourth quarter of 2001 compared to the previous year. During that quarter, the organization had a net income of $187 million on revenues of $5 billion, up from $105 million net income on revenues of $4.6 billion in 2000. Considering all of 2001, net income grew 17 percent to $681 from $584 million in 2000. Revenues increased by $2 billion to $19.7 billion from $17.7 billion. The bottom line figures for 2001 reflect the second straight year Kaiser posted a net income after recording three consecutive years of net losses from 1997 through 1999.

HISTORY

Kaiser Permanente had its beginnings during the Great Depression when Dr. Sidney R. Garfield opened Contractors General Hospital, a 12-story facility designed to care for the thousands of workers who were building the Los Angeles Aqueduct. Establishing his hospital in the middle of the Mojave Desert, six miles outside the small town of Desert Center, Garfield began treating sick and injured contract workers. The doctor soon ran into financial difficulties as the insurance companies were slow in paying claims and some of the men he treated held no coverage.

Insurance agent Harold Hatch offered Garfield a possible solution, suggesting that the insurance companies could pay in advance a flat-rate daily fee for every worker covered. The upfront money would solve the hospital's immediate need for cash, and Garfield would be able to focus on health maintenance and safety rather than after-the-fact medical treatment. Thus, prepayment insurance coverage was introduced, a form of business that Kaiser continues to practice. The insurance company agreed to pay $.05 per day for each worker covered. Garfield offered workers the option of paying another $.05 out of their own pockets to gain coverage for non-work-related accidents and illnesses. The pre-

FAST FACTS:
About Kaiser Permanente

Ownership: Kaiser Permanente is a privately held, not-for-profit organization.

Officers: George C. Halvorson, Chmn. and CEO; L. Dale Crandall, EVP and CFO; Richard G. Barnaby, Pres. and COO

Employees: 55,300

Principal Subsidiary Companies: Kaiser Permanente is an organization of three business segments that are linked by exclusive contracts: Kaiser Foundation Health Plans, Inc.; Kaiser Foundation Hospitals; and Permanente Medical Groups.

Chief Competitors: Kaiser competes against for-profit health maintenance organizations on a national and regional level. Important competitors include Aetna, Blue Cross, CIGNA, Humana, Pacificare, and Well-Point Health Networks.

pay concept worked, and soon Garfield's hospital was back in the black.

When work on the aqueduct was coming to a close, Garfield, who was planning to start a private practice in Los Angeles, was contacted by an employer in need of health coverage for the 6,500 workers who were building the Grand Coulee Dam in Colorado. Jumping at the chance, Garfield transformed a run-down hospital into his headquarters and recruited other physicians to join him in a group prepaid practice. Once again the formula was a success and was affirmed by the physicians, the workers, the employer, and the insurance company.

As this project wound down, the United States was entering World War II, and Garfield's next project was even bigger than his last. Henry Kaiser, who owned Kaiser Shipyards in Richmond, California, saw his business increase due to the demand for ships, aircraft carriers, and other vessels. However, the many new workers brought in to step up production were inexperienced and often in poor health. With 30,000 employees to care for, Kaiser turned to Garfield for help. Garfield obliged and set up his third prepaid group practice for Kaiser's workers. At its peak, when employee numbers reached their highest, Garfield's plan covered approximately 200,000 shipyard workers and their families.

CHRONOLOGY:
Key Dates for Kaiser Permanente

1933: Dr. Sidney R. Garfield establishes a prepayment health plan for workers on a construction project in the Southern California desert

1938: Henry Kaiser persuades Dr. Garfield to set up a group practice prepayment plan for Grand Coulee Dam construction workers

1942: Dr. Garfield establishes group practice prepayment plans for workers and their families at Kaiser-managed shipyards in the San Francisco Bay Area; membership reaches 200,000 during World War II

1955: Kaiser Permanente is reorganized; membership reaches 500,000

1963: Membership reaches 1 million

1968: Membership reaches 2 million

1976: Membership reaches 3 million

1985: Membership nears 5 million; the organization includes 12 regions

1997: Membership approaches 9 million; the organization, overwhelmed by rapid expansion, posts a net loss for the year

1999: Membership declines to slightly more than 8 million; organization posts third consecutive annual net loss

2001: Organization posts second consecutive annual net income, announces plans to withdraw from unprofitable markets

At the end of the war, workers vacated the shipyards by the thousands, and only about 12 of Garfield's physician team of 75 remained. However, Kaiser was duly impressed by the prepaid plan and wanted to continue it. To that end, the Permanente Health Plan was formed on October 1, 1945 and officially opened to the public. Within ten years, membership reached more than 300,000. Growth was due in large part to support from several major unions that endorsed the plan for their members.

In 1952 the health plans and hospitals changed the name from Permanente to Kaiser to build on Kaiser Industries' national recognition. The physician group voted to keep the Permanente name. Thus, the entire organization became known as Kaiser Permanente. From the 1970s, Kaiser Permanente expanded its regional coverage with varied success, but membership grew rapidly until the organization became the largest single HMO in the United States.

STRATEGY

Kaiser focuses its appeal to the public on the tag line, "In the Hands of Doctors." The organization's strategy is to distinguish itself from competitors by emphasizing Kaiser's integrated care system that empowers members' physicians to act as the ultimate decision-makers at every level of care. Because of the partnership between Permanente doctors and Kaiser Foundation Health Plans and Hospitals, physicians are able to manage patients' care without interference from health plan administrators. The organization also promotes the overarching influence its physicians have on the entire network of care and services. For example, physicians dictate the drugs that are placed on the organization's recommended list, participate in developing clinical guidelines for most effective treatments, and address the value of new medical technology or procedures.

Six principles guide Kaiser's business model: social purpose, partnership, integration, prevention, comprehensive benefits, and choice. As a not-for-profit organization, Kaiser envisions the social benefit of its services beyond the scope of the profit line, and the company is involved in a wide range of activities beyond direct patient care, including a strong investment in medical research. Partnership is the cornerstone of Kaiser. It is what distinguishes it from its competition. According to Kaiser's organizational vision, integrated care is more effective and efficient than segmented care for both the patient and the administrator and allows for better quality and more innovative care.

Kaiser was a driving force in the introduction of preventive care. By allowing generous benefits, members are able to seek care before medical problems arise or become serious. Comprehensive benefits address the broad spectrum of medical issues, including well-baby care, emergency room visits, hospitalization, surgery, allergy treatment, lab services, and home health care. Choice is the final principle that governs Kaiser's operational strategy. Members choose a personal physician within the Permanente network who provides and coordinates all their care, including specialists, diagnostics, medications, therapy, and hospitalization. A member's physician alone has the authority to make all medical decisions; no administrative or outside authority is necessary.

INFLUENCES

Centering its image on its physicians, Kaiser steers away from negative images of HMO management, to which Kaiser itself had contributed. In 1997 the organization instituted a money-saving program that rewarded nurses for cutting costs. The practice received widespread negative attention as critics claimed that such a strategy could only lead to a decline in the quality of care. In fact, Kaiser was subsequently involved in two wrongful-death suits based on negligence caused by cost-cutting.

Kaiser had few friends between 1997 and 1999. In 1998 the organization posted a loss of $288 million, and losses between 1997 and 1999 totaled $560 million. Its poor financial performance was blamed on Kaiser's surge of new members who were enticed to join when Kaiser lowered rates to expand its membership base. However, membership grew too rapidly, rising by 20 percent. Kaiser found it could not accommodate the increased numbers, which resulted in expensive referrals to non-Kaiser physicians and decreased member satisfaction with the quality of services.

To right the sinking ship, Kaiser raised its monthly premiums, which helped revenues grow but did little to improve relations with members. The organization also took action to improve its operational efficiencies and abandoned several regions into which Kaiser had expanded without positive results, including Texas, North Carolina, and Kansas. To appease members, new and improved customer services were added, including decreased wait time on customer service telephone lines, the introduction of the option to make appointments online, and the taking of steps to improve the quality of care.

The most significant influence on Kaiser's operations is the rapid rise of medical costs. Also, unlike most HMOs, the organization is burdened with substantial fixed expenses, including a largely unionized workforce and a capital-intensive infrastructure of hospitals and medical facilities. Additionally, as medical technology advances, new procedures and treatments become available but they are accompanied by large price tags. Kaiser must decide how to conduct business so that its members receive quality care and yet it keeps its operations financially solvent.

CURRENT TRENDS

Kaiser attempted to extend its regional coverage but, in several cases, was unsuccessful. In the mid-1990s, under pressure to improve its profits, the organization began pulling out of regions that were not performing well. David Lawrence, who served as Kaiser's chairman and chief executive officer from 1991 until May of 2002, told the *San Francisco Chronicle*, "We had the naive belief that we were good people, we believed in what we were doing and it had worked in California, Oregon, Colorado, Hawaii, and by God it was going to work elsewhere. Expansion is hard to do and do well. You've got to be very systematic about it, and I don't think we were."

Despite its several failed attempts to extend its territory, Kaiser has succeeded in growing its membership base. In California, Kaiser covers one out of every three insured individuals. During the organization's 10 years under Lawrence's leadership, membership increased from 6.5 million in 16 states and the District of Columbia to 8.2 million in 8 states and the District of Columbia. Membership growth under James Vohs, Lawrence's predecessor, was even more dramatic, tripling in just 15 years.

Another recent trend is the move to integrate advanced technology. Kaiser invested nearly $2 billion in an electronic medical records system that is scheduled to be operational in Northern California in the fall of 2002. The system will then be gradually phased into other areas and regions. The goal of the new technology is to increase quality of care and reduce medical mistakes and missteps.

In March 2002 Kaiser announced that it would drop coverage of 7,800 low-income HMO members in Colorado as of June 1 due to a payment dispute with the state's health officials. Having lost $4.4 million on Medicaid plans in 2001 and approximately $2 million in each of the prior two years, Kaiser warned officials that unless reimbursement rates increased, the organization would be forced to withdraw. Kaiser will maintain roughly 2,300 disabled and elderly patients.

PRODUCTS

Kaiser offers a wide range of health plans that cover individuals of all ages and companies of all sizes. Its policies are divided within five primary divisions: individual and family coverage, Medicare eligible, small businesses, mid-sized and large employers, and nationwide employers. Individual plans include the Personal Advantage, which provides individual and family options; Cares for Kids Child Health Plan-1, which targets uninsured children; continuing coverage, which transitions group coverage into individual policies; and Steps Plan, which provides options for individuals whose income is too high to qualify for federal or state-funded programs or those who cannot afford a full-priced plan. Senior Advantage is tailored for Medicare-eligible members. Members have easy access to specialists and continuous, around-the-world coverage for urgent care. Kaiser's plans require virtually no paperwork.

Kaiser's business options no longer require qualifying medical exams, and the application process was streamlined. A traditional plan for a small business (defined as 2 to 50 employees) requires no deductibles and offers low cost office visit co-payments, low prescription drug co-payments, worldwide coverage for emergency care, and hospitalization. Large group coverage provides a wider range of plan options, including an HMO plan, a Dual-Choice PPO plan, an Added-Choice

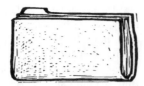

TO YOUR HEALTH

Kaiser's award-winning Web site offers a rich array of health information under three sections. "To Your Health" addresses topics such as nutrition, preventative measures, and exercise; "Just for Kids" features health-themed games and activities for children; and "Food and Nutrition" includes tips for good health and recipes. Several health-related educational videos are also offered for a small price. Each Kaiser region offers its own individual Web site, accessible through the main site at http://www.kaiserpermanente.org. Regional sites provide health tips as well as information on local opportunities for health education and screenings.

POS plan, as well as supplemental coverage, occupational coverage for work-related injuries, and options for those who live outside the Kaiser coverage area. Nationwide business plans can be customized to the needs and specifications of the employer.

CORPORATE CITIZENSHIP

A commitment to community has been a long-standing tradition of Kaiser. In 1996 the organization adopted an official policy of direct community benefit investment (DCBI) with the goal of improving the health of communities in which Kaiser is a presence and increasing access to affordable health care. The DCBI policy focuses on three major areas: improving children's health, improving the health of the uninsured via subsidized coverage, and advancing medical knowledge through research. The DCBI program also provides opportunities for education and training programs in the health sciences through grants, equipment, expertise, and volunteerism.

EMPLOYMENT

Approximately 1,000 of Kaiser's more than 26,000 employees are based at Kaiser's national headquarters in Oakland, California. Corporate career opportunities are primarily within the national leadership team and as high-level consultants who work with divisions on business management issues such as quality, finance, marketing, and governmental relations. Staffing within regional offices is handled locally. Kaiser does actively recruit specialists in information technology to assist in advancing its capabilities in management and medical information technology.

SOURCES OF INFORMATION

Bibliography

Colliver, Victoria. "David M. Lawrence: CEO Led Kaiser Through Storm." *The San Francisco Chronicle*, 31 March 2002.

"Kaiser Foundation." *Hoover's Company Profiles*, 2002. Available at http://www.hoovers.com.

"Kaiser Paring Down Its Medicaid Patients." *PR Newswire*, 22 March 2002.

"Kaiser Permanente Awards $285,000 in Scholarships for Nursing Students." *Business Wire*, 13 March 2002.

Kaiser Permanente Home Page, 2002. Available at http://www.kaiserpermanente.org.

"Kaiser Permanente: Improved Operations Helped Net Surge 78% in 4th Period." *The Wall Street Journal*, 1 March 2002.

"A Positive Financial Performance in 2001 Prepares Kaiser for Future Challenges." Company Press Release, 28 February 2002. Available at http://www.kaiserpermanente.org.

For additional industry research:

Investigate companies by their Standard Industrial Classification Codes, also known as SICs. Kaiser Permanente's primary SIC is:

6324 Hospitals and Medical Health Service Plans

Also investigate companies by their North American Industry Classification System Codes, also known as NAICS codes. Kaiser Permanente's primary NAICS code is:

524114 Direct Health and Medical Insurance Carriers

Kimberly-Clark Corp.

FOUNDED: 1872

Contact Information:
HEADQUARTERS: PO Box 619100
  Dallas, TX 75261
PHONE: (972)281-1200
URL: http://www.kimberly-clark.com

OVERVIEW

Kimberly-Clark manufactures and distributes consumer tissue products, personal care products, feminine care products, and baby care products. Kimberly-Clark products include Huggies diapers and Pull-Ups training pants, Scott paper towels, Kotex products, Kleenex, and Depends personal protection garments. Kimberly-Clark products are sold in more than 150 countries globally, and approximately 1.3 billion people around the world use their products.

COMPANY FINANCES

Kimberly-Clark's financial performance has been consistently strong. Even in 2001, one of the most difficult financial years in two decades, the company's cash operations grew by 6 percent to $2.3 billion. Net sales grew 3.9 percent from $13.98 billion in 2000 to $14.52 billion in 2001. In early 2002 shares were $63.67, having reached a 52-week high of $68.96 and a 52-week low of $52.06. In 2001 earnings per share were $3.04, down from $3.34 the previous year, and Kimberly-Clark shares paid cash dividends of $1.11, up from $1.07 in 2000.

Kimberly-Clark's CEO Wayne Sanders stated that several factors impacted the company's performance in 2001. The high cost of natural gas and electricity, along with a strong U.S. dollar, cost investors $.18 per share. The sluggish economy impacted Kimberly-Clark's newly-developed business-to-business division. A weak global economy also contributed to the decline in profits. Operating profit in Latin America and Asia fell from

FINANCES:
Kimberly-Clark Corp. Net Incomes, 1997-2001 (million dollars)

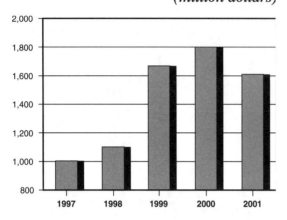

Kimberly-Clark Corp. 2001 Stock Prices (dollars)

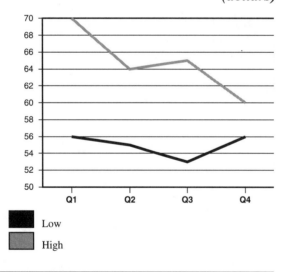

■ Low

■ High

$329.7 million in 2000 to $245.2 million in 2001. Financial difficulties in Latin America, particularly in Argentina and Brazil, prompted Kimberly-Clark to streamline in 2001, and the company closed four small plants. The company also closed a technical paper mill in North America.

Kimberly-Clark management remained optimistic and predicted the delivery of sales growth of 6 to 8 percent annually, as it had consistently done in the past. The company's strategy included a continued global expansion, particularly in the emerging economies of Latin America and Asia.

ANALYSTS' OPINIONS

Standard & Poor's rated Kimberly-Clark's conservative, diverse approach favorably, and the company maintained an AA/Stable/A-1+ credit rating in 2001. Although the paper products industry only grows by a small amount annually, between 2 and 3 percent, growth remains stable. The company's global sales and opportunity for growth, particularly in the health care industry, combined with its relatively low debt, were deemed positive in S&P's rating of Kimberly-Clark.

HISTORY

In 1872 four young business men: John Kimberly, Havilah Babcock, Charles Clark, and Frank Shattuck, combined their ideas and with $30,000 established Kimberly, Clark and Company in Neenah, Wisconsin. By 1880 Kimberly, Clark and Company had grown and incorporated under the name Kimberly & Clark Company, with $400,00 in capital stock. Nine years later, the company built a town around Kimberly Mill, just east of Appleton, Wisconsin. In 1879, brothers Irvin and Clarence Scott, formed a paper company with $300 cash and $2,000 borrowed from Irvin's father-in-law.

Both companies grew and were leaders in the paper products industry. Scott Paper introduced the first paper towel in the United States in 1907, and Kimberly-Clark set up the Cellucotton Products Company to sell Kotex feminine pads in 1920. Scott Paper's strategy for building brand loyalty used catchy slogans such as "It's the counted sheet that counts," for its toilet tissue ads in 1916, and the catchy title of "Thirsty Fibre," for its cross-weave paper towels in 1921.

The two companies merged in 1995, and the new company became a Fortune 100 global consumer products company with annual revenues upwards of $13 billion.

STRATEGY

Kimberly Clark's formula for success lay in diverse products. The company introduced the disposable cold cream towel, Kleenex facial tissue, in 1924. Six years later, the company marketed the tissues as disposable handkerchiefs and sales skyrocketed. Kimberly-Clark became an industry leader once again in 1978 when it introduced Huggies diapers. The brand has consistently been the top selling disposable diaper since it hit the market shelves. The company hit two more sales jackpots in 1989 with Pull-Ups training pants and in 1998 with Huggies Little Swimmers disposable swim pants.

Another important factor in Kimberly-Clark's strategy has been their ability to go global. Through brand marketing and global acquisitions, the company has consistently sold brands that rank first or second in their markets around the globe. Between 1993 and 2001, the company made more than 40 acquisitions around the world which helped Kimberly-Clark establish leading market shares in 80 countries. By working with global retailers such as Wal-Mart, Carrefour, Ahold and Costco, the company further strengthened its global sales.

CURRENT TRENDS

Growing and developing global economies drove many of Kimberly-Clark's business decisions and acquisitions through the 1990s and early 2000s. After establishing brand loyalty in the United States, and securing a modest, but predictable growth rate, the company expanded abroad and predicted their greatest growth would be in countries whose economies were still improving, such as Latin America and Asia.

In 2002 the company predicted growth in the global markets, as only 10 percent of Asian consumers and 30 percent of Latin American consumers used tissue products. In 2001 nearly two-thirds of the company's sales came from outside the United States, compared to one-third 10 years earlier.

PRODUCTS

Kimberly-Clark is the manufacturer and distributor of a variety of paper and personal care products including: Huggies and Goodnites diapers, Pull-Ups training pants, Little Swimmers swim diapers, Scott towels and toilet tissue, Kotex feminine pads, Kleenex facial tissues, Depend and Poise adult undergarments, Scott toilet tissue, Andrex tissue, Page tissue, and Safeskin latex gloves.

Kimberly-Clark also has a non-consumer division, which it developed into its business-to-business (B2B) division in 2001. The B2B division manufactures and markets health care products and technical paper products, and comprises 25 percent of the company's global sales. The rest of the company's sales are in its personal care division, which makes up 40 percent of sales, and consumer tissue, which makes up 35 percent of sales, divisions.

CORPORATE CITIZENSHIP

Kimberly-Clark established it charitable arm, the Kimberly-Clark Foundation, in 1952. The foundation supports programs and organizations in the communities where it operates. Since 1993 the foundation has contributed more than $4 million to schools and non-profit organizations, has awarded more than $16 million

FAST FACTS:
About Kimberly-Clark Corp.

Ownership: Kimberly Clark is a publicly traded company on the New York Stock Exchange.

Ticker Symbol: KMB

Officers: Wayne R. Sanders, Chmn. and CEO, 55, 2001 base salary $950,000, bonus $1,110,304; John W. Donehower, SVP and CFO, $440,000; Thomas J. Falk, Pres. and CEO, 58, $675,000; Kathi P. Seifert, EVP, 53, $480,000; O. George Everbach, SVP, Law and Govt. Affairs, $455,000

Employees: 64,000

Chief Competitors: Kimberly-Clark's key competitors include Playtex and Proctor & Gamble.

in scholarships, and has awarded $16.5 million in employee matches to the United Way and other non-profit organizations.

GLOBAL PRESENCE

When Kimberly-Clark purchased Scott Towels in 1995, overnight it became a global Fortune 100 company. Kimberly-Clark operates in nearly every country on the planet and has manufacturing facilities in 42 countries. Its global presence has helped the company to quickly expand its overseas markets and, in 2001, two-thirds of the company's sales came from outside the United States, compared with one-third in 1990. Kimberly-Clark established its global presence in part due to acquisitions like the 2001 purchase of Italian diaper business, Lines. The company made 40 such acquisitions between 1993 and 2001, helping it to increase its global reach.

EMPLOYMENT

Kimberly-Clark was ranked number 92 in 2001 on *Fortune* magazine's "Best 100 Companies to Work for." The company offers better than average salaries, with the average entry-level production worker garnering more than $30,000 a year, and an entry-level engineer earning more than $50,000 annually. Kimberly-Clark says its

CHRONOLOGY:
Key Dates for Kimberly-Clark

1872: Kimberly, Clark and Company is established in Neenah, Wisconsin; John A. Kimberly, Havilah Babcock, Charles B. Clark, and Frank C. Shattuck joined to start the company with $30,000 in capital

1879: Brothers Irvin and Clarence Scott formed Scott Paper Company with $300 and another $2,000 they borrowed from Irvin's father-in-law

1880: Kimberly, Clark and Company changes its name to Kimberly & Clark Company, and incorporates with a capital stock of $400,000

1889: Kimberly Mill builds and develops a town three miles east of Appleton, Wisconsin; the town was built along the Fox River, and the company constructed 60 houses and a hotel

1890: At a time when toilet tissue was still an "unmentionable" product, Scott Paper had become the nation's leading producer

1906: Kimberly & Clark is reorganized and incorporated as Kimberly-Clark

1907: Scott Paper introduces the first paper towel in the country, the Sani-Towel, for use in Philadelphia classrooms to prevent the spread of the common cold

1915: Kimberly-Clark begins to manufacture Cellucotton, which was first used as bandage material for soldiers in World War I

1920: After the war, Kimberly-Clark found another use for Cellucotton and began production and sales of Kotex feminine pads; because the company was afraid the move might tarnish its reputation during a time when people didn't openly discuss menstruation, the company formed a subsidiary, Cellucotton Products Company, under which to manufacture and market the products

1955: Scott Paper becomes the first company to advertise toilet tissue on national television

1978: Kimberly-Clark introduces Huggies diapers, and they soon become the top selling disposable diaper in the country

1980: Kimberly-Clark introduces Depend incontinence products and hired actress June Allyson for the ad campaign, "Get back into life"

1989: Without the benefit of a test-marketing program, Kimberly-Clark invents and markets Pull-Ups training pants, which became an instant hit with parents

1995: Scott Paper and Kimberly-Clark merge in a $9.4 billion deal, creating a Fortune 100 company with annual revenue of more than $13 billion

2000: Kimberly-Clark posts a sales record for the fourth quarter and full year of 2000; the company's fourth quarter sales were $3.6 billion, an increase of 5.1 percent over the previous year

---

work environment is casual, comfortable, professional, and respectful, and the company values teamwork, integrity, and respect.

SOURCES OF INFORMATION

Bibliography

Harris, Lori. "Kimberly-Clark Corp. Ratings." *Standard & Poor's*, 4 October 2001.

"Snapshot Report." *Market Guide*, 22 March 2002.

Stenqvist, Alf. "Stable Outlook for European Forest Products Despite Challenging Market Conditions." *Standard & Poor's*, 13 March 2002.

For an annual report:
on the Internet at: http://www.kimberly-clark.com

For additional industry research:
Investigate companies by their Standard Industrial Classification Codes, also known as SICs. Kimberly-Clark Corp.'s primary SIC is:

2676 Sanitary paper products

Also investigate companies by their North American Industry Classification System codes, also known as NAICS codes. Kimberly-Clark Corp.'s primary NAICS code is:

322291 Sanitary Paper Product Manufacturing

Kmart Corporation

OVERVIEW

Alternately praised and ridiculed for its "blue-light" special offers, and oft-criticized for extremely generous salary and benefits to its top company officers, Kmart Corporation is a large discount retail chain in the United States. In 2002 the struggling corporation had numerous detractors, and *The New York Times* speculated whether the company would be bought out by an international conglomerate, miraculously find a way to redefine itself and stop its expanding losses, fold, or merely continue to flounder as Wal-Mart and Target collectively steal away Kmart's once-impressive market share. Kmart has never been able to quite shed its low-status image, although it has been actively trying to do so.

Just a few years ago, it looked as if the company had reversed its ill fortune. After reporting staggering losses in 1995 and 1996, Kmart returned to profitability in 1997, only to flounder badly in the 2000s. Its strategy of returning to the company's core business as a discount retailer and mass merchandise retailer seemed to be paying off for a brief time, but Wal-Mart's intense competition, and Kmart's inability to rekindle enough former customer loyalty, proved to be the company's financial undoing. In January 2002, Kmart Corporation filed for reorganization under Chapter 11 of the U.S. Bankruptcy Code, claiming that it intends to rebound by 2003, a date that company officials and Kmart creditors soon acknowledged was likely unrealistic to meet. On March 9, 2002, then-Kmart Chairman Charles C. Conaway resigned under fire, drawing statewide headlines when it revealed his last estimated compensation package could be worth as high as $11 million.

FOUNDED: 1899 as S.S. Kresge Company

Contact Information:

HEADQUARTERS: 3100 W. Big Beaver Rd.
  Troy, MI 48084
PHONE: (248)643-1000
FAX: (248)643-5249
TOLL FREE: (800)635-6278
URL: http://www.Kmart.com

FAST FACTS:

About Kmart Corporation

Ownership: Kmart is a publicly owned company traded on the New York, Chicago, and Pacific Stock Exchanges.

Ticker Symbol: KM

Officers: James B. Adamson, Chmn. of the Board, Pres., and CEO, 53, $1.5 million salary , $2.5 million signing bonus (additional incentive bonuses up to $5.2 million will be paid if Kmart emerges from bankruptcy in timely fashion); Julian C. Day, Pres. and COO, 49, base salary $775,000, $2.66 million bonus; Albert Koch, 59, EVP and CFO, employed through Jay Alix & Associates at $640 an hour; Ted Stenger, 44, Treas., employed through Jay Alix & Associates at $620 an hour

Employees: 250,000

Chief Competitors: Kmart Corporation's primary competitors are other discount retailers, including Wal-Mart and Target.

The news that the company filed for bankruptcy was disappointing for investors who had hoped that Kmart had already rebounded from its economic woes of the 1990s after it decided in 1993 to sell all its non-core businesses and nearly all its international operations to focus on serving customers in the United States. Puerto Rico, Guam, and the U.S. Virgin Islands. Among the biggest changes customers noticed was the closing of all Penske Auto Centers located at 550 Kmart stores and their conversion to additional space for shopping items; the move led to 4,000 jobs lost by Penske employees. All told, analysts predicted that Kmart would close up to 600 of its least profitable stores in the early 2000s-a substantial chunk of the 2,114 stores that were open in January 2002. In March 2002, Kmart officials confirmed that at least 284 stores would be closed in an "orderly" fashion, but a nationwide network of about 1,000 employees formed an Internet site to express their grievances against Kmart management.

According to the annual *Kmart Fact Book*, "Kmart's primary target customer group is women between the ages of 25 and 45 years old, with children at home and with household incomes between $20,000 and $50,000 per year." To better serve its core customers and to attempt to lose a reputation for stocking "cheap" products, Kmart introduced new product lines such as the Martha Stewart Everyday and Sesame Street lines in 1997, while it implemented hundreds of initiatives aimed at improving customers' shopping experience and the overall performance of the company. By 2002 the company had expanded its partnerships with celebrity and name brand product lines; it attracted other name brands such as Hewlett Packard computer products and Black & Decker electrical tools for home workshops. The company did away with its automobile repair alliance with the Penske Corporation, instead concentrating on expanding grocery shopping operations and sales merchandising areas to attract Kmart customers. In March 2002 the company parted ways with Mark S. Schwartz, its president and chief operating officer for less than one year; a bankruptcy court ruled that Kmart could retain its working agreements with partners such as Martha Stewart Everyday, Jaclyn Smith apparel, Kathy Ireland exercise equipment and clothing line, JOE BOXER apparel, and Disney's line of children's and infant's clothing. To replace Schwartz, on March 11, 2002, Kmart hired its non-executive chairman of the Board of Directors, 53-year-old James B. Adamson, best known for restoring the reputation of Denny's after he assumed control as CEO of the parent company Advantica in 1995. After Adamson took control, more than one dozen top national executives with the companies were terminated and received unusually high severance packages of three years' pay (plus bonuses and some forgiven loans), and Julian C. Day was appointed President and Chief Operating Officer.

In the 1990s, Kmart converted many of its traditional stores into a new prototype called "Big Kmart." Big Kmart stores feature a new layout, an expanded consumable goods section, brighter lighting, wider aisles, and a bigger assortment of goods. In addition, the corporation's Super Kmart centers have about 12.5 million square feet of selling space and offer full-service shopping convenience from groceries to general merchandise. They are open 7-days-a-week, 24-hours-a-day.

COMPANY FINANCES

After reporting net losses of $571 million in 1995 and $220 million in 1996 on relatively flat sales of $31.7 and $31.4 billion, Kmart attempted a financial turnaround in 1997 with a net income of $249 million on sales of $32.2 billion. Successful product introductions, such as Martha Stewart Everyday home fashions and Sesame Street children's apparel, also contributed to the company's improved financial performance. In 1997 the stock was trading in the $10-$15 range, buoyed by the company's short-term return to profitability. The company's fourth quarter profits in 1997 were the best in five years, prompting analysts to begin recommending Kmart stock. However, the company's profits plummeted from 2001 to 2002 when stock closed at a low of $1.60 in January, compared to a 2001 high of $13.55. In 2001 Kmart disclosed a second-quarter loss of $22 million and, over the course of the next year's meetings, the board of directors agreed to make wholesale changes in company leadership in 2002.

ANALYSTS' OPINIONS

Early in 2002, analyst Wayne Hood of Prudential Securities strongly urged dumping Kmart stock and rightly forecast almost-certain bankruptcy ahead for Kmart. Shortly, Kmart stock closed down 13 percent at $4.74. After Kmart hired a marketing firm to revamp its tattered image following Chapter 11 hearings, Matt Miller, a media analyst for *The Daily Deal* and one of Kmart's many harsh critics, wrote this: " Word this week that bankrupt Kmart Corp. is hiring Creative Artists Agency for a marketing makeover left us momentarily nonplussed. Isn't CAA a talent agency primarily for overpaid movie stars? Isn't Kmart a retail store primarily for underpaid workers?"

HISTORY

Sebastian S. Kresge founded the S.S. Kresge Company in 1899. It became one of the largest dime-store chains in the United States. The company opened the first Kmart discount department store in 1962 in Garden City, Michigan, a suburb of Detroit. In 1966 company sales topped the $1 billion mark for the first time. There were 162 Kmart stores and 915 total stores in operation. In 1976 S.S. Kresge opened a record 271 Kmart stores in one year. The next year, 15 years after opening the first Kmart store, the company name was changed from S.S. Kresge Co. to Kmart Corporation.

In the late 1970s the company bought the Walden Book Company and in the 1980s bought Builders Square, a chain of home improvement stores. In 1981 the two-thousandth Kmart store was opened. By 1985 Kmart owned PayLess Drug Stores Northwest and Bargain Harold's Discount Outlets in Canada. Kmart also ventured into warehouse club retailing, opening PACE Warehouse with a company called Makro. In 1987 it sold most U.S. Kresge and Jupiter stores. Kmart bought The Sports Authority in 1990 and sold PACE Warehouse to Wal-Mart in 1994.

In the early 1990s, Wal-Mart bounded ahead of both Kmart and Sears as the leader in the industry. By 1991 Kmart's older and less attractive stores with slimmer merchandise shelves couldn't keep up with Wal-Mart's ultra-modern reputation. Kmart's sales and market share fell behind this mega-merchandiser.

Kmart fought on and bought a large portion of OfficeMax in 1991. In 1992 Kmart purchased 76 percent of Maj, a Czechoslovakian department store. It also

CHRONOLOGY:
Key Dates for Kmart Corporation

1962: S.S. Kresge opens the first Kmart discount department store in Garden City, Michigan

1966: Sales top $1 billion for the first time

1976: Kresge opens a record 271 stores in one year

1977: The S.S. Kresge Co. becomes Kmart Corporation

1984: Kmart acquires Walden Book Company and Builders Square

1990: Kmart purchases The Sports Authority

1992: The first Super Kmart opens; Purchases Borders Group, a book chain

1994: The company begins to sell off its non-core business by spinning off Office Max and the Sports Authority

1995: Sells Borders Group

1997: Enters into an agreement with Little Caesars for its KCafe

1999: Kmart initiates partnerships with food giants Supervalu Inc. and Fleming Companies Inc. to stock Kmart shelves with groceries

2000: Ex-CVS exec Charles Conaway takes over from Floyd Hall as chairman and chief executive officer and shuts down 72 Kmart stores

2001: In November Kmart's $224 million loss leads to Standard & Poor's reduced rating of Kmart in view of staggering debts

2002: Stock analysts nationwide suggest in January that clients unload Kmart stock in view of apparently irreversible debt service problems; Kmart changes executive leadership and files for Chapter 11 bankruptcy protection

announced plans to build 100 stores in Mexico with Grupo Liverpool. Also in that year, the company bought Borders, a chain of bookstores, but that venture proved ill advised. In 1994-1995, Kmart spun off OfficeMax and The Sports Authority as public companies through initial public offerings (IPOs) of stock. Proceeds to Kmart were $1 billion for OfficeMax and $405 million for The Sports Authority. It also sold its interest in Coles Meyer in Australia. Facing falling profit margins, Kmart continued to sell its investments. In 1995 Borders Group became a publicly traded company through an IPO; proceeds to Kmart were $566 million.

Searching for a new strategy, Kmart brought in a new CEO, Floyd Hall (who stayed at the helm only to 2000), and a new management team and board of directors, either highly paid or overpaid depending on one's view, were put in place. More than 200 stores closed by the mid-1990s, and the company tried to restructure itself and focus on its core business, but stock prices fell even more. Rumors of bankruptcy swarmed Wall Street, but Kmart seemed to right itself for a time.

In 1996 and 1997 Kmart continued to divest itself of its non-core businesses and its international operations, including its Czech and Slovak stores. Thrifty/Payless was spun off as a public company in 1996. In 1997 Kmart sold its interest in Kmart Mexico and all of its Kmart Canada stores. Finally, it divested itself of Builders Square in 1997. In 1999 the company signed an agreement with Martha Stewart Retail to carry her line of products. Hoping to reclaim past glory, the Blue Light Special sales gimmick so popular in the 1980s was restored after a decade-long absence in 2001. Mark S. Schwartz, a former Wal-Mart executive, became the president and chief operating officer of Kmart in March 2001, but he stayed barely long enough to use his shopper discount at Christmas, getting the heave-ho in January 2002 when Kmart became the largest retail chain in history ever to file for Chapter 11, according to *The New York Times*. His replacement, James B. Adamson, has earned a reputation by turning around beleaguered companies. In 2002, with rumors swirling through the business community that Kmart was a company ripe for purchase by a conglomerate or rival retail chain, Adamson was charged with the responsibility of trying to find a way to keep the now slimmed-down 1,900-store chain in business first, then to restore it to profitability. Adamson in 2002 found few analysts who thought the bankrupt company could regain the shopper and investor confidence Kmart once enjoyed. If Adamson can not pull off a minor financial miracle, his last job as chief executive officer might be to extinguish Kmart's famed blue lights.

STRATEGY

Kmart was originally a general merchandise discount store. The company sputtered financially after it tried to diversify into a variety of specialty stores, from book stores to home improvement centers. However, even after Floyd Hall became head of the company in 1995, and Kmart refocused on its core business, it became readily apparent that rivals Wal-Mart and Target had fashioned too big a lead to catch. Kmart conducted a study to determine a profile for the target Kmart shopper: women between the ages of 25 and 45 years old, with children at home and with household incomes between $20,000 and $50,000 per year. Of the 180 million people that shop at Kmart each year, 57 percent are women and 43 percent are men. The core mart shopper visited the store an average of 4.3 times a month and made an average purchase of $40 each visit. These core shoppers accounted for 60 percent of total store revenues. In 2000, when Charles C. Conaway took the top Kmart position, he pushed to strengthen marketing efforts to serve mothers and their children, but failed when the store took too long to replenish out-of-stock items. In short, Conaway tried, but not without failing, and he was quickly replaced as CEO. The Kmart chain reported a $244 million net loss for the fiscal year ending Jan. 31, 2001.

According to Kmart's annual report, the company is focused "on improving our customers' shopping experience through stronger assortments, better stores, convenient service and quality products at great prices." The company's merchandising strategy was focused on three areas: frequently purchased goods, popular national brands, and high-quality private label offerings. Its strategy was to improve its assortment of dominant national brands and be aggressive in pricing them. It wanted to complement that with a strong line of private label products, which included the Martha Stewart Everyday line of home fashions, the Sesame Street collection for children, and Jaclyn Smith and Kathy Ireland apparel, as well as Penske Automotive products and more. In 2002 the company kept all of the above except for Penske which proved an unprofitable partnership.

Part of the company's strategy of improving its customers' shopping experience was to convert its older, gone-to-seed stores into Big Kmart stores, with brighter lighting, wider aisles, bigger assortments, and an expanded consumable goods section. Super Kmart centers now feature about 12.5 million square feet of selling space, a broad selection of general merchandise and apparel, and a full assortment of groceries. Super Kmart centers are open 24-hours-a-day, 7-days-a-week. The first Super Kmart center opened in 1991 and numbered nearly 100 by the end of 1997, a number that dipped in 2002 as the company dumped many of its least profitable store operations nationwide.

Another aspect of Kmart's real estate strategy was to develop a five-year plan for each of the company's top 30 metropolitan markets. Within each of those regions, made up of both urban and suburban areas, Kmart planned to expand its presence. The 2002 store closings, however, demonstrated certain patterns of regional sales weaknesses. Kmart closed 33 stores in Texas; 21 in Illinois; 18 in Michigan; 16 in both California and Florida; 14 in Georgia; and 10 in Ohio.

INFLUENCES

Kmart's poor financial performance and bankruptcy in 2002 was attributed to poor management and an inabil-

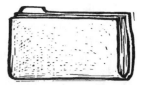

ity to cut the huge sales advantage Wal-Mart and Target had built since the 1990s. Kmart's strategy in 2002 was yet to be announced by yet another CEO, James B. Adamson, but most analysts agreed that the company needed to learn from mistakes of the past or die. Stores had to keep better inventory, not sending customers away disappointed with rain checks tucked inside their purses or wallets. It must focus on providing its core shoppers with a better shopping experience and surprise them with brighter, cleaner stores and helpful clerks hovering somewhere in plain sight. It must continue to provide an assortment of general merchandise at discounted prices, but some analysts feel that the company must play its Martha Stewart trump card more often and a whole lot better to compete with Target and Wal-Mart.

The company is also influenced by the strong performance of other mass merchandisers, especially Wal-Mart, Target and to a lesser extent, Sears. It will compete with them in the area of general merchandise, attempting to offer a bigger and better assortment that is more aggressively priced than its competitors. It is unlikely that Kmart will again try to branch out into specialty stores, and it even has cut loose from its Penske in-store auto repair operations. However, as of 2002, the company continued to retain its in-store Kmart Pharmacy Centers to fill prescriptions, a holdover from Kmart's attempt to take business away from the large drugstore chains such as CVS.

In spite of reverses, Kmart remains an extremely high volume retail store. Its 2000 sales amounted to $37 billion and its earnings the same year were $244 million. But losses in the third quarter of 2001 compared to the same quarter of 2000 were problematic as net sales declined 2.2 percent from $8.2 billion to $8.0 billion.

CURRENT TRENDS

In the mid-to-late 1990s, Kmart divested its specialty stores and all of its international operations, and in 2002 the company continued its practice of shutting down unprofitable store operations across the United States. First and most important, the company must shed its bankruptcy status by 2003 as first announced, or no later than 2004 if it hopes to maintain what is left of fast-dwindling creditor, supplier, and customer confidence. Whatever strategies Adamson's new marketing team in 2002 chooses to adopt, Kmart must implement initiatives to draw customers into stores and heighten their positive experiences while shopping.

The company had a more aggressive Internet marketing program in the 2000s, selling low-cost goods and even $12,000+ luxury Toshiba televisions through a Bluelight.com Web site. In the 2000s it offered customers a special Kmart MasterCard with 0 percent interest for six months on Kmart-purchased merchandise. However, the company's best-known marketing strategy was its

SOMETHING FOR EVERYONE

You're taking care of the last-minute packing for your spring break trip, and suddenly you realize you forgot to pick up suntan lotion. Chances are you're included in the 80 percent of the U.S. population who are within a 15-minute drive of a Kmart store. More than 180 million people shop each year at Kmart, and odds are that if you're a middle-income parent, they're carrying what you need. Each year, Kmart stores stock more than 100,000 items, everything from candy bars to camping gear. Need to do some planting? Kmart sells 83,000 tons of potting soil each year. Or perhaps your house needs a fresh coat of paint. Kmart sells enough paint each year to paint a foot-wide line around the globe 35 times. On the other hand, Kmart never has shed a popular misconception that it is a place where "losers" go to shop. That image caused movie goers in 1988 to crack up hysterically when a character played by Tom Cruise uttered an expletive about Kmart quality in the movie *Rain Man*. Can Kmart, which for some years has stocked well-known lines such as Black & Decker, find a way to demolish this stereotype that rightly or wrongly has stuck to it? It better.

return to the Blue light special, "unannounced" in-store sales on merchandise, but this strategy clearly was insufficient to stop Kmart's downward spiral into bankruptcy court.

PRODUCTS

The company continues to tout its Martha Stewart Everyday line of home fashions, Black & Decker workshop electric tools, and Sesame Street and Disney lines of children's apparel. Other specialty lines the company prominently displays in its print and online advertising include DeLonghi, Nickelodeon, Panasonic, Philips, and Hewlett Packard.

CORPORATE CITIZENSHIP

Kmart has an impressive record of sponsorship, particularly in programs that support infant and child health such as the March of Dimes WalkAmerica. Kmart has participated faithfully and has consistently been the nation's leading team in this program since 1985, raising $33 million through 2001. Kmart alone raised $3.3 million for the March of Dimes in 2001. Kmart, since 1999, has been a major supporter of the American Red Cross and supplied store space and supplies to help lifesaving and cleanup efforts in New York following the September 11, 2001 terrorist attacks.

Kmart also hosts holiday programs for the raising of funds at Christmas by encouraging the in-store fundraising efforts of the U.S. Marines and local law enforcement authorities.

A self-proclaimed supporter of K-12 education, Kmart in 2001-2002 began a new fund-raising opportunity for enrolled schools called the Kmart School Spirit Program. The program donated about $10 million to member schools during the 2001-2002 school year.

GLOBAL PRESENCE

As of 1998, Kmart stores were located only in the United States, Puerto Rico, Guam, and the U.S. Virgin Islands. The company divested itself of international holdings in Canada, Mexico, and Europe during the 1990s. The company clearly has positioned itself in the 2000s as an American-owned and run company that serves the interests of lower- and middle-income families. It also has strongly positioned itself as a corporate good citizen to back causes that aid in the fight against children's diseases.

EMPLOYMENT

With some 275,000 Kmart employees (called "associates" by the company) through 1999, Kmart was the sixth largest employer in the United States. That number dropped dramatically in the spring of 2002 as the company announced plans to let go of more than 20,000 employees in addition to earlier mass layoffs in the decade, With a renewed emphasis on customer service, Kmart has demonstrated that it is committed to attracting, retaining, and developing the most talented and highly motivated associates in retailing. Associates may work in a store, distribution center, or at Kmart's headquarters. They are hired and retained on the basis of high standards of performance. Kmart provides equal employment opportunities regardless of race, religion, color, national origin, sex, or disability. However, in 2002, a Web site devoted to the concerns of disgruntled Kmart employees boasted nearly 1,000 members, a sign that the company has a long way to go before employee confidence in management can be restored. Much of the

employee anger was directed toward multi-million dollar settlements with top management officials in spite of their roll in leading the company to Chapter 11 bankruptcy status.

Bibliography

Brauer, Molly. "Kmart Earnings Point to Recovery." *Detroit Free Press*, 14 May 1998.

Gaffney, John. "Kmart's Marketing Miscues." *Business2.0*, 28 January 2002. Available at http://www.business2.com.

Hays, Constance L. " Is Kmart Out of Stock in Answers?" *The New York Times*, 17 March 2002.

"Kmart's Bright Idea." *Businessweek Online*, 9 April 2002. Available at http://www.businessweek.com.

"Kmart Cutting 22,000 Jobs." *CNNMoney Online*, 8 March 2002. Available at http://money.cnn.com.

Kmart Fact Book. Troy, MI: Kmart Corporation, 1999.

Kmart Home Page, 11 May 2002. Available at http://www .Kmart.com.

Miller, Matt. " Singing the Blue Light Special." *The Daily Deal*, 1 May 2002.

Preddy, Melissa, and David Howes. "Kmart Crafts a Comeback Team." *The Detroit News*, 2 February 1996.

Strom, Stephanie, and Leslie Kaufman. "Kmart Is On Verge of Filing a Claim for Bankruptcy." *The New York Times*, 22 January 2002.

For an annual report:

telephone: (248) 643-1040 **or** write: Investor Relations, Kmart Corp., 3100 W. Big Beaver Rd., Troy, MI 48084-3163

For additional industry research:

Investigate companies by their Standard Industrial Classification Codes, also known as SICs. Kmart Corporation's primary SICs are:

5261 Retail Nurseries And Garden Stores

5331 Variety Stores

5411 Grocery Stores

5651 Family Clothing Stores

5912 Drug Stores And Proprietary Stores

Also investigate companies by their North American Industry Classification System codes, also known as NAICS codes. Kmart Corporation's primary NAICS codes are:

444190 Other Building Material Dealers

444220 Nursery and Garden Centers

445110 Supermarkets and Other Grocery (except Convenience) Stores

446110 Pharmacies and Drug Stores

448140 Family Clothing Stores

452990 All Other General Merchandise Stores

Knight Ridder

FOUNDED: 1974
VARIANT NAME: KRI

OVERVIEW

Knight Ridder, the third largest newspaper publisher in the United States, operates a number of the country's most distinguished newspapers, including the Philadelphia Inquirer, the Miami Herald, and the San Jose Mercury News. The company's Newspaper Division oversees the publication of 32 daily newspapers in 28 U.S. markets. The circulation of these daily properties totals 8.7 million readers daily and 12.9 million on Sunday. In addition, Knight Ridder publishes 26 non-daily newspapers as well as special publications and shoppers.

In 2001, 17.3 percent of the company's newspaper operating revenue was accounted for by its Philadelphia properties, the Philadelphia Inquirer and the Philadelphia Daily News; the Miami Herald and its Spanish-language sister publication, el Nuevo Herald, brought in 10.9 percent; and the Kansas City Star accounted for 9 percent of newspaper operating revenue in 2001. Other major newspaper properties and their share of total newspaper operating revenue in 2001 include the San Jose Mercury News, 8.7 percent; Fort Worth Star-Telegram, 7.7 percent; Charlotte Observer, 6 percent; Contra Costa Newspapers, 4.4 percent; St. Paul Pioneer Press, 3.9 percent; and Akron Beacon Journal, 3.1 percent.

Knight Ridder Digital, the company's other major division, is responsible for Knight Ridder's online ventures, the most prominent of which is the Real Cities Network, 58 regional Web sites that offer extensive local coverage. Among the Web sites in the Real Cities Network are 16 in the nation's top 25 markets. Each of the Real Cities sites offers a broad range of services, including classified advertising, local news, weather, sports,

Contact Information:

HEADQUARTERS: 50 W. San Fernando Street
    San Jose, CA 95113
PHONE: (408)938-7700
FAX: (408)938-7766
URL: http://www.kri.com/

FINANCES:

Knight Ridder Inc.
Operating Revenues, 1997-2001
(million dollars)

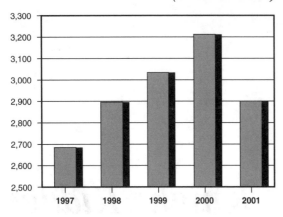

entertainment guides, directories of local civic institutions and businesses, and job postings.

COMPANY FINANCES

An advertising recession and the terrorist attack on America combined to sharply depress revenue and income at Knight Ridder—as well as the newspaper industry in general—in 2001. The company posted 2001 net income of $184.8 million on revenue of $2.9 billion, plummeting sharply from income of $314.4 million on revenue of $3.2 billion in 2000. The company's performance in 2000 was down slightly from its results in 1999 when it posted net income of $339.9 million on revenue of just over $3.2 billion. Total advertising revenue for 2001 was down 8.5 percent. Although retail advertising was up modestly, at least until the terrorist acts of September 11, help wanted and general advertising were particularly hard hit. With unemployment rising throughout the year, help wanted advertising revenue fell almost 36 percent. The company reported that the impact of the help wanted advertising slump was particularly hard in some of its larger markets, including Philadelphia and San Jose.

Despite the company's disappointing financial performance in 2001, Knight Ridder stock outperformed all other companies in its publishing peer group, climbing just over 14 percent over the year as a whole. By mid-February 2002, its stock had hit an all-time high of $68.73. The company's online division, Knight Ridder Digital, experienced substantial growth in 2001, adding 19 sites to its Real Cities Network.

ANALYSTS' OPINIONS

Although the prolonged downturn in the advertising market, stretching from 2001 into the early months of 2002, affected all newspaper publishers across the board, there were some security analysts who suggested that Knight Ridder was struggling even more than some of its industry peers. One of the most prominent of that fraternity, Michael Beebe of Goldman, Sachs & Co., downgraded the company's stock in mid-2001, indicating that he expected a tough second-half 2001 and little recovery in 2002. At the same time, Beebe downgraded the stock of two other prominent newspaper publishers, the Gannett Company and the Tribune Company. However, he singled out the New York Times Company, Pulitzer Publishing Company, and Dow Jones as likely "market outperformers." Beebe expressed some doubt about Knight Ridder's projected earnings for 2001, suggesting that the company was perhaps relying too heavily on cost cuts to make up some of the anticipated shortfall in revenue.

Of Knight Ridder CEO Tony Ridder's attempts to keep costs down even if it meant cuts in editorial staffing, most analysts have been generally positive, although some have suggested that even more could be done. Wrote Merrill Lynch analyst Lauren Fine: "There are any number of their papers that are incredibly overstaffed. Yet employees are sitting there complaining that Tony's cutting costs. It's just one of the great ironies-these guys don't realize how great they have it." Echoing her sentiments was Bear Stearns analyst Kevin Gruneich, who said, "I think newspapers are a special business as long as they are not asking Wall Street for capital. If they want Wall Street capital, they have to play by the rules. If they don't, they can try to take themselves private."

HISTORY

Knight Ridder, Inc., was formed in 1974 through the merger of Knight Newpapers, Inc. and Ridder Publications, Inc. Both of the merging newspaper publishing companies had enjoyed long and prestigious histories before the merger. Ridder Publications was born in 1892 when Herman Ridder purchased New York City's German-language Staats-Zeitung, while Knight Newspapers was founded in 1933 when John S. Knight inherited the Akron Beacon Journal from his father, Charles Landon Knight, who had founded the paper in 1903. Both newspaper chains grew quickly, and both Knight and Ridder took their stock public in 1969. Although Knight Ridder was originally incorporated in Ohio in 1974, it was reincorporated in 1976 in Florida, home of the company's headquarters in Miami.

Knight Ridder stock split two for one in 1978 and a year later, the company became a partner with Cox Newspapers and Media General in the ownership of a newsprint mill in Dublin, Georgia. The merged company continued to expand, acquiring new properties throughout the late 1970s and 1980s. Among its more notable acquisitions during this period were television stations in Providence, Rhode Island, Albany, New York, and Flint, Michigan in 1978; book publisher HPBooks in Tucson, Arizona in 1979; the Fort Wayne News-Sentinel in 1980; American Quotation Systems in 1981; Tradecenter, Inc., in 1984; and Dialog Information Services, Inc. in 1988. In the late 1980s, the company sold all eight of the television stations under its control as well as the Pasadena Star-News. During this same period, Knight Ridder launched Viewtron, America's first full-scale consumer videotext system, but abandoned the project three years later.

During the latter half of the 1990s, Knight Ridder moved aggressively to capitalize on the opportunities presented by the Internet while continuing to selectively expand its newspaper chain into new markets. By 1996, most Knight Ridder daily newspapers had launched their own Web sites. The following year, the company acquired four of the Walt Disney Company's newspaper properties: the Kansas City Star, Fort Worth Star-Telegram; Belleville (IL) News-Democrat, and Wilkes-Barre (PA) Times Leader. That same year, Knight Ridder swapped Boulder (CO) Camera for two of E. W. Scripps Company's California newspapers, the San Luis Obispo Telegram-Tribune and Monterey County Herald. KnightRidder.com, launched in 2000 as a separate division responsible for the company's online ventures, was renamed Knight Ridder Digital in 2001.

STRATEGY

Knight Ridder's corporate strategy focuses on "the two Vs: Vision and Value." Recognizing consumer demand for ever-increasing value, particularly now that technology has made possible a constant flow of new services and products, Knight Ridder seeks to be "preeminent" in advertising, information technology, and news delivery in all its markets. According to its strategy statement, "We will do this by developing our own high-value products and service to complement our traditional businesses. In our markets, we will grow reader and advertising share every year; we will reach a majority of adults every day; and we will have the dominant share of local online consumer and advertiser business. We will grow revenue, profit, and economic value added."

Knight Ridder has not lost sight of its historic mission, informing the communities in which it operates. The company looks upon this mission as "a privilege, responsibility, and source of competitive strength." It considers its commitment to its own employees and its customers fundamental to the company's success and has pledged to strive to reflect the diversity of the markets it serves in both content of its products and the makeup of its work force.

FAST FACTS:
About Knight Ridder

Ownership: Knight Ridder is a publicly owned company traded on the New York and Frankfurt Stock Exchanges.

Ticker Symbol: KRI

Officers: P. Anthony (Tony) Ridder, Chmn. and CEO, 61, 2001 base salary $935,720; Stephen B. Rossi, Pres. Newspaper Division, 52, 2001 base salary $613,250; Mary Jean Connors, SVP Human Resources, 49, 2001 base salary $518,533

Employees: 19,000

Principal Subsidiary Companies: Knight Ridder's major subsidiaries include Career Builders, Inc. and Classified Ventures, Inc. Career Builders, Inc., jointly owned with the Tribune Company, operates an online network of more than 60 career-oriented Web sites that operate as forums where employers and potential employees can make contact with each other. Classified Ventures, Inc., a joint venture operated with six other publishers, seeks to capitalize on the revenue growth in the online classified advertising categories of automotive, apartments and rentals, and real estate. Knight Ridder, partnered with the Gannett Company and Landmark Communications, Inc., also owns one third of InfiNet Company, a Web hosting and application service provider for online publishers.

Chief Competitors: As the nation's third largest newspaper publisher, Knight Ridder's major competitors are the Gannett Company, Inc., publisher of USA Today and more than 90 other newspapers with a combined circulation of close to 8 million, and the Tribune Company, which publishes the Chicago Tribune and Los Angeles Times. Another significant Knight Ridder competitor in the newspaper industry is Cox Enterprises, which publishes 18 daily newspapers, including the Atlanta Journal-Constitution.

INFLUENCES

One of the biggest challenges facing Knight Ridder in recent years has been the prolonged slump in advertising sales that began in the latter part of 2000 and continued into the early months of 2002. There were few bright spots in a generally gloomy advertising outlook,

ers quit in protest over the cuts, particularly those in the newsrooms of the chain's newspapers. On the other side of the coin, several Wall Street analysts suggested that the cuts had not been nearly deep enough.

CHRONOLOGY:

Key Dates for Knight Ridder

1974: Merger of Knight Newspapers and Ridder Publications creates Knight-Ridder Newspapers, Inc.

1978: Entrance into television business with purchase of 3 TV stations.

1979: Acquisition of HPBooks of Tucson, Arizona

1983: Knight Ridder forms Business Information Services division

1985: Launches Knight-Ridder Graphics

1987: Sells HPBooks

1988: Acquires Dialog Information Services Inc.

1989: Sells off all television stations

1996: Web sites launched by most Knight Ridder newspapers

1998: Corporate name changed to Knight Ridder

2001: KnightRidder.com renamed Knight Ridder Digital

---

although prior to the September 11, 2001 attack on America, retail advertising had shown some modest gains. Those were wiped away after the terrorist attack as Americans across the country sharply cut back their shopping, forcing many retailers to cancel scheduled advertising.

For Knight Ridder newspapers as a group, general advertising—including telecommunications, national automotive, dot-coms, airlines, and finance—was down 10.3 percent in 2001, and the decline was greatest in the larger urban markets. Hardest hit among the advertising sectors was help-wanted advertising, which plummeted 35.9 percent in the company's Newspaper Division. Again, the larger urban markets were hardest hit. With the national jobless rate rising from 4 percent in December 2001 to 5.8 percent in December 2001, it was inevitable that job listings would tumble precipitously, but that knowledge hardly eased the pain.

Knight Ridder's response to the sharp decline in advertising revenue was to aggressively cut back on its costs. CEO Tony Ridder's decision to reduce the company's work force won him few friends but helped to stanch the flow of red ink onto the company's books. A couple of the company's most widely respected publish-

CURRENT TRENDS

The phenomenal growth of the Internet over the last several years has not been lost on Knight Ridder executives who early on positioned the company to take full advantage of this new market. By 1996, almost all of the chain's daily newspapers had Web sites up and running.

Even more ambitious in scope is Knight Ridder Digital, which is responsible for all of the company's Internet operations; and by far the most ambitious of those operations is the Real Cities Network of regional Web sites serving 58 major U.S. markets. The goal of the Real Cities Network, according to Dan Finnigan, president of Knight Ridder Digital, is to take the lead in local news and information service on the Internet. Real Cities sites were visited by 9.6 million unique Web surfers in the month of December 2001 alone. As 2001 ended, the Real Cities Network was second only to the combined online properties of AOL Time Warner.

Knight Ridder's presence on the Internet extends beyond its newspapers' sites and the Real Cities Network to include the operations of CareerBuilder, Inc. and Classified Ventures. CareerBuilder, jointly owned with the Tribune Company, operates a network of more than 60 career Web sites that supplement their own job listings with the local help wanted ads of all Knight Ridder and Tribune newspaper markets, as well as additional ads from other cooperating newspaper publishers. Classified Ventures, Inc., a joint venture operated with six other publishers, concentrates on the online classified advertising categories of automotive, apartments and rentals, and real estate.

PRODUCTS

Knight Ridder's principal product is information, delivered in its daily and non-daily newspaper products as well as on line through its Real Cities Network and other ventures on the World Wide Web. The company is justifiably proud of its reputation for quality journalism, which has won for the newspapers of the chain more than 80 Pulitzer Prizes as well as numerous honors.

CORPORATE CITIZENSHIP

All of Knight Ridder's local newspaper properties take an active role in the affairs of the communities in which they operate, as does the company itself. In addition to active participation in charitable causes through in-house fundraising, employee volunteerism, and corporate donations, the Knight Ridder Promise pledges the company "to contribute to the quality of life. . .of the communities that sustain us" and ensure that its employees enjoy "a clean and safe workplace."

GLOBAL PRESENCE

Although Knight Ridder correspondents staff news bureaus in the major capitals of the world, most of Knight Ridder's business is domestic. As its online products evolve and grow, it can be expected that the company's international presence will eventually expand.

EMPLOYMENT

Knight Ridder's employees totaled 19,000 at the end of 2001, a decline of 13.6 percent from December 31, 2000.

SOURCES OF INFORMATION

Bibliography

Knight Ridder 2001 Annual Report. San Jose, CA: Knight Ridder, 2002.

Knight Ridder Home Page, 2002. Available at http://www.kri.com.

"Knight Ridder Inc." *Hoover's Online*. Available at http://www.hoovers.com.

Mullins, Robert and Sharon Simonson. "Knight Fighting Talk of a Major Slump." *Silicon Valley/San Jose Business Journal*, 29 June 2001.

"Newspapers Stung in Fourth Quarter by Sagging Ad Market." *Reuters Business Report*, 24 January 2002.

Pasick, Adam. "Knight-Ridder Says Ad Slump to Hurt Earnings." *Reuters Business Report*, 16 November 2001.

———. "Knight Ridder, Washington Post Feel Ad Market Pain." *Reuters Business Report*, 25 January 2002.

For an annual report:

on the Internet at: http://www.kri.com **or** write: Knight Ridder, Corporate Relations, Suite 1500, 50 W. San Fernando St., San Jose, CA 95113

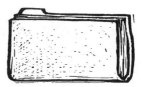

BALANCING QUALITY WITH PROFITABILITY

Knight Ridder's somewhat controversial response to 2001's sharp decline in advertising revenue was to pare the company's workforce, including cuts in editorial staffing. Not surprisingly, the move produced howls of protest from journalists, who had somehow adopted the notion that the newsroom was sacrosanct and unlikely to feel the sorts of cutbacks suffered by other departments when times got tough. Unhappily for CEO Tony Ridder, those newsroom howls of protest were not the only criticism of his moves to cut costs. Wall Street analysts and investors complained that the cuts should have been even deeper. Writing in the company's 2001 annual report, Jerry Ceppos, vice president of news, sought to clarify the company's struggle to balance quality with profitability. He observed: "The 'balance' we seek is to generate enough profit to keep the newspapers and Knight Ridder healthy and growing but not so 'healthy' that product is subordinated to profit. We seek margins that are in the first tier of newspaper companies, but not out in front. Balance requires a generous news hole, ample staffing and support for a challenging agenda, but also a recognition that in a year such as the one just concluded, less-than-tight operations could imperil the whole enterprise."

For additional industry research:

Investigate companies by their Standard Industrial Classification Codes, also known as SICs. Knight Ridder's primary SICs are:

2711 Newspapers

7375 Information Retrieval Services

7383 News Syndicates

Also investigate companies by their North American Industrial Classification System Codes, also known as NAICS codes. Knight Ridder's primary NAICS codes are:

511110 Newspaper Publishers

514110 News Syndicates

514191 Online Information Services

Krispy Kreme Doughnuts, Incorporated

Contact Information:

HEADQUARTERS: 370 Knollwood Street, Suite 500
    Winston-Salem, NC 27103
PHONE: (336)725-2981
FAX: (336)733-3794
EMAIL: marketing@krispykreme.com
URL: http://www.krispykreme.com

OVERVIEW

Based in Winston-Salem, North Carolina, Krispy Kreme Doughnuts is a leading branded specialty retailer of premium quality doughnuts. In 2001, it was estimated that it sold five million donuts a day and more than two billion a year.

Founded in 1937, Krispy Kreme operates a chain of 218 shops in 33 states and Canada that offer its signature doughnuts, including its best-known offering, the Hot Original Glazed. Each shop has the capacity to produce from 4,000 dozen to over 10,000 dozen doughnuts daily. Shop sites are located in Alabama, Arizona, California, Colorado, Delaware, Florida, Georgia, Illinois, Indiana, Iowa, Kansas, Kentucky, Louisiana, Maryland, Michigan, Mississippi, Missouri, Nebraska, Nevada, New Mexico, New York, North Carolina, Ohio, Oklahoma, Pennsylvania, South Carolina, Tennessee, Texas, Utah, Virginia, Washington, West Virginia, Wisconsin, and Ontario, Canada.

Besides serving its sweet offerings to customers, Krispy Kreme also sells its food products to supermarkets and convenience stores. In 2001, approximately 123 of the company's stores sold to major grocery store chains like Food Lion and Acme Markets, as well as to local and national convenience stores and select co-branding customers. Krispy Kreme also sells its ingredients and equipment to its franchisees.

Krispy Kreme's organizational structure includes three reportable segments: company store operations, franchise operations, and Krispy Kreme Manufacturing and Development (KKM&D). Company store operations include company stores and consolidated joint venture stores that make and sell doughnuts and complementary products through on-premise and off-premise sales channels. Franchise operations include the associate program and the area developer program. KKM&D involves the buying and processing of ingredients to produce doughnut mixes. Also, this unit manufactures doughnut-making equipment that all of Krispy Kreme's stores are required to purchase, and it makes and sells all supplies necessary to operate a Krispy Kreme store, including all food ingredients, juices, Krispy Kreme coffee, signage, display cases, uniforms and other items.

COMPANY FINANCES

For the fiscal year that ended February 3, 2002, the company's revenues rose 31 percent to $394.4 million. Company revenue in 2001 was $300.7 million. Net income increased 79 percent to $26.4 million, up from $14.7 million in 2001. For the full fiscal year 2002, system-wide sales of $621.7 million rose 38.7 percent versus the previous year. Company store sales for all of fiscal year 2002 increased 24.6 percent over 2001. This topped sales growth of 9.7 percent in 1999 and 12.7 percent in 1998. The company attributed the rise in revenues from increased comparable store sales and new franchise stores as well as improved operating efficiencies and lower interest expense.

ANALYSTS' OPINIONS

Krispy Kreme stock soared when the company expanded beyond the South in the mid-1990s. This led some investors to think the franchise had the potential to be another Starbucks. However, others were skeptical, and analysts expressed caution. When Starbucks had expanded, it faced little competition. Krispy Kreme, on the other hand, had many competitors, including the strong Dunkin' Donuts chain. Plus in recent years, other high-profile franchise enterprises had failed, including Boston Chicken, Discovery Zones, and TCBY. Some analysts were waiting to see how Krispy Kreme handled the franchiser-franchisee relationship and what effect its aggressive expansion would have.

HISTORY

Krispy Kreme Doughnuts' beginnings go back to 1933, when Vernon Rudolph, the company founder, bought a doughnut shop in Paducah, Kentucky. With the purchase, he acquired the rights to a secret yeast-raised doughnut recipe that would provide the foundation for the company's hugely successful product. At first, the small business primarily sold and delivered doughnuts to local grocery stores. Buoyed by early success, Rudolph

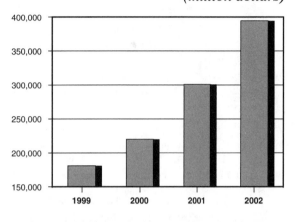

FINANCES:

Krispy Kreme Doughnuts, Inc.
Revenues, 1999-2002
(million dollars)

and his partner went after a larger market. In 1937, they moved their operations to Nashville, Tennessee, where they opened a doughnut shop and took on the name Krispy Kreme Doughnuts. The company was officially established.

Eventually, Rudolph opened a shop in Winston-Salem, North Carolina, which would become the headquarters of the company. Short on cash, Rudolph borrowed money from a local grocer, promising to pay him back once he sold enough doughnuts. The grocer didn't have to wait long. With other family members brought into the business, the company branched out to Charleston, West Virginia, and Atlanta, Georgia.

By the 1960s, Krispy Kreme had developed and established its trademark look: a store topped by a green roof and emblazoned with the "Marching Ks" symbol. By this time, the coffeehouse had been added, and a large window gave customers a close-up look at Krispy Kreme's unique doughnut-making process.

Vernon Rudolph died in 1973. Soon after, the company was sold to a large food service business that implemented many changes—not all for the best. New and different ingredients were used to make the doughnuts, diluting the distinctive Krispy Kreme flavor. Also, quality further suffered as attention to detail diminished. Eventually the company was resold and former workers returned to the fold, bringing with them knowledge of the "old ways." Krispy Kreme was back on track.

In 1977 the company made a pivotal hire that would prove crucial to Krispy Kreme's future success. That was the year Scott Livengood, the company's current CEO, came on board. He became president in 1992 and CEO

FAST FACTS:

About Krispy Kreme Doughnuts, Incorporated

Ownership: Krispy Kreme Doughnuts, Incorporated is a publicly owned company that is traded on the New York Stock Exchange.

Ticker Symbol: KKD

Officers: Scott A. Livengood, Chrmn., Pres. and CEO, 48, 2001 base salary $375,000; John N. McAleer, VChmn., EVP Concept Development, 42, 2001 base salary $214,000; John Tate, COO, 50, 2001 base salary $83,769; Paul J. Breitbach, VP Finance, Administration, and Support Operations, 2001 base salary $252,000

Employees: 3,200

Principal Subsidiary Companies: Krispy Kreme Doughnuts, Incorporated sells doughnuts and related items through company-owned stores, and sells doughnut-making equipment and mix to company-owned and franchised stores. The company operates through three business segments: company store operations, franchise operations, and Krispy Kreme Manufacturing and Distribution (KKM&D). The KKM&D business unit produces doughnut mixes and manufactures doughnut-making equipment. The company operates a chain of 218 shops in 33 states and Canada.

Chief Competitors: As Krispy Kreme operates in the service sector of the restaurant industry, technically its competition includes any restaurant, from a Lone Star to a TGIF. However, its most significant competition comes from the chains that serve pastries and coffee, particularly Starbucks and especially Dunkin' Donuts. As a matter of fact, Krispy Kreme faces competition from any small independent restaurant that has a breakfast counter or any coffee shop.

---

in 1998. In 1999, he was also elected chairman of the board.

For more than 60 years, the company had been a Southern institution. However, by the mid-1990s, it had made some encroachments into Northern territory, led by Livengood. The move proved a resounding success, as the company's distinctive recipe gained new fans in other parts of the country. The company had become such a

favorite that in 1997, some Krispy Kreme artifacts were added to the Smithsonian Institution's National Museum of American History. In 1999, the company incorporated.

STRATEGY

Krispy Kreme's success can be attributed to five elements: marketing, a vital business model, attention to quality, a balanced financial model, and aggressive expansion.

In recent years, Krispy Kreme's marketing strategy has been to capitalize on the strong market existing for doughnuts by establishing itself as a leader using the power of its recognized brand name, turning out a high volume of product, and entering targeted markets through several sales channels.

Krispy Kreme employs a unique and successful business model. The company is divided into two business units that complement each other: store operations (which includes the company store segment and the franchise store segment) and manufacturing and development or the KKM&D unit. Its main source of revenue is the sale of doughnuts produced and distributed by store operations, a highly automated, high-volume producer of product. KKM&D, with its strong operating competencies and capabilities, supports the stores.

In the area of quality, the company sets itself apart from competitors by using the best ingredients and a vertically integrated production process designed to create consistent quality in an efficient manner. Quality control efforts include state-of-the-art laboratories in its manufacturing plants. These labs perform quality tests on all key ingredients and each batch of mix.

With its financial model, Krispy Kreme creates sales and income from its stores, franchise fees and royalties, and a vertically integrated supply chain that supports its operations.

Krispy Kreme also employs an aggressive expansion campaign. Sixteen new stores opened in 2000, while 25 opened in 2001. By 2000, area franchisees were contractually obligated to open 250 new stores between January 2001 and January 2006.

INFLUENCES

Krispy Kreme blossomed in the late 1990s thanks largely to the guidance of its CEO, Scott Livengood, who was instrumental in transforming it from a regional wholesaler into a nationally recognized and leading brand specialty retailer. In guiding the company through its expansion, he has developed markets for Krispy Kreme doughnuts across the United States, and he has taken the company into Canada while planning for even more inter-

A worker operates the apple filling station at a Krispy Kreme Doughnut factory in Alexandria, Virginia. (AP Photo/Ricky Carioti)

national growth. The company began expanding in 1996, when it only had 95 stores. By the turn of the century, it had more than 200.

CURRENT TRENDS

As far as the future is concerned, Krispy Kreme believes there are no boundaries. After a strong year in 2002, Krispy Kreme felt it had exceptional growth potential and opportunities, thanks to new initiatives that included the development of the small-format doughnut and coffee shop, international opportunity, and an expanded beverage program. The company also revealed plans to open a new manufacturing and distribution facility in Illinois that would facilitate its expansion into the Midwest, West, and Canada.

Krispy Kreme also designed and perfected a new doughnut machine, about the size of a small car, that could help the company open even more outlets in places like center city locations, train stations, and small towns. The machine's smaller size makes it possible for the company to open smaller stores that could be operated more cheaply and in spaces about one-fifth the size of its

CHRONOLOGY:

Key Dates for Krispy Kreme Doughnuts, Incorporated

1933: Company founder Vernon Rudolph buys his first doughnut shop, in Paducah, Kentucky

1937: The company is officially founded when Rudolph names his business enterprise Krispy Kreme Doughnuts

1937: Rudolph expands his business into Tennessee and North Carolina

1973: Vernon Rudolph passes away

1977: Scott Livengood is hired

1997: Krispy Kreme artifacts are placed in the Smithsonian Institution's National Museum of American History

1998: Scott Livengood is named CEO of Krispy Kreme Doughnuts

1999: Krispy Kreme Doughnuts is incorporated

2001: Krispy Kreme announces its international expansion plans

typical 4,500-square-foot store. As a result, company officials believe they can open thousands of new stores across the country.

PRODUCTS

Krispy Kreme is best known for fresh, glazed, yeast-raised doughnuts, especially the "Krispy Kreme Original Glazed," its first and best-known doughnut. All of its doughnuts are made from a secret recipe that has been in the company since 1937.

Unlike other doughnut shops and restaurants, Krispy Kreme serves its doughnuts hot, which has undoubtedly added to their popularity. Along with the original glazed, company stores offer a variety of doughnut styles including chocolate iced, chocolate iced with sprinkles, maple iced, chocolate iced creme filled, chocolate iced custard filled, raspberry filled, lemon filled, cinnamon apple filled, powdered blueberry filled, glazed creme filled, traditional cake, chocolate iced cake, glazed cruller, powdered cake, glazed devil's food, chocolate iced cruller,

DOUGHNUT HOLES

When Krispy Kreme Doughnuts founder Vernon Rudolph opened a shop in Winston-Salem, North Carolina, he planned on selling the doughnuts he made to local grocery stores. However, the product became so popular that people began stopping by and asking if they could buy doughnuts on site. Rudolph obliged. The demand for customer service then became so great that Rudolph had to cut a hole in the shop's wall to serve more people. That somewhat crude innovation foreshadowed Krispy Kreme's modern-day window service.

cinnamon bun, glazed blueberry, and glazed sour cream. Krispy Kreme also makes fruit pies, cinnamon buns and several varieties of snack foods. Its shops also serve coffee and juices.

Krispy Kreme not only sells its doughnuts in its shops, it also packages and markets its products for sale in supermarkets, convenience stores and other retail outlets throughout the country.

CORPORATE CITIZENSHIP

Since 1937, Krispy Kreme has been active in community fundraising. Through the years, it developed successful fundraising programs for schools and community clubs and organizations. The company helps fundraising efforts by supplying quantities of doughnuts for sale.

GLOBAL PRESENCE

Since the 1930s, Krispy Kreme had been a uniquely American business. However, encouraged by increasing and phenomenal success in the last decades of the twentieth century, the company began setting its sights on international markets. In 2001, Krispy Kreme hired an executive, Donald Henshall, to plot its global expansion strategy, and it entered a partnership to expand into Canada, its first venture outside U.S. borders. According to the plan, Krispy Kreme Doughnuts Eastern Canada, Inc. would open 32 stores over six years in eastern provinces including Ontario and Quebec. At the time, the company had no immediate plans to open a store overseas, although that was certainly a future goal.

EMPLOYMENT

By 2001, Krispy Kreme had 3,200 employees filling various roles in its stores throughout the country. Positions include "Krew leader," retail specialist, processing specialist, coffee specialist, route salesperson, route sales manager, and sanitation specialist. The company offers employees a benefits package that includes medical, dental and life insurance plans, as well as paid training and vacation, a 401(k) savings plan, advancement potential, discounted products, and disability programs.

For career development, Krispy Kreme offers a management training course that involves classroom training followed by on-the-job training. Upon completing the training, students are ready run a store.

SOURCES OF INFORMATION

Bibliography

Associated Press. "Krispy Kreme Profits a Delicious Double," Daily News.com, 9 March 2002. Available at http://dailynews .com/business/articles/0302/09/biz04.asp.

BusinessWeek Online. "Krispy Kreme Doughnuts." Company Profile/S&P Business Summary, 9 April 2002. Available at http://research.businessweek.com.

Craig, Michael. "The Hole Nine Yards," Business 2.0, 4 June 2001. Available at http://business20.com.

Deck, Stewart. "Krispy Kreme: The Doughnuts That Keep on Giving," Taquitos.net, 2002. Available at http://www.taquitos .net/yum/kk.shtml.

Hoover's Online. "Krispy Kreme Doughnuts, Inc. Profile," 10 April 2002. Available at http://www.hoovers.com.

Icon Partnerships. "Krispy Kreme Doughnuts," 2002. Available at http://www.icon.com/partners/partners_krispy_kreme.html.

Investors.com. "Scott A. Livengood," 2002: A Business and Economic Outlook. Available at http://www.investors.com/2002conference/ScottLivengood.html.

Yahoo! Profiles. "Profile-Krispy Kreme Doughnuts," 10 April 2002. Available at http://biz.yahoo.com.

For an annual report:
on the Internet at: http://199.230.26.96/kkd/annrep.shtml

For additional industry research:
Investigate companies by their Standard Industrial Classification Codes, also known as SICs. Krispy Kreme Doughnuts, Incorporated's primary SICs are:

2051 Breads, Cakes and Related Products; Doughnuts Except Frozen

2053 Doughnuts Frozen; Frozen Bakery Products Except Bread

3556 Food Products Machinery

5461 Retail Bakeries

Also investigate companies by their North American Industry Classification System Codes, also known as NAICS codes. Krispy Kreme Doughnuts, Incorporated's primary NAICS codes are:

311812 Bread Products, Fresh, Made in Commercial Bakeries; Doughnuts Made in Commercial Kitchens

311813 Doughnuts Frozen, Manufacturing

333294 Bakery Machinery and Equipment Manufacturing

Lockheed Martin Corporation

FOUNDED: 1926

Contact Information:
HEADQUARTERS: 6801 Rockledge Drive
    Bethesda, MD 20817
PHONE: (301)897-6000
FAX: (301)897-6704
URL: http://www.lockheedmartin.com

OVERVIEW

Lockheed Martin Corp. is the largest defense contracting company in the world. It is a major contractor to the U.S. Department of Defense (DoD), civil agencies of the U.S. federal government, foreign governments, and private companies. The U.S. federal government is Lockheed Martin's single largest client—by far. In 2001, it was responsible for over three quarters of all Lockheed's net sales. Lockheed operates a chain of facilities, including plants, laboratories, service centers, administrative centers, and warehouses throughout the world. Most are located in the United States. Lockheed Martin is headquartered in Bethesda, Maryland.

Lockheed Martin is divided into four main corporate segments: Systems Integration, Space Systems, Aeronautics, and Technology Services. Systems Integration manufactures electronic systems for surface, sea, undersea, and air applications. These include radar and other surveillance systems, tactical missile systems, high performance sensor systems, and so-called C4I systems—command, control, communications, computers, and intelligence systems. Systems Integration is based in Bethesda Maryland. The Space Systems segment produces space systems for both the government and civilian sectors. Its products include communications and surveillance satellites, launch vehicles, ground systems for space launches, and space-based missile systems. The segment is involved with various joint ventures, including United Space Alliance, LLC, which manages and operates NASA's space shuttles. The segment is based in Denver, Colorado. Lockheed's Aeronautics segment produces a broad line of combat and transport aircraft, including the F-35 Joint Strike Fighter, the F-16 multi-role fighter, the F-22 Raptor fighter, and the C-130J tactical airlift aircraft. The segment is based in Fort Worth, Texas. The Technology Services segment produces a line of scientific, engineering, and logistic products and services. They include software modernization services, data management, engineering, and scientific consulting for NASA, training, maintenance and logistical support for government and civilian systems, and R&D in connection with government nuclear weapons and reactor programs. Technology Services is headquartered in Cherry Hill, New Jersey. Lockheed Martin had a fifth segment, Global Telecommunications, which it discontinued at the end of 2001.

COMPANY FINANCES

Lockheed Martin reported about $24 billion in net sales in 2001, down 2 percent from 2000. Its largest customer, the U.S. federal government, accounted for about 78 percent of Lockheed's sales in 2001, or about $18.6 billion. In comparison, foreign governments made $3.89 billion in purchases from Lockheed in 2001. The commercial sector brought up the rear, accounting for just under $1.5 billion of Lockheed Martin's net sales that year, primarily space launch services, satellites, and information technology services. Systems Integration accounted for more of Lockheed's net sales than any other segment in 2001 with about $9 billion generated. Space Systems was second in sales with $6.84 billion, 87 percent of sales were to the federal government. The Aeronautics segment made about $5.35 in net sales in 2001; sixty-five percent of those sales were to the U.S. government and 35 percent to foreign governments. Technology Services was responsible for 12 percent of Lockheed's 2001 sales. At the end of 2001, the company had just under $71.3 in backlog, or firm orders from clients, an increase of almost 30 percent from 2000. Most of those orders would not be filled by the end of 2002.

Lockheed's 2001 operating profit was $888 million, down from $1,251 million in 2000 and $1,997 million in 1999. In the end the company reported a net loss of $1.05 billion in 2001, which worked out to a loss of $2.42 per share, almost double the loss in 2000. The loss was attributable in part to the write-off of its discontinued Global Telecommunications segment and to a change in the company's accounting procedures. Lockheed Martin's share price remained relatively stable during 2001, but jumped at year end following the terrorist attacks on the World Trade Center and the Pentagon.

ANALYSTS' OPINIONS

Analysts were confident that 2002 marked a new chapter for Lockheed Martin, and a recovery from its woes of the late 1990s. Value Line predicted an "earnings surge" as the result of new contracts received from

FINANCES:

Lockheed Martin Corporation
Net Sales, 1999-2001
(million dollars)

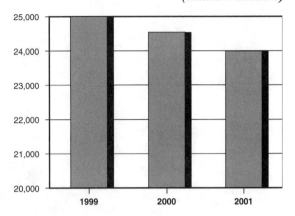

Lockheed Martin Corporation
2001 Stock Prices
(dollars)

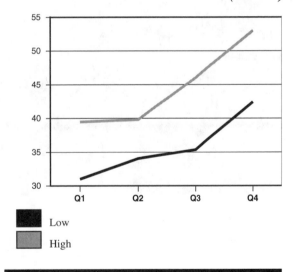

the federal government and foreign governments. For example, Lockheed received orders for its new F-35 fighter from Britain, Canada, Turkey, the Netherlands, and Denmark. Value Line predicted a continuing rise in the company's stock price until the mid-2000s.

HISTORY

The company known today as Lockheed Martin was formed by the merger of two smaller firms, each founded

At the Lockheed Martin plant in Marietta, Georgia, workers assemble an F-22 Raptor fighter jet. (AP Photo/Lockheed Martin, John Rossino)

in the early 1900s: The Lockheed Company and the Martin Company.

The Lockheed Company grew out of the Alco Hydro-Aeroplane Company founded in 1912 by Allan and Malcolm Loughead, who pronounced their name "Lockheed." In 1916 they established the Loughead Aircraft Manufacturing Company in Santa Barbara, California and were producing flying boats. The company made its first sale to the U.S. Navy in 1918, the same year the firm built the first twin engine bomber, the MB-2. In 1926, the company was reestablished as the Lockheed Aircraft Company, this time spelled phonetically—the brothers were tired of people getting

it wrong. The company was sold in 1932 to Detroit Aircraft Company.

In the 1930s, the company manufactured a series of innovative planes, including the model flown by Amelia Earhart in 1932 when she made the first transatlantic flight by a woman. It supplied the Army Air Force with bombers during World War II, and in the 1950s developed, among other products, the U-2 spy plane, the Polaris submarine-launched ballistic missile, and the Titan I rocket used in the U.S. space program. In 1958 Lockheed introduced the flight recorder—the so-called black box—that is now standard equipment on all commercial and military air-

craft. After attempting to break into the market for planes for commercial airlines, Lockheed experienced financial problems that almost drove it out of business in 1971. It survived with the aid of guaranteed loans from the federal government. In the later 1970s, Lockheed's relationship with certain foreign governments unleashed a bribery scandal that toppled governments in Japan and Italy. In the 1980s, it did much of the development work on the Hubble Space Telescope and the F-117A stealth fighter jet.

The other half of the organization that would become Lockheed Martin, was founded in 1909. Glenn L. Martin founded a company that supplied training aircraft to the U.S. Army Signal Corporations. It manufactured bombers and flying boats during the First World War. In the 1930s it developed new planes for military and commercial use, including the famous China Clipper, the model Pan Am used to make its first transpacific commercial flights. It supplied the military with bombers during World War II—including the two planes that dropped the atomic bombs on Hiroshima and Nagasaki—and with missiles and nuclear systems in the 1950s. After its merger with American Marietta in 1961 it became Martin Marietta. The company was the target of a hostile takeover by Bendix in 1980, but was able to avert the corporate action. The cost of the takeover defense left the company deep in debt and forced it to sell off a number of holdings.

Lockheed and Martin Marietta merged in 1995, a deal valued at $10 billion. A year later it acquired the defense electronics businesses of the Loral Corporation. With the end of the Cold War defense spending was cut 35 percent between 1985 and 1998. The company purchased the Consat Corporation hoping to break into the commercial telecommunications market and lessen its dependence on government contracts.

In the late 1990s problems emerged. Some of the company's space projects suffered catastrophic failures, including the very public loss of two Mars spacecraft in 1999. The failures were blamed on the lack of management oversight. Lockheed Martin also experienced difficulties during its attempts to integrate the operations of 17 recently acquired companies. An attempt to buy major competitor Northrop Grumman was blocked by government regulators on antitrust grounds. Lockheed's stock price dropped from $49 a share in 1998 to $16.62 in 2000. Profits had dropped 66 percent, and only large orders from the Pentagon, Greece, and the United Arab Emirates saved the firm. Meanwhile CEO Vance Coffman initiated a reorganization of the firm in 1999, which split it into four operating segments. Some of the company's holdings were also sold. A new program was implemented in 2001 to streamline operations. The company was back on the road to profitability in 2001 when it won the Joint Strike Fighter contract from the Department of Defense (DoD). Valued at $200 billion, it was the largest defense contract ever awarded.

FAST FACTS:
About Lockheed Martin Corporation

Ownership: Lockheed Martin Corporation is a public company traded on the New York Stock Exchange.

Ticker Symbol: LMT

Officers: Vance D. Coffman, Chmn. and CEO, 2001 base salary $1,409,615; Robert J. Stevens, Pres. and COO, 50, 2001 base salary $766,154; Dain M. Hancock, EVP Aeronautics, 2001 base salary $561,538; Robert B. Coutts, EVP Systems Integration, 2001 base salary $561,538; Albert E. Smith, EVP Space Systems, 2001 base salary $561,538

Employees: 125,000

Principal Subsidiary Companies: In late 2001 Lockheed Martin had facilities in 384 locations in more than 50 countries, although most of them are in the United States. United Space Alliance LLC, which Lockheed Martin owns jointly with Boeing, has been contracted by NASA to manage the Space Shuttle fleet. Lockheed Martin's Technology Services segment runs the federal government's Sandia Laboratories in California.

Chief Competitors: Lockheed Martin has a number of competitors in the aerospace and defense sectors. Some of its most important competitors are: Alliant Techsystems, BAE Systems, DaimlerChrysler, General Dynamics, Northrop Grumman, Raytheon, The Boeing Company, EADS, MBDA, and Honeywell International.

STRATEGY

Lockheed Martin's strategic plan was initiated and implemented by Chairman and CEO Vance D. Coffman as a response to the company's decline in the late 1990s. It called for the company to focus on key areas such as active phased arrays, photonics and optical computing, virtual environments, systems integration, advanced sensors, advanced software technology, advanced structures and materials, and data transmission and communication, which supported advanced military platforms. An important corollary to this was the divestiture of non-core businesses and Lockheed's reorganization into four core areas, with strong lines of accountability and an emphasis on product quality. Lockheed's goal was to realize $3.7 billion in annual savings.

CHRONOLOGY:

Key Dates for Lockheed Martin Corporation

1916: Loughead Aircraft Manufacturing Co. is founded by Loughead brothers in Santa Barbara California

1917: Glenn L. Martin Co. is founded in Cleveland, Ohio

1926: Loughead Aircraft Manufacturing becomes Lockheed Aircraft

1929: Lockheed is acquired by the Detroit Aircraft Company

1945: Lockheed produces nearly 20,000 aircraft for war effort-9 percent of the total U.S. production

1961: Martin Company merges with American Marietta

1971: Lockheed receives government loan to avoid going into bankruptcy

1980: Martin is the object of a hostile takeover attempt by the Bendix Corporation

1995: Martin and Lockheed merge

1996: Lockheed Martin acquires the Loral Corporation's defense electronics business

1998: The U.S. government blocks a merger with Northrop Grumman

2001: Lockheed Martin is awarded a DoD contract for the Joint Strike Fighter

INFLUENCES

The events of September 11, 2001 had a great impact on Lockheed Martin. The resulting focus on civil defense, as well as the war in Afghanistan created a political climate that supported the modernization and expansion of the nation's defense infrastructure. The new political climate resulted in a proposed 2003 federal budget which included increases for defense procurement and research and development. After more than a decade of budget cuts, Lockheed Martin saw itself as the beneficiary of an increase in defense spending. The new emphasis on homeland defense may also spur demand for other Lockheed products, such as air traffic systems, biohazard detection systems, and other security systems.

CURRENT TRENDS

The defense budgets of foreign governments declined in the late 1990s and the early 2000s. The result was not only fewer contracts, but a general consolidation of the industry, particularly in Europe. The companies that remained were larger and possessed the cream of the talent from the constituent firms. They were also more able competitors. The consolidation of the European defense community signaled less demand for American manufactured products.

PRODUCTS

Lockheed Martin's most significant product, in size and long-term impact, is the Joint Strike Fighter. The Joint Strike Fighter, commissioned by the largest defense contract in history, is an aircraft designed with certain basic features—stealth technology and the capability of supersonic speeds—that can be modified to meet the individual needs of each branch of the military. The Marine version, for example, will be able to land vertically, like a helicopter. The British military is taking part in the specifications for the aircraft as well. The first 14 planes, which cost about $30 million each, are scheduled for completion in 2008. Lockheed Martin is the leading contractor on the Joint Strike Fighter project. Other firms, such as Northrop Grumman and BAE SYSTEMS are working on it as well. Other important Lockheed products include the F-16 multi-role fighter, the F-22 Raptor, and the C-130J tactical airlift aircraft.

CORPORATE CITIZENSHIP

Lockheed Martin Corporation supports a variety of efforts to help minority students in the areas of math, science, and engineering. It sponsors Math, Engineering and Science Achievement (MESA) Grants which are given to African-American, Native American, and Latino students. Similarly the Inroads program helps prepare minority students for roles in their communities and the corporate world. The company provides participating high school graduates with career-related summer jobs for three summer terms. Lockheed Martin provides financial support and volunteers to organizations such as the American Red Cross, the American Cancer Society, and the Multiple Sclerosis Association.

Lockheed Martin encourages its employees to volunteer for educational and environmental initiatives in the communities in which they work and live. They tutor disadvantaged or at-risk elementary and high school students, rehabilitate housing for the poor and elderly, organize food drives, work at senior citizens centers, take part in environmental clean-up projects, and support public television.

GLOBAL PRESENCE

Lockheed Martin's international business consists primarily of sales of its products to foreign governments in Europe, the Middle East, and Asia. In late 2001, Israel purchased 52 F-161 fighter jets worth $1.3 billion. Sales are sometimes made directly to foreign governments, but frequently they are mediated by the U.S. government. In 2001 the company was involved in various joint ventures with foreign companies. It worked with Alenia Marconi Systems of Italy, European Aeronautic Defence and Space (EADS), and LFK—Lenkflugkorpersysteme GmbH of Germany—on the development of the Medium Extended Air Defense System for NATO. Its Aeronautics segment was part of a joint U.S.-Japanese venture to produce F-2 jets. Lockheed is the majority owner of Lockheed-Khrunichev-Energia International (LKEI), a joint venture with two space firms owned by the Russian government, to organize and market commercial space launches from sites in Kazakhstan. Lockheed Martin's Aircraft and Logistics Center is a partner in a joint venture with the Chinese government that provides aircraft maintenance engineering. It also provides Lockheed's international customers with aircraft maintenance and other related services.

EMPLOYMENT

Lockheed's workforce of 125,000 includes approximately 45,000 of the world's most talented engineers and scientists. Lockheed encourages its employees to supplement their skills through continuing education and training.

SOURCES OF INFORMATION

Bibliography

Anselma, Joseph C. "Vance Coffman: With great tenacity, the low-key CEO of Lockheed Martin guided the defense contractor out of stormy weather and into sunnier skies." *Washington Techway*, 7 January 2002.

Flight in America 1900-1983: From the Wrights to the Astronauts. Baltimore: The Johns Hopkins University Press, 1984.

Guccione, Jean. "Lockheed Settles With Residents For $5 Million." *Los Angeles Times*, 18 October 2000.

Scott, William B. "Lockheed Martin Hangs Onto Space Science Missions." *Aviation Week & Space Technology*, 10 December 2001.

THE LAST TITAN ROCKETS

In April 2002 Lockheed Martin ended the most successful production program in the history of its work with the U.S. space program—it manufactured its last Titan rocket. The Titan, the most powerful U.S. rocket, was developed in 1959 for intercontinental ballistic missiles (ICBMs). However, it became famous as a vehicle for launching two-man Gemini missions into space in the 1960s, and many of the unmanned Viking and Voyager expeditions in the 1970s. Beginning in 1986, the U.S. Air Force began converting Titans from its ICBMs into rockets for weather satellites and the like. Titans never caught on as launch vehicles for communication satellites and other commercial payloads—they were simply too powerful. Lockheed's smaller Atlas rockets were preferred for such missions. Lockheed produced 528 Titan rockets, and the last Titan-launched mission was scheduled for 2003.

Smith, Bruce. *The Sky's the Limit.* London: Macmillan, 1979.

Sutton, Oliver, and Michael Taverna. *Conquest of the Skies.* Boston: Little Brown, 1979.

For an annualreport:

on the Internet at: http://www.lockheedmartin.com/investor *or* write: Lockheed Martin Investor Relations, 6801 Rockledge Drive, Bethesda, MD 20817

For additional industry research:

Investigate companies by their Standard Industrial Classification Codes, also known as SICs. Lockheed Martin Corporation's primary SICs are:

3721 Aircraft

3760 Guided Missiles & Space Vehicles & Parts

Also investigate companies by their North American Industrial Classification System codes, also known as NAICS codes. Lockheed Martin Corporation's primary NAICS codes are:

336411 Aircraft Manufacturing

336414 Guided Missile and Space Vehicle Manufacturing

L'Oréal SA

FOUNDED: 1909

Contact Information:

HEADQUARTERS: 41, rue Martre
   Clichy, 92117 France
PHONE: 33147567000
FAX: 33147568002
URL: http://www.loreal.com

OVERVIEW

L'Oréal SA may be the world's largest cosmetic company, but it is hardly content to rest on its laurels. The international cosmetics giant has more than 2,500 scientists hard at work in laboratories at the company's Paris headquarters, constantly searching for new products to help beautify and enhance the physical appearance of L'Oréal's millions of customers around the world. Each year these researchers file for hundreds of patents on their latest discoveries and concoctions.

Although the name L'Oréal is instantly recognizable to most consumers on the strength of the popular cosmetics products marketed under the company's name, there are a number of other equally well-known brand names that are part of L'Oréal's product line. These include the cosmetic products of Biotherm, Laboratoires Garnier, Redken, Maybelline, Lancome, Helen Rubinstein, and Vichy, as well as the designer perfume lines of Ralph Lauren and Giorgio Armani. L'Oréal also owns a number of specialty cosmetic companies, including Matrix Essentials, which produces beauty salon products; Soft Sheen/Carson Products, a manufacturer of cosmetic products for ethnic markets; and Kiehl's Since 1851, which produces natural cosmetic products.

L'Oréal's products fall into one of the company's four divisions: Active Cosmetics, skin care and related cosmetic products); Luxury (fragrances and other beauty products); Professional (hair care products for beauty salons); and Consumer (makeup and hair and skin care products).

L'Oréal's largest stockholder is Liliane Bettencourt, one of the richest women in the world and the daughter of L'Oréal's founder, Eugene Schueller. Bettencourt and her family own 51 percent of Gesperal, the holding company that owns 54 percent of L'Oréal. The remaining shares of Gesperal are owned by Nestle SA.

COMPANY FINANCES

Through good times and bad, the demand for products to enhance our physical appearance seems to remain strong. This fact of life has given L'Oréal, the world's largest cosmetic company, one of the most enviable financial records around. The Paris-based company had no more than posted its 16th consecutive year of double-digit profits for 2001 when it announced that it expected to do it once again in 2002. For 2001 L'Oréal reported a profit of almost $1.1 billion on revenue of about $12.2 billion. This compared with net income of almost $968 million on sales of slightly more than $11.9 billion in 2000. In 1999 L'Oréal posted a profit of almost $702 million on revenue of $10.8 billion.

In 2001, 54 percent of L'Oréal's sales were generated by the company's Consumer division. The Luxury division accounted for 27 percent of total sales in 2001, while the Professional division brought in 14 percent of total revenue. Bringing up the rear with 5 percent of total sales was L'Oréal's Active Cosmetics division. Geographically, European markets accounted for 49 percent of total 2001 sales, followed by North America with 23 percent and other markets with 19 percent.

For L'Oréal, the year 2002 got off to a promising start. The company in early April 2002 posted a first quarter sales increase of 8.5 percent, excluding acquisitions and currency effects. This was substantially above the 7 percent estimate for first-quarter sales growth. In announcing the first-quarter results, Lindsay Own-Jones, L'Oréal's chairman and CEO, said: "The first-quarter results deepen our confidence for 2002. . . .After 17 years of growth, another is starting to emerge. What can we say? In the short term, it isn't looking bad at all."

ANALYSTS' OPINIONS

Given its glittering record of profitability over more than a decade and a half, it's difficult to find a security analyst anywhere with an unkind word to say about L'Oréal SA. After all, it's tough to argue with success. L'Oréal's 7.1 percent increase in sales during 2001, despite a worldwide economic slowdown, slightly exceeded the predictions of a JCF Group poll of 25 analysts that had predicted the company would post a 7 percent increase in sales in 2001. Of the company's 2001 performance, one Paris analyst observed: "Their weak point is luxury in the United States, but that is compensated for by a very good performance in the younger markets."

Analysts were equally positive about L'Oréal's prospects for 2002. After the company announced a jump

FAST FACTS:
About L'Oréal SA

Ownership: L'Oréal SA is a publicly-owned company traded over the counter.

Ticker Symbol: LORLY

Officers: Lindsay Owen-Jones, Chmn. and CEO; Jean-Pierre Meyers, VChmn.

Employees: 49,150

Principal Subsidiary Companies: L'Oréal SA owns a number of subsidiaries worldwide. One of its largest subsidiaries is L'Oréal USA, Inc., formerly known as Cosmair. Some of the best-known cosmetic product lines in the United States and around the world are produced under the banner of L'Oréal USA. These include Biotherm, Redken, Maybelline, Lancome, L'Oréal, Helena Rubenstein, as well as the designer cosmetics lines of Ralph Lauren and Giorgio Armani. Also owned by L'Oréal USA are Kiehl's Since 1851, which produces natural cosmetic products; Soft Sheen/Carson Products, a producer of ethnic beauty products; and Matrix Essentials, the manufacturers of a wide range of beauty salon products. Other L'Oréal subsidiaries include Sanofi-Synthelabo, a pharmaceuticals company in which L'Oréal holds a stake of about 20 percent, and Galderma, a manufacturer of skin products.

Chief Competitors: The world's largest cosmetics company, L'Oréal SA faces competition from Revlon, Estee Lauder, and Procter & Gamble. Other competitors include Chanel, Bath & Beauty Works, Mary Kay, Clarins, Alberto-Culver, Unilever, Merle Norman, and Body Shop.

of 8.5 percent-excluding currency effects and acquisitions-in its sales for the first quarter of 2001, Aurel Leven analyst Marina Boutry-Cuypers said that "everything leads us to expect that internal growth will largely exceed that [L'Oréal's 7.1 percent sales growth in 2001] this year." Boutry-Cuypers said she was encouraged by the outlook for improved economic conditions in the second half of 2002.

Analysts also seemed to look positively on the growing rumors in early 2002 that L'Oréal wold soon make a bid for Germany's Beiersdorf, which produces the popular Nivea brand of cosmetics and skin care products.

CHRONOLOGY:

Key Dates for L'Oréal

1907: Eugene Schueller invents first synthetic hair dye

1909: Schueller founds Societe Francaise des Teintures Inoffensives pour Cheveux, which is soon renamed L'Oréal

1953: L'Oréal sets up U.S. licensee, Cosmair, to distribute its products in the United States

1963: L'Oréal goes public

1984: L'Oréal acquires Ralph Lauren and Gloria Vanderbilt brands

---

Observed Andy Smith, Citigroup's consumer products analyst: "There is a fantastic fit between L'Oréal and Beiersdorf. By buying the German group, L'Oréal would be inheriting a brand it could do a lot with. It could give Nivea a huge exposure to the North American market."

HISTORY

L'Oréal traces its roots to French chemist Eugene Schueller's 1907 invention of the first synthetic hair dye. After Schueller had developed a market—largely among the hair salons of Paris—for his product, he founded a company he called Societe Francaise des Teintures Inoffensives pour Cheveux. Not long thereafter Schueller's company changed its name to L'Oréal. After it had firmly established its hold on the market for hair dye, L'Oréal added soaps and shampoos. Within only a few years of the company's founding, L'Oréal had expanded its sales outside France. By 1912 its products were being sold in Austria, Holland, and Italy. Eight years later, L'Oréal products were available in 17 countries, including Bolivia, Brazil, Chile, Ecuador, the Far East, Peru, the Soviet Union, and the United States, as well as the European countries in which L'Oréal had begun selling earlier. The company, still headquartered in Paris, had a staff of 10 sales representatives and three research chemists. In the 1920s L'Oréal was the first major French cosmetics maker to begin advertising on radio.

After World War II the demand for L'Oréal's products grew rapidly. To serve its ever-growing market in the United States, the company in 1953 established a U.S. subsidiary called Cosmair (renamed L'Oréal USA in

2000) to oversee the distribution of L'Oréal's hair products to U.S. hairdressing salons. Before long, Cosmair added L'Oréal's makeup and perfume to its product offerings in the United States. Francois Dalle, a close associate of Eugene Schueller, took over the direction of the company after the death of the L'Oréal founder in1957. Dalle in 1963 took the company public, although Schueller's daughter, Liliane Bettencourt, held on to a majority interest in her father's company. An important step in the company's diversification came in 1965 when L'Oréal acquired Lancome. In the early 1970s L'Oréal gained a foothold in the pharmaceuticals industry with its purchase of Synthelabo.

The 1980s saw L'Oréal emerge from the shadows of the international cosmetic business to become the industry's biggest manufacturer. This was accomplished largely through strategic acquisitions, including the 1984 purchase of Warner Communications' cosmetics operations, including the Gloria Vanderbilt and Ralph Lauren brand names; Helena Rubinstein and Laboratoires Pharmaeutiques Goupil in 1988; and an investment in Lanvin in 1989. In 1994 L'Oréal purchased control of its Cosmair U.S. licensee from Nestle SA and the Bettencourt family. In 1995, L'Oréal purchased Maybelline for $508 million, thus becoming the second largest U.S. cosmetics producer, trailing only Procter & Gamble, which manufactures Cover Girl and Max Factor brand-name products. In 1997 the company purchased the sun protection brand Ombrelle; the following year it acquired Soft Sheen Products, a manufacturer of ethnic hair care products. In 2000 L'Oréal added another ethnic beauty products producer, Carson, which has since been combined with L'Oréal's Soft Sheen and renamed Soft Sheen/Carson Products. The company in 2000 also acquired Kiehl's Since 1851, a family-owned producer of natural cosmetic products, and Matrix Essentials, which produces products for use in beauty salons.

STRATEGY

Key elements in L'Oréal's strategy for 2002 and the short-term future include (1) dedication to a profession of enduring relevance; (2) staking its success on innovation and quality; (3) focus on a limited number of worldwide brands with diverse origins; (4) development of promising new reservoirs of growth; (5) organic growth as a core priority; (6) full involvement of company personnel; (7) respect for fundamental values; and (8) sustainable growth.

Writing of the corporation's dedication to its core profession in L'Oréal's 2001 annual report, Chairman Lindsay Owen-Jones observed that "our profession, which has existed since the earliest societies, is constantly changing and reinventing itself, enabling us to anticipate the future with confidence." As to the importance L'Oréal attaches to innovation and quality, its chairman wrote that "by producing ourselves over 94 percent of the product ranges we sell, we recognize the part played by our own manufacturing sites in delivering overall quality."

To avoid spreading itself too thin, L'Oréal has resolved to focus on a limited number of worldwide brands. In recent years, the company's core products of French heritage have been joined by a second group of products of American origin. The company has recognized the emergence of New York as a second center of global creativity in the cosmetics business. Some of the more influential L'Oréal brands of American origin are Redken, Maybelline, Ralph Lauren, Matrix, and Kiehl's. Although L'Oréal's principal business will continue to be cosmetics, dermatology has emerged as a market offering significant potential for the company.

Central to the success of L'Oréal's blueprint for the future is the full involvement of all company employees. Explaining this aspect of the company's strategy in its 2001 Annual Report, Chairman Owen-Jones wrote: "L'Oréal has a clear aim to enable company staff to benefit from the company's economic success. For example, a manual worker in France on an average salary of 23,400 euros received a profit sharing bonus of 3,950 euros in 2001." And L'Oréal has not forgotten the important contributions made by the communities in which the company operates. To help repay those communities for their support, the company has undertaken a number of initiatives in cultural, humanitarian, and scientific fields.

INFLUENCES

One of the more significant adverse factor facing L'Oréal in 2001 was the weakness in the U.S. cosmetics market, particularly for luxury-type products. The company managed, however, to make up for the softness in U.S. sales by concentrating more of its marketing efforts in emerging markets. The success of this strategy was reflected in L'Oréal's 7.1 percent in sales growth during 2001, this despite an economic slowdown worldwide.

CURRENT TRENDS

A significant trend for L'Oréal over the last two or more decades has been its expansion through strategic acquisition. In 2001 the company purchased Colorama, Revlon's makeup and hair care brand in Brazil, and CosMedic Concepts' line of 60 BioMedic products, which are distributed to dermatologists in 60 countries. In early 2002, rumors circulated that L'Oréal was planning to make a bid for Germany's Beiersdorf consumer care group, producer of Nivea skin care products. L'Oréal executives declined to disclose whether such an acquisition was planned.

To stay abreast of changing tastes and styles, L'Oréal maintains an extensive research and development operation. The company has research centers on three continents: Europe, North America, and Asia. These centers are staffed by some 2,700 employees who originate from 26 different countries and work in 30 different areas of specialization.

PRODUCTS

L'Oréal's product line is spread out over four different divisions: Active Cosmetics, Consumer Products, Luxury Products, and Professional. Within the Active Cosmetics division, the major brand names are La Roche-Posay and Vichy. Brand names marketed by the Consumer Products division include Gemey, Laboratoires Garnier, L'Oréal, Plenitude, and Maybelline. Luxury Products brand names include Biotherm, Cacharel, Lancome, Lanvin, Guy Laroche, Giorgio Armani, Helena Rubinstein, Ralph Lauren, and Paloma Picasso. The Professional division offers such brand names as Kerastase, Inne, Redken, and L'Oréal Professional. L'Oréal also offers pharmaceuticals, luxury goods, and dermatological products through its Galderma, Lanvin, and Vich Laboratoires subsidiaries.

CORPORATE CITIZENSHIP

L'Oréal feels strongly that if its growth is to be sustained, it must be based on both a winning strategy and an awareness of the company's responsibility to everyone who plays a part in the company and in the wider environment in which L'Oréal operates. More than a decade ago, the company set ambitious targets to limit the impact of its operations on the environment, this in an industry that consumes only small amounts of natural resources. In a portion of its corporate Web site devoted to environmental policy, L'Oréal offers these views on its responsibility to the environment: "Respecting the environment is a civic responsibility and a duty for the company. For years, the L'Oréal Group has been made acutely aware of these issues and has made significant efforts to master the environmental impact of its activities, as well as those of its suppliers and contractors." In 2001 nearly 8 percent of the company's industrial investments were for the environment and security.

As part of its perceived responsibilities to the communities in which it operates, L'Oréal has taken a number of initiatives in cultural, humanitarian, and scientific fields. Additionally, the company has formed a partnership with UNESCO that is targeted specifically at helping bring more women into scientific careers worldwide and promoting the role played by women in scientific research.

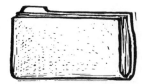

L'ORÉAL'S R&D TEAM GETS DOWN TO BASICS

L'Oréal each year allocates one-third of its research and development resources, including staff, to fundamental research projects. These include intensive study of hair structure to learn more about how and why hair changes, turns grey, or falls out. Such research into the characteristics of hair has turned up some interesting findings about the fragility of hair of African origin, which will form the basis of innovative products for L'Oréal's ethnic hair products. To improve its understanding of skin, L'Oréal researchers have been exploring the phenomenon of pigmentation through studying the characteristics of the melanocyte cells responsible for skin color. Researchers' findings about the workings of melanocyte have been passed along to L'Oréal chemists, and it is hoped that in time these research studies will enable chemists to develop more effective products to correct blemishes and dull skin.

GLOBAL PRESENCE

L'Oréal operates in 130 different countries. In recent years the growth of cosmetic markets in developed countries has stabilized at about 5 percent annually. The growth rates in emerging markets, however, are far more vigorous. Major growth areas for L'Oréal have been Latin America, where the cosmetics market grew 14 percent in 2001; Asia outside Japan with 2001 growth of 17 percent; and Eastern Europe with a growth rate of 21 percent.

EMPLOYMENT

At the end of 2001, L'Oréal SA had a workforce of 49,150 people worldwide. L'Oréal feels that it has a responsibility to enable its workers to benefit from the company's success. Its Worldwide Profit Sharing program is gradually extending these benefits to all company employees worldwide. For those already in the program, the company's 2001 results were expected to yield a bonus payment equivalent to one week's salary. Providing the company is able to meet its profit targets, it hopes to increase the size of such profit-sharing bonuses to the equivalent of one month's salary or even more. In addition the company's stock option plan, as of early 2002, was available to more than 2,500 of L'Oréal's managers, about one-quarter of its global management staff.

SOURCES OF INFORMATION

Bibliography

"Because They're Worth It." *Sunday Independent,* 19 May 2002, 1.

Brothers, Caroline. "L'Oréal Says Sales Herald Yet More Profit Growth." *Reuters,* 4 April 2002.

"Kiehl's Since 1851 LLC." *Hoover's Online,* 2002. Available at http://www.hoovers.com.

"L'Oréal Expects 17th Year of Strong Profit Growth." *Reuters,* 23 January 2002.

"L'Oréal—History." *Gale Business Resources,* 2002. Available at http://galenet.galegroup.com/servlet/GBR.

L'Oréal SA 2001 Annual Report. Paris: L'Oréal SA, 2002.

"L'Oréal SA." *Hoover's Online,* 2002. Available at http://www.hoovers.com.

"L'Oréal Silent on Beiersdorf Talk; Sources Skeptical." *Reuters,* 20 May 2002.

"L'Oréal USA, Inc." *Hoover's Online,* 2002. Available at http://www.hoovers.com.

"Recession-Resistant L'Oréal Posts 2001 Sales Rise." *Reuters,* 23 January 2002.

For an annual report:
on the Internet at: http://www.loreal-finance.com

For additional industry research:
Investigate companies by their Standard Industrial Classification Codes, also known as SICs. L'Oréal's primary SIC is:

2844 Toilet Preparations

Also investigate companies by their North American Industry Classification System codes, also known as NAICS codes. L'Oréal's primary NAICS code is:

325620 Toilet Preparation Manufacturing

Lowe's Companies, Inc.

OVERVIEW

Lowe's Companies, Inc. is the second largest home improvement chain in the world, with more than 740 stores located in 42 states serving over six million individual and commercial customers. The 55-year-old company, headquartered in Wilkesboro, North Carolina, employs over 100,000 people across the nation. States with the largest number of Lowe's stores include North Carolina (77), Texas (63), Ohio (48), Florida (47), and Virginia (42). Typically, a Lowe's store consists of a sales floor approximately 120,000 square feet in size, as well as a lawn and garden center consisting of another 30,000 square feet. Lowe's offers a wide range of products and services in the areas of home improvement, home decor, home maintenance, home repair and remodeling, and maintenance of commercial facilities.

During 2000, 75 percent of Lowe's sales revenues were generated by do-it-yourself and buy-it-yourself consumers, and 25 percent came from commercial business. Retail customers include all personal-use shoppers who buy products and services for home building, repair, and maintenance. Commercial customers are professional contractors in such fields as remodeling, electrical work, landscaping, painting, plumbing, and maintenance professionals. To meet customers' wide variety of needs, all Lowe's stores provide a home fashions and interior design center; a lawn and garden center; a selection of appliances; a hard goods and hardware store; an air conditioning, heating, and plumbing supply center; and a building materials center.

FOUNDED: 1957

Contact Information:

HEADQUARTERS: PO Box 1111
   North Wilkesboro, NC 28656
PHONE: (336)658-4000
FAX: (336)658-4766
TOLL FREE: (800)445-6937
URL: http://www.lowes.com

FAST FACTS:

About Lowe's Companies, Inc.

Ownership: Lowe's Companies, Inc. went public in 1961. It is traded on the New York, Pacific, and London Stock Exchanges.

Ticker Symbol: LOW

Officers: Robert L. Tillman, 57, Chmn. and CEO, 2001 base salary $935,000, 2001 bonus $1.9 million; Larry D. Stone, 49, EVP Store Operations, 2001 base salary $600,000, 2001 bonus $983,000; William C. Warden, Jr., 48, EVP Administration, 2001 base salary $470,000, 2001 bonus $770,000; Thomas E. Whiddon, EVP Logistics and Technology, 2001 base salary $470,000, 2001 bonus $770,000; Dale C. Pond, EVP Merchandising, 2001 base salary $450,000, 2001 bonus $737,000

Employees: 100,000

Principal Subsidiary Companies: Lowe's primary subsidiaries are Lowe's Home Centers, Inc.; The Contractor Yard, Inc.; Sterling Advertising, Ltd.; LF Corp.; LG Sourcing, Inc.; and Lowe's Home Centres (Canada), Inc.

Chief Competitors: Lowe's Companies, Inc.'s competitors also cater to the do-it-yourself home improvement market. Although Lowe's receives its principal competition from Home Depot, it also competes against Ace Hardware, Best Buy, Menard, Payless Cashways, Sears, Sherwin-Williams, Sutherland Lumber, and Wal-Mart as well as regional and local chains.

COMPANY FINANCES

For fiscal year 2001, ending February 2, 2002, Lowe's reported a net income of $1.02 billion on $22.1 billion in revenues. This compares favorably to net income in fiscal 2000 of $810 million on revenues of $18.8 billion. Earnings in fiscal 2001 translated into $1.30 per share versus $1.05 per share in fiscal 2000. In fiscal 1999, the company generated $15.9 billion in sales, resulting in a net profit of $673,000.

Both income and sales have grown steadily since 1994. The nearly 18 percent increase in sales during fiscal 2001 was driven by a 19 percent increase in square footage from new and relocated stores and a 2.4 percent increase in same-store sales. Stock prices closed in January of 2000, 2001, and 2002 at $22.21, $26.68, and $46.07 respectively. Lowe's made a particularly strong showing in the fourth quarter of fiscal 2001 with net earnings increasing 55 percent and same-store sales increasing over 7 percent compared to the same period in 2000.

ANALYSTS' OPINIONS

Analysts consider Lowe's to be a solid company with significant and consistent growth potential. During the first quarter of 2002, most analysts marked Lowe's as a Strong Buy with a target stock price of $50. In fact, some analysts believed that Lowe's own estimates for upcoming years possibly were too conservative. Based on plans for expansion in square footage, along with ongoing cost controls and inventory management, they looked for Lowe's to top its expected 20 percent increase in total sales. Those analysts who see a bright future for Lowe's stock consider the company an excellent long-term investment opportunity.

HISTORY

In 1921, L.S. Lowe opened a hardware store in North Wilkesboro, North Carolina. Upon his death, Lowe's son James and James' brother-in-law, Carl Buchan, continued to operate the family business until both men were called into military service during World War II. For several years, Lowe's sister and mother ran the store. Before the end of 1943, Buchan was wounded and returned to North Carolina. Taking a 50 percent interest in the store, Buchan sold off much of the existing merchandise and reorganized the business as a wholesale warehouse specializing in hardware and building supplies. Lowe returned from military service in 1946 to assist Buchan. The operation produced enough revenue to allow the two men to open a second store as well as purchase an automobile dealership and a cattle ranch.

In 1952 Buchan traded the automobile dealership and the cattle ranch for Lowe's half-interest in the two stores. In the same year, Buchan opened a third store in Asheville, North Carolina. In 1955, with six stores now in operation, Buchan incorporated the business as Lowe's North Wilkesboro Hardware, Inc. During the 1950s, the business grew rapidly, primarily as a result of the postwar building boom that created an endless demand for hardware and building supplies. Between 1952 and 1959, sales increased from $4.1 million to $27 million. The company's business philosophy was simple: buy products directly from the manufacturer to avoid paying higher wholesale prices from distributors. Customers were primarily building contractors and construction companies. Stores were generally small with limited inventory and a lumberyard behind the store near railroad tracks that provided easy access to delivery.

Buchan died in 1960, and the following year, with sales reaching $30.7 million, the company went public and was renamed Lowe's Companies, Inc. By 1969, the company operated 50 stores and revenues neared $1 billion. Just two years later, the company posted a net income of $170 million; and by 1979, 200 Lowe's stores were producing in excess of $900 million in profits.

Despite its rapid growth, Lowe's noticed that revenues paralleled increases and declines in the housing market. During the 1970s when the price of homes and homebuilding rose considerably and the cost of professional remodeling became prohibitive, homeowners began taking on fix-it projects themselves. When the housing market came to a near dead stop in the late 1970s, Lowe's made the decision to realign the company to target do-it-yourself consumers rather than commercial contractors. Correctly, Lowe's management expected that the company would be more protected from economic swings that traditionally affected the housing industry.

To attract consumers, stores were redesigned to resemble a supermarket. Seasonal and nonessential products were placed at the front of the store on the assumption that customers would come in for basic hardware supplies but buy more when exposed to such departments as home dÈcor and appliances. Product selection was upgraded and expanded, store hours were extended, and the advertising budget was increased. The strategy was a spectacular success. By 1982, sales topped $1 billion and the following year became the first that Lowe's consumer sales outdid its commercial sales.

By the end of the 1980s, the do-it-yourself home improvement market was clearly here to stay. Home Depot arrived on the scene and quickly surpassed Lowe's to lead the industry. Modeling Home Depot's much larger floor plan, in 1989 Lowe's began greatly expanding its own square footage from 20,000 square feet to 60,000 square feet, which was still significantly smaller than Home Depot's standard 100,000-plus square feet stores. Becoming more aggressive in its expansion efforts between 1991 and 1995, Lowe's remodeled or relocated approximately half of its stores, bringing the square footage to between 85,000 and 115,000.

After focusing for several years on restructuring, Lowe's began to expand into new markets again in the mid-1990s. The company operated 520, 576, 620, and 744 "warehouses" in 1998, 1999, 2000, and 2001, respectively. In 1999, Lowe's purchased Washington-based Eagle Hardware for $1 billion and converted its stores over to the Lowe's name. Although the majority of Lowe's stores are located in the Midwest and Southeast, Lowe's has increased its presence in other regions, especially on the West Coast with 35 stores in California and 20 stores in Washington.

CHRONOLOGY:
Key Dates for Lowe's Companies, Inc.

1921: L.S. Lowe opens a hardware store in North Wilkesboro, North Carolina

1943: Lowe's son, James Lowe, runs the business with brother-in-law Carl Buchan

1952: Buchan buys out Lowe, who trades his interest in the company for an auto dealership and a cattle farm

1959: Post-war construction boom generates sales of $27 million, up from slightly more than $4 million in 1952

1961: Lowe's goes public with most customers being contractors and construction workers

1971: Company is operating over 50 stores with revenues reaching $170 million

1983: For the first time, sales to consumer do-it-yourselfers surpasses sales to contractors and sales reach $1.43 billion

1990: Lowe's is operating 309 stores located primarily in the southern United States

1995: Web site launched, featuring do-it-yourself tips and locations of stores

1996: Initiation of major expansion project by opening 37 new stores

1998: Dedication of $1.5 billion to opening 100 new stores in western United States

2001: Fiscal year 2001 sees net earnings increase 21 percent to $1.05 billion on total revenues of $22.1 billion

STRATEGY

Customer satisfaction is at the heart of Lowe's retail strategy. Using the tag line, "Improving Home Improvement," the company is constantly looking to improve its warehouses and increase its line of products and available services in order to provide a customer-friendly environment that offers the products consumers want. For example, after researching consumer preferences, Lowe's discovered that important aspects of Lowe's warehouses included a bright, friendly store environment, informative displays, and a practical store layout. This

IN-STORE AND ONLINE SPECIAL HELPS

Lowe's offers a variety of free in-store services to its customers. Complimentary computer project design is available to those who need help detailing the plans of a project such as designing a deck or storage building, or redesigning a kitchen. Regularly scheduled How-To clinics teach customers skills in a range of areas from home repair, installation, and remodeling projects to lawn and garden topics. Lowe's also offers computerized color matching. Using a sample of the desired color, Lowe's color-matching software will mix paint to the exact shade. If a local store isn't a convenient destination for information, Lowe's Web site provides extensive How-To tips on such topics as indoor and outdoor projects, home décor, energy solutions, home safety, moving and relocation. The site also offers tools such as project calculators and buying guides.

information helped Lowe's determine product display, design, and location. Lowe's also provides goods and services to consumers with a broad range of needs, tastes, and budgets. The company attempts to include a variety of offerings within a product line with clear information on individual features.

An important factor in Lowe's profitability is inventory management, which is based on the company's network of distribution centers. The key is to maintain minimal levels of merchandise on the warehouse shelves without sacrificing selection choice or availability. Regional distribution centers allow for rapid restocking of individual stores, which means better customer service while minimizing distribution and inventory costs. Lowe's operates seven regional distribution centers along with nine smaller support operations that handle merchandise with unique shipping requirements due to size or packaging, such as lumber, special imports, and some building materials. Approximately 50 percent of a store's merchandise arrives from a Lowe's distribution facility. The remainder is shipped directly from suppliers.

INFLUENCES

Lowe's is a leader in the phenomenon of the do-it-yourself home improvement trend. Along with being the

second largest home improvement retailer, it is the 14th largest retailer in the United States and the 30th largest retailer in the world. However, despite its big chain status and direct competition with industry leader Home Depot, 80 percent of Lowe's competition comes from smaller and regional chains. With the home improvement industry generating an estimated $400 billion annually, the impact of local competition is significant.

Customer type also influences Lowe's strategy for sales growth. The company wants to appeal to Baby Boomers who are in the process of upgrading their housing by moving or remodeling as well as Gen-Xers who are preparing to purchase their first house. The company continues to upgrade special order options and installation services to accommodate a range of needs and preferences. Additionally, women shoppers have become increasingly important as more and more women become the decision-makers in home improvement projects.

One specific reason for a positive outlook is Lowe's increasing strength in appliances in the wake of Circuit City removing its appliance product line and Montgomery Ward going out of business altogether. With Sears as Lowe's lone remaining national competition, analysts expect the company to increase its share of the appliance market. Of interest will be comparable same-store sales of appliances at Sears and Lowe's locations. Appliances comprise 10 percent of Lowe's sales, representing its largest product line.

CURRENT TRENDS

Lowe's has expanded its square footage consistently and significantly. Between 1998 and 2001, total square footage increased from 47.8 million to 80.7 million, and average store size grew from 92,000 square feet to 121,000 square feet. Continued store expansion over the next several years has been targeted to grow by 10 to 15 percent annually. Traditionally, Lowe's has located in small and medium-sized markets. However, future growth will be focused primarily in major metropolitan areas. New stores will account for the majority of growth. Some store relocations will also continue to take place as smaller, older warehouses are moved into new, larger facilities.

Reacting to a change in its customer base, Lowe's began providing services for what it calls "buy-it-yourselfers," those consumers with the money to purchase products but without the time for delivery and installation. Quick to target this new consumer group, Lowe's began offering delivery and installation services as well as providing Web-based tools, also staffing its locations with professionals with home improvement knowledge, skills, and practical experience to provide assistance and guidance to customers. The increase in buy-it-yourselfers has also fueled the growth of Lowe's commercial-based business.

PRODUCTS

Lowe's offers a broad range of home improvement and maintenance products. Major product lines consist of tools, books and videos, home organization, home dÈcor, outdoor living, paints and painting supplies, cleaning supplies, appliances, hardware, lighting and ceiling fans, moving supplies, plumbing, outdoor equipment, electrical supplies, fencing, safety equipment, lawn and garden products, and lumber and building supplies. An average Lowe's warehouse stocks approximately 40,000 items, with hundreds of thousands more available via special order. Excluding special order suppliers, the company contracts for goods from nearly 7,000 vendors, many of whom supply name-brand merchandise. No single vendor claims more than 4 percent of a typical store's total sales. Along with name-brand selection, Lowe's offers an exclusive line of products including Lowe's Top Choice Lumber, Kobalt Tools, and Alexander Julian at Home décor products.

A limited selection of products can be purchased on line at the company's Web site. Purchases are available for pickup at a local Lowe's store or may be delivered. Visitors to the Web site can also find how-to advice and information as well as specialized services for commercial customers. The company offers two Lowe's credit cards, one for individual customers and another for commercial accounts.

CORPORATE CITIZENSHIP

Lowe's is an active member of the communities in which its warehouses are located through support of local programs and volunteer involvement, including the Lowe's Heroes program and Lowe's Charitable and Educational Foundation. The company also provides financial support to such well-known nonprofit organizations as the American Red Cross and United Way.

As a major U.S. supplier of lumber, Lowe's has taken steps to phase out the purchase of lumber from endangered forests as these areas are identified. In 2000, the company placed an immediate ban on lumber purchases from the endangered Great Bear Rainforest of British Columbia. Lowe's is also a founding sponsor of the National Garden, a three-acre area adjacent to the U.S. Botanic Garden Conservatory located in Washington, D.C.

EMPLOYMENT

Lowe's considers its employees as the key to customer satisfaction, which in turn relates directly to the company's success. Committed to diversity and inclusion, Lowe's provides comprehensive, ongoing training that provides its employees with product knowledge, home improvement know-how, and people skills to better serve customers. Lowe's wants its friendly, knowledgeable associates to separate the company from competitors. Newly hired store personnel are provided with a one-on-one mentor as well as group orientation programs.

Employment benefits include competitive pay, performance incentives, stock options, and career development opportunities. Store managers can benefit from a bonus program based on the store's performance. All employees are eligible to participate in the Buy, Own, Save stock program, which provides company stock at a discounted price. After one year, employees are automatically enrolled in an employee stock ownership plan into which the company makes annual contributions of Lowe's stock. A 401(k) employee investment plan is also available.

SOURCES OF INFORMATION

Bibliography

"Analysts See Lowe's Growth." *Pacific Business News*, 11 January 2002.

Benjamin, Jeff. "Lowe's Builds a Solid Foundation for Profit Growth." *Investment News*, 18 February 2002.

Grant, Tina, and Jay P. Pederson, eds. *International Directory of Company Histories*, Vol. 21. Detroit: St. James Press, 1998.

Lowe's Companies, Inc. Home Page, 2002. Available at http://www.lowes.com.

"Lowe's CEO Tillman Tells Vendors What it Will Take to Do Business with the Big Box Chain in the Future." *Do-It-Yourself Retailing*, March 2002.

"Lowe's Companies, Inc." *Hoover's Company Profiles*. Available at http://www.hoovers.com.

"Lowe's Concentrates on Metro Markets." *Home Textiles Today*, 4 March 2002.

"Lowe's Fourth-Quarter Earnings Surged 55.1 Percent to $218.4 Million." *Chain Store Age Executive Fax*, 1 March 2002.

"Lowe's Reports Record Earnings for Fourth Quarter and Fiscal Year." *PR Newswire*, 25 February 2002.

For an annual report:
on the Internet at: http://www.lowes.com

For additional industry research:
Investigate companies by their Standard Industrial Classification Codes, also known as SICs. Lowe's Companies, Inc.'s primary SICs are:

2431 Millwork

3442 Metal Doors, Sash And Trim

5031 Lumber, Plywood And Millwork

5039 Construction Materials, Not Elsewhere Classified

5072 Hardware

5211 Lumber And Other Building Materials

5251 Hardware Stores

5261 Retail Nurseries And Garden Stores

5722 Household Appliance Stores

Also investigate companies by their North American Industry Classification System Codes, also known as NAICS codes. Lowe's Companies, Inc.'s primary NAICS codes are:

321918 Other Millwork (Including Flooring)

332321 Metal Window and Door Manufacturing

421310 Lumber, Plywood, Millwork and Wood Panel Wholesalers

421390 Other Construction Material Wholesalers

421710 Hardware Wholesalers

443111 Household Appliance Stores

444130 Hardware Stores

444190 Other Building Material Dealers

444220 Nursery and Garden Centers

Lucasfilm Ltd.

FOUNDED: 1971

OVERVIEW

George Lucas is the visionary behind the phenomenally successful *Star Wars* saga and the epic adventure Indiana Jones films. Lucas is one of the most influential filmmakers of the twentieth century, transforming the way movies are made, marketed and experienced by audiences. With five of the top 20 grossing films of all time, Lucasfilm is one of the most powerful and influential independent movie empires in all of filmdom. One of the six companies owned by filmmaker George Lucas, Lucasfilm's productions have struck Academy Awards gold 17 times.

The installment in the *Star Wars* saga, *Star Wars: Episode I—The Phantom Menace*, released in May 1999, topped the box office at $920 million, finishing number two behind *Titanic*.

Through Lucasfilm, created in 1971, commander Lucas handles all of the business affairs in his empire. Lucasfilm is a self-contained multimedia production enterprise that along with its subsidiaries runs completely independent of Hollywood influence.

In addition, Lucas has developed computer software for use in classrooms, and has put his name and fame behind many less successful filmmakers over the past two decades.

Contact Information:
HEADQUARTERS: 5858 Lucas Valley Rd.
   Nicasio, CA 94946
PHONE: (415)662-1800
FAX: (415)662-2437
URL: http://www.lucasfilm.com

COMPANY FINANCES

Lucasfilm Ltd., a private company, estimated 2001 sales of $1.5 billion, including sales from international business, up 36.4 percent from the previous year. Thanks

FAST FACTS:

About Lucasfilm Ltd.

Ownership: Lucasfilm Ltd. is a private company owned and operated by filmmaker George Lucas.

Officers: George W. Lucas, Jr., Chmn. and CEO; Gordon Radley, Pres.; Micheline Chau, CFO; Lynne Hale, Dir. of Public Relations

Employees: 2,000

Principal Subsidiary Companies: Lucasfilm is a parent/holding company established to handle the business affairs of each company in the Lucas empire. Its subsidiaries include: George Lucas Educational Foundation, Lucas Digital Ltd. LLC, Lucas Learning Ltd., Lucas THX, and LucasArts Entertainment Company LLC.

Chief Competitors: Lucasfilm is the sixteenth largest motion picture producer in the United States, ranked by revenues. Some of its chief competitors are Dreamworks SKG, Universal Studios, and Walt Disney.

to Lucas' strong self-belief, his deal with Twentieth Century Fox to finance *Star Wars* made him extremely wealthy. The studio originally offered Lucas a flat fee for writing and directing the film, anticipating he would ask for a higher salary. Instead, he asked only for sequel rights and full ancillary rights, giving him a large portion of the profits from sale of toys, games, soundtrack albums, posters, costumes, and any product bearing the *Star Wars* name.

Profits from *Star Wars* memorabilia, books and comics, estimated at $2.6 billion worldwide by 1991, allowed Lucas to fully finance subsequent films and retain a higher portion of film profits. Additionally, Lucas expanded the company's reach into postproduction facilities and multimedia research. With a third *Star Wars* prequel slated and Spielberg's agreement to direct the fourth Indiana Jones film, Lucasfilm seems poised for continued intergalactic good fortunes.

HISTORY

Lucasfilm Ltd. is a motion picture, television and distribution company created by celebrated filmmaker George Lucas. Company founder Lucas was born in 1945

in Modesto, California and attended the University of Southern California's film school. Lucas won a scholarship to observe Francis Ford Coppola direct the film *Finian's Rainbow*, which had a profound effect on the young filmmaker. In 1970 Coppola produced Lucas' sophomore film effort, the futuristic *THX 1138*. The following year, Lucas created his own film company, Lucasfilm Ltd., in Hollywood across from Universal Studios. In 1973, Lucas got his first taste of commercial success with the movie *American Graffiti*, a comedic look at a night in the lives of high school graduates in the 1960s, which he co-wrote and directed. The film netted five Academy Award nods, a Golden Globe award, and awards from the New York Film Critics and National Society of Film Critics.

Lucas became well known in Hollywood and began company expansion. For example, he founded Skywalker Sound, a full service audio and post production facility. He also set up Industrial Light and Magic (ILM), now the world's foremost visual effects production facility, to develop spectacular effects for his upcoming science fiction *Star Wars* epics.

Lucas wrote and directed the first *Star Wars* movie in 1977 for Twentieth Century Fox, at a cost of $6.5 million. *Star Wars* became a number one box-office smash, and an important part of American culture and film history. Over the next six years, Lucas wrote and produced the Star Wars sequels *The Empire Strikes Back* (1980) and *Return of the Jedi* (1983).

As Lucasfilm continued to profit, Lucas began to distance himself from Hollywood, and moved his offices to Skywalker Ranch, a secluded 3,000-acre facility in San Rafael, California. Despite his detachment from Hollywood, Lucasfilm continued creating successful films, producing the popular Indiana Jones movies, directed by Lucas colleague Steven Spielberg. *Raiders of the Lost Ark* (1981), *Indiana Jones and the Temple of Doom* (1984), and *Indiana Jones and the Last Crusade* (1989) all achieved wide financial success.

STRATEGY

Lucasfilm is an independent, multimedia company that seeks to develop technology and create film and television projects. Lucasfilm Ltd. oversees the business affairs of each company in the ever-expanding motion picture, television, and distribution empire. The company includes all of George Lucas' feature film and television projects as well as the business activities of the THX Group and Lucas Licensing. Lucasfilm pioneered film-oriented computerized nonlinear electronic editing for picture and sound with the creation of the EditDroid and SoundDroid, which premiered at the National Association of Broadcasters in 1984. Lucasfilm recently sold the technology to AVID and has teamed up with them on the next generation of editing

CHRONOLOGY:

Key Dates for Lucasfilm Ltd.

1971: Lucasfilm Ltd. incorporates; the movie *THX 1138* is released

1973: *American Graffiti* is released and later receives five Academy Award nominations

1975: Industrial Light and Magic is created to produce visual effects for *Star Wars*; Skywalker Sound is established to edit and mix *Star Wars*

1977: *Star Wars* opens May 25, becomes the largest-grossing film of all time to that date, and later receives six Academy Awards for original score, film editing, sound, art and set decoration, costume design and visual effects, as well as a Special Achievement Academy Award for sound effects creations

1980: *The Empire Strikes Back* opens May 21, becomes the third largest grossing film of all time, and receives an Academy Award for best sound and a Special Achievement Academy Award for visual effects

1981: *Raiders of the Lost Ark* is released June 21, becomes the largest-grossing film of the year and one of the most popular movies ever made, and receives Academy Awards for art direction, sound, film editing and visual effects, as well as a Special Achievement Academy Award for sound effects editing

1983: *Return of the Jedi* premieres May 25 and breaks industry records for a single day with the largest opening in history, $6.2 million

1984: *Indiana Jones and the Temple of Doom* opens May 23 and receives an Academy Award for visual effects

1989: *Indiana Jones and the Last Crusade* is released May 24, passes the $100 million mark in the weekend before June 13, and receives an Academy Award for sound effects editing; Industrial Light and Magic completes *Body Wars*, another attraction for Disney's Epcot Center; LucasArts Entertainment Company is established, including the Games Division

1992: The first season of *The Young Indiana Jones Chronicles* airs on ABC; George Lucas is presented with the Irving Thalberg Award by The Academy of Motion Picture Arts and Sciences

1997: *Star Wars* Special Edition premieres on January 31 to a record opening and becomes the first movie to break $400 million in domestic grosses and reclaim its title as the highest-grossing film of all time

1998: Making the American Film Institute's list of America's 100 greatest movies are *Star Wars, Raiders of the Lost Ark,* and *American Graffiti*

1999: *Star Wars: Episode I—The Phantom Menace* is released to record-breaking business across North America on May 19, shatters opening weekend box office records in 28 countries and ends the year with ticket sales of $922 million, becoming the second-highest grossing film ever released

2002: *Star Wars: Episode II—The Attack of the Clones* is released

equipment. THX is at the forefront of quality film presentation in the exhibition and consumer electronics industry. The Professional THX Sound System is currently in more than 2,500 theaters and mixing stages worldwide.

For quality assurance, Lucasfilm initiated the Theatre Alignment Program (TAP) as a service to filmmakers and movie studios. TAP's service has covered over 500 film releases, including many of the top box office films of the past decade. The THX Digital Mastering Program was first created to certify laser discs, but has gone on to include VHS and, most recently, DVD. Lucas Digital Ltd. includes the divisions of Industrial Light & Magic (ILM) and Skywalker Sound, which is committed to servicing the digital needs of the entertainment industry for visual effects and audio postpro-

duction. ILM has created special effects for eight of the top 15 box office hits of all time, winning 14 Academy Awards for Best Visual Effects and 16 Technical Achievement Awards. ILM is at the forefront of the digital revolution, and is the world's largest digital production facility. Skywalker sound has pioneered innovative picture and sound editing technologies and has received ten Academy Awards.

INFLUENCES

Around the year 2000, there were high hopes at Lucasfilm that up to 2,000 screens could be converted to digital projection in time for *Star Wars: Episode II—*

Master model maker, Lorne Peterson, displays his "Star Wars" model of the Millennium Falcon at the Museum of Fine Arts in Houston, Texas. (AP Photo/David J. Phillip)

Attack of the Clones. The reality is that there are only 20 digital screens nationwide and little prospect of adding more by the picture's scheduled May 16, 2002 release. In recent years, industry insiders have gone from talking about digital cinema as a possibility to something more of an inevitability. Its not a question of whether some portion of exhibitors will convert to digital, just a question of when.

The actual debut of the technology has been hampered by two main problems. First, there is still no uniform set of engineering standards for digital camera systems; and exhibitors have had other problems, such as a dozen bankruptcy filings amid industry over-expansion. Lucas had hoped that several hundred digital screens would be in place by the time *Attack of the Clones* premiered. The second Star Wars prequel was shot entirely on digital video. Now the feeling is perhaps several dozen theaters could convert to digital projection by the time *Clones* premieres, but it is doubtful that anyone will step up to provide the multi-million dollar funding necessary.

Digital productions come along rarely and usually involve computer generated-cartoons such as Dream-Works' *Shrek* or Disney/Pixar's *Monsters, Inc.*. Lucas plans a third *Star Wars* prequel for release in three years. Industry insiders predict *Episode III* could be distributed entirely in the digital format.

CURRENT TRENDS

George Lucas' long term plans to move his ILM digital f/x house and other digital operations to San Francisco's Presidio are moving ahead. Planning and design of the Letterman Digital Arts Center (LCD) has progressed to the schematic drawing stage and has been submitted to the Presidio Trust for public review. The Presidio Trust released a draft implementation plan and environmental impact statement for the 1,450-acre San Francisco park in July 2001. The draft concentrates new development in the former Army base's northeast corner, near the Palace of Fine Arts and newly restored Crissy Field. The plan limits total structural space to 5.6 million square feet.

In August 2001, the Presidio Trust and Lucasfilm inked an agreement to allow the company to develop a 23-acre office and movie production campus at the site of the abandoned Letterman Military Hospital. The 900,000 square-foot Lucasfilm campus would house about 2,500 workers, which Presidio Trust officials see as the park's financial backbone. The buildings themselves are designed to blend in with the original Spanish-style military structures, in accordance with the Presidio's design rules. The structures would be made of red brick and stucco with pitched red roofs and range from two to four stories high. Lucas' $5 million annual

lease payments would assist in the park's plan to achieve economic self-sufficiency by 2013.

"Hopefully," said Lucasfilm President Gordon Radley, "together we'll build a presence so the Presidio not only signifies a geographic location, but can also signify the creative vision of all the people here who are engaged in figuring out the issues of the 21st century."

PRODUCTS

Lucas Learning is an extension of the company's successful multimedia activities. It draws on George Lucas' dedication to technological excellence with the focus on children's educational products for the home and school. LucasLearning's six titles have received worldwide acclaim.

LucasArts is a leading international developer and publisher of interactive entertainment software for computer and home video consoles. The company's games have been honored with over 150 industry awards for excellence and are among the best-selling. Fans long requested a bounty hunter game from LucasArts, and they complied with the "Father of Legendary Bounty Hunter Boba Fett Highlights Action Game" for PlayStation 2. Nintendo GameCube was planned for release in the fall of 2002. And fans will "feel the force" as the *Star Wars' Jedi Starfighter* for the Xbox video game system is released in May 2002 to coincide with the premiere of *Star Wars: Episode II —Attack of the Clones.*

Lucas Licensing represents one of the most solid core brands in the entertainment industry. It consists of licensing and merchandising activities of the *Star Wars* and *Indiana Jones* films, properties and trademarks. Like intergalactic marauders, *Star Wars* fans scour the globe for toys and memorabilia, from the newest action figures to vintage, classic toys. For example, while *Star Wars* fans awaited the latest film, the American International Toy Fair in New York City gave a glimpse of the 2002 product lines of related toys and games from Hasbro, including the release of limited edition collectible "fossil" watches to help fans know just how long it will be until *Episode II* comes out. And handset maker Nokia and Lucas Licensing have signed a multiple-year deal that will let Nokia distribute *Star Wars*-themed wireless messages, cell phone logos, and screensavers.

CORPORATE CITIZENSHIP

When *Star Wars: Episode I—The Phantom Menace* was released in May 1999, it didn't have the usual celebrity premiere in Hollywood. Instead, the film opened in 11 cities as a benefit for local children's charities raising a total of $5.3 million. Then, to celebrate the

A TASTE OF SPACE: *STAR WARS* Pics in Frito-Lay's Packs.

Jedi masters Anakin Skywalker, Obi-Wan Kenobi, and Yoda were among the galaxy of stars featured in Frito-Lay's "Find the Hero Inside" campaign that kicked off in April 2002. The "3D Star Pic" plastic puzzle pieces was spotlighted as the snackmaker's tie-in with Lucasfilm's *Star Wars: Episode II—Attack of the Clones.* The plastic collectibles were found in Chee-tos, Cracker Jack, 3Ds, Doritos, 3Ds Ruffles, and the variety pack. The puzzle pieces served as trading cards. There were nine standard pieces, with four colors apiece, and a limited edition "Clone Trooper" tenth piece. Each piece featured highlighted a holographic image of a character in the movie. When the puzzle was completed, hidden characters were revealed. Star Pics targeted 8 to 12-year-olds, and had holes so they could be clipped to backpacks and tied to shoelaces.

A four to five week TV blitz was planned to tout the Star Pics and was expected to reach 90 percent of kids. The ads portrayed an 11-year-old boy who transformed into a hero thanks to his Star Pic. The ads ran on the ABC Family Cartoon Network, Nickelodeon, and in the newspaper *USA Today.* Frito-Lay was hoping for a strong performance from the undisclosed multi-million dollar effort. It spent $106 million on media in 1999, the year it teamed with *Star Wars: Episode I—The Phantom Menace,* and $81 million on media in 2001. Supporting the ads were heroic *Star Wars* imagery special offers for the Frito-Lay Web site, Eploids.com. "We want to make sure we make our business goals selling more chips, but we're also excited about getting this generation reconnected to the *Star Wars* sagas," said Lora DeVuono, vice president of retail marketing at Frito-Lay in Plano, Texas.

holiday season, *The Phantom Menace* was re-released for one week beginning December 3, 1999. One hundred percent of the box office proceeds from the encore charity release were contributed to local charities selected by theater owners. This marked the first time in history that total revenues generated from the exhibition of a film in movie theaters were contributed to charitable causes. Lucasfilm, Twentieth Century Fox, and local theater owners came together in about 358 cities in the U.S. and Canada to benefit 184 different charities. George Lucas

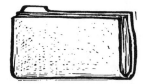

SEND IN THE CLONES

Audiences can't wait for more *Star Wars*. So much so that director George Lucas and Twentieth Century Fox decided that *Clones* would attack a day earlier than scheduled. *Star Wars: Episode II—Attack of the Clones* premiered in North America on Thursday, May 16, 2002 in a move to jump-start the *Clones'* box office assault over Memorial Day weekend, considered the official kickoff of the summer blockbuster season.

When *Star Wars: Episode I—The Phantom Menace* opened on May 19, 1999, it scored the biggest single-day theatrical gross ever, taking in $28.5 million, and eventually earning $105.7 million in its first five days, which were before Memorial Day weekend. Over that holiday period, the film rang up another $66.9 million.

Clones "invaded" the U.S. and Canada on the same day it debuted overseas in the United Kingdom, Russia, Germany, Jordan, Hong Kong, Thailand and Hungary. Other countries, including France, Belgium, Italy, Spain, Israel, West Africa, and Bulgaria, will have to wait one day longer. The decision came from fans of the Force who complained in 1999 about *The Phantom Menace* opening earlier in North America than the rest of the world. Of course, some fans in Korea, India, Japan, Latin America and the Caribbean felt left in a galaxy far, far, away as *Clones* was not slated to open in those countries until June or July 2002 at the earliest.

commented, "Throughout the years, *Star Wars* films have entertained generations of children. We are delighted that these premieres will provide an opportunity to benefit the children who need it the most."

In addition to these activities, a *Star Wars* charity run took place on November 22, 1999, benefiting 360 charities of all types. And in July 1999, starwars.com's official chat provider, Talk City, auctioned off exclusive *Star Wars: Episode I—The Phantom Menace* theatrical one-sheet posters signed by George Lucas. Those proceeds benefited the Southern California Chapter of the National Multiple Sclerosis Society.

In a repeat performance, Lucasfilm and Twentieth Century Fox announced that *Star Wars: Episode II—Attack of the Clones* would premiere May 12, 2002 in 11 cities in the U.S. and Canada to benefit children's charities. At each premiere, portions of theater seating will be available to disadvantaged kids.

Lucas is involved in arts and education, serving as chairperson of the George Lucas Educational Foundation as well as on the board of directors of the National Geographic Society Education Foundation, the Artist Rights Foundation, The Joseph Campbell Foundation and The Film Foundation. He is also a member of the USC School of Cinema-Television Board of Councilors.

EMPLOYMENT

Lucasfilm provides eligible employees with an extraordinary workplace as well as an excellent variety of benefits. The company offers two internship sessions annually for students in an undergraduate or graduate degree program. Lucasfilm generally offers positions related to its business affairs, not in film productions. Positions are offered in various business activities including the THX professional and consumer audio systems and the management of its corporate headquarters, Skywalker Ranch.

In 1994, for the fourth year running, *Working Mother* magazine named Lucasfilm, Lucas Digital, and LucasArts Entertainment among the top one hundred workplaces for working mothers. The magazine commended the companies' child-care centers, flexible working hours, and profit sharing plans as well as equal treatment in matters of salary. Additionally, the companies subsidized 100 percent of health care costs for employees and 75 percent rates for their families. For these reasons, Lucas companies boast a low turnover rate.

SOURCES OF INFORMATION

Bibliography

Diorio, Carl. "Digital Gurus Can't 'Send In The Clones.'" *Brandweek*. 25 March 2002.

Hein, Kenneth. "Frito-Lay Supplies Pieces to the Star Wars Puzzle." *Brandweek* 25 March 2002.

"Lucas, George Walton, Jr." *Jones Telecommunications and Multimedia Encyclopedia*, 1999. Available at http://www.digitalcentury.com.

"Lucasfilm Ltd." Hoover's Online. Available from http://www.hoovers.com.

Lucasfilm Ltd. Home Page, 2002. Available at http://www.lucasfilm.com.

"Lucasfilm Ltd's Star Wars: Episode II - Attack of the Clones Premieres To Benefit Children's Charities in 11 Cities on May 12, 2002." *Canadian Corporate News*, 27 February 2002.

Pollock, Dale. *Skywalking: The Life and Films of George Lucas*. New York: Samuel French, 1990.

"The Presidio Trust Released a Draft." California Planning and Development Report, September 2001.

Stein, Todd. "Will the Trust Be with Him?" *San Francisco Business Times*, 4 August 2000.

For additional industry research:

Investigate companies by their Standard Industrial Classification Codes, also known as SICs. Lucasfilm's primary SICs are:

6794 Patent Owners and Lessors

7372 Prepackaged Software

7812 Motion Picture, Video Tape Production

7819 Services Allied To Motion Pictures

7822 Motion Picture and Video Distribution

7829 Services Allied to Motion Picture Distribution

Also investigate companies by their North American Industry Classification System Codes, also known as NAICS codes. Lucasfilm's primary NAICS codes are:

512110 Motion Picture and Video Production

512190 Postproduction and Other Motion Picture and Video Industries

512199 Other Motion Picture and Video Industries

Luxottica Group S.p.A.

FOUNDED: 1961

Contact Information:
HEADQUARTERS: Via Valcozzena 10
    Agordo, Belluno 32021 Italy
PHONE: 39 0437 6441
FAX: 39 0437 63223
URL: http://www.luxottica.com

OVERVIEW

Italy's Luxottica Group S.p.A. is the largest eyewear company in the world. The firm designs its own eyeglass frames and sunglasses and manufacturers them via six plants in Italy. In 2002, Luxottica had the capacity to produce up to 130,000 eyeglasses per day. Through 29 wholly-owned subsidiaries, as well as various sales representatives and independent wholesalers, Luxottica distributes its products in 115 countries. The firm also operates more than 2,500 retail outlets, mainly Lenscrafters and Sunglass Hut units, in North America.

COMPANY FINANCES

Sales in 2001 reached $2.8 billion, a 27 percent increase over 2000 sales of $2.26 billion. Earnings totaled $290 million, also a substantial increase over 2000 earnings of $239.7 million. In fact, both sales and earnings have increased every year since 1992. Luxottica's profit margins exceeded 10 percent in both 2000 and 2001. While this margin was an improvement over margins in the mid and late 1990s, it was lower than Luxottica's record 15.4 percent profit margin of 1994. Stock prices in 2000 ranged from a record high of $17.06 per share to a low of $7.91 per share. Stock had also reached record highs in 1998 ($9.76 per share) and 1999 ($10.69 per share). In early 2002, as analysts remained positive about the firm's outlook despite the lagging North American economy, prices hovered near $20.00 per share.

ANALYSTS' OPINIONS

Along with Luxottica's strong financial performance throughout the late 1990s and early 2000s, many analysts were also impressed by the firm's move into North American retail sales, which allowed it to eliminate many middlemen from its supply chain in that region. After the purchase of LensCrafters in 1995, Luxottica was able to control the sale of its designs at the 700 LensCrafters stores operating throughout North America. The purchase of Sunglass Hut in 2001 furthered the firm's North American reach. As stated in a March 2001 issue of *DSN Retailing Today*, Luxottica's purchase of Sunglass Hut "will wed its existing LensCrafters prescription business in North America with mass market sunglasses." According to Ladenburg, Thalmann & Co. analyst Eric Beder, "In some respects, it's a dream acquisition. . .Luxottica now controls both the high and the lower end in the malls."

FINANCES:

Luxottica Group S.p.A. Revenues, 1996-2000 (million dollars)

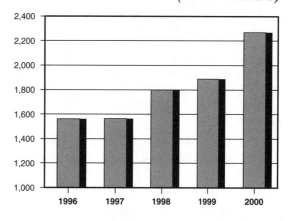

HISTORY

Leonardo del Vecchio and two partners established Luxottica s.a.s. in 1961. At first, the Agordo, Italy-based factory manufactured parts for eyeglass frame makers. Employees totaled ten. To increase earnings, the firm began to make finished frames in 1967. Production practices were modeled after those used by jewelry makers. Luxottica began selling its frames in the United States via a licensing agreement with Avant Garde in 1970, discontinued the sale of eyeglass parts in 1971 to focus its efforts solely on finished frames, and the Luxottica brand made its debut that year at the International Exhibition of Optics, Optometry and Opthalmology in Milan.

In 1974, Luxottica acquired Scarrone, a distribution company based in Italy. The acquisition of Avant Garde in the early 1980s boosted Luxottica to the number one spot among U.S. eyeglass manufacturers. In 1982, del Vecchio's son Claudio was sent to New York to oversee the new U.S. branch of Luxottica. The firm spent most of the 1980s expanding its international distribution networks by creating distribution subsidiaries around the world. For example, Luxottica founded Fashion Brillen Gmbh in Germany in 1981. Luxottica U.K., Luxottica France, and Luxottica Canada emerged mid-decade.

After securing a licensing agreement from Giorgio Armani in 1988, Luxottica designed and manufactured a line of Giorgio Armani eyeglasses. Similar agreements with firms like Giugiaro, Genny, and Byblos in 1989, Valentino in 1990, and Yves St. Laurent in 1991, allowed Luxottica to increase its designer eyeglass offerings.

Luxottica completed its initial public offering (IPO) on the New York Stock Exchange (NYSE) in January of 1990, raising $80 million in fresh capital. The IPO was particularly newsworthy because it marked the first time an Italian firm had listed its shares on the NYSE prior to listing them on the Milan Stock Exchange. Del Vecchio

had made this decision in an effort to highlight Luxottica's international reach. It wasn't until December of 2000 that Luxottica's shares were listed on the Milan exchange.

To gain access to LensCrafters, a chain of 700 retail shops selling prescription lenses and a wide range of eyeglass frames, Luxottica paid $1.4 billion in a hostile takeover of LensCrafter's parent company, U.S. Shoe, in 1995. Eventually, Nine West bought the shoe operations of U.S. Shoe for $600 million. Del Vecchio folded the apparel arm of U.S. Shoe, which included chains such as Casual Corner, into a separate family business. Luxottica also acquired Italian sunglasses maker Persol that year.

In 1999, Luxottica gained access to Ray-Ban, Revo, Killer Loop, and other designer sunglasses via its $640 million purchase of the sunglasses operations of Bausch & Lomb. The firm also become the first distributor licensed to sell the Chanel brand after it convinced Chanel to forge its first ever brand licensing agreement.

Luxottica paid $462 million for Sunglass Hut International, another North American retail chain, in 2001. In an effort to strengthen its position in the managed care market, Luxottica also acquired First American Health Concepts that year and folded it into its recently established Eyemed Vision Care, LLC unit.

STRATEGY

Fully centralized production has been a key strategy for Luxottica since its inception. By keeping the manu-

FAST FACTS:
About Luxottica Group S.p.A.

Ownership: Luxottica Group S.p.A. is a public company traded on the New York Stock Exchange and the Milan Stock Exchange. Founder Leonardo Del Vecchio holds a 70 percent stake in the firm.

Ticker Symbol: LUX

Officers: Leonardo Del Vecchio, Chmn.; Luigi Francavilla, Co-CEO; Roberto Chemello, Co-CEO; Enrico Cavatorta, CFO

Employees: 31,000

Principal Subsidiary Companies: Headquartered in Belluno, Italy, Luxottica owns and operates six manufacturing plants in Italy as well as 29 wholly-owned subsidiary companies throughout the world. Some of Luxottica's more well known subsidiaries include LensCrafters and Sunglass Hut.

Chief Competitors: Competitors to Luxottica include Marchon Eyewear, National Vision, Eye Care Centers of America, and other eyewear manufacturers, distributors, and retailers.

CHRONOLOGY:
Key Dates for Luxottica S.p.A.

1961: Leonardo del Vecchio and two partners establish Luxottica

1967: Luxottica begins making finished eyeglasses

1974: Scarrone, based in Italy, becomes Luxottica's first distributor

1988: Giorgio Armani licenses its brand name to Luxottica

1990: Luxottica lists its shares on the NYSE

1995: Luxottica acquires LensCrafters

1999: The firm acquires the sunglass operations of Bausch & Lomb

2000: The Milan Stock Exchange begins to list Luxottica's shares

2001: Luxottica pays $462 million for Sunglass Hut International

facture of all eyeglass components in house, the firm has maintained both quality and cost control. It has also maintained control of its distribution network. Luxottica acquired its first distributor in 1974. Throughout the 1980s, the firm created several of its own distribution units, believing that close contact with its resellers allowed for an increased understanding of its market. This strategy was taken a step further in the 1990s when Luxottica moved into retail sales for the first time.

The reason for Luxottica's strategic move into retailing was the emergence of large discount retailers selling eyewear in the United States, a market that had accounted for more than 50 percent of Luxottica's revenues since the early 1990s. Because the United States had proved to be one of the firm's most important markets, Del Vecchio was determined to maintain market share there. According to a February 2002 article in *Forbes*, Del Vecchio believed the purchase of LensCrafters, via U.S. Shoe, "was the only way to prevent Luxottica from being squeezed by such discount chains as Wal-Mart—even if it meant competing with his best customers, the small opticians that then provided 90% of his sales." When the purchase was completed, Del Vecchio began to demand

price cuts from LensCrafters' suppliers. Less profitable brands were discontinued in favor of Luxottica brands. In fact, by 2002, frames manufactured by Luxottica accounted for 70 percent of LensCrafters' sales, compared to 5 percent prior to the takeover.

Luxottica implemented a very similar strategy with Sunglass Hut. When the takeover of Sunglass Hut was completed in 2001, Del Vecchio began to exact discounts from Sunglass Hut's ten suppliers and to increase the number of Luxottica brands sold by the chain.

To improve the profitability of the Ray-Ban, Revo, and Killer Loop sunglass brands it acquired from Bausch & Lomb in 1999, Luxottica undertook several strategic moves designed to lower production costs and increase demand for the brands. For example, the firm began limiting the distribution of the Ray-Ban brand to department stores and shops specializing in sunglasses (under Bausch & Lomb, Ray-Ban sunglasses had been sold by nearly 13,000 outlets, including discount retailers). In addition, Luxottica closed four Ray-Ban factories, internalizing the manufacture of the sunglasses. Consequently, Ray-Ban production costs were nearly cut in half by 2000. The lower costs, coupled with Luxottica's decision to raise the price of Ray-Bans, boosted profitability despite fewer Ray-Ban sales over the next two years.

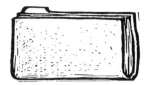

EYEWEAR GIANTS CLASH

When Luxottica founder Leonardo del Vecchio asked Sunglass Hut suppliers to reduce their prices shortly after Luxottica had purchased Sunglass Hut, most agreed. However, Oakley, Inc. CEO James Jannard refused, pointing out that because Oakley accounted for nearly one quarter of all Sunglass Hut sales, it should not be required to cut its prices. Increasingly tense meetings between the two billionaires in both May and July of 2001 resulted in Jannard's decision to lower prices modestly. However, when Del Vecchio slashed the Oakley order by roughly 66 percent shortly after the July meeting, Jannard responded by retracting his offer to cut prices. Del Vecchio then refused to carry the Oakley brand at all.

In November 2001, Oakley sued Luxottica, alleging that the firm had violated an Oakley patent on a particular lens coating called Iridium. As a result, a judge issued a preliminary injunction ordering Luxottica to stop producing Iridium lenses. When Del Vecchio and Jannard met again in December, shortly before the injunction had been issued, Del Vecchio agreed to Jannard's demands that Sunglass Hut restock the Oakley Brand while Jannard granted Sunglass Hut increased price concessions.

PRODUCTS

Luxottica sells both traditional and designer eyeglass frames, sunglasses, and related eyewear products. Along with the Luxottica brand, the firm owns the following lines: Ray-Ban, Vogue, Persol, Arnette, Killer Loop, Revo, Sferoflex, Luxottica, and T3. The firm also licenses several brands, including Giorgio Armani, Emporio Armani, Chanel, Ferragamo, Bulgari, Byblos, Genny, Ungaro, Tacchini, Moschino, Web, Anne Klein, and Brooks Brothers.

GLOBAL PRESENCE

Luxottica's North American subsidiaries, which account for more than half the firm's sales, include Avant Garde Optics, Inc., Lenscrafters, Inc., and Sunglass Hut International, Inc. Additional subsidiaries are located in countries such as India, Brazil, Argentina, South Africa, Japan, Hong Kong, Australia, Belgium, Portugal, Sweden, Poland, the Netherlands, France, and the United Kingdom.

SOURCES OF INFORMATION

Bibliography

Kroll, Luisa. "Lens Master." *Forbes*, 4 February 2002. Available at http://www.forbes.com.

Kroll, Luisa. "The Son Also Rises." *Forbes*, 17 September 2001. Available at http://www.forbes.com.

"Luxottica Group S.p.A." *International Directory of Company Histories*. Detroit: Gale Research, 1997.

Luxottica Group S.p.A. Home Page, 2002. Available at http://www.luxottica.com

"Sunglass Hut." *DSN Retailing Today*, 5 March 2001.

For an annual report:

on the Internet at: http://www.luxottica.com/english/investor_relations/index_annual_report.html

For additional industry research:

Investigate companies by their Standard Industrial Classification Codes, also known as SICs. Luxottica's primary SIC is:

3851 Ophthalmic Goods

Also investigate companies by their North American Industry Classification System Codes, also known as NAICS codes. Luxottica's primary NAICS code is:

339115 Ophthalmic Goods Manufacturing

Martha Stewart Living Omnimedia, Inc.

FOUNDED: 1982
VARIANT NAME: MSLO

Contact Information:

HEADQUARTERS: 20 W 43rd St., 25th Fl.
   New York, NY 10036
PHONE: (212)827-8000
FAX: (212)827-8204
EMAIL: customerservice@marthastewart.com
URL: http://www.marthastewart.com

OVERVIEW

Martha Stewart Living Omnimedia, Inc. (MSLO) is one of today's foremost authorities on the domestic arts for homemakers and lifestyle aficionados. The company is a media and merchandising firm that provides how-to content and related products to create a beautiful home and garden environment. MSLO pioneered the lifestyle category, combining what had previously been small niche markets into one power genre. MSLO cross-promotes and distributes the brand across a wide spectrum of media and retail outlets, providing consumers with an array of how-to home décor options. Led by celebrated style arbiter Martha Stewart, the familiar brand is synonymous with tasteful entertaining and home decorating. Through the award winning magazine, *Martha Stewart Living*, best-selling books, an Emmy-Award winning top-rated television show, Web site, syndicated newspaper column, national radio show, mail order catalog, and product lines, Martha Stewart shares the ideas that have made her brand one of the highest-profile names in home arts.

MSLO has eight core content areas: Home, Cooking and Entertaining, Gardening, Crafts, Holidays, Baby, Keeping, and Weddings. The creative experts at MSLO continuously strive to develop innovative ideas to maintain the high quality image the ever-expanding brand is known for. The company has two business objectives. The first objective is providing original, detailed information to the wide target audience. The second objective is turning audiences into "doers" by providing an array of products and projects. MSLO distributes its content over what is referred to as an "omnimedia" platform, which includes *Martha Stewart Living* magazines, the television show, books, a radio show, a newspaper column, and a Web site. MSLO distributes its products over what is referred to as an "omnimerchandising" platform, which includes the mass market discount channel in the United States and Canada, the national department store channel, craft and fabric stores, the *Martha by Mail* catalog, and bluelight.com.

COMPANY FINANCES

Martha Stewart Living Omnimedia, Inc. is comprised of four business segments: publishing, television, merchandising, and Internet. Publishing accounts for 60 percent of revenue, television makes up 10 percent, and merchandising's tally is 14 percent. The Internet segment accounts for the remaining 16 percent.

In 2001, retail sales of the Martha Stewart Everyday brand reached $1.6 billion worldwide, up 26 percent from the prior year. Revenues for the fourth quarter of 2001 were $85.1 million, compared to $85.5 million in the previous year's quarter. Fourth quarter earnings fell 3.3 percent and operating income was off 9 percent due to a harsh advertising and retail climate. The Earnings Before Interest, Taxes, Depreciation, and Amortization (EBITDA) for the fourth quarter increased 21 percent to $13.2 million, compared to $10.9 million in the same period the year before. Earnings per share were $.12 for both 2000 and 2001 quarters. For the year ending December 31, 2001, revenues increased 4 percent to $295.6 million, up from $285.8 million in 2000. MSLO stock ranged from a low of $12 to a high of $25 over a 52-week period, and the company's price-earnings ratio was 44.38.

The company is closely evaluating its exclusive merchandising deal with Kmart, since the Troy, Michigan-based retailer filed for bankruptcy protection on January 22, 2002. MSLO's accounts receivable totaled $13 million at the time of the filing, and the company will make adjustments to their fourth quarter and full year balance sheets, as necessary.

ANALYSTS' OPINIONS

Martha Stewart Living Omnimedia, Inc. reports that prospects continue to develop for 2002 and beyond as they build on the solid foundation that their brand has established and as they develop new alliances and product launches. MSLO is a well-established, diversified, and financially strong multimedia company. In 2001, MSLO delivered fourth quarter results that matched expectations but warned it expects 2002 earnings per share to be at the low end of Wall Street estimates. Net income for fourth quarter 2001 was $5.73 million, or $.12 a share. For 2002 the company is forecasting revenue growth of 10 percent and earnings per share of $.50 to $.55, below analyst EPS' expectations of $.61; that outlook is based on an estimate that Kmart will close 284 underperforming stores.

FINANCES:
Martha Stewart Living Omnimedia, Inc.
Net Sales, 1998-2001
(million dollars)

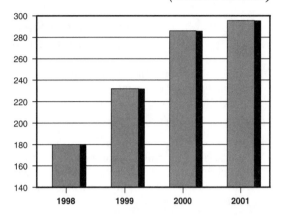

Martha Stewart Living Omnimedia, Inc.
2001 Stock Prices
(dollars)

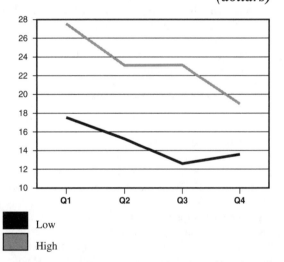

HISTORY

Martha Stewart was born in Nutley, New Jersey, a suburb near New York City, on August 3, 1941. Upon graduation from Barnard College, Martha pursued a successful career as a stockbroker on Wall Street. In 1972, Martha, along with her husband and daughter Alexis, moved to Westport, Connecticut, where she turned her considerable talents to a new venture, a catering business. The recipes and unique visual presentations for her business became the basis for her landmark book, published in 1982 *Entertaining.*

FAST FACTS:

About Martha Stewart Living Omnimedia, Inc.

Ownership: Martha Stewart Living Omnimedia, Inc., is a publicly owned company traded on the New York Stock Exchange.

Ticker Symbol: MSO

Officers: Martha Stewart, Chmn. and CEO, 60, 2001 base salary $2.7 million; James Follo, CFO, 41; Suzanne Sobel, EVP, Marketing and Sales; Sharon Patrick, Pres. and COO, 58, 2001 base salary $1.3 million; Lori Riordan, Director of HR

Employees: 585

Chief Competitors: Martha Stewart Living Omnimedia, Inc. is a multimedia content and commerce company with a variety of competition including retail merchandising stores, such as Wal-Mart and Target; series television programs, such as how-to and home decorating shows; and book and magazine publishers, including those producing decorating, lifestyle, and cooking magazines.

The first issue of her trademark magazine *Martha Stewart Living* rolled off the presses in 1999 when Stewart joined with Time Publishing Ventures, Inc. The monthly lifestyle magazine offers the company's particular brand of homestyle panache to readers, gaining a loyal audience of 2.1 million. The *Martha Stewart Living* syndicated television show premiered in September 1993 as a half-hour weekly series. In September 1997, the show became a daily program with a weekend edition. Hosted by Stewart, *Martha Stewart Living* covers a wide variety of subjects and projects for the home and garden. Her guest list includes experts in various fields, including chefs, gardeners, and artisans. The show expanded to an hourly program in January 1999, featuring new segments like "Cookie of the Week," "Cooking 101," and her trademark "Good Things." Stewart's state-of-the-art Connecticut studio provides the backdrop for her detailed and visually appealing presentations. The show is produced by Stewart and distributed by King-World Productions, Inc., boasting domestic viewership of 88 percent of households. The family-oriented, educational format has netted Stewart 6 Daytime Emmy Awards and 29 Emmy nominations since the show's premiere. In May 1998, *Martha Stewart Living* garnered the

prestigious James Beard Foundation Award for the Best National Cooking Segment. Martha Stewart Omnimedia, Inc. was formed in 1997 and became a publicly-owned company in 2000.

In 1997, marthastewart.com was little more than a fledgling enterprise but, in the past five years, it has become a major dot-com destination that boasts more than 1 million viewers per month who can filter through MSLO content from television shows, newspaper columns, and magazines. Viewers can also buy gifts and housewares from MSLO's burgeoning merchandising business—Martha By Mail. With a registered user file of 1.6 million viewers and revenues exceeding $33 million in 2000, Internet and direct commerce are the fastest growing segments of the MSLO media empire.

MSLO has had a business relationship with Kmart since they approached Stewart in 1987. MSLO has exclusive merchandise contracts with Kmart in the United States and Zellers in Canada. MSLO also designs various other products for such retailers as: Sears, Kmart, Canadian Tire, specialty paint stores, Jo-Ann Fabrics, and Crafts and Calico Corners. In September 1999, HFN's Brand Awareness Survey named Martha Stewart the number one brand in the Textile area. Martha Stewart Everyday/Sherwin Williams were honored with Edison Awards for Best New Products in 1998.

STRATEGY

MSLO developed the "omni" business model. The company believes that this plan effectively distributes talent and investment across multiple platforms for maximum economic efficiency. In the center of the model are MSLO's eight core content areas, which produce original how-to content. They then distribute the cost of research and development across their 3 business platforms, Omnimedia (publishing and television), Omnimerchandising, and Omni Internet/Direct Commerce. Through the Omnimedia platform, MSLO offers their how-to information to educate, inspire, and create demand. The Omnimerchandising platform supplies a wide array of products to satisfy consumer demand. Finally, the Omni Internet/Direct Commerce platform supplies high-end merchandise in an interactive setting for their loyal core audience.

INFLUENCES

MSLO creates growth strategies through spinoffs and extensions. The company creatively cross-promotes their brand across multiple media vehicles. Their publications include: *Martha Stewart Living, Martha Stewart Weddings*, and a continuing special issue series including *Martha Stewart Baby, Martha Stewart Holiday*, more than 30 books, continuity programs, and the *askMartha* newspaper column and radio show. Each venture is separate but consistent with the familiar Martha Stewart brand formula. The company's objective is to be available in all mediums to teach, inspire, and generate consumer demand.

CURRENT TRENDS

MSLO saw across-the-board expansion in 2000. The company expanded their content library, increased products at mass market and online, added Baby and Kids as a new core content area, and continued international growth. In merchandising, MSLO added a new major product line, Martha Stewart Everyday Kitchen. In publishing, *Martha Stewart Living* magazine reached record sales and a millennium milestone, their tenth anniversary issue featuring the "Best of the Past Decade." This issue also signaled a move to a 12-issue yearly frequency. Another special issue of *Martha Stewart Holiday,* for Halloween, topped newsstand sales at 430,000 copies and is now to be extended into a comprehensive Holiday series. In television, *Martha Stewart Living* won its sixth Emmy Award for Outstanding Service Show. Rounding out the menu, *From Martha's Kitchen*, a compilation show, began airing in the United States and Canada, and the *Martha Stewart Living* television show entered the international markets in Brazil and Japan. In March 2002, a new daily half-hour television show *From Martha's Garden* premiered weekdays on Home & Garden Television (HGTV). In Internet commerce, there has been steady growth in product sales and ad and royalty revenue. The introduction of new features like Recipe Finder, Encyclopedia of Plants, and marthascards, an online greeting/holiday card service, has helped MSLO double their buyer file in 2000.

PRODUCTS

MSLO designs products that are manufactured by their business partners, Kmart in the United States and Zellers in Canada. These retailers distribute Martha Stewart Everyday Home, Martha Stewart Everyday Garden, Martha Stewart Everyday Baby, and Martha Stewart Everyday Kitchen. MSLO launched a multitude of products successfully in 2001. MSLO introduced a major new product line for mass market distribution, Martha Stewart Everyday Kitchen, which includes dinnerware, flatware, beverageware, cookware, bakeware, and utensils. The Martha Stewart Everyday Garden collection was expanded to include 1,300 garden and outdoor products, including assorted seeds and live plants. The company introduced the Martha Stewart Signature Color Palette with coordinating punch-out cards at Sherwin Williams stores, as well as a new line of paint to the Martha Stew-

CHRONOLOGY:
Key Dates for Martha Stewart Living Omnimedia, Inc.

1972: Martha Stewart develops catering business in Westport, Connecticut

1982: Martha Stewart publishes landmark volume *Entertaining*

1991: Martha Stewart and Time Publishing Ventures Inc. publish flagship lifestyle magazine *Martha Stewart Living*

1993: *Martha Stewart Living* syndicated television show premieres

1996: MSLO strikes its first international media and merchandising deal

1998: Martha Stewart named one of the "50 Most Powerful Women" by *Fortune* magazine

2000: *Martha Stewart Living* television show honored with sixth Daytime Emmy Award for Outstanding Service Show

2000: MSLO partners with GloboSat TV to air the *Martha Stewart Living* program in Brazil

2001: MSLO signs media and merchandising deal with Japanese retail giant, The Seiyu Limited

2002: The company celebrates the 100th issue milestone of *Martha Stewart Living* magazine

art Everyday collection. A fourth collection of specialty fabrics was added to the Martha Stewart Home collection in the specialty channel. In 2001 the company expanded the Martha Stewart Everyday line to include products from the Keeping and Home categories. In publishing, MSLO's tenth anniversary cookbook topped the *New York Times* and *L.A. Times* cookbook bestseller lists.

Martha by Mail has evolved from a magazine insert to a high-end consumer direct business. The catalog includes finished products such as patio furniture, bedding, and home furnishings, as well as craft kits and marthasflowers. Available through marthastewart.com, marthasflowers is a full-service florist, providing monthly selections, seasonal arrangements, grower's bunches, and fresh roses. The catalog was originally created to coordinate with the how-to projects presented by MSLO's other divisions. Other accomplishments for 2000 included adding 1,500 Martha by Mail products, and the introduc-

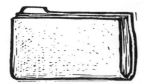

MARTHA STEWART
MARTHA—It's a Good Thing

In July 2001 Martha Stewart Living Omnimedia, Inc. announced that they had inked a deal with Japanese retailer The Seiyu Ltd. to debut Martha Stewart Everyday brand merchandise, as well as a publishing venture, in Japan. The brand will be carried in 226 Seiyu stores and include 1,500 home, cooking, and entertaining products. MSLO formed a jointly owned company and premiered its first issue of *Martha Stewart Martha*, the name of the Japanese edition of MSLO's trademark magazine, which is read from the back page to the front. Stewart said of the magazine's unusual title, "the Japanese people like repetition."

tion of the Martha Stewart Everyday microsite on Blue-Light.com, which links to marthastewart.com, offering 4,000 bed, bath, garden, and kitchen products.

CORPORATE CITIZENSHIP

As chairman and chief executive officer of MSLO, Martha Stewart is a regular speaker on the lecture circuit in support of various charities including the National Chapter of the March of Dimes and the Lupus Foundation. In the past, MSLO has donated furniture and housewares to furnish Habitat for Humanity built houses. To celebrate the tenth anniversary of *Martha Stewart Living* magazine, MSLO donated a portion of the advertising proceeds to three children's charities: Campaign for America's Children, Help's Mentoring USA, and The Children's Hearing Institute. MSLO also promotes education about the health and welfare of animals in television segments featuring animal expert Mark Marrone.

GLOBAL PRESENCE

MSLO continues to increase their global presence. In January 1996, MSLO signed its first international media and merchandising deal. The *Martha Stewart Living* cable television program debuted in Canada on the Life Network, a division of Your Channel Television Inc.

MSLO distributes merchandise in Canada through Zellers and Canadian Tire. In May 2000, MSLO partnered with Globo-Sat TV Network. The *Martha Stewart Living* program, dubbed in Portuguese, airs in 2 million cable households in Brazil. In October 2000, MSLO entered the Japanese market through an agreement with Jupiter Programming Co. The show is dubbed in Japanese and shown three times daily and twice on weekends on LaLa TV, a women's cable channel. MSLO also has merchandising deals with Japan's Shop Channel and Home ShoppingNetwork, and several MSLO books are to be translated into Japanese.

EMPLOYMENT

MSLO employs a variety of creative experts who research and develop all of the company's editorial content. Experts in each of their eight core areas create original material to support the high standards and unique look required by the MSLO brand. Once developed, ideas and projects are presented by writers, art directors, and stylists who work together for a seamless presentation. MSLO likens their employee training system to a university. Their core content experts and their deputies are like professors who teach new classes of employees about their fields the "Martha brand" way. These employees then become teachers for the next group of students. Moreover, the company teaches employees "brand standards," a technique that applies to all areas of the company, enabling future cross-development in other areas.

SOURCES OF INFORMATION

Bibliography

"About MSO." Martha Stewart Living Omnimedia, Inc., March 2002. Available at http://www.marthastewart.com.

Driver, Anna. "Martha Stewart Net Falls; Sales Not Hurt by Kmart." *Reuters*, 20 February 2002.

Kilgore, Tomi. "Martha Stewart Hits Q4, To Miss 2002 Est." *CBS Marketwatch*, 20 February 2002. Available at http://www.CBS.Marketwatch.com.

"MSLO, Inc. Announce Fourth Quarter and Full-Year results." *PRNewswire—FirstCall*, 20 February 2002.

Perman, Stacy. "E-Business the Martha Stewart Way." *eCompany Now*, January 2000.

Sellers, Patricia. "The 50 Most Powerful Women in Business." *Fortune*, October 2000.

———. "First: Kmart, It's Not a Good Thing, Kmarts Woes Threaten to Taint Martha Stewart's Image—and Business." *Fortune*, 4 February 2002.

Shrage, Michael. "Martha Stewart." *ADWEEK Eastern Edition*, 14 February 2000.

Wells, Melanie. "Overcooked." *Forbes*, 19 March 2001.

For an annual report:

on the Internet at: http://www.marthastewart.com **or** write: Martha Stewart Living Omnimedia, Inc., 20 W 43rd St., 25th Fl., New York, NY 10036

For additional industry research:

Investigate companies by their Standard Industrial Classification Codes, also known as SICs. Martha Stewart Living Omnimedia, Inc.'s primary SICs are:

2721 Periodicals Publishing & Printing

3952 Lead Pencils and Art Goods

5023 Home Furnishings

Also investigate companies by their North American Industry Classification System codes, also known as NAICS codes. Martha Stewart Living Omnimedia, Inc.'s primary NAICS codes are:

339942 Lead Pencil and Art Good Manufacturing

421220 Home Furnishing Wholesalers

511120 Periodical Publishers

Marvel Enterprises

FOUNDED: 1939
VARIANT NAME: Marvel Comics

Contact Information:

HEADQUARTERS: 10 East 40th Street
    New York, NY 10016
PHONE: (212)696-4000
FAX: (212)576-8598
URL: http://www.marvel.com

OVERVIEW

Marvel Enterprises is best known for the Marvel comic book characters that it has developed for more than half a century. Over the years, characters such as Spiderman, the X-Men, the Incredible Hulk, the Fantastic Four, the Avengers, Daredevil, the Mighty Thor, Captain America, the Submariner, the Silver Surfer, Iron Man, Dr. Strange, and Ghost Rider have become some of the most readily identifiable comic heroes in the world. They have been featured in comic books, TV shows, feature films, and cartoons. They have been reproduced on posters, T-shirts, lunch boxes, and as action figures. By 2001 the Marvel library of characters had reached 4,700 in number. The primary vehicle for these characters is Marvel's line of comic books, which are sold throughout the United States and the world. The primary markets for Marvel comics are people between the ages of 13 and 35, some of whom simply buy the comics to read, others who also purchase the comics as collectible goods. Marvel's toy line is aimed at the global pre-teen market.

Marvel Enterprises is divided into three business units. Marvel Licensing, MARVEL Publishing and Toy Biz. The Toy Biz division designs, develops, manufacturers, markets and distributes toys. Its primary products are the action figures based on Marvel comic book characters and the characters in movies such as *Lord of the Rings*. Toy Biz includes the Spectra Star division, which produces and sells kites. Marvel Licensing licenses Marvel's various comic characters for use in a variety of products, including TV shows, feature films, cartoons, theme parks, toys, games, clothing, Web sites, and other computer media. A noteworthy licensing coup was the *X-Men* characters produced by Twentieth Century Fox in

2000. The final unit, Marvel Publishing, develops and produces comic books.

COMPANY FINANCES

Marvel's customer base varies from product line to product line. Its comic books are directed primarily at consumers between the ages of 13 and 35. They are sold via three channels. The first, the "direct market," consists of stores that specialize in comic books. Marvel sells its products to them on a non-returnable basis. In 2001, about 80 percent of Marvel's comic book sales were made to the direct market. The second channel consists of traditional retail stores that stock magazines and other periodicals. They include newsstands, drug stores, supermarkets, and bookstores. Marvel distributes its publications to this market on a returnable basis—any books left unsold after a certain period of time can be returned to Marvel for credit. The retail returnable market accounted for 8 percent of Marvel's book sales in 2001. The third channel is subscriptions, which were responsible for 3 percent of comic sales in 2001.

Marvel sells its toy products primarily through retail stores. Its largest customers in 2001 were Toys 'R' Us Inc., Wal-Mart Stores Inc., Kmart Corporation, Target Stores Inc., and Kay-Bee Toy Stores. These chains together accounted for 56 percent of Marvel Enterprise's toy sales in 2001. About 77 percent of the company's sales were made in the United States. In 2001 about three-quarters of Marvel's toys were not based on Marvel characters. The company expected this percentage to drop in 2002 as it prepared a line of toys to coincide with the release of the Spiderman motion picture.

Marvel Enterprise's experienced a period of growth and decline in the late 1990s and early 2000s. Revenues increased from $150 million in 1997 to $320 million in 1999 and then shrunk to $181 million in 2001. Despite the lull in sales, 2001 saw the company report a profit for the first time in five years. It reported profits of about $5 million, up from a loss of $90 million the previous year. Nonetheless the company's common stock holders took a loss of $0.31 per share.

ANALYSTS' OPINIONS

Although Marvel had begun to turn around its comic book sales through the introduction of more "realistic" subject material, financial observers were still taking a wait-and-see stance toward the firm's future performance. *Publishers Weekly* pointed out the company's $250 million in bond debt that had not been reduced by sales increases, and the lien on its trademarks and copyrights held by loan-giver Tot Funding. The consensus was that Marvel Enterprises should shed its money-

FINANCES:

Marvel Enterprises Inc.
Net Sales, 1997-2001
(million dollars)

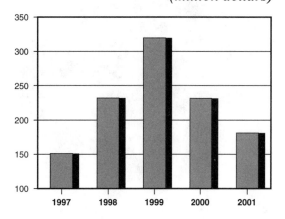

Marvel Enterprises Inc.
2001 Stock Prices
(dollars)

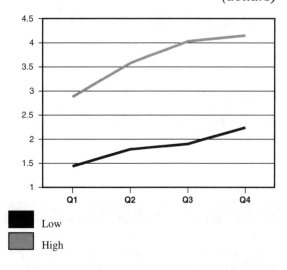

losing toy business and concentrate on realizing the true value of its licensing opportunities. Despite successes such as the *X-Men* film and the fact that it is one of the largest most popular comic book franchises in the world, the company's licensing record is woeful. "Many a comic book rival, large and small," *Forbes* wrote, "has proved more adept at exploiting its properties." *Forbes* went on to blame the company's transformation to a public company for many of Marvel's current problems. Suddenly accountable to stockholders, the company tried to squeeze every drop of profit from every phase of its business, ultimately to its detriment. It increased the number

Marvel Comics' Spider-Man character, created in 1962, is finding a new generation of fans thanks to the 2002 relase of a Spider-Man movie. (AP Photo/Courtesy *Marvel Comics*)

of monthly titles, raised the prices of some books to nearly $5. *Forbes* observed that the best thing that could happen to Marvel might be another takeover, by Sony for example, who could use the Marvel cast of characters for its Playstation.

HISTORY

Marvel was founded in 1939 after a group of comic book writers and artists persuaded pulp magazine publishers Martin Goodman that comics could be a profitable area of expansion. The creative people, represented by Funnies, Inc., provided the stories and art. Goodman arranged to have them printed and distributed. The arrangement was a success. Goodman's first issues, titled *Marvel Comics*, were hits. Soon he had formed a new company called Timely Publications that added new titles. By the end of World War II, Timely was publishing a profitable line of comics that featured characters that would become perennial favorites: the Submariner, the Human Torch, and Captain America; as well as humorous comics, comics with animal stories for younger children, and romance comics for teenage girls.

Timely was doing well as the 1950s began. The company changed its name to Atlas Publishing and

began handling its own national distribution. However, by the mid-1950s there was a public backlash against the alleged harmful influence of comic books, in particular the horror genre, on young minds. The result was the establishment of the Comics Code Authority, which reviewed comics for appropriateness prior to publication. Safe, homogenized tales that were not nearly as popular among readers replaced the anarchic, often gruesome stories of the early fifties. Marvel's sales took a dive. It cut back its publication schedule and closed its distribution operations. Matters turned finally around in 1961 with the introduction of the Fantastic Four comics. They introduced a formula that would be the mainstay of Marvel for the remainder of the century—stories driven by the frequently maladjusted personalities of their superheroes. They were a hit, and were soon joined by two other social outcasts, the Incredible Hulk and Spiderman. Later in the 1960s the X-Men, the Avengers, and Daredevil were introduced. All Marvel's superheroes inhabited the same world, the so-called Marvel Universe, in which they were able to interact with each other. The comics first bore the name "Marvel Comics" on their covers in 1963.

Marvel's success in the 1960s allowed it to branch out into other media. Cartoons were produced for syndication. The company released other related items such as games and shirts. By 1968 Marvel reported sales figures for 50 comic publications annually. Martin Goodman sold the firm that year to Cadence Industries. His timing was good. The comic book boom was coming to an end. Titles were dropped, and new distribution schemes were tried. One Marvel success was publishing anti-drug issues of Spiderman over the objection of the Comics Code Authority; a move which eventually led to greater openness in comic book storytelling. The business reached new financial lows in the mid-1970s, going $2 million into debt. The 1977 hit TV show, *The Incredible Hulk,* created some new readers as well as tapping the profits to be made from licensing Marvel's stable of characters. Another favorable trend in the early 1980s was the growth of comic sales to collectors and the rise of specialty stores that sold predominantly comic books. By 1982 these stores made up half of Marvel's sales.

By 1986 Marvel was reporting annual revenues of $100 million and attracted a buyer, New World Pictures. Only two years later, New World sold the firm to the Andrews Group, Inc., for $82.5 million. In 1992 the company made its first stock offering and became a public firm. It also purchased the Fleer Corporation, a maker of trading cards the same year. In 1993 it acquired a 46 percent share of Toy Biz, a company that introduced a successful line of Marvel character action figures. Marvel expanded its publishing schedule in the early 1990s, almost doubling its monthly titles from 1989. By mid-decade Marvel was on the skids once more, and in 1996 it filed for bankruptcy protection. When the dust cleared the firm had been acquired by Toy Biz Inc., Marvel's one-time holding. After the acquisition, Toy Biz changed its name to Marvel Enterprises and made plain its goal to capitalize on Marvel's huge collection of characters. Among the results were the 2001 film *X-Men* by Twentieth Century Fox and plans with the Sony Corporation for a Spiderman film.

STRATEGY

Under CEO, Peter Cuneo, Marvel Enterprises has moved away from toy manufacturing—once the primary activity of the company—and into licensing which is lower risk and potentially more lucrative. A licensing strategy has the added benefit of ultimately creating more exposure for Marvel comic characters which will lead to an increase of comic book sales, and create new opportunities for toy sales . The greatest opportunities for Marvel's licensing efforts lies in the motion picture industry. This was illustrated in May 2002 when the *Spiderman* film opened to record box office numbers. In its opening weekend the movie grossed an astounding $114 million dollars. Two sequels to the hit movie are already in the works with a scheduled 2003 release for the next installment.

INFLUENCES

The release of the movie *X-Men* at the end of 2000 proved to be a turning point for Marvel's comic book business. The company expected the film to revitalize sales of its *X-Men*comics, and possibly other titles as well. To the company's dismay, although the movie was a box office smash, it had virtually no effect at all on comic sales. When it examined its product, it realized that the comic book *X-Men* had very little to do with the movie *X-Men*. Some of the characters were different; the uniforms had been changed in the movie from the original comic book outfits; and the stories—in practically *all* Marvel comics had become too complicated for fans to follow. Fans had to be familiar with 30 to 40 issues in order to follow the story in any particular book. In addition, the basic premises of most Marvel comics remained unchanged from the 1960s and young readers found it harder and harder to relate to the characters. As a result, Marvel re-conceptualized many of the company's most popular characters. For example, Spiderman was transformed from a high school science geek to a brooding teenager with an interest in computers. The new stories have been published under the banner of *Ultimate Spider-Man*. That, and the revamped *Ultimate X-Men* were Marvel's most popular comic titles in late 2001, with increased sales 500 to 600 percent each, compared with increases of around 30 percent for other titles.

FAST FACTS:
About Marvel Enterprises

Ownership: Marvel Enterprises is a publicly owned company traded on the New York Stock Exchange.

Ticker Symbol: MVL

Officers: F. Peter Cuneo, Pres. and CEO, 57, 2001 base salary $750,000; Avi Arad, Chief Creative Officer and CEO of Marvel Studios, 54, 2001 base salary $450,000; Alan Fine, Pres. and CEO of Toy Biz Inc., 51, 2001 base salary $500,192

Employees: 500

Principal Subsidiary Companies: Marvel Enterprises is an entertainment company that publishes comic book, manufactures toys, and licenses its products. Marvel is headquartered in New York City and has office and manufacturing facilities in Arizona, Washington State, California, and Mexico. The company's Marvel Publishing division produces the famous line of Marvel comics which include characters such as Spiderman, the X-Men, Captain America, the Incredible Hulk, and the Fantastic Four.

Chief Competitors: Marvel Enterprises has a number of competitors in the toy and comic book industries. Some primary competitors are: DC Comics, Stan Lee Media, Walt Disney, Hasbro, Mattel, and Acclaim Entertainment.

CURRENT TRENDS

The end of the 1990s and the start of the 2000s saw a general decline in the comic book industry, and readership fell off at a rate of seven to ten percent a month. The trend was exacerbated by the closure of a large number of comic book stores across the United States. In addition fewer of the traditional retail sources of comic books—drug stores, convenience stores, super markets—continue to stock comic books. These factors have made the decade long drop in Marvel comic book sales even more serious. The company hopes reverse this trend with the development of new story-lines in its most popular books and the regular publication of collections of older stories in trade paperback "graphic novels" that tell a complete self-contained story.

CHRONOLOGY:

Key Dates for Marvel Enterprises

1939: Martin Goodman publishes the first issue of Marvel Comics and founds Timely Publications

1941: Captain America is introduced

1951: Timely Publications renamed Atlas News Company

1961: The Fantastic Four first appear, followed soon afterwards by Spiderman and the Incredible Hulk

1963: "Marvel Comics Group" appears on Marvel comics for the first time

1966: Marvel Super Heroes cartoon series first appears on TV

1968: Martin Goodman sells Marvel to Cadence Industries

1975: Marvel publishes the first *Giant Size X-Men*

1977: *The Incredible Hulk* TV series debuts

1986: Marvel sold to New World Pictures

1988: Marvel sold to Andrews Group, Inc.

1991: Marvel makes its first public stock offering

1992: Marvel acquired Fleer Corporation

1996: Marvel files bankruptcy

1998: Marvel acquired by Toy Biz, Inc.

2001: Twentieth Century Fox releases film *X-Men*

PRODUCTS

In addition to completely revamped versions of its most successful and revered series, Marvel introduced other products which proved a hit with comic fans. One new product is a series of trade paperback "graphic novels," each containing reprinted stories. The trade book line was an alternative to reprinting comic books when they were sold out during their first release. This new format increased their value as collectibles and increased demand for the initial print run. In fall 2001, Marvel introduced a program to print twelve graphic novels a month. Another innovative product is the free sample stories that Marvel offers for downloading on

MARVEL LEADS AMERICA TO WAR

As his new superheroes were battling foes in the Marvel universe, Martin Goodman was becoming concerned about more serious threats in the real world. Nazi Germany had invaded Poland around the time he was forming his comic book empire. For the first two years of World War II the United States maintained a careful neutrality. Marvel, on the other hand, was fighting hard for the Allies. In February 1940 the Submariner singlehandedly captured a Nazi U-boat. Just a year later, Captain America hit the scene, a hero whose specialty was battling Hitler. His comics were a resounding success—the premier issue sold an amazing one million copies. Nine months later, the rest of the United States entered the war against Germany, and three and a half years later, Hitler was defeated.

its Web site to attract new readers to the Marvel universe.

GLOBAL PRESENCE

Foreign markets accounted for more than 20 percent of Marvel Enterprise's sales in 2001. Marvel maintains an office in Hong Kong, which oversees the production of toys in the People's Republic of China. It also has a Hong Kong subsidiary, which sells the company's products in markets outside the United States. A subsidiary in Mexico, Compania de Juguetes Mexicanos. S.A. de C.V., manufactures kites for Spectra Star.

EMPLOYMENT

Marvel Enterprises has a full-time staff of about 500 employees. This include editorial staff at Marvel Publishing and production and development staff in the Toy Biz division. In addition, Marvel employs a contingent of approximately 500 freelancers. Toy Biz works with freelance toy inventors; Marvel Publishing relies on an army of freelance writers, pencil artists, inkers, and colorists. Much of the actual work on each Marvel comic book takes place outside Marvel's own facilities. Free-lancers are paid on a per page basis. They may also qualify for a percentage of issues sold.

SOURCES OF INFORMATION

Bibliography
Brownstein, Charles. "Revamped Marvel Looks to Sell Books," *Publishers Weekly*, September 24, 2001.

Bryant, Adam. "Pow! The Punches That Left Marvel Reeling." *New York Times*, May 24, 1998.

"Comic Book Publisher Marvel Emerges From Bankruptcy." *Los Angeles Times*, October 2, 1998.

Daniels, Les. *Marvel: Five Fabulous Decades of the World's Greatest Comics*. New York: Harry N. Abrams, Inc., 1991.

Elder, Robert K. "Suddenly, Marvel Comics Have 'X' Appeal."*Pittsburgh Post-Gazette*, July 18, 2000.

Massari, Paul. "Marvel's Superheroes Fight Their Way Back From Comic Disaster." *Boston Globe*, December 2, 2001.

"Marvel Enterprises." *Hoover's Company Profiles*, 2002. Available at http://www.hoovers.com.

"Marvel Entertainment." *Hoover's Company Profiles*, 2002. Available at http://www.hoovers.com.

"Marvel Entertainment Group Inc." *International Directory of Company Histories*. Detroit: Gale Research, 1994.

Marvel Home Page, 2002. Available at http://www.marvel.com.

Powers, Kemp. "Wanted: Superhero." *Forbes*, 11 November 2001.

Yan, Ellen. "Superheroes to Take On Illiteracy." *Newsday*, 22 July 2001.

For an annualreport:
write: Marvel Enterprises, 10 East 40th Street, New York, NY 10016

For additional industry research:
Investigate companies by their Standard Industrial Classification Codes, also known as SICs. Marvel Enterprises' primary SICs are:

2721 Periodicals Publishing & Printing

2731 Book Publishing & Printing

3944 Games, Toys, And Children's Vehicles

Also investigate companies by their North American Industrial Classification System codes, also known as NAICS codes. Marvel Enterprises' primary NAICS codes are:

339932 Game, Toy, and Children's Vehicle Manufacturing

339999 All Other Miscellaneous Manufacturing

Maytag Corporation

FOUNDED: 1893

Contact Information:

HEADQUARTERS: 403 West Fourth Street
    Newton, IA 50208-0039
PHONE: (641)792-7000
FAX: (641)787-8376
URL: http://www.maytag.com

OVERVIEW

Maytag Corporation, in business since 1893, is the third largest manufacturer of major household appliances in the United States, trailing Whirlpool Corporation and GE Appliances. Originally founded as a manufacturer of farm implements, the company today concentrates on the production of clothes washers and dryers, dishwashers, electric ranges and ovens, and refrigerators. Its full line of home appliances is marketed under the brand names of Admiral, Amana, Dynasty, Jenn-Air, Magic Chef, and Maytag. Through its Hoover subsidiary, the company is the market leader in floor care products.

In addition to its full range of household appliances, Maytag manufactures a wide range of products for commercial applications, including cooking, floor care, laundry, and vending. Maytag sells specially modified washers and dryers for use in coin laundries, restaurants, hotels, health care facilities, athletic clubs, apartment buildings, and colleges and universities. Its Hoover subsidiary produces a number of floor care products designed for use in office buildings, hotels, restaurants, and schools.

One of Maytag's subsidiaries, Dixie-Narco, is a major U.S. manufacturer of soft drink bottle and can vending machines. The vending machines are primarily sold by Dixie-Narco to soft drink bottlers, including Coca-Cola and Pepsico. Another Maytag subsidiary, Jade Range, manufactures premium-priced commercial ranges and refrigerators, as well as commercial-style ranges for the home market.

COMPANY FINANCES

Maytag executives voiced some disappointment with the company's financial performance in 2001. Although revenue climbed to $4.3 billion in 2001, the company's profit fell sharply to $47.7 million, or $1.41 per share, from $201 million, or $2.44 per share, in 2000, when revenue totaled $4.2 billion. Reasons for the decline in net income included higher marketing, distribution, and support costs; coupled with low price points in the household appliance market. Other factors contributing to the drop in profit included lower volume in the floor care business and reduced revenue in the company's vending machine business. In the 52 weeks ended May 24, 2002, Maytag's stock traded between a low of $22.25 and a high of $47.94. The company's price earnings ratio, as of May 24, 2002, was 24.83. During 2001, Maytag took a number of special charges against income, including a restructuring connected with the company's reduction in its salaried workforce and the discontinuation of some of its operations. In 2000, Maytag posted net income of $201 million, or $2.44 a share, on sales of $4.2 billion, down from a 1999 profit of almost $329 million, or $3.66 per share, on revenue of $4.3 billion.

After the first quarter of 2002, things were looking up for Maytag, although company executives were quick to point out that they didn't expect the first quarter buoyancy in their key markets to be sustained throughout the year. In the first quarter of 2002, the company's earnings per share jumped to 75 cents per share, compared with 46 cents a share in the first quarter of 2001. Net income for the first quarter in 2002 totaled $56.7 million, compared with $36.6 million a year earlier. When interviewed by Bill Griffeth on cable television's CNBC business network, Ralph Hake, Maytag's chairman and chief executive officer, attempted to temper optimism for the remainder of 2002, based on the company's performance in the first quarter by offering his analysis. "The first quarter in our industry was up 9.5 percent, really quite a surprise to everyone. Next quarter it will be up about 5 and for the year it will be up 2 or 3. So the environment is going to mitigate performance here going forward."

FINANCES:

Maytag Corp.
Net Sales, 1998-2001
(billion dollars)

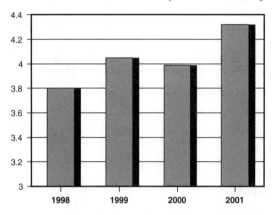

Maytag Corp.
2001 Stock Prices
(dollars)

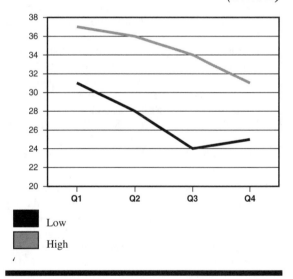

ANALYSTS' OPINIONS

After the announcement of Maytag's earnings for the first quarter of 2002, Lawrence Horan, research director at Parker/Hunter Inc., said it appeared that the company might be cutting prices. "Gross margin was considerably below a year ago, so I suspect that they are pumping the volume to get the units out. Under their interim CEO [Leonard A. Hadley, who served as president and CEO from November 2000 until June 2001] last year, they were vehement about holding the minimum suggested retail price. Maybe they are looking the other way to move the stuff." As of mid-April 2002, analysts'

full-year estimates of Maytag earnings per share ranged from $2.45 to $2.60, with a mean of $2.52, according to First Call.

Reacting to a February 2002 prediction from Maytag Chairman Ralph Hake that the company's 2002 earnings would increase 20 percent on a sales increase of 12 to 15 percent, analyst Nicholas P. Heymann of Prudential Securities sounded a cautiously optimistic note. "They're moving along, getting work done. They're getting more products, trying to upmix. They're doing all the right stuff."

FAST FACTS:
About Maytag Corporation

Ownership: Maytag is a publicly owned company traded on the New York Stock Exchange.

Ticker Symbol: MYG

Officers: Ralph F. Hake, Chmn. and CEO, 53, 2001 base salary $409,821; Steven H. Wood, EVP and CFO, 44, 2001 base salary $260,000; William L. Beer, Pres. Maytag Appliances Division, 49, 2001 base salary $275,000

Employees: 21,755

Principal Subsidiary Companies: Maytag owns a number of subsidiaries in North America, the majority of which are based in the United States. One of its best-known subsidiaries is Hoover Company, the designer and manufacturer of floor care products for both home and commercial applications based in North Canton, Ohio. Other subsidiaries include Maytag Appliances, Newton Laundry Products, Herrin Laundry Products, Jackson Dishwashing Products, Galesburg Refrigeration Products, Cleveland Cooking Products, Jefferson City Component Parts, Amana Refrigeration Products, Florence Cooking Products, Searcy Laundry Products, and Jade Products Company. Subsidiaries based in Canada and Mexico include Maytag Canada, Hoover Canada, and Maytag Mexico Appliance Products.

Chief Competitors: As the third largest manufacturer of home appliances in the United States, Maytag faces its primary competition from Whirlpool Corporation, which is the number one U.S. appliance manufacturer; GE Appliances, number two in the United States; and Sweden's Electrolux AB, the world's largest manufacturer of household appliances.

HISTORY

Founded in 1893 by Frederick Louis Maytag and three partners, Maytag Company was originally a manufacturer of farm implements, specializing at first in the production of threshing machine band cutters and self-feeder attachments. Before long the company added other farm equipment to its product line, some of it of questionable quality. Rampant customer complaints about the company's Success corn husker caused a rift between Maytag and his partners. He bought them out in 1907 and vowed that from that point on, Maytag products would be known for their quality and dependability.

In 1907 Frederick Maytag added a clothes washer to his company's product line, mostly to provide some sort of balance for the company during its off-season when farming equipment sold slowly. Maytag's washer quickly caught on with consumers, and by 1922 its revolutionary Gyrofoam washer, which had an agitator at its bottom rather than at the top, pushed Maytag into first place among U.S. washing machine companies. So successful had Maytag's washing machine business become that in the early 1920s its farm equipment business was discontinued. In 1925 the company was incorporated, and its stock was listed on the New York Stock Exchange. A year later the presidency of the company passed from L.B. Maytag, son of the founder, to another of his sons, E.H. Maytag, who remained in the presidency until his death in 1940.

Under the direction of E.H. Maytag, the company managed to weather the Great Depression fairly well, even managing to eke out a profit while scores of other companies went under. After the death of E.H. Maytag in 1940, the leadership of the company passed to his son, Fred Maytag II. During the years of World War II, Maytag produced nothing but parts for military equipment. The production of washers resumed in 1946, and the company began marketing a line of refrigerators and cooking ranges that were manufactured by other companies under the Maytag brand name. During the 1950s, a decade of rapid growth for the home appliance industry, Maytag began manufacturing equipment for the commercial self-service laundry businesses as well as institutional laundry operators. The 1950s also saw increased competition from full-line appliance companies, including General Electric, Frigidaire, and Whirlpool. Despite the increased competition, Maytag continued to manufacture only clothes washers and dryers, which were marketed alongside ranges and refrigerators manufactured by other companies. During this period the Maytag line of laundry equipment acquired a reputation as a premium brand.

In 1955 Maytag dropped cooking ranges from its product line and five years later it dropped refrigerators, returning to its core products of washing machines and dryers. After the death in 1962 of Fred Maytag, the direction of the company passed into the hands of non-family members. George Umbreit was named chairman and chief executive officer, while E.G. Higdon was appointed president. After laundry equipment sales peaked in the early 1970s, the company began pricing its washers and dryers more competitively, but beginning in 1980, under the direction of Chairman Daniel J. Krumm, Maytag started its return to the marketing of a full line of household appliances. To accomplish this transformation and maintain the corporate reputation for quality and dependability, Maytag began to acquire a number of appliance manufacturers that had also established a reputation for quality products. Acquired in 1981 was Hardwick Stove Company, followed in 1982 by the Jenn-Air Corporation, a leading manufacturer of indoor electric grills with stove-top ventilation systems. In 1986 Maytag took over Magic Chef, giving the company a means to re-enter the refrigerator and freezer market through Magic Chef's Admiral division. Other Magic Chef brand names included Toastmaster, Norge, and Magic Chef. At about the same time, Maytag moved into the soft drink vending industry in a big way with the purchase of Dixie-Narco Inc., the biggest player in the U.S. soft drink vending market.

In 1989 Maytag moved into the floor care equipment market in a big way with the purchase of Chicago Pacific Corporation, primarily to acquire Chicago Pacific's Hoover division. The company's almost frenzied acquisition pace during the 1980s eventually caused acute financial problems, forcing the company, now under the direction of Chairman and CEO Leonard Hadley, to back away from most of its overseas operations and focus on putting its North American house in order.

Maytag's retrenchment in the early 1990s paid off in the latter half of the decade. In 1996 the company posted a healthy profit of $162 million, its best showing up to that point in the 1990. The following year, Maytag acquired G.S. Blodgett Corporation, manufacturer of commercial ovens, fryers, and charbroilers for the food service industry. In 2001 Blodgett was sold by Maytag to Middleby Corporation, and the company acquired the Amana major appliance and commercial microwave oven businesses from Goodman Manufacturing.

STRATEGY

Maytag looks to the future with optimism, hoping to ensure business success "by building on our traditions, continuously improving those, and seeking even greater opportunities for our innovation and operational excellence strategies," according to the company's 2001 Annual Report. For Maytag, innovation is not limited to the development of new products but also about finding new and creative ways to manage its business operations. Examples of this type of innovation in Maytag's management of its business include LeanSigma, a program that pinpoints ways to eliminate waste in operations and variations in parts and processes that can undermine product quality.

Maytag also hopes to extend its dominance in the laundry and floor care businesses into the kitchen sector. A major step toward this ambitious goal came in 2001 with the acquisition of Amana, part of Maytag's initiative to "own the kitchen." A strong result for the company's major appliance business in 2001 was expected

CHRONOLOGY:
Key Dates for Maytag Corporation

1893: Maytag Co. founded as farm implement manufacturer

1907: Maytag markets its first washing machine

1921: Maytag begins selling its products nationwide

1941: Maytag suspends washer production to make parts for military aircraft

1948: Maytag introduces automatic washers

1981: Purchase of Hardwick Stove Co. sets off Maytag acquisition frenzy

1982: Maytag acquires Jenn-Air

1986: Maytag acquires Magic Chef group of companies

1989: Maytag acquires Hoover Co.

2001: Maytag acquires Amana

to be followed in 2002 by still further growth. To support its initiative to "own the kitchen," Maytag plans an expanded advertising and marketing effort "designed to build presence and identity with customers."

Another important element in Maytag's strategy is its effort to develop world-class logistics. To that end, the company contracted with Exel Direct in late 2001 to handle the distribution of Maytag's major appliances to retail and builder customers. Exel Direct is also providing direct home delivery and installation of Maytag appliances to customers who desire that service. In its 2001 Annual Report, the company observed, "Teaming up with Exel has improved the quality of our service to customers and consumers, and we are experiencing cost benefits associated with having a single third party perform this part of our logistics function."

INFLUENCES

For much of its history, Maytag has adjusted its corporate strategy to reflect changing trends in the marketplace as well as outside forces exerting an influence on retail sales in the company's markets or retail markets in general. In its earliest years, Maytag Company, originally founded to manufacture farm implements, added the

Maytag Corp. teamed up with Ford Motor Co. to create a concept Winstar van that includes a microwave and washer/dryer. (AP Photo/Charles Bennett)

production of clothes washers to help balance the company's year-round business and offset the sharp drop in demand for farming equipment during the off-season. By 1920 Maytag's success in the laundry market prompted a decision to abandon the farm equipment market altogether.

As the household appliance industry grew rapidly during the 1950s and competition became keener, particularly from full-line appliance manufacturers, Maytag expanded its product line to include cooking ranges and refrigerators produced by other companies but marketed under the Maytag brand name. Within a few years, however, the company decided to return to its core product line of clothes washers and dryers, although it soon added to those a portable dishwasher and food-waste disposable systems manufactured in its own plants.

After sales in the laundry equipment market peaked in the 1970s, the company once again began to move towards marketing a full line of household appliances. To accomplish this, Maytag embarked on an ambitious campaign of acquisition, looking specifically for manufacturers of appliances that, like Maytag, had earned a reputation for producing dependable, high-quality products. During the 1980s, Maytag acquired Hardwick Stove Company, Jenn-Air Corporation, and Magic Chef. Also acquired during this period was vending machine manufacturer Dixie-Narco Inc., giving Maytag a leading position in the soft drink vending equipment market. In 1989 the company purchase Chicago Pacific Corporation,

mostly to gain entry into the floor-care industry, in which Chicago Pacific's Hoover Division was a major player.

By the early 1990s Maytag's frenetic acquisition pace led to hard times for the company during the economic recession of that period. Maytag trimmed back its overseas operations sharply, choosing to focus instead on its North American markets. More recently, however, the company has begun to add to its product line through selective acquisitions and to expand its operations abroad. In 2001 Maytag acquired Amana's major appliance business from Goodman Manufacturing, although only after selling its G.E. Blodgett commercial cooking equipment manufacturer to Middleby Corporation.

CURRENT TRENDS

Perhaps the most significant trend for Maytag in recent years has been its carefully studied transformation from its core business of clothes washers and dryers into a full-line household appliance manufacturing. The company has made clear its intention to continue this transformation in 2002, stating in a recent corporate release: "Now we need to move into the kitchen to own it the way we own the laundry room and floor care. To the extent we can develop elegant, innovative kitchen products, we can own the most active and involved room in the household-the kitchen."

The information explosion that has accompanied the rapid spread in popularity of the Internet has resulted in changes in Maytag's marketing strategy. In his letter to shareholders in the company's 2001 Annual Report, Chairman Ralph Hake commented: "We will continue to build our relationship with consumers in other ways, particularly with the Internet where close to 30 percent of all appliance shoppers-nearly 11 million consumers-research products before going to a retail outlet to make their purchase. The influence of the Internet as a valuable resource will grow exponentially over the years, and Maytag will be there to help educate and influence shoppers online."

PRODUCTS

Today, in addition to its core laundry equipment business, Maytag markets a broad range of major household appliances. These products include cooking ranges and ovens, microwaves, dishwashers, and refrigerators, as well as numerous specially designed products for commercial applications. These products are marketed under the following brand names: Maytag, Amana, Jenn-Air, Dynasty, Magic Chef, and Jade Range. A wide range of floor care products are produced and sold by Maytag's Hoover subsidiary, and its Dixie-Narco subsidiary is a leader in the production and sale of vending equipment.

CORPORATE CITIZENSHIP

Maytag takes seriously its responsibilities to the communities in which it operates. The three main areas of Maytag's social commitment are community involvement, its contributions program, and environmental efforts. In the realm of community involvement, Maytag endeavors to give back to the community through company-sponsored programs and the efforts of Maytag employees who volunteer for community service. In Canton, Ohio, more than 300 Hoover Company employees built a Habitat for Humanity home. A similar project for Habitat for Humanity was undertaken by employees at Maytag's plant in Cleveland, Tennessee.

Through its contributions program, Maytag has sought to finance programs and projects that make a difference in people's lives. The company in 2000 contributed more than $4 million in cash and products through its foundation and direct giving program to meet some of the needs and support worthy causes in Maytag's operating communities. Of this sum, approximately 43 percent supported education, while 35 percent was dedicated to community improvement, largely through youth programs and arts and culture. Most of the remainder was committed to community support, including the United Way.

LEANSIGMA HELPS TRIM WASTE

In its quest to keep down the costs of manufacturing operations while maintaining high quality and finding new efficiencies, Maytag has turned to LeanSigma. This program helps identify waste in operations, as well as variations in parts and processes that can undermine product quality. A shining example of LeanSigma's benefits can be found at Maytag's plant in Jackson, Tennessee. The program resulted in the transformation of a half-mile-long, continuous-line dishwasher assembly line operation into seven separate assembly cells capable of a wide range of product-mix capabilities. This transformation improved productivity at Jackson by 22 percent and freed up 43,000 square feet of manufacturing floor space. Perhaps most importantly, the changes resulted in an improvement in product quality of 55 percent. To achieve similar efficiencies elsewhere, Maytag is implementing LeanSigma at all its major manufacturing facilities.

In the area of environmental responsibility, Maytag has taken the lead within the appliance industry in pushing for stronger energy and water standards. The company has worked closely with the Department of Energy to develop new Energy Star criteria for appliances. Maytag has twice been named Energy Star Appliance Partner of the Year by the Department of Energy and the Environmental Protection Agency.

GLOBAL PRESENCE

Responsible for the coordination of Maytag's presence in foreign markets is Maytag International, headquartered in Chicago. Maytag International directs all the corporation's international efforts, including export sales and marketing and the licensing of brands and joint ventures. Maytag's presence in overseas markets includes direct sales operations in Mexico, the United Kingdom, Australia, and Puerto Rico.

EMPLOYMENT

According to its 2001 annual report, Maytag Corporation employed a workforce of 21,755 people, as of

December 31, 2001. This represented an increase of about 18.5 percent from its workforce of 18,350 at the end of 2000 and is explained largely by the company's acquisition of Amana during 2001, which added roughly 4,000 employees to the corporate payroll.

Maytag's Web site carries this profile of the type of employee the company is looking for: "At Maytag, we reach out for the best people. . .people with a need to succeed, people who make things happen, people committed to quality, people who understand innovation."

SOURCES OF INFORMATION

Bibliography

"Business Description: Maytag Corporation." *Multex Investor*, 2002. Available at http://www.marketguide.com.

Cohen, Rachel. "Maytag Earnings to Top Estimates; Shares Surge." *Reuters Business Report*, 12 March 2002.

———. "Maytag Net Income Falls; Sees Slower Sales Growth." *Reuters Business Report*, 16 April 2002.

Griffeth, Bill. "Maytag-Chmn. & CEO-Interview." *CNBC/Dow Jones Business Video*, 16 April 2002.

"Maytag Corp.—History." *Gale Business Resources*, 2002. Available at http://galenet.galegroup.com/servlet/GBR

"Maytag Corporation." *Hoover's Online*, 2002. Available at http://www.hoovers.com.

Maytag Corporation 2001 Annual Report. Newton, IA: Maytag Corporation, 2002.

Maytag Corporation Home Page, 2002. Available at http://www.maytag.com.

For an annualreport:

on the Internet at: http://www.maytag.com **or** write: Shareholder Relations, Maytag Corporation, 403 W. 4th St. N., Newton, IA 50208

For additional industry research:

Investigate companies by their Standard Industrial Classification Codes, also known as SICs. Maytag Corporation's primary SICs are:

3581 Automatic Vending Machines

3582 Commercial Laundry Equipment

3589 Service Industry Machinery NEC

3631 Household Cooking Equipment

3633 Household Laundry Equipment

3635 Household Vacuum Cleaners

3639 Household Appliances NEC

Also Investigate companies by their North American Industrial Classification System codes, also known as NAICS codes. Maytag Corporation's primary NAICS codes are:

333311 Automatic Vending Machine Manufacturing

335212 Household Vacuum Cleaner Manufacturing

335221 Household Cooking Appliance Manufacturing

335224 Household Laundry Equipment Manufacturing

The MCI Group

OVERVIEW

MCI is the second-largest long-distance provider in the United States after AT&T, but that position was in jeopardy in the second half of 2002 as number three Sprint aggressively went after MCI Group customers to become a provider of services. It is a leader and innovator in the telecommunications industry. MCI was instrumental in forging an opening in that industry for companies to compete with AT&T. It continued through mid-2002 to lead all others except for AT&T, which had held an industrywide monopoly until the 1980s.

In 1997, the global long-distance company World-Com Inc. made a $30-billion bid to buy MCI. GTE made a $28 billion offer. After some negotiation, MCI agreed to a $37-billion purchase by WorldCom. The merger was announced November 10, 1997 and the new company became the MCI Group under the WorldCom parent company.

COMPANY FINANCES

Scrutiny—both internal and external—of MCI and WorldCom finances was underway in mid-2002, and analysts have predicted either the bankruptcy of the entire company or the selling off of MCI to satisfy billions of dollars in unsecured bank loans. In July 2002, WorldCom announced plans to sell more than $1 billion of its subsidiaries, but made no mention of selling MCI Group. The debacle occurred in mid-2002 when World-Com revealed that it had removed $3.8 billion in "ordinary expenses" by unethically calling them capital

FOUNDED: 1968

Contact Information:
HEADQUARTERS: 500 Clinton Center Dr..
   Clinton, MS 39056
PHONE: (601)460-5600
FAX: (601)460-8269
URL: http://www.mci.com

FAST FACTS:
About The MCI Group

Ownership: MCI is a publicly owned corporation traded on NASDAQ.

Ticker symbol: MCIC

Officers: Bert C. Roberts Jr., Chmn., 60; John W. Sidgmore, VChmn., CEO, and Pres., 52

Principal Subsidiary Companies: Among the many subsidiaries of MCI are MCI Systemhouse Inc., MCI Metro Inc., Nationwide Cellular Service Inc., and The News Corp. Ltd.

Chief Competitors: The MCI Group competes directly with AirTouch, AT&T, Bell Atlantic, BellSouth, EDS, GTE, NYNEX, and Sprint.

---

expenditures, which get deducted over years instead of in one year. WorldCom reported bogus profits of $1.5 billion for 2001 and $130 million for the 2001 first quarter, and accountants for WorldCom and MCI were asked by a House investigation committee to account for cooking company books.

ANALYSTS' OPINIONS

According to Andrew Backover of *USA Today*, analysts feel that the poor ethical judgment that led WorldCom and the MCI Group to falsify accounts was a reaction to industry and shareholder pressures in November 2000 when the entire telecommunications industry started, in the words of many, to "melt down."

HISTORY

MCI began when John Goeken wanted to provide a radio link between Chicago and St. Louis. In 1966, AT&T held a virtual monopoly over what would later be called the telecommunications industry. Goeken had to go before the Federal Communications Commission (FCC) to obtain permission to set up his link. He formed an enterprise called Microwave Communications, Inc., which became MCI Communications in 1968. By this time Goeken had departed, and William McGowan had taken the helm of the new company.

Throughout the 1970s, MCI fought one legal battle after another in a drama that cast it as "David" to AT&T's "Goliath." However, by the end of the decade, it had won almost full competition rights and become a Goliath itself to rivals. MCI found its position further improved when the breakup of AT&T into several "Baby Bells" was ordered in the 1980s.

In 1982 MCI bought Western Union, once a telecommunications giant in the era when people regularly sent telegrams, from Xerox. A year later, it became the first telephone company to involve itself in the new high-tech version of the telegram, e-mail, when it launched MCI Mail in 1983. This was long before most Americans had ever used the Internet. In 1988 it acquired RCA Global Communications, a major phone-service provider in Asia, from General Electric. Two years later, MCI bought Telecom USA, at that time the fourth-largest long-distance carrier in the United States.

During the 1990s, MCI became heavily involved in the Internet. It also launched several successful marketing programs, including 1-800-COLLECT and Friends & Family. In 1993, MCI and British Telecom (BT) formed a joint venture called Concert Global Communications, which would sell telecommunications services worldwide.

When MCI merged with WorldCom, the company planned to enter new markets and offer local phone service. According to the terms of the agreement, MCI owned 45 percent of the newly formed company. The WorldCom marriage with MCI Group showed itself to be disastrous in 2002 as company fraud at the executive level caused hardship to rank-and-file employees as layoffs of WorldCom (including MCI Group) workers began with 17,000 layoffs in late June 2002. At this writing in July 2002, MCI's lucrative long-distance business may be ordered sold by banks that hold nearly $3 billion in unsecured loans obtained by WorldCom. What is certain is that Sprint in July 2002 has aggressively launched a campaign to take away MCI customers and to challenge for the number two telecommunications leader position long enjoyed by MCI.

STRATEGY

MCI has adopted a "When all else fails, come clean" strategy in July of 2002 as MCI Group and its parent WorldCom try to restore Wall Street and shareholder confidence. But owing to the fact that WorldCom was audited by Andersen, itself reeling from scandal following the Enron crisis, it was uncertain in mid-2002 if the company could avoid bankruptcy and the selling off of MCI Group, by far its prize asset. John Sidgmore, WorldCom President and CEO, and Bert Roberts, WorldCom Chairman of the Board, have pledged to cooperate fully with House and SEC requests for an inspection of company books. In effect, WorldCom and MCI have thrown themselves at the mercy of the federal government, but whether such openness is too little, too late or in time to save the company remains unknown in mid-2002. Stock was nearly worthless—83 cents in June 2002, more than $20 below stock prices in mid-2000.

CURRENT TRENDS

The future of MCI Group may be out of parent company WorldCom's hands before the end of 2002. According to the New York Times, banks holding the paper on nearly $3 billion worth of unsecured loans may force the company to sell bankable assets such as MCI. In addition, Worldcom and MCI past and present executives are facing a house investigation that could lead to indictments if wrongdoing is substantiated. In addition, the number three provider, Sprint, has approached all MCI corporate customers with an offer to serve as a backup if MCI folds, and early indications in 2002 were that a number of MCI corporate customers were switching to Sprint.

PRODUCTS

In the 2000s, MCI competes in the long distance, local, Internet, wireless, and systems integration markets. MCI One is a one-stop package for residential customers to combine all these types of services. NetworkMCI One is the business equivalent of MCI One. MCI's Internet division, InternetMCI, offers access service and software. In the area of wireless communication, the company claims to have the largest combined service area, "or wireless footprint," in the nation.

GLOBAL PRESENCE

As of July 2002, MCI provided worldwide direct-dial service to 146 foreign countries.

SOURCES OF INFORMATION

Bibliography

Backover, Andrew. "Pressure to Perform Felt as Problems Hit." *USA TODAY,* 1 July 2002.

Comerford, Mike. "MCI's Free Fall Concerns Customers." *Chicago Daily Herald,* 27 June 2002.

Dillon, Nancy. "Bush Slams WorldCom on Fraud." *The Washington Post,* 27 June 2002.

Emling, Shirley. "The Bell Tolls for Long Distance." *The Atlanta Journal and Constitution,* 28 June 2002.

MCI Home Page, 1 July 2002. Available at http://www.mci.com/.

Noguchi, Yuki. "Employees In Area Wait For Layoffs." *The Washington Post,* 28 June 1995.

Swartz, John. "MCI Customers Should Watch for Danger Signs." *USA TODAY,* 28 June 2002.

CHRONOLOGY:
Key Dates for The MCI Group

1966: John Goeken sets up Microwave Communications, Inc.

1968: Goeken departs and the company becomes MCI Communications

1982: Western Union buys Western Union

1983: MCI Mail is launched as the first company to provide e-mail services

1984: AT&T is forced to break up its monopoly, strengthening MCI's position in the market

1990: Purchases Telecom USA

1993: MCI launches 1-800-COLLECT

1998: WorldCom Inc. and MCI announce merger

2002: WorldCom fires top employees or accepts their resignation as the company learns some $3.8 billion was wrongly stated as company profits for the 2001 annual report; MCI Group's parent company hires a consultant, William McLucas, former Chief of the Enforcement Division of the Securities and Exchange Commission, to investigate allegations of corruption and false reporting; House Financial Services Committee orders WorldCom's CEO John W. Sidgmore and other head executives (including fired executives) to testify; banks holding WorldCom's nearly $3 billion in unsecured loans may force the company to sell MCI to satisfy the debt

For an annual report:
on the Internet at: http://www.mci.com/ **or** write: MCI Communications, Investor Relations, 1801 Pennsylvania Ave., Washington, D.C. 20006

For additional industry research:
Investigate companies by their Standard Industrial Classification Codes, also known as SICs. MCI's primary SIC is:

4813 Telephone Communications Except Radio

Also investigate companies by their North American Industry Classification System codes, also known as NAICS codes. MCI's primary NAICS code is:

513310 Wired Telecommunications

Microsoft Corporation

FOUNDED: 1975

Contact Information:

HEADQUARTERS: 1 Microsoft Way
  Redmond, WA 98052-6399
PHONE: (206)882-8080
FAX: (206)936-7329
URL: http://www.microsoft.com

OVERVIEW

Microsoft Corporation is the world's leading independent software company. If the company were like a toy giant, it could accurately call itself "Computers 'R Us." On any given day that a person anywhere in the world uses a computer, chances are almost 100 percent that a Microsoft product was employed. With such pervasiveness, profits have not only been staggeringly high but so has antagonism toward the company-much of that directed toward Bill Gates whose personal wealth stems from owning a 12 percent share of Microsoft. One measure of Microsoft's size is that the Apple Computer television ad campaign hopes to win defectors from the 95 percent of computer users who now use Microsoft operating systems.

COMPANY FINANCES

According to the company which cites prominent analysts, Microsoft Corporation for the end of 2002 and beginning of 2003 is expected to do better than its rivals and is a relatively low-risk stock. Nonetheless, earnings by July of 2002 have sagged drastically in a slowed economy from booming profits in January 2000. At the start of 2001, Microsoft had the rare chore of telling investors it had overestimated revenue for the year. Nonetheless, Microsoft is a proven company with proven results over nearly a quarter-century. Taken as a whole, registered Microsoft products such as Windows XP, the Xbox game, and MSN Internet Access services brought in 2001 revenues of $7.7 billion in the fourth quarter of 2001. However, on May 30, 2002, newspapers announced that Microsoft's reported earnings for 2001 made the company the latest giant to be accused of "smoothing its [earnings] results by setting aside artificially large reserves to reduce revenues with the idea of reversing that procedure to record the revenues in less profitable future periods," according to the *Deseret News* and other newspapers. Microsoft has agreed to cooperate with the SEC but still may face civil charges, according to the Deseret News, citing copyrighted information and sources claimed by the Wall Street Journal. The 2001 annual report for Microsoft noted revenue of $25.3 billion, and operating income of $11.72 billion.

HISTORY

Microsoft was founded in 1975 by high school friends Bill Gates and Paul Allen. While students at Harvard, the two developed the programming language called BASIC, which was used in the first commercial microcomputer, Altair. Gates dropped out of Harvard when he was 19 years old in order to sell a variation of BASIC with his friend. After moving to Albuquerque, the two men used a hotel room to launch Microsoft, originally called Micro-soft. The company continued to grow because they adapted their BASIC program to work on other computers.

In 1980, International Business Machines (IBM) chose Microsoft Over competing Digital Research to write its operating system (software that commands a computer's standard functions) for its new personal computer (PC). Under pressure, Microsoft purchased rights to QDOS, or quick and dirty operating system, for less than $100,000 from Seattle programmer Tim Paterson. They renamed it the Microsoft Disk Operating System, or MS-DOS.

IBM's PC was an instant hit and became the standard for PC operating systems in the 1980s. When other personal computer companies wanted to be compatible with IBM, MS-DOS became a dominant force in the industry. Microsoft continued to grow, creating software for IBM, Apple, and Radio Shack computers. In 1982 Microsoft opened its first European offices and, in 1983 the company expanded its horizons to include West Germany, France, Australia, and Korea.

Microsoft introduced its first Windows operating system in the mid-1980s, starting an avalanche of demand for PCs in the workplace and, finally, in the home. Windows opened up the world of computers to people with little technical background and allowed the PC industry to flourish in the late 1980s and early 1990s. By the mid-1990s, Windows was the world's leading operating system.

Allen left the company in 1983 due to an illness but remained on the Microsoft board. Taking the company public in 1986, Gates instantly became the personal com-

FAST FACTS:
About Microsoft Corporation

Ownership: Microsoft is a publicly owned company traded on NASDAQ.

Ticker symbol: MSFT

Officers: William H. (Bill) Gates III, Chmn. and Chief Software Architect, 47; Steven A. Ballmer, Pres., 46

Employees: 31,746

Chief Competitors: Microsoft not only produces operating systems and computer application software, but also offers an online service and is partner in a cable news operation. Some primary competitors include America Online, Apple Computer, AT&T Corp., IBM, MCI, Netscape, Computer Associates, Applied Microsystems Corp., and Novell.

puter industry's first billionaire, holding 45 percent of the company's shares.

In 1997 the U.S. Department of Justice threatened to charge Microsoft with unfair business practices as a result of complaints from Internet browser developers that consumers using Windows 95 and the soon-to-be-released Windows 98 would be given Internet Explorer as part of their operating system. This was expected to make it difficult for consumers to choose a Microsoft competitor for their Internet browser. The Justice Department alleged that this constituted a monopoly and alerted the company that it faced possible anti-trust charges unless it unbundled certain applications, including the browser, from its operating systems. This action postponed the release of Windows 98. In June 1998, a federal appeals court lifted the injunction, allowing the sale of Microsoft's operating systems with the browser, and Windows 98 was rolled out in July.

The government case wasn't beneficial to either the image of Microsoft or Bill Gates, especially after Gates floundered and looked uncomfortable during questioning. The government ended up settling the case against the company. The company was forced to make the Windows operating system friendlier to competitors' software so that a competing browser could be launched by the user if so desired. Microsoft barely escaped having to break the company in half literally to comply with antitrust laws, but the court did find the company in violation of antitrust laws, paving way for AOL Time

CHRONOLOGY:

Key Dates for Microsoft Corporation

1975: Microsoft is founded by Bill Gates and Paul Allen

1979: Company headquarters move from Albuquerque, New Mexico to Bellevue, Washington

1981: IBM launches its Personal Computer run by Microsoft's MS-DOS; Microsoft incorporates

1985: The first version of Windows hits the market

1986: Microsoft goes public

1988: Apple sues Microsoft and its Windows system for copying the look and feel of a Macintosh

1995: Windows 95 is launched

1997: The Department of Justice investigates an antitrust action against Microsoft

1998: Windows 98 is released after a delay because of the investigation

2002: Rick Belluzzo, Microsoft Corp.'s president and chief operating officer, announced he was stepping down; Sun Microsystems takes Microsoft to court for alleged infringement of Java programming language and alleged antitrust practices; AOL Time Warner also sues Microsoft over what it terms unfair monopolistic practices; The Department of Justice finds a way to settle with Microsoft in spite of press, public, and some states' opposition to the done deal; the company agreed to share Windows software code with rival companies so that competing products can compete with Microsoft even while using Microsoft's operating system; unhappy with federal settlement, nine state prosecutors vow to seek antitrust penalties against Microsoft; *The Wall Street Journal* reports that Microsoft accounting practices are under scrutiny by the SEC; the company defended its accounting practices

Warner and its Netscape Communications Corp. to pursue a civil suit that claimed the company's so-called "bundling" of its Internet Explorer browser in its own Windows operating system constituted unfair competition. That 2002 suit may take some years to come to a conclusion or settlement. Microsoft also has been taken to court by Sun Microsystems, maker of the Java Platform, which contends that Microsoft committed copyright infringement and violated additional antitrust laws; these civil matters also are likely to drag through the courts for years.

In the late 1990s and 2000s, Windows NT5 (rechristened Windows 2000) became the most familiar system in the global business world. In 2001, the company released Windows XP, a product with so many bugs in its storage system and other areas that a chastened Microsoft promised future releases would be more friendly to users and more bug-free. Microsoft also helped its bottom line during the softer economy of the 2000s with the release of a video game called Xbox.

STRATEGY

Microsoft's success is largely due to its founder, chairman, and CEO, William H. Gates. His goal, the company says, has been to work toward improving and advancing his software, making it affordable and easy to use, although competitors harshly criticize the Windows operating system for frustrating flaws and crashes. According to the company, its mission is to "create software for the personal computer that empowers and enriches people in the workplace, at school and at home. Microsoft's early vision of a computer on every desk and in every home is coupled today with a strong commitment to Internet-related technologies that expand the power and reach of the PC and its users." In 2001, Microsoft's much ballyhooed publicity campaign took a serious public relations and credibility hit when the company was forced to admit Windows XP has serious security flaws.

INFLUENCES

Microsoft's first major success—developing MS-DOS—began the company's reputation as the one to beat. As a dominant power in the industry, Microsoft has been accused of, and even taken to court for, questionable practices and ruthless tactics aimed at squashing its competition. Critics, and the U.S. Department of Justice, have accused it of creating a monopoly, or an economic good controlled by a single power. In other words, with Microsoft's financial status, coupled with its ability to "bundle" its own products inside the Windows operating system package, many competitors felt they did not have a chance to compete on the same playing field, and the Department of Justice in 2002 got a company settlement which proved as much.

What is admirable about the company is the way it has taken failure and moved on until success came. Microsoft's huge size has meant it could afford experimentation and failure. Philip Elmer-Dewitt was quoted in *Time* as saying, "the company never gives up." The reporter cited Microsoft's chief executive officer, Steve Ballmer, as saying, "It doesn't matter if we bang our heads and fail. We keep right on banging and banging and banging and banging." The mission to always be ahead or way ahead of the competition proved successful when Microsoft took over Software Arts, which created the electronic spreadsheet. This strategy rang true once again when Microsoft, after several delays, introduced Windows 95, a modern version of a 10-year-old product.

Of course, along with its quest for power came times of frustration. Tough economic times even took their toll on Bill Gates' checking account. In 2000, Forbes reported Gates' personal fortune at $92.7 billion. In 2001, that total was reduced to $54.4 billion, and in 2002 to $34.5 billion, just enough to still make him the world's richest person. Much of his "lost" income was in stock contributed to charities that he and his wife support.

Instead of being ahead of the competition in the world of the Internet, Microsoft spent time chasing Netscape, a leading power in the Internet arena. To meet this challenge, Microsoft programmers developed new products devised to entice Internet users in their direction. Microsoft released its web-browsing software, Internet Explorer, as part of Windows 95, and its upgrade with Windows 98. As a result, in 2002, the U.S. Department of Justice settled with Microsoft which had, in effect, used its monopoly power to prevent its rivals from selling its products when it made its own browser part of its operating system. The fact that Internet Explorer was offered free to purchasers of Windows products made it difficult for Netscape and other browser producers to sell their products. In 2002, AOL Time Warner elected to take Microsoft to court charging unfair competition over the browser flap. In its defense, Microsoft and gates maintained that state and federal governments have stripped Microsoft of its right to software and other intellectual properties that were the result of expensive research, development, and employee hirings.

CURRENT TRENDS

Microsoft continues to try to corner every aspect of the Internet market. It has developed products to allow people to conduct business over the Internet, including Microsoft Internet Information Server, Microsoft SQL Server, and the BackOffice family of products. In June of 2002, Bill Gates announced that absolute computer security has become the next big challenge for the company, and that his goal is to make all transactions by computer "trustworthy." Under the code name Palladium, named for the statue of Athena which guarded ancient Troy, Microsoft has vowed to redesign "the architecture of PCs" in order "to dramatically improve our ability to

control and protect personal and corporate information," says Newsweek magazine. In other words, not only will sender identity and cash transactions finally be made truly secure, but spam, hacker-sent viruses, and unintentional meltdowns caused by internal bugs will also be dreaded problems of the past if Bill Gates' latest ambitious goal can be met.

PRODUCTS

Microsoft software is compatible with most PCS, including Intel microprocessor-based computers and Apple computers which have software for the Mac (Macintosh). Because of Department of Justice action, Microsoft in 2002 has been forced to allow rivals a more sporting competitive edge.

CORPORATE CITIZENSHIP

According to its corporate Web site, Microsoft's credo is that "amazing things happen when people get the resources they need." This belief is the foundation of the company's community affairs initiative. Microsoft contributes cash and software to non-profit organizations, supports education through many programs, supports efforts to improve learning and expand diversity in higher education, supports organizations in communities where its employees live and work, supports major arts organizations, and more.

In 2001, Microsoft and Microsoft employees donated $215 million "to help people and communities realize their potential," boasts the Microsoft Web site. In addition, after Bill Gates authored two books (*Business@ the Speed of Thought* and *The Road Ahead*) that were New York Times best sellers for many weeks, he donated all profits to non-profit corporations advancing computer technology in education. Bill and wife Melinda have started and maintained a $21 billion foundation to support projects related to global health and learning. The Gates family has spent $500 million to bring computer Internet capabilities to low-income communities.

GLOBAL PRESENCE

Microsoft is highly dependent upon foreign markets, although its revenue base is clearly in the United States. With offices in West Germany, France, Australia, Korea, and Great Britain, Microsoft is the world's largest software manufacturer and has employees all over the world. According to Microsoft's corporate Web site, the company maintains offices in 60 countries. It would be impossible to find a country on earth that didn't have Microsoft products somewhere on its soil. Microsoft in

2001 and 2002 has lobbied Congress to cut taxes on global profits from 35 percent to 5 percent, saying that such a move would be good for the overall economy and lead to at-home investments that would jumpstart the U.S. economy.

EMPLOYMENT

Microsoft employs 31,746 people worldwide. Microsoft has established many cultural groups to support its diverse workplace population, and Microsoft executives regularly speak on ways to ensure minority participation in business. These groups include: Blacks at Microsoft; Chinese at Microsoft; Gay, Lesbian, and Bisexual Employees at Microsoft; Microsoft Women's Group; Jews at Microsoft; Microsoft Grupo Unido Ibero-Americano; and Native Americans at Microsoft. In addition, Microsoft sponsors scholarships and organized cultural activities available to all of its employees.

SOURCES OF INFORMATION

Bibliography

"Apple Woos Potential Windows Defectors." *Newhouse News Service*, 8 April 2002.

Levy, Stephen. "The Big Secret." *Newsweek*, 1 July 2002.

"Microsoft Corporation." *Hoover's Online*, 2 July 2002. Available at http://www.hoovers.com.

Microsoft's Home Page, 2 July 2002. Available at http://www.microsoft.com.

"Microsoft Is Negotiating with SEC, Journal Reports." *The Deseret News*, 30 May 2002.

"Microsoft, P&G Seek U.S. Tax Break for Global Profits." *Bloomberg News*, 9 November 2001.

Moltzen, Edward F. "Salary Survey." *Computer Reseller News*, 24 June 2002.

"Timeline." *Washington Post Online*, July 2002. Available at http://www.washingtonpost.com/wp-dyn/technology/specials/microsoft/timeline.

For an annual report:
on the Internet at: http://www.microsoft.com

For additional industry research:
Investigate companies by their Standard Industrial Classification Codes, also known as SICs. Microsoft's primary SICs are:

7372 Prepackaged Software

7375 Information Retrieval Services

7383 News Syndicates

Also investigate companies by their North American Industry Classification System codes, also known as NAICS codes. Microsoft's primary NAICS code is:

511210 Software Publishers

Motorola Inc.

OVERVIEW

Motorola Inc. is one of the world's leaders in providing integrated communications solutions and embedded electronic solutions. The company's principal business sectors include Broadband Communications; Commercial, Government, and Industrial Solutions; Global Telecom Solutions; Integrated Electronic Systems; Personal Communications; and Semiconductor Products.

Motorola's Broadband Communications sector markets end-to-end systems for the delivery of interactive digital voice, video, voice, and high-speed data solutions for broadband operators. The company's Commercial, Government, and Industrial Solutions sector is a leading integrator of communication and information solutions for work teams in business and government enterprises. The sector's solutions are designed to enhance and transform operations by delivering rapid, mobile intelligence to meet mission-critical needs.

The Global Telecom Solutions sector provides the network services, infrastructure, and software to meet the needs of operators worldwide while offering a migration route to next-generation networks that will enable them to provide innovative, revenue-generating applications and services to their customers. Customers in the automotive, industrial, Telematics, telecommunications, and portable energy systems markets look to Motorola's Integrated Electronic Systems sector to provide a wide range of embedded systems and products. The company's Personal Communications sector manufactures and markets wireless subscriber and server equipment, including wireless handheld devices for cellular and iDEN integrated digital-enhanced networks, advanced messaging

FOUNDED: 1928

Contact Information:

HEADQUARTERS: 1303 E Algonquin Rd.
    Schaumburg, IL 60196
PHONE: (847)576-5000
FAX: (847)576-5372
TOLL FREE: (800)262-8509
EMAIL: invest1@email.mot.com
URL: http://www.motorola.com

FAST FACTS:
About Motorola Inc.

Ownership: Motorola Inc. is a publicly owned company traded on the New York Stock Exchange.

Ticker Symbol: MOT

Officers: Christopher B. Galvin, Chmn. and CEO, 51, 2001 base salary $1,275,000; Edward D. Breen Jr., Pres. and COO, 45, 2001 base salary $733,654

Employees: 111,000

Principal Subsidiary Companies: Motorola operates a vast network of subsidiaries worldwide. A number of the company's foreign-based subsidiaries oversee the marketing of Motorola products and services in the countries in which they are based, as well as neighboring countries that have no Motorola sales subsidiary. Some of the company's other subsidiaries include Metrowerks Inc., Next Level Communications Inc., Printrak International Inc., Starfish Software Inc., and Symbian Inc.

Chief Competitors: Competition within the wireless communications industry is extremely intense. Motorola faces keen competition in each of the market segments in which it is active. Principal competitors for the company's Personal Communications sector include Nokia, Ericsson/Sony, Siemens, and Samsung. Competitors for Motorola's Global Telecom Solutions sector include Ericsson, Nokia, Lucent, Nortel, Siemens, Alcatel, NEC, Samsung, and LG International. The leading competitors for the Commercial, Government, and Industrial Solutions sector include Tyco, M/A-Com, Nokia, Kenwood, and E.F. Johnson. Thomson/RCA, Toshiba, Terayon, COM21, Pioneer, Sony, and Scientific Atlanta lead the competition for Motorola's Broadband Communications sector. Competitors for the company's Integrated Electronic Systems sector include Delphi, Intel, Visteon, Sony, Panasonic, Sanyo, Toshiba, Sun Microsystems, and Radisys.

devices, personal two-way radios, and a broad range of mobile data services, servers, and software solutions, with related software and accessory products.

Motorola's Semiconductor Products sector is the world's largest producer of embedded processors. The sector provides DigtalDNA system-on-chip solutions for a connected world. The sector's strong focus on wireless communications and networking enables customers to develop smarter, simpler, faster, and synchronized products for the individual, work team, home, and automobile.

On the heels of a disappointing financial performance in 2001 and a discouraging start to 2002, the company was pinning some of its hopes for an upturn on a line of hip new mobile phones and an innovative advertising campaign. The first of the company's new phone models—the V70—features a rotating cover, circular display, and translucent keypad and was introduced in May 2002. Interviewed by the *Toronto Star*, Geoffrey Frost, head of global marketing for Motorola, said: "From a marketing standpoint, this was the right time to start going on offense. We are the underdog, no question about it."

COMPANY FINANCES

For the first time in 71 years, Motorola Inc. reported an operating loss in 2001. And things were looking somewhat dicey for 2002, despite the company's assurances that it would return to profitability in the second half of the year. For 2001 Motorola posted a net loss of about $3.9 billion on revenue of $30 billion. This compared with a profit of $1.3 billion on sales of almost $37.6 billion in 2000. The company attributed its disappointing performance to general economic weakness, as well as sluggish demand from most of the end markets Motorola serves. The company, however, expressed optimism that Motorola would get back into the black in the third quarter of 2002, thanks to its campaign of cost cutting and the expectation of improved profit margins in the mobile phone and semiconductor businesses.

In announcing the company's results for 2001, Edward Breen, president and chief operating officer of Motorola, said: "While the end markets Motorola serves continue to be weak, the company is making good progress in improving its strategic focus and in reducing its cost structure. We are particularly pleased with the improving profitability in the Personal Communications segment. We are also pleased with the Broadband Communications and Commercial, Government, and Industrial Systems segments' ability to maintain a strong level of profitability under current market conditions. We made great progress in strengthening our balance sheet by generating $1.9 billion in positive operating cash flow and reducing net debt by more than one-half, from $7.2 billion to $3.1 billion during 2001. We are confident we are taking the right steps to position the company to return to the level of profitability that it is capable of generating as its end markets recover."

In April 2002, Motorola announced a net loss of $449 million for the first quarter of 2002, the company's fifth consecutive money-losing quarter. Observers attributed the company's disappointing performance to continued weakness in the cell phone and semiconductor businesses. Motorola Chairman Christopher Galvin held out hope for recovery in the second half. "These are challenging and turbulent markets worldwide, and economic and political instability makes predictions uncertain," Galvin said. "Still, we continue to believe that Motorola will return to profitability during the second half of 2002 and be profitable for the full year, excluding special items and barring any unforeseen political or economic disruptions."

ANALYSTS' OPINIONS

Security analysts expressed skepticism in the spring of 2002 about Motorola's predictions of a return to profitability in the second half of the year. On the heels of the company's report of its fifth consecutive quarterly loss in the first quarter of 2002, Todd Bernier, an analyst for Morningstar, said the company's results showed little promise of a turnaround in the near future. "With numbers like this, there's no reason to believe that," he said. "It's just weakness right across the board." Equally skeptical was UBS Warburg analyst Jeffrey Schlesinger, who said, "It's hard to. . .buy into it. You can't put a lot into that until they start to show us the leverage. We haven't seen it yet other than in [mobile phones]."

When a handful of frustrated Motorola shareholders expressed dissatisfaction with Christopher Galvin's leadership of the company at the company's annual meeting in May 2002, analysts were quick to offer their two-cents worth. Galvin, grandson of the company's founder, can't win, according to Edward Snyder, an analyst with J.P. Morgan. "If the company turns around, there will be a neutral stance to him." Needless to say, the calls for Galvin's removal are certain to increase if Motorola's performance continues to lag. Another analyst who declined to be named said that a handful of large institutional investors refuse to buy Motorola stock as long as Galvin is chairman and CEO. "You have quite a few buyside accounts who don't like him at all and a couple which will never buy the stock as long as he's involved," he said.

HISTORY

Motorola's history began in 1928 with the founding by Paul V. Galvin of Galvin Manufacturing Company in Chicago. Galvin's first new product was the "battery eliminator," a device that allowed the owners of early battery-operated radios to operate them directly from household current instead. The demand for this pioneering Galvin product quickly dried up when radio manufacturers phased out their battery-powered products. Casting about for a new product idea, the company began to work on producing a car radio that provide decent

CHRONOLOGY:
Key Dates for Motorola Inc.

1928: Paul Galvin founds Galvin Manufacturing Company in Chicago

1947: Galvin Manufacturing Company changes its name to Motorola

1948: Motorola establishes semiconductor development group

1959: Paul Galvin dies and is succeed as chairman and CEO by his son, Robert

1999: Christopher Galvin, grandson of the founder, becomes chairman and CEO

2000: Motorola merges with General Instrument Corporation

2001: Edward Breen is named president and COO

reception. The company's first commercially successful car radio, introduced in the early 1930s, was marketed under the brand name Motorola. Later in the decade the company branched into the production of home radios and police radios.

Convinced that war was imminent after a 1936 trip to Europe, Galvin directed his company's researchers to look for products that might be useful to the military. This research effort produced the Handie-Talkie two-way radio and its successor, the Walkie-Talkie, which were widely used by the U.S. military during World War II.

In 1947 the company officially changed its name to Motorola. The company also introduced the first Motorola television that year. Largely on the strength of the television's compact size and reasonable price, Motorola soon became the fourth largest U.S. television manufacturer. Still later in 1947, Motorola bought Detrola, a failing car radio company that had produced car radios for Ford Motor Company. One of the conditions Motorola attached to its purchase of Detrola was retention of the contract with Ford. The Detrola acquisition proved a shot in the arm for Motorola's car radio business. The company went on to supply half of all the car radios produced for Ford and Chrysler, as well as all of the car radios for American Motors.

On the heels of the invention of the transistor in 1948, Motorola established a semiconductor development group. The group's first product was a 3-amp power

The Motorola Museum located in Schaumburg, Illinois, has on display the first car radio, the portable "handie-talkie" developed for U.S. troops in WWII, the transponder that relayed Neil Armstrong's first words from the moon, and the first cell phone. (AP Photo/Motorola, Inc., HO)

transistor. Not long thereafter, the company opened a semiconductor plant in Arizona. Soon the company was supplying transistors for use in some of the products manufactured by its competitors. By the mid-1950s Motorola's operations had become so widely diversified that its founder decided it was too large for one man to manage. He created a number of divisions, giving each

its own engineering, purchasing, manufacturing, and marketing departments. When Paul Galvin died in 1959, he was succeed as chairman and CEO by his son, Robert, who had previously served as president.

Robert Galvin took Motorola global in a big way during the 1960s. He also moved the company away from its focus on consumer electronics and redirected it to high-technology markets in commercial, government, and industrial sectors. By the end of the 1980s, the company had become the leading worldwide supplier of cellular telephones, a lead it has since surrendered to Nokia. In 1999 Christopher Galvin, grandson of founder Paul Galvin, who had served as CEO of Motorola since 1997, was named chairman. He retained his responsibilities as CEO. In 2000 Motorola merged with General Instrument Corporation to provide integrated video, voice, and data networking for Internet and high-speed data services. In 2002 Edward D. Breen was elected president and chief operating officer.

STRATEGY

Faced with one of the worst financial showings in its history, Motorola in 2001 implemented a five-point strategy designed to improve the company's performance. The strategy calls for Motorola to (1) revitalize its management team; (2) stabilize its balance sheet and improve financial flexibility; (3) reduce costs and manufacturing capacity; (4) produce innovative products and software applications and improve customer relationships; and (5) evaluate and re-evaluate its strategy as the high-tech environment changes.

In its 2001 annual report, the company reported this progress on the goals set forth in its corporate strategy: "While we are not done, we are delivering on this plan. We implemented a world-class leadership supply system to ensure we have the right managers in the right positions. We also have hired new managers. We reduced our net debt and improved our working capital. We reduced costs throughout the company. We describe our major cost-reduction programs by business segment below, but in summary we closed and consolidated manufacturing facilities to reduce our manufacturing capacity, we exited businesses that did not fit with our strategy, and we significantly reduced the number of employees. Our businesses are introducing new customer-driven products and solutions. Finally, we are continuously evaluating our strategies and adjusting our business to focus on the areas we believe will provide the opportunity for profitable growth and to take advantage of growth in our marketplace."

One high-profile executive change at Motorola that won approval from Wall Street was the appointment on January 1, 2002, of Edward Breen as president and chief operating officer. Breen succeeded Robert L. Growney in the position. Breen, who was CEO at General Instrument when that company merged with Motorola in early 2000, more recently had served as president of Motorola's networks sector. Wall Street observers seemed to feel that Breen was the type of executive who may just be able to get Motorola's floundering business sectors stabilized and growing once again.

INFLUENCES

The biggest challenge facing Motorola in the early years of the new millennium was a pronounced slowdown in several of its key markets, a slowdown that reflected general economic weakness worldwide. So sharp was the decline in demand in several of the company's markets that Motorola in 2001 posted its first operating loss in 71 years. Revenue in 2001, at approximately $30 billion, was down roughly 20 percent from nearly $37.6 billion in 2000. For 2001 as a whole, the company posted a net loss of more than $3.9 billion, compared with a profit of about $1.3 billion the previous year.

Even before 2001 was over, the company had moved aggressively to cut costs. Between August 2000 and the end of 2001, more than 48,000 jobs were eliminated, cutting Motorola's workforce by almost a third from its peak employment of 150,000 in August 2000. Despite the company's rather drastic cost cutting, analysts seemed to feel that more could be done, possibly by selling off its infrastructure unit, the performance of which has been particularly weak. In the spring of 2002 rumors circulated that Motorola was engaged in talks to sell the unit to Nortel Networks of Canada or Siemens of Germany.

CURRENT TRENDS

The wireless communications industry in mid-2002 was in the midst of upheaval as new handset technologies and consumer demands for ever more sophisticated and intuitive products cause profound changes in the way industry participants will do business. Motorola executives felt confident that by leveraging "the most comprehensive cellular knowledge in the industry," the company can stay on top of changing trends and demands in the marketplace and manage to increase its share of the highly competitive mobile phone market.

Some confirmation that their confidence is not misplaced came in May 2002 when a Gartner report indicated that Motorola's mobile phones had increased their share of the market during the first quarter of 2002. While Motorola's market share edged up from 14.7 percent to 15.5 percent during the first quarter, market leader Nokia lost market share, falling from 36.9 percent to 34.7 percent. The Gartner report showed that South Korea's Samsung Electronics had overtaken Germany's Siemens for third place in the cellular phone competition, jumping to

a market share of 9.6 percent from 7.9 percent in the fourth quarter of 2001.

Early reaction to Motorola's new V70 wireless phone has been extremely positive. The V70 is one of the first products to reflect the company's efforts to add style to products created in its engineering-driven culture. The phone, which features a "switchblade" cover and white-on-black display, offers text messaging, always-on Internet access, voice activation, and an optional radio headset.

PRODUCTS

Motorola markets a broad range of communications and electronics products. The company's lineup of products and services includes software-enhanced wireless telephones and messaging, two-way radio products and systems, as well as networking and Internet-access products for consumers and network operators as well as commercial, government, and industrial customers. Motorola also markets end-to-end systems for the delivery of interactive digital video, voice, and high-speed data solutions for broadband operators. Other products include embedded semiconductor solutions for customers in wireless communications, networking, and transportation markets, and integrated electronic systems for the automotive, Telematics, telecommunications, computing, and portable energy systems markets.

CORPORATE CITIZENSHIP

Motorola believes that as a major international corporation, its responsibilities extend beyond its shareholders to its customers, employees, business partners, and the communities in which it operates. The company's Code of Business Conduct is used as the guide for its treatment of all the diverse groups and communities with which it deals.

Motorola reaches out to the local communities in which it has a presence through charitable donations and volunteerism. In the company's *2000 Global Corporate Citizenship Report*, Motorola provided some examples of the many contributions it had made to its communities in 2000. The company and its employees pledged $7.2 million to United Way in 2000. In Arizona, Motorola partnered with local community groups to build and repair homes for those in need. Motorola engineers in India mentored young people to help them complete their studies.

The Motorola Foundation provides funding to a number of education projects. The foundation has partnered with First Inspiration and Recognition of Science and Technology (FIRST) to sponsor FIRST's Robotics Competition, a challenge that teams high school students

dom; Motorola Semiconducteurs S.A. of France; Motorola GmbH of Germany; Motorola Asia Ltd. of Hong Kong; Motorola de Mexico S.A.; Motorola Electronics Pte. Ltd. of Singapore; and Motorola Electronics Taiwan Ltd.

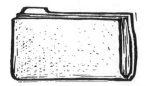

BUSINESS CODE OF CONDUCT GUIDES MOTOROLA

Virtually everything that Motorola and its employees do in business and its dealings with customers, stockholders, and local communities is guided by the company's Business Code of Conduct, the centerpiece of which is two key beliefs. In the introduction to its Business Code of Conduct, Motorola observes: "Times will change. Our products will change. Our people will change. Our customers will change. What will not change is our commitment to our key beliefs." Those two key beliefs are uncompromising integrity and constant respect for people. As outlined in the company's code of conduct, the former means "staying true to what we believe. We adhere to honesty, fairness, and 'doing the right thing' without compromise, even when circumstances make it difficult." For Motorola and its employees, constant respect for people dictates that every individual with which the company interacts be treated with dignity.

with engineers from business and academia. The company also supports Project Hope, an initiative that provides continuing education for children who have dropped out of school in China's rural areas. Motorola and its employees also support Junior Achievement chapters across the United States and in Ireland, Hungary, and Russia.

GLOBAL PRESENCE

Motorola markets its products and services worldwide. The company also maintains an extensive network of sales subsidiaries and manufacturing facilities outside the United States. Motorola's foreign subsidiaries include Motorola Australia Proprietary Ltd.; Motorola (China) Electronics Ltd.; Motorola Telcarro de Puerto Rico Inc.; Motorola S.A. of France; Motorola Electronic GmbH of Germany; Motorola B.V. of the Netherlands; Motorola Communications Israel Ltd.; Motorola SpA of Italy; Nippon Motorola Ltd. of Japan; Motorola Electronics Sdn. Bhd. of Malaysia; Motorola Philippines Inc.; Motorola Espana S.A. of Spain; Motorola A.B. of Sweden; Motorola Canada Ltd.; Motorola Ltd. of the United King-

EMPLOYMENT

As of December 31, 2001, Motorola had a workforce of approximately 111,000 people worldwide. This represented a sharp reduction from the company's peak employment of 150,000 people in August 2000. Once the company detected signs of a slowdown in its key markets, it moved aggressively to reduce costs and, in the process, eliminated more than 48,000 jobs.

SOURCES OF INFORMATION

Bibliography

Carpenter, Dave. "Motorola Posts $449 Million 1Q Loss." *AP Online*, 16 April 2002.

Iwatani, Yukari. "It Ain't Easy Being the Founder's Grandson at Motorola." *Reuters Business Report*, 12 May 2002.

———. "Motorola to Face Tough Questions at Annual Meeting." *Reuters Business Report*, 2 May 2002.

Klayman, Ben. "Motorola Bets on New Phones, Edgy Advertising Campaign." *Toronto Star*, 30 March 2002.

Klayman, Ben, and Yukari Iwatani. "Motorola Sees Return to Profit in Third Quarter." *Reuters*, 23 January 2002.

"Motorola Inc." *Gale Business Resources*, 2002. Available at http://galenet.galegroup.com/servlet/GBR.

"Motorola Inc." *Hoover's Online*, 2002. Available at http://www.hoovers.com.

Motorola Inc. 2000 Global Corporate Citizenship Report. Schaumburg, IL: Motorola Inc., 2001.

Motorola Inc. 2001 Annual Report. Schaumburg, IL: Motorola Inc., 2002.

Motorola Inc. Home Page, 2002. Available at http://www.motorola.com.

"Motorola Plans More Cost-Cutting." *London Free Press*, 24 January 2002.

"Motorola Sees No Net Profit in 2002." *Reuters Business Report*, 4 April 2002.

Roman, Monica. "In Business This Week: And the Winner at Motorola is—Breen." *Business Week*, 15 October 2001.

For an annual report:

on the Internet at: http://www.motorola.com **or** write: Motorola, Inc., Investor Relations, 1303 E. Algonquin Rd., Schaumburg, IL 60196

For additional industry research:

Investigate companies by their Standard Industrial Classification Codes, also known as SICs. Motorola Inc.'s primary SICs are:

3812 Search and Navigation Equipment

3571 Electronic Computers

3575 Computer Terminals

3612 Transformers Except Electronic

3661 Telephone and Telegraph Apparatus

3663 Radio and TV Communications Equipment

3674 Semiconductors and Related Devices

4812 Radiotelephone Communications

5065 Electronic Parts and Equipment, NEC

7373 Computer Integrated Systems Design

Also investigate companies by their North American Industry Classification System codes, also known as NAICS codes. Motorola Inc.'s primary NAICS codes are:

334210 Telephone Apparatus Manufacturing

334220 Broadcasting and Wireless Communications Equipment Manufacturing

334413 Semiconductor and Related Device Manufacturing

341110 Electronic Computer Manufacturing

MTV Networks, Inc.

FOUNDED: 1984

Contact Information:

HEADQUARTERS: 1515 Broadway
   New York, NY 10036
PHONE: (212)258-8000
URL: http://www.mtv.com

OVERVIEW

MTV Networks, Inc. (MTVN) includes MTV: Music Television in the United States, Europe, and Latin America; Nickelodeon in the United States, Europe, Asia, and Latin America; Nick at Nite in the United States; VH1 in the United States, United Kingdom, and Germany; MTV2: Music Television in the United States and Europe; and TV Land in the United States. MTV targets viewers from the ages of 12 to 34 with programming that includes music videos, comedy, animated programs, news specials, interviews, documentaries, and other youth-oriented programming. MTV2: Music Television, a 24-hour, seven-days-a-week spinoff of MTV, targets a segment of the 12 to 34-year-old audience with music videos that cover a variety of musical genres. MTVN also includes "The Suite from MTV Networks," a package of digital television program services, which currently consists of six music program services.

Individual network survival often depends on staying current with trends. Nickelodeon, for instance, has been successful with innovative programming for children of all ages. In 1998 MTV decided to overhaul its programming. Management's concern was that the company had become too corporate, interested more in profit than its original design of music programming; that it was alienating the target audience with increasing levels of non-music programming, which had originally been designed to raise ratings. Due to this evaluation, MTV decided to cut back on its non-music programming and scheduled a return to more music and music/news.

COMPANY FINANCES

MTV's profits steadily increased throughout the 1990s at a rate of approximately 25 percent per year. Its cash flow margin was 40 percent in 1995 and 41 percent in both 1996 and 1997, which is considered a high percentage in the industry. While about one third of MTV's revenue comes from cable subscription fees, advertisers will pay high rates to get the 12- to 34-year-old audience despite low Nielsen ratings. The rates for advertising on MTV have grown an average of 10 percent per year.

In 2000, MTVN reported sales of $3.895 million, reflecting growth of 73.1 percent. In 2001, MTVN had revenues of $2.25 billion and operating income of $816.9 million, reflecting respective increases of 21 and 24 percent. The increase in revenues was due to higher worldwide advertising revenues, higher affiliate fees, and the success of MTVN's consumer products licensing programs. The previous year, MTVN had revenues of $1.9 billion and operating income of $660.1 million.

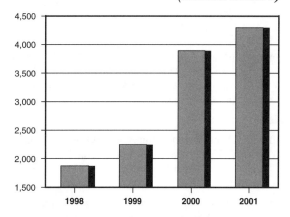

FINANCES:

*MTV Networks Inc.
Revenues, 1998-2001
(million dollars)*

ANALYSTS' OPINIONS

Observers have noted a huge irony about MTV: It is a network for 20-year-olds run by people in their 40s and 50s. Proponents of educational or moral improvement have blamed MTV for the intellectual or spiritual "dumbing down" of America. A criticism leveled at MTV since its inception, it reached a crescendo in 2001, thanks to MTV's bizarre show "Jackass," which involved a group of guys who enjoyed videotaping each other as they performed ridiculous and often quite dangerous stunts. That year, a teenager was badly burned when he tried to imitate a stunt he saw on the show. He had his friends pour gasoline on him and then set him on fire. During the ensuing outcry, Senator Joseph Leiberman, Al Gore's vice presidential candidate the previous year, asked Viacom to implement some programming changes. By 2002, "Jackass" was off the air.

HISTORY

MTV was the creation of a small group of people who sought to take advantage of the new industry in rock videos. It began with a $15-million investment from Warner Amex Satellite Entertainment. The debut video of the network in August of 1981 was *Video Killed the Radio Star*, by the Buggles.

In 1984, the year MTV held its first Video Music Awards, MTV and children's network Nickelodeon, established in 1979, were brought together as MTV Networks. On the first day of 1985, with the establishment of VH1, a 24-hour video network appealing to an older audience, MTV Networks had an audience that ranged

in age from preschool to the late 40s. Meanwhile, Warner put MTV Networks up for sale in order to raise cash. In September 1985, it was purchased by entertainment conglomerate Viacom International. The next year, Viacom itself was bought by National Amusements, Inc., largely owned by multi-millionaire investor Sumner Redstone.

Under its new ownership, Nickelodeon went from last place among basic cable channels to first place. The network adopted some of the same graphic-intensive qualities of MTV, which proved to be successful. The flagship network, however, entered a slump in the late 1980s, as the novelty of the video craze wore off. The network moved away from videos and toward game shows to stem this decline. It began with the launch of *Remote Control* in December 1987. News and other types of programming, such as the acoustic concert series called *MTV Unplugged*, were introduced in 1990.

During the 1990s, MTV became heavily involved with politics, starting with the "Rock the Vote" campaign, and continuing with the "Choose or Lose" election coverage in 1992. Also in 1992, MTV premiered the popular show *The Real World*. In 1993, *Beavis and Butt-Head* was introduced. MTV established a strong presence in cyberspace with the launch of MTV Online, in cooperation with America Online, in 1994. In 1996, MTV created a sister channel, MTV2: Music Television.

Also in 1996, MTV Productions in association with Paramount Pictures released the feature film *Beavis and Butt-Head Do America*. Following that initial success, MTV and Paramount Pictures have produced a successful string of films aimed at the MTV demographic that includes *Varsity Blues* and *The Wood*.

FAST FACTS:

About MTV Networks, Inc.

Ownership: MTV Networks, Inc. is a wholly owned subsidiary of Viacom International, Inc., a publicly owned company whose stock is traded on the American Stock Exchange.

Ticker Symbol: VIA

Officers: Tom Freston, Chmn. and CEO; Judy McGrath, Pres. MTV, Chmn. MTV Interactive; Mark Rosenthal, COO; Richard J. Bressler, CFO Viacom/MTV Networks

Principal Subsidiary Companies: The major subsidiaries of MTV Networks are MTV Music Television, VH1, Nickelodeon, and MTV Films (in association with Paramount Pictures).

Chief Competitors MTV Networks compete with television and cable stations broadcasting music and children's shows. Major competitors include ABC, CBS, NBC, Fox, and The Family Channel.

In July 1999, MTV formed its Original Movies for Television Division and its first film, *2gether*, which first aired in February, 2000, garnered high ratings. Also in 1999, MTV introduced a line of home videos, consumer products and books, all featuring MTV programming and personalities.

STRATEGY

MTV's strategic focus has been its awareness of its core audience's preferences and tastes. MTV and its networks spin off products in order to hold the attention of their focus age group. Movies, new networks, and merchandise keep the brand name in front of consumers. As far as MTV itself, videos are not the product; MTV is the product. By the late 1990s, MTV was working to define itself and to keep viewers. With 50 to 100 cable channels available to the average household, competition was fierce. Videos, too, were available to any network. MTV had to be unique to hold on to a respectable market share.

MTV goes beyond the usual focus groups to stay on the cutting edge. The network sends researchers into the field to go through the closets, rooms, and CD collections of young adults, looking at anything that could pro-

vide a clue to their tastes. The age range chosen was 18 to 24 because younger teens want to be seen as older and older adults want to be seen as younger.

The Networks' Nickelodeon channel opened an animation studio in California in early 1998, the first in Los Angeles in 35 years. This was expected to allow Nickelodeon more flexibility in programming. The network also started a comic strip based on the *Rugrats* show in 1998, continuing the strategy of spinning off brands.

Overall, MTV Networks, Inc. commands an impressive spectrum of age groups. Rounding out MTV's demographic on each side are Nickelodeon, which was originally geared toward the under-16 age group, and VH1, which appeals to viewers 18 to 49 years old. Nick at Nite and Nick at Nite's TV Land, with their nostalgic offerings of television shows from the 1950s into the 1980s, further solidified MTV Networks' hold on the older age group.

As would be expected, a "cutting edge" organization such as MTVN rode on the wave of the information and communication technologies revolution in the late 1990s. In 1998, the company launched "The Suite from MTV Networks," a package of digital television program services offered for distribution by digital technologies. The following year, it formed the MTVi Group, L.P., an Internet music network.

INFLUENCES

MTV's popularity created a contradiction. In its early days, part of the appeal to a young audience was the underground nature of the network. This sensation was heightened by the obvious fact that it did not have much money. Soon, MTV was realizing tremendous profits - and found itself in an ironic situation. It promoted rebellion and anti-materialism, yet it was an extremely profitable corporate entity. This irony was heightened in 1985 when it became the property of the conglomerate Viacom.

Soon the complaints rolled in. An "MTV Hater's Web site" even surfaced on the Internet. The general opinion was that there was too much non-music programming. The shows that had been hits were running their course and nothing substantial was replacing them. The public decided the network was not in touch with the trends.

A document, referred to as the "Melissa Memo," served to change MTV's direction. Written by two interns named Melissa, the memo made its way to Judy McGrath, MTV's president. It said in effect that MTV had become too dark, too lame, not happy, clean and bright. They wanted their MTV back. McGrath immediately acted on the critique, which happened to coincide with her latest research.

MTV underwent a makeover. It got rid of the shows considered dull and replaced the VJs with people who knew music. A new animation series, *Daria*, debuted to enthusiastic responses. A new studio in Times Square was built, with music hours shown live for the first time. Interviews with and programs about musicians, along with more focus on news, brought back the networks' popularity.

CURRENT TRENDS

In the 1990s, three of the leading trends at MTV were politics, the Internet, and the tension between musical and non-musical programming. The focus on politics began with the 1990 "Rock the Vote" advertising campaign, which featured performers such as Madonna urging young viewers to go out and vote for the candidate of their choice in the national elections held that year. In 1992 and 1996, MTV stepped up its involvement in the presidential elections with its "Choose or Lose" campaign. Then Governor Bill Clinton gained huge points with the youth vote by telling MTV viewers that he had tried marijuana but "didn't inhale." Even such conservative politicians as Senator Bob Dole and House Speaker Newt Gingrich appeared on MTV. According to a *Rolling Stone* article, however, it appeared that neither "Rock the Vote" or "Choose or Lose" had any noticeable impact on getting out the youth vote.

In addition to its political involvement, MTV became heavily involved with the Internet. In addition to its own Web site, in 1994, the network joined with America Online in establishing MTV Online, which offered users an opportunity to have an online MTV chat and to gain a direct link to "The MTV Beach House."

Non-musical programming such as The MTV Beach House raised charges from critics that MTV was no longer a music network. In August 1996, exactly 15 years to the minute after the launch of MTV, the network introduced MTV2: Music Television, a "free-form" 24-hour music station with a broad play list of artists and a heavy concentration on music.

By the late 1990s and early 2000s, MTVN became heavily oriented toward technology to strengthen its appeal to an emerging audience of young people, who as Brian Graden, President of MTV Programming, put it, "have had a remote control the entire time they've been alive." Accordingly, MTVN developed programming that was of a more participatory nature, featuring programs like "Total Request Live," where viewers could choose videos as well as see themselves on screen, and "Fanatic," where the viewer could interview a celebrity.

PRODUCTS

MTV and VH1 began developing networks to suit the tastes of different people and keep up with competi-

CHRONOLOGY:
Key Dates For MTV Networks, Inc.

1981: MTV is born

1984: MTV holds its first Video Music Awards; MTV launches VH1, a music channel aimed at older listeners

1985: Viacom International buys MTV

1987: To keep up with its audience's changing tastes, MTV shifts its programming away from music videos

1992: MTV goes political and covers the 1992 presidential campaign; MTV introduces the raunchy cartoon "Beavis and Butt-Head"; MTV enters cyberspace with MTV Online

1996: MTV Productions in association with Paramount Pictures releases the feature film "Beavis and Butt-Head Do America"

1999: MTV's Original Movies for Television Division airs its first film

tors. The company created several new products, including: MTV Ritmo, Latino music; MTV Indie, college and independent label music; MTV Rocks, hard rock and heavy metal; VH1 Soul; VH1 Country; and VH1 Smooth, featuring jazz. In 1997, MTV introduced *MTV News Unfiltered*, which allows for audience participation. In 1998, MTV had 20 pilots in development for original programming, including "Ultra Sound" and "True Life," both documentary series.

Nickelodeon planned to extend its prime time programming in 1998. Since the network began primetime programming for children in September of 1996, over 2.5 million children were tuning in each night, more than any competitor attracted. Nickelodeon acquired the rights to the *Peanuts* series in 1998, and launched new cartoon *OhYeah! Cartoons!* featuring new characters each week. The network also opened three Nickelodeon stores in 1997, selling clothes, games, videos, and other merchandise stamped with Nickelodeon characters.

In 2001, MTV's regular series included "Total Request Live," "The Real World," "Road Rules," and the ever-popular "Celebrity Deathmatch," which showcases Claymation likenesses of celebrities ripping each other apart in WWF-inspired wrestling matches.

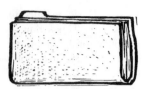

IN THE LAND OF OZ

Years from now, when pop culture observers inevitably write their high-minded histories about mass entertainments, they'll no doubt refer to the first years of the twenty-first century as the era of reality TV programming.

Reality TV is a concept MTV helped advance with "The Real World," a sort of docu-soap opera that served as a model for the CBS game show "Big Brother," which, like the mega-popular "Survivor" (another CBS hit), added its own elements to the prototype.

As the CBS programs demonstrated, the reality concept easily attached itself to other genres. But leave it to MTV to come up with the most compelling and most watched hybrid: a "reality sitcom" called "The Osbournes"—a "day in the life" account of heavy metal rocker Ozzy Osbourne and his eccentric family.

Actually, the true antecedent for "The Osbournes" is not really "The Real World"; rather, the adventures of Ozzy and Sharon and the foul-mouthed little Osbournes harken back to a 1970 PBS show called "An American Family," a weekly cinema verite that, among other things, revealed the real-life dissolution of a marriage and allowed one son a very public platform on which to stage his coming out of the closet.

The appeal of "An American Family" certainly resided in the viewing audiences' innate voyeuristic impulses. The same is true of "The Osbournes." However, there is a much stronger sense of sideshow voyeurism attached to the MTV show. What compels viewers who watch "The Osbournes" is the same kind of curiosity that attracted crowds to carnival freak shows, and that is what is largely responsible for its phenomenal popularity (the show is watched by those well outside of the traditional MTV demographic). A viewer may sometimes wonder what kind of test tube spawned the children, and Osbourne, who once gained a great deal of notoriety when he bit the head off of a live bird, is very much a modern version of the old-time carnival "geeks," desperate people in the last stages of chronic alcoholism who were exhibited in traveling carnivals as wildmen. Among other gross acts, "geeks" would chew the heads off of live chickens. As compensation for their degradation, "geeks" were given a warm place to sleep and a daily bottle of liquor.

Of course, Osbourne, 53 years old in 2002, is far from destitute (he lives in Beverly Hills), and he is a reformed alcoholic. But "The Osbournes" often depicts him wandering around his mansion in a somewhat addled and oblivious state, trying to make sense of all of the craziness surrounding him. Watching him, one can't help think of the dissipating lifestyle embraced by many heavy metal rockers. And therein lies its humor.

What also makes the show so funny is that Osbourne represents a hilarious anachronism. He is as out of place in Beverly Hills as Jethro Bodine. Also, at times, he can be a walking set of contradictions. He'll admonish his children for their sometimes bad behavior as well as their outlandish sense of style, despite his own bad boy past and his former rock star flamboyance. Osbourne, as music fans will recall, was lead singer of Black Sabbath, one of the most notorious heavy metal bands in the most lunkheaded of musical genres. Osbourne later claimed that at one point during the band's career, he was in an "altered" state of mind every day. When Osbourne went solo, his reputation became even more notorious and, just like the geeks of old, he was legally forbidden to perform in various communities. (Staid old Boston and conservative San Antonio wanted nothing to do with his brand of entertainment).

Despite his inclinations and antics, his marriage has proven stable and lasting. He married Sharon Arden in 1982. Their children, Kelly and Jack, are 17 and 16 years old, respectively. Reportedly, the idea for the show was Sharon's.

As it turned out, "The Osbournes" became MTV's highest rated program ever. On March 26, 2002, in its regular Tuesday night-time slot, the show attracted 4.1 million viewers. Success was so great that MTV started airing the show as many as 15 times a week. The advantage this provided MTV is obvious: the network can use "The Osbournes" as a way to promote the rest of its schedule.

One of the most interesting consequences of the show's success is that for members of the viewing audience who are over 40—those who sneered down their noses at "Sweet Leaf" and laughed out loud with derisive pleasure at the lyrics of "Iron Man"—it is actually cool to like Ozzy.

The MTV Interactive network, MTVi, offers music via MTV.com, VH1.com and SonicNet brands, as well as 13 international sites for music lovers in regions such as Latin America, the United Kingdom and Japan. MTV.com is targeted at the12 to 24 age group, while VH1.com targets an audience 25 years or older.

CORPORATE CITIZENSHIP

MTV devotes millions of dollars of air time each year to programming that serves the community by highlighting issues such as teenage violence, AIDS, drugs, education, and the environment. VH1's "Save the Music" campaign aims to restore music programs to public schools. Since its inception in 1997, the program has restored music classes to 91 schools, affecting 27,000 children.

GLOBAL PRESENCE

Into the late 1990s, the MTV Networks reached viewers all over the world. MTV alone was viewed by 68 million households in America. By the new century, it was reaching more than 340 million households in 140 countries through 31 TV channels and 17 Web sites. Affiliates include MTV Australia; MTV Brazil; MTV Europe, an English-language network that reaches viewers in 38 countries; MTV India; MTV Japan; the Spanish-language MTV Latin America, based in Miami; MTV Mandarin; and MTV in the United Kingdom, launched in 1997. Nickelodeon's networks reach the Australian, British, German, and Latin American markets. VH1 has German and British affiliates.

In 2000, MTVN Europe introduced MTVF, a programming service targeted at French-speaking viewers in France, Switzerland, and Belgium. That same year, MTV Polska was launched, offering 24-hour, Polish-language music programming. Also in 2000, MTV España was introduced to 1.5 million homes in Spain, the Balearics, and the Canary Islands. In 2001, MTV launched a new 24-hour, Korean-language music channel for Korean audiences.

EMPLOYMENT

The corporate culture at MTV Networks is non-existent in the expected sense. Employees are generally young and dress casually. Bosses are friendly co-workers, not critical overseers. Those at the top of MTV's management believe that work should be fun and everyone's ideas should be encouraged and examined by all.

Brian Graden, President of MTV Programming, once remarked that anyone signing up to work at MTV as an executive had to care deeply about "what it's like to be 21 years old and to see the world from their point of view and to celebrate the art that they celebrate."

SOURCES OF INFORMATION

Bibliography

Boehlert, Eric. "Rock the Vote." *Rolling Stone*, 23 January 1997.

Gunther, Marc. "This Gang Controls Your Kid's Brains." *Fortune*, 27 October 1997.

James, Caryn. "'Party Pitch' and 'Politically Incorrect' Put Their Spin on Convention." *The New York Times*, 15 August 1996.

Lewis, Michael. "The Herd of Independent Minds." *The New Republic*, 3 June 1996.

Murphy, Mary. "Defying Convention." *TV Guide*, 31 August 1996.

Seabrook, John. "Rocking In Shangri-La." *The New Yorker*, 10 October 1994.

"Star Woes." *Economist*, 11 April 1998.

Stein, Joel. "The M is Back in MTV." *Time*, 1 December 1997.

Wild, David. "Television: Techno, Anyone?" *Rolling Stone*, 6 February 1997.

Macavinta, Courtney. "Viacom's MTV Makes Major Net Music Drive." *Tech News-CNET.com*, 14 November 1999. Available at: http://news.com.com.

"Teen Burned Imitating MTV Stunt." *Your1voice.com*, 29 January 2001. Available at: http://www.your1voice.com/CtTeen.htm.

"Viacom's MTV Networks and Cablevision Sign Long-Term Affiliation Agreement." *Yahoo! Finance*, 29 January 2001. Available at: http://biz.yahoo.com.

"The Merchants of Cool." PBS Interview of Brian Graden on *Frontline*, 12 October 2001. Available at: http://www.pbs.org.

For an annual report:

on the Internet at: http://www.mtv.com or write Investor Relations, Viacom, 1515 Broadway, New York, NY 10036

For additional industry research:

Investigate companies by their Standard Industrial Classification Codes, also known as SIC codes. MTV's primary SIC is:

4841 Cable and Other Pay Television Stations

Also investigate companies by their North American Industry Classification Codes, also known as NAICS codes. MTV Networks, Inc.'s primary NAICS code is:

513220 Cable and Other Program Distribution

National Railroad Passenger Corporation

VARIANT NAME: Amtrak

Contact Information:

HEADQUARTERS: 60 Massachusetts Avenue N.E.
  Washington, DC 20002
PHONE: (202)906-3000
FAX: (202)906-3306
TOLL FREE: (800)872-7245
URL: http://www.amtrak.com

OVERVIEW

Amtrak provides inter-city rail service for the United States. It operates approximately 600 facilities in 46 states utilizing a rail network encompassing 22,000 miles, most of which is owned and operated by freight railroads. Amtrak pays a fee to the freight railroads in exchange for use of their networks. Amtrak's most important service areas are the Northeast Corridor, which extends from Massachusetts to Virginia, and Amtrak West, which operates primarily in California, Oregon, and Washington. Amtrak operates about 265 passenger trains every day and serves more than 20 million passengers each year. In addition to its regular passenger service, Amtrak acts as a contractor for various commuter rail lines, performing rail and train maintenance, and in some cases operating the service. Although it was originally founded to provide passenger rail service, freight and mail delivery have become important to Amtrak's selection of services.

Amtrak is a private corporation, owned by the U.S. government through the Department of Transportation. The President of the United States appoints the Amtrak board of directors. They appoint the president of the company. The company is organized into four strategic business units (SBUs) set up along primarily geographical lines. The Northeast Corridor SBU manages Amtrak's eastern seaboard service that serves Boston, New York City, Philadelphia, Baltimore, and Washington DC. The Amtrak West SBU runs Amtrak's West Coast service, which includes daily schedules in southern California and the Pacific Northwest. Amtrak's Intercity SBU operates the vast rail network in the center of the nation, including traffic into and out of Amtrak's Mid-Western hub in

Chicago and its long-distance service between the coasts and the Gulf of Mexico. The fourth SBU, Mail and Express, operates Amtrak's freight and mail transport business.

COMPANY FINANCES

Amtrak reported revenues of $2.1 billion for 2001. Amtrak had 23.5 million passengers in 2001 and ticket sales accounted for more than one-half of the firm's total revenues. In 2000 Amtrak's revenues totaled $2.11 billion. That year the Northeast Corridor SBU alone was responsible for more than 50 percent of Amtrak's revenues. Broken down by activity, passenger traffic accounted for approximately $1.28 billion of Amtrak's 2000 revenues, more than 60 percent of the total. The greatest growth in the passenger sector took place in Amtrak's Northeast Corridor service. Commuter service brought in about $274 million. Mail and freight shipping accounted for $122 million in 2000 revenues, an increase of 24.8 percent over 1999. Other activities, mainly the provision of maintenance and operational services to other railroads, real estate operations, and rail access fees, brought in about $326 million in 2000.

Amtrak had operating expenses totaling $2.88 billion in 2000, up 8 percent from $2.66 billion in 1999. In its 30-year history, Amtrak has never had a year in which it turned a profit. In 2000 only a single service route, the high-speed-rail Metroliner between New York City and Washington DC generated a profit. Amtrak recorded a net loss of $768 million in 2000, up from 1999's loss of $702.2 million. In 2000 about $112 million of Amtrak's revenues came from the federal and state governments. The federal subsidy was the lowest in the company's history. Amtrak has publicly stated its belief that some level of financial support from the U.S. government will always be necessary. However, a law passed in 1997 requires Amtrak to operate without benefit of aid by the beginning of 2003. If it cannot achieve this goal, the company can be reorganized or liquidated.

ANALYSTS' OPINIONS

The General Accounting Office's (GAO) outlook for Amtrak is bleak. Like the rail service itself, the GAO is convinced that the company will not be able to support its operations without ongoing financial support from the federal government. A GAO report in mid-2001 pointed out that between 1996 and 2001, Amtrak was able to move $83 million closer to self-sufficiency. However, the firm would have to make up another $281 million in order to be completely self-sufficient by the end of 2002, as mandated by federal law. "The outlook for it achieving operational self-sufficiency," the GAO report commented dryly, "is dim." The GAO went so far as to

FINANCES:

Amtrak Total Revenues, 1996-2000 (million dollars)

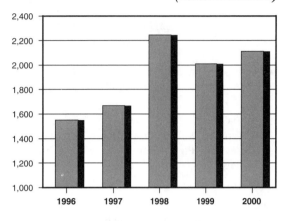

question the very basis of Amtrak's existence, maintaining that the benefits sometimes attributed to a passenger rail system might be illusory. Passenger trains play only a minor part in the U.S. transportation system; *Newsweek* once estimated that Amtrak carries less than one percent of intercity travelers in the United States. "If that role were greater", the GAO writes, "Amtrak would have to make its prices, schedules, and travel times competitive with airlines, buses, and other transportation modes. That would entail putting more trains and faster trains into service, a large investment Congress might be unwilling to make without an honest, comprehensive study of the future of passenger trains in the United States."

HISTORY

Amtrak was founded by Congress as a response to the collapse of the U.S. passenger rail industry after World War II. By 1970 train riding had fallen to about one-half of its 1940 level. Railroads were losing millions of dollars annually and wanted out of the business; however, in order to operate their profitable freight services, they were required by law to offer passenger service as well. President Richard Nixon suggested the formation of a semi-public corporation that would take over all passenger rail service in the United States. Proponents of the plan claimed that if the company reorganized, about 80 percent of the existing U.S. system could operate profitably. In October 1970 Congress passed the Rail Passenger Service Act which established the National Railroad Passenger Corporation. Amtrak was officially launched in April 1971.

FAST FACTS:

About National Railroad Passenger Corporation

Ownership: National Railroad Passenger Corporation is a private company almost wholly-owned by the U.S. government.

Officers: George D. Warrington, Pres. and CEO; Edward V. Walker, Pres. Amtrak Inter-city; E.S. Bagley, Jr., Pres. Northeast Corridor; Gilbert O. Mallery, Pres. Amtrak West

Employees: 24,000

Chief Competitors: Some primary competitors include Greyhound, Delta Airlines, and AMR.

CHRONOLOGY:

Key Dates for The Amtrak Corporation

1970: Congress passed the Rail Passenger Service Act establishing the National Railroad Passenger Corporation

1971: First Amtrak trains run

1979: Amtrak asks to be restructured as a public service rather than a profit-making company

1985: David Stockman calls for Amtrak's dissolution

1986: Special interest alliance persuades Congress to renew Amtrak's subsidy

1997: Congress passes Amtrak Reform and Accountability Act

2002: Congress urges Bush administration to formulate a plan for Amtrak's future

Plans for streamlining the U.S. passenger service were challenged almost immediately. Various members of Congress demanded priority for their respective states when rail services were being restored. Some states contributed funds of their own to guarantee that service would continue. The first Amtrak trains ran on May 1, 1971. The first year was difficult. Under-funded, under-staffed, and unable to compete with airlines, the railroad flirted with bankruptcy. In 1975 Amtrak estimated that it would lose $75 million a year even if it sold every seat on every train. Only the geographically compact Northeast Corridor, where trains offered a viable alternative to the airlines, was relatively successful. This sector represented only two percent of the entire rail system. In 1975 a plan to bring European or Japanese-style high-speed trains to the Corridor routes was developed; the first high-speed trains went into service in December 2000.

In 1979 Amtrak's president proposed, unsuccessfully, that Congress undertake a radical reexamination of Amtrak's mission and allow it to be run as a public service rather than as a money-making venture. Recommendations from the Secretary of Transportation and the Office for Management and Budget urged the government to cut Amtrak's subsidies. The corporation continued to operate after President Ronald Reagan assumed office. In 1985 the Director of Management and Budget, David Stockman, called for its complete dissolution. An alliance of Congressmen, railroad workers and train buffs took action and persuaded Congress to renew Amtrak's subsidy in 1986. The mid-1990s saw a jump in Amtrak riders, from 149 million to 441 million. Nonetheless,

financial shortfalls continued to threaten the service with discontinuation.

Despite a general organizational restructuring, Amtrak's losses grew in the latter half of the 1990s. The Amtrak Reform and Accountability Act of 1997 altered the mission of the service substantially. The Act repealed the requirement that Amtrak operate a "basic route system" which enabled the company to unilaterally shut down unprofitable lines. The law also permitted the company to use contractors for certain work and established the Amtrak Reform Council to evaluate Amtrak's performance.

Still plagued by losses, Amtrak's future was very much in question in early 2002. Still bound by the requirements of the 1997 Reform and Accountability Act, the company needs to operate independently by January 2003. If this does not happen, the Reform Council could recommend closing down the service. In 2002, Congress urged President George W. Bush to formulate a plan for the railroad's future. Various Congressmen proposed plans including options for higher subsidies, privatization, and dissolution of the service.

STRATEGY

Amtrak's Network Growth Strategy, inaugurated in 2000, was a plan to expand and diversify the firm's rail services. A new business unit created Mail and Express to oversee Amtrak's growing freight and mail transport business. The company also entered into an agreement with ExpressTrak LLC that provided Amtrak with 350 refrigerated railcars over a 15-year period. In 2000 Amtrak expanded its Northeast Corridor service with the addition of the United States' first high-speed train, the Acela Express, running between Boston and Washington DC. In 2002 Amtrak proposed a series of strategic cutbacks as a way out of its finance crisis. If put in place, the cutbacks would abolish virtually all of Amtrak's long-distance routes.

INFLUENCES

The terrorist attacks on September 11, 2001, caused Amtrak's number of riders to increase temporarily. It declined after the government approved an aid package for the airlines. The firm's 30-year financial crisis will come to a head in 2002 as it nears the self-sufficiency deadline, mandated by Congress in 1997. Various plans have been proposed as alternatives if the company does not achieve financial independence by the deadline. Amtrak mortgaged part of Penn Station in New York City for $300 million and threatened to end long-distance rail service in the United States in response to the seriousness of its financial situation.

CURRENT TRENDS

A large part of Amtrak's plan for the future is the introduction of high-speed rail service, similar to services offered in Europe and Japan. High-speed rail, which means that trains travel at up to 150 miles per hour on special tracks, is a key element in Amtrak's plan to make rail service competitive with airline travel. Amtrak began testing high-speed rail service in 2000 and by early 2002 had 20 trains in service between Boston and Washington DC. Amtrak hopes to eventually introduce high-speed service on the West Coast and in other important intercity lines in the country.

PRODUCTS

In addition to its passenger, mail, and freight services, Amtrak offers its 30 years of equipment expertise to railroads and other rail-related bodies. Its services include equipment design and engineering, locomotive and passenger car repairs and overhauls, specialized train components, and wreck repair. Its customers include three railroads, six commuter rail authorities, a state department of transportation, and two private rail companies.

GETTING STATES INVOLVED

Individual states have proven to be valuable partners to Amtrak. Rather than lose local rail service altogether, some states stepped in with money of their own to supplement Amtrak's declining federal subsidies. Washington State, for example, owns its own trains and pays Amtrak to operate inner-state lines. Similarly, North Carolina owns an entire railroad and hires Amtrak to run the trains and maintain the stations. Other states, like Texas, provided financing so that Amtrak would not discontinue its existing service.

GLOBAL PRESENCE

Amtrak offers daily rail service from Chicago and Detroit, through Southeastern Ontario to Toronto, Canada. Amtrak also partners with the Canadian National Railroad for mail delivery.

EMPLOYMENT

About 90 percent of Amtrak employees are unionized, and more than half of Amtrak's annual budget is for salaries, wages, pensions, and other benefits. Amtrak offers its onboard employees comprehensive training in guest services.

SOURCES OF INFORMATION

Bibliograhpy

Amtrak Home Page, 2002. Available at http://www.amtrak.com.

Arnold, Lawrence. "Proposed Long-distance Cuts Would Spell End to National Rail System." *Associated Press Business News*, 5 February 2002.

Clinger, Robert. "Amtrak Reformists Should Learn from UK." *Financial Times*, 8 March 2002.

"Coming Soon: The Death of Passenger Trains?"*U.S. News & World Report*, 29 April 1985.

Hecker, JayEtta Z. "Intercity Passenger Rail: The Congress Faces Critical Decisions About the Role of and Funding for Intercity Passenger Rail Systems." Washington DC: General Accounting Office, 2001.

Hightower, Brendan. "Break-up and Partial Sell-off Put Forward as Way to Rescue U.S. Railways." *Financial Times*, 14 February 2002.

"Intercity Passenger Rail." Washington, DC: General Accounting Office, 1998.

"McCain Proposes Abolishing Amtrak, Turning Rail over to Private Sector." *Associated Press*, 15 February 2002.

Moore, Stephen. "Scamtrak." *The Weekly Standard*, 24 December 2001.

Noah, Timothy. "How Amtrak Can Save Itself?" *Slate Magazine*, 25 November 2001.

Perlman, Ellen. "Rail's Resurgence." *Governing Magazine*, September 1999.

Samuelson, Robert J. "The Parable Of Amtrak." *Newsweek*, 3 November 1997.

———. "Why Amtrak Must Go." *Newsweek*, 7 March 1988.

Sanchez, Humberto. "Senate Committee Leaders Push Bush Administration for Rail Plan." *Bond Buyer*, 15 March 2002.

Shaw, Russell. "Amtrak Offers Budget Cuts to Avoid the End of the Line." *Insight on the News*, 23 January 1995.

Sobel, Robert. *The Fallen Colossus*, New York, 1977.

Vranich, Joseph. *Derailed*. New York, 1998.

———. "Q: Should Congress Phase Out the Amtrak System Within the Next Two Years?; Yes: Halt Amtrak's Money-losing System and Let Private Operators Handle the Rails." *Insight on the News*, 24 November 1997.

For an annual report:

on the Internet at: http://www.amtrak.com/about/reports.html **or** write: Amtrak, 60 Massachusetts Avenue N.E., Washington, DC 20002

For additional industry research:

Investigate companies by their Standard Industrial Classification Codes, also known as SICs. National Railroad Passenger Corporation's primary SIC is:

3743 Railroad Equipment

Also investigate companies by their North American Industry Classification System codes. National Railroad Passenger Corporation's primary NAICS code is:

482111 Line-Haul Railroads

Newport News Shipbuilding, Inc.

OVERVIEW

Newport News Shipbuilding for more than a century has designed, built, and repaired a wide variety of vessels for the U.S. Navy as well as commercial customers. A subsidiary of Northrop Grumman Corporation since late 2001, the company is the only shipyard in the United States that designs, builds, and refuels nuclear-powered aircraft carriers. Another important area of its business is the design and construction of nuclear-powered submarines. Although the bulk of its business is for the military, the shipyard provides after-market services, including overhauls and repairs, for commercial vessels as well.

Headquartered in the Virginia city for which it is named, the shipyard's main production facility sprawls across more than 550 acres that stretch along two miles of waterfront in the Hampton Roads port area. Although its specialty vessels are nuclear-powered aircraft carriers and submarines, the shipyard has the capability to design, build, and maintain every type of ship in the fleet of the U.S. Navy.

Northrop Grumman's acquisition of Newport News Shipbuilding in November 2001 climaxed a bitter battle between two of the country's biggest defense contractors. Although Newport News stockholders were initially partial to the advances of another "suitor," General Dynamics Corporation, government opposition to the combination and a Justice Department suit to block the acquisition eventually prompted Newport News to drop its plan. The bid from Northrop Grumman was at first regarded as hostile, although shortly after abandoning its plans to combine with General Dynamics, Newport News began serious discussions with officials of Northrop

FOUNDED: 1886

Contact Information:

HEADQUARTERS: 4101 Washington Ave.
   Newport News, VA 23606
PHONE: (757)380-2000
FAX: (757)380-4713
TOLL FREE: (800)753-8790
URL: http://www.nns.com

FAST FACTS:

About Newport News Shipbuilding, Inc.

Ownership: Newport News Shipbuilding is a wholly-owned subsidiary of Northrop Grumman Corporation.

Ticker Symbol: NNS

Officers: Thomas C. Shievelbein, Pres., 2001 base salary $435,000

Employees: 17,000

Principal Subsidiary Companies: As a subsidiary of Northrop Grumman Corporation, Newport News Shipbuilding and its former subsidiaries have all been integrated into the parent company.

Chief Competitors: In its principal area of business—the design, construction, and repair of nuclear-powered aircraft carriers—Newport News Shipbuilding stands alone, with no competition at all. In its secondary area of specialization—the design and construction of nuclear-powered submarines—the shipbuilder's principal competitor is General Dynamics' Electric Boat Corporation headquartered in Groton, Connecticut. In addition to its construction of military vessels, the company also provides after-market services for both naval and commercial ships; and in this business, it competes with a wider number of U.S. shipbuilders and ship repair companies.

Grumman. Federal opposition to the acquisition of Newport News by General Dynamics centered on fears that the merger would give General Dynamics a monopoly in the construction of nuclear-powered submarines. The only U.S. shipyards involved in the nuclear submarine business are Newport News and the Electric Boat Corporation, already part of the General Dynamics family.

Under the acquisition agreement, signed November 8, 2001, the shareholders of Newport News had the option of receiving $67.50 in cash per share or an equivalent value in Northrop Grumman stock. In announcing the definitive agreement, Kent Kresa, Northrop Grumman's chairman and CEO, said, "We are very pleased with our strategic acquisition of Newport News. With Newport News, we are creating a $4 billion world class, fully capable shipbuilding enterprise with expertise in every class of nuclear and non-nuclear naval vessel. Newport News' long and distinguished history and reputation

for innovation and excellence in shipbuilding are highly regarded worldwide."

Although plans called for Newport News to be operated as a separate sector of Northrop Grumman in the short term, long-range plans envision the eventual integration of its operations with those of Northrop Grumman's Ship Systems Sector, which includes the Ingalls and Avondale shipyards located on the Gulf Coast.

COMPANY FINANCES

As a subsidiary of Northrop Grumman, Newport News is not required to disclose details of its financial performance. However, in the three full years before its acquisition by Northrop Grumman, the shipbuilder had managed to post a profit each year. In 2000, net income was $90 million on revenue of nearly $2.1 billion, compared with a profit in 1999 of $97 million on revenue of nearly $1.9 billion. The company's profit in 1998 was $66 million on sales of $1.86 billion. For Northrop Grumman, the combined acquisition of Newport News and Litton Industries earlier in 2001 paid off in the final quarter of the year, when the company reported revenue almost doubled to $4.3 billion from $2.2 billion in the fourth quarter of the previous year.

ANALYSTS' OPINIONS

Although Newport News Shipbuilding is no longer traded publicly, the struggle between General Dynamics and Northrop Grumman for the shipyard during the spring, summer, and fall of 2001 drew plenty of comments from security analysts. The bid for Newport from Northrop Grumman followed by only two weeks the announcement from General Dynamics of its plan to acquire the shipbuilder. Many analysts believed that Northrop Grumman was more motivated by a desire to block the General Dynamics' takeover than any genuine interest in Newport. Earlier in the year, Northrop had spent $3.8 billion to acquire Litton Industries, which included major shipbuilding and defense electronics operations. Typical of analyst comments was this observation from Paul Nisbet of JSA Research, Inc.: "I suspect the concerted effort by Northrop Grumman to persuade the Justice Department this was a monopoly situation that would kill Litton over the long term bore fruit and they in turn went to the Defense Department."

HISTORY

Newport News Shipbuilding was established in 1886 by railroad magnate Collis P. Huntington, who had founded the Chesapeake & Ohio Railroad to move coal from the Ohio River Valley to port facilities at Newport News, Virginia. Seeing the need for a ship repair facility in the Hampton Roads port area, Huntington opened one of his own, naming it the Chesapeake Dry Dock & Construction Company. Its name was later changed to Newport News Shipbuilding. The shipyard delivered its first vessel, a tugboat, in 1891. By 1897, the company had built three warships for the U.S. Navy.

The pace of naval ship construction accelerated in the early 1900s. To demonstrate America's naval might, President Teddy Roosevelt in 1907 sent the Great White Fleet of American battleships on a round-the-world tour. Seven of the 16 vessels in the fleet were built by Newport News. Between 1907 and 1923, the shipyard turned out six of 23 dreadnoughts produced for the U.S. Navy.

During the difficult years of the Great Depression, Newport News began turning out aircraft carriers. Two of the most famous fighting ships of World War II were the Yorktown and the Enterprise, both of which were built by Newport News. In 1940, a syndicate of underwriters bought the company for $18 million and took its stock public. The years preceding America's entry into World War II saw a frenzied pace of shipbuilding for Newport News. By 1940, the shipyard's order book included seven aircraft carriers and four cruisers for the U.S. Navy. Before long, it was forced to deal with additional requests for so-called Liberty ships, merchant vessels that were pressed into military service during the war. To accommodate this overwhelming workload, the shipyard opened an emergency production facility on the Cape Fear River in North Carolina. Its first Liberty ship was launched by the end of 1941. In all, the company built 239. In the years following the war, Newport News focused on repair work and conversions as well as some new construction challenges, including the building of the famous passenger liner United States.

Shipbuilding experienced a general slump in the late 1950s and early 1960s, but Newport News managed to avoid the worst of it because of its decision to get involved in nuclear-powered shipping. Working with the U.S. Navy and Westinghouse, the company in 1954 had developed and built a prototype nuclear reactor for a carrier propulsion system. In 1960, the shipyard, in partnership with the Navy, launched the Enterprise, the world's first nuclear-powered "super" aircraft carrier. Only a year before, Newport News had launched it first nuclear-powered submarine.

As competition intensified in the late 1960s, Newport News decided to merge with Tenneco Corporation in 1968. In the 1970s, its shipbuilding operations were substantially expanded with the opening of a new North Yard. It was in this new yard that the company built two of the largest tankers ever built as well as three huge carriers to transport liquefied natural gas. Toward the end of the 1970s, commercial shipbuilding demand began to weaken, and Newport News again turned its attention largely to naval construction.

CHRONOLOGY:

Key Dates for Newport News Shipbuilding, Inc.

1886: Collis Huntington establishes shipyard

1891: Shipyard delivers first ship, a tugboat

1923: Last of six dreadnoughts for U.S. Navy completed

1930: Company goes public, trading on the NYSE

1959: First nuclear submarine launched

1960: First nuclear-powered "super" aircraft carrier launched

1968: Tenneco Corp. acquires Newport News

1996: Newport News once again goes public

2001: Northrop Grumman acquires company

In 1996, Newport News went public once again. However, in the early years of the new millennium, as the consolidation trend among major defense contractors accelerated, the need for change was apparent. General Dynamics sought to acquire the shipyard, but when the federal government expressed its opposition to such a union, an agreement was struck with rival suitor Northrop Grumman.

STRATEGY

The heart of Newport News Shipbuilding's strategy is its corporate Principles of Leadership, which call upon management and employees collectively to demonstrate uncompromising ethics and integrity; show foresight while striving for continuous improvement; exhibit respect and dignity for all employees; and motivate, develop, and empower employees to give their very best. Other major tenets of the corporate leadership principles encourage managers to build teamwork and diversity within and across functional boundaries; show compassion yet have the strength to make tough decisions; exhibit strong personal commitment and accountability toward achieving company objectives; communicate clearly and often, listen well, give recognition, seek feedback, and encourage candor; and take action based on sound planning and relevant facts.

NEWPORT NEWS MANAGES VASCIC

Established in 1998 by Virginia's General Assembly, the Virginia Advanced Shipbuilding and Carrier Integration Center, or VASCIC, works to promote the quality and competitiveness of Virginia's shipbuilding industry. Appointed to manage the center was Newport News Shipbuilding. With its partners from U.S. Navy laboratories, Virginia colleges and universities, and suppliers of electronic systems and software, Newport News works through VASCIC to develop new technologies for aircraft carriers and advanced shipbuilding. The center's benefits to the state of Virginia include job creation, a cornerstone for Newport News urban development, creation of a state technology hub, and an opportunity for industry, government, and academia to work together. For the U.S. Navy and other potential shipbuilding customers, the center provides a state-of-the-art research and development integration facility, transitions technology across multiple platforms, and builds infrastructure and relationships for a long term, world class collaborative center.

INFLUENCES

During the 1970s, Newport News Shipbuilding focused a great deal of its energy on the construction of commercial vessels, specifically tankers for the transport of petroleum products. However, by the early 1980s, much of the demand for such tonnage had faded, which caused the company to refocus on its design and construction of naval vessels. It is the only U.S. shipyard to design, build, and repair nuclear-powered aircraft carriers and one of only two American shipyards involved in the design and construction of nuclear submarines. This concentration on its core defense products has allowed Newport News to weather the weakness in demand for commercial vessels and the barriers to competition with other world shipbuilders because of cost differentials.

CURRENT TRENDS

The most profound trend of the late twentieth century and the early twenty-first century has been the sharp decline in domestic demand for commercial tonnage, which reflects the basic weakness of the U.S. maritime sector. Newport News has chosen to focus on its core defense products, including the nuclear-powered aircraft carrier and nuclear submarine.

PRODUCTS

The most important of the shipyard's products are the nuclear-powered aircraft carrier and the nuclear submarine. In addition to the design, construction, overhaul, and repair of such vessels, Newport News provides a wide variety of after-market services for commercial vessels.

CORPORATE CITIZENSHIP

Newport News seeks to involve itself in the affairs of the communities in which it operates, believing that "an investment in communities where we have facilities supports both our strategic business goals and our responsibility as a good corporate citizen and neighbor." To help make its communities "a better place to live," the company makes donations of money, volunteer time, and materials. Local organizations to which corporate support is directed include those involved in education, culture, and health and human services. Cash donations from the corporation have surpassed $1 million annually, which is supplemented each year by more than $2 million of in-kind contributions from Newport News employees.

In the area of education, Newport News believes its support is one of the best ways the company can invest for the future and help the country achieve its ideals. To that end, the company has contributed generously to a number of universities, including the University of Virginia, William & Mary, Virginia Tech, Old Dominion University, Hampton University, Christopher Newport University, and Norfolk State. Through its corporate membership in CHROME (Cooperating Hampton Roads Organizations for Minorities in Engineering), the company helps to encourage minority students to pursue careers in engineering and science.

In the realm of civic and community activities, Newport News employees have volunteered their time to a number of organizations through the company's Volunteer Opportunity Listing, a monthly publication used to coordinate volunteer projects around the company.

Through the United Way, the company, its employees, and retirees have contributed nearly $1.5 million to 51 different agencies. Company blood drives each year collect nearly 1,200 units of blood for the American Red Cross. Cultural organizations that have benefited from the company's generosity include the Virginia Living Museum, Mariner's Museum, Virginia Symphony, Virginia Stage Company, Peninsula Fine Arts Center, Virginia Air and Space Museum, and WHRO Public Radio and Television.

GLOBAL PRESENCE

Although Newport News' products sail the seven seas, the bulk of its business is domestic, most of it focused on the American defense sector.

EMPLOYMENT

As of December 31, 2000, the last full year before the company was acquired by Northrop Grumman, Newport News Shipbuilding employed approximately 17,000 employees. About 4,000 of these employees were design and engineering professionals.

SOURCES OF INFORMATION

Bibliography

"General Dynamics-Newport Deal Off." *Associated Press*, 26 October 2001.

"Newport News Shipbuilding." *Hoover's Online*, 2002. Available at http://www.hoovers.com.

Northrup Grumman Newport News Home Page, 2002. Available at http://www.nns.com.

Scheider, Greg. "Rivals Compete to Buy Newport News Shipbuilding." *Washington Post*, 20 August 2001, E14.

VASCIC Home Page, 2002. Available at http://www.vascic.com/.

For additional industry research:

Investigate companies by their Standard Industrial Classification Codes, also known as SICs. Newport News Shipbuilding's primary SIC is:

3731 Ship Building and Repairing

Also investigate companies by their North American Industrial Classification System (NAICS) Codes. Newport News Shipbuilding's primary NAICS code is:

336611 Ship Building and Repairing

News Corporation Limited

FOUNDED: 1923
VARIANT NAME: News Corp.

Contact Information:

HEADQUARTERS: 2 Holt Street
    Sydney, N.S.W. 2010 Australia
PHONE: 61 (2) 9288 3000
FAX: 61 (2) 9288 3292
URL: http://www.newscorp.com

OVERVIEW

Rupert Murdoch's News Corporation Ltd. is a media presence that extends to nearly every corner of the globe, and into nearly every type of communications medium: film, broadcast, and print. The company is a true conglomerate of corporate divisions, fully and partly owned subsidiaries, and joint ventures. The company is responsible for some of the most successful films and TV shows as well as the some of the world's best-known magazines and newspapers. It is a full or part owner of three iconic U.S. sports franchises, the Los Angeles Dodgers baseball team, the New York Knicks of the National Basketball Association, and the New York Rangers of the National Hockey League. Although Murdoch became a U.S. citizen in the mid-1980s in order to purchase U.S. TV stations, News Corp. is an Australian firm, headquartered in Sydney.

News Corp. is comprised of seven operating segments. The Filmed Entertainment segment is made up of companies that produce films for theatrical release and programming for television. The segment's centerpiece is the Twentieth Century Fox Film Corporation which turned out blockbusters like Star Wars: The Phantom Menace and Moulin Rouge. Twentieth Century Fox Television is the only studio creating programming for all six U.S. broadcasting networks, and at the end of 2001 it was responsible for more primetime programming than any other studio. Other studios in the segment include Fox 2000 Pictures, Fox Searchlight Pictures, Fox Television Studios, a group of independently-run production houses, Regency Television, and Blue Sky Studios. The Fox group also includes film studios in Australia and Mexico.

The News Corp. Television segment is made up of the The Fox Broadcasting Company which broadcast hit shows such as The Simpsons, Ally McBeal, and The X-Files. The chain of Fox stations is the foundation of the network—over thirty local stations in almost every major market in the United States; in seven markets News Corp. has two television stations. The company's other global television operations include British Sky Broadcasting, Sky Global Networks, STAR and the Channel [V] Music Networks in Asia, News Broadcasting Japan, Canal Fox in Latin America, and Fox Sports Australia. The firm's third corporate segment, Cable Network Programming, is anchored by the Fox Cable Networks which include FX, the Fox Movie Channel, Fox Sports Networks, the National Geographic Channel and others.

News Corp. purchased the Los Angeles Dodgers, and shares of the New York Knicks and New York Rangers to bolster its cable sports offerings. By 2002 the Fox News Channel was a close second in viewership behind CNN.

News Corp. is well-represented in the print media. Its Magazine & Inserts segment includes Gemstar-TV Guide International, which publishes *TV Guide*, the most popular magazine in the United States as well as an inter-active program guide for cable TV. Other magazines include *Weekly Standard, In-Store,* the *Times Literary Supplement,* the *Times Educational Supplement,* and others in the United States, Canada, Australia and Asia. News Corporation's Newspapers segments publishes the *New York Post* in the United States, four of the UK's most popular newspapers the *Times of London, Sunday Times, Sun,* and *News of the World* in the U.K., and the *Australian* and scores of other newspapers in Oceania. The Book Publishing segment, which produces books for both adults and children, is anchored by HarperCollins and a long list of imprints including Perennial Books, the Ecco Press, HarperTorch, William Morrow and Avon. News Corp.'s Other segment includes NDS, a producer of digital TV technology, the News Corp. Music Group which is active in Asia and Australia, the Australian National Rugby League, and various software and Internet ventures.

FAST FACTS:
About News Corporation Limited

Ownership: News Corporation is a publicly owned company traded on the New York, Australian, New Zealand, and London Stock Exchanges.

Ticker Symbol: NWS

Officers: K. Rupert Murdoch, Managing Dir., CEO, and Chmn., 70, 2001 base salary $4,357,000; P. Chernin, Executive Dir., Pres., and COO, 50, 2001 base salary $7,000,000; D.F. DeVoe, CFO and Finance Dir., 54, 2001 base salary $1,675,000

Employees: 30,000

Principal Subsidiary Companies: News Corporation is a multinational media company with offices and subsidiaries in North America, Europe, Australia, Asia and Latin America. Its interests include news-papers, broadcast media, film studios, book publishing, and software development. Particularly noteworthy is its Fox Film Entertainment group which 6 of the top 10 grossing films of all times as of the year 2000. About 30 percent of News Corporation is owned by the family of the company's founder, Rupert Murdoch.

Chief Competitors: Because of its broad media holdings, News Corporation competes with a number of multinational companies in a variety of industries including book and magazine publishing, film production, and cable, satellite and traditional broadcasting. Some primary competitors are AOL Time Warner, Bertelsmann, Walt Disney Company, CBS, NBC, Hearst Corporation, and Tribune Company.

COMPANY FINANCES

News Corp. products are sold the world over. The company finances are reported in Australian dollars, except when it is specified otherwise. The company had $25.58 billion in sales revenues in 2001, up from $22.44 billion the previous year. The United States accounted for 75 percent of the 2001 revenues with $19.1 billion. The United Kingdom brought in 16 percent of the firms' revenues, $4.18 billion in all. Australian and Asian revenues totaled $2.3 billion, 9 percent of the company's total.

News Corp's TV segment led all industries with $7 billion in sales revenue in 2001. Films were a close sec-ond with $6.63 billion, followed by Newspapers with $4.6 billion, Cable Network Programming with $2.7 billion, Book Publishing with $1.92 billion, Magazines & Inserts with $1.68 billion, and Other with $1.07 billion. The Fox News Channel reported a profit in 2001, the first in its five year history, while STAR TV boosted its operating income by 24 percent. Thanks to strong video and DVD sales, Twentieth Century Fox Home Entertainment reported its first billion dollar year, with (US) $1 billion in net sales, a clear indication of the firm's importance to News Corp's overall film businesses. News Corp. reported an operating loss in 2001 of $746 million, which translated to a basic loss of $0.10 per share. The loss was in large part the result of a

CHRONOLOGY:

Key Dates for News Corporation

1923: News Corporation is founded

1955: Rupert Murdoch inherits *Adelaide News* in Australia from his father

1956: Murdoch makes his first acquisition, the *Perth Sunday Times,* in Australia

1958: Murdoch acquires his first television station, TV-9, in Adelaide Australia

1960: Murdoch enters first major Australian market with acquisition of *Sydney Mirror* newspaper

1964: Murdoch establishes *The Australian*, the first Australian newspaper of national scope.

1969: Murdoch purchases Britain's *News of the World*

1970: Murdoch acquires Britain's *Sun* newspaper

1973: Rupert Murdoch acquires first U.S. holdings, the *San Antonio Express and News* newspapers

1974: Murdoch acquires the *National Star*, which he renames the *Star*

1976: Murdoch acquires the *New York Post*

1981: Murdoch acquires the *Times of London* and the *Sunday Times*

1983: Murdoch establishes Inter-American Satellite, Inc.

1985: Rupert Murdoch becomes a U.S. citizen

1985: Murdoch acquires 20th Century Fox Film Corporation

1986: Murdoch acquires seven U.S. television stations and establishes Fox Television Network

1987: Acquisition of U.S. publishing house Harper & Row Publishers and British publishers, William Collins & Sons

1988: Murdoch establishes Sky Television, a satellite TV provider serving Europe

1993: Star Television Ltd., based in Hong Kong, is founded

1995: Murdoch finances the establishment of *The Weekly Standard* by William Kristol

1996: Sky Television begins serving France and Germany

1997: News Corp. purchases Los Angeles Dodgers major league baseball team

2001: The FCC approves the sale of ten ChrisCraft TV stations to News Corp.; News Corporation is unable to purchase DirecTV from Hughes Electronics

worldwide drop in advertising. The company had had a profit of over $1.2 billion in 2000, and more than doubling its profits between 1997 and 1999. Its stock price in 2001 went as high as (US) $57.50 and as low as (US) $28.63

ANALYSTS' OPINIONS

In 2002, analysts saw News Corporation as the victim of a weak advertising market, which impacted the profitability of its television, newspaper, and magazine businesses. Value Line expected the hard times to continue in advertising and to affect News Corp.'s operations. The analysts believed News Corporation's advertising-dependent units faced challneges in the coming quarters, as did the entire company, which itself depended on those units for a great deal of revenue. At the same time, income from News Corp.'s book, cable TV, and films businesses—those which did not derive their income from advertising sources—remained strong,

and helped counterbalance other weaker performers. "News Corp. shares offer moderate appeal," Value Line wrote, noting that the company's diversity exposed it to most trends in the overall economy. "Although results have been down," it concluded, "we feel a pickup in the economy will spawn a solid earnings rebound through 2004-2006."

HISTORY

News Corporation was founded in 1923 by Keith Murdoch, the father of Rupert Murdoch. By 1952, when the elder Murdoch died, the company consisted of a chain of papers that stretched across Australia. They were taken over by Rupert, whose single-minded pursuit of a media empire would frequently draw comparisons to another media mogul of the early twentieth century, William Randolph Hearst. In 1954, after a brief apprenticeship in Britain, Murdoch took over as the publisher of two News Ltd. papers, the *Sunday Mail* and the *Adelaide News.* To boost circulation, Murdoch made over the two papers in a way that would later become his trademark. They started reporting the news in an entertaining, accessible manner and they focused on the sensational—crime sex scandals, gossip. The formula worked. With the spoils of his success, Murdoch began buying other Australian newspapers and in 1958 his first TV station in Adelaide. Over the course of the next decade, he purchased a chain of TV stations in Australia.

A Murdoch pattern was emerging: an almost obsessive drive to expand the business empire with new acquisitions. Even as the company grew, Murdoch retained control of all executive decision-making, a factor that gave News Corp. the ability to quickly outmaneuver more traditionally organized competitors. In 1960, with the purchase of the *Sydney Mirror*, he penetrated the Australia's largest media market for the first time; in 1964 he founded the country's first national newspaper, *The Australian*. He entered the British market, with the 1969 purchase of *News of the World*, the English-language paper with the largest readership in the world, and expanded it with 1970 acquisition of the *Sun*, both of which adopted his tried and true formula of mayhem-and-sex—the *Sun* also introduced the infamous "Page Three girl"—a daily photo of an attractive woman with her shirt off. News Corp. topped off its U.K. newspaper empire in 1981 with the acquisition of the venerable *Times of London* and the *Sunday Times*. Murdoch was also acquiring U.S. newspapers. In 1974 he purchased the tabloid *National Star*, in 1976 the *New York Post*, and the *Boston Herald*, and the *Chicago Sun-Times* in 1982 and 1983 respectively.

In the 1980s Murdoch turned his attention to the lucrative U.S. television market. He first focused on cable and satellite TV and later—after Murdoch became a U.S. citizen in 1985—a group of six local broadcast stations which he christened the Fox Network. It was the first major challenge to the three major networks, CBS, NBC, and ABC since the late 1940s. The network took its name from the Twentieth Century Fox film studios which News Corp. purchased in 1985.

News Corp. moved into book publishing in the late 1980s, acquiring the U.K. house William Collins Publishing and the U.S. publisher Harper & Row in 1987, and in 1988 the religious publisher Zondervan. By 1990 News Corp. was also involved in magazine publishing with the *Times Literary Supplement*, *Times Educational Supplement*, and *TV Guide*. In 1995 Murdoch bankrolled William Kristol's *Weekly Standard*.

In the late 1980s and the 1990s News Corp. began creating a truly global media empire with the establishment of the firm's various satellite television ventures. Sky Television, a system servicing Europe, was launched in late 1988. The service was limited to the United Kingdom and Ireland until state television monopolies were dismantled in much of continental Europe. Finally in 1996, News Corp. forged pacts with France's Canal Plus and Germany's Bertelsmann AG, and Sky TV was

beamed into those countries as well. In 2000, News Corp. acquired a 24 percent share of the German KirchGruppe's Kirch PayTV, which was subsequently renamed TaurusHolding. In 1993 News Corp. purchased Star Television Ltd, a five-channel network based in Hong Kong, and extended its service to most of Asia. A major area not served by STAR—the People's Republic of China—was conquered by News Corp. in 1996 when the company and the Chinese government established a joint venture. That same year, following the purchase of TV Asahi, News Corp. began broadcasts into Japan. With the establishment of Canal Fox, the company's Latin American satellite network, News Corporation had achieved penetration into every continent but Africa. News Corp. unified its satellite companies under the umbrella of Sky Global Networks. In 2001, an attempt to purchase DirecTV failed along with a plan to merge its Italian pay-TV service Stream with another Italian pay-TV service, Telepiu.

In the United States, News Corp. acquisitions continued apace, frequently to the dismay of Murdoch's critics. With (US) \$2.7 billion from the spin-off of Fox Entertainment, the company bought the Los Angeles Dodgers of Major League Baseball—News Corp already owned the Australian National Rugby League—and later added significant shares in the NBA's New York Knicks and the NHL's New York Rangers. In 2001 News Corp.'s plan to purchase 10 local U.S. stations from Chris-Craft was approved by the Federal Communications Commission. An attempt to purchase DirecTV from the General Motors subsidiary Hughes electronics fell through in late 2001.

STRATEGY

The hallmark strategy of News Corp. has been attention to cost-cutting and the bottom line of its companies day-to-day operations. There have been exceptions, for example, its decision to bid over \$400 million for the rights to the European Champions League soccer broadcasts in Europe to launch a new German cable channel, TM3. But that illustrates another trait of News Corp.—the willingness to pull out all the stops to make a success of a venture. Sports have always been an important means of creating instant viewership, as in the middle 1990s when the upstart Fox Network went after and obtained the rights to NFL broadcasts. Another strategy that News Corp. used from its earliest days under Rupert Murdoch, was to use the value of his existing companies to finance continued growth. Under-performing firms or ineffective companies were sold off and the proceeds put back into new acquisitions.

News Corp. is famous for focusing unapologetically on the lowest common denominator of public taste, for example the *New York Post*, the*Sun*, the *Star*, and some of its Fox Network televisions shows. Crime, sex, and

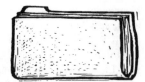

NEWS CORP. CONQUERS BULGARIA

Rupert Murdoch made headlines when he bought four of the leading British newspapers; likewise, when he launched his upstart Fox Television in the United States. The media did not take as much notice, however, when Murdoch conquered one of the last European frontiers—Bulgaria. Financial problems caused News Corp. to miss out on the first wave of Eastern European investment in the early 1990s. But at the end of the decade, in February 2000, New Corporation was awarded the country's first commercial TV license. The news service, Balkan News Corporation, went into operation in summer 2000. It seemed an unlikely acquisition for a man with Murdoch's multi-million-dollar ambitions. Bulgaria is a nation with few resources and it is not clear where advertising revenues will come from. However, News Corp. has bigger plans for the station. The firm wants to make it the base for a TV service that will eventually cover the entire Balkan region, including Romania, Serbia, Croatia, and Macedonia.

celebrity scandals are found everywhere. Despite the rebuke of critics, the formula has usually worked for the company. Despite his well-known conservative leanings, Murdoch does not to let politics interfere with a business deal. Hence, despite years of zealous anticommunism, he was willing to become a partner in a satellite TV venture with the government of the People's Republic of China.

INFLUENCES

Although many companies successfully embraced the Internet revolution, News Corp was unable to break into the Internet economy in any significant manner. All of its attempts to do so failed. Murdoch's son, James suffered a great loss in 1995 when communications company, MCI pulled out of a planned alliance that would have backed a Web site called iGuide. His deal to buy another Internet company, Pointcast—whose software later proved to have fatal flaws—broke down at the eleventh hour. The elder Murdoch also brokered a deal to enter the Internet business. He bought into a Japanese Internet firm, Soft Bank, which went out of business when the Internet bubble burst in late 2000. Despite Mur-

doch's 1999 promise that News Corporation would be based squarely on Internet businesses, by 2002 News Corporation had largely abandoned efforts at quick expansion into cybermedia and refocused its sights on satellite television.

CURRENT TRENDS

News Corp. has continued efforts to expand its television network in the United States. In 2001 the FCC approved the sale of ten Chris Craft owned television stations to News Corporation. The sale was the first one approved under new rules permitting a company to own two stations in the same market. The ChrisCraft sale gave News Corp. two stations—duopolies, the company calls them—in three major U.S. markets, New York City, Los Angeles, and Phoenix. Newscorp would have had two stations in Salt Lake City, but the law bars owning two stations where there are four or fewer stations. Other deals with Viacom and ClearChannel Communications gave News Corporation duopolies in four other U.S. TV markets: Dallas, Houston, Washington D.C., and Minneapolis. Murdoch also attempted to purchase DirecTV in 2001. If it had succeeded, the U.S. company would have closed a major gap in Murdoch's international satellite TV network. The deal with Hughes Electronics fell apart.

PRODUCTS

News Corporation has been responsible for many of the most popular and successful television programs in the late 1990s and early 2000s. The hit TV shows Fox has produced include *The Simpsons*, *The X-Files*, *Ally McBeal*, *King of the Hill*, *Buffy the Vampire Slayer*, and *Malcolm in the Middle*. Fox Filmed Entertainment and News Corporations other film businesses gave the world hit movies such as *Titanic*, *Moulin Rouge*, *Star Wars Episode One: The Phantom Menace*, *Fight Club*, and *Quills*. These News Corp. products created unique ongoing synergies. After the theatrical release, Fox films were re-released on video and DVD by Fox Home Entertainment. Similarly, Fox's television shows have frequently gone into profitable syndication on its own stations.

GLOBAL PRESENCE

News Corporation's global arms extends into virtually every corner of the world—only Africa remains outside its reach. In Europe British Sky Broadcasting is growing, along with Stream in Italy. In 2001 News Corp. inaugurated the Balkan News Corporation based in Bulgaria. STAR, News Corp.'s Pan-Asian service has a viewership that extends from the Middle East, through the Indian subcontinent, into Southeast Asia and beyond. The service was particularly successful in India where STAR Plus was the number one Hindu station in 2001 with 39 of India's top 50 television shows. Canal Fox provides programming for Latin America. Seventy percent of all British adults read a News Corp. newspaper. The firm is strongly represented in Australia, New Zealand and the South Pacific islands. In Australia it owns and operates more than 100 newspapers, the National Rugby League, and music, software, Internet, and technology companies. It has interests in Fox Studios Australia, which made *Moulin Rouge* and produced *Star Wars Episode Two*, Fox Sports Australia, and many other companies.

EMPLOYMENT

News Corporation employs some 30,000 people in all areas of entertainment and media, including producers, directors, writers and actors, and technicians for film and television; journalists, editors, and printing workers for the firm's magazines and newspapers; programmers and software writers.

SOURCES OF INFORMATION

Bibliography

Auletta, Ken. "The Pirate." *New Yorker*, November 13, 1995.

Black, Larry. "LA's Dodgers Accepts Dollars 350m Murdoch Bid." *Daily Telegraph*, September 6, 1997.

Brooks, Richard. "Love, marriage and the real Rupert Murdoch." *Observer*, November 8, 1998.

Crainer, Stuart and Des Dearlove. *Business the Rupert Murdoch Way: 10 Secrets of the World's Greatest Deal-Maker*. AMACOM, 1999.

Cromie, Ali. "James Awaits His Digital Kingdom." *Business Review Weekly*, December 10, 1999.

"Family." *Independent*, November 16, 1999.

"From Murdoch, a Health Bulletin." *Business Week*, December 20, 1999.

Hickey, Neil. "Is Fox News Fair?" *Columbia Journalism Review*, March, 1998/April, 1998.

James, Steve. "Murdoch's Dodgers Start Era of Rupert Ball in L.A." *Detroit News*, April 8, 1998.

Kuczynski, Alex. "TV Guide Sold for $9.2 Billion in Stock Deal." *New York Times*, October 5, 1999.

"Murdoch's Newest GOOOOAAAAL." *Time*, September 12, 1998.

Neil, Andrew. "Murdoch and Me." *Vanity Fair*, December 1996.

"News Corporation." *Hoover's Company Profiles*, 2002. Available at http://www.hoovers.com.

Roberts, Johnnie L. "The Man Behind Rupert's Roll." *Newsweek*, July 12, 1999.

"Rupert Murdoch," *American Decades CD-ROM*. Farmington Hills, MI: Gale Research, 1998.

"Rupert Murdoch." *Encyclopedia of World Biography:* 2nd ed. Farmington Hills, MI: Gale Research, 1998.

"Rupert Does the Cyberhustle." *Business Week*, July 12, 1999.

"Rupert Murdoch Picks Sides Between Money and Honesty." *Herald*, March 3, 1998.

"Rupert's Misses." *Economist*, July 3, 1999.

Shah, Diane K. "Will Rupert Buy L.A.?" *Los Angeles Magazine*, December 1997.

Shawcross, William. "Rupert Murdoch." *Time International*, October 25, 1999.

————. *Murdoch*. New York: Simon and Schuster, 1992.

Tuccille, Jerome. *Rupert Murdoch.* New York: Fine, 1989.

For an annual report:

on the Internet at: http://www.newscorp.com/public/ir/index *or* write: News Corporation, 1211 Avenue of the Americas, New York, NY 10036

For additional industry research:

Investigate companies by their Standard Industrial Classification Codes, also known as SICs. News Corporation Limited's primary SICs are:

2711 Newspapers: Publishing or Publishing & Printing

4833 Television Broadcasting

7812 Motion Picture, Video Tape Production

Also investigate companies by their North American Industrial Classification System codes, also known as NAICS codes. News Corporation Limited's primary NAICS codes are:

511110 Newspaper Publishing

513120 Television Broadcaaasting

Nextel Communications Inc.

FOUNDED: 1987

Contact Information:

HEADQUARTERS: 2001 Edmund Halley Dr.
   Reston, VA 20191
PHONE: (703)433-4000
FAX: (703)433-4343
URL: http://www.nextel.com

OVERVIEW

Launched in 1987 to take advantage of the specialized mobile radio (SMR) market, Nextel Communications today is one of the major digital mobile phone operators in the United States. The company provides digital mobile communications throughout the United States by offering integrated wireless services under the Nextel brand name, targeting primarily business users. Nextel's digital mobile network is one of the largest integrated wireless communications systems utilizing a single transmission technology in the United States. Referred to as integrated Digital Enhanced Network, or iDEN, this technology was originally developed by Motorola.

Customers who use Nextel's digital mobile network are able to access digital mobile telephone service, including such advanced calling features as conference calling, voice mail, speakerphone, and call forwarding, and Nextel Direct Connect service, allowing subscribers within the same local calling area to contact one another instantly. Other services accessible to customers using Nextel's network include international roaming capabilities (marketed as Nextel Worldwide), as well as Internet services, mobile messaging services, e-mail, and advance Java-enabled business applications (marketed as Nextel Wireless Web services).

As of the end of 2001, Nextel had nearly 8.7 million digital handsets in service in the United States. Nextel's iDEN network, along with the compatible digital mobile network of Nextel Partners, were operational in 195 of the top 200 metropolitan statistical areas of the United States as of December 31, 2001.

COMPANY FINANCES

It might not seem it to look at Nextel's bottom line for 2001, but company executives were clearly pleased with its accomplishments for the year. Writing in the company's 2001 Annual Report, Timothy M. Donahue, president and chief executive officer, observed, "Nextel delivered its best financial results ever in 2001. We met our goals, adding nearly 2 million new domestic subscribers, and generating $1.9 billion in EBITDA (earnings before interest, taxes, restructuring and impairment charges, depreciation and amortization) for domestic operations. We continue to lead the national carriers with the highest monthly revenue per unit and have the highest customer loyalty rate. In fact, Nextel ranks first in Customer Lifetime Value, according to the Yankee Group."

Nextel posted a net loss of almost $2.9 billion for 2001 on revenue of about $7.7 billion, compared with a net loss of slightly more than $1 billion on revenue of $5.7 billion in 2000. In 1999 the company reported a loss of more than $1.5 billion on sales of about $3.8 billion. However, a glance at some of the company's other key data provides a somewhat brighter picture of the company's progress over those three years. Domestic service revenue totaled nearly $6.6 billion in 2001, compared with just under $5 billion in 2000 and $3.2 billion in 1999. The company's operating cash flow in 2001 totaled $1.9 billion, up from about $1.4 billion in 2000 and $700 million in 1999. Nextel's domestic subscribers increased to nearly 8.7 million in 2001, a big jump from 6.7 million in 2000 and 4.5 million in 1999.

The announcement in May 2002 that Nextel's international subsidiary, NII Holdings, Inc., had filed for protection from the U.S. Bankruptcy Court cast something of a shadow over Nextel's financial picture. A good part of Nextel's 2001 loss was directly attributable to the problems of its global subsidiary, which had defaulted on most of its $2.7 billion in debt. Earlier in 2001 Nextel had written off $1.7 billion in debt it was owed by NII. Under the terms of NII's Chapter 11 filing, Nextel's stake in NII was to be reduced from 95 percent to less than 50 percent, with most of the equity transferred to NII bondholders. Additionally, Nextel has agreed to contribute up to $65 million in new capital to NII, with an additional $75 million or more coming from a consortium of NII bondholders. Nextel will also give NII $50 million in funding as part of an existing agreement under which the two companies share wireless spectrum in Mexico and the United States.

Nextel's performance in the first quarter of 2002 cheered investors and analysts alike. The company's revenue and cash flow rose on the strength of vigorous subscriber growth. Nextel added slightly more than a half-million new customers in the United States, surpassing the projections of security analysts that had forecast subscribers would increase between 475,000 and 500,000 during the quarter. As of March 31, 2002, Nextel's subscribers totaled 9.2 million. The company's revenue rose

FAST FACTS:
About Nextel Communications Inc.

Ownership: Nextel Communications is a publicly owned company traded on the NASDAQ Stock Exchange.

Ticker Symbol: NXTL

Officers: William E. Conway, Chmn., 52; Timothy M. Donahue, Pres. and CEO, 53, 2000 base salary $465,174; Paul N. Saleh, EVP and CFO, 45

Employees: 17,000

Principal Subsidiary Companies: Nextel Communications Inc.'s major subsidiaries include Nextel Partners, Inc. and NII Holdings, Inc. Nextel Partners, in which Nokia Communications holds a share of 32 percent, provides digital wireless communications services under the Nextel brand name in mid-sized and tertiary U.S. markets. Formerly known as Nextel International, NII Holdings is a substantially wholly owned subsidiary of Nextel Communications. The subsidiary exports Nextel's brand of wireless service to overseas markets, most notably Latin America and the Philippines.

Chief Competitors: Nextel's primary competitors on a national scale are AT&T Wireless Services, Cingular Wireless, Sprint PCS, Verizon Wireless, and VoiceStream Wireless Corporation. In addition to its competitors in the nationwide market, Nextel competes with a number of regional providers of mobile wireless voice communications, including such companies as Southern LINC.

to $2.16 billion from $1.74 billion in the same quarter the previous year. However, Nextel's net loss increased $654 million, compared with a loss of $428 million the previous year. The company's first-quarter 2002 results included a charge of $355 million related to goodwill accounting changes, as well as a restructuring charge of $40 million. Excluding these extraordinary charges, Nextel's net loss was $279 million, or $.35 a share, better than the average $.40 loss predicted by analysts.

ANALYSTS' OPINIONS

Nextel's cash flow improvement in the first quarter of 2002 won praise from most security analysts. Typical of their reactions was this comment from Jeffrey Hines, an analyst with Deutsche Bank Securities: "It was a great quarter across the board." Comments from investment banks SoundView Technology and Williams Capital Group indicated that Nextel's cash flow figure surpassed their expectations.

Analysts also seemed to look with favor on Nextel's positioning in the market for walkie-talkies, an old technology revived by wireless operators in their search for new customers and higher revenue. Nextel had introduced a radiotelephone combination in the late 1990s, giving it a leg-up in the competition for the consumers' walkie-talkie dollar. While cell phone calls generally take several seconds to connect, do not support instant group links, and are more expensive, most walkie-talkie chats are finished before a phone call could have been connected. Trucker Consolidated Freightways uses Nextel's Direct Connect walkie-talkie technology to stay in touch with its drivers. According to Brownlee Thomas, an analyst with Giga Information Group, "it's a group thing. It doesn't cost me what it would cost to set up a conference call. . . ." Michael Doherty, a wireless analyst with Ovum, observed that Nextel has already got such a strong foothold on the market that other entrants would have to come up with something pretty innovative to make a serious bid in the walkie-talkie market. "Depending on how the newer entrants bundle push-to-talk in with their other product lines, that's where they could start to do some damage to Nextel."

HISTORY

In the mid-1980s the Federal Communications Commission, realizing that the cellular phone industry had matured to a point where it could withstand greater competition, opened the door to the development of specialized mobile radio (SMR). Morgan O'Brien, a prominent telecommunications attorney, decided to try his fortune in the emerging SMR industry. Partnering with accountant Brian D. McAuley, O'Brien founded a company called Fleet Call to acquire SMR properties. In its first year Fleet Call financed the acquisition of 10 mobile radio companies and began making plans to construct communications networks in major markets. The SMR business had been dominated for years by Motorola, which manufactured the radio systems and also operated dozens of networks. Fearing that Motorola would block Fleet Call's efforts to build a new SMR communications network, O'Brien and McAuley arranged to meet with Motorola Chairman to outline their proposal to him in person. Much to their surprise, Motorola's chairman not only supported the idea but also asked if Motorola could become a partner in the venture. An agreement was worked out, giving Motorola an equity stake in Fleet Call, and Motorola began working on components for the new communications network. Only a month after meeting with Fisher, Fleet Call had increased its holdings to 74

mobile radio companies in major metropolitan areas, including Chicago, Dallas, Houston, Los Angeles, New York, and San Francisco. At this point all of Fleet Call's mobile radio businesses were operated as radio dispatch systems utilizing old analog transmission technology.

In early 1991 Fleet Call petitioned the FCC for permission to design and build digital communications systems that would operate on the SMR bands. By going digital, the systems would allow many more calls to be made while still providing access to existing fleet dispatchers. The FCC unanimously approved Fleet Call's request. After getting the green light from the FCC, Fleet Call brought in other partners to help Motorola build the network. These new participants in the project included Canada's Northern Telecom and Matsushita of Japan. Partners O'Brien and McAuley took Fleet Call public in January 1992, raising $112.5 million. From Motorola, Northern Telecom, and Matsushita, Fleet Call got $345 in equipment financing, and cable television operator Comcast provided another investment commitment of $230 million in exchange for a 30 percent interest in the company.

Although Fleet Call's communications system attracted wide interest from investors, it did have one significant drawback-its incompatibility with other cellular networks. To turn this into an advantage, Fleet Call decided to significantly expand its already completed Los Angeles cell site (completed in May 1992), extending coverage south to the Mexican border, east to Palm Springs, and north to Santa Barbara. And the company pledged to extend service to all of California by mid-1994. Facilitating Fleet Call's expansion was its merger in December 1992 with Dispatch Communications. The combination gave Fleet Call coverage in nine of the country's 10 largest markets. In early 1993 Fleet Call hired John Caner, who previously had been director of wireless data development at PacTel Cellular. Two months later Fleet Call changed its name to Nextel, which seemed more in keeping with the new-wave technologies the company was using.

Throughout the early 1990s, Nextel continued to extend its network of radio bands, acquiring most of them through merger. Of particular importance was the company's alliance with long-distance provider MCI in February 1994, giving Nextel nationwide long-distance coverage. By the end of 2001, Nextel had become the fifth largest wireless communications operator in the United States.

STRATEGY

Nextel's business strategy focuses on the differences that distinguish its wireless service offerings from those of the competition. The company's strategy emphasizes five main points: (1) Nextel provides a differentiated, integrated package of wireless services, including its unique Nextel Direct Connect feature; (2) Nextel focuses on the business customer; (3) Nextel's nationwide upgrade to the iDEN digital mobile network, already under way, will effectively double the operator's voice capacity for interconnect calls and leverage the company's investment in its existing infrastructure; (4) Nextel's pricing strategy, marketing program, and distribution channels; and (5) the company's strategic relationships with Motorola, Craig O. McCaw, and Nextel Partners.

Nextel's bundled product offering, accessible through a single handset, consists of digital mobile telephone service, including advanced features; Nextel Direct Connect service; Internet services; and international roaming capabilities. The company believes its Direct Connect service more than any other service sets it apart from the competition. Nextel also believes its focus on business customers positions the company well to handle the specific needs of this market. The company's deployment of the iDEN technology gives Nextel one of the most comprehensive wireless coverage networks in the United States. Nextel also believes its pricing packages offer customers simplicity and predictability in their wireless communications billings. Finally, Nextel touts the value of its close relationships with Motorola, wireless maven Craig O. McCaw, and Nextel Partners in giving the company the technological counsel it needs to help develop new technologies and improve existing products.

INFLUENCES

As the wireless mobile communications business has become increasingly competitive, all the major players have sought new and innovative ways to market their services and products. Nextel, the fifth largest wireless communications operator in the United States, is no exception. In 2001 the company moved aggressively to target "the right customer through the right channel at the right price" in order to reduce its customer acquisition costs while at the same time achieving a higher rate of return.

Through its acquisition in May 2001 of the "Let's Talk Cellular & Wireless" retail chain, the 200 outlets of which were re-branded Nextel stores, the company opened up an important new marketing channel and also helped to facilitate service and repairs for its existing customers. The company said it planned to add another 200 retail outlets in 2002. Based on its experience in 2001, the average revenue per unit at Nextel stores was even higher than that generated through the company's other sales channels.

In 2001 Nextel's TeleSales channel, accessible by telephone at 800-NEXTEL9, experienced an increase in calls of more than 80 percent over the previous year. But that jump pales in comparison with the increase in pro-

CHRONOLOGY:
Key Dates for Nextel Communications Inc.

1987: Morgan O'Brien and Brian D. McAuley form Fleet Call, Inc.

1992: Fleet Call goes public

1993: Fleet Call changes name to Nextel Communications Inc.

1994: Nextel agrees to buy all of Motorola's SMR licenses in the United States

2002: Nextel increases U.S. subscribers to total of 9.2 million

ductivity of the TeleSales line in 2001. More than 209 percent more phones were sold through this sales channel than in 2000. The company attributes at least part of this spectacular growth to its decision to outsource its telemarketing operations to outside companies with greater experience in this form of marketing.

Another key marketing channel for Nextel is the Internet. The company's 2001 sales through its Web site were up more than 240 percent from the previous year. The sharp increase in sales is particularly heartening to Nextel since the customer acquisition costs for this channel are among the company's lowest.

CURRENT TRENDS

Significant trends in the wireless communications industry include the move towards greater consolidation. Many observers have identified Nextel as a likely candidate for merger with a larger, more financially stable partner sometime within the foreseeable future. The likelihood of such a merger is expected to grow as the Federal Communications Commission continues to relax its limits on how much of the wireless spectrum can be controlled by a single company. The FCC limits are scheduled to disappear altogether by January 2003, making Nextel a likely target for several potential buyers.

The wireless communications industry, like most industries in the United States, has been moving aggressively to reduce its costs. In 2001 Nextel reduced its payroll substantially when it decided to farm out its customer

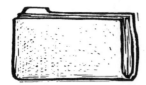

NEXTEL HELPS MINNESOTANS TRACK WEATHER

A new Nextel service is helping alert Minnesotans to weather changes. The service, developed by Nextel primarily for business customers, is offered via cell phone by Digital Cyclone of Minnetonka, Minnesota. The customized weather service, introduced in early 2002, is proving particular popular with building contractors, landscapers, and others whose work schedules are dictated by the vagaries of the weather. The service provides real-time weather data and animated radar screens that show the direction and speed of weather conditions on a cell-phone display. To obtain the service, customers must have a Java-enabled cell phone, which are sold by Nextel for about $75 to $250. The weather service itself costs $12.95 a month for black-and-white display. Color service was to be introduced in the summer of 2002.

relations operations and its technical functions to IBM and EDS Corporation.

Recognizing the consumer appetite for something new and different in wireless services, Nextel has been aggressively marketing its new version of the walkie-talkie, an alternative to cellular service. Nextel had actually introduced a radio/phone combination in the late 1990s, giving it a decided advantage in this emerging market. The push-to-talk technology, using radio frequencies, provides almost instantaneous connections, while cellular calls typically take several seconds to connect.

PRODUCTS

Nextel's products fall into two principal categories: wireless services and mobile phones. The company's services and their features include Nextel Direct Connect, which uses radio frequencies to provide almost-instant connections and costs sharply lower than those for cellular service; Wireless Web services, which allow users to access the Internet on their mobile phones; and Nextel Mobile Messaging. Other popular Nextel services include Nextel Worldwide, which allows subscribers to stay connected in a number of countries outside the

United States, and Email Services, giving subscribers easy access to their home and business e-mail accounts. Nextel also offers Java applications on a number of its mobile phones.

Mobile phones marketed by Nextel include nine models, including the top-of-the-line i90c, its smallest full-feature phone, and the i2000plus, which offers worldwide capabilities and a vibrating signal of incoming calls. All Nextel mobile phones are Internet ready and equipped for such features and services as digital two-way radio, voice mail, call waiting, caller ID, mobile messaging, and call hold.

CORPORATE CITIZENSHIP

Nextel is proud of its reputation as a responsible corporate citizen. The company has undertaken a number of initiatives to support the communities in which it operates. In April 2002, Nextel partnered with APS Wireless Communications of Bensalem, Pennsylvania, to raise money for the ALS Association in the fight against Lou Gehrig's disease. APS Wireless announced it would contribute $5 to the ALS Association for every unit sold in its nine stores during the month of April. Nextel agreed to contribute an additional $5 to ALS for every Nextel phone sold by APS Wireless during the month.

In March 2002 Nextel underwrote the CBS-TV show "9-11," a two-hour documentary account of the terrorist attack on New York's World Trade Center September 11, 2001. The company devoted its television time during the show to raise public awareness and funds for charitable causes, as well as to pay tribute to America's public safety workers.

GLOBAL PRESENCE

Much of Nextel's international operations are handled by its global subsidiary, NII Holdings, Inc., previously known as Nextel International. However, NII experienced some serious financial setbacks in 2001 and in May 2002 was forced to seek bankruptcy protection from its creditors in order to reorganize. NII, sells the Nextel brand of wireless communications, in Latin America and the Philippines, in which regions it has slightly more than 1 million subscribers. Under the terms of NII's reorganization plan, Nextel's stake in its subsidiary will be reduced from 95 percent to less than 50 percent, with most of the equity being transferred to NII bondholders.

In addition to the Nextel services marketed abroad, the company's domestic subscribers have access to international services when they travel abroad. Subscribers using Nextel's i2000plus phone can make calls in more than 80 countries worldwide. Even those subscribers who don't have an i2000plus phone can make calls outside the United States in the countries of Argentina, Brazil, Canada, Israel, Mexico, Peru, and the Philippines.

EMPLOYMENT

At the end of 2001, Nextel employed approximately 17,000 employees worldwide, about 13,000 of whom work in the United States. In its 2001 Annual Report, the company described its employees as "the power behind our performance and results. They anticipate our customers' needs. They push innovation. They create wireless solutions to business challenges. They form one national team."

Recognizing the importance of continuing education for its employees, Nextel in 2002 planned significant enrichment initiatives with Nextel University and Quarterly Career & Development Planning. These company programs are designed to ensure that Nextel's employees are equipped with the industry-leading skills and knowledge to help the company advance in today's increasingly competitive marketplace.

SOURCES OF INFORMATION

Bibliography

"Business Summary: Nextel Communications." *Multex Investor.* Available at http://www.marketguide.com.

Carew, Sinead. "Nextel Rises on Strong First-Quarter Results." *Reuters Business Report*, 17 April 2002.

———. "Telecom Goes Back to the Future with Walkie Talkies." *Reuters*, 22 May 2002.

Meyerson, Bruce. "Nextel Unit Files for Bankruptcy." *AP Online*, 24 May 2002.

"Nextel Communications Inc." *Hoover's Online*, 2002. Available at http://www.hoovers.com.

Nextel Communications Inc. 2001 Annual Report. Reston, VA: Nextel Communications Inc., 2002.

"Nextel Communications Inc.—History." *Gale Business Resources*, 2002. Available at http://galenet.galegroup.com/servlet/GBR.

"Nextel Partners Inc." *Hoover's Online*, 2002. Available at http://www.hoovers.com.

"NII Holdings, Inc." *Hoover's Online*, 2002. Available at http://www.hoovers.com.

Peterson, Susan E. "The Digital Forecast."*Minneapolis Star Tribune*, 22 April 2002.

For an annual report:

on the Internet at: http://www.corporate-ir.net/ireye/ir_site.zhtml **or** write: Investor Relations, 2001 Edmund Halley Dr., Reston, VA 20191

For additional industry research:

Investigate companies by their Standard Industrial Classification Codes, also known as SICs. Nextel Communications Inc.'s primary SICs are:

4812 Radiotelephone Communications

5999 Miscellaneous Retail Stores, NEC

6719 Holding Companies, NEC

Also investigate companies by their North American Industrial Classification System codes, also known as NAICS codes. Nextel Communications Inc.'s primary NAICS codes are:

513320 Wireless Telecommunications Carriers (except Satellite)

551112 Offices of Other Holding Companies

Nissan Motor Company Ltd.

FOUNDED: 1933

Contact Information:

HEADQUARTERS: 17-1 Ginza 6-chome, Chuo-ku
    Tokyo, 104-8023 Japan
PHONE: 81-3-3543-5523
FAX: 81-3-3546-2669
URL: http://www.nissan-global.com

OVERVIEW

Nissan Motor Company Ltd., the third largest automobile manufacturer in Japan behind Toyota and Honda, produces 2.6 million vehicles annually that are sold in more than 190 countries around the world. Its product line includes the Maxima and Sentra mid-ranged passenger cars, the upscale sedans Altima and Infiniti, Frontier trucks, and Pathfinder and Xterra SUVs. With plans for 22 new models to hit the market between 2000 and 2005, consumers can expect to see a new and expanded product line. Nissan has also diversified into a variety of nonautomotive industries, including aerospace, marine, and textile equipment production and financial and real estate services. Headquartered in Japan, Nissan maintains regional offices in the United States and The Netherlands. Marketing and sales operations are conducted through 172 national sales offices and an extensive network of over 7,700 automobile dealers worldwide.

Experiencing financial difficulties since the early 1990s, the company managed to make a net profit in fiscal year 1996, but posted net losses for the following three fiscal years. By 1999 the company was faltering and in desperate need of a financial boost. Although DaimlerChrysler showed interest in acquiring part of the company, the French automobile maker Renault stepped up first and purchased a 37-percent stake in Nissan, making it the majority stockholder.

As soon as the stock purchase was completed, Renault instigated the appointment of Carlos Ghosn as the new head of Nissan. Known for his ability to cut costs effectively, Ghosn undertook a series of measures to stop the financial drain. He closed outdated plants, laid off employees, and abandoned suppliers who refused to renegotiate high prices. He also helped the company develop a comprehensive three-year reorganization called the Nissan Revival Plan. With the new influx of cash and under the strong leadership of Ghosn, results began to materialize quickly. The company posted net gains in fiscal 2000 and during the first half of fiscal 2001. In March of 2002 Renault increased its share of Nissan from 37 percent to 44.4 percent, and Nissan announced intentions to purchase a 15 percent interest in Renault.

COMPANY FINANCES

Fiscal 1999, ending March 31, 2000, was a plainly terrible year for Nissan. The company posted a net loss of ¥684.4 billion. ($5.7 billion; based on an average exchange rate of ¥120 = $1.) Nissan had posted losses, albeit less substantial, in fiscal 1998 and fiscal 1999 of ¥14 billion and ¥27.8 billion, respectively. In fiscal 2000 the numbers began to turn around, with the company generating a net income of ¥331 billion on revenues of ¥6.1 trillion. During the first two quarters of fiscal 2001, the company continued to post profits. Net sales for the period totaled ¥3 trillion ($24.8 billion), representing a decrease of 1.4 percent from the same time period of the previous year. Despite the slight decline in overall sales revenues, Nissan was able to post a net income for the first half of fiscal 2001 of ¥230.3 billion, an increase of nearly 34 percent year-on-year. The company was also able to reduce its debt load by ¥154 billion to ¥799 billion. This represents a significant decrease in debt from the debilitating amount of ¥2.3 trillion the company held in 1997. Stock prices, which closed in October of 1994 at $15.83 per share on NASDAQ, had fallen to $4.52 per share by October of 1998. After the announcement of the Renault deal, stock prices began to slowly creep back up, reaching $14.96 per share by close of March of 2002. Net income for fiscal 2001 was expected to be approximately ¥330 billion.

ANALYSTS' OPINIONS

Clearly Renault's influx of cash helped revitalize Nissan's prospects for the future. Analysts describe the deal as pulling Nissan "back from the brink," and Ghosn likened the scenario to moving out of the operating room into the recovery room. The introduction of a new subcompact model at the beginning of March, a weak yen, positive U.S. sales, and a promising outlook from Ghosn prompted investors to take notice. By April of 2002 Ghosn's strong leadership combined with consistently improving bottom-line numbers finally began to convince analysts that Nissan's turnaround might be real. Although the company faces ongoing challenges, including a weak Asian economy, the company's progress toward financial recovery has garnered considerable praise from the analysts.

FAST FACTS:
About Nissan Motor Company Ltd.

Ownership: Nissan Motor Company Ltd. is a publicly held company that is traded on the Tokyo, Frankfurt, and NASDAQ Stock Exchanges.

Ticker Symbol: NASNY

Officers: Yoshikazu Hanawa, Chmn.; Carlos Ghosn, Pres. and CEO; Itaru Koeda, EVP; Hisayoshi Kojima, EVP; Norio Matsumura, EVP; Thierry Moulonguet, EVP and CFO; Nobuo Okubo, EVP

Employees: 30,750

Principal Subsidiary Companies: Nissan's numerous subsidiaries include Nissan Capital of America Inc.; Nissan Design International; Nissan Motor Acceptance Corporation; Nissan Motor Company USA; Nissan Motor Manufacturing Corporation USA; Nissan North America Inc.; and Nissan Textile Machinery Corporation.

Chief Competitors: Nissan battles all major automobile manufacturers for a piece of the automobile market share. In the United State competitors include General Motors and Ford. In both the Japanese and U.S. market, Nissan competes with Honda and Toyota.

HISTORY

In 1911 Masujiro Hashimoto, a U.S.-educated engineer, founded the Kwaishinsha Motor Car Works in Tokyo. In order to finance the production of the first Japanese car, Hashimoto took on three investors. Using the initials of their last names, Hashimoto named his creation DAT. The second model introduced was referred to as a Datson, meaning "son of dat." In 1926 Hashimoto merged his company with fellow Japanese automaker Jitsuyo Jidosha Seizo Company to create the Dat Jidosha Seizo Company. The company changed hands in 1931, but the name Datson stuck, although the spelling was changed to Datsun in 1932. The following year the company's name became Nissan.

Sales of the Datsun were not exceptional in Japan during the 1930s because Ford and General Motors, who had already established production facilities in Japan, dominated the market. During World War II Nissan operated under government orders to cease production of passenger cars to produce trucks for the war effort. After the

CHRONOLOGY:

Key Dates for Nissan Motor Company Ltd.

1918: Kwaishinsha Motor Company in Tokyo introduces the Datson, a two-seat sports car

1932: Name is changed to Datsun

1933: Company is renamed and incorporated as Nissan Motor Company

1951: Becomes a publicly traded company

1958: Nissan enters the U.S. market by establishing the Nissan Motor Company U.S.A

1975: Revenues top $5 million

1981: Changes name of U.S operations from Datsun to Nissan

1992: Posts a pre-tax loss for the first half of 1992 of ¥108.1 billion

1999: Posts a net loss of ¥791 billion for the fiscal year; Renault buys a 37 percent interest in the company; Carlos Ghosn is named chief executive officer

2000: Company restructuring under the Nissan Revival Plan leads to a net income of ¥187 billion for the fiscal year

2001: Posts a net income for the second year in a row

2002: Introduces to the Japanese market the Moco, the company's newest minicar

war ended it took several years for the company to rebuild its business as the entire nation of Japan struggled to recoup from the devastation of the war.

By the mid-1950s with sales still slow in Japan, Nissan became increasingly convinced that its future lie in exporting its small, inexpensive cars to the United States. After an unsuccessful attempt to contract with several American auto dealers, Nissan decided to create its own U.S.-based company to market and sell its product. In 1960 Nissan Motor Company U.S.A. had 60 dealerships within its organization and annual car sales of 1,640 units. The Datsun pickup, one of the first small trucks on the market proved particularly popular. The success of the pickup was followed by the introduction of the 240Z to the American market. By 1975 revenues topped $5 million.

During the 1980s Nissan expanded its production facilities into Italy, Spain, Germany, and the United Kingdom, and in 1981 changed the name under which it conducted business in the United States from Datsun to Nissan. New luxury models were introduced to the company's line of affordable passenger cars, and Nissan invested heavily in research and development of advancements and technological innovations. In 1989 Nissan introduced its top-of-the-line Infiniti luxury sedans.

During the 1990s the Asia economy became increasingly unstable. An increase in the value of the yen made export to the United States costly. As a result, Nissan could no longer compete with success against U.S. automakers. At the same time, U.S. manufacturers were increasing production, decreasing costs, and improving efficiency. Because its pockets were not nearly as deep as Toyota's, who could sustain a larger economic hit without undermining the company's viability, Nissan began to lose its financial footing. The company posted a net loss four out of five years between 1995 and 1999. However, after Renault purchased a substantial interest in the company, Nissan's fortunes began to turn, posting a net profit in both fiscal 2000 and fiscal 2001 as well as significantly reducing the company's debt load.

STRATEGY

The three-year Nissan Revival Plan, instituted in 1999, set out three basic promises for change: return to net profitability in fiscal 2000; achieve a minimum operating income to sales margin of 4.5 percent by fiscal year 2002; and reduce consolidated net automotive debt to less than ¥700 billion by fiscal year 2002. Upon enacted of the plan, the company's executive company guaranteed fulfillment of all three goals by the specified date, or they promised to resign. To drastically reduce operating costs, Nissan made significant reductions in jobs. Managers were also instructed to request that suppliers reduce their prices by 20 percent over a three-year period or face losing Nissan's business. In tandem with cost-cutting measures, Nissan began moving toward a goal of introducing 22 new models to its global markets.

Reducing its overhead and expanding its product line is the major focus of the company's reorganization. Within the context of completing those tasks, Nissan is also pushing to enhance the Nissan image, increase efficiency at all facilities, and develop and implement new technologies that make the company's vehicles more attractive to consumers by providing convenience and safety as well as being ecologically sound. With completion of the Nissan Revival Plan well underway, the company planned its strategy for the years beyond 2003. The three areas of focus are growth, profitability, and debt reduction. The post-Revival plan calls for production of units to grow by 1 million by 2005, fueled by the planned addition of 22 new models by the same year. Sustained profitability is vital to the company's long-term financial health, which will be based on increased volume, quality vehicle selection, competitive pricing, and a cooperative economy. Finally, Nissan plans to eliminate its debt by 2005.

INFLUENCED

The most substantial influence on Nissan's financial position is the general state of the world economy. As a global player in a heavily competitive market, Nissan's profit margin is affected by upswings and downturns of national and regional economies. Unfortunately for Nissan, its own economic homeland of Japan has suffered a long period of recession. With no end in sight for the foreseeable future, decreased car sales in Japan continues to adversely affect Nissan. As the United States emerges from a recessive economy there is hope that it will be the bright spot for improving sales figures. Another factor, also uncontrollable, that directly affects Nissan's business is the exchange rate. In the first few months of 2002, the value of the yen dropped to ¥135 per dollar. However, a weak yen is a double-edged sword. Although a weak yen provides an exchange rate that translates into increased profits for Nissan, the situation also points to the continuing weakness of the Japanese economy.

CURRENT TRENDS

Even accounting for Nissan's no-less-than-spectacular recovery, in its home market it continues to lag well behind the results it posted during its peak in the 1970s, at which time it commanded more than 33 percent of the Japanese car business, compared to 18 percent in 2000. With U.S. sales accounting for approximately three quarters of Nissan's revenues in fiscal 2001, the company continues to work to expand and strengthen both its domestic and U.S. market shares.

Nissan launched seven new models in Japan in 2002. Three new models were aimed at first times buyers: the Moco, representing the company's entrance into the minicar market; the March, a new compact; and a remodeled version of the compact Cube. Nissan, who is getting into the minicar sector late, behind by Honda and Toyota, received a positive response to the introduction of the March in Japan, where minicars and subcompacts are hot sellers. Within three weeks of its launch on March 5, 2002, Nissan sold 40,000 March models, and monthly sales are targeted at 8,000 units.

PRODUCTS

Nissan produces numerous models within various product lines under a variety of names depending on the market. Sedans include Sunny (Sentra), Cima (Infiniti

Nissan's gallery show-room building towers prominently above downtown Tokyo.

(AP Photo/Shizuo Kambayashi)

Q45) Cefiro (Maxima QX), Primera, March, and Cedric. The sporty line includes Skyline GT-R, Skyline, and Silvia. Trucks, SUVs, and minivans include Datsun (Frontier), Terrano (Pathfinders), Quest, and X-TRAIL. The top five sellers in Japan in 2000 were the Cuba, Serena, March, Sunny, and AD Van. In North America top sellers in 2000 were the Ultima, Maxima, Sentra, Frontier, and Xterra. Top sellers in the European market in 2000 were the Micra, Almera N16, Primera, Almera N15, and the D22 pickup.

With 22 new models promised by 2005, consumers can expect to see Nissan's product list change substantially.

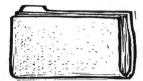

ON THE CUTTING EDGE

Nissan is on the cutting edge of advanced technology in automobile design and equipment. For example, the Nissan Cima (marketed as the Infiniti Q45 outside Japan) introduced the world's first lane-keeper technology. The lane-keeper system helps a driver stay in the correct lane under normal driving operation. The system also assists the driver in keeping the car running true on a stretch of highway where direction may be influenced by such factors as banking or crosswinds. The X-TRAIL, Nissan's new SUV introduced to the Japanese market with success, offers advancement in the four-wheel drive system. The vehicle operates under normal driving conditions as front-wheel drive, thereby reducing fuel consumption compared to the standard rear-wheel four-by-fours. When roads become rough or slick, the electronic sensor equipment automatically shifts the vehicle into four-wheel drive.

On April 10, 2002, the company introduced its newest minicar, the Moco, named after the Japanese "mokomoko," an expression of a warm and cute feeling. Scheduled to arrive on the North American market in 2003 are three new models: the 350Z, a remake of the classic 1970s sports car; the Frontier Open Sky, which offers a convertible feature to the SUV; and the Murano, a stylist hybrid car/SUV built for the urban driver.

GLOBAL PRESENCE

Nissan is headquartered in Japan with North American and European regional offices located in the United States and The Netherlands respectively. Seven domestic manufacturing plants operate in Japan, of which four assemble vehicles, and three produce engines and other major components. In North America, Nissan has an operational presence in the United States and Mexico including production and research, design, development, and testing facilities. In Europe production facilities are located in the United Kingdom and Spain. The United Kingdom and Germany are home to design and technical centers. In Asia Thailand and Taiwan are home to production facilities, with assembly plants located in China, the Philippines, Malaysia, and Indonesia. African assembly facilities are located in Egypt, Kenya, and Zimbabwe, and a production plant operates in South Africa.

Nissan's Middle Eastern presence includes two assembly plants in Iran. The company maintains consumer finance operations in Japan, the United States, and Canada.

Nissans markets its vehicles in approximately 140 countries around the world. Of the 2.65 million units sold in 2000, Japan accounted for the sales of 861,411; the United States and Canada accounted for 662,501; and Europe accounted for 548,292. The remaining units were sold in other regions. Of the total production of 2.65 million units, 1.53 million were produced in Japan; over 279,000 were produced in the United States; more than 276,000 were produced in the United Kingdom.

CORPORATE CITIZENSHIP

As a global citizen, Nissan works continually to develop and improve its products and manufacturing process to be as ecologically friendly as possible. Nissan was the first automobile manufacturer to install systems to recycle chlorofluorocarbons and hydrofluorocarbons at all its U.S. dealerships and was one of the first in the industry to stop using these harmful substances. The company has been honored by the U.S. Environmental Protection Agency twice, receiving the "Best of the Best" award for efforts to protect the ozone layer as well as the 1999 Climate Protection Award. Goals of the Nissan research and development team include creating a zero-emissions vehicle and developing a viable fuel cell system by which a vehicle could function on electrical power. Nissan also supports programs that encourage used vehicle recycling. To focus its community involvement, Nissan set out three basic priorities: fostering the imagination of children, nurturing creativity with respect for diversity and promoting a better understanding of environmental protection. To that end, the company sponsors and supports a wide array of nonprofit organizations.

SOURCES OF INFORMATION

Bibliography

Burt, Tim. "Nissan Motor Plans Design Centre in London." *The Financial Times,* 1 March 2002.

Ibison, David, and Tim Burt. "Renault's Nissan Deal Begins to Come Up Trumps." *The Financial Times,* 17 October 2001.

"Infiniti Vehicles Receive Telematics Technology." Company Press Release, 29 March 2002. Available at http://www.nissan-global.com.

Kepos, Paula, ed. *International Directory of Company Histories.* Vol. 11. Detroit: St. James Press, 1995.

"Nissan Announces 187 Billion Yen Record Half-Year Operating Profit." Company Press Release, 18 October 2001. Available at http://www.nissan-global.com.

Nissan Motor Company Ltd. Global Home Page, 2002. Available at http://www.nissan-global.com.

"Nissan: Saying Sayonara. It's Closing Plants and Cutting Jobs at Home—And Facing Little Protest." *BusinessWeek Online,* 24 September 2001.

Uniworld Business Publications Inc. *Directory of Foreign Firms Operating in the United States*. New York: Author, 2000.

For an annual report:

on the Internet at: http://www.Nissan-global.com

For additional industry research:

Investigate companies by their Standard Industrial Classification Codes, also known as SICs. Nissan Motor Company Ltd.'s primary SICs are:

3537 Industrial Trucks And Tractors

3711 Motor Vehicles And Car Bodies

3713 Truck And Bus Bodies

3714 Motor Vehicle Parts And Accessories

6719 Holding Companies, Not Elsewhere Classified

Also investigate companies by their North American Industry Classification System codes, also known as NAICS codes. Nissan Motor Company Ltd.'s primary NAICS codes are:

327211 Flat Glass Manufacturing

333924 Industrial Truck, Tractor, Trailer and Stacker Machinery Manufacturing

336111 Automobile Manufacturing

336211 Motor Vehicle Body Manufacturing

336399 All Other Motor Vehicle Parts Manufacturing

522298 All Other Non-Depository Credit Intermediation

Nokia Corporation

FOUNDED: 1865

Contact Information:
HEADQUARTERS: Keilalahdentie 4
    Espoo, FIN-00045 Finland
PHONE: (358)7180-08000
FAX: (358)7180-38226
URL: http://www.nokia.com

OVERVIEW

One of the largest industrial enterprises in Scandinavia, Nokia, headquartered in Finland, is a world leader in the mobile communications business. In 2001 the company enjoyed worldwide sales of $27.8 billion, down about $900 million from the previous year. Structurally Nokia is broken into three main operational components: Nokia Networks, Nokia Mobile Phones, and Nokia Ventures Organization.

Nokia Networks, responsible for about 24 percent of the corporation's total 2001 revenue, supplies mobile, fixed broadband, and IP network infrastructure and related services. Nokia Mobile Phones is the world's largest manufacturer of mobile phones. Accounting for 74 percent of Nokia's total revenue in 2001, the mobile phones division offers a broad range of products covering all consumer segments and cellular protocols. Nokia Ventures is ever vigilant for new business opportunities for Nokia, based on technological developments. This division generated approximately 2 percent of the corporation's total revenue in 2001.

In the spring of 2002, Nokia was closing in on its goal of a 40 percent market share, this despite the pressures of a global economic slump. Although it's only a matter of time before Chairman Jorma Ollila's market share goal is reached, most observers doubt that the Finnish-based company will ever be able to get much beyond that point, largely because cell phone service operators are hesitant to let any single handset maker become too dominant. Some have suggested that carriers may push phones from rival manufacturers to keep Nokia from capturing an even larger share of the market.

COMPANY FINANCES

Despite intense competition within the telecommunications market, Nokia managed to turn in a very creditable performance in 2001. Because of the strong U.S. dollar, Nokia's 2001 financial performance looked even better when expressed in terms of Euros. For 2001 as a whole, the company posted a profit of almost $2 billion on revenue of $27.8 billion. This was down from 2000's net income of $3.7 billion on sales of $28.6 billion, but surprisingly good considering the inhospitable economic climate of 2001. In 1999 Nokia posted a profit of $2.6 billion on revenue of almost $20 billion.

In his assessment of the company's 2001 performance, Nokia Chairman and CEO Jorma Ollila said: "The year was characterized by intense competition, extreme volatility, and a weakened global economy. Even in this environment, with our strong and focused team, we increased sales, sustained solid profitability, and achieved extraordinarily strong operating cash flow. . . .As we enter 2002, our strategic position is better than ever backed by a very strong brand, product range, and operational ability."

Although the global economy remained sluggish and the telecommunications sector continued to experience weakness in early 2002, Nokia executives were heartened by the company's first quarter showing. According to Chairman Ollila, "the company put in a solid overall performance for the first quarter 2002, with mobile phone profitability exceeding all expectations. The strong bottom line in our mobile handset business continues to be driven by Nokia's global leadership. Based on Nokia's preliminary research for the first quarter 2002, we believe we have at least maintained our estimated 37 percent share of the overall mobile phone market, in line with our long-term 40 percent share target."

The new millennium has not been particularly kind to the stocks of most telecommunications companies. As of early May 2002, Nokia's stock was down 74 percent from its peak in June 2000. However, this was a better stock performance than that of most of Nokia's competitors. The Finnish company's price-earnings ratio of 40 has kept investors interested.

ANALYSTS' OPINIONS

Security analysts were generally positively impressed by Nokia's announced plans to introduce 20 new mobile phone models during the first half of 2002. Of Nokia's strategy, analysts at Strategy Analytics said: "Nokia is attempting to battle brand fatigue with innovation." To tap more heavily into the high-end of the mobile phone market, Nokia in January 2002 announced plans to offer a new range of hand-crafted telephones, some of which will be adorned by precious and semiprecious gemstones. To handle these new high-end mod-

FAST FACTS:
About Nokia Corporation

Ownership: Nokia Corporation is a publicly owned company traded on the New York Stock Exchange.

Ticker Symbol: NOK

Officers: Jorma Ollila, Chmn. and CEO, 52; Pekka Ala-Pietila, Pres., 45; Olli-Pekka Kallasvuo, EVP and CFO, 49

Employees: 53,849

Principal Subsidiary Companies: Nokia Corporation's major subsidiaries include Nokia Ventures and Symbian Ltd. Nokia Ventures, headquartered in Menlo Park, California, is on the lookout for new business opportunities for Nokia as a whole. Symbian Ltd., based in London, is a joint venture with Psion, Motorola, Sony Ericsson, Siemens, and Matsushita Communications Industrial. The company markets an operating system for hand-held devices.

Chief Competitors: The world's leading manufacturer of mobile phones, Nokia also supplies mobile, fixed, and Internet protocol (IP) networks and related services and multimedia terminals. Its major competitors in the mobile phone market are Ericsson, Motorola, Samsung, and Siemens. In the networks market, Nokia faces competition from Alcatel, Ericsson, Motorola, Nortel, and Siemens.

els, the company launched a new subsidiary called Vertu. Ben Wood, senior mobile communications analyst at Gartner, observed: "It is a way for Nokia to differentiate its product range further as part of its ongoing brand strategy. People are willing to pay a premium for this, just like they are for exclusive watches."

Analysts were also positively impressed with Nokia's decision to go head to head with computer software giant Microsoft in a battle for the market for software for mobile telephones. As mobile phones rapidly turn from mere instruments of convenient communication into miniature computers with a multitude of capabilities, the need for more sophisticated operating systems and software becomes apparent. To tackle this emerging market, Nokia in 2001 set up its own mobile software unit. "Nokia's strong point is their ability to evolve," said Len Morris, a communications technology consultant with the Accenture Group.

CHRONOLOGY:

Key Dates for Nokia Corporation

1865: Nokia Co., a wood pulp maker, is founded

1967: Nokia Co. merges with Finnish Rubber Works and Finnish Cable Works to form Nokia Corporation

1982: Nokia introduces first fully digital local telephone exchange in Europe

1984: Nokia introduces car phone for Nordic Mobile Telephone analog standard

2001: Nokia acquires Ramp Networks and Amber Networks, both of the United States

HISTORY

Although it's now the world's leading mobile phone manufacturer, Nokia began nearly 140 years ago as a pulp and paper maker. Founded in 1865 in the small central Finnish town for which it is named, Nokia pioneered many innovations in paper production and even constructed its own power plants. It was not until after World War II that the company began to make its presence known outside Scandinavia. As Finland and its Scandinavian neighbors began to trade more extensively with other western countries, Nokia became a major exporter.

In the 1960s Nokia moved to strengthen its economic base through diversification. Seeing little opportunity for such expansion within Finland, the company began to look outside for possible acquisitions. However, the Finnish government encouraged Nokia to merge with a couple of under performing Finnish companies. Bowing to government pressure, Nokia merged in 1967 with Finnish Rubber Works, a Finnish producers of tires, rubber boots, and other rubber products for both the consumer and industrial markets, and Finnish Cable Works, a manufacturer of cable for power transmission and telephone and telegraph networks, to form Nokia Corporation. Through this merger, Nokia entered the telecommunications market. In 1960 Finnish Cable Works had set up an electronics department to focus on the production of radio transmission equipment. Products developed by this electronics department included a radio telephone and cable modems, long before the general public had even heard of such products.

Nokia's management, which early on had identified the potential for telecommunications and personal electronics, in the early 1980s moved to strengthen its position in these markets, both through the creation of new divisions and the acquisition of outside companies in these businesses. The company in 1982 introduced Europe's first fully digital local telephone exchange and in 1984 offered a car telephone to operate on the Nordic mobile telephone analog standard. Three years later, in 1987, Nokia purchased the consumer electronics business and part of the components business of Germany's Standard Elektrik Lorenz and the French consumer electronics company, Oceanic. By the end of the decade, Nokia had become the largest information technology company in Scandinavia through its purchase of Ericsson's information systems division in 1988.

The early 1990s brought a strategic decision by Nokia's management to concentrate on telecommunications as its core business. Once this decision had been made, the company began to divest its basic industry and non-telecommunications businesses. The company's rise to prominence in its chosen business has been substantially aided by Finland's competitive business climate and the emphasis on innovation. Technological advancements have also played a significant role in Nokia's success. The development in the mid-1980s of the Global System for Mobile communication (GSM) provided a technology that allowed the transmission of data as well as high-quality voice communications. In 1987 European countries resolved to adopt GSM as the continent's digital standard by July 1, 1991. Finland met the deadline, and the first GSM call was placed over the Nokia-built network of Radiolinja using a Nokia mobile phone.

In 2001 Nokia made two strategic acquisitions. The company purchased Ramp Networks, a U.S.-based provider of purpose-built Internet security appliances designed for small office applications. Also acquired was Amber Networks, also based in the United States. Amber, the first to develop a fault-tolerant routing platform, was integrated with Nokia Networks' network platforms business division.

STRATEGY

The primary objective of Nokia's business strategy is to strengthen the company's position as a leading provider of systems and products. In its 2001 annual report, Nokia said its "strategic intent, as the trusted brand, is to create personalized communication technology that enables people to shape their own mobile world. We innovate technology to allow people to access Internet applications, devices, and services instantly, irrespective of time and place. Achieving interoperability of network environments, terminals, and mobile services is a key part of our objective."

A bird's eye view of the Nokia headquarters, which looks out on an icebound inlet of the Baltic Sea in Keilaniemi, Espoo, Finland. (AP Photo/Markku Ulander)

Key elements in Nokia's strategy include "being the preferred provider of products and solutions for mobile communications; creating personalized communication technology; driving open mobile architecture, enabling a non-fragmented global mobile services market; strengthening and leveraging Nokia, the trusted brand; and expanding our business and market position on a global basis," according to the company's 2001 annual report.

INFLUENCES

Nokia in 2001 had to contend with keen competition in its key markets as well as the effects of a global economic slowdown. Some of these influences were clearly being felt in the early months of 2002 as well, although optimism was expressed that prospects for Nokia would improve in the second half of the year. After several years of rapid growth, the mobile phone industry in 2001 appeared to be undergoing a technology transition, resulting in lower sales volumes worldwide and a decrease in capital spending by service operators. For the year, the total cellular network market decelerated and was down slightly from the previous year; the GSM market remained flat. This reflected some fundamental changes under way at telecommunications networks, which are converting from circuit-switched to packet-switched IP connectivity and from single-purpose net-

works supporting mainly voice transmissions to multi-service networks facilitating a variety of voice and non-voice applications and interactions.

Even more ominous for Nokia, the mobile phone market in 2001 experienced an unprecedented slowdown in growth. Factors behind the slowdown included a technology transition, related to the same transition being experienced in the cellular network market, and challenging economic conditions. Both of these factors were reflected in a depressed replacement market and lower sales volumes. The size of the mobile phone market, for obvious reasons, is closely tied to the number of cellular subscribers worldwide. Nokia estimated the global mobile phone subscriber base at about 930 million as of the end of 2001. This figure was expected to top 1 billion by the middle of 2002 and to reach 1.5 billion sometime in 2005.

CURRENT TRENDS

Undoubtedly the most significant trend in 2001 was a transition in mobile communications technology that depressed both the mobile phone and mobile communications network markets. The beginning of 2002 witnessed the beginning of third generation (3G) wireless. This newest stage in wireless technology is expected to reach its maturity sometime between 2003 and 2005. The

NOKIA TO DEVELOP MOBILE SOFTWARE

Now that Nokia is king of the mountain in the mobile phone business, it has no intention of turning a blind eye to Microsoft Corporation's attempts to capture the lead in the emerging field of wireless software. The Finnish-based mobile phone giant has set up its own mobile software unit to develop operating systems and other software for mobile phones that are rapidly being transformed from convenient communications devices into multi-capable mini-computers. Nokia's new software unit, headed by Niklas Savander, is being staffed with some 1,600 employees, and Nokia also ramped up its research and development budget in 2001 by 16 percent to $2.6 billion. As early as 1995, Nokia Chairman Jorma Ollila presaged the current developments when he told the Associated Press: "We aren't far off from a palmtop that can store information, receive TV pictures, and can also be used as a telephone."

prospects for sales of 3G mobile devices will depend to a large extent on the timely and successful build-out of 3G networks and the development of related services.

Features and capabilities of 3G mobile devices will ultimately include enhanced multimedia (voice, data, video, and remote control); usability on all popular modes, including cellular telephone, e-mail, paging, fax, Web browsing, and videoconferencing; broad bandwidth and high speed (upwards of 2 Mbps); routing flexibility; operation at transmit and receive frequencies of approximately 2 GHz; and roaming capability throughout Europe, Japan, and North America.

PRODUCTS

Nokia markets two main categories of products: mobile phones, handled by the company's Nokia Mobile Phones division, and communications networks, for which Nokia Networks division is responsible. A more recent addition to the company's product line is software for mobile devices.

The product matrix of Nokia Mobile Phones has six style dimensions (basic, expression, active, classic, fashion, and premium) and five functional dimensions (voice, entertainment, media, imaging, and business applica-

tions). The matrix helps Nokia's product developers to identify potential new products in each cross-section of the two dimensions. By combining each of the styles with each of the functionalities, the company is better able to address specific user needs.

Nokia Networks supplies mobile, fixed broadband, and Internet protocol (IP) network infrastructure and related services. In the fall of 2001, Nokia Networks began the rollout of third generation (3G) wireless network coverage.

CORPORATE CITIZENSHIP

In the realm of corporate responsibility, Nokia is an active participant in a number of international initiatives, including the International Youth Foundation, World Business Council for Sustainable Development, United Nations ICT Task Force, Global Compact, and the World Wildlife Fund.

GLOBAL PRESENCE

Nokia products—both mobile phones and mobile communications networks and services—are marketed worldwide. As of December 31, 2001, the company operated a number of manufacturing facilities in nine countries around the world. Seven of those production plants were operated by the Nokia Networks division. Of those, four were located in Finland and three were in China. The Nokia Mobile Phones division operated nine manufacturing plants in eight countries: Brazil, China, Finland, Germany, Hungary, Mexico, South Korea, and the United States.

EMPLOYMENT

At the end of 2001, Nokia Corporation had on its payrolls 53,849 employees worldwide. Recognizing the importance of its employees to the company's business success, Nokia has instituted the "Nokia Way," a philosophy of attracting and retaining the best personnel and ensuring continuous renewal. The company seeks to instill in each of its employees a set of four core values—customer satisfaction, respect for the individual, achievement, and continuous learning—that it believes are essential for an international corporation such as Nokia to operate efficiently. Management also seeks to cultivate in Nokia's employees an attitude of trust, responsibility, and open-mindedness that allows them "to build teams of independent entrepreneurs that are permitted to take chances and even make occasional mistakes. The result is a culture in which decisions can be, and are, made quickly, and employees are energized and driven by a desire to win. We believe that this type of corporate culture is essential for us to prevail in the rapidly changing mobile communications industry."

SOURCES OF INFORMATION

Bibliography
de Bendern, Paul. "Nokia Targets Rich with Luxury Mobile Phone Range." *Reuters*, 11 January 2002.

Gamel, Kim. "For Cell Phone King, Challenge Turns to Mobile Software." *AP Worldstream*, 12 March 2002.

"GPRS: Flop or Kingdom Come for Sluggish Telecom Sector?" *Agence France Presse*, 9 May 2002.

"Nokia Corp.—History." *Gale Business Resources*, 2002. Available at http://galenet.galegroup.com/servlet/GBR.

"Nokia Corporation." *Hoover's Online*, 2002. Available at http://www.hoovers.com.

Nokia Corporation 2001 Annual Report. Espoo, Finland: Nokia Corporation, 2002.

Nokia Corporation Home Page, 2002. Available at http://www.nokia.com.

"Nokia Losing Market Share to Cell Phone Rivals, Study Says." *Toronto Star*, 17 May 2002.

Reinhardt, Andy. "European Business: Finland: Has Nokia Run Out of Rocket Fuel?" *Business Week International*, 6 May 2002.

"Snapshot Report: Nokia Corporation." *Multex Investor*, 2002. Available at http://www.marketguide.com.

For an annual report:
on the Internet at: http://www.nokia.com/aboutnokia/downloads/index.html.

For additional industry research:
Investigate companies by their Standard Industrial Classification Codes, also known as SICs. Nokia Corporation's primary SICs are:

3679 Electronic Components, NEC

4812 Radiotelephone Communications

4813 Telephone Communications Except Radiotelephone

Also investigate companies by their North American Industrial Classification System codes, also known as NAICS codes. Nokia Corporation's primary NAICS codes are:

334419 Other Electronic Component Manufacturing

513322 Cellular and Other Wireless Telecommunications

Oracle Corporation

FOUNDED: 1977

Contact Information:

HEADQUARTERS: 500 Oracle Pkwy
   Redwood Shores, CA 94065
PHONE: (650)506-7000
FAX: (650)506-7200
TOLL FREE: (800)672-2531
EMAIL: investor@us.oracle.com
URL: http://www.oracle.com

OVERVIEW

Founded in 1977 by computer programmers Lawrence J. Ellison and Robert N. Miner, Oracle Corporation is today the world's largest supplier of information management software and the second largest independent software company in the world, second only to Microsoft Corporation. With revenue of nearly $10.9 billion in fiscal 2001, the company has expanded beyond its original database products into a variety of business applications and online services, including human resource and supply chain management applications.

Headquartered in Redwood City, California, Oracle was established by founders Ellison and Miner to take commercialize the technology for a relational database, the company's core product. That technology, as well as new Oracle applications developed in the years since its founding, can be found in nearly every industry around the world today. Of the Fortune 100 companies, 98 use Oracle software in their everyday operations. The company was the first software company to develop and market 100 percent Internet-enabled enterprise software across its entire product line.

For aspiring computer technology entrepreneurs, colorful Oracle Chairman and CEO Ellison has few words of encouragement. In an interview with the *Financial Times* in mid-December 2001, he offered this advice: "Get out of the tech business. It's too late. There won't be any more big companies. Our business in on its way to being like the car business; it's going through a massive consolidation. There is this fantasy that the computer industry will always be young. I think that's ridiculous. Companies have been disappearing at a very high rate; there's a very high level of extinction. You may have a cool piece of technology like a new chip design or a cute little switch. But the days of building a giant new tech company are over. Try to build a giant new auto company. We're going into a much more mature industry. Every industry matures. Is the technology industry unique; will it ever mature? Sure, it will mature. The railroads were like this; the oil industry was like this."

COMPANY FINANCES

Fiscal 2001 (ended May 31, 2001) saw a significant slowdown in revenue growth for Oracle. Against a backdrop of worldwide economic recession, the company posted an increase in sales of 7.2 percent, up to almost $10.9 billion from just over $10.1 billion in fiscal 2001. Revenue in fiscal 2000 had jumped to $10.1 billion from $8.8 billion in fiscal 1999, an increase of about 14.8 percent. Even more alarmingly, Oracle's profit in fiscal 2001 dropped to about $2.6 billion, down sharply from almost $6.3 billion in fiscal 2001. Net income in fiscal 1999 was $1.3 billion. Despite their disappointment with fiscal 2001's performance, company executives expressed optimism that the worst was over. Jeff Henley, Oracle's chief financial officer, said: "Hopefully we hit the bottom in our fiscal fourth quarter." Chairman Ellison also expressed cautious optimism. "Barring any further decline in the economy, we think our sales will pick up. . . .We're cautiously optimistic that we might beat those numbers."

A recovery in sales and profit proved elusive, however. Oracle's revenue for the third quarter of fiscal 2002, ended February 28, 2002, slipped to $2.23 billion, down 17 percent from the $2.7 billion reported in the same quarter of fiscal 2001. The company's net income for the quarter was down to $507.9 million from $582.7 million the previous year. Perhaps the most alarming development from the quarter was a drop of 30 percent in the company's sales of software licenses, the sharpest decline during four consecutive quarters of falling software sales. Oracle's management blamed the slowdown almost exclusively on a worldwide recession that prompted businesses around to cut back their spending on software and other technology.

ANALYSTS' OPINIONS

Despite some misgivings about Oracle's financial rough patch in fiscal 2001 and 2002, most security analysts remained essentially bullish on the company. The consensus of analysts in early June 2002 was positive, with five of 35 analysts rating Oracle stock a Strong Buy, 15 rating it Buy, and another 15 advising investors to "hold" the stock. As to its more immediate problems, analysts did express concern about Oracle's precipitous decline in software licensing sales during the third quar-

FAST FACTS:
About Oracle Corporation

Ownership: Oracle Corporation is a publicly-owned company traded on the NASDAQ Stock Exchange.

Ticker Symbol: ORCL

Officers: Lawrence J. Ellison, Chmn. and CEO, 58; Jeffrey O. Henley, EVP and CFO, 57, 2001 base salary $825,000

Employees: 42,927

Principal Subsidiary Companies: Oracle operates a network of more than 60 foreign subsidiaries to market its products outside the United States. The subsidiaries license and support Oracle's products in their local countries as well as in neighboring countries in which the company has no direct sales subsidiary. The company's foreign subsidiaries are based in more than two dozen countries worldwide. In addition to its foreign sales subsidiaries, Oracle operates a number of U.S.-based subsidiaries. Three of the more prominent of these domestic subsidiaries include Liberate Technologies, New Internet Computer Company, and OracleMobile.com.

Chief Competitors: Competition for the consumer's computer software business is extremely intense. Oracle competes in a number of specific markets within the computer software business, including the database, business applications and services, and application development tools sectors. The company's principal competitors in the enterprise database management system (DBMS) market are IBM and Sybase Inc. In the work group and personal DBMS market, the company competes with a number of desktop software vendors, including Microsoft Corporation. In the ERP (enterprise resource planning) business applications software market, Oracle competes with J.D. Edwards, PeopleSoft Inc., and SAP Aktiengesellschaft.

ter of fiscal 2002. Since it was in the same quarter of fiscal 2001 that the company's softening sales first became evident, the fiscal 2002 quarter should have been "a layup, and they missed the lay-up, so everyone is really surprised," said Mark Verback, an analyst with Think Equity Partners.

Oracle executives have insisted that the company's slowdown in sales was almost entirely attributable to the

CHRONOLOGY:

Key Dates for Oracle Corporation

1977: Programmers Lawrence Ellison and Robert Miner found Oracle Corporation

1979: Oracle markets first relational database management system

1982: Oracle begins marketing its software abroad

1985: Oracle's annual revenue tops $23 million

1987: Oracle's sales top $100-million mark

1988: Oracle introduces first family of CASE application development tools

1990: 12 stockholders sue Oracle, charging forecasts were false and misleading

1991: Oracle's annual revenue tops $1-billion mark

1998: Oracle launches Business Online

1999: Oracle integrates Java and XML in an application development tool

worldwide economic recession. Most analysts agreed that the recession was a significant factor but suggested that the company had created some of its own problems. Particularly damning was this observation from analyst Robert Austrian of Bank of America Securities: "About 80 percent of Oracle's problems are from self-inflicted wounds, and 20 percent are from the economy."

The spring of 2002 brought persistent reports that Oracle had lost its lead in total database sales to IBM, which bought Infomix in 2001. According to reports from Dataquest, IBM's revenue from database sales grew to $3.06 billion in 2001, compared with sales of $2.83 billion for Oracle. Dataquest analyst Betsy Burton said she believed that IBM had edged ahead of Oracle on the strength of its purchase of Infomix. "They bought market share." Oracle CFO Jeff Henley cautioned analysts against jumping to conclusions on the basis of limited data. "You can't take a one-year snapshot and say Oracle is losing share," he said.

HISTORY

Oracle Corporation was born in 1977 when computer programmers Lawrence J. Ellison and Robert N.

Miner pooled their $1,500 savings to rent office space in Belmont, California, and start a company dedicated to the development and marketing of database management systems (DBMS) software. The fledgling company's first big contract called for the development of a special database program for the Central Intelligence Agency. While researching the CIA project, Ellison began looking at some of IBM's work on relational databases, which in theory would allow computer users to retrieve corporate data from virtually any form. IBM had developed a computer language called Structured Query Language (SQL) that would tell a relational database what data to retrieve and how to display it. Ellison and Miner then set out to develop an SQL relational database software program for use on Digital minicomputers and other hardware. Oracle's first relational database management system (RDBMS) was first marketed in 1979, two years after IBM debuted its first RDBMS program. Oracle quickly became profitable. By 1984 the company posted annual sales of almost $2.5 million. Encouraged by its success domestically, the company began reaching out beyond to markets outside the United States. Its first foreign subsidiary, Oracle Denmark, was opened in 1982.

Competition in the market for DBMS software began intensifying in the early 1980s, but Oracle managed to keep its edge on the strength of its reputation for innovation and its aggressive advertising style. By 1985 the company's annual sales had climbed to more than $23 million. The following year saw an even more impressive upsurge in revenue, as sales climbed to $55.4 million. That same year, the company made its initial public offering of stock. Never one to shy away from self-promotion, Ellison later that year publicly touted Oracle as the fastest growing software company in the world, citing its record of revenue growth of 100 percent or more in eight of its first nine years. By the end of 1986, the company's customer base had swelled to some 2,000 mainframe and minicomputer users in a wide range of industries, including aerospace, automotive, pharmaceutical, and computer manufacturing, as well as a number of government agencies. Also, by the end of 1986 Oracle's network of foreign sales subsidiaries had grown to 17, marketing the company's products in 39 countries.

Largely on the strength of Oracle's selection to supply the relational DBMS software for most major computer manufacturers, the company in 1987 topped the $100-million mark in revenue and officially became the world largest database management software company. As more and more software companies used Oracle products as a platform for their applications, the company in 1987 established its VAR (Value-Added Reseller) Alliance program, designed to build cooperative selling and product-planning alliances with other software producers. The following year Oracle introduced a line of accounting programs for corporate bookkeeping and its first family of computer-aided systems engineering (CASE) application development tools.

Oracle employees gather around a lake at company headquarters in Redwood City, California, as part of the national day of remembrance for those lost in the September 11th terrorist attacks. (AP Photo/Paul Sakuma)

When Oracle announced a sharp jump in earnings but essentially flat net income for the third quarter of fiscal 1990, Wall Street analysts turned cool to its former darling. Shortly thereafter, a handful of Oracle's shareholders sued the company, charging that it had made false and misleading forecasts of its earnings. Matters were exacerbated a couple of months later when Oracle announced record revenue of $970.8 million but a profit of only $117.4 million, below the company's own estimates. Later that year Oracle reported its first-ever quarterly loss, and the company's stock plummeted to $6.25 a share, bringing the six-month loss in the stock's market value to more than $2.7 billion. By the end of fiscal 1992, Oracle's earnings had begun to rebound. Only two years later, the company's annual sales had topped the $2-billion mark. By 1997, annual sales had skyrocketed to $5.7 billion. Continuing its long record of innovation, Oracle in 1998 launched Business Online, the first hosting service for enterprise applications to be run over the Internet, and offered full Web deployment of all its applications. The following year Oracle became the first software company to integrate Java and XML (Extensible Markup Language) into an application development tool. For fiscal 1999, the company posted a profit of nearly $1.3 billion on revenue of $8.8 billion.

In fiscal 2000, ending May 31, 2000, Oracle's revenue soared 14.8 percent to more than $10.1 billion, and the company reported a profit of nearly $6.3 billion. The

worldwide economic recession and other factors slowed the company's revenue growth in fiscal 2001, with sales reaching nearly $10.9 billion, but net income was down to $2.56 billion.

STRATEGY

Using Internet technology, Oracle is in the process of transforming itself into an e-business. Its corporate strategy calls for the company to (1) streamline and integrate its entire organization; (2) globalize its business systems; (3) simplify and standardize business practices; (4) implement a complete suite of fully integrated products; (5) base corporate decisions on information that flows continuously from the sell side to the inside to supply and back again; and (6) provide self-service applications to customers and employees.

The rationale for implementing a complete suite of fully integrated products is intended to bring to an end the custom of paying once to buy software, again to have expensive integration consultants to squeeze it into a unique information architecture, and still again to endlessly customize it to accommodate outdated business processes. As for supplying self-service applications to customers and employees, it is hoped that this will lower operating costs and improve accuracy.

Oracle believes the transformation into an e-business allows an organization to make the best possible use of its capital expenditures by permanently reducing operating costs and eliminating complexities from its business processes and infrastructure.

Already, the company's move into the new economy through its transformation to e-business has resulted in an improvement of greater than 10 points in its operating margin. According to an update on its Web site, "every improvement Oracle has made was a result of the same strategy. The company standardized its business processes and moved to the Internet, consolidated all separate databases into a single global database, and unified all separate computer systems using E-Business Suite. Shared information enabled people to communicate more clearly and work together more effectively. Since the organizations were interdependent, groups using those systems become dependent upon one another. Along with that interdependency came cooperation among groups, specialization, and economies of scale. When Oracle globalized its business, operational inefficiencies began to melt away."

INFLUENCES

In the wake of the terrorist attacks on the World Trade Center and Pentagon on September 11, 2001, software customers became increasingly concerned about security and reliability. In an interview with Richard Waters of the *Financial Times* in December 2001, Oracle Chairman Lawrence J. Ellison shared his thoughts about how the shift in consumer sentiment might affect Oracle. "Oracle's tag line used to be 'Oracle: Software powers the Internet.' Now it's 'Oracle: Unbreakable.' Our heritage is in military intelligence, building military systems. They're not allowed to break; they're not allowed to lose data. That's much more important now."

Asked by Waters what he saw beyond the Internet as a method of deploying e-business applications, Ellison said: "Nothing. Nothing. The basic architecture of the telephone network hasn't changed for 100 years. [The basic architecture of the Internet] won't change. We will have wireless connections to the Internet, it will be cheaper, but it will still be the Internet."

CURRENT TRENDS

Many software companies in recent years have marketed "best-of-breed" systems combining the leading software of each type into one system. Scott R. Smith, interviewing Oracle CEO Lawrence J. Ellison for *American Way* magazine, asked how Oracle's business software suites could compete effectively with "best of breed" since some of the individual applications inte-

grated in the Oracle suites were not really the best available. Ellison replied: "People want you to engineer everything to work together. In fact, SAP was the first ERP company that had all the pieces of the back office put together. We're the first to have the back office, the middle office, and the front office put together effectively, automation extending from suppliers through the legal department and contracting to the customer. History has shown that the more complete the suite is, the more successful you become: It trumps 'bastard-breed.' The cycle always begins there, but ultimately the specialist companies die out. That's the way evolution works."

PRODUCTS

Oracle's product lineup is broken into a number of different segments, the core of which is its relational database management system (RDBMS), which in turn is the key component of the company's Internet platform. The RDBMS system enables the storage, manipulation, and retrieval of relational, object-relational, multidimensional, and other types of data. In the spring of 1999, the company introduced Oracle8i, a database specifically designed as the foundation for Internet development and deployment. The Oracle8i database extended Oracle's technology in the areas of data management, transaction processing, and data warehousing. In June 2001, Oracle introduced Oracle9i, which was designed to run any packaged application with unlimited scalability and reliability across multiple computers clustered together.

Another major segment of Oracle's product lineup is the Oracle International Application Server 8i, introduced in June 2000, which in October of that year was joined by Oracle9i Application Server, an open software platform that makes it easier for developers to build Internet Web sites and applications.

Other important products in the Oracle product mix include the Oracle Internet Developer Suite, a complete and integrated suite of development tools for rapidly developing Internet database applications and Web services. The company also offers Oracle E-Business Suite Release 11i, a fully integrated and Internet-enabled set of Customer Relationship Management (CRM) and Enterprise Resource Planning (ERP) software applications for the enterprise. The E-Business Suite is available in more than six platforms and approximately 30 languages.

In addition to its lineup of software applications, Oracle provides a broad range of related services, including consulting, support, education, and online services.

CORPORATE CITIZENSHIP

Oracle clearly recognizes its corporate responsibilities to the communities in which it operates. It seeks to fulfill those responsibilities through programs in the following areas: education, charitable contributions, volunteerism, community partnerships, and diversity and compliance. The company's educational initiatives include the Oracle Help Us Help Foundation, which provides computer equipment to schools and youth organizations that provide educational service in economically challenged communities, and Oracle Academic Initiative, supplying software, curriculum, training, and Oracle certification to colleges and universities. Other educational initiatives include Think.com, a collaborative learning environment provided free of charge to primary and secondary schools; Oracle Internet Academy, which provides technology skills training to high school students; and Oracle Workforce Development Program, which makes software, curriculum, training, and certification available to workforce development communities.

In the realm of charitable contributions, Oracle financially supports the efforts of nonprofit organizations working in the following fields: environmental protection; protection of endangered animals; K-12 math, science and technology education; and medical research. To stimulate volunteerism among its worldwide employees, the company in 1991 established Oracle Volunteers. Its purpose is the formalization of volunteer opportunities for company employees. Oracle Community Partners provides support to local and state agencies; energy, planning, and other commissions; and chambers of commerce. Oracle's Diversity and Compliance program is designed to ensure that the company complies with federal, state, and local regulations and promotes a work environment that values diversity and is inclusive of all employees.

GLOBAL PRESENCE

Oracle is a truly international operation with subsidiaries in some 60 other countries around the world. Most of those subsidiaries operate not only in their local country but also in neighboring countries where Oracle has no foreign marketing subsidiary. Foreign countries and U.S. territories in which Oracle operates include Argentina, Australia, Austria, Barbados, Belgium, Brazil, Canada, Cayman Islands, Chile, Colombia, Costa Rica, Croatia, Czech Republic, Denmark, Ecuador, Egypt, Finland, France, Germany, Greece, Hong Kong, Hungary, India, Indonesia, Ireland, Israel, Italy, Japan, Malaysia, Mexico, the Netherlands, Netherlands Antilles, New Zealand, Norway, Peru, Philippines, Poland, Portugal, Puerto Rico, Saudi Arabia, Singapore, Slovakia, Slovenia, South Africa, South Korea, Spain Sweden, Switzerland, Thailand, Turkey, United Arab Emirates, United Kingdom, U.S. Virgin Islands, Uruguay, Venezuela, and Vietnam.

ELLISON THINKS TOO MUCH SPENT ON IT

Business is spending entirely too much money on information technology, according to Larry Ellison, cofounder and CEO of Oracle Corporation. Interviewed by Richard Waters of the *Financial Times*, Ellison said: "The more money you spend, the worse it gets." He said companies are storing their information in too many different systems "so you've no idea what's going on. Every additional system fragments your data. We believe all of a company's information should be on one database." He added that when a company talks about "investing" in IT, "that's a code word for spending more money. Companies have spent far more money on IT than they should already. IT is way too expensive; it delivers far too little value." He said Oracle would be "happy to go to any of our largest customers and give them all of our software, give them all of our services, and install them for nothing. We will guarantee their IT budget will go down by 5 percent a year. But they have to become an Oracle customer."

EMPLOYMENT

As of May 31, 2001, the end of Oracle's 2001 fiscal year, the company employed a workforce of almost 43,000 people, including 29,422 in sales and services, 1,230 in marketing, 7,926 in research and development, and 4,349 in general and administrative positions. Of these employees, 22,008 were located in the United States, with the remaining 20,919 employed in some 60 other countries.

SOURCES OF INFORMATION

Bibliography

Baertlein, Lisa. "Oracle Edges Past Expectations, Sees Rebound." *Reuters Business Report*, 19 June 2001.

"Business Summary: Oracle Corporation." *Multex Investor*, Available at http://www.marketguide.com.

Liedtke, Michael. "Oracle Reports 13 Percent Drop in Profit, 30 Percent Decline in Software Sales." *AP Worldstream*, 14 March 2002.

"Oracle Corp.—History." *Gale Business Resources*, Available at http://galenet.galegroup.com/servlet/GBR.

"Oracle Corporation." *Hoover's Online*, 2002. Available at http://www.hoovers.com.

Oracle Corporation 2001 Annual Report. Redwood Shores, CA: Oracle Corporation, 2001.

Oracle Corporation Home Page, 2002. Available at http://www.oracle.com.

Pain, Steve. "E-business: Oracle Is Trailing IBM, Say Figures." *Financial Times*, 14 December 2001.

Smith, Scott S. "The Oracle Speaks." *American Way*, 1 May 2002.

Waters, Richard. "Answers from Oracle's Larry Ellison." *Birmingham Post*, 14 May 2002.

For an annual report:

on the Internet at: http://www.oracle.com **or** write: Investor Relations, Oracle Corporation, 500 Oracle Parkway, Redwood Shores, CA 94065

For additional industry research:

Investigate companies by their Standard Industrial Classification Codes, also known as SICs. Oracle Corporation's primary SICs are:

2731 Book Publishing

3571 Electronic Computers

3572 Computer Storage Devices

7371 Computer Programming Services

7372 Prepackaged Software

7379 Computer Related Services, NEC

Also Investigate companies by their North American Industrial Classification System codes. Oracle Corporation's primary NAICS code is:

511210 Software Publishers

Owens Corning

OVERVIEW

Probably best known for its fiber glass (trademarked name Fiberglas) and foam insulation product line, Owens Corning produces a broad range of other construction materials, including everything from vinyl siding and windows to patio doors, roofing materials, and rain gutters. The company is divided into two major operating segments: Building Materials Systems and Composite Solutions. The Building Materials Systems division accounts for about 80 percent of the company annual sales, with the rest generated by Composite Solutions, which produces composite materials used in the electronics, telecommunications, and automotive industries.

Headquartered in Toledo, Ohio, Owens Corning was founded in the 1930s as a joint venture of Owens-Illinois and Corning Glass. The company was originally established to research and manufacture glass fiber, for which both Owens-Illinois and Corning Glass saw great potential as an insulation material. Shortly after its incorporation as Owens-Corning Fiberglas Corporation in 1938, the fledgling company was granted the patent for glass fiber. The company's products are marketed worldwide through its network of subsidiaries and joint licensees in more than 30 countries on six continents.

Owens Corning, in the 1950s, became involved in the asbestos business when it entered into an agreement to distribute Owens-Illinois' Kaylo-brand high-temperature calcium silicate insulation containing asbestos. In the late 1950s Owens Corning bought all Kaylo's assets and began manufacturing the insulation product as well as distributing it. As the dangers of asbestos became better known in the 1970s, Owens Corning removed asbestos from Kaylo but continued to market the product. The

FOUNDED: 1938

Contact Information:

HEADQUARTERS: 1 Owens Corning Pkwy
   Toledo, OH 43659
PHONE: (419)248-8000
FAX: (419)248-5337
TOLL FREE: (800)GET-PINK
EMAIL: investor@owenscorning.com
URL: http://www.owenscorning.com

FAST FACTS:

About Owens Corning

Ownership: Owens Corning is a publicly owned company traded on the New York Stock Exchange.

Ticker Symbol: OWC

Officers: Michael H. Thaman, Chmn. and CFO, 36, 2001 base salary $425,000; David T. Brown, Pres. and CEO, 52, 2001 base salary $400,000

Employees: 19,000

Principal Subsidiary Companies: Oracle operates a number of domestic and foreign subsidiaries. These include Advanced Glassfiber Yarns, LLC; Alcopor Owens Corning AG; Amiantit Fiberglass Industries Ltd. in Saudi Arabia; Arabian Fiberglass Insulation Company Ltd.; Fiberteq LLC; Flowtite Argentina; Flowtite (Botswana) Pty. Ltd.; Flowtite Iberica SA in Spain; Owens Corning Energy LLC; Owens Corning (India) Ltd.; Owens Corning (Nanjing) in China; Owens Corning Yapi Merkezi Boru Sanayi Veticaret A.S. in Turkey; Owens-Corning Eternit Rohre GmbH in Germany; Siam Fiberglass Co. Ltd. in Thailand; Stamax B.V. in the Netherlands; Stamax NA LLC ; and Vitro-Fibras SA in Mexico. Advanced Glassfiber Yarns, headquartered in Aiken, South Carolina, is a leading manufacturer of glass yarns, used in electronic products, automotive equipment, and other industrial applications.

Chief Competitors: The two main operating segments of Owens Corning are Building Materials Systems, which accounts for roughly 80 percent of the company's annual revenue, and Composite Solutions, which generates the remainder of the company's sales. The company's leading competitors include Andersen Corporation, G-I Holdings, and Guardian Industries.

company's involvement in the asbestos business eventually resulted in a billion-dollar asbestos liability for Owens Corning. Struggling under the growing demands of these lawsuits on its cash flow, Owens Corning on October 5, 2000, filed a petition for reorganization under Chapter 11 of the U.S. Bankruptcy Court. The filing enables the company "to refocus on operating its business and serving its customers, while it develops a plan of reorganization that will resolve its asbestos and other liabilities and provide a suitable capital structure for long-term growth."

COMPANY FINANCES

Owens Corning eked out a profit of $39 million in 2001, a significant improvement from its results in 2000 when it reported a net loss of $479 million for the year. The company managed to get back into the black in 2001 despite a slight decline in revenue to $4.76 billion from $4.94 billion in 2000. In 1999 Owens Corning posted a profit of $270 million on revenue of slightly more than $5 billion.

For some years Owens Corning has faced a significant legal liability related to the company's involvement in the asbestos business decades earlier. In late 2000, the company, along with 17 of its subsidiaries, filed for protection from its creditors under Chapter 11 of the U.S. Bankruptcy Code. It was hoped that such protection would enable the company to continue operating its existing businesses and serving its customers while it formulates a plan of reorganization that will resolve its asbestos liability and provide a suitable capital structure for long-term growth.

To further enhance its liquidity, Owens Corning obtained a debtor-in-possession financing commitment of $500 million from the Bank of America shortly before it filed its petition for reorganization. The company hopes to use these funds to help meet its future needs and fulfill obligations related to the operation of its business, including payments under normal terms to suppliers and vendors for all goods and services. The company has confirmed that its pension plan for retirees and vested employees is fully funded and protected by federal law.

Owens Corning narrowed its net loss in the first quarter of 2002, reporting a shortfall of $6 million, compared with a loss of $10 million in the same quarter the previous year. The company's revenue for the first quarter edged up slightly to $1.11 billion from $1.07 billion the previous year.

ANALYSTS' OPINIONS

Much of what security analysts were saying about Owens Corning in late 2001 and the first half of 2002 centered on the substantial asbestos-related claims against the company, which triggered its bankruptcy filing in October 2001. Other companies that previously had been involved in the asbestos business-including Johns Manville-were forced to seek similar relief. At the time Owens Corning filed its petition for reorganization under Chapter 11 of the U.S. Bankruptcy Code, the company said the number of asbestos-related claims against it had risen to 7,800 in the third quarter of 2001, up sharply from 4,200 the previous quarter.

Looking at the rapidly mounting number of asbestos-related lawsuits against U.S. construction and manufacturing companies, analyst Scott Davis of Morgan Stanley said: "I view asbestos as a big black hole. It's a problem for many sectors now, not just the traditional spaces." As of early 2002, U.S. companies had paid about $20 billion in asbestos claims and related costs, according to the Asbestos Alliance, a group of corporate asbestos defendants and their trade associations. Security analysts estimated that the cost of the remaining asbestos liability in January 2002 ranged from $20 billion to as high as $200 billion. And, according to A.M. Best analyst Gerald Altonji, the insurance industry has only about half the money it needs in reserves to cover these long-running asbestos and pollution claims.

The outlook was gloomy for relief through acquisition or merger for companies facing asbestos-related liability, according to Morgan Stanley analyst Davis. "Companies with asbestos liability have effectively been put in the penalty box on M&A," he said.

HISTORY

Owens Corning had its origins in the pioneering work of Owens-Illinois Glass Company and Corning Glass Company into glass fiber technology. Much of the research behind the fiberglass technology for which Owens Corning later became famous was conducted in the early 1930s by Games Slayter, Dale Kleist, and Jack Thomas. Kleist, a young researcher who worked for Thomas, Slayter's research assistant, one day in 1932 was welding architectural glass blocks together to form a vacuum-tight seal when a jet of compressed air accidentally hit a stream of molten glass. The result was the creation of fine glass fibers. Later that same year, the process was refined by using steam rather than compressed air to attenuate glass fibers. The result was a glass fiber material that was thin enough to be used as a commercial fiber glass insulation.

In the mid-1930s Owens-Illinois and Corning Glass struck an agreement for a joint venture operation to share the costs of continuing glass fiber research and development. In 1938 the companies decided it might be better to operate the joint venture as a separate company. That same year the patent for glass fiber was granted to Dale Kleist and Jack Thomas. On November 1, 1938, the formation of Owens-Corning Fiberglas Corporation was announced.

During the first half of the 1940s, Owens Corning partnered with the U.S. military to develop and manufacture products for use in the construction of aircraft and ships, as well as for insulation. In 1949 the company built it first plant designed specifically for the manufacture of insulation. In the 1950s, Owens Corning, in partnership

CHRONOLOGY:
Key Dates for Owens Corning

1938: Owens-Corning Fiberglas Corporation is founded

1944: Owens-Corning develops the first Fiberglas-reinforced plastic boat hull

1949: Owens-Corning opens first plant specially built for production of insulation

1953: Owens-Corning and GM introduce auto body made entirely of Fiberglas-reinforced plastic

1976: Owens-Corning annual sales top $1 billion

1992: Company unveils a new corporate logo

1996: Company formally changes name to Owens Corning

2000: Owens Corning files for reorganization under Chapter 11

with General Motors, announced the first production automobile with a body made entirely of Fiberglas-reinforced plastic, the Chevrolet Corvette. By the end of the 1950s, the company's annual revenues had topped $211 million.

In late 1960 Owens Corning opened its Granville Technical Center in Granville, Ohio, and transferred its research and development operations to the new facility from their previous home in Newark, Ohio. Armstrong Rubber Company in 1966 introduced its Fiberglas-reinforced automobile tire, developed jointly with Owens Corning. The 1970s saw a rapid expansion in Owens Corning's overseas operations as well as a multitude of glass-reinforced plastic innovations. The Pontiac Silverdome, covered by a 10-acre Fiberglas-fiber roof, opened in 1975, and in 1976 Owens Corning topped the $1-billion mark in annual sales. By the end of the decade, annual revenue had climbed to more than $2 billion.

In 1980 Owens Corning adopted the Pink Panther, the lovable United Artists cartoon character, for use in its advertising campaign for PINK Fiberglas insulation. The 1980s saw an extensive expansion of the company's manufacturing facilities around the world. Owens Corning in 1986 rejected a hostile takeover offer from Wickes Companies Inc. As the decade closed, the company's annual revenue had reached $3 billion.

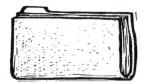

OWENS CORNING FRIENDLY TO THE ENVIRONMENT

Owens Corning took the occasion of Earth Day 2002 to outline what it is doing to help preserve the environment. Some of the company's best-selling products are environmentally friendly—in addition to environmentally friendly manufacturing processes. Some of the "green" products cited by Owens Corning are its insulation products, Strataguard roof boards, and TruPave paving mat. The main raw material in the company's fiber glass insulation products is sand, a renewable resource, and 30 percent of its content comes from recycled materials. Owens Corning's foam insulation products are made of 20 percent recycled content. The company's Strataguard roof boards are composed of 95 percent recycled material, while Owens Corning's metals business manufactures all of its metal trip coil out of 95 percent recycled aluminum.

In January 1992 Glen H. Hiner took over as the new chairman and CEO of Owens Corning and announced that his top three priorities for the company were "customer satisfaction, individual dignity, and shareholder value." In June 1993 the company unveiled PINKPLUS, a new polyethylene encapsulated glass fiber insulation product for the residential market. In early 1996 the company officially changed its name from Owens-Corning Fiberglas Corporation to Owens Corning.

In the late 1990s and the beginning of the twenty-first century, Owens Corning was inundated with liability claims related to the company's involvement in the asbestos business decades earlier. On October 5, 2000, the company filed a petition for reorganization under Chapter 11 of the U.S. Bankruptcy Code. The move was undertaken to give the company protection from its creditors while it developed and implemented a plan to reorganize.

STRATEGY

Established by then-Chairman and CEO Glen Hiner in 1992, Owens Corning's Core Values make up the framework on which the company's strategy is based. These guiding principles are composed of three key components: customer satisfaction, individual dignity, and shareholder value.

To Owens Corning, customer satisfaction means more than simply selling quality products at an attractive price. The company thinks it is essential to understand-and even anticipate-customers' needs. The company's focus on individual dignity has made the company a preferred place of employment worldwide. It emphasizes the importance of respect for every individual, regardless of race, creed, color, religion, gender, or national origin. The final component in its Core Values is shareholder value, which is a recognition on the company's part that its stockholders expect the company to be managed efficiently and profitably and to produce an acceptable rate of return.

Although it's not a formal part of the company's Core Values, Owens Corning's October 2000 petition to reorganize under the protection of the U.S. Bankruptcy Code was an important strategic move taken to help preserve cash flow in the face of its extensive asbestos-related liability.

INFLUENCES

Undoubtedly the biggest challenge to have faced Owens Corning in recent years has been the flood of asbestos-related claims tracing back to the company's involvement in the asbestos business between the 1950s and the 1970s. Although the first such claims against Owens Corning were filed in the early 1980s, they were few in number and not perceived to be a major threat to the company.

By the early 1990s, Owens Corning had become a target defendant for asbestos litigation. Towards the end of the 1990s, the National Settlement Program (NSP) was announced, incorporating 176,000 cases settled with more than 50 law firms. To meet its payments to NSP, Owens Corning was forced in 1999 to sell off some of its assets to raise cash. Under pressure to meet its payments to NSP, the company's burden was further increased by the filing of asbestos suits by law firms that had not participated in the NSP. Unfortunately this surge in additional claims coincided with a slowdown in the U.S. economy in the first half of 2000, further hampering the company's ability to generate the strong cash flow needed to meet these demands. Left with few other options, Owens Corning in October 2000 filed a petition for reorganization under Chapter 11 bankruptcy protection.

PRODUCTS

The products and services of Owens Corning fall into two separate categories: Building Materials Systems and Composite Solutions. The former accounted for roughly 83 percent of the company's total sales in 2001, with the remainder being generated by Composite Solutions.

Within the company's Building Materials Systems division are two distinct categories of products: glass fiber, foam, and mineral wool insulation and exterior systems for the home, including siding and roofing systems. All of these products are used primarily in the home improvement, new residential construction, manufactured housing, and commercial construction markets. Building Materials Systems products include insulation systems, asphalt products, roofing shingles, windows and patio doors, vinyl siding, and housewrap.

Owens Corning is the world's largest manufacturer of glass fiber materials used in composites, which are made up of two or more component materials and used in a variety of applications to replace traditional materials, such as wood, steel, and aluminum. A typical composite might be made up of a plastic resin and a fiber, usually a glass fiber. The company's Composite Solutions division provides composite materials for use in the manufacture of automotive products, bathtubs and showers, electronics and telecommunications systems.

CORPORATE CITIZENSHIP

Owens Corning makes a concerted effort to enhance and enrich the local communities in which it operates around the world. The company's program of corporate responsibility includes civic and environmental projects, monetary contributions, and the donation of materials, expertise, and volunteer time. Each year the company gives more than $1 million in monetary gifts, as well as product donations, volunteer time, and expertise. The company's program is an extension of its core value of Individual Dignity, which calls for respect for every individual, regardless of race, color, creed, religion, gender, or national origin.

GLOBAL PRESENCE

Owens Corning markets its products around the world. The company operates foreign sales subsidiaries in a number of countries, including Argentina, Botswana, Canada, China, Germany, India, Mexico, Netherlands, Saudi Arabia, Spain, Thailand, and Turkey.

EMPLOYMENT

As of December 31, 2001, Owens Corning had a workforce of 19,000 people worldwide. The company maintains operations in the United States and more than 30 other countries on six continents.

One of the company's three Core Values is Individual Dignity, which stresses the importance of respect for every individual, regardless of race, creed, color, religion, gender, or national origin. Owens Corning's pursuit of this value has made the company a preferred place of employment worldwide. The company is always on the lookout for bright, highly motivated individuals and offers career opportunities in a number of fields, including administrative support, communications, customer service, engineering, finance, health and safety, human resources, information systems, management, marketing and sales, production management, research and development, supply chain management, and transportation/logistics.

SOURCES OF INFORMATION

Bibliography

"Business Summary: Owens Corning." *Multex Investor*, 2002. Available at http://www.marketguide.com.

MacIntosh, Julie. "Asbestos Worries Snare Wider Range of U.S.Firms." *Reuters Business Report*, 12 December 2001.

"Owens Corning." *Gale Business Resources*, 2002. Available at http://galenet.galegroup.com/servlet/GBR.

"Owens Corning." *Hoover's Online*, 2002. Available at http://www.hoovers.com.

"Owens Corning 1st-Quarter Net Loss Narrows." *Reuters Business Report*, 23 April 2002.

Owens Corning 2001 Annual Report. Toledo, OH: Owens Corning, 2002.

Owens Corning Home Page, 2002. Available at http://www.owenscorning.com.

Seewer, John. "Owens Corning Names New CEO." *AP Online*, 18 December 2001.

For an annual report:

write: Owens Corning World Headquarters, Investor Relations, 2-E, 1 Owens Corning Parkway, Toledo, OH 43659

For additional industry research:

Investigate companies by their Standard Industrial Classification Codes, also known as SICs. Owens Corning's primary SICs are:

2821 Plastics Materials and Resins

2891 Adhesives and Sealants

2899 Chemical Preparations, NEC

2951 Asphalt Paving Mixtures and Blocks

2952 Asphalt Felts and Coatings

3089 Plastics Products, NEC

3229 Pressed and Blown Glass, NEC

3231 Products of Purchased Glass

3272 Concrete Products, NEC

3296 Mineral Wool

3442 Metal Doors, Sash and Trim

Also investigate companies by their North American Industry Classification System codes, also known as NAICS codes. Owens Corning's primary NAICS codes are:

313210 Broadwoven Fabric Mills

325211 Plastics Material and Resin Manufacturing

327212 Other Pressed and Blown Glass and Glassware Manufacturing

327993 Mineral Wool Manufacturing

Pacific Gas & Electric Corporation

OVERVIEW

The PG&E Corporation is an energy-based holding company with headquarters in San Francisco, California. PG&E has a number of subsidiaries, including Pacific Gas and Electric Company, PG&E National Energy Group, Inc., PG&E Energy Trading, PG&E Gas Transmission Corporation, a gas pipeline manufacturer, and PG&E Generating Company, LLC, which builds and manages power plants. The firm's gas and electric utility subsidiary, Pacific Gas and Electric Company, delivers electric service to approximately 4.8 million customers and natural gas service to approximately 3.7 million gas customers in an area of California that reaches from Bakersfield in the south to Eureka in the north, and from the Sierra Nevada in the east to the Pacific Ocean in the west. The company operates 131,000 miles of electric lines and 43,000 miles of natural gas pipelines. The utility subsidiary filed for bankruptcy following the California energy crisis of the early 2000s.

During the latter half of the 1990s the PG&E Corporation began diversifying its core utility business in California to business in national and international energy markets. PG&E Energy Trading buys and sells energy in various markets in North America. It also owns and operates California's Diablo Canyon Nuclear Power Plant. The PG&E National Energy Group provides a broad range of energy products and services in various North American markets. Among its activities are power generation, transmission of natural gas, and energy trading. It is based in Bethesda, Maryland.

FOUNDED: 1905
VARIANT NAME: PG&E

Contact Information:

HEADQUARTERS: One Market St., Spear Tower, Suite 2400
San Francisco , CA 94105
PHONE: (415)267-7000
FAX: (415)267-7262
TOLL FREE: (888)263-3269
URL: http://www.pgecorp.com

FINANCES:

PG&E Corporation
Operating Incomes, 1996-2000
(million dollars)

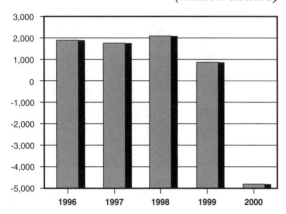

PG&E Corporation
2001 Stock Prices

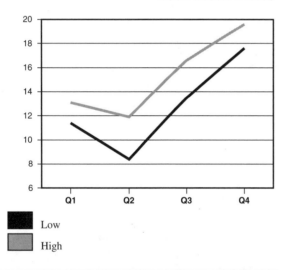

■ Low

■ High

COMPANY FINANCES

Through its various subsidiaries PG&E Corporation sells energy, in the form of gas and electricity, to residential and commercial customers in the Untied States and Canada. It also buys and sells energy and related financial instruments. PG&E Corporation had $22.96 billion in revenues in 2001, down from $26.23 billion in 2000, but up from $20.82 billion in 1999, and $9.61 billion in 1996. Conversely, the company's income fell steadily between 1996 and 2000. The company reported $1.9 billion in 1996, $878 million in 1999, and a loss of $4.81 billion in 2000. A significant portion of the loss

was attributable to the skyrocketing cost of energy during the California energy crisis. It only picked up again in 2001 when it reached $2.74 billion. Much of the 2001 profit was attributable to the PG&E utility company in California that was allowed to raise rates in the wake of the state's energy crisis. PG&E Corporation's stock price ranged from a high of $20.94 in 2001 to a low of $6.50. Down from a range of $31.81 to $17.00, the share price clearly reflected the impact of the energy crisis and PG&E Corporation's unsuccessful attempt to spin off its utility subsidiary.

The firm's California utility subsidiary, PG&E Company, sells gas and electricity throughout most of central and northern California. Forty-nine percent of its electricity customers are residential, 41 percent commercial, 7 percent industrial; 75 percent of its gas customers are residential, 24 percent commercial and 1 percent industrial. The firm's largest customer for gas and electricity is the petroleum refining industry. PG&E Company generates an ever declining share of its parent's revenue base. In 1997 the utility's revenues made up fully 67 percent of PG&E Corporation's; by 2000 the reported revenues had shrunk by almost half, to 37 percent. PG&E Company's 2000 loss of $5.2 billion was single-handedly responsible for the loss its parent reported that year.

ANALYSTS' OPINIONS

As a result of its descent into bankruptcy court, there has been tremendous uncertainty about PG&E utility's future and how it would impact the fortunes of its parent, PG&E Corporation. PG&E Corp. attempted unsuccessfully to spin the subsidiary off, and there were cries from the California press and consumer groups that the government of the state of California should take over the strapped utility. Further complicating PG&E Corporation's position, the California attorney general brought suit against PG&E Corporation, claiming that it had illegally siphoned money from the utility. These factors and others combined to create an unstable climate for investment in PG&E Corporation. A report from Value Line stated that an extensive reorganization plan proposed by PG&E Corporation would, if approved by the Federal Regulatory Commission, go a long way towards rehabilitating the company's credit. "But the timing is unpredictable, and some revisions in the plan are likely," Value Line wrote. "Major changes could have an important impact on the company's future. Because of the uncertainties here, the stock is best-suited for risk-tolerant investors."

HISTORY

PG&E's first half-century is the history of small gas, electric, and water companies, being founded, compet-

ing, and eventually consolidating. The San Francisco Gas Company, the city's first, was founded by Peter Donahue in 1854. It merged with the City Gas Company in 1873 to form the San Francisco Gas Light Company. Meanwhile electric companies were also being formed. In 1879 George Roe opened California Electric Light Company, which built the first power plant in the nation to offer central station electric service to the public, beating Thomas Edison's plant in New York by several years. Around 1890, Roe's company merged with the Edison General Electric Company, which had spread west, to form the Edison Light and Power Company. Realizing it was more efficient to combine their operations, Edison Light and Power merged with San Francisco Gas Light Company in 1892 to form the San Francisco Gas and Electric Company. By the end of the century, hydro-electric companies, built to capitalize on the water resources of the Sierra Nevada, were transmitting power to Sacramento and other California cities. In 1905 a number of these smaller companies formed California Gas and Electric Company, which in 1905 merged with the San Francisco Gas and Electric Company and formed the Pacific Gas and Electric Company.

By 1920 there were three major gas and electricity companies serving central and northern California: the Great Western Power Company, San Joaquin Light and Power, and PG&E. In 1924 Great Western acquired San Joaquin; it was then itself acquired by the North American Company. In March 1930 PG&E acquired a controlling interest in San Joaquin and Great Western North American in exchange for $114 million in PG&E stock. As a result of the deal PG&E won control of nearly all gas and electric service in central and northern California. In the 1930s, the company began developing its reserves of natural gas in California; in later decades it sought and developed natural gas deposits in other states. In the 1950s the company pioneered the commercial use of atomic power, with the world's first privately owned atomic power plant in 1957. In 1980 PG&E put the Diablo Canyon nuclear plant into operation despite protests from environmental groups who were concerned about its location, which was dangerously close to an earthquake fault.

By the late 1980s PG&E was losing many of its industrial customers, leading the company to eliminate thousands of jobs in 1987. In 1993 residents of the California town of Hinkley sued PG&E claiming the utility had released cancer-causing chromium into their groundwater. The company paid $333 million in an out-of-court settlement. The case was later the basis of the 2000 film *Erin Brockovich*. PG&E was the target of similar environmental suits later in the 1990s.

By the mid-1990s, a serious movement was underway—led by power companies in large part—to deregulate the utility industry. By 1996, when it experienced a major power outage, PG&E had already begun diversifying into smaller, unregulated companies, such as U.S. Generating and PG&E Energy Services. PG&E Corpo-

FAST FACTS:

About Pacific Gas & Electric Corporation

Ownership: PG&E Corporation is a public company traded on the New York Stock, Pacific, and Swiss Exchanges.

Ticker Symbol: PCG

Officers: Robert D. Glynn, Jr., Chmn., CEO, and President, 59, 2001 salary $2,081,700; Thomas G. Boren, EVP, 50, 2001 salary $1,369,478; Peter A. Darbee, SVP and CFO, 49, 2001 salary $783,578

Employees: 21,000

Principal Subsidiary Companies: PG&E Corporation is an energy-based holding company. It markets energy services throughout North America through business groups, PG&E National Energy Group and Pacific Gas and Electric Company.

Chief Competitors: PG&E competes with a variety of energy providers throughout the United States. Among its most significant competitors are Duke Energy, Dynegy, Reliant Energy, Mirant, TXU, Exelon Corporation, Sempra Energy, American Electric Power, and Calpine Corporation.

ration was established in 1997 as a holding company with Pacific Gas & Electric and other companies as its subsidiaries. Billions in debt after the California energy crisis of 2000, the PG&E utility initiated bankruptcy proceedings, and PG&E Corporation began looking for a reorganization plan that could restore the company's credit and satisfy state regulatory bodies. Despite its utility's bankruptcy, PG&E Corporation reported record profits in 2001 and proposed $17.5 million in bonuses for company executives. This drew criticism from shareholders and in 2002 the California attorney general sued PG&E Corporation for fraudulent management of the utility's money.

STRATEGY

PG&E Corporation is lowering its profile as a California utility and expanding its activities in the national wholesale energy market. This strategy is being realized primarily through its subsidiary, the PG&E National Energy Group, which is an energy broker, a builder of

CHRONOLOGY:

Key Dates for PG&E

1852: San Francisco Gas Company is founded

1879: California Electric Light Company is founded

1905: California Electric and SFG&E merge to form Pacific Gas and Electric

1957: Vallecitos atomic power plant is opened

1960: PG&E constructs North America's first geothermal plant

1980: Diablo Canyon atomic power plant begins operations

1987: PG&E founds U.S. Generating, an independent producer of electricity

1993: PG&E settles a lawsuit for polluting groundwater with residents of Hinkley, California, for $333 million, a case later dramatized in the movie *Erin Brockovich*

1995: PG&E Energy Services is founded

1997: PG&E Corporation founded with Pacific Gas and Electric its subsidiary

2001: Pacific Gas & Electric utility seeks bankruptcy relief

power plants and an owner and operator of pipelines for the transmission of natural gas. PG&E Corporation sold most of the fossil-fuel power plants that formerly supplied its California grid when the electric market there was deregulated in the late 1990s.

INFLUENCES

Deregulation of energy markets on both the state and federal levels had profound impacts—both positive and negative—on PG&E Corporation as well as other energy companies. No longer a regulated monopoly, PG&E had to compete on the open market—to sell to retail consumers in California who were now free to choose to get their electricity from alternate power companies. Ultimately PG&E will be able to buy power at the lowest price it can find and will no longer have to charge prices fixed by utility regulators. For its part in California utility deregulation, PG&E agreed to a temporary price cap

for consumer energy prices at the same time it was selling off most of its power plants. The consequences of these two decisions were momentous. When wholesale energy costs skyrocketed in 2000, PG&E could neither raise its rates nor produce cheap energy on its own. It was forced to purchase energy on the open market from unregulated outside suppliers at grossly inflated rates. As a result, California was plunged into an energy crisis and the utility PG&E, billions in debt, filed for bankruptcy in 2001. PG&E Corporation devised a reorganization plan that would have spun off some holdings and provided a basis for credit, however in early 2002 a federal judge rejected the plan. PG&E was still making its case in bankruptcy court in mid-2002.

CURRENT TRENDS

Construction on new PG&E energy plants slowed down due to a general decline in projected wholesale energy prices and the general economic slowdown that hit the United States. The outlook for several stalled projects was uncertain, although PG&E maintained it intends to complete the projects regardless of the economic climate.

As a result of the California energy crisis and the apparent bankruptcy of the PG&E utility, PG&E Corporation has developed a reorganization plan that would spin off assets such as the utility to help restore PG&E Corporation's credit rating. While welcomed by the investment world, critics claimed the plan was a device to protect PG&E Corporation's assets from the utility's creditors. The plan was rejected by a federal court. An alternative was put forth by the California Public Utilities Commission, but as of mid-2002 no agreement with PG&E had been reached.

PRODUCTS

PG&E Corporation offers products in two broad ranges. The Pacific Gas and Electric Company, based in San Francisco, California, delivers electricity and natural gas to retail customers, both residential and commercial, in California. The PG&E National Energy Group, based in Washington D.C., builds and operates power plants and natural gas pipelines, as well as trading energy on a wholesale basis on the national market.

GLOBAL PRESENCE

In 2000 PG&E Corporation's National Energy group began building a natural gas pipeline from Ehrenburg, Arizona to Tijuana, Mexico with the Mexican firm, Próxima Gas, S.A. de C.V., and Sempra Energy International.

PG&E planned to have the pipeline in operation by 2003. PG&E Corporation subsidiaries purchase natural gas from suppliers in Canada and pump it to the United States via company owned pipelines. PG&E Company is interconnected with power systems in western Canada and Mexico.

CORPORATE CITIZENSHIP

PG&E's corporate policy is to promote environmental justice in all its activities. To this end it endeavors to comply with both the letter and the spirit of all environmental laws and to maintain high standards for limiting environmental impacts; to make environmental considerations an essential consideration when building or purchasing new facilities; to work with communities on environmental issues; and to accept responsibility for corporate actions. PG&E Corporation is also committed to maintaining a culturally and ethnically diverse workforce.

SOURCES OF INFORMATION

Bibliography

Berthelsen, Christian. "PG&E earned $1.1 billion last year." *San Francisco Chronicle*, 6 March 2002.

"California Attorney General Sues PG&E Corp. for Unfair Business Practices," *Transmission & Distribution World*, February 2002.

Coleman, Charles. *PG.& E of California: The Centennial Story of Pacific Gas and Electric Company, 1852-1952.* New York: McGraw-Hill, 1952.

"Consumer Advocacy Group Blasts PG&E'S Reorganization Plan." *Foster Electric Report*, 30 January 2002.

"CPUC Pushes Alternate Bankruptcy Reorganization Plan for PG&E *Foster Natural Gas Report*, 21 February 2002.

Davis, Kathleen. "PG&E to Gov. Davis: We're busted." *Electric Light & Power*, May 2001.

Glantz, Aaron. "No Power For The People." *In These Times*, March 5, 2001.

Hamilton, Martha M. "PG&E Plans to Move Its Headquarters to D.C." *Washington Post*, 13 March 2000.

Hood, Julia. "Public Awareness - PG&E Powers Up Big Voter Victory." *PR Week*, 11 February 2002.

"PG&E Corporation." *Hoover's Company Profiles*, 2002. Available at http://www.hoovers.com.

Lazarus, David. "PG&E Cast as Villain in New True-Story' Movie." *San Francisco Chronicle*, 16 March 2000.

————. "PG&E's Eco-Friendly Image Falls on Its Face—Company's nonanswers fail to satisfy shareholders." *San Francisco Chronicle*, 20 April 2000.

Mitchell, Russell. "PG&E: One step ahead of future shock." *Business Week*, 14 November 1994.

ERIN BROCKOVICH

In early 2000, as the California energy crisis was just starting to rock PG&E's corporate reputation, along came the movie *Erin Brockovich*. It could hardly have been worse for the firm's image. *Erin Brockovich* told the true story of Hinkley, California's struggle to win damages from a company (PG&E) that had polluted the town's ground water with cancer—causing chromium, a fight the town eventually won. The film made Brockovich, the woman who led the fight, into a national celebrity, and shattered PG&E's image as a firm concerned about the environment. So apprehensive was PG&E about the film's possible repercussions that, according to the *San Francisco Chronicle*, it considered paying the producers to change the name of the bad-guy company in the movie. With Julia Roberts in the lead role, the film was a blockbuster hit.

Reason, Tim. "Ring Around the Subsidiary." *CFO The Magazine for Senior Financial Executives*, October 2001.

"Uncharted Territory is the Only Consensus So Far On PG&E Bankruptcy." *Electric Utility Week*, 16 April 2001.

For an annualreport:
on the Internet at: http://www.pgecorp.com **or** write: Investor Relations PG&E Corporation, PO Box 193722, San Francisco, CA 94119-3722

For additional industry research:
Investigate companies by their Standard Industrial Classification Codes, also known as SICs. Pacific Gas & Electric Corporation's primary SICs are:

4923 Gas Transmission and Distribution

4931 Electric and Other Services Combined

4932 Gas And Other Services Combined

6719 Holding Companies, Not Elsewhere Classified

Also investigate companies by their North American Industrial Classification System codes, also known as NAICS codes. Pacific Gas & Electric Corporation's primary NAICS codes are:

221119 Other Electric Power Generation

221121 Electric Bulk Power Transmission and Control

221122 Electric Power Distribution

221210 Natural Gas Distribution

Panavision, Inc.

FOUNDED: 1955

Contact Information:
HEADQUARTERS: 6219 De Soto Ave.
   Woodland Hills, CA 91367
PHONE: (818)316-1000
FAX: (818)316-1021
URL: http://www.panavision.com

OVERVIEW

Panavision, Inc. is the top designer, supplier and manufacturer of high-precision cinematography cameras, both analog and digital, used in the motion picture and television industries. In 2000, the company's equipment was used in the making of about 75 percent of all movies produced by major film studios. Panavision's equipment includes camera systems comprised of cameras, lenses, and accessories. Essentially, Panavision's innovations through the years changed the way motion pictures were made.

Throughout the years, Panavision has worked directly with producers, directors and cinematographers to design and produce systems and accessories that meet the film industry's creative needs.

Panavision's equipment is not available for sale. it can only be rented through the company's domestic and internationally owned and operated facilities and a network of independent agents. Panavision has rental offices and maintenance facilities throughout North America, Europe and the Asia Pacific region.

Panavision, which incorporated in 1990, also has rental operations that offer lighting, lighting grip, power distribution and generation, and related transportation equipment. These operations include Lee Lighting, a lighting rental company in the United Kingdom, as well as other owned and operated facilities in Chicago, Dallas, Orlando, Toronto and Australia. The company manufactures and sells lighting filters and other color-correction and diffusion filters through its Lee Filters operation. In 2000, camera rental accounted for 63 percent of Panavision's revenues, while lighting rental accounted for 20 percent.

COMPANY FINANCES

Panavision, Inc. revenue for the 12 months ending December 31, 2001 was $190.8 million, down from $204.6 million in 2000. Revenue was $202.8 million in 1999, $192.9 million in 1998, and $176.9 million in 1997.

Operating income for 2001 was $21.9 million as compared to $30.8 million in 2000. Camera rental revenue for 2001 was $124.6 million. Camera rental revenue for 2000 was $130.0 million. Revenue decreased $0.8 million, or 0.6 percent, compared to 1999.

Lighting rental revenue for 2001 was $31.7 million, a decrease of $8.6 million, or 21.3 percent, compared to 2000. The decrease was primarily due to considerably lower levels of feature film production in the U.K. Lighting rental revenue for 2000 was $40.3 million, an increase of $4.1 million, or 11.3 percent, compared to 1999.

ANALYSTS' OPINIONS

On April 4, 2002, Panavision's price hit a new 52-week low at $3.80 per share. At the time, VectorVest, a stock analysis organization, reported that Panavision had well-below-average safety with well-below-average upside potential, making it a stock which was likely to give well-below-average, inconsistent returns over the long term. The firm's estimation reflected a general consensus among many observers.

HISTORY

Panavision, Inc. was started in 1955 by Robert Gottschalk, a camera pioneer, to meet the needs of motion picture producers who wanted to make movies in a wide-screen format. The company's first product was an anamorphic projection lens, a high-quality spherical optic mounted in a housing that holds a pair of anamorphic prisms. That year, MGM studios began preproduction on the movie spectacle "Ben Hur." The studio's Chief of Research and Development, Douglas Shearer, asked Gottschalk to develop a camera process that would accommodate MGM's wide-screen plans for the epic. Wide-screen formats were still relatively new and MGM wanted to film "Ben-Hur" in the best available system. That led to the development of the anamorphic 65/70 mm process known as MGM Camera 65, or Ultra Panavision.

In 1957, Ultra Panavision was ready for use before the studio was ready to begin filming "Ben-Hur," so MGM used it on the film "Raintree County." Around the same time, the company introduced the Ultra Panatar variable anamorphic lens that could be used with either 35mm or 70mm films.

In 1959, the Ultra Panavision process was premiered with the release of "Ben-Hur." The film won a record 11

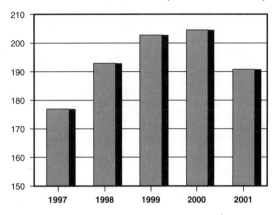

FINANCES:

Panavision Inc.
Total Revenues, 1997-2001
(million dollars)

Academy Awards, including best color cinematography and a special technical Oscar, awarded to MGM and Panavision, for the development of the Camera 65 process. This success paved the way for MGM's remake of "Mutiny on the Bounty." Released in 1962, the film was the first credited as being filmed in Ultra Panavision 70. During this period, MGM sold its camera department to Panavision and rented back the cameras and lenses from Panavision for the production of the film. In the meantime, Panavision refined both the lenses and cameras, making them lighter and more portable.

In 1965, Panavision was purchased by Banner Productions, headed by Sy Weintraub, which allowed Panavision to expand geographically. Gottschalk remained president and Weintraub became chairman of the board. Until that year, the company had only been supplying Hollywood with its equipment. Gottschalk now provided Panavision equipment for rental companies all over the world.

The company changed hands again in 1968 when it was taken over by the Kinney National Service, Inc. conglomerate. Again, Gottschalk remained president. In 1971, Kinney was renamed Warner Communications, Inc. During this period, Gottschalk had an idea for a new camera and hired Albert Mayer, an engineer from Mitchell Cameras, to design a 35mm hand-held camera system that would also be silent. The project resulted in the Panaflex, which weighed under 100 pounds, enabling better location filming. "The Sugarland Express" (1973), an early Steven Speilberg film, was the first production filmed entirely with Panaflex cameras.

During the mid-1970s, Panavision developed a video camera called the Panacam, which featured Panav-

FAST FACTS:

About Panavision, Inc.

Ownership: Panavision, Inc. is a publicly owned company traded on the New York Stock Exchange. Up until 2002, Chairman Ronald Perelman, who is also chairman of Revlon, owned 86 percent of the company.

Ticker Symbol: PVI

Officers: Ronald O. Perlman, Chmn. of the Board; John S. Farrand, CEO, Pres., and Dir., 58, 2000 salary $900,000; Scott L. Seybold, EVP and CFO, 56, 2000 salary $243,058; Barry F. Schwartz, EVP and Gen. Counsel

Employees: 1,284

Principal Subsidiary Companies: Panavision, Inc. has a network of rental offices and maintenance facilities throughout North America, Europe and the Asia Pacific region. It serves as the parent company for the following subsidiaries: Panavision UK, Panavision Australia, Panavision New Zealand, Panavasion Alga Paris, Panavision Merchandise/Expendables, and Panavision New York. The Lee Filters subsidiary makes and sells lighting, color-correction, and diffusion filters. The Lee Lighting subsidiary rents lighting equipment in the United Kingdom.

Chief Competitors: Panavision's two primary competitors are Arriflex, based in Munich, Germany, and Moviecam, based in Vienna, Austria. It is also in competition with Eastman Kodak Company, ParkerVision, Inc., and Vari-Lite International, Inc.

---

ision lenses and an optical viewfinder. In 1976, the company developed the Panaflex Gold, an improvement over the Panaflex because of its electronic features. In the late 1970s, Panavision introduced the Panaglide, a harness enabling the camera operator to walk with the Panaflex attached in front, which eliminated the need for the dolly track. Also during that decade, Panavision introduced the Panastar, a high speed camera.

In the 1980s, the company introduced the Panaflex 16, a 16mm camera with all the features of the Panaflex. It was developed for low-budget photography, music videos and television commercials.

When Robert Gottschalk passed away in 1982, Jac Holzman assumed the chairmanship of Panavision, now a wholly-owned subsidiary of Warner Communications. By this time, Panavision was in financial trouble, but Holzman helped turn the company around. While Holzman was at the helm, Panavision introduced an advanced system of 16mm cinematography called the Platinum Panaflex, and the company began a new program of optical design resulting in the acclaimed Primo Series lenses. It also created a comprehensive management information system to track the whereabouts of rental equipment throughout the world. This proved necessary, as Panavision's reach had expanded considerably.

In 1985, Panavision was sold to a group of investors headed by John Farrand, the company's current CEO, and Ted Field, for more than $70 million. After five months, Field and Farrand bought the other investors out and Panavision started two new projects. The result was the Platinum, a new Panaflex camera, and the Primo lenses, which featured color-matching. In 1988, Panavision developed a relay optical system that combined its lenses into the one-inch image format of the Sony high definition HDC-300 camera.

In 1990, Panavision incorporated to become Panavision, Inc. In 1994, the company entered a five-year renewable licensing agreement with Lockheed Missiles and Space Company for the exclusive worldwide use of the Lockheed liquid lens technology.

Heading into the new century, Panavision joined the digital revolution. In 1999, it began collaborations with Sony to develop high definition, digital camera systems. In 2000, the two organizations formed a new company to supply Sony and Panavsion technology. In 2001, Panavision entered a partnership with EFILM, a firm that operates an advanced digital laboratory and serves the motion picture and television industries. Also, Panavision partnered with Viewpoint Digital, a leader in 3D digital modeling, to provide a solution for scanning and modeling feature film sets and locations.

STRATEGY

As stated by Panavision's president and CEO John Farrand, "Panavision's mission has always been to provide clients with the best equipment and services. Along with that, the company's goals include developing a series of extremely high-performance lenses, specifically for digital cinematography; producing a complete system of cameras, lenses, and accessories to satisfy the needs of cinematographers and directors, and to present this in a form that is both familiar and unobtrusive to their creative needs."

The company has found that renting rather than buying equipment is more cost-effective for feature film, television and commercial producers because of periods of inactivity between productions. Panavision has geared its business strategy accordingly. With Panavision's rental arrangement, producers have continual access to equipment.

Panavision cinematographic equipment includes cameras, lenses and accessories which clients rent on a project-by-project basis. The company's rental inventory includes more than 1,000 cameras, 5,000 lenses, and associated accessories. The company has designed its camera systems so clients have an integrated design with compatible products. Typical camera rental packages include a number of camera systems including a camera, lenses and accessories such as eyepieces, viewfinders, cables and brackets. Specific needs are met through equipment such as sync-sound cameras, including the Platinum Panaflex. The lighting rental operations offer a large inventory of lampheads. The company also manufactures and sells lighting filters through its Lee Filters operations in the United Kingdom and the United States. In addition, Panavision sells various consumable products such as light bulbs and gaffer tape.

Panavision's rental policy has been the strategy that has allowed the company to stay in business. The fact that the equipment remains the property of the company provides several advantages. At first, Panavision sold projection attachments and some anamorphic 35mm taking lenses. However, it soon decided to limit its operations to equipment rental. The initial reason was that the company saw that the anamorphic taking lenses were complicated and needed constant tuning and maintenance work, but the company then realized that it could drive itself out of business by selling equipment. The rental arrangement worked out best for everyone involved. A film producer could write off the cost of lenses on one production and Panavision could, during the equipment maintenance process, upgrade the equipment to clients' needs and requests.

The policy of customer engineering is one of the most significant elements of the Panavision business model. Panavision can spend a lot of money developing an improved product because it is not limited by a sales price. For example, if Panavision designs a lens to sell, the lens cannot cost more than a certain amount of money in the development and manufacturing phases. If it did cost more, the company would see no profit. On the other hand, if the lens is developed and manufactured for rental only, the company can spend as much money as it wishes on it because, over a certain period of time, the costs will be covered by rental fees and a profit will eventually be realized by continued rentals. As a result, Panavision can spend money to get the best materials to manufacture its equipment, and customers know that they are renting the best.

INFLUENCES

Profits in the motion picture industry can be influenced by any number of unforeseen and uncontrollable

CHRONOLOGY:
Key Dates For Panavision, Inc.

1955: Panavision is started by camera pioneer Robert Gottschalk

1957: Panavision develops Ultra Panavision, which is used in the films "Raintree County" and "Ben Hur"

1959:" Ben Hur" is released and wins 11 Academy Awards, including awards for Panavision technology

1965: Panavision is purchased by Banner Productions

1968: Panavision is bought by Kinney National Services, Inc.

1973: Panavision's Panaflex is used in the film "The Sugarland Express"

1982: Robert Gottschalk dies

1985: Panavision is sold to a group of investors, including current CEO John Farrand

1990: Panavision incorporates

1999: Panavision begins collaborations with Sony

factors. Panavision's decreased revenue in recent years can be attributed to such factors, specifically threatened labor disruptions and threatened strikes by the Writers Guild of America and the Screen Actors Guild as well as the World Trade Center attack of 9/11, all of which contributed to a decline in production in the second half of 2001.

Panavision president and CEO John Farrand described the situation as it related to Panavision late in 2001: "As of the end of September, major studio feature film production starts on a year-to-date basis were below the levels of the first nine months of 2000. The market environment in our other two key market segments was mixed. We continue to have good results in North American series television; however, our revenue in the television commercial segment has been constrained throughout the year by a weak commercial advertising market worldwide. The features and commercial segments have also been adversely impacted by the tragic events of September 11."

Other factors that can, and have, affected fortunes within the industry in recent years include competitive pressures resulting from changes in technology, customer

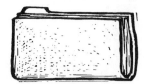

"I'M READY FOR MY CLOSE-UP, MR. DEMILLE"

Before Panavision and MGM put their heads together to come up with their own wide-screen process, the rage of the movie industry was CinemaScope. However, that process featured a significant flaw. The center of the filmed image received less horizontal squeeze when lenses were focused at short distances, and that played havoc with closeups. The face of any actor caught in that portion of the frame looked distorted. This resulted in what was called the "Cinemascope Mumps." The MGM/Panavision collaboration, with its anamorphic lenses, eliminated that problem.

requirements and industry standards, increased expenses related to new product initiatives and product development, and unfavorable foreign currency fluctuations.

Company revenues and income are affected also by factors like seasonality and market risk. In North America, Panavision points out, episodic television programs cease filming in the second quarter for several months and typically resume production in August. Feature film production activity typically reaches its peak in the third and fourth quarters. About market risk, Panavision indicates that it is exposed to risk from changes in foreign currency exchange rates and interest rates, which could affect its business, results of operations, and financial condition.

CURRENT TRENDS

Besides modifying existing products for its clients, Panavision, Inc. has been at the vanguard of industry innovation. In the past, new products that it designed and manufactured include Panaflex, the Panaglide and the Panaflex 16, all pioneering inventions that advanced the art of motion pictures.

As it heads into the future, Panavision is moving in the direction of digital technology. To do this, it has been entering into partnerships and agreements with appropriate organizations. In 2000, Sony Electronics, Inc. and Panavision, Inc. established a strategic relationship to form a new company to supply Sony's 24P CineAlta high definition video cameras with Panavision's advanced Primo Digital lenses for use in the motion pictures industry. The companies saw the partnership as a way to

advance implementation of digital cinematography. The equipment was soon being used by filmmaker George Lucas for two installments of his *Star Wars* film series, "Episode I" and "Episode II." In 2001, Panavision further strengthened its digital strategy by entering a partnership with EFILM, a firm that operates an advanced digital laboratory that serves the motion picture and television industries.

Also, Panavision formed a strategic relationship with Viewpoint Digital, a leader in 3D digital modeling, to provide a solution for scanning and modeling feature film sets and locations. This would accelerate the adoption of set scanning with digital modeling as the fastest, most accurate way to integrate live-action photography with computer-generated imagery.

Panavision also integrated new information systems and telecommunications capabilities into its services to provide more options for its customers. In 2001, Panavision entered into an exclusive agreement with Picture PipeLine, LLC to make available Pipeline's file transfer, synchronized playback and annotation applications at Panavision locations worldwide. The service allows production crews to use broadband to transmit film footage and allow digital collaboration. Further, production personnel can drop off dailies to Panavision locations, where they are encoded in MPEG 1 or MPEG 2, encrypted at the highest level of security, and delivered electronically to another Panavision location or to another PipeLine facility. When sent to the Panavision location, the footage can then be delivered to the desired film location or the production staff can collaborate at Panavision facilities using Picture PipeLine's synchronized playback and annotation features (voice and text).

PRODUCTS

Panavision's revenue is generated by camera rental operations, lighting rental operations, and sales and other revenue. Camera equipment rentals include camera systems, lenses and accessories. Lighting rental operations include the leasing of lighting, lighting grip, transportation and distribution equipment, and mobile generators. Sales and other revenue include the manufacture and sale of lighting filters through Lee Filters in the United Kingdom and the United States; EFILM's operations, which provide high-resolution scanning of film, digital color timing, laser film recording of digital video, and high-definition images to film and digital mastering services used by the motion picture and television industries; and sales of various consumable products, such as film stock, light bulbs and gaffer tape.

GLOBAL PRESENCE

Panavision, Inc. is truly an international corporation. Its main subsidiaries, located around the world, include

Panavision UK, Panavision Australia, Panavision New Zealand, Panavasion Alga Paris, Panavision Merchandise/Expendables, and Panavision New York. Subsidiaries Lee Filters and Lee Lighting operate in the United Kingdom.

CORPORATE CITIZENSHIP

Panavision, Inc. often contributes its resources toward educational purposes. In recent years, it has joined Kodak in an initiative, called the Panavision/Kodak Outreach Program, to provide university film students with free access to cameras, lenses, films, and digital technology. For several years, Kodak and Panavision have worked together in the program, which travels to four to six colleges and universities each year to conduct an extensive 16 mm hands-on camera workshop. The equipment remains at the school for the making of a faculty-nominated student film project.

Panavision is also a major supporter of F.O.C.U.S. Institute of Film, a California organization dedicated to the discovery of new film talent and the development of charitable feature film production. Proceeds go to educational and vocational scholarship funds for the underprivileged, orphaned and foster children.

EMPLOYMENT

In 2000, Panavision, Inc. had 1,284 employees. It only hires highly qualified and specialized people capable of designing and manufacturing the most complex equipment.

In the motion picture industry, its is very hard to break into various sectors and companies. In recent years, prospective candidates may have found it particularly hard to find employment at Panavision. The company's 2000 employee count only represented a less-than-one-percent growth rate (0.8) over the previous year. In 2001, Panavision undertook certain cost reduction initiatives that included reductions in headcount.

SOURCES OF INFORMATION

Bibliography

Bijl, Adriaan. "The Importance of Panavision: The Diffusion Phase." *70MM Newsletter*, March 2002. Available at http://hjem.get2net.dk.

Business.com. "Panavision Information," 11 April 2002. Available at http://www.business.com.

Hart, Martin. "Solving the Mysteries of MGM Camera 65 and Ultra Panavision 70." *Wide Gauge Film and Video Monthly*, Aug-Dec. 1997. Available at http://www.widescreenmuseum.com/widescreen/c65story.htm.

MSN Money.com. "PVI Company Report: Investing," 11 April 2002. Available at http://moneycentral.msn.com/investor/research/profile.asp?Symbol=PVI.

WRSN.com. "Company Info: Panavision Inc.," 11 April 2002. Available at http://www.wsrn.com/apps/companyinfo.

Yahoo! Finance. "Profile: Panavision, Inc.," Yahoo! Market Guide, 11 April 2002. Available at http://biz.yahoo.com/p/p/pvi.html.

For an annual report:
on the Internet at: http://biz.yahoo.com/e/010330/pvi.html

For additional industry research
Investigate companies by their Standard Industrial Classification Codes, also known as SICs. Panavision's primary SIC is:

3861 Photographic Equipment and Supplies

Also investigate companies by their North American Industry Classification System Codes, also known as NAICS codes. Panavision's primary NAICS code is:

333315 Photographic and Photocopying Equipment Manufacturing

PETsMART Inc.

FOUNDED: 1987

Contact Information:

HEADQUARTERS: 19601 N. 27th Ave.
    Phoenix, AZ 85027
PHONE: (623)580-6100
FAX: (623)580-6502
URL: http://www.petsmart.com

OVERVIEW

PETsMART is the largest U.S. provider of supplies and services for animals and household pets. It currently operates more than 500 stores in North America and plans to increase this number annually. The stores offer the customary items such as dog and cat food, grooming supplies, and accessories. In an effort to move beyond traditional retail products the company has become a pioneer in the pet services industry. Customers can take their pets to many locations and schedule a pet grooming session, an obedience class, or an appointment with a licensed veterinarian. PETsMART hopes to carve out an identity as the company that cares about animals and provides services for the entire lifespan of pets.

Merchandise sales account for more than 95 percent of the company's North American revenues. There are three broad categories of products that fuel sales in the pet care industry: pet food, pet supplies and live pets. The pet food sector includes food and treats, and nets about 44 percent of PETsMART's total retail sales. The company stocks only high quality name brands, as well as premium style pet foods not found in discount stores. The pet supplies category offers a large selection of goods for many different types of pets, large and small. Toys, furniture, collars, leashes, and even aquariums are staples of this line that accounts for almost 50 percent of North American retail sales. PETsMART does not sell puppies or kittens, but some smaller creatures may be purchased in most centers. Tropical fish, birds, hamsters and reptiles are available to take home as pets. Sales of live animals account for only three percent of retail sales.

PETsMART Inc. is the leading provider of pet supplies and services in the United States. The company was founded in 1987 and now includes retail stores, catalogues, and an Internet shopping site. PETsMART operates more than 560 stores in North America, which provide pet supplies, pet grooming, training, and veterinary services. PETsMART stores allow pets to stroll the aisles with their human parents. PETsMART stores provide space in retail stores for animal shelters to promote pet adoption.

COMPANY FINANCES

PETsMART claimed $39.6 million in net income on $2,501 million in revenues for the fiscal year ending in January 2002. Although this represents a profit margin of only two percent, it was a marked improvement from the previous year's losses. In 2001 the company posted a net loss of $30.9 million on sales of $2,224 million. Ninety five percent of all revenues were derived from the sale of merchandise. Pet foods and pet supplies each account for 45 percent of the merchandise revenues with the remainder coming from live pets. Pet services account for five percent of total sales and represent the largest growth sector for the company. Revenues from pet training and grooming increased nearly 30 percent in fiscal year 2001.

ANALYSTS' OPINIONS

PETsMART appeared on Investor's Business Daily 52-Week New Highs list in January 2002. Stock prices for the company quadrupled in 2001 from a lowly $2.50 to $11.00 a share. Hans Utsch of the Federated Kaufmann Fund described the improved financial picture: "You don't cut back on your pet. You spend whatever it takes. It's not like fashion, it's not cyclical. This is a turnaround story. New management, remodeled stores and rising cash flow showed us it was not going out of business." PETsMART also received positive reviews from David Mann, a specialty retailer analyst, reporting for Zack's Investment Research. He recommended the company as a stock to hold in 2002. He cited the potential to increase market share as a factor in his analysis, "a growing part of their business is in the grooming and training areas. The grooming business alone is seeing an increase around 20 to 25 percent per year." Absent any strong competition in the field, PETsMART's future appears promising.

HISTORY

The origins of PETsMART can be traced to Las Vegas in the mid 1980s. A wholesale pet food supplier decided to make business more profitable by selling his

FINANCES:

*PETsMART
Revenues, 1999-2001
(million dollars)*

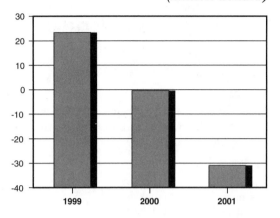

*PETsMART
2001 Stock Prices
(dollars)*

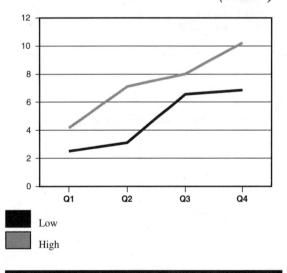

wholesale goods in his own retail environment. He hired Jim and Janice Dougherty to open an outpost in Las Vegas, far away from his California customer base. The experiment was a success and two PetFood Warehouse stores were opened in 1987 in Arizona. The Doughertys added a business partner, Ford Smith, and expansion of the pet food stores was underway. The company added stores in Arizona and branched out to Texas and Colorado. The name was officially changed to PETsMART.

By the early 1990s new management had replaced the Doughertys at the reins of PETsMART. The original

FAST FACTS:

About PETsMART Inc.

Ownership: PETsMART Inc. is a publicly traded company on the NASDAQ Stock Exchange.

Ticker Symbol: PETM

Officers: Philip L. Francis, Chmn. and CEO, 54, salary $619,750, bonus $285,600; Robert F. Moran, Pres. and COO, 50, salary $433,520, bonus $100,000

Employees: 20,450

Principal Subsidiary Companies: PETsMART Inc. is a publicly traded company with several subsidiary units. PETsMART Direct controls the company's catalog businesses. PETsMART.com Inc. is the popular Internet pet supply site.

Chief Competitors: PETsMART is the largest U.S. retailer of pet supplies and services. Its primary competitors include pet store rival Petco Inc. and discount retailers Wal-Mart, Kmart, and Target.

stores were renovated and some of the warehouse features were eliminated in favor of a more appealing design. PETsMART began offering pet services such as grooming and obedience classes. New stores opened annually and the company operated in states stretching from Georgia to Utah. In order to implement its plan for sustained growth, the company made an initial public offering (IPO) of stock in 1993. PETsMART earned $125 million from its IPO and began trading on the NASDAQ exchange.

PETsMART blossomed into a bona fide money maker operating over 100 stores in 19 states. The company's ambitious growth strategy no longer relied on single store expansion. The company began acquiring other retail chains. In 1994, PETAZZ, a midwestern retailer with stores in five states, became the first major acquisition, with others soon to follow. Petstuff Inc., The Pet Food Giant, Sporting Dog Specialties Inc., and State Line Tack became part of the PETsMART brand. State Line Tack represented a move into a new industry, equine supplies.

In 1999 there were 500 PETsMART stores throughout the country, but the company was poised to enter an even greater market: cyberspace. PETsMART.com was launched and became the most popular online pet store. The company had some difficult financial times in the

years 2000 and 2001 due to inventory and distribution inefficiencies. Improved technology and delivery systems remedied these problems and PETsMART prospered again by early 2002.

STRATEGY

PETsMART has developed a strategy that recognizes the important role pets play in the family unit. The strategy targets pet owners who are appropriately labeled "pet parents". These customers treat their pets as loved ones and spare no expense in obtaining the highest quality pet care necessities. In order to attract this type of loyal customer, the company adopted certain best practices. Value and selection are two critical elements in the PETsMART strategy. Stocking the stores with the widest selection of quality goods at a reasonable price is the overall goal. In order to remain competitive PETsMART attempts to undersell grocery stores by a 10 percent margin and to remain within a five percent differential with the discount and warehouse clubs.

Expanding pet services is a crucial point in the growth strategy. Pet grooming and pet training classes are unique to the PETsMART experience. Pet owners cannot find these services at the local discount store and this creates a reason to visit a PETsMART center. The company has invested time and resources to develop a caring, professional staff of pet handlers who will foster the trust of committed pet owners. Providing exceptional customer service in all areas of operation, not just the pet services, is another focal point of the organization. All associates are trained to answer questions and anticipate the needs of customers. Finally, the design and layout of all stores maximizes the shopping experience and invites pet families to spend time browsing.

INFLUENCES

PETsMART was arguably the first bricks and mortar pet "super store." The original management team copied the concept pioneered by successful toy retailer, Toys "R" Us. The business plan translated well and provided a solid foundation upon which the fledgling company built an empire. PETsMART quickly became a "category killer," a term used to describe powerhouse retailers who drive smaller independent stores in their industry out of business. Winning the fight for domination in the shopping mall scene was not the only challenge the company faced.

The emergence of e-retailing brought with it a host of online pet supply sites that would garner more attention than any other competitors. In 1999 PETsMART launched its dot-com outlet in partnership with PetJun-

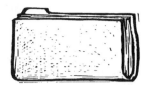

I WANT TO BE LIKE SPIKE!

Gatorade—for dogs. Rebound, a pet sports drink, is a new product for active dogs. The beverage, designed to counter dehydration in pets, is being distributed by PETsMART Inc. and grocery store, Kroger Inc. The company expected sales to break the $1 million mark in the year 2000. The drink has received national publicity in *Rolling Stone* and *Maxim* magazines. PETsMart hopes to expand to more retail outlets in the future.

gle.com and touched off a fierce competition with Pets.com for online supremacy in the pet care industry. PETsMART would eventually acquire struggling rival Pets.com despite the popularity of Pets.com's sock puppet spokespooch. The high profile advertising campaign waged by Pets.com, and its subsequent failure, underscored the PETsMART belief that value and customer service were more effective than a gimmicky sales pitch.

CURRENT TRENDS

Moving forward PETsMART's emphasis is on creating a lifestyle for pets. Beginning in 2001 the company rolled out a new slogan in its advertisements that read: "PETsMART: All you need for the life of your pet." Grooming and training services have been identified as an untapped market for the store. PETsMART intends to capitalize on this niche. Stylists and pet handlers are recruited and enrolled in a 15 week training program that teaches them grooming skills ranging from shampooing to nail clipping.

PRODUCTS

PETsMART offers extensive product lines for virtually every creature great and small. Dog and cat food and treats are a top sales item in all stores. The company tries to encourage the use of high quality, nutritious foods for animals. Supplies are an equally important segment. Shampoo, toys, pet carriers, beds, aquariums, and cages are popular buys. Live pets can be purchased at PETs-

CHRONOLOGY:
Key Dates for PETsMART Inc.

1987: The first PETsMART store opens in Phoenix, Arizona

1990: PETsMART expands chain which now has more than 15 stores

1993: PETsMART becomes a publicly traded company on the NASDAQ Stock Exchange

1994: PETsMART Charities is formed to help homeless pets

1995: PETsMART acquires State Line Tack and enters the field of equine care

1999: PETsMART.com is launched

2001: The PETsMART adoption program completes its one millionth adoption

MART locations, but are limited to small pets. This includes reptiles, gerbils, birds, and fish. At the other end of the spectrum, the company has entered the equine supply market and sells riding gear and apparel.

Pet and veterinary services are also offered at many locations. In 2002, almost 300 locations offered veterinary care for pets. Routine physical examinations, vaccines, and dental care are available in a safe, hospital environment. The in-store hospitals operate under the name of Banfield and are owned by Medical Management International. PETsMART owns 38 percent of Medical Management International.

GLOBAL PRESENCE

PETsMART is primarily a North American retailer with operations in most major markets of the United States and Canada. Less than 10 percent of total sales were generated from Canada or any other non U.S. region. The company attempted global expansion in 1996 when it acquired Pet City Holdings, a pet supplier in the United Kingdom. The complications associated with international operations affected overall company profitability and in 1999 PETsMART sold Pet City to Pets At Home to refocus on domestic operations.

Phoenix-based PetsMart has more than 560 stores in the United States and Canada, catering to a wide variety of pets and their owners. (AP Photo/Matt York)

A TALE OF TWO KITTIES

The eighth annual Spay Day USA was held February 26, 2002. Spay Day is national campaign launched by the Doris Day Animal Foundation. The foundation's goal is to end pet over-population by altering dogs and cats. The theme for 2002's event is "A Tale of Two Kitties—Don't Let Fluffy Breed Like the Dickens." PETsMART Charities sponsored the event for the third consecutive year. For the record, eight of every ten cats that enter a shelter are killed; likewise six of every ten dogs are killed. For more information on this program, visit www.1888pets911.org.

ally to worthy animal training programs and campaigns to spay and neuter pets. In a time of crisis, PETsMART is also willing to lend a hand. Following the terrorist attacks in New York and Washington, D.C. in September 2001, PETsMART donated dog food, supplies, paw protectors, and ear and eye cleaners to police canine units and search and rescue coordinators for use in their efforts.

EMPLOYMENT

In 2002, the number of PETsMART employees reached 22,375. Almost 11,000 of these employees were full time staff members. PETsMART provides training for employees interested in the pet services area. The company has initiated incentive programs designed to increase employee retention and pays above minimum wage rates. Employees also receive a generous benefit plan including major medical coverage and tuition assistance programs.

CORPORATE CITIZENSHIP

PETsMART Charities was formed in 1994 to save the lives of homeless pets and facilitate animal population control. The company offers space in its retail stores for local animal shelters to promote pet adoption to its customers. In 2001, the millionth pet was adopted through in store adoption programs. PETsMART also participates in local community events to help raise funds for rescued animals. The PETsMART Charities Foundation donates millions of dollars annu-

SOURCES OF INFORMATION

Bibliography

"A Tale of Two Kitties, Don't Let Fluffy Breed Like the Dickens." *Business Wire,* 24 December 2001.

"Doner Breaks its First PETsMART Campaign." *AdWeek,* 23 February 2001.

Moreau, Dan. "Retail Stocks Offering Up Mixed Bag. . . ." *Investor's Business Daily,* 22 January 2002.

"PETsMART Sends Supplies to Canine Rescue Teams." *Business Wire*, 14 September 2001.

Reyes, Sonia. "Dreyer's PETsMART on Spot." *Brandweek*, 20 November 2000.

Waldrop, Libby. "Sports Drinks for Pooches Leaps Over National Hurdle." *The Business Journal*, 10 December 1999.

Williamson, Deborah Aho. "A Dog's Life: Despite its Popular Icon. . . ." *Advertising Age*, 7 August 2000.

"Zacks All Star Analyst Issues Recommendations." *PR Newswire*, 2 April 2002.

For an annual report:

on the Internet at: http://www.irconnect.com/petm

For additional industry research:

Investigate companies by their Standard Industrial Classification Codes, also known as SICs. PETsMART's primary SIC is:

5999 Misc. Retail Stores

Also investigate companies by their North American Industry Classification System codes, also known as NAICS codes. PETsMART's primary NAICS code is:

453998 All Other Misc. Store Retailers Except Tobacco

Pfizer Inc.

FOUNDED: 1849

Contact Information:
HEADQUARTERS: 235 E. 42nd St.
   New York, NY 10017-5755
PHONE: (212)573-2323
URL: http://www.pfizer.com

OVERVIEW

Pfizer Inc., a global pharmaceutical company, develops, manufactures, and markets drugs and consumer health products for humans and animals. In mid-2000 Pfizer acquired in a hostile takeover one of its competitors, Warner-Lambert, nearly doubling its net income from $3.7 billion in 2000 to $7.8 billion in 2001.

Pfizer Inc.'s largest segment, its pharmaceutical division, produces cholesterol-lowering drug Lipitor; impotence treatment drug Viagra; antibiotic Zithromax; seratonin up-take inhibitor Zoloft; and allergy medicine Zyrtec.

COMPANY FINANCES

Revenues for 2001 were $32.3 billion, a 10 percent increase over the previous year. Net income in 2001 grew to $8.3 billion, a 28 percent increase over 2000. Diluted earnings per share in the same period increased 28 percent, to $1.31, an increase that was more than double the overall pharmaceutical industry. The company's pre-tax operating margins were 34 percent, a 4 percent improvement over 2000, placing them at the highest level in the pharmaceutical industry.

According to Pfizer Inc.'s 2001 annual report, the company's performance capped a spectacular decade of growth in which sales more than tripled, net income doubled, and research and development spending more than quadrupled. The report stated that Pfizer stock had outperformed the Dow Jones industrial Average and the Standard & Poor's 500 during the previous one-, five-, and ten-year periods. The company's stock had split four times since 1990, and the company's annual dividend had increased for more than 30 consecutive years.

Although Pfizer anticipated continued growth, shares in 2002 were on a slight downtrend and, at the end of the first quarter, were trading at $42.44 per share, with resistance at $42.50 per share. Still, Pfizer predicted at the end of the quarter shares would up to $45.00 by the end of the second quarter.

ANALYSTS' OPINIONS

Despite heavy industry competition, Pfizer's financial outlook was strong through 2010. Its diverse portfolio and eight products, which generate more than $1 billion in annual sales each is led by Lipitor, which sold more than $6.4 billion in 2001.

Standard & Poor's rated gave Pfizer a AAA/Stable/A-1+ rating due in part to the company's diverse product lines and in part because none of its major product patents expire until 2004, which will keep some competitors at bay for several years. Its top seller, Lipitor, is protected by patent until 2010; Norvasc until 2007; Zoloft until 2005; and Viagra until 2011.

Standard & Poor's also looked favorably on Pfizer because the company plans to continue to remain active in research and development, which is crucial to staying ahead of competition in the pharmaceutical industry. Pfizer spent more than $4 billion in research in 2001 and had plans to increase research spending the following year. Further strengthening its financial status was Pfizer's repurchase of $5 billion of its common stock through 2000 and 2001.

However, according to *Forbes*, the merger could pose some undesirable side effects and "swallowing Warner-Lambert almost whole may give Pfizer a stomachache that will last several years." Typically for three years after a merger, drug companies spend less on research, which can put their finances in jeopardy as current patents expire. Pfizer stated that the company would increase, not decrease, its research activity.

HISTORY

Pfizer Inc. got its start years before cousins Charles Pfizer and Charles Erhart emigrated to the United States from Germany. Charles Pfizer had trained as an apothecary apprentice, and Charles Ehrhart learned the confectioner trade. The two left their lives of privilege in search of excitement and opportunity, and moved to America in the mid-1840s.

Once in the states, they opened a chemical firm in Brooklyn in 1849, Charles Pfizer & Company. Their first

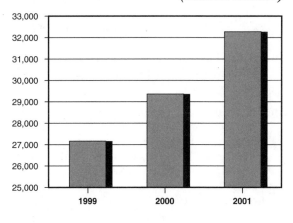

FINANCES:
Pfizer Inc. Revenues, 1999-2001 (million dollars)

breakthrough product came from a combination of both cousins' expertise. They made santonin, a bitter-tasting treatment of parasitic worms, a palatable medicine by blending it with almond-toffee flavoring and shaping it into a candy cone. The product was immediately successful. Less than 10 years later, the company was producing a dozen other products, including borax, camphor, and iodine.

The company's continued success relied on further innovation. Late in the nineteenth century, Pfizer's staple product was citric acid, used in cleaning solutions, for medicinal purposes, as flavoring and an ingredient in soft drinks. The raw materials to produce the acid had until 1880 primarily been imported from Italy. However, political instability, price fluctuation, and supply had affected Pfizer's ability to consistently profit from production. The company then faced a dire shortage of raw material supply and needed to either find a solution or close the business.

By 1914 the Italian imports stopped entirely, as the United States engaged in war in Europe, and Pfizer found other sources, although they were limited. Chemist James Currie joined Pfizer in 1917 and quickly applied his expertise in fermentation. He had discovered one of the by-products of cheese fermentation was citric acid, and began a series of experiments, conducted under extreme security, before discovering how to mass-produce the acid using molasses and processing them in a revolutionary deep-tank fermentation process.

The process set the company up for future success. In 1928 Dr. Alexander Fleming discovered the antibiotic uses for penicillin. Because he had no way to produce

FAST FACTS:
About Pfizer Inc.

Ownership: Pfizer Inc. is a publicly owned company traded on the New York Stock Exchange.

Ticker Symbol: PFE

Officers: Henry A. McKinnel, Chmn. and CEO, 59, 2001 salary $1,516,667, 2001 bonus $2,780,800; John F. Niblack, VChmn, 63, 2001 salary $944,600, 2001 bonus $1,062,700; David L. Shedlarz, CFO and EVP, 53, 2001 salary $722,800, 2001 bonus $736,900; C.L. Clemente, EVP, Sec., and Corporate Counsel, 64, 2001 salary $679,500, 2001 bonus $680,900

Employees: 90,000

Chief Competitors: Pfizer Inc. is the largest pharmaceuticals and consumer health care company in the world. Its competitors include Merck & Company Inc., Johnson & Johnson, Bristol-Meyers Squibb Company, American Home Products Corporation, Abbott Laboratories, and Eli Lilly and Company.

the bacteria in any large quantity, his discovery was dismissed by most of the scientific world. Scientists at Oxford University revisited Fleming's work a decade later and went to the United States to seek production options. Pfizer's John Davenport and Gordon Cragwall heard about the antibiotic at a symposium, and immediately saw the possibilities.

When the U.S. Government made an appeal to pharmaceutical companies to find a way to mass produce, Pfizer stepped up and invested heavily in using their deep-tank technology to mass-produce the antibiotic. The company purchased an ice plant and in fewer than four months converted it into a deep-tank fermentation facility. Pfizer supplied 90 percent of the penicillin for the Allied forces at Normandy on D-Day in 1944 and more than 50 percent of all the penicillin used during World War II.

After the company's breakthrough with penicillin production, Pfizer discovered a new antibiotic in soil. To find the antibiotic substance, the company conducted some 20 million tests and collected 135,000 soil samples before hitting "pay dirt." The drug that Pfizer developed was Terramycin and, although the company had always sold its products in bulk to other companies that sold them under their own brand names, Pfizer went into the

pharmaceutical business for themselves and packaged and marketed Terramycin.

In the 1950s Pfizer began to expand globally, first establishing a small network of sales agents in a few countries, then developing offices and subsidiaries around the world. The world was divided into four regions: Europe, Western Hemisphere, Far East, and Middle East. Representatives in each of the regions were urged to immerse themselves in their markets and learn the languages, customs, and make contacts. They were given the autonomy to make quick decisions on behalf of the company, therefore rapidly establishing global presence.

During the last 50 years, Pfizer has continued to forge ahead through innovation, more so than through mergers and acquisitions. The company spends some $2.5 billion annually on research and development and has aggressively marketed its pharmaceuticals, quickly making some of its new drugs familiar to healthcare professionals and consumers.

STRATEGY

Pfizer's success has traditionally hinged on marketing, research, and development. However, a mega-merger in 2000, in which the company acquired Warner-Lambert through hostile takeover, placed the new Pfizer on top of the pharmaceutical industry. After the merger, Pfizer garnered a 7.0 percent global market share, making it the largest pharmaceutical company in the world.

Although prior to the merger, some analysts thought Pfizer may become a less nimble company, the first quarter of 2002 proved them wrong. Pfizer reported at the end of the 2002 first quarter it had earnings of $2.356 billion, or $.37 per share, compared with $1.93 billion and $.30 per share the previous year. Post-merger earnings rose 14 percent, or $.39 per share, excluding merger-related costs.

As part of the merger, Pfizer cut some $1.6 billion in operating costs in 18 months, starting with cutting about 10 percent of its workforce. At the same time, the company planned to more efficiently use its sales staff, which could effectively sell two formerly-competing drugs at the same time.

INFLUENCES

From the company's origins in the nineteenth century, Pfizer has had a history of taking risks and making them pay handsomely. The most recent substantial risk was the merger with Warner-Lambert. Some analysts stated that the move was purely strategic in nature, and Pfizer did not need the merger to improve its value. The

CHRONOLOGY:

Key Dates for Pfizer Inc.

1849: Charles Pfizer & Company, a chemical business, opens and produces its first medical product, candied santonin, an antiparasitic

1862: Pfizer launches the first domestic production of tartaric acid and cream of tartar, both vital to the food and chemical industries

1868: Pfizer opens corporate offices in Manhattan's Wall Street district to accommodate growth during the Civil War, when the company produced and supplied many drugs used by the Union forces

1880: Pfizer begins manufacturing citric acid, and it quickly becomes the company's mainstay, as well as the launching pad later when the company becomes involved in penicillin production

1882: Pfizer opens its first location outside of New York, in Chicago

1919: Pfizer perfects mass production of citric acid, freeing it from dependency on European citrus growers

1928: Alexander Fleming discovers the medical qualities of the penicillin mold

1941: Pfizer is the only pharmaceutical company to use fermentation technology and begins mass-producing penicillin, at the urging of the U.S. Government, to treat soldiers in World War II

1942: Pfizer incorporates, with an initial offering of 240,000 shares of common stock

1946: Pfizer buys Electric Boat Victory Yard and builds the world's largest citric acid fermentation plant

1950: Terramycin, an antibiotic, becomes the first pharmaceutical sold in the United States under the Pfizer label

1952: Pfizer opens (in Terre Haute, Indiana) its first facility dedicated to research

1954: Pfizer discovers Tetracyn (tetracycline), the first synthetic broad-spectrum antibiotic

1955: Pfizer goes global and expands its worldwide operations; the company had since 1951 facilities in England, Cuba, Mexico, India, and Puerto Rico; in 1955 Pfizer opens a fermentation plant in England and partners with Japanese company, Taito (Pfizer would acquire the company nearly 40 years later, in 1993)

1963: Pfizer purchases Desitin Chemical Co. Inc., which remains part of its Consumer Health Division

1971: Pfizer establishes its Central Research Division, combining pharmaceutical, agricultural and chemical research and development

1972: Pfizer reaches the $1 billion sales mark

1982: Pfizer's anti-inflammatory medication, Feldene, becomes the first product to reach $1 billion in sales

1992: Pfizer introduces three major new drugs: Zoloft, Norvasco, and Zithromax

1993: Pfizer introduces its Sharing the Care drug donation program; the program provides more than 500,000 low-income and uninsured patients in the United States with prescription medicines

1994: Pfizer invests more than $1 billion in research and development

1998: Pfizer launches Viagra; the company invests nearly $2.5 billion in research

2000: Pfizer acquires competitor Warner-Lambert, creating the world's fastest growing pharmaceutical company

takeover was motivated by the opportunity to become the largest pharmaceutical company in the world, a position that would increase Pfizer's leverage in contracts with wholesale drug buyers.

Along with the clout of being the largest drug company in the world, the merger also brought Pfizer some baggage, most notably its pending suits over Rezulin, which had been produced and marketed by Warner-Lambert. Suits were pending in five states in 2002, and Pfizer was appealing a nearly $12-million judgment against the company late in 2001. The suits claimed that the drug caused liver failure in some patients who used the drug.

PRODUCTS

Pfizer has three major product divisions: Human Pharmaceuticals, Consumer Health Care, and Pfizer Animal Health.

The pharmaceuticals division accounted for some 79 percent, or $25.5 billion, of the company's total 2001 revenues. Lipitor, the company's top-selling drug, grew by 28 percent in 2001, to $6.4 billion. The company's fastest sales growth in 2001 was produced by Norvasc. Sales leapt 28 percent in 2001, from $5.0 billion to $6.4 billion.

Batotu Yetu dancers partcipate in a sendoff of Pfizer's donation of Zithromax, a sight-saving drug, to be distributed among African nations. *(AP Photo/Jeff Brand)*

The Consumer Healthcare division saw a 6 percent increase in 2001, with sales of $2.4 billion. The segment's fastest sales growth was achieved by Sudafed, Benedryl, and Listerine mouthwash. The launch of the Listerine PocketPaks also positively impacted the division's sales.

Animal Health increased 13 percent in 2001, to $1 billion, after a 20 percent decrease in 2000. The decrease was primarily due to foreign currency exchange factors and to the weak livestock markets amid the mad cow disease scare.

CORPORATE CITIZENSHIP

Established in 1953, the Pfizer Foundation is Pfizer's charitable organization. The foundation's mission is to "promote health care and education, to nurture innovation, and to support the community involvement of Pfizer people." In 2001 the Pfizer Foundation donated more than $400 million in products and money to organizations and people in the United States.

GLOBAL PRESENCE

Although Pfizer has established a presence in more than 150 countries worldwide, most of its growth has been in North America. In 2000 approximately 68.0 percent of Pfizer's sales were generated in North America, compared with its closest competitor GlaxoSmithKline, which had 56.6 percent of its revenues generated in North America. In 2001 Pfizer's U.S. revenues increased 10 percent to $32 billion, and international revenues climbed 6 percent to $12 billion. Revenues exceeded $500 million in seven countries outside the United States, and the United States was the only country to contribute more than 10 percent of the company's total revenue, according to Pfizer's 2001 annual report.

EMPLOYMENT

Pfizer Inc. offers employees in its research facilities opportunities that afford "the high visibility and responsibility available only in a small, entrepreneurial organization, yet your efforts will have the support of one of the world's largest and most respected pharmaceutical enterprises." In its recruitment efforts, Pfizer offers scientists an opportunity to work in state-of-the-art facilities and to work toward the development of life-saving drugs.

SOURCES OF INFORMATION

Bibliography
"FTC Grants Final Clearance for Pfizer/Warner-Lambert Merger." Available at http://www.pfizer.com.

Galewitz, Phil. "Warner-Lambert Begins Merger Talks with Pfizer." *Business News*, 14 January 2000.

Pfizer Analysis, 30 July 2001. Available at http://www.standardandpoors.com.

"Pfizer Profits Surge on Strong Sales." *Reuters*, 17 April 2002.

Herper, Matthew. "Pfizer's Warner-Lambert Acquisition Has Side Effects." *Forbes*, 21 June 2000.

"Pfizer Still Ahead Following GlaxoSmithKline Merger." *IMS Health*, 4 January 2001.

Shook, David. "Pfizer-Warner: One Drug Merger that Might Just Deliver." *BusinessWeek*, 17 May 2000.

"Significant Developments, Pfizer Inc." *Market Guide*, 25 March 2002.

For an annual report:
on the Internet at: http://www.pfizer.com

For additional industry research:
Investigate companies by their Standard Industrial Classification Codes, also known as SICs. Pfizer Inc.'s primary SICs are:

2833 Medical Chemicals & Botanical Products

2834 Pharmaceutical Preparations

2879 Pesticides & Agricultural Chems, Not Elsewhere Classified

3842 Surgical Appliances & Supplies

5122 Drugs, Proprietaries, & Sundries

Also investigate companies by their North American Industry Classification System codes, also known as NAICS codes. Pfizer Inc.'s primary NAICS codes are:

325320 Pesticide and Other Agricultural Chemical Manufacturing

325411 Medicinal and Botanical Manufacturing

325412 Pharmaceutical Preparation Manufacturing

339113 Surgical Appliance and Supplies Manufacturing

Polaris Industries, Inc.

FOUNDED: 1954

Contact Information:
HEADQUARTERS: 2100 Hwy. 55
    Medina, MN 55340-9770
PHONE: (763)542-0500
FAX: (763)542-0599
URL: http://www.polarisindustries.com

OVERVIEW

Polaris Industries is the largest snowmobile maker in the world. Snowmobiles account for 25 percent of the firm's sales. All-terrain vehicles (ATVs) bring in more than 50 percent of sales; parts, gear, and apparel, 13 percent; personal watercraft, 5 percent; and motorcycles, 1 percent. To sell its recreational and utility vehicles, Polaris uses roughly 2,000 North American dealers as well as 52 distributors across the world. The firm is listed on the Standard & Poor's SmallCap 600 stock index.

COMPANY FINANCES

The year 2001 marked the tenth consecutive year of sales growth for Polaris. Sales exceeded $1 billion for the first time in 1995, having grown more than threefold since 1991. In 2000, revenues reached $1.42 billion, and despite recessionary economic conditions, they grew 6.1 percent to $1.51 billion in 2001. Net income growth during this time period was a bit less consistent. After peaking in 1994 at $129 million, net income fell to $60.8 million in 1995. After climbing to $65.4 million in 1997, net income fell to $31 million in 1998. By 2001, however, net income had recovered to $91.4 million. The firm's profit margin was 10.4 percent that year, second only to the 15.6 percent profit margin realized in 1994. Stock prices in 2000 ranged from a high of $42.06 per share to a low of $25.56 per share, resulting in earnings per share of $3.50 that year.

ANALYSTS' OPINIONS

Despite the economic slowdown in North America, sales of ATVs continued to grow in 2001. Healthy ATV sales helped to boost revenues for Polaris in a year that proved to be disastrous for many other businesses marketing recreational wares. However, analysts were mixed about the firm's outlook in 2002. Some believed that price cuts by rivals like Honda would undermine sales for Polaris, and that ATV sales, which reached 700,000 units industrywide in 2001, had peaked. Other analysts, however, predicted that the market would continue to grow and fuel revenues for ATV manufacturers like Polaris and Arctic Cat.

HISTORY

Edgar Hetteen and David Johnson created Hetteen Hoist & Derrick in 1945. Based in Roseau, Minnesota, the business focused on repairing farm machinery for nearby farmers. A gas-powered sled Johnson built to travel to various hunting spots during the winter months attracted the attention of a neighbor, who asked to buy the machine. Realizing that a market for a motorized sled existed, Hetteen Hoist & Derrick began to manufacture early snowmobiles. The company changed its name to Polaris Industries, Inc. in 1954. Polaris, another name for the North Star, reflected the firm's northern Minnesota location. That year, the number of snowmobiles manufactured reached five. In 1956, Polaris shipped its snowmobiles to Canadian distributor H.C. Paul. The machines were dubbed "Autoboggans." By 1957, Polaris was manufacturing 300 snowmobiles each year.

In the late 1950s, Polaris distributed machines known as "Sno-Travelers" in Alaska, which proved to be a significant market for the firm's early snowmobiles. To generate publicity for Polaris machines, Edgar Hetteen and three companions rode three Sno-Tavelers from Bethel to Fairbanks, Alaska, covering 1,200 miles in three weeks. At the age of 31, Allan Hetteen, brother of Edgar, took over as president. In 1962, Polaris shipped its snowmobiles to dealers in Sweden for the first time. Two years later, the firm unveiled a sportier snowmobile, the Mustang, which helped to promote the recreational use of snowmobiles.

Textron acquired Polaris in 1968. That year, the firm began to make use of engines supplied by Fuji Heavy Industries. By the early 1970s, all Polaris snowmobiles were outfitted with Fuji engines. Sales in 1971 neared the 500,000-unit mark. Throughout the remainder of the decade, however, snowmobile sales began to wane despite attempts to spark interest with new model releases and sponsorships of snowmobile races. In 1979, Polaris developed the first independent front suspension (IFS) snowmobile, the TX-L Indy. When Textron revealed its plans to shutter its snowmobile subsidiary in 1981, sev-

FINANCES:

*Polaris Industries Inc.
Revenues, 1997-2000
(million dollars)*

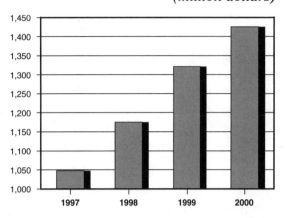

*Polaris Industries Inc.
2001 Stock Prices
(dollars)*

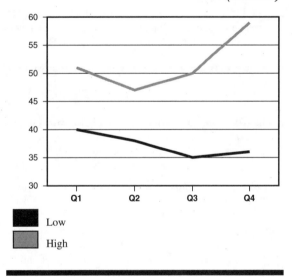

eral Polaris managers, led by president W. Hall Wendel, Jr., bought the firm back from Textron. Along with Hall Wendel, Jr., the new owners of Polaris included company chairman William H. Wendel, Sr. as well as several junior and senior executives.

In 1984, Polaris purchased the snowmobile operations of John Deere. The following year, the firm decided to reduce its reliance on snowmobiles by diversifying into all-terrain vehicles (ATVs). A limited partnership called Polaris Industries, L.P. acquired Polaris in 1987 and listed Polaris stock on the American Stock

FAST FACTS:

About Polaris Industries, Inc.

Ownership: Polaris Industries, Inc. is a public company traded on the New York Stock Exchange and the Pacific Stock Exchange.

Ticker Symbol: PII

Officers: W. Hall Wendel, Jr., Chmn., 58, 2001 base salary $240,000; Thomas C. Tiller, Pres., CEO, and Dir., 39, 2001 base salary $450,000; Michael W. Malone, Vice Pres. Finance and CFO, 42; Jeffrey A. Bjorkman, VP Operations, age 41

Employees: 35,600

Principal Subsidiary Companies: Polaris Industries operates manufacturing plants in Iowa, Minnesota, and Wisconsin.

Chief Competitors: Polaris Industries' competitors include other snowmobile and all-terrain vehicle makers like Arctic Cat, Suzuki, Honda, and Yamaha, as well as motorcycle makers like Harley-Davidson.

Exchange, using the symbol "SNO," for $20.00 per share. Eventually, the firm's stock was listed on the New York Stock Exchange as well as the Pacific Stock Exchange.

Ken Larson replaced Hall Wendel as President in 1988; however, Wendel remained chairman and CEO. *Snowmobile* magazine named the Polaris Indy 500 the "Snowmobile of the Decade'' in 1989. Polaris expanded operations with a new production plant in Wisconsin in 1990. By then, the firm was the largest maker of snowmobiles in the world. Polaris diversified into personal watercraft in 1991 with the launch of the SL 650. The firm opened a third plant in Spirit Lake, Iowa in 1994. Sales exceeded $1 billion for the first time in 1995. That year, Fuji Heavy Industries and Polaris created Robin Manufacturing, a joint venture dedicated to engine manufacturing. In 1997, Polaris established a facility in Vermillion, South Dakota, to distribute parts, clothing, and gear. The firm also introduced its first motorcycle, the Victory, and full-scale production on Victory Cruisers began in 1998. *CycleWorld* magazine named the Victory V92C its "Cruiser of the Year" that year. Tom Tiller took over as president and CEO in 1999 and Wendel remained chairman. In 2001 Polaris developed the All Surface Loader, a landscaping machine.

POLARIS MACHINES MAKE HISTORY

Polaris Sno-Traveler machines, introduced in the late 1950s, were among the first snowmobiles in the world. In 1958 the U.S. Air Force used a Polaris Sno-Traveler to get within 400 miles of the North Pole, despite a temperature of 48 degrees below zero.

STRATEGY

When Polaris entered the ATV market in the 1980s, it faced fierce competition from established players like Honda and Suzuki. However, the firm's strategy of marketing its ATVs as utility vehicles versus recreational vehicles helped to differentiate Polaris from the competition. As a result, the firm found itself second only to Honda in the U.S. ATV market in the late 1980s. The firm retained its position as leader in ATV sales into the early 2000s.

A marketing strategy employed by Polaris throughout its history was its intense promotion of new product releases. For example, to publicize its move into ATVs, Polaris asked the governor of Minnesota, Rudy Perpich, to ride the firm's first ATV as it exited the assembly line. When the firm unveiled its first motorcycle, the Victory, it hired famous race car driver Al Unser, Jr. to ride the first Victory into Planet Hollywood at the Mall of America.

In 2000, sluggish snowmobile sales prompted the company's founders, Edgar Hetteen and David Johnson, to plan a snowmobile trip across Alaska with company CEO Tiller. The trio hoped that the publicity surrounding the trip would spark increased interest in snowmobiling in the same way that Hetteen's 1,200-mile, three-week trip across Alaska had boosted sales in the early 1960s. The publicity generated did help to boost snowmobile sales from 22 percent of Polaris' revenues in 2000 to 25 percent of revenues in 2001. This growth took place despite a mild winter throughout most of the United States.

INFLUENCES

The firm's decision to diversify into ATVs in the mid-1980s was the result of its reliance on snowmobiles, which limited the lion's share of production and sales to the winter months. Later diversification moves into personal watercraft and motorcycles were also sparked by sluggish snowmobile sales and the goal of reducing Polaris' reliance on any single vehicle.

CURRENT TRENDS

According to a March 2002 issue of *Business Wire*, "Quality and reliability continue to be key factors in the success of the Polaris snowmobile line, but innovation plays an increasingly important role in this competitive market." To maintain its position as a pioneer of technological developments that enhance snowmobile performance, Polaris invests millions of dollars into new product development efforts. For example, in 2002, Polaris introduced a snowmobile with an engine that exceeded the Environmental Protection Agency standards scheduled to take effect in 2010. The new machine's lower center of gravity increased stability and handling for drivers. The firm also put in place a program called Snow Check, which allows customers visiting the firm's Web site to design a snowmobile with the features they want and order it from their local Polaris dealer.

PRODUCTS

The Polaris Indy 600 XC SP snowmobile was the world's bestseller in 2001. Along with 28 other snowmobile models, Polaris sells a variety of four-wheel and six-wheel ATV models; a line of personal watercraft; two motorcycle models; apparel and gear including gloves, hats, helmets, jackets, sweaters, and boots; and accessories including tow hitches, hand warmers, lubricants, luggage, and cargo racks.

GLOBAL PRESENCE

While most of Polaris' engineering and manufacturing activities take place in the United States, the firm distributes its products in 121 countries. Polaris also operates subsidiaries in Canada, Australia, and New Zealand.

CHRONOLOGY:
Key Dates for Polaris Industries, Inc.

1945: Edgar Hetteen and David Johnson create Hetteen Hoist & Derrick

1954: Hetteen Hoist & Derrick changes its name to Polaris Industries, Inc.

1968: Textron acquires Polaris

1981: Polaris managers buy Polaris back from Textron

1985: Polaris begins manufacturing ATVs

1991: Polaris begins making personal watercraft

1995: Sales exceeded $1 billion for the first time

1998: Polaris begins manufacturing motorcycles

SOURCES OF INFORMATION

Bibliography

Black, Sam. "ATV Makers Predict Continued Growth; Analysts Take More Conservative Stance." *Minneapolis-St. Paul City Business*, 28 September 2001.

"Polaris Gives Snowmobile Dealers Reasons for Optimism." *Business Wire*, 25 March 2002.

Polaris Industries, Inc. Corporate History. Available at http://www.polarisindustries.com.

Polaris Industries, Inc. Home Page, 2002. Available at http://www.polarisindustries.com.

For additional industry research:
Investigate companies by their Standard Industrial Classification Codes, also known as SICs. Polaris Industries' primary SICs are:

3732 Boat Building and Repairing

3799 Transportation Equipment, Not Elsewhere Classified

Also investigate companies by their North American Industry Classification System Codes, also known as NAICS codes. Polaris Industries' primary NAICS codes are:

336120 Boat Building

336999 All Other Transportation Equipment Manufacturing

priceline.com, Incorporated

FOUNDED: 1998

Contact Information:
HEADQUARTERS: 800 Connecticut Ave.
    Norwalk, CT 06854-9998
PHONE: (203)299-8000
FAX: (203)299-8948
EMAIL: info@priceline.com
URL: http://www.priceline.com

OVERVIEW

priceline.com gave the public the power to "Name Your Own Price" online for the first time on goods and services in four areas: travel, with airline tickets, hotel rooms, cruises, and rental cars; personal finance, with home mortgages, refinancing and home equity loans; automotive, offering new cars; and telecommunications, with long distance calling service and calling cards. As long as a customer was flexible and prepaid, he/she could soon be airborne for far less money than ever before. priceline.com founder and former vice chairman, Internet commerce pioneer Jay S. Walker, came up with the innovative idea of patenting priceline.com's method of doing business, along with a slew of other patents granted and pending, that could revolutionize industries outside the Internet as well. Walker is also founder, chairman and CEO of Walker Digital Corp., the largest intellectual property laboratory dedicated to business methodology.

COMPANY FINANCES

During the technology boom, the company went public and its March 29, 1999 Wall Street debut was a huge success. The offer price of $16.00 per share ended the first day of trading at $69.00, making it one of the most successful initial public offerings ever, giving the company a $9.8 billion market value and making founder Walker an instant billionaire. The stock reached to more than $82.00 on the next day. At its all-time high, the company's stock reached $165.00 a share. Just over a year later, the stock reflected the deflated technology market at nearly $30.00 a share.

Though the company had yet to post a profit, like many other former high-flying technology companies, analysts predicted priceline.com would be in the black by 2001. It in fact posted a quarterly profit for the first time in late 2001. It's 2000 sales stood at more than $1.2 billion and its loss narrowed to $315 million. Year 2001 revenues were $1.17 billion, a five percent drop from the previous year. priceline.com stock ranged from a low of $1.80 to a high of $10.35 over a 52-week period and its price-earnings ratio was 66 as of August 2001.

ANALYSTS' OPINIONS

After Walker's departure in late 2000, priceline.com struggled amid publicity regarding complaints about customer satisfaction and increased competition from other Internet businesses. In September 2000, the Better Business Bureau expelled the company due to complaints that it didn't adequately explain the restrictions on its discount airline tickets, but it was reinstated two months later when the company changed its disclosure policy. Its stock price stood at about $4.00 as of early 2002.

Due to priceline.com's better than expected 2001 fourth quarter earnings and revenues, analyst Scott Kessler reiterated a "hold" recommendation on the company's stock. Kessler also noted priceline.com's partnership with eBay to create travel-booking service for airline tickets, car rentals, hotel reservations and vacation packages on auction and said that "Buy It Now" formats on the auction Web site were a positive and significant move for priceline.com. Lehman Brothers had similar opinions about the company and noted that its solid, better than expected 2001 fourth quarter results and continuing profitability for three consecutive quarters in a challenging economic environment warranted the company a "market perform" rating. Several analysts also recognized priceline.com's future potential in and beyond the travel sector, especially as the travel industry and economic climate improved.

HISTORY

priceline.com founder Jay S. Walker started in business with a catalog venture, Catalog Media Corp., which saw its first success in 1985 when he made a deal between hundreds of catalog vendors and Federal Express. The deal was that the catalog merchants would subsidize Fed-Ex overnight delivery of their products to customers, thereby extending the Christmas holiday shopping season for the merchants until the day before December 25.

Fresh from his first big business achievement, Walker then partnered with Michael Loeb in a company they called NewSub Services, which began operation in 1991. Walker's aim for the company was to offer an

FINANCES:

priceline.com Inc.
Revenues, 1998-2001
(million dollars)

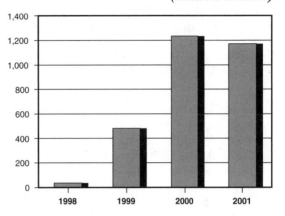

priceline.com Inc.
2001 Stock Prices
(dollars)

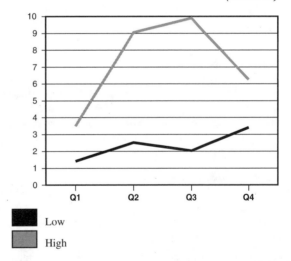

Low

High

indefinite renewal service for magazine subscriptions by charging customers' credit cards automatically each year. A common procedure in other countries, the practice had not yet been introduced in the United States. He came up with a software program, which later received a patent in 1999, that allowed publishers to renew subscriptions automatically to a customer's stored credit card number, with the customer's permission. Loeb, whose father was the financial journalist and editor Marshall Loeb, had connections in the publishing industry and the company sold half a million subscriptions within one year. By 1998, the company, later renamed Synapse Group, Inc.,

FAST FACTS:

About priceline.com, Incorporated

Ownership: priceline.com, Incorporated is a publicly owned company traded on the NASDAQ Stock Exchange.

Ticker Symbol: PCLN

Officers: Richard S. Braddock, 59, Chmn. and CEO, 2000 base salary $1,700,000; Jeffery H. Boyd, 44, Pres. and COO, 2000 base salary $5,800,000; Robert Mylod, 34, CFO; Brett Keller, Chief Marketing Officer; Ronald V. Rose, CIO; Trey Urbahn, 43, Pres. Airlines, 2000 base salary $978,000; Christopher L. Soder, Pres. Lodging, Automotive and Business Development; Jeanne D. Wisniewski, EVP Human Resources; Lisa Gillingham, SVP Customer Service and Operations; Mitch Truwit, EVP Operations; Thomas P. D'Angelo, 41, SVP Finance and Controller, 2000 base salary $683,000; Peter J. Millones, Jr., SVP and Gen. Counsel

Employees: 359

Chief Competitors: priceline.com's competitors include traditional travel agencies; consolidators and wholesalers of airline tickets and other travel products; operators of travel reservation databases, including Worldspan and Sabre; and other Internet travel service companies, including Expedia, Orbitz, Hotwire, and Travelocity.com.

---

had sold 30 million magazine subscriptions and had sales of nearly $300 million.

Walker was already looking for a new challenge to conquer in the early 1990s and set his eye on the Internet as his medium. At first, Walker had the idea to start an Internet casino. Then he began to wonder if he could simply profit from ownership of the idea of Internet gaming. He followed up with patent lawyers who assured him he could patent his idea. Business, at the time, invented many things, like credit cards and frequent flyer programs, and Walker was amazed to learn no one had ever tried to patent these original ideas. With that in mind, Walker began his next business, Walker Digital Corp. in 1994. He hired a group of computer engineers, cryptographers, and other technical personnel to devise new methods of doing business on the Internet and develop the corresponding technology. Patent lawyers were also retained to secure ownership

of any ideas that the research division of the company developed.

On April 6, 1998, Walker started his online business, priceline.com, with $20 million from the sale of a third of his ownership of NewSub and $100 million from outside investors, including Paul Allen, co-founder of Microsoft; George Soros, a financier; Jim Manzi, a computer-software executive; and John C. Malone, a cable television executive. Four months later, Walker was granted a patent for development of a "buyer-driven" business method and the corresponding software. The method entailed allowing prospective customers of goods and services to send a binding purchase offer to a prospective seller over the Internet. This was the driving force behind priceline.com.

The first priceline.com offering to consumers was the opportunity to bid for airline tickets. Users would indicate their travel dates and the price they wanted to pay, enter their credit card number, and participating airlines would review the bids and decide whether to accept the traveler's offer. If they agreed on the price, the traveler was obligated to purchase the ticket. Prospective travelers stood to gain by receiving discounted tickets while airlines gained by being able to fill any as yet unsold seats.

priceline.com sold an estimated 40,000 tickets in the first three months of business. The idea caught on because of the appeal of discounts as well as the humorous ad campaigns that starred former *Star Trek* cast member William Shatner. Some early complaints noted that the success rate was only about 10 percent but it rose as more airlines gradually participated in the process.

During the technology boom, the company went public, and its March 29, 1999 Wall Street debut was a huge success. The offer price of $16.00 per share ended the first day of trading at $69.00, making it one of the most successful initial public offerings ever, giving the company a $9.8 billion market value and making Walker an instant billionaire. The stock reached to over $82.00 the next day. At its all-time high, the company's stock reached $165.00 a share. Just over a year later, the stock reflected the deflated technology market at nearly $30.00. Though the company had yet to post a profit, like many other former high-flying technology companies, analysts predicted priceline.com would be in the black by 2001. In fact, it posted a quarterly profit for the first time in late 2001. Its 2000 sales stood at more than $1.2 billion and its loss narrowed to $315 million.

While 2001 revenue dropped 5.1 percent to 1.17 billion, fourth quarter results for the company were strong, with hotel room unit sales up 115 percent year over year; rental car sales up 38 percent; and pro forma net income of $3.3 million compared with fourth quarter 2000 pro forma net loss of $25 million. priceline.com's customer base also grew to nearly 12.7 million and a record 63.3 percent repeat offer rate.

priceline.com soon grew beyond merely airline tickets, with customers being able to name their price on home financing, hotel rooms, new cars, rental cars, and telephone long distance. Some argued that the system behind priceline.com wouldn't work with the new products and services it added, but Walker firmly defended his idea to invent new business methods and patent them.

Walker suffered a setback when he left the day-to-day operations of priceline.com to others in November 1999 to launch WebHouse Club. The company was not affiliated with priceline.com but was a licensee that used Walker's patented technology to allow people to bid on gasoline and groceries. The business shut down in October 2000 because of insufficient operating funds. Walker then stepped down as priceline.com's vice chairman in late 2000, selling off most of his stake in the company and retaining about 10 percent ownership. He left priceline.com to focus on the company he started that came up with priceline.com's business model, Walker Digital, where he is now chairman and CEO.

STRATEGY

As its annual reports states, "priceline.com has established itself as one of the most recognized e-commerce brands through an aggressive marketing and promotion campaign." The company launched its memorable television ads in 1999 with former *Star Trek* star William Shatner. The campaign, called "Troubadour," showed Shatner as a kind of lounge singer crooning such tunes as "Two Tickets to Paradise" and "Age of Aquarius" in his unique and humorous off-key style. priceline.com spent $67.2 million in advertising during 2000.

In an attempt to regain financial momentum as the company's stock plunged, priceline.com decided to position itself as more "cutting edge" with a new national advertising strategy that didn't include Shatner but instead in early 2001 featured the slogan "Spend less. Live more." The new ads, which were done with a significantly reduced advertising budget, featured animation and live-action sequences and were intended to be more consumer-focused than the Shatner ads.

In July, 2001, priceline.com took the campaign one step further, utilizing director Quentin Tarantino along with singer Billy Idol and actor Tony Randall as the television pitchmen for their new "Let's Jet Set" campaign, which ran on the MTV and E! cable channels. The ads also featured the animation/live-action theme and used celebrities' voices to personify traveling to such places as Orlando, London, and New York. The campaign launched with the voice of actress Sarah Jessica Parker.

Recognizing that it was Shatner's commercials that helped make it one of the most recognized brands in the travel industry, priceline.com renewed its affiliation with Shatner in early 2002, launching a string of

CHRONOLOGY:

Key Dates for priceline.com, Incorporated

1998: Jay S. Walker founds priceline.com, Inc.

1999: priceline's initial public offering one of the most successful in history

1999: Launching of WebHouse Club with gasoline and home grocery delivery services

2000: Walker steps down as priceline.com's vice-chairman; WebHouse Club closed

2000: Memorable television ads with former *Star Trek* star William Shatner launched

2000: Sales reach more than $1.2 illion.

2001: priceline posts a quarterly profit for the first time

2001: priceline allies with online service giant American Online (AOL)

2001: New priceline.com cruise service launched

2001: priceline partners with online auctioneer eBay

radio ads with the actor interacting with the company's super computer that worked to find customers the best deals on airline tickets, hotels, and other travel products. The company found the new fun ads also underscored what differentiated it from others in the travel industry.

INFLUENCES

The closing of the disastrous priceline.com licensee WebHouse Club, Inc., which offered discount groceries and gas, the rise of negative reaction in the company's service and customer service areas, and the company's plunging stock price forced the company to revamp its strategy in 2000. priceline.com outlined its new goals in its 2000 annual report: focusing on core businesses, especially travel; strengthening its products and customer services; building international relationships; and motivating and retaining employees. With its new strategy in place, priceline.com was able to not only improve on all the issues mentioned but also strengthen the company's balance sheet, turning in three consecutive quarters of profitability by early 2002.

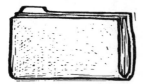

TO BOLDLY GO WHERE NO PITCHMAN HAS GONE BEFORE

If you missed the quirky stylings of *Star Trek's* own original Captain Kirk extolling the virtues of priceline.com the first time around on television, you can now catch four of the ads, entitled *Age of Aquarius, Convoy, The King* and *Paradise*, on http://www.priceline.com/media/plmedia.htm. Foregoing a paycheck, the actor instead accepted 125,000 shares of priceline.com pre-IPO stock. The crooning pitchman's portfolio was at one time worth an estimated $20.6 million when priceline.com's stock peaked at $165.00 per share but ebbed considerably when the company's stock sank to around $4.00. Shatner did, though, manage to exercise 35,000 options the following year at about $95.00 a share for a total of more than $3 million.

As the company's stock began to nosedive during the technology bust, priceline.com quickly revised its advertising campaign to reflect a more serious, consumer-oriented attitude - in contrast to the lighthearted, self-parodying Shatner television spots - and focused on characterizing the company's early tremendous success. While priceline.com temporarily shelved Shatner in favor of young, hipper entertainment personalities and cutting-edge animation in their commercials, the company recognized the power of the affiliation with Shatner and began utilizing the actor in a new and more serious yet still characteristically lighthearted manner with a string of radio ads. The new ads still conveyed the unique Shatner quality while emphasizing priceline.com's own unique strengths in the travel service market.

CURRENT TRENDS

priceline.com continued expanding its travel products, launching the priceline.com cruise service with partner National Leisure Group in February 2002. The service offered fixed-price cruises to worldwide destinations at discounted prices. Users could choose from all the largest cruise lines, a variety of worldwide destinations, and a range of time spans.

Early 2002 also saw priceline.com grow its non-travel products with an expansion of the priceline Long Distance's Name Your Own Price service. The expanded service boasted a unique Name Your Own Price phone card and the addition of Qwest Communications International and CNM Network as service partners. The new phone card, which could save users up to 40 percent or more over other phone cards, could be purchased in blocks of time up to 1,000 minutes for calls anywhere in the U.S. and users could print out the phone cards instantly using their own computers.

In February 2002, the company also entered into a long term worldwide technology agreement with Worldspan, the world's number one reservation system and e-commerce provider for the travel industry. The agreement would make Worldspan the preferred global distribution system (GDS) for processing fare searches and reservation requests and allow priceline.com access to greater travel technology, including Worldspan ePricing and enhancements to Worldspan Hotel Select, among other things.

The company also heightened marketing and consumer security protection efforts with Visa U.S.A. by implementing Verified by Visa, an authentication system utilizing passwords for Visa cardholders. Additionally, priceline.com allied with online service giant American Online (AOL) in December 2001 to allow AOL users access to priceline.com's many travel-related services and products through AOL's Travel Channel, including promotion on related sites across CompuServe, Netscape, and MapQuest.

PRODUCTS

priceline.com offers goods and services in the following four areas: travel, including airline tickets, hotel rooms and rental cars; personal finance, including home mortgages, refinancing and home equity loans; automotive, offering new cars; and telecommunications, with a long distance calling service. The company also added two new products in 2002, offering cruises in the travel category and an innovative new long distance calling card that allows users to prepay, pick the amount of calling time, and print the card out from their home computers. Teaming up with online auctioneer eBay in 2002, priceline.com has expanded its travel services beyond the priceline.com Web site.

GLOBAL PRESENCE

With hotel and resort property affiliations in the U.S., the U.S. Virgin Islands, Puerto Rico, the Bahamas, Canada, and Mexico, the launch of priceline Europe in October 2001 expanded the company's worldwide presence, allowing U.S. customers to reserve hotel rooms in fifty cities and towns in Europe through its Web site.

Countries include Austria, Belgium, England, the Czech Republic, France, Germany, Holland, Ireland, Italy, Scotland, Spain, Switzerland, and Wales. The service increased priceline.com's airline ticket service from the U.S. to 250 international sites. Since June 2000, the company entered several Asian markets, including Japan, in an agreement with subsidiaries of Hutchison Whampoa Limited, forming Hutchison-Priceline Limited.

CORPORATE CITIZENSHIP

Priceline strongly believes in giving back to the community. Employees of the company may become involved in a number of charitable events, including the AmeriCares Homefront program.

EMPLOYMENT

The company employs about 359 full-time employees, as well as a number of independent contractors in its customer service and system support areas. The company considers its relations with its employees to be good. Since priceline.com considers intellectual capital its most important asset, it continues efforts to attract, retain, and motivate highly qualified technical and management personnel in a highly competitive environment. The company also organizes events such as local softball, basketball, and golf leagues for its employees.

SOURCES OF INFORMATION

Bibliography

"Beam Me Up?" *Canadian Business*, 16 April 2001.

Grossberg, Joshua. "The Price (line) Isn't Right for Shatner." E! Online, 12 December 2000. Available at http://www.eonline.com.

"Priceline Makes European Move." FT.com, 12 October 2001. Available at http://news.ft.com.

"Priceline Revamps Ad Strategy, Sans Shatner." *ADWEEK Eastern Edition*, 8 January 2001.

Priceline.com Home Page, 2002. Available at http://www.priceline.com.

"priceline.com Incorporated." Hoover's Online, 25 February 2002. Available at http://www.hoovers.com.

"Priceline.com Inc." Gale Group, 2002. Available at http://www.galenet.galegroup.com.

"Profile@emdPriceline.com Inc." Yahoo! Finance. Available at http://biz.yahoo.com.

"S&P Says Hold Priceline." Business Week Online, 5 February 2002.

"Shatner Returns in Priceline Radio Spots." *ADWEEK Eastern Edition*, 19 February 2001.

"Tarantino's Travels." *ADWEEK Eastern Edition*, 30 July 2001.

"William Shatner Takes Center Stage in New Priceline.com Advertising Campaign Launching Today." Newstream, February 2002. Available at http://www.newstream.com.

"Worldspan, Priceline.com Announce New Long-Term Worldwide Agreement." *PR Newswire*, 5 February 2002.

For an annual report:

on the Internet at: http://www.priceline.com **or** write: priceline.com Inc., 800 Connecticut Ave., Norwalk, CT 06854

For additional industry research:

Investigate companies by their Standard Industrial Classification Codes, also known as SICs. priceline.com's primary SICs are:

7373 Computer Integrated Systems Design

7389 Business Services, Not Elsewhere Classified

Also investigate companies by their North American Industry Classification System Codes, also known as NAICS codes. priceline.com's primary NAICS code is:

541512 Computer Systems Design Services

Publix Super Markets, Inc.

FOUNDED: 1930

Contact Information:

HEADQUARTERS: 1936 George Jenkins Blvd.
   Lakeland, FL 33815
PHONE: (863)688-1188
FAX: (863)284-5532
URL: http://www.publix.com

OVERVIEW

With 534 stores in Florida, Publix is the state's largest grocery store chain. Publix also operates 127 stores in Georgia, 23 stores in South Carolina, and 4 stores in Alabama. Operations, most of which are located in Florida, also include eight distribution centers, three dairy processing plants, a deli processing plant, and a bakery. Publix is one of the largest employee-owned companies in the United States and the largest private company in Florida.

COMPANY FINANCES

After more than ten years of consecutive growth, sales for Publix reached $15.3 billion in 2001. Earnings for Publix also grew consistently throughout the 1990s, reaching $530.4 million in 2000 and remaining the same in 2001. The firm's profit margin climbed to a record 3.6 percent in 2000. Publix stock, which is sold only to Publix employees and directors, hovered around a price of $41.00 per share in the early 2000s.

ANALYSTS' OPINIONS

Florida Monthly magazine rated Publix "The Best Grocery Store" in 2001. The firm also ranked number one on a national customer satisfaction survey completed by the University of Michigan Business School and the American Society for Quality Control in 2002. That year,

FINANCES:

Publix Super Markets Inc.
Revenues, 1996-2000
(million dollars)

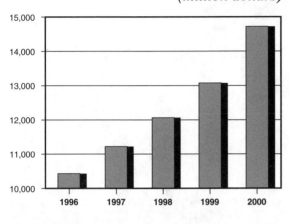

Fortune magazine named Publix on its "List of Most Admired Companies."

HISTORY

Publix was founded in 1930 when 22-year-old George W. Jenkins left his position as manager of a Piggly Wiggly store and opened his own small grocery store in Winter Haven, Florida. With five employees, the store made roughly $500.00 during its first year of operation. Jenkins added a second Publix store in 1935. Five years later, he replaced his two smaller stores with a larger Publix Market. In an effort to expand, Jenkins purchased a 19-unit grocery store chain from a Lakeland businessman looking to retire in the mid-1940s. After relocating headquarters to Lakeland, the company constructed a 70,000-square-foot store there in 1950.

In an effort to attract more customers, Publix put in place an S & H Green Stamp collection program, allowing shoppers to trade completed stamp books for discounts. Expansion continued in the late 1950s with the purchase of seven stores near Miami and surrounding areas. The firm also began selling its stock to employees. By the decade's end, Publix was operating 62 grocery stores in 32 of Florida's cities. To serve stores located in southeastern Florida, Publix established a southeast division headquarters unit and distribution center in Miami. Sales reached $500 million in 1970.

During the early 1970s, Publix established a bakery plant and produce distribution center in Lakeland. In addition, another distribution center and division head-

FAST FACTS:

About Publix Super Markets, Inc.

Ownership: Publix Super Markets, Inc. is a private company. Employees, both current and former, own 85.5 percent of the firm, while executives and directors own the remaining 14.5 percent.

Officers: Howard M. Jenkins, Chmn., 50, 2001 base salary $373,750; Hoyt R. Barnett, VChmn., 57, 2001 base salary $279,625; Charles H. Jenkins, Jr., CEO and COO, 58, 2001 base salary $356,800; W. Edwin Crenshaw, Pres., 50, 2001 base salary $337,900; David P. Phillips, CFO, 41

Employees: 122,000

Principal Subsidiary Companies: Publix Super Markets operates roughly 700 grocery stores in the southeastern United States.

Chief Competitors Competitors to Publix include Winn-Dixie, Albertson's, Kroger, and other grocery store chains, as well as retailing giants like Wal-Mart.

quarters office opened in Jacksonville. Sales reached $1 billion in 1974. By then, stores in operation had reached nearly 200. Publix added a dairy processing plant to its Lakeland facilities in 1980. Sales grew to $2 billion in 1982. Four years later, Publix opened a joint grocery store and pharmacy in Orlando. Along with constructing a dairy processing plant in Deerfield Beach, Publix also opened 30 new stores in 1988. George Jenkins handed managerial control of Publix to his son Howard in 1989.

Publix stores began to take on a new look in the 1990s. In 1991, the firm unveiled its first 65,000-square-foot store. Publix also expanded into Georgia for the first time with a 65,000-square-foot store in Savannah. Sales in 1992 exceeded $6 billion. Publix was named one of the top ten companies in *Fortune's 100 Best Companies to Work for in America* in 1993. By then, the firm had established itself as one of the top ten supermarket chains in the United States. Expansion into Georgia continued in the early 1990s, and Publix moved into South Carolina as well.

In 1995, a CBS program called *American Journal* alleged that Publix beef included sheep meat. Publix refuted the charges. In 1996, the firm moved into Alabama for the first time. Also that year, 12 women

Publix Supermarket's South Beach, Florida, store includes a 40-foot-high escalator that carries customers and their groceries to cars parked in a circular garage. (AP Photo/Marta Lavandier)

suing Publix for sexual discrimination in its hiring, promotion, and salary determination practices were granted class action status. Rather than go to trial, Publix agreed to an $85 million settlement in 1998. The firm also paid $3.5 million to settle a racial discrimination charge. The firm's legal woes continued in 1999 when it became the target of a class action racial discrimination lawsuit. That case was settled for $10.5 million in 2000.

Despite these problems, growth continued. Publix acquired nine stores in Atlanta from the A&P supermarket chain in 1999. By then, the firm was not only the sixth largest U.S. grocery store chain, it had also become the nation's tenth largest food company. Charles Jenkins succeeded his cousin, Howard Jenkins, as CEO in 2001.

STRATEGY

The success of Publix is due at least in part to its strategy of offering innovative services to its customers. For example, the first Publix Market, constructed in

1940, offered Florida grocery shoppers air conditioning for the first time. In the 1970s, Publix became the first grocery store chain in Florida to use bar code scanning technology to speed the checkout process. The firm also began offering ATM machines before Florida banks did. In 1988, Publix put in place an automated checkout system for customers who wanted to scan their own groceries. While other grocery store chains focused on offering the lowest prices, Publix differentiated itself by promoting these and other services as well as a friendly staff.

Historically, the firm had limited its growth efforts to Florida. That strategy changed in the 1990s, however, when Howard Jenkins succeeded his father as CEO. Publix moved into Savannah, Georgia, in the early 1990s and the firm's expansion efforts in Georgia intensified throughout the 1990s. By 1998, the company operated 70 stores near Atlanta, holding roughly 22 percent of the grocery market there. According to *Florida Trends* writer John Finotti, although this aggressive expansion strategy did boost sales, it also caused some problems. "Building that base in such a short period of time has been taxing . . . For one, marketing costs have climbed as Publix introduced itself to Atlanta shoppers. In addi-

PUBLIX MARKET SETS ITSELF APART

At the age of 32, George Jenkins decided to close his two small Publix grocery stores and build a larger supermarket. The Publix Market, which opened its doors in 1940, was the first supermarket in Florida to offer air conditioning. The store also attracted attention with its electronic doors, florescent lights, pastel colors, and music.

tion, Publix has struggled to replicate its culture of friendly store employees and customer service as the expansion stretched the ranks of experienced managers thinner and thinner." Despite these difficulties, Publix maintained its expansion strategy with plans to open 300 new stores by 2006.

CURRENT TRENDS

In the late 1990s, some analysts predicted that online grocery stores like Webvan and Peapod would pose a serious threat to traditional grocery store chains like Publix. Although that threat failed to materialize, Publix decided to launch its own online grocery service in September of 2001. The firm had seen a drop in sales in Atlanta after Webvan opened there. When Webvan went bankrupt, Publix decided that although the immediate threat was gone, the trend of online shopping was likely to continue, particularly as high-speed Internet connections became less expensive and more commonplace and as people continued to look for ways to save time. Rather than wait for another competitor to launch such a service, the firm developed its own Internet-based operation. Known as PublixDirect, the new unit operated a fleet of 38 trucks and made roughly 2,500 deliveries per week in January of 2002.

PRODUCTS

Along with traditional groceries, Publix stores sell flowers, baked goods, dairy products, ethnic foods, heath and beauty care products, housewares, meats, produce, and seafood. Services include photo processing and banking. Some stores also include pharmacies.

CHRONOLOGY:
Key Dates for Publix Super Markets, Inc.

1930: George Jenkins opens a grocery store named Publix

1940: Jenkins opens the first Publix Market

1964: Publix opens its one-hundredth store

1991: Expanding outside Florida for the first time, Publix opens a store in Georgia

2001: Publix launches PublixDirect, an online grocery store service

CORPORATE CITIZENSHIP

Each year, Publix supports the Special Olympics, March of Dimes, Children's Miracle Network, United Way, and Food Industry Crusade Against Hunger. In 2001, the firm donated $2.1 million to the March of Dimes. It also raised $600,000 for Children's Miracle Network; $651,000 for the Special Olympics; $14.5 million for United Way; and $900,000 for Food Industry Crusade Against Hunger. Publix also makes cash and non-cash donations to a variety of local charities.

SOURCES OF INFORMATION

Bibliography

Gibbs, Lisa. "Virtual Paper or Virtual Plastic." *Florida Trend*, March 2002.

Finotti, John. "Publix's Battle for Atlanta." *Florida Trend*, March 1999.

"Publix Announces Annual Results." *Business Wire*, 1 March 2002.

Publix Super Markets, Inc. Home Page, 2002. Available at http://www.publix.com.

"Publix Super Markets, Inc." *Notable Corporate Chronologies*. Farmington Hills: Gale Research, 1999.

For an annual report:

write: Publix Super Markets, Corporate Office, Attention Consumer Relations, PO Box 407, Lakeland, FL 33802-0407 **or call:** (800) 242-1227

For additional industry research:

Investigate companies by their Standard Industrial Classification Codes, also known as SICs. Publix Super Market's primary SICs are:

2013 Sausages and Other Prepared Meat Products

2051 Bread and Other Bakery Products

5411 Grocery Stores

Also investigate companies by their North American Industry Classification System Codes, also known as NAICS codes. Publix Super Markets' primary NAICS codes are:

311812 Commercial Bakeries

312111 Soft Drink Manufacturing

445110 Supermarkets and Other Grocery (except Convenience)

Qualcomm, Inc.

FOUNDED: 1985

OVERVIEW

Listed on the Standard & Poor's 500, the Fortune 500, and the Fortune e-50 Stock Index, San Diego, California-based Qualcomm is a leading provider of wireless technology chips. The firm holds more than 600 patents. Qualcomm's efforts to position its Code Division Multiple Access (CDMA) technology as a standard in the wireless industry paid off in the mid-1990s when cellular service providers began to embrace CDMA, considered one of the most efficient ways to allow wireless technology users to share airwaves without interference. Licensing CDMA technology to firms like Samsung, Kyocera, and LG Electronics accounts for more than one-third of revenues. Qualcomm also develops satellite-based tracking systems.

Contact Information:
HEADQUARTERS: 5775 Morehouse Dr.
  San Diego, CA 92121-1714
PHONE: (858)587-1121
FAX: (858)658-2100
EMAIL: ir@qualcomm.com
URL: http://www.qualcomm.com

COMPANY FINANCES

Throughout the 1990s, sales for Qualcomm grew explosively. Less than $200 million in the early 1990s, revenues reached more than $2 billion in 1997. After climbing to $3.3 billion in 1998 and peaking at $3.9 billion in 1999, sales fell to $3.1 billion in 2000 and to $2.6 billion in 2001. Earnings also skyrocketed during the 1990s, growing from $12.1 million in 1993 to a record $670 million in 2000. That year, earnings per share reached a noteworthy 21 percent. However, Qualcomm posted a $548.7 million loss in 2001. Stock prices, which had jumped from a high of $49.75 per share in 1999 to a high of $200 per share in 2000, fell to a high of $107.81 per share in 2001.

FINANCES:

Qualcomm Inc.
Revenues, 1997-2001
(million dollars)

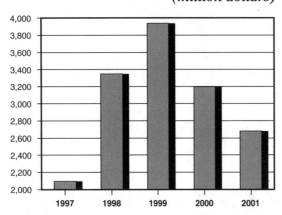

Qualcomm Inc.
2001 Stock Prices
(dollars)

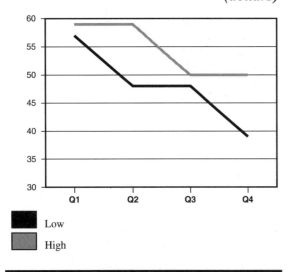

- Low
- High

ANALYSTS' OPINIONS

Although Qualcomm stock tumbled in 2001, as did the stock of most major telecommunications technology players, analysts pointed out that its per share price remained significantly higher than many of its rivals. According to an October 2001 issue of *Forbes*, "That owes largely to Qualcomm's extensive and pricey portfolio of patents on a wireless transmission scheme known as CDMA (code division multiple access). Analysts estimate the firm collects a 4 percent royalty on the cost of a cell phone, reaping profits on a big share of the 400 million cell phones sold every year." Rather than continuing to rely on licensing fees, however, some analysts believe the firm must expand its chip sales, particularly in Europe, if it wants to continue growing.

HISTORY

Irwin M. Jacobs and Andrew Viterbi, both graduates of the Massachusetts Institute of Technology (MIT), created a company called Linkabit in 1968. Based in San Diego, California, the new firm sold digital communications processing equipment. Jacobs and Viterbi began working to develop satellite communications applications for the television industry. Sales in 1980 reached $100 million and employees exceeded 100,000. Linkabit merged with M/A-COM that year to create M/A-COM Linkabit., and company activities included developing cable television and data transmission technology.

In 1985, believing that wireless communications would prove to be a boom market in the near future, Jacobs and Viterbi left M/A-COM to create Qualcomm, Inc. Initially, the pair worked on developing digital satellite communications technology into commercially viable products. In the late 1980s, Jacobs and Viterbi decided that the trucking industry would benefit from advances in wireless, long distance communications, and they began working on a wireless messaging and tracking system that would allow trucking companies to monitor trucks along their routes and allow drivers and dispatchers to communicate with each another. The new system was dubbed OmniTRACS, and it linked with existing communications satellites to offer access across North America. Drivers were outfitted with keyboards, terminals, and software that allowed them to contact dispatchers via a massive network managed at the Qualcomm's headquarters in San Diego.

The OmniTRACS system proved highly successful and Qualcomm eventually created similar satellite-based systems for use in Canada and Europe. Qualcomm completed its initial public offering in 1991. The trucking industries in both Brazil and Japan ordered OmniTRACS systems in 1992. The following year, *Fleet Owner* magazine named Jacobs "The Man Who Changed Trucking."

Jacobs and Viterbi then began to eye the U.S. cellular phone industry, which had started to develop in the 1980s. In fact, nearly 300,000 Americans were using cellular car phones in 1985. Jacobs and Viterbi believed that digital signals, which converted the electrical signals used by conventional telephones into the zeros and ones used by computers, would replace the early analog transmission technology adopted by the cellular industry. As a result, they turned Qualcomm's focus to creating a new standard for cellular technology. However, cellular technology developer Ericsson, based in Sweden, convinced the Cellular Telecommunications Industries Association

(CTIA) to adopt its cell phone standard, called time division multiple access (TDMA), in 1989. TDMA parceled phone conversations into data chunks that were transmitted, one at a time, over specific radio frequencies. Although time division multiple access (TDMA) was more efficient than the analog system, it proved to be less so than the code division multiple access (CDMA) standard developed by Jacobs and Viterbi. CDMA assigned codes to every phone call. These coded calls were then divided into ten different data chunks and transmitted at the same time across all available cell phone channels. In fact, CDMA proved twice as efficient as TDMA and nearly 10 times as efficient as analog systems.

In 1990, both NYNEX and Ameritech agreed to adopt code division multiple access (CDMA) technology. Eventually, Qualcomm convinced the Cellular Telecommunications Industries Association (CTIA) to consider making CDMA a cellular phone standard. Because the infrastructure necessary to implement CDMA simply did not exist at that time, Qualcomm decided to conduct its initial public offering in December of 1991. The firm used the $53 million it raised to create a base station and an extensive network system for CDMA.

Jacobs and Viterbi also explored other technologies in the early 1990s. In 1991, the firm released its Eudora email software, which secured users over the next five years. It also began working with Loral Corp. on a satellite telecommunications system called Globalstar.

Sales of OmniTRACS doubled in 1992. The following year, the trucking industry in Mexico requested the OmniTRACS system, as did J.B. Hunt, the largest U.S. truckload hauler. It was then that the Cellular Telecommunications Industries Association formally adopted code division multiple access (CDMA) as a cellular standard in North America. As a result, three regional Bell companies and Alltel Mobile Communications ordered CDMA handsets and infrastructure equipment. In addition, leading telecommunications companies began to conduct tests of CDMA service, and firms in Korea and the Philippines placed CDMA orders.

CDMA made its official debut in 1995. By July, 11 of the 14 largest U.S. telephone carriers had adopted CDMA. Twelve of the world's largest cellular phone companies, such as Motorola, Inc., NEC Corp., and Sony Corp., each paid Qualcomm $1 million to license its CDMA technology. Six leading telecommunications equipment makers, including AT&T Corp. and Northern Telecom, paid $5 million to gain rights to manufacture CDMA network equipment.

Along with licensing the CDMA standard, Qualcomm also began to manufacture its own wireless phones. However, Qualcomm's ties to the CDMA standard undermined its competitiveness as a cellular phone maker because rivals tended to manufacture phones for each cellular standard. By the middle of 1997, more than

FAST FACTS:
About Qualcomm, Inc.

Ownership: Qualcomm, Inc. is a public company traded on the NASDAQ Stock Exchange.

Ticker Symbol: QCOM

Officers: Irwin M. Jacobs, Chmn. and CEO, 66, 2001 base salary $936,557; Anthony S. Thornley, Pres. and COO, 54, 2001 base salary $529,241; Franklin P. Antonio, EVP and Chief Scientist, 48; Roberto Padovani, EVP Chief Technology Officer

Employees: 6,500

Principal Subsidiary Companies: Qualcomm, Inc. operates offices in 17 countries, including the United States.

Chief Competitors: Competitors to Qualcomm include Nokia, Ericsson, Motorola, and other leaders in the wireless technology industry.

half of all digital wireless systems under construction used the CDMA standard. Sales that year more than doubled to $2.09 billion. Legal wrangling between Ericsson and Qualcomm over the adoption of CDMA as an industry standard came to an end in 1999 when the two companies agreed to license one another's technology. The following year, Qualcomm sold its cellular phone operations to Japan's Kyocera Corp. The Chinese government granted permission for Qualcomm and China Unicom to establish the first CDMA network in China in 2001. The firm reached a similar deal with Vespers, based in Brazil.

STRATEGY

When Qualcomm was ready to release its first version of the OmniTRACS satellite-based vehicle tracking system in 1988, the firm's founders decided to demonstrate the new technology directly to those who would have the authority to make such a purchase. To this end, they invited 300 trucking industry leaders to San Diego to demonstrate OmniTRACs. The marketing tactic paid off when Wisconsin-based Schneider National, Inc., a leading U.S. long haul trucking firm, ordered an OmniTRACS system a few months after the presentation. Because Schneider operated a fleet of more than 5,000

CHRONOLOGY:

Key Dates for Qualcomm Inc.

1985: Jacobs and Viterbi found Qualcomm

1989: Qualcomm releases its first version of CDMA

1991: Qualcomm completes its initial public offering

1993: The Cellular Telecommunications Industry Association adopts CDMA as a North American wireless communications standard

2000: Kyocera Corp. acquires the cell phone operations of Qualcomm

trucks, the contract proved to be worth $20 million. As a result, Qualcomm's revenues grew to $32 million in 1989.

Marketing tactics were at the core of Qualcomm's success with CDMA as well. While Jacobs and Viterbi were working on developing the new cellular phone standard in the late 1980s, rival Ericsson convinced the Cellular Telecommunications Industries Association (CTIA) to adopt its new cell phone standard, time division multiple access (TDMA). This proved to be quite an obstacle for Qualcomm. Not only had the CTIA found another standard, Qualcomm had yet to test CDMA, leaving many authorities convinced it was nothing more than a theory. Despite the lukewarm response he got while presenting CDMA to the CTIA, Jacobs began to make presentations to companies like Nynex, Bell Atlantic, Motorola, and Nokia, hoping to convince them to fund testing of CDMA, which would demonstrate its superiority over TDMA. Eventually, Pacific Telesis offered $2 million to fund a CDMA trial. In fact, by the end of 1989, Jacobs had secured roughly $30 million to create trial CDMA networks in San Diego and New York City.

While testing the quality, capacity, and reach of the CDMA networks, Qualcomm continued to aggressively market CDMA to industry leaders. In 1990, both NYNEX and Ameritech agreed to use the CDMA standard. The following year, Nokia, Motorola, and AT&T agreed to fund additional testing and development of CDMA networks.

A successful November 1991 test of Qualcomm's CDMA technology, accomplished in conjunction with 14 international and domestic cellular service providers and equipment manufacturers, prompted the CTIA to consider adopting CDMA as a standard. Two years later, CDMA was officially named a North American wireless

communications standard by CTIA. Marketing efforts continued in the mid-1990s as the new networks were actually built. In the late 1990s and early 2000s, Qualcomm began promoting CDMA in areas such as Asia and South America by agreeing to form partnerships with leading wireless service providers there.

CURRENT TRENDS

The growing popularity of the Internet in the late 1990s prompted many wireless service providers and manufacturers to begin creating technology that offered wireless access to the Internet. In 1998, Microsoft Corp. and Qualcomm created Wireless Knowledge, a wireless Internet access technology joint venture. Two years later, Wireless Knowledge became a wholly owned subsidiary of Qualcomm after Microsoft sold its stake in the venture back to Qualcomm. In the early 2000s, Qualcomm developed Binary Runtime Environment for Wireless (BREW) software, which allowed for access to all sorts of Web-based and electronic business applications via wireless devices.

PRODUCTS

Along with licensing its CDMA technology, which accounts for nearly one-third of sales, Qualcomm also sells integrated circuits and systems software. In fact, various CDMA-based technology products account for more than half of Qualcomm's revenues. Wireless and Internet systems and services—such as Globalstar, Omni-TRACs, Eudora email, and BREW software—bring in 20 percent of sales.

CORPORATE CITIZENSHIP

Along with encouraging volunteerism among its employees, Qualcomm also makes cash and non-cash donations to non-profit organizations focused on math and education, arts and culture, and health and human services. The firm also awards a "Young Women Who Mean Business" scholarship annually.

GLOBAL PRESENCE

Qualcomm operates offices in Argentina, Australia, Brazil, China, France, Germany, India, Indonesia, Israel, Italy, Japan, the Netherlands, Russia, South Korea, Thailand, the United Kingdom, and the United States. The firm has struggled to push its CDMA standard in Europe as most wireless firms there have chosen the General Packet Radio Service standard in favor of paying what they believe are hefty CDMA royalties to Qualcomm. Roughly 35 percent of Qualcomm's sales take place in the United States while another 35 percent happen in Korea. Other countries account for the remaining 30 percent.

SOURCES OF INFORMATION

Bibliography

Qualcomm, Inc. Home Page, 2002. Available at http://www.qualcomm.com.

"Qualcomm Hits the Big Time." *Fortune*, 15 May 2000.

"Qualcomm's Dr. Strangelove." *The Economist*, 17 June 2000.

Williams, Elisa. "When the Chips are Dow." *Forbes*, 29 October 2001.

For an annual report:

on the Internet at: http://www.qualcomm.com/IR/annualreport/ar2001

For additional industry research:

Investigate companies by their Standard Industrial Classification Codes, also known as SICs. Qualcomm's primary SICs are:

3633 Radio and TV Broadcasting and Communication Equipment

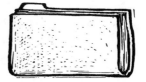

HUMBLE BEGINNINGS FOR QUALCOMM

In 1985, when Irwin Jacobs and Andrew Viterbi founded Qualcomm (the name was a combination of the words "quality" and "communication"), they based their operations above a pizza restaurant located in a strip mall. Within four years, the firm had landed more than $15 million in defense contracts.

6794 Patent Owners and Lessors

Also investigate companies by their North American Industry Classification System Codes, also known as NAICS codes. Qualcomm's primary NAICS codes are:

334220 Radio and Television Broadcasting and Wireless Communications Equipment Manufacturing

334290 Other Communication Equipment Manufacturing

513322 Cellular and Other Wireless Telecommunications

RadioShack Corporation

FOUNDED: 1919 as Hinckley-Tandy Leather Company
VARIANT NAME: Tandy Corporation

Contact Information:

HEADQUARTERS: 100 Throckmorton St.
   Fort Worth, Texas 76102
PHONE: (817)415-3700
FAX: (817)390-2774
URL: http://www.radioshack.com

OVERVIEW

In early 2001 RadioShack Corporation offered more than 22,000 different electronics products and planned to add another 10,000 throughout the course of the year. The firm's products can be purchased through its Web site and catalog as well as through its retail outlets. Its varied product line includes virtually everything connected with electronics, and RadioShack has become famous as the source for electronics parts that cannot be found anywhere else. In addition to electronic parts and accessories, RadioShack sells cellular, PCS, and conventional telephones; audio and video equipment, such as stereo systems, radios, and televisions; home satellite systems; personal computers and accessories; and a number of specialized items such as weather radios. RadioShack also acts as a middleman for services offered by firms with which it has forged strategic alliances, including DirecTV Inc., Microsoft Corporation, Sprint Communications, Thomson Multimedia, and Verizon Wireless.

Headquartered in Ft. Worth, Texas, RadioShack maintained a network of 7,199 stores in the United States at the beginning of 2001, of which 5,109 were owned outright by RadioShack Corporation. The rest were dealer franchises that sold RadioShack products together with other retail lines. RadioShack stores are usually located in shopping malls and strip malls, although some are stand-alone buildings. Virtually all RadioShack stores are leased by the firm. In addition to its stores, the company also owns and operates seven facilities in the United States and one in China that manufacture RadioShack products including telephones, antennas, wire and cable products, and a variety of other hard-to-find consumer electronic parts and accessories. There are 56 Radio-Shack Service Centers that repair all products purchased at RadioShack stores. The ten regional distribution centers ship more than 1 million cartons of goods to RadioShack stores monthly. Four of the centers also fill orders made through the RadioShack Web site.

COMPANY FINANCES

Number 360 in the *Fortune* 500, RadioShack Corporation reported $4.794 billion in sales in 2000, an increase of 16.2 percent from 1999 results. The growth was partly the result of the addition of 22 new stores to the RadioShack chain. On the other hand, RadioShack's sales per employee ratio dropped precipitously during the latter half of the 1990s, reaching only $33,840 in 2000—a 31 percent drop from 1997. The company's gross profits ($2,369 million in 2000) grew at a slightly slower rate than they had in 1999.

In 2000 telephones and other communications products were RadioShack's leading product area, accounting for nearly 28 percent of the company's total sales. Electronic parts and accessories were second with just under 25 percent. With 22.5 percent of 2000 sales, audio and video merchandise showed the greatest improvement, up more than 5 percent from 1999. The rest of RadioShack's sales were personal electronics, seasonal merchandise, computers and peripherals, and services. Long a favorite of hobbyists and other consumers, RadioShack has also begun attracting a significant number of clients in the business, governmental, and educational sectors, thanks in particular to its presence online. Most of the firm's sales were made within the United States.

RadioShack's common stock price fluctuated from a low of $35.06 to a high of $72.94 in fiscal year 2000. Its price-earnings ratio for 2000 was 16.1.

ANALYSTS' OPINIONS

Analysts saw RadioShack facing a challenging period in 2002. Sales growth in 2001 was below levels targeted by the firm and, in the view of Merrill Lynch analysts, those goals were likely to remain frustrated partly because of structural changes in the marketplace in which RadioShack operates. The company, they predicted, would be hurt by a downturn in wireless communication sales—one of RadioShack's most important sales sectors—which had "already peaked." Personal computer sales were very weak, "largest rate of decline of any of the major consumer electronic retailers," in part because of RadioShack's decision not to stock notebook computers. Personal electronics sales would continue to suffer, analysts at Merrill Lynch speculated, unless RadioShack lowered its relatively high prices. Electronic

FINANCES:

RadioShack Corporation Net Sales, 1998-2000 (million dollars)

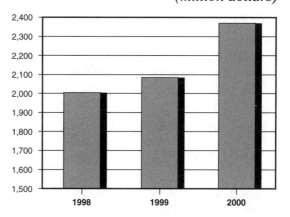

RadioShack Corporation 2000 Stock Prices (dollars)

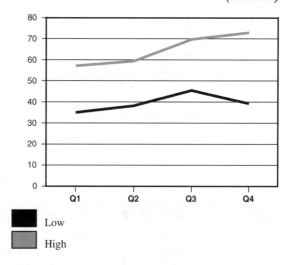

parts continued to perform well; however, those customers were not purchasing items from other parts of RadioShack stores. Robertson Stephens found fault with RadioShack's plan to cut costs by reducing inventory at its stores, pointing out that "the RadioShack brand stands as a resource for hard to find electronic connectors, batteries, and accessories. . . .We remain concerned about the possibility that the company's inventory turn improvement goals are at odds with its ability to satisfy customers, which requires an increasingly deep and broad product assortment."

FAST FACTS:

About RadioShack Corporation

Ownership: RadioShack Corporation is a publicly owned company traded on the New York Stock Exchange.

Ticker Symbol: RSH

Officers: Leonard H. Roberts, Chmn. and CEO, 53, 2000 base salary $1,000,000; David J. Edmondson, Pres. and COO, 41, 2000 base salary $420,000

Employees: 32,000

Principal Subsidiary Companies: RadioShack has more than 7,200 retail outlets in the United States, more than 5,000 of which are owned by RadioShack Corporation Its Amerilink subsidiary provides services to RadioShack as RadioShack Installation Services. In June 2001 InterTAN Canada, a former division of RadioShack, operated 833 RadioShack stores in Canada.

Chief Competitors: RadioShack competes with a number of companies in the areas of consumer electronics, computers, and communication devices. Some of its primary competitors include Best Buy, Circuit City Stores Inc., CompUSA, Sears, Home Depot, Wal-Mart, Target, and Sprint PCS Group.

HISTORY

RadioShack was founded in 1919 as Hinckley-Tandy Leather Company, a firm that distributed products for the manufacture and repair of shoes. After World War II, the firm switched its focus from shoe repair to leathercraft and hobbyists, a market that would later be important to RadioShack. Renamed the Tandy Leather Company, the company was acquired by American Hide and Leather in the early 1950s; by the end of the decade, however, Charles Tandy, the son of Tandy's founder, had won control of American Hide and rechristened the firm the Tandy Corporation.

In 1963 Tandy made the most important move of its history—it purchased RadioShack, a east coast chain of nine stores that sold radio and hi-fi equipment to the home and hobby markets along with a line of electronic parts for do-it-yourselfers. By the early sixties, the chain was on the verge of a bankruptcy; however, by 1965

Tandy Corp. had turned the chain around and made it profitable once more.

The 1970s were a key period for the Tandy Corp. In 1974 it decided to focus exclusively on electronics and sold off its leather business. By 1976 when the citizens band (CB) radio craze hit and RadioShack's radio sales increased dramatically, that decision looked like a stroke of genius. The following year RadioShack marketed a major innovation—the first mass-produced, pre-assembled computer for home use, the TRS-80. Priced at $599.99, the TRS-80 was a sensation. It made RadioShack a household name and sold more than 200,000 units between 1977 and 1981. By 1983, however, other companies, such as IBM, were bringing out their own more sophisticated personal computers. Sales of the TRS-80 plummeted. In 1984 the company held on to less than nine percent of the computer market. In response Tandy introduced two new IBM-compatible computers, as well as setting up its own specialized computer centers where brand name computers were sold. During the 1980s RadioShack launched other innovative products, including a mobile/portable cellular that consumers could install themselves and a TV satellite system for do-it-yourselfers.

The 1990s were a time of reorganization for Tandy Corp. In 1993 it separated its retailing and manufacturing operations. A year later it sold off the manufacturing side completely and diversified its operations. In 1994 it launched two new retail chains: Incredible Universe, a store that specialized in science and nature items, and Computer City. By the end of the 1990s, the company had begun paring back to its original tight focus on electronics. In 1998 it sold Incredible Universe to Fry's Electronics, and it sold Computer City to CompUSA. In 2000 the company changed its name to RadioShack Corporation. The early 2000s saw RadioShack exploring new outlets for its electronics stores, including a later-abandoned plan to expand into Blockbuster video stores. In December 2001 the firm announced a reorganization plan that included the closure of 35 stores that were not performing up to expectations and the trimming of a number of products from its line of merchandise, including televisions larger than 27 inches, car stereos, security systems, and pagers. At the same time, the company announced that it was building a new headquarters in Ft. Worth, Texas.

STRATEGY

RadioShack's basic strategy is to offer a vast line of electronics products, both third party brands and its own in-house Realistic brand, in one place. For many years RadioShack carried only Realistic products. However, since the 1980s, partly in response to the failure of its in-house line of personal computers, RadioShack has also sold third-party brand names. In line with its stated mis-

CHRONOLOGY:

Key Dates for RadioShack Corporation

1919: Charles Tandy takes over his family's leather store, soon expanding into the hobby market

1960: The Tandy Corp. begins trading on the New York Stock Exchange

1963: Tandy purchases Radio Shack, a bankrupt chain of electronics stores

1965: Radio Shack turns a profit

1975: Tandy spins off its leather line and a related wall and floor covering business into separate companies

1976: Radio sales rise significantly with the CB-radio craze

1978: Charles Tandy dies; Phillip North steps in as interim president and CEO

1983: Sales of Radio Shack's house-brand personal computer prove dismal

1984: Radio Shack's market share plummets to under nine percent; the company introduces and begins selling two new IBM-compatible computers

1985: Radio Shack establishes a series of specialized computer centers; Tandy enters the name brand retail market with the acquisitions of Scott-McDuff and Videoconcepts, two electronic equipment chain stores

1993: Tandy announces that it will divide its manufacturing and retail operations; TE Electronics Inc. will develop computers and home electronics equipment for Tandy's Radio Shack Stores; company announces plans to open four

new store formats, Famous Brand Electronics and Energy Express Plus (new stores) and Radio Shack Express and Computer City Express (smaller versions of the existing stores), raising questions about their market strategy and commitment to their traditional large-store format; Tandy sells Memtek Products and its licensing agreement with Memorex Telex, N.V., to Hanny Magnetics (B.V.I.) Ltd. for $62.5 million

1994: Tandy divests its ready-to-assemble furniture manufacturing and marketing business for approximately $350 million; Tandy sells its computer manufacturing operations to AST Research, Inc. for $90 million; opens new high-sales-volume retail chains—Incredible Universe and Computer City—in response to more competition in the consumer electronics industry

1995: Tandy closes 173 Video Concept stores, 20 McDuff Supercenters, and 40 McDuff mall stores; Tandy announces plans to purchase five million shares of its stock to increase stock dividends

1997: Tandy transfers Incredible Universe chain stores to Fry's Electronics

1998: Tandy sells its subsidiary Computer City to CompUSA Inc. for $211 million

1999: Tandy acquires AmeriLink Corp.

2000: Tandy Corp. changes its name to RadioShack Corporation, a moniker that more accurately reflects the company's single focus and gives it greater visibility among investors

---

sion to demystify technology for Americans, RadioShack established a chain of stores that extends into most neighborhoods in the United States and put in place a highly trained force of workers, who are able to answer virtually any question a customers might have about products or services.

INFLUENCES

Following a year of disappointing sales, as well as the collapse of its "store within a store" plans with the Blockbuster Video chain, RadioShack underwent a major reorganization in late 2001. It closed 35 stores nationwide, including RadioShack Installation Services, its commer-

cial installation business. It discontinued a number of product lines, including large screen TVs, home security systems, car stereo systems, and pagers. The moves were an attempt to cut costs and get rid of high-price, low-margin lines that did not turn a profit. The product cuts also opened up floor space for other goods. Overall, few people lost jobs in the reorganization. Most affected workers were transferred to other areas. It also announced plans to build a new corporate headquarters in downtown Fort Worth.

CURRENT TRENDS

As 2000 began RadioShack was pushing ahead vigorously with its "Store Within a Store" concept, in which

THE RADIOSHACK TRS-80

RadioShack introduced its groundbreaking personal computer, the TRS-80, in August 1977. There had never been a personal computer like the TRS-80. It was a complete package, pre-built and tested, that included a full keyboard, a video display, cassette storage system, a microprocessor—and 4K of memory! (The operating system was provided by a then-unknown young software designer named Bill Gates.) Although it was the most expensive RadioShack product of all time (the system listed at $599.95) thousands of customers were soon signing onto waiting lists for the revolutionary new product. By 1981 more than 200,000 units had been sold. The success came as a complete surprise to many at the firm. Chairman Charles Tandy doubted that anyone would be interested in buying a computer; he only authorized the production of the first 1,000 units because he figured when they did not sell they could be used in RadioShack stores.

an outside firm sells its own products in a designated area of RadioShack stores. The Microsoft Network@RadioShack was introduced in 2000, followed by the Sprint Store (in partnership with Sprint PCS) and the RCA Digital Entertainment Center. RadioShack and Verizon Wireless began working together in late 2001. The results of the "Store Within a Store" idea have been positive for the most part. RadioShack expects the strategy to have reached its full potential by 2005.

PRODUCTS

RadioShack sells a broad variety of consumer electronic goods at its stores and through its thick catalogue. Among its popular product lines are wireless phones and service plans, home satellites for TV, and computers. The store is most famous for its line of hard to find electronic items, including cables, jacks, outlets, and circuits. With the rise of CDs, RadioShack has been one of the only sources for phonograph parts, like styluses and arms.

CORPORATE CITIZENSHIP

RadioShack stores participate in the "Rechargeable Battery Recycling" program sponsored by the Recharge-

able Battery Recycling Corporation. Under the program RadioShack stores accept for recycling nickel cadmium, nickel metal hydride, lithium ion, and small sealed lead acid batteries that are found in many home and office products, such as wireless phones, notebook computers, and cameras.

GLOBAL PRESENCE

Until the mid-1980s, RadioShack had a network of stores in Canada, the United Kingdom, and Australia that were managed by Tandy Corp.'s international division, InterTAN. Looking to diversify its U.S. business, Tandy spun the division off in 1987, divesting its interest completely. The now-independent InterTAN kept control of all of Tandy's international retail outlets. Tandy maintained a close relationship with InterTAN, nonetheless, supplying it with most of its products and licensing it to use the names "RadioShack" and "Tandy" for its stores. By 2001, in increasingly dire financial straits, the Toronto-based InterTAN had sold off all of its U.K. and Australian holdings. There was speculation in the Canadian press whether the U.S. RadioShack, sharply focused on electronics retailing once again, would repurchase InterTAN.

EMPLOYMENT

RadioShack employs a large workforce of sales associates in its stores. Before starting work, sales associates are required to complete the new associates training program, the so-called "Fast Track to the Sales Floor." The program, which is taught via manuals and CD-ROMs, covers sales skills and the RadioShack product line. Prospective associates study the material on their own at their own pace, usually for one to two-and-a-half weeks. Store managers hold monthly Saturday morning classes to brief employees on new products and products featured in RadioShack monthly flyers. Training for managers is ongoing as well. Six months after their initial training, managers attend "Answers University" in their local district to reinforce their background in people skills and merchandising. After five years managers can attend the "Masters Class" at the RadioShack central office in Ft. Worth, an intense seminar that cover topics such as conflict resolution, hiring and firing procedures, and other specialized management topics.

SOURCES OF INFORMATION

Bibliography

Ahles, Andrea. "RadioShack Revises Its Focus." *Fort Worth Star-Telegram*, 20 December 2001.

"Blockbuster Deal Fizzles." *Chain Store Age Executive*, February 2002.

Grant, Lorrie. "RadioShack Uses Strategic Alliances to Spark Recovery." *USA Today,* 26 March 2001.

Krause, Reinhardt. "RadioShack Finds New Role As Cell Phone, Satellite Shop." *Investor's Business Daily*, 14 December 2000.

"RadioShack." *Hoover's Company Profiles*, 2002. Available at http://www.hoovers.com.

Schnurman, Mitchell. "InterTan May Be Looking for Buyer." 26 January 2001. Available at http://www.star-telegram.com.

For an annual report:

on the Internet at: http://www.radioshackcorporation.com **or** write: RadioShack Investors Relations, 100 Throckmorton Street, Suite 1800, Ft. Worth, TX 76102

For additional industry research:

Investigate companies by their Standard Industrial Classification Codes, also known as SICs. RadioShack Corporation's primary SICs are:

5731 Retail Radio TV & Consumer Electronics Stores

6719 Offices of Holding Companies, NEC

Also investigate companies by their North American Industry Classification System codes, also known as NAICS codes. RadioShack Corporation's primary NAICS code is:

443100 Electronics and Appliance Stores

Roadway Corporation

FOUNDED: 1930

Contact Information:

HEADQUARTERS: 1077 Gorge Blvd.
 Akron, OH 44310
PHONE: (330)384-1717
TOLL FREE: (800)257-2837
URL: http://www.roadwaycorp.com

OVERVIEW

Roadway Corporation, a holding company, was formed in May of 2001 to expand and diversify the company's interests through acquisitions, mergers, and partnerships in the transportation and delivery industry. It holds two subsidiaries: Roadway Express Inc. and Roadway Next Day Corporation. The corporate structure is limited as all subsidiaries operate autonomous businesses.

Founded in 1930, Roadway Express Inc., the primary subsidiary of Roadway Corporation, is a less-than-truckload (LTL) carrier that caters to industrial, commercial, and retail businesses requiring transportation services in the two- to five-day region and long-haul markets across the United States. Reimer Express Lines Ltd., based in Winnipeg, Manitoba, is a subsidiary of Roadway Express. Operating 22 terminals in Canada, it is Canada's largest common carrier. Roadway S.A. de C.V., also a subsidiary of Roadway Express, operates in Mexico. In January of 2002 Roadway Express announced the addition of a third subsidiary to its portfolio: Roadway Air, which provides expedited, on-time deliveries via air.

In 2001 Roadway entered the next-day delivery service with the acquisition of Arnold Industries, which included New Penn and Arnold Transportation Services (ATS). Arnold Industries was restructured to become Roadway Next Day Corporation, of which New Penn and ATS are subsidiaries. New Penn provides LTL next-day service in the northeastern region of the United States. Florida-based Arnold Transportation Services provides regional and short-haul irregular route and truckload deliveries in a 37-state region.

COMPANY FINANCES

In 2001 Roadway generated $2.8 billion in revenues resulting in a net income of $30.8 million, down from $3 billion in revenues and $56.5 million net income in 2000. Along with revenues dropping 8.2 percent and net income dropping 45.5 percent, basic earnings per share also decreased, from $3.03 in 2000 to $1.67 in 2001. Poor performance continued into 2002 as Roadway reported a first quarter loss of $1.7 million, or 9 cents per share, down from $5 million net income, or 26 cents per share, posted for the same period in 2001. Revenues fell 2 percent year-on-year from $650.5 million to $637.2 million. During the downward trend, stock prices remained steady, closing in March 2002 at $37.00 per share, up from $21.84 at same time of the previous year.

ANALYSTS' OPINIONS

Roadway's performance during the fourth quarter of 2001, down 46 percent from 2000, was actually slightly better than analysts had predicted. Expectations are that Roadway will eventually recover from its losses in 2001, but at least some analysts believe that the stock, priced at $37.00 a share at the close of the first quarter of 2002, was higher than its true value. Due to the slow economy in the United States, Roadway's tonnage was down double figures. In addition LTL companies began edging into pricing competition at the beginning of 2002 in order to retain the freight business that they still had. With prices dropping and no short-term recovery of the economy in view, analysts' recommendations ranged between a cautious nod toward buying Roadway stock to encouraging investors to sell in order to take advantage of the inflated stock prices. Others recommended investors hold the stock until it is clear which direction the company will go in the medium-range future. Analysts view the acquisition of Arnold Industries as a positive step as next-day delivery services generate a higher profit margin than LTL services.

HISTORY

In 1930 when the trucking industry was in its infancy, brothers Galen and Carroll Roush founded Roadway Express in Akron, Ohio. Starting with 10 owner-operators, Roadway Express hauled LTL shipments between Chicago, Houston, and Kansas City. Within months terminals were opened in additional locations, including Atlanta, Baltimore, Indianapolis, Nashville, New York, and Philadelphia. By 1935 the trucking industry had expanded sufficiently to cause deep concern among railroaders, who were still the dominant force in production transportation. The railroad industry successfully lobbied Congress, which passed the Motor

FAST FACTS:
About Roadway Corporation

Ownership: Roadway Corporation is a publicly held company and trades on the NASDAQ Stock Exchange.

Ticker Symbol: ROAD

Officers: Michael W. Wickham, 54, Chmn. and CEO, 2001 compensation $1,300,000; James D. Staley, 51, Pres. and COO (Roadway Express), 2001 compensation $894,000; J. Dawson Cunningham, 53, EVP and CFO, 2001 total pay $776,000

Employees: 28,000

Principal Subsidiary Companies: Roadway Corporation's main transportation arm is Roadway Express. Roadway Air, Reimer Express Lines Ltd. (Canada) and Roadway S.A. de C.V. (Mexico) are subsidiaries of Roadway Express. Roadway Corporation's other subsidiary is Roadway Next Day Corporation. New Penn and Arnold Transportation Services are subsidiaries of Roadway Next Day.

Chief Competitors: Roadway Corporation's primary competitors include Airborne, American Freightways, Consolidated Freightways, DHL, FedEx, UPS, U.S. Postal Service, and USFreightways.

Carrier Act in 1935. The act created the Interstate Commerce Commission (ICC) to oversee standards and rates. The new law also limited the right to operate trucking operations to those already in existence and any new ones that could prove convenience and necessity. Although Roadway Express was required to justify its operations and abide by the ICC's rulings, the regulation of the trucking industry also served to limit the company's competition and thus allow it to gain a dominant position in many key markets.

The trucking industry expanded rapidly in the booming post-World War II economy. In 1945 Roadway Express began replacing owner-operators with company drivers. The company also began to focus on the LTL business, charging customers three times more per ton than if shipped by the full truckload. During the 1950s, with a substantial loan from Chase Manhattan Bank, Roadway Express underwent extensive expansion of its terminal system. Between 1958 and 1968, the company's operations network grew from 60 to 135 terminals. From

CHRONOLOGY:

Key Dates for Roadway Express, Inc.

1930: Brothers Galen and Carroll Roush open Roadway Express in Akron, Ohio, and by the end of the year have terminals open in nine states

1941: World War II causes a substantial increase in demand for truck transportation

1945: Owner-operator drivers are replaced with hired company drivers

1956: Carroll Roush sells his half of the business to the public for $5 million

1975: Roadway Express is the number-one trucking company in the United States, producing high profit margins by specializing in less-than-truckload shipments and operating 300 terminals in 40 states

1982: Profits decline and Roadway falls to third in the industry behind Yellow Freight and Consolidated Freightways; Roadway Services, Inc. is established as a holding company with Roadway Express as its primary subsidiary

1985: Launches Roadway Package System, which struggles at first but eventually becomes profitable

1990: Moves into European market with subsidiary Roberts Express, serving Belgium, France, Luxembourg, the Netherlands, and Germany

1993: Becomes second largest freight-moving company in the United States with sales nearing $3 billion

1996: Roadway Express separates from Roadway Services, Inc. and becomes a publicly held company

1997: Expands market arena by purchasing Canadian trucking firm, Reimer Express Lines, and by launching Asian Roadway Express to service Indonesia, Malaysia, Singapore, and Thailand

2001: Reorganizes by creating Roadway Corporation as a holding company with Roadway Express as its primary operating subsidiary

---

the 1950s into the 1970s Roadway Express was the largest LTL carrier in the United States.

In 1956 Carroll Roush, at serious odds with his brother, decided to sell his shares to the public for $5 million. Solely in charge, Galen Roush pushed his company aggressively with spectacular results, and by the

1970s the debt from rapid expansion during the previous decade was paid off. Operating with a return on investment that averaged 20 percent, Roadway Express was becoming a giant in the LTL carrier business.

The market environment changed dramatically in 1980 when the trucking industry underwent deregulation. This paved the way for a multitude of new competitors to stream into the market. Even though new companies were offering cut-rate prices to attract business, for several years Roadway Express kept its high-end prices and boasted of its higher quality services. The strategy failed, and by 1982 Roadway Express had slipped to third in market share. In response, the company decided to reduce its rates and increase its exposure by developing the first advertising campaign in company history.

In 1982 the company reorganized, creating the holding company Roadway Services Inc. with Roadway Express as its main subsidiary. The company then moved to grow its business through acquisitions, some of which proved successful while others failed and were subsequently sold off. During the 1990s Roadway Services increased its international presence, setting up service networks in The Netherlands, Belgium, France, Luxembourg, England, and Germany as well as Mexico. In 1991 a depressed economy pushed the big three trucking firms, Roadway Services, Yellow, and Consolidated Freight into a price war and profits were adversely affected by a very narrow profit margin. In 1994 Roadway Express' unionized workers went on strike for over three weeks. The work stoppage resulted in the company posting a net loss of $68 million for that quarter.

In 1995 Roadway Express spun off as a separate, publicly traded company. Analysts suspected that the parent company was trying to rid itself of Roadway Express due to the high cost of unionized labor. Few held out hope that Roadway Express would prevail on its own. However, the company posted a profit of $21.8 million in 1996, just a year after the spinoff. Management aggressively cut costs and worked with the union to reach cooperative agreements. The strategy paid off and Roadway Express continued to expand through organic growth and acquisition. Profits increased accordingly, growing from $36.9 in 1997 to $56.5 in 2000, before falling off sharply in 2001 due to a downturn in the economy. During 2001 the company underwent reorganization; Roadway Corporation was established as a holding company with Roadway Express once again becoming a subsidiary.

STRATEGY

Roadway's strategic focus is multifaceted and includes special attention to information technology and customer service, safety, and remaining competitive. Information technology is a fundamental ingredient in Roadway's ability to provide top-rated services to its customers. The company takes advantage of technologies related to e-commerce in order to integrate scheduling and transit management to provide optimum routing and real-time delivery information. At Roadway Express' Web site, customers are able to check shipment status information as well as obtain online quotes, pick up and delivery notification, and pick up requests. Customers can obtain real-time information on their orders via my.roadway.com, a secure site accessible only to Roadway customers by password. Over two terabytes of shipment data are stored online, and over 99 million transactions are processed daily by the information technology systems. On average, the online shipment tracking systems processes 1,100 requests per second.

The safety of both the public and employees is another strategic priority for Roadway. Tractors, trailers, and other machinery undergo regular inspection and maintenance, and Roadway acknowledges its drivers that go without preventable accidents for extended periods.

To remain competitive in the transportation market, Roadway invests in technology that improves efficiency in its management systems that result in decreased transit times. The company has also increased its competitiveness in regional transit routes through its "Express From" service, which usually delivers in two days. In its LTL long-haul business, Roadway relies on its seamless border crossing into Canada and Mexico, as well as specialized services such as on-time guarantees, volume shipments, and cold-storage loads.

INFLUENCES

Roadway was negatively impacted by the economic recession that took hold during the first half of 2001 and was further exacerbated by the terrorist's attacks on Washington, D.C. and New York on September 11. During the first quarter of 2002, daily tonnage carried by Roadway Express was 14 percent below year-on-year levels. A decrease in commercial and industrial activity during an economic downturn translates into a decrease in transportation needs; on the other hand, during economic boons, the LTL industry profits from extended needs for product delivery. Another factor that influences Roadway's bottom line is the variable and unpredictable price of fuel. Although fluctuations in price are somewhat offset by a variable-rate fuel surcharge, fuel costs can be either a negative or positive factor. Labor relations are also a factor in Roadway's business. Over 70 percent of its 28,000 employees are represented by a labor union, primarily the International Brotherhood of Teamsters.

CURRENT TRENDS

With the acquisition of Arnold Industries in 2001, Roadway marked its clear intentions to move into the

next-day LTL shipping business. Other acquisitions are expected to follow in the future to expand Roadway's next-day business region by region. Because next-day hauling is the fastest growing segment of the trucking industry as well as a more profitable endeavor than medium- and long-hauls, Roadway is committed to carving out a niche in the market by acquiring successful regionally-based companies and building on the proven strategies already marked out by New Penn. Roadway further expanded its portfolio with the introduction of Roadway Air in 2002.

Because the LTL industry follows certain cyclical business trends in which certain periods of the year tend to be busier whereas other periods product fewer revenues, Roadway has worked for several years to convert fixed costs into variable costs that could be reduced during off seasons or during economic downturns that reduce the tonnage. For example, instead of purchasing new tires to outfit its trucks and trailers, Roadway began leasing tires on a per mile basis. The company also began moving its long-haul loads on railroad flatcars, thus reducing the number of trucks and drivers that needed to be retained during slow business periods. More than 25 percent of all ton miles are via the rails. Consequently, cost is always relative to the revenues: more revenue equals more cost, and reduced revenue equals reduced cost. Other cost-cutting measures have included a 12 percent reduction in work force between 2001 and 2002, and some tractors and trailers have been taken out of service to avoid maintenance costs.

PRODUCTS

Along with nationwide coverage in the United States, Roadway Express also provides delivery into and out of Canada and Mexico, as well as export services to 66 countries worldwide. The company maintains 379 terminals—257 company-owned and 122 leased. On an average day, Roadway Express' fleet of 34,500 trailers and 10,700 tractors are in transit with over 50,000 shipments. In 2001, the company delivered 7.4 million tons of freight, and its drivers logged over 500 million miles. Reimer Express Lines provides primarily LTL services to destinations throughout Canada, the United States, and Mexico as well as export services to over 65 other countries. Through its 19 terminals in Mexico, Roadway S.A. de C.V. provides LTL services to the electronics, automotive, and textile industries as well as other consumer sectors. With access to nearly 3,000 planes, over 12,000 daily flight departures, and over 40,000 trailers coordinated through a partnership with Integres Global Logistics, Roadway Air provides expedited on-time, hour-specific or day-specific delivery services. Its services are available in all 50 states and Puerto Rico.

New Penn, based in Lebanon, Pennsylvania, specializes in loads of several hundred pounds or more and

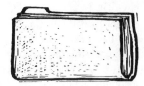

SAFETY FIRST

At the beginning of 2002, more than 1,600 active Roadway drivers had logged more than 1 million accident free miles; 227 drivers had logged more than 2 million accident-free miles; and 55 active drivers had logged more than 3 million accident-free miles. In 1998 Roadway honored its drivers with more than 3,000 safe miles by presenting them their own new Volvo tractors. In the same year Roadway Express driver Gary Ott was named National Champion at the ATA National Truck Driving Championships.

95 percent of its deliveries are next-day. As such the company does not directly compete with United Parcel Service or FedEx Corporation, both of which primarily ship loads of 50 pounds or less. ATS is an irregular route and dedicated truckload hauler with an average destination of 450 miles. Based in Jacksonville, Florida, it competes in the truckload sector in a 37-state area of midwestern and eastern states.

GLOBAL PRESENCE

All Roadway Express shipments originate from the United States, all Reimer Express Lines originate from Canada, and all Roadway S.A. de C.V. originate in Mexico, but destinations for all shipments range from the United States, Canada, and Mexico, to more than 65 other countries around the world. Asian Roadway Express, a joint venture, provides services between North America and Singapore, Indonesia, Malaysia, and Thailand. Services are also provided to Africa, Australia, Europe, and the Middle East.

CORPORATE CITIZENSHIP

Corporate citizenship focuses on highway safety, children's health and educational needs, and the United Way. Program participation and support are offered in numerous community service projects. To promote highway safety, Roadway displays "No Zone" signs on its trailers to warn motorists of the driver's blind spots. Children are supported through such programs as Christina's Smile Dental Trailers, a mobile dentistry service that

travels in two 48-foot trailers, and St. Jude's Children's Research Hospital. Roadway also participates in a variety of driver education and training programs. Roadway addresses environmental issues through employee training, recycling, employment of fuel-efficient machinery, use of alternative fuels, and advanced leak detection systems for its underground fuel storage tanks.

EMPLOYMENT

Roadway acknowledges that its employees are its greatest asset. Accordingly, the company is deliberate in its efforts to provide a positive working environment that promotes cooperation, diversity, and professional growth. As a unionized carrier Roadway provides highly competitive wages and excellent benefits that allow the company to attract and hire quality drivers and support staff. Driver retention is 98 percent, and average length of employment is 11.5 years, which provides the company with an experienced and well-trained workforce. Along with drivers Roadway hires individuals to work in an array of fields, including accounting and finance, customer service, information technology, management trainee, marketing, communications, mechanics, and sales.

SOURCES OF INFORMATION

Bibliography

Kiernan, Pat, and Ali Velshi. "Roadway Express CEO—Controlling Costs, Excess Capacity Help Hold Profits Up." *CNN,* 23 January 2002.

"Roadway Corporation," *Hoover's Company Profiles,* 2002. Available at http://www.hoovers.com

"Roadway Corporation," *The Wall Street Journal,* 10 April 2002.

Roadway Corporation Home Page, 2002. Available at http://www.roadwayCorporationcom.

"Roadway Express Launches Roadway Air Service as a Unique Solution for Customer Shipping Needs." *Business Wire,* 2 January 2002.

"Roadway Reports a Loss." *The New York Times,* 9 April 2002.

"Roadway Swung to Fiscal 1st-Quarter Loss, Hurt by Weak Demand." *Dow Jones Business News,* 9 April 2002.

Winter, Ralph. "Roadway Steers Toward Growth in Next-Day Game," *The Wall Street Journal,* 27 December 2001.

For additional industry research:

Investigate companies by their Standard Industrial Classification Codes, also known as SICs. Roadway Corporation's primary SICs are:

4213 Trucking, Except Local

4731 Arrangement Transport Freight & Cargo

6719 Holding Companies, Not Elsewhere Classified

Also investigate companies by their North American Industry Classification System codes, also known as NAICS codes. Roadway Corporation's primary NAICS codes are:

484121 General Freight Trucking, Long-Distance, Truckload

488510 Freight Transportation Arrangement

551112 Offices of Other Holding Companies

Ronco Inventions, LLC

Contact Information:
HEADQUARTERS: 21344 Superior St.
    Chatsworth, CA 91311
PHONE: (818)775-4602
FAX: (818)775-4664
URL: http://www.ronco.com

OVERVIEW

Ronco Inventions sells things like pasta makers, rotisseries, and food dehydrators via infomericals, which are televised commercials that last up to 28 minutes and 30 seconds. The firm's founder, Ron Popeil, is considered a pioneer of the infomercial. In early 2001, Popeil revealed that his firm was up for sale.

COMPANY FINANCES:

Sales for Ronco Inventions grew 11.1 percent to a record $250 million in 2000.

HISTORY

Ronald Popeil first began selling housewares at places like county fairs and state fairs and at stores like Woolworth's. He purchased the majority of his merchandise from his father, a profitable manufacturer based in Chicago. After learning that television commercials were much less expensive than he imagined, Popeil headed to a television station in Tampa, Florida to film his first commercial. Featuring the Ronco Spray Gun, a hose spraying device that consumers could use to wash and wax their automobiles as well as to fertilize their lawns, the commercial made its debut in 1962. At the time, rather than have people call him directly, Popeil arranged for the Ronco Spray Gun to be available at select stores, the names of which he mentioned on the air. Eventually, consumers were able to mail their orders

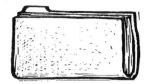

INFOMERCIALS PAYOFF IS HIGH FOR RONCO

During a single day in late 2000, infomercials starring Ronco founder Ron Popeil sold 40,000 Showtime Rotisseries, 18,000 Ronco Food Dehydrators, and 800 Popeil Automatic Pasta Makers. Popeil had first developed his selling skills working at various carnival booths.

---

and payment directly to Ronco via a post office box. By 1966, more than one million spray guns had been sold.

Popeil continued to sell his father's products, including the Chop-o-Matic and the Vego-o-Matic, as well as products other manufacturers began to send him. Sales in the late 1960s reached $8.8 million. Under the name Ronco Teleproducts, the firm completed its initial public offering in 1969, selling 22 percent of its shares for $5.5 million. The firm raised another $750,000 via an offering on the American Stock Exchange in 1970.

Heavy debt forced Ronco into bankruptcy in 1984. Popeil agreed to repurchase the firm's inventory from the bank for $2 million. In 1991 Popeil agreed to sell 200,000 of his Ronco Electric Food Dehydrators on USA Direct, a television shopping channel owned by U.S. mail order giant Fingerhut. A few years prior, the Federal Communications Commission (FCC) had relaxed regulations that limited commercials to 30- second, 60-second, 90-second, and two-minute segments. Home shopping channels like QVC had emerged, helping to boost the popularity of television-based shopping. Eventually, Popeil decided to develop his own infomercial for his food dehydrator, a move that resulted in the creation of Popeil's second company, Ronco Inventions.

In 1998, the firm introduced the Showtime Rotisserie and Barbeque Oven. More than 2.5 million units were sold for a total of $400 million by mid-2001. While continuing to work on new products and expanding into new markets, Popeil began looking to sell his company in the early 2000s.

STRATEGY

Throughout Ronco's history, Ronald Popeil maintained control of nearly every aspect of operations. While at first he sold his father's products, eventually

FAST FACTS:
About Ronco Inventions, LLC

Ownership: Ronco Inventions, LLC is a private company owned by founder and president Ronald Popeil.

Officers: Ronald Popeil, Pres.; Stuart Rosenblum, CFO; Robert Nordlicht, COO

Employees: 200

Chief Competitors: Competitors to Ronco Inventions include Sunbeam and other housewares manufacturers. The firm also competes with housewares retailers such as Williams-Sonoma and Linens 'n Things.

Popeil began to invent his own devices and gadgets. According to a June 2001 issue of *Sales & Marketing Magazine*, "Popeil is not just Ronco's president and pitch man. He invents each and every product. He does his own testing and all the research and development. He's head of packaging and manufacturing. He is the sales and marketing manager. He oversees media buys. No detail is left unPopeiled. He conceives the infomercials, then helps shoot them, write them, and ultimately stars in them."

This strategy appeared to work for Ronco. By the beginning of the twenty-first century, the firm had sold more than $1 billion in products via television advertising. In addition, because Popeil chose not to hire producers, actors, and an extensive team of executives, Ronco's operating costs remained low. Ronco's plans for the early 2000s included marketing the Showtime Rotisserie and Barbeque Oven—introduced in the United States in 1998—in Europe.

CURRENT TRENDS

The use of television to sell products directly to consumers grew in the 1980s and 1990s, particularly as television shopping channels like QVC became increasingly popular. In fact, by 1999, QVC had become the tenth largest retailer of housewares in the United States, with profits of $564.2 million. Ronco founder Ron Popeil is credited for helping to launch this trend.

The growth of electronic commerce in the late 1990s prompted Ronco to build its own Web site. As a result,

CHRONOLOGY:
Key Dates for Ronco Inventions, LLC

1962: Ron Popeil makes his first commercial

1979: Ronco conducts its initial public offering

1984: Ronco declares bankruptcy

1991: Popeil forges an agreement with Fingerhut to sell electric food dehydrators on Fingerhut's television shopping network

2000: Sales reach a record $250 million

in addition to calling in their orders, Ronco customers were able to make purchases via the Internet. Increased online shopping was a trend that worked in Ronco's favor as sales completed via the Internet were less expensive for Ronco to process than those completed with phone calls simply because they eliminated the need for customer services representatives. In addition, because the firm was already shipping products directly to customers, its transition to Internet retailing proved much smoother than it did for many traditional retailers.

PRODUCTS

Ronco Inventions sells housewares including food dehydrators, rotisseries, pasta makers, sausage makers, and vegetable choppers. Other products include heath and beauty items such GLH Formula #9, a spray designed to cover bald spots. Key product release dates include the Veg-O-Matic in 1963, the Pocket Fisherman in 1972, the Miracle Broom in 1973, the Inside the Egg Shell Scrambler in 1977, both Mr. Microphone and the Smokeless Ashtray in 1980, the Ronco Electric Food Dehydrator in 1991, both GLH Formula #9 and and Popeil's Pasta and Sausage Maker in 1992, the Ronco Grip Spatula in 1997, and the Showtime Rotisserie and Barbeque Oven in 1998.

WARNING LABEL SPURS ADDITIONAL SALES FOR RONCO

When advertising his new Rotisserie Oven on an infomercial in 1998, Ronco founder Ron Popeil developed the catch phrase, "Just set it. . .and forget it," in an effort to convey the convenience of his $160.00 appliance. A short while later, however, Popeil became concerned that leaving the oven completely untended might prove dangerous. As a result, he began placing warning labels on each of the ovens, and he mailed a similar caveat to his entire database of customers. Along with the warnings, Popeil included print advertisements for some of his other products, the result of which was $2 million in additional sales.

SOURCES OF INFORMATION

Bibliography
Donoho, Ron. "One-Man Show." *Sales & Marketing Management*, June 2001.

Graham, Jefferson. *The Salesman of the Century*. New York: Delacorte Press, 1995.

Porter, Thyra. "Ron Popeil Ronco: He's a Successful Inventor and a Savvy Merchandiser. . .But Wait, There's More." *HFN: The Weekly Newspaper for the Home Furnishing Network.*, 27 November 2000.

Ronco Inventions, LLC Home Page, 2002. Available at http://www.ronco.com.

For additional industry research:
Investigate companies by their Standard Industrial Classification Codes, also known as SICs. Ronco Inventions' primary SIC is:

3634 Electric Housewares and Fans

Also investigate companies by their North American Industry Classification System Codes, also known as NAICS codes. Ronco Inventions' primary NAICS code is:

335211 Electric Housewares and Household Fans Manufacturing

Samsonite Corporation

OVERVIEW

Samsonite Corporation, headquartered in Denver, Colorado, is one of the world's largest and most influential designers, manufacturers, and distributors of luggage. Its products are marketed under a number of brand names, the best known of which are Samsonite and American Tourister. The company manufactures a wide range of luggage and luggage-related products, including suitcases, garment bags, business cases and portfolios, computer cases, sports bags, and casual bags. The company's line of luxury luggage, casual bags, shoes, and accessories is marketed under the Hedgren and Samsonite Black Label brand names. In addition to its own line of manufactured products, Samsonite licenses its brand names for use on such products as travel accessories, leather goods, clothing, furniture, and handbags.

Most of Samsonite's products are designed at the company's research and development and design centers in the United States and Europe. The products themselves are manufactured either at one of the company's 12 global manufacturing facilities or by third-party suppliers. Samsonite's products are marketed in more than 100 countries worldwide at a wide range of retail outlets, including department stores, mass merchants, specialty stores, warehouse clubs, and catalog showrooms, as well as at the chain of about 200 Samsonite-operated stores in the United States, Canada, Latin America, Europe, and Asia. Customers may also purchase Samsonite products through the Web sites of several of the company's retailers.

FOUNDED: 1910

Contact Information:
HEADQUARTERS: 11200 E. 45th Ave.
   Denver, CO 80239
PHONE: (303)373-2000
FAX: (303)373-6300
URL: http://www.samsonite.com

FINANCES:

Samsonite Corp. Net Sales, 1999-2001 (million dollars)

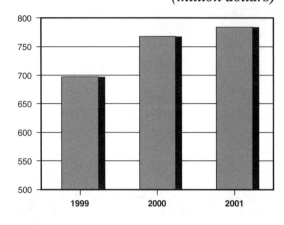

COMPANY FINANCES

Economic and market conditions have colored Samsonite's financial performance in recent years, obscuring to some extent the positive progress the company has achieved. For example, although net sales in 2001 climbed 2.1 percent to $783.9 million from $767.7 million in 2000, the company's bottom line showed a net loss of $6.8 million compared with a net loss of $1.9 million the previous year. Part of the company's loss can be attributed to the weakness of most European currencies against the U.S. dollar. The company's sales in Europe jumped almost 12 percent in 2001, the third consecutive year of double-digit sales growth in Europe. However, taking the currency differential into account, European sales were $9.8 million behind their performance in 2000. The company also managed to scratch out a 1.7 percent sales gain in the United States, against the backdrop of an economy in recession. Samsonite's sales in Mexico and Canada climbed 16 percent and 18 percent respectively. Sales in Asia were also strong, climbing 50 percent in 2001, on the heels of a 55 percent increase in 2000.

In 1999, Samsonite reported a net loss of $88.8 million on revenue of $697.4 million. In the 52 weeks ended March 31, 2002, the company's stock traded in a range of $0.85 to $4.00.

ANALYSTS' OPINIONS

As of early 2002, most security analysts were essentially neutral in their rating of Samsonite Corporation, which translates to a recommendation of "hold" on the company's stock.

HISTORY

Samsonite has its roots in Colorado, where Colorado native Jesse Shwayder in 1910 founded the Shwayder Trunk Manufacturing Company using his life savings of $3,500. Shwayder quickly used up his modest start-up capital and was forced to borrow money to keep his company going. He was later joined by his brothers, Maurice, Sol, Ben, and Mark, each of whom took over a specific segment of the company's operations. By 1917, the company was selling $76,000 of luggage annually throughout the American West, forcing the Shwayders to expand their manufacturing facility to keep pace with soaring demand for their products. To better convey the strength and durability of their luggage products, the Shwayders dubbed their product line "Samson." In 1918, the company took its products national, and by 1924, annual sales had soared to $300,000. That same year, the brothers moved their manufacturing operations into an 80,000-square-foot factory in South Denver. Demand for their products continue to climb, and by the end of the 1920s, annual revenue had jumped to more than $1 million.

With the arrival of the Great Depression, demand for the Shwayders' luggage collapsed, dropping by 50 percent within just a few years. To help face the challenge of the Depression, the brothers diversified their product lineup to include card tables, license plates, sandboxes, and stilts, and changed the company name to Shwayder Brothers, Inc. Their strategy paid off, and the company survived the lean years of the 1930s. In 1939, the company introduced a unique suitcase that was marketed under the name "Samsonite." The suitcase, which was a predecessor to the company's Samsonite Streamlite line, was covered with a durable vulcanized fiber that was used with a leather binding.

To meet the needs of American armed forces, much of the Shwayders' manufacturing capacity was converted during World War II to the production of war materiel. But when the war ended, the brothers quickly got back to the business of making luggage and folding furniture, incorporating some of the tricks they'd picked up during the years of wartime production. Annual sales climbed to $7 million in 1946.

During the 1950s and early 1960s, the company continued to market its popular line of Samsonite luggage, expanding its product line to include attaché cases and specialized travel cases. In 1965, the company's name was officially changed to Samsonite Corporation to capitalize on the growing popularity of its Samsonite product line. By the early 1970s, Samsonite had established itself as the world's largest manufacturer of molded luggage and attachÈ cases. Global distribution was made easier through a number of factories and sales offices that had been established in Europe and Japan during the previous decade. As demand continued to soar, Samsonite opened a growing network of manufacturing facilities throughout the United States and abroad.

In 1973, corporate giant Beatrice Foods acquired Samsonite from the Shwayder family. For the rest of the decade, Samsonite continued to grow through the introduction of new products and aggressive overseas expansion. However, the growth surge had ended by the early 1980s, as Samsonite began to feel the impact of low-cost foreign competition. In 1983, Beatrice brought in British-born Malcom Candlish to whip the company into shape. Candlish cut the size of Samsonite's work force and launched an aggressive program of cost-cutting. In 1986, Beatrice sold Samsonite to Kholberg, Kravis & Roberts, who 15 months later spun the company off into a newly established company dubbed E-II. Six months later, E-II was bought out by American Brands, which itself was purchased not long thereafter by billionaire Meshulam Riklis. Through it all, Candlish hung on as CEO.

After E-II filed for bankruptcy and was reorganized in the early 1990s, Samsonite ended up as a subsidiary of a new company called Astrum International Corporation. Steve Green took over as Samsonite's CEO, and under his direction the company purchased American Tourister, another major U.S. luggage manufacturer. The company regained its independence in 1995 when Astrum announced it would split into two companies, one of which would be the independent, publicly owned Samsonite Corporation.

STRATEGY

Samsonite's strategy is to use its existing assets, including its quality products, strong brand names, and global capabilities, to expand sales and improve profitability. Key tactics in the company's strategy include expanding its channels of distribution, expanding product offerings, creating innovative products, enhancing brand image, continuing international expansion, and improving its product marketing execution.

In the realm of distribution channels, the company has moved to increase its presence in those channels in which it is presently underrepresented. This will be done by using targeted sales efforts that are tailored to each specific channel. As to the expansion of product offerings, Samsonite is designing, manufacturing, and marketing more casual and sports bags, luxury luggage, computer cases, clothing, shoes, and accessories. In recent years, the company has added the upscale brand names of Hummer, Hedgren, and Samsonite Black Label to its product lineup. Recent innovations in the company's product line have included Ziplite, a lightweight, hard-sided luggage made from ultra-thin, flexible polypropylene, and Carbon 2010, a hybrid luggage that

FAST FACTS:
About Samsonite Corporation

Ownership: Samsonite is a publicly owned company traded on the NASDAQ small cap market.

Ticker Symbol: SAMC

Officers: Luc Van Nevel, Pres. and CEO, 55, 2001 base salary $382,041; Richard H. Wiley, CFO, Treas., and Sec., 45, 2001 base salary $275,000; Thomas R. Sandler, Pres. The Americas, 55, 2001 base salary $325,000

Employees: 7,150

Principal Subsidiary Companies: To properly oversee its worldwide business, Samsonite has a number of subsidiary or joint venture companies outside the United States. These include Samsonite Mercosur, Ltd. headquartered in the Bahamas; Samsonite Asia, Ltd. based in Hong Kong; Samsonite Mauritius, Ltd. on the island of Mauritius; Samsonite Singapore Pte., Ltd. in Singapore; Samsonite AG in Switzerland; and Lonberg Express S.A. in Uruguay.

Chief Competitors: Competition within the worldwide luggage market is very fragmented. In the U.S. market, Samsonite competes based on brand name, product innovation, consumer advertising, product quality, differentiation, customer service, and price. In Europe, competition in the luggage market is based on the company's premium brand name, product design, product quality, access to established distribution channels, new product offerings, and price. Because manufacture of soft-sided luggage is labor intensive but not capital intensive, the barriers to entry into this segment of the luggage market are relatively few, which means that competition for Samsonite in this market is relatively intense. Because the manufacture of hard-sided luggage is much more capital intensive, the number of competitors in this market segment are considerably fewer. Some of the company's major competitors worldwide are LVMH, Moet Hennessy, Louis Vuitton S.A., Brown-Forman Corporation, which produces Hartmann luggage, and Land's End, Inc.

CHRONOLOGY:

Key Dates for Samsonite Corporation

1910: Shwayder Trunk Manufacturing Co. founded

1918: Shwayder begins marketing nationally

1941: Shwayder introduces Samsonite Streamlite

1946: Annual sales top $7 million

1965: Shwayder changes name to Samsonite

1973: Samsonite is acquired by Beatrice Foods

1995: Samsonite regains corporate independence

incorporates attractive features of both hard-sided and soft-sided luggage.

To enhance its brand image, Samsonite plans to introduce more upscale products under its Hummer, Hedgren, and Samsonite Black Label brand names and to open flagship stores in major international cities. Although it has enjoyed an international presence for decades, Samsonite hopes to expand further abroad, focusing on the emerging foreign markets of India, China, Latin America, and the Pacific Rim. To improve product marketing execution, the company is concentrating its resources on the improvement of forecasting, brand positioning and advertising, product development, and customer service.

INFLUENCES

Serving a global marketplace has required Samsonite to quickly adjust its marketing strategies to changing buying patterns in its various markets. In Europe, for example, the company has seen consumer preferences shift from hard-sided luggage, beauty cases, and attachÈ cases to soft-sided suitcases and casual bags. To stimulate and revive sales of its hard-sided products, the company has devoted considerable capital to the development of innovative, lightweight, hard-sided suitcases, including its Ziplite, Hardlite, and D'Lite brand names.

Another negative factor in the European market has been the weakness of European currencies against the U.S. dollar in recent years. To lessen the negative effects of this foreign exchange differential, Samsonite has

moved more of its production from the Far East to plants in Eastern Europe to take advantage of the resulting savings in production costs.

In the domestic market, Samsonite has seen U.S. demand for hard-sided luggage deteriorate significantly. This prompted the company to discontinue manufacturing operations at its Denver facility. The company will continue to market hard-sided luggage in the United States but the product will be sourced from Samsonite's foreign-based manufacturing facilities. To further address the problem of weaker demand in the United States, Samsonite plans to reduce the total number of retail outlets it operates by eliminating those that have proven unprofitable.

CURRENT TRENDS

A growing trend worldwide has been the decline in demand for Samsonite's hard-sided products. The company's sales of soft-sided suitcases and garment bags accounted for 46 percent of total sales in 2001, compared with 21 percent for hard-sided luggage. So sharply has the company's U.S. demand for hard-sided luggage declined that Samsonite in 2001 halted manufacturing at its Denver facility. The much-diminished demand for hard-sided product will henceforth be met with supplies from the company's foreign-based manufacturing facilities.

In the company's view, part of the reason for the sharp drop in demand for hard-sided product has been the growing consumer preference for lighter weight luggage. To satisfy this consumer preference while continuing to produce a hard-sided suitcase line, Samsonite has invested heavily in research and development to come up with innovative new materials to meet customers' needs. Some of the so-called hybrid products that have emerged from such research include the company's Hardlite, D'Lite, and Ziplite product lines. These hard-sided products are made with newly developed materials and production processes, and satisfy consumer demands for a lighter weight product.

PRODUCTS

Although Samsonite is most closely identified with its luggage products, the company produces a wide range of other products, including casual bags, business and computer cases, footwear and clothing, and other products. Approximately two-thirds of the company's sales in 2001 were accounted for by hard-sided and soft-sided luggage products. Soft-sided suitcases and garment bags accounted for 46 percent of total sales, while hard-sided suitcases made up 21 percent of total sales. Casual bags accounted for 11 percent of sales, while

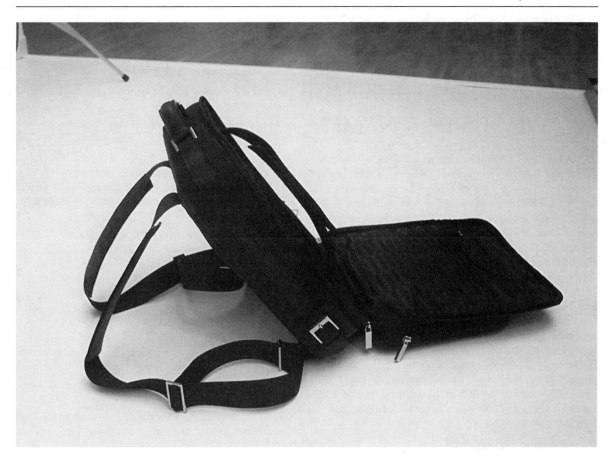

A trendy laptop back pack is part of Samsonite's Black Label Fall 2002 collection. *(Godfrey Deeny-Fashion Wire Daily)*

business and computer cases made up another 8 percent. Footwear and clothing accounted for 3 percent of sales, with the remaining 11 percent made up by other products.

The company's products are marketed under a number of brand names. Samsonite Black Label products are directed at the high-end luxury market, while Lark products target the luxury market. Products bearing the Samsonite label are directed to consumers looking for high-quality, innovative goods. The sport luxury market is targeted by products bearing the Hedgren brand name and American Tourister products are targeted at consumers seeking quality and value.

GLOBAL PRESENCE

More than half of Samsonite's annual sales are made in markets outside the United States. To meet this worldwide demand for its products, the company operates a network of 12 company-owned manufacturing facilities. Another large segment of its product line comes from third-party suppliers, most of whom are located in the Far East, Eastern Europe, and Dominican Republic. In 2001, less than 40 percent of Samsonite's revenue from soft-sided luggage products came from products manufactured in its own facilities. The rest was supplied by third-party vendors outside the United States. Company-owned manufacturing facilities are located in Belgium, France, Hungary, Italy, the Slovak Republic, Mexico, Spain, India, and China.

EMPLOYMENT

Samsonite employed approximately 7,150 employees worldwide as of Decemer 31, 2001. Of those, about 1,850 worked in the United States. While most of the company's 2,780 European employees are unionized, only a small percentage of those in the United States belong to a union.

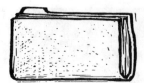

WHAT'S IN A NAME?

When Jesse Shwayder and his brothers first began marketing luggage from their Denver factory, they dubbed it "Samson" after the super-strong character in the Bible. This, they felt, would reflect well upon their products and give potential customers a sense of their quality and durability. To further demonstrate the strength of their suitcases, four of the Shwayder brothers and their father posed for an advertising picture standing on a wooden plank that had been positioned atop one of their suitcases. The caption read, "Strong Enough to Stand On." The Shwayer brothers' luggage was first marketed nationally in 1918. The name "Samsonite" first appeared as the brand name of a unique new suitcase introduced by the Shwayders in 1939. Their company had developed a sturdy vulcanized covering for the new product. It was the birth of a name that was to outlast the name of Shwayder. In 1965 the Shwayder Trunk Manufacturing Company officially changed its name to Samsonite Corporation.

SOURCES OF INFORMATION

Bibliography

2001 Annual Report of Samsonite Corporation. Denver: Samsonite Corporation, 2002.

"Samsonite Corporation." *Hoover's Online*. Available at http://www.hoovers.com.

"Samsonite Corporation - History." *Gale Business Resources*. Available at http://galenet.galegroup.com/servlet/GBR.

Samsonite Corporation Home Page, 2002. Available at http://www.samsonite.com.

"Snapshot Report: Samsonite Corporation." *Multex Investor* Available at http://www.marketguide.com.

For an annual report:

on The Internet at: http://www.samsonite.com/global/ **or** write: Investor Relations, 11200 E. 45th Ave., Denver, CO 80239.

For additional industry research:

Investigate companies by their Standard Industrial Classification Codes, also known as SICs. Samsonite's primary SICs are:

3089 Plastics Products NEC

3131 Footwear Cut Stock

3161 Luggage

3171 Women's Handbags and Purses

3172 Personal Leather Goods Except Women's Handbags and Purses

3199 Leather Goods, NEC

Also investigate companies by their North American Industrial Classification System (NAICS) Codes. Samsonite's primary NAICS codes are:

316992 Luggage Manufacturing

316993 Personal Leather Goods Manufacturing

316999 All Other Leather Goods Manufacturing

Sanrio Co. Ltd.

FOUNDED: 1960

Contact Information:
HEADQUARTERS: 1-6-1 Osaki 1-chome, Shinagawa-ku
    Tokyo, 141-8603 Japan
PHONE: 81337798111
FAX: 81337798054
URL: http://www.sanrio.co.jp

OVERVIEW

Sanrio Co. is best known for its "Hello Kitty" brand of merchandise. The Hello Kitty character, along with other characters created by Sanrio, appears on stationary, apparel, school supplies, and a multitude of other products typically purchased by children and teenagers. These products, called social communication gifts by Sanrio, account for 92 percent of the firm's sales. Greeting cards account for another 4.9 percent, while movies, video, and publications bring in 1.6 percent, and restaurants secure 1.3 percent. Theme park operations account for less than 1 percent of total revenues. Sanrio sells its own merchandise in roughly 200 Sanrio outlets; however, the majority of sales take place at retailers licensed to sell Sanrio products.

COMPANY FINANCES

After growing from $1.26 billion in 1999 to $1.3 billion in 2000, sales for Sanrio dropped 17.9 percent to $1.08 billion in 2001. Earnings followed a similar pattern, growing from $43.1 in 1999 to $193.6 in 2000, and then falling to a loss of $21.1 million in 2001.

HISTORY

Shintaro Tsuji created Yamanashi Silk Center Co., Ltd. in 1960. The firm developed Strawberry, its first character design, in 1962. Seven years later, Yamanashi Silk opened a specialty store in San Francisco, Califor-

FINANCES:

Sanrio Co. Ltd.
Revenues, 1999-2001
(million dollars)

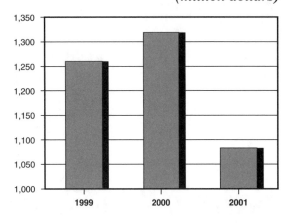

FAST FACTS:
About Sanrio Co. Ltd.

Ownership: Sanrio Co. Ltd. is a public company traded on the Tokyo Stock Exchange.

Officers: Shintaro Tsuji, Chmn. and CEO; Kunihiko Tsuji, Senior Managing Dir.; Tetsuo Uohashi, Managing Dir. and CFO; Yoshihiko Kaneda, Managing Dir.

Employees: 947

Principal Subsidiary Companies: Japan-based Sanrio Co. operates several domestic subsidiaries, including Sanrio Puroland Co., a theme park operator; Sanrio Far East Co., an importer and exporter of gift items, and Sanway Co., a restaurant operator. The firm also operates subsidiaries in the North America, South America, Europe, and other parts of Asia.

Chief Competitors: Competitors to Sanrio Co. include Mattel, Hasbro, and other manufacturers of merchandise for children and teenagers.

nia, named the Strawberry Shop, to sell merchandise with the Strawberry character. Another retail outlet, called the Gift Gate, opened in Tokyo in 1971. Yamanashi Silk changed its name to Sanrio Co. Ltd. in 1973. Sanrio launched its first publication, *Shi to Meruhen*, or *Poetry and Fairytales*, in May of that year.

The Hello Kitty character was first drawn in 1974. Two additional characters, Patty and Jimmy, were developed as well. That year, Sanrio diversified into film production and distribution with the establishment of Sanrio Communications Inc. in Los Angeles, California. The company published *Strawberry News* for the first time in 1975. The following year, Sanrio completed its first film, *Little Jimbo*.

Various manufacturers began to license Hello Kitty, Strawberry, and other characters created by Sanrio in the mid-1970s. A U.S. subsidiary, Sanrio Inc., was created in 1976 to oversee U.S. operations, including those of Sanrio Communications. In 1978, the firm received an Academy Award for its documentary, *Who Are the Deadbolts and Where Did They Get 19 Kids?* Another film, *Glacier Fox*, was released that year as well.

Expansion into Europe first took place in 1980, when Sanrio opened an office in West Germany. That year, the company also created the Sanrio Theater to show family-oriented films made by Sanrio and other film producers. Sanrio GmbH was established to oversee German operations in 1983. By then, Hello Kitty had started to gain popularity with teenage girls. UNICEF named Hello Kitty its child ambassador in the United States, and the firm diversified into video sales. International expansion continued when Sanrio created San-

rio do Brasil Comercio e Representacoes Ltd. in 1987. To handle the import and export of its merchandise, Sanrio established Sanrio Far East Co. Ltd. in 1990. The company also opened Sanrio Puroland, its first theme park. Another theme park, Harmonyland, opened in 1991.

Subsidiaries in both Taiwan and Hong Kong opened in the mid-1990s. Hello Kitty became the child ambassador for UNICEF in Japan in 1994. Sanrio began to license Hello Kitty to mass markets in the late 1990s. In 2000, a Hello Kitty store opened in New York City. The following year, the firm announced its intent to open three Hello Kitty stores in Madrid, Spain.

STRATEGY

Throughout most of the 1980s and 1990s, Sanrio limited distribution of Hello Kitty products, by far its best selling merchandise, to specialty stores and department stores. In 1999, however, the firm launched several brand building tactics, such as pushing Hello Kitty products into mass market stores like Target. To this end, Sanrio also forged a joint marketing venture with

Sanrio Company's Hello Kitty promotional dolls on display at a McDonald's restaurant in Taiwan, where demand is so great that there is a black market for the toy. (AP Photo/Wally Santana)

McDonald's, which agreed to feature Hello Kitty products in select areas throughout its popular fast food restaurant chain. Sales soared as a result. To maintain the sense of exclusivity it had worked for years to develop for Hello Kitty products, Sanrio continued its practice of only offering new products for a few months a time. Because it released nearly 100 new products a month, the firm was able to continually rotate which products were available for sale.

CURRENT TRENDS

Hello Kitty products began to appeal to a new market in the United States in the late 1990s. The reason for this, according to a September 2001 article in *Business Week*, was the character's appeal to various celebrities: "Supermodels Tyra Banks and Laetitia Costa love it. Christina Aguilera, Mariah Carey and the gals from *Sex and the City* are avid collectors. The newest couture line? No-rather, purses, bags, and T-shirts adorned with Hello Kitty. All the rage for decades in Japan and once merely the domain of little girls in the U.S., the round-faced cat is suddenly cheap chic in the fashion world." Celebrity sightings at the Hello Kitty store in New York City helped to fuel the fad. This trend wasn't merely a stroke of luck for Sanrio, however. Sanrio had begun to target the U.S. teen market in 1998 with a national marketing

campaign that included advertisements in magazines like *Seventeen*.

PRODUCTS

Although Sanrio has developed roughly 400 different characters, it's Hello Kitty that produces nearly half the firm's profits. More than 15,000 Hello Kitty products, including bags, purses, clothing, and school supplies, are sold in stores across the world. Other characters include a penguin named Badtz-Maru and Hello Kitty's boyfriend, Dear Daniel. Sanrio also sells greeting cards, produces movies, and operates theme parks and restaurants.

GLOBAL PRESENCE

Latin America proved to be the most lucrative market for Sanrio's Hello Kitty character merchandise in the early 2000s. With 76 Hello Kitty stores, Venezuela accounted for 23 percent of Sanrio's Hello Kitty sales. North America also proved to be a growth area for the firm. As U.S. celebrities began to embrace Hello Kitty merchandise, North American sales grew more than threefold to $300 million in the late 1990s. Sanrio operates

CHRONOLOGY:

Key Dates for Sanrio Co. Ltd.

1960: Sanrio's predecessor company is founded

1974: Hello Kitty is created

1976: Sanrio begins licensing its characters for merchandise

1980: Sanrio expands into Germany

1987: Sanrio opens a subsidiary in Brazil

1992: Sanrio opens a subsidiary in Taiwan

2000: Sales reach a record $1.3 billion

international subsidiaries in the United States, Germany, Brazil, Taiwan, and Hong Kong.

SOURCES OF INFORMATION

Bibliography

Betzold, James. "Hello Kitty: Bill Hensley." *Advertising Age*, 8 October 2001.

"Character Company on a Roll with Cute Hello Kitty." *South China Morning Post*, 17 January 2001.

Cosgrove, Julia. "Cat on a Hot Thin Model." *Business Week*, 10 September 2001.

"Hello Kitty Finds Another Life in Drugstores." *Women's Wear Daily*, 21 January 2000.

HELLO KITTY AT MCDONALD'S INCITES FIGHTS

In 2000, as part of its plan to push its Hello Kitty merchandise into the mass market, Sanrio decided to sell Hello Kitty dolls for a limited time at McDonald's restaurants in Hong Kong. Demand proved so high that fights erupted between some of the patrons waiting to purchase the dolls.

Sanrio Co. Ltd. Home Page, 2002. Available at http://www .sanrio.co.jp.

"Taking Kitty Beyond Kiddies." *ADWeek Eastern Edition*, 6 July 1998.

"Your Money: Trends: Hello Kitty." *AsiaWeek*, 9 March 2001.

For additional industry research:

Investigate companies by their Standard Industrial Classification Codes, also known as SICs. Sanrio's primary SICs are:

5091 Sporting & Recreational Good & Supplies

5092 Toys & Hobby Goods & Supplies

Also investigate companies by their North American Industry Classification System Codes, also known as NAICS codes. Sanrio Co.'s primary North American Industrial Classification System, also known as NAICS codes are:

421910 Sporting & Recreational Goods & Supplies

421920 Toys & Hobby Goods & Supplies

Scientific-Atlanta, Inc.

OVERVIEW

Scientific-Atlanta is the second largest U.S. manufacturer of the set-top boxes used with cable television and cable-based online services, such as high-speed Internet access. A member of the Standard & Poor's 500, Scientific-Atlanta also manufactures cable modems and broadcasting transmission and distribution equipment. Customers include cable operators, broadcasters, and telephone operators. The firm's three largest clients—Adelphia; AOL Time Warner (owner of Time Warner Cable) and Charter Communications-account for nearly 60 percent of sales.

COMPANY FINANCES

Scientific-America's sales reached $1.2 billion in 1999, grew to $1.7 billion in 2000, and surpassed the $2 billion mark the following year. In 2001, sales jumped another 46.5 percent, reaching $2.51 billion. Net income also skyrocketed between 1999 and 2001, growing more than threefold from $102.3 million to $333.7 million. The firm's earnings per share grew from 64 cents to $1.99 over the same time period. Weakening economic conditions began to undercut sales during the first half of fiscal 2002. As a result, the firm's stock price, which had neared record highs early in 2001, began to tumble. In March of 2002, stock hovered at roughly $22 per share.

In the late 1990s and early 2000s, Scientific-Atlanta began to gain ground on arch rival Motorola. In the first half of 2001, Scientific-Atlanta had secured a 37 percent share of the digital set-top box market. Although this still

FOUNDED: 1951

Contact Information:
HEADQUARTERS: 5030 Sugarloaf Pkwy.
    Lawrenceville, GA 30044
PHONE: (770)903-5000
FAX: (770)236-6777
URL: http://www.scientificatlanta.com

FINANCES:

Scientific-Atlanta Inc. Revenues, 1999-2001 (million dollars)

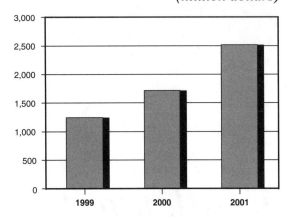

Scientific-Atlanta Inc. 2001 Stock Prices (dollars)

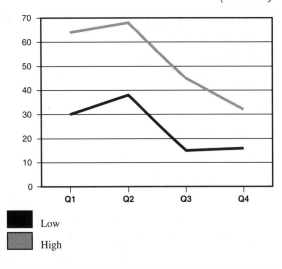

Low

High

According to an October 2001 article in *Broadcasting & Cable*, Scientific-Atlanta's stock, "a hot pick on Wall Street just nine months ago, has been battered this summer, largely by a serious slowdown in the growth of digital TV sales by cable operators." The firm began to trim operating costs in October of 2001, which prompted some analysts to look more favorably upon its outlook. However, when digital set-top box shipments remained low, analysts again downgraded the stock, and prices continued to fall.

Some believed that the firm would be well positioned for growth once the economy improved. Scientific-Atlanta's newest set-top box was considered better equipped to handle interactive services, a potential growth market for cable operators and equipment makers, than those of its rivals. According to Wachovia Securities Analyst George Hunt, as quoted in *Broadcasting & Cable*, Scientific-Atlanta is "the best technology company in the cable television space."

HISTORY

Six Georgia Institute of Technology professors created Scientific-Atlanta on October 31, 1951, with plans to sell an instrument that recorded antennae patterns. The young firm began to manufacture electronic testing equipment for the space and defense industries in the 1960s. By the early 1970s, products included telephone testing devices, as well as various electronic implements designed specifically for federal government use. Sales totaled $16 million a year.

Sidney Topol left Raytheon Co. to become president of Scientific-Atlanta in 1971. He focused the firm on telecommunications products, and in 1973, Scientific-Atlanta unveiled a portable satellite station at a large communications convention, and shortly thereafter, Scientific-Atlanta began to market its portable satellite stations to the fledgling cable television industry. The satellite allowed cable television operators to transmit their programming to a large number of stations in different locations. Growth in the cable industry intensified in the mid- to late 1970s, and sales at Scientific-Atlanta began to soar, reaching $45 million. The firm held a 66 percent share of the cable television satellite stations market during the 1970s. The firm also began to make and market other cable television system devices, as well as products not related to the cable industry, such as testing and measuring devices for telecommunications and industrial industries. In 1978, Scientific-Atlanta paid $17.4 million for Spectral Dynamics Corp., a maker of laboratory implements with operations throughout Europe. The following year, the firm bought automatic testing devices maker Adar Associates Inc.

By 1980, Scientific-Atlanta was the largest cable satellite stations supplier in the world. Early in the decade, the firm paid $5.5 million for coaxial cable

lagged behind the 58 percent share held by Motorola, it was higher than the 30 percent market share Scientific-Atlanta held in the late 1990s.

ANALYSTS' OPINIONS

Analysts started to downgrade Scientific-Atlanta stock in mid-2001. Digital set-top box growth had slowed as the North American economy worsened, and Scientific-Atlanta's shipments began to decline.

manufacturer Systems Communications Cable, Inc. Quality control issues with set-top boxes (units placed on top of television sets to receive cable channel broadcasts) began to plague the firm; in 1982, these problems resulted in Scientific-Atlanta's first quarterly loss in 13 years. Scientific-Atlanta eventually stopped making set-top boxes in its U.S. plants; instead, the firm hired Matsushita, an electronics company based in Japan, to handle the manufacturing. Early in the 1980s, growth in the U.S. cable television industry began to slow, and demand for cable-related equipment weakened. In 1984, leading cable broadcasters Home Box Office (HBO) and Showtime chose MA/Com, Inc. over Scientific-Atlanta to develop signal scrambling equipment that would prevent homeowners without cable subscriptions from gaining access to cable transmission via satellite dishes. Attempts to diversify into other markets failed, prompting Topol, by then chairman, to hire an outside consultant, William E. Johnson, to restructure operations.

Johnson decided that Scientific-Atlanta had grown too rapidly. He sold off several assets and narrowed the firm's focus to a few promising markets, such as satellite communications networks. To boost its foothold in this fledgling industry, Scientific-Atlanta acquired Advanced Communications Engineering. At the same time, cable television began to catch on in Europe, which helped bolster the firm's sales. In an effort to keep pace with rivals, Scientific-Atlanta began to allocate more resources for research and development. The firm cut costs by laying off 1,000 workers, and eliminating pay increases. Scientific-Atlanta also eliminated 75 percent of its senior-level management, hoping to revitalize its corporate culture and streamline operations. Productivity increased, and earnings in 1989 reached $36 million.

In the 1990s, Scientific-Atlanta continued to focus on staying abreast of cutting edge technologies in an effort to grow its market share. Despite new product releases in 1991, sales fell 20 percent, due to reduced spending throughout the cable industry and a weak North American economy. Earnings tumbled to $1.1 million. Demand for set-top boxes began to grow as the economy improved, and Scientific-Atlanta and General Instrument (later part of Motorola) emerged as the two leaders of the set-top box industry, which was worth $3 billion by 1999.

Digital technology began to replace analog technology in the cable industry in the mid-1990s. As a result, firms like General Instrument and Scientific-Atlanta began to develop digital set-top boxes. General Instrument introduced the first commercially viable digital set-top box in 1996. Three years later, Scientific-Atlanta unveiled the Explorer 2000, a box that was considered technologically superior to rival products. In 2001, America Online Inc. and Scientific-Atlanta began working together on making AOL TV compatible with Explorer 2000 boxes.

FAST FACTS:
About Scientific-Atlanta, Inc.

Ownership: Scientific-Atlanta is a public company traded on the New York Stock Exchange.

Ticker Symbol: SFA

Officers: James F. McDonald, Chmn., Pres., and CEO; Conrad J. Wredberg Jr., SPV and COO; Wallace G. Haislip, SVP, CFO, and Treas.

Employees: 8,000

Principal Subsidiary Companies: Scientific-Atlanta operates offices in 70 countries across the globe.

Chief Competitors: Scientific-Atlantic's chief rival in the set-top box industry is Motorola Inc. Other competitors include Pioneer Electronic Corp., Samsung Co. Ltd., and Sony Corp.

STRATEGY

When Sidney Topol, a proponent of strategic planning, joined Scientific-Atlanta in the early 1970s, he put in place a long-term plan designed to increase the firm's profitability. First, he decided to divest all money-losing operations, particularly those outside of Scientific-Atlanta's area of expertise. He focused the firm on new markets he believed offered substantial growth potential and the opportunity to manufacture low-cost, high-volume products. To increase the firm's competitiveness, he expanded research and development and marketing budgets. Rather than targeting certain markets based on products Scientific-Atlanta had already developed, Topol decided to concentrate on pinpointing growth markets and then developing products for those markets. Believing that the cable television industry was poised for substantial growth, Topol steered Scientific-Atlanta's development of the satellites that eventually became the backbone of the cable industry. By 1980, due to Topol's successful implementation of his strategy, Scientific-Atlanta had become the largest cable satellite stations supplier in the world.

In the 1990s, Scientific-Atlanta again used the strategy of developing a product to target a specific growth market: interactive cable services. In the cable industry, digital technology was first embraced for its ability to offer a clearer picture, crisper sound, and a greater number of channels. Eventually, firms began to

CHRONOLOGY:

Key Dates for Scientific-Atlanta Inc.

1951: Scientific-Atlanta is founded

1971: Sidney Topol takes over as president

1973: Scientific-Atlanta unveils its portable satellite station

1980: Scientific-Atlanta is the world's largest supplier of portable satellite stations for the cable industry

1999: Scientific-Atlanta releases the Explorer 2000 digital set-top box

examine ways to use digital technology to offer interactive services such as high-speed Internet connections and video-on-demand. Believing that these interactive services would emerge as a huge growth market, Scientific-Atlanta began developing technology toward that end as early as 1993. This strategy resulted in the release of the Explorer 2000, the first set-top box able capable of handle high-speed Internet access, email, electronic commerce, video-on-demand, and other interactive services. If interactive services in the early 2000s become the high growth market some analysts anticipate, Scientific-Atlanta will have a product ready to serve that market.

INFLUENCES

When William E. Johnson took over in the mid-1980s, he determined that Scientific-Atlanta had grown too rapidly and become involved in too many new technologies. Too many layers of management had burdened operations and added unnecessary costs. At the same time, competition had intensified, undercutting sales. These problems prompted Johnson to embark up a full-scale restructuring that included the sale of seven business units and the elimination of 75 percent of senior management positions.

PRODUCTS

While set-top boxes account for the majority of Scientific-Atlanta's revenues, the firm also sells broad-

SCIENTIFIC-ATLANTA'S FIRST DIGITAL SET-TOP BOX

In the early-1990s, Scientific-Atlanta began working to develop a digital set-top box. The resulting product, completed in the mid-1990s, cost roughly $3,000 to make. Although the box made use of cutting edge technology, it proved far too expensive to release to the general public and was considered ahead of its time.

band access products, such as digital head end equipment, cable modems, trunk stations, amplifiers, and digital compression devices. Via its SciCare unit, Scientific-Atlanta offers network installation and related services.

CORPORATE CITIZENSHIP

Scientific-Atlanta makes donations every year to organizations like nature conservancies and botanical gardens, zoos and humane societies, and chambers of commerce.

SOURCES OF INFORMATION

Bibliography

Grotticelli, Michael. "Battle of the Set-Top Boxes." *Broadcasting & Cable*, 11 June 2001.

Haley, Kathy. "Gaining Ground." *Broadcasting & Cable*, 29 October 2001.

"Scientific-Atlanta." *International Directory of Company Histories*. Detroit: Gale Research, 1992.

Scientific-Atlanta Inc. Home Page, 2002. Available at http://www.scientificatlanta.com.

Upbin, Bruce. "My Box Can Beat Your Box." *Forbes*, 8 February 1999.

For an annual report:

on the Internet at: http://www.scientificatlanta.com/investors/ar_2001.pdf

For additional industry research:

Investigate companies by their Standard Industrial Classification Codes, also known as SICs. Scientific-Atlanta, Inc.'s primary SIC code is:

3663 Radio & TV Broadcasting & Communications Equipment

Also investigate companies by their North American Industrial Classification System codes, also known as NAICS codes. Scientific-Atlanta, Inc.'s primary NAICS code is:

334220 Radio and Television Broadcasting and Wireless Communications Equipment Manufacturing

Siemens AG

FOUNDED: 1966

Contact Information:

HEADQUARTERS: Wittelsbacherplatz 2, D-80333
   Munich, Germany
PHONE: 49-89-234-0000
FAX: 49-89-234-4242
URL: http://www.siemens.com

OVERVIEW

Siemens AG, headquartered in Munich, Germany, is a large and diversified company with a network of more than 400 companies and over 450,000 employees located in 190 countries. Specializing in electronics and electrical engineering, the company is organized into 14 business groups within 7 business segments: Information and Communication, Automation and Control, Power, Transportation, Medical, Lighting, and Financial and Real Estate. Information and Communications is comprised of three groups: Information and Communications Networks (ICN), Information and Communications Mobile (ICM), and Siemens Business Services (SBS). Automation and Control contains four groups: Automation and Drives (A&D), Industrial Solutions and Services (I&S), Siemens Dematic (SD), and Siemens Building Technologies (SBT). The Power business segment contains two groups: Power Generation (PG) and Power Transmission and Distribution (PTD). The Transportation segment is comprised of Transportation Systems (TS) and Siemens VDO Automotive (SV). Other segments are Medical Solutions; Lighting, which does business as Osram; and Siemens Financial Services.

After a banner year in 2000 in which Siemens rode the wave of an explosion in the mobile telecommunications market, the company was roughed up during 2001 as the mobile phone and semiconductor business suddenly dried up. Siemens, who had invested in the U.S. market heavily since 1997, was hit hard by the dissolution of the U.S. economy after the terrorist attacks on New York and Washington, D.C. in September of 2001.

In the Siemens plant in Dresden, Germany, a worker performs pre-production tests for a bigger silicon wafer. (AP Photo/Matthais Rietschel)

COMPANY FINANCES

In fiscal 2001, ending September 31, 2001, Siemens posted a net income of 2.1 billion euro on 87 billion euro in net sales, down from a net income of 8.9 billion euro on 77.5 billion euro in fiscal 2000. (Average currency exchange rate for fiscal 2001: 1.09 euro = $1.) However, the fiscal 2000 profits were significantly inflated due to substantial divestments made during the year. Siemens' bottom line in 2001 was adversely affected by its 50 percent interest in the computer chip company Infineon, which recorded a profit of 1.2 billion euro in 2000 but posted a loss of 591 million euro in 2001. Additionally, the company incurred 1.9 billion euro in restructuring charges and asset write-downs during the year. Siemens' Operations (i.e., core business segments of Information and Communication, Automation and Control, Power, Transportation, Medical, and Lighting) posted earnings before interest, taxes, and amortization (EBITA) of 1.3 billion euro in fiscal 2001. In fiscal 2000 EBITA was 2.8 billion euro; however, if the 1.9 billion euro in restructuring and write-down of assets is removed from the equation, EBITA from Operations in fiscal 2001 jumps to 3.2 billion euro, an increase of 400 million euro over the previous fiscal year.

During fiscal 2001, Siemens' stock posted a high per share price of $80 on the New York Stock Exchange on May 2, and low per share price of $32.52 on September 21, closing the fiscal year at $38.40. Prices began to rebound during the first two quarters of fiscal 2002, posting a high of $70.48 per share on January 9, closing the second quarter on March 28 at $65.85.

During the first quarter of 2002, ending December 31, 2001, Siemens generated sales of 21 billion euro, up slightly from 20.5 billion euro posted during the same period in fiscal 2001. However, year-on-year net income was down almost half from 1 billion euro in fiscal 2001 to 538 million euro in 2001 due to increased cost of sales and over 100 percent increase in contract orders in the Transportation group.

ANALYSTS' OPINIONS

Because Siemens is such a large conglomeration of companies and interests, analysts tend to use a sum-of-the-part methodology. Examining each of the 14 business groups separately, analysts then total the overall positive or negative impact of all the units combined. In fiscal 2002 most advisors remained neutral toward Siemen's prospects for upcoming performance as positive and negative factors tended to cancel out each other. The most commonly expressed concern focused on Information and Communications. As a result of the sluggish economy especially in the United States, ICN posted a year-on-year decline in sales of 13 percent for the first quarter of fiscal 2002, and

FAST FACTS:
About Siemens AG

Ownership: Siemens AG is an international publicly traded company that is listed on numerous stock exchanges including Amsterdam, Brussels, Dusseldorf, Frankfurt, Geneva, New York, Paris, Vienna, and Zurich.

Ticker Symbol: SI

Officers: Karl-Hermann Baumann, M.D., Chmn., 66; Heinrich von Pierer, M.D., Pres. and CEO, 60; Heins-Joachim Neuburger, CFO, 48

Employees: 477,100

Principal Subsidiary Companies: As Europe's largest electrical and electronics company, Siemens AG has more than 400 production sites in 40 countries. Its wide array of subsidiaries are located around the globe, including Paris, London, New York, Tokyo, Bombay, Madrid, Zurich, Athens, and Brussels.

Chief Competitors: Siemens generates the third highest revenues worldwide in its industry, behind General Electric and IBM, respectively. Two Japanese companies, Matsushita and Hitachi occupy the fourth and fifth spots on the revenue ladder. Other lesser competitors include Hewlett Packard, Toshiba, and Fujitsu.

---

analysts suggest a need for further restructuring in this segment.

Profitability in PG was well ahead of analysts' predictions for fiscal 2001, and PTD greatly increased its number of orders, which will eventually translate into increased revenues as long-term orders are filled. However, analysts warn that the power generation market is at a peak and will likely fall off in the foreseeable future. Segments of Automation and Control also performed well in fiscal 2001, and analysts expect the divisions to continue post positive numbers. Medical Solutions is the group seen as having the most potential for significant growth in the future.

HISTORY

In 1847 Warner Siemens and J. G. Halske formed Siemens & Halske in Berlin to produce and install tele-

graph systems. By 1853 the company was prospering as it benefited from a burst of activity in the communications industry. In 1867 Siemens & Halske received a contract to build a telegraph line between London and Calcutta, totaling 11,000 miles. Three years later the job was complete and the first telegraph message was relayed between London and Calcutta. Through the remainder of the 1800s, innovation followed innovation. In 1875 the company laid the first transatlantic cable, connecting Ireland and the United States. The following year it built the first electric power transmission system in Europe. The next year Siemens patented an improved version of Alexander Graham Bell's telephone. The company built one of the world's first electric elevators in 1880 and produced its first electric trolley car in 1882.

Into the early twentieth century Siemens & Halske remained busy; however at the onset of World War I, orders for the organization's various products and services dropped off and the company retooled to manufacture war-related items, such as military communication devices as well as explosives and airplane engines. The company also provided the German Navy with an advanced fire control system that was instrumental in the sinking of at least two British ships. After the war Siemens & Halske continued to build its influence in electrical engineering. By 1930 the company supplied one third of Germany's electrical manufacturing industry.

Having survived the Great Depression by cutting costs and laying off significant numbers of employees, Siemens & Halske was revitalized by the onset of World War II. Once again the company turned its attention to military products, including the design and production of an automatic pilot system for airplanes and the V 2 rocket. Siemens & Halske's involvement in the Nazi's activities is somewhat unclear. Although Carl Friedrich von Siemens, then head of the company, was quoted as being disgusted by the Nazi's anti-Semitism, without a doubt Siemens & Halske benefited from the war due to increased business and the use of slave labor, a practice employed by many German manufacturers at the time. The company was also accused of importing slave labor from occupied territories and providing the Nazis with gas chamber equipment. The charges, which were never substantiated, were denied by Siemens & Halske.

After recouping from damages and losses suffered during the war, Siemens & Halske refocused on its railroad, medical, telephone, and power generation businesses. With offices already in the United Kingdom, Russia, and Japan, in 1954 Siemens & Halske opened an office in New York. At the same time, the company expanded into the new field of computers, producing its first mainframe in 1955. Growing rapidly in numerous fields and markets, the company decided to reorganize in 1966. All businesses entities became subsidiaries of the new parent company, Siemens AG. During the 1970s the newly restructured company continued to expand its businesses and increase its revenues. During the late 1970s an unsuccessful and costly attempt was made to enter the microchip business. Despite an influx of $1 billion for research and development, Siemens fell behind in both research and production and had to buy chips from another vendor to fill its orders.

During the 1980s the company dedicated massive amounts of money to acquisitions and research, spending $24 billion between 1983 and 1988. A new era for Siemens was marked in 1992 when Dr. Heinrich von Pierer was named as head of the company. Von Pierer brought a new mentality of global vision, and he set out to upend the slow, methodical, and process-laden system of manufacturing traditional to German culture. He cut costs, pushed into new markets including Asia and an increased presence in the United States, and encouraged his management team to be innovative and aggressive. The strategy paid off; by 1994 Siemens AG was Germany's third-largest public corporation and the third-largest manufacturer of electrical products and power generation systems. The company continued to post positive numbers until an already slow economy in 2001 was decimated by the events of September 11.

STRATEGY

Siemens set its strategy by assigning goals for growth in profitability to each of its operational groups through steady and measurable progress. Siemens' primary method of tracking success is by looking at its economic value added (EVA). EVA measures the difference between return and cost. To motivate management leaders to achieve goals, incentive pay is tied directly to EVA. Impacted by a sharp decline in the telecommunication industry, as well as the overall economy, Siemens developed "Operation 2003," a plan that will drive the company toward its medium-range goals in spite of a hostile economic environment. Because significant growth is not expected to come from increase revenues from sales, the fundamental strategy for Operation 2003 is to reduce costs in a variety of areas. Operations will be targeted for streamlining, employee numbers will be cut by up to 17,000, and corporate spending will be reduced by 15 percent. U.S. operations, which were deeply affected by the downturn in the economy in the second half of 2001, are specifically targeted for increased profit return.

In the continually evolving process of diversifying and acquiring new business interests, Siemens made a significant transaction in 2001 when it began to divest itself of Infineon. In fiscal 2000 the Munich-based chipmaker posted a net income of 1.1 billion euro; in fiscal 2001 the company posted a net loss of 591 million euro as the semiconductor market fell off drastically. Although Infineon was spun off as a separate company in 2000, Siemens retained just over 50 percent. By the end of 2001 Siemens had reduced its interest in the company to 41.4 percent, and stated intentions to continue to divest of the floundering company. In addition, in March of 2002

CHRONOLOGY:
Key Dates for Siemens

1847: Werner Siemens and J. G. Halske found Siemens & Halske in Berlin to manufacture and install telegraphy systems

1857: Receives a major contract to establish a telegraph system in Russia

1867: Lays 11,000 miles of telegraph line, connecting London and Calcutta, India

1875: Lays the first transatlantic cable from Ireland to the United States

1909: Develops and installs first automatic telephone exchange

1914: Shifts focus to military contracts during World War I

1930: Provides one-third of all Germany's electrical manufacturing capacity

1941: Focuses once again on military contract during the war years

1954: Establishes a U.S.-based subsidiary to manufacture electron microscopes

1966: Reorganizes as Siemens AG, bringing all its subsidiaries under its umbrella

1978: Becomes second largest manufacturer of electrical equipment in the world

1992: Establishes a $16 million research and development laboratory in New Jersey

2000: Announces plans to invest $1.5 billion by 2003 to expand its operations in Asia; annual sales top $67.5 billion with a world-wide workforce of 447,000

Siemens announced that it would divest itself of approximately 50 low-performing companies.

INFLUENCES

Numerous factors influence the performance of Siemens as a whole and the profitability of individual business areas. The Information and Communications segment is primarily affected by two factors. First, it

SAY CHEESE

Siemens has developed a real-time 3D and color face-recognition camera that provides advances in the accuracy, speed, and lower cost. The device used cutting edge technology to generate 3D images by determining coordinates of scene points by intersecting lines of view of a standard color camera which combines with planes of light generated by a slide projector. Image acquisition rate is up to 12 images per second and a distance accuracy of 1 millimeter to 1 meter. Siemens expects that the new camera will revolutionize face-recognition technology, making it decisively accurate (up to 100 percent) and widely used for such applications as airport security.

operates in a highly competitive market of electronics and communications and is thereby subject to the trends in pricing and volatile markets. During fiscal 2001, price pressure and a depressed market were apparent in semiconductors, telecommunications, and automobile production. Second, because Siemens works on the cutting edge of highly advance technology, the company must invest heavily in research and design. Some research may not evolve into a viable product, or the product may not prove to be marketable.

Because a significant portion of Siemens' business is tied to long-term fixed price contracts, the company may be either positively or negatively affected by actual productivity and production costs. Cost overruns can negate profitability, and coming in under expected costs can increase estimated profits. Also, Siemens often relies heavily on third parties to supply parts or assemble products. If a third party fails to meet its obligations, Siemens may be unable to meet its own commitments. Also because the company operates around the world, it is subject to trends in currency exchange, which can result in either expanded or decreased value.

CURRENT TRENDS

To survive and prosper in a highly competitive industry, Siemens has moved to distinguish itself from its competitors by moving beyond simply offering products and services to providing comprehensive solutions to its customers' problems. By combining products, systems, and services into an integrated package, Siemens hopes to offer what its competitors cannot: a total pack-

age that provides customers with a complete and integrated answer to their needs, from design to installation to management. For example, Medical Solutions not only provides cutting edge technology in state of the art medical systems used in diagnosis and therapy, but also includes options for professional consulting services, technology systems for clinical and administration use, and remote processing services.

Another trend has been the significant increase in Siemens' presence in the United States. Between 1997 and 2002, Siemens invested $9 billion in U.S.-based acquisitions, making the United States Siemens' largest single market. In March of 2001 Siemens cross-listed 12 percent of its shares on the New York Stock Exchange and established a headquarters in New York. The company also invested in an advertising campaign and sponsored the U.S. Open in order to gain exposure in the United States.

PRODUCTS

Siemens' Information and Communications segment focuses on next-generation Internet, wireless communications, and advanced electronics. One of the largest producers in the world of mobile phone handsets, Siemens provides a wide range of products, services, and solutions in innovative voice, data, and video communications devices. ICN develops and markets communication systems to the public and private sectors; ICM designs, manufactures, and markets mobile network devices, such as mobile and cordless phones and radio base stations; and SBS designs, builds, and sells information and communications systems to business in sectors such as industry, transport, and utilities.

Automation and Control focuses on products and services that optimize production, cost efficiency, and productivity. A&D products and services include low voltage control and installation technology, manufacturing automation, drive systems, and process automation; I&S provides advanced electronic products and services designed to improve infrastructure facilities throughout the entire life cycle of the facilities; SD designs, produces, and markets factory automation and logistics automation equipment; and SBT provides products and services related to monitoring and maintenance of temperature, safety, electricity, lighting, and security for commercial and industrial properties.

Siemens' Power segment provides a full range of power generation, transmission, and distribution. PG offers power plant technology, including production of key components and power plant design and construction; PTD provides equipment, systems, and services that assist in moving electrical power from generation point to consumer destination, including power system controls, transformers, and high voltage products. Within Transportation, STS specializes in the rail industry, producing heavy rails, locomotives, and trains as well as associated services; SV manufactures and sells electrical and electronic systems and devices used in automobiles, including powertrain safety, chassis communication, multimedia, and cockpit controls.

Siemens' Medical Solution researches, designs, and develops high-tech medical products and services related to diagnosis and treatment. Products include medical imaging systems and electromedical systems such as patient monitoring equipment and life support systems. Osram develops and markets lighting sources and controls, including general lighting products, automobile lighting, special photo-optic lamps, and display lighting. The Financial and Real Estate group operates as Siemens Financial Services GmbH, which specializes in corporate financing, risk management, investment financing, fund management and insurance services.

CORPORATE CITIZENSHIP

Siemens' environmental policy operations on the concept of sustainability. Through careful use of natural resources and with a constant eye for the ecological impact during the life cycle of any given product, Siemens is committed to achieving zero pollution if at all possible, and if not, then reducing the impact to the environment as much as possible. Along with regulation requirements imposed by numerous governments and agencies, Siemens maintains ongoing in-house environmental standards and objectives that are routinely assessed.

Key aspects to Siemens' citizenship goals include learning and research, public welfare, and arts and culture. Siemens works with schools, colleges, and university both in Germany and around the world to promote interaction between research and industry. The company sponsors numerous learning and scholarship programs aimed at generating interest in technology. Concerning public welfare, Siemens focuses its community initiative on education and training to help alleviate the underlying problems of poverty. The company attempts to offer assistance on a local level, specific to local needs. Siemens also promotes the arts by supporting museums and artists through private foundations as well as through the Siemens Arts Program.

GLOBAL PRESENCE

Operating through hundreds of companies in 140 countries around the world, Siemens is truly an international company. Employees are primarily located in Europe, with 199,000 in Germany and 118,000 in other European countries. The Americas has 107,000 Siemens employees; the Asia-Pacific has 53,000; and Africa and the Middle East have 7,000. The United States is

Siemens' single largest market, accounting for over half of PG and Medical sales worldwide, as well as over 40 percent of SD and Osram sales. Much of Siemens' business is conducted in Europe with a strong market for ICM in the Asia-Pacific region. In all, during fiscal 2001 sales by region were as follows: Germany, 22 percent; Europe excluding Germany, 30 percent; The Americas, 30 percent; Asia-Pacific, 13 percent; and Africa/Middle East, 5 percent.

EMPLOYMENT

Of the 450,000 persons employed by Siemens during fiscal 2001, 191,900 worked in manufacturing jobs; 143,200 worked in sales and marketing; 58,800 worked in administration; and 56,100 worked in research and development. Distribution of employees worldwide is as follows: 42 percent in Germany; 25 percent in Europe excluding Germany; 22 percent in the Americas; 11 percent in the Asia-Pacific; and 1 percent in Africa/Middle East. Of all employees, 38 percent had a college degree, and of that total, 78 percent received their education in the fields of natural science or technology. In fiscal 2001, Siemens spent 500 million euro on employee training and apprenticeships. The single most important area for staff recruitment is in research and development. Because much of the company's success depends on the development of highly advanced, innovative technology, Siemens actively recruits the best and brightest prospects for its research and development positions.

SOURCES OF INFORMATION

Bibliography

Aston, Adam. "He's Putting Siemens on the American Map." *Business Week*, 4 February 2002.

Grant, Tina, ed. *International Directory of Company Histories.* Vol. 14. Detroit: St. James Press, 1996.

Karnitschnig, Matthew. "Siemens Stages Turnaround as Profit Beats Forecasts—Sale of Infineon Stake Boosts Net to $477 Million; Outlook Is Still Clouded." *The Wall Street Journal*, 24 January 2002.

Kueppers, Alfred. "Siemens Posts Losses, Shuffles Management in Ailing Tech Unit." *The Wall Street Journal*, 15 November 2001.

McHugh, David. "Siemens Reduces Stake In Chip Maker Infineon to 41.4 Percent, Selling 40 Million Shares." *AP Newswire*, 8 January 2002.

Pringle, David. "Spending by China Mobile-Phone Operators Will Be Cut as Slump in Demand Spreads." *The Wall Street Journal*, 29 March 2002.

Siemens AG Home Page, 2002. Available at http://www.siemens.

Uniworld Business Publications, Inc. *Directory of Foreign Firms Operating in the United States*. New York: Author, 2000.

For an annual report:

on the Internet at: http://www.siemens.com

For additional industry research:

Investigate companies by their Standard Industrial Classification Codes, also known as SICs. Siemens AG's primary SICs are:

1731 Electrical Work

3511 Turbines And Turbine Generator Sets

3519 Internal Combustion Engines, Not Elsewhere Classified

3531 Construction Machinery

Also investigate companies by their North American Industrial Classification System codes, also known as NAICS codes. Siemens AG's primary NAICS codes are:

235310 Electrical Contractors

333120 Construction Machinery Manufacturing

333131 Mining Machinery and Equipment Manufacturing

333298 All Other Industrial Manufacturing

Six Flags Inc.

FOUNDED: 1989

OVERVIEW

Six Flags Inc. is the world's second largest theme park operator. It is second in size only to Walt Disney. Unlike Disney's parks, Six Flags' parks are meant to be experienced in a single day. The 39 parks are spread throughout the world and each reflects a unique regional personality. Most of Six Flags' customers live within in a 150-mile radius of its parks. Each park offers different themes and attractions. The parks operate on a seasonal basis, usually from Memorial Day until Labor Day. Some parks have longer operating seasons depending on the local climate. The company generates the majority of its revenues during the second and third quarters of each year, which is optimal park season. Attractions include thrill rides, water rides, live entertainment, and concerts.

Contact Information:
HEADQUARTERS: 11501 Northeast Expwy.
  Oklahoma City, OK 73131
PHONE: (405)475-2500
FAX: (405)475-2555
URL: http://www.sixflags.com

COMPANY FINANCES

Six Flags posted a net loss of $58.1 million on $1.1 billion in revenues in fiscal year 2001, which represents the third consecutive year that the company has lost money. In 2000 the losses totaled $52 million on revenues of nearly $1.1 billion—an increase on the 1999 loss of $30 million. In 2000 some 54 percent of revenues were derived from admission fees, while 46 percent was derived from sales of food and merchandise.

ANALYSTS' OPINIONS

Six Flags ended 2001 falling slightly short of analysts' predictions; however, much of the downturn can

FINANCES:

Six Flags Inc. Net Income, 1998-2001 (million dollars)

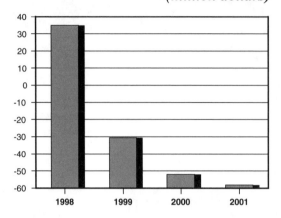

Six Flags Inc. 2001 Stock Prices (dollars)

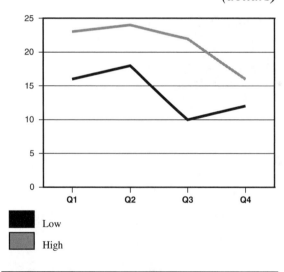

Low

High

that a seven to eight percent growth in earnings was possible for 2002.

Tierco Group Inc., the original company behind Six Flags Inc., got into the theme park business almost by accident. Tierco, an Oklahoma City-based developer of commercial property, in 1982 bought Frontier City, a run-down Oklahoma City theme park, with the intention of razing the park to make way for an office complex. The Oklahoma economic slump intervened, putting the local real estate market into a tailspin. Generating more money as a theme park than it would if converted into commercial real estate, Frontier City was saved.

A whole new enterprise began to take shape in 1989 when Tierco's major shareholder took direct control of the troubled company in a financial restructuring. As part of the restructuring, all of Tierco's assets were relinquished to lenders, except Frontier City. Soon after assuming control, the new management team embarked on a two-year capital program to reposition and revitalize the 30-year-old Frontier City. By 1990 Tierco was transformed from a real estate developer into the operator of a single theme park. However, Frontier City was not to remain the company's sole attraction for long. In 1991 the company purchased White Water Bay, a winter adventure park in Oklahoma City. The following year the company went out of the hometown market and acquired Wild World Amusement Park, located between Baltimore and the District of Columbia. The park's name was changed to Adventure World in 1994.

The fledgling operator of theme parks changed its name to Premier Parks Inc. in 1994. In 1995 Premier purchased Ohio-based Funtime Parks Inc., acquiring Geauga Lake, Wyandot Lake, and Darien Lake theme parks in the process. Things really took off for Premier Parks in 1996 when the company raised nearly $70 million in an initial public offering. Armed with fresh capital, company officials went searching for new acquisitions. That year alone, Premier purchased Elitch Gardens Amusement Park in Denver, Colorado; Waterworld USA water adventure parks in Concord and Sacramento, California; and Great Escape and Splashwater Kingdom in Lake George, New York.

Premier pursued a vigorous program of expansion into 1997, purchasing Riverside Amusement Park in Agawam, Massachusetts. A secondary public offering in early 1997 raised another $200 million for Premier. In April 1997, the company assumed management of Marine World Africa USA. Later this year Premier acquired Kentucky Kingdom theme park in Louisville and purchased the site of the Old Indiana in Indianapolis for redevelopment as a theme park. In fall 1997, Premier announced that it had negotiated a definitive agreement to purchase Walibi Family Parks in Western

be attributed to the September 11, 2001, terrorist attacks. Prior to the events of that day, the company had been building momentum going into the fall. Frederic E. Russell, a Tulsa money manager, said that the setback should not be surprising. Attendance at theme parks and destination vacation resorts collectively plunged during the final months of 2001. By March 2002 the financial landscape showed signs of improvement. The company posted a smaller than expected fourth quarter loss for fiscal year 2001. Goldman Sachs analyst Chris Cox upgraded the company to a "trading buy" and predicted

Europe. In December 1997, the company's stock, which had been traded on the NASDAQ Exchange since the company first went public in 1996, began trading on the New York Stock Exchange.

All that had gone before was dwarfed by the company's stunning 1998 acquisition of the Six Flags theme parks from Time Warner Entertainment and an investor group led by Boston Ventures for nearly $1 billion in cash and an assumption of about $900 million in debt. In one fell swoop, the company added to its stable 12 of the most popular regional theme parks in the country. A short time later, Premier finalized its acquisition of Walibi, which operates six theme parks in Western Europe—three in France, two in Belgium, and one in the Netherlands.

As the world entered the twenty-first century, Six Flags Inc. entered the world. Beginning in 2000 the company focused on non-U.S. acquisitions. Six Flags Mexico, Warner Brothers Movie World Madrid, Montreal's La Ronde, and Warner Brothers Movie World Madrid were all integrated into operations. International parks accounted for 15 percent of gate revenues in 2001.

STRATEGY

Six Flags holdings consist of a diverse set of properties around the world. Despite the size and scope of operations, management has devised and implemented a global marketing strategy. National marketing programs are designed to promote the Six Flags brand name. To further enhance this strategy, 11 parks have been re-branded under the Six Flags name since 1998. Three of the renamed parks were international holdings. In 2000 Six Flags entered into a marketing agreement with America Online (AOL)/Time Warner. America Online promised to feature Six Flags prominently in its sites and include Six Flags as its official theme park sponsor. Six Flags will provide ticket discounts and special offers to AOL customers and use its software in its U.S. theme parks. This alliance provides Six Flags with exposure to a worldwide audience.

In addition to global brand marketing, parks are promoted through local media outlets. The emphasis is placed on the individual park and its unique features and specific attractions. Regional companies are often approached to distribute discounts or premium offers to customers in the local area of a park. This strategy allows geographic or cultural themes to be featured in advertising.

Direct marketing and telemarketing are also key components in the campaign for customers. Group sales constituted 34.5 percent of sales in 2001. Each park has its own group sales team that targets different markets in the area. The season pass is also a profitable marketing channel. Pre-sold attendance instruments assure revenues regardless of unexpected changes in the economy or inclement weather. Discount tickets, coupons, and other

FAST FACTS:
About Six Flags Inc.

Ownership: Six Flags Inc. is a publicly traded company on the New York Stock Exchange.

Ticker Symbol: PKS

Officers: Kieran E. Burke, Chmn. and CEO, 43, salary $773,240; Gary Story, Pres., COO, and Dir., 45, salary $587,423; James F. Dannhauser, CFO and Dir., 48, salary $459,289

Employees: 43,081

Principal Subsidiary Companies: Six Flags Inc. is a multi-national corporation with operations in 39 locations throughout the United States, Canada, and Europe.

Chief Competitors: Six Flags Inc. is the second largest amusement and theme park operator in the world. Its primary competitors are in the entertainment and theme park industries, including Walt Disney, Universal Studios, Viacom Entertainment, Cedar Fair Ltd., and Anheuser Busch.

offers are also effective in bolstering attendance. Historically, in-park spending by consumers offsets the revenue loss on a discount ticket.

INFLUENCES

All marketing or promotional campaigns are updated or completely changed each season. The company faces an ongoing challenge to keep its image fresh and exciting. A number of elements are combined to produce a plan for each park. Six Flags owns licensing rights to a number of well-known fictional and cartoon characters including Warner Brothers and DC Comics animated characters, including Superman, Batman, Bugs Bunny, and Daffy Duck. Additionally, the company has acquired rights to some Cartoon Network and Hanna-Barbera characters for use in Europe and Latin and South America; these characters include Scooby Doo, the Flintstones, and Yogi Bear. Ownership of these characters allows the company to take advantage of trends and capitalize on marketing opportunities. In 2002, a live action Scooby Doo film is expected to resurrect interest in that character and his cohorts. Many comic book heroes are receiv-

CHRONOLOGY:

Key Dates for Six Flags Inc.

1982: Tierco purchases a run-down amusement park, Frontier City, with intentions to build an office complex in its place

1989: Tierco's major shareholder assumes control and begins to revitalize Frontier City

1990: Tierco abandons real estate development and focuses on theme parks

1994: Tierco becomes Premier Parks

1996: Premier Parks goes public

1998: Purchases Six Flags theme parks from Time Warner; begins global expansion with purchase of Walibi Parks

2000: Changes name to Six Flags Inc.

2002: Opens Warner Brothers Movie World Madrid

ing the large screen treatment, and Six Flags will utilize all avenues of promotion presented.

Local and regional customs are also critical in creating appeal for park guests. Food, music, concerts, and theme events are designed to reflect the culture and appetite of the area.

CURRENT TRENDS

Six Flags has created a vast empire of theme parks largely through purchasing and revitalizing existing sites. It is highly likely that this will continue to be the model for any planned expansion. Analysts at Six Flags have determined that it would cost more than $200 million and take at least two years to design and build a regional theme park comparable to its holdings. In addition, it has become more difficult to secure the necessary permits to undertake such a project. Environmental regulations are increasingly stringent, and compliance with all appropriate codes and laws can be extremely costly.

In 2002 Six Flags is focused on increasing attendance at each park and maximizing customer spending at each venue. In order to achieve this goal, the company attempts to rotate attractions every two years, which allows an attraction to remain new and exciting to the

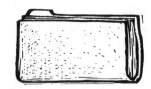

MAKING THE GRADE

Six Flags isn't talking about the rate of the inclines on its latest thrill rides when it talks about grades. It has partnered with a local insurance agency in the Washington DC area to encourage kids to do well in school. As part of an incentive program, children who received A's and B's in their classes are rewarded with a trip to the Six Flags America theme park in Largo, Maryland. The reward program entices the students to work harder to achieve the grades necessary to make the trip, which is held at the end of the school year.

thrill-seeking public. The development of new rides is also a continuous process that helps to maintain interest in the parks.

PRODUCTS

In 2002 Six Flags operated 39 theme parks in North America and Europe serving more than 46 million visitors. The parks are designed for single day visitation, as opposed to a resort destination park designed for stays of a week or longer. All of the parks provide family-oriented entertainment and attractions. Depending on the regional climate, the attractions range from water parks and thrill rides to concert venues and regional theme shows. Collectively, the parks boast more than 1,430 different rides, which are rotated between parks. Roller coasters are the centerpiece of theme park attractions, and Six Flags owns 185 separate rides guaranteed to thrill even the most seasoned rider. Six Flags theme parks account for 16 of the most popular parks in North America. A complete list of parks and their locations can be found on the company's Web site.

CORPORATE CITIZENSHIP

Six Flags considers itself to be a vital part of the communities surrounding its many parks. In an effort to contribute to the quality of life and give back to the residents, Six Flags participates in many local charitable events. The company donates free passes to many worthy organizations and sponsors events to raise funds and awareness for many causes. In June 2001 Six Flags New

England joined forces with the Leary Firefighters Foundation to provide a family night out at the park. The event was held to honor firefighters who died in a tragic fire in 1999 and to demonstrate appreciation for the many firefighters who continue to risk their lives in the protection of others.

GLOBAL PRESENCE

Six Flags operates 39 theme parks in the United States and Belgium, Canada, France, Germany, Holland, Mexico, the Netherlands, and Spain. In 2001 approximately 84 percent of sales originated in the United States, with the remainder attributed to international operations. There are 10 international properties, but this number is expected to increase. The most recent addition to the international roster is Warner Brothers Movie World Madrid. Six Flags is developing the park, which was slated to open in April 2002.

EMPLOYMENT

During the 2001 operating season, Six Flags employed 3,000 full-time employees and 44,000 seasonal workers. A large number of the seasonal employees are teenagers who fall under the jurisdiction of child labor laws. Seven percent of the company's full-time employees are participants in a labor agreement with a national union. These agreements are slated for renewal in 2002 and 2003, and management expects this relationship to continue uninterrupted.

SOURCES OF INFORMATION

Bibliography

Bunyan, Clytie. "Acquisitions Boost Company; Parks Operator's Formula Keeps Firm Growing." *The Oklahoman*, 15 October 1997.

Laval, Kevin. "Shareholder Takes Control of Tierco: Some Assets Relinquished; Frontier City Is New Priority." *The Oklahoman*, 21 October 1989.

Martin, Stacy. "Theme Park Firm Getting Big Boost from Acquisitions." *The Oklahoman*, 15 October 1995.

McDowell, Edwin. "Premier Parks Is the New Monster of the Midway." *New York Times*, 21 June 1998.

"Meltzer Group Pays Off Insurance Policy for Good Grades." *PR Newswire*, 21 August 2001.

Meltzer, Mark. "Six Flags to Go on Spending Ride." *Atlanta Business Chronicle*, 1 June 1998.

X MARKS THE SPOT

The extreme sports craze is everywhere and Six Flags is no exception. In an attempt to capitalize on the youth-oriented movement, Six Flags Magic Mountain in Los Angeles has been christened as the home of the "Xtreme" park. "Xperience the Xtreme" is the slogan and the "X" is the premier attraction. The "X" is billed as a one of a kind, first of its kind thrill ride. Unlike traditional roller coasters that operate with the cars running parallel to the track, this ride offers a second axis of rotation. The ride is described as a "prototype vehicle that spins independently 360 degrees forward and backward on a separate axis." Passengers whip through a 3,600-foot track, traveling in a 20-foot-wide winged vehicle that plummets 200 feet to the ground head first, face down, spinning backward and forward, head over heels. Xtra seatbelts required for this ride!

Payne, Charles, and Rhonda Schaffler. "Upgrades & Downgrades: Six Flags Waving Strong." *CNNfn*, 20 March 2002.

"Premier Parks Agrees to Buy Six Flags from Time Warner Entertainment and Boston Ventures for $1.9 Billion." *Business Wire*, 9 February 1998.

"Six Flags Blames Terror Attacks for Earnings Shortfall." *AP Wire*, 8 November 2001.

"Six Flags Inc." *Hoover's Online*, 2002. Available at http://www.hoovers.com

"Six Flags New England and The Leary Firefighter Foundation Unite for June 8, 2001 Benefit." *PR Newswire*, 14 May 2001.

For an annual report:
on the Internet at: http://www.sixflags.com/forinvestors/

For additional industry research:
Investigate companies by their Standard Industrial Classification Codes, also known as SICs. Six Flags Inc.'s primary SICs are:

7996 Amusement Parks

7999 Amusement and Recreation

Also investigate companies by their North American Industry Classification System codes, also known as NAICS codes. Six Flag Inc.'s primary NAICS code is:

713110 Amusement and Theme Parks

Skechers U.S.A., Inc.

FOUNDED: 1992

Contact Information:

HEADQUARTERS: 228 Manhattan Beach Blvd.
  Manhattan Beach, CA 90266
PHONE: (310)318-3100
FAX: (310)318-5019
URL: http://www.skechers.com

OVERVIEW

Skechers U.S.A., Inc. is an emerging global mega-brand in the lifestyle footwear industry that markets casual fashionable footwear to trend-conscious men, women, and children. The company's formula for success combines a top-quality product that meets customer expectations and an innovative global marketing strategy driven by fashion-forward print and television advertising. Also essential to the company's growth scheme is its broad range of domestic and international distribution channels: department stores, specialty and athletic stores, the Internet, and company-owned retail stores.

Since Skechers was established in 1992, the company's product offerings have grown from utility-styled workboots to include sport, casual, dress, dress casual, and its latest addition, roller skates. Celebrity endorsements have further increased Skechers brand profile. Teen pop icon Britney Spears began appearing in international Skechers Sport print ads in January 2001, followed by worldwide endorsement deals with actors Rob Lowe and Matt Dillon.

Skechers sells its products to numerous department and specialty stores including Nordstrom, Macy's, Dillards, Robinsons-May, JCPenney, Footlocker, Famous Footwear, Genesco's, Journeys, and FootAction USA. The company also sells direct to consumers through more than 80 company-owned and operated Skechers USA retail stores, from New York and Los Angeles, to London, Paris, and Germany. Skechers sells its footwear in more than 100 countries though more than 35 major distributors. Additionally, Skechers sells its products to customers through its official online Web site.

COMPANY FINANCES

In fiscal 2001 Skechers reported record full-year results. For the year ending December 31, 2001, net sales climbed 42.3 percent to $960.4 million, up from $675 million the previous year. Net earnings rose 8 percent from $43.8 million or $1.20 per share to $47.3 million or $1.24 per share. Skechers Chairman and CEO Robert Greenberg remarked, "With a 42.3 percent increase in sales over 2000 and annual sales at nearly a billion dollars, we believe 2001 was an impressive year for Skechers. We are delighted that we continue to build the brand in 2001—across all channels of distribution and within each of the categories that we offer, and we increased market share both domestically and internationally." In a 52-week period, stock prices ranged from a low of $10.00 to a high of $40.30 and had a price earnings ratio of 12.3 for 2000.

Net sales for the fourth quarter 2001 rose 24.4 percent to $214.1 million compared to $172 million in fourth quarter 2000. Net earnings for the fourth quarter were $2 million versus net earnings of $9.7 million for the same period in 2000. Earnings per share in the fourth quarter were $0.05 compared to $0.26 per share in the comparable period of 2000. Gross margin in the quarter was 39.7 percent.

Skechers also implemented cost-cutting initiatives designed to cut general and administrative expenses. As of December 31, 2001, the company had $140.0 million in working capital, $29.6 million in long-term debt, and stockholder's equity of $199.0 million.

ANALYSTS' OPINIONS

Skechers has experienced rapid growth since its inception, increasing net sales at a compound annual growth rate of 39.7 percent from $90.8 million in 1994 to $675 million in 2000. This momentum increased into 2000 with a 60 percent increase in sales and a 109.3 percent increase in earnings compared to 1999. Analysts at Wedbush Morgan Securities predicts that Skechers will be in demand among middle-class customers in 2002 and benefit from assertive advertising and new product launches. Analysts project revenues of $1.15 billion for full-year 2002, a 20 percent increase, as well as earnings per share at $1.60 and price earnings ratio of 9.2. Skechers continues to build their brand with the unique approach of offering comfortable, stylish footwear at reasonable prices for all demographics, maximizing advertising dollars. Sales remain strong, particularly in Skechers Sport for Women, Skechers USA for Women, Skechers Collection, and Skechers for Kids. Additionally, Skechers by Michelle K. and Somethin' Else from Skechers were initially well-received.

FINANCES:

Skechers U.S.A., Inc.
Net Sales, 1998-2001
(million dollars)

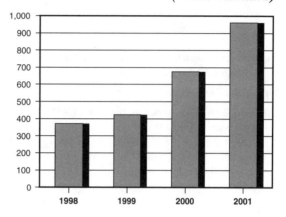

Skechers U.S.A., Inc.
2001 Stock Prices
(dollars)

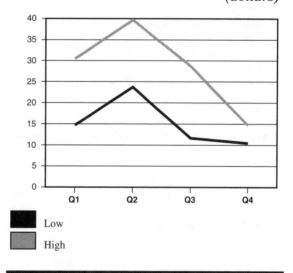

HISTORY

Skechers founder Robert Greenberg, the self-proclaimed king of brand-building, has created a major league footwear label in a relatively short amount of time. The chairman and CEO of Skechers turned a strong promotional sense and a keen eye for trends into a household name. Moving out of the fashion industry in 1983, Greenberg stepped into footwear at the height of the aerobics craze, which became the birth of his new business, L.A. Gear. Greenberg spotted missed opportunities in the

FAST FACTS:

About Skechers U.S.A., Inc.

Ownership: Skechers U.S.A., Inc. is a publicly owned company traded on the New York Stock Exchange.

Ticker Symbol: SKX

Officers: Robert Greenberg, Chmn. and CEO, 60, 1999 base salary $289,000; David Weinberg, CFO, 49, 1999 base salary $421,000; Jeff Greenberg, Dir. of Marketing; Clay Irving, Dir. of Management Information Systems; Marcee Mackey, Dir. of Human Resources

Employees: 1,666

Chief Competitors: Skechers U.S.A., Inc. competes with other branded products within their product category as well as private label products sold by retailers. The company's utility footwear competes with such companies as The Timberland Company, Dr. Martens, Kenneth Cole Productions, Steven Madden, and Wolverine World Wide, Inc. The company's athletic shoes compete with footwear from such companies as Nike, Reebok International Ltd., Adidas-Salomon AG, and New Balance. Their children's shoes compete with brands offered by The Stride Rite Corporation.

---

women's and teen's athletic shoe markets, segments ignored by other manufacturers. Greenberg rode out the trend, resulting in revenues exceeding $900 million within 7 years. During a period of financial difficulty, Greenberg was ousted from L.A. Gear.

Undeterred, he established Skechers in Manhattan Beach, California, and began distributing R. Griggs Ltd. and other brands in 1992. Skechers filed suit against R. Griggs the following year for breach of contract and eventually the two firms canceled their licensing agreement. Greenberg then began designing his own brand of street-wise shoes for young trend-conscious men, one of the only markets not dominated by industry heavyweights. In 1993 the firm introduced the grunge-look "Chrome Dome," a worn-looking shoe that was picked up by Nordstrom and Foleys, among other retailers. The company signed licensing agreements for clothes and expanded operations to Europe and Asia. Skechers started to focus on athletic footwear and, in June 1999, conducted its initial public offering, selling seven million shares at $11 a piece. Greenberg

and his family control about 80 percent of Skechers voting power.

Since 1999 Skechers has increased retail stores and in-store boutiques, expanded women's shoes, and diversified into children's shoes. In 2000 *Business Week* placed Skechers fifth on their "100 Best Small Companies" list and was named "Company of the Year" by *Footwear News*.

STRATEGY

Skechers business plan for 2001 was "Strategy, Focus, Growth." The result was a record year from increased net sales to wholesale and retail expansion, and a burgeoning international business. The company's long term plan is to capitalize on their premier brand status by continuing to capture an increased share of the global footwear market, which is estimated at $43 billion worldwide. Skechers took specific measures in 2001 to achieve this goal; the company assumed direct control of international business in parts of Europe, opened retail stores in key locations, introduced three new lines of shoes, and added styles to existing lines of Skechers Sport, Skechers Collection, Skechers USA, and Skechers Kids. The company also tightened its management team and increased their infrastructure to allow for the company's future growth. For 2002, the California-based firm will focus on further development of product lines, expanding new categories, broadening retail operations, and driving business through licensing deals.

INFLUENCES

Skechers marketing philosophy is "Unseen. Untold. Unsold." Skechers believes in the power of their advertising, and they promote the idea that Skechers is simply a must-have product. As an industry leader, Skechers goal is to maximize brand impact by keeping their message on consumers minds and the shoes on their feet. Focusing on Skechers cutting-edge attitude and streetwise image, the company utilizes an aggressive marketing approach that uses multiple mediums for maximum effectiveness. This integrated approach is based on advertising and supported by alternative direct mediums. Skechers places print advertising in up to 90 magazines a month including: *Cosmopolitan, In Style, People, Vogue, GQ, Maxim, Us Weekly, Mens Fitness, Rolling Stone, Teen People*, and *Sports Illustrated*. Skechers places broadcast advertising on ABC, CBS, NBC, FOX, MTV, WB, ESPN, and Nickelodeon.

Skechers uses the term "alternative direct" mediums to describe their in-store presence, their at-home presence, and their special promotions. In company stores, Skechers' signature look is consistent throughout the retail environment creating a lasting brand image for consumers.

There are more than 80 Skechers stores in Los Angeles, Boston, San Francisco, and New York, including the high-traffic, high-tourist locations of Melrose Avenue, Universal CityWalk, and Third Street Promenade in Los Angeles and 34th Street and SoHo in New York. Skechers are available through 3,500 accounts representing 25,000 sales outlets in the United States alone. The company's catalog and the interactive Web site provide convenience and around-the-clock access for the at-home customer. These direct-to-consumer operations also allow those not near a company-owned store to experience the Skechers lifestyle, see the extensive product selection, and utilize a store finder that directs customers to the nearest locations for brand purchases. To further promote e-commerce, Skechers has signed a deal with America Online (AOL) that allows shoppers to directly access the Skechers Web site through Shop@AOL.com, AOL's shopping destination. The company's promotion team gets their message across through various agreements with well-known brands who's images are compatible with the company. In summer 2000, Skechers teamed with McDonalds for a promotion that placed the Skechers name and picture of a shoe on drink cups and french fry boxes in more than 13,000 restaurants. The company also teamed with Wherehouse Music for a special in-store promotion.

CURRENT TRENDS

Each year presents new opportunities for Skechers to build on their brands' ever-increasing popularity. For the first time, the company had signed endorsement deals with major celebrities to tie-in the brand with recognizable faces. Starting with one of the biggest teen icons in the world, singer Britney Spears appeared in Skechers Sport ads in international teen, young women, and pop culture magazines. For 2002 the pop princess inked a three-year deal to represent signature Britney 4 Wheelers by Skechers, the company's new funky, techno-fashion roller skates. Balancing out the companies image, actors Matt Dillon and Rob Lowe can be seen in separate ad campaigns running in domestic and international men's and pop culture magazines. Capitalizing on the trend, in 2002 the company signed worldwide endorsement deals with L.A. Lakers star Rick Fox and award-winning actor Robert Downey, Jr.

Supplementing the print ads, Skechers picks up the pace with lively and memorable broadcast campaigns for men and women centered on Skechers Sport and bright energetic spots for Skechers Kids. The ads run on television and cable networks in the United States, Canada, Europe, and Asia.

PRODUCTS

Skechers product lines include Skechers Sport, Skechers Collection, Skechers USA, and Skechers Kids.

CHRONOLOGY:
Key Dates for Skechers U.S.A., Inc.

1992: Greenberg establishes Skechers in Manhattan Beach, California, distributing Doc Martens and other footwear

1993: Greenberg begins designing his own brand of street-wise shoes for young fashion-conscious men

1995: Skechers signs licensing deal with Signal/American and Genova Inc. to make casual clothes for men and boys

1997: The company expands into international markets, selling shoes in Europe and Asia

1999: Skechers conducts its initial public offering, selling seven million shares for $11 a piece

1999: Begins construction on two new stores: one in New York City and one in Universal City, California

2000: *Business Week* places Skechers fifth on their "100 Best Small Companies" list

2001: Opened flagship Skechers U.S.A. store in Tokyo, Japan

2001: Skechers sales climb more than 40 percent and reach nearly $1 billion

Two new women's lines that premiered in 2001 are Somethin' Else from Skechers and Skechers by Michelle K. With more than 900 styles, Skechers offers a broad range of styles cutting across gender lines and age ranges. Started in 1998 Skechers Sport has become a vital part of the company's business. Their line is promoted by extensive domestic and international print and broadcast campaigns. Skechers Collection is a line of mens dressy casual shoes, sandals, and boots that takes the fashion-savvy guy from the office to a night on the town. Chosen to represent this stylish line are two actors who embody the Skechers attitude, Rob Lowe and Matt Dillon. Skechers USA is a line of men's and women's casual shoes that concentrates on comfort without sacrificing style. Easy-going and casual, the line appeals to a wide variety of customers. These shoes are more-than-basic black and brown shoes, boots, and sandals. Although children's feet are small, kids make a big impression at Skechers. From infants to toddlers to active boys and girls, Skechers wants to fill the shoes of a stylish new

THE BRITNEY EFFECT: FIT ME SKECHERS, ONE MORE TIME

Britney Spears has hip-hopped her way to footwear fame. Envious marketing executives the world over wondered how a manufacturer holding only 2 percent of the home market could attract such a musical mega-star as Britney Spears. So why hadn't Ms. Spears gone after industry giants like Nike or Reebok, who spend billions on advertising and sponsorship each year? According to Skechers, the answer is simple: Britney approached them. The singer had worn the trendy trainers for personal use and performances, resulting in her decision to become their first celebrity endorsee. Skechers believes that the Britney Spears print campaign was an important catalyst behind their international growth, which rose 50 percent in 2001, and had wall-to-wall customers at store openings clamoring for "the Britney shoe." CEO Robert Greenberg remarked, "It was natural to broaden her impact on the company's business to the United States and reach more consumers overseas through a new agreement promoting Britney Spears 4 Wheelers, Skechers hot, hip line of roller skates. We think the Britney Spears collection of 4 Wheelers will result in consumers worldwide requesting the 'Britney skate,' which we believe will fly off shelves as people roll out of the stores."

generation. The kid's line features unique fabrics and colorful upper treatments, as well as lighted footwear, S-Lights. Somethin' Else is designed with the trendy teen in mind, while Michelle K. is a designer line featuring the latest high-fashion looks.

GLOBAL PRESENCE

To achieve brand expansion, Skechers has taken a comprehensive international approach to all aspects of their business. Skechers' international business has grown 75 percent over the past year and reached $100 million at year's end 2001. Boldly moving into the European marketplace, Skechers is seizing opportunity for growth potential, and the company now handles marketing and merchandising in France and distribution, marketing, and merchandising in Germany, Switzerland, and the United Kingdom. In 2001 the company opened

European flagship stores in London, Dusseldorf, and Tokyo. In Japan Skechers' business has nearly doubled in the past year and is a key market in their international growth scheme. Skechers sees vast potential for increased sales considering the tremendous populations of Japan, Asia, and the Pacific Rim. To accommodate this expansion, the company incorporated Skechers S.a.r.l., a Swiss company that now runs international sales, marketing, and operations. The company's foreign business is handled by 35 distributors who sell products in more than 100 countries worldwide. To support its global efforts, Skechers runs extensive print and broadcast ads. The company's goal is to grow their international business from 12 percent to 25 percent of their total sales by 2007.

EMPLOYMENT

Skechers' corporate culture is a stimulating, energized, and creative environment that is reflected in their offices, stores, products, and ads. Skechers credits their success to their extended employee family, from the designers who create their signature products to the innovative marketing staff, the sales representatives who distribute the product to the sales staff at their retail stores who interact with customers daily, and provide valuable feedback. From their ocean-view corporate offices in Manhattan Beach, to the field as a sales rep, distributor, or visual merchandise associate, Skechers is a fun-filled and inspiring atmosphere for career development.

SOURCES OF INFORMATION

Bibliography

Abel, Katie. "Skechers Takes Control in France." *Footwear News,* 4 February 2002.

Lenetz, Dana. "Skechers USA, Saucony Report Disparate Results." *Footwear News,* 18 February 2002.

Pitman, Simon. "Fit Me Trainers One More Time: Britney Spears Endorsement of Skechers Sports Shoes Is a Major Scoop." *Brand Strategy,* September 2001.

Skechers Home Page, 2002. Available at http://www.skechers .com.

"Skechers U.S.A., Inc." *Hoovers Online*, 2002. Available at http://www.hoovers.com.

Thompson, Kelly. "Green Days: Robert Greenberg Talks Candidly about the Pitfalls and Triumphs of Brand-Building." *Footwear News,* 17 December 2001.

For an annual report:

on the Internet at: http://www.skechers.com **or** write: Skechers, 228 Manhattan Beach Blvd., Manhattan Beach, CA 90266

For additional industry research:

Investigate companies by their Standard Industrial Classification Codes, also known as SICs. Skechers U.S.A. Inc.'s primary SICs are:

3021 Rubber and Plastics Footwear

5139 Footwear

Also investigate companies by their North American Industry Classification System codes, also known as NAICS codes. Skechers U.S.A. Inc.'s primary NAICS code is:

316211 Rubber and Plastics Footwear Manufacturing

Snap-On Inc.

FOUNDED: 1920

Contact Information:

HEADQUARTERS: 10801 Corporate Dr.
    Pleasant Prairie, WI 53158-1603
PHONE: (262)656-5200
FAX: (262)656-5577
URL: http://www.snapon.com

OVERVIEW

Snap-On, Inc. is a leading U.S. manufacturer and distributor of hand tools, power tools, shop equipment, and automotive diagnostic equipment. The firm, a member of the Standard & Poor's 500, targets the industrial, automotive, and aerospace industries, and its clients typically include automotive manufacturers, car mechanics, and various government operations. To sell its products, Snap-On uses franchised truck drivers-nearly 4,000 of them-to purchase tools and equipment at wholesale prices and then market and deliver products directly to clients. Because Snap-On trucks are stocked with a wide variety of the firm's merchandise, customers are able to take delivery of many of their tools and equipment immediately upon purchase.

COMPANY FINANCES

Sales for Snap-On, which totaled $1.48 billion in 1996, grew steadily throughout the late 1990s, reaching a peak of $2.17 billion in 2000. Earnings growth proved less consistent. After climbing from $131.5 million in 1996 to $150.4 million in 1997, earnings plummeted in 1998 due to weak sales in Asia, where the economy had collapsed, as well as problems Snap-On experienced while implementing a new computerized operations system. That year, the firm posted a $4.8 million loss. Earnings recovered in 1999 to $127.2 million, and they grew to $148.5 million in 2000. Both sales and earnings dropped in 2001, however, to $2.9 billion and $19 million, respectively, due to a particularly weak North American economy. As a result, earnings per share, which had reached a high of $2.53 in 2000, fell to 33 cents in 2001. Stock prices, which ranged from a high of $46.44 per share and a low of $25.50 per share in 1998, ranged from a high of $34.21 per share to a low of $21.65 per share in 2001.

ANALYSTS' OPINIONS

Many analysts became concerned about Snap-On's outlook in mid-2001, when company officials revealed that third quarter earnings would be roughly 68 percent lower than in the third period of the previous year. To bolster earnings, the firm announced its intent to reduce its workforce by 4 percent and to undertake measures to improve efficiency in both domestic and international operations. The plan seemed to reassure investors, and stock prices rose 4.6 percent on the day following the news. According to an August 2001 issue of *The Business Journal-Milwaukee*, many analysts believed the firm's earnings per share would recover in 2002.

A member of *Entrepreneur*'s Franchise 500, Snap-On was lauded by many industry publications for the strength of its franchised operations . In 2002, *Entrepreneur* magazine ranked Snap-On 14th among its list of the top 500 franchise opportunities. In fact, the firm had placed among the top 20 of the Franchise 500 since 1994. In 2002, the *Franchise Times* ranked Snap-On 32nd on its list of the top 200 franchises.

HISTORY

After coming up with an idea for an "interchangeable sockets," Joe Johnson and William A. Seidemann created Snap-On in 1920. Interchangeable sockets, which allowed multiple sockets to be "snapped on" to various handles, proved more efficient than the one-piece socket wrenches traditionally used by mechanics. To sell this product, as well as several others, the partners demonstrated the many uses of Snap-On tools directly to potential customers. Snap-On published its first catalog, listing 50 items, in 1923. More than 150 sales representatives were marketing and distributing Snap-On tools by 1925. Two years later, international operations were launched when Snap-On opened an office in Montreal. The firm created a Canadian subsidiary to oversee operations there in 1931. Sales reached $1 million in 1935, and Snap-On conducted its initial public offering six years later.

By 1945, all salespersons carried stock and made immediate deliveries to their customers. Eventually, Snap-On decided to convert its direct sales staff into a fleet of independent representatives serving assigned territories. International expansion continued in the 1950s, with the creation of a subsidiary in Mexico. The firm also diversified by acquiring specialized companies which

FINANCES:
Snap-On Inc. Revenues, 1997-2001 (million dollars)

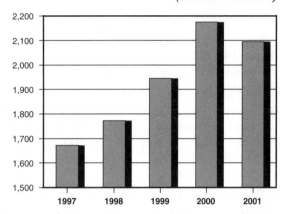

Snap-On Inc. 2001 Stock Prices (dollars)

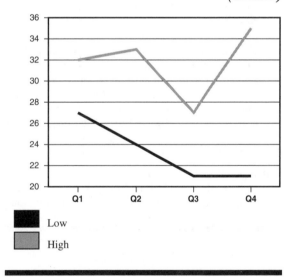

manufactured diagnostic tune-up and maintenance equipment for the automotive industry. In 1964, the firm replaced its punch-card order processing equipment with an IBM computer-based system. Direct sales operations expanded into the United Kingdom in 1965. That year, Snap-On secured a patent, after years of legal wrangling, for its ""flank drive'' design, which improved the grip of wrenches operating in high torque conditions. The firm had developed the flank drive wrench in response to grip problems the U.S. Navy had experienced while removing small fasteners from aircraft.

FAST FACTS:
About Snap-On Inc.

Ownership: Snap-On Inc. is a public company traded on the New York Stock Exchange.

Ticker Symbol: SNA

Officers: Robert A. Cornog, Chmn.; Dale F. Elliott, Pres., CEO, and Dir.; Donald S. Huml, SVP and CFO; Richard V. Caskey, VP Marketing; Alan T. Biland, VP and CIO

Employees: 13,500

Principal Subsidiary Companies: Snap-On Inc. operates an extended network of subsidiaries, dealers, and representatives throughout North America, including Snap-On Tools Co.; mechanical collision repair equipment maker Nu-Tech Industries, Inc.; torque measuring products and calibrating equipment maker Consolidated Devices, Inc.; mechanical collision repair equipment maker Hein-Werner Corp.; Mitchell Repair Information Co., which handles vehicle repair information and business management systems; industrial power tool maker Sioux Tools, Inc; Snap-On Industrial Group; Snap-On/Sun de Mexico S.A. de C.V.; Snap-On Tools of Canada Ltd.; Snap-On Tools Puerto Rico; Snap-On Diagnostics; and Wheeltronic Ltd., which manufactures vehicle lifts. Snap-On also operates subsidiaries in South America, Europe, Asia, and Africa.

Chief Competitors: Competitors to Snap-On Inc. include Black & Decker, Stanley Works, and other tool and equipment manufacturers and distributors.

Growth in the 1970s was substantial. Compared to $66.2 million in 1969, sales reached $100 million in 1972, and grew to $373.6 million in 1979. Over the same time period, net income jumped from $6 million to $42.6 million. Sales representatives numbered more than 3,000 by the middle of the decade. In 1978, the New York Stock Exchange began listing Snap-On stock.

Recessionary economic conditions in the 1980s prompted a modest fall in both sales and profits. Snap-On launched cost cutting measures and stepped up marketing efforts. As a result, growth resumed. NASA named Snap-On the exclusive supplier of tools for the space shuttles. The firm purchased a 34 percent stake in engine diagnostic and wheel service equipment Balco,

Inc. in 1984. Snap-On acquired the remainder of Balco for $21.2 million in 1991. It was at this time that Snap-On began converting its independent sales force network into a franchise network. The firm also centralized distribution operations, condensing the operations of 51 warehouses into four regional distribution facilities. The company itself was reorganized into three segments: Finance; Manufacturing and Technology; and Marketing and Distribution.

Snap-On expanded into Japan in 1992. The following year, sales exceeded $1 billion for the first time. In an effort to broaden its offerings further, the firm began to search for new markets. To this end, it acquired diagnostics equipment maker Sun Electric Corp. in 1992. The following year, the firm added industrial hand tools maker J.H. Williams, industrial power tools maker Sioux Tools, Inc., and vehicle lift manufacturer Wheeltronic Ltd. to its mix. In 1995, Snap-On acquired Eurotools S.A., its first hand tool manufacturing facility in Europe. The firm also created an intranet that allowed dealers electronic access to inventory, prices, and information on new products. The new system also allowed dealers to place orders and file sales reports electronically.

The purchase of the automotive service operations of FMC in 1996 allowed Snap-On boost its under-car equipment operations. That year, the firm also acquired Automotive Data Solution, a telephone-based diagnostic service for car mechanics. Thomson Corp.'s Mitchell Repair Information and Snap-On created Mitchell Repair Information Co., one of North America's largest vehicle repair information providers, in 1997. That year, Snap-On entered the collision repair industry for the first time with the purchase of Nu-Tech Industries Inc. Additional acquisitions included a German wheel balancing equipment manufacturer and an Italian vehicle lift manufacturer.

In 1998, for the first time in its history, Snap-On moved into the retail market by developing tools for Lowe's Home Improvement Warehouse.. Problems with the adoption of a new computer-based inventory and order processing system that year undercut earnings. Weak Asian sales also posed a problem. To improve its performance, Snap-On eliminated roughly 4 percent of its sales force. It also shut down a handful of manufacturing plants and warehouses, discontinued certain products, consolidated related businesses, and shuttered several sales offices in both North America and Europe. Eventually, the computer glitches were resolved, and Snap-On was able to launch extensive online operations, including the sale of its tools on the Internet. Additional layoffs were announced in 2001, after weaker demand hurt sales. In 2002, Snap-On was ordered to pay SPX Corp. $44 million in damages related to a patent infringement case.

STRATEGY

Direct contact with customers has been a key component of Snap-On's marketing strategy since its inception. Recognizing the importance of this contact, Snap-On asked its salespersons to increase their contact with clients from once a month to at least twice a month in 1962. By the mid-1980s, some dealers were visiting customers weekly. A typical Snap-On van carried $50,000 to $200,000 of inventory. Along with simply selling products, Snap-On representatives also offered extra services, such as free Snap-On tool and equipment cleaning every six months, to their clients. Along with impressing customers, services like this allowed Snap-On dealers to identify any tools or parts that needed replacement. Due to the services it offered, as well as the strong relationships its dealers had forged with clients, the firm was able to avoid lowering its prices despite increased competition from companies like Sears, Roebuck & Co., Mac Tools (a subsidiary of Stanley Works), and several Japanese firms.

Also instrumental to the firm's success were its 350-page catalogs. By the mid-1980s, Snap-On dealers were distributing roughly two million catalogs each year, and they found that when clients experienced mechanical difficulties, they would quite often look through the catalogs for a solution.

In the mid-1990s, Snap-On began to examine the ways in which technology could allow dealers to offer additional services to customers. In 1998, the firm began working on an e-commerce strategy with the goal of giving customers 24-hour-a-day access to their dealers. According to a July 2000 article in *Forbes*, the firm's new e-commerce strategy team "figured they could use the interactivity of the Internet to create a Web site that could do most of the things a sales rep did: help customers find the right socket wrench for a particular job, tell them what was in stock and when they could have it, recommend alternatives to out-of-stock products." By the end of 2000, nearly all of the firm's 4000 dealers had been connected to the Internet and more than 14,000 products were available for sale on the firm's Web site. Within a year, more than 10,000 orders had taken place online.

INFLUENCES

The late 1980s were marred for Snap-On by the growing number of lawsuits filed by former and current U.S. dealers, who alleged things like misrepresentation of potential profits and various contract violations by Snap-On. Other suits claimed than Snap-On pressured dealers to extend credit to clients. Between 1989 and 1991, the firm paid $40.7 million in settlement costs. This problem prompted the firm to begin enrolling all new U.S. dealers as franchisees in the early 1990s. In addition, existing dealers were given the opportunity to apply for a franchise as well. Along with gaining more control over its dealer network, Snap-On believed that converting to a franchise program would allow for more cohesive marketing efforts and a more unified brand image.

CHRONOLOGY:
Key Dates for Snap-On Inc.

1920: Snap-On is founded

1923: The first Snap-On catalog lists 50 products

1941: Snap-On completes its initial public offering

1945: Via a fleet of vans, all Snap-On sales reps transport stock to their customers, who can take immediate delivery of the products they order

1965: Snap-On secures a patent for its ""flank drive'' wrench design

1972: Sales reach $100 million

1978: Snap-On lists its stock on the NYSE

1991: Snap-On creates its franchise system

1993: Sales exceed $1 billion for the first time

2000: Snap-On is ordered to pay SPX Corp. $44 million in damages related to a patent infringement case

PRODUCTS

Snap-On's products include wrenches, sockets, pliers, ratchets, screwdrivers, and other hand tools, as well as pneumatic (air) and corded (electric) drills, sanders, polishers and other power tools. The firm also makes wheel balancing and alignment equipment for cars, tool chests and cabinets, and engine and emission analyzing equipment.

GLOBAL PRESENCE

International expansion for Snap-On first took place in the 1920s, and it continued throughout the firm's development. By the early 1990s, Snap-On subsidiaries operated in Australia, Canada, Germany, Japan, Mexico, the Netherlands, and the United Kingdom. International sales accounted for 17 percent of total revenues.

In 2002, European operations include Sweden's Bahco Group AB; Italian wheel service equipment manufacturer G.S. S.r.l; Spain-based automotive and industrial hand tools maker Herramientas Eurotools, S.A.; Hofmann Werkstatt-Technik and Hofmann Sopron Kft, two automotive equipment manufacturers based in Hun-

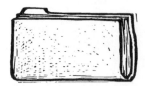

SNAP-ON STRUGGLES WITH NEW TECHNOLOGY

When Snap-On paid $54 million for a new enterprise software system, it expected to see an immediate upturn in productivity. However, several glitches with the new system resulted in thousands of delayed orders, which cost the company an estimated $50 million in sales in 1998.

gary; Snap-On Equipment France; Netherlands-based Snap-On Europe Holding B.V.; United Kingdom-based Snap-On Tools Ltd.; Snap-On Tools Germany; and Italian vehicle and motorcycle lift manufacturer Texo.

In Africa, the firm operated Africa Snap-On Tools/PST Africa (Pty.) Ltd. Asian operations included Snap-On Tools (Australia) Pty. Ltd.; Snap-On Tools China; Snap-On Tools Japan, K.K.; Snap-On Tools Korea Ltd.; Snap-On Tools New Zealand, and Snap-On Tools Singapore Pte Ltd. In South America, Snap-On Inc. also operated Sun Electric do Brasil.

SOURCES OF INFORMATION

Bibliography

Copple, Brandon. "It's a Snap." *Forbes*, 17 July 2000.

"Genuine Parts, Snap-On Form Alliance." *Aftermarket Business*, February 2002.

Itoi, Nikki Goth. "Metamorphosis of the Middleman." *Industry Week*, September 2001.

Fellman, Michelle Wirth. "Snap out of It." *Marketing News*, 28 September 1998.

"Midwest 100 Regional Stock Analysis." *The Business Journal-Milwaukee*, 10 August 2001.

"Snap-On Inc." *International Directory of Company Histories.* Detroit: Gale Research, 1993.

Snap-On Inc. Home Page, 2002. Available at http://www.snapon.com.

"Snap-On's Franchise Opportunity Recognized in Recent Rankings." *Business Wire*, 25 March 2002.

For an annual report:
on the Internet at: http://www.snapon.com/investor/annual01/2001_snapon_annual_report.pdf

For additional industry research:
Investigate companies by their Standard Industrial Classification Codes, also known as SICs. Snap-On Inc.'s primary SICs are:

3411 Metal Cans

3423 Hand & Edge Tools

3546 Power Driven Hand Tools

3825 Instruments to Measure Electricity

3829 Measuring & Controlling Devices, Not Elsewhere Classified

6719 Holding Companies, Not Elsewhere Classified

Also investigate companies by their North American Industrial Classification System codes, also known as NAICS codes. Snap-On Inc.'s primary NAICS codes are:

332116 Metal Stamping

332212 Hand and Edge Tool Manufacturing

332431 Metal Can Manufacturing

333991 Power-Driven Hand Tool Manufacturing

334515 Instrument Manufacturing for Measuring and Testing Electricity and Electric Signals

334519 Other Measuring and Controlling Device Manufacturing

551112 Offices of Other Holding Companies

Sotheby's

FOUNDED: 1744

OVERVIEW

Sotheby's, with 98 offices in 38 countries, is one of the world's leading auction houses. The company divides its business activities into three segments: the auction segment, the finance segment, and the real estate segment. Sotheby's primary activity is the auctioning of art, antiques, and collectibles in more than 90 categories, including paintings, sculpture, jewelry, ceramics, furniture, rare books and manuscripts, and other objects. Sotheby's holds auctions in its auction rooms in North America, Europe, Asia, and Australia. Its staff of internationally recognized specialists identify, evaluate, and appraise works of art before they go up for auction. Once appropriate works have been selected and their value and authenticity established, Sotheby's utilizes various marketing techniques, including glossy catalogues, public and private exhibitions, and personal contact between Sotheby's staff and individual collectors to generate interest in an auction. Finally, Sotheby's brings buyers and sellers together at auctions. Sotheby's holds auctions in New York and London, as well as in 14 other countries including Australia, Italy, India, Japan, and China. Sotheby's also conducts online auctions on its Web site.

Sotheby's acts as the agent of its sellers. It accepts the seller's property on consignment, bills the purchaser, and pays the seller. Sotheby's receives a commission from sellers based on the so-called "hammer price," the last offer made before the auctioneer's hammer fell and closed bidding on the item, known as a "lot." The rate of the commission is based on a sliding scale or may be negotiated individually with particularly valued sellers. Buyers must also pay Sotheby's a premium equal to ten percent of the hammer price. Occasionally, for example,

Contact Information:
HEADQUARTERS: 1334 York Avenue
    New York, NY 10021
PHONE: (212)606-7000
FAX: (212)606-7027
TOLL FREE: (800)700-6321
URL: http://www.sothebys.com

FINANCES:

Sotheby's Auction Sales, 1996-2000 (million dollars)

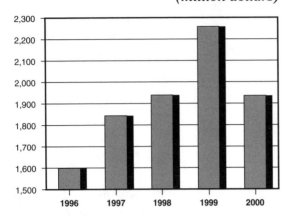

to secure the rights to auction particularly prestigious works or collections, Sotheby's will guarantees a seller a minimum price for an item. If that amount is not bid at auction, Sotheby's must pay the seller the difference.

Sotheby's finance segment provides sellers and buyers with financing, usually guaranteed with works of art as collateral. The company extends advances to sellers based on the anticipated selling price of objects or collections. More controversially, in the past Sotheby's also extended loans to buyers prior to auctions, a practice that critics claimed made Sotheby's a not-wholly-disinterested auctioneer. Sotheby's real estate segment, represented by its subsidiary Sotheby's International Realty, Inc. (SIR), assists clients throughout the world in the purchase of so-called luxury properties. Such properties include resorts, ranches, farms, and residences. SIR operates 16 of its own brokerage offices in the United States, Britain, France, and Australia. Sotheby's also has five regional offices in Manhattan; Palm Beach, Florida; Newport Beach, California; Boston, Massachusetts; and Munich, Germany; as well as a representative in Hong Kong.

COMPANY FINANCES

Two and a half years of criminal scandal, lawsuits, and expensive class action settlements have shattered Sotheby's bottom line and sent its stock price plummeting. Sotheby's $1.94 billion in total auction sales in 2000 was down from $2.26 billion in 1999—a fourteen percent drop. Sotheby's 2000 revenues totaled $397.79 mil-

lion and marked the second year of decline after climbing to $447.05 million in 1998. Along with the drop in revenue, Sotheby's reported a whopping after-tax loss of $189.7 million in 2000. The loss was due largely to the discovery of Sotheby's involvement in a massive price-fixing scheme, which resulted in millions of dollars in civil and criminal fines. The 2000 loss translated to a loss in earnings of $3.22 per share. Sotheby's share price did not fare well in the atmosphere that surrounded the price-fixing investigation either. It plunged from a high of $46.75 in the second quarter of 1999 to slightly higher than $10 in November 2001, just before the trial of Sotheby's former chairman, A. Alfred Taubman began. The stock recovered and hovered around $15 for a couple weeks in early 2002, fueled by rumors that Taubman was going to sell his controlling share in the company. The price subsequently dropped again in February 2002.

Fine arts accounted for 57 percent of Sotheby's auction sales in 2000; decorative arts accounted for about 27 percent; jewelry, rare books, and other areas accounted for 16 percent. Approximately 54 percent of the firm's auction sales were made in North America, primarily at its New York City auction rooms. About 41 percent were made in Europe and a little more than 5 percent were in Asia. Those numbers remained more or less constant from 1999.

ANALYSTS' OPINIONS

Wall Street analysts took a highly cautious stance toward the beleaguered auction house in 2001. On the positive side, by spring 2001, Sotheby's had settled the civil litigation that followed the accusations of price-fixing with Christies, litigation that had threatened to force Sotheby's into bankruptcy. Furthermore, the company had installed new upper management, replacing convicted chairman A. Alfred Taubman and self-confessed conspirator president Diana D. Brooks. Its online auction site was up and running as well. Nonetheless, a Dain Rauscher Wessels report bleakly stated, "The outlook ahead is troubling." Auction sales continued to drop going in to 2001, "the continuance of a disappointing trend of missed (or perhaps mismanaged) expectations," as the report put it. Market forces were conspiring against Sotheby's as well. Demand for million dollar paintings that were not top-line was drying up, and Sotheby's continued speculation in that area was a questionable strategy. Phillips Auctioneers, although still a distant third behind Sotheby's and Christie's, was backed by a parent company with deep pockets and had positioned itself as a legitimate challenger to the long-established duopoly. In all, Dain Rauscher Wessels painted a bleak picture of Sotheby's future, citing "a loss of confidence in the predictability of the business model. . . .a justifiable concern over operating inefficiencies." The report concluded by bluntly warning investors off from Sotheby's: "We believe the only reason the stock

Originating in London in 1774 and based in the U.S. since 1983, Sotheby's new Paris location marks the end of a 400-year-old monopoly of the market by French auctioneers.
(AP Photo/Michel Euler)

should be held is on the hope of a buyer surfacing—otherwise avoid it."

HISTORY

Sotheby's traces its history back to 1744, to the firm of Samuel Baker, who sold antiquarian books at first through catalogues and later in his own premises in London England. It was not until 1778—12 years after Sotheby's twentiethth century arch-rival Christie's was founded—that Baker and his partner George Leigh invited John Sotheby to join their business. By 1823 the other partners had died without heirs, and Sotheby's grandson Samuel was the business' sole proprietor. The same year the firm made news when it auctioned the collection of books that Napoleon had taken into exile on St Helenas. By mid-century, the company had branched out into autographs and prints, but not until the twentieth century did it venture to auction paintings or other works of fine art.

In 1861 the last Sotheby died without leaving an heir, and the company passed into other hands. The name had acquired a reputation by then, and it was kept, even as new partners added theirs to it. In 1909 a partnership led by Montague Barlow purchased the business. Over the next ten years, Barlow engineered a series of coups

for the firm, the most noteworthy of which was the 1913 auction of the love letters of poets Robert Browning and Elizabeth Barrett. In 1917 Barlow oversaw Sotheby's move into new quarters just blocks from Christie's in London's Mayfair district. It was not until after World War I that Sotheby's diversified into paintings, in particular the venerable Old Masters that had been Christie's stock in trade for the better part of two centuries. That unleashed a cutthroat competition that had the bitter flavor of a blood feud in which the two sides could scarcely bring themselves to utter the other's name. It continued unabated—even as the two firms were secretly fixing prices together to avoid destructive price wars—into the twenty-first century. One of Barlow's most significant innovations was to hire acknowledged experts in specific areas of art to evaluate and appraise works that were up for auction at Sotheby's. Their careful, scholarly descriptions in Sotheby's catalogues won the company unprecedented levels of trust among buyers.

Peter Wilson is acknowledged as the individual who forged Sotheby's into the internationally renowned global company that made headlines in the latter half of the twentieth century. Wilson was a classic success story, starting as a lowly porter and working his way up quickly to become a director and eventually Sotheby's chairman and president. He inaugurated a period that one employee of later called "one long party." The "party" was characterized by the aggressive

FAST FACTS:
About Sotheby's

Ownership: Sotheby's is a publicly owned company traded on the New York and London Stock Exchanges.

Ticker Symbol: BID

Officers: William F. Ruprecht, Pres. and CEO, 46, 2000 base salary $500,000; Robin Woodhead, EVP and CEO Sotheby's Europe and Asia, 50, 2000 base salary $383,598; William S. Sheridan, EVP and CFO, 47, 2000 base salary $350,000

Employees: 2,048

Principal Subsidiary Companies: Sotheby's has facilities and subsidiary companies in North America, Europe, Asia, and Australia. Sotheby's International Realty, Inc., its real estate subsidiary, is headquartered in New York City. Its English auction house, Sotheby's (U.K.), is based in London.

Chief Competitors: Sotheby's faces competition in both its auction business and its real estate business. Its real estate segment competes almost exclusively with small, local real estate agents. Its auction segment competes with numerous private art dealers, auction houses, and online auction sites. It main competitors in this area are Christie's and Phillips Auctioneers.

pursuit of art and collectibles to auction—most notably the vast collection of King Farouk of Egypt, which Sotheby's auctioned over a 27-day period in 1954 for £750,000. The auction of the modern art collection of Wilhelm Weinberg, a collection that included several Van Goghs and brought in over £326,000, put Sotheby's on the map for good. In the 1958-1959 season, Sotheby's for the first time had more turnover than its rival Christie's, a lead it would widen dramatically over the next two decades. Wilson also oversaw Sotheby's growth into an international auction house. In 1964 he engineered the takeover of the Parke Bennet auction house in Manhattan. By the time Wilson retired in 1979, Sotheby's had offices for both auction and real estate in several European countries, Asia, Canada, and on both coasts of the United States, and its sales had increased tenfold since the middle 1960s. It had also gone public, making a stock offering in 1977.

When Wilson left, Sotheby's was deep in the throes of an economic downturn brought about by the international economic recessions of the 1970s, as well as by an overly relaxed corporate management style leftover from the first half of the century when the company had a staff in the low two figures instead of the thousands. Wilson's departure only exacerbated a bad situation. With no strong leader at the helm, losses mounted even more quickly and the share price dropped. Abruptly, in 1982, the company was faced with a hostile takeover by two American businessmen who had made their fortunes in the carpet business. The British Parliament intervened rather than allow a national institution to be taken by such buyers. The firm found its savior in the person of A. Alfred Taubman, a real estate magnate from Michigan who had become wealthy many times over building upscale shopping malls. In 1983 Taubman obtained a controlling interest in Sotheby's.

Taubman introduced modern, efficient business practice to Sotheby's. He also set about to get rid of the British snobbishness that he had found so off-putting himself when he first attended auctions there. As a result of Taubman's changes—along with the bullish art market of the 1980s—Sotheby's returned to profitability. Indicative of its recovery was its auction in 1987 of a Van Gogh for £30 million. But the sale also foreshadowed troubles when it was later revealed that Sotheby's had lent half the cost of the painting to the buyer—who later reneged on the payments! Other scandals followed in the 1990s. It was revealed that for many years Sotheby's had routinely looked the other way when art works were smuggled into Britain, or they even encouraged or assisted sellers in breaking export laws. It was also revealed that Sotheby's had sold numerous furniture forgeries in mid-decade, some of which had drawn record prices. The most damaging revelation came in 2000 when the U.S. Justice Department launched an investigation into allegations of a conspiracy between Sotheby's and Christie's to fix their commission rates. By the time the criminal and civil litigation ended in December 2001, both houses had to pay millions in fines and damages. Diana D. Brooks, the company's charismatic president was forced to resign and turn state's evidence. A. Alfred Taubman, Sotheby's 71-year-old chairman and majority share holder was eventually convicted on antitrust counts.

STRATEGY

Historically, Sotheby's clientele was comprised almost exclusively of a relatively small coterie of international art collectors, and personal contact with such collectors was Sotheby's most important tool. From the 1980s on, however, as the number of large private collections of noteworthy art has declined, Sotheby's has relied more and more on drawing middle class collectors to its auctions. They have added lower-priced objects as well as popular culture objects, such as the Jacqueline Kennedy Onassis estate or various bits of Hollywood memorabilia. The Internet is also expected to draw a number of first-time buyers from the middle-brow segment to Sotheby's. The challenge for Sotheby's in this strategy is to reach less affluent buyers without tarnishing the company's upper-crust patina. Britain is seen as presenting greater opportunities in the middle market. Sotheby's primary focus in the United States will continue to be high end buyers.

INFLUENCES

In a misguided attempt to negotiate a way out of the recession they found themselves in following the 1991 Gulf War, executives of Sotheby's and Christie's held secret meetings in which they hammered out a plan to end their self-destructive price wars: they would set fixed commission rates that both companies would thereafter abide by. The conspiracy came to light in 1999 when the U.S. Justice Department discovered documents detailing the negotiations and naming names. Christie's made a deal with the Justice Department to avoid prosecution. Later, Sotheby's president Diana D. Brooks agreed to cooperate with prosecutors as well. She became the star witness in the trial of A. Alfred Taubman, Sotheby's majority stockholder and chairman. It ended with Taubman's conviction of conspiracy to fix prices. Earlier, a huge class action suit against both auction houses resulted in damages of $256 million each. Criminal fines against Sotheby's were subsequently lowered so as not to force the firm into bankruptcy, which would have left Christie's—which had been given amnesty for its role— the only big auction house.

The case, nonetheless, will continue to have important consequences for Sotheby's. Even before his conviction, Taubman seemed resigned to selling his controlling share in the company. The one factor that delayed the sale was probably the extremely depressed price of Sotheby's stock as a result of the scandal—it dropped from more than $46 a share in 1996 to a low of about $10 in late 2001. The trial will have repercussions for Sotheby's relations with sellers for some time that go beyond general skepticism about auction industry practices. Previously, the details of contracts with sellers were closely kept secrets. In order to snare a prestigious collection, Sotheby's was often willing to forgo part of or even all of a commission, as well as to make sizable loans to collectors against the promise (or likelihood) of a future auction. Many of those delicate details were described in detail in the New York courtroom. The case will cause regulators in New York State to scrutinize Sotheby's and other auction houses more carefully after a decade or more of leaving them to their own devices.

CHRONOLOGY:
Key Dates for Sotheby's

1744: Samuel Baker begins selling books in London England

1778: On death of Samuel Baker, John Sotheby becomes a partner in Leigh and Sotheby

1823: Samuel Sotheby sells Napoleon's collection of books

1842: Samuel Leigh Sotheby takes full control of the book business

1909: Montague Barlow, Felix Ware, and Geoffrey Hobson take over Sotheby Wilkerson and Hodge

1924: Company reorganized as Sotheby & Co.

1913: Elizabeth Barrett-Robert Browning letters are auctioned by Sotheby Wilkerson & Hodge

1958: Peter Wilson becomes Sotheby's chairman

1964: Sotheby's acquires Parke-Bernet in New York City

1977: Sotheby Parke Bernet Group goes public

1983: A. Alfred Taubman acquires company and changes its name to Sotheby's

1996: Sotheby's auctions the estate of Jacqueline Kennedy Onassis

2000: Sotheby's chairman A. Alfred Taubman and president Diana D. Brooks resign amidst allegations of conspiring with Christie's to fix prices on commissions

2001: A. Alfred Taubman is convicted of conspiring to fix prices

CURRENT TRENDS

Sotheby's has extended its auction rooms into virtual space. It has started holding online auctions of works of art and other collectibles on its Web site, Sotheby's .com. An important difference between Sotheby's Internet auctions and those at eBay, for example, is that the provenance of Sotheby's objects has been authenticated by the company's staff of experts. Sotheby's online auctions began in 2000. Another more disturbing trend for Sotheby's is the rise of Phillips, de Pury & Luxembourg as a legitimate force in the auction world. Phillips is controlled by Bernard Arnaud, owner of the luxury goods

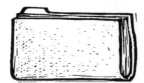

PAUL CÉZANNE'S *BOY IN A RED WAISTCOAT*

The first of Sotheby's modern day blockbuster pictures was a Cézanne painting put up for auction by collector Erwin Goldschmidt in October 1958. The picture, *Boy in a Red Waistcoat*, was part of a group of Impressionist masters, and the auction drew the attention of the world. Among the audience at Sotheby's the day of the auction were actor Kirk Douglas, writer Somerset Maugham, and dancer Margot Fonteyn. Before the bidding opened, experts believed the Cézanne would bring in at most £30,000. By the time bidding had concluded, the Cézanne had reached a breathtaking £220,000. Auctioneer Peter Wilson drew laughter from the crowd when he asked in surprise, "Will no one offer any more?" It was the most money paid for a painting up to that time.

group LVMH, a man with the financial resources to make a run at the supremacy of the Sotheby's-Christie's duopoly.

PRODUCTS

Constantly searching for new markets for its auctions, Sotheby's has expanded its offerings to attract collectors who do not have the resources (or perhaps the interest) to purchase fine art or antiquities. They have organized so-called "theme" sales, such as the auctions of possessions once belonging to Lady Diana or Jackie Kennedy Onassis. They have also auctioned Arabian horses, sport pictures, guns, and movie memorabilia.

GLOBAL PRESENCE

Sotheby's maintains offices on five continents. Besides its main auction rooms on York Street in Manhattan and New Bond Street in London, it also has auction facilities in Amsterdam, Geneva, Madrid, Milan, Munich, Paris, Rome, and Zurich. Sotheby's also has auction rooms in various Asian cities, including Hong Kong, Seoul, Singapore, Taipei, and Tokyo, as well as in Australia, South America, and Canada. Sotheby's International Realty has offices in North America,

Europe, and Australia. Sotheby's global reach is important for more than simply snagging important collections that are scattered across the world. Certain types of objects command higher prices if auctioned in a particular country rather than New York or London. For example, Chinese antiquities sell for significantly more money if auctioned in the Far East.

EMPLOYMENT

Sotheby's employed 2,048 workers at the beginning of 2001—916 worked in North America, 777 in Great Britain, and 355 worked elsewhere in the world. Most of Sotheby's employees were active in the auction segment (1,709). These employees ranged from administrators to experts in various areas of arts and crafts to porters, the menial laborers of the auction world. Sotheby's real estate segment employed 110 people. The finance segment had a staff of eight people. In addition, the company counted 221 employees who were not tied to any particular segment.

SOURCES OF INFORMATION

Bibliography

Bennett, Will. "After the Scandal Comes a Crisis of Succession—The Future of Sotheby's." *Daily Telegraph (London)*, 10 December 2001, 16.

Chaffin, Joshua. "Would Sotheby's Hear any Bids with Itself under the Hammer?" *Financial Times (London)*, 15 January 2001, 30.

Faith, Nicholas. *Sold: The Rise and Fall of the House of Sotheby*. London: Macmillan, 1985.

Lacey, Robert. *Sotheby's—Bidding for Class*. Boston: Little Brown, 1998.

Lieberman, Paul. "The Bold and the Dutiful." *Los Angeles Times*, 23 November 2001.

"Sotheby's." *Hoover's Company Profiles*, 2002. Available at http://www.hoovers.com.

Sotheby's Home Page, 2002. Available at http://www.sothebys.com.

Span, Paula. "The Bidding War." *Washington Post*, 21 February 1998, C1.

Stewart, James B. "Bidding War." *New Yorker*, 15 October 2001.

Surowiecki, James. "Price-Fixing For Dummies." *New Yorker*, 4 December 2000, 40.

Ungoed-Thomas, Jon, and Christopher Owen. "Sotheby's Sold Fakes for Years." *Sunday Times (London)*, 5 September 1999.

Vogel, Carol. "Auction Houses Are Set Back By Conviction In Price-Fixing." *New York Times*, 7 December 2001, D1.

Watson, Peter. "A Damning Catalogue of Evidence." *Observer*, 9 February 1997, 5.

————. *Sotheby's: The Inside Story*. New York: Random House, 1997.

For an annual report:

write: Investor Relations, Sotheby's, 1334 York Avenue, New York, NY 10021

For additional industry research:

Investigate companies by their Standard Industrial Classification Codes, also known as SICs. Sotheby's primary SICs are:

5999 Miscellaneous Retail Stores Not Elsewhere Classified

6719 Offices of Holding Companies

Also investigate companies by their North American Industry Classification System codes, also known as NAICS codes. Sotheby's primary NAICS codes are:

453920 Art Dealers

453998 All Other Miscellaneous Store Retailers (except Tobacco Stores)

551112 Offices of Other Holding Companies

Southwest Airlines Company

FOUNDED: 1971

Contact Information:

HEADQUARTERS: 2702 Love Field Dr.
    Dallas, TX 75235-1611
PHONE: (214)792-4000
FAX: (214)792-5015
TOLL FREE: (800)435-9792
URL: http://www.southwest.com

OVERVIEW

Southwest Airlines Co. is the United States' only major carrier that provides short haul, high frequency, point-to-point low fare service. Southwest was established in 1971 with three Boeing 737 aircraft serving three Texas cities: Dallas, Houston, and San Antonio. The fledgling carrier's business then took off, with Southwest becoming the fourth largest domestic airline. Today, Southwest flies 57 million passengers a year to 57 cities all over the Southwest and beyond, on over 2,700 flights a day. Customers can rest assured of flying the friendliest skies because Southwest has one of best overall productivity, service, and safety records in the industry. The airline maintains the lowest operating cost structure of any airline as well as economical fares.

Fiscal year 2001 marked Southwest's 29th consecutive year of profitability. *Fortune* magazine has consistently rated Southwest as one of the top ten places to work and one of the most admired companies and airlines in the world. Southwest also earned top ranking in the National Aviation Quality Rating study, conducted annually at the W. Frank Barton School of Business at Wichita State University and the University of Nebraska's Omaha Aviation Institute.

Three decades ago, Southwest Airlines reinvented air travel with its no-reserved-seats, no-frills, low-cost approach and groundbreaking, innovative management style. The airline, once viewed as a maverick, is now seen as a model in an industry struggling for survival since the terrorist attacks of September 11, 2001. The airlines stock exchange symbol is LUV, chosen to represent their home at Dallas Love field as well as the theme of their employee and customer relationships.

COMPANY FINANCES

Southwest Airlines announced fourth quarter earnings and its 29th consecutive year of profitability for year-end 2001. It was also the airline's ninth consecutive year of increased profits. Sales for the year totaled $5.5 billion, slightly down from year 2000 sales of $5.6 billion. The airline had an annual net income of $511.1 million compared to $625.2 million in 2000. Net income per diluted share was $.63 in 2001, down from $.79 per diluted share the previous year. In a 52-week period, the airline's stock ranged from a low of $11.25 to a high of $22.00. Accordingly, Southwest's employees earned $214.6 million in contributions to profit sharing and savings plans. The company's 2001 net income included a special pre-tax gain of $235 million from a federal grant received following the Air Transportation Safety and System Stabilization Act and special pre-tax charges of $48 million in the wake of the terrorist attacks on September 11, 2001.

Southwest Airlines' net income for fourth quarter 2001 was $63.5 million, down 58.9 percent from fourth quarter 2000 earnings of 154.7 million. Net income per diluted share was $.08 for fourth quarter 2001, compared to $.19 for the same period a year earlier. The company again benefited from a special pre-tax gain of $67 million from the federal grant, and the company's board of directors amended the profit-sharing plan to take that amount into consideration, increasing profit-sharing expense by $28 million. James F. Parker, vice chairman and CEO remarked, "We are grateful that the company's financial position has been stabilized. Our liquidity remains strong and our revenue trends improved in the fourth quarter."

ANALYSTS' OPINIONS

In 2001 some analysts believed Southwest would be the only airline to make a profit for the year as a whole due to the events that rocked the airline industry since events of September 11. In October 2001, its market capitalization rose to $11 billion, topping the combined equity valuations of American Airlines, United Airlines, Delta, Continental, Northwest Airlines and US Airways. As the strongest carrier, both financially and operationally, Lehman Brothers anticipated a strong performance for Southwest in 2002. They believed that Southwest would benefit from the weak environment by further strengthening its employee culture and would experience growth opportunities from other airlines' capacity reductions. Analysts at Merrill Lynch believed that Southwest's ability to report a profit in a weak environment was evidence of a strong business model. Its operating costs were less than predicted; and while capacity cuts at other major airlines were still occurring, Southwest's market share was already showing improvement.

FINANCES:

Southwest Airlines Co.
Net Sales, 1999-2001
(million dollars)

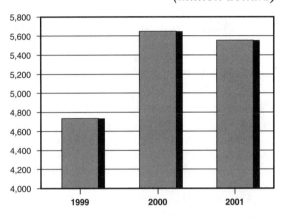

Southwest Airlines Co.
2001 Stock Prices
(dollars)

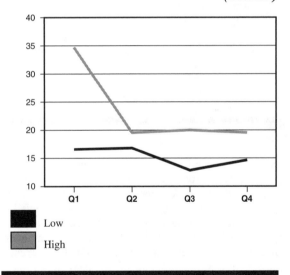

In December 2001, it ranked fourth next to the other major carriers.

HISTORY

Thirty years ago, a simple idea took flight: to create a new kind of airline; to get passengers to their destinations when they want to get there, on time, at the lowest price and making sure they have a good time in the process. A group of Texas investors including Rollin

FAST FACTS:

About Southwest Airlines Company

Ownership: Southwest Airlines Company is a publicly owned company traded on the New York Stock Exchange.

Ticker Symbol: LUV

Officers: Herbert D. Kelleher, Chmn. of the Board; James F. Parker, VChmn. and CEO, 54, 2000 base salary $558,000; Colleen C. Barrett, Pres., COO, and Dir., 56, 2000 base salary $558,000; John Denison, EVP Corporate Services, 56, 2000 base salary $524,000; Gary C. Kelly, EVP and CFO, 45, 2000 base salary $361,000

Employees: 31,850

Chief Competitors Southwest Airlines is the world's biggest budget carrier, an alternative to full service carriers. Southwest is the fifth largest domestic airline, and its primary competitors are United Air Lines, American Air Lines and Delta. United Air Line's main subsidiary is United Airlines, the world's number one air carrier based on revenue and passenger miles. American Air Lines is the number two U.S. air carrier, followed by Delta Air Lines.

King, Lamar Muse, and Herb Kelleher pooled $560,000 to form the Air Southwest Company to serve commuters between three Texas cities: Dallas, Houston and San Antonio. Although the Texas Aeronautics Commission (TAC), the state regulatory body, granted the company permission to fly in February 1968, three competing airlines filed suit to keep the company grounded. Kelleher, an attorney whose stake in the company was a mere $20,000, took the case all the way to the Supreme Court, which ruled in favor of Air Southwest in December 1970. Six months later, after numerous legal battles, a name change to Southwest Airlines, and going public with its stock, the airline kicked off operations on June 18, 1971.

With President Lamar Muse at the helm, the airlines offered daily round-trip flights between Dallas and San Antonio and 12 daily round-trip flights between Dallas and Houston. A one-way ticket cost $20.00. Foregoing traditional frills, flight attendants wore go-go boots and hot pants and served "love potions" and "bites" (drinks and peanuts) to primarily business commuters. By the end of 1973, Southwest had racked up its first profitable year, carrying half a million passengers. Company expan-

sion began in 1976, when the airline commenced service to the Rio Grande Valley. By year's end, it acquired a fifth plane, carried its five-millionth passenger, and its stock was listed on the New York Stock Exchange as "LUV."

In 1978, Congress passed the Airline Deregulation Act, legally freeing Southwest to greatly expand its operations. In 1979, Southwest introduced self-ticketing machines in many airports to simplify passenger ticketing, and introduced service to New Orleans. In September, 1981, president Howard Putnam resigned and was succeeded by the flamboyant Herb Kelleher. Kelleher picked up the pace of the airline's expansion despite a national recession and air traffic controllers strike. In early 1982, Southwest entered the western air markets and California.

As a result of steady growth, the company entered the 1990s as a major airline, with a fleet of 94 planes serving 27 cities. Counting on conservative financial management, the company was able to avoid the crippling debt of other carriers. In 1995 the company reached $2.8 billion in operating revenues, boasted its twenty-fifth year of posting a profit, and debuted Internet ticket sales. By 2000 service to New York, New Hampshire, and Florida were added.

STRATEGY

The secret to Southwest's financial success is its low-cost business model, which emphasizes modest debt and stockpiling cash. Southwest had $1 billion in cash on September 11, 2001, and access to a line of millions of dollars in credit, which it drew on on September 12, before other airlines lined up for aid. Its debt-to-capital ratio in 2001 was only 33.3 percent in an industry that averaged 71 percent, giving Southwest the heartiest finances of the country's ten largest carriers. Any economic slowdown was offset by the fact that Southwest currently provides 90 percent of all low-fare airline service within the U.S. In previous economic downturns, Southwest's traffic levels were sustained by an increase in cost-conscious air travelers.

Southwest concentrates primarily on point-to-point rather than hub-and- spoke service in markets with frequent, conveniently-timed flights and low fares. The company's 360 airplanes provide service between 60 cities in 30 states across the nation. To maintain low maintenance and training costs, the airline uses only Boeing 737s. Southwest offers ticketless travel and operates its own reservation system, keeping office costs down. Southwest's average aircraft trip length in 2001 was 514 miles with an average flight duration of one and a half hours. At year-end 2001, Southwest had over 344 one-way, non-stop city-to-city flights. The company services many conveniently located satellite or downtown airports including Dallas Love Field, Houston Hobby, Chicago

Midway, Baltimore-Washington International, Burbank, Manchester, Oakland, San Jose, Providence, Ft. Lauderdale/Hollywood, and Long Island, airports which are generally less crowded than hub airports.

INFLUENCES

In the months following the September 11, 2001, terrorist attacks, there were sweeping changes in airline day-to-day business practices. In some cases, customers had to be patient while the airlines adjusted their daily business affairs. After September 11, the airlines received more than 50 new directives from the Federal Aviation Administration that had to be implemented within hours, sometimes creating a difficult learning curve for employees. Southwest met the challenge by making facility changes, adding new screening devices, and designating employees to help customers adjust to new procedures. These measures were designed to help enhance customer relations and reduce long lines.

When the federal government took over the responsibility of airport and airline security, another transition period took place. While a loose framework for the government takeover had been established, details were still being worked out. During this time, Southwest explored new technologies and methods while still providing the kind of customer service Southwest Airlines is known for to minimize inconvenience and maximize security.

CURRENT TRENDS

Southwest has always stood out by doing things its own way. For years the flight attendants' uniforms included hot pants when conservative suits were the industry norm. Its pilots are expected to clean cabins on busy days.

Illustrating the creative license Southwest gives the advertising agencies it works with is a whale of a tale, the Killer Whale custom-painted plane, Shamu One. The artscape was devised by the ad agency GSD&M. Championed by vice president and creative director Tim McClure, the project was to secure a promotional partnership between Sea World and Southwest. Those who knew were sworn to secrecy and the plan was dubbed "Project Friend." After three days of a sophisticated painting process in an isolated World War II hanger, the brand-new 737 was secretly flown to Ellington Air Force Base in Houston. Later that day, Shamu One made its spectacular debut in San Antonio flying over Sea World of Texas and dazzling hundreds of cheering spectators below. Shamu One then went on a 27-day tour that included each of Southwest's cities.

Since the overwhelming public response to Shamu One, Southwest has spent $140 million in airplane bill-

CHRONOLOGY:
Key Dates for Southwest Airlines Company

1971: With President Lamar Muse at the helm, Southwest takes off on its maiden voyage with service to three Texas cities

1977: Southwest carries its five-millionth passenger; Southwest stock is listed on the New York Stock Exchange as "LUV"

1978: Lamar Muse steps down as President; Howard Putnam is unanimously elected President and CEO; Herb Kelleher becomes permanent Chairman of the Board

1981: Southwest celebrates a decade of "Love Southwest Style" with fun, games, and more savings

1982: Herb Kelleher takes the reins as President, CEO, and Chairman of the Board; Southwest wings its way to new cities San Francisco, Los Angeles, San Diego, Las Vegas, and Phoenix

1990: Southwest hits the billion dollar mark and becomes a "major" airline; Lone Star One takes off as Southwest's Twentieth Anniversary tribute plane

1994: Southwest introduces ticketless travel in four cities; Morris Air is merged with Southwest; seven new cities open, including Spokane, Portland, and Boise

1997: Southwest starts the year with service to its fiftieth city and accepts delivery of the first Boeing 737-700, the next- generation Boeing

2000: The airline introduces "SWABIZ," a tool that assists company travelers; the company holds the first annual Phoeniz LUV Classic Golf Tournament, an addition to the same event held in Dallas every fall

2002: Herb Kelleher steps down as CEO, chooses GC Jim Parker as his successor

boards: Shamu Two and Three; Lone Star One, painted to represent the Texas flag; and two other "flag" planes, Arizona One and California One. The Lone Star was unveiled in 1991 to mark Southwest's twentieth anniversary. Arizona One and California One joined the fleet in

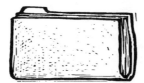

MALICE IN DALLAS: THE BATTLE OF THE BUSINESS TYCOONS

Setting the scene: The Sportatorium, a wrestling palace in Dallas, March 1992. Cheerleaders chant, the crowd whistles and cheers. In one corner, a burly 37-year old weightlifter, dressed in pants and a dark shirt, wearing a confident scowl, and displaying a "Born to Raise Capital" tattoo on his massive arm. Strutting in to the blaring trumpets of the theme from *Rocky* is the opponent, a grinning, skinny 61-year-old cigar-chomping lawyer decked out in a t-shirt and red satin boxing trunks and accompanied by a handler carrying rows of airline-sized liquor bottles. This was expected to be a battle royal, a one-on-one battle of the biceps. Actually, it was just a friendly contest between Southwest Airlines CEO Herb Kelleher and Stevens Aviation chairman Kurt Herwald to decide the rights to a slogan.

Stevens Aviation had been using "Plane Smart" as its slogan a year before Southwest unknowingly began infringing by using "Just Plane Smart" in its ads. Instead of an expensive, drawn-out trial, the companies agreed to send their top titans to settle the dispute in an arm-wrestling match held in front of the media and employees. The best two out of three matches would win the rights to the slogan, and the loser would donate five thousand dollars to a charity of the winner's choice.

Round One saw "Smokin Herb Kelleher" send in a ringer, a one-time arm wrestling champ who bested Herwald. In Round Two, Kelleher was quickly thrashed by "Kurtsey Herwald's" ringer, a tiny customer service rep. Finally, it was Kelleher against Herwald, and in a matter of seconds, it was all over. Kelleher was defeated, but Herwald announced that Southwest could keep using the slogan.

Everybody won. The companies got publicity, the media got a great story, and two charities, The Muscular Dystrophy Association and the Cleveland Ronald McDonald House, got big checks. The companies' hijinks even caught the Oval Office's attention. Then-President Bush wrote them a note congratulating the pair for their charitable deeds, and comedic antics.

May 1994 and August 1995. In June 1996, Southwest unveiled Silver One, the seventh of the painted planes, which featured a matching interior. Later additions were the Triple Crown One, dedicated to the company's employees; Nevada One, a high-flying tribute to the state of Nevada; and New Mexico One.

Southwest's painted planes offer more than good PR value," notes Tim McClure. "They have delighted people, children in particular, for years. And, while you generally don't think about the plane you're getting on, when people see these, they point them out. So I think it keeps the spirit alive out there. These planes speak to the Spirit of Southwest. What other company would have the guts to take the lead in painting one of these big monsters and having fun with it?"

CORPORATE CITIZENSHIP

Southwest Airlines is the proud sponsor of some of America's favorite sports, including professional baseball, basketball, hockey and football. The airline was the Official Airline of Super Bowl XXXV. The company is also the Official Airline of the NHL and NHLPA. In 2001, for the first time, Southwest ran a series of commercials during prime-time sports to point out to fans and customers that when it comes to major league hockey, "Its Tougher Than It Looks."

The Ronald McDonald House program, the cornerstone of the Ronald McDonald Children's Charities, is the primary corporate charity of Southwest Airlines. The company sponsors the Southwest Airlines LUV Classic golf tournament, the proceeds of which benefit the Ronald McDonald Houses and has raised more the $4.8 million over the past 16 years. *Business Ethics* magazine lists Southwest Airlines among its "100 Best Corporate Citizens" and Southwest was listed in *Hispanic*-magazine's "Corporate 100" for providing minority opportunities. The Secretary of Defense presented the Employer Support of the Guard and Reserve (ESGR) 2001 Employer Support Freedom Award to Southwest Airlines. And First Lady Laura Bush sent Southwest a personal recognition letter celebrating the success of the Adopt-A-Pilot program, which has reached over 25,000 students since 1997.

EMPLOYMENT

Southwest Airlines boasts a highly interactive corporate culture. In the company's 30-year history, it only had one strike. The airline values people as the company's greatest asset and designates much time and energy to hiring people with winning attitudes. Because Southwest Airlines is known as an exceptional place to work, many people apply for jobs yearly, giving them the edge in a tight job market. In 2001, the company received 194,821 resumes and hired 6,406 new employees. Once hired, Southwest provides a supportive work environment that gives employees freedom to be creative, have fun and make a positive difference. Although the airline offers competitive compensation packages, they feel its employees' sense of pride in their team accomplishments that keeps the Southwest spirit alive and productive. Although many companies ban inter-office romance, the airline boasts 928 married couples on staff.

For these reasons, Southwest Airlines was included on *Fortune* magazine's annual "Best 100 Companies to Work for in America" ranked in the top five for over four straight years. In May 1998, Southwest was the first airline to win the coveted Triple Crown for a month: Best On Time Record, Best Baggage Handling, and Fewest Customer Complaints. Since that time, the company has won it more than thirty times, as well as five times annually from years 1992 through 1996. At Southwest, prices are low, but morale flies high.

SOURCES OF INFORMATION

Bibliography

Freiberg, Kevin and Jackie. "Nuts! Southwest Airlines' Crazy Recipe for Business and Personal Success." *Austin: Bard Press, Inc.,* 1996

McNulty, Sheila. "Southwest Airlines: Short on Frills, Big on Morale." 30 October 2001. Available at http://www.financialtimes.com.

Shaw, Daniel. "The Quiet Man: Flamboyant Herb Kelleher Is a Tough Act to Follow as Southwest Airlines Chief. But Jim Parker Gets High Marks in Tough Times." *Corporate Counsel.,* March 2002.

"Southwest Airlines Co." Gale Group, March 2002. Available at http://galenet.galegroup.com.

"Southwest Airlines Co." *Hoover's Online,* 20 March 2002. Available at http://www.hoovers.com.

Southwest Airlines Co. Home Page, 2002. Available at http://www.southwest.com.

"Southwest Airlines Reports Fourth Quarter Earnings and 29th Consecutive Year of Profitability." *PRNewswire,* 17 January 2002.

For an annual report:

on the Internet at: http://www.southwest.com **or** write: Southwest Airlines Co., Investor Relations, PO Box 36611, Dallas, TX 75235

For additional industry research:

Investigate companies by their Standard Industrial Classification Codes, also known as SICs. Southwest Airlines' primary SIC code is:

4512 Air Transportation, Scheduled

Also investigate companies by their North American Industry Classification System Codes, also known as NAICS codes. Southwest Airlines' primary NAICS code is:

481110 Scheduled Air Transportation

Spanish Broadcasting System Inc.

FOUNDED: 1983

Contact Information:

HEADQUARTERS: 2601 Bayshore Dr.
  Coconut Grove, FL 33133
PHONE: (305)441-6901
FAX: (305)466-5148
URL: http://www.spanishbroadcasting.com

OVERVIEW

Based in Coconut Grove, Florida, Spanish Broadcasting System is the second-largest U.S. operator of Spanish-language radio stations. With 26 radio stations in the United States and Puerto Rico, Spanish Broadcasting is the largest Spanish-owned radio broadcasting company. These stations, which target Hispanic adults from 18 to 49 years of age, are located in the top ten Hispanic markets, including New York City; Los Angeles and San Francisco, California; Miami, Florida; Chicago, Illinois; and San Antonio and Dallas, Texas. Music formats include Spanish adult contemporary, regional Mexican, and contemporary salsa, merengue, and cumbia. The firm reaches roughly 61 percent of the Hispanic population in the United States.

COMPANY FINANCES

Although sales grew nearly 10 percent in 2001 to $134.3 million, Spanish Broadcasting posted a $7.6 million loss that year. The firm had also posted a loss, totaling $10.7 million, in 2000, on sales of $122.7 million. In 1999, the year that the firm completed its initial public offering (IPO), earnings had reached $5.8 million on sales of $97.4 million. Stock prices, which had jumped to $27.75 immediately following the IPO, fell to a low of $4.95 per share in September of 2001 after a sluggish North American economy prompted companies in nearly every industry to trim their advertising budgets. Earnings per share in both 2000 and 2001 were negative.

FINANCES:

Spanish Broadcasting Inc. Revenues, 1999-2001 (million dollars)

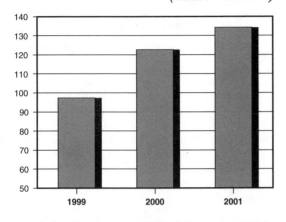

ANALYSTS' OPINIONS

According to an October 1997 issue of *Broadcasting & Cable*, "although Hispanic radio has moved into the listener mainstream...the industry's share of ad revenue continues to lag behind the share of audience it attracts." This gap continued to exist in 2002. Some analysts questioned whether advertisers would begin to spend more dollars targeting this market. Those who predicted advertising dollars would eventually make their way to Hispanic broadcasters believed that Spanish Broadcasting was positioned for growth.

HISTORY

Spanish Broadcasting was founded in 1983 when Cuban emigree Pablo Raul Alarcon acquired an AM radio station in New York City. In February of 1989, Spanish Broadcasting acquired WEVD-FM, another radio station serving New York. The firm changed the station's call letters to WSKQ-FM and its format to tropical, which included popular salsa, merengue, and cumbia music. Eventually, this station grew to be one of the largest in New York's broadcast market. In fact, by the mid-1990s, WSKQ's morning show was second only to the Howard Stern Show.

Spanish Broadcasting incorporated in 1994. As Spanish radio broadcasting throughout the 1990s grew in popularity, advertising sales for Spanish Broadcasting began to climb. The firm added to its New York holdings in 1996 with the purchase of easy listening station

FAST FACTS:

About Spanish Broadcasting System Inc.

Ownership: Spanish Broadcasting System Inc. is a public company traded on the NASDAQ Stock Exchange.

Ticker Symbol: SBSA

Officers: Raul Alarcon, Jr., Chmn., Pres., and CEO, 45, 2001 base pay $1.9 million; Joseph Garcia, EVP and CFO, 56, 2001 base pay $380,000; William Tanner; EVP, Programming, 57, 2001 base pay $703,000

Employees: 500

Principal Subsidiary Companies: Spanish Broadcasting System Inc. operates 26 radio stations in the United States and Puerto Rico. The firm also owns an 80 percent stake in JuJu Media, which operates LaMusica.com, a Spanish music Web site that broadcasts various Spanish Broadcasting radio stations via the Internet.

Chief Competitors: Spanish Broadcasting System's major rival is Hispanic Broadcasting Corp. The firm also competes with Infinity Broadcasting, Radio Unica, and other radio broadcasting companies.

WPAT-FM. Spanish Broadcasting changed its new station's format to Spanish adult contemporary, which included ballads, pop music, and love songs. Headquarters moved from New York to Miami in 1997. By then, Spanish Broadcasting operated 12 radio stations. Along with rival Heftel Broadcasting, the firm accounted for 85 percent of the Hispanic radio market.

In April of 1999, Spanish Broadcasting acquired LaMusica.com, a Spanish-English Web site featuring Latin music reviews, interviews, news, contests, videos, and shopping. As a result, LaMusica.com began broadcasting the Spanish Broadcasting's radio stations via the Internet. In October of that year, the firm conducted its initial public offering, selling 21.7 million shares for a total of $435.8 million. Spanish Broadcasting used the fresh capital to pay down debt and to purchase more radio stations. In fact, in January of 2000, the company acquired eight radio stations in Puerto Rico from AMFM Inc. A few months later, Spanish Broadcasting also bought Rodriguez Communications Inc. for $165.2 million in cash and stock. The deal added the following stations to the firm's holdings: KFOX-FM and KREA-FM,

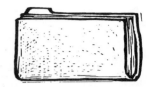

CHRONOLOGY:

Key Dates for Spanish Broadcasting System Inc.

1983: Spanish Broadcasting is founded

1994: Spanish Broadcasting is incorporated

1999: Spanish Broadcasting completes its IPO

1997: Headquarters move from New York to Miami

1999: Spanish Broadcasting acquires LaMusica.com

2000: Spanish Broadcasting acquires eight radio stations in Puerto Rico

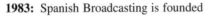

SPANISH BROADCASTING FORMATS

Radio stations owned by Spanish Broadcasting make use of a wide variety of formats. For example, radio stations with a Tejano format play Mexican music that was produced in Texas. The Spanish Tropical format includes salsa, merengue and cumbia dance music. A Regional Mexican format can include ranchera, nortena, banda, and other music played in different regions of Mexico. Spanish adult contemporary includes ballads, pop, and Latin rock.

both serving Los Angeles, California, and surrounding areas; KXJO-FM, based in San Francisco, California; KSAH-FM, serving San Antonio, Texas; and KTCY-FM and KXEB-AM, both serving Dallas, Texas, and nearby areas. Growth continued in November, when Spanish Broadcasting paid $250 million to purchase KFSG-FM from International Church of Foursquare Gospel.

The firm formed an alliance with America Online Inc. in January of 2001. The cross-marketing deal called for Spanish Broadcasting to include AOL advertisements in its broadcasts in exchange for AOL's promotion of LaMusica.com. By then, the firm operated 26 radio stations.

increasing in terms of its population, but also in terms of its purchasing power, growing three times faster than the U.S. total consumer spending. One thing we want to emphasize to our advertisers is that the Hispanic consumer needs the basic necessities of life like everybody else...our listeners fit very well the advertisers' target audience."

To maintain its competitiveness, the firm uses a 14-person team to perform market research on a regular basis. These individuals are responsible for things like creating listener focus groups and conducting telephone surveys in order to determine the success of each of the stations.

STRATEGY

Spanish Broadcasting's strategy is to target the top ten Spanish markets in the U.S., with a particular focus on the top four: Los Angeles, New York, Miami, and Chicago. This has helped the firm differentiate itself from rival Hispanic Broadcasting Corp., which operates in both the leading markets and the smaller markets. The reason for the firm's focus on the top four markets is the fact that Hispanic populations are growing more quickly there than anywhere else in the United States. By the early 2000s, Hispanics made up more than 45 percent of the population in Los Angeles, more than 65 percent of the population in Miami, and more than 25 percent of the populations in Chicago and New York. In addition, the Hispanic populations in those areas were becoming more affluent. According to Joseph Garcia, the firm's chief financial officer, "The Hispanic market is not only

CURRENT TRENDS

The growing popularity of Spanish music, even among non-Spanish cultures, helped to boost the number of Spanish Broadcasting's listeners in the late 1990s and early 2000s. One reason for this trend was the emergence of Hispanic music stars like Ricky Martin and Jennifer Lopez.

PRODUCTS

Spanish Broadcasting operates 26 stations, including WRMA-FM, a Ft. Lauderdale, Florida-based station serving the Miami area with Spanish adult contemporary programming; WLEY-FM, an Aurora, Illinois-based station serving the Chicago area with regional Mexican music; KLEY-FM, a regional Mexican and South Texas-style station serving San Antonio, Texas; WCMQ-FM, a Spanish oldies station serving Miami; WXDJ-FM, a contemporary salsa and merengue station serving Miami; and KXOL-FM, a Spanish adult contemporary station serving Los Angeles.

CORPORATE CITIZENSHIP

After the September 11th terrorist attacks on the World Trade Center Towers in New York City and the November 12th crash of an American Airlines flight in Queens, New York, Spanish Broadcasting sponsored a benefit concert to raise funds for the families of victims. Performed in the Music Square Garden in December of 2001, the concert raised roughly $400,000.

SOURCES OF INFORMATION

Bibliography

Bachman, Katy. "SBS Expands West." *MEDIAWEEK*, 22 May 2000.

"CFO of Spanish Broadcasting System Comments on the Size of the Spanish Market." *The Wall Street Transcript*, 23 July 2001. Available at http://www.twst.com.

Fakler, John T. "Spanish Broadcasting Looks to Buy Stations, Expand Reach." *South Florida Business Journal*, 22 December 2000.

Haley, Kathy. "Radio Rides Hispanic Population Boom; Stations Moving into Listener Mainstream as Ratings Grow." *Broadcasting & Cable*, 6 October 1997.

"Spanish Broadcasting Announces Acquisition of Full-Market FM Signal in Los Angeles." *PR Newswire*, 3 November 2000.

"Spanish Broadcasting System and America Online Announce Strategic Promotional Alliance with LaMusica.com, the Popular Site for Latino Entertainment." *Business Wire*, 2 August 2000.

Spanish Broadcasting System, Inc. Home Page, 2002. Available at http://www.lamusica.com.

For an annual report:

write: Spanish Broadcasting System, 2601 S. Bayshore Dr., Coconut Grove, FL 33133

For additional industry research:

Investigate companies by their Standard Industrial Classification Codes, also known as SICs. Spanish Broadcasting's primary SIC code is:

4823 Radio Broadcasting

Also investigate companies by their North American Industry Classification Codes, also known as NAICS codes. Spanish Broadcasting's primary NAICS code is:

513112 Radio Stations

Subway Restaurants

FOUNDED: 1965

Contact Information:
HEADQUARTERS: 325 Bic Dr.
    Milford, CT 06460-3059
PHONE: (203)877-4281
FAX: (203)876-6695
TOLL FREE: (800)888-4848
URL: http://www.subway.com

OVERVIEW

Subway is the world's largest sandwich chain, with more than 16,242 independently owned and operated locations in 73 countries. Its restaurants offer a variety of submarine sandwiches and salads as well as snacks and beverages. Subway is the leader in the "non-traditional branded fast food" category, meaning that it does not offer hamburgers, pizza, or fried chicken. While a substantial amount of Subway's business is in carryout orders, most of the chain's stores offer seating areas where customers can eat their sandwiches and salads. About 2,900 of the Subway outlets are smaller units operating in convenience stores, truck stops, railroad stations, college and high school campuses, military bases, airports, grocery stores, department stores, hospitals, and other locations.

COMPANY FINANCES

Subway grew rapidly during the 1990s, with the number of stores increasing from about 5,000 in 1990 to about 13,200 in 1998, second only to McDonald's. System-wide gross sales increased from about $1.1 billion to approximately $3.2 billion over the same period. As of 1998, owners DeLuca and Buck split about $320 million in annual profits. The store failure rate in 1999 was only 1 percent, down from 2 percent in earlier years. By 2000, sales had climbed to $4,720 million. In 2002, Subway finally overtook McDonald's as the largest restaurant chain in the country with 13,247 stores (148 more than McDonald's).

ANALYSTS' OPINIONS

From 1994 to 1997, Subway franchises were voted America's favorite sandwich chain according to a poll conducted by *Restaurants and Institutions* magazine. In the 1997 poll, more than 70 percent of U.S. restaurant customers surveyed voted for Subway as their favorite sandwich restaurant. The chain received the highest rankings overall in the sandwich category and scored top marks for value, service, cleanliness, and convenience. Subway is also a fixture on *Entrepreneur* magazine's "Franchise 500" list.

However, many store owners became dissatisfied with their relationship with the company, accusing Subway of damaging their sales by opening too many stores in the same area. DeLuca felt that clustering stores increases customer awareness and boosts everyone's sales. However, he did establish a site review committee, charged with preventing new stores from opening if they would reduce a neighboring store's sales by more than 10 percent.

By 2001, apparently having worked out its grievances with its franchisees, Subway was named "number one" franchise opportunity by *Entrepreneur* magazine. Its fare was also cited with some choice recognitions: Subway won the gold award for the sandwich category in the Restaurants and Institutions Choice in Chains Award and earned the MenuMasters Award for best menu/line extension from *Nation's Restaurant News*.

HISTORY

Subway traces its roots to August 1965 when Fred DeLuca, then 17 years old, opened Pete's Super Submarine, a sandwich shop in Bridgeport, Connecticut. DeLuca opened the shop on the advice of Dr. Peter Buck, a nuclear physicist and family friend who also provided a $1,000 loan for the new business. A year later the two partners opened their second unit, and soon after that a third store. The third store was highly successful and is still operating today.

Buck and DeLuca shortened the name of the operation from Pete's Subs to Subway and introduced the now familiar bright yellow Subway logo. They also began franchising the Subway concept. The first Subway franchise opened in Wallingford, Connecticut in 1974. Franchising worked well for the Subway chain and the operation began to grow rapidly.

In 1983 Subway restaurants began baking bread in their stores, a feature that would become a central part of the company's image. Baking units in Subway outlets are located behind the counter in direct view of the customers. The chain cites in-store baking as one of the key reasons for its strong growth in the 1980s and 1990s.

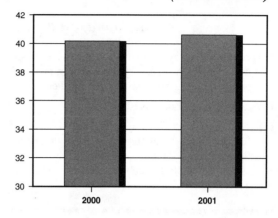

FINANCES:
Subway Restaurants Systemwide Sales, 2000-2001 (billion dollars)

In 1984 the first international Subway restaurant opened in the island country of Bahrain off the coast of Saudi Arabia. In August of 1995, the Subway chain celebrated 30 years in business and opened its 11,000th restaurant, with Fred DeLuca still serving as president of the company.

By 1998, Subway opened its 2,500th non-traditional unit. The year included several significant firsts, including its first restaurants in Hong Kong, Italy, Northern Ireland, Norway, Pakistan and the United Arab Emirates. The following year, Subway opened its 14,000th store.

In 2000, the year of its 35th anniversary, Subway became the first U.S. quick-serve food chain in Tanzania. In 2001 Subway was becoming more of a global presence as it now had 15,000 restaurants worldwide.

In 2002, Subway scored a particularly significant achievement: it passed McDonald's as the largest restaurant chain in the country.

STRATEGY

Subway is exclusively a franchise operation. It does not own or operate any corporate restaurants. The Subway chain was built on the concept of franchising units to independent owner/operators who establish freestanding stores in high-traffic areas such as shopping centers and strip malls.

Simplicity of concept and a strong brand have proven to be a cornerstones of Subway's success. The operation itself doesn't require much space and very lit-

FAST FACTS:

About Subway Restaurants

Ownership: Subway Restaurants is a franchise business operated by Doctor's Associates, Inc., a private corporation owned by Fred DeLuca and Peter Buck.

Officers: Fred DeLuca, Pres., 50

Chief Competitors: Subway competes with other fast food and pizza restaurant chains, including Blimpie, Burger King, Domino's Pizza, Little Caesar's, McDonald's, Papa John's, Sbarro, Taco Bell, Tubby's, and Wendy's.

---

tle cooking is involved, which allows it to easily fit into areas that larger restaurants are forced to avoid, and it has earned a reputation for quality, good service, convenience, and attention to hygiene. Simplicity of concept is also applied to its menu, which includes basic items like its trademark submarine sandwiches as well as salads and deli sandwiches.

Subway is also an easily identifiable commodity. Its stores are easy to recognize. When a customer sees the familiar Subway sign, he or she knows exactly what they'll get before entering the store.

INFLUENCES

Military bases are another growth area for Subway. In January 1997 the company was awarded a license agreement with the Navy Exchange Service Command (NEXCOM) to develop Subway restaurants on all qualified U.S. Navy installations around the world. The agreement was to run for five years. Subway franchisees were licensed to operate all of the sandwich shops on 26 naval installations, with 38 sites around the world and the potential of developing Subway sandwich shops in more than one hundred installations.

The Navy contract was not Subway's first experience in the military market. The first Subway sandwich shop on a military base opened in July 1989 at the Pearl Harbor Naval Station in Honolulu, Hawaii. Subway actively developed sandwich shops on military installations in the United States and abroad throughout the 1990s, and by early 1997 there were Subway restaurants operating on 17 military bases around the world.

In the early to mid-1990s, Subway restaurants targeted amusement parks as another avenue for sales growth, and the chain was expanding that effort in the late 1990s. As of 1997, 27 Subway outlets were open and operating in park and recreational facilities across North America, with more units being planned. Two successful, established units included the Museum of Natural History in New Mexico and Clyde Peeling's Reptileland in Allenwood, Pennsylvania.

CURRENT TRENDS

In the late 1990s, Subway attempted to address the trend toward low-fat eating by promoting existing sandwich products that customers could make low-fat by eliminating certain condiments and food items while continuing to offer its traditional sandwiches that were higher in fat. In a promotion launched in early 1997, Subway marketed seven of its sandwiches as low-fat alternatives by stressing their good taste. Subway's Low Fat Challenge advertised the seven sandwiches, which contained six grams of fat or less, by comparing them to competitors' burgers and tacos that contained as much as 30 grams of fat. The low-fat subs did not include cheese, oil, or mayonnaise.

To further address the trend, in 2000 Subway began promoting the story of Jared Fogle, a 425-pound man who reportedly lost 245 pounds through what he called his "Subway diet." Fogle said the diet consisted of little more than a six-inch turkey sub for lunch and a foot-long veggie sub for dinner. By further limiting his diet to a few soft drinks and a small bag of chips, his diet totaled less than 10 grams of fat and about 1,000 calories a day. Although Subway did not officially endorse this diet, no doubt for possible liability considerations, it nevertheless trumpeted Fogle's success; and Fogle attained something of a celebrity status as he appeared on national TV commercials for Subway and on programs like the "Oprah Show" and NBC's "Today."

Another trend affecting Subway in the mid to late 1990s had nothing to do with food. An increasing number of franchisees in many U.S. businesses were suing their franchisors over various disagreements and Subway was no exception. Legal problems of various types have plagued the company, which has more legal disputes registered with the Federal Trade Commission than its seven largest competitors combined.

In December 1995, Doctor's Associates, Inc. (DAI), chain founders Buck and DeLuca, and the affiliated leasing company, Subway Sandwich Shop, Inc., were found guilty in federal court of breach of contract and fraud in a dispute with a landlord. DAI, Buck, and DeLuca were assessed punitive damages of $3 million each, while Subway Sandwich Shop, Inc. was assessed a $1 million judgment. The jury, after hearing from Subway's top contract lawyer Leonard Axelrod, whose nickname is "Lenny the

Ax," found that DAI illegally used Subway Sandwich Shop, Inc. as a front to shield itself from liabilities.

A group of 32 Subway franchisees filed suit the following year against Subway for $100 million in damages, charging that the sandwich chain misused advertising funds. They claimed that Subway Franchisee Advertising Trust Fund members and Subway owners used the fund to pay for ads recruiting more franchisees and to evict delinquent franchisees. Franchisees contributed 2.5 percent of their sales to the fund at the time. The fee has since been raised to 3.5 percent.

Subway franchisees pay eight percent of their gross sales in royalties, the highest in the food business, where four or five percent is more common. But the high fees don't buy a corresponding amount of power. One tactic the company uses is to lease property and then sublet it to store owners. Controlling the lease means that Subway can (and does) evict the franchisee if a dispute arises.

PRODUCTS

Subway's U.S. menu consists of 7-under-6 sandwiches, select sandwiches, classic sandwiches, salads, wraps, cookies, party subs, soft drinks, and the Kids-Pak. Its regular six-inch subs are made with meat, onions, lettuce, tomatoes, pickles, green peppers, and olives on fresh baked bread. Sandwiches include the Veggie Delite, ham, roast beef, the Subway club, roasted chicken breast, turkey breast, and turkey breast and ham. Subway Classics include the Cold Cut Tri, Italian B.M.T., tuna, and the Seafood and Crab. Salads include turkey breast, the Veggie Delite, chicken breast and tuna. Wraps include Asiago Caesar, chicken, steak and cheese and turkey breast and bacon.

CORPORATE CITIZENSHIP

Doctor's Associates, Inc., the franchisor of Subway restaurants, supports a wide variety of charitable organizations on national and local levels. Some of the groups supported by DAI include The American Cancer Society, Big Brothers/Big Sisters, the Muscular Dystrophy Association, and the United Way. Owners of individual Subway franchises also provide support to the communities in which they operate.

In addition, the company has established the Micro Investment Lending Enterprise (MILE), a volunteer-run, non-profit organization that lends money to people so they can start their own businesses. DeLuca has also developed the Micro Enterprise Hall of Fame, which honors entrepreneurs who started small and raises awareness of the micro-credit movement.

CHRONOLOGY:
Key Dates for Subway Restaurants

1965: Fred DeLuca opens Pete's Super Submarine sandwich shop

1966: Pete's Super Submarine is changed to Subway

1974: The first Subway franchise opens

1983: Subway restaurants begin baking their own bread in the stores

1984: The first international Subway opens in Bahrain

1992: Subway introduces a co-branding strategy to work with local grocery stores and college food store operations

1997: Subway gets a licensing agreement with the Navy Exchange Service Command to develop Subway restaurants on Navy bases

2000: Subway becomes first U.S. quick-serve food chain in Tanzania

2002: Subway overtakes McDonald's as the largest restaurant chain in the country

GLOBAL PRESENCE

Subway pursues an aggressive international growth strategy. In 1996 the chain had 300 sandwich shops in 29 countries outside the United States and Canada. By mid-1998 that number had doubled, to 602 in 62 countries. The international growth strategy includes co-branding smaller Subway units with convenience stores in Central and South America, Europe, Australia, New Zealand, and Asia. Australia is one of Subway's largest markets, having celebrated the opening of its 100th Subway restaurant in January of 1997.

In January 2000, Subway became the first U.S. quick-serve food chain in Tanzania, and the company had plans to open stores in Poland, Finland, India, Bangladesh and Croatia. Subway's global success hinged on its providing travelers with a familiar, core menu that ensures the same quality found in the United States. However, the company often adapts the menu to the cultural or religious variations of the regions in which it operates.

By 2001 Subway had 15,000 restaurants worldwide including 100 locations in Puerto Rico, 300 in Australia, 50 in Venezuela and the United Kingdom. That same

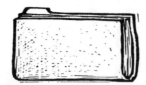

DID YOU KNOW THAT. . .

- There are nearly two million different sandwich combinations available on Subway's menu?

- Subway customers consume about 60 million pounds of lunch meat every year?

- Subway restaurants have been featured in many motion pictures, including *Lethal Weapon, Happy Gilmore,* and *Ransom?*

- Subway is the world's largest sandwich chain with more than 16,242 stores in 73 countries?

- That at $10,000, Subway's initial franchise fee is lower than that of Burger King ($40,000), Kentucky Fried Chicken ($25,000), McDonald's ($45,000), Taco Bell ($45,00), and Wendy's ($25,000)?

year, it opened its first restaurants in France, Oman and Croatia.

EMPLOYMENT

Subway's independently owned and operated locations each hire their own staff. As with most fast food restaurant chains, many of the positions are part time.

Some of Subway's legal problems have stemmed from its relationships with its franchisees and employees. Its 220 development agents work with potential franchisees to get new Subway locations in place. They have organized for leverage in dealing with DeLuca, who they say has broken contracts with them. The company requires that agents meet ambitious new store quotas or risk losing their territories. This puts them into conflict with franchisees, who worry about new stores cropping up nearby.

Subway markets itself to potential franchisees by stressing its low startup costs. It requires an initial fee of $10,000, in contrast to some competitors' requirement of nearly $50,000, and doesn't insist that franchisees have any minimum net worth. As a result, it is the franchise of choice for many immigrants, who comprise 30 to 50 percent of its owners. These franchisees are often extremely motivated, anxious to own a business, prepared to work hard, and are seeking to take part in the

"American Dream." But in general they have not had experience in evaluating contracts. In fact, according to the company's own survey, only 10 percent of its franchisees even read the contracts. Some are surprised when they discover that they are expected to pay royalties. In fact, some 35 percent failed a math and English proficiency test Subway instituted in 1997.

SOURCES OF INFORMATION

Bibliography

Allen, Robin Lee. "Subway Ordered to Pay $10M in Punitive Damages to Ex-Landlord." *Nation's Restaurant News,* 11 December 1995.

Behar, Richard. "Why Subway Is 'The Biggest Problem in Franchising.'" *Fortune,* 16 March 1998.

Brooks, Steve. "Can Low-Fat Sell? Two Fast-Feeders Give It Yet One More Try." *Restaurant Business,* 15 February 1997.

Casper, Carol. "Sub Sales: Sandwich Shops Hope Customers Will Pick Up Lunch at Breakfast." *Restaurant Business,* 10 February 1996.

Page, Heather. "No Sub-Stitute: Any Way You Slice It, Subway Comes Out on Top." *Entrepreneur,* January 1996.

Pollack, Judann. "Subway Slapped with $100 Million Suit: Franchisees Claim Management Siphons Ad Funds for Other Uses." *Advertising Age,* 26 August 1996.

Prather, Michelle. "No. 1 With Everything." *Entrepreneur,* January 2002. Available at http://www.entrepreneur.com.

"Subway Restaurants Add Seasonal Appeal to Amusement Parks." *PR Newswire,* 11 July 1997.

Hoover's Online. *Doctor's Associates, Inc. Capsule,* 15 April 2002. Available at http://www.hoovers.com.

Bujol, Jessica. "Subway Outlets Overtake McDonald's."*The Honolulu Advertiser.com,* 2 February 2002. Available at http://the.honoluluadvertiser.com.

"Subway Franchise Opportunity."*FranchiseDirect.com,* 2001. Available at http://www.franchisedirect.com/news/subway.htm.

"Two Subway Restaurants Are Targeted by Robber." *Chicago Tribune,* 4 March 1997.

For additional industry research:

Investigate companies by their Standard Industrial Classification Codes, also known as SIC codes. Subway's primary SIC codes are:

5812 Eating Places

6794 Patent Owners and Lessors

Also investigate companies by their North American Industry Classification System Codes, also known as NAICS codes. Subway's primary NAICS code is:

722110 Full Service Restaurants

Sunoco, Inc.

FOUNDED: 1886

OVERVIEW

Sunoco, Inc., headquartered in Philadelphia, Pennsylvania, is one of the largest independent oil refining and marketing companies in the United States. Its five domestic refineries have a combined processing capacity of 730,000 barrels of crude oil per day, and the company has stakes in more than 10,000 miles of crude oil and refined product pipelines and 35 product terminals. Sunoco also owns and operates a petrochemical facility in Philadelphia that produces phenol and acetone. Sunoco sells its gasoline through more than 4,100 retail outlets, primarily in the Northeast and upper Midwest.

Sunoco's refineries are located in Marcus Hook, Pennsylvania; Philadelphia, Pennsylvania; Toledo, Ohio; Tulsa, Oklahoma; and Yabucoa, Puerto Rico. The Marcus Hook, Philadelphia, and Toledo refineries produce fuels and petrochemicals. The Tulsa and Yabucoa refineries concentrate on lubricant production.

Sunoco's petroleum refining and marketing operations manufacture and market a full range of petroleum products, including fuels, lubricants, and petrochemical feedstock. These operations are conducted principally in the eastern half of the United States. Employing a patented technology, Sunoco also annually manufactures two million tons of high-quality metallurgical-grade coke for use in the steel industry. Its coke-making facilities operate in Virginia and Indiana.

In recent years, Sunoco has expanded its chemical business. In 2001, it bought the Aristech Chemical Corporation, a wholly owned subsidiary of Mitsubishi Corporation. The acquisition included Aristech's five chemical plants and a research center.

Contact Information:

HEADQUARTERS: Ten Penn Center, 1801 Market Street
  Philadelphia, PA 19103
PHONE: (215)977-3000
FAX: (215)977-3409
EMAIL: sunoco_online@sunoil.com
URL: http://www.sunocoinc.com

FINANCES:

Sunoco, Inc.
Net Incomes, 1998-2001
(million dollars)

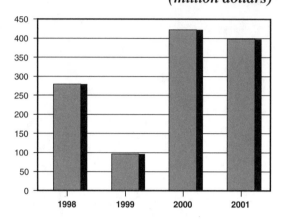

Sunoco, Inc.
2001 Stock Prices
(dollars)

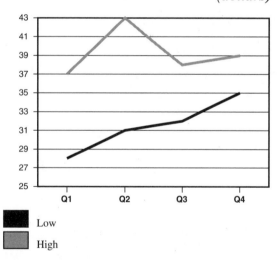

COMPANY FINANCES

Even though Sunoco posted a loss in the income column in 2001, it was still a strong year for the company, especially when you look at numbers posted before the turn of the century. For the fiscal year ended December 31, 2001, revenues for Sunoco's petroleum refining and marketing operations fell 4 percent to $14.14 billion. Net income from continuing operations fell 3 percent to $398 million. Sunoco's net income for 2000 was $422 million. Prior to the enormous jump in income in 2000, Sunoco

had posted fluctuating figures. Its net income in 1997 was $263 million. In 1998, income rose to $280 million. It fell steeply in 1999 to $97 million.

The 2001 losses reflected lower margins in Sunoco's northeast U.S. refining system, higher refinery fuel costs, and higher volume-related marketing expenses. Sunoco CEO John Drosdick also attributed the figures to the combined effects of warm temperatures and a weak economy.

ANALYSTS' OPINIONS

Even though Sunoco's earnings dropped in 2001, the company still did better than Wall Street analysts had expected. During the final quarter of 2001, the company's net income dropped sharply to $4 million, or $.05 per share. In the same quarter of 2000, Sunoco's net income was $154 million, or $1.80. Analysts had predicted that Sunoco would earn just $.02 per share in 2001.

In 2001, analysts noted that energy prices had been strong in previous quarters, which resulted in large profits for oil companies. They did expect energy prices to drop, leading many to speculate that earnings for the upcoming quarters would not show big increases. One analyst-Michale Young, with Gerard Klauer Mattison & Company-remarked that the first half of 2001 was the peak of the oil industry's earnings for the foreseeable future.

Still, oil company executives and financial analysts realize that the industry marketplace is highly volatile, and they expect rapid fluctuation. Also, analysts say that if Sunoco continues moving forward in the strategic direction it adopted in the late 1990s—to streamline its organization and focus on its core business practices—it could realize sustained improved earnings for a substantial amount of time.

HISTORY

The genesis of Sunoco began in 1886, when Joseph Newton Pew and Edward O. Emerson, partners in The Peoples Natural Gas Company in Pittsburgh, Pennsylvania, started exploring for more oil in Ohio and Pennsylvania. Wanting to diversify their business, the partners acquired new pipelines, leases, and storage tanks. By 1890, their company was one of the leading oil suppliers in Ohio, as it transported and stored oil and refined, shipped, and marketed petroleum products. The growth was accompanied by a name change, as the company became The Sun Oil Company of Ohio. The company continued growing when, in 1894, the partners bought the Diamond Oil Company in Toledo, Ohio.

In 1899 the partnership ended when Pew bought out Emerson's interests. Two years later, with Pew alone at the helm, the company was incorporated in New Jersey as Sun Company. At the time, Pew secured more leases and oil from a Texas field, and he purchased 82 acres in Marcus Hook, Pennsylvania.

When Joseph Pew died in 1912, the company was taken over by his son J. Howard Pew. Howard became president while his brother, Joseph N. Pew, Jr., became vice president. Together, the brothers took the company through a period of growth and innovation. In 1920, they changed the name to Sun Oil Company and started opening service stations in Ohio and Pennsylvania. By 1929, the brothers took the company into the oil field equipment business. In 1937, Sun built the world's first large-scale, commercial catalytic cracking plant in Marcus Hook. In 1941, Sun went into the mining business and formed the Cordero Mining Company in Nevada. More than just a side business, the mining company supplied mercury for Sunoco motor oils.

When J. Howard Pew resigned in 1947, he was succeeded by Robert G. Dunlop, who steered the company through expansion in the north and south and overseas in the 1950s. In 1953, Sun opened a refinery in Sarnia, Ontario, and, in 1957, one in Venezuela.

In 1956, Sun introduced the Custom Blending Pump, which revolutionized gasoline marketing. The pump gave customers a choice of several octane grades of gasoline from a single pump.

In 1968, Sun merged with the Sunray DX Oil Company of Tulsa, Oklahoma. The new Sun Oil company moved from its Philadelphia headquarters to St. Davids, Pennsylvania.

The 1970s saw some major restructuring of the company. In 1975 Sun was organized into 14 operating units, 2 property companies, and a non-operating parent company, and it moved its headquarters to Radnor, Pennsylvania. The following year, the Sun Oil Company was renamed Sun Company in 1976.

The company saw some major transitions in the 1980s. In 1981 it scored two key acquisitions when it bought the oil and gas properties of Texas Pacific Oil Company, Inc. and Viking Oil Limited. Viking owned 20 percent interest in production blocks in the North Sea. In 1982 Sun sold all of its shipbuilding interests. A year later, it introduced Sunoco Ultra, which was the highest octane premium unleaded gasoline available from a major U.S. supplier. Also during the decade, the company expanded into the North Sea and offshore China, and it acquired the Exeter and Victory oil companies, the Whitaker Coal Corporation, and purchased interests of the Petro-Lewis Corporation.

Sun underwent some more major restructuring of its organization in 1988 when it stopped all of its domestic oil and gas exploration and chose to focus on refining and marketing. As part of this shift in focus, it bought the Atlantic Petroleum Corporation. The acquisition brought with it a network of service stations and a pipeline system. In 1994, the company made another major acquisition when it bought Chevron's Philadelphia

FAST FACTS:
About Sunoco, Inc.

Ownership: Sunoco, Inc. is a publicly owned company traded on the New York Stock Exchange.

Ticker Symbol: SUN

Officers: John Drosdick, Chmn. and CEO, 58, $2,900,000; Thomas Hofmann, CFO and SVP, 50; Charkes Valutas, SVP and CAO, $690,000; Robert Owens, SVP of Marketing, 48, $798,000; Michael Dingus, SVP, 53

Employees: 14,200

Principal Subsidiary Companies: Sunoco has organized its operations into seven business units, including Sun Northeast Refining, Sunoco Northeast Marketing, Sunoco Chemicals, Sun Lubricants, Sunoco MidAmerica Marketing & Refining, Sunoco Logistics, and Sun Coke. The company also includes a holding company and a shared services organization.

Chief Competitors: Sunoco's main competitors are in the energy sector in the oil and gas operations industry: Amerada Hess, Marathon Ashland Petroleum LLC, Motiva Enterprises, Shell Oil Products, and Tosco Corporation.

Refinery. Sun combined the Chevron and Atlantic facilities into a single, more efficient refining complex and linked it into its Marcus Hook Refinery.

Also during the 1990s, Sun shifted it strategic direction toward its "value-added businesses." As part of this new direction, Sun divested itself of its real estate interests, including Radnor Corp.; its Canadian subsidiary, Suncor; the Cordero Mining Company; and its international oil and gas production business.

In 1996 Sun's board elected John G. Drosdick President and Chief Operating Officer, the first Sun president to come from outside the company. Two years later, the company changed its name yet again—this time to Sunoco, Inc.

In 2001 Sunoco acquired the Aristech Chemical Corporation of Pittsburgh, a purchase that included five Aristech chemical plants and a research center. This doubled the size of Sunoco's chemicals business and strengthened Sunoco's position in the global chemical markets.

CHRONOLOGY:
Key Dates for Sunoco, Inc.

1886: Joseph Newton Pew and Edward O. Emerson form The Peoples Natural Gas Company, which will become Sunoco

1890: The Peoples Natural Gas Company becomes the Sun Oil Company of Ohio

1912: Joseph Pew dies and his son, J. Howard Pew, becomes president of the Sun Company

1937: Sun builds the world's first large-scale, commercial catalytic cracking plant in Marcus Hook, Pennsylvania

1956: Sun introduces the Custom Blending Pump, which revolutionizes gasoline marketing

1968: Sun merges with the Sunray DX Oil Company of Tulsa, Oklahoma

1983 Sun introduces Ultra, the highest octane premium unleaded gasoline available in the United States

1988: Sun restructures its organization to focus on refining and marketing

1996: John G. Drosdick is named company president and COO, and Sun changes its name to Sunoco, Inc.

2001: Sunoco acquires the Aristech Chemical Corporation of Pittsburgh

STRATEGY

Sunoco's strategic plan involves focusing company efforts on extracting the maximum value and efficiency from its existing assets "while opportunistically and prudently utilizing financial resources to further grow the company and enhance the value for Sunoco shareholders." A stated strategic action employed in recent years has been to evaluate its portfolio of assets to achieve the kind of mix that enables it to maintain "a return on capital employed in excess of its weighted-average cost of capital." Sunoco's investment strategy focuses on growth in its retail marketing, chemicals, logistics, and coke-making operations.

In particular, Sunoco sought to expand its chemical operation. In that direction, it bought the Pittsburgh-based Aristech Chemical Corporation with its five chemical plants located at Neal, West Virginia; Haverhill,

Ohio; Neville Island, Pennsylvania; Pasadena, California; and LaPorte, Texas, as well as a research center in Pittsburgh. The plants could produce 1.5 billion pounds per year of polypropylene and more than 1.6 billion pounds per year of phenol and related derivatives. Phenol is a raw material for the production of resins used in adhesives primarily in the construction industry. It is also a raw material for bisphenol-A, which is used to make rapidly growing polycarbonate resins for compact discs and high impact automobile parts. Polypropylene is a thermoplastic used in a wide variety of applications, including fibers, injection molded plastics, and films.

Sunoco felt that the acquisition would provide enhanced earnings power as well as a platform for expansion in product lines having high demand growth and with less capital intensity than traditional refining. The polypropylene and phenol businesses, it believed, would integrate well with existing chemical operations.

INFLUENCES

Essentially, what happened with Sunoco in the latter half of the twentieth century was that it had spread itself a bit thin and its focus had become too diffuse. Like other large companies that found themselves in the same situation, Sunoco embraced the corporate streamlining and cost-cutting trend of the late 1990s and, like other corporations that moved in that direction, Sunoco shrank the number of its operations and concentrated on what it deemed its core business practices.

The company was already heading in this direction in 1988 when it disposed of all domestic oil and gas exploration to concentrate on refining and marketing. This meant that the company would focus on its value-added businesses: gasoline marketing, lubricants, chemicals, and logistics.

As part of its new direction, Sunoco made a drastic departure from tradition when it hired someone from outside the organization to be its president. That man was John Drosdick, an executive who had developed a strong reputation as an aggressive cost-cutter and expert streamliner.

CURRENT TRENDS

The most significant aspect of Sunoco's restructuring and streamlining involved the organization of seven business units, designed to charge the units with increased accountability for bottom line performance and to let each unit focus on innovating its operations in the industry's characteristic volatile environment. The business units compete in three primary market segments: petroleum products, petrochemicals, and coke-making.

In the 12-month period following the business unit reorganization, results were mixed. Operating income for 2001 was $391 million versus $438 million for 2000. However, the company pointed out that the decrease was largely due to lower margins in Sunoco's northeast U.S. refining system, higher refinery fuel costs, higher volume-related marketing expenses, lower chemical operations income, and higher net financing expenses as a result of financing costs attributable to the Aristech acquisition. On the positive side, all of this was offset by higher refinery production and retail gasoline sales volumes, as well as improved margins in Sunoco's mid-continent refining centers and retail marketing operations.

Net income for 2001 included net after-tax benefits of $7 million associated with special items. The year also saw a $21 million after-tax gain from an income tax settlement; $26 million of after-tax charges associated with employee termination and exit costs related to the disposal of certain company businesses; an environmental accrual associated with Sunoco's retail marketing and distribution operations; and $1 million of after-tax income from value added and Eastern lubricants operations. Looking back at 2000, net income included a net after-tax charge of $16 million associated with special items.

PRODUCTS

Each of Sunoco's seven business units is involved in different product categories. The Sun Northeast Refining business unit business manufactures petroleum products, including gasoline, middle distillates (jet fuel, heating oil, and diesel fuel), residual fuel oil, and petrochemical feedstocks. The unit sells the products to other Sunoco business units and to wholesale and industrial customers.

The Sunoco Northeast Marketing unit is involved in the retail sale of gasoline and middle distillates, and it operates convenience stores that dispense gasoline in the eastern United States, primarily in a 13-state region from Maine through Tennessee. At retail locations, Sunoco Northeast Marketing offers four grades of gasoline including Ultra 94, the highest octane premium gasoline commercially available in the United States, and 93, 89, and 87 octanes.

The Sunoco Chemicals unit manufactures, distributes, and markets base commodity and intermediate petrochemicals including olefins and their derivatives (ethylene, ethylene oxide, refinery-grade propylene, and polypropylene), aromatics and their derivatives (benzene, cumene, cyclohexane, toluene, xylene, phenol, acetone, bisphenol-A, and anilene), and plasticizers (phthalic anhydride, 2-ethylhexanol, and phthalate plasticizers). The unit also produces polymer-grade propylene and polypropylene and petrochemicals.

The Sun Lubricants unit manufactures fuel and lubricant products, which are then sold to the processed oil, wholesale base oil, and wax markets. The business also manufactures and sells base oils and related fuels produced at the Puerto Rico refinery.

Sunoco MidAmerica Marketing & Refining sells gasoline and middle distillates and operates convenience stores in the Midwest. It also manufactures, distributes, and sells fuels and petrochemicals produced at the Toledo refinery. It markets five grades of retail Sunoco gasoline products, including Ultra 94. The unit's chemical operations manufactures base commodity and intermediate petrochemicals including aromatics, spirits, nonene, and tetramer.

The Sunoco Logistics business unit consists of crude oil and refined product pipeline operations; domestic lease crude oil acquisition and related trucking operations; crude oil terminalling; and product terminalling and transport operations.

The Sun Coke unit manufactures blast furnace coke at facilities in East Chicago, Indiana, and Vansant, Virginia.

CORPORATE CITIZENSHIP

Sunoco is a staunch advocate of environmental responsibility. It has developed a strategic focus that champions operating safe, reliable facilities in an environmentally sound manner. Sunoco is part of the CERES Coalition, a network of more than 70 organizations that includes environmental, investor, and advocacy groups working together for a sustainable future. It adheres to CERES principles, which include protection of the biosphere, sustainable use of natural resources, reduction and safe disposal of wastes, energy conservation, risk reduction, and environmental restoration.

As part of its own efforts, Sunoco undergoes a regular Health, Environment, and Safety (HES) report that enables it to measure its own performance. In 2000, Sunoco developed processes and systems to improve its HES performance. Elements include employing research, planning, and analysis to minimize the environmental impact and health and safety hazards of its products and services; counseling employees and customers in the safe use and handling of its products; and eliminating the use of purchased products that pose known environmental hazards. Sunoco also makes it a policy to inform officials, employees, contractors, customers, and the public about significant health, safety, or environmental hazards related to its facilities in a timely manner. The company actively seeks dialogue with neighboring communities and their residents.

GLOBAL PRESENCE

When Sunoco ventured into the international business arena, its efforts could be described as tentative at

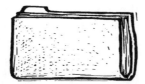

SUNOCO LOGO: WHAT'S OLD IS NEW

The new Sunoco Logo made its debut in 1998. However, it is essentially the same familiar logo that has been in use since 1920. The logo was last revised in 1954 when the arrow was moved from a horizontal to a diagonal position; also, the lettering was changed slightly. In the new design all elements are retained including the blue and yellow colors, the famous diamond shape, the Sunoco name, and the red arrow. The company felt that the new version of the logo had a more contemporary look.

best. By the end of the twentieth century, the company made a business decision to concentrate only on domestic enterprises.

In the 1950s, Sunoco—or Sun, as it was then known—had a refinery in Canada and one in Venezuela. In the 1960s, it had a subsidiary in Canada. In the 1980s it had expanded into the North Sea and offshore China; however, during the restructuring and streamlining of the 1990s, Sunoco chose to focus on domestic business, and it quit any international exploration. During that decade, it sold its international oil and gas production business. Today, all of its facilities are located in the United States.

EMPLOYMENT

Sunoco's employment policy affords equal employment opportunities to all qualified individuals, without regard to their race, color, religion, sex, national origin, age, physical or mental disability, citizenship status, veteran status, sexual orientation, or any other characteristic or status that is protected by federal, state or local law.

Sunoco offers a comprehensive benefit package that includes annual success-sharing bonuses, a 401K savings

plan, medical and dental plans, and an educational assistance plan. It also engages employees in regular career expectation discussions.

SOURCES OF INFORMATION

Bibliography

Bishop, Todd. "Drosdick to Become Top Gun at Sunoco." *Philadelphia Business Journal*, 28 April 2000. Available at http://philadelphia.bizjournals.com.

Business 2.0. "Web Guide-Sunoco, Inc.," 1 April 2002. Available at http://www.business2.com.

Forbes.com. "Company Details: Sunoco, Inc.," 1 April 2002. Available at http://www.forbes.com.

Hoover's Online. "Company Capsule-Sunoco, Inc.," 2002. Available at http://www.hoovers.com.

"Sunoco Shows Off New Technology and Commercial Center." *The Business Journal Online*, 10 December 2001. Available at http://www.businessjournal.com.

Yahoo! Finance. "Profile-Sunoco, Inc.," 28 March 2001. Available at http://biz.yahoo.com.

Yahoo! Finance. "Sunoco Company News," 28 March 2002. Available at http://biz.yahoo.com.

For an annual report:
on the Internet at: http://www.sunocoinc.com/shareholder

For additional industry research:
Investigate companies by their Standard Industrial Classification Codes, also known as SICs. Sunoco, Inc.'s primary SICs are:

1221 Bituminous Coal & Surface Mining

1311 Crude Petroleum And Natural Gas

2911 Petroleum Refining

5172 Petroleum Products, Not Elsewhere Classified

Also investigate companies by their North American Industry Classification System codes, also known as NAICS codes. Sunoco, Inc.'s primary NAICS codes are:

211111 Crude Petroleum and Natural Gas Extraction

212111 Bituminous Coal and Lignite Surface Mining

324110 Petroleum Refineries

422720 Petroleum and Petroleum Products (except Bulk Stations and Terminals) Wholesalers

The Swatch Group Limited

FOUNDED: 1983

OVERVIEW

The Swatch Group is known for its trademark watches and time pieces. It is the largest watchmaker in the world and is responsible for the manufacture of many name brand watches and clocks. The company was formed through multiple mergers of smaller Swiss companies, which are now all operating under the Swatch umbrella. Although the main focus of the company is consumer sales of wristwatches, the company does have interests in battery making, telecommunications components and timing and scoring devices.

COMPANY FINANCES

The Swatch Group has posted double digit profit margins for nearly a decade. The company had a record setting year in 2000 posting $2,563 million in revenues and $403.9 million in net income. The resulting 16 percent net profit margin was an increase over the 12 percent margin established in 1999. During 2001 the company was forced to revise its prediction of continued double-digit growth. The decline was attributed to an overall poor global economy and the slowdown of in the sales of luxury items. The forecast for 2001 was dropped from a projected 10 to 12 percent sales growth to a more modest 5 to 8 percent increase. Management indicated in its statement that this revision is not a sign of more serious problems.

ANALYST'S OPINIONS

Analysts reporting on Swatch are optimistic about the future of the company. Although it has not met expec-

Contact Information:
HEADQUARTERS: Seevorstadt 6
2502 Biel, Bern Switzerland
PHONE: +41-32-343-68-11
FAX: +41-32-343-69-11
URL: http://www.swatchgroup.com

FAST FACTS:

About The Swatch Group Limited

Ownership: Swatch is a publicly owned company traded on exchanges around the world including London, Frankfurt, Munich, Berlin, and the New York Stock Exchanges.

Ticker Symbol: UHRZ.S

Officers: H.C. Nicolas G. Hayek, Chmn. and CEO; Edgar Geiser, CFO

Employees: 17,719

Principal Subsidiary Companies: The Swatch Group is the largest watchmaker in the world. It is the parent company to many subsidiaries including: Longines, Omega, Tissot, and Endura.

Chief Competitors: The Swatch Group is primarily in the business of making watches. The company also has interests in chip manufacturing and electronic components. The main competition for Swatch products is other watch manufacturers, most notably Timex, Fossil, Guess and Rolex.

tations in recent months, at least one analyst observed that the company was too optimistic in its forward looking statements. Christoph Bohli, an analyst at Bank Sarasin, questioned the outlook for the remainder of 2001, but concluded that there was no concrete reason to be concerned about long term prospects. Also in 2001 Swiss analyst, Gina-Luca Manca, of HSBC downgraded her rating from a "buy" to a "hold". She stated, "The company is wary of a deteriorating U.S. economy, and weak demand from Japanese tourists." Martine Rogonon of Banque Bordier offered a different opinion noting that Swatch does not have great exposure to Japan and that the decline in sales in 2001 was due to overall bad economic conditions worldwide.

HISTORY

The Swatch group was formed in 1983 by the merger of two Swiss watchmakers: ASUAG and SSIH. ASUAG was founded in 1931 with the goal of building and expanding the Swiss watch industry. SSIH was founded in 1930 as a result of a merger between Omega and Tissot. Both companies grew by acquiring other local companies, but struggled during difficult economic times. In addition, each company controlled so many small subsidiaries it was difficult for either to maintain consistent policies throughout operations.

In the 1970s both companies were in financial trouble. Japanese watchmakers were mass producing inexpensive watches and gaining valuable market share. Nicolas Hayek, who was the Chief Executive Officer at a consulting firm bearing his name, was asked to evaluate the situation. The Swiss financial community wanted to preserve the rich Swiss tradition of watchmaking and hoped a recovery strategy could be developed. Hayek completed his work, which would be known as the Hayek Study, and recommended that the two rival firms would benefit by joining forces.

In 1983 SSIH and ASUAG merged and became SMH (Societe Suisse de Microelectronique & d'Horlogerie). The first year the newly minted conglomerate posted $124 million in losses on $1.1 billion in sales. The company countered the Japanese domination of the low cost watch market by introducing the now famous Swatch Watch. It was high tech, low cost and much more appealing to the younger crowd. The launch was a huge success and did not diminish the polished reputation of the more upscale brands owned by the company. Nicolas Hayek apparently liked the potential of this new company he helped create. He soon took over the majority of shares and was named CEO of the new company. He revitalized the company, introduced new ideas, and is widely credited with salvaging the failing Swiss watch industry. The next ten years were very profitable for Swatch and Hayek, its new leader.

In 1998 the company officially changed its name to Swatch to increase visibility and create brand identity. SMH was a rather non-descriptive name and was often not even recognized by the buying public. Hayek decided to raise the company's profile in the United States by holding a gala event, a glitzy three day event in Las Vegas at Caesar's Palace, to publicize its new product lines. A group of international journalists were then transported by Swatch bus to a resort in Death Valley. Dinner was provided by celebrity chef, Wolfgang Puck, and the entertainment by the Cirque du Soleil.

The next few years would be all about marketing and brand development. There was never any doubt that the watches produced by the Swiss conglomerate were some of the finest timepieces in the world. The company merely needed to formulate a plan to keep new ideas flowing and the brand name in the public consciousness.

STRATEGY

Swatch developed its own strategy for presenting its merchandise to the watch buying public. Hayek felt strongly that U.S. department stores did little to enhance the image of his product. In most instances, department

CHRONOLOGY:

Key Dates for Swatch Group

1930: SSIH was founded

1931: ASUAG was founded

1983: The Swatch Group was founded by the merger of SSIH and ASUAG

1985: Nicolas Hayek acquires a majority interest in the company and becomes CEO

1998: Swatch Group sells its participation in Daimler Benz

2001: Swatch enters partnership with AOL Time Warner to cross promote products; Swatch signs multi-year contract to be official timekeeper for the Olympics

BRAINS, BRAWN, AND BOND

Swatch has designed several advertising campaigns aimed at attracting young male customers. There is something for everyone, no matter who your hero. NBA star Shaquille O'Neal is featured in a campaign scheduled to roll out in spring of 2002. The theme of the ads is "I want to be." James Bond will also be a mainstay in one of the new promotions. Swatch plans to sponsor Bond nights at movie theaters, and will release a set of collectible theme watches. Twenty different watches will be created in honor of various movies. The watches will be released in set throughout the year and will commemorate the 40th anniversary of the Bond series. Finally, for the young man with more cerebral interests, Swatch will sponsor a chess match between two of the world's highest ranked players: Gary Kasparov and Judit Polgar. The game will be played on a Swatch chessboard and use Swatch timers.

stores arranged multiple display cases in one crowded area with little means of differentiating one brand from the next. The company announced a plan outlining a major expansion of monobrand retail stores in locations worldwide. Hayek's plan called for 500 new stores to open globally. One hundred of the new stores were given U.S. addresses. The chain of stores allowed the company to create a unique atmosphere surrounding its products. In addition, management wanted to emphasize the high tech aspect of Swatch gear, which was often overshadowed by the attention dedicated to the colorful designs. It was able to implement this strategy in its own retail space.

INFLUENCES

The Internet, wireless technology, and entertainment outlets influence even the oldest and most traditional industries. Swatch is not immune to the wave of new products that continue to reach the market. Despite having roots steeped in tradition, Swatch is generally perceived as a youth oriented brand. In order to reach the youth in America and keep time with them, Swatch took to the net, the Internet. In a bold move, the company created a concept called "Internet time". The idea came from Nick Hayek Jr. Internet time is a standard time established online. It doesn't require mental arithmetic to determine conversion times in different zones. CNN.com has adopted the time for use on its Web site to schedule chats or games. Ericsson incorporated the feature into its

latest cell phone prototypes to obtain a competitive advantage over its rivals.

Swatch's partnership with the Internet doesn't end with the time concept. Swatch and AOL/Time Warner have signed a marketing deal agreeing to collaborate on promotional activities. It is possible that one day soon the Internet will be accessible by wristwatch.

CURRENT TRENDS

The company continues to forge partnerships with technology providers to create new products aimed at the youth market. The majority of the company's brands, such as Omega and Tissot have long histories and are well respected among the customer base. They are impervious to trends and fads and never seem to go out of style. Brand loyalty is strong for the established company brand names. The company continues its efforts to market innovative products to a new generation of consumers.

PRODUCTS

The Swatch group produces wristwatches in every price range. The group controls more than two dozen brand name watchmakers: Longines, Omega, Renata,

MAKE YOUR OWN TIME

Swatch is encouraging customers to make their own time, or at least their own advertisement for time. The company is one of a growing number of cutting edge firms that are turning their advertising campaigns over to the customers. It asked animators to log on and design an ad campaign promoting its revolutionary concept of "Internet Time." Internet time is a standardized timekeeping system that allows users around the world to be on the same time clock. The company received original work from more than 300 artists in 30 different countries.

Rado, and Tissot. In addition the company creates sophisticated time keeping devices for and held interests in automobile maker Daimler Chrysler. In the year 2000 watches accounted for 73 percent of total sales, watch production and components 17 percent, and electronic systems 10 percent.

GLOBAL PRESENCE

The Swatch Group is the largest watchmaker in the world today, garnering about one quarter of the global market for time pieces. The watches are made in factories and production centers located in Malaysia, China, Thailand, Italy, Germany, France, United States, Virgin Islands and Switzerland. Watches are sold in "monobrand" Swatch stores worldwide, as well as upscale brand boutiques for the luxury items. In an effort to expand its global appeal Swatch has signed on to become the official timekeeper of the International Olympic Committee. The company has signed a long term contract to provide timing and results reporting services through 2010. The company will also work with the ParaOlympic games in a similar capacity.

CORPORATE CITIZENSHIP

Since its formation almost 20 years ago, the Swatch Group has worked to be a role model for corporate citizenship. Much of the company's philosophy originates with CEO Nicholas Hayek. Hayek has long been vocal on the international scene and does not hesitate to take a stand on the issues. In 1992 Swatch marketed a special watch to commemorate the United Nations Conference on Environment and Development. Swatch also designed a self-winding watch in honor of Earth Day and called it "Time to Move." The company is also a supporter of the Olympics. Nicolas Hayek discussed his firm's partnership with the IOC and offered the following comments, "they are more than a sporting event-the Games are an emotional festival and the most perfect, peaceful and warmhearted competition between youth. The Olympic Games fit perfectly with Swatch's strategy."

EMPLOYMENT

The Swatch Group boasts over 17,000 employees worldwide. Almost 60 percent of all workers are based in Switzerland and another 30% are in Asia. The remaining 15 percent are housed in offices throughout Europe and in the United States. The workforce has grown each year for the past ten years beginning in 1990. In 1990 the company claimed approximately 12,500 employees.

SOURCES OF INFORMATION

Bibliography

Dolbow, Sandra. "Swatch Bonds next mission with 007, Shaq." *Brandweek* 21 January 2002.

Ellis, Kristi. "Swatch at 15: A New Identity." *Women's Wear Daily*6 July 1998.

Freeman, Laurie. "User Created Ads Catch On" *Advertising Age*, 18 September 2000.

Hall,William "Swatch halves its target for sales growth." *Financial Times*21 August 2001.

"It's about Time." *The Online Reporter*, 13 November 2000

Lynn, Matthew. "Clock is Ticking as corporate Switzerland loses its sheen." *Sunday Business*, 26 August 2001

Shuster, William George. "Swatch Group's net profits fall." *JCK's High-Volume Jeweler*, November 2001

"Swatch Higher on FY Sales Figures." *AFX European Limited*, 6 February 2002.

Underwood, Elaine. "A self-winding eco-pitch." *Adweek's Marketing Week*, 13 April 1992.

For an annual report:

on the Internet at: http://www.swatchgroup.com/investor

For additional industry research:

Investigate companies by their Standard Industrial Classification Codes, also known as SICs. The Swatch Group Limited's primary SIC is:

3873 Watches

Also investigate companies by their North American Industry Classification System codes, also known as NAICS codes. The Swatch Group Limited's primary NAICS code is:

334518 Watch, Clock, and Part Manufacturing

Target Corporation

OVERVIEW

The Minneapolis-based Target Corporation is among the largest general merchandise companies in the United States. It employs more than 281,000 people in 47 states and operates approximately 1,400 stores nationwide.

Formerly Dayton Hudson, Target Corporation developed the concept of the "upscale discounter," and it promotes its Target stores as an inexpensive department store that offers more selection and class than similar retail outlets such as Kmart and Wal-Mart.

The Corporation is an acknowledged retail empire and the Target stores are the centerpiece of its operations. Target Corporation's three operating divisions include Target, Mervyn's, and the Department Store Division (DSD), which consists of Dayton's, Hudson's, and Marshall Field's. In 2001, the Target division generated about 80 percent of retail sales and operating profits, while Mervyn's generated about 12 percent of revenues and 8 percent of profits, and the Department Store Division generated about 9 percent of sales and 12 percent of profits.

Target Corporation has regional offices in Los Angeles, Dallas, Richmond and Minneapolis. Its distribution centers are located in Huntsville, Alabama; Maumelle, Arkansas; Fontana, California; Ontario, California; Woodland, California; Pueblo, Colorado; Tifton, Georgia; Indianapolis; Fridley, Minnesota; Albany, Oregon; Tyler, Texas; Stuarts Draft, Virginia; Oconomowoc, Wisconsin and Wilton, New York.

FOUNDED: 1902

Contact Information:

HEADQUARTERS: 1000 Nicollet Mall
    Minneapolis, MN 55403
PHONE: (612)304-6073
FAX: (612)304-5104
TOLL FREE: (888)304-4000
EMAIL: investorrelations@target.com
URL: http://www.targetcorp.com

FINANCES:

Target Corporation Revenues, 1998-2002 (million dollars)

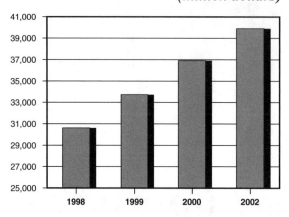

(2001 figures were not available)

Target Corporation 2001 Stock Prices (dollars)

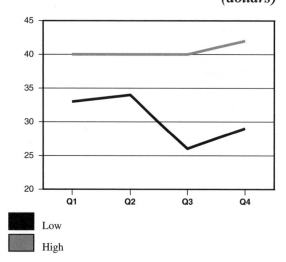

■ Low

■ High

COMPANY FINANCES

For the fiscal year that ended February 2, 2002, Target Corporation's revenues rose 8 percent to $39.89 million. Net income rose 9 percent to $1.37 billion. Revenues reflected increased revenues at Target due to the opening of new stores. Earnings also benefited from improved operating margins. Revenues for 1999 were $36.903 million. In 1998, they were $33.702 million. In 1997, rev-

enues were $30.662 million, and were $27.487 million in 1996.

ANALYSTS' OPINIONS

Overall, analysts have commented that Target has attractive value on the market because of its ability to keep capital costs within reason, which results from the fact that it does not have an excessive amount of financial leverage. A high degree of combined leverage indicates a company might be in financial trouble. Target, with its low degree of combined leverage, has lower financial risk and increased market value. The corporation's earnings per share have grown around 15 percent each year, which represents a low level of risk.

Indeed, Wall Street has liked Target's continued growth and earnings. One analyst from www.NYSE.com remarked that Target Corporation "is a wonderful company. They have a great growth vehicle in Target stores, which have a significant amount of growth potential left."

Value Line and Standard & Poor's also rated Target high because of its average earnings growth over the past decade, and they indicated the company had projections for 15 to 17 percent growth over its next five years.

HISTORY

The Target Corporation's history dates back to 1902, when a man named George Dayton opened a store called Goodfellows in Minneapolis, Minnesota. He changed the name of his business to the Dayton Company in 1910. Later, in 1956, the company would create a milestone in the retail industry when it built the world's first fully-enclosed shopping mall.

The seeds for the Target concept were planted in 1961, when Dayton's saw a demand for a store that sold less-expensive goods in a quick, convenient format. A year later, the first Target discount store was opened in Roseville, Minnesota. It became the first retail store to offer well-known national brands at discounted prices.

The Dayton Company initial public offering (IPO) took place in 1967. In 1969, the Target Corporation, as it is known today, really came into existence when the Dayton Company merged with Hudson Company, another department store organization, to form the Dayton-Hudson Company (DHC). Like the Dayton Company, the Hudson Company started in the early 1900s. And also like the Dayton Company, Hudson's founder became successful by replacing bargaining with price marking, and offering return privileges and liberal credit. Target now controls Dayton's and Hudson's stores along with the Target, Mervyn's, and Marshall Field's stores.

By 1971 revenues topped $1 billion, and DHC acquired Mervyn's of California to become the seventh

Minnesota Gov. Jesse Ventura lights the Governor's home with mini-lights donated by Target Stores for Halloween safety. (AP Photo/Dawn Villella)

largest retailer in the United States. During the decade, the Target stores broke new ground for the industry when they implemented electronic cash registers storewide to monitor inventory and speed up service. Target also began hosting an annual shopping event for seniors and people with disabilities.

The 1980s were marked by rapid growth. Revenues in 1982 topped $5 billion. By 1987, that figure doubled.

In 1990, DHC acquired Marshall Field's. By 1994, revenues topped $20 billion. Also during the decade, DHC launched the first Target Greatland store, and its Club Wedd bridal gift registry went nationwide in 1995. In 1996, Target's Mervyn's subsidiary was forced to cut costs or face restructuring. Within its one-year deadline, it replaced 70 percent of its senior management, improved customer services, and reintroduced discontinued product lines such as women's dresses. The efforts paid off and Mervyn's survived.

The decade also saw the opening of the first SuperTarget store, which combined groceries and special services with a Target Greatland store. The Target Guest Card was also introduced during that period. In the meantime, revenues kept climbing. In 1996, they hit $25 billion. In 1998, they reached $30 billion. That same year DHC acquired Rivertown Trading, the direct marketing company. In 1999 the company ventured into e-commerce when www.target.com was launched.

In 2000 DHC changed its name to Target Corporation. Early that same year, target.direct, the direct merchandising and electronic retailing organization of Target Corporation, was launched. The enterprise involved the merging of Target's e-commerce team with its direct merchandising unit into one integrated organization.

STRATEGY

Target Corporation's principal operating strategy is to provide exceptional value to consumers through multiple retail formats ranging from upscale discount and moderately priced to full service department stores. Target's financing strategy is to ensure liquidity and access to capital markets, to manage the amount of floating-rate debt, and to maintain a balanced range of debt maturities.

Target's growth strategy involves achieving average annual earnings per share growth of 15 percent or more over time. Heading into 2001, the company had consistently demonstrated growth. In the previous five years, its earnings per share had increased to around 13 to 15 percent each year. It was expected, by both the company and analysts, that it would achieve 15 to 17 percent growth over the next five years.

FAST FACTS:

About Target Corporation

Ownership: Target Corporation is a publicly owned company traded on the New York Stock Exchange.

Ticker Symbol: TGT

Officers: Robert Ulrich, Chmn. and CEO, 57, 2001 salary $2.2 million; Gerald Storch, VChmn., 44, 2001 salary $1.1 million; Douglas Scovanner, CFO and EVP, 45; Gregg Steinhall, Pres. of Target Stores, 46, 2001 salary $1.6 million; James Hale, VP, Gen. Counsel and Sec., 60

Employees: 281,000

Principal Subsidiary Companies: Target Corporation operates stores under three business divisions including Target, a discount chain with more than 1,000 stores; Mervyn's of California, mid-range department stores; and the Department Store Division, which includes Marshall Field's, Dayton's, and Hudson's. The Target chain includes subsidiaries SuperTarget and Target Greatland. Target Corporation also owns catalog retailer Rivertown Trading and apparel supplier Associated Merchandising Corporation, and it operates an electronic retailing organization, targetdirect.

Chief Competitors: Target Corporation operates in the service sector of the retail industry. Its top competitors include Ames, Federated Department Store, J.C. Penney, Kmart, Kohl's Corporation, Sears & Roebuck, and Wal-Mart.

One of the ways that Target Corporation keeps its revenues and earnings growing is through its commitment to store expansion, which it achieves primarily through its Target and SuperTarget stores. Another way is by setting itself apart from the competition through its differentiated merchandise and its multiple retail segmentation. Target stores offer more upscale merchandise than similar organizations like Wal-Mart or K-Mart. The result is that Target reaches a broader and more affluent consumer base.

Further, the company's e-commerce efforts have helped fuel its growth. At first, Target was reluctant to try and skeptical about the Internet, but by 2001 it was operating seven Web sites that supported store and catalog brands.

9/11 AFTERMATH

Following the September 11, 2001 attack on New York City and subsequent terrorist threats against symbols of U.S. capitalism, Target Corporation announced that it planned on retiring its very recognizable logo: a big red bull's eye.

INFLUENCES

Target's business model combined with its approach has proven to be effective. It has a formula that other retailers wish it would bottle: Target Corporation provides a traditional retail business offering good customer service, and it combines this with excellent financial standing, tremendous growth and profit potential, superb financial ratios, management that is business savvy, and a demonstrated ability to adapt to changing times.

CURRENT TRENDS

Target plans on increasing its number of new stores. At the same time, sales in its existing stores are rising. Industry observers say that this combination will result in even more growth for Target Corporation. The company opened 74 new stores in 2000 and planned on opening about 70 more in 2001, despite a weakened economy. Actually, Target seemed somehow impervious to the country's economic situation. While other large retailers experienced slower sales growth or even negative sales growth, Target Corporation consistently showed gains. Observers reasoned that since Target customers tended to be more affluent than the typical Wal-Mart or Kmart shopper, a national spending downturn didn't impact the corporation too significantly. True, the corporation's other divisions weren't quite as strong as the Target stores, but they still provided the Corporation with access to even more affluent shoppers. This gives Target Corporation a decided advantage over Wal-Mart.

PRODUCTS

Products available in the Target Corporation stores include men's, women's and children's apparel; toys;

---

small appliances; dress, casual and athletic shoes; health and beauty aids; school and office supplies; jewelry and accessories; candy, snacks, and soda; stationery, party home decor and gifts; cameras, phones, and automotive accessories; housewares, commodities, audio and video equipment; hardware, paint, and wallpaper; bicycles, outdoor sports and fitness accessories; music, movies, and books; bath and bedding supplies; rugs; luggage; pet supplies; furniture and lighting; patio and lawn care products; pharmacy services; holiday and seasonal products; and food service.

For the Target stores, the focus is on basic merchandise: the everyday items that consumers use and need most. Products sold include all merchandise categories, from apparel to personal care, and home decor to automotive. The merchandise focus for Marshall Field's is fashion. Mervyn's merchandise focus is on moderately-priced apparel and home fashions.

CORPORATE CITIZENSHIP

Target Corporation has established the Target Foundation to maintain its history of five-percent giving in the Minneapolis/St. Paul metropolitan area. The foundation supports the arts and social services.

Target also established the Family of Giving programs at Target Stores, Marshall Field's, Mervyn's and Target Foundation. The programs support nonprofit organizations in the Minneapolis/St. Paul metropolitan area.

The company has been recognized for its philanthropic efforts. In 1998, it was named one of "America's 25 most generous companies" by *The American Benefactor* magazine. In 1999, it received the American Association of Museums Medal for Distinguished Philanthropy, which honors organizations or people who have made outstanding contributions to museums. It has also been named as one of *Business Ethics* magazine's "100 Best Corporate Citizens."

Target also embraces positive environmental stewardship. Through its environmental initiative, it seeks healthy, long-term corporate growth through energy conservation, increased efficiency, recycling, waste reduction and respect for the ecosystems of the communities its serves.

GLOBAL PRESENCE

Target Corporation's Associated Merchandising Corp (AMC) subsidiary is a global sourcing organization that works with other global sourcing companies to source garments and other goods for the parent company. AMC, which employs 1,200 people, has 27 full-service

CHRONOLOGY:
Target Corporation

1902: George Dayton opens the Goodfellows store in Minneapolis, Minnesota

1910: Goodfellows becomes the Dayton Company

1956: Dayton opens the world's first fully enclosed retail mall

1962: The first target store opens in Roseville, Minnesota

1969: The Dayton Company merges with the Hudson Company to form the Dayton-Hudson Company (DHC)

1971: DHC revenues hit the $1 billion mark

1990: DHC acquires Marshall Fields

1998: DHC acquires Rivertown Trading

1999: DHC goes online

2000: DHC changes its name to Target Corporation

offices, 48 quality-control offices and seven commissionaires around the world.

EMPLOYMENT

Target Corporation is among America's top 20 employers in the private sector, with over 280,000 employees. It has received national recognition for its comprehensive team member benefits, productive work environment, and commitment to diversity. The company provides training, development and advancement, and family-friendly benefit programs. Diversity efforts are monitored by its board of directors.

Each of the organization's three divisions has its own program of human resources policies and benefits, but they all have several common features that include pretax salary set-asides to help pay for dependent care; child care resource and referral information; alternative work arrangements (telecommuting, job-sharing, work-at-home, flextime, part-time); sick leave and pregnancy leave; 401(k) plan and stock option/stock ownership plans; a pharmacy discount program, including mail order access for maintenance prescriptions; a vacation values program; and automobile/homeowners insurance through payroll deduction.

SOURCES OF INFORMATION

Bibliography

Hoover's Online. "Target Corporation Capsule," 10 April 2002. Available at http://www.hoovers.com/co/capsule/0/0,2163, 10440,00.html

Catron, V., Culver, A., Demore, M., et al. "Financial Analysis: Target Corporation," August 2000. Available at http://www .history-=buff.org/Target%20Corporation.ppt

Forbes.com. "Company Details: Target Corporation," 10 April 2002. Available at http://www.forbes.com/finance/mktguideapps/ compinfo/CompanyTearsheet.jhtml?tkr=TGT

U.S. Business Reporter. "Target Corporation Business Description," 2000. Available at http://www.activemedia-guide.com/ pkg_target.htm

Henssler.com. "Target Corporation." *Money Talks with Dr. Gene*, 2001. Available at www.henssler.com/market/equity/topten-stocks/ target.htm

Yahoo! Finance. "Target Corporation," Yahoo! Market Guide, 10 April 2002. Available at http://biz.yahoo.com/p/t/tgt.html

DPI. "Target Corporation Announces Emergency Logo Change." *Susannah's Soap Box*, 2001. Available at http://www.susannas-soapbox.com/nstarget.html

For an annual report:

on the Internet at: http://www.targetcorp.com/targetcorp_group/ investor-relations/investor-relations.jhtml

For additional industry research:

Investigate companies by their Standard Industrial Classification Codes, also known as SICs. Target Corporation's SICs are:

5311 Department Stores

5331 Variety Stores

5651 Family Clothing Stores

5399 Misc. General Merchandise Stores

5961 Mail Order Houses

Also investigate companies by their North American Industry Classification System Codes, also known as NAICS codes. Target Corporation's NAICS codes are:

448140 Family Clothing Stores

452110 Department Stores

452990 All Other General Merchandise Stores

Tenneco Automotive Inc.

OVERVIEW

One of the largest North American manufacturers of shock absorbers, Tenneco Automotive also makes exhaust systems and related parts for automobiles and trucks. The auto parts industry also has two primary sectors: the original equipment sector, which includes parts for new car manufacturers; and the aftermarket parts sector, which includes replacement parts for cars and trucks. Nearly two-thirds of Tenneco Automotive's revenues come from sales to new car manufacturers, while the remaining one-third is secured in the automotive aftermarket.

COMPANY FINANCES

In 1997 Tenneco Automotive held a 25 percent share of the global shocks and mufflers market. The firm sold its products to nearly every original equipment manufacturer in the world, and its sales reached a record $2.94 billion, nearly double the total in 1992. Despite this promising growth, however, Tenneco Automotive's performance since its emergence as an independent public company in November of 1999 has suffered. The newly independent firm has yet to achieve profitability. It posted a $423 million loss on sales of $3.27 billion in 1999. Performance the following year improved a bit as sales grew to $2.54 billion, and the firm's losses diminished to $42 million. Losses increased, however, in 2001 to $130 million as sales fell to $3.36 billion. Stock prices, which reached roughly $10 per share in 2000, had fallen to less than $2 per share by November of 2001.

FOUNDED: 1977

Contact Information:

HEADQUARTERS: 500 North Field Dr.
 Lake Forest, IL 60045
PHONE: (847)482-5000
FAX: (847)482-5940
URL: http://www.tenneco-automotive.com

FINANCES:

*Tenneco Automotive Inc.
Revenues, 1999-2001
(million dollars)*

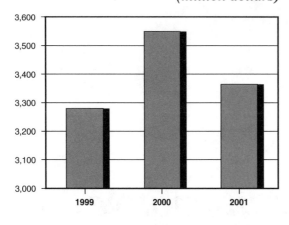

ANALYSTS' OPINIONS

Although recessionary economic conditions were largely to blame for Tenneco Automotive's weak financial performance in 2001, the firm's 1.5 billion debt load, the highest in the industry, also posed problems. The company had inherited the debt when it split from its packaging operations in 1999. According to a December 2001 issue of *Crain's Chicago Business*, "While analysts say the company's brands-Walker mufflers and Monroe shock absorbers-are strong, and the company should bounce back when the economy and auto industry rebound, they agree that the big challenge for Tenneco is to whittle down its debt."

HISTORY

Tenneco Automotive began as part of Tenneco Corp. a conglomerate with interests in everything from oil to shipbuilding. Tenneco Corp. was founded in 1960 to oversee the growing oil and gas subsidiaries of publicly owned Tennessee Gas Transmission Co., which had been created in 1943 to create a 1,200-mile gas pipeline in the United States. In 1961, Tenneco diversified into chemicals with the purchase of Heyden Newport Chemical Corp. and into paperboard and packaging material with the purchase of Packaging Corporation of America. Between 1950 and 1966, Tenneco acquired 22 companies, including Walker Manufacturing and Monroe, both of which would form the core of Tenneco Automotive.

In 1967, Tenneco added farm machinery manufacturer J.I. Case to its holdings. The firm restructured along geographical lines, creating two major divisions: Tenneco West and Tenneco Virginia. The following year, Tenneco Virginia bought Newport News Shipbuilding & Drydock Co. Tenneco continued to grow and diversify, purchasing British chemical company Albright & Wilson Ltd., Philadelphia Life, Southwestern Life Insurance, and Danish company Lydex in the 1970s.

Management thwarted efforts by shareholders to split and sell the firm's several divisions in 1982. Two years later, Tenneco acquired Ecko Housewares and Ecko Products. The farm machinery operations of Navistar were purchased and folded into the Case division in 1985. The following year, Tenneco divested its insurance arm to I.C.H. Corp. In 1991, Tenneco posted record losses of $723 million. Michael Walsh took over as president and launched a $2 billion restructuring plan that included the closing of several plants, the layoff of more than 10,000 employees, and the divestment of several holdings. For example, Tenneco sold its Case farm machinery subsidiary in 1995. That year, the firm also spun off its Albright & Wilson chemicals unit as a public company listed on the London Stock Exchange. The spinoff raised $819 million in fresh capital for Tenneco. Headquarters moved from Houston, Texas, to Greenwich, Connecticut.

To bolster its lucrative plastic packaging and consumer products operations, Tenneco paid $1.27 billion for the plastics division of Mobil Chemical Co. in 1995. However, the firm's divestment efforts continued when El Paso Energy Corp. acquired Tenneco Energy in 1996. By then, Tenneco had decided to focus on two major business segments: packaging and automotive parts. To this end, Tenneco also sold off its shipbuilding operations.

Between 1993 and 1997, Tenneco Automotive doubled its sales, mainly due to its purchase of more than 20 automotive parts suppliers. To cut costs, Tenneco Automotive laid off 1,000 employees and consolidated the management of its two strongest automotive parts brands: Walker and Monroe. In 1998, plans to merge with Tower Automotive Inc. fizzled. That year, Tenneco Inc. announced its intent to split into two separate firms: automotive and packaging. The split was completed in 1999, when Tenneco Automotive Inc. and Pactiv Corp. began trading as independent companies on the New York Stock Exchange.

Among the largest 150 North American automotive parts suppliers, Tenneco Automotive ranked 37th, according to *Automotive News* in 1999. The following year, the firm agreed to jointly manufacture emission control parts and systems with both Futaba Industrial Co. and Tokico Ltd. A sluggish North American economy undercut revenues in 2001. The firm also struggled with a heavy debt burden. Between mid-2000 and early 2002, the firm cut its salaried workforce by 28 percent, which resulted in roughly $62 million in savings. To achieved additional savings, Tenneco Automotive launched cost cutting efforts in early 2002 that included trimming 4 percent of its North American and European work force and shutting down eight plants.

STRATEGY

The split of Tenneco Inc. into two independent companies was a strategic move designed to improve the performance of each company. As a conglomerate, Tenneco Inc. had struggled with heavy debt, bureaucracy, and low profits. Management reasoned that its automotive arm would operate more efficiently as a smaller, independent entity able to focus solely on the automotive parts markets and respond quickly to various market trends.

One of Tenneco Automotive's strategies in the early 2000s was the expansion of international operations, particularly in emerging growth markets. Tenneco's presence in the mature markets of both North America and Western Europe was strong, and the firm wanted to expand into areas where growth looked more promising. According to a March 2001 *PR Newswire* release, "Tenneco Automotive's long-term strategy is to expand its global capabilities through niche acquisitions, joint ventures, and strategic alliances. With the increasing globalization of the automotive industry, the company is strategically expanding its operations in Eastern Europe and emerging markets in order to take advantage of lower operating costs, and to be better positioned to serve its original equipment customers in these growing markets." To this end, despite its desire to cut costs and pare down debt, the firm paid $20 million for a shock absorber manufacturing plant in Poland in 2001.

INFLUENCES

The decision to spin Tenneco Automotive off as an independent company came after Tenneco Inc.'s efforts to sell its automotive arm to Grand Rapids, Michigan-based Tower Automotive Inc. failed. Along with creating a $5 billion auto parts giant, the merger would have allowed Tenneco Automotive to offer a more comprehensive product line by giving it access to Tower's suspension systems. When the two firms were unable to agree on how to best manage the merger, negotiations halted.

CURRENT TRENDS

Traditionally, during periods of economic recession, original equipment demand drops, while sales in the auto-

FAST FACTS:
About Tenneco Automotive Inc.

Ownership: Tenneco Automotive Inc. is a public company traded on the New York Stock Exchange.

Ticker Symbol: TEN

Officers: Mark P. Frissora, Chmn., Pres., and CEO; Mark A. McCollum, SVP and CFO; Timothy R. Donovan, EVP

Employees: 20,000

Principal Subsidiary Companies: Tenneco Automotive Inc. operates 75 plants in more than 20 countries.

Chief Competitors: Major rivals of Tenneco Automotive Inc. include ITT Industries, Lear Corp., Arvin-Meritor Inc., and other manufacturers of automotive parts.

motive aftermarket remain level and frequently strengthen as cost conscious car owners tend to fix and repair their cars rather than buy new. Because Tenneco tended to rely more heavily on the original equipment market, it remained vulnerable to this trend. When the North American economy began to weaken in the early 2000s, the automotive industries there began to feel the pinch. A surplus problem in North America prompted auto manufacturers to shut down assembly plants for days and, in some cases, weeks during the first quarter of 2001. Although automakers were able to maintain sales growth throughout the year with no-interest financing programs, many began slowing production in anticipation of reduced demand in 2002. Consequently, automotive parts players like Tenneco Automotive saw demand for their products slow.

PRODUCTS

Under the Walker and Monroe brand names, Tenneco Automotive manufactures Sensa-Trac and Reflex shocks and struts, Rancho shock absorbers, Walker Quiet Flow Mufflers (first introduced in 1998), DynoMax performance exhaust products, and Monroe Clevite vibration control components. The firm also manufactures catalytic converters, engine mounts, and steering stabilizers.

CHRONOLOGY:

Key Dates for Tenneco Automotive Inc.

1943: Tennessee Gas Transmission Co. is created

1960: Tenneco Corp. is founded to oversee the holdings of Tennessee Gas

1991: Tenneco posts a record losses of $723 million

1996: Tenneco begins to focus on two major segments: packaging and automotive parts

1999: Tenneco splits into two independent companies, one of which is Tenneco Automotive Inc.

FORMER TEXAS GIANT MOVES TO THE NORTHEAST

In the early-1990s, Tenneco Inc was the largest public company in Houston, Texas. After relocating headquarters to Greenwich, Connecticut, and then selling off its Houston-based ship building and energy operations in the mid- to late 1990s, Tenneco Inc. virtually disappeared from Houston.

GLOBAL PRESENCE

Tenneco Automotive began its global expansion efforts in earnest in the mid-1990s. Between 1995 and 1997, Tenneco Automotive spent $1.8 billion on operations in Argentina, Australia, Brazil, China, Czechoslovakia, India, Japan, Mexico, Spain, and Turkey. By 1998, the firm operated 67 plants, offices, or branches in 21 countries. In the early 2000s, Europe accounted for 35 percent of total revenues.

SOURCES OF INFORMATION

Bibliography

Arndorfer, James B. "Tenneco Struggles to Pare Down Debt." *Crain's Chicago Business*, 3 December 2001.

Murphy, Tom. "Aiming High for the 21st Century." *Ward's Auto World*, June 1997.

Richards, Don. "Tenneco, a Houston Force, out of Chemicals, and Town." *Chemical Market Reporter*, 13 January 1997.

Sedgwick, David. "Tenneco Offspring Expected to Survive Parent's Breakup." *Automotive News*, 27 July 1998.

Sherefkin, Robert. "Caution Flag; Tenneco is Lean and Focused, But Analysts Warn of Softening Market." *Automotive News*, 13 November 2000.

Sherefkin, Robert. "Tenneco, Lear Post Losses; Both Will Close Plants." *Automotive News*, 4 February 2002.

Tenneco Automotive Inc. Home Page, 2002. Available at http://www.tenneco-automotive.com.

For an annual report:

on the Internet at: http://www.shareholder.com/tenneco/annual.cfm

For additional industry research:

Investigate companies by their Standard Industrial Classification Codes, also known as SICs. Tenneco Automotive Inc.'s primary SIC is:

3714 Motor Vehicle Parts and Accessories

Also investigate companies by their North American Industrial Classification System codes, also known as NAICS codes. Tenneco Automotive Inc.'s primary NAICS code is:

336399 All Other Motor Vehicle Parts Manufacturing

Tiffany & Co.

FOUNDED: 1837

OVERVIEW

Founded more than 160 years ago and the nation's preeminent jeweler for more than 50 years, Tiffany & Co. is a uniquely American symbol of elegance and style. Tiffany pioneered what would become a classic engagement ring style, the raised solitaire diamond, six-prong "Tiffany Setting." Tiffany has catered to everyone from the likes of Presidents, including Abraham Lincoln and John F. Kennedy; European royalty; preeminent American families, including the Vanderbilts and the Astors; and various celebrities. The company's trademarked Tiffany Blue Boxes and shopping bags have become familiar and enduring American icons of wealth and luxury to this day.

Tiffany & Co.'s main product lines are fine jewelry, timepieces, sterling silver goods, crystal, china, writing instruments, fragrances, and personal accessories. Jewelry accounts for a majority of the company's sales, at 78 percent in fiscal 2000. Tiffany's products can be acquired through its three areas of distribution: the company's 125 branch stores in the United States and worldwide, its trademarked Tiffany blue catalog, and the company's Web site, which offers about 1,350 products. Marketing, merchandising, distribution, and customer service are the keys to the company's growth. Product development is an important part of that strategy, introducing new products such as the Lucida diamond engagement ring, three-stone rings, and band rings, and distributing them worldwide in 2000. Tiffany's long-standing mission has to be being "the world's most respected jewelry retailer" and key beliefs are what drive the company's strategy. These beliefs include that Tiffany is not just a brand name, but a physical location

Contact Information:
HEADQUARTERS: 600 Madison Ave.
   New York, NY 10022
PHONE: (212)755-8000
FAX: (212)230-6633
URL: http://www.tiffany.com

therein lies the secret of their longevity and sustainability. Tiffany is about things that last."

FINANCES:

Tiffany & Co.
Net Sales, 1998-2001
(million dollars)

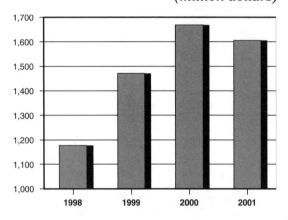

Tiffany & Co.
2000 Stock Prices
(dollars)

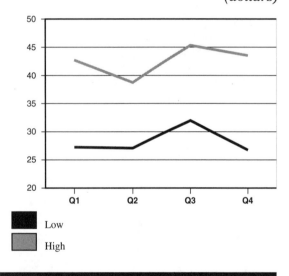

COMPANY FINANCES

Tiffany & Co. brand jewelry accounts for more than 75 percent of the company's sales. Tiffany's flagship Fifth Avenue store in New York accounted for approximately 12 percent of the company's sales in 2000. U.S. retail sales as a whole, at $833.2 million, made up 50 percent of the company's total net sales of $1.66 billion in 2000. Worldwide, net sales totaled $679.2 million and accounted for 41 percent of Tiffany's total net sales, with Japan representing about 28 percent of net sales Tiffany that made internationally in 2000. Direct marketing made up the remaining 9 percent of total net sales that year at $155.5 million. The company's sales dipped by 3.7 percent in 2001, ending the year at $1.60 billion, with net income also decreasing nearly 9 percent to $173.6 million.

Domestic sales increased 12 percent in 2000 and 25 percent in 1999. Similarly, international retail sales rose 15 percent in 2000 and 27 percent in 1999. Net earnings rose 31 percent in 2000 and have grown at a 37 percent compound annual growth rate in the past five years. Tiffany stock ranged from a low of $19.90 to a high of $39.01 over a 52-week period. The annual dividend was four cents per share and Tiffany's price-earnings ratio was 31. The company estimates that it will experience moderate 2002 growth of five to nine percent in 2002.

ANALYSTS' OPINIONS

The year 2000 saw the company raise the quarterly dividend rate for the fifth consecutive year. Due to the company's past success and favorable outlook, Tiffany & Co. was added to Standard & Poor's S&P 500 Index. Despite the challenging economic climate for high end businesses in 2001, several analysts remained positive on Tiffany stock. Merrill Lynch recommended the stock in a January 2002 report, believing that the company will perform better than other high-end retailers, noting the company's variety of products at various prices, its strong brand positioning, healthy Japanese sales, and its emphasis on expanding its watch collection. Lehman Brothers reported that due to Tiffany's better than expected 2001 holiday sales and continued positive outlook, the company would raise its earnings estimates for early 2002. Salomon Smith Barney similarly raised its earning estimates for Tiffany due to its 2001 holdiay sales, its plans to open three additional stores in 2002, and a new jewelry-only store model that would bring higher sales per square foot. Morgan Stanley maintained its Neutral rating on the company, citing a slowdown in tourist sales,

where customers can experience products in person and experience excellent service. More than just a retailer, Tiffany is also a manufacturing jeweler, with craftsmanship and design at the core of the business and serving as the competitive edge. As a product-driven company, Tiffany believes that the product is the "hero," and its blue box a representation of the company's unwavering focus on products of superior quality, value, and design. Finally, the company also believes that the superiority of its products and service drive its success. To that point, the company's 2000 annual report states, "Our strategies have never been about fashion or luxury or excess. And

a drop in Japanese sales, and a recent run-up in shares, as reasons.

HISTORY

On September 18, 1837, with a thousand dollars borrowed from his father, Tiffany and friend John B. Young opened Tiffany & Young at 259 Broadway in New York City. The store originally sold stationery supplies and fancy goods, including costume jewelry. Business conditions were less than ideal at the time with the Panic of 1837 and some thought the company's uptown location would be bad for patronage. The first three days of sales totaled $4.98, but after that rocky start, the business soon took off. Tiffany's store was unique for its time, offering fixed prices on items, thus removing the bartering process. The company also refused to extend credit to customers, which had become a problem for many businesses of the day. By 1839 Tiffany added glassware, cutlery, porcelain, and clocks to the company's line of products.

The company soon had a new partner, J. L. Ellis, and then became known as Tiffany, Young & Ellis. With the funds Ellis brought to the firm, the company was able to rent the adjoining room, doubling its floor space. Ellis, who brought strong experience in the European jewelry market, became the company's chief overseas operator after his buying trip to the Continent. In 1844 the company was importing quality Italian and English jewelry, adding to its already well-respected reputation. That year the company discontinued its costume jewelry line as demand for the imported gems escalated along with their reputation for offering expensive, quality pieces. The company, which focused very little on gems at the time, published its first catalogue in 1845 that some speculate was the country's first mail-order catalogue.

The company's trademark shade of robin's egg blue was also established during the early years of the company and appeared on all company catalogues, shopping bags, boxes, and promotional materials. Regarding the now familiar Tiffany Blue boxes, the company's Web site quoted a 1906 article in the *The New York Sun:* "Tiffany has one thing in stock that you cannot buy of him for as much money as you may offer; he will only give it to you. And that is one of his boxes. The rule of the establishment is ironclad, never to allow a box bearing the name of the firm, to be taken out of the building except with an article which has been sold by them and for which they are responsible." The tradition has continued to this day, with the Tiffany Blue boxes becoming a symbol of elegance and sophistication.

In 1847 the company also began selling silverware. The following year, the company benefited from revolutionary movements in Europe, enabling Tiffany's to acquire historic European jewels from important aristocrats over the next several decades, including some of

FAST FACTS:
About Tiffany & Co.

Ownership: Tiffany & Co. is a publicly owned company traded on the New York Stock Exchange.

Ticker Symbol: TIF

Officers: William R. Chaney, Chmn., 68; Michael J. Kowalski, Pres. and CEO, 49; James E. Quinn, VChmn., 49; Beth O. Canavan, EVP, 46; James N. Fernandez, EVP and CFO, 45; Victoria Berger-Gross, SVP, Human Resources, 45; Patrick B. Dorsey, SVP, Gen. Counsel and Sec., 50; Linda A. Hanson, SVP, Merchandising, 40; Fernanda M. Kellogg, SVP, Public Relations, 54; Caroline D. Naggiar, SVP, Marketing, 43; John S. Petterson, SVP, Direct Marketing, 42

Employees: 5,960

Principal Subsidiary Companies: Tiffany & Co. operates approximately 125 branch stores in the United States, Canada, Mexico, Europe, Japan, and elsewhere worldwide.

Chief Competitors: Tiffany & Co. competes with other jewelers and retailers based on quality and value, unlike companies who compete mainly through advertised price promotion. Competition from other companies is significant throughout all of Tiffany's brands, some who specialize in just one area of Tiffany's many product lines. Some of Tiffany's main competitors include Rolex, Bulgari, and Cartier.

crown jewels from the French Empire in 1887 when the pressed dubbed Tiffany the "King of Diamonds." After the European acquisitions, the company's reputation greatly broadened. In 1850 Tiffany opened another store in Paris and hired John C. Moore, a silversmith, to craft silverware exclusive to Tiffany's and also began manufacturing gold jewelry, aided by the California gold strike in 1850. Tiffany was the first U.S. company to use the 925 parts silver per thousand standard for sterling that later became the United States Sterling Standard. The company underwent another reorganization when Tiffany's partners, Young and Ellis, retired and, in 1853, the company was renamed Charles L. Tiffany & Company. Tiffany had a huge statue of Atlas beneath a clock installed at the company's new headquarters at 550 Broadway. The statue, which moved three more times,

CHRONOLOGY:

Key Dates for Tiffany & Co.

1837: Charles Lewis Tiffany and John Young established Tiffany & Young

1845: Tiffany's published its first catalogue

1850: Began making silverware exclusive to Tiffany's

1853: Company renamed Tiffany & Co. after his partners retire

1867: First American firm to win an award for its silverware at the Paris Exposition

1878: Purchased the 128.54 carat Tiffany Diamond

1886: Introduced the "Tiffany Setting"

1887: Acquired some of the French Crown jewels

1905: Tiffany & Co. moves to Fifth Ave. and 37th in New York, which became a National Landmark in 1978

1926: Tiffany's platinum became the official standard for all platinum in the United States

1940: Tiffany makes its final move to its current location at Fifth Ave. and 57th in New York

1969: The company introduced Tanzanite, a unique blue gemstone, to the world

1986: Tiffany goes public on the New York Stock Exchange

1999: Tiffany creates the Lucida engagement ring

---

may still be seen above the company's Fifth Avenue store entrance.

Tiffany was skilled in promotion, and steered the company to further growth throughout the rest of the 1850s. Tiffany was able to generate publicity for his company in association with P.T. Barnum on several occasions. Once he crafted a special jeweled horse and carriage as a wedding gift for the marriage of Barnum's Tom Thumb. The most publicized promotional event occurred in 1858 when Tiffany's sold sections of the first transatlantic cable as souvenirs; this generated so much interest that the police were called to keep frenzied buyers in line. In 1861 Tiffany was hired to design a presentational pitcher for the inauguration of President Abraham Lincoln. President Lincoln later gifted wife Mary Todd Lincoln with a seed-pearl jewelry suite from Tiffany's.

In support of the Union forces during the ensuing Civil War, Tiffany manufactured patriotic items, including flags, medals, surgical implements, and swords, and he allowed his store to serve as a depot for military supplies. Tiffany also designed jewel-encrusted presentation swords for Generals Grant and Sherman. After the war, the company, which was incorporated in 1868, opened a London store that year. Tiffany, who served as the company's president and treasurer, also found a building for its New York operations on Fifth Avenue after several other sites were tried. In addition to jewelry, the company also then began producing clocks and watches.

As the company's reputation for quality and excellence grew, Tiffany attracted more than 20 crowned heads of state among its worldwide range of customers. In 1867 Tiffany's was the first American company to win the gold medal for jewelry and the grand prize for silverware at the Paris Exposition. The company opened a factory in Newark, New Jersey, which produced Tiffany's silverware, stationery, and leather goods. Tiffany-designed copper, silver, and niello pitchers were acquired by the Boston Museum of Fine Arts, the first of many of the company's designs currently in museum collections worldwide. Charles Tiffany continued to enhance his company's reputation by acquiring the 128.54 carat fancy yellow Tiffany Diamond in 1878, one of the largest diamonds of its kind in the world. It was later worn by Audrey Hepburn in publicity photos for the 1961 movie classic, *Breakfast at Tiffany's*. The gem can be seen to this day on the first floor of Tiffany's Fifth Avenue store.

Innovative jewelry design became a Tiffany trademark early on. The 6-prong diamond solitaire engagement ring was created using the "Tiffany Setting," which raised the stone up from the setting, thus allowing the maximum amount of light to set off the diamond's brilliance. Tiffany's son, Louis Comfort Tiffany, established a special department within the company called Tiffany Art Jewelry in 1902.

Charles Tiffany died of pneumonia on February 18, 1902, in Yonkers, New York. At the time of his death, his personal fortune was valued at $35 million and the company was capitalized at $2.4 million. Son Louis took the position of vice president and artistic director of Tiffany & Co. after his father's death and became an accomplished jeweler in addition to the fame he would later acquire for designing stained glass.

In 1905 the store moved again, to a sixteenth century Venetian-style building on Fifth Avenue at 37th, which later became a National Landmark in 1978. In 1940 the company moved its New York headquarters to its own building, designed by Cross & Cross, on Fifth Avenue and 57th Street, where it exists today. The company, which went public on the New York Stock Exchange in 1986, continued after Tiffany's death to set standards in the jewelry industry: In 1926 Tiffany's platinum became official standard for all platinum in the United States; the company introduced Tanzanite, a unique blue gemstone to the world in 1969; and the company innovated a new engagement ring, the Lucida, with a patented cut in 1999.

STRATEGY

The company's ongoing strategy is to open three to five new U.S. stores per year and open stores in selected locations internationally. Tiffany is also renovating its Manhattan store throughout a three-year period to increase selling space by 25 percent. To ensure ongoing quality, Tiffany plans to expand internal manufacturing and develop existing relationships with external suppliers with the goal of maintaining a healthy product development program and support the distribution of existing products.

Tiffany makes use of a wide variety of channels to reach prospective customers, including advertisements in magazines, newspapers, television, catalogs, and the Internet in order to ensure that they go to Tiffany for luxury products and a superior shopping experience. Through these advertisements, Tiffany seeks to communicate the relevance of the company and its products in the consumer's life. Promotional activities remain an important aspect of Tiffany's business in order to maintain consumer awareness. The company's annual *Blue Book* displays Tiffany fine jewelry and other wares; its New York store's window displays aid in the company's promotional efforts; and Tiffany Design Director John Loring has authored several books featuring the company's products. The company spent approximately $65 million on worldwide advertising in 2000.

INFLUENCES

Since *Breakfast at Tiffany's*, the 1961 movie that prominently featured the company, Tiffany has continued to reap promotional benefits through the medium of film. The company's new Tiffany Lace collection of platinum and diamond jewelry was exclusively worn by movie star Julia Roberts in the 2001 film *Ocean's Eleven*. Other Tiffany accessories, including a watch and cuff links from the Tiffany Atlas collection, were worn by the another of the film's stars, Andy Garcia. The company has also expanded its Internet product selection, enhanced the site's overall functionality, and created an online bridal registry.

CURRENT TRENDS

To focus wholly on company-operated stores and increase profitablity, Tiffany has eliminated wholesale trade and fragrance distribution, including the sale of its products in department stores and non-company-owned jewelers in the United States and Europe. Tiffany's goal is to distribute only through company-operated stores in significant markets and through direct selling. In keeping with that decision, Tiffany plans to open three to five new stores in the United States each year, as well as one to two new locations per year, and expanding or renovating existing stores in Japan, along with opening additional stores worldwide. Plans for 2002 included opening stores Bellvue, Washinton; St. Louis, Missouri; and Orlando, Florida. Tiffany's will also open a large jewelry manufacturing center in Rhode Island in order to meet future demand for products.

PRODUCTS

In addition to the wide variety of Tiffany brand jewelry, the company offers products in various categories, including timepieces and clocks; sterling silver products, including flatware, hollowware, trophies, key holders, picture frames, and desk accessories; stainless steel flatware; crystal, china, glassware, and tableware; writing instruments; custom engraved stationery; and fashion accessories. The company also sells other brands of tableware and timepieces in the United States and is the sole licensee for jewelry designed by Paloma Picasso, Elsa Peretti, and Jean Schlumberger. Fragrances include Tiffany, Trueste, and Tiffany for Men. The company also sells a line of commercial glassware under the Judel trademark.

The 2000 Lucida three-stone and band rings were created to build on U.S. success of the 1999 Lucida engagement ring, and its distribution was extended worldwide. The Streamerica and Petal jewelry collections, Palladium dinnerware, and the company's first stainless steel flatware collection were also introduced in 2000. To commemorate the twentieth anniversary of Tiffany's relationship with Paloma Picasso, a new line of her designs were launched that year. In 2001 the Tiffany Lace collection was featured in the film *Ocean's Eleven,* worn by star Julia Roberts. The line was inspired by designs from the company's archives, including necklaces designed by Louis Comfort Tiffany from 1906-1910.

CORPORATE CITIZENSHIP

Tiffany believes that its company image benefits from its charity sponsorships, grants, and merchandise donations. The Tiffany & Co. Foundation is a private foundation designed to support other charitable organizations with a focus on the preservation and conservation of the arts.

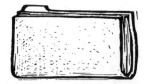

DIAMONDS ARE A GIRL'S BEST FRIEND

Although Holly Golightly might not have gotten the Tiffany diamond she craved, film legend Audrey Hepburn, who played the character in the 1961 film, *Breakfast at Tiffany's*, was indeed lucky enough to wear not just *a* Tiffany diamond, but *the* Tiffany Diamond, albeit briefly, during a publicity shoot for the movie. The Tiffany Diamond, discovered in the Kimberley diamond mines in South Africa in 1877, is among the world's largest fancy yellow diamonds. Purchased by Charles Lewis Tiffany in 1878, it may be seen today on the first floor of Tiffany's flagship Fifth Avenue store in New York. The rough diamond crystal was 287.42 carats before it was cut into a cushion-shaped brilliant diamond, weighing in at 128.51 carats and featuring 90 facets—which exceeds the facets of a traditional brilliant-cut stone by 32 facets.

GLOBAL PRESENCE

With international sales accounting for 41 percent of Tiffany's 2000 total sales of $1.66 billion and Japan representing about 28 percent of net sales made internationally in 2000, Tiffany believes that the name Tiffany & Co. is known internationally. Although Tiffany operated retail outlets in London and Paris before World War II, the company did not re-establish stores in Europe post-war until 1986 and accordingly, awareness of the brand is not as high as in the United States or Japan. As of 2000 the company had approximately 42 U.S. stores, 4 in Canada and Mexico, 8 in Mexico, 44 in Japan, and 21 elsewhere. Leading Japanese department store Mitsukoshi and Mitsukoshi operated 27 of Tiffany's boutiques there, and the success of the somewhat declining department store industry in Japan will have a major impact on Tiffany's growth in that country. Tiffany plans to continue to open stores internationally. Plans for 2001 included opening three new boutiques in Japan, one in Melbourne, Australia, one in Sao Paulo, Brazil, one store in Rome and one new London store.

EMPLOYMENT

Tiffany employs approximately 5,950 full- and part-time personnel, with 4,932 located in the United States. Salaried employees numbered 2,250; 572 persons were employed in manufacturing; and 2,887 were employed in retail stores. No Tiffany employees are represented by a union.

SOURCES OF INFORMATION

Bibliography

"About Tiffany." *Tiffany & Co.*, 2002. Available at http://www.tiffany.com.

"Tiffany & Co." Gale Group, 2002. Available at http://www.galenet.galegroup.com.

"Tiffany & Co." *Hoover's Online*, March 2002. Available at http://www.hoovers.com.

"Tiffany & Co. Adorns Ocean's Eleven Star Julia Roberts in Dazzling Jewels Including New Tiffany Lace." *Business Wire*, 6 December 2001.

"Tiffany Announces Plans to Open Stores in Bellevue, St. Louis, and Orlando." *Business Wire*, 8 January 2002.

For an annual report:

on the Internet at: http://www.tiffany.com **or** write: Tifffany & Co., 727 Fifth Ave., New York, NY 10022

For additional industry research:

Investigate companies by their Standard Industrial Classification Codes, also known as SICs. Tiffany & Co.'s primary SIC is:

5944 Jewelry Stores

Also investigate companies by their North American Industry Classification System codes, also known as NAICS codes. Tiffany & Co.'s primary NAICS code is:

448310 Jewelry Stores

The Topps Company

OVERVIEW

The Topps Company, or Topps as it is commonly known, produces a broad array of candy, comic books, and trading cards. Originally produced for children, Topps trading cards—especially baseball, football, basketball, and hockey cards—now appeal just as much to adult collectors. With a price tag of nearly $10 a pack, some Topps trading cards are marketed specifically with the adult buyer in mind. Some Topps cards, like the 1952 Mickey Mantle card, are now highly sought after collector's items worth tens of thousands of dollars.

The Topps Company is divided into three main production segments, confectionery, collectible sports products, and entertainment products. The confectionery division manufactures a variety of non-chocolate candy products aimed primarily at the children's market. Topps' candy brands include lollipops such as Ring Pop, Push Pop, and Baby Bottle Pop, and what is arguably the company's most famous candy, Bazooka Bubble Gum. In 2000 Topps began marketing Pokemon products under license from Nintendo of America. They include Pokemon Pops, Pokemon Popzoids, and Pokemon Treasure Pops. Topps also sells seasonal lines of candy as well as novelty candies. Topps' collectible sports products include its annual lines of trading cards that feature pictures of athletes from Major League Baseball, the National Football League, the National Basketball Association, and the National Hockey League. By 2001 Topps was producing more than 10 lines of baseball cards, including brands such as Bowman, Bowman Chrome, Bowman's Best, Bowman Reserve, Topps Chrome, Topps Finest, Topps Gallery, Topps Gold

FOUNDED: 1938
VARIANT NAME: Topps

Contact Information:
HEADQUARTERS: One Whitehall Street
    New York, NY 10004-2109
PHONE: (212)376-0300
FAX: (212)376-0573
URL: http://www.topps.com

FINANCES:

The Topps Company Net Sales, 1998-2001 (million dollars)

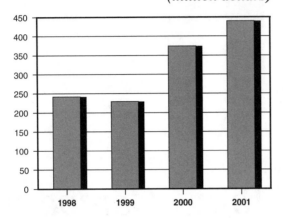

The Topps Company, 2001 Stock Prices (dollars)

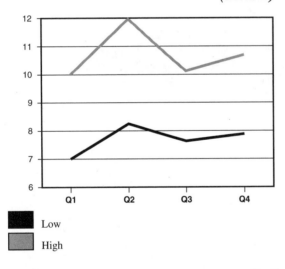

Label, Topps Heritage, Topps Stadium Club, and the traditional Topps line. The Etopps line, introduced in 2001, is available only through the Topps Web site. Sports trading cards are sold in packs whose cost ranges from $.99 to $7.00. Full series can also be purchased. The entertainment products segment produces trading cards and sticker albums based on current films, television programs, comic books, musical celebrities, and the like. Topps also develops its own lines of comic characters for stickers and cards, such as Wacky Packs and Garbage Pail Kids.

COMPANY FINANCES

The Topps Company's sales nearly doubled between 1999 and 2001, rising from $229.41 million to $439.27 million. This growth followed a series of declines in the late 1990s, which also saw the company's net income sink into the red. Income has also recovered in the meantime, climbing from $15.57 million for 1999 to $88.49 million for 2001, an increase of more than 500 percent. The Topps Company's stock ranged from a low of $7.63 in the third quarter of 2001 to a high of $10.69 in the fourth quarter. The stock earned $1.97 net per share in 2001, up from only $0.34 two years earlier.

Despite the firm's public image, sports trading cards were Topps' lowest selling segment in 2001. The company's confectionery products led in sales with $172.53 million, about 39 percent of the total. Entertainment products followed with $143.82 million or almost 33 percent of the total. This represented a mighty surge for Topps' entertainment segment—in 1999 its sales were a mere $9.32 million. The increase was due to the overwhelming success of Topps' Pokemon cards and stickers in both the United States and Europe. Collectible sports products, mainly trading cards, brought up the rear with $122.92 million, down about 8 percent.

ANALYSTS' OPINIONS

As 2002 began, analysts were skeptical about Topps' near term prospects. At the beginning of the year, sales of Topps' Pokemon products had plunged by close to 95 percent from the previous year, which resulted in large declines for both the entertainment and confectionery segments. Those losses merely segued with problems in other areas of the company. As a Value Line report put it in February 2002, "Topps doesn't have much to cheer about. The collectibles division continues its downward trend as the traditional card collecting business seems to have reached a plateau, and perhaps entered a contractionary cycle. As the company tries to ramp up demand by offering autographs and other value-added materials, costs have risen sharply, thus putting even more pressure on margins. Confectionery sales are holding up, though. Ring Pop and Push Pop products have been drawing greater demand from consumers." Valueline considered etopps, the company's online offering, a step in the right direction, but inadequate to turn the firm's fortunes around—at least in the short term.

HISTORY

The Topps Chewing Gum Company was founded in Brooklyn in 1938 by four brothers, Abram, Ira, Philip, and Joseph Shorin. Starting out with regular chewing gum, it was not until after World War II that the company introduced its most famous and successful product, Bazooka Bubble Gum. From 1953, comics that could be redeemed for premiums were included with each piece of gum. Over the years, almost 700 different comic gags were written for the comics. They are recycled every seven years or so.

A milestone occurred in 1947 with the hiring of Sy Berger. On Berger's initiative, Topps began producing baseball trading cards in 1951. The following year, it released its first major set, the legendary 1952 series. At that time, Topps was going head to head with another baseball card maker, the Bowman Gum Company, to sign major league players to annual trading card contracts. By 1956, when Topps acquired Bowman, it had established itself as the clear leader in baseball cards. By 1957 Topps had added football, basketball, and hockey cards as well. For 20 years, Topps enjoyed a virtual monopoly in the trading card field. In 1975, Fleer brought suit against Topps, claiming that its exclusive contracts with players violated antitrust laws. Topps was found guilty in U.S. District Court, and it was enjoined from enforcing the exclusivity clauses in its contracts with athletes.

Topps continued to expand its confectionery line over the years, adding grape, strawberry shake, and sugarless flavors of Bazooka Bubble Gum. Ring Pops (a lollipop that is worn on the finger) were introduced in 1977, while Push Pops hit the market in 1986. Since they were launched in 1998, Baby Bottle Pops (a bottle of powdered candy topped with a lollipop nipple) have been one of Topps best selling candy items.

Topps was acquired in a management-led buyout in 1984, and three years later made its first public stock offering. At the same time, it changed its name to The Topps Company Inc. The company reported sales of $268 million the following year, with about 69 percent coming from the sale of sports cards. By 2001, that percentage had dropped to about 28 percent. In 1995 Topps acquired Merlin Publishing International Limited, a company that produces sticker albums. Called Topps Europe since March 1997, the subsidiary continues to market stickers and albums featuring players from various European soccer leagues. In the late 1990s, the company stepped up Far Eastern distribution of its confectionery products. In 2000, in cooperation with Nintendo of America, Topps introduced a Pokemon line of candy and trading cards, products that gave a significant boost to the sales of Topps Entertainment segment in 2000 and 2001.

STRATEGY

In its early years, Topps marketed its products—especially Bazooka Bubble Gum and its packs of baseball cards—to children. By 2000, the company still saw children as its primary customers, calling itself "a serious player in the kids' candy market" in its 2001 annual report. It designs its candy products specifically to appeal to kids;

FAST FACTS:
About The Topps Company

Ownership: The Topps Company is a publicly owned company traded on the NASDAQ Stock Exchange.

Ticker Symbol: TOPP

Officers: Arthur T. Shorin, Chmn., Pres., and CEO, 65, 2001 base salary $838,082; Ronald L. Boyum, VP Marketing and Sales and GM Confectionery, 49, 2001 base salary $277,308; Scott A. Silverstein, EVP, 39, 2001 base salary $245,692

Employees: 420

Principal Subsidiary Companies: The Topps Company's European subsidiary, Topps Europe Ltd., makes stickers and albums that feature players from major European soccer leagues. Topps also has subsidiaries in Canada, Brazil, and Argentina.

Chief Competitors: The Topps Company competes with other firms primarily engaged in making confectionery products and trading cards. Some primary competitors include Fleer/Skybox International, Donruss Trading Cards Inc., and Spangler Candy Company.

it makes an effort to get its candy products into stores where kids are likely to see them; and, its TV advertising is produced with the children's audience in mind.

In its sports collectibles area, however, Topps has oriented itself increasingly to adults collectors who make up 70 percent of the market for trading cards and frequently purchase them with an eye toward their future value. During the 1990s, Topps issued a number of new lines of trading cards, whose design and pricing—some as high as $7 a pack—were geared specifically toward the adult collector. Ironically, the trading cards were originally conceived as an incentive to for kids to buy Topps bubble gum. However, in 1992, the gum was discontinued at the behest of collectors who complained that it marred the cards, rendering them less collectible.

INFLUENCES

The Topps Company is greatly influenced by changes in popular culture and it must carefully plan new

CHRONOLOGY:

Key Dates for The Topps Company

1938: The Topps Chewing Gum Company was founded in Brooklyn New York

1947: Topps introduces Bazooka Bubble Gum

1951: Topps produces its first set of baseball cards

1953: Topps includes comics with Bazooka Bubble Gum for the first time

1975: Fleer sues Topps for antitrust practices and as a result Topps is forbidden from signing players to exclusive contracts

1984: Topps acquired in management buyout

1987: Topps makes first public offering of stock on NASDAQ national market

1992: Gum no longer included with trading cards

1995: Topps acquires Merlin Publishing International Limited

2000: Topps introduces its Pokemon line

THE TOPPS 1952 SET

Topps released its first baseball cards—two 52-card sets called the Blue Backs and Red Backs—in 1951. But it was with the release of Topps' first major set the following year that the company hit stride. The 1952 Topps set, which consisted of 407 cards with hand-colored black and white photos, is now the most coveted set of baseball cards of all times. A 1952 Mickey Mantle rookie card reputedly sold for $49,000; a complete 1952 set in near-mint condition is listed at $62,000. But it wasn't always that way. Despite the initial popularity of the series, at the end of the 1952 season, a large number of unsold packs languished in Topps' warehouse. For much of the next decade, Topps tried to sell them off. By 1959 demand was so low that Topps couldn't sell ten of the cards for a penny. A decision was made to get rid of the old 1952 cards rather than have them clog the warehouse. As a result approximately 500 cases of 1952 Topps baseball cards were loaded onto a barge, hauled out to sea, and dumped in the Atlantic Ocean. Those cards would have been worth millions of dollars today!

product releases (especially in its trading card lines) to coincide with the narrow window of popularity generated by current movies and television programs. Like yesterday's newspaper, a box of trading cards for a movie just out of circulation seems old and pointless. For example, Topps' Pokemon products, the company's best-selling line in 2000 and 2001, had worn out its welcome by the end of 2001, and sales dropped by 95 percent. The products developed to replace it—series based on films such as *Planet of the Apes*, *Lord of the Rings*, *Jurassic Park III*, and Marvel comic book superheroes—didn't come near to matching Pokemon's earlier popularity. Collectors of Topps sports cards also continuously demand new and different products. By 2001, the firm had no fewer than 12 lines of baseball cards, including its new, Internet-only etopps line.

of-a-kind collectible items from its business files, including contracts and cancelled checks to players, signature cards, and the original photos used on cards. Around the same time, it brought out a new line of sports cards, Etopps, also in cooperation with eBay. Etopps is modeled on a stock market, right down to making IPOs, in this case Initial Player Offerings. Etopps cards can only be purchased online for a limited period of time; they are only sold individually, not in packs. The price of a card depends on the particular player and estimated demand. After a purchase Topps will ship all or part of the order to a collector. Collectors can also opt to establish a "portfolio" at Topps. The company stores the cards in its own vaults, guaranteeing their mint condition if the owner wants to sell them later on the Etopps trading floor at eBay. Etopps was expected to expand the market for trading cards by drawing in participants in other online sports activities, such as rotisserie league baseball. Etopps is essentially open only to adult collectors since buyers must have a credit card.

CURRENT TRENDS

In the 2000s, Topps began using the Internet in unique ways to create new avenues for marketing sport collectible items. In March 2001, for example, the company initiated a series of unique auctions on eBay: one-

PRODUCTS

Through the years, Topps has kept up a constant search for new ideas to add to its trading card line.

Besides its sports cards from baseball, football, basketball, and hockey, the company has produced successful sets of cards with images from movies, television, and comics. They have ranged from *Hopalong Cassidy*, *Bring 'Em Back Alive*, and *Davey Crockett* sets in the early 1950s to Marvel Superheroes, Pokemon, *Star Wars*, and *Lord of the Rings* in the 2000s. A more unusual set, "Enduring Freedom" was released following the terrorist attacks on the World Trade Center and the Pentagon. It chronicled many of the events and personalities connected with the attacks: New York Mayor Rudolf Giuliani, the American flag, an F-117 stealth fighter, White House National Security adviser Condoleezza Rice, even Osama Bin Laden—whose card, Topps CEO Arthur Shorin said, could be stamped on or ripped apart. To avoid possible controversy, there were no images of the attacks themselves. However, a card that portrayed Yasser Arafat giving blood drew fairly bitter complaints nonetheless. Topps said it hoped the cards would help educate children about the attacks. A portion of the sales was donated to the WTC relief fund.

GLOBAL PRESENCE

Topps gradually extended its market internationally, until by 2001 it distributed its products in 60 countries and about half of all sales were made outside the United States. In 1995 it acquired a U.K. company, Merlin Publishing International Limited, which two years later was renamed Topps Europe. Topps Europe produces collectible stickers and albums. Topps has negotiated licenses with two major U.K. soccer leagues, the Premier League Soccer and England National Soccer, as well as with some Italian soccer leagues. Soccer stickers and albums are sold in Europe and in Asia under both the Merlin and Topps brands. In 2001 the sticker products were produced in conjunction with an Italian company. In 2000 and 2001, Topps' candy made inroads in Asian markets, particularly Japan.

EMPLOYMENT

Topps employed about 420 workers in 7 countries in 2001. In addition to employees in its various produc-

tion facilities, photos of athletes used on the trading cards are taken by company and freelance photographers. Graphics work on trading cards is performed both by in-house artists as well as by design agencies contracted for specific projects.

SOURCES OF INFORMATION

Bibliography

"50 Years of Topps." *Tuff Stuff presents Topps*, 2001.

Joseph, Dave. "He's Topps in His Trade." *Newsday*, 24 July 2001, A54.

Sindrich, Jackie. "Topps Turns Attack into Trading Cards." *San Diego Union-Tribune*, 9 November 2001, E7.

The Topps Company Home Page, 2002. Available at http://www.topps.com.

"The Topps Company, Inc." *Hoover's Company Profiles*, 2002. Available at http://www.hoovers.com.

Wadler, Joyce. "Now (Still) Cleaning Up: Topps Company." *New York Times*, 27 October 2000, B2.

For an annual report:

write: The Topps Company, One Whitehall Street, New York, NY 10004-2109

For additional industry research:

Investigate companies by their Standard Industrial Classification Codes, also known as SICs. The Topps Company's primary SICs are:

2064 Candy and Other Confectionery Products

2067 Chewing Gum

2759 Commercial Printing, Not Elsewhere Classified

Also investigate companies by their North American Industry Classification System codes, also known as NAICS codes. The Topps Company's primary NAICS codes are:

311330 Confectionery Manufacturing from Purchased Chocolate

311340 Nonchocolate Confectionery Manufacturing

323119 Other Commercial Printing

Travelocity.com Inc.

FOUNDED: 1996

Contact Information:

HEADQUARTERS: 15100 Trinity Blvd.
   Fort Worth, TX 76155
PHONE: (817)785-8000
URL: http://www.travelocity.com

OVERVIEW

Travelocity.com Inc. is the Internet's leading travel service provider and the sixth-largest travel agency in North America, offering bargains, one-stop shopping, and reservations on plane travel through more than 700 airlines, some 55,000 hotels, more than 50 rental car companies, 8 major cruise lines, and more than 6,500 vacation packages. Other travel features include MapQuest, Frommers, Lonely Planet, World Travel Guide, Meterologix, and an online video library on many vacation destinations.

The Travelocity.com site is offered in English, German, and French and, in addition to serving the United States, the company also offers Web sites tailored to customers in Canada, the United Kingdom, Asia, and Europe. Although competitor Orbitz, a consortium of airlines joined to provide online airfare deals, is gaining fast on Travelocity's lead, the online travel service still boasts an industry-leading 32 million members who have registered free of charge on the Web site and had gross travel bookings of $3.1 billion in 2001. Travelocity.com Inc.'s goal is to increase the power and efficiency of its online shopping service and continue to promote customer satisfaction and loyalty through its customer service centers. Travelocity.com Inc.'s parent company, Sabre Inc. with a 70 percent share in the company, bought the remaining 30 percent ownership of Travelocity in early 2002.

COMPANY FINANCES

Travelocity.com Inc. enjoys a diversified revenue mix, with 2001 revenues consisting of approximately

48.8 percent in air transactions; 19.5 percent in non-air transactions, such as hotels, car rentals, cruises, and vacation packages; 20.8 percent in advertising; and 10.9 percent in other revenues. Travelocity has enjoyed financial growth even through the tough economic climate, particularly suffered by the travel industry, in late 2001. Sales for 2001 totaled $301.8 million, up 56.6 percent from sales of $192.7 million in 2000 and a big jump from the company's 1999 sales of $90.9 million.

Travelocity stock has varied from a low of $11.69 to a high of $37.90 over a 52-week period. No cash dividends were declared or paid during 2000 or 2001, and the company does not intend to pay cash dividends in the foreseeable future but will use any future earnings to finance business growth.

ANALYSTS' OPINIONS

Since Travelocity.com Inc. has established itself as a leader in the online travel agency field, many analysts consider it an attractive stock. Thomas Weisel Partners reported in late 2001 that the stock was an attractive buy due to its 35 percent share of the online agency market, $2.5 billion of travel sold in 2000, and its surprisingly positive outlook for 2002. Weisel also noted in early 2002 that acquiring the remaining 30 percent share of Travelocity was critical for Sabre. Some analysts had a slightly different view, with Robertson Stephens noting in late August of 2001 that although the company reported better-than-expected results, the increasingly competitive market, including Orbitz and Expedia, may negatively affect Travelocity's market share. Nonetheless, they remained positive about the company's long-term outlook. Now fully owned by Sabre, Travelocity's position as a leader in the travel segment seems further cemented.

HISTORY

Travelocity's innovation and leadership in the travel industry began with its parent company, Sabre, who launched the online travel agency with 70 percent ownership and went on to fully acquire it in 2002. Sabre has a long history in revolutionizing the travel business, beginning with their first computer reservation system developed and implemented in 1960, when the first state-of-the-art Sabre system was installed on two IBM computers and was able to process some 84,000 telephone calls each day. In 1964 the final Sabre system was complete: the biggest, private, real-time data processing system with a telecommunications network stretching across the entire United States and providing huge savings for American Airlines, giving it a competitive boost for the next five to seven years.

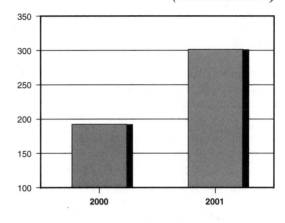

FINANCES:
Travelocity.com Inc. Revenues, 2000-2001 (million dollars)

The next decade saw Sabre upgrading its system and consolidating its computer facilities in Tulsa, Oklahoma, where all of American Airlines' data processing was now handled. The Sabre system was eventually utilized by 86 percent of the top 100 agencies who used automated systems in the most competitive markets. By 1978 the Sabre system had stored 1 million fares.

Sabre expanded internationally when Canadian travel agents began using the Sabre computer reservation systems in 1983. The following year, the company introduced the ground-breaking Bargain Finder pricing, a low-fare search feature enabling travel agents to advise which class of service was the cheapest for the flight booked. EasySabre was launched in 1985, enabling consumers with personal computers to access the Sabre system online to book air travel, hotel, and automobile rental services. The next year, Sabre installed the first automated yield management system for use by the airline industry. The system was designed to generate prices of airline seats for the optimum revenue per flight. Sabre also extended service into the United Kingdom around that time, a move that would herald Sabre's international growth in the next decade.

The company expanded its products and services to the airlines in the late 1980s, with consulting, systems management services, and software designed to aid yield management, crew scheduling, and revenue accounting. The Sabre system had, by then, grown to store 36 million fares. In 1992 the company introduced its Sabre Air-Flite scheduling system and, in 1994, developed a systems for railroad reservations in France and later, the United Kingdom.

FAST FACTS:

About Travelocity.com Inc.

Ownership: Travelocity.com Inc. is a wholly-owned subsidiary of Sabre Inc., a publicly owned company traded on the New York Stock Exchange.

Ticker Symbol: TSG

Officers: William J. Hannigan, Chmn., 42; Sam Gilliland, Pres. and CEO; Eric J. Speck, EVP and Chief Mktg. Officer; Ramesh K. Punwani, CFO and EVP, 59, 2001 base salary $216,000; James D. Marsicano, EVP, Sales and Services, 59, 2001 base salary $243,230; Andrew B. Steinberg, EVP, Admin., Gen. Counsel, and Corp. Sec., 43, 2001 base salary $233,200; Christopher McAndrews, SVP, Leisure Travel and Media, 38, 2001 base salary $235,224; Peter Cardell, SVP, Transportation and Hospitality, 51; Susan Carmichael, SVP of HR, 49

Employees: 1,554

Principal Subsidiary Companies: Travelocity.com Inc. is wholly owned by parent Sabre Inc., a travel reservations and information technology services company. In addition to Travelocity, Sabre also owns GetThere, Inc. with the corresponding travel Web site GetThere.com.

Chief Competitors: Travelocity.com rivals other companies in the extremely competitive online travel services market, including Expedia, and agencies formed by travel suppliers such as Orbitz, Hotwire, and Hotel Distribution Systems. The company also faces additional competition from wholesalers and consolidators of airline tickets and related travel services; traditional local, regional, national, and international travel agencies; and airlines, hotels, and auto rental companies, some of whom are suppliers to Travelocity.com, via their own Web sites.

Sabre launched Travelocity.com in March 1996. The revolutionary Web site was the first to provide travel reservations and extensive destination and event details online. Travelocity was incorporated in September 1999. In 2000 the company merged with Preview Travel and began trading on the NASDAQ Stock Exchange under the symbol TVLY. Along with partner and leading direct marketer Otto Freizeit und Touristik GmbH, the company launched its Travelocity Europe in 2001, a multi-channel travel company that is one of the top European online Agencies. Travelocity.ca, a French and English language site, was also developed FOR Canadian customers.

In March 2002 Sabre Holdings Corporation purchased all the outstanding shares of common stock of Travelocity and became sole owner of the company. Travelocity's symbol, TLVY, was delisted from NASDAQ in April of that year and is now traded under the umbrella of parent company Sabre's symbol, TSG. In early 2002, Travelocity agreed to form a one-stop online travel site in Japan, Tabini. Some of the site's suppliers include Nippon Airways, Japan Airlines, United Airlines, Japan Air Systems, and a consortium of 13 other large international airlines.

STRATEGY

Travelocity.com Inc. seeks to leverage its existing strengths to become a world leader in travel products and services. The company's ultimate goal is to make shopping online for travel a better experience than in the physical world. With more consumers shopping online for travel, the company seeks to enhance their products, services, and features to take advantage of the growing market. With a highly recognizable brand name and 32 million members, the company is able to target customers via e-mail regarding private sales, special fares, and promotions. The company also made significant gains from its member base by the ability to supply key merchandising and advertising opportunities for their travel suppliers. Travelocity also plans to continue its global reach by utilizing Web sites tailored for specific international markets. They balance the risk in these markets by sharing investments with partners. The company stresses that its customer service efforts are key for maintaining customer loyalty.

In an effort to promote travel products and service and increase brand awareness, part of Travelocity's aims include entering into strategic relationships. With that in mind, Travelocity acquired Site59.com, a private online travel service with merchant hotel and vacation packages, as a subsidiary in 2002. The company also has exclusive agreements with online giants America Online (AOL) and Yahoo!. Travelocity also has agreements with a number of their travel suppliers, which include major airlines. With its Web sites now available to about 50 percent of the U.S. wireless market, the company has entered into agreements with AT&T Wireless, Sprint PCS, Palm, and Nextel Communications to keep their brand in people's hands everywhere they go.

INFLUENCES

Travelocity has benefited from efforts to broaden its product offerings, including engaging in partnerships and strategic relationships with travel partners, online vendors, and a variety of organizations. The success of international, market-based sites has spurred the company to continue to seek growth in these areas, with the intended goal of becoming a leader worldwide.

One of Travelocity's biggest challenges is the rapid growth and increasing competition in the online travel services market from rival online companies and even travel partners. Some of Travelocity's competitors have recently made use of advanced "off-host" technology, which has spurred the company to meet or exceed those technological advancements. As a result, Travelocity launched the Intelli-Deck technology, designed to enhance the purchase of cruise vacations through viewable deck plans and interactive tours of the ships. By constantly improving products and services and continuing to focus on brand awareness, the company hopes to keep its leadership status in the field.

In late May 2002, the company launched a new $40 million television, radio, print, and online advertising campaign called "Travelocity Can." The ads focus on the travel possibilities available through the Web site that they suggest is unparalleled in the industry: more like a "travel dream factory" servicing all travel needs at a highly individual level. The ads feature real people describing how Travelocity has helped them plan their dream trips.

CURRENT TRENDS

The company intends to continue to utilize technology to enhance their online services and user friendliness. Travelocity gets its booking capability from utilizing Sabre's technology, with its long history of innovation. Along these lines, the company implemented a new fare search technology that will aid customers in finding even lower fares and increase the range and scope of fare searches by looking for combinations of "local" fares that outmatch traditional, published, nonstop or connecting fares between the user's requested cities. The new search is able to check millions of fare combinations, ensuring the best options for the customer.

With existing partnerships in place with such organizations such as HRN, AOL, Yahoo!, AT&T Wireless, Sprint PCS, Palm, Nextel Communications, and companies in international markets, Travelocity continues to pursue such beneficial alliances and diversifying in new markets worldwide. The company is also seeking growth through recent acquisitions and mergers.

PRODUCTS

The company offers a variety of travel products and services, including airfare, hotel, car rental, cruises, and

CHRONOLOGY:
Key Dates for Travelocity.com Inc.

1960: The first Sabre computer reservations system is installed

1972: The upgraded Sabre system handles all of American Airlines' data processing

1976: The first Sabre system is installed in 130 travel agencies

1978: The Sabre system stores 1 million fares

1984: Bargain Finder, the first low-fare search system is introduced

1985: EasySabre, the first online consumer reservations system, is implemented

1996: Travelocity.com is launched

1999: Travelocity is incorporated

2000: Travelocity merges with Preview Travel to become the number one online travel destination; Travelocity goes public on NASDAQ under the symbol TVLY

2001: Travelocity Europe and Travelocity.ca are launched

2002: Sabre acquires the remaining 30 percent of Travelocity that it did not previously own; Travelocity acquires Site59.com

vacation packages. The services may be accessed via the company's Web site or via online providers, including AOL. Additionally, Travelocity is also able to target customers with its newsletters, including *INSIDER,* which has a bi-weekly circulation of about nine million, and *REAL DEALS* with a monthly circulation of about nine million.

Among its new developments, a deal was struck with Walt Disney Parks and Resorts in early 2002 that allows Travelocity to market Disney theme-park tickets and hotel rooms directly from Disney, bypassing third-party wholesalers. Users can buy Disney vacation products and bundle them with other Travelocity products, including airline tickets, under the company's Travelocity Vacations. This may allow the company to offer better prices and access to Disney resorts, parks, and hotels and is the first such agreement made by an online travel vendor with Disney. In a related move, Travelocity entered into

I DREAM OF VACATIONING

Travelocity.com ads launched in 2002 featured the theme of ordinary people doing the things that they only dreamed about, of course using the variety of products and services available on Travelocity's one-stop shopping site. For example, one of the ads, "Elephant," showed a customer riding on one of the African beasts rented through Travelocity.com. Travel tools like Dream Maps, are also featured, which offer a variety of destinations and flight fares for whatever budget is specified by the consumer. Intellideck is yet another innovative tool shown in the ads that allows customers to virtually "tour" a cruise ship so that they can book the perfect cabin on the perfect ship of their dreams. Maybe one day the virtual tour will replace the actual tour?

a marketing agreement with the Orlando/Orange County Convention & Visitors Bureau, Inc. to create a one-stop shopping service dubbed the "Orlando Super Site" within the Travelocity.com Web site, also accessible through www.orlandoinfo.com, for travelers to the popular vacation destination.

CORPORATE CITIZENSHIP

After the September 11 disasters, Travelocity and Sabre worked to help stranded travelers and local travel agencies. Sabre and its network suppliers worked overtime in New York and throughout the Northeast to reroute network traffic and offer alternative connections to the reservation system. The company also provided equipment, including software and office space in Manhattan to help displaced agencies get up and running again. Along with a major travel agency, Sabre participated in setting up and staffing the agency's government call center that would book flights for U.S. military troops for deployment. Within days after the attacks, Sabre designed and launched the Travel Bulletin Central (TBC) as an information source for stranded travelers that included travel alerts, restrictions, changes in security procedures, contact information, and answers to a variety of most-asked questions. Sabre also gave airlines booking fee credits for canceled flights in the following days, waived normal fees for accessing premium Sabre services through the end of 2001, and aided air-

lines in calling for U.S. government support of the travel industry.

GLOBAL PRESENCE

Travelocity has created Web sites specific to certain internationals markets, keeping in mind the distinctive cultures, travel purchasing, and supplier inventory in various regions of the world. The creation of a Canadian site, www.travelocity.ca, also brought arrangements with the Canadian Internet brands Yahoo! Canada and AOL Canada. The company also has agreements with various local customer service partners and agencies, enabling international customers to make reservations on the Travelocity Web site to pick up their tickets at participating Sabre travel agencies. With such a variety of channels, Travelocity has been able to make sales in more than 90 countries.

The company's joint ventures, Travelocity Europe, serving the growing European market, and Tabini, in Japan, has allowed Travelocity to extend its global reach, while spreading risk. Tabini, powered by the company's technology, offers booking on nearly all airlines serving Japan, more than 55,000 hotels, and more than 50 car rental companies in the region and worldwide. Additionally, Travelocity intends to join in another venture along with several airlines to create Zuji, offering a wide range of travel services serving the Asian-Pacific region beginning in 2002.

EMPLOYMENT

Travelocity.com Inc. employs some 1,554 people. None of the company's employees are represented by a labor union, and Travelocity considers relations with their employees to be good. In such a competitive field, the company places a priority on attracting qualified personnel and preserve good working relationships with them. Travelocity seeks a variety of resourceful professionals, including Internet application programmers, marketing and promotion specialists, travel industry relations leaders, database specialists, system integrators, designers, and project managers.

SOURCES OF INFORMATION

Bibliography

Sabre Home Page, 2002. Available at http://www.sabre.com.

Travelocity.com Home Page, 2002. Available at http://www.travelocity.com.

"Travelocity.com Inc." *Hoover's Online*, June 2002. Available at http://www.hoovers.com.

"Travelocity.com Inc." Gale Group, June 2002. Available at http://galenet.galegroup.com.

"Travelocity.com to Buy Site59.com for $43 Million." *The Wall Street Journal*, 26 March 2002.

"Travelocity.com to Announce Marketing Pact with Disney, Cutting Out Third Parties." *The Wall Street Journal*, 11 February 2002.

"Travelocity.com to Create Orlando Super Site; Exclusive Marketing Agreement With Orlando/Orange County Convention & Visitors Bureau, Inc. Means Better Deals and Expanded Orlando Content On Travelocity.com." *PR Newswire*, 20 May 2002.

"Travelocity and The Richards Group Break New Branding Campaign: 'Travelocity Can'." *PR Newswire*, 28 May 2002.

For an annual report:

on the Internet at: http://www.sabre.com **or** write: Sabre Inc., 3150 Sabre Drive, Southlake, Texas 76092

For additional industry research:

Investigate companies by their Standard Industrial Classification Codes, also known as SICs. Travelocity.com Inc.'s primary SICs are:

4724 Travel Agencies

7375 Information Retrieval Services

7812 Motion Picture, Video Tape Production

Also investigate companies by their North American Industry Classification System codes, also known as NAICS codes. Travelocity.com Inc.'s primary NAICS codes are:

512110 Motion Picture and Video Production

514191 Online Information Services

561510 Travel Agencies

Ty, Inc.

FOUNDED: 1986

Contact Information:

HEADQUARTERS: 280 Chestnut Ave.
   Westmont, IL 60559
PHONE: (630)920-1515
FAX: (630)920-1980
EMAIL: contact@ty.com
URL: http://www.ty.com

OVERVIEW

Ty Warner created a billion dollar industry based on an idea for a $5.00 pellet-filled toy cat that turned into a line of hundreds of avidly collected and traded Beanie Babies. Ty, Inc. rose to the rank of number one toy maker in 1998 and currently ranks as the third highest selling toymaker in the world, using Warner's unique marketing techniques, which kept his company shrouded in mystery and his Beanie Babies in high demand with limited volumes of an ever-changing lineup of cuddly characters. The Beanie frenzy of the late 1990s created an entire industry around the aftermarket sales of the toys, including trading clubs and auction Web sites, sometimes fetching $5,000 and more for rare or most-wanted Beanies. Selling toys with names like Legs the Frog and Chip the Cat made Warner himself a billionaire, ranked on The *Forbes* 400 list, while his company ranks consistently in The *Forbes* Private 500.

COMPANY FINANCES

Sales of the company in 2000 were estimated at $800 million, rising an estimated 36 percent from 1999. The company enjoys the third largest toy sales worldwide, behind Mattel and Hasbro. Ty also has the highest sales margin of the leading four toy makers, which includes Lego, Mattel, and Hasbro.

FAST FACTS:

About Ty, Inc.

Ownership: Ty, Inc. is a privately owned company solely owned by H. Ty Warner.

Officers: H. Ty Warner, Pres.; Michael W. Kanzler, CFO; Diane Digangi, Dir. of Human Resources

Employees: 1,000

Chief Competitors: Leading competitors of Ty, Inc. include toymakers Hasbro, Mattel, Applause, and Play-By-Play.

HISTORY

1962 was the year Ty Warner got his start in the toy business working with his father as a salesman at Dakin toy company. His former boss told *People*, "He was probably the best salesman I ever met." At Dakin, Warner learned the ins and outs of the toy business by selling the company's plush animals. He began dabbling in unorthodox marketing techniques, arriving at distributors in a white Rolls-Royce convertible he had purchased and dressed in a fur coat with a top hat and cane. He guessed, correctly, that it would intrigue retailers enough to see what he had for sale.

After eighteen years at Dakin, Warner was making more than $100,000 at the company but left in 1980. Warner told *People* he left to pursue other interests, but his former boss told the magazine he was fired for creating a competing line of toys.

Warner traveled to Sorrento, Italy, where he was inspired by the number of unique stuffed toy cats he saw there. Upon his return in 1983, his father died of a heart attack and left Warner $50,000. With that money, in addition to his savings from his time at Dakin and a second mortgage on his condo home, Warner began to develop a line of toys. In 1986 he formed Ty, Incorporated, and after working out of his home, moved to a small office in Oakbrook, Illinois. He hired two employees and found a production plant to manufacture his stuffed animals on a trip to Korea.

His first toy was a white Himalayan cat named Angel. In the first line, there were ten cats, all with different names like Peaches and Smokey, and in all different colors. "Kids identify with names. In the beginning, I thought of the cute names. Now I take them into the office and everyone makes suggestions," Warner told *People*. He was able to get buyers through his old Dakin contacts and sold the small, loosely filled pellet animals for $20.00. They sold well. At the Atlanta Toy Fair, Warner sold 30,000 in one hour.

After his success in Atlanta, Warner moved out of the little Oakbrook office and into a 12,000 square foot warehouse in Lombard, Illinois. He began a new line of toys, the Collectable Bears Series, in 1991. They were limited edition bears, each with a numbered stripe on their right foot. Ty, Inc.'s 1992 catalogue featured these bears and the original cats, in addition to a variety of new animals like dogs and monkeys in the $5.00 to $20.00 range.

Warner then decided to put his focus on a toy that children could easily afford and would like to collect. He wanted to create a quality toy line for the retail price of $5.00, which he felt to that point didn't exist.

In 1993, the first Beanie Babies were born: Brownie the Bear and Pinchers the Lobster. After tweaking these early attempts, there were nine Beanie Babies altogether in the first line unveiled at the New York Toy Fair. Warner called the flagship Beanies Chocolate the Moose,

Cubbie the Brown Bear, Flash the Dolphin, Legs the Frog, Patti the Platypus, Pinchers the Lobster, Splash the Whale, Spot the Dog, and Squealer the Pig. By early 1994 the little toys with the characteristic heart-shaped tag were in stores.

Warner's marketing genius was keeping stores from carrying all the different kinds toys in the line. That way, people went hunting for them and kept demand high. He shunned all advertising and the toys weren't carried by toy retail giants like Toys "R" Us or Wal-Mart, yet soon Beanies were flying off the shelves of Hallmark stores and smaller retailers that carried the line. Warner also limited each store to a certain number of Beanies it could order each month. Making supply scarcer, he knew, would increase demand from avid collectors.

In 1995, he came up with another scheme: retiring certain styles after a while and putting out new styles to keep interest up. Warner himself designed all the different Beanies, except one, Spook, now called Spooky, that was designed by Jenna, his girlfriend's daughter.

The mystique Warner likes to keep around his products, his company, and himself is well known. He has no sign anywhere surrounding his Illinois headquarters and no listed phone number, sometimes frustrating retailers wishing to reorder. Warner claims the unlisted phone number is simply because he can't keep up with demand. He swears his employees to secrecy regarding the company and himself and has only agreed to a very limited number of interviews with the press.

In 1998, Ty was named the leading toy maker in the country. That year, Ty, Inc. partnered with Cyrk, Inc., a corporate promotion company, to form the Beanie Baby Official Club. The club kit offered a chance to buy the exclusive Clubby Bear. The next year, the partnership

CHRONOLOGY:

Key Dates for Ty, Inc.

1962: H. Ty Warner begins career in toys at Dakin

1980: Warner leaves Dakin after 18 years

1986: Ty, Inc. formed

1993: First Beanie Babies created

1994: Beanie Babies hit the market

1998: Ty named number one toy maker

1999: Warner buys Four Seasons Hotel in Manhattan—city's tallest hotel

1999: Ty announces retirement of all Beanie Babies; company holds online vote on whether to discontinue Beanies

2000: People vote to continue Beanies

2001: America Bear premieres, with all proceeds donated to victims of the September 11 attacks

began producing BBOC Trading Cards, but only lasted for four series of the cards, and another kit offering the new Clubby II Bear. Cyrk also produced a number of promotional items, including calendars, trading card accessories, and the special club bears. Cryk was unable to produce the Clubby Beanie Buddies in the time advertising, which is illegal, and was fired by Ty.

In August 1999, Ty, Inc. enigmatically announced on its Web site that it would discontinue making all the 325 different Beanie Babies after December 31 of that year. Collectors, who sometimes paid in the thousands for Beanies in aftermarkets like auction sites eBay and Beanienation.com, went wild. Fans emailed frantic messages to the company and prices bid online for the Beanies rose. Even the company's own employees were baffled. Some speculated that the reason behind the decision was that the secondary market had ebbed recently and it was an attempt to boost sagging sales. Although Ty did not gain from secondary sales, many retailers purchased the Beanies based on the aftermarket values, which were dropping. Stores began stocking up in droves after the announcement. When December 1999 finally arrived, Ty, Inc. decided to let the public vote on whether the company should produce Beanies in 2000. The vote was overwhelmingly pro-Beanie with 91 percent in favor of continuing Beanie production in the new millennium. Votes cost 50 cents each with Ty donating the proceeds

to the Elizabeth Glaser Pediatric AIDS Foundation. Year 2000 sales were up 36 percent at $800 million.

In 2001, a special edition America Bear appeared with 100 percent of the profit from sales donated to the Disaster Relief Fund of the American Red Cross in honor of the victims of the attacks of September 11, 2001.

Warner's personal fortune has allowed him to embark on a second career as a hotelier. He purchased prestigious real estate, including the Four Seasons Hotel in New York City, the city's tallest hotel, the Four Seasons Resort in Montecito, and the San Ysidro Ranch near Santa Barbara, the honeymoon destination of John F. and Jacqueline Kennedy. He has renovated the New York and Santa Barbara hotels, with plans of expansion for the latter.

STRATEGY

Warner honed his unorthodox marketing techniques early in his toy career at Dakin and the unique sales style he cultivated there proved invaluable for his own business. Ty does not advertise its plush wares and keeps production numbers limited. The result has fueled collectors and has proven to be an ingenious way to keep people interested in new lines. The company relies on small, specialty retailers to distribute the toys instead of retail giants Wal-Mart or Toys "R" Us. Warner also prevents stores from carrying all the different kinds toys in the line. That way, people go hunting for them and keep demand high. The company also limits each store to a certain number of Beanies they can order each month. Making supply scarcer, the company knew, would increase demand from avid collectors. In 1995, Warner came up with another scheme: retiring certain styles after a while and putting out new styles to keep interest up.

Ty's strategy and intense privacy, however, also left some retailers feeling frustrated. Citing reasons including lack of communication, shipping issues, and invoicing problems, some disappointed retailers have opted out of carrying the line.

INFLUENCES

Due to the enormous success of its products, the company's ordering system became quickly outdated in 1997. With approximately 100,000 daily orders called in per day, Ty immediately issued orders to its technology employees to create a new system or it would suffer millions in losses. Given an unlimited budget to do so, an estimated $750,000 to $1 million was eventually spent on the new system and training, which served to cut order implementation time by two-thirds.

Ever the marketing genius, Ty generated a wealth of free publicity when the toymaker threatened to end production of Beanies December 31, 1999. Shortly thereafter, it announced it would let the public decide the fate of the stuffed toys in a worldwide online vote that year. The results were tallied with a resounding 91 percent in favor on continuing the line. Some in the media speculated that the announcement was merely a publicity stunt and that the company had planned to keep making Beanies all along, as there were factory expansion plans still in the works and several Beanie names submitted for trademark at the time.

CURRENT TRENDS

Ty has explored expansion in several ways. The company's introduction of Beanie Kids signaled growth beyond its traditional lines of beanbag animals only. Beanie Kids also have proven that Ty can produce a more sophisticated type of toy, with an emphasis on craftsmanship, detail and diversity found throughout the new line.

Exploring new markets with the help of the newly formed Ty Asia, Ty sought to expand distribution of its beanbag creations in Malaysia, Singapore, and Japan in addition to its existing sales channels in Germany, Canada, England, and the U.S. Its release of a Japan-only limited edition bear also signaled a move to solidify its presence in the region.

Ty responded to the widespread counterfeit of its Beanies by developing new, harder to copy holographic tags. The company also legally disputed the name of the Windermere Company's Web site named Ilovebeanies.com, which Ty claims encroaches on its own Web site, www.beaniebabies.com. Windermere also retails a number of other similar beanie toys, including Meanie Beanies, Salvino's Bammers, and the Grateful Dead Bean Bears. A copyright infringement lawsuit was also filed against HolyBears, Inc. in 1999 for creating a similar product. No stranger to lawsuits, Ty has gone after approximately 70 companies making Beanie look-alikes, successfully settling a majority of its cases.

PRODUCTS

To implement its line of Beanie animals, in 2000, Ty introduced Beanie Kids dolls, which were created from the likenesses of children. There are 13 different dolls in the line, which measure about 10 inches long, including Angel, Boomer, Buzz, Calypso, Chipper, Cookie, Curly, Cutie, Ginger, Precious, Princess, Rascal, and Tumbles. The line features soft bodies and a variety of skin, hair and eye colors. The dolls, praised for their detail and craftsmanship, are clad in Ty Gear, outfits that exemplify each doll's culture and origin. In continuing efforts to discourage the widespread problem with coun-

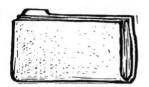

BEANIE MANIA

Certain rare Beanie Babies, which originally retailed for about $5.00, have been known to sell in aftermarkets for up to $6,000 to avid collectors. The most expensive Beanie ever, however, known as Number One, is a numbered, limited edition given to 253 Ty representatives. It has sold for more than $10,000 at Beanie shows and on Internet auction sites. Rare Beanies continue to rise in value, if they are in mint condition with the original Ty tag affixed.

---

terfeit Beanies, the company has developed holograms which are difficult to duplicate or forge.

CORPORATE CITIZENSHIP

Ty's success has also allowed the company to show its philanthropic side. The specially-designed Princess Bear raised more than $15 million for the Diana, Princess of Wales Memorial Fund. Beanies were donated to refugee children in Kosovo. Votes to keep Beanie's in business at 50 cents each in 1999 were donated to the Elizabeth Glaser Pediatric AIDS Foundation and all proceeds from the special edition America Bear created in 2001 were donated to the Disaster Relief Fund of the American Red Cross in honor of the victims of the attacks of September 11, 2001. The company promised at least $1 million to the Red Cross but expects worldwide sales of the America Bear to greatly surpass that number.

GLOBAL PRESENCE

Ty markets its Beanie creations in the U.S., Canada, England, Germany and Japan. A desire to further expand into the Asian market resulted in the formation of Ty Asia in 2000, which rated a 12 percent market share in Malaysia and Singapore. A limitededition pink bear, Sakura, was introduced exclusively in Japan by Ty Asia in March 2000 to great success, with bids for the bear going as high as 60 times above its retail price. The company announced in October 2001 that it would open its first store in Korea in November of that year. Ty plans to sell Beanie Babies and Beanie Buddies, two of its seven lines of toys, in the Korean market.

EMPLOYMENT

Famed for its uniquely insular culture, Ty employees are sworn to secrecy and Warner rarely gives interviews. The company's phone number was even made unlisted at one point. Ty does share the wealth from its Beanie empire with its workers, however. In 1998, Warner handed out bonuses to all 300 Ty employees equal to their annual salaries and often gives out special edition Beanies to them as well. As of 2000, employee numbers were estimated at 1,000.

SOURCES OF INFORMATION

Bibliography

"Bean There, Done That." *People Weekly*, 20 September 1999.

"Beaned! Locals Sued by Toymaker." *Orlando Business Journal*, 12 November 1999.

"Beanie Babies Blitz IS." *Computerworld*, 28 April 1997.

"Beanie Babies Firm to Let Public Decide Toys' Fate." *The Wall Street Journal*, 27 December 1999.

"Beanie Kids' KL Debut." *New Straits Times*, 15 November 2000.

"Beanie-Mania." *People Weekly*, 1 July 1996.

"Consumers Vote for More Beanie Babies." *The New York Times.*, 3 January 2000.

"Mystique Marketing." *Forbes*, 21 October 1996.

"New Kids' in Town." *New Straits Times*, 11 November 2000.

"Time is Money." *Computerworld*, 5 May 1997.

"Ty Advances Into Korean Toy Market." *Korea Herald*, 30 October 2001.

"Ty Asia Sees RM12M Sales in Beanie Babies." *Business Times (Malaysia)*, 9 November 2000.

"Ty Inc." Gale Group, 2002. Available from http://www.galenet .galegroup.com

"Ty Inc." Hoover's Online, February 2002. Available at http://www.hoovers.com.

"Ty to Sell Fundraising Beanie Baby America." *Gifts & Decorative Accessories*, October 2001.

"Update on Small Business: Beanie Babies Bears Down in Suit Against Religious Firm." *The Wall Street Journal*, 12 October 1999.

For additional industry research:

Investigate companies by their Standard Industrial Classification Codes, also known as SICs. Ty, Inc.'s primary SIC is:

3942 Dolls and Stuffed Toys

Also investigate companies by their North American Industry Classification System Codes, also known as NAICS codes. Ty Inc.'s primary NAICS code is:

339931 Doll and Stuffed Toy Manufacturing

Unilever

FOUNDED: 1930

OVERVIEW

Unilever is one of the world leaders in packaged consumer goods. Its many products include personal hygiene products, frozen foods, margarine, tea, and washing powders. According to the company, 150 million people choose their brands every day to "feed their families and clean their homes." Despite being one of the most successful corporations, and having a global presence, Unilever is a company whose brand names are more well-known than that of their producer. Unilever manufactures and sells products like Slim-Fast, Dove, Ben & Jerry's, Q-Tips, Wisk and Lipton.

When Unilever purchased Bestfoods, famous for the Hellmann's and Skippy brand names, it became one of the world's top three food companies, behind Nestlé and Kraft. It is also the world's second largest packaged consumer goods company, behind Procter & Gamble. Today, Unilever is based in two global divisions: Unilever Bestfoods and Home and Personal Care. Both divisions have an executive board, responsible for divisional strategy and global implementation. Truly a multinational corporation, Unilever sells its products in over 150 countries.

Contact Information:

HEADQUARTERS: Lever House, 390 Park Avenue
New York, New York 10022-4698
PHONE: (212)888-1260
FAX: (212)906-4666
EMAIL: paul.wood@unilever.com
URL: http://www.unilever.com

COMPANY FINANCES

At the end of fiscal year 2000, Unilever reported sales of $44,813,000,000, which represented sales growth of 2.7 percent.

FAST FACTS:
About Unilever

Ownership: Unilever is a joint venture of Unilever NV (The Netherlands) and Unilever PLC (UK), the parent companies. The two companies have operated as one since 1930. They trade separately but have one board of directors. Unilever's corporate centers are London and Rotterdam. In the United States, it is traded on the New York Stock Exchange.

Ticker Symbol: UN

Officers: Niall Fitzgerald, Chmn., Unilever PLC, VChmn., Unilever NV, 56; Antony Burgmans, Chmn., Unilever, VChmn., Unilever PLC, 54; Clive Butler, Corporate Development Dir., 54; Rudy Markham, Financial Dir., 54

Employees: 295,000

Principal Subsidiary Companies: Unilever, a multinational organization, operates over 300 companies in 90 different countries. Its United States operations consolidated into two main companies, specializing in foods and home and personal care. Unilever has 104 offices and manufacturing sites in 27 states and Puerto Rico.

Chief Competitors: Unilever's main competition comes from the consumer non-cyclical sector of the food processing industry. Major competitors include ConAgra Foods, Inc., Kraft Foods, Nestle, Proctor & Gamble, Sara Lee Corp., and Tyson Foods, Inc.

ANALYSTS' OPINIONS

At the turn of the century, Unilever was ranked as the top FMCG company in the Dow Jones Sustainability Index 2000. At the same time, investors were concerned about Unilever's performance when the company bought Bestfoods in 2000. In fact, the integration caused Credit Suisse First Boston to downgrade Unilever from a "hold" to a "sell" rating. Unilever, however, expressed optimism, pointing out that its sales rose 35 percent by June 2001. It estimated that the acquisition would produce an annual savings of $32 million. Further, Unilever said it expected to realize low double-digit growth in earnings per share for the full year of 2002. Analysts on Wall Street were expecting Unilever to earn $3.09 per share in that same period.

HISTORY

Unilever's roots go back to the nineteenth century, when Lever Brothers, a British soapmaking company, was founded in 1885 by William Hesketh Lever. In 1917, the company diversified into food products, including fish, ice cream and canned goods. In 1930 that company merged with Margarine Unie, a Dutch Margarine company, to form Unilever. The move seemed a logical one, as both companies competed for the same raw materials and consumer market. During the 1920s, Margarine Unie had grown through mergers with other margarine companies. Between them, Lever and Maragarine Unie now had operations in 40 countries.

Throughout the next three decades, Unilever improved its technology, and its business grew and diversified and it expanded its reach into Latin America. It also tried out different business areas. During World War II, the company helped make tank periscopes and soldiers' food rations. Unilever entered the synthetic detergent market in 1954, when it introduced Omo, a blue detergent powder. From there, the company developed brands like Persil and Skip, and it has vied with Proctor & Gamble for top positions in the market.

Throughout the 1950s, Unilever entered into chemicals, packaging, and market research and advertising. At the beginning of the Lever-Unie merger, soap products accounted for 90 percent of Unilever's profits, but as the company moved into other areas that figure decreased. By 1980, soap products only contributed to 40 percent of its profits.

In the latter half of the twentieth century, the company began streamlining its operations. It rid itself of its packaging companies, its chemicals business, and some of its agricultural enterprises, and it concentrated on personal hygiene and food products. In the 1980s, it scored several important acquisitions including the Brooke Bond tea company, Chesebrough-Pond's Inc., and the Faberge/Elizabeth Arden brand lines. In buying Brooke Bond, it strengthened its position in the tea market. When it bought Chesebrough-Pond's, Unilever became a leader in the world's skin care market.

In the 1990s, Unilever sold much of its remaining agribusiness interests and it began to focus on what it considered its core products and activities. In 1999, Unilever further streamlined its organization, as it announced that it would focus on fewer and stronger brand names. This, it believed, would spark faster growth. At one point, Unilever had 1,600 brands. The figure is now down to about 400.

In 2000, Unilever bought Slim-Fast, which became one of its top sellers. That same year, Unilever implemented corporate initiatives to further spark growth, including organizational restructuring and the splitting of the company into two global units (food and home products, and personal care products). As part of this strategy, it also started selling the subsidiary businesses that weren't turning enough profit.

STRATEGY

Unilever's declared strategy is to focus on research and development-which it invests billions of dollars a year into-and marketing of brands most popular with consumers. Despite the streamlining the organization has experienced in recent years, it intends to continue developing new brands in anticipation of future consumer needs. At the same time, it seeks to foster growth by focusing on key brands and simplifying its business systems. It hoped to accomplish these aims when it consolidated its best-selling brands into two global divisions: Foods, and Home and Personal Care. So far, the company has been pleased with the results.

As part of its strategy, Unilever institutionalized a corporate structure designed to be effective. Specifically, the purpose of the structure is to clarify roles, responsibilities, and decision making. One of its critical elements is the executive committee, which is responsible for agreeing company priorities and allocating resources; setting overall corporate targets; agreeing and monitoring business group strategies and plans; identifying and exploiting opportunities created by Unilever's scale and scope; managing external relations at the corporate level; and developing future leaders. The committee is led by the chairmen of Unilever PLC and Unilever N.V.

The structure also includes regional presidents, advisory directors, and senior corporate officers. Regional presidents are responsible for delivering business results in their respective regions. Advisory directors are the principal external presence in Unilever's government. One of their key roles is assuring that government provisions are adequate and reflect best practices. They attend quarterly meetings, committee meetings, conferences of the directors and the Executive Committee, as well as meetings with the Chairmen. Senior corporate officers see to it that board meetings and board committee meetings are supplied with the information they need.

Underlying the corporate structure is a strict code of business principles. Main principles include a high standard of conduct, avoidance of conflicts of interest, product assurance, and reliable financial reporting, among others.

INFLUENCES

To a large extent, the growth and success that Unilever has achieved in result years results from recognition of its diversity as well as a faithfulness to its own mission statement. The company's stated purpose is to meet "the everyday needs of people everywhere," which refers to its expansive global reach. In keeping with its mission statement, Unilever regularly adapts it line of products as to target different cultures in different parts

CHRONOLOGY:
Key Dates for Unilever

1885: Lever Brothers is founded by William Hesketh Lever

1917: Lever Brothers diversifies its product line to include food items

1930: Lever merges with Margarine Unie to form Unilever

1954: Unilever entered the synthetic detergent market

1999: Unilever begins a radical streamlining of its organization.

2000: Unilever purchases Slim-Fast, which becomes one of the company's top sellers; Unilever sells 27 business as part of its organizational restructuring; Unilever purchases Bestfoods

of the world. The organization's radical restructuring in the last years of the 20th century was part of this plan. One of the aims of the restructuring was to decentralize responsibility and move it to specific international regions and product areas.

CURRENT TRENDS

The most significant part of Unilever's reorganization is the strategic plan it calls "The Path to Growth." Essentially, this involves a significant streamlining of its product portfolio. As it headed into the twenty-first century, the company felt it necessary to reduce its brands from 1,600 to 400. When it made the decision, in September 1999, the company reasoned that focusing on fewer and stronger brands would promote faster growth. The stated goal of the strategy was to accelerate top line growth and step up the rate of margin improvement in five years.

"The Path to Growth" involved a shake-up at the top level of management, splitting the company into two global units, and selling off any subsidiary businesses making less than average profits. The concentration on core brands resulted in the selling of 27 businesses during 2000. At the same time, Unilever acquired several well-known companies, including Bestfoods, Ben & Jerry's, and Slim-Fast.The restructuring resulted in specific changes in its divisions. Unilever's Foods division

FRANKENBEANS

Not all of Unilever's products have been resounding successes. One notorious failure was its Beanfeast line, marketed in the late 1990s. With Beanfeast, Unilever became the first multinational company to use genetically modified (GM) products. Beanfeast contained soy beans manufactured from the genetic material of a virus. When this was learned, the company was inundated with thousands of angry calls from consumers in the United Kingdom. By 1999 Unilever decided to withdraw Beanfeast and get out of GM foods.

was renamed Unilever Bestfoods. Its categories now included dressings, beverages, spreads and cooking, health and wellness, frozen foods, and ice cream. Home and Personal Care division categories now included deodorants, hair care, household care, laundry, skin care and cleansing, oral care and prestige products.

At the start of the new century, Unilever also decided to venture into cyberspace-that is, it deemed e-commerce a key component of its growth strategy. As part of this, Unilever formed alliances with companies like Compaq, IBM, and Microsoft. Also, in February 2000, Unilever and iVillage formed a new Internet company.

PRODUCTS

Unilever's products include a large number of well-known name brands listed under several categories. Its cosmetics include Rimmel, Cutex, Elizabeth Arden, and Sensiq. Beauty products include Ponds, Vaseline Intensive Care, and Close-up. Shampoos include All Clear, Cream Silk, Dimension, Pears, Sunsilk, and Salon Selectives. Soaps include Dove, Knights Castile, Lifebouy, Lux, Pears, and Sunsight. Toothpastes include Shield, Signal, and Mentadent. Some it its aftershaves include Lynx, Axe, Rexona, Degree, and Suave. Washing powders and laundry liquids include Persil, Radion, Surf, and Wisk. Its oils, fats, and margarines include Cookeen, Dante, Delight, and Outline, among others. Teas and coffees include Lipton, Lyons, and Red Mountain. Undoubtedly, Unilever's best known products are its food products and brand names like Slim-Fast, Ragu, Skippy, Good Humor, Breyers, and Ben & Jerry's.

GLOBAL PRESENCE

With 300 locations in 90 countries, Unilever is truly part of the global community. Its international business unit, DiverseyLever, has locations in Asia, Europe, Latin America and North America. The company's home and personal care regions include Africa, Middle East & Turkey Home. Its Unilever Bestfoods regions include Africa, Asia, Europe, the Middle East, and North America.

CORPORATE CITIZENSHIP

Unilever proudly points out that it is internationally recognized as one of the world's most environmentally responsible businesses. It has established a corporate policy that commits the company to meeting the needs of customers and consumers in an environmentally sound and sustainable manner. The strategy focuses on achieving its goals through eco-efficiency, eco-innovation and three sustainability initiatives on agriculture, fish and water. Around the world, it has set up various environmental initiatives to ensure minimum impact on local environments. By 2001, 73 of its factories reached the international environmental management system standard ISO 14001.

Unilever recognizes its social responsibility and, as such, it has established the Social Review 2000, which maps out the major areas of the company's social interaction including wealth creation, employment values and practices, consumer commitment, and its responsibilities towards the environment and the communities in which its operate.

As a member of the global community, Unilever is concerned with the health, education, and welfare of the populations of local communities. Each of its operating companies are involved in projects and programs that include dental services for remote communities, funding for hospitals, care for disabled people, and teaching people young and old the importance of personal hygiene. Unilever is also involved in projects and initiatives to raise standards of education in the local communities.

EMPLOYMENT

Unilever believes that success requires the highest standards of corporate behavior toward employees, consumers and communities. To that end, it has created a work environment that embraces diversity and doesn't compromise integrity or professional excellence. As a result, the company consistently ranks among the world's top employers. Corporate leaders are encouraged to foster the pursuit of excellence, while employees are challenged to pursue goals, develop professionally, and maintain a balance between their professional and personal lives.

When recruiting employees, Unilever seeks individuals who can demonstrate leadership, team commitment, integrity, innovation, and drive; and who have a passion for achievement. It seeks experienced professionals for senior positions, and it offers a graduate development program for recent graduates or students nearing graduation. The aim of the program is to develop future business leaders within the organization.

Unilever offers career management processes that provide professional development and recognition. It also provides learning opportunities and has installed feedback systems that ensures individuals are on target with their performance, development and career plans.

SOURCES OF INFORMATION

Bibliography

BBC News. "Unilever: A Company History." *BBCi*, 22 February 2000. Available at http://news.bbc.co.uk.

Parker, Kay. "Old-Line Goes Online." *Business 2.0*, June 2000. Available at http://www.business2.com.

Semilof, Margie. "Unilever Tackes E-Logistics." *Internet Week*, 30 October 2001. Available at http://www.internetweek.com.

"Nestle and Unilever Go to War" *Management First*, 14 May 2001. Available at http://www.managementfirst.com.

For an annual report:

on the Internet at: http://www.unilever.com/investorcentre/financialreports

For additional industry research:

Investigate companies by their Standard Industrial Classification System Codes, also known as SICs. Unilever's primary SICs are:

2038 Frozen Specialties, Not Elsewhere Classified

2099 Food Preparations, Not Elsewhere Classified

2841 Soap & Detergents

2842 Specialty Cleaning Polishing

Also investigate companies by their North American Industry Classification System Codes, also known as NAICS codes. Unilever's primary NAICS codes are:

311412 Frozen Specialty Food Manufacturing

325611 Soap and Other Detergent Manufacturing

325612 Polish and Other Sanitation Good Manufacturing

325620 Toilet Preparation Manufacturing

Union Pacific Corporation

FOUNDED: 1862
VARIANT NAME: UP

Contact Information:
HEADQUARTERS: 1416 Dodge St., Rm. 1230
   Omaha, NE 68179
PHONE: (402)271-5000
FAX: (402)271-6408
URL: http://www.up.com

OVERVIEW

Union Pacific Corporation (UP) is the country's leading railroad carrier through its Union Pacific Railroad, a rail system that covers much of the western and midwestern United States, as well as Canada and Mexico. In addition to transporting coal, chemicals, and other cargo through 23 states along its 33,000 route miles of rail lines, UP also moves freight on the roads with its trucking operations. UP's trucking segment is made up of Overnite Transportation, offering less-than-truckload (LTL) shipments throughout the eastern U.S. and Motor Cargo Industries, the LTL carrier covering the western United States.

Famed for its role in building a significant part of the country's first transcontinental railroad in 1869, Union Pacific survived early years of scandal and financial uncertainty to emerge as perhaps the most respected U.S. railroad. Blessed with valuable land and mineral rights along its many miles of track, UP has built a substantial business in natural resources. At one time in the 1970s, it appeared that its energy holdings might eventually overshadow UP's rail business, and some day they may well do so, but the heart and soul of Union Pacific Corporation remains its railroad.

COMPANY FINANCES

Union Pacific's revenue for the year 2001 stood at $11.9 billion, a .8 percent increase from the previous year. Net income, at a record $966 million, grew 14.7 percent, however, during the same year, due to revenue growth, productivity gains, cost control, lower non-operating expenses, and lower fuel prices. Rail revenue totaled $10.4 billion, while trucking accounted for $1.1 billion of UP's total revenues for the year.

Over the last three years, UP profits have essentially remained flat. Over a 52-week period, UP stock ranged from a low of $43.75 to a high of $60.70. The company has paid dividends to its common shareholders during each of the past 102 years, and the annual dividend for 2001 was $.80 per share. UP's price-earnings ratio was 15.46 as of June 2002.

ANALYSTS' OPINIONS

A Fortune 500 company, Union Pacific will tell any potential investor that they have the most powerful franchise in the rail industry and offer stability and have proven solid financial results in difficult economic times. Analysts generally would agree with UP's statements. Salomon Smith Barney noted that UP's earnings were above estimates in early 2002 but that lower than expected fuel prices were most of the reason, which is outside management's control. They also noted that the rail industry in general offers slow growth characteristics. Similarly, Morgan Stanley, Dean Witter reported in early 2002 that UP was the only railroad in the United States to beat consensus earning expectations but that the lack of non-fuel productivity gains was a concern as the company's expenses actually increased $20 million during a quarter in which revenue remained flat. Analysts at Merrill Lynch generally agreed, but they noted that the higher than expected earnings were due to a variety of factors, including better than expected operating income from trucking subsidiary Overnite. Through focus on market, price, and penetration combined with solid service, UP believes that it will continue to grow revenue faster than the economy.

HISTORY

Union Pacific came into existence when U.S. President Abraham Lincoln signed the long-anticipated Pacific Railroad Act of 1862, which created a rail link between the established eastern states and the rapidly growing states of the far West. The act called for the creation of a public corporation, called Union Pacific Railroad Company, to build a railroad from Nebraska to the California-Nevada border and there to meet the Central Pacific, building east from Sacramento, California, and later linked with San Francisco. Later, the meeting place of the two railroads was set at Promontory Summit, Utah Territory. The government retained the right to inspect each section of track laid before releasing the allotted number of bonds, and it would keep two directors on UP's board, but the company was to be otherwise a venture of the private sector.

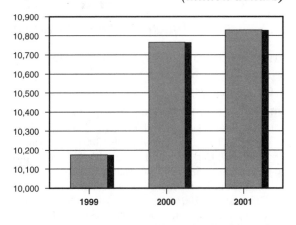

FINANCES:
Union Pacific Corp.
Operating Revenues, 1999-2001
(million dollars)

Leadership of the UP fell chiefly to Thomas C. Durant and the Ames brothers, Oliver and Oakes, who sought to make handsome profits off the railroad's hurried construction. Durant was the vice president and dominant figure in the company's early years, and it was he and a handful of others who formed a construction company called Credit Mobilier of America (CMA) to receive contracts from Union Pacific for the building of its vast railroad. Estimates vary as to precisely how inflated these contracts were, but later congressional investigations left no doubt that the backers of CMA intentionally siphoned off far more of the UP's capital than was fair to its investors or good for its future financial health. The investigations of the early 1870s also revealed that the CMA principals bribed members of Congress with company stock.

Still, the railroad they built was a splendid success, and so vast a project might never have been undertaken without the promise of equally vast profits to be made. In five years the UP crews laid more than 1,000 miles of rail between Omaha, Nebraska, and Promontory Summit, Utah Territory, where on May 10, 1869, a golden spike completed the first transcontinental rail line. The railroad's completion supplied a critical impetus to the development of the U.S. West, which to that time had been settled only on the Pacific Coast and in areas of unusual mineral wealth, such as Colorado. With the coming of the railroad, farmers, ranchers, and manufacturers were able to transport their goods to the great eastern metropolitan markets cheaply and quickly, and the West began to fill with pioneers. As the area's most significant railroad for almost 15 years, Union Pacific enjoyed rapid growth and excellent earnings for its scandal-ridden promoters, who

FAST FACTS:

About Union Pacific Corporation

Ownership: Union Pacific is a publicly owned company traded on the New York Stock Exchange.

Ticker Symbol: UNP

Officers: Richard K. Davidson, Chmn. and CEO, 60, 2001 base salary $1,100,004; Ivor J. Evans, Pres. and COO of the Railroad, 59, 2001 base salary $683,340; Carl W. von Bernuth, SVP, Gen. Counsel and Sec., 58, 2001 base salary $421,900; James R. Young, EVP Finance of UPC and CFO of the Railroad, 49, 2001 base salary $400,008; Dennis J. Duffy, EVP Operation of the Railroad, 51, 2001 base salary $400,008; Leo H. Suggs, Chmn. and CEO of Overnite, 62

Employees: 48,000

Principal Subsidiary Companies: Union Pacific has subsidiaries, including Union Pacific Railroad Company, Union Pacific Resources Company, and Overnite Transportation, serving the eastern United States, and Motor Cargo Industries, serving the western United States. Subsidiary Fenix manages four technology companies in telecommunications, wireless software products, and transportation management.

Chief Competitors: Union Pacific competes with other companies in the railroad and trucking industries, primarily the railroad companies Burlington Northern Santa Fe, Norfolk Southern, and CSX.

---

were dominated from 1873 to the mid-1880s by financier Jay Gould. The Credit Mobiler scandal began in 1872, when several UP officials received $23 million in dividends from the bogus construction company, Credit Mobiler, and gave a portion of its stock to members of Congress. Gould bought into the UP in 1873 and rescued the railroad from near bankruptcy.

In 1884 Union Pacific completed the Oregon Short Line (OSL) to the Pacific Northwest from the connection with the Union Pacific at Granger, Wyoming. OSL gave UP access to Portland, Oregon. The company logo, the railroad's shield, debuted in February 1889. Since its inception, UP has had four non-shield logos and eleven variations of the shield logo. In 1890 UP's first subsidiary, Union Pacific Coal Co., was established to sup-

ply coal from the Wyoming coal mines for UP's steam locomotives. After years of struggling with debt, efficiency problems, and increasing competition from three rival lines, Union Pacific filed for bankruptcy in 1893. The company was put in receivership in 1897 and sold for $110 million to a group of investors at an Omaha, Nebraska, auction where it was reorganized as the Union Pacific Railroad. The sale is significant in the company's history as one of the investors is Edward H. Harriman, then president of the Illinois Railroad.

Beginning in 1898, Harriman and Judge Robert S. Lovett run Union Pacific, and Harriman's leadership over the next ten years was the key to rebuilding the Union Pacific into the most modern railroad of its day. After a failed attempt to purchase the Central Pacific Railroad from parent Southern Pacific Railroad (SP), UP bought 38 percent of Southern Pacific's stock and assumed control over SP in 1901. In 1905 Union Pacific gained access to Los Angeles when the San Pedro, Los Angeles, and Salt Lake Railroad was completed. The same year, in an attempt to cut passenger train operation costs, the company ordered the first gasoline-powered McKeen Motor Car, a railroad motor car (bus), which would replace light density steam-powered passenger trains and were widely used by UP and SP over the next decade. In 1906 the subsidiary Pacific Fruit Express was created to haul fruits and vegetables with a fleet of 6,000 iced refrigerator cars.

Harriman died in 1909 and Lovett, then elected Chairman of the Executive Committee, later became president of Union Pacific and Southern Pacific. Harriman's two sons, Averell Harriman and Roland Harriman along with Lovett's son, Robert Abercrombie Lovett, continued their fathers' legacy, eventually running the company until 1969. In 1912 the U.S. Supreme Court ordered UP to sell its now 46 percent stake in SP and relinquish control of Southern Pacific. Under Judge Lovett, UP reorganized in 1920 with Union Pacific Company in New York now limited to major financial matters, policy decisions, and government regulations with all other management decisions made by Omaha's Union Pacific Railroad headquarters. Carl R. Gray, one of UP's most notable presidents, is named president of Union Pacific Railroad System.

In the late 1920s, subsidiary Union Pacific Stages was formed and introduced the country's first transcontinental bus service in a joint agreement with Chicago & Northwestern Railroad (C&NW). Innovation marked the next two decades when the first streamlined passenger train in the country, Union Pacific's M-10000, made its first run in 1932 and, in 1941, when UP took delivery of the No. 400, the first locomotive of the Big Boy class of steam locomotives and the largest steam locomotives ever built. The last of its kind, No. 844, was built for UP in 1944, and it continues to serve the UP from Cheyenne, Wyoming to this very day.

UP faltered in the late 1950s, its income, dividend, and stock price all falling between 1956 and 1961. Part of the problem lay in the rapid depletion of the company's best oil well, outside Los Angeles, and part lay in the continuing loss of railroad freight sales to the trucking industry. In response, UP restructured its holdings into three divisions—transportation, land development, and natural resources—and in the mid-1960s began a concentrated program of mineral, oil, and gas exploration. In 1969 UP acquired Champlin Petroleum Company and Pontiac Refineries from Celanese Corporation for $240 million, thus completing the formation of a fully integrated oil and gas business. UP also signed a joint-venture agreement allowing a subsidiary of Standard Oil Company of Indiana to drill for oil on its acreage, with UP getting royalties and retaining a quarter interest in whatever oil was found. The beginning of 1960s also marked the beginning of the longest and most intensely challenged railroad merger proposal's in the history of the United States when Union Pacific filed to merge with Chicago, Rock Island & Pacific Railroad (CRI&P) into Union Pacific. In 1969 Union Pacific Corporation was established as a holding company with headquarters in New York City. Union Pacific Railroad is one of its operating companies, with headquarters remaining in Omaha. The end of the 1960s also brought with it the end of the Harriman-Lovett dynasty at the company when Roland Harriman and Robert A. Lovett retired from active roles in the company, but remained on the board of directors until 1978, when Harriman died and Lovett resigned.

In 1974, fifteen years after UP's application to merge with CRI&P, it was approved. UP, however, terminated it offer three months later resulting from CRI&P's financial decline, which eventually forced them into bankruptcy. Pacific Fruit Express, jointly owned by UP and SP since 1906, has its assets split between the two companies as subsidiaries Union Pacific Fruit Express (UPFE) and Southern Pacific Fruit Express (SPFE).

The 1980s were a time for more growth when UP acquired the Missouri Pacific Railroad and Western Pacific Railroad, giving it access to the San Francisco Bay area for the first time since 1912. The year 1986 brought about the consolidation of all 40 of its regional customer centers into one National Customer Service Center in St. Louis. The company also forged into the trucking industry, buying Overnite Transportation Service, a nationwide trucking operation, to further intermodal service. In the early 1990s, UP seemed to be balanced between a streamlined, comprehensive rail and truck carrier and a natural resources division capable of considerable expansion or contraction depending on the market price of commodities.

Growth abounded, as the company acquired Chicago & North Western Railroad in 1995, but it failed in an attempt to purchase the Santa Fe from competitor Burlington Northern Santa Fe Corp. In 1996 the company merged with Southern Pacific Railroad, forming Union Pacific Railroad Corp., the largest railroad operation in the United

CHRONOLOGY:

Key Dates for Union Pacific Corporation

1862: The Pacific Railroad Act is signed by Pres. Abraham Lincoln and Union Pacific is formed to build a transcontinental railroad

1869: The first transcontinental railroad is completed and marked in a ceremony with a golden spike driven at Promontory Summit, Utah

1873: Jay Gould rescues UP from near bankruptcy

1889: Union Pacific's first logo is unveiled

1893: UP files for bankruptcy

1897: UP is sold to a group of investors, including the legendary Edward H. Harriman; Harriman and Judge Robert S. Lovett become longtime leaders of UP

1901: UP assumes control over competitor Southern Pacific Railroad

1912: Supreme Court orders UP to sell its controlling stake in Southern Pacific Railroad

1927: Subsidiary Union Pacific Stages launches the first transcontinental bus service in the United States

1941: UP acquires locomotive No. 400, the first of the Big Boy class and largest of the steam locomotives

1960: UP requests to merge with the Chicago, Rock Island, & Pacific Railroad (CRI&P), which becomes the longest and most severely challenged railroad merger proposal in U.S. history

1969: Union Pacific Corp. is established as a holding company with Union Pacific Railroad as one of its operating companies

1981: UP acquires the Missouri Pacific Railroad and the Western Pacific Railroad

1986: UP acquires Overnite Transportation Service, a trucking service with nationwide operations

1996: Union Pacific Railroad merges with Southern Pacific Railroad forming the largest rail company in the United States

1997: A "transportation emergency" is declared when UP services grind to a halt resulting from merger-related problems

Workers in London, Ontario, apply a U.S. flag decal to the side of a Union Pacific Corp. locomotive. (AP Photo/HO/UnionPacific)

States. Union Pacific Railroad is kept as a wholly-owned subsidiary of Union Pacific Corp. Due to the merger, the following year brought a number of problems, including computer glitches, labor disputes, equipment shortages, and safety issues that effectively shut down operations within a matter of months. A transportation emergency was declared in 1997 by the Surface Transportation Board (STB) to move 40,000 cars off the rail, acquire more locomotives, and hire additional personnel to aid the cause, which cost the United States an estimated $2 billion in lost production. The same year, UP absorbed the Missouri Pacific Railroad and invested in the Mexico City Terminal Co. to operate lines in Mexico. Union Pacific then moved its headquarters to Dallas, Texas.

Union Pacific showed improvement in 1998, with the STB declaring that a renewal of the emergency service order was unnecessary. The company cut 2,400 employees and organized into northern, southern, and western divisions, including 22 local offices. In 1999 the company moved headquarters once again, this time to Omaha, Nebraska. As the millennium drew to a close, UP leased 1,000 new diesel-electric locomotives to replace 1,500 older trains. The year 2000 saw the company place its bets on technology, bringing an alliance with Canadian Pacific Railway Co., CSX Corp., and Norfolk Southern Corp. to invest in Arzoon, an Internet-based tranportation management system.

STRATEGY

Union Pacific has identified the components that it believes will ensure continued revenue growth: market, price, penetration, and customer service. With a franchise that has access to some of the fastest growing markets, including the southwestern U.S. and Mexico, UP believes that it will have an advantage over the rest of the slower growing markets. They plan on an aggressive pricing strategy, based on products and value-added services. To increase market share, UP intends to convert highway business to railroad business. To penetrate new markets, UP believes that the key is reliable, consistent customer service.

Union Pacific also plans to proceed with more emphasis on efficiency in its operations. With employee productivity at an all-time high in 2001, the company plans on building on this strength as the economy rebounds. Union Pacific also has plans to increase its implementation of technology to increase customer service and grow revenue. UP's trucking subsidiary Overnite, with some of 2001's best financial results in the industry, will continue to focus on on-time performance and profitable revenue growth for future success. Overnite's improved transit times in more than 3,000 lanes and improved one- and two-day service lanes will provide opportunities for future growth and efficiency. The acquisition of Motor Cargo Industries in 2001 also enhances the company's strategy of growth within its trucking unit.

To highlight the company's prestigious 140 years of helping build a prosperous nation, UP launched an advertising campaign in April 2002 called "Building America." The ads consisted of two television spots narrated by actor Sam Elliott who spoke of the connection between Union Pacific and the country's way of life while showing images of majestic landscapes filmed on UP tracks near Moab, Utah, and Santa Maria, California, to highlight the campaign's theme of UP and its employees helping build America.

INFLUENCES

One of the successes enjoyed by UP in 2001 was the locomotive modernization program. In order to make their assets more productive, UP acquired 500 new units and retired more than 700 units. As a result, maintenance costs decreased dramatically and the fuel consumption rate attained its best level in the company's history.

A fundamental component for revenue growth, UP continues efforts to keep things running quickly and smoothly. Although the company seeks to use new technology to play a major role in its future, some of their methods have come under fire. In 2002 UP announced plans to bring its unmanned locomotives, using remote controlled operations, to Houston despite many safety and efficiency issues. With several accidents involving UP locomotives that operate without a Locomotive Engineer on board in Des Moines, Iowa, Hinkle, Oregon, and Kansas City, Missouri, the Brotherhood of Locomotive Engineers (BLE)in the Houston area voiced concerns that the company is sacrificing safety by using less than the most qualified personnel to operate the locomotives. The BLE's main concern was that UP's major involvement in shipping potentially deadly chemicals and hazardous materials makes the use of individuals who are not Locomotive Engineers as remote control operators as allowing potential safety problems. There are no Federal Railroad Administration (FRA) regulations in place regarding remote control, merely voluntary guidelines that are not enforceable, so UP continues to implement the technology at many of its major switching yards.

CURRENT TRENDS

The company continues to establish alliances with other railroads to introduce new, competitive services and meet customer needs more effectively. UP partnered with CSX, for example, to establish the "Express Lane" service that transports perishables from California and the Pacific Northwest to the East coast. The service enjoyed revenue growth of 12 percent and was 90 percent on time.

In partnership with leading competitor Norfolk Southern, UP started the "Blue Streak" intermodal service with routes from Los Angeles to Atlanta and beyond and has been nearly sold out since its launch, owing to a 99 percent on-time status.

The increasing use of technology is also another trend seen by the company in 2001. UP implemented a voice recognition system at the National Customer Service Center, enabling customers to release cars 24 hours a day with a mere phone call. Receiving extremely good customer response, UP plans to add more functionality in the coming years. Similarly, after receiving negative feedback from the company's Internet site, UP streamlined its Web pages, resulting in a 95 percent increase in online transactions and earning the company *B2B* magazine's top ranking for transportation/shipping Web site.

Finally, in an effort to cut costs and preserve natural resources, Union Pacific installed multiple EnergySaver systems as the first part of a multi-tiered program to conserve energy on lighting in their facilities nationwide. The first EnergySaver installation at their Chicago locomotive repair warehouse resulted in 20 percent energy saving levels with no noticeable reduction in lighting levels. To achieve maximum energy efficiency in its lighting system, UP will also contract to receive high efficiency ballasts and lamps that will take place later in 2002.

PRODUCTS

Union Pacific offers services in the two main categories of Railroad and Trucking. Rail operations, serving the western two-thirds of the country, have more than 33,000 route miles linking the Pacific Coast and Gulf Coast ports to the Midwest and eastern United States. They also provide several north/south corridors to important Mexican gateways. By maintaining coordinated schedules with other carriers, the company also handles freight to and from the Atlantic Coast, the Pacific Coast, the Southeast, the Southwest, Canada, and Mexico. Rail freight consists of six commodities: automotive, agricultural, chemicals, energy, industrial products, and intermodal. Some of the newer and more successful services introduced in this segment include the "Express Lane," in partnership with CSX, which moves fresh and frozen fruits and vegetables in refrigerated equipment across the Untied States. The success of this service led the company to expand service to additional U.S. locations in 2002.

The company's trucking segment includes the operations of Overnite and Motor Cargo. Overnite services specializes in less-than-truckload (LTL) shipments serving all 50 states and parts of Mexico and Canada. With 170 service centers throughout the United States, Overnite provides regional, inter-regional, and long haul service. Overnite cargo consists of a variety of goods,

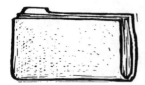

CONNECTING A NATION

Union Pacific's 2002 advertising campaign, "Building a Nation," highlights some of the company's greatest assets: leadership and history. In one of the two featured television ads, a gravelly-voiced Sam Elliott says, "In 1869 we connected a nation—east to west, west to east. Today we connect a nation—past to present, present to future. So you might say that the road to the future, isn't a road at all." In another ad, depicting gorgeous shots of the vast American vistas along Union Pacific's routes, Elliott says, "33,000 miles of timber and steel—from Portland to New Orleans, from Los Angeles to Chicago—and the beauty of the land that spans half the continent. Its been said that in those 33,000 miles of rail you can feel America's pulse." These ads can be viewed at the company's Web site.

including machinery, tobacco, plastics, textiles, paper products, and electronics. To expand its trucking services, Union Pacific acquired Motor Cargo in 2001. Motor Cargo is now a regional LTL carrier serving 10 of America's western states. General commodities' Motor Cargo carries consumer goods, packaged foodstuffs, industrial and electronic equipment, and auto parts.

CORPORATE CITIZENSHIP

Union Pacific Foundation has been the philanthropic arm of Union Pacific Corporation and Union Pacific Railroad since 1959. The company's activities are centered in the communities where there is a significant corporate presence in a effort to improve the quality of life in the areas in which their employees live and work. In 1999 the Foundation distributed $7.5 million to more than 700 institutions across the United States in education, health and human services, community and civic causes, and the arts. Several U.S. organizations supported by the Foundation benefiting women, minorities, and the physically disabled include: the American Institute for Managing Diversity, the Cardinal Glennon Children's Hospital, Cay-Uma-Wa Youth Services, El Museo Latino, Hispanic Scholarship Fund, Neighborhood Centers Inc., PUENTE Learning Center, and Self-Enhancement Inc.

GLOBAL PRESENCE

United Pacific is the primary rail connection between the United States and Mexico, providing several north/south corridors to principal Mexican gateways. Its Mexico Markets group aims to facilitate market share growth in the land transportation of commodities to and from Mexico and to establish efficient border and operations processes. The company will continue to increase the focus on the growing international intermodal market. Additionally, UP interchanges traffic with the Canadian rail system. Export and import traffic is conveyed through Gulf Coast and Pacific Coast ports and across the Mexican and, mostly through interline connections, Canadian borders. The company also maintains an International Customer Service Center (ICSC), with a branch office in Mexico city, in addition to their successful National Customer Service Center. UP also entered into a 2001 joint agreement with the Canadian National Railway to introduce a new truck-competitive service for intermodal shipments between Central Canad, Michigan, Texas, and Mexico City.

EMPLOYMENT

Union Pacific outlines several values and leadership behaviors among its company culture, including safety, quality principles, respect for employees, commitment, accountability, simplicity, and communication. The company maintains that it acts with respect for all employees; addresses employees' developmental needs and builds on their strengths through coaching and training; and promotes and rewards managers for their leadership skills, technical knowledge, and abilities. UP's corporate policy provides equal opportunity to all employees and supports diversity. Support groups within Union Pacific include the Black Employee Network, begun in Omaha in 1979, boasting more than 700 employee members; the Women's Network, founded in March 1989; and the Latino Employee Network. About 87 percent of UP's 48,000 employees are represented by 14 major rail unions.

The company strives to retain and motivate their workforce and looks for innovative approaches to work/life issues company-wide. Alternative work arrangement and flexible benefits the company employs include Rest Easy, an in-home alternative for dependent care when an emergency arises; Life Care Services, to help management employees with prenatal planning, adoption, adult care, and related services; and Employee Assistance, designed to assist employees and their families with a range of personal problems. *Working Mother* recognized the company's efforts in 2001 by naming the company as on of the top 100 employers for working mothers.

SOURCES OF INFORMATION

Bibliography

"Union Pacific Builds in Energy Conservation with Electric City." *PR Newswire*, 3 June 2002.

"Union Pacific Corp." The Gale Group, June 2002. Available at http://galenet.galegroup.com.

"Union Pacific Corporation." *Hoover's Online*, June 2002. Available at http://www.hoovers.com.

Union Pacific Corporation Home Page, 2002. Available at http://www.up.com.

"Union Pacific's Unmanned Locomotives: A Danger to Public Safety." *PR Newswire*, 11 June 2002.

For an annual report:

on the Internet at: http://www.up.com **or** write: Union Pacific Corporation, 1416 Dodge St., Rm. 1230, Omaha, NE 68179

For additional industry research:

Investigate companies by their Standard Industrial Classification Codes, also known as SICs. Union Pacific Corporation's primary SICs are:

4011 Railroads, Line-Haul Operating

4213 Trucking, Except Local

6719 Holding Companies, Not Elsewhere Classified

Also investigate companies by their North American Industry Classification System codes, also known as NAICS codes. Union Pacific Corporation's primary NAICS codes are:

213112 Support Activities for Oil and Gas Field Operations

482111 Line-Haul Railroads

484121 General Freight Trucking, Long-Distance, Truckload

United Airlines

FOUNDED: 1931
VARIANT NAME: UAL Corp.

Contact Information:

HEADQUARTERS: PO Box 66100
   Chicago, IL 60666
PHONE: (847)700-4000
FAX: (847)700-5229
URL: http://www.ual.com

OVERVIEW

United Airlines in 2001 moved from the number one air passenger carrier in the world to number two in number of daily departures, number of destinations (both domestic and international), and jet fleet size. United Air Lines Corporation (UAL Corp.), its parent company, is the largest majority employee-owned company in the world. In 2002 United's operating fleet totaled 567 aircraft, and, in 2001, the company noted that its average age of aircraft is eight years. However, the troubled company cancelled delivery contracts with Boeing and Airbus for all 18 aircraft ordered for 2003 delivery. In 2002, United flew destinations in the United States and 27 other countries. Like other major airlines, United has established "hubs" or major route and passenger transfer centers in Chicago, Denver, San Francisco, Los Angeles, and Washington, D.C. (Dulles) to fly passengers between North America and the Pacific, and Latin America and Europe. In 2001, United cancelled service to Hong Kong from New York. In 2001 United averaged more than 210,000 passengers per day compared to 230,000 passengers per day in 1997. In 2001 UAL flew about 108 billion passenger miles, down from more than 121 billion revenue passenger miles in 1997, according to UAL Corp.'s 1997 and 2001 annual reports. Besides its domestic and international passenger flights, United also operates a cargo service, but problems in operations saw a 24 percent decline in cargo revenue in 2001 compared to 2000, according to company disclosure statements. The airline currently has two main cargo centers: one a consolidation center in Charlotte, North Carolina, to serve the southeastern and mid-Atlantic states; and a transfer center at JFK Airport in New York. A new cargo transfer center started operating in Honolulu in 1998, which serves as a major cargo connection point for Japanese air cargo coming into and out of the United States and for domestic cargo to and from Hawaii. In 2001 through 2002, new cargo facilities opened in Miami, Newark and Chicago.

Besides its domestic passenger flight operation serving major cities and hubs around the United States, United is able to "feed" or provide flights to smaller cities or shorter distances through its Shuttle by United service and through its United Express program. The latter program is a marketing arrangement with small, independent carriers, In June of 2002, the United Express regional component serviced 150 destinations in the United States, totaling about 1,800 daily flights.

COMPANY FINANCES

Like many other companies in the airline industry, United saw its financial operations plummet in 2001, so much so that a former chief executive officer sent a message to all employees that there was danger of the company perishing. By June of 2002, the company's financial situation was most precarious, and it was again without a CEO after turnaround expert John W. Creighton turned around and left the top position after only a half year in command. "The troubled carrier has been a graveyard of failed executives who have tried to save it," said the Seattle Post-Intelligencer. In addition, a writer for Financial Times in 2002 predicted that the cash-strapped company might have to declare for Chapter 11 bankruptcy for relief from creditors, following news that the company abruptly cancelled all deliveries for new planes slated for 2003. However, other analysts dispute that claim, saying that the company, though clearly in trouble, may be able to get through its current crisis with the aid of loans only.

Before quitting his newly accepted job as chief executive officer, according to the Chicago Daily Herald, Jack Creighton gave UAL shareholders a quotation from Ben Franklin that summed up UAL's economic woes, union worker disputes, and the fallout of the human and economic effects of the September 11 terrorist attacks: "That which hurts, also instructs."

UAL placed too much emphasis in 2001 on its expected merger with USAir, but the consolidation was stopped cold by announced opposition by the U.S. Justice Department which said the merger would result in unfair competition advantages. The merger of the two financially ailing companies would have created the biggest air corporation ion the world. Also in 2001, the company saw two of its flights go down with passengers and crew aboard on September 11 in commandeerings engineered by international terrorists. Trying to stop losses that totaled some $2.1 billion in 2001, the employee-owned company ironically had to force 20,000 workers to accept layoffs.

FAST FACTS:
About United Airlines

Ownership: United Airlines is the principal subsidiary of UAL Corporation, a publicly owned company traded on the New York, Chicago, and Pacific Stock Exchanges.

Ticker symbol: UAL

Chief Competitors: United Airlines competes with both domestic and international airlines, chief among them being American Airlines; USAir; British Airways; and Delta.

The only good news for UAL shareholders in 2002 was that the bleeding of the victim was only half as bad as it had been the year before. Instead of the $10 million a day losses incurred the end of 2001, UAL lost $5 million a day or $510 million for the first quarter of 2002, according to self-disclosures. The company expected losses to continue at lease until the end of 2003, but some analysts said normal air traveler patterns for all airlines could be as far away as 2007. Shares of UAL continued to plummet in 2002, selling for under $12 a share.

ANALYSTS' OPINIONS

In spite of staggering losses, managerial problems, and employee layoffs, some analysts point to United's long previous successes as evidence the company can fly out of the turbulence it has been experiencing in the early 2000s. In short, the analysts are buying the airline's slogan carted out for print and broadcast commercials in 2002: "A reason to believe in United." If business travelers who purchase higher-end tickets find that reason to believe, analyst Michael Friedman of American Express Financial Corp. thinks a turnaround is possible before 2003. Perhaps the analyst least optimistic about United's chances of reversing its misfortunes is aviation industry analyst Sam Buttrick of UBS Warburg. "With its current cost structure, it is unlikely that UAL will be profitable until 2004 or even 2005," Buttrick informed the San Francisco Chronicle in May of 2002. "It is further unlikely that UAL will ever be able to earn attractive returns on capital on any consistent basis with its current cost structure." Most optimistic is Michael Boyd, principal of the Boyd Group, who told the San Francisco

CHRONOLOGY:
Key Dates for United Airlines

1927: Boeing Air Transport begins offering passenger routes to its air mail routes

1931: Boeing, National Air Transport, Pacific Air Transport, Varney Air Lines, and Stout Air Services begin working together to eliminate competition calling themselves United Airlines

1934: Boeing, National, Pacific, and Varney officially merge as United Airlines and Transport

1943: The company name becomes United Airlines

1954: United is the first airline to use flight simulators as part of its pilot training

1961: United acquires Capital Airlines

1967: Becomes the first airline to surpass $1 billion in annual revenue

1969: UAL becomes the holding company for United Airlines

1979: United loses $72 million largely attributable to a month-long labor strike

1985: Acquires Pan Am's Asian traffic rights; loses number one ranking in passenger volume to American Airlines

1994: United employees become majority shareholders of United

2001: On September 11, two United Airlines planes that had been hijacked by terrorists went down in New York and Somerset, Pennsylvania, killing all aboard; following an announcement that the U.S. Justice Department planned to block a merger between USAir and UAL that would have raised airline fares and hurt competition, US Airways Group Inc. and UAL Corp. ended plans to consolidate operations; UAL union workers oust CEO and chairman Jim Goodwin, and Jack Creighton becomes CEO

2002: Newly named UAL CEO Jack Creighton hands in his resignation and the beleaguered airline looks for a successor

Chronicle. "I'm high on United Airlines. . .They have cleared the deck and are getting rid of a lot of excess baggage."

HISTORY

The company traces its roots back to the Boeing Company. Between World War I and World War II, the former Boeing Air Transport established the first international air mail route between Seattle and neighboring British Columbia. Starting in 1927 other routes were established, including passenger routes. Boeing Air Transport was merged with National Air Transport, Pacific Air Transport, and Varney Air Lines in 1931 to form United Air Lines and Transport.

Over the years United has pioneered important innovations in the air travel industry. These include flight attendant service, an in-flight kitchen, non-stop coast-to-coast service, and in 1971 the automated reservation system.

In July 1994 United's shareholders approved an historic stock ownership plan, in which United's employees became the majority shareholders in the company—owning 55 percent of United. This resulted in tremendous cost savings for the company in the areas of pay, benefit, and work rules. The most important result of this was that for about six years it strengthened the company's presence in an increasingly competitive airline market. But that advantage unraveled in the 2000s as unions representing baggage carriers, stewardesses and other employees fought management for wage increases and largely won all concessions they had demanded by 2002. Coupled with top management turnover, fewer air traffic after September 11, 2001, and a failure to merge with USAir following U.S. Department of Justice opposition of the plan, UAL experienced a turbulent business economy expected by analysts to continue for years to come.

CURRENT TRENDS

Traditionally, economic downturns have especially affected the airline industry directly impacting passenger ticket sales. Another influence on airline revenues has been fare wars. In 2002, for example, United tried to raise tickets on many domestic flights by $20, only to drop the plan when Northwest Airlines announced it was keeping lower fares and used that as a marketing plus. Another trend has been that wage demands from employees not only contributed to United's economic woes in 2002 but also led to the so-called "furloughing" of more than 20,000 employees. Battles between unions and United are hardly over, according to analysts. "Labor is unlikely to agree to permanent wage rollbacks," analyst Sam Buttrick of UBS Warburg in New York told the *San Fran-*

cisco Chronicle. "They have worked hard to get the wage structure where it is."

CORPORATE CITIZENSHIP

Through its United Airlines Foundation, United Airlines supports such charitable causes as the Alzheimer's Association, Make a Wish Foundation, Fulbright Scholars Programs, Habitat for Humanity, Inner-city Games, Museum of Science and Industry, Orbis Flying Eye Hospital, the United Negro College Fund, the United Way, and others. In addition, the company makes travel donations to numerous health organizations and supports schools throughout the country. The company's employees have won high praise for their volunteerism all season long, but the December "Fantasy Flights" have long drawn media notice. Employees arrange trips for disadvantaged children to locations disguised as the North Pole.

GLOBAL PRESENCE

United Airlines expanded to include international service in 1983 with flights to Tokyo. In 1986 the company took over the now defunct Pan Am's Pacific routes and thus added 11 cities in 10 nations to its flight schedules. Four years later the company began flights to Europe from Washington D.C. and further expanded in 1991 when it took over PanAm's flights from London's Heathrow airport, adding 13 more routes to its growing list of destinations. In 1992 the company began Latin American service with flights between Miami and Caracas, Venezuela. Soon after, United added flights to 11 more countries. In 1997 the airline was flying to nearly 30 nations. However, the addition of flights seemed more and more unlikely in 2001 and 2002 as United's financial situation worsened. In fact, in 2001, UAL cancelled its New York to Hong Kong route.

According to its 2001 annual report, United's Pacific operations were responsible for 16 percent of the company's revenues that year, down from 20 percent in 1997. Through its Tokyo hub, United provides passenger service between its U.S. gateway cities: Chicago, Honolulu, Los Angeles, New York, and San Francisco, and Bangkok, Beijing, Hong Kong, Seoul, Shanghai, and Singapore. Within Asia, United provides service between Osaka and Seoul.

EMPLOYMENT

Worldwide, United Airlines employs more than 80,000 persons, but some 20,000 were furloughed in 2002 and not all will be rehired or will be available for rehiring once the economy rebounds. Because United Airlines is an employee majority owned company, its management places particular importance in operating within a consensus framework to gain employee trust and loyalty, which has resulted in increased productivity. But by 2002, employees joined shareholders in expressing frustration with UAL top management and gave the non-binding demand that all future pay to executives be tied to company profits, a demand that made the vacant job of CEO in 2002 most unattractive to superior executives approached by headhunters for UAL.

SOURCES OF INFORMATION

Bibliography

Armstrong, David. "Flying into turbulence." *San Francisco Chronicle,* 9 May 2002.

Comerford, Mike. "Creighton Quits the Top Post at UAL." *Chicago Daily Herald,* 17 May 2002.

Earle, Julie. "Creighton Quits the Top Post at UAL." *Financial Times,* 1 May 2002.

Kesmodel, David. "UAL Workers Suspicious of Concessions." *Rocky Mountain News,* 4 May 2002.

Labich, Kenneth. "When Workers Really Count." *Fortune,* 14 October 1996.

Merrion, Paul. "Flight Paths Divulge for Airline Rivals." *Crain's Chicago Business,* 3 June 2002.

Lott, Steve. "Former United CEO Takes Home $5.7 Million After Resignation." *Aviation Daily,* 28 March 2002.

"UAL Corp." *Hoover's Company Profiles,* 2002. Available at http://www.hoovers.com.

UAL Home Page, June 2002. Available at http://www.ual.com.

United Airlines Annual Report, 2002. Available at http://www .google.com/

Wallace, James. "Creighton Quits the Top Post at UAL." *Seattle Post-Intelligencer,* 6 June 2002.

Williamson, Tammy. "UAL Investors Vent Frustration." *Chicago Sun-Times,* 17 May 2002.

Wong, Edward. "United's Lame-Duck Chief May Have to Move Fast." *The New York Times,* 19 May 2002.

———. "UAL Loses $510 Million." *New York Times,* 20 April 2002.

For additional industry research:

Investigate companies by their Standard Industrial Classification Codes, also known as SICs. United Airlines' primary SICs are:

4512 Air Transport, Scheduled

4522 Air Transport, Non-scheduled

Also investigate companies by their North American Industry Classification System codes, also known as NAICS codes. United Airlines' primary NAICS code is:

481110 Scheduled Air Transportation

United States Postal Service

FOUNDED: 1971

Contact Information:

HEADQUARTERS: 475 L'Enfant Plaza SW
    Washington, DC 20260-0010
PHONE: (202)268-2000
FAX: (202)268-2392
URL: http://www.usps.gov

OVERVIEW

Many people think of the United States Postal Service (USPS) as just another part of the federal government, like the Department of Agriculture or the FBI. But in fact, the USPS, although an independent agency of the federal government, is largely self-supporting financially; and though it enjoys a monopoly in some areas of its services, particularly First Class mail, it faces competition in other areas, especially package delivery.

The USPS is the planet's largest postal system, delivering 41 percent of the world's mail. By contrast, the second-largest system, Japan's, handles only 6 percent. It also delivers the mail more cheaply than the postal systems of industrialized nations such as Germany and Japan, whose citizens pay $.58 and $.63 respectively for First Class postage as opposed to the $.34 rate in effect in the United States in 2001. According to the USPS, it delivers more mail in one day than its chief competitor, Federal Express, delivers in a year.

COMPANY FINANCES

The USPS reported revenues of $65.9 billion in 2001, $64.6 billion in 2000, and $62.7 billion in 1999. Total net income for 2001 was $1.7 billion compared to $199 million in 2000 and $363 million in 1999.

ANALYSTS' OPINIONS

In 1997, a war of words between the USPS and competitor Federal Express began an ongoing battle, a battle that the USPS may have won in the short term. Federal Express had complained about USPS television commercials that stated that the USPS's Priority Mail was far cheaper than comparable services of Federal Express or United Parcel Service (UPS). The complaint was that the ads were misleading because the USPS "can't match their delivery record or track a piece of Priority Mail from shipper to receiver," according to *Time* magazine. In January 1997, the National Advertising Review Board rejected the complaint, but the two rivals continued to face each other in lawsuits.

Another controversy surrounded the USPS's attempt in 1997 to secure an increase in the price of a First Class stamp. Although the USPS had not gotten such an increase since 1995 and although the increase was only to be for $.01, arguments against it were raised. With record profits in the ledgers of the USPS, competitors such as UPS said that an increase amounted to unfair competition by the USPS against rival companies. Although the price increase was approved, it was offset by decreases in other areas. The independent commission approving the increase reportedly did so reluctantly because it may have felt misled by previous dire warnings by the USPS that the increase was needed to keep the USPS from drowning in "red ink," warnings that never came to be.

However, all was not negative or controversial. At the beginning of the new century, USPS reported that it had scored high marks on *Government Executive* magazine's Federal Performance Report, earning A's in managing for results, financial management and physical assets management. Also, it had received more White House "Closing the Circle" awards for environmental achievement, which brought its total to 37 awards since the recognition began in 1995. Further, *Fortune* magazine ranked USPS among the nation's top 20 employers for minorities.

In a significant development, USPS formed an alliance with its top rival Fedex to create an air transportation network. The effect of this network was to increase the market reach of the Postal Service's Express Mail Next-Day and Priority Mail Two-Day services.

HISTORY

The ancient Greek historian Herodotus wrote admiringly of how Persian messengers of his day got the mail delivered: "Neither snow/nor rain/nor heat/nor gloom of night stays these couriers from the swift completion of their appointed rounds." These lines were inscribed on the front of New York's central post office.

The postal systems of Herodotus' time, and those of the Roman Empire (by far the most advanced in the ancient world), were chiefly for the use of governments and influential persons. This was also the case with major

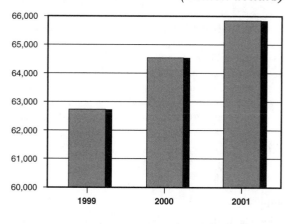

FINANCES:
United States Postal Service Revenues, 1999-2001 (million dollars)

non-Western postal systems of ancient and medieval times, notably those of the Chinese, the Mongols, and in the New World, the Aztecs and Incas. Even when Europe emerged from the Middle Ages and its postal system, like many other aspects of daily existence, came back to life, use of mail was confined to those who were very wealthy. And in fact, prior to the invention of the printing press and the spread of reading, there were few literate persons outside of the nobility and the clergy.

The British postal system that began to develop in the 1600s, particularly with the establishment of the London Penny Post, was more democratic and accessible. In America, a country founded on British-inspired ideals of government, the postal system was from the beginning conceived as a cheap, efficient means for all people to communicate with other people throughout the country. Before the age of electronic communications and rapid transportation, this was a particularly necessary facet of life. Even today in the era of the Internet, America would be handicapped without its postal system. In the 1990s, the USPS continued the tradition of efficient delivery for a cost much lower than the postage in other developed countries.

America's postal system has its roots in the British postal system. In the 1600s, the British colonies in America got their first postal operations, which at that time were still privately operated, though under authority of the British monarch. As the colonies matured into a larger unit that would eventually be called the United States, Benjamin Franklin became their Deputy Postmaster General in 1753. Twenty-two years later, when the colonies revolted against England, they made Franklin the first U.S. Postmaster General.

FAST FACTS:

About the United States Postal Service

Ownership: The United States Postal Service is an independent agency in the executive branch of the U.S. Federal Government. As such, it is not owned in a traditional way by shareholders but is managed with a corporate structure similar to that of large U.S. companies.

Officers: John E. (Jack) Potter, Postmaster General and CEO, 50; Robert F. Rider, Chmn.; Richard J. Strasser, EVP and CFO

Employees: 767,795

Chief Competitors: By law, the United States Postal Service (USPS) has a monopoly on the transport and delivery of First Class letters. In all other areas of its operation, however, especially in package and parcel delivery, the USPS faces increasing competition. Some competitors are: United Parcel Service, Federal Express, Airborne Express, Burlington Air Freight, DHL Worldwide Express, Emery Worldwide, and Republic Package Express.

It was not until 1847, however, that Congress actually issued the first postage stamps, an indication of how haphazard the new country's postal system remained. The era before railroads often required heroic means of delivering the mail, such as the fabled Pony Express, which only operated for a period of a few months during 1860 and 1861, prior to the completion of the transcontinental railroad. Railways greatly enhanced the efficiency of the postal system, and by the first year of the twentieth century, the United States had 77,000 post offices.

In 1911, the first airmail flight took mail between two towns in New York, introducing a major innovation in mail delivery. New systems of designating addresses also enhanced the efficiency of delivery. In 1943, the Post Office began dividing major cities into numbered postal zones, and 20 years later it introduced the much more comprehensive Zoning Improvement Plan (ZIP) Codes for the entire country.

Slightly less than 200 years after its founding, the Post Office Department, whose postmaster general had been a member of the President's Cabinet, ceased to exist. On August 12, 1970, President Nixon signed legislation creating the United States Postal Service, an independent agency in the executive branch of the federal government. Established in 1971, the USPS continued to enjoy some government subsidies but it no longer held a monopoly over delivery of packages. Thus the 1970s saw the emergence of competitors, primarily UPS and Federal Express. In the decades that followed, competition would become a significant theme for a "company" that had not previously had to face it.

The late 1970s and 1980s saw other changes as well, especially in the areas of mechanization and automation. In 1978, to offset rising costs and reduce the amount of mail piece handlings, the USPS began expanding the ZIP Code, which required new equipment. In 1982, it installed a computer-driven single-line optical character reader. The following year, the USPS further increased efficiency by introducing the ZIP+4 Code, which included a hyphen and four more digits. The first five numbers still sent the mail to the region and delivery office, while the sixth and seventh numbers zeroed the mail into a delivery sector, and the final two indicated a delivery segment that further defined the destination. That same year, the Governors of the Postal Service approved price incentives for First Class Mail bearing the ZIP+4 code.

By the 1990s, the USPS introduced more complex equipment that virtually changed the way mail traveled, including multi-line optical character readers that read the entire address on an envelope, placed a barcode on the envelope, then sorted mail at a rate of more than nine per second. In 1991, USPS started using an 11-digit ZIP Code, which helped sort mail into a delivery sequence for postal carriers. Also in the 1990s, the USPS began placing automated equipment in its office lobbies.

Despite all of the efficiency-increasing automation, the USPS encountered even more financial pressure because of the economic climate of the 1990s and a drop in mail volume. Competition increased as well, due to technological advancements in the areas of telecommunications and broadcasting as well as the rise of fax machines and home computers. In response, the USPS began restructuring. It began contracting out some work, sought more customer feedback, and began streamlining its bureaucracy. It also worked on improving service through measures such as expanded retail hours. The steps had impact, the Postal services finances improved, and it became more competitive.

STRATEGY

In 1997 the USPS created a Five-Year Strategic Plan. Its goals mirrored the risks and challenges that lay ahead for the world's largest postal service. The plan aimed to improve customer service, enhance the workplace for its employees, and improve relations with business. The plan acknowledged that electronic mail could

CHRONOLOGY:

Key Dates for the United States Postal Service

1639: First official postal system is established in Boston, Massachusetts

1753: Benjamin Franklin becomes Deputy Postmaster General in Colonial America

1775: Franklin becomes the United States' first Postmaster General

1794: Letter carriers begin delivering mail in cities

1800: The Post Office headquarters is moved from Philadelphia, Pennsylvania, to Washington, DC

1847: Congress issues the first postage stamps

1860: The Pony Express begins operations

1861: The Pony Express ceases operations

1863: Standard postage rates introduced; free city delivery began

1896: Free rural delivery introduced

1911: First airmail flight delivers mail in the state of New York

1913: Parcel post introduced

1920: First transcontinental airmail is delivered

1935: Regular trans-Pacific airmail begins

1939: Regular trans-Atlantic airmail begins

1943: Post Office begins dividing cities into numbered postal zones

1950: Residential deliveries cut from two to one a day

1963: The Zoning Improvement Plan (ZIP) Codes introduced

1970: President Nixon signs legislation to make the United States Postal Service (USPS) an independent agency

1971: The USPS is established

1977: Express mail service introduced

1982: Government subsidies are no longer given to the USPS

1995: Global Package Link introduced

1998: Postal Rate Commission approves a $.01 increase in first class postage

2000: USPS revises its five-year strategic plan

2001: USPS and FedEx Express form business alliance involving air transportation and retail business agreements; USPS releases stamp honoring heroes of September 11, 2001

---

substantially cut into the First Class mail delivery of the USPS; that at least 38 billion e-mails being sent at that time would previously have been posted by mail. The plan also looked toward important congressional legislation to reform the USPS. If passed by Congress, the way that the USPS set prices would change dramatically.

From 1997 through 2002, the USPS was to spend $17 billion for capital improvements. The money would be spent on new technologies to produce labor savings and on customer service programs that would increase revenue or enhance competitiveness.

Central to any strategy of the USPS is the cost of stamps. In 1998, the independent Postal Rate Commission approved the USPS's request for a $.01 increase in First Class stamps. Because of record income of the USPS, however, the Commission recommended cutting other costs. The Commission also delayed the implementation of the increase until 1998. In total it cut $2.4 billion in requested increases by about one third. The penny increase would bring in about $1 billion a year to the USPS.

Key to the automation strategy of the USPS was bar coding, the coded addition of address information to a letter. In 1997, 82 percent of First Class letters were bar coded. The USPS's goal was to be the first completely bar- coded, fully automated carrier. Also important to that goal was the continued development of handwriting recognition technology, vital to an agency that is at the mercy of handwritten addresses.

Three years into its Five-Year Strategic Plan, the USPS called into question some of the core assumptions of the plan and it realized it needed to revise some thinking. During the 1999 congressional hearings on postal reform, hearing stories of future mail volume declines, the USPS decided to conduct surveys and perform research. The results suggested to the USPS that its strategic planning would have to be more flexible.

To that end, in 2000, it developed a new plan (2001-2005) that set new performance goals placed in three categories: "Voice of the Customer," "Voice of the Employee," and "Voice of the Business." For the first category, the USPS set a five-year goal to earn cus-

THE FABLED PONY EXPRESS

In March of 1863, the following advertisement appeared: "Wanted. Young, skinny, wiry fellows not over 18. Must be expert rider willing to risk death daily. Orphans preferred." And so was born the Pony Express. Mail to the western coast was notoriously slow, often taking months to get there. The Los Angeles *Star* had mournfully asked, "Can somebody tell us what has become of the U.S. mail for this section of the world?" The Pony Express promised to change all that—and it delivered. The first run began on April 3, 1863 in St. Joseph, Missouri and ended in Sacramento in under 10 days, a then unheard of feat. It was accomplished by an amazing relay of riders and horses. A rider would gallop full tilt for 15 miles, then at a relay station switch to a fresh horse in under two minutes and dash on. He would continue like this for 75 to 100 miles, at which point he was relieved by a rested rider who would gallop on.

Newspapers everywhere praised the Pony Express and printed sensational stories about it. The populace was captivated. Mark Twain, while on a stagecoach in Nevada, once saw a rider speed by. "A hurrah from our upper deck, a wave of the rider's hand, and a man and horse burst past our excited faces and went swinging away like a belated fragment of a storm." Historian David Nevin: "The Pony Express was an ongoing story of thrill, speed, and lone daring."

Make no mistake, there was danger enough between the vicious snowstorms of the mountains and various native North American Indians, some of whom had conflicts, often violent, with white settlers. One rider was waylaid by Indians in the Utah Territory but he completed his run even though his jaw was broken by an arrow and his arm shattered by bullets. Another rider struggled for more than a day through a raging blizzard in a mountain pass that took him usually just a few hours to traverse. Only once did a rider lose his life to an Indian attack—and his horse escaped, finishing the run.

Heroics like the above made the riders romantic figures. The image of the daring horseman captivated the people's imagination. Young women adored them and young men wished that they, too, could taste some of that adventure and danger.

With the completion of the transcontinental telegraph in October of 1861, the Pony Express was doomed. With the last run in November of that year, a colorful and heroic chapter in U.S. postal history came to a close. The California *Pacific* wrote a fitting epitaph: "A fast and faithful friend has the Pony been to our far-off state. . . Goodbye, Pony! We looked to you as those who wait for the morning, and how seldom did you fail us! When days were months, and hours weeks, how you thrilled us out of our pain and suspense, to know the best or know the worst. You have served us well!"

---

tomers' business in a competitive marketplace by providing its world-class service at competitive prices. For the "Voice of the Employee" category, the USPS intended to foster an "inclusive and welcoming workplace consistent with the values of fairness, opportunity, safety, and security" that would offer encouragement and education. The USPS goal for "Voice of the Business" was to achieve a financial performance that demonstrated the continuing commercial viability of its service.

Specific "Customer" goals included timely, consistent, and accurate delivery of all categories of mail, and achievement of high levels of customer satisfaction. Specific "Employee" goals included training for each employee, safety improvements, better workplace relations, improvements in diversity, and a high level of employee satisfaction. Specific "Business" goals included achieving net income, investing in future improvements in service and productivity by making substantial capital investments, and controlling costs by making productivity gains. A hard task lay ahead. The

USPS realized it would be more and more difficult to achieve results under business goals that involved financial self-sufficiency, net income, affordability, and continuing high levels of capital investment.

Specific means to achieving its plan included stronger focus on issues of productivity and cost control by developing an integrated operating plan across five broad areas of concern: organizational infrastructure, work-force, pricing, revenue generation, and effectiveness of capital investment.

INFLUENCES

Though the Postal Service is no longer a full part of the U.S. Government, it is still highly influenced by federal government policy, in part because Washington still plays a role in reimbursing some Postal Service activities -that is, paying for cost overruns. This is particularly the case with mail other than First Class, which costs more to deliver than the sender actually pays for postage, as well as congressional and other government mail. Hence the government pays for the difference. Also, the Postal Service has authorization to borrow as much as $10 billion from federal funds.

Obviously these are advantages that most businesses would envy, as they would envy the USPS' continued monopoly over many aspects of mail delivery, including First Class mail. However, the present USPS setup reflects a sharp turn toward privatization of the service, beginning with President Nixon's signing into law the Postal Reorganization Act in 1970. In the years since then, particularly in the 1990s, the USPS has seen heated competition from private enterprise because companies that have to make a profit have a greater incentive to move packages quickly and treat their customers well. Hence the Postal Service has worked to adopt many of the methods of private enterprise, and it proudly touts the fact that unlike government agencies, every year it takes in as much as it spends.

As a result of privatization, costs of postage—which were once kept artificially low by government subsidies—have steadily increased. In 1974 the price of a First Class stamp jumped from $.08 to $.10; in 1985, from $.20 to $.22; and in 1995, from $.29 to $.32—four times the cost 21 years before. In 1999 the price of a First Class stamp was raised to $.33. Overall, the average increase across all classes of mail in 1999 was 2.9 percent, the smallest ever. The modest increases represented the longest period of rate stability in 27 years of postal service

But optimism didn't run high at the start of the new millennium. The year 2001 was particularly challenging, as a weakening economy and inflation combined to negatively affect the USPS's financial performance. The organization expected 2002 to be even more of a challenge due to increasing economic uncertainty as well as anxieties created in the wake of the terrorist attacks on the country. In addition, Postal Service operations were critically affected by the anthrax threat that followed the attacks.

On top of the security fears, economic woes, and rising labor costs, the USPS was worried about the apparent slowing down of mail volume growth, as much of First Class and Standard Mail was increasingly being conducted by the electronic alternatives such as email. By 2001, Internet-based bill payment systems had become well entrenched.

CURRENT TRENDS

Facing increased competition from private enterprise, the Postal Service worked harder in the 1990s to present itself as an ordinary business, one which had to worry about the bottom line. Symptomatic of this was an article in *Industry Week* about the furor former Post-

master General Marvin Runyon caused among the American Postal Workers Union with his declaration that the USPS would hire more private sector labor because it is cheaper and more efficient.

An article in *Postal Life* magazine, found on the USPS Web site, indicated that labor-management problems were still dominant in 1998. In 1996, the General Accounting Office, the investigative arm of Congress, found that persistent labor problems "generally contributed" to tense working conditions and decreased production. Unresolved employee grievances against the USPS rose from 68,000 in 1996 to 108,000 in 1998.

Employment issues were addressed in the revised Five-Year Strategic Plan (2001-2005), which indicated that USPS had developed innovative training programs that helped employees improve skills in their jobs and to meet the challenges of the new workplace. Further, and especially in light of the anthrax threat in 2002, the USPS was more intent on providing a safe and secure workplace. To help insure this, management compensation was connected in part to safety performance. At the height of the anthrax fears, the USPS worked with the top public health officials in the country to implement an aggressive and far-reaching employee protection program.

But if the Postal Service trend toward imitating private enterprise attracted the ire of unions, it had features that were bound to win the approval of customers. In the wake of feverish competition, particularly with Federal Express and UPS, the Postal Service attempted to make its deliveries quicker and to encourage its personnel to treat customers as though they have a choice of doing business elsewhere.

Another trend facing the USPS was the increasing use of electronic mail. Seeking to capitalize on the boom and to stem its losses, the USPS created postmarks for email, which, for a fee, could certify that an email was delivered. In the 2001-2005 Strategic Plan update, the Postal Service admitted that it needed to respond much more quickly and effectively to such changes. Part of the new five-year plan involved cutting costs and seeking new revenue sources within the current regulatory structure if its attempts at electronic diversion did not demonstrate sufficient impact.

PRODUCTS

In October 1996, *Advertising Age* reported that the USPS was working to increase its stamp collectors market, particularly among children between the ages of 8 and 12. In April of that year, the USPS launched its Global Priority Mail service through its International Business Unit. This put the USPS into a heavily contested market, the global courier business. Also, in January 1997, the USPS announced an experimental plan to test the market for bulk usage of nonletter-size business reply mail.

The USPS has several types of delivery service, though most persons receive mail either through city delivery or rural delivery (persons without a permanent address may receive their mail via general delivery at the nearest post office—e.g., "John Smith, General Delivery, Atlanta, GA 30303"). Persons sending mail can choose from a number of services. First Class mail is for written material such as letters and postcards, and Priority Mail is for First Class material weighing from 11 ounces to 70 pounds. Periodical-rate mail is for magazines and newspapers the delivery of which is subsidized by the U.S. government because it costs more for the USPS to deliver it than the sender pays for postage. Standard Mail (A) includes all packages and printed material not included in either of the two preceding classes (in order to qualify for a periodical-rate designation, the sender has to prove that printed material is not primarily for the purposes of advertising, whereas Standard Mail (A) includes advertising circulars). Standard Mail (B) is for packages that weigh more than one pound but are not considered Priority Mail. Express Mail is the fastest form of mail, usually guaranteed for next-day delivery.

In addition, the Postal Service sells stamps, both for mailing and for collectors; money orders; and a variety of forms of protection against losing valuable items such as insurance and certificates of mailing. Some facilities also rent post office boxes and perform other functions for their customers.

CORPORATE CITIZENSHIP

The USPS is involved in several different public issues, as evidenced by a visit to its Web site. From the USPS site, users can be linked automatically to sites for the Bone Marrow Foundation or the National Center For Missing and Exploited Children. There is also information about breast cancer, for which the USPS issued a breast cancer awareness stamp in the mid-1990s.

For at least three years, the USPS has hosted the Environmental Stakeholders Conference, which promotes environmental awareness. The USPS has long been a leader in recycling programs and in the use of alternative fuel vehicles.

Postal employees also do their part. Letter carriers in more than 10,000 cities collected food donations in May 1998. This was billed as the largest single-day effort to end hunger. In 1999, they collected 73 million pounds of food. The annual food collection was again successful in years 2000, 2001 and 2002.

GLOBAL PRESENCE

U.S. mail can be delivered to any of the 170 countries that participate in the Universal Postal Union, or UPU. The UPU, a United Nations organization, oversees mailing agreements between nations and sets international law regarding the postal service.

EMPLOYMENT

With more than 767,795 stateside employees, the USPS is one of the largest employers in the United States. Employee recruitment is decentralized and based on local postal needs. Positions include clerks, carriers, mail handlers, custodians, maintenance technicians, operations research analysts, engineers, attorneys, ergonomics specialists, chemists, information systems specialists, real estate specialists, economists, accountants, human resources analysts and specialists, safety and risk management specialists, and marketing specialists. The USPS benefits include health and life insurance, a retirement plan, a savings/investment plan with employer contribution, a flexible spending account, flextime scheduling of core work hours, and annual and sick leave.

SOURCES OF INFORMATION

Bibliography

Blackmon, Douglas A., and Glenn Berkins. "Advertising: Post Office Ads Worked, But Creator Is Out of a Job." *Wall Street Journal*, 22 October 1996.

Bradley, Sam. "USPS Launches First Global Courier Service." *Brandweek*, 1 April 1996.

"Complaint Rejected On Postal Service." *New York Times*, 29 January 1997.

Fehr-Snyder, Kerry. "New Postal Centers to Lighten the Load." *Arizona Republic*, 8 May 1998.

Greenwald, John. "Zapping the Post Office." *Time*, 19 January 1998.

Hodges, Jane. "Postal Service Thinks Young to Interest Kids In Stamps." *Advertising Age*, 7 October 1996.

"How the Postal Service Plans to Stop ëGoing Postal'." *Government Executive*, December 1996.

Knutson, Lawrence L. "A Penny Not Saved: Stamp to Rise to 33 Cents." *Associated Press*, 12 May 1998.

"A Looming Battle?" *Industry Week*, 3 February 1997.

"Postal Service Files Experimental Case For Business Reply Mail." *Direct Marketing*, January 1997.

U.S. Postal Service Home Page, May 1998. Available at http://www.usps.gov.

Hoover's Online. United States Postal Service Capsule, 15 April, 2001. Available at http://www.hoovers.com/co/capsule/7/0,2163,40507,00.html

USPS Five Year Strategic Plan. United States Postal Service Home Page, 15 April, 2001. Available at http://www.usps.com/common/category/5yearplan.htm

"William J. Henderson Named 71st Postmaster General." U.S. Postal Service Press Release, 12 May 1998. Available at http://www.usps.gov/fyi/welcome.htm.

Zvirgzdins, Ilze. "Labor-Management Peace?" *Postal Life*, May/June 1998. Available at http://www.usps.gov/history/plife/pl041698/labor.htm.

For an annual report:

on the Internet at: http://www.usps.com/financials/ **or** write: United States Postal Service, 475 L'Enfant Plz. SW, Rm. 10431, Washington, D.C. 20260-3100

For additional industry research:

Investigate companies by their Standard Industrial Classification Codes, also known as SIC codes. The United States Postal Service's primary SIC is:

4311 United States Postal Service

Also investigate companies by their North American Industry Classification System Codes, also known as NAICS codes. The United States Postal Service's primary NAICS code is:

491110 Postal Service

United States Steel

FOUNDED: 1901

Contact Information:
HEADQUARTERS: 600 Grant Street
    Pittsburgh, PA 15219-2800
PHONE: (412)433-1121
URL: http://www.ussteel.com

OVERVIEW

United States Steel produces a variety of steel products, including sheet steel, steel plate, and tubular steel. United States Steel's main steel plants are the Gary Works, one of the largest steel producing complexes in the world, located in northern Indiana; the Mon Valley Works in Pennsylvania; the Fairfield Works in Alabama; and through its foreign subsidiary USSK, the Koşice Works in the Slovak Republic. United States Steel has an annual raw steel production capability of 17.8 million tons. United States Steel is a so-called integrated steel company—it produces steel primarily from iron ore, in contrast to minimills that make steel from recycled scrap steel. Although integrated mills are able to manufacture steel of a higher quality, their production costs per ton are higher and they face stiff competition from minimills. In addition to steel, United States Steel is one of North America's top two makers of tin mill products, primarily for the container industry.

United States Steel is active in virtually every activity connected with the production of steel, including the mining of iron ore and coal, coke production, and transportation. The company's Minntac division mines taconite from which iron ore is then extracted. United States Steel mines are located in Mountain Iron, Minnesota. The firm operates coal mines in West Virginia and Alabama. It main coke works are located in Gary Indiana, Koşice, Slovakia, and the Clairton Works near Pittsburgh. United States Steel's Transtar subsidiary runs the company's truck and barge operation, which is used in large part to transport steel and raw materials. In 2001 Straightline Source was launched, an online service through which customers could place steel orders, regardless of size, directly with United States Steel. United

States Steel is also engaged in real estate development, technology licensing, and consulting services.

COMPANY FINANCES

United States Steel has experienced troubled financial times for the better part of two decades, the result of heated foreign competition, aging facilities, and increasing fragmentation in the American steel industry. The years between 1997 and 2001 have been up and down at best. Total revenues declined from $7.16 billion in 1997 to $5.47 billion in 1999. By 2001, however, they had recovered, reaching $6.37 billion. That recovery disguised continuing declines in revenues for some of United States Steel's key products though; between 1997 and 2001 revenues from sheet and semi-finished steel products dropped from $3.92 billion to $3.16 billion, while raw materials (coal, coke, and iron ore) declined from revenues of $796 million to $485 million. These losses were made up by growth in tubular products revenues, which increased from $596 million in 1997 to $755 million in 2001. The company also experienced noteworthy growth in its plate and tin mill products, as well as its engineering and consulting services and its real estate development segment between 1999 and 2001.

Between 1997 and 2001, United States Steel's output fell in most key areas: coke production, coke shipments, iron ore pellet shipments, coal shipments, and domestic steel shipments. Domestic steel production declined from 12.35 million tons in 1997 to 10 million tons in 2001. Overall production only reached 14.14 million tons in 2001 because of the acquisition of VSZ in the Slovak Republic. Lower prices for steel in Central Europe offset those gains however—$260 for Slovakian steel in 2001 compared with $427 in the United States. United States Steel's year-end share price fluctuated at the end of the 1990s: $31.25 in 1997, $23 in 1998, $33 in 1999, and $18 in 2000. It seemed to level off in 2001 at $18.11.

ANALYSTS' OPINIONS

Analysts differ on the effects of United States Steel's spin off from the USX Corporation at the end of 2001. Hoover's speculated that the steel firm would miss the deep pockets of its former parent, particularly during the difficult times that continue to beset the U.S. steel industry. Labor and legacy costs, mainly pensions and insurance for retirees, place a huge burden on the company's bottom line. A Value Line report, on the other hand, acknowledged that the restructuring could hardly happen at a worse time in the steel industry. However it believed that United States Steel would be able to survive the separation, indeed it would be strengthened by it, maintaining its earning power. Value Line saw "momentum" in

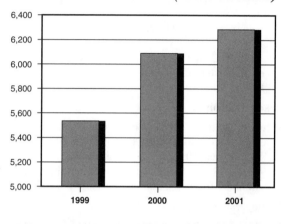

FINANCES:
United States Steel
Revenues, 1999-2001
(million dollars)

United States Steel's recovery and predicted that 2002 would be a transitional year leading to stronger future results.

HISTORY

United States Steel was the outcome of a mammoth consolidation of the American steel industry in 1901, a merger masterminded by banker J.P. Morgan, industrialist Andrew Carnegie, Charles Schwab, and Elbert Gary. Carnegie's company, U.S. Steel was acquired by Gary and Morgan and then combined with the Federal Steel Company. By the time the dust settled, a number of other companies had been added to the conglomerate, including American Steel & Wire Co., National Tube Company, American Tin Plate Co., American Steel Hoop Co., and the American Sheet Steel Co. When it was founded, United States Steel was capitalized at more than $1.4 billion, a sum equivalent to about $80 billion in 2001 dollars. It was the first billion-dollar corporation and the largest corporation in the world at the time.

In its first year of existence, United States Steel produced 67 percent of the steel made in the United States and 29 percent of the steel made in the world. The Gary Works in northern Indiana, begun in 1906, was the first major expansion of the company. The plant, which in 2001 was still the largest integrated steel plant in the western hemisphere, was comprised of four blast furnaces and had an annual capacity of 7.8 million tons. It was almost inevitable that in 1911 the U.S. Justice Department brought suit against United States Steel for

FAST FACTS:
About United States Steel

Ownership: United States Steel is a publicly owned company traded on the New York, Chicago, and Pacific Stock Exchanges.

Ticker Symbol: X

Officers: Thomas J. Usher, Chmn., CEO, and Pres., 59, 2001 base salary $1,400,000; John P. Surma, VChmn. and CFO, 47, 2001 base salary $416,667; Dan D. Sandman, VChmn. and Chief Legal and Admin. Officer, 53, 2001 base salary $481,677

Employees: 35,600

Principal Subsidiary Companies: United States Steel has subsidiary companies and facilities in the United States, Slovakia, and Mexico. In addition to activities directly related to steel production, such as iron mining, coal mining, and coke making, the firm and its subsidiaries are also involved in consulting services, transportation, and real estate.

Chief Competitors: In addition to domestic and foreign steel makers, United States Steel competes with firms that manufacture a diverse array of other materials such as aluminum, cement, composites, glass, plastics, and wood, which compete with steel in construction and manufacturing. Some primary competitors are Nucor Corporation, Nippon Steel Corporation, Pohang Iron and Steel Co., Arbed SA, Alcoa, and Bethlehem Steel.

---

antitrust violations, charging that the company had been formed specifically to dominate the U.S. steel industry. The case dragged on until 1920. In the end United States Steel was exonerated, a decision influenced, among other things, by the fact that far from dominating the U.S. steel trade, the company's market share had actually dropped from 67 percent in its first year to about 50 percent in 1911.

In the course of its history, United States Steel chalked up an impressive list of firsts. It was the first U.S. corporation to issue an annual report, to hold an annual shareholders' meeting, to adopt the eight-hour workday, and to establish an employee stock program. In 1917 it became the first company to reach $1 billion in revenues. It played a crucial roll in World War II by producing about one-third of the total U.S. steel produc-

tion, about 156 million tons altogether. Immediately after the war started, while the federal government was prohibited by law from selling armaments, United States Steel bought $37 million worth and resold them to Britain and France.

The postwar years were a time of long decline for United States Steel. Imports, made in more modern factories by foreign workers who were paid less than unionized U.S. steelworkers, began increasing. Between 1958 and 1959 alone, imports jumped from 1.70 million tons to 4.39 million tons. By the end of the 1970s, the steel industry as a whole was facing a major depression that only deepened during the course of the decade. Finally, in spring 1979, David Roderick took over as United States Steel chairman and began the long painful turnaround. He initiated plant closures—and painful layoffs—that reduced the firm's overall capacity by two-thirds. Roderick ordered the long-overdue modernization of U.S. Steel facilities, a move that increased the firm's continuous casting capacity from 35 percent in 1989 to nearly 100 percent in 1992. He entered joint ventures with foreign competitors, such as Japan's Kobe Steel and South Korea's Pohang Iron & Steel. He also sold off holdings unrelated to steel production, in particular chemical and agri-chemical businesses.

Nonetheless United States Steel had to find ways to shore up its sagging bottom line. With that in mind, the company moved into the energy business. In 1982 it acquired the Marathon Oil Company and, in 1986, the Texas Oil & Gas Co. By 1986 steel accounted for less than one-third of the company's revenues. It was reorganized under the name USX. The new firm had four operating units, Marathon Oil Company, Texas Gas & Oil Corp, USS, and U.S. Diversified Group. In 1991 USX recognized the important distinction in its core businesses when it issued a new common stock, USX-U.S., for its steel related businesses. At the end of 2001, USX underwent a major reorganization. Its steel-related businesses were spun off into a new independent company called the United States Steel Corporation. The rest of USX (its energy segments) were renamed Marathon Oil Corporation.

STRATEGY

At a time of increasingly fierce competition in the highly fragmented domestic market, United States Steel has adopted a strategy of consolidating and streamlining its vast infrastructure. It is modernizing the productive facilities that are most productive and closing down the rest. Significant modernization projects include new degasser facilities at the Mons Valley Works, a new hot-dip galvanized line at PRO-TEC and upgrades at the Gary Works. Its modernization efforts focused on producing high-quality specialty steels for specific markets, such as the automobile and construction industries. The company also recognizes the importance of globalization to its long-term health. Beginning in 2000, United States Steel made its first significant move into the global economy with the purchase of VSZ in the Slovak Republic. It is also involved in joint ventures with Japanese and Mexican firms. United States Steel's globalization strategy has various goals: To be closer to foreign workforces, to broaden the company's base of customers, and, as with domestic plant upgrades, the production of high-quality steel with special characteristics.

INFLUENCES

Imported steel presented United States Steel with a major challenge during the latter half of the twentieth century. Less developed nations in particular are able to produce steel at costs that U.S. companies—largely because of wage and benefit agreements with organized labor—are unable to match. As a result, by 1999, the United States was importing nearly one-third of all the steel it consumed. Some of that was steel which foreign producers "dumped" (or sold at an artificially low cost, often lower than the cost of producing it) on the American market. Dumped steel frequently came from countries whose steel industries were government subsidized. In both 2000 and 2001, United States Steel filed complaints with the International Trade Commission (ITC) and the U.S. Department of Commerce charging 24 countries with unfair trade practices and, in some cases, dumping. The ITC found in United States Steel's favor in the 2000 cases. In addition, the firm has urged the administration of George W. Bush to establish rules with foreign governments for steel trade and the elimination of government subsidies. The Bush administration responded in March 2002 with new quotas and tariffs on steel imports.

CURRENT TRENDS

The late 1990s witnessed the rise of a number of online steel exchanges such as Metal Suppliers, MetalSite, Metal Network Exchange Services, and eSteel. Steel consumers could visit their sites, get the best price for a type and quantity of steel, and place an order. United States Steel's response in October 2001 was to found a new division, Straightline. Specializing in carbon flat-rolled steel, Straightline enables customers, including customers whose orders would previously have been too small to place directly with United States Steel, to order online at Straightline's Web site. The site manages every aspect of the order: finding the steel at one of United States Steel's facilities, giving a quote and placing the order, meeting the

CHRONOLOGY:
Key Dates for United States Steel

1901: United States Steel is founded in Pittsburgh, Pennsylvania

1906: Construction of Gary Works

1911: Antitrust suit brought against United States Steel by U.S. Justice Department

1917: United States Steel is the first company in history to have revenues of $1 billion

1942-45: United States Steel produces 156 tons of steel for war effort

1979: United States Steel begins series of plant closures

1982: United States Steel acquires Marathon Oil Company

1986: United States Steel acquires Texas Gas & Oil Corp

1986: United States Steel reorganized as USX

2000: USX acquires VSZ in the Slovak Republic

2001: USX spins off its steel-related companies as United States Steel Corporation

specifications of the customer, and delivery. By the end of 2001, it offered delivery in North Carolina, South Carolina and parts of Florida, Tennessee, Illinois, Indiana, Michigan, and Wisconsin. New areas were planned for 2002.

PRODUCTS

With competition for steel customers at a high pitch, United States Steel in 2001 began focusing on the production of specialty steels with unique characteristics. Special tubular goods were developed for the oil industry and higher quality tin products for containers. The automotive industry—one of the world's largest buyers of steel—was targeted in particular with new kinds of steel, such as bake-hardenable and coated steels. In 2001 DUAL-TEN automotive steel was introduced, which possessed an unprecedented combination of plasticity for shaping, lightness for fuel efficiency, and strength for safety.

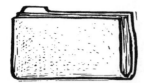

HELMETS FOR THE WAR

World War II was called, among other things, a war of steel. It was a war of steel ships, steel tanks, steel planes, and steel guns. Unique new steel alloys were required to meet the demands of warfare, many of which were developed by United States Steel. These special steels sometimes had to possess seemingly impossible characteristics. For example, United States Steel was instructed by the U.S. government to develop a steel alloy for helmets worn by soldiers. It had to be light enough to wear, flexible enough to be mechanically stamped into shape from sheet metal without tearing, and tough enough to deflect a .45-caliber bullet. The company pulled it off. By war's end, United States Steel had turned out enough of the alloy to make 21 million helmets.

CORPORATE CITIZENSHIP

In February 2002 United States Steel's domestic steelmaking facilities were registered under the environmental management systems standard of ISO 14001, administered by the International Standards Organization in Geneva Switzerland. The ISO standards were implemented in 1996 as a means of reducing pollution and improving the environment. Registration established United States Steel's commitment to adhere to existing environmental standards and to continuously develop new projects in the area. The company was the first integrated steelmaker to have all facilities registered under the ISO standard. In 2000 United States Steel was recognized by the Wildlife Habitat Council for its work in rehabilitating the site of its Clairton Works plant in Pennsylvania. The company was cited for its work as an environmental steward and in supporting biodiversity on the site.

GLOBAL PRESENCE

United States Steel made its first move into the global market in November 2000 when it purchased VSZ, a.s., a steelmaking company in Koşice the Slovak Republic. The company, renamed USSK (United States Steel-Koşice), gave United States Steel an added 4 million tons in annual steel producing capacity. The Slovak venture was undertaken to give the firm a foothold in the European market. United States Steel also participates in var-

ious international joint ventures, including a U.S. steel plant it operates with the South Korean firm Pohang Iron & Steel Co., Ltd., and another with the Japanese firm Kobe Steel, Ltd. The company's Mexican subsidiary, United States Steel Export Company de Mexico, participates in Acero Prime with two Mexican companies, Feralloy Mexico, S.R.L. de C.V., and Intacero de Mexico, S.A. de C.V. The joint venture operates slitting and warehouse operations in Mexico. Walzwerk Finow GmbH in Germany is a wholly owned subsidiary of United States Steel that produces precision steel tubes and other specialty steel.

SOURCES OF INFORMATION

Bibliography

Apelt, Brian. *The Corporation: A Centennial Biography of United States Steel Corporation*. Pittsburgh: Cathedral Press, 2001.

Berglund, Abraham. *The United States Steel Corporation: a study of the growth and influence of combination in the iron and steel industry*. New York: AMS Press, 1968.

Berner, Robert. "Finally Forging Ahead." *Business Week*, 14 January 2002.

"A Centennial History of United States Steel Corporation." *Pittsburgh Magazine*, February 2001.

Fisher, Douglas A. *Steel Serves the Nation, 1901-1951: the Fifty Year Story of United States Steel*. New York: United States Steel Corp, 1951.

Lee, Jennifer. "An Echo of Big Dreams Of a World With Big Steel." *New York Times*, 5 December 2001.

"United States Steel Corporation." *Hoover's Company Profiles*, 2002. Available at http://www.hoovers.com.

United States Steel Home Page, 2002. Available at http://www.ussteel.com.

For an annual report:

on the Internet at: http://www.ussteel.com/corp/investor_shareholders **or** write: Shareholder Services, 600 Grant Street, Room 611, Pittsburgh, PA 15219-2800

For additional industry research:

Investigate companies by their Standard Industrial Classification Codes, also known as SICs. United States Steel's primary SICs are:

1011 Iron Ore Mining

1231 Anthracite Mining

3312 Blast Furnaces & Steel Mills

Also investigate companies by their North American Industry Classification System codes, also known as NAICS codes. United States Steel's primary NAICS codes are:

331110 Iron and Steel Mills

331513 Steel Foundries (except Investment)

336414 Iron and Steel Forging

Universal Music Group

OVERVIEW

Universal Music Group (UMG) is the largest music company in the world. UMG develops, manufactures, markets, sells, and distributes the full spectrum of recorded music in 63 countries worldwide through its numerous subsidiaries, joint ventures, and licensees that represent a dominating 98 percent of the world's music market. Through its subsidiaries, UMG also engages in music publishing and mail order music/video clubs. The leading U.S. music company also is the market leader in three-quarters of the international market it operates in, including the United Kingdom, Canada, Germany, France, and Brazil. Parent company Vivendi Universal, also owner of Hollywood's Universal Studios, bought UMG from former owner Seagram in 2000.

Covering the classical music market, Universal Classics Group includes such labels as Deutsche Grammophon, the world's oldest recording company; industry legend Decca Records, which controls the world's biggest opera catalogue; and Philips Classics. UMG's Verve Music Group is the largest jazz recording company in the world, including legendary jazz artists Louis Armstrong, Count Basie, John Coltrane, Ella Fitzgerald, Diana Krall, and Al Jarreau. Subsidiary Universal Music Enterprises (UME) is responsible for music catalog management of all UMG labels. The label also owns the world's leading Broadway catalog through Decca Broadway. Universal Music Publishing Group, with 43 offices in 40 countries, is one of music's leading publishers and manages the eminent Rondor Music Catalogue. The prestigious company also operates such diverse labels as MCA Records, MCA Nashville, Mercury Nashville, Motown Record Company, Barclay, Interscope Geffen

VARIANT NAME: UMG; Polygram Records

Contact Information:

HEADQUARTERS: 1755 Broadway
    New York, NY 10019
PHONE: (212)841-8000
FAX: (212)331-2580
URL: http://www.umusic.com

FAST FACTS:

About Universal Music Group

Ownership: Universal Music Group is a subsidiary of Vivendi Universal S.A., a publicly owned company traded on the New York Stock Exchange.

Ticker Symbol: V

Officers: Doug P. Morris, Chmn. and CEO; Zachary I. Horowitz, Pres. and COO; Nick Henny, EVP and CFO; Glen Sanatar, CFO, Universal Music Enterprises; Dan McGill, CFO North America

Employees: 12,000

Principal Subsidiary Companies: Universal Music Group has some 15 record labels, including Interscope Records, The Island Def Jam Group, MCA Records, Inc., and Pressplay. Subsidiary Universal Music Publishing Group is one of the world's leading music publisher and its Universal Music Enterprises manages all of the company's labels' catalogs. Universal Music Group itself is a subsidiary of Vivendi Universal S.A., the French media and utility company.

Chief Competitors: Universal competes with other companies in the music industry, including Sony Music Entertainment, BMG Entertainment, and Warner Music.

A&M, Island Def Jam Music Group, Motor Music, Polydor, Universal Records, and Verve Music Group. Some well-known names on UMG's artist roster are Sting, Sheryl Crow, Eminem, Dr. Dre, Vince Gill, Melissa Etheridge, Bon Jovi, Andrea Bocelli, Cranberries, Elton John, U2, and Enrique Iglesias.

Other major UMG subsidiaries are Pressplay, a Sony Music UMG joint venture, offering on-demand online music by subscription though affiliates like MP3.com and Yahoo!; GetMusic, along with the getmusic.com Web site, one of the Web's most visited music content sites; and MusicUwant, the first big music company to offer customized music programming for high-speed Internet access and interactive television.

COMPANY FINANCES

The maker of one of every four albums sold worldwide in 2001, UMG has approximately a 22.7 percent share of the music market worldwide and leads the industry in 70 percent of the markets where it has operations. Owned by French media firm Vivendi Universal, UMG's financial data is reported in euros. Revenues for 2001 were down 6.6 percent from the previous year at $6.5 billion euro, which translates to about $5.8 billion. The United States accounts for 42 percent of UMG's total revenue, another 40 percent comes from Europe, and the remaining 18 percent comes from the rest of the world. During a 52-week period, Vivendi Universal stock ranged from a low of $26.75 to a high of $65.55 and had a price-earnings ratio of 231.15.

ANALYSTS' OPINIONS

Clearly a world leader in the field, UMG's financial performance for the first quarter of 2002 represented a decline of 6 percent. The company attributes this to a lighter release schedule than the previous year, with most of its major releases due out in the latter part of 2002. Also working against the company was the overall worldwide decline in the music industry in early 2002, estimated at 8 percent, attributed to a slimmer release schedule than in the prior year. In that light, UMG fared better than the music industry as a whole, with its market share holding steady. Trends that plague UMG and the industry as a whole include rampant CD-copying and Internet music file-swapping services. The International Federation of the Phonographic Industry (IFPI) valued pirated music activities at $4.2 billion in 2001. Analysts estimate that music sales were off 10 percent in 2001, with poor sales in the largest two markets, the United States and Japan. Media analysts predict that the pirated music trend will only continue and worsen as a new generation of listeners becomes accustomed to seeking out music in this way. Many analysts predict that UMG's newly launched Internet subscription services, including Pressplay, will take no fewer than five years to make a marked difference in sales and eradicate existing free competition.

HISTORY

The company's long and varied history can be understood by tracing the evolution of the two main companies that eventually came together in 1998 to form UMG, Polygram and Universal. Polygram's beginnings date all the way back to 1898, When the Siemens Company founded Deutsche Grammophon Gesellschaft. In 1924 the company introduced its second brand name to be used abroad, Polydor. In 1962 Siemens entered into a joint venture to create a record company with a Netherlands-based company called Philips Electronics N.V., with subsidiary Philips Phonographische Industries (PPI), who had established the Phillips Classics label in

1951 and acquired Mercury Records in 1960. The agreement gave Siemens 50 percent ownership of PPI, and Philips an equal share of Deutsche Grammophon. The two subsidiaries reorganized as PolyGram in 1972, the same year they acquired Verve Records. The company expanded throughout the 1980s, first acquiring the London-based classical music label Decca in 1980. Philips and PolyGram introduced the music world's first compact disc in 1982, and PolyGram Music Publishing began operations in 1986. Philips gained full ownership of subsidiary PolyGram in 1987. Two years later saw PolyGram's initial public stock offering and its acquisition of Island Records. Growth continued through the 1990s with the acquisitions of A&M Records in 1990 and Motown Records in 1993. The following year PolyGram acquired 50 percent of Def Jam Recordings and established a subsidiary in Russia, the first western record company to do so. In 1995 the company moved into Latin America when it bought Rodven Records, the region's largest independent record company. In 1996 PolyGram acquired another 10 percent of Def Jam.

Universal, meanwhile, was founded in Chicago some years later, in 1912, by pioneer filmmaker Carl Laemmle under the name Universal Film Manufacturing Co. Universal relocated to Southern California in 1915. The U.K.-based Decca Record Co., which launched Decca Records in the United States, acquired a controlling interest in Universal Pictures in 1952, while Music Corporation of America (MCA), acquired the Universal Studios property for its newly created TV division, MCA Inc. Universal Pictures and MCA Inc. merged in 1962 when MCA acquired Decca Records. The year 1964 marked the beginning of MCA Music Publishing with MCA's purchase of Leeds Music and Duchess Music, while Universal began opening its Universal City lot doors for visitors, marking the birth of its recreation and theme park operations. The company opened the Universal Amphitheatre in 1972, initiating the company's interests in owning and operating concert venues and live entertainment promotion. Decca merged into MCA Records in 1973, along with ABC Records, acquired in 1979. MCA continued to grow, with the acquisition of Chess Records in 1985 and Geffen Records and GRP Records in 1990. The next year, MCA Inc. was, itself, bought by Matsushita Electric Industrial Co. Four years later, in 1995, ownership of MCA Inc. was passed again when the Seagram Company Ltd. acquired 80 percent of the company. The same year, 1995, MCA established Rising Tide (later renamed Universal Records). In 1996 MCA Inc. was renamed Universal Studios, Inc., and the MCA Music Entertainment Group was renamed Universal Music Group. That year Hip-O Records was also founded, and a 50 percent interest in Interscope Records was acquired.

In 1998 the separate histories of these two groups came together when Universal owner Seagram acquired PolyGram and renamed the newly combined music operations of the two Universal Music Group. The newly

CHRONOLOGY:

Key Dates for Universal Music Group

1898: The Siemens Company founds Deutsche Grammophon Gesellschaft

1962: Siemens enters into a joint venture with Philips Electronics N.V., owner of the Phillips Classics label and Mercury Records

1972: The company reorganizes as PolyGram in 1972, the same year they acquired Verve Records

1980: Polygram acquires classical music label Decca

1989: PolyGram has its initial public stock offering and acquires Island Records

1990: PolyGram acquires A&M Records

1993: Polygram acquires Motown Records

1998: Universal owner Seagram acquires PolyGram and renames the newly combined music operations of the two Universal Music Group

1999: UMG becomes sole owner of Def Jam; GetMusic and getmusic.com is launched; UM3, a division of Universal Music International, is created; Universal Music Enterprises (UME) is created; the company acquires additional shareholdings in Universal Music Turkey, Nese Muzik, Mars Musik, and S Musik; launches Universal Music India; invests in the Latin music Web site eritmo.com; MCA Music Publishing is renamed Universal Music Publishing

2000: Acquires Rondor Music; Vivendi Canal Plus merges with Seagram in 2000, resulting in Vivendi Universal, now parent to UMG

merged UMG continued its long history of expansion—embarking on unprecedented growth as the millennium drew to a close. Highlights from 1999 include UMG's purchase of the remaining portion of Def Jam; partnering with BMG to form the GetMusic Internet content and commerce entity with e-commerce Web site, getmusic.com; the launch of UM3, a division of Universal Music International covering all areas of catalog marketing outside North America; the creation of Universal Music Enterprises (UME); expansion in Turkey with the acquisition of additional shareholdings in Universal Music Turkey, Nese Muzik, Mars Musik, and S Musik;

launch of Universal Music India; launch of UMG's Jimmy and Doug's Farm Club label; investment in the Latin music Web site eritmo.com; and the renaming of MCA Music Publishing to Universal Music Publishing. Among its acquisitions in 2000 was Rondor Music, International Publishing Company. French company Vivendi Canal Plus merged with Seagram in 2000, with the resulting conglomerate becoming known as Vivendi Universal, now parent to UMG.

STRATEGY

Going into the difficult climate for the music industry in 2002, the goals of UMG were to try and develop a balance between the investment in artist development and effective cost control measures. The company planned to remain focused on costs, artist development, and beginning legitimate digital music offerings for the public. To cover a variety of media, UMG also partnered with *Popstars* television shows in several European countries in 2001. Popstars artists produced major hits in France, the United Kingdom, and Germany.

Vivendi's strategy for the company as a whole is based on a consumer-focused attitude, committed to anticipating consumer needs and building consumer loyalty to create and deliver high-quality services and products that satisfy consumers worldwide. Vivendi hopes to strengthen leadership in each of their markets; concentrate on internal growth, which it noted should be above 10 percent for the year; continue restructuring when necessary; finish integrating teams; and reinforce the synergies in their businesses. As an example of revenue synergies, Vivendi launched Universal Music Mobile in France, which drew on their strength's in telecommunications and music to target a younger audience.

Universal launched its "Universal Best" campaign, running from June to August 2001, which offered music fans a selection of 40 "Best Of" albums from a wide variety of artists in diverse genres at discounted prices. Music included selections from rock, R&B, dance, pop, and New Age. The goal was to reintroduce some of the company's greatest songs and showcase collectible editions by the company's headlining acts at affordable prices. The strategy was implemented, in part, to help combat music piracy and attract music lovers with limited disposable income.

INFLUENCES

UMG was built through acquisitions, a tradition the company has continued into 2000 and beyond. Through strategic acquisitions, UMG hopes that through its latest acquisitions, it will find the right business model to realize profits via the Internet. One of the most significant developments in that area was the founding of Pressplay, a subscription, on-demand online music service that allows consumers to stream, download, and burn music onto compact discs. Artist development will also be key for the company moving into 2002 and beyond as the overall slump in the music industry forces the company to come up with "the next big thing" that will stimulate record sales in the United States and worldwide.

Internationally, UMG continued the trend of gaining market share in other countries. In 2001 UMG purchased legendary Latin and Tropical label RMM Records founded by Ralph Mercado 14 years ago and has delved into the Latin music genre in recent years. Following major structural and personnel changes at all levels, Universal Music Latin Maerica/Iberian Peninsula, Universal became the market leader in Spain and Portugal during the year 2001. The company aims to be the clear number one label in the region.

CURRENT TRENDS

Looking to the Internet as the way of the future, UMG became the world's leading Internet music publisher through a variety of growth strategies. The company acquired a stake in online music leader ARTISTdirect, Inc.; expanded its e-commerce activities by creating Universal eLabs and Global e; invested in Listen.com, the Internet's online directory to legal downloadable music; and launched Pressplay, a joint venture with Sony Music Entertainment, all in 2000. Universal eLabs was formed to provide research and strategies for developing and implementing global e-business and new technology distribution for UMG. With pirated music on the Internet a growing problem in the music industry, UMG's Pressplay offers on-demand, digital music online that may be downloaded and burned on to compact discs from artists represented by Universal, Sony, EMI, and several independent labels. Pressplay's services are also offered by subscription through affiliates MSN, Yahoo!, and sister company MP3.com. MP3.com, acquired in 2001, contained more than 1.2 million song and audio files, 185,000 artists, and had 5 million visitors. MP3.com Europe had more than 3 million registered users with sites adapted the markets in the United Kingdom, France, Germany, and Spain.

Another sign that UMG seeks to leverage Internet profits is by purchasing the remaining 50 percent of Get-Music from former partner BMG in 2002. The company's ventures, which include GetMusic and MusicUwant also offer a range of online, high-speed online, offline, and television music options. UMG also struck a non-exclusive licensing deal with Streamwaves, the leading digital music subscription company, which would add U.S. Universal Music titles to Streamwaves' on-demand subscription music service.

PRODUCTS

UMG supplies a diverse mix of music products and services, including the manufacture, marketing, sales, and distribution of the full spectrum of recorded music in 63 countries worldwide through its numerous subsidiaries, joint ventures, and licensees worldwide. Through its subsidiaries, UMG also engages in music publishing; online, on-demand subscription music services; and mail order music/video clubs.

Toward their goal of maximizing catalog repertoire through non-traditional and alternative channels, the company's Universal Music Enterprises (UME) entered into an agreement with alternative marketing company Disc Marketing, Inc. in 2002 to create E-CDS for corporate clients that will contain content including video and animated content, music tracks, television commercials, product information, and links to Web sites where products are sold and/or promoted, and more. With speedy, high-quality sound and video downloading, the E-CD may be used alone or along with a Web site in the corporate client's marketing campaign with print, TV, radio, and online elements. Disc Marketing uses new media and music to aid in marketing its clients brands, which include Target, NASA, Toyota, Betty Crocker, General Mills, Princess Cruises, Kellogg's, and Sears. Disc Marketing also supplies audio programming for United Airlines, Air Force One, and Air Force Two.

CORPORATE CITIZENSHIP

The company encourages employees to contribute their time and money in volunteer initiatives and other ways that reflect their personal values and interests. The Vivendi Universal Foundation is the philanthropic arm of the organization, with the main goals of supporting the under-privileged in the United States, France, and elsewhere. Fondation Vivendi Universal in France was created in 1996 to aid in the causes of unemployment and inequality of opportunity. Over the following five years, its funding created or maintained 18,000 jobs in local services—1,377 jobs created in 2001 alone. Another interest of the foundation includes narrowing the digital divide, a modern form of inequality. Vivendi Universal foundation in Berlin funded some 40 projects, which created 122 jobs and secured another 50. The Vivendi Environment team Water Force aided the Red Cross in providing water to 100,000 people in Afghanistan. The company subsidiaries in Hungary team with UNICEF helped launch a program to equip all children's hospitals with free TV sets, computers, and access to the Internet.

Vivendi's philanthropic focus in the United States is on young people, especially those with limited resources, in four major areas: education, music, the arts,

and new technologies. The foundation supported some 54 programs and donated more than $15 million. One of the many programs the company supports is Reach Out and Read, a project that combines pediatric check-ups with literacy in an effort to encourage avid reading at a young age. The project distributes more than 550,000 books in the manner. Another U.S. program the company participates in helps children learn about the consequences of racism and prejudice for the benefit of society.

GLOBAL PRESENCE

UMG is the leading global music company, enjoying a 22.7 percent share of the world market in 2001 and operations in 63 countries worldwide. The company's numerous subsidiaries, joint ventures, and licensees represent a dominating 98 percent of the world's music market. UMG also owns the largest music catalog and one of the leading global music publishing companies, Universal Music Publishing Group. One of every four albums sold worldwide in 2001 was a Universal album. UMG is also the world leader in classical music, with a 41 percent share worldwide. Sales outside the United States account for 58 percent of the company's total revenue. The company is a market leader in three-quarters of the international market it operates in, including the United Kingdom, Canada, Germany, France, and Brazil.

Of late, the company has been expanding even further into the Latin market with the 2001 acquisition of legendary Latin and Tropical label RMM Records. The company's UM3, a division of Universal Music International, is designed to maximize the value and profile of Universal Music's catalog outside North America. Its three main areas of concentration are Catalog Marketing; Commercial and Consumer Marketing; and TV Merchandising. With more than 2 million subscribers, UMG also maintains the largest mail order music/video club in Europe, Britannia, a UK-based operation founded in 1969. The company also operates DIAL, the largest music/video club in France founded in 1970.

EMPLOYMENT

As a an international company with 12,000 employees, UMG recognizes and prizes cultural diversity within the organization. They believe their multi-cultural background is a unique strength to be drawn upon to preserve, promote, and protect the distinct cultural character in the countries, communities, and local regions that it serves. They also value the variety of their musical content, which serves to represent their own heritage and the cultural diversity worldwide.

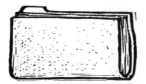

UMG IS MUSIC TO YOUR EARS

Universal Music Group's talent roster boasts some of the most well-known and popular recording artists in the world. Evidence of that could be found at the 44th Grammy Awards ceremony held in February 2002, where UMG snagged 32 awards. Some of the company's most successful artists of 2001 included Shaggy, boasting UMG's best selling album of the year at more than 10 million copies; India.Arie, nominated for seven Grammy awards and whose debut album sold 1.3 million copies; Enrique Iglesias, boasting the hit single, *Hero* and selling more than 4 million albums; and Mary J. Blige, with 2.7 million Grammy-nominated albums sold and a chart-topping single. In other musical genres, Andrea Bocelli won the best-selling album of the year at 3.6 million copies, and Diana Krall sold 2.1 million copies of her Grammy winning best-selling jazz album of the year. The U.S. number one selling country album was also a Universal album, *O Brother, Where Art Thou?* which also ranked as best-selling soundtrack of the year, sold 4.5 million copies, and received four Grammy Awards.

Other major characteristics that the company prizes in its employees are creativity, and the company seeks to promote imaginative, initiative, individual expression and creative freedom, which not only reflects the company's enterprising spirit, but drives their continued growth and innovation. Teamwork, observation of strict ethical standards, value creation, and social responsibility are also named by the company as part of its value system.

SOURCES OF INFORMATION

Bibliography

"Bronfman, Vivendi Look Forward." *Billboard*, 22 December 2001.

"Labels to Count Cost of Pirates' Plunder." *Reuters*, 16 April 2002.

"Universal Acquires The Remaining 50% Share of GetMusic From BMG." *Billboard*, 5 May 2001.

"Universal Best for Less." *New Straits Times*, 9 July 2001.

"Universal Hays Latin Label." *Los Angeles Business Journal*, 2 July 2001.

"Universal Music Enterprises and Disc Marketing, Inc. Join Forces in the CD Music Premium Market." *PR Newswire*, 23 May 2002.

"Universal Music Group." The Gale Group, June 2002. Available at http://galenet.galegroup.com.

"Universal Music Group." *Hoover's Online,* June 2002. Available at http://www.hoovers.com.

Universal Music Group Home Page, 2002. Available at http://www.umusic.com.

"Universal Purchases Tropical Indie RMM." *Billboard*, 7 July 2001.

"Universal Reports Improved Cash Flow." *Billboard*, 10 November 2001.

"Universal Settles into New Rhythm With Lopez," 1 September 2001.

Vivendi Universal Home Page, 2002. Available at http://www.vivendiuniversal.com.

For an annual report:
on the Internet at: http://www.vivendiuniversal.com

For additional industry research:
Investigate companies by their Standard Industrial Classification Codes, also known as SICs. Universal Music Group's primary SIC is:

3652 Phonograph Records Tapes & Disks

Also investigate companies by their North American Industry Classification System codes, also known as NAICS codes. Universal Music Group's primary NAICS code is:

334612 Prerecorded Compact Disc (except Software), Tape, and Record Reproducing

Vans Inc.

FOUNDED: 1966

OVERVIEW

Vans Inc. makes and sells footwear, clothing, and accessories for skateboarders and snowboarders. To target this market, which consists primarily of youths ranging from 10 to 24 years of age, Vans sponsors various skateboarding and snowboarding competitions. In the early 2000s, the firm also began operating several large skateboarding facilities. Since the mid-1990s, manufacturing has taken place primarily in Mexico and South Korea. In addition to its 150 retail outlets, Vans sells its products at department and specialty stores such as Nordstrom's, Sears, JC Penney, and Footlocker, as well as through independent distributors in nearly 50 countries.

COMPANY FINANCES

Sales exceed $100 million for the first time in 1996. By 1999, sales had more than doubled to $205.1 million, and profits had grown to $8.7 million. Sales in 2000 grew 33.3 percent to $273.5 million, while profits grew 38.5 percent to $12.1 million. Earnings per share grew from 64 cents to 84 cents over the same time period. Despite a weakening economy, sales in 2001 grew 24.8 percent to $341.2 million, and profits grew 24 percent to $15 million. Earnings per share reached 99 cents. Sales and profits for Vans began to slow in early 2002.

ANALYSTS' OPINIONS

Although revenues for Vans paled in comparison to the sales secured by Nike and other athletic shoe makers,

Contact Information:
HEADQUARTERS: 15700 Shoemaker Ave.
    Santa Fe Springs, CA 90670
PHONE: (562)565-8267
FAX: (562)565-8406
URL: http://www.vans.com

FINANCES:

Vans Inc.
Revenues, 1999-2001
(million dollars)

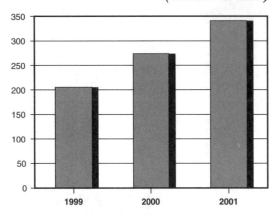

many analysts believed the firm's success was due to its persistence in targeting a much smaller market than its larger competitors. According to a May 2001 article in *Business Week*, "by staying true to its base of alternative-sports fanatics, the company has built an intensely loyal customer base." However, other analysts viewed this narrow focus as a liability, reasoning that if the popularity of sports like skateboarding and snowboarding faded, so would sales for Vans.

HISTORY

In the mid-1960s, shoe manufacturer Paul Van Doren decided to create a company that not only manufactured shoes, but also sold them directly to customers. Along with partners Serge D'Elia, Gordy Lee, and Jim Van Doren, Paul Van Doren moved from his East Coast home to Southern California. He oversaw the creation of a factory and a 400-square-foot retail store, which opened for business in March of 1966. The new business was named Van Doren Rubber Co.

As they grew in popularity, Van Doren's shoes came to be known simply as Vans. In 1967, the firm opened a new retail outlet nearly every week. In the early 1970s, skateboarding emerged in California as a popular alternative to surfing, and Vans developed a new shoe that quickly became popular with skateboarders. The firm expanded its skateboard shoe offerings with new color combinations and patterns. In 1979, Vans released a slip-on version of the shoe that became one of the hottest fads in California. The trend spread throughout the United

States after Sean Penn, the lead actor in *Fast Times at Ridgemont High*, wore a pair of checkerboard slip-ons throughout the 1982 hit movie. As a result, department stores, as well independent retailers, began to carry Vans.

By the early 1980s, Vans was also making shoes for the growing numbers of BMX bicyclers. Growing demand prompted Vans to build a new 175,000-square-foot plant in Orange, California. Employees exceeded 1,000 for the first time. The firm began to forge licensing deals with companies who wanted to manufacture things like Vans sunglasses, notebooks, and other products that would appeal to the youth market. Vans also began to expand into shoes for sports like baseball, football, basketball, and soccer, a move that caused production costs to soar. These high costs, coupled with increased competition and pressure to lower prices, eventually forced the firm into Chapter 11 bankruptcy.

Vans emerged from bankruptcy in 1986. Although Vans slip-ons were no longer all the rage, demand for Vans shoes remained strong. Sales reached $50 million in 1987, and the firm returned to profitability. By then, international sales, mainly in Mexico and Europe, accounted for 10 percent of revenues. Despite the fact that nearly all major manufacturers of athletic shoes had shifted production to Asia, Vans remained committed to domestic production. Although this strategy did allow the firm to fulfill orders more quickly, it also added to operating costs.

Investment firm McCown De Leeuw & Co. paid $74.4 million for Vans in 1988. Although Paul Van Doren remained chairman, the firm's new owner hired Richard Leeuwenberg to take over as president and CEO of Vans. Sales reached $70 million in 1990. International sales grew to account for 25 percent of total revenues. Vans completed its initial public offering the following year, offering 4.1 million shares for $14 apiece.

Despite recessionary economic conditions in the early 1990s, sales grew to $91 million, and profits jumped to $6.5 million in 1992. International sales accounted for 32 percent of revenues. Although Vans catalogs showcased more than 200 different shoe styles, the firm's original canvas and rubber shoe continued to garner 50 percent of revenues. Sales and earnings began to wane in 1993, falling to $86.5 million and $2.7 million, respectively. The following year, sales tumbled to $80.5 million, while earnings dropped to $1.4 million. Walter Schoenfeld replaced Leeuwenberg in 1994. Along with moving some of the firm's production to Asia, Schoenfeld also closed several under performing stores. To help strengthen the Vans brand name, he also hired a new team of designers and marketers. In 1995, Vans closed its plant in Orange, California, laying off nearly 1,000 workers. Although some domestic production continued to take place at a plant in Vista, California, the bulk of manufacturing was handled by South Korean factories.

Vans began manufacturing snowboarding boots for the first time in 1995. The firm also diversified into women's and children's lines. With manufacturing being handled by outside contractors, Vans began to focus on its marketing efforts. The firm started to sponsor various skateboarding and snowboarding events. In 1999, Vans built three skateboarding parks in Southern California. The firm began selling its products online in 2000. By the end of 2001, ten skateboarding parks had been completed.

FAST FACTS:
About Van's Inc.

STRATEGY

Paul Van Doren's decision to create a company that combined manufacturing and retailing activities allowed him to not only eliminate the costs of a middleman; it also helped him remain in close contact with customers. This direct contact with clients paid off in the late 1960s when several complaints over cracked soles prompted the firm to revamp its rubber sole design. Realizing that the simple diamond pattern it had used cracked too easily along the edges, the firm began to incorporate vertical lines into the pattern; this design was eventually patented as Vans' waffle sole. In the early 1970s, after skateboarders began requesting new shoe colors and patterns, Vans hired two professional skateboarders to develop new designs; one of their first creations, a red and blue shoe called the Era, became the best selling shoe among skateboarders.

In the mid-1990s, CEO Gary Schoenfeld worked to change the focus of Vans. After moving manufacturing overseas, Vans was able to turn its attention to strengthening the Vans brand. To this end, the firm became more market-oriented, attempting to pinpoint what its key market, teenagers, wanted, as well as how to best sell to this market. According to Schoenfeld, as quoted in a December 1999 issue of *Inc.*, "You have to strategically commit to the teen market and them tactically find the things that are relevant to teens and cost-effective for the company. Kids don't relate to direct hard-sell advertising. They see through a company that's just spending a lot of money to attract their attention. Our strategy is to ingratiate ourselves more into their lifestyles. Rather than pour money into advertising, we invest in sports and music and entertainment, sponsoring music festivals and events in our core sports."

INFLUENCES

Efforts to diversify into footwear for more mainstream sports in the mid-1980s proved disastrous. Because the firm continued to manufacture its products in the United States, its production costs were much higher than those of competitors who had moved production to Asia. When cheap imitations of Vans shoes began to flood the market, the firm, already struggling to contain costs, was forced to lower prices to compete.

Ownership: Vans Inc. is a public company traded on the NASDAQ Stock Exchange.

Ticker Symbol: VANS

Officers: Gary H. Schoenfeld, President and CEO; Andrew J. Greenbaum, EVP and CFO; Craig D. Strain, VP Marketing; Joseph D. Giles, VP and CIO

Employees: 1,690

Principal Subsidiary Companies: Vans Inc. operates 150 stores in the United States and Europe, as well as several indoor skateboarding parks.

Chief Competitors: Major rivals of Vans Inc. include athletic shoe makers, such as Converse and Nike. The firm also competes with Billabong International Ltd. and other manufacturers of apparel and gear for skateboarders and snowboarders.

Debt mounted, and in 1984, after defaulting on its payment to a creditor, the firm was forced into Chapter 11 bankruptcy reorganization. When Vans emerged from bankruptcy two years later, management resolved to focus only on alternative sports.

CURRENT TRENDS

Skateboarding and snowboarding continued to grow in popularity in the early 2000s, boosting sales for Vans. In fact, according to an American Sports Data super study of Sports Participation, snowboarding and skateboarding both saw participation levels jump by a minimum of 25 percent in 2001. As these once "underground" sports evolved into more mainstream activities, they were considered increasingly viable industries as well. As a result, firms like Vans continued working to position themselves as top selling brands.

PRODUCTS

Vans sells footwear, clothing, outerwear, gear, and accessories for snowboarders and skateboarders. In the late 1990s, the firm began to manufacture girl's footwear.

CHRONOLOGY:
Key Dates for Vans, Inc.

1966: The first Vans store opens

1979: Vans creates its slip-on shoe for skateboarders

1984: Vans files for Chapter 11 bankruptcy

1986: Vans emerges from bankruptcy

1991: Vans completes its IPO

1995: Manufacturing is moved to Asia

1999: The first Vans skateboarding park is built

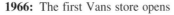

In 2002, Vans launched two lines of juniors' sportswear. One of the lines, which includes t-shirts and fleece items, is manufactured by Van Pac LLC, a joint venture between Pacific Sunwear and Vans.

GLOBAL PRESENCE

Van's products are distributed in nearly 50 countries. Most of the firm's manufacturing activities take place in Mexico and South Korea.

SOURCES OF INFORMATION

Bibliography

Bowers, Katherine. "Skating Its Way to the Top." *WWD*, 7 February 2002.

Cole, August. "Vans Slammed in After-Hours Trading." *CBS.MarketWatch.com*, 19 December 2001. Available at http://www.marketwatch.com.

Gonzales, Angela. "Vans Inc. Continues Skate Park Expansion, Despite Economic Worries." *The Business Journal - Serving Phoenix & the Valley of the Sun*, 2 November 2001.

"Still Awesome After All These Years." *Inc.*, December 1999.

Vans Inc. Home Page, 2002. Available at http://www.vans.com.

FIRST ATTEMPTS AT RETAILING

When Vans opened its first store, three shoe models, ranging in price from $2.49 to $4.99, were on display. Unsure of how many orders it would receive, two of the store's founders, Paul Van Doren and Gordy Lee, had decided to fill its shelves with empty boxes. On the first day of business, 12 customers placed orders for shoes, and Van Doren and Lee asked them to come back a few hours later to retrieve their orders; however, when the customers returned to pick up the newly manufactured shoes, Van Doren and Lee, neither of whom had prior experience with retailing, realized they had no money available to make change. Rather than make the customers wait, Van Doren and Lee gave them the shoes and asked them to return the following day to make payment. Fortunately, all 12 customers complied.

Weintraub, Arlene. "Vans: Chairman of the Board." *Business Week*, 28 May 2001. Available at http://www.businessweek.com

For an annual report:
write: Vans Inc., 15700 Shoemaker Ave., Santa Fe Springs, CA 90670

For additional industry research:
Investigate companies by their Standard Industrial Classification Codes, also known as SICs. Vans Inc.'s primary SICs are:

3021 Rubber and Plastics Footwear

3143 Men's Footwear, Except Athletic

3144 Women's Footwear, Except Athletic

5661 Shoe Stores

Also investigate companies by their North American Industrial Classification System Codes, also known as NAICS codes. Vans Inc.'s primary NAICS codes are:

316211 Rubber and Plastics Footwear Manufacturing

316213 Men's Footwear (except Athletic) Manufacturing

316214 Women's Footwear (except Athletic) Manufacturing

Verizon Communications Inc.

OVERVIEW

A company with more than $67 billion in revenues, Verizon Communications Inc. is the leading local phone company in the United States, the second-leading provider of telecommunications services, and the number one U.S. wireless provider with 132.1 million access lines and nearly 30 million customers. Internationally, Verizon provides service in more than 40 countries with 39 million wireless customers and 10 million access lines. Formed by a 2000 merger of Bell Atlantic and GTE Corp., Verizon is one of the ten largest private U.S. employers with some 247,000 workers. The company is also the world's leading print and online directory publisher.

The company is organized into four segments, each operating as a strategic business unit: Domestic Telecom, Domestic Wireless, Information Services, and International. The Domestic Telecom segment covers local, long-distance, and other telecommunication services. Domestic Wireless includes wireless voice and data services, equipment sales, and paging services. The Information Services segment publishes U.S. and international print and electronic directories and Internet-based shopping guides and also covers Web site creation and related electronic commerce services and products. The International unit includes wireline and wireless communications, investments, and management contracts extending to more than 40 countries in the Americas, Europe, Asia, and the Pacific.

FOUNDED: 1885

Contact Information:

HEADQUARTERS: 1095 Avenue of the Americas
    New York, NY 10036
PHONE: (212)395-2121
FAX: (212)869-3265
TOLL FREE: (800)621-9900
URL: http://www.verizon.com

FINANCES:

Verizon Communications Inc.
Net Income, 1998-2000
(million dollars)

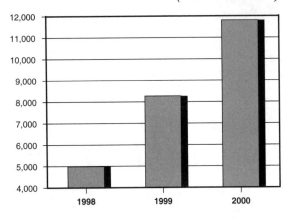

COMPANY FINANCES

Verizon's total revenues for the year 2001 were $67.2 billion, which marked a 3.8 percent increase from the previous year, and up nearly $9 billion from 1999. Domestic Telecom sales accounted for 65 percent of total revenues at $43.1 billion; Domestic Wireless accounted for 26 percent at $17.4 billion; International, with 4 percent, brought in $2.3 billion; and Information Services, with 6 percent, sold $4.3 billion in 2001.

Net income, reported at $389 million, declined significantly for the company in 2001, down 96.7 percent from the previous year, due in part to the losses from circumstances associated with the events of September 11, 2001. Verizon stock ranged from a low of $43.80 to a high of $57.40 over a 52-week period. The annual dividend was $1.54 per share, and Verizon's price-earnings ratio was 14.1. One of the company's stated financial goals, after the 2000 merger was complete, was to realize $2 billion in cost savings and merger synergies by 2003. In early 2002, Verizon stated that it did not expect any major economic turnarounds until 2003 and looked for 0 to 1 percent revenue growth for 2002.

ANALYSTS' OPINIONS

As one of the largest phone companies in the United States and a member of the four organizations that dominate the telecommunications industry, several analysts agree that Verizon's long-term financial outlook remains positive. Morgan Stanley reported in April 2002 that some of the company's strengths were its market leadership, strong balance sheet, and the most desirable combination of value, competitive position, and safety in the telecommunications group. The report further stated that Verizon's core local business would offer a steady stream of revenue over the next few years and, despite increased competition in the field and an extended recession, believed Verizon's local companies would prove more resilient to those factors. Stable revenue growth in the 0-3 percent range in the next few years, strong cash flow and an attractive dividend yield were also mentioned in the company's favor. U.S. Bancorp's Piper Jaffray made similar observations in an April 2002 report, praising the company's expense management, cost cutting, and free cash flow but noted that the economic climate and competition in the telecommunications industry negatively affected the company's financial performance, with declining revenue in the first quarter of 2002.

HISTORY

Telecommunications giant Verizon has gone through numerous incarnations from its prestigious origin more than 115 years ago, evolving from the American Telephone and Telegraph Company (AT&T), which was founded in 1885. The company's history mirrors the history of telephone service itself in the United States.

With Alexander Graham Bell's historic transmission of the first telephone message to his assistant Thomas A. Watson in 1876, the Bell Telephone Company was formed the following year. Later renamed American Bell Telephone Company, the company and its subsidiaries became known as the Bell System. The Bell subsidiary, Newark District Telegraph Company, opened the first New Jersey exchange of the Bell Telephone Company in Newark. AT&T was incorporated in New York in 1885, a wholly owned American Bell Telephone Company subsidiary formed for the purpose of managing and expanding the growing long-distance operation of American Bell. When American Bell reorganized in 1899, AT&T became the parent company of the Bell System, assuming all the business and property of American Bell.

Soon Bell Systems were springing up all over the country. Service in Delaware began in 1897 and 1916 marked the beginning of what is now Verizon West Virginia, then known as the Chesapeake and Potomac (C&P) Telephone Company of West Virginia. In 1904 AT&T acquired the Delaware and Atlantic Telegraph and Telephone company, which serviced southern New Jersey. New York Telephone Company, another AT&T subsidiary, served northern New Jersey. Newark customers were the first to dial local calls in the first modern dial exchange in 1915. From 1927 to 1984, the company today known as Verizon Communications changed its name from the Delaware and Atlantic Telegraph and Telephone company and incorporated as New Jersey Bell

Telephone Co. (NJB), a subsidiary of AT&T. By 1927 the newly renamed NJB handled an average of more than 2.2 million calls a day and had more than half a million telephones in service.

In 1929 NJB relocated its headquarters to 540 Broad Street in Newark, New Jersey, where the Verizon New Jersey still resides. The company installed the first coaxial cable system across New Jersey in 1936, connecting New York and Philadelphia. The year 1944 marked the end of competing service in New Jersey when the last two independent telephone companies, Eastern Telephone and Telegraph Company and the Camden and Atlantic Company, were purchased by NJB. Two years later, NJB installed the one-millionth telephone in Union City. The telephone industry's first nationwide strike occurred at NJB in 1947 and lasted 39 days. The beginning of the next decade brought the introduction of area codes for long-distance calls, with New Jersey getting its 201 designation in 1951. That year also saw the first coast-to-coast, direct dial long-distance call in the nation, between the mayors of Englewood, New Jersey, and Alameda, California. Highlights from the 1960s included the introduction of the princess telephone, the first electronic central office in Succasunna, the launch of the first U.S. touch-tone service, and the introduction of the electronic Traffic Service Position System (TSPS), which would later replace cord-type switchboards. Atlantic City became the first in the nation to provide 911 emergency calling service in 1970.

Some of the company's more innovative developments over the next decade included the first tests for cellular mobile phones in Newark in 1977; the introduction of the cordless telephone to NJB customers in 1982; and the first call utilizing NJB's state of the art laser-powered lightwave communications system, also in 1982. As a result of a 1974 antitrust suit filed by the U.S. Department of Justice, the Bell System was forced to reorganize with final plans approved by U.S. District Court Judge Harold H. Greene in 1983. After 100 years of providing telephone service, AT&T divested and the Bell System was officially dismembered in 1984. NJB became a subsidiary of the Bell Atlantic Corp., one of the seven "Baby Bell" holding companies.

As the home computer trend was ushered in, NJB began the first service to send and receive data via the home personal computer in 1986. The following year NJB's new CLASS Calling Services were approved, which included call waiting, call forwarding, and three-way calling. In 1994 after nearly 70 years as the New Jersey Bell Telephone Company, NJB's name was changed to Bell Atlantic-New Jersey (BA-NJ). Bell Atlantic Corp. acquired "Baby Bell" Nynex in 1997 to form the second largest telephone company in the United States behind AT&T. Another historic merger occurred the very next year, in 1998, when Bell Atlantic and GTE Corp. announced their merger, one of the largest corporate mergers ever in the United States, creating one of the largest communication companies in the world.

FAST FACTS:
About Verizon Communications Inc.

Ownership: Verizon Communications Inc. is a publicly owned company traded on the New York, Philadelphia, Boston, Chicago, Pacific, London, Swiss, Euronext Amsterdam, and Frankfurt Stock Exchanges.

Ticker Symbol: VZ

Officers: Charles R. (Chuck) Lee, Chmn.; Ivan G. Seidenberg, Pres., Dir., and CEO; Doreen A. Toben, EVP and CFO; Lawrence T. Babbio, Jr., VChmn. and Pres., Telecom; Frederic V. Salerno, VChmn.; Michael T. Masin, VChmn. and Pres.; Dennis F. Strigl, EVP, Pres., and CEO of Verizon Wireless

Employees: 247,000

Principal Subsidiary Companies: Verizon operates in more than 40 countries in the Americas, Europe, Asia, and the Pacific. Verizon's joint venture, Verizon Wireless Inc., is the leading U.S. wireless provider.

Chief Competitors: As a provider of local phone service, long-distance, and wireless services, Verizon Communications Inc. competes with other telecommunications companies in the United States and worldwide, most notably AT&T, Sprint, and WorldCom. Wireless competitors include Sprint PCS, AT&T Wireless, Cingular Wireless, Nextel Communications, and VoiceStream.

The company continued innovating the industry under the Bell Atlantic name. Bell Atlantic-New Jersey's telecommunications became all digital in 1999, and the company also won approval from the FCC that year to begin offering long distance service in the New York area. On April 3, 2000, the company announced that its new moniker resulting from their prominent union would be Verizon. The next day, Bell Atlantic merged with Vodafone Airtouch to create Verizon Wireless. On June 30, 2000, the Bell Atlantic and GTE merger became complete and Verizon Communications Inc. was officially in business, trading on the New York Stock Exchange under the new symbol, VZ. Of all the Baby Bells of history, all that remained of the Bell names by 2000 was Bell South.

CHRONOLOGY:
Key Dates for Verizon Communications Inc.

1885: AT&T incorporates as a subsidiary of the American Bell Telephone Company

1899: AT&T becomes the parent company of the Bell System

1904: AT&T acquires the Delaware and Atlantic Telegraph and Telephone company

1927: The company today known as Verizon changed its name from the Delaware and Atlantic Telegraph and Telephone company and incorporated as New Jersey Bell Telephone Co. (NJB), a subsidiary of AT&T

1929: NJB moves its headquarters to 540 Broad Street, Newark

1944: NJB purchases the last two independent telephone companies, Eastern Telephone and Telegraph Company and the Camden and Atlantic Company

1946: NJB installs the one-millionth telephone

1951: NJB enables first coast-to-coast long-distance dialing

1969: NJB's introduces the electronic Traffic Service Position System (TSPS), replacing the old cord switchboards

1974: Antitrust suit filed by the U.S. Department of Justice, calling for dismantling of the Bell System

1984: Final reorganizations plans approved; AT&T divests and the Bell System is officially dismembered; NJB became a subsidiary of the Bell Atlantic Corp., one of the seven "Baby Bell" holding companies

1994: New Jersey Bell Telephone Company (NJB) changes name to Bell Atlantic-New Jersey (BA-NJ)

1997: Bell Atlantic Corp. acquires "Baby Bell" Nynex in 1997 to form the second largest U.S. telephone company, behind AT&T

1998: Bell Atlantic and GTE Corp. merge, one of the largest corporate mergers ever in the United States, creating one of the largest communication companies in the world

2000: The company announces that its new moniker resulting from their merger would be Verizon; Bell Atlantic merges with Vodafone Airtouch to create Verizon Wireless

STRATEGY

Preferring to use the word "promise" over "strategy" or "performance," the Verizon Promise incorporates Verizon's core purpose: to bring the benefits of communications to everybody. Their corresponding core goal is to create the most respected brand in communications. Building on their heritage to create their future, Verizon lists their values as integrity, respect, imagination, and passion, and they single out service as a value that spans their past and future as well as capturing their reliability, quality, and excellent performance for customers. Verizon believes it will be a successful company when they make and keep their promise to customers, communities, shareholders, and employees. These promises include: promising the world of communications that they will lead it; promising customers and all their stakeholders that they absolutely can rely upon them; and promising themselves that they are going to settle for nothing less than greatness.

Verizon's core operational strategy in 2001 focused on reducing costs, managing complex networks, introducing new products, and delivering superior service to customers. With increasing competition and changes in technology on the horizon, Verizon plans to concentrate on the basics in 2002 to solidify their position as an industry leader, building on a prestigious brand name, existing customer relationships, and dedication to customer service. The company's long-term strategy consists of ushering in new technology, including the next generation of broadband wireless data, and related products and services. Their continued innovation will ultimately be the key to any future success within the telecommunications industry.

INFLUENCES

With profits dwindling in 2001 due to economic factors, the company also noted a significant decrease in local communications services, a large part of their business, since more consumers were giving up second phone lines for Internet connections in favor of high-speed lines and wireless access. The leader in local phone service due to years of innovation in the telecom industry, Verizon began offering long-distance service in 2000 to better compete in the overall telecom landscape. The move benefited the company by having a more diverse revenue base and increasing the largest segment of its company, Domestic Telecom. Ranking as the country's fourth largest long-distance company, Verizon had 8.2 million long distance customers in early 2002. By merging with Vodaphone, Verizon Wireless became the instant leader in wireless communication and has spurred the company to extend its wireless reach even further. As unprecedented innovators, Verizon made sure they remained so, increasing their DSL lines by 88 percent for the year 2001, totaling 1.35 million lines. A back to basics approach, including cost cutting from years of steady growth, is one of Verizon's reactions to the disappointing profits in 2001 and early 2002. The company cut 16,000 full-time jobs and 13,000 part-time positions in 2001 and planned to cut another 10,000 in the year 2002.

CURRENT TRENDS

Verizon continues to expand their range of services by entering the long-distance game. The company began such service in New York in 2000 and the following year in Massachusetts, Connecticut, and Pennsylvania. More than two-thirds of all Verizon access lines offered long-distance service by early 2002. The wireless segment of the company continued its growth trend, combining business operations with Price Communications Wireless in late 2001. As the controlling partner, Verizon Wireless will gain a significant 560,000 customers.

With the formation of the business unit Global Solutions Inc., Verizon began an initiative in early 2001 to expand its presence in the carrier and large business markets worldwide. The unit will offer a network that connects commercial centers worldwide and offer a range of data, Internet, and voice services.

PRODUCTS

Verizon's Domestic Telecom segment covers local, long-distance, and other telecommunication services. The company's Domestic Wireless unit includes wireless voice and data services, equipment sales, and paging services. Products and services in the Information Services segment include U.S. and international print and electronic directories and Internet-based shopping guides, and it also covers Web site creation and related electronic commerce services and products. Some of the company's directories are the print *Verizon SuperPages* white and yellow pages and the online Internet directory SuperPages.com. The segment also provides sales, publishing,

Drivers travel Verizon's service area from Texas to New England in station wagons equipped with banks of cell phones and computers to check reception. (AP Photo/Lou Krasky)

and related services to nearly 2,300 directory titles worldwide with total circulation of about 106 million copies in the United States and 44 million internationally.

In early 2002 Verizon began offering bill payment services for its telephone customers, as well as purchases of long-distance minutes through a link to Verizon's customer Web site on 7-Eleven Stores Inc.'s Vcoms—Web-based multifunction automated teller machines. The Vcom machines, which offer Western Union money

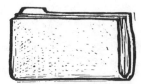

GIVE PEACE A CHANCE

With the first three letters of its name borrowed from the Latin word "veritas," meaning truth, and the second part of its name derived from the world "horizon," Verizon not only conveys images of honesty, trustworthiness, dependability, leadership, and possibilities with the merger of the two words, but it also signifies the historic merger between the two companies, Bell Atlantic and GTE, that formed one of the world's leading communications companies. Capitalizing on the first letter of its name, the "V" became the peace sign flashed by numerous people in the Verizon Wireless ads of early 2000. Initial reaction to the name was mixed—some found it refreshing and new, while others didn't like that it broke from tradition by not describing or invoking any kind of telecommunications lingo.

orders and automated check-cashing, have been tested in Texas and Florida.

CORPORATE CITIZENSHIP

The Verizon Foundation is the philanthropic arm of Verizon Communications, serving the nonprofit community. The Foundation aims to invest $75 million and benefit more than 14,000 nonprofit organizations in various communities served by the company across the country, making it one of the ten biggest U.S. corporate foundations. The Foundation focuses on four main funding areas, emphasizing innovative technology solutions to solve problems: Literacy; Community Technology Development; Workforce Development; and Employee Volunteerism. With more than $10 million in grants earned by Verizon employees who volunteer their time and money for nonprofit organizations, Verizon is one of the biggest supporters of employee volunteerism in the world. Some of the organizations supported by Verizon employees each year include the United Way, Literacy Volunteers, Junior Achievement, the mentoring program Aspira, and international programs to benefit disaster victims and cancer and AIDS patients and research. The mission of the foundation is to offer an online philanthropic community network dedicated to supporting the 700,000 nonprofit organizations in the United States.

GLOBAL PRESENCE

Verizon's International segment incorporates wireline and wireless telecommunications operations in the Americas, Europe, Asia, and the Pacific. In Asia, Verizon has a presence in India, Indonesia, Japan, the Philippines, Taiwan, and Thailand. Verizon's European operations include Italy, Greece, the Czech Republic, Gibraltar, the United Kingdom and elsewhere as the company poises for additional opportunities in the region as technology progresses and regulations alter there. Verizon cites the rapidly growing markets of the Americas and the Caribbean as an important part of its current operations and future strategy, with a presence in Argentina, Canada, Mexico, Puerto Rico, and the Dominican Republic. With about 10 million access lines and wireless service to approximately 39 million customers, the International segment accounted for $2.3 billion in revenues in 2001 and experienced 18.3 percent growth over the previous year.

The company also has a number of consolidated international investments, including Grupo Iusacell in Mexico; CODETEL in the Dominican Republic; CTI Holdings, S.A. in Argentina; Micronewsian Telecommunications Corporation in the Northern Mariana Islands; and Global Solutions Inc.

EMPLOYMENT

Verizon boasts a unique environment of talented and diverse employees. The company is committed to hiring, training, and developing professionals from diverse backgrounds, races, and creeds. They offer performance-based bonuses, tuition reimbursement, and career and growth opportunities. Employees are encouraged to grow professionally through attending training classes, conferences, and seminars and are also offered a broad internal training curriculum.

The company offers a variety of options for medical, dental, and life insurance, as well as reimbursement accounts. Other benefits include a generous time off plan, Employee Assistance Program, Adoption Benefits, and Dependant Life Insurance with some locations additionally offering Day Care Assistance.

SOURCES OF INFORMATION

Bibliography

"Verizon Communications Inc." Gale Group, June 2002. Available at http://galenet.galegroup.com.

"Verizon Communications Inc." *Hoover's Online,* June 2002. Available at http://www.hoovers.com.

"Verizon Has A Deal With 7-Eleven on the Horizon." *Cardline,* 2 November 2001.

Verizon Home Page, 2002. Available at http://www.verizon.com.

For an annual report:

on the Internet at: http://www.verizon.com **or** write: Verizon Communications Inc., 1095 Avenue of the Americas, New York, NY 10036

For additional industry research:

Investigate companies by their Standard Industrial Classification Codes, also known as SICs. Verizon Communications Inc.'s primary SICs are:

4812 Radiotelephone Communications

4813 Telephone Communications Except Radiotelephone

6719 Holding Companies, Not Elsewhere Classified

Also investigate companies by their North American Industry Classification System codes, also known as NAICS codes. Verizon Communications Inc.'s primary NAICS codes are:

513310 Wired Telecommunications Carriers

513322 Cellular and Other Wireless Telecommunications

551112 Offices of Other Holding Companies

VF Corporation

FOUNDED: 1899

Contact Information:

HEADQUARTERS: PO Box 21488
  Greensboro, NC 27408
PHONE: (336)547-6000
FAX: (336)547-7630
TOLL FREE: (888)836-3971
URL: http://www.vfc.com

OVERVIEW

VF Corporation is the leading making of jeanswear in the world and markets its products in the United States and Europe, as well as other international markets. Its brand name jeans, Lee, Rustler, Brittania, Chic, and Wrangler, hold over 20 percent of the U.S. jeans market, with Lee and Wrangler products available in countries around the world. VF Corporation also manufactures and markets intimate apparel, occupational apparel, knitwear, outdoor apparel and equipment, children's playwear and other apparel. The company is organized into four business segments: Consumer Apparel, Occupational Apparel, Outdoor Apparel and Equipment, and All Other.

VF Corporation's Consumer Apparel segment, which includes its jeanswear, intimate apparel, and children's wear, is its largest business group, accounting for nearly three quarters of the company's sales. In 2001, business conducted with the company's ten largest customers accounted for 43 percent of all sales. Wal-Mart is VF Corporation's largest single buyer, accounting for over 14 percent of total sales in 2001.

COMPANY FINANCES

Net sales in 2001 totaled $5.52 billion, a four percent decline from the previous year's record total of $5.75 billion. If the financial impact of acquisitions and divestitures are removed from the equation, sales declined by six percent. Net income posted for 2001 was $138 million, down from $260 million in 2000 and $336 million in 1999. Net sales in 2001 for the Consumer Apparel segment totaled $4.02 billion, compared to $4.23 billion in 2000. Occupation Apparel and All Other segments were also down from $662 million to $538 million and $490 million to $464 million, respectively. Only Outdoor Apparel and Equipment showed improved profits of $492 million compared to $368 million in the previous year. Basic earnings per share for 2001 fell by $1.06 to $1.19 from $2.25 in 2000. Stock prices reached the year's high of $42.70 during the second quarter of 2001 and hit the year's low of $28.15 in the fourth quarter. During the fourth quarter of 2001, year-on-year net sales slumped over 11 percent to $1.3 billion down from $1.46 billion the previous year, resulting in a net loss for the quarter of $113 million.

ANALYSTS' OPINIONS

Working in favor of the future success of VF Corporation, according to analysts, is its positive record of surviving economic recessions. During the economic slowdowns of both the early 1980s and early 1990s, VF Corporation significantly outperformed the market. The company's substantial sales to Wal-Mart, which are expected to do well despite the economy's health, place VF Corporation in a good position to weather a recession in the short- to medium- time range. Analysts also see the company's move to divest itself of unprofitable businesses and significantly reduce overhead costs as positive signs for the future. VF Corporation announced in the fourth quarter of 2001 that it would undergo restructuring and divest itself of several smaller businesses that represented approximately 5 percent of sales, including swimwear, private label knitwear, and a small work wear business. Although analysts anticipate the future benefit of the company's return to core businesses of jeanswear, intimate apparel and outdoor wear, restructuring costs as well as a continuing decline in demand are expected to affect the bottom line in 2002.

Because VF Corporation's major brands are mature and are experiencing rapidly increasing competition from mass market private label jeanswear outfitters, some analysts expect that growth, if consistent, will not be dramatic. In order to drive sales and profits more aggressively, the company will look to new acquisitions to push sales up at a faster rate. However analysts' opinions vary on the likely outcome of this strategy. Some view VF Corporation's mature core business as a solid foundation to generate growth. Recently acquired businesses, including Bestform, Eastpak, CHIC Jeans, Gitano, and The North Face, have all performed better than expected so far. Other analysts warn that growth through acquisition can be risky and often unsuccessful. Nonetheless, the consensus among analysts is that VF Corporation has made positive moves to restructure, and supported by a solid core of businesses, should continue to be a viable investment.

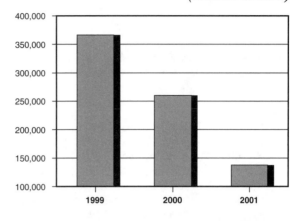

FINANCES:
VF Corporation Net Incomes, 1999-2001 (million dollars)

HISTORY

In 1899 a group of six men formed the Reading Glove & Mitten Manufacturing Company in Reading, Pennsylvania to produce knit and silk gloves. After a decade of slow sales, one investor, John Barbey, bought out his partners and renamed the company Schuylkill Silk Mills. In 1914 Barbey, along with his son J.E. Barbey introduced a line of silk lingerie. Three years later they ran a contest to find a brand name for the lingerie products. With a prize offering of $25, the contest was conducted and the name Vanity Fair won. Barbey then undertook an aggressive marketing campaign to promote Vanity Fair brand apparel, a unique strategy in the lingerie industry at the time as most intimate apparel was sold without brand names.

In 1919 the company's name changed to Vanity Fair Silk Mills Inc. With the intimate apparel business outperforming the glove business during the 1920s; gloves were discontinued. Vanity Fair began making its first acquisitions in 1969, including the purchase of H.D. Lee, a jeanswear manufacturer established in 1860, and Berkshire International, a hosiery company. As a result of the acquisitions, the company was reorganized; VF Corporation was established as a holding company, and Vanity Fair became a subsidiary. In 1979 VF Corporation, becoming serious about global expansion, opened an International Division. During the sluggish market of the early 1980s, VF Corporation responded by continuing to diversify through acquisitions. At the same time, the company tried to distinguish itself from its competitors by being the first to market separate product lines for men and women, and excelled as one of the first jeans

FAST FACTS:
About VF Corporation

Ownership: VF Corporation is a publicly held company and trades on the New York Stock Exchange.

Ticker Symbol: VFC

Officers: Mackey J. McDonald, 55, Chmn., CEO, and Pres., 2001 salary $960,000, 2001 bonus $530,400; Robert K. Shearer, 50, VP and CFO, 2001 salary $360,000, 2001 bonus $151,500; T.L. Lay, 54, VP and Chmn., 2001 salary $495,000, 2001 bonus $194,600; J.P. Schamberger, 53, VP and Chmn., 2001 salary $495,000, 2001 bonus $194,600; E.C. Wiseman, 46, VP and Chmn., 2001 salary $345,000, 2001 bonus $161,500

Employees: 75,000

Principal Subsidiary Companies: VF Corporation is the parent of numerous well-known activewear, jeanswear, and intimate apparel, including Wrangler, Lee, Riders, Gitano, Rustlers, C.H.I.C., Healthtex, Eastpak, Brittania, JanSport, Lee Jeans, Vanity Fair Mills Inc., and Bestform Intimates, Inc.

Chief Competitors: The apparel market is highly competitive, and VF Corporation competes with a range of manufacturers. Sara Lee Corporation, maker of Leggs and Hanes, has sales that top VF Corporation's, and is the company's largest competitor in the intimate apparel market. Levi Strauss is the company's long-standing main rival in the jeanswear sector. In addition, because the company markets its different lines of apparel to a variety of markets, including specialty, department, and discount stores, it also competes with a broad range of apparel manufacturers, including Fruit of the Loom, The Gap, Guess?, Levi Strauss, The Limited, OshKosh B'Gosh, Reebok, Russell Corporation, and Warnaco Group.

makers to offer high-end and stretch jeans. The Ms. Lee brand became the best-selling line of women's jeans in the United States.

In 1986 VF Corporation greatly expanded its operations, becoming the largest U.S. apparel manufacturer, through the acquisition of Blue Bell Holding Company, owner of the Wrangler, Rustler, Jantzen, and Red Kap brands. In the late 1980s in order to boast sagging sales

VF Corporation made the costly strategic decision to sell Lee jeans to mass marketers, angering its retail customers who stopped carrying the Lee brand in protest of its lower-level image. Not only did the company alienate the department store industry, it entered the already saturated market of mass merchandise in which it could not successfully compete. By the early 1990s VF Corporation sales and income figures had fallen. To make matters worse, Levi Strauss introduced the very successful Dockers brand, offering casual wear pants, which cut significantly into the sales of Lee jeans.

VF Corporation realized that it had stumbled and successfully recovered over the next several years. Sales grew from $2.95 billion in 1991 to $4.97 in 1994. During the second half of the 1990s, revenues rose steadily up from $5 million, and the company posted record sales in 2000 of $5.75 billion. Net income reached its peak in 1998 when the company reported $388 million. When the U.S. economy slid suddenly into an economic slump in 2001, VF Corporation found itself burdened by excessive inventory, which the company worked throughout the year to reduce. Having diversified outside its core businesses to sustain itself during the downturn in its jeanswear sales, the company outlined a new plan in 2001 to return to its main businesses and seek growth through acquisitions within the framework of the consumer apparel industry.

STRATEGY

VF Corporation's core strategies are: build strong brands that consumers know and want, focus on high volume basic apparel categories, expand international presence, and follow conservative financial practices and policies. The company's long-term financial objectives include: achieving sales growth of 6 percent, a return on capital of 17 percent, an operating margin of 14 percent, a debt-to-capital ratio below 40 percent, and dividend payouts of 30 percent. Growth by adding new businesses to the company's portfolio is expected to come in two forms of acquisitions: smaller brands valued around $100 million that can be quickly and easily integrated into VF's core businesses and lifestyle brands valued up to $500 million.

To achieve its objectives VF Corporation will slim down its operations, exit under performing businesses, and focus on its major business segments. The company announced in the fourth quarter of 2001 that as part of its restructuring plan it would cut 13,000 jobs worldwide, close approximately one fifth of its plants, and move more production to low-cost contracts outside the United States and Europe. Facing increasing competition from private label jeans makers, the company plans to cut its prices on Rustler, Wrangler, Riders, and Lee brands, although the cuts will not be across-the-board but depend on the competition levels in individual markets. In

Europe, where jeans sales are strong, VF Corporation will introduce a new line of high-end Lee jeans in 2002. Marketing budgets in all five business segments are also slated for increases.

INFLUENCES

VF Corporation is facing a two-pronged challenge. First, the apparel market in the United States, which accounts for 82 percent of all sales, remained soft into 2002. Second, as demand has decreased, competition has increased. Private label brands offer consumers more choices, often at lower prices than VF Corporation's name brand products. In 2001 approximately 569 million pairs of jeans were sold in the United States. VF Corporation held 21 percent of the market primarily with its Wrangler, Lee, and Rustler lines, which held the second, third, and fourth largest market shares of brand name jeans, respectively. However, private label jeans sold by major retailers held approximately 40 percent of the entire market. In order to remain competitive in this economic and market environment, VF Corporation has committed to reducing its costs in all areas of its operations. Resulting actions taken in 2000 resulted in $45 million of cost reduction, with anticipated savings of $100 million in 2002 and $30 million in subsequent years.

CURRENT TRENDS

As part of the 2001 restructuring plan, VF Corporation undertook actions to exit three under performing business, the most significant of which is the Private Label knitwear business that marketed fleece and T-shirt apparel to large U.S. retailers and other operating units within the VF Corporation family. The company will also shed its Jantzen swimwear business, a high-end, seasonal business with consistently low returns, and a small specialty work wear business that was negatively impacted by the downturn in the high tech industry. During the three years preceding 2001, the three businesses' total operating profit was $9 million, but all reported losses in 2001.

In its efforts to reduce its operations base, the company closed 21 higher cost North American manufacturing facilities to reduce total production capacity and transition into a higher rate of outsourcing of manufacturing. The company obtains its products via two methods: VF businesses purchase raw material from suppliers, which are used to create finished products at company-owned manufacturing facilities; or the company contracts third-party companies to provide finished goods. VF Corporation has begun to rely more heavily on its company-owned facilities outside the United States and Europe where labor costs are significantly less expensive. The company is also using more contractors to supply its

CHRONOLOGY:
Key Dates for VF Corporation

1899: A group of six investors in Pennsylvania form the Reading Glove & Mitten Manufacturing Co.

1911: John Barbey buys out his five partners and changes the name to Schuylkill Silk Mills

1914: Barbey conducts a contest to rename his business, awarding the winning contestant $25 for the name "Vanity Fair"

1937: Operations move from Reading to Monroeville, Alabama, later relocating to Greensboro, North Carolina

1943: Purchases H. D. Lee Co., Inc. and Berkshire International

1948: Introduces an innovative new material, nylon tricot, which revolutionizes the lingerie industry

1950: Vanity Fair receives the Coty Award for Design

1969: Reorganizes at VF Corporation and Vanity Fair becomes a subsidiary

1979: An international division is established in Europe

1986: Becomes largest apparel manufacturer in the United States after acquiring Blue Bell Holding Company, maker of Wrangler Jeans as well as Rustler jeans, Jantzen and JanSport Swimwear, Red Kap occupational clothing

1991: Acquires Health-tex, Inc., a manufacturer of children's clothing

1992: Sales exceed $3 billion for the year

1995: Annual sales reach $5 billion

2000: Purchases Eastpak, Chic and H.I.S. jeans brands, and outdoor retailer The North Face

2001: Announces plans to cut 13,000 jobs, close one fifth of its 150 U.S. plants, and move production to lower cost facilities overseas

products. In 2001, 78 percent of all VF Corporation's products sold in the United States were produced internationally, and the company intends to increase that number to 85 percent in the future, leaving only 15 percent to U.S. domestic production. In 2001, 45 percent of all international merchandise was manufactured in com-

NYLON TRICOT

During the 1940s Vanity Fair pioneered the use of innovative material in its lingerie because of an embargo on silk during World War II. The company began using rayon and in 1948 introduced nylon tricot, which revolutionized the intimate apparel industry. The material was strong, durable, elastic, and easy to care for, and could be dyed a wide range of popular colors.

pany-owned facilities in Mexico and the Caribbean basin, and 40 percent was provided by contractors primarily located in Mexico, the Caribbean, and Asia.

Despite efforts to reduce costs and increase marketing, VF Corporation estimates a sales decline of 8 percent for 2002. Approximately half of the expected loss stems from business closures. The company also anticipates lower revenues as a result of the bankruptcy filing by K-Mart, one of its five largest customers, and the continued poor performance of sluggish market.

PRODUCTS

Within its Consumer Apparel segment, VF Corporation maintains three product-related groups: jeanswear, intimate apparel, and children's wear. The company's leading U.S. jeanswear products are Lee, Wrangler, Rustler, and Rider brands. Other jeanswear labels are Chic, Gitano, and Brittania as well as casual cotton pants and shirts under the Lee Casuals and Timber Creek by Wrangler names. By the end of 2002 the company plans to be complete owner of H.I.S., a jeanswear company in which it began investing in 2000. Lee and Wrangler are the most widely marketed brands around the world. Lee brands are generally sold through department and specialty stores, and Wrangler westernwear is distributed to western specialty stores. Hero by Wrangler, Rustler, and Riders brands are sold via the mass merchants as well as national and regional discount chains such as Wal-Mart. Chic, Gitano, and Brittania are also marketed to discount chains.

Intimate apparel is manufactured and marketed for distribution to domestic department, chain, and specialty stores under the names Vanity Fair, Lily of France, Exquisite Form, and licensed Tommy Hilfiger and Natori labels. Apparel includes bras, panties, day-

wear, shapewear, robes, and sleepwear. Vassarette and Bestform are brands produced for the discount store market.

The Children's Playwear division manufactures and markets Healthtex and Lee brands as well as licensed Nike and Michael Jordan apparel. Products are distributed primarily department and specialty stores. Healthtex is also available directly to consumers at its Web site, www.healthtex.com.

Occupational Apparel is marketed in the United States under the Red Kap name. More than half of all sales are to industrial laundries that supply work clothes primarily on a rental basis to companies who require on-the-job clothing for production and service employees. Apparel items include work pants, slacks, work and dress shirts, overalls, jackets, and smocks. VF Corporation also supplies restaurant and safety uniforms under the brand names Penn State Textiles and Bulwark, respectively. Corporate image apparel is marketed through VF Solutions. VF Corporations maintains Web-based catalogs and online ordering services for several of its major customers, including FedEx, American Airlines, and the U.S. Customs and Immigration and Naturalization Services.

Outdoor Apparel and Equipment markets products under three brand names: The North Face, Jansport, and Eastpak. The North Face, which is sold in the United States, Europe, and Asia, provides high performance outerwear, snowsports wear and functional sportswear and equipment such tents, sleeping bags, backpacks, and daypacks. The North Face is sold to specialty outdoor and high-end sporting goods stores. In the United States, the brand is also sold through ten company-owned showcase retail stores. Daypack manufacturer Jansport, which holds the leading market share in the United States, is sold through department and sporting goods as well as college bookstores. Jansport is also available in Europe and Asia. Eastpak, also specializing in daypacks, was acquired in 2000 and merged into Jansport operations in the United States. Jansport products are distributed to mass market and specialty stores in the United States and Europe.

The All Other segment consists primarily of knitwear apparel including sports apparel under licenses granted by major American professional sports leagues. Also included in this group is a chain of approximately 50 retail outlet stores located across the United States that sells primarily overruns of first quality products.

CORPORATE CITIZENSHIP

VF Corporation sponsors various sporting, music and other special events, including Wrangler National Finals Rodeo and the Lee National Denim Day fundraiser for the Susan G. Komen Breast Cancer Foundation. The company requires all contractors to abide by strict standards covering hours of work, age of workers, health and safety conditions, and conformity to all laws and regulations. VF Corporation periodically audits its contractors to check for compliance.

GLOBAL PRESENCE

VF Corporation owns manufacturing operations in several countries outside the United States including France, Spain, Malta, Tunisia, Poland, and Turkey. Internationally VF Corporation is the largest jeanswear manufacturer in Western Europe. Where its products are not directly marketed, the company markets its merchandise via licenses and distribution contracts. Branded jeanswear sold internationally include Lee, Wrangler, Hero by Wrangler, Maverick, and Old Axe. Products sold in Europe tend to be more fashion-driven, higher-end apparel. Lee brand products are marketed in China with plans to introduce the Wrangler brand to the country in 2003. Lee and Wrangler brands are marketed in Canada and Mexico and in South America through company-owned operations in Brazil, Argentina, and Chile. In Europe intimate apparel is sold to department and specialty stores under the names Lou, Bolero, Gemma, Intima Cherry, and Belcor. Discount stores brands in the European market include Variance, Vassarette, and Bestforms. Vanity Fair and Exquisite Form products are also available in Europe. All three outdoor apparel brands, The North Face, Jansport, and Eastpak, are available in Europe and are marketed in Asia via licensees and distributors.

EMPLOYMENT

At the end of 2001, VF Corporation's workforce totaled approximately 71,000. However, 13,000 jobs are slated for dissolution according to the restructuring plan set out in 2001.

SOURCES OF INFORMATION

Bibliography

Clark, Evan. "VF Losses Hit $112.6M in Quarter." *WWD*,13 February 2002.

Cunningham, Thomas. "VF in Major Restructuring; Firm to Take Up to $320 Million in Charges, Increase Offshore Sourcing, Tighten Focus." *Daily News Record*, 19 November 2002.

Grant, Tina, ed.*International Directory of Company Histories*. Vol. 17. Detroit: St. James Press, 1997.

Malone, Scott, and Joshua Greene. "Denim Dish." *WWD*, 14 February 2002.

"VF Corporation." *Hoover's Company Profiles*. Available at http://www.hoovers.com.

"VF Corporation." *Multex.com*. Available at http://www .multex.com.

"VF Cuts a New Pattern." *Business Week*, 26 November 2001.

VF Corporation Home Page, 2002. Available at http://www .vfc.com.

For an annual report:

on the Internet at: http:\\www.vfc.com.

For additional industry research

Investigate companies by their Standard Industrial Classification Codes, also known as SICs. VF Corporation's primary SICs are:

2325 Mens & Boys Separate Trousers & Slacks

2339 Womens Misses & Jr Outerwear, Not Elsewhere Classified

2253 Knit Outerwear Mills

2254 Knit Underwear & Nightwear Mills

Investigate companies by their North American Industry Classification System Codes, also known as NAICS codes. VF Corporation's primary NAICSs are:

315191 Outerwear Knitting Mills

315192 Underwear and Nightwear Knitting Mills

315224 Men's and Boys' Cut and Sew Trouser, Slack and Jean Manufacturing

315999 Other Apparel Accessories and Other Apparel Manufacturing

WebMD Corp.

FOUNDED: 1995

Contact Information:

HEADQUARTERS: 669 River Dr., Center 2
    Elmwood Park, NJ 07407
PHONE: (201)703-3400
FAX: (201)703-3401
TOLL FREE: (877)469-2163
URL: http://www.webmd.com

OVERVIEW

WebMD Corp. is best known for its popular Internet site of the same name, but providing online health care information to consumers is only a small piece of the business. The company was founded in 1995 and has grown rapidly, largely due to mergers and acquisitions. It is now one of the largest companies specializing in electronic healthcare solutions and technology services. WebMD operates in three distinct sectors: transaction services, medical practice management systems, and Internet content for health-related sites.

COMPANY FINANCES

In 2001 WebMD Corp. posted $6,684.3 million in losses on $706.6 million in revenues. This was the result of losses from continuing operations and one-time charges associated with restructuring. These numbers are somewhat worse than the 2000 fiscal year that saw the company post a nearly $3.1 billion loss on $517.2 million in revenues. The company was seriously impacted by the dot-com collapse in the year 2000, and the most recent financial statements reflect these events.

ANALYSTS' OPINIONS

In 1999 WebMD was one of the top ranked Internet stocks on the market, trading at an eye popping $126 per share. In 2000, when Internet stocks tumbled, WebMD had a long way to fall. It bottomed out at $3.22

a share. Since that time the company has begun a major reorganization effort. Company officials are claiming that they will be able to show positive operating income before the end of 2002. Analysts are taking a "wait and see" attitude with the health care company. David Risinger, an analyst at Merrill Lynch looked at the company in early 2002 and described its rebuilding efforts as "herculean." Michael J. Barrett, a health care analyst with Forrester Research, said about the company, "Without question, WebMD is the leading health care consumer portal." Analysts and physicians alike will need more evidence that the company can deliver its products, and do it profitably, before they endorse it.

HISTORY

WebMD (formerly Healthscape) is a conglomerate of numerous healthcare companies formed through a series of corporate actions. The origins of the company can be traced back to 1995 when Healthscape was founded. The three founding partners each specialized in either medicine or information technology. Jim Clark came to the venture as the founder of both Netscape and Silicon Graphics. Pavan Nigam was an executive at Silicon Graphics and came with Clark. David Schnell was a medical doctor with a degree from Harvard Medical School. He was formerly a partner in biotech company Kleiner Perkins. Together the three men represented the union of medicine and technology. Not long after the launch of the company, the name was changed to Healtheon to avoid confusion with another firm using the name Healthscape in its title.

Healthscape attempted to streamline the cumbersome enrollment process required by most health care plans by offering online enrollment services that could be customized to meet differing needs of employers. While this appeared to be a sound business premise, it never gained popularity and, by 1997, the business was in decline. The founders made the decision to shift the company's focus to electronic transactions and data exchange protocols. David Schnell departed in 1997 to become a partner in a venture capital firm and a new CEO was hired. Michael Long was a seasoned executive from the world of technology and brought the expertise required to manage Healtheon's transition to a high-end medical technology outfit. Beginning in 1998 the company initiated a string of acquisitions that would continue for several years. One of the first purchases was ActaMed, an electronic data company.

The partners believed that the company was once again on the path to profitability and announced plans to make a public stock offering. Market conditions deteriorated, and the IPO was postponed. Instead, the company was able to secure the necessary financing from private venture capitalists. The following year would prove to be a pivotal year in the short history of the company. Cashing in on the Internet phenomenon, Healtheon real-

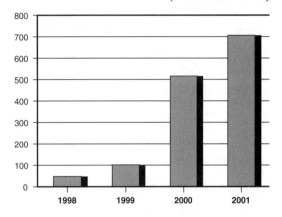

FINANCES:
WebMD Corp.
Revenues, 1998-2001
(million dollars)

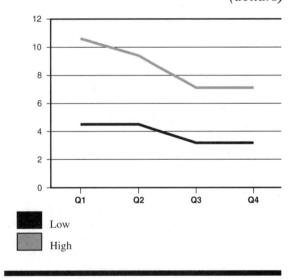

WebMD Corp.
2001 Stock Prices
(dollars)

Low
High

ized its goal of becoming a publicly traded corporation. The initial stock offering netted more than $40 million and provided the resources to continue the company's expansion plans. It was in 1998 that Healthscape merged with the first company to bear the name of WebMD. This company was founded in 1996 by Jeffrey Arnold, a pharmaceutical salesman turned Internet entrepreneur. The new entity was renamed Healtheon/WebMD and Arnold assumed the title of CEO for both firms.

The next several years would be marked by a series of acquisitions and agreements designed to establish

FAST FACTS:
About WebMD Corp.

Ownership: WebMD Corp. is a publicly traded company on the NASDAQ Stock Exchange.

Ticker Symbol: HLTH

Officers: Martin J. Wygood, Chmn. and CEO, 61; Thomas P. Apker, COO, 45; Kevin Cameron, EVP, 34

Employees: 4,700

Chief Competitors: WebMD Corp. is a healthcare information and technology company that provides online medical content to consumers and business solutions for medical practice management. Its primary competitors are online service providers and electronic transaction firms such as America Online, Health Management Systems, iVillage, and EDS.

superiority in each of the areas of operations. The electronic transaction division continued to grow with the addition of several firms including MEDE America and ENVOY, the medical transaction unit of Quintiles Transnational, and Kinetra, a joint venture of EDS and Eli Lilly. The latter two deals cost the company more than $1 billion in fees. The Internet portal business was also the beneficiary of noteworthy partnership deals. Healtheon/WebMD initiated an arrangement to receive medical news from the Greenberg News Networks and worked with News Corporation to license information and take advantage of the branding services afforded by the larger media company. To complete the string of corporate actions, Medical Manager and its subsidiary, CareInsite were purchased to strengthen the physician management software division. This last transaction cost the company billions of dollars but increased its overall presence among physicians and within medical practices.

In September 2000 this new conglomerate shortened its name to WebMD Corp. Although the company name was smaller, operations had become unwieldy. The changes to the organizational structure had happened rapidly and without a plan for maximizing efficiency or managing integration. Management was forced to begin the difficult task of restructuring the organization in an effort to stem escalating costs of operations and the resulting loss of revenues. Efforts to streamline operations did not come without a price. By the end of fiscal

year 2000, the company had accrued $452.9 million dollars in charges related to the reorganization, including expenses such as moving and relocation fees, severance packages for terminated employees, and penalties assessed for marketing or licensing agreements that were cancelled.

Three prominent partnerships were redefined during this time in accordance with WebMD's newly created strategic plan. A contract with News Corporation Limited, which called for the parties to exchange media services and Internet content, was trimmed. Plans for several future joint ventures, including a cable health network, were tabled. An agreement with E.I. du Pont de Nemours was suspended completely, but a future joint venture in the area of food and nutrition remained a possibility. WebMD's relationship with software giant Microsoft was also revised to better meet the needs of the revamped conglomerate. A series of new joint ventures with Microsoft were outlined and scheduled in conjunction with new product developments at both firms. Numerous other deals with other smaller vendors were also revisited, all with the end goal of making WebMD a leaner and more efficient corporation.

The year 2000 also marked significant personnel changes for the medical technology firm. Amidst the many operational changes, key company officials departed. Pavan Nigam, Jeffrey Arnold, and Jim Clark, who was now serving as a member of the board of directors, left the company they had created. In early 2001, CEO Mike Long also ended his tenure with the organization and was replaced at the helm by Martin Wygood. In the first eighteen months at the controls, Wygood and company closed some of the unprofitable divisions and repurchased more than 77 million shares of WebMD stock. At the close of 2001, the company purchased the main business unit of its largest competitor, MedicaLogic/Medascape for only $10 million. This acquisition gave WebMD a virtual monopoly in the area of online healthcare. Ability to generate revenues will pose the greatest challenge to future financial health of the company.

STRATEGY

Following the consolidation of new business units, WebMD planned to move forward with a slate of strategic initiatives designed to position the company as a leader in its field. Improving connectivity, increasing the frequency of electronic transactions, and more rapid processing of transactions (timeliness) are constant priorities. Specific initiatives that the company plans to implement include: the introduction of handheld devices for physicians, strengthening relationships with pharmaceutical companies, marketing a single solution for

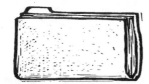

DOOGIE HOWSER, MD

The notion of a teenage Marcus Welby was once the subject of a popular television series starring Neil Patrick Harris as the young physician. Each episode ended with Doogie typing his thoughts into his computer journal. Teenagers today aren't becoming doctors, but they are flocking to their computers to find answers to their most personal questions. Thousands of teenagers surf the Internet to gather information and articles about issues they are reluctant to discuss with their parents. The topics include general, sexual, and emotional health issues. Sites like WebMD are popular with adults, but teenagers are visiting sites especially designed for them. Some popular options include: www.teengrowth.com, www.kidshealth .com, www.iemily.com, and www.zaphealth.com.

claims processing, and using the Internet portal to expand the company's customer base.

INFLUENCES

The Internet and wireless markets impact significantly on company operations. Despite the collapse of many companies in the technology sector, WebMD is still focused on expanding and improving its services utilizing technology. Strategic partnerships will be evaluated for compatibility with the company's overall goal of becoming a leader in selected markets. Moving forward, the company plans to pay special attention to the level of acceptance of technology by its users and target markets.

CURRENT TRENDS

WebMD is positioning itself to be dominant in wireless and handheld devices for medical management and physician practices. However this roll out must not occur without first achieving a high level of interest from the medical community. The creation of advanced technologies such as electronic prescription writing capabilities are worthless if physicians prefer to use a pad and pen.

CHRONOLOGY:
Key Dates for WebMD Corp.

1995: Healthscape is founded, but soon changes its name to Healtheon

1997: Company changes strategic direction as online enrollment does not gain popularity

1999: Healtheon becomes a publicly traded company; Healtheon merges with WebMD and the new company eventually adopts the WebMD name

2000: WebMD begins a major rebuilding effort in the wake of dot-com collapse

As an online health care information provider for consumers, WebMD faces the same challenges as any Internet service provider. It must find new methods of generating revenues while providing free information to users. The company plans to develop sponsorship opportunities, fee based services, and increase revenues from advertising.

PRODUCTS

WebMD is an online health care information and technology company. The company provides transaction services for physicians, pharmacies, insurance companies, hospitals, billing services, state and federal agencies, and other participants in the healthcare profession. Virtually every application involved in the practice of medicine can be automated and conducted electronically: lab ordering, prescription writing, tracking of medical and x-ray charts, billing, and insurance verification. WebMD provides online information for consumers. Physician search tools, diet and fitness journals, calorie counters, online management of family health records, and e-mail newsletters are only a handful of the tools available to users of the site.

CORPORATE CITIZENSHIP

WebMD believes in supporting community and charity events. It is particularly inclined to donate time or services to medical causes and research. The company co-sponsored a large charity event to benefit the Elton

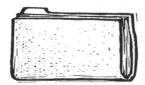

BEAM ME UP!

Crew members on the popular television series *Star Trek Voyager* needed to only push a button or issue a voice command and the perfect doctor materialized before their eyes uttering his pre-programmed line, "Please state the nature of the medical emergency." Not the best bedside manner, but not bad for a hologram. Star Trek technology like that doesn't really exist, but companies like WebMD are hoping to make it a reality. E-health companies are all in search of the "killer app" that will revolution doctor's office visits and generate huge streams of revenues for its inventor. Before the "killer application" can rock the medical community, doctors need to agree on what they need. Online health companies collapsed in 2000 because physicians were not enticed to enter the world of e-mail and browsers to conduct business with the expensive tools that were developed. Many doctors claim to be computer illiterate or simply can't type. This was a valuable lesson for future product development. The search for the ultimate solution is still a work in progress.

John AIDS Foundation. A star-studded tennis tournament held in Atlanta featured appearances by Andre Agassi and Pete Sampras and was presented by WebMD and Dupont. WebMD welcomes opportunities to participate in fundraising events.

GLOBAL PRESENCE

WebMD is accessible to Internet users worldwide, but operations are largely conducted in the United States. Company operations are designed to serve medical practices, insurance providers, and consumers who are a part of the U.S. medical system and subject to its insurance practices and regulations. At this time, international markets are not a primary consideration.

EMPLOYMENT

WebMD employs about 4,700 employees and 180 independent contractors. In the year 2000, the company terminated more than 1,000 employees as part of the restructuring effort. In 2002 the company recruited employees to strengthen its new organization. The company looks for individuals who are highly trained, innovative, and creative. The self-described corporate culture is a "casual work environment, but very serious about business". WebMD offers a competitive benefits package that includes education assistance, adoption assistance, and medical and dental insurance.

SOURCES OF INFORMATION

Bibliography

Chin, Tyler. "In Search of the Killer App that Will Bring Physicians Online." *amednews.com*, 9 October 2000.

Elton John AIDS Foundation/Press Release, 23 August 2000.

Hoovers Company Profiles, 2002. Available at http://www.hoovers.com.

Rothman Morris, Bonnie. "Teenagers Find Health Answers with a Click." *The New York Times*, 20 March 2001.

For an annual report:
on the Internet at: http://www.webmd.com/corporate

For additional industry research:
Investigate companies by their Standard Industrial Classification Codes, also known as SICs. WebMD Corp.'s primary SIC is:

7372 Prepackaged Software

Also investigate companies by their North American Industry Classification System codes, also known as NAICS codes. WebMD Corp.'s primary NAICS codes are:

511210 Software Publishing

514191 Online Information Services

Weight Watchers International, Inc.

FOUNDED: 1963

OVERVIEW

Weight Watchers International, Inc. is one of the premier weight loss service organizations in the world. Despite several changes in ownership, the company has maintained the same basic approach to weight loss for nearly 40 years. Artal Luxembourg S.A., a private European investment firm, purchased 80 percent of the company from H.J. Heinz Inc. in June 1999. The current corporate structure of the company includes several divisions: weight management, products, publishing, and the packaged food. Artal Luxembourg controls the first three, while Heinz retained licensing rights to the latter. The weight management division, which owns about 65 percent of the franchises, remains the strongest performer for the company.

The Weight Watchers weight management plan is comprised of four central elements: group meetings, behavior modification, exercise, and diet. The fee-based group meetings account for the majority of the company's income and generated in excess of $400 million in 2001. The meetings are considered critical to the success of the outfit and the statistics are impressive. In 2001 there were nearly 40,000 meetings held in more than 30 countries boasting attendance of more than 1 million members. The behavior modification component teaches members to evaluate and improve their eating habits. The company produces dietary aides such as leaflets, manuals and videotapes to track progress. Exercise is another element of the program, though Weight Watchers does not operate fitness centers. Physical activity is encouraged and members are given guidelines for exercise that are endorsed by the American College of Sports Medicine. Diet is the fourth and perhaps most critical aspect

Contact Information:
HEADQUARTERS: 175 Crossways Park West
    Woodbury, NY 11797-2055
PHONE: (516)390-1400
FAX: ((516)390-1334
TOLL FREE: (800)651-6000
URL: http://www.weightwatchers.com

FINANCES:

Weight Watchers Inc.
Net Incomes, 1999-2001
(million dollars)

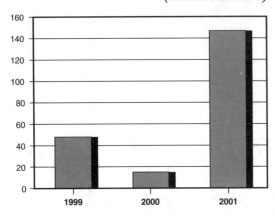

covering the stock, and all had ties to the initial public offering. Lauren Rich Fine, an analyst at Merrill Lynch, praised the company saying: "This company generates and gushes free cash flow." Others point to the poor track record of weight loss companies that have entered the public markets. Jenny Craig and Nutri-System have both performed poorly, but they suffered in the aftermath of the fen-phen controversy. (Fen-phen is a diet drug that was pulled from the market by the FDA in 1997.) Both companies had recommended this drug as part of their programs. Weight Watchers managed to steer clear of this problem.

HISTORY

Weight Watchers International, Inc. is perhaps the most well-known name in the world of weight management programs. Its origins can be traced back to the early 1960s when a homemaker from Queens, New York, told her friends about her battle to lose unwanted pounds. Jean Nidetch had struggled with her weight for years and had experimented with all available diet plans, but none of them produced the desired results. At 5-feet 7-inches and 214 pounds, she knew that she was at risk for developing a variety of medical conditions if she did not change her lifestyle.

Nidetch did not create a new or revolutionary diet plan. She picked up a copy of the program recommended by the New York City Department of Health's Obesity Clinic and began to use it as her guide. It was very similar to any sensible diet regimen that might be prescribed by a doctor or health care practitioner. What made the difference this time? Discussing her failures with other women proved to be the secret to her success—personally and professionally. Jean discovered that many women were frustrated with their pattern of lifelong dieting. The women shared stories and encouraged each other to persevere. These informal support sessions formed the basis for what would one day become an international corporation created to encourage healthy weight loss.

of the program. Over the years various systems have been used to fashion sensible and easy-to-follow meal plans. Members can prepare fresh food meals or select Weight Watchers brand packaged frozen entrees and snacks. The most recent incarnation of the Weight Watchers plan is based on a points system, which assigns numeric values to various foods. Points are calculated for each item consumed, frozen or fresh. The numbers are tallied at the end of the day with the objective of achieving a daily point goal.

Weight Watchers also operates two smaller units: a publishing division and licensed products ranging from snacks to CDs and videotapes. This unit produces a wide variety of Weight Watchers cookbooks and food guides, as well as a monthly magazine: *Weight Watchers*.

COMPANY FINANCES

Revenues for 2001 were record setting. Weight Watchers posted a net income of $147.2 million on $623.9 million in revenues for a profit margin of 23.6 percent. This was a dramatic increase over the year 2000, which saw a profit margin of only 5 percent.

ANALYSTS' OPINIONS

Weight Watchers became a publicly traded company in November 2001. It has not established a history in the financial markets. In early 2002, only five analysts were

By 1962 Jean Nidetch was holding weekly meetings in her living room for overweight men and women. She even managed to recruit her husband, Marty, an overweight bus driver, to participate in the program. The size of the group grew while the size of the individual members began to shrink. Soon the meetings had to be moved to a larger location and finally settled in a space above a movie theater in Little Neck, Long Island. Jean brought her own bathroom scale to the meetings and charged each member two dollars a week to cover the cost of the rental space. In two years Jean and her husband Marty each managed to lose 70 pounds. Motivated by the success of the group, and with her slimmed down body as her most persuasive advertising, Nidetch secured a business partner in 1963. Albert Lippert, a former business executive, joined Nidetch to launch Weight Watchers Inc. The group meeting format was well-received and the partners decided to expand the company by offering franchise opportunities.

A decade after introducing the Weight Watchers plan to the world, Nidetch and Lippert sold the company to H.J. Heinz in 1978. Weight Watchers became a wholly owned subsidiary of the Heinz Corporation, but Nidetch and Lippert retained majority ownership, and the basic tenets of the program remained intact. The weekly group meetings continued to be synonymous with the Weight Watcher's name.

Weight Watchers entered the 1980s posting small, but consistent, growth numbers. While the company remained the same, the public mentality had begun to change. "Skinny" was in and baby boomers were willing to pay big money for anything that would help melt the excess pounds and slow down the aging process. The diet industry as a whole was pulling in an estimated $3 billion dollars a year, and demand for services continued to grow. Market research conducted at the time showed that about 60 percent of all women considered themselves heavy or overweight. This was not even the best news for the diet programs. Detailed research revealed that 40 percent of the women who wanted to lose weight did not believe they could achieve their goals without professional assistance. In prior studies only 25 percent of the respondents had indicated a need for outside counseling. All in all there were more overweight people and fewer and fewer of them believed that they could make a change in their lives without paying for a service.

Weight Watchers was no longer the only option when it came to weight reduction. Others had entered the field and shifted the emphasis away from strict weight loss and calorie counting programs. Healthy and fit lifestyle choices were now the buzzwords of the industry. Overweight housewives were not the core audience for marketers who were anxious to attract affluent, upscale, professional women with money to spend on food and fitness programs.

By 1986 it was evident that Weight Watchers needed a face lift. Heinz mounted a campaign to revive the aging franchise. The weekly meetings remained central to the program, and there was little that needed changing in that area. The same could not be said of the other components of the program. Perhaps the most important element in any successful weight loss regime is the food. Weight Watchers had its work cut out for it in this discipline. The Weight Watchers plan required members to perform lengthy calculations to determine appropriate calories and food portions for each meal or snack. Compared to the fad diets of the time, which were often liquid diets, Weight Watchers was labor intensive. Members had the ability to go to the supermarket and purchase prepared foods that could popped into the microwave, but this was not a popular option. More specifically, Weight Watchers frozen foods were no longer a popular option.

Though the company was a pioneer in the field of low calorie frozen meals, competitors were quick to cash

FAST FACTS:
About Weight Watchers International, Inc.

Ownership: Weight Watchers is a publicly owned company traded on the New York Stock Exchange.

Ticker Symbol: WTW

Officers: Raymond Debbane, Chmn., 46; Linda Huett, Pres., CEO, and Dir., 56, salary $236,565, bonus $283,351; Thomas S. Kiritsis, VP and CFO, 57, salary $130,798, bonus $160,035

Employees 34,400

Prinicpal Subsidiary Companies European Investment firm Artal Luxembourg purchased 80 percent of the company from H.J. Heinz in 1999. Heinz retains a stake in the food products division.

Chief Competitors Weight Watchers International, Inc. is primarily a weight loss and weight management company. Its competitors include Jenny Craig, Diet Centers, and Nutri-System. The company also produces low calorie frozen entrees and desserts. In this market the company's rivals include Stouffers Lean Cuisine and Healthy Choice frozen entrees.

in on the demand for no fuss, no fat food. Stouffers introduced a line of meals under the Lean Cuisine banner. Sales of the line skyrocketed. Weight Watchers had generated interest in this type of offering, but Lean Cuisine executed the idea brilliantly. The package design and marketing were geared to an upscale, fitness conscious audience. The recipes and entree selections reflected current tastes in food and were generally more attractive to consumers. Weight Watchers foods were handicapped by their very own brand identity. The name suggested no fat, no taste foods intended for overweight dieters.

Heinz dedicated itself to improving the taste of the food and changing the overall image of the line. The bright pink packages were toned down and new script lettering was added to lend a touch of elegance. Television advertising was also modified to reflect a more contemporary attitude toward health and fitness. Gone were the spots that chided viewers for poor eating habits replaced by more encouraging and inspirational messages. The ads were strategically placed during some of the most popular television shows of the decade, including *The Cosby Show* and *Magnum P.I.* The overall goal

CHRONOLOGY:
Key Dates for Weight Watchers

1963: Weight Watchers founded by Jean Nidetch

1978: Weight Watchers is sold to H.J. Heinz Co.

1986: Campaign to overhaul frozen food line is launched

1991: Burger King offers Weight Watchers foods

1997: 1-2-3 Success Points system debuts; Sarah Ferguson, the Duchess of York, signs on as spokesperson

1999: Artal Luxembourg SA buys Weight Watchers

2001: Weight Watchers goes public

of the marketing plan was to associate the Weight Watchers program with a healthy, active lifestyle versus strict weight loss and calorie counting.

Packaging and ad campaigns alone were not enough. The executives at Weight Watchers was finally forced to realize that consumers could be enticed to try a product by a slick promotional campaign, but they would not come back for seconds if the food was not appetizing. The research staff worked to reformulate the recipes for many of the products. The public wanted low calorie foods that tasted good and were made from natural ingredients. Products were pulled from store shelves and altered to satisfy the public's demand for flavor-filled foods.

The early 1990s saw the United States enter the Gulf War and the economy face a recession. Revenues for the weight loss industry dropped, but dieting remained a lucrative industry. The preference for healthy eating versus weight loss dieting continued to grow. Consumers once again demanded more of the diet foods available at the supermarkets. New competitors entered the arena. ConAgra, Inc. launched a line of Healthy Choice frozen foods and watched it become an industry giant. In only two years, the company achieved $500 million in sales. Slim-Fast and Kraft Foods also realized huge gains in market share. Slim-Fast expanded its offerings, which had been limited to liquid shakes, to include energy bars and snacks. Kraft was offering a wide variety of fat free products such as mayonnaise and salad dressings. Weight Watchers' investment in the food business was too large to allow the venture to be outsold so handily. The marketing team again found itself playing catch up. Dieti-

TCBY

Talk show host, Rosie O'Donnell is not a paid Weight Watcher's spokesperson, but she could fill the bill. Every day the company benefits from free publicity as O'Donnell recounts her food struggles from the day before and tallies her points. By her own admission, she has not shed a significant amount of weight, but her efforts were not for nothing. After daily lobbying from the set of her television show, Weight Watchers finally added TCBY ice cream treats to its list of acceptable goodies. How many brownie points is that worth?

cians worked to decrease the fat and sodium in the food items, but the marketers decided this would not be enough to stem the tide. A separate brand with an identity that was not so openly fused with the Weight Watchers name was needed. The result was an entirely new line of entrees called Smart Ones.

In addition to new products, Weight Watchers also experimented with distributing their food products through an unlikely venue: Burger King. In 1991 Burger King agreed to offer hot Weight Watchers entrees in its restaurants and sell frozen entrees as take out items. The idea never gained popularity with the customers and the trial was suspended.

Weight Watchers also turned its attention to more sophisticated advertising in the 1990s. Actress Lynn Redgrave had served as a celebrity spokesperson for more than a decade, but the company decided to replace her with a more contemporary personality. In 1997 Sarah Ferguson the Duchess of York signed on as the new face of Weight Watchers. In exchange for a 1 million dollar salary, Ferguson agreed to lose 5 pounds. In 1999 Heinz had finally had enough of Weight Watchers and sold the brand to Artal Luxembourg. Two years later, the company enjoyed a successful public offering.

STRATEGY

Weight Watchers found the formula for success in 1997—literally. It introduced a new plan called "1-2-3 Success," which used the points system to monitor food intake. This plan simplified the process enormously for members. The point system continues to be the foundation for the company's diet plan. The program was mod-

U.S. spokesperson for Weight Watchers Duchess of York, Sarah Ferguson, admires a man's 110-pound weight loss at a convention in Houston, Texas. (AP Photo/David J. Phillip)

ified and the name changed to Winning Points in the year 2000. Non U.S. operations were also re-named. In the United Kingdom, the plan is known as Pure Points, and in Europe it is simply the Points Plan.

INFLUENCES

Many diet plans were rocked by complications associated with prescribing diet pills in the mid-1990s. Weight Watcher's weight loss programs have never relied upon drugs of any type. In light of recent information collected and new concerns about dietary supplements, Weight Watchers advocates a drug free weight loss plan. Instead the company advocates healthy eating, exercise, and support meetings. Recognizing that not everyone can attend a meeting at any time of the day, Weight Watchers developed a comprehensive Web site. Members are able to log on to the site and chat with others and receive encouragement. The site also includes many useful tools to assist in the weight management programs.

CURRENT TRENDS

Weight Watchers has developed several new methods of delivering its programs to members. The At Work program offers classes in the workplace for employees;

this option has increased in popularity as more employers realize the benefits of a healthy staff. The At Work classes are particularly popular in the United States. The company has also developed CD-ROMs for those who cannot attend normal classes. The CDs contain copies of the diet plan and weight loss guidance.

PRODUCTS

The Weight Watchers name is attached to a number of products. The weight management programs generate the majority of revenues. Sixty-five percent of weight loss revenues are derived from company-owned operations. The remaining thirty-five percent of weight loss revenue is generated by franchises. Products such as calculators, books, CD-ROMs, and snack bars accounted for 27 percent of total revenues in 2001. The Weight Watchers name is also licensed for cookbooks, a magazine, and other published items. The Heinz company continues to hold the rights to manufacture Weight Watchers frozen food products.

GLOBAL PRESENCE

Weight Watchers is a global brand name and maintains operations world wide. By December 2001, the

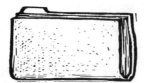

A LESS TAXING WEIGHT LOSS PLAN

In 2002 the Internal Revenue Service ruled that weight loss programs are now tax-deductible. The decision is based on the fact that obesity is considered a disease and treatment is a legitimate medical expense. In order to qualify for the benefit, individuals must be diagnosed by a doctor as obese. Analysts who follow Weight Watchers stock did not herald this ruling as a reason to celebrate. The impact on enrollment will likely be minimal, and the tax break is only good in the United States. Members in the United Kingdom will continue to fork over pounds to lose the pounds.

company had established 8,900 international meeting locations in more than 15 countries. International attendance in 2001 was 23.5 million and revenues were $153 million. Programs are customized from country to country in keeping with local cuisine.

CORPORATE CITIZENSHIP

Weight Watchers is committed to corporate citizenship and supports the communities in its areas of operations.

EMPLOYMENT

In 2001 the company had 34,400 employees in locations around the world. The geographic breakdown of employees reports 13,300 are in the United States, 13,200 in the United Kingdom, 3,500 in Europe and 4,400 in Australia and New Zealand. There are about 9,300 program leaders moderating classes on a part time basis.

SOURCES OF INFORMATION

Bibliography

Cliff, Jennifer, and Dan Moreau. "Change Agents, Jean Nidetch Knew that Weight Watchers Success Hinged on More Than a Diet." *Changing Times*, August 1989.

Fannin, Rebecca. "Shape Up!" *Marketing & Media Decisions*, February 1986.

Leder, Michelle. "Investing: Real Belt Tightening as Part of Portfolio." *The New York Times*, 20 January 2002.

Pender, Kathleen. "Weight Watchers Stays Flat." *The San Francisco Chronicle*, 7 April 2002.

Tascarella, Patty. "Heinz Tips Scales on Low Cal Fare." *Pittsburgh Business Times*, 26 December 1997.

Thompson, Stephanie. "Two Ad Pitches for Weight Loss Gain More Heft." *Advertising Age*, 4 December 2000.

Thresher, Alison. "Girth of a Nation." *Nation's Business*, December 1986.

"Wall Street in Busiest Week for IPOs Since Mid-May." *Los Angeles Times*,14 November 2001.

Warner, Fara. "Weight Watchers Focuses on Eating." *Adweek's Marketing Week*, 19 August 1991.

"Weight Watchers Profile." *Hoovers Company Profiles*, 2002. Available at http://www.hoovers.com

Wilson, Steve. "Fashionable Plan Brings Weight Watchers Back." *Advertising Age*, 8 March 1999.

For an annual report:
on the Internet at: http://www.weightwatchers.com

For additional industry research:
Investigate companies by their Standard Industrial Classification Codes, also known as SICs. Weight Watchers International, Inc.'s primary SIC is:

7299 Miscellaneous Personal Services, Not Elsewhere Classified

Also investigate companies by their North American Industry Classification System codes, also known as NAICS codes. Weight Watchers International, Inc.'s primary NAICS code is:

812990 All Other Personal Services

WestPoint Stevens, Inc.

OVERVIEW

WestPoint Stevens, Inc. is a manufacturer, marketer and distributor of bed and bath home fashions products. The company's trademark brands include Atelier Martex, Chatham, Grand Patrician, Martex, Patrician, Utica, Stevens, Lady Pepperell, Luxor and Velux. The company also has licensing agreements with Ralph Lauren Home, Dr. Scholl's, Designers Guild, Beautyrest, Joe boxer, Glynda Turley, Sanderson, Disney Home and Martha Stewart. In 2001, the company held the largest market share in domestic blankets, and had one of the largest market shares in domestic sheets and pillowcases and domestic bath towels. WestPoint Stevens has 34 manufacturing facilities, 16 distribution centers, and 52 outlets.

FOUNDED: 1813

Contact Information:

HEADQUARTERS: 507 West 10th Street, PO Box 71
    West Point, GA 31833
PHONE: (706)645-4000
FAX: (706)645-4772
URL: http://www.westpointstevens.com

COMPANY FINANCES

Westpoint Stevens' revenues for 2001 were $1.7 billion, down from $1.8 billion in 2000 and $1.88 billion in 1999. The company's sales were negatively affected by an unfavorable economy in nearly every segment but its basic bedding division. Gross profits fell from $550 million in 1999 to $469 million in 2000.

As sales began to slip, so did the company's earnings per share, which were $.84 in 1999, –$1.28 in 2000, and –$0.55 in 2001. Stocks hit a 52-week low in 2001 at $0.96 per share from a high price for the year at $10.15. At year end, the price was $2.45 per share, and by the end of the first quarter of 2002, it was $1.95 per share. The stock's 2001 high price was $19.63 and the low was

FAST FACTS:

About WestPoint Stevens, Inc.

Ownership: WestPoint Stevens is a publicly owned company traded on the New York Stock Exchange.

Ticker Symbol: WXS

Officers: Holcombe T. Green, Jr., Chmn. of the Board and CEO, 62, $899,444; M.L. "Chip" Fontenot, Pres. and COO, 58, $443,365; Joan E. Amberg, SVP, 40, $285,000; Lester D. Sears, SVP, 53, $226,666; Lanny L. Bledsoe, SVP, 65, $265,000; Michael J. Velsmid, Jr., SVP, 58, $300,000

Employees: 15,337

Chief Competitors: WestPoint Stevens' main competitors include Pillowtex, Dan River, and Springs Industries.

$5.94, ending the year at $7.49. In 1999, the price per share had reached a high of $37.56.

In March 2002, a lawsuit was filed against WestPoint Stevens alleging that some of its directors and officers had breached their duties, had acted in bad faith, and had wasted corporate assets. The Complaint against the company named CEO Holcombe Green and was similar to a class action suit filed in October 2001, which alleged that during 1999 and 2000l, the directors and officers issued misleading statements regarding inventories and capacity in the towel products division. The March 2002 lawsuit alleged that company press releases were misleading because the company did not state it knew sales "would be adversely affected in future years and quarters."

The suit followed some tough financial news: in January 2002, one of WestPoint Steven's largest customers, Kmart Corporation, filed for bankruptcy protection. More than half of the company's sales in 2001 were to large retailers such as Kmart, J.C. Penney Company, Inc., Sears Roebuck & Company, Wal-Mart and Target, but WestPoint Stevens stated the bankruptcy would not likely have a long-term negative effect on the company. According to WestPoint Stevens' annual report, no single brand license comprises more than 12 percent of the company's sales. In 2000, Kmart and Target each accounted for approximately 14 percent of the company's sales.

Operating margins remained stable through the difficult financial times at WestPoint Stevens. Margins were

in the 17 to 20 percent range through 2001, although they had slipped briefly to 15.7 percent late in 2000.

ANALYSTS' OPINIONS

In the late 1990s and early 2000s, textile companies had a difficult time increasing sales and profits, and WestPoint Stevens was no exception. The weak economy had caused sales to drop 2.8 percent in 2001, and 3.6 percent in 2000. Standard & Poor's lowered the company's ratings twice between October 2000 and October 2001 due to "poor operating results and financial measures that were significantly below Standard & Poor's expectations. A sluggish and highly promotional retail environment, manufacturing downtime to reduce inventories, and high debt levels all contributed to weak operating results and the related negative impact on profitability and cash flow measures."

Standard & Poor's stated that despite the company's decreased rating, it was generally an extremely efficient manufacturer and had become a full- service supplier for its largest customers, global mass merchandisers, who increasingly favored full-service vendors.

Further, S&P looked favorably on the company's Eight Point Program for restructuring, as well as its steep ($700 million in six years), investments in modernizing its production facilities.

HISTORY

Stevens, the first textile company which would later become part of WestPoint Stevens, was opened in Massachusetts in 1813. Lady Pepperell Manufacturing Company, Inc. followed in 1815, opening in Biddeford, Maine. The Chattahoochee Manufacturing Company, which soon became the West Point Manufacturing Company, was established in Georgia in 1873.

West Point was founded at a time when textile milling in the post-war South was ready for takeoff. Lafayette Lanier is credited with much of the company's early success. Lanier quickly replaced old equipment with new machines to increase productivity in producing a canvas-type material called "flat duck." Before mill construction was widespread, he pursued large commercial accounts through a large Boston sales agent.

When "mill fever" became contagious throughout the South, West Point was already well established and ready to expand. In 1880, only 20 percent of all textile mills were located in the South. By 1920, the percentage had leapt to 60 percent. During that time, West Point had built three new mills just across the Chattahoochee River in Alabama.

Throughout the early twentieth century, the mill prospered under the leadership of Lafayette Lanier's son.

George H. Lanier initiated a massive expansion in the 1930s, while the country was in the throes of an economic recession. In 1933, West Point acquired the Dixie Cotton Mill.

In 1965, West Point merged with Pepperell, Inc. and in 1988, it acquired Stevens. Soon after, the company defaulted on several financial obligations and filed for Chapter 11 bankruptcy in June 1992. By September of that year, the company had restructured and emerged from bankruptcy protection. In December 1993, West Point-Pepperell had merged into WestPoint Stevens.

In June, 2001, three banks—the Bank of Nova Scotia, First Union National Bank, and Bank One—seized 9.3 million shares of WestPoint Stevens stock. The shares had been offered as collateral in 1997 for a $130 million loan by a group of banks. The loan was to pay off debt held by the company's investors.

STRATEGY

In 1999, WestPoint Stevens examined strategies and financial efficiency. In 2000, the company announced it would acquire the company in a leveraged buyout at $21 per share, which would value the company at $1.15 billion. However, by May, the company's board terminated the plan, which would have paid $22 per share to stockholders. Following the board's announcement, shares plummeted. The board also announced at the same time that it would discontinue examination of a merger or sale and approved a regular dividend of $0.02 as well as a special dividend of $2.00 per share, which was paid in June 2000.

In June, 2000, the company also unveiled its Eight Point Program to restructure WestPoint Stevens. The plan included a $195 million pretax restructuring impairment charge to cover the cost of implementing the plan. The plan addresses expansion of brands; exploration of the new licensing opportunities; rationalization of manufacturing operations; reduction in overhead expense; increase in global sourcing; improvement of inventory utilization; enhancement of supply chain and logistics functions; and improvement in capital structure. Four plant closings to be completed under the plan were announced.

WestPoint Stevens would also examine, under the plan, expanding its global market. In 2001, sales to retail establishments within the U.S. made up some 85 percent of its total sales. International sales accounted for only 5 percent of the company's total sales.

CURRENT TRENDS

The home fashions industry is becoming increasingly competitive. According to WestPoint Stevens' annual report, the company believes it will face greater competition from foreign markets. In order to remain

CHRONOLOGY:
Key Dates for WestPoint Stevens, Inc.

1813: Stevens Textile Company opens in Massachusetts

1815: Lady Pepperell Manufacturing Company, Inc. opens in Biddeford, Maine

1873: Chattahoochee Manufacturing Company opens in Georgia

1880: Chattahoochee becomes West Point Manufacturing Company at beginning of big textile manufacturing boom in the South

1933: West Point Manufacturing Company acquires the Dixie Cotton Mill

1965: West Point merges with Pepperell, Inc.

1988: West Point acquires Stevens

1992: West Point files for Chapter 11 bankruptcy, restructures, and emerges from bankruptcy protection

1993: West Point-Pepperell merges into WestPoint Stevens, Inc.

2000: WestPoint Stevens announces its Eight Point Program, a $195 million restructuring plan

2001: Three banks seize 9.3 million shares of WestPoint Stevens stock that had been used as collateral in 1997 for a $130 million loan to pay off debt of company investors

competitive, WestPoint Stevens stated that the company would likely increase its foreign sourcing.

PRODUCTS

WestPoint Stevens holds the country's largest market share of bed and bath fashions. Their product line includes sheets, comforters, bed accessories, towels, shower curtains, draperies and decorative pillows.

The company's brands include its best-selling brand Martex, Grand Patrician, Patrician, Stevens, Lady Pepperell, Utica and Veliux. WestPoint Stevens also holds licenses on Ralph Lauren Home, Disney Home, Joe Boxer, Sanderson, Designer's Guild, Simmons Beautyrest, Dr. Scholl's, Glynda Turley, and Martha Stewart Bed and Bath.

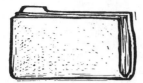

AT HOME AWAY FROM HOME

WestPoint Stevens has made a home in the away-from-home business, supplying hospitals, nursing homes, and hotel chains with bedding and linens.

Some of the company's larger clients include Hilton, Hyatt, Mirage, Adams Mark, Embassy Suites, Doubletree, Wyndham Hotels, Ramada and LaQuinta Inns.

WestPoint Stevens produces enough sheets to make 36 million beds every year, which, according to the company, averages out to 330 items for the bed every minute its plants are in operation. The company's plants produce more than 5,000 miles of cloth every week, which WestPoint Stevens calculated in one year is enough to reach the moon with 20,000 miles of fabric left over.

Its products are largely marketed through partnerships with major global retailers such as Target and Kmart. The company also sells its products in specialty stores, catalogs, warehouse clubs, television shopping networks and supermarkets. The remainder is sold to large commercial customers such as healthcare clients and hospitality chains.

CORPORATE CITIZENSHIP

The charitable arm of WestPoint Stevens is the WestPoint Stevens Foundation. Through the foundation, employees may contribute money and volunteer time. The foundation's primary benefactors are the United Fund, United Way, and the American Red Cross. The foundation donates blankets, towels and bed linens to the Red Cross during disasters. It also helps to sponsor arts programs and scholarships. Associates are encouraged to volunteer in literacy programs, as well as hospice or emergency aid programs.

GLOBAL PRESENCE

While only 5 percent of WestPoint Stevens' sales were generated outside the United States, the company began examining, as part of its plan, expansion in Europe, Australia, Canada, Mexico, the United Kingdom, the Middle East and the Far East.

WestPoint Stevens has had a long history of global sourcing, purchasing specialty yarns and fabrics from around the globe. In 2001, it imported materials and finished products from 20 countries, compared to 14 in 2000.

The company established strict policies on global sourcing. It doesn't purchase any merchandise produced in whole or in part by "indentured, prison or illegal immigrant or child labor." WestPoint Stevens requires proof from its vendors that they do not violate human rights or engage in labor practices prohibited in the policy.

EMPLOYMENT

"Corporate responsibility starts with being a good employer," states the WestPoint Stevens Web site. The company describes itself as diverse and strongly committed to embracing workplace diversity and to empowering its associates to achieve on their own merit.

According to the company's 2001 annual report, WestPoint Stevens had not experienced a labor dispute in 20 years. Approximately 10 percent of its workforce is unionized.

SOURCES OF INFORMATION

Bibliography

"Banks seize shares of WestPoint CEO." *CFO*, 20 July 2001.

Marino-Nachison, Dave. "WestPoint Stevens Shredded." *The Motley Fool*, 22 May 2000. Available at http://www.fool.com.

McPike, Joanne. "WestPoint Stevens officers sued for breach of duty." *Dow Jones Newswires*, 29 March 2002.

Ross, Jayne M. "WestPoint Stevens Analysis." *Standard & Poor'*, 30 November 2000.

"Textile firm linked to 'Negro cloth' for slaves." *Money*, 20 February 2001.

Turner, Julie. "Industrial history of Troup County." *Travels Through Troup County: A guide to its Architecture and History*. Published by the Troup County Historical Society, Troup County, GA, 1996.

"WestPoint Stevens announces manufacturing restructuring." *Hoover's*, 21 March 2002.

For an annual report:

on the Internet at: http://www.westpointstevens.com.

For additional industry research:

Investigate companies by their Standard Industrial Classification Codes, also known as SICs. WestPoint Stevens' primary SIC is:

2392 Housefurnishings Except Curtains

Also investigate companies by their North American Industry Classification System Codes, also known as NAICS codes. WestPoint Stevens' primary NAICS code is:

314129 Other Household Textile Product Mills

Weyerhaeuser Company

OVERVIEW

The Weyerhaeuser Company, a leader in the international forest products business, is the largest international owner of merchantable softwood timber and the largest producer of softwood and hardwood lumber and engineered lumber products. Incorporated in 1900, the company primarily grows and harvests trees and produces and sells forest products. It also builds homes, develops land, and recycles paper products. Many of its products are used in the manufacturing and construction industries. In North America, it is the second-largest producer of structural panels and second-largest distributor of wood products. In the United States, it is the top forest products exporter and it ranks among the top exporters overall.

Headquartered in Federal Way, Washington, the Weyerhaeuser Company has offices or operations in 18 countries and customers across the world. Its principal business segments are timberlands and wood products; pulp, paper, and packaging; and real estate and related assets.

As may be expected, Weyerhaeuser's land holdings are great. In North America, it manages 5.9 million acres of company-owned and a half-million acres of leased commercial forestland in North America. The company also has renewable, long-term licenses on 32.6 million acres of forestland in five Canadian provinces managed by its Canadian operations.

COMPANY FINANCES

In the first quarter of 2002, the company's revenues rose 13 percent to $4.01 billion. Net income before extra-

FOUNDED: 1900

Contact Information:

HEADQUARTERS: 33663 Weyerhaeuser Way S.
   Federal Way, WA 98003
PHONE: (206)924-2345
URL: http://www.weyerhaeuser.com

Created by U.S. lumber producer, Weyerhaeuser, The Pacific Rim Bonsai Collection is the largest of its kind in the Northwest United States. (AP Photo/Ralph Radford)

ordinary item fell 50 percent to $53 million. Results reflect an improved performance at the real estate division, offset by non-recurring charges related to facility closure. In 2001 the company's sales totaled $14.5 billion. Accounting for 19 percent of this total were sales outside of the United States, including exports. Its timberlands business segment accounted for 7 percent of sales, while the wood products segment accounted for 44 percent. The pulp, paper, and packaging segment accounted for 39 percent. In 2000 wood products accounted for 42 percent of revenues; pulp, paper, and packaging, 41 percent; real estate and related assets, 9 percent; and timberlands, 7 percent.

ANALYSTS' OPINIONS

Heading into 2002, analysts felt that Weyerhaeuser Company may be in a somewhat difficult financial position. However, it was also acknowledged that the company demonstrated aggressive growth in the past several years, and that that kind of approach can involve significant financial risks. Many wouldn't be surprised if the company's fortunes assumed an upward trajectory, especially following the major acquisition of Williamette Industries in 2002. In the first quarter of 2002, Weyerhaeuser earned $.27 per share. The earnings were above Wall Street forecasts. According to the

research firm of Thomson Financial/First Call, nine analysts had expected the company to earn an average of $.15 per share.

HISTORY

Though not incorporated until 1900, the Weyerhaeuser Company's beginnings go back to the mid-eighteenth century, when a man named Frederick Weyerhaeuser, who was born in 1834 and died in 1914, emigrated to America in 1852 at the age of 18. Weyerhaeuser worked at a succession of menial jobs, but he saved his money and eventually bought a sawmill in 1857 in Rock Island, Illinois. Weyerhaeuser was a hard worker and a smart businessman, and the mill became a great success. This allowed him to purchase more sawmills on the Mississippi and to buy forests in Wisconsin, Minnesota, Idaho, Washington, and Oregon. By the turn of the century, Weyerhaeuser owned more timberland than anyone in the country. Also, he had taken on several partners. This group turned its eyes from the American Midwest to the Northwest, one of the greatest areas of timber on the face of the Earth, and the company was well on its way to becoming a global leader in the industry.

Officially, the Weyerhaeuser Company was founded in 1900, when it was incorporated. It didn't take long for the enterprise to extent itself into the international realm. Company sales to Japan started in 1923, when the island needed Weyerhaeuser lumber to rebuild Tokyo and Yokohama following an earthquake. But it wouldn't be until 1963 that the company opened its first Asia-based office, located in Tokyo. The company would spread itself out through the region during the rest of the decade and into the 1970s.

The company's Asian connection was strengthened when former U.S. President Richard Nixon initiated partial relations with China in 1971. Weyerhaeuser became the first U.S. forest products company to develop business in the Communist country. That same year, the company opened its first-ever corporate headquarters, in Federal Way, Washington.

As the company headed into the new millennium, it began demonstrating an aggressive approach to growth, as it made some significant acquisitions and business moves. In 2001 in acquired a 50 percent interest in Southern Cone Timber Investors Limited, a joint venture with institutional investors focusing on plantation forests in the Southern Hemisphere. Principal assets include 68,000 acres of eucalyptus and pine tree plantings. In July, the Weyerhaeuser Company bought the remaining 50 percent interest in Cedar River Paper Company, a manufacturer of liner and medium containerboard from recycled fiber, for $261 million. In January 2002 Weyerhaeuser entered into a merger agreement with Willamette Industries, a premium and low-cost forest products company focused on producing white paper, brown paper, and building materials.

STRATEGY

The Weyerhaeuser Company's overall stated strategies are to achieve total quality, maintain managerial excellence, pursue full customer satisfaction, empower its employees, and produce large returns for shareholders. These strategies are designed to help the company achieve its ultimate vision of becoming "the best forest products company in the world." To achieve its aims, the company is implementing business metrics and improved work processes.

Specifically, as the company headed into 2002, management placed strong focus on what it considered to be two key business metrics: safety and return on net assets (RONA). Safety, the Weyerhaeuser leaders believe, is not only about protecting employees. It also results in increased productivity and product quality.

To improve its RONA, the company has developed a "road map" that includes three elements: PACE, PIE, and process reliability. PACE (Process to Achieve Capital Excellence), the company explains, is a business metric designed to help reduce capital spending and maximize effectiveness. Weyerhaeuser

FINANCES:
Weyerhaeuser Company Net Earnings, 1998-2001 (million dollars)

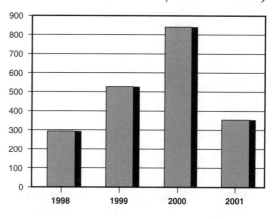

puts each of its projects through a PACE analysis, which helps determine if the project provides the correct solution in the first place and then it helps keep the project on track. PIE, or Purchasing Improvement Effort, is designed to help decrease spending on goods, services, and capital equipment; to reduce inventories; and to simplify purchasing transactions. The third element, process reliability, is designed to insure that the company's products are produced in the safest and most efficient manner possible. The company is also focusing on improving work systems throughout the organization and the internal delivery of services, and on streamlining its core services. The company estimates that these efforts will result in more than $150 million in annual savings.

The Weyerhaeuser Company is also focusing on the issue of increased globalization. To deal with this, the company says it is important that its internal companies develop proper scale and scope through consolidation. In this way, they can better serve the changing customer base resulting from globalization, which will improve returns for shareholders. As far as the future of international trade, the company says the global demand for forest products will outweigh supply for most of the next decade. To deal with this situation, it is developing strategic partnerships with international companies. These include entering a joint marketing agreement with Svenska Cellulosa Aktiebolaget of Sweden, creating a partnership with the World Timberfund, and opening its first packaging plant in Mexico.

FAST FACTS:

About Weyerhaeuser Company

Ownership: The Weyerhaeuser Company is a publicly owned company operating in the forestry, wood products, and paper sectors of the materials industry. It is traded on the New York and Toronto Stock Exchanges.

Ticker Symbol: WY

Officers: Steven Rogel, 59, Chmn., Pres., and CEO, 2001 salary $2,100,000; William Stivers 63, CFO, EVP, 2001 Salary $761,00; William Corbin, 60, EVP Wood Products, 2001 Salary $885,000; Richard Hanson, 58, EVP Timberlands, 2001 Salary $655,000; Steven Hill, 54, SVP of Human Resources

Employees: 60,000

Principal Subsidiary Companies: The Weyerhaeuser Company has three wholly owned subsidiaries: Weyerhaeuser New Zealand Inc., Weyerhaeuser Australia Pty. Ltd., and Weyerhaeuser Forestlands International. Through Weyerhaeuser New Zealand Inc., the Company runs the management and marketing activities of a New Zealand joint venture, Nelson Forests Joint Venture, which consists of 151,000 acres of Crown Forest License cutting rights, 42,000 acres of freehold land and the Kaituna sawmill. Through Weyerhaeuser Australia Pty. Ltd., the company owns a 70 percent interest in Pine Solutions, an Australian softwood timber distributor. It also owns two sawmills and 16,800 acres of cutting rights. Through Weyerhaeuser Forestlands International, the company is a 50 percent owner and managing general partner in RII Weyerhaeuser World Timberfund, L.P. (WTF), a limited partnership that makes investments outside the United States. WTF owns 58,500 acres of radiata pine plantations, two softwood lumber mills, a pine molding remanufacturing plant, a chip export business, and a 30 percent interest in Pine Solutions. This partnership also owns a Uruguayan venture, Colonvade, S.A. The company is also involved in real estate development, construction, and other real estate-related activities through its real estate subsidiary, Weyerhaeuser Real Estate Company, and its financial services subsidiary, Weyerhaeuser Financial Services, Inc.

Chief Competitors: The Weyerhaeuser Company's major competitors include International Paper and Georgia Pacific.

INFLUENCES

One of the ongoing strategies that has helped put the Weyerhaeuser Company where it is today is its proactive approach to its business. Obviously, a company that primarily makes its money by manufacturing and marketing wood products must ensure that raw materials remain plentiful. To this end, Weyerhaeuser strongly focuses on activities designed to increase the yield from its fee timberland acreage. These activities include extensive planting, suppression of non-merchantable species, pre-commercial and commercial thinning, fertilization, and operational pruning. Success in this area requires effective forest management, and Weyerhaeuser has dedicated itself to learning more about a forest's natural cycles. Specifically, the company applies principles of science and sustainable forestry to protect natural resources and increase forest productivity.

With the increasing globalization that began in the 1990s, Weyerhaeuser has applied these same strategies and standards to its international land holdings. In areas where it is only involved in the importation of wood products, it only conducts business with companies who operate responsibly managed forests.

CURRENT TRENDS

The merger agreement with Willamette Industries, completed in January 2002 and described as a "hostile takeover," was the most significant development in the company's recent history. Analysts estimated the total value of the transaction to be somewhere between $6 and $8 billion. Many repercussions resulted from the acquisition. As Weyerhaeuser began aligning its operations with Williamette, it closed three facilities (in Oregon, Louisiana, and Colorado) which eliminated 206 jobs, a move that was part of the consolidations and cuts intended to help Weyerhaeuser save $300 million a year over the next three years. It also closed two Williamette facilities and a Weyerhaeuser packaging facility in Denver, Colorado. Other job cuts and downsizing measures were expected.

Weyerhauser's first quarter profits for 2002 fell, in part because of the charges for its acquisition of Williamette and the resulting plant closures. For the first quarter, Weyerhaeuser reported net earnings of $30 million. At the same time in 2001, it reported net earnings of $107 million.

Still, Weyerhaeuser felt confident following the prolonged, 14-month process to acquire Williamette. The company said it expected the market for wood products to improve in the second quarter. Also, at the time, the industry had been in a year-long downturn and was beginning to show signs of a recovery. Weyerhaeuser CEO Steven Rogel said the company was still on its way to meeting the goal of saving $300 million at the end of three years.

PRODUCTS

The Weyerhaeuser Company is divided into business segments that include timberland and wood products; pulp, paper, and packaging; and real estate and related assets. The company's wood products segment produces and sells engineered, hardwood, and softwood lumber; plywood and veneer; composite panels; oriented strand board; doors; treated products; logs; and chips and timber.

Its pulp, paper, and packaging division is further divided into businesses that include pulp, which manufactures chemical wood pulp; newsprint, which manufactures newsprint at the company's North Pacific Paper Corporation mill; paper, which manufactures and markets a range of coated and uncoated fine papers; containerboard packaging, which manufactures linerboard and corrugating medium and manufactures and markets industrial and agricultural packaging; paperboard, which manufactures and markets bleached paperboard, used for production of liquid containers; recycling, which operates a wastepaper collection system and markets it to company mills and worldwide customers; and chemicals, which produces chlorine, caustic, and tall oil.

Weyerhaeuser's real estate and related assets businesses are involved in real estate development and construction through its real estate subsidiary, Weyerhaeuser Real Estate Company, and in other real estate-related activities through its financial services subsidiary, Weyerhaeuser Financial Services, Inc.

CORPORATE CITIZENSHIP

Frederick Weyerhaeuer reputedly was a very philanthropic individual. In keeping with the spirit of its founder, the Weyerhaeuser Company established the Weyerhaeuser Company Foundation in 1948, which has donated more than $100 million to humanitarian causes, public outreach, and education programs.

The company itself assumes the highest degree of environmental responsibility. In 1971 it established an environmental policy that outlined its commitments and codes of behavior toward the environment, as well as to the surrounding communities and its employees. In 1999 the company began aligning all of its timberlands and manufacturing operations to the ISO 14001 Environmental Management System standard. It expects to complete this process by 2005. By adhering to these standards, the company expects that it will improve upon its already solid environmental performance and meet regulatory and stakeholder requirements. It also believes the standards will improve its efforts toward practicing sustainable forestry, reducing pollution, and conserving natural resources.

CHRONOLOGY:
Weyerhaeuser Company

1852: Frederick Weyerhaeuser comes to America

1857: Weyerhaeuser buys his first saw mill, in Rock Island, Illinois

1900: Weyerhaeuser and partners incorporate as the Weyerhaeuser Company

1914: Frederick Weyerhaeuser dies

1923: The company makes its first sale in Japan

1948: The philanthropic Weyerhaeuser Company Foundation is established

1963: The company's first Asian-based office is opened

1971 Weyerhaeuser becomes the first U.S. forest products company to do business in China

2001: Weyerhaeuser acquires a 50 percent interest in Southern Cone Timber Investors Limited

2002: Weyerhaeuser acquires Willamette Industries

GLOBAL PRESENCE

The Weyerhaeuser Company has operations throughout North America, as well as in the British Virgin Islands, New Zealand, Germany, Hong Kong, Japan, and Korea. Its Canadian operations are located in Alberta, the Atlantic Region, British Columbia, Ontario, and Saskatchewan. The company has sales offices in Japan, China, Korea, Hong Kong, Singapore, Taiwan, Switzerland, and Belgium.

The company's Weyerhaeuser Australia Pty Limited operates facilities in the Tumut region of New South Wales and in the Caboolture area, located north of Brisbane, Queensland. The Tumut operations include a sawmill that handles more than 500,000 cubic meters of logs a year, as well as the Gilmore Operations, which include finger-jointing, kiln drying, molding, and treatment plant facilities. The Caboolture operations include a sawmill, plantation, and chip export business.

EMPLOYMENT

The Weyerhaeuser Company offers its employees a wide range of benefits including health and dental

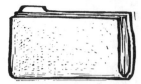

THE ENRON AFTERMATH

Following the Enron Scandal of 2002, things became tough for the Texas corporation's public accounting firm Arthur Andersen. After it was indicted on criminal charges in connection with Enron's collapse, the Chicago-based Arthur Anderson immediately lost more than 200 clients—including the Weyerhaeuser Company.

After dropping the Andersen account, Weyerhaeuser named KPMG LLP as its independent public accountant. Weyerhaeuser claimed that its decision to change auditors didn't result from any disagreement on accounting issues. In fact, Weyerhaeuser praised Arthur Andersen for its quality service and professionalism. The decision came after a review process by the Audit Committee of the Weyerhaeuser board of directors and Weyerhaeuser management.

Andersen's involvement with Weyerhaeuser became particularly problematic during Weyerhauser's takeover of Williamette—in the eyes of many, a hostile takeover that generated questions of merger accounting and conflicts of interest, issues of great concern in the Enron debacle.

benefits, life insurance, short- and long-term disability, 401(k) plans, and performance share and pension plans. The benefits package is designed to create a mutually beneficial arrangement for the company and employees. The reason that the company offers such an attractive benefits package is that it feels it is the best way to recruit and retain top-quality employees and to manage costs in a competitive environment. On the other side, the employees are protected against financial loss and are ensured a secure financial future.

The company also actively seeks vigorous employee involvement as well as good labor relations. Moreover, employee safety is the company's top priority. Many of its facilities have been recognized for their outstanding health and safety programs. The company also takes employee concern to a higher level, as its prevention focus is designed to help reduce preventable diseases, such as hypertension, heart disease, substance abuse and diabetes. To this end, the company offers an employee and family assistance program that provides free and confidential assistance in the areas of personal, financial, family or work-related problems, and a wellness program that provides comprehensive health and wellness resources and health screenings.

In fact, the company is quite innovative and forward thinking in regards to its company culture, which even includes a work/life balance element. Believing that there is more to life than just work, the company provides resources for employees to help them focus on themselves, their families, and their community. These resources include adoption and adult/elder care assistance, employee support groups, employee and family assistance program, exercise facilities, family events, financial planning workshops, flexible spending accounts, flexible working arrangements, recreation services, and scholarships.

SOURCES OF INFORMATION

Bibliography

Davitt Publications. "Weyhaeuser, Frederick (1834-1914)." *German-American Corner*, 2002. Available at http://www.german-heritage.com.

Dcipher Reports. "Corporate Snapshots-Weyerhaeuser Company." *Business Week Online*, 13 June 2002. Available at http://host.businessweek.com

Parrish, Bill. "Enron Lessons for Weyerhaeuser, Willamette Industries, the SEC and Arthur Andersen." *Parrish and Company*, 24 January 2002. Available at http://www.billparish.com/20020124willamette.html.

Verespej, Michael A. "Who Owns Trees?," *IndustryWeek.com*, 20 March 2000. Available at http://www.industryweek.com

Yahoo! Finance. "Profile-Weyerhaeuser Company." *Yahoo! Market Guide*, 2002. Available at http://biz.yahoo.com/p/w/wy.html

For an annual report:
on the Internet at: http://investor.weyerhaeuser.com

For additional industry research:
Investigate companies by their Standard Industrial Classification Codes, also known as SICs. Weyerhaeuser Company's primary SICs are:

0811 Timber Tracts

2421 Sawmills & Planing Mills, General

2611 Pulp Mills

2621 Paper Mills

2631 Paperboard Mills

2679 Converted Paper & Paperboard Prod, Nec

Also investigate companies by their North American Industry Classification System codes, also known as NAICS codes. Weyerhaeuser Company's primary NAICS codes are:

233110 Land Subdivision and Land Development

321113 Sawmills

322110 Pulp Mills

322130 Paperboard Mills

Whirlpool Corporation

OVERVIEW

Whirlpool originally operated as a family-owned small town business, but it eventually grew into the world's largest manufacturer and marketer of major home appliances, including washers and dryers, refrigerators, freezers, dishwashers, ranges, compactors, room air conditioners, and microwaves. The company also manufactures portable appliances including stand mixers, hand mixers, and blenders. The company's major brands—Whirlpool, KitchenAid, Roper, Bauknecht, Ignis, Brastemp, and Consul—are marketed in more than 170 countries. The firm is also Sears, Roebuck and Co.'s largest supplier, providing the department store with major appliances under the Kenmore brand name. In fact Sears accounted for more than 20 percent of sales in 2001.

Intense competition, slowing economies in several of its key markets, and industry consolidation forced Whirlpool to revamp its strategy early on in the new millennium. The company's focus included restructuring certain operations, expanding globally, developing new and existing products, and fostering customer loyalty.

COMPANY FINANCES

Whirlpool's sales in 2001 were $10.34 billion, less than 1 percent higher than the previous year. Sales had increased from $6.5 billion in 1991 to $10.5 billion in 1999, but fell in 2000 to $10.32 billion. The home refrigerators and freezers product segment and the home laun-

FOUNDED: 1911

Contact Information:
HEADQUARTERS: 2000 N. M-63
    Benton Harbor, MI 49022-2692
PHONE: (616)923-5000
FAX: (616)923-5443
EMAIL: info@whirlpool.com
URL: http://www.whirlpoolcorp.com

ANALYSTS' OPINIONS

As a market leader, Whirlpool believes it is well positioned to secure future revenue and profit growth. Agreeing with that assessment, Standard & Poor's (S&P) analysts rated the stock a "buy", due to favorable demographics, cuts in interest rates, strong housing activity, and economic improvement in the United States during early 2002. S&P also favored the company because it continued to grow faster than its domestic counterparts. In addition, a larger portion of the company's sales are stemming from higher profit margin products.

HISTORY

Whirlpool began as a small, family-owned business in St. Joseph, Michigan. Lou Upton established the Upton Machine Co. to manufacture electric motor-driven wringer washing machines. The company's first years were rocky, and it found itself producing toys, camping equipment, and automotive accessories to stay afloat. Upton's first big break came in 1916, when it landed a contract with Sears, Roebuck & Co. to supply the store with washing machines. The firm's good fortune continued through the first World War, and in 1925, it launched its own brand name of washers.

Upton merged with New York-based Nineteen Hundred Washer Co. in 1929 to form Nineteen Hundred Corp. The company made it through the Depression and World War II, when most of its facilities were used to manufacture weapon parts. In 1948, Nineteen Hundred launched the Whirlpool brand of automatic washers, which it began manufacturing along with the Sears' Kenmore brand. The following year, a complete line of Whirlpool appliances—including wringers, washers, and dryers—was introduced.

The firm officially adopted the name Whirlpool Corp. in 1950 to promote its new line of home appliances. Whirlpool added automatic dryers to its product line and then began a series of acquisitions in order to expand further. In 1951, Whirlpool purchased Clyde Porcelain Steel of Ohio, gaining access to one of the largest washing machines plants in the world. In 1955, the firm purchased Seeger Refrigerator Co. and started manufacturing refrigerators, as well as air conditioning units and cooking ranges. Vacuum cleaners were also added to Whirlpool's product mix when Birtman Electric Co. was merged into the company's operations.

Expansion continued into the 1960s, and the firm established a 24-hour toll-free hotline for consumers. It also constructed a new manufacturing facility in Findlay, Ohio. By the end of the decade, sales had reached $1 billion, and Whirlpool had expanded into the Canadian market through the purchase of an interest in Inglis Ltd. International expansion had started in the late 1950s

FINANCES:

*Whirlpool Corp.
Revenues, 1998-2001
(million dollars)*

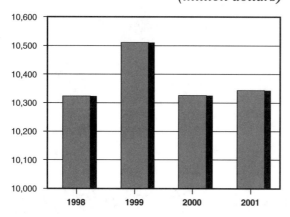

*Whirlpool Corp.
2001 Stock Prices*

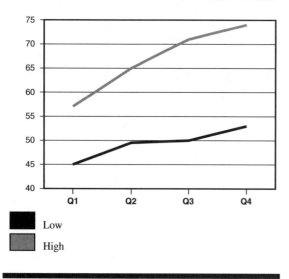

Low

High

dry appliances division both accounted for 30 percent of sales, while home cooking appliances brought in 16 percent of sales. Other products, including room air-conditioning equipment and hand appliances, secured 24 percent of total sales in 2001.

Whirlpool's net income fell from $367 million in 2000 to $21 million in 2001 due to restructuring charges. The firm's stock ranged from a low of $45.87 per share to a high of $74.20 per share over a 52-week period. Its annual dividend in 2001 was $1.36 per share and its operating profit margin was three percent.

when Whirlpool began investing in the Brazilian market. In 1976, the firm acquired Consul S.A. and Embraco S.A.

Well on its way to becoming a leading force in the appliance industry, Whirlpool began manufacturing trash compactors, microwave ovens, and Whirlpool vacuum cleaners in the 1970s. The firm also introduced the first solid-state electronic washing machines. Revenues climbed to $2 billion in 1978.

Growth continued in 1986 with the purchase of the KitchenAid division of Hobart Corp. Whirlpool also expanded into Italy with the purchase of compressor manufacturer Aspera s.r.l. The company entered the Indian market the following year when it teamed up with Madras-based Sundaram-Clayton Ltd. In 1987, David Whitwam was named president and CEO of Whirlpool, and he set out to turn the company into an international powerhouse. That year, Whirlpool partnered with McDonnell Douglas Astronautics Company to develop appliances used in space. In 1988, Vitromatic S.A. de C.V. was created as a joint venture with Vitro S.A. of Monterrey, Mexico. One year later, the company joined with N.V. Philips in partnership that gave Whirlpool greater access to the European market.

The company continued its global expansion throughout the 1990s with a focus on European and Asian operations. Subsidiaries were created in Hungary, Poland, and the Czech Republic. The company also began producing washers in Slovakia, and continued its expansion in Latin America. In 1997, the firm restructured its operations to capture greater profit from its overseas businesses. It also divested its appliance financing business and organized its North American operations into two major segments: brand management and product delivery.

Whirlpool continued to focus on global expansion and reorganization in the new millennium. In 2000, it purchased the remaining shares in its two Brazilian subsidiaries, Brasmotor S.A. and Mutlibras S.A. In early 2002, it set plans in motion to acquire Polar S.A., a major home appliance manufacturer in Poland. Amid fierce competition, industry consolidation, and a weakening global economy, Whirlpool's long-standing history of success left management confident that the company would remain a leader in the appliance industry.

STRATEGY

Whirlpool's strategies of product diversification and global expansion have persevered through much of the firm's history, and they remain part of its long-term business plan. According to Whirlpool, many appliance manufacturers utilize similar strategies that focus on lowering costs, increasing product quality, expanding distribution, and increasing the share of floor space at retail locations. A cornerstone to Whirlpool's strategy in the new millennium, however, was building customer loyalty, a strat-

FAST FACTS:
About Whirlpool Corporation

Ownership: Whirlpool is a public company traded on the Chicago and New York Stock Exchanges.

Ticker Symbol: WHR

Officers: David R. Whitwam, Chmn. and CEO, 59; Jeff M. Fettig, Pres., COO and Dir., 44; Mark E. Brown, EVP and CFO, 50

Employees: 59,000

Principal Subsidiary Companies: Whirlpool has subsidiary companies and facilities in North and South America, Europe, and Asia. Its products are marketed in over 170 countries. The company's main subsidiaries are Whirlpool Europe B.V., Whirlpool Properties Inc., Whirlpool Patents Company, Brasmotor S.A., and Multibras S.A. Eletrodomesticos.

Chief Competitors: As the world's largest manufacturer and marketer of major home appliances, Whirlpool competes with other appliance manufacturers on the basis of product features, price, product quality and performance, service, warranty, advertising, and promotion. Its primary competitors are Electrolux AB, GE Appliances, and Maytag Corp.

egy that the company believed was quite different from its competitors' business plans.

Whirlpool revamped its research and development strategy in 1999 and began to focus on consumer behavior. Company engineers went to the homes of consumers to study behavior. The findings were then used to develop new products believed to be well suited to consumer lifestyles. Roughly 20 percent of the firm's $400 million capital budget was reserved for the creation of these new products. In addition, executive pay was linked to the revenue that stems from new products or services. By 2003, the company expected to spend 35 percent of its budget on new product development.

Whirlpool also employs innovative consultants who help to turn employee ideas into new products. The company has an intranet site where employees can post a product idea. The site averages about 300,000 hits per month. Once an idea gets approval from senior management, employees and innovative consultants are given 100 days and $100,000 to test the idea, conduct market research,

CHRONOLOGY:

Key Dates for Whirlpool Corp.

1911: Upton Machine Co. is established

1916: The company begins supplying washing machines to Sears, Roebuck and Co.

1929: Upton merges with the Nineteen Hundred Washer Company

1948: The Whirlpool brand is launched

1950: The company adopts the name Whirlpool Corp.

1976: Brazil-based Consul S.A. and Embraco S.A. are acquired

1986: The KitchenAid division of Hobart Corp. is acquired

1997: The company launches a restructuring effort designed to improve competitiveness

2000: Whirlpool acquires the remaining shares of its two Brazilian subsidiaries: Brasmotor S.A. and Multibras S.A.

and develop initial prototypes. Whirlpool believes its aggressive strategy of new product development will allow it to remain one step ahead of competitors.

INFLUENCES

The company's strategy is influenced by intense competition. For example, in the late 1990s, competitor Maytag Corp. beat Whirlpool to market with its Neptune front-loading washing machine. Shortly thereafter, the company launched its aggressive product innovation campaign.

Whirlpool also saw its competitors become stronger in 2001 due to industry consolidation. Maytag purchased Amana Appliances in August of that year, while Italy-based Merloni Elettrodomestici acquired a 50 percent stake in General Domestic Appliances, a large UK appliance supplier. Then in early 2002, Elco Holdings Inc. acquired Brandt, one of France's largest home appliance manufacturers. Influenced by its competitor's actions, Whirlpool continues to focus heavily on its global operations.

PRODUCTS

Whirlpool has operations in North America, Asia, Latin America, and Europe. Its supplies its North American market with air purifiers, dryers, washers, built-in ovens, countertop appliances, dehumidifiers, dishwashers, freezers, hot water heaters, ice makers, jetted and soaking tubs, microwaves, ranges, refrigerators, room air conditioners, and trash compactors. In the late 1990s and early 2000s, the company introduced several new products in North America, including the AccuBake Duo System, new energy efficient refrigerators, the Calypso wash motion clothes washer, the Senseon clothes dryer, and the Duet front-loading washer and dryer.

The company provides washers, compressors, microwaves, and refrigerators to the Asian market under the Whirlpool brand name. During 2001, Whirlpool launched a vertical axis clothes washer, the Fire Genie microwave, Whitemagic Hotwash clothes washer, Ice Magic refrigerator, QuickChill frost-free refrigerator, and the MagiCook microwave oven and gas cooking ranges.

In Latin America, the company supplies washers, compressors, countertop appliances, dishwashers, freezers, microwaves, refrigerators, and room air conditioners under the Whirlpool, Brastemp, Consul, Embraco, and Eslabon de Lujo brand names. The firm launched several new appliances in this region during 2001.

In Europe, the Middle East, and Africa, Whirlpool sells washer and dryers, ovens, compressors, dishwashers, free-standing cookers, freezers, microwaves, ranges, and refrigerators. During 2001, the company introduced the Whirlpool Maximo compact microwave in these markets, and it also launched the Bauknecht brand of built-in ovens and ranges, and the Dialogue line of dishwashers, washers and dryers, and refrigerators and freezers. In each of its markets, Whirlpool completes extensive consumer research before launching a product to ensure the design and function meets with regional expectations and design tastes.

CORPORATE CITIZENSHIP

Whirlpool believes that by manufacturing efficient appliances, it will help create self-reliant individuals who are socially and environmentally responsible. During 2001, Energy Star named Whirlpool Partner of the Year for its energy efficient products. Its dedication to the environment was applauded by the Environmental Protection Agency during a ceremony in Washington D.C. in March 2001.

The firm also works with nonprofit organizations, governments, schools, and businesses to enrich the communities in which it operates. In 1951, the Whirlpool Foundation was created to focus on quality of family life, cultural diversity, and lifelong learning. During 2000, the foundation awarded $6.7 million in grants.

GLOBAL PRESENCE

While North America accounted for $6.6 billion of Whirlpool's $10.34 billion in sales during 2001, the company's brand was a leader in all of its international markets. Because of the firm's overseas exposure, however, it had to contend with a variety of turbulent economies during 2001. An economic crisis in Argentina and an energy shortage in Brazil challenged the firm's growth in Latin America. A recession in Germany weakened its European sales. The economy in India—one of the firm's largest growth markets—began to experience a decline as well, due in part to the military action in South Asia. Nevertheless, Whirlpool continues to invest in its global operations.

EMPLOYMENT

Because of its focus on new product development, Whirlpool hires creative people. The company believes it will achieve its vision—to have a Whirlpool product is every home, everywhere—by creating pride in its employees. The firm is also dedicated to workplace diversity and believes that it can make use of each employee's talents. Nearly two-thirds of company employees are located outside of the United States.

SOURCES OF INFORMATION

Bibliography

Arndt, Michael. "Whirlpool Taps its Inner Entrepreneur." *Business Week*, 7 February 2002.

Beatty, Gerry. "A Whole New Range of Options." *HFN: The Weekly Newspaper for the Home Furnishing Network*, 4 February 2002.

Stovall, Sam. "A Positive Spin on Appliance Stocks." *Business Week*, 7 March 2002.

Tatge, Mark. "Firestorm." *Forbes*, 21 January 2002.

Whirlpool Corp. Home Page, 2002. Available at http://www.whirlpoolcorp.com

"Whirlpool Corp." *Appliance Manufacturer*, October 2001.

DOING THE RIGHT THING

Whirlpool's corporate culture regarding quality and "doing the right thing" for its consumers and suppliers was set in place by founder Lou Upton. One of Upton Machine's first orders came from Federal Electric in 1911. The company shipped 100 washing machines to its first major customer; however, a cast iron gear in each and every machine proved to be faulty. Lou Upton personally worked with the Federal's management to fix the problem and replaced each gear with a new cut-steel piece. Federal, so impressed with Upton's integrity, placed another order for 100 additional machines.

For an annual report:

write: Whirlpool Corp., 2000 M-63 North, Mail Drop 2800, Benton Harbor, MI 49022

For additional industry research:

Investigate companies by their Standard Industrial Classification Codes, also known as SICs. Whirlpool's primary SICs are:

3631 Household Cooking Equipment

3632 Household Refrigerators and Home and Farm Freezers

3633 Household Laundry Equipment

Also investigate companies by their North American Industry Classification System Codes, also known as NAICS codes. Whirlpool's primary NAICS codes are:

335221 Household Cooking Appliance Manufacturing

335222 Household Refrigerator and Home Freezer Manufacturing

335224 Household Laundry Equipment Manufacturing

White Castle System, Inc.

FOUNDED: 1921

Contact Information:

HEADQUARTERS: 555 West Goodale Street
  Columbus, Ohio 43215
PHONE: (614)228-5781
FAX: 614)464-0596
TOLL FREE: (800)843-2728
URL: http://www.whitecastle.com

OVERVIEW

White Castle first sold hamburgers for a nickel in 1921 in Wichita, Kansas. Today, the company claims, its sells 500 million hamburgers a year and has sold more than 7 billion in total. That's not bad for a company that is essentially a regional operation that has never franchised any of its units. White Castle remains a family-owned company with a chain of restaurants. The company operates 348 restaurants in 12 states and 17 cities in the Midwest and Northeast. White Castle System Inc.'s signature product is its distinctively shaped and flavored burger, which measures a mere 2.5 inches, has 5 holes, and is served on a steamed bun. The burger's unique flavor results from the patty being grilled on a bed of onions and having the bun placed on top of the burger while its cooking. In this process, the bun absorbs the onion flavor (as well as a good deal of grease). It has been said that consumers either love or hate the White Castle burger.

Long before McDonald's, White Castle became the first-ever hamburger chain in the country. However, it would later become supplanted by McDonald's in the collective American consciousness, as the Ingram family chose to keep the business a regional and family-operated enterprise. Despite this seemingly non-aggressive approach, White Castle is a highly profitable business.

The White Castle hamburger, a bite-sized square served on a soft and steamy bun (some would call it "soggy") often has been called a "cult" food item. It has even been judged an acquired taste and is subject to frequent put-downs. The company itself is deemed an also-ran in the American hamburger sweepstakes. The somewhat demeaning terms cannot erase the fact that, from its inception, the company has demonstrated steady growth. True, it is a slow growth. McDonald's, founded in 1954 and expanded by the franchise route, had 25,000 restaurants across the world by 2001. By comparison, White Castle, which was founded in 1921 and never franchised, had only 351 stores in 2001. Indeed, a slow and conservative approach is the creed the owners live by. New restaurants only open when profits make it possible. The owners have never borrowed to expand; the only time borrowing was ever involved was when founder Edgar Ingram borrowed $700 to start the operation. As a result, White Castle only opens about 10 to 20 new restaurants a year. Still, this approach has kept the company, which consistently posts $1.2 million in daily sales, in business for 80 years.

COMPANY FINANCES

Because it is a privately owned company, detailed financial data about White Castle is unavailable. However, this much is known: the business brings in about $1.2 million a day in sales. In 1999 annual sales reached the $420 million mark. That same year, it posted a one-year sales growth of 5.0 percent.

HISTORY

Before White Castle came along, ground beef-or hamburger meat-was regarded as the lowest of meat products. That started to change in 1916, when short-order cook J. Walter Anderson essentially invented the hamburger. It was Anderson's idea to cook ground beef as a flat patty and serve it on a bun. This approach proved popular enough that Anderson opened three hamburger stands in Wichita, Kansas, between 1916 and 1920.

In 1921 Anderson and Edgar Waldo "Billy" Ingram, a real estate and insurance agent, became partners and opened a fourth location, this one called White Castle. Ingram reportedly had to borrow $700 to go into the hamburger business. With the founding of White Castle, the hamburger was well on its way to becoming the quintessential American sandwich. In 1924 the company was incorporated as the White Castle System of Eating Houses.

That same year, Anderson and Ingram opened another hamburger stand in Kansas City. At first, expansion happened rapidly as throughout the rest of the decade the partners opened up restaurants in 12 major cities in the eastern region of the country, serving its small, square, and inexpensive burgers from five-stool hamburger stands.

In 1931, to assure the quality of its product, White Castle began using frozen beef patties and developed crush-resistant cardboard carton specially lined to keep

FAST FACTS:
About White Castle System, Inc.

Ownership: White Castle is a privately held company that is owned by founder's (E.W. Ingram) family.

Officers: E.W. (Bill) Ingram III, Chmn, Pres., and CEO; William A. Blake, CFO; Dean Cromer, Area Manager

Employees: 7,000

Principal Subsidiary Companies: In addition to its restaurants, White Castle System, Inc. owns and operates three bakeries in Rensellaer, Indiana; Evendale, Ohio; and Carteret, New Jersey. The bakeries produce hamburger buns for the restaurants. The company also operates two meat-processing plants that supply the restaurants with their hamburgers and factories that produce snack foods. White Castle also owns and operates a subsidiary, the Porcelain Steel Building (PSB) Company, originally created to manufacture the stainless steel fixtures found in the restaurants. The subsidiary later solicited outside jobs, and it eventually attracted major industrial customers. Services include sheet metal fabrication, welding, powder painting, assembly, packaging, storage, and shipping. Its other subsidiary, White Castle Distributing, Inc., markets a line of frozen, microwavable hamburgers.

Chief Competitors: White Castle System Inc.'s top competitors include major hamburger franchises including McDonald's, Wendy's, and Burger King.

the burgers hot. The following year, with a campaign first used in St. Louis, Missouri, White Castle became the first fast-food enterprise to promote its product through coupon advertising.(The deal offered five hamburgers for the price of two.)

In 1933 Ingram bought out Anderson's share of the company. A year later, with the business now his alone, Ingram established a company headquarters in Columbus, Ohio. That same year, White Castle Systems founded its PSB subsidiary.

The company's expansion came to a standstill during the 1940s, due to World War II and the rationing of food products such as meat and sugar. Expansion resumed after the war but never at its previous pace. By the end of the decade, in 1949, the company added the

CHRONOLOGY:

White Castle Systems Inc.

1921: J. Walter Anderson and Edgar Waldo "Billy" Ingram found White Castle in Wichita, Kansas

1924: The company is incorporated as the White Castle System of Eating Houses

1931: White Castle starts using frozen beef patties

1933: Ingram purchases Anderson's share of the company

1934: White Castle implements a food-coupon promotion

1934 Ingram establishes the company headquarters in Columbus, Ohio

1954: White Castle patents its five-holed burger, calling it the "Slyder"

1961: White Castle sells its one-billionth hamburger

1982: White Castle establishes its own frozen food distribution company

2001: White Castle celebrates its eightieth anniversary

---

distinctive, trademark five holes to its patties. The holes helped the hamburgers cook faster as the patties were cooked within the bun. (Five years later, the company would even patent its five-holed burger, which it called the "Slyder.")

During the next two decades, the company initiated several significant changes including curb-side service, more menu items, larger buildings in more suburban locations, and drive-through service. In 1950, as if anticipating the emergence of frozen food products, White Castle began freezing hamburgers for sale to customers to eat whenever they wished. In 1956 White Castle added milk shakes to its menu. By 1961 White Castle reached the one-billion-hamburgers-sold plateau. At that time, no other hamburger chain had sold as many. A year later, the restaurants began serving cheeseburgers. In 1968 White Castle hit the two-billion-burger mark. In 1982 White Castle established its own frozen food distribution company. It publicized this move by sending its hamburgers to marines stationed in Beirut. During this period, White Castle became a 24-hour, quick-service restaurant.

In 1992 the company built a hamburger plant in Covington, Kentucky, that produced 200,000 hamburgers a

day. These sandwiches were frozen and sold in convenience stores. In 1993 White Castle even began selling its hamburgers and cheeseburgers in vending machines. A year later, the first White Castle hamburgers were exported to Mexico. In 1999 White Castle went online with a Web site at www.Whatyoucrave.com. In 2001 the company celebrated its eightieth anniversary.

STRATEGY

Through the years, White Castle's strategy has involved adhering to its stated mission, which is to serve the finest products, for the least cost, in the cleanest surroundings, with the most courteous personnel. Facility hygiene is extremely important to the company, who says that the two elements of its name—"White" and "Castle"—were selected to suggest to customers that they were eating in a clean and safe environment. To advance the idea of cleanliness, the company moved its kitchens from the back of its restaurants to the front, so that customers could actually see how their food was being prepared.

At the same time, White Castle has always been savvy in the ways of marketing and promotion. All efforts toward safety and purity of product were publicized. It openly claimed that fresh raw hamburger was delivered to its restaurants twice a day. Also, the company once hired a scientist from the University of Michigan to evaluate the nutritional value of its hamburgers. In a somewhat dubious test, the scientist fed a student nothing but White Castle hamburgers and water for three months. At the end, the student was examined and pronounced healthy. Though the methodology—and especially the rationale—behind such a test seems highly questionable, it made for great press.

Other marketing ideas were innovative and successful. White Castle was the first fast food restaurant to package its products in a take-out style. It was also the first restaurant to promote its business via coupons. The campaign was an overwhelming success, and it helped the company introduce its hamburger to a larger market. As far back as 1932, the company implemented a program that allowed consumers to tour restaurants and receive free samples of food products. Such goodwill gestures had a positive impact on consumers' perceptions about the organization. Other marketing innovations included publishing menu books and printing up free hand-outs (such as score pads for bridge, golf, and bowling) that advertised all of its products and locations.

Such promotional strategies proved to be far ahead of their time and would be later employed, with variations, by fast-food chains that would come after World War II. The company also proved to be forward thinking when establishing its organizational policies. Essentially the first-ever fast-food franchise, White Castle established a written set of standards for its restaurant operations, food preparations, and employee conduct. These policies formed the basis of the company's expansion, as White Castle replicated all of the elements that made the company so successful in the first place. The familiar White Castle restaurant faÁade came to represent a recognizable commodity in the eyes of the consumers (just as the golden arches would later do for the McDonald's chain).

INFLUENCES

White Castle's influence of the huge fast-food industry cannot be underestimated. Large chains that established themselves after World War II employed White Castle's strategies and innovations. Ironically, these companies would surpass in size and success the company that served as their business model.

That's not to say that White Castle became a dinosaur that couldn't survive in the emerging new world of mega fast-food franchises. Rather, White Castle has demonstrated continued growth and success. It just chooses to move at a slower pace and won't allow itself to be consumed by any over-ambitious stratagems. White Castle has retained a loyal clientele through the years, and it has attracted new devotees of its cult product, while other, larger fast-food franchises—such as Gino's and Jack in the Box—have come and gone.

In order to maintain its level of success and its modest but effective growth rate, the company continues to implement technical and organizational improvements. In 1993 Ingram issued a mandate to all of its stores to speed up its service while maintaining the highest level of food quality. In 1996 the company opened a computerized meat processing plant in Indiana that produces 16 million pounds of beef a year.

CURRENT TRENDS

At the start of the new century, White Castle envisioned opening 150 more restaurants in a ten-year period. Expansion includes new locations in Illinois, Ohio, Michigan, Indiana, Kansas, Kentucky, Minnesota, Tennessee, New Jersey, New York, Pennsylvania, and Missouri.

In 2001 White Castle started experimenting with a new design and logo for its restaurants. All locations would retain the trademark castle motif. However, the new design will be brighter, more colorful, and easier to read, and it is aimed at making the restaurants more "warm and appealing."

PRODUCTS

White Castle's best-known product is, of course, its square burgers with five holes served on a steamed bun.

The inexpensive, bite-sized burgers (nicknamed "Slyders") can be bought singly or in packaging promotions such as the "Sack of Ten."

However, just like other purveyors of fast food, the company has expanded its offerings throughout the years. Menu items include cheeseburgers, jalapeño burgers, fish sandwiches, chicken sandwiches, chili, French fries, onion chips, cheese sticks, soft drinks, milk shakes, coffee, hot chocolate, frozen Coke and cherry drinks, and a limited breakfast menu. A recent addition to its menu is its Chicken Rings, a variation on the popular onion ring, and created, no doubt, in response to competitors' similar offerings such as Chicken McNuggets.

CORPORATE CITIZENSHIP

Company founder Billy Ingram firmly believed in treating people fairly, sharing his success with the community, and investing in the future of others. Accordingly, in 1949, the Ingram family established the Ingram-White Castle Foundation. In 1999, to celebrate its fiftieth year, Mary and E. W. Ingram, Jr. gifted $11 million to the foundation to provide financial resources for grants. Over the years, the Ingram family has donated $35 million to the foundation. The grants funded by the Ingram generosity support arts, education, health and human services, primarily in Ohio communities. The foundation has awarded more than $8 million in grants to support scholarships to college students and awards to outstanding teachers, as well as to increase community support of education.

GLOBAL PRESENCE

As a regional operation, White Castle System, Inc. has little interest in global expansion. However, it does have restaurants in Japan and Malaysia.

EMPLOYMENT

White Castle adheres to a "hire from within" employment policy, and it has committed itself to providing substantial growth opportunities for its workers. It points out that many people now employed at the upper levels of the organization got their start by working at restaurant counters or on factory floors. The community also actively seeks input from its employees, and it provides them with open communication through a toll-free employee hot line. According to the company, more than 15 percent of its employees have been with the organization for more than ten years. With an envisioned expansion of 150 stores over a ten-year period, the company expects its management ranks to grow by

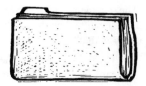

SO WHY A CASTLE?

In its early years, White Castle restaurants were really just five-stool hamburger stands. In order to make the stands more recognizable in the consumers' eyes, as well as to protect company investment in the structures, employee Lloyd Ray designed a moveable, all-steel frame structure that enclosed the stands. For the design, Ray used a castle motif. Though it looked medieval in its concept, the motif was actually based on the famous old Water Tower in Chicago. (The Water Tower is one of the few structures remaining from "Old Chicago," which was largely destroyed by the famous "great fire," the one allegedly started by Mrs. O'Leary's cow). These structures had exterior and interior enamel panels. Enamel panels had never before been used in a building design. After 1934 all of these steel and porcelain structures were produced by the Porcelain Steel Building Company, the White Castle Subsidiary. In the beginning, company founder Billy Ingram wanted to use the motif of a white castle, because he felt it would represent purity of product (white) and safety (castle) to its customers. To this day, the castle motif remains the company's trademark visual façade.

50 percent, and it intends to fill the new positions with current employees.

The company offers both full- and part-time positions. Benefits and incentives include paid pension and profit sharing, health and life insurance, sickness and vision benefits, dental plan, free meals while working, uniforms, flexible hours, on-the-job training, performance appraisals, paid holidays and vacations, competitive salaries, and sales bonuses.

SOURCES OF INFORMATION

Bibliography

American Business Journals Inc. "White Castle Testing New Look." *Columbia Business First,* 10 August 2001. Available at http://columbus.bizjournals.com

BBCi.co.uk. "White Castle Hamburgers," *h2g2,* 5 February 2002. Available at http://www.bbc.co.uk.

Chenoweth, Doral. "White Castle Still a Cult Hit in 80th Year." *The Columbia Dispatch,"* 12 September 2000. Available at http://www.dispatch.com.

The Greater Greenfield Chamber of Commerce. "Chamber Profiles." *Greenfield Chamber,* 2002. Available at http://www.greenfieldcc.org

Hoover's Capsule Profiles. "White Castle Systems Inc." *Hoover's Online,* 2002. Available at http://www.hoovers.com.

Ohio Historical Society. "MSS 991-White Castle System, Inc. Records, 1921-1991," 2002. Available at http://www.ohiohistory.org.

"White Castle Opens Plant in Indiana." *Central Ohio Source,* 30 August 1996. Available at http://centralohio.thesource.net.

For additional industry research:

Investigate companies by their Standard Industrial Classification Codes, also known as SICs. White Castle System Inc.'s primary SICs are:

2599 Furniture Fixtures, Not Elsewhere Classified

5812 Eating Places

Also investigate companies by their North American Industry Classification System codes, also known as NAICS codes. White Castle System Inc.'s primary NAICS codes are:

337127 Istitutional Furniture Manufacturing

722110 Full Service Restaurants

Whole Foods Market, Inc.

OVERVIEW

Whole Foods Market (WFM) is the largest natural and organic supermarket chain in the world. In February 2002, it had 129 stores in 23 states and the District of Columbia. The company planned to open three to five stores in each quarter of 2002, about 25 percent of them in new markets such as Toronto and Las Vegas. Its stores are supported by regional distribution centers, bakeries, commissary kitchens that supply prepared foods, a seafood processing facility, a produce procurement and field inspection office, and a coffee roasting operation.

Year 2001 store openings included Whole Foods Market's first foray into Manhattan, a 40,000 square foot store in Chelsea, which it reports has become one of its ten highest volume stores—along with new stores opened in Denver and Washington, D.C. Whole Foods Market is a *Fortune* 1000 company, ranked in April 2002 by *Fortune* magazine the 633rd largest U.S. company, ranked the 41st largest U.S. supermarket company by *Supermarket News* in 2001, and ranked for five consecutive years as one of the Top 100 Companies to Work For by *Fortune* magazine.

Whole Foods Market nutrition departments display a wide offering of vitamins, supplements, herbs and teas, homeopathic remedies, and information on alternative healthcare. Departments are staffed with team members having product knowledge and are organized and well-marked not only by product but by purpose, such as Joint Health, Stress Reduction, and Men's Health. Included with many brands are products under the Whole Foods and 365 labels.

In the Whole Foods Market *2001 Annual Stakeholder's Report*, Board Chairman, President, and CEO

FOUNDED: 1980

Contact Information:

HEADQUARTERS: 601 North Lamar, Suite 300
    Austin, TX 78703
PHONE: (512)477-4455
FAX: (512)476-1069
URL: http://www.wholefoodsmarket.com

FINANCES:

Whole Foods Market, Inc.
Net Sales, 1998-2001
(million dollars)

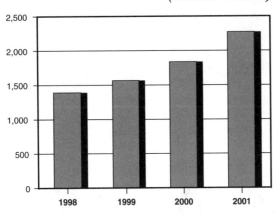

John Mackey cited the company's mission, core values, and national quality goals, saying "We do not carry natural and organic products to help boost our sales. We carry natural and organic products because we believe that food in its purest state—unadulterated by artificial additives, sweeteners, colorings and preservatives—is the best tasting and most nutritious food available. We actively support organic farming because we believe it is the best method for promoting sustainable agriculture as well as for protecting the environment and farm workers. It is our authenticity as a wellness lifestyle brand that is our major competitive advantage. . .To understand and truly appreciate Whole Foods Market one must recognize that we are a mission-driven company. . .Our motto—Whole Foods, Whole People, Whole Planet—emphasizes that our vision reaches far beyond just being a food retailer."

COMPANY FINANCES

Whole Foods Market's net sales have been steadily increasing since 1998 and this was projected to continue through 2002. To illustrate, 1998 net sales were nearly $1.4 billion; net sales in 1999 were nearly $1.6 billion; 2000 net sales were approximately $1.8 billion; net sales in 2001 were nearly $2.3 billion; and 2002 net sales were projected to reach $2.6 billion.

Value Line, Fortune, and Stockgroup in company profiles describe World Foods Markets Inc. as the world's largest retailer of natural and organic foods, *Fortune* adding that WFM pioneered the health foods super-

market concept. Since its initial public offering on the NASDAQ at $8.50 per share in 1992, Whole Foods Market has twice announced a two-for-one stock split, the second coming in recession-plagued 2001. On April 4, 2002, its stock price was $44.58 with all cash dividends still being reinvested. It was classified by Value Line in February 2002 as a mid cap stock with a $2.3 billion market cap.

ANALYSTS' OPINIONS

On March 25, 2002, CBS MarketWatch reported its most recent analyst recommendations on Whole Foods Market stock: Bear Stearns rated it attractive, setting a $49 price target; REC Capital Markets rated it a top pick; and Merrill Lynch rated it an intermediate-term buy, setting a $50 price target.

Amy Schatz of Knight-Ridder/Tribune Business News reported on February 14, 2002 that Whole Foods Market profits for first quarter 2002 rebounded and were up 34 cents per share, or $20 million, due to stronger than expected sales. Her article indicated that this strong performance surprised analysts and was particularly significant because of WFM's failed ventures into mail-order vitamins and Internet sales leading to a loss of $49 million in 2000, and added, "The company's success at reaching beyond natural food junkies comes when its smaller competitors, notably Denver-based Wild Oats Market, Inc., have struggled."

Also in February 2002, Value Line raised its revenue estimates for Whole Foods Market based on its acquisition of the three Atlanta-area Harry's Food Markets perishable superstores. While cautioning that WFM's bottom line probably wouldn't benefit until at least fiscal 2003 because of Harry's recent negative comparable store sales and its former owner's financial inability to retain and attract customers, Value Line cited the Harry's acquisition as part of WFM's trend to larger-format stores, which shows strong sales performance. Value Line also expressed confidence in Whole Foods Market by increasing its estimate of the company's fiscal 2002 performance based on more than a ten percent increase in comparable store sales in 2001's faltering economy, the company's cautious setting of 2002 store growth at five to eight percent, and its increased recognition as a "lifestyle" brand by a loyal and economically stable customer base. Value Line ranked Whole Foods Market shares highest for year-ahead price performance and speculated that because WFM share earnings were near the top of their historical range, profit-taking might result.

HISTORY

In September 1978, John Mackey, Whole Foods Market Co-founder, Chairman, President, and CEO,

opened SaferWay, a small health foods store in Austin, Texas; in 1979, the Clarksville Natural Grocery was opened in Austin by Craig Weller and Mark Skiles; and in September 1980, the three men joined forces to open the two stores as Whole Foods Market with a staff of 19.

Expansion began with the opening in August 1984 of a store in Houston and to April 2002 includes: the purchase of Bluebonnet Natural Foods in Dallas; the acquisition of three Wellspring Grocery stores in Raleigh, Durham, and Chapel Hill, North Carolina; the purchase of six stores from Bread & Circus, then the largest natural food retailer in the Northeast; the acquisition of Mrs. Gooch's Natural Foods Markets; the purchase of the San Francisco Bread of Life stores; the purchase of 22 Fresh Fields stores located in Washington, D.C./Baltimore, Philadelphia, New York/New Jersey/Connecticut, and Chicago markets; the acquisition of Florida Bread of Life stores; the acquisition of Amrion of Boulder, Colorado; the purchase of Allegro Coffee Company and Merchant of Vino stores; the acquisition of Nature's Heartland in Boston; the acquisition of Food for Thought in Northern California; the acquisition of three Natural Abilities, Inc. food stores in Sonoma County, California; and the merger of WholePeople.com with e-retailer Gaiam.com.

When Chairman and CEO John Mackey was asked about future growth, he said, "One of the concerns that has been expressed since we went public is: How big is this market? How big can it get? Seven or eight years ago, we didn't have any stores making $380,000 a week. Now that's the average. We're appealing to a broader range of customers. To me, this is all good news and it means we have a lot of expansion possibility ahead."

FAST FACTS:
About Whole Foods Market, Inc.

Ownership: Whole Foods Market, Inc. is a publicly owned company traded on the NASDAQ Stock Exchange.

Ticker Symbol: WFMI

Officers: John Mackey, Chmn., CEO, Pres., and Co-Founder, 48, $265,000; Glenda Flanagan, EVP and CFO, 48, $215,000; A.C. Gallo, EVP, 48, $220,000; Walter Robb, EVP, 48, $224,000; James Sud, EVP, 49, $215,000

Employees: 23,000

Principal Subsidiary Companies: Through mergers and acquisitions, Whole Foods Market owns and operates some stores under the following names: Wellspring, Fresh Fields, Bread & Circus, and Harry's Farmers Market.

Chief Competitors: Whole Foods Market, Inc.'s top competitors include other natural foods supermarkets, conventional and specialty supermarkets, other natural foods stores, small specialty stores, and restaurants. *Fortune* magazine in April 2002 named GNC, Trader Joe's Company, and Wild Oats Markets, Inc. as Whole Foods Market's three top competitors.

STRATEGY

In the mid-1990s, Whole Foods Market began to shift the purchase of products for retail sale from the store level to regional and national wholesale suppliers and vendors for better negotiation of volume discounts. In 2002, eight regional distribution centers distributed natural products, produce, and private label products to WFM stores in their respective regions. A Whole Foods Market seafood wharf, produce procurement center, specialty coffee roaster and distributor, and regional prepared food commissaries and bake houses also distribute products to stores.

In 1994 WFM's growth strategy turned to opening larger stores of between 30,000 to 50,000 square feet with expanded perishable departments, which in 2002 accounted for close to 65 percent of store sales. WFM believes that this larger store format with emphasis on high-quality perishables appeals to a broader customer base and is largely responsible for the strong new store performances it has been experiencing. The company also feels these larger stores are less vulnerable to competition over the longer term. In October 2001, to continue enlarging and improving its appeal to a more diverse customer base, WFM acquired three Harry's Farmers Markets—very large perishable superstores in the Atlanta area averaging more than 70,000 square feet each with approximately 75 percent of sales in perishables.

Because at year end 2001 Whole Foods Market regarded the natural foods retailing industry as highly fragmented into many smaller local and regional chains, its plan to open or acquire 15 to 20 stores in both fiscal 2002 and 2003 included the acquisition of smaller chains with desirable locations, markets, and experienced team members; relocation of existing stores; and new store openings. It also believed at that time that more future growth would come from developing new stores on premier real estate sites than from acquisition of existing stores.

New stores are generally located in high-traffic shopping areas, often in urban high-population locales,

CHRONOLOGY:

Key Dates for Whole Foods Market, Inc.

1980: Two Whole Foods Market (WFM) stores open in Austin, Texas

1984: WFM's first expansion outside Austin with store opening in Houston

1991: WFM launches its Whole Foods premium private label

1992: Whole Foods Market, Inc. goes public and is traded on NASDAQ; WFM purchases six Bread & Circus stores—the then largest natural foods retailer in Northeast

1993: WFM stock splits two for one

1997: WFM adds its 365 Every Day Value product line

1998: First of five consecutive years that *Fortune* magazine names WFM one of its Best 100 Companies To Work For; WFM launches Whole Kids product line

2001: WFM opens first store in Manhattan; Whole Foods Market stock splits two for one again

and are either free standing or in a strip center. Site selection is through internal analysis of potential markets based on criteria such as education levels, population density, and income levels. In 2002, about 95 percent of existing stores were located in the top 50 metropolitan areas.

A part of its mission and a major component of its growth strategy is the company's use of what it calls a "team approach" to store operations to promote a strong company culture, which it believes empowers employees much more than traditional supermarket operations. Whole Foods Market stores employ "team members" who are organized into up to 11 teams, each led by a team leader. There is also a store team leader (manager). Each team is responsible for a different product category or aspect of store operations. In this decentralized team approach where many personnel, merchandising, and operating decisions are made by teams at the individual store level, Whole Foods Market emphasizes that an effective store team leader is critical to the success of the store. Store team leaders are paid a salary plus an Economic Value Added-based bonus and are eligible to receive stock options. There also is a gainsharing program rewarding a team's labor productivity. Team members are eligible for stock options through seniority, promotion, or at the discretion of senior regional or national leadership. Team members can purchase restricted stock at a discount through payroll deductions. WFM stock is an investment option within the company 401(k) plan.

In fiscal year 1999, Whole Foods Market, Inc. adopted an Economic Value Added (EVA) management and incentive system. EVA is equivalent to net operating profits after taxes minus a charge for the cost of capital necessary to generate that profit. WFM corporate management credits EVA with improved business decisions across the company's decentralized culture, where decisions are made at the store level, close to the customer, and considers it one of WFM's strongest competitive advantages. Says Chairman and CEO John Mackey, "Rather than taking decision-making authority away from local areas as we grow, we instead are developing tools for our team members to use to help them make better decisions. As a result, EVA is strengthening financial discipline in decisions made throughout the company." At fiscal year-end 2001, more than 350 leaders throughout the company were on EVA-based incentive plans that cover senior executive leadership, regional leadership, and the store leadership team in all stores.

Whole Foods Market says it spends less on advertising than conventional supermarkets, instead relying primarily on word-of-mouth recommendations from customers. Stores spend most of their marketing budgets on in-store signs and other printed material and store events such as taste fairs, classes, and product samplings. WFM promotes a natural and organic lifestyle by customer education initiatives beyond the store, including proactive public relations programs. WFM also seeks generation of customer appreciation and loyalty through in-store education about natural and organic foods, health, nutrition, and the environment as well as on its corporate Web site.

INFLUENCES

The success of Whole Foods Market, Inc.'s corporate strategy was described by Chairman and CEO John Mackey in the company's *2001 Annual Stakeholder's Report*: "We believe that much of our success to date is because we remain uniquely mission driven. We are highly selective about what we sell, we believe in providing an empowering work environment for our team members and are committed to sustainable agriculture. Our motto is Whole Foods, Whole People, Whole Planet. We obtain our products locally and from all over the world, often from small, uniquely dedicated food artisans. We strive to offer the highest quality, least processed, most flavorful and naturally preserved foods.

We recruit the best people we can to become part of our team. We empower them to make many operational decisions, creating a respectful workplace where team members are treated fairly and are highly motivated to succeed. We look for team members who are passionate about food but who are also well-rounded human beings who can play a critical role in helping to build our stores into profitable and beneficial parts of their communities." Mackey went on to say: "We believe companies, like individuals, must assume their share of responsibility for our planet. On a global basis, we actively support organic farming, which we believe is the best method for promoting sustainable agriculture and protecting the environment and farm workers. On a local basis, we are actively involved in our communities by supporting food banks, sponsoring neighborhood events, compensating our team members for community service work, compensating our team members for community service work and contributing at least 5 percent of our after-tax profits in cash or products to not-for-profit organizations."

PRODUCTS

Whole Foods Market stores sell an average of 20,000 food and non-food items with a heavy emphasis on perishable foods designed to appeal to both natural, organic, and gourmet shoppers. Most products are natural or organic, but a limited selection of conventional national brands that meet Whole Foods Market quality goals are also sold. Product categories include produce, grocery, meat and poultry, seafood, bakery, prepared foods, beer/wine/cheese, nutritional supplements, body care, pet products, floral, household products, and educational products such as books.

WFM product quality goals and standards include evaluating every product sold; carrying featured and prepared foods free from artificial preservatives, colors, flavors, and sweeteners; a passion for great tasting food and for sharing it with each other; a commitment to foods that are fresh, wholesome, and safe to eat; using no genetically-modified organisms in WFM private-label products; seeking out and supporting sources of organically-grown foods; maintaining that seafood, poultry, and meat are free of added growth hormones, antibiotics, nitrates, or other chemicals; and featuring grains and grain products that have not been bleached or bromated. WFM does not sell food that has been irradiated and sells only household and personal products that have been proven safe through non-animal testing methods.

In 1991, Whole Foods Market launched its Whole Foods premium private label of products made by small producers with a regional focus and a reputation for authentic and flavorful food. There are more than 400 Whole Foods premium brand products, including organic chocolate from Switzerland, apple butter made by one of the last small cider mills in Pennsylvania, organic pastas from Italy, and an organic micro-brewed beer. Other

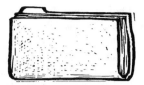

NATURAL/ORGANIC FOODS: WHAT ARE THEY AND WHO BUYS THEM?

Whole Foods Market defines natural foods as "minimally processed, largely or completely free of artificial ingredients, preservatives and other non-naturally occurring chemicals, and as near to their whole, natural state as possible." Organic is defined as a production management system based on minimal use of off-farm inputs and practices that restore, maintain, and enhance ecological harmony.

In April 2002, Julie Huntemann, Director of Business Development of The Hartman Group, a consumer research and consulting firm, said that in a Spring 2001 study asking 4,942 representative households what motivates their organic food and beverage purchases, 67 percent said reasons of health and nutrition, 38 percent said taste, 30 percent said food safety, and 26 percent said concern for the environment. Participants could choose more than one reason. These findings had been consistent for 10 years, prompting the conclusion that people are buying organic for health rather than environmental concerns.

Patrick Rea, Rgbesearch Director of the *Nutrition Business Journal*, a natural and organic foods trade journal, said that in 2001, estimated U.S. natural and organic food sales amounted to $12.9 billion, $6.95 billion organic and $6.25 billion natural. He stated that U.S. organic fruit and vegetable sales were $2.7 billion in 2001 or 40 percent of total organic food sales, explaining that many people purchase only organic produce to help sustain the planet through reduction of pesticides and commercial fertilizers.

Rea said further that the $12.9 billion in natural/organic U.S. food sales represented 2.5 percent of the total U.S. food sales of $503 billion in 2001. However, he indicated, organic/natural foods are a small market that is growing between 9 and 12 percent each year versus total food market growth of between 1 and 4 percent annually. He attributed the larger organic/natural growth rate to increased consumer awareness about health issues, rising worry about the integrity of the conventional food supply and available disposable income, adding that more conventional food manufacturers like General Mills have started to introduce and sell organic products to increase their growth above 1 to 4 percent.

Whole Foods Market product lines include 365 Every Day Value, which are all-natural commodity products that meet company quality standards; Whole Kids, the country's first organic product line developed just for kids, with a kids pre-production tasting panel to address the risk of toxic pesticides in the country's vegetables and fruits; the Lex Alexander Handpicked Selection line of international products; and the Allegro Coffee Company line of specialty and organic coffees, teas, and brewing equipment.

CORPORATE CITIZENSHIP

In March 2001, *Business Ethics* magazine ranked Whole Foods Market one of the country's "100 Best Corporate Citizens." To create good will and maintain a high profile within its community, each store has a separate budget for making contributions to a variety of philanthropic and community activities, contributing in 2001 at least 5 percent of after-tax profits in the form of cash or products to not-for-profit organizations.

GLOBAL PRESENCE

Whole Foods Market, Inc. makes global purchases for its Whole Foods premium private label food products. In 2002, its first store outside of the United States was scheduled to open in Toronto.

EMPLOYMENT

Whole Foods Market believes that many of its team members regard their job as an extension of their personal philosophy and lifestyle—that they are contributing to the good of others by selling clean and nutritious foods and contributing to long-term sustainable agriculture by promoting a pesticide-free and healthier environment. WFM provides paid time off to team members for working with qualified community service organizations.

SOURCES OF INFORMATION

Bibliography

"Analysts Information, Whole Foods Market, Inc.," 25 March 2002. Available from www.CBS.Marketwatch.com.

"Upgrades/Downgrades, Whole Foods Market, Inc.," 25 March 2002. Available from www.CBS.Marketwatch.com.

2001 Whole Foods Market, Inc. Annual Stakeholders Report. Austin, TX: Whole Foods Market, Inc., 20 December 2001.

Schatz, Amy. "Profits Rebound, Rise 34 Percent for Austin, Texas-Based Whole Foods Market." *Austin American Statesman, Texas Knight Ridder/Tribune Business News*, 14 February 2002.

Van Liew, Nils C. "Whole Foods Market." *Value Line*, 8 February 2002.

"The 2002 Fortune 500," 7 April 2002. Available at http://www.Fortune.com.

"Company Information, Whole Foods Market, Inc.," 7 April 2002. Available at http://www.Fortune.com.

"The Street Likes Whole Foods Market, Inc," 8 May 2001. Available at http://www.Stockgroup.com.

"Whole Foods Market At A Glance," 4 April 2002. Available at http://www.CNNMoney.com.

"Whole Foods Market, Inc. Quarterly Financials," 7 April 2002. Available at http://www.Hoovers.com.

Whole Foods Market Reports First Quarter Fiscal Year 2002 Results: Comparable Store Sales Increase Over Nine Percent for the Fourth Consecutive Quarter. Austin, TX: Whole Foods Market, Inc., 13 February 2002.

For additional industry research:

Investigate companies by their Standard Industrial Classification Codes, also known as SICs. Whole Foods Market's primary SICs are:

5411 Grocery Stores

5499 Miscellaneous Food Stores

Also investigate companies by their North American Industry Classification System codes, also known as NAICS codes. Whole Foods Market's primary NAICS codes are:

445110 Supermarkets and Other Grocery (except Convenience) Stores

445299 All Other Specialty Food Stores

446191 Food (Health) Supplement Stores

Williams-Sonoma, Inc.

OVERVIEW

With 2002 sales of more than $2 billion, Williams-Sonoma, Inc. is one of the top retailers of home products, including cookware, through the Williams-Sonoma chain, and contemporary tableware and home furnishings via their Pottery Barn chain. The company has two segments, made up of the retail segment and its four chains, including Williams-Sonoma; Pottery Barn; Pottery Barn Kids, selling children's furnishings; and Hold Everything, selling storage items; and the direct-to customer segment with its six direct-mail catalogs, including Williams-Sonoma; Pottery Barn; Pottery Barn Kids; Pottery Barn Bed+ Bath; Hold Everything; and Chambers, a bed and bath product seller; along with four Web sites, which includes an online bridal registry. Williams-Sonoma merchandise may be found at its 415 stores located in 41 states, Washington DC, and Toronto, Canada. Of these 415 stores, Williams-Sonoma is the largest, with 214 retail outlets, 145 Pottery Barn stores, 27 Pottery Barn Kids, 15 Hold Everything, and 14 outlet stores.

FOUNDED: 1956

Contact Information:

HEADQUARTERS: 3250 Van Ness Ave.
   San Francisco, CA 94109
PHONE: (415)421-7900
FAX: (415)616-8359
URL: http://www.williams-sonomainc.com

COMPANY'S FINANCES

The retail segment of the company accounted for 59.3 percent of net revenues in 2001, while the direct-to-customer segment accounted for the remaining 40.7 percent of revenue. Sales for the fiscal year ending February 3, 2002 were nearly $2.1 billion—a 14.1 percent increase from the previous year. 2002 net income stood at $75.1 million, up 32.2 percent from 2001.

Williams-Sonoma has shown a consistent increase in profits over the past five years. The company's stock

FINANCES:

Williams-Sonoma, Inc.
Net Revenues, 1999-2001
(million dollars)

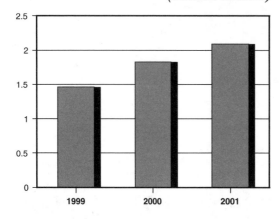

ranged from a low of $21.73 to a high of $46.00 over a 52-week period. Williams-Sonoma's price-earnings ratio was 76.87.

ANALYSTS' OPINIONS

As a leading home products retailer with a growing business, Williams-Sonoma will tell any potential investor that it is a solid investment. Several analysts also agree the retail home products industry is a growing one and in which Williams-Sonoma is a strong leader. In a 2002 report, U.S. Bancorp Piper Jaffray upgraded Williams-Sonoma stock to Strong Buy, based on stronger than expected sales and the belief that the company is in the middle of a beneficial operational turnaround which would allow it to outperform others in the retail market. A 2002 Lehman Brothers report concurred, noting that Williams-Sonoma's cost cutting measures, strong sales, increased store expansion, and extremely positive customer response to new Pottery Barn merchandise in particular has made the company's stock a very attractive buy. Robertson Stephens noted that with a proven growth track record, the company that began with a single concept begun in 1956 has now expanded to include six distinct brands that enjoy strong brand recognition that holds meaningful potential for continued long-term growth.

HISTORY

The first Williams-Sonoma store opened, aptly enough, in Sonoma, California in 1956 by founder

Charles E. Williams, currently vice chairman and one of the company's directors. The store's first product offerings were a small variety of cookware imported from France. Williams then moved the store to its current headquarters location, San Francisco, California. That year, the store began its first in-store bridal registry service.

Williams-Sonoma's direct-to-customer business began with the introduction of the company's first catalog in 1971, called *A Catalog For Cooks,* marketing some of the company's products. The company was incorporated the next year. In 1973, the second Williams-Sonoma store opened in Beverly Hills, California. The store began expanding throughout the Golden state, with a third store opening in Palo Alto, and a fourth in Costa Mesa. The company's first distribution center was opened in 1977, in Emeryville, California.

Williams then sold his fledgling retail chain in 1978, to Howard Lester and Jay McMahan. Currently, Chairman Lester owns almost 9 percent of the company, while McMahan has a 10 percent stake. The company also opened its first out-of-state store in Dallas, Texas the year of its sale. Another effort to expand its direct-to-customer reach came with the acquisition of the *Gardeners Eden* catalog, which was eventually sold in 1999.

The company went public in 1983 as Williams-Sonoma, Inc., trading on the NASDAQ under the symbol WSGC. That year, the company also began distribution of its Hold Everything catalog, offering storage solution products. To sustain its growing operations, the company built a 450,000 sq. ft. distribution center in Memphis, Tennessee, which opened in 1984. The next year, the company's first Hold Everything store was launched in Corte Madera, California, but the company's acquisition of the 21 Pottery Barn chain of stores in 1986 was what really signaled that Williams-Sonoma intended to become a retail force to be reckoned with. The Pottery Barn chain sold retail and direct-to-customer merchandise, including casual home furnishings, flatware, and table accessories from around the world. Ever expanding its brand, the company issued a Williams-Sonoma cookbook in 1986, as well.

Following their proven business plan of establishing retail and direct channels, the company began mailing out the first Pottery Barn catalogs in 1987. Two years later, the company issued its Chambers catalogs, offering a variety of high quality linens, towels, robes, soaps, and accessories for the bed and bath. With all the new business, the company began to outgrow its Memphis distribution center, and finished expansion of the center in 1991, extending it 307,000 sq. ft. At the same time, the company dove into technology with its launch of a nationally-linked, computerized bridal registry hitting all Williams-Sonoma stores. Building on its publishing presence, the first of the Williams-Sonoma Kitchen Library cookbooks hit the bookshelves in 1992, the same year innovative founder Chuck Williams received the first annual Retailer of the Year award at the San Francisco Gourmet Products Show.

By 1993, Williams-Sonoma stores numbered more than 200, nearly half its current total. The company proceeded to launch new store formats, Williams-Sonoma Grande Cuisine, which featured upscale cookware, and Pottery Barn Design Studio in 1994. Williams, who was then named to the Who's Who of Food and Beverage by the James Beard Foundation, issued his *Simple American Cooking and Gifts from the Kitchen,* books. The following year, Pottery Barn launched its gift registry and Williams was lauded again, this time received the Lifetime Achievement Award by the Beard Foundation.

As the company celebrated its fortieth anniversary, the new Customer Care Center opened in Summerlin, Nevada, in 1996. The Williams-Sonoma cookbook became the best-selling cookbook series of the 1990s, when its ten millionth copy was printed that year. Building on the successful venture, Williams published another book in 1997 about the history of food in the United States entitled, *Celebrating the Pleasures of Cooking.*

In 1998 the company reached $1 billion in sales and Williams-Sonoma, Inc. was listed on the New York Stock Exchange (NYSE) under the symbol WSM, which it stands today. The corporate Web site was also launched that year and a second Customer Care Center was opened in Oklahoma City, OK. The company launched both its Williams-Sonoma Internet wedding and gift registry Web site, wsweddings.com, and its Williams-Sonoma e-commerce site, williams-sonoma.com, in 1999. Additionally, Williams-Sonoma began its Pottery Barn Kids catalog, offering stylish, quality children's furnishings. The next year, the first of the Pottery Barn Kids stores opened nationwide followed a year later by its own Web site. In 2000, the company introduced its Pottery barn Web site, potterybarn.com, and launched Pottery Barn Bed+Bath, a catalog offering bed and bath goods. The company's *TASTE* magazine was also published. 2001 brought the company's Pottery Barn online gift and bridal registry along with a Pottery Barn Kids online gift registry. The company also expanded internationally with five new retail outlets opening in Toronto, Canada, including two Williams-Sonoma, two Pottery Barn, and one Pottery Barn Kids.

STRATEGY

The overall corporate vision consists of enhancing the quality of life at home. As part of its 2002 growth strategy, Williams-Sonoma plans expand businesses that have done well or exceed expectations, including the Pottery Barn Kids and the company's direct-to-customer segment. The company will open 66 new stores throughout the year, including 25 new Pottery Barn Kids, adding to its existing 27 PBK stores; 23 Williams-Sonomas, 15 Pottery Barns, one Hold Everything and two clearance stores. The company will also close 16 underperforming locations. The new stores include the three additional

FAST FACTS:
About Williams-Sonoma, Inc.

Ownership: Williams-Sonoma, Inc. is a publicly owned company traded on the New York Stock Exchange.

Ticker Symbol: WSM

Officers: W. Howard Lester, 66, Chmn., 2001 base salary $899,787; Dale W. Hilpert, CEO, 2001 base salary $754,038; Charles E. Williams, Founder and VChmn., 86; Laura J. Alber, Pres. Pottery Barn Brands, 33, 2001 base salary $407,700; James E. Boike, EVP and COO, 55, 2001 base salary $544,462; Patrick J. Connolly, EVP and CMO, 55, 2001 base salary $506,065; Patrick Cowell, Pres., Williams-Sonoma Brand, 52; Sharon L. McCollam, SVP and CFO, 39

Employees: 27,000

Principal Subsidiary Companies: Williams-Sonoma has subsidiaries including Pottery Barn, Pottery Barn Kids, and Hold Everything.

Chief Competitors: Williams-Sonoma competes with other companies in the cookware and housewares industry, including Bed Bath & Beyond, Euromarket Designs, and Pier 1 Imports.

stores in Toronto, Canada, adding to its existing five Canadian locations. Toward goals in the direct-to-customer category, Williams-Sonoma plans to increase catalog circulation by 10 percent, mailing out 270 million catalogs. Other plans include a private label credit card launch in May 2002 and expanding their seasonal gift assortment.

Williams-Sonoma will further efforts to streamline supply chain operations and lower expenses begun in 2001, with inventories down 10 percent from the previous year. The company plans to reduce merchandise costs by increasing purchasing volumes and pursuing possible new supply channels. Also, through increased sourcing quality, the company hopes to reduce customer returns.

INFLUENCES

With a history of building distinct brands, Williams-Sonoma's success in that area has led them to aggressively pursue new retail sectors and create new brands to

CHRONOLOGY:

Key Dates for Williams-Sonoma, Inc.

1956: Chuck Williams founds Williams-Sonoma in Sonoma, California

1958: Store moves to San Francisco; in-store bridal registry launched

1971: First catalog is mailed

1972: Williams-Sonoma incorporates

1978: Williams-Sonoma is bought by Howard Lester and Jay McMahan

1983: Williams-Sonoma goes public on the NASDAQ

1985: First Hold Everything store is opened

1986: Williams-Sonoma acquires Pottery Barn, with stores

1987: Launch of Pottery Barn catalog

1995: Pottery Barn gift registry launched

1998: Williams-Sonoma listed on the New York Stock Exchange under new symbol WSM; corporate Web site is launched

1999: Williams-Sonoma.com is launched; Williams-Sonoma online bridal registry is launched; Pottery Barn Kids catalog introduced

2000: Pottery Barn Bed+Bath catalog introduced; PotterBarn.com launched; Pottery Barn Kids stores open

2001: Opens first Canadian stores in Toronto; Pottery Barn online gift and bridal registry launched; Pottery Barn Kids online gift registry introduced

2002: Launch of West Elm catalogs

reflect new times and new customers. Building on the success of Pottery Barn, the company built 27 Pottery Barn Kids stores. The stores outperformed expectations, and as a result, will be one of the main areas of new growth for the company, which plans on opening another 25 in one year alone. While Williams-Sonoma and Pottery Barn are relatively mature brands, Pottery Barn Kids is exactly what the company foresees will keep its name fresh and attractive to new consumers. The creation of the West Elm catalog, the company's answer to more affordable home furniture, is another way for the company to build on the success of Pottery Barn, while forg-

ing out another niche—a lower-priced, alternative Pottery Barn. Enjoying sales success in late 2001 and 2002 while other retailers were struggling, growth in these areas will most likely continue in these areas.

CURRENT TRENDS

Along with many old-school retail chains, one trend that Williams-Sonoma is following is that of e-commerce. Launching its first e-commerce segment in 1999, the company took many of its key brands online—not an easy task for a retailer with such diverse products and segmented corporate structure. Challenges arose due to the lack of communication between the retail side of the company and the catalog division. The two had different shipping methods from the warehouse and had unique compensation systems. The company soon established a cohesive online strategy, however, coupling its retail houses, direct marketing and online selling along with its wide range of brands from Pottery Barn, Pottery Barn Kids, to Williams-Sonoma. The trend has proved successful, with direct-to-customer sales, which include Internet and catalog revenue, increasing 15.4 percent in the second quarter of 2001. With several cutting-edge Web sites, the company, however, does not plan to focus on enhanced technology to bring them future success, preferring, instead the more tried and true strategy of improving customer service.

PRODUCTS

The company offers a variety of merchandise through its four retail chains, catalogs, and Internet Web sites. Chains include Williams-Sonoma, selling hundreds of high-end products for kitchen and entertaining, including cookware, serveware, tools, linens, food products, cooking ingredients, and a large cookbook library; Pottery Barn, offering a variety of contemporary home furnishings, bedding/bath, rugs, window treatments, ledges and lighting for the home, tableware, flatware, and decorative accessories; Pottery Barn Kids, selling stylish, quality children's furnishings and decorative accessories for children aged 0-12; and Hold Everything, selling a range of storage solution items. Pottery Barn has also adopted the Design Studio, a service that helps customers plan their living spaces. Additionally, the company's Grand Cuisine specializes in upscale cookware. Its six direct-mail catalogs include Williams-Sonoma; Pottery Barn; Pottery Barn Kids; Pottery Barn Bed+Bath; Hold Everything; and Chambers, a bed and bath product seller. Four company Web sites sell the company's merchandise and offer online bridal and gift registry. Williams-Sonoma merchandise may be found at its 415 stores located in 41 states, Washington DC, and Toronto, Canada.

Williams-Sonoma plans to test a new catalog in 2002 called West Elm. The new brand will offer quality items at accessible prices and target young, design conscious consumers seeking home furnishings and accessories for their apartments, lofts, or first homes. Product categories in the new brand will include, furniture, decorative accessories, table top items and a wide range of textile collections. Williams-Sonoma will launch the catalog nationwide in the summer of 2002 and, if proven successful, may expand the brand into retail outlets beginning in 2003.

GLOBAL PRESENCE

The company opened its first stores outside of the United States in 2001, launching three Williams-Sonoma, three Pottery Barn, and two Pottery Barn Kids in Toronto, Canada. Three locations were chosen for the stores, which opened in late 2001 and early 2002. The company acknowledged that many Canadians already shopped at the U.S. retail stores and that their entry into Canada was a response to the demand of the company's home products in the country. To help penetrate its new market, Williams-Sonoma plans to be competitive pricewise and offer good value. The company also plans to use the newly opened Canadian stores as benchmarks for possible future international expansion, and as of March 2002, had exceeded the company's expectations. They further estimate another 15 to 20 location there are feasible.

EMPLOYMENT

With 27,000 employees, Williams-Sonoma offers many career opportunities in their various corporate departments, including the corporate headquarters; customer care centers; data center; distribution center; retail stores; Canadian retail stores; and through the Corporate Internship Program for college juniors seeking retail experience. The company is an Equal Opportunity Employer and offers a benefits package that includes an Associate discount program; paid vacations and holidays; health, life, and travel insurance; short- and long-term disability programs; health and dependent care tax-free spending accounts; medical, family and bereavement leave; tuition reimbursement; same-sex domestic partner benefits; and a stock incentive plan.

Williams-Sonoma seeks employees with skills in the following areas: critical thinking, planning and organization, decision making, business knowledge, people skills, customer focus, job knowledge, interpersonal communication, and commitment to please customers and continuous long-term financial growth. Additionally,

THE MAN BEHIND THE COMPANY NAME

Beginning with a 1952 trip to Europe, Chuck Williams became fascinated with French food. With a desire to recreate it in his hometown of Sonoma, California, the then-carpenter purchased a run-down hardware store in Sonoma and began stocking professional-quality, imported French cookware in his store—now the cookware and home furnishings giant known as Williams-Sonoma. Eventually weeding out hardware in favor of cookware, the store attracted a following of inquisitive epicures to the newly relocated San Francisco Bay Area store. The rest is (a long and prosperous) history. Although penning numerous cookbooks, Williams, as the company's vice chairman, is still a vital part in guiding the company's successful growth.

they list their corporate values as people, customers, quality, shareholders, and ethical sourcing.

SOURCES OF INFORMATION

Bibliography

"Old Retailer Whips Up New Recipe." *San Francisco Business Times*, 19 October 2001.

Williams-Sonoma Home Page, 2002. Available from http://www.williams-sonomainc.com.

"Williams-Sonoma, Inc." *Hoover's Online*, June 2002. Available at http://www.hoovers.com.

"Williams-Sonoma, Inc." The Gale Group. Available at http://galenet.galegroup.com.

"Williams-Sonoma Outlines Overall Growth Plan." *Home Textiles Today*, 4 March 2002.

"Williams-Sonoma Sets Foot in Canada." *DSN Retailing Today*, 10 December 2001.

"Williams-Sonoma Tries a New Recipe." *Business Week*, 6 May 2002.

For an annual report:
on the Internet at: http://www.williams-sonomainc.com **or** write: Williams-Sonoma Inc., 3250 Van Ness Ave., San Francisco, CA 94109

For additional industry research:

Investigate companies by their Standard Industrial Classification Codes, also known as SICs. Williams-Sonoma's primary SICs are:

5719 Miscellaneous Homefurnishings Stores

5261 Retail Nurseries And Garden Stores

5961 Mail Order Houses

6719 Holding Companies, Not Elsewhere Classified

Also investigate companies by their North American Industry Classification System codes, also known as NAICS codes. Williams-Sonoma's primary NAICS codes are:

442299 All Other Home Furnishings Stores

444220 Nursery and Garden Centers

454110 Electronic Shopping and Mail-Order Houses

551112 Offices of Other Holding Companies

Yahoo! Inc.

OVERVIEW

Yahoo! Inc. is an Internet company that provides a wide variety of services to more than 200 million consumer and business customers. It can be accessed at www.yahoo.com, which is the company's U.S. address on the World Wide Web. The site was designed to make the Internet user-friendly, even for individuals with little computer or technology experience. Yahoo! offers directories of other sites along with a description of the content. The company has moved beyond its modest beginning as a search engine and now offers news, shopping, e-mail, chat rooms, and media services.

Yahoo! was created in 1994 by two graduate students at Stanford University. Within two years of the company's development, the founders, David Filo and Jerry Yang, had abandoned their academic careers and were working full time as managers of this fledgling venture. Yahoo! became a publicly traded company in a 1996 initial public offering that was a success by any standard. The stock opened at $13 a share and ended its first day of trading up 154 percent at $33 a share.

Yahoo! is a member of the Standard & Poor's 500 Index and operates a global network of 24 international sites produced in 13 languages. The company offers services in the following areas: listings, media, finance and information, commerce, communications, enterprise solutions, and access and distribution. Yahoo! has entered into partnerships or agreements with numerous corporations and media outlets that provide content and listings for the site. This comprehensive network of strategic alliances has transformed Yahoo! from a simple search engine to a full-service Internet portal placing a multitude of information at the fingertips of the public.

FOUNDED: 1994

Contact Information:

HEADQUARTERS: 701 First Ave.
   Sunnyvale, CA 94089
PHONE: (408)349-3300
FAX: (408)349-3301
EMAIL: yahoocc@yahoo-inc.com
URL: http://www.yahoo.com

FINANCES:

Yahoo! Inc.
Revenues, 1998-2001
(million dollars)

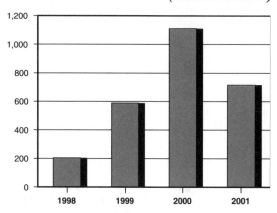

Yahoo! Inc.
2001 Stock Prices
(dollars)

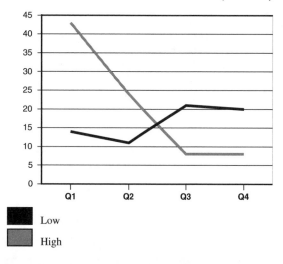

to the disbelief of Wall Street firms, Yahoo! stock was trading at a whopping 745 percent increase from its original price on the day of the 1996 IPO.

ANALYSTS' OPINIONS

Analysts are applauding Yahoo!'s efforts to diversify and generate new sources of revenue. The recent addition of HotJobs.com and the completion of several other deals are considered a solid beginning for recovery. John Corcoran, an analyst with CIBC World Markets Inc. is quoted as saying, "Things are improving for them. We think the stock is more than halfway back to where it should be." Holly Becker, an analyst for Lehman Brothers is more cautious in her review, "Yahoo! is dependent on new business initiatives, which are just beginning to impact the bottom line and remain somewhat uncertain." Fred Moran an analyst at Jeffries & Co. States, "Yahoo is in a transition. They have maintained a course of adding new revenue, such as subscription-based services, but the revenues from these services is materializing very gradually." Expectations for the company are positive for 2002 and beyond.

HISTORY

Yahoo! was developed by two Ph.D. candidates enrolled in Stanford University's electrical engineering program. David Filo and Jerry Yang were both computer programmers, but the creation of Yahoo! had little to do with programming or technology. It began life as a list of favorite sites entitled "Jerry's Guide to the World Wide Web." They published this list on the Internet to serve as a navigation tool for other users. Prior to 1994 the Web was not browser capable, which severely limited the number of users to those who possessed enough technical expertise to manipulate the required codes. In 1994 a program named Mosaic, which would later be renamed Netscape Navigator, was released. This new browser allowed nonscientists to view information on the Web with ease. Filo and Yang provided the public with a neatly organized address book of the best sites to visit.

The single most pivotal event in the history of this young company may have occurred the day the founders' Ph.D. advisor ordered them to move the extracurricular project off-campus. The site had become enormously popular, receiving hundreds of thousands of visitors daily, and the incredible growth was placing a strain on the university's computer network. When both AOL and Netscape offered the partners jobs at their respective organizations, the two grad students began to consider a future as entrepreneurs. When venture capital dollars were offered in February 1995, they couldn't resist. Sequoia Capital fronted them more than $1 million dol-

COMPANY FINANCES

The company reported profits soon after its launch and was widely regarded as the first bona fide Internet success story. In 2001 Yahoo! posted annual revenues of $717.4 and a net loss of 92.8 million dollars compared with $1,110.2 million in revenues and a net income of $70.8 million in 2000. Investors did not focus on the daily activities of the start-up. Stock prices for the company were astonishing. In 1997 the company grew 242 percent and the stock rose 500 percent. By the following year, the price had jumped 584 percent. In 1998, almost

lars to turn their pet project into a business. In return, Sequoia would acquire 25 percent of the operation. Filo and Yang left Stanford University six months short of completing their degrees. A management team was formed (including new CEO Tim Koogle), staff was hired, and a business strategy was hatched. Yahoo! generated its first revenues in 1995 by selling advertising space on its pages. The company adhered to its user-friendly policies and did not overload its site with a multitude of banner ads or pop-up ads, which required users to click through to access a listing.

In 1996 SOFTBANK of Japan invested $100 million dollars in the start up company. Despite the large infusion of cash, Yahoo! registered to make its initial public offering (IPO) in April 1996. In most cases, the goal of an IPO is to generate enough cash to finance the continued growth and expansion of the company. Yahoo! did not need the money. The offering was rooted in its desire to gain respect as a leader in this new field. The initial offering was a success, due in part to the very small amount of stock actually released to the public. As a result, demand for the stock was high, supply was low, and the price climbed dramatically.

The company actively developed new features for the portal, which promoted the feeling of community among users. Geographically themed sites were introduced for members in Los Angeles, Chicago, New York, and Washington DC. International expansion was also a priority in 1996. Using the funds and expertise provided by the investors at SOFTBANK, Yahoo! Japan and Yahoo! Europe were launched.

Beginning in 1997, the company increased its presence in cyberspace through strategic acquisitions. Internet directory firm Four11; Viaweb, an e-commerce software organization; and Yoyodyne Entertainment, a marketing company, joined forces with Yahoo! Growth continued for the next several years, and the popular sites Broadcast.com and GeoCities were purchased as part of the growing Internet consolidation trend. Smaller firms were being swallowed by stronger competitors as market conditions began to slow down. When the dot-com bubble burst in 2000, Yahoo was able remain in business, but revenues and investor goodwill disappeared quickly.

In 2001 CEO Tim Koogle left his post and was replaced by former Hollywood executive, Terry Semel. Semel had no experience in the field of technology, but his personal connections, and skill in navigating the entertainment industry, made him an attractive candidate. As the World Wide Web embraces new media services, such as music and video streaming, Semel can be a valuable asset to the firm. He faces this challenge without the help of longtime Yahoo! executive Jeff Mallett. Mallett stepped down from his position in April 2002. Despite the changes in the executive offices, Yahoo! continues to move forward with ambitious plans to offer new features and revitalize the flow of revenue.

FAST FACTS:
About Yahoo! Inc.

Ownership: Yahoo! Inc. is a publicly traded company on the NASDAQ Stock Exchange.

Ticker Symbol: YHOO

Officers: Terry S. Semel, Chmn. and CEO, 58, 2001 base salary $254,853; Jerry Yang, Chief Yahoo!, 32; David Filo, Chief Yahoo!, 35

Employees: 3,259

Principal Subsidiary Companies: Yahoo! Inc. is the parent company for subsidiaries HotJobs.com, Launch Media, GeoCities, and a number of smaller technology firms.

Chief Competitors: Main competitors to Yahoo! Inc. include America Online (AOL)/Time Warner, Microsoft MSN, Terra Lycos, and Amazon.com.

STRATEGY

Yahoo!'s goal is to be the home page for every Internet user. A home page is the first page that a browser opens to whenever a user logs onto the Web. Once the user has entered cyberspace via the Yahoo! portal, the goal is to keep all "eyes" on related company sites, filled with company-provided content and services. In 1996 Yahoo! was reporting 20 million page views a day and, by June 2000, this number had multiplied to 685 million pages a day. The number of pages viewed on an Internet site correlates directly with the amount of revenues generated. Sustained profitability is the ultimate challenge of any company, but it is particularly important for Internet firms.

From its inception, Yahoo! realized that it was necessary to be more than just a search engine to be successful. It wanted to provide useful, quality content to its users in a simple and understandable manner. The company forged agreements with respected business and media firms, thus avoiding the high costs and risks of producing content in-house. It then hired employees known as "surfers" to personally review and categorize all Web sites that requested inclusion in the Yahoo! directories. The management of the company did not want the site to be automated and impersonal.

Current strategies address the needs to expand services offered domestically, develop in depth information

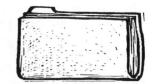

CHRONOLOGY:

Key Dates for Yahoo! Inc.

1994: David Filo and Jerry Yang begin construction on the site working from a trailer on the Stanford University campus

1995: The company is incorporated and funded by venture capitalists

1996: Yahoo! Inc. becomes a publicly traded company in a highly successful IPO

1999: Acquires Broadcast.com and Geocities

2000: Stock reaches its highest level, trading at $250.06 a share

2001: Internet bubble bursts, revenues decline, stock price tumbles to a low of $7.75, and CEO Tim Koogle steps down

2002: Hollywood executive Terry Semel leads the organization as it begins to offer fee based services in attempts to generate revenue.

about current user preferences, create Yahoo! online properties in international markets, and identify new methods of producing revenues.

INFLUENCES

Yahoo! pioneered navigation on the World Wide Web and is arguably the most dominant company formed strictly as an Internet venture. Ironically, the efforts of traditional media and technology companies may be exerting the greatest influences on its operations. The merger of Time Warner and America Online, as well as the evolution of Microsoft's MSN have created formidable competitors for the startup. Together America Online and Time Warner possess an enormous customer base drawing from both AOL's Internet customers and Time Warner's subscribers from cable networks and publishing ventures. In addition they have already established a fee-paying relationship with these customers and have collected demographic information for targeted marketing. Time Warner also provides AOL with content, global distribution networks, and vast financial resources. Yahoo! recognizes the advantages in this model and will adapt its strategies accordingly to remain competitive.

YAHOOLIGANS!

Hooligans and hooliganism usually mean there's trouble afoot. These slang terms are used to describe young "ruffians" or hoodlums and the mischief they cause. Yahoo! decided to change that notion when it coined the term "Yahooligans" and used it as the name of its children's site. Yahooligans! can be found on the Yahoo! home page and offers fun, safe, and educational activities for children. Young Internet users can read news stories of the day written in an understandable and non-threatening style. Movie reviews are limited to films that are suitably rated for children and young adults. The site also provides an instant messaging service for chatting with friends online.

CURRENT TRENDS

Yahoo! has been able to post profits by charging advertising and sponsorship fees for site placement. However, faced with stiff competition and a soft economy, the company is moving quickly to establish fee-based services. It is exploring the possibility of subscription-based streaming media, which would offer audio and video programming at a fee. Sporting events, news, and movies on demand would be offered for a monthly fee or on a pay-per-view basis. Yahoo! is also considering tacking on user fees for its previously free e-mail, data storage, and photo-sharing services. The company is also working to expand its business to business products and enterprise information solutions.

PRODUCTS

Yahoo!'s products include search and directory tools that allow users to browse listings for real estate, automobiles, and even careers. It became a major factor in the online job search market with its acquisition of HotJobs.com in 2001. Web surfers can also find information on books, movies, investments, health, and weather by accessing personalized pages. Media services allow consumers to download music, videos and even concert feeds with a personal computer. Commerce and shopping services are also popular Yahoo! destinations. Yahoo! offers online shopping, auctions, and travel planning. Communication is a premier benefit of the World Wide Web, and Yahoo! offers some of the most popular systems. E-mail, instant messaging, calendars, and chat rooms are heavily trafficked applications. Enterprise Solutions focuses on the business and corporate community. Yahoo! provides platforms, which allow companies to integrate content into their own intranets or extranets. Other business tools include conferencing and meeting capabilities and online training classes.

GLOBAL PRESENCE

The Internet is rapidly gaining users around the world, and Yahoo! has plans to greet them all in every language. The first international sites were launched in Japan in 1996, and the company now boasts the largest worldwide community of users. Yahoo! is aware of the risks of entering global markets but has confidence that it will be successful in its quest for worldwide acceptance. The company places a great deal of importance on global citizenship and attempts to respect and comply with local cultures, customs, and laws in any market it enters. The network of Yahoo! sites now extends to 24 countries with many custom-built sites. The company maintains offices in Europe, Asia, Latin America, Australia, and Canada. Sunnyvale, California, remains Yahoo! central.

CORPORATE CITIZENSHIP

Yahoo! employees are encouraged to volunteer time to local community causes. Each year the company organizes opportunities for the staff to participate in special events as a group. Yahoo! staff members have pledged time to the environment by working to beautify the California coastline as well as local elementary schools. Commitment to children is also a priority. Volunteers have signed up to be classroom buddies in elementary schools, leading activities such as reading, sports, and computers. Other projects centered on the need for animal rights, assisting elderly citizens, and participating in career and employment mentoring days.

EMPLOYMENT

You don't have to be a technical genius to be a Yahoo! employee, or Yahoo!, at least not according those who have made the commitment. Candidates are encouraged to search for their dream job in the Yahoo! database of open positions. It is even possible to become an international Yahoo! and see the world. Employees are encouraged to be innovative, creative, fun-loving, and dedicated. The Silicon Valley offices are very casual and boast foosball and video games. The "team" theme is evident throughout the corporate headquarters, which are

A ROOM WITH AN ATTITUDE

The corner office was once a status symbol that helped define our corporate culture. Times have changed. The Internet revolution created a new way of communicating and doing business for everyone. Internet companies have taken it even one step further and are breaking with many work place traditions. Jeans and T-shirts are in. Video games and foosball tables replace lunchroom tables. Even the meeting rooms aren't immune to the new trends. Conference rooms are often designated with numbers, letters, or a combination of the two. Yahoo! and many other Silicon Valley companies decided that the room names should reflect the often quirky personalities of the employees. If you are invited to a meeting at Yahoo!, you may be assigned to a meeting room named after one of the ten Biblical plagues: "Frogs," "Boils," "Blood," or even "Pestilence." The room dubbed "Darkness" houses comfortable couches for sleeping. Another set of rooms proudly proclaim the company's attitude: "Decent, Definitely, and Disposed." Yes, one of the favorite jokes is to tell lost souls who are searching for a meeting, "We're in Decent!"

bathed in the company colors: purple and yellow. Parties are scheduled regularly for holidays including a Halloween party day nicknamed YaBoo!. The downturn in Internet fortunes has been felt at the Yahoo! headquarters, and management has been forced to institute a company-wide lay off impacting hundreds of employees.

SOURCES OF INFORMATION

Bibliography

Barlas, Pete. "Analysts Cheer Yahoo's Efforts to End Reliance on Advertising." *Investor's Business Daily*, 10 April 2002.

Beckett, Jamie. "Making Meetings Merry." *The San Francisco Chronicle*, 30 July 1998.

Boardman, Bruce. "Yahoo—185 Million Users Served." *Network Computing*, 30 October 2000.

"Do You Believe How Yahoo! Became A Blue Chip: A tale of how Wall Street and the rest of us learned to stop worrying and love an insanely valued Internet stock." *Fortune*, 7 June 1999.

Hoovers Company Profiles, 2002. Available at http://www .hoovers.com.

Lardner, James. "Search No Further: Its Share Price May Be Crazy, But Yahoo! Remains Sane." *U.S. News & World Report*, 18 May 1998.

Noglows, Paul. "Taking Stock of the Internet Phenomenon." *Interactive Week*, 25 October 1999.

Yahoo! Home Page, 2002. Available at http://www.yahoo.com.

"Yahoo Tacks Fee Onto E-mail, Storage." *CNET News.com*, 21 March 2002.

"Yahoo Tests Paid-Programming Waters." *CNET News.com*, 18 March 2002.

For an annual report:

on the Internet at: http://docs.yahoo.com/info/investor/inv-info.html

For additional industry research:

Investigate companies by their Standard Industrial Classification Codes, also known as SICs. Yahoo! Inc.'s primary SIC is:

7373 Computer Integrated Design

Also investigate companies by their North American Industry Classification System codes, also known as NAICS codes. Yahoo! Inc.'s primary NAICS code is:

514191 On-line Information Services

Yellow Corp.

OVERVIEW

Yellow Corp. is a less-than-truckload (LTL) freight carrier that offers regional, national, and international freight transportation services. Compared to heavy truckload freight, which typically fills an entire truck, LTL freight weighs less than 10,000 pounds. In addition, while heavy truckload freight is hauled directly from sender to receiver, LTL freight is usually transported to one or two sorting terminals before reaching its final destination.

The largest LTL freight company in the United States, Yellow Corp. is a Fortune 500 company with more than $3 billion in annual sales. Yellow Corp.'s largest subsidiary, Yellow Transportation, serves more than 300,000 corporate clients with a fleet of roughly 8,400 tractors and 36,300 trailers. Yellow Transportation offers traditional freight transportation services, such as next-day delivery, as well as a variety of premium services. For example, time specific delivery services allow businesses to choose both the time and date they would like to receive shipments. In addition, online tracking services allow clients to monitor the movement of their freight via the Internet. Another subsidiary, Duluth, Georgia-based Saia Motor Freight, offers both overnight and next-day delivery services to its 98,000 customers via 1,900 tractors and 6,200 trailers. With 10,000 customers and a fleet of 1,400 tractors and 2,800 trailers, Jevic Transportation, headquartered in Delanco, New Jersey, is the third largest unit of Yellow Corp.

FOUNDED: 1924

Contact Information:

HEADQUARTERS: 10990 Roe Ave.
    Overland Park, KS 66207
PHONE: (913)696-6100
FAX: (913)696-6116
TOLL FREE: (800)610-6500
EMAIL: webcorp@yellowcorp.com
URL: http://www.yellowcorp.com

FINANCES:

*Yellow Corp.
Revenues, 1999-2001
(million dollars)*

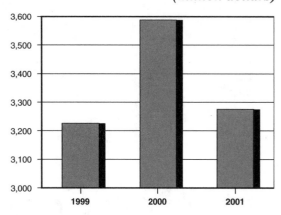

*Yellow Corp.
2001 Stock Prices
(dollars)*

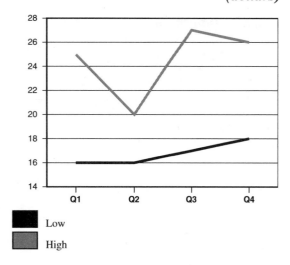

Low

High

COMPANY FINANCES

Following two years of significant growth in 1999 and 2000, Yellow Corp. saw weaker sales and profits in 2001. Sales fell 8.7 percent from $3.588 billion to $3.276 billion, while earnings dropped 77.5 percent from $68 million to $15.3 million. The poor performance was mainly due to the general economic downturn in North America, which undercut demand for most trucking companies. High fuel prices also eroded profits. Yellow Transportation accounted for 76 percent of Yellow

Corp.'s total revenues in 2001, while Saia Motor Freight secured 15 percent, and Jevic Transportation brought in the remaining 9 percent. Between March 2001 and March 2002, stock fluctuated from a low of $15.50 per share to a high of $27.57 per share.

ANALYSTS' OPINIONS

Between 1998 and 2002, *Fortune* magazine ranked Yellow Corp. as one of America's most admired companies, placing the firm first it its category for both "Innovation" and "Quality of Products and Services." However, despite favorable reviews such as this one, Yellow Corp. found itself vulnerable to the North American economic downturn of the early 2000s. In 2001, the firm's daily load volume fell 13 percent to its lowest level since the mid-1980s. Share prices dropped as a result, and industry analysts were mixed in their analysis of Yellow Corp. stock. Some pointed out that the stock, like the that of other leading freight movers, was simply a reflection of a temporarily weak economy; as such, it would likely rebound as economic conditions improved. Other analysts expressed concern that Mexican truckers, who were expected to gain access to the U.S. market in mid-2002, would undercut the prices of freight haulers like Yellow Corp. Along with unstable fuel prices, these new low-cost competitors could pose problems for the firm even in robust economic times.

One area that still offers room for growth, according to most industry experts, is Internet-based logistics, which is essentially the use of Internet technology to coordinate all aspects of freight shipping, from ordering and pick-up to payment and delivery. This bodes well for Yellow Corp. According to AMR Research analyst Chris Newton, as quoted in a June 2001 issue of *InternetWeek*, Yellow Corp. "has a head start on most of its competitors in terms of technology deployment. They have invested more dollars in e-business than most carriers, and they're now at the forefront of the new wave of logistics and transportation services coming to the industry."

HISTORY

Yellow Cab franchise operator A.J. Harrell created the Yellow Transit trucking company in 1924. Based in Oklahoma City, Oklahoma, the new firm started out by offering short-run LTL shipping services to and from Tulsa, Oklahoma. By the mid-1940s, Yellow Transit was overseeing more than 50 small units, many of which were located in the Midwest.

Larger trucking firms started to replace smaller, independent operations in the late 1940s. The increased competition from these more efficient operators, along with the rising costs associated with leasing trucking equipment, forced Yellow Transit into bankruptcy in

1951. George E. Powell and a team of investors bought the firm from Harrell and began to restructure operations. By the end of the following year, Yellow was once again operating profitably. The firm purchased Michigan Motor Freight Lines in the late 1950s, and sales grew to $15 million. In 1965, Yellow doubled its size when its paid roughly $13 million for Watson-Wilson Transportation System. The following year, the firm changed its name to Yellow Freight System, Inc. With sales in excess of $200 million in 1969, Yellow was the third-largest trucking company in the United States.

Yellow began to embrace computer technology in the early 1970s when it installed its first computerized monitoring system in the Kansas City-based command center. The system greatly enhanced Yellow's ability to accurately track each shipment and improved communications, not only within the company but also with clients. The mid-1970s were marked by a series of acquisitions designed to expand the firm's geographic reach. Purchases included Adley Express, Republic Freight Systems, and Braswell Motor Freight. In 1976, Yellow diversified from trucking into oil when it invested roughly $4 million in Overland Energy Company; however, Overland racked up $60 million in losses by the end of the decade, prompting Yellow to refocus on its core freight hauling operations.

The deregulation of the U.S. trucking industry in 1980 caused a series of problems for Yellow. For example, Yellow had made roughly $34 million per year from trucking companies willing to pay fees to use its routes. When deregulation eliminated restrictions on truck routes, Yellow saw this portion of its revenues simply disappear. In addition, increased competition from rivals like Consolidated Freightways and Roadway Express cost Yellow market share in the early 1980s. As a result, the company reduced its workforce by 20 percent. In an effort to strengthen its position, Yellow upgraded its facilities with new technology in 1983. To increase efficiency, the firm added new sorting centers (facilities at which packages are grouped together by destination location and loaded onto the appropriate trucks). Yellow also increased its number of terminals to 600. In 1987, Yellow expanded into Alaska by establishing a terminal there.

International expansion began in the early 1990s as Yellow moved into Canada, Puerto Rico, and Mexico. Yellow Freight Mexicana was created in 1991. The following year, Yellow paid $24 million for regional and interregional LTL hauler Preston Trucking Company, gaining access to regional markets in the northeastern and southern states. Yellow Freight restructured as a holding company for its subsidiaries in 1993; the new holding company changed its name to Yellow Corp., of which Yellow Freight remained the largest unit.

A one-day strike by the Teamsters Union in April of 1994 cost Yellow Freight $7.9 million in net sales. To resolve the dispute, Yellow Freight agreed to a 5 percent

FAST FACTS:
About Yellow Corp.

Ownership: Yellow Corp. is a publicly owned company traded on the NASDAQ Stock Exchange.

Ticker Symbol: YELL

Officers: William D. Zollars, Chmn., Pres., and CEO, 54, 2001 base salary $700,000; Donald G. Barger, Jr., SVP and CFO, 58, 2001 base salary $335,000; William F. Martin, Jr., SVP Legal and Corporate Sec., 2001 base salary $267,750; Gregory A. Reid, SVP and Chief Mktg. Officer, 2001 base salary $226,375

Employees: 32,000

Principal Subsidiary Companies: Yellow Corp. is the parent company of Yellow Transportation. Other Yellow Corp. subsidiaries include Yellow Global, an international shipping logistics operation, and regional carriers Saia Motor Freight Line, Inc. and Jevic Transportation, Inc.

Chief Competitors: Yellow Corp. competes with traditional trucking companies, as well as with railroads and air freight companies. Major rivals include Roadway Express Inc., Arkansas Best Corp., and Consolidated Freightways Corp.

wage increase for its employees, most of whom were represented by the union. Growth continued in the mid-1990s with the purchase of Phoenix, Arizona-based regional hauler Johnson's Freightlines. Yellow Corp. changed the name of its new unit to WestEx, Inc. and shifted its focus to providing overnight and two-day delivery services. In 1997, Yellow Freight reorganized operations along geographic lines and laid off 70 administrative employees. As a result, the firm achieved profitability for the first time in three years.

Increased competition among LTL trucking companies prompted Yellow Corp. to continue looking for ways to improve customer service; as a result, the firm began to expand beyond traditional LTL services into areas like logistics. With an eye toward additional international growth, Yellow Corp. created YCS International in 1998. Regional LTL services were bolstered by the purchases of Action Express in 1998 and Jevic Transportation in 1999. Believing that Internet technology would allow for more streamlined operations among all industry players, Yellow Corp. created Transportation.com, an online hub

CHRONOLOGY:
Key Dates for Yellow Corp.

1924: Yellow Transit trucking company is founded in Oklahoma City, Oklahoma

1965: The purchase of Watson-Wilson Transportation System doubles Yellow's size

1968: Yellow Transit changes its name to Yellow Freight System, Inc.

1981: The firm lays off 20 percent of its workforce

1992: Yellow purchases Preston Trucking Company

1993: Yellow Freight restructures as a holding company named Yellow Corp.

1998: Yellow Corp. creates YCS International and acquires Action Express

1999: Jevic Transportation is purchased

2000: Two venture capitalists and Yellow Corp. jointly create Transportation.com

2001: Action Express and WestEx are consolidated into Saia Motor Freight Line

2002: Yellow Freight changes its name to Yellow Transportation. Saia Motor Freight and Jevic are placed into a new holding company, SCS Transportation, which Yellow Corp. plans to spin off as a public company

for trucking and other transportation companies, in 2000. While the marketplace was originally created in conjunction with two venture capital firms, Yellow Corp. eventually became the sole owner.

Action Express and WestEx were consolidated into Saia Motor Freight Line in 2001. Yellow Freight changed its name to Yellow Transportation the following year to reflect its broader service offerings. Saia Motor Freight and Jevic, both non-unionized regional carriers, were placed into a new holding company, SCS Transportation, which Yellow Corp. planned to spin off as a public company in late 2002.

STRATEGY

One of the first key shifts in Yellow Corp.'s corporate strategy came in 1992 when the firm bought Pre-

ston Trucking, a struggling regional and interregional LTL hauler. The purchase allowed Yellow Corp., which had specialized in long-haul LTL services for several decades, to move into regional and interregional LTL hauling for the first time. Management had made the decision to diversify after coming to the realization that customers were looking for freight haulers who could offer both regional and national hauling services. Along with paying $24 million for Preston, Yellow Corp. also assumed $116 million in debt. Although management was able to restore Preston to profitability within a year of the acquisition, the performance of the Preston unit remained unstable. As a result, Yellow divested a large portion of Preston in 1998. Although the purchase itself posed problems for Yellow Corp., the decision to diversify into new services served the company well in the late 1990s, as rivals continued to increase the comprehensiveness of their freight transportation services.

The corporate strategy devised by Maurice Myers, who took the helm of Yellow Corp. in 1996, remained in place in the early 2000s. Myers began expanding the firm's focus from LTL trucking to global transportation services by moving into things like logistics. This proved a successful strategy for the firm, particularly when cost-conscious companies began looking to logistics firms to help manage inventory. According to a January 2001 article in *Business Week*, "Indeed, Corporate America's rush to minimize inventories is keeping the nation's freight companies rolling faster than ever, effectively turning their fleets into warehouses on the go. Traditional trucking companies such as Yellow and Roadway Express Inc. are pushing into realms once controlled by overnight shipping companies."

William Zollars, who succeeded Myers in 1999, continued to look for new growth areas for Yellow Corp. In mid-2000, Yellow Corp. launched Operation Slingshot, a strategic plan designed to put the firm's use of Internet technology on par with the likes of United Parcel Service (UPS) Corp. and FedEx Corp. Key to the new initiative was the rapid expansion of Yellow's Web site, dubbed MyYellow, which launched in early 2000 to allow customers to track their shipments online. Yellow added a rate calculator to its site to help clients to determine prices based on variables such as delivery times. In addition, Yellow developed technology to allow clients to do things like file damage claims and make payments online. Within a year, the number of customers using MyYellow increased from 4,300 to roughly 37,000 people.

CURRENT TRENDS

The trend of intermodalism, whereby trucking services work in conjunction with trains, boats, and airplanes to perform long-haul deliveries, became increasingly important to firms like Yellow Corp. in the late 1990s. Using other modes of transportation to complete deliveries (typically via alliances with other shipping companies) have allowed the firm to diversify to the extent it has. For example, Exact Express time-specific delivery services make use of both air and ground transportation modes. In addition, Yellow Global uses both air and sea freight forwarding services to deliver products to their final destination.

Yellow Corp. continues to focus on using technology to streamline its productivity and to offer innovative services to its clients. In 2001, Yellow Corp. transformed Transportation.com from an online transportation marketplace to a marketer of the transportation management software developed internally by Yellow Corp. Transportation.com also began offering logistics and transportation management consulting services. In 2002, Yellow Corp. created transportation technology management unit Meridian IQ.

PRODUCTS

Yellow Freight offers national, regional, and international freight transport. Goods hauled typically include industrial, commercial, and retail products. Along with traditional services like Standard Ground, Yellow Freight also offers premium services like Exact Express, a delivery service that allows clients to specify their desired delivery time on any given date. Definite Delivery is a guaranteed on-time shipping service that allows clients to track shipments from the moment they are picked up until they are delivered. Saia Motor Freight offers regional LTL delivery services, including both overnight and next-day delivery services to 21 U.S. states, as well as to Canada, Mexico, and Puerto Rico. Jevic Transportation offers regional and interregional freight transport services within the United States.

GLOBAL PRESENCE

Yellow Corp. continued to expand internationally into the early 2000s. The firm changed the name of its international arm from YCS International to Yellow Global, believing the new name would capitalize on the strong image of the Yellow brand. In an effort to boost international sales, which were less than 1 percent of total sales in 1999, Yellow Corp. also planned to more closely align the sales and marketing efforts of Yellow Global with Yellow Corp. In 2001, the firm began offering its Exact Express service in Mexico. The following year, Yellow Corp. and Road Air Distribution B.V., based in the Netherlands, agreed to

YELLOW CORP. DELIVERS HARRY POTTER BOOKS JUST IN TIME

Thanks to its use of just-in-time technology, Yellow Corp. was able to coordinate the delivery of 150,000 copies of the new Harry Potter release, *Harry Potter and the Goblet of Fire*, to book stores across the United States shortly before midnight on July 8, 2001. The publisher, Scholastic, had developed a marketing campaign that centered around the book's specific release time and date; as a result, deliveries too early or too late could have undermined the entire campaign. Yellow Corp.'s Exact Express service proved equal to the task, which pleased not only Scholastic executives, but also the thousands of children waiting in line to buy the book.

work together to handle one another's shipments in their home countries.

SOURCES OF INFORMATION

Bibliography

Anderson, James A. "Clipped Wings and Broken Wheels." *Business Week*, 18 April 2001. Available from www.businessweek.com.

Arndt, Michael. "Industry Outlook 2001-Transportation." *Business Week*, 2 January 2001. Available from www.businessweek.com.

Haddad, Charles. "Transportation: A Long Haul to Recovery?" *Business Week*, 14 January 2002. Available from www.businessweek.com.

Kirkwood, Heather. "Yellow Buys Local Trucker to Fortify Long-Term Plans." *The Kansas City Business Journal*, 24 September 1999.

Wilson, Tim. "Portal, Exchange Deliver Goods for Freight Carrier." *InternetWeek*, 11 June 2001.

"Yellow Corp." *International Directory of Company Histories.* Detroit: Gale Research, 1996.

Yellow Corp. Home Page, 2002. Available at http://www.yellowcorp.com.

For an annual report:

on the Internet at: http://media.corporate-ir.net/media_files/nsd/yell/annual2000/index.htm

For additional industry research:

Investigate companies by their Standard Industrial Classification codes, also knows as SICs. Yellow Corp.'s primary SICs are:

4213 Trucking, Except Local

4731 Arrangement Transport Freight & Cargo

6719 Holding Companies, Not Elsewhere Classified

Also investigate companies by their North American Industry Classification System codes, also known as NAICS codes. Yellow Corp.'s primary NAICS codes are:

484121 General Freight Trucking, Long-Distance, Truckload

488510 Freight Transportation Arrangement

551112 Offices of Other Holding Companies

Appendixes, Glossary, & Master Index

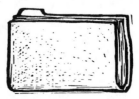

Industry Profiles

Air Transportation, Scheduled, and Courier Services

Overview

The scheduled passenger airline segment of the air transportation industry grew out of the U.S. airmail services into a multi-billion dollar industry. According to the December 2001 edition of *Standard & Poor's Industry Surveys*, revenues for the 10 largest airlines reached $98.8 billion in 2000, resulting in operating profits of $5.8 billion. However, profits fell 10 percent from 1999 levels due to increased operating expenses, including higher fuel prices. The air travel industry experienced renewed growth in the mid- to late 1990s, stemming from the country's economic prosperity. However, by the summer of 2001, the nation's leading airlines were losing money. *Airline Business* revealed that collective net losses for the leading carriers amounted to approximately $1 billion in the first half of 2001.

On September 11, 2001, terrorists hijacked four commercial jets and used them to attack the Pentagon and New York's World Trade Center towers. The attacks shut down all U.S. air traffic for nearly one week, caused devastating human and financial losses, and increased existing concerns about safety and security. According to *Airline Business*, the nation's leading airlines lost more than $2 billion in the fourth quarter of 2001. Signs of improvement were evident in March of 2002 when air travel began to increase and stock prices for several leading U.S. airlines finally reached or exceeded pre-September 11 closing prices.

The air courier industry segment includes services that ship freight (generally under 100 pounds) and express mail. Two kinds of companies provide air courier services in the United States. These include integrators or all-cargo companies such as Federal Express (FedEx) and DHL. Integrators have a fleet of planes, carry cargo only, usually fly at night, and have ground transportation and personnel for door-to-door pick up and delivery. On the other hand, some passenger airlines, such as American Airlines and Northwest Airlines, also provide air courier services. These companies transport cargo (freight, express, and mail) in the holds of their passenger aircraft. They fly during the day since passenger traffic is their first priority. Passenger airlines have provided service similar to integrators, except most airlines have to subcontract ground transportation. Several factors, including competition from trucking companies and integrators, economic factors, and the terrorist attacks of September 2001, caused some passenger airlines to scale back or eliminate certain cargo services in the early 2000s.

The Federal Aviation Administration (FAA) reported that domestic freight and express services reached 12.1 billion revenue ton-miles (RTMs) in 2000, an increase of 5.3 percent over 1999. Domestic mail RTMs totaled 2.5 billion in 2000, an increase of 3.2 percent. A revenue ton-mile (RTM) equals one ton of revenue traffic transported one mile. Domestically and internationally, cargo RTMs grew an average of 3.4 percent and 7.2 percent, respectively, from 1995 to 2000.

History of the Industry

The passenger and courier air transportation industry resulted from the development of the aviation industry, which began with the first successful sustained flight by Wilbur and Orville Wright in Kitty Hawk, North Car-

FINANCES:

Passenger Revenues
1996-1999
(millions)

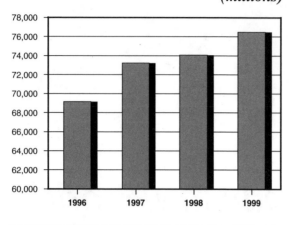

by the integrators. From 1982 to 1990, the domestic air express market grew at an annual rate of nearly 19 percent. In 1996, the air express industry continued to grow along with air cargo. According to a recent report issued by the Boeing Company, an annual growth rate of 6.6 percent is predicted for air cargo, including air courier services.

By the late 1990s, leading industry concerns included safety, security, and competition, according to *Air Transport World*. Two crashes thrust the first two issues directly into the country's view. The 1996 ValuJet flight 592 crash, which occurred in the Florida Everglades, first set the stage. Later, the TWA 800 crash spawned anti-terrorist panic and brought about a number of expensive and time-consuming preventative measures. However, after examining the evidence, experts believed a mechanical failure caused the crash, not terrorism.

Significant Events Affecting the Industry

Labor problems, increasing fuel costs, and a sluggish economy were beginning to impact the air transportation industry in the early 2000s. However, the terrorist attacks that took place on September 11, 2001, turned the industry completely upside down. The attacks brought all U.S. air traffic to a complete halt for four days and then resulted in significant decreases in flights, passengers, and freight. In its December 2001 *Transportation Indicators* report, the U.S. Department of Transportation's Bureau of Transportation Statistics revealed the tragedy's immediate effects on the nation's transportation system. Revenue passenger miles (one fee-paying passenger transported one mile) for domestic flights in September 2001 were 32 percent below levels for September 2000. Rates for international flights were down 29 percent. During the same time period, revenue ton-miles for domestic flights and international flights dropped 24 percent and 31 percent, respectively.

These conditions took an immediate financial toll on the industry. Costs quickly began to exceed revenues and airlines soon began to lose millions of dollars each day. By January of 2002, fourth quarter losses for the leading passenger airlines totaled more than $2 billion, according to *Airline Business*. Some airlines, including Swissair, went bankrupt. For the entire year 2001, United Airlines' parent, UAL Corporation, lost $2.14 billion. American Airlines' parent, AMR Corporation, lost $1.76 billion. In its February 21, 2002 issue, *Purchasing* reported that according to the Air Cargo Management Group, worldwide freight traffic was approximately eight to ten percent lower in 2001 than in 2000.

The federal government eventually authorized grants totaling $5 billion to help air transportation companies compensate for the mandatory four-day shutdown. According to *Air Transport World*, by February 2002 the U.S. Department of Transportation had received more than 300 applications for financial assistance and had paid more than $3.8 billion to 131 of the applicants. In

olina, in 1903. The popularity of air travel exploded with the successful overseas flight of Charles Lindbergh on May 20, 1927. Various air transport holding companies were created, such as Aviation Corporation, launched by financiers W. Averill Harriman and Robert Lehman. The air transport division of this company was called American Airways. In 1928, another holding company, United Aircraft and Transportation Corporation, was created by Boeing and its air transport division. By 1931, United Air Lines was created as the management company for United Aircraft's four transport companies.

The passenger industry remained heavily regulated by the government until 1978 when the Carter administration brought free market conditions to the industry. As a result, route structures and price setting became the decisions of the domestic carriers, not the U.S. government. A "hub and spoke" route system was quickly created and airlines had the right to expand internationally as they saw fit.

The U.S. airmail system was the forerunner to the air courier or express mail industry. Yet the air courier industry and the time-sensitive delivery of letters and parcels remained dormant until the late 1970s. Following deregulation, the air cargo industry underwent dramatic changes as air forwarders and ground transportation operators acquired their own aircraft and became integrators. Several passenger airlines also began to pick up some market share, but it was the all-cargo carriers that created the express delivery service that has been most commonly known as air courier service.

The rapid growth of the air courier industry during the 1980s was primarily due to the success of express delivery service. This particular service has been dominated

addition to the grants, President George W. Bush signed the Air Transportation Safety and System Stabilization Act on September 22, 2001, in order to guarantee loans for air carriers affected by the attacks.

After September 11, more stringent security measures were implemented for both passenger airlines and air freight companies. These measures included an FAA rule that required indirect air carriers to verify the credibility and identity of shippers based on specific criteria. Security also was bolstered at the nation's airports, resulting in longer lines and more thorough searches. At one point, National Guard troops were on hand to provide added security. On the recommendation of President Bush, leading airlines, including United and American, began installing steel bars on cockpit doors shortly after the attacks. Additionally, United announced that it would place stun guns in the cockpits of its planes for pilots to use in case of future emergencies.

In the late 1990s, airlines around the world started to establish alliances in an effort to help the industry balance its transportation capacity with the country's demand for services. By reducing some global competition, alliances can reduce the need for larger fleets. In 2002, the leading alliance was the Star Alliance. Formed by Lufthansa, it involved 15 airlines including Air Canada, Thai Airways, Air New Zealand, United, and Varig. Other alliances included oneworld, involving American and British Airways, and SkyTeam, involving Delta Airlines and Air France. Alliances also existed in the cargo industry.

In addition to alliances, airlines came together in other ways. For example, in the early 2000s, Delta, Continental, United, Northwest, and American partnered to form an online travel site called Orbitz, and American and United combined their electronic ticketing systems to simplify travel for customers who utilized both airlines. There also were initiatives such as the U.S. "open skies" agreements to open up foreign markets to competition. The United States negotiated its first such agreement in 1992 with the Netherlands and, by the year 2000, had entered into agreements with 52 nations.

Key Competitors

In the passenger air transportation segment, AMR Corporation, the parent company of American Airlines, ranked number one with 2001 sales of $18.9 billion. This represented a 3.8 percent decrease from 2000. After the events of September 11, AMR reported a net loss of $1.7 billion. American Airlines resulted from the consolidation of companies owned by the Aviation Corporation (AVCO). Formed in 1929, AVCO acquired enough small transportation companies by 1930 to form a coast-to-coast network called American Airways. In 1934, American Airways developed a more integrated route system and became American Airlines. By the late 1930s, American passed United and became the leading U.S. airline. On May 19, 1982, a plan for reorganization under the

newly established AMR Corporation was approved at the American Airlines annual meeting. American absorbed competitor TWA in 2001 after that airline went bankrupt. In the early 2000s, American served approximately 160 destinations in North America, South America, the Pacific Rim, and Europe.

United Airlines (a subsidiary of the UAL Corporation) ranked second in the industry with 2001 sales of $16.1 billion. However, it posted an industry record loss of $2.1 billion. Headquartered in Chicago, Illinois, United in 2001 serviced approximately 130 destinations in 28 countries and employed 84,000 workers. On July 12, 1994, the airline's plan to turn over 53 percent of the company's ownership to its employees in exchange for wage concessions was finally approved by United stockholders.

United began in 1926 as Varney Airlines, the nation's first scheduled service. Varney, along with Pacific Air Transport and National Air Transport, eventually merged with Boeing Air Transport (including Boeing Airplane Company and Pratt and Whitney). United Airlines was formed as a management company for Boeing's airline division, but became an independent business when the Boeing Air Transport combination was dissolved. United had planned to enter into a $4.3 billion merger with US Airways in 2001, but the deal never materialized due to regulatory problems.

FDX Corporation, the outcome of Federal Express's purchase of Caliber System, was the world's largest express transportation company in the early 2000s. Each day, Federal Express (FedEx) delivers approximately 3 million items in 211 countries via its fleet of 642 aircraft and more than 45,000 vehicles. The company began operations in 1973 and is known as the creator of the hub system of distribution. In 2001, FedEx reached an agreement with the U.S. Postal Service (USPS) allowing it to place drop boxes outside of USPS locations. The company also entered into a major transportation agreement with the USPS and began transporting USPS Express Mail and Priority Mail between airports. By 2002, Federal Express had 143,500 employees worldwide. The company's FedEx Express Web site automated transactions for more than 2.5 million customers. David J. Bronczek was president and chief executive officer of the company. Worldwide headquarters of Federal Express are located in Memphis, Tennessee. The company posted sales of $19.6 billion in 2001.

United Parcel Service of America, Inc. (UPS), headquartered in Atlanta, Georgia, is the second largest express courier in the United States and the world's largest package delivery company. UPS operates 88,000 vehicles, including package cars, vans, tractors, and motorcycles. The company operates 253 jets and utilizes 346 chartered aircraft. In the early 2000s, UPS had 1,748 operating facilities. As of 2002, Michael L. Eskew was the company's chairman and chief executive officer. In 2001, UPS had sales of $30.6 billion on a volume of 3.4 billion packages and documents. In the early 2000s, the company was involved in e-commerce through its e-Ventures unit and in corporate supply chain management.

Industry Projections

According to the Air Transport Association of America's (ATA) 2002 *State of the U.S. Airline Industry Report*, net profits for U.S. scheduled airlines amounted to about $2.6 billion in 2000, a significant drop from 1999 levels of $5.3 billion. Passenger volumes, which remained relatively steady throughout 1999 and 2000, began to decline along with the slumping economy into mid-2001. The attacks of September 11 caused a significant drop in both air traffic and earnings. ATA figures indicate that net income for U.S. scheduled airlines fluctuated around $5 billion from 1997 to 1999 and then dropped below $3 billion in 2000. Because of worsening economic factors, a $3 billion loss was expected in 2001. The events of September 11 brought this figure closer to $7 billion. Because the terrorist attacks were unprecedented and no basis of comparison existed, estimating their impact on many facets of the industry was extremely difficult for analysts. However, in its report the ATA estimated that the industry would return to profitability in late 2003. In March 2002, the FAA forecast airline passenger traffic would return "to more normal levels of growth by Fiscal Year (FY) 2004." The FAA further forecast that traffic would grow an average of four percent through 2013, eventually reaching one billion passengers.

In 2001, the air freight industry was in fine shape, having benefited from a 10-year period of economic prosperity. All of the major air express carriers experienced growth through the late 1990s. Cargo revenues for the 10 largest U.S. airlines, which reached $3.61 billion in 1999 and was estimated at $3.97 billion the following year, were expected to be $4.20 billion in 2001 according to estimates from Standard & Poor's. However, by the third quarter of 2001, the worsening economy and terrorist attacks of September 11 had a worldwide impact on the air freight industry. In November, *Air Cargo World* reported that growth had ceased or begun to decline for express carriers in the United States. This was an unprecedented occurrence. The publication revealed that worldwide air freight traffic, which achieved growth of six percent in 2000, had declined by approximately five percent midway through 2001.

Considering the events of September 11, *Air Cargo World* indicated that industry conditions might not improve until the third quarter of 2002 or sometime later. Prior to September 11, The Colography Group indicated that based on 4.4 percent growth in domestic air shipments, the overall volume of expedited shipments would increase 3.2 percent from 2001 to 2002, reaching 6.9 billion shipments, and *The MergeGlobal 2001 World Air Freight Forecast* reported that world air freight volume would grow through 2005 at an annual rate of 5.2 percent, eventually reaching 38 million tons.

Courier-only services, or integrators, control most of the domestic market for envelopes, packages, and freight. The leading companies in this segment include FedEx, UPS, and Airborne Express. At the end of 2001, FedEx was the industry leader with more than 39 percent of the air courier market, according to Valanium Associates. Next in line were UPS (30 percent), the U.S. Postal Service (19 percent), and Airborne Express (11 percent).

Global Presence

As home to the world's top two airlines, American and United, the United States had the largest air transportation market in the early 2000s. In terms of revenue passenger kilometers, the country was the leader among the world's airlines with 35.5 percent of the market, according to *Air Transport World*. Europe ranked second with 31.1 percent, followed by Asia/Pacific with 22.5 percent, Latin America/Caribbean with 4.2 percent, the Middle East with 2.7 percent, Canada with 2.3 percent, and Africa with 1.7 percent.

U.S. cargo air transportation services also rank among the world's leaders. According to the Boeing Company's *World Air Cargo Forecast for 2001*, world air freight is expected to grow 6.5 percent annually through 2019, exceeding the growth rate of mail. Boeing estimates that U.S. world market share will decrease from 31.5 percent through 2019. The strongest growth prospects are expected in markets linked to Asia. At the end of 2001, Valanium Associates reported that United States-based DHL International, the longest established operator in the international market, held the largest market share in Asia (20 percent). DHL operates the world's largest air express network, reaching approximately 228 countries via 36 hubs and more than 250 aircraft.

Employment in the Industry

In 2002, total employment by the major carriers was approximately 463,400 workers. Despite layoffs and salary cuts, airline employees remain one of the best paid workforces in the United States, with the average wage and compensation package exceeding $73,000 per year. This was significantly higher than the national average due to the strong presence of labor unions. The Air Transport Association estimated this figure would surpass $76,000 in 2002. Although many air courier companies operate in the United States, the three leading firms— FedEx, UPS, and Airborne, Inc.—employed 536,027 employees worldwide in 2002. According to the U.S. Department of Labor, from 2000 to 2010, 25 percent growth is expected in the air transportation industry, both cargo and passenger traffic, in both wage and salary jobs.

Sources for Further Study

"Air Transport Industry." *Valueline*, March 1997.

"Air Transportation." *Career Guide to Industries 2002-03 Edition*. U.S. Department of Labor, 13 March 2002. Available at http://www.bls.gov/oco/cg/cgs016.htm.

"Airline Industry Changed Forever." *Airwise*, 20 February 2002. Available at http://news.airwise.com.

"Airlines Industry Survey." *Standard & Poor's Industry Surveys*. New York: The McGraw-Hill Companies, December 2001.

Airports Council International, May 1997. "The Economic Benefits of Air Transport."

"BTS Indicators Report Shows Impact of September 11 on Airlines." U.S. Department of Transportation, 9 March 2002. Available at http://www.dot.gov/affairs/bts0102.htm.

"Consolidation Trend." *Travel Weekly*, 16 June 1997.

Dinell, David. "Cargo Traffic at 10-Year High." *Wichita Business Journal*, 8 November 1996.

"FAA Forecasts Continued Drop in Air Traffic This Year, Strong Recovery in 2003." U.S. Department of Transportation, Federal Aviation Administration, 12 March 2002. Available at http://www.faa.gov. http://www.bls.gov/oco/cg/cgs016.htm.

Henderson, Danna K., and Lisa H. Ray. "The World Airline Report: 1997 Edition." *Air Transport World*, July 1997.

Henterly, Meghan. "DHL Bracing for Competition on Its Overseas Turf." *Gannett News Service*, 11 June 1996.

State of the U.S. Airline Industry, 2002. Washington: Air Transport Association, 13 March 2002. Available at http://www.airlines.org.

"UAL Loses $2.1 Billion in 2001; An Airline Record." *Monitor Daily*, 1 February 2002. Available at http://www.monitordaily.com.

U.S. Department of Transportation. *Federal Aviation Administration Forecasts, Fiscal Years 1991-2002*. Washington, DC, GPO.

Walker, Karen. "US Alliance Opens the Floodgates." *Airline Business*, March 1998.

Aircraft

Overview

The aircraft manufacturing industry began to turn around in the late 1990s, as sales increased from $55.0 billion in 1995 to $60.3 billion in 1996. This increase reversed a five-year period of declining aircraft sales. Sales continued to increase into the early 2000s, reaching $84.1 billion in 2001. Civil aircraft make up about 60 percent of industry sales, with military aircraft accounting for the remainder. The Aerospace Industries Association (AIA) reported that in 2001, shipments of civilian aircraft (including transports, general aviation, and rotocraft) reached 3,483 units with a value of $43.6 billion.

Commercial aircraft deliveries were expected to number 3,254 in 2002. The commercial jet fleet, which is projected to reach 23,600 by the year 2016, numbered approximately 16,000 in the early 2000s, 75 percent of which were aircraft manufactured by the Boeing Company. The industry entered 2001 with almost $90 billion in unfilled orders. Boeing aircraft accounted for 96 percent of these backlogs. According to the Teal Group, business jet deliveries eclipsed the 700 mark in 2000, an

industry record. This increase was attributable to a number of factors, including higher levels of profit in the corporate sector as well as an increased emphasis on productivity. The value of these aircraft exceeded $10 billion. However, Teal forecasts indicated, fewer business jets would be produced through the mid-2000s, with unit totals falling from the 700 range to approximately 600 by 2005.

History of the Industry

On December 17, 1903, bicycle makers Orville and Wilbur Wright earned credit as the first to produce an aircraft capable of powered, sustained, and controlled flight. Such a lofty honor was coveted around the world, and the early development of the "flying machine" was hindered by bickering and fierce legal battles. For example, Gabriel Voisin, who along with his brother Charles was the first to build aircraft in France on a commercial basis, scoffed at the influence of both the Wright brothers and other aviation pioneers.

A company founded by Glenn Curtiss made the first commercial sale of an aircraft in 1909 to the Aeronautic Society of New York. In the same year, one of the Wright brothers succeeded in meeting U.S. Army specifications for an aircraft which sold for $30,000. The Wrights promptly sued Curtiss for patent infringement, thus smothering the development of the aircraft industry in the United States until World War I. Later, U.S. Army war surplus Curtiss JN-4 "Jenny" trainers and the de Havilland Moth in Great Britain would carry a postwar barnstorming craze across both countries. The Piper Cub, introduced in 1937, became the best seller of all time in the general aviation category.

Although Leonardo da Vinci had sketched a helicopter design in 1483, the first sustained helicopter flight was not achieved until 1935, in a coaxial model built by Louis Breguet and Rene Dorand in France. Within the next five years, Igor Sikorsky would perfect his single-rotor type in the United States, opening the door for practical applications.

The early companies formed by pioneers were eventually merged into giant defense and aerospace companies. For example, the Wright Company, formed in 1909 when a group of New York investors bought the Wright brothers' patents for $100,000 in cash, was sold to another group in 1915, then merged with the Glenn L. Martin companies to form the Wright-Martin Aircraft Corporation. Wright-Martin Aircraft later became the Wright Aeronautical Company, which merged in 1929 with the Curtiss Aeroplane and Motor Company to form the Curtiss-Wright Corporation, which was controlled by North American Aviation.

Large conglomerates dependent upon government support continued to dominate the aircraft industry throughout World War II and the postwar period. The "Great War," World War I, had demonstrated the possibilities of aircraft in wartime. By World War II, they had become an integral part of modern warfare. Much of the phenomenal advancements in aircraft design—jet engines, swept-back wings, electronic flight controls, and composite materials—were funded by governments, often in time of war. Air Force One, a Boeing 747, illustrates how important aircraft have become to national security. Converted to serve as a mobile command post for the president of the United States in time of nuclear war, the aircraft has phone, fax, computer, and escape capabilities. The technological improvements in military aircraft have been accompanied by a proportional increase in price. A typical 1945 fighter plane cost about $51,000. By the 1990s, the F-16 jet fighter was selling for approximately $25 million.

Significant Events Affecting the Industry

Environmental groups in the United States, Europe, and Australia have focused on noise pollution. The Airport Noise and Capacity Act of 1990 (ANCA), which went into effect December 31, 1993, ordered U.S. airlines to make their fleets meet quieter noise specifications by January 1, 2000. Smaller business jets were exempted from this rule. Although the act was successful in reducing noise levels, by the early 2000s it had fallen short of reducing opposition to airport expansion and the continuing need for government funds. According to the October 2001 issue of *Noise Regulation Report*, "Community opposition on the basis of noise remains the primary obstacle to airport expansion and applications for federal noise mitigation funding have held steady." The report also indicated that calls to restrict and remove older, noisier aircraft from service were increasing. These aircraft require special modification to meet noise reduction standards. In addition to ANCA, the International Civil Aviation Organization imposed similar noise reduction standards, which were adopted by European countries in April 2002.

Because of heavy congestion in airports, a perceived need for large, 600-to-800-seat, ultra-high capacity aircraft (UHCA) or very large commercial transport (VLCT) arose. However, the extent to which very large planes would be required was a source of debate in the early 2000s. At that time, Airbus was moving forward with its plans to introduce the 555-passenger A380 in 2006. Boeing, on the other hand, changed its earlier plans to move in that direction. Citing weak demand for UHCA, the company stopped producing its 568-passenger 747-400 Domestic aircraft after manufacturing nineteen of them and instead began development of the Sonic Cruiser, a high-speed civil transport that is capable of flying near the sound barrier. Boeing's new plane is expected to enter service sometime between 2006 and 2008.

Key Competitors

The Boeing Company has earned a considerable reputation for quality both in its commercial aircraft and military aircraft such as the Clipper series of flying boats and the B-17 and B-29 bombers produced in World War II. Another successful military bomber was the B-52. Boeing's 707, 727, and 737 airliners have been well received. Its 747 has become a status symbol among world airlines, with 1,000 sold in its 25-year production run. The 737, the best selling aircraft in history, has dominated the medium-size/medium-range category and has remained Boeing's best-selling plane. The 2,500th 737 was delivered in 1993 and by mid-2002 more than 4,250 had been delivered. Literally no one has sold more jet airliners than Boeing. More than 12,000 were sold by the early 2000s, accounting for about 75 percent of the world's airliner fleet.

In 1997, Boeing increased its hold on the aircraft market by acquiring one of its leading competitors, McDonnell Douglas Corporation, formerly the third largest manufacturer of airplanes. With the merger, Boeing controlled about 50 percent of the aircraft industry. McDonnell Douglas, formed by the 1967 merger of The McDonnell Company and Douglas Aircraft, made such illustrious transports as the DC-3, named the C-47 by the U.S. military. In 1951, Douglas produced 56 percent of the world's airliners. In 2001, Boeing posted revenues of $58.2 billion and employed 188,000 people.

Airbus S.A.S. began as a five-nation European consortium conceived as a European answer to America's domination of the large commercial transport market. France and Great Britain had been discussing such a venture as early as 1965, but Britain dropped out of the project due to political disputes. In 1969, with the formation of Airbus Industrie, the West Germans agreed with France to build the A300, a wide-body, twin-engine airliner. Airbus' initial shareholders included Aerospatiale, Construcciones Aeronauticas SA (CASA) of Spain, Deutsche Airbus, and British Aerospace, which joined in 1979. Fokker and Belairbus of Belgium was an associate member that participated in some of the company's projects. By the early 2000s, Airbus Industrie was restructured into a corporation named Airbus S.A.S. The company's majority shareholder (80 percent) is the European Aeronautic Defence & Space Company. BAE SYSTEMS of the United Kingdom holds the remaining 20 percent interest. The company's main aircraft assembly plant is located in Toulouse, France.

Airbus has succeeded in capturing a substantial market share, becoming the second largest manufacturer of jets in the world. In 2001, the company recorded $18.2 billion in sales and received approximately 60 percent of the industry's orders for large aircraft, outpacing Boeing for the second time in three years. Airbus' key models include the twin-engine jets A300 and A310; the single-aisle twin-engine jets A319, A320, and A321; and the four-engine jet A340 produced for leading airlines around the world. Airbus also has developed the A380, a super jumbo jet capable of transporting 550 passengers, which it expects to introduce by 2006.

Industry Projections

In the early 2000s, the aircraft industry continued to achieve strong growth. However, according to the Aerospace Industries Association (AIA), industry sales ($84.1 billion in 2001) were expected to drop considerably in 2002, falling to an estimated $76.1 billion, because of high jet fuel prices, a weak economy, and the September 11 terrorist attacks that wreaked havoc on the profitability of air transportation providers in 2001. According to the Teal Group, the retirement of Boeing 747-400s will begin in 2005 and be in full swing by 2009, at which time the demand for larger planes is expected to increase.

The military market was somewhat stagnant in the early 2000s, held back in part by a reduction in exports, but the Teal Group predicted relatively steady growth for fixed-wing military aircraft through 2005. Industry production levels were expected to climb from 214 units in 2001 (worth $10.9 billion) to 395 units in 2005 (worth $18.1 billion).

The general aviation market looked promising as well, according to the Teal Group. Production of these aircraft was expected to reach 439 in 2001, worth nearly $6.3 billion. Through 2005, the Teal Group forecast the production level to remain around 380 units with an average value of approximately $5.8 billion. Cessna, Bombardier, and Dassault led the industry in the early 2000s.

The outlook for the civil helicopter market was more or less flat in the early 2000s. According to the Teal Group, the market will achieve small percentage annual growth rates and reach about $1.2 billion by 2010. Between 2001 and 2014, deliveries of nearly 820 helicopters are expected, valued at approximately $12.4 billion. Growth in the corporate aircraft segment was expected to partially drive the demand for certain models of high-end helicopters used for executive travel.

Aircraft manufacturing has historically been one of the most consistently profitable and successful of American industries, and by all indications this trend is likely to continue. Led by companies such as Boeing and Lockheed Martin Corporation, the aircraft industry collects a higher amount of export earnings than any other American industry. Until recently, no foreign manufacturer has been able to keep up with the pace of technological achievement or unit output achieved by American firms.

Global Presence

The U.S. industry maintains a positive balance of trade with exports exceeding imports by about $10 billion, although this balance dropped in the mid to late 1990s. Airbus Industries, a European consortium, and Montreal-based Bombardier, Inc. have moved into competition with the American giants and growing companies in the Far East, especially Japan, threaten to absorb some of the demand for commercial and military aircraft. Some industry analysts suggest that future growth in the aircraft manufacturing industry will cross national borders as more and more companies engage in joint ventures with competitors from around the world, taking advantage of the strengths of the individual companies to provide the most competitive product available.

The value of all aircraft exports declined from $35.2 billion in 1998 to $24.7 billion in 2000. At the same time, the value of imports rose considerably, climbing from $4.7 billion in 1998 to $12.4 billion in 2000. According to the AIA, military aerospace exports declined for the third straight year in 2001, while civil aircraft exports increased after two years of declines. Demand in world commercial markets, particularly the expanding economies of Asia and the Pacific Rim, is expected to increase over the next 10 to 15 years. In fact, the larger share of the commercial transport market is now overseas. The U.S. share, as a percentage of the world market, is expected to shrink.

Employment in the Industry

The total number of workers in the aircraft industry stood at 184,698 in 2000, with 88,200 employed as production workers. The industry's production workers earned an average wage of close to $24.00 per hour the same year. According to the U.S. Bureau of Labor Statistics, employment in the large aircraft and parts sector of the industry is expected to achieve a healthy growth rate of 23 percent between 2000 and 2010. Reductions in defense spending and cuts in aircraft purchases by troubled commercial airline carriers, which led to the elimination of thousands of jobs in the industry prior to the late 1990s, remain factors that affect employment levels. In 2002, industry leader Boeing had plans in place to eliminate as many as 30,000 jobs from its employee base of 188,000.

Sources for Further Study

"A Boom Ends?" *The Economist*, 17 January 1998.

Aboulafia, Richard. "Helo Challenge: Consolidation." *Aviation Week & Space Technology*, 12 January 1998.

Aerospace Industries Association, Washington, DC, 8 June 2002. *2001 Year-End Review and 2002 Forecast.* Available at http://www.aia-aerospace.org.

"Aerospace Manufacturing." *Career Guide to Industries 2002-03 Edition.* U.S. Department of Labor, 8 June 2002. Available at http://www.bls.gov.

"Airbus Outsells Boeing in 2001." *Air Transport World*, February 2002.

"Airplane Makers Say Soaring Sales Made 1997 a Record Year." *Knight-Ridder/Tribune Business News*, 12 February 1998.

Annual Survey of Manufacturers. Washington, DC: U.S. Bureau of Census. GPO, 1996.

Annual Survey of Manufacturers. Washington, DC: U.S. Department of Commerce, Economics and Statistics Administration, U.S. Census Bureau, February 2002.

Aviation Week & Space Technology, 8 June 2002.

2002 Aerospace Source Book, 2002. Available at http://www.aviationnow.com.

Kelly, Emma. "EU Adopts International Noise Rules." *Flight International*, 2 April 2002.

Noise Regulation Report, October 2001.

Proctor, Paul. "New Models, New Capabilities Spark Civil Helicopter Demand. *Aviation Week & Space Technology*, 17 March 1997.

Taverna, Michael A., and Pierre Sparaco. "Eurocopter Boosts Production, Expands Market Share." *Aviation Week & Space Technology*, 16 February 1998.

Woolsey, James P. "A New Buying Cycle?" *Air Transport World*, January 1996.

Amusement Parks

Overview

After stagnant years in the early 1990s because of the country's recession, the amusement park industry entered a period of renewed growth that began in the mid-1990s and continued into the early 2000s. During this period, amusement park attendance continued to rise along with amusement park revenues. Furthermore, amusement park operators took advantage of this renaissance to upgrade their parks, adding new rides and amenities and opening up new parks. In 2001 a record 319 million people visited major U.S. theme parks, and industry revenues were approximately $9.6 billion, according to conservative estimates from the International Association of Amusement Parks and Attractions (IAAPA). That year, industry leader Walt Disney Parks & Resorts posted revenues of $7 billion.

Since the U.S. market already contained a high number of amusement parks, U.S. amusement park operators such as Disney and Six Flags began to expand globally, setting up new parks in Europe and Asia. In the late 1990s, Asia became the hottest market for new amusement parks, especially in China. Nonetheless, several new U.S. amusement parks opened up in the late 1990s including Disney's Animal Kingdom and Universal Studio's Islands of Adventure, both in Orlando, Florida. The industry also continued to unveil new attractions within parks to lure visitors. In North America, 14 new roller coasters were expected to debut in 2002. This number was much greater in Europe, where 22 new rides were to open that year.

On September 11, 2001, terrorist attacks against the United States raised concerns about the safety of air travel. Along with an economy that was already slowing down, the attacks added to lower levels of consumer confidence. Consequently, the amusement park industry saw a reduction in business in the last quarter of 2001. This was especially true of amusement parks like Disney because most of these parks' visitors travel by air from afar. The impact was not expected to be as bad on regional parks, such as those operated by Six Flags, because visitors can reach these parks by driving shorter distances.

History of the Industry

According to *The Great American Amusement Parks,* the earliest amusement parks were the European pleasure gardens of the seventeenth and eighteenth centuries. But only with the technological advances of the industrial revolution did the mechanical rides of the modern amusement park come into being. In this area of development, American parks led the way.

Jones's Wood in New York City, established in the early nineteenth century, was probably the first major U.S. amusement park. But its humble attractions—including billiards, bowling, and donkey rides—were soon eclipsed by Coney Island. This legendary resort first began to expand dramatically in the 1870s, when a railway line to it was constructed. In 1920 the extension of the New York subway system to Coney Island put city residents a nickel away from the resort's attractions. Indeed, before the advent of the automobile, ease of travel played a crucial role.

Mechanized rides of the kind taken for granted in modern amusement parks reached Coney Island in 1884, with the advent of LaMarcus Adna Thompson's Switchback Railway, the first roller coaster. From their inception, roller coasters proved to be the most popular attractions at these parks, as well as the largest and most expensive to build and maintain.

The first ferris wheel made its appearance at the 1893 Chicago World's Fair Colombian Exposition. It was named for George Ferris, not because he invented the concept, but because his engineering talents produced the first such ride made of steel rather than wood and built on a huge scale. Coney Island and the many other amusement parks that sprang into being in response to its success faced hazards from fire and water. Rainy weather discouraged attendance because most of the attractions were outdoors. Initial reliance for construction on such cheap but highly flammable materials as lath and staff, a combination of plaster of Paris and hemp fiber, meant that fires were frequent and caused great damage.

Other problems such as noise, dirt, and criminality often found in the early amusement parks became more apparent as larger numbers of middle- and upper-class Americans owning cars gained the freedom to seek their entertainment elsewhere. The formation of the International Association of Amusement Parks and Attractions (IAAPA) in 1920 was motivated in part by the industry's concern over its reputation. Individual parks, such as Cincinnati's Coney Island and Rye, New York's, Playland, also sought to create a more family-oriented image by making sure that structural damage, litter, and graffiti were swiftly removed from sight.

Disney was, however, the most significant creator of family amusement in its innovative theme parks. The first of these, Disneyland, opened its doors in 1955. An instant success, the park initially proved hard to imitate; but Six Flags Over Texas, opened in 1961, found a winning formula, leading to the construction of additional

Six Flags complexes. Other Disney competitors also began to find new angles on the theme park concept.

Significant Events Affecting the Industry

The industry's largest merger took place in 1998 when Premier Parks bought second-ranked Six Flags for $1.9 billion. Time Warner and an investment group led by Boston Ventures previously owned Six Flags, which had benefited from the relationship with Time Warner by creating Warner Bros. themes for its parks. As part of the acquisition agreement, Premier gained the exclusive long-term licensing rights to Warner Bros.' cartoons and characters as well as to DC Comics' comic book characters at its North American theme parks. Premier announced it would not only keep the Six Flags name and licensed characters at many of the chain's existing parks, but also change the names of the existing Premier Parks to "Six Flags." The move launched Premier to the top of the industry, becoming the world's largest regional theme park with attendance of roughly 50 million. In 2000 Premier Parks changed its corporate name to Six Flags Inc.

Key Competitors

Disney properties leads the present-day amusement park industry. In the United States, Disney World's Magic Kingdom, Epcot Center, and Disney-MGM Studios Theme Park, located in Lake Buena Vista, Florida, controlled a sizeable share of the market. However, the company's reach extends overseas as well. According to the International Association of Amusement Parks and Attractions, Disney operated 7 of the world's 10 most visited parks in 2001. Leading the list was Tokyo Disneyland, with 17.7 million visitors. Although Disney World's Magic Kingdom and Disneyland (both located in the United States) ranked second and third, Disneyland Paris came in fourth with 12.2 million visitors. Overall, Disney's amusement parks posted sales of $7.0 billion in 2001. In 1998 Disney added to its amusement park empire by opening the $1-billion Animal Kingdom in Orlando, Florida. In 2002 the company was moving forward with plans to open Hong Kong Disneyland by 2005.

Formerly known as Premier Parks, Six Flags Inc. ranked second in the industry in 2002 by using Warner movie tie-ins to boost attendance. That, and the fact that 98 percent of all Americans were able to drive to one of the company's parks, gave Six Flags a 20-percent attendance increase in the mid-1990s. Annual attendance levels at the company's 38 parks totaled approximately 50 million in 2001. Most of Six Flags' parks (29) are located in North America, while eight are located Europe, and one is located in Mexico. In 2001 the company reported sales of $1 billion, and a loss of $58 million.

By 2002 the amusement parks of Universal Studios Inc. had grown beyond Orlando, Florida, and Hollywood, California, to include international locations. Among these was Universal Studios Japan, which ranked among the world's 10 most visited parks with 9 million visitors in 2001. The company also operated Port Aventura in Barcelona, Spain, and the Universal Experience in Beijing, China. Busch Entertainment Corporation, a subsidiary of beverage giant Anheuser-Busch, is one of the leading U.S. operators of adventure parks. The company's nine parks, including SeaWorld Orlando, have more environmentally oriented themes.

Industry Projections

With the exception of 1994 when poor summer weather had a negative impact, the amusement park industry has achieved relatively steady increases in attendance since 1990. According to the International Association of Amusement Parks and Attractions (IAAPA), in the early 2000s attendance levels increased slightly from 317 million visitors in 2000 to 319 million in 2001. At the same time, revenues increased steadily between 1990 and 2000 and then remained flat in 2001 at $9.6 billion. In addition to weather, economic conditions and the availability of disposable income also are key factors affecting the industry. The weakening economy and terrorist acts of the early 2000s were a setback for amusement parks in 2001. According to some industry analysts, conditions were expected to improve sometime in 2002.

The IAAPA indicated that, in the early 2000s, several categories of attractions were especially popular at amusement parks. These included attractions that allowed visitors to become more involved in entertainment experiences by incorporating new sensory elements such as touch and smell. Thematic attractions based on popular movies and comic book characters, as well as an increasingly advanced offering of roller coasters, also remained popular. Finally, amusement parks were relying on new reservation systems that reduced the amount of time visitors had to spend waiting in lines to go on rides, as well as technology that allowed parents to remotely locate their children within parks.

Global Presence

In the early 2000s, the United States represented more than half of the industry's global revenues. As the U.S. market filled, amusement and theme park operators began tapping markets such as Europe and Asia. In Asia, according to *The Economist,* more free time and increased income was spurring a leisure revolution. Shopping malls have become theme parks, with more than 40 opened in China alone during the 1990s. Unlike their American counterparts, amusement parks in Asia often tend toward a cultural, historical, or environmental theme. Bangkok, Singapore, and Kuala Lumpur all would like to become hubs of tourism, and theme parks have figured into that future. In the early 2000s, Latin America represented the smallest market within the amusement park industry according to the IAAPA. However, as the fastest-growing market, it had considerable potential. Based on information from the IAAPA, of the 10 most visited parks in 2001 five were located in the United

States, four were located in Asia, and one was located in Europe.

Employment in the Industry

The amusement park industry employs mostly high school and college students and senior citizens as seasonal workers. Pay at amusement parks usually starts at minimum wage, and returning workers receive an extra $0.75 to $1.00 per hour depending on the number of years with the company. In addition, some amusement parks offer bonuses and other incentives to reduce employee turnover. These incentives include bonuses for working on the busiest days of the year.

Besides the standard jobs related to the day-to-day operation of amusement parks such as ticket and concessions sales, maintenance, security, and ride operation, amusement parks also offer positions for actors. In fact, major celebrities, such as Steve Martin and Teri Garr, herald from amusement park theater positions. Many amusement parks provide scheduled performances, giving actors, dancers, and singers an opportunity to practice their art and job security relative to other fields in the entertainment industry.

Sources for Further Study

"Asians at Play." *The Economist*, 21 December 1996.

Benz, Matthew. "Amusement Industry's Financial Forecast for '02 Remains Cloudy." *Amusement Business*, 7 January 2002.

Blank, Christine. "Parking It for Fun." *American Demographics*, April 1998.

Coulter, Dick. "Father of Ride Safety Program Talks State of the Industry." *Amusement Business*, 22 April 2002.

Emmons, Natasha. "Industry Looks to Second Half for Rebound." *Amusement Business*, 7 January 2002.

———. "Park Execs Address Attendance Issues." *Amusement Business*, 17 December 2001.

"EuroDisney Posts 77% Surge in Yearly Earnings." *New York Times*, 20 November 1996.

Frankel, Mike. "Welcome to Euro-World!" *Newsweek*, 12 June 1995.

Grover, Ronald, Gail DeGeorge, Robert Neff, and Stewart Toy. "Thrills and Chills at Disney." *Business Week*, 21 June 1993.

"Industry Information." International Association of Amusement Parks and Attractions, 15 May 2002. Available at http://www.iaapa.org.

Jensen, Jeff. "Movies Star in Connection with Major Theme Parks." *Advertising Age*, 27 September 1995.

Kyriazi, Gary. *The Great American Amusement Parks*. Secaucus, NJ: Citadel Press, 1976.

"Let's Make a Deal." *Amusement Today*, March 1998. Available at http://www.amusement-today.com/FramBody.htm.

McGraw, Dan. "America's Theme Parks Ride High." *U.S. News & World Report*, 26 June 1995.

O'Brien, Tim. "Parks Worldwide to Spend Record Amounts in 1998 for Improvements." *Amusement Business*, January 1998.

Apparel and Accessory Stores

Overview

During the decade of the 1990s, the performance of apparel and accessory stores fluctuated with the industry. Because the country faced an economic recession in the early 1990s, apparel sales remained sluggish during this period. However, most of the industry's segments began to recover by the mid-1990s as the U.S. economy turned around. The apparel industry continued to strengthen in the late 1990s with strong prices and apparel demand. Brand names and fashion also played a more prominent role in the industry in the late 1990s, since consumers became less interested in discount apparel than they had been earlier in the decade. By 2001, the nation's economy had taken a turn for the worse. Large numbers of workers were victims of unemployment, which has a significant impact on consumer spending. According to the *Daily News Record*, retail sales of men's and women's apparel fell nearly seven percent, from $150.4 billion in 2000 to $140.2 billion in 2001.

With a saturated market in the United States and economic growth in countries such as Mexico, U.S. clothing retailers began tapping new markets around the world in the mid to late 1990s. This trend continued in the early 2000s. Furthermore, changes in the makeup of the U.S. population spurred these expansions abroad. People aged 50 and over tend to buy less clothing, and in the United States the baby boomer generation started to reach that age. According to *WWD*, women, who account for 70 percent of all apparel and accessory purchases, tend to reduce their apparel spending by 20 percent around the age of 55. The *Daily News Record* indicated that in 2001, shoppers aged 55-64 reduced their spending on apparel by approximately six percent. This number was much higher (14 percent) for consumers over 65.

History of the Industry

Retail clothing stores emerged in the United States during colonial times. In those early days, stores were extensions of tailor shops. There were few stores relative to the size of the growing population, however, because owning a variety of clothes was considered a luxury. During the 1800s, with the expansion westward, clothing retailers were mostly manufacturers who sold their merchandise through catalogs. It was not until the late 1800s, with innovations in mass manufacturing and the growth of cities, that most retail clothing stores began operating exclusive of tailor shops.

Samuel Slater built the first textile mill in a locale convenient for sailors coming off ships who needed ready-to-wear clothing when they arrived in port. As the seamen could not afford custom-tailored clothing, tailors in port cities like New Bedford, Boston, and New York made standard-size suits for them to wear as soon as they arrived on land. These early garments were made of the roughest cloth and were also frequently purchased by southern plantation owners for their workers. The industry continued to develop as the demand for ready-to-wear clothing increased. The steady stream of immigrants to the United States, the Gold Rush in 1849, and the Civil War all stimulated the industry. When the Civil War ended, opportunities in the industry continued since people moving to newly-opened land in the West purchased ready-made clothing before they departed.

The invention of the sewing machine, the rise of mass production, and the increase of retail stores by the late nineteenth century led increasingly more people to rely on ready-made clothing as a reliable means of obtaining fashionable clothing. In the 1890s, ready-to-wear clothing came into its own, and by the turn of the century, ready-made apparel was available in abundance in the United States. By the 1920s, it was considered more fashionable to buy clothing from a store than to make it at home; and as the population continued to move toward urban and industrial centers, apparel and accessory stores spread across the country.

Casual and sportswear stores, a new segment of men's and boys' retailers, developed in the 1960s. Changes in lifestyle and increased demand for more variety in men's wear led to the decline of many tailored-wear retailers. By the 1970s, leisure wear was the fastest-growing segment of men's and boys' retailing.

Like other retailing that benefited from the country's growing population, shoe stores did well from the beginning of this century through the 1920s. The industry expanded rapidly as the economy strengthened and became highly competitive by the 1950s, when fashion trends changed and footwear styles grew more diverse. The retail shoe industry experienced another boom during the late 1970s and the 1980s, as athletic footwear sales increased dramatically along with America's infatuation with fitness and sports.

For many years, the department store and the downtown women's shop were the mainstays of women's wear retailing. Along with the growth of women's wear retailing came the increasing importance of fashion, and focused outlet stores like The Gap and The Limited began luring customers away from department stores. Retailers such as Bloomingdale's and Dayton Hudson department stores re-examined the big picture in 1995 and revamped their women's apparel collections in an effort to win back shoppers.

During the twentieth century, family retail clothing stores moved from small, individually-run stores to regional chains and then, in the 1990s, to nationwide chains of large stores. According to the National Retail Federation, the vast majority of family clothing outlets in the mid-1990s were chain stores.

Key Competitors

The leaders in the women's clothing store retail industry in the United States are The Gap, Inc. and The Limited, Inc. The Gap, founded in 1969, is an international specialty retailer specializing in men's, women's, and children's casual clothing and accessories. The Gap operated 4,200 stores throughout the world in 2002, including 2,966 Gap stores (Gap Adult, GapKids, GapBody, and babyGap), approximately 450 Banana Republic stores, and about 800 Old Navy locations. In 2002, the company's sales totaled $13.8 billion.

The Limited had 4,600 stores in the United States in 2002 and brought in $9.4 billion in sales. The Limited focuses mainly on women's clothing with its Limited, Express, and Lerner New York stores. However, its Structure stores sell men's clothing as well. In the early 2000s, The Limited was in the process of re-naming Structure to Express Men's. The Limited's subsidiary, Intimate Brands, Inc., operates Victoria's Secret lingerie stores, Bath & Body Works, and the White Barn Candle Company. Victoria's Secret experienced success in the 1980s by introducing a new approach to lingerie sales. The Victoria's Secret concept was originated by Roy Raymond in San Francisco. After studying the lingerie market, Raymond saw an opportunity to target men who liked to buy lingerie for their wives or girlfriends, yet were embarrassed to venture into the intimate apparel section of a department store.

In the early 2000s, Spiegel, Inc. and its Eddie Bauer stores remained one of the industry's leading retailers of men's and women's clothing. Eddie Bauer's retail and mail order businesses were growing rapidly. During this period, the company operated 560 Eddie Bauer stores as well as a number of Spiegel Ultimate Outlets and Newport News stores. However, Speigel's sales totaled $3.1 billion in 2001, a decline of more than 17 percent from the previous year.

Another industry leader involved in retail and manufacturing is Brooks Brothers, the oldest men's retail store in America. This company was started in 1818 by Henry Sands. Brooks Brothers was the company that invented the button-down shirt and the argyle sock. The company outfitted notable early Americans like Abraham Lincoln and Franklin D. Roosevelt and continues as the last retailer of truly conservative apparel in the men's clothing industry. As of 2001, the company also was selling apparel for women. That year, Brooks Brothers posted sales of $635 million, up less than one percent from the previous year.

The following retail companies led the footwear segment of the industry in sales in the early 2000s: Foot Locker, Inc. with 2002 sales of $4.4 billion; Payless ShoeSource, Inc. with 2002 sales of $2.9 billion; Footstar, Inc. with 2001 sales of $2.5 billion; Brown Shoe Company, Inc., recording approximately $1.8 billion; and The Athlete's Foot Group, Inc. with 2000 sales of $248 million.

Industry Projections

The men's clothing and accessory store industry includes many small, independently-owned businesses and dozens of larger chain stores. These companies carry different product lines, including tailored clothing, work clothes, and heavy outerwear. Stores specializing in men's clothing accounted for almost nine percent of all clothing store sales in 2001. Growth has been relatively flat in this category, with sales averaging $9.8 billion from 1992 to 1996 and $10.5 billion between 1997 and 2001. In 2001, sales totaled $10.6 billion.

Because growth rates in men's and boy's wear apparel stores were below the rates for the total apparel and accessory industry, these stores re-evaluated product lines and pricing strategies in an effort to improve their financial performance in the mid to late 1990s. Consumer demand for value- priced clothing caused changes in brand name pricing and marketing. In the early 2000s, one trend affecting this category, as well as the women's clothing category, was the increasing popularity of casual work environments. According to *Standard & Poor's*, the number of professional workers allowed to wear casual apparel at work increased from only 20 percent in 1995 to more than 50 percent by 2000.

Stores specializing in women's clothing accounted for about 27 percent of all clothing store sales in 2001. Growth also had been relatively flat in this category, with sales averaging $30.4 billion from 1992 to 1996, and $30.4 billion between 1997 and 2001. In 2001, sales totaled $32.8 billion. Although the weak economy had a negative impact on this segment of the apparel industry in the early 2000s, one strong category was intimate apparel. In *Textile World*, Vanity Fair Intimates President Ellen Rohde called intimate apparel "replenishable and almost recession-proof." Because of a renewed American spirit in the wake of the September 11, 2001 terrorist attacks against the United States, patriotic themes joined other strong fashion trends in this category in the early 2000s.

The family clothing store segment accounted for more than 47 percent of all clothing store sales in 2001. Growth was the strongest in this category, with sales averaging $37.7 billion from 1992 to 1996 and $52.5 billion between 1997 and 2001. In 2001, sales totaled $57.3 billion. This segment of the industry is highly competitive, and marketing research and sales promotions are central to companies' operations. Other factors affecting sales in this industry segment include national economic trends, regional population growth, seasonal factors such as weather and holidays, and dramatic changes in fashion and clothing trends.

While retail businesses of all types were expected to grow in the United States, family clothing stores had a slower growth rate in the 1990s than in previous years. Other types of retail stores, such as specialty stores, discount stores, and hypermarkets, took business away from this industry segment. However, while the number of stores has decreased, individual stores have grown in size, on average doubling both their inventory and floor space.

The children's and infants' wear segment of the industry consists of hundreds of small independently-owned shops and dozens of larger retail chains. This industry segment's sales managed to grow at an annual average rate of approximately 6.6 percent in the 1990s despite the country's recession, which negatively affected overall retail sales. Fueling this growth was a rise in birth rates in the late 1980s and mid-1990s, which increased demand for infants' and toddlers' wear. By the early 2000s, this demographic trend had caused growth in the number of retailers catering to children, including The Talbots, Inc. (Talbots Kids), The Gap, Inc. (babyGap and GapKids), Gymboree Corporation, and the Children's Place Retail Stores, Inc. Census Bureau data indicates that the number of children under five years of age will continue to grow through the 2000s, which likely will fuel additional growth in this particular apparel industry segment.

The shoe stores segment of the industry benefited from the widespread popularity of athletic shoes, which helped shoe stores through the recession that affected other apparel stores more drastically during the late 1980s and early 1990s. In the mid-1990s, the U.S. athletic footwear market stood at almost $11.4 billion and accounted for approximately 40 percent of all shoes purchased. Furthermore, this segment's overseas markets expanded rapidly through the first half of the 1990s. Overall growth in the shoe stores category has been steady, with sales averaging $19.3 billion from 1992 to 1996 and $21.5 billion between 1997 and 2001. In 2001, sales totaled $21.7 billion.

While the apparel industry as a whole faced sluggish sales in the early 1990s, miscellaneous apparel and accessory stores, which sell items such as belts, bathing suits, and sports apparel, continued to have slow sales even after the rest of the industry started to recover in the middle of the decade. Into the early 2000s, discount stores and home shopping have provided direct competition for specialty stores and have taken business away from all clothing stores, but especially from miscellaneous apparel stores.

Global Presence

As the industry moved into the mid-1990s, efforts to establish specialty retail operations abroad were beginning. Manufacturers of clothing and accessories were well aware of the opportunities abroad, and many had established joint ventures in foreign markets. The retailers, however, found it more difficult to penetrate foreign markets. The North American Free Trade Agreement (NAFTA) was ratified in 1993 to create a free trade zone between the United States, Mexico, and Canada. In the early 2000s, international expansion was still an important growth strategy for U.S. firms, which operated in a mature domestic market.

In addition, mid-priced U.S. apparel retailers were doing well in Japan, according to *U.S.A. Today*. The new trend in the Japanese market was a push toward affordable casual clothing and convenience. In 2002, Eddie Bauer operated a Web site especially for its Japanese customers. At that time, the company also had a strong retail presence in Japan, as well as in Germany and the United Kingdom, made possible through licensing agreements and joint ventures. The Gap opened four stores in Tokyo and opened its first freestanding store in 1996. By 2002, the retailer's overall international presence had expanded considerably, to more than 650 stores in Japan, Germany, France, Canada, and the United Kingdom.

Employment in the Industry

The U.S. Department of Labor reported that in 2000, the number of people employed in this industry was estimated at 1.2 million and that they were paid an average hourly wage of $9.68 per hour. Wages for those in the industry's managerial portion were somewhat higher, averaging out at $27.29 per hour. Family clothing stores employed the most people, with a workforce of roughly 464,510 people. The next largest categories were women's clothing stores, which employed 280,460 workers, shoe stores (191,430), and men's clothing stores (82,020).

Overall, the Department of Labor estimated that employment in department, clothing, and accessory stores will increase 4.2 percent between 2000 and 2010. However, many part-time positions in this industry are often available due to a high turnover rate. In addition, salespeople are often hired on a temporary basis during peak selling periods such as Christmas and tourist seasons. Other occupations supported by this industry include bookkeepers, accountants, and secretarial and clerical personnel.

Sources for Further Study

Arbitman, Jacob, et al. "Apparel Industry." *The Value Line Investment Survey*, 21 November 1997.

Borland, Virginia. "Shape of Things to Come; Part 1 of a Two-Part Feature Focusing on the Intimate Apparel Industry, Including Fiber, Yarns, and Fabric, as well as Forecasts and Trends." *Textile World*, March 2002.

Brady, Jennifer. "Analysts Predicting a Bang-up 2nd Half for Apparel Retail." *WWD*, 16 September 1996.

Chirls, Stuart. "Analyst Sees More Change Ahead for Domestic Industry." *WWD*, 16 December 1997.

Larson, Kristin. "Trend Outlook: Feminine Looks and Patriotic Themes." *WWD*, 5 December 2001.

Lazich, Robert S. *Market Share Reporter 1996*. Detroit, MI: Gale Research, 1996.

———. *Market Share Reporter 1997*. Detroit, MI: Gale Research, 1997.

"Occupational Employment Statistics." Bureau of Labor Statistics, U.S. Department of Labor, 24 May 2002. Available at http://www.bls.gov.

"Retailing: Specialty Industry Survey." *Standard & Poor's Industry Surveys*. New York: The McGraw-Hill Companies, December 2001.

Russo, David A., et al. "Apparel Industry." *The Value Line Investment Survey*, 20 February 1998.

Schneiderman, Ira P. "The $3.8 Billion Plunge; Skittish Consumers Sunk Men's Wear Sales in 2001, But Outerwear Beat the Trend." *Daily News Record*, 4 March 2002.

U.S. Department of Commerce, Economics and Statistics Administration, U.S. Census Bureau. *Annual Benchmark Report for Retail Trade and Food Services: January 1992 Through March 2002*. Washington, May 2002.

U.S. International Trade Commission. "Forces Behind Restructuring in U.S. Apparel Retailing and Its Effect on the U.S. Apparel Industry." Washington, 11 November 1996. Available at http://www.usitc.gov/332/ittrexmp.htm.

"U.S. Retailers Set Fashion Trend." *U.S.A. Today*, 18 June 1996.

Catalog and Mail-Order Houses

Overview

Mail-order and catalog houses serve the busy lifestyles of many U.S. citizens as well as the less mobile lifestyles of the aging. Mail-order shopping allows customers to purchase the whole gamut of merchandise: home furnishings, electronics, clothing, lawn and garden supplies, books, music, videos, and even groceries—almost anything practically saleable is available through mail-order houses. The industry includes firms who sell almost exclusively via mail, as well as those who rely on additional channels (including physical retail stores) for generating revenue. By the early 2000s, e-commerce was an accepted way of doing business. "Threesellers" were an emerging category of merchants who utilized catalogs, physical stores, and the Internet to serve their customers. Although catalog retailers initially were slow to integrate the Internet into their operations, almost all of the industry players had a Web site by 2002. Beyond general economic fluctuations, increasing postage rates were a key concern for mail order business. According to the Direct Marketing Association (DMA), catalog sales grew at an annual rate of approximately 12 percent during the latter half of the 1990s, reaching an estimated $111 billion in 2000.

History of the Industry

Venician book merchant Aldus Manutius provided one of the first mail-order services in 1498, selling Greek and Latin books via a catalog, according to Ronald Vanderwey in *The Journal of Lending & Credit Risk Management*. In the United States, Benjamin Franklin used catalogs to sell scholarly literature in 1744. As people moved across the country and began dwelling in rural areas, catalog shopping offered a convenient alternative to traveling long distances to shop at general stores. In the 1800s, catalogs such as Orvis and Montgomery Ward sprang up and started to flourish. Since 1856 Orvis has marketed fishing gear and, since 1872 Montgomery Ward has sold general merchandise. As railway transportation improved, connecting the East Coast with the Midwest,

FINANCES:

*Catalog Sales
1997-2000
(billion dollars)*

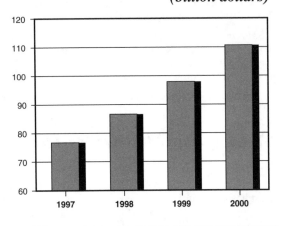

Richard Sears and Alvah Roebuck teamed up to offer a general merchandise catalog in 1887.

Technological advances of the twentieth century propelled the industry to even greater success. In 1913 the U.S. Postal Service began offering parcel package delivery and, in 1928 it introduced third-class bulk mail, creating an inexpensive method of sending packaged goods. The Diners Club offered the first credit card in 1950, ushering in increased demand for mail-order and catalog shopping. The credit card provided users with a convenient and safe means of payment and hence facilitated catalog shopping. Later, AT&T made mail-order shopping one step easier by introducing toll-free phone numbers and the computer era of the 1990s allowed some mail-order houses to offer CD-ROM catalogs to replace the mailing and manufacturing of costly print catalogs.

The 1980s were a period of rapid growth for the industry. During that decade, catalog sales rose briskly and the industry expanded by approximately 300 percent. Mail-order houses and catalog-based retailers continued to experience growth in the mid- to late 1990s, although sales did not rise as they did during the previous decade. Driving growth during the 1990s were advances in marketing based on knowledge of consumer spending patterns and demographics.

Significant Events Affecting the Industry

In the mid- to late 1990s, the industry turned to niche marketing or segmentation, discontinuing large general merchandise catalogs, which it relied on in previous decades. Instead, catalog and mail-order houses created small, specialized catalogs based on demographic and marketing research information. Sears got rid of its "Big Book" catalog in the early 1990s, marking the end of this form of catalog marketing and replaced it with 18 specialized catalogs that catered to the different tastes of its 24 million customers, according to Vanderwey. With rising postage and catalog production costs, general catalogs no longer offered a cost-efficient way to market mail-order products. Moreover, the increase of mail-order houses brought about a glut of catalogs and promotions, which failed to excite consumers and led to sluggish sales in the early 1990s. Consequently, mail-order houses worked to make their products stand out or match the buying patterns of their catalog recipients in the mid-1990s and early 2000s. This was more challenging for catalog marketers who sold products to business clients. Catalogs of business products, such as computers and accessories, often look very much alike and therefore lose their differential among potential buyers. Because of this, the need for creativity was paramount for business-to-business catalog marketers.

With the popularity of the Internet in the mid- to late 1990s, mail-order houses and general retailers alike set up World Wide Web sites to sell their products over the Internet. With millions of Internet users throughout the world, companies saw great potential for sales via this new medium. Initially, security concerns and tax uncertainties hindered the industry. Some users remained wary of providing their credit card numbers on the Internet, fearing hackers might intercept them. This led to the creation of secure servers that scramble confidential information. By 2000, e-commerce had exploded in popularity, and e-sales to consumers were estimated to be approximately $38 billion, according to *eMarketer.*. Catalog companies discovered that their print catalogs could be effective means of increasing sales on their Web sites and vice versa. This was good news for an industry that can be adversely affected by rising postal rates. According to the DMA, the percentage of industry net sales attributed to the Internet increased from two percent in 1999 to 13 percent in 2000. The share of net sales attributed catalogs declined from 80 percent to 68 percent during the same time period.

The industry also faced the challenge of reducing waste because of its approximately 100-billion advertising pieces mailed annually throughout the world. With growing consumer environmental awareness U.S. consumers voiced strong concern for the environment, calling for the reduction of advertisement and packaging materials and doing business with companies that held similar views on the environment. To shed this negative image and to save money, some mail-order companies started to reduce the amount of paper used by viewing on-screen before printing, verifying addresses before mailing advertisements, using recycled paper and recycling paper, and publicizing their commitment to environmental protection.

Key Competitors

Although approximately half of its sales come via the Internet, Dell Computer Corporation has achieved enormous success using mail-order techniques, ranking number one in terms of directly marketed computer sales. Headed by founder Michael Dell, the company established itself as the world market share leader in the early 2000s. Dell caters to consumers, as well as the business and government market. In 2001 the computer system company posted revenues of $31.2 billion.

United Services Automobile Association (USAA), a worldwide insurance and financial services institution headquartered in the United States, was another leading company in the mail-order industry. The company emphasizes telephone and direct mail sales to professional, well-educated consumers paid by the U.S. military. Given its primary clientele, the company is less susceptible to economic recession than most retailers. USAA is a leader in the use of advanced database marketing and management techniques. In 2000 the company's sales reached $8.6 billion.

Leading apparel catalog and mail-order retailers include L.L. Bean, Lands' End, J. Crew, and Blair. L.L. Bean Inc. issues about 14 different catalogs per year and specializes in outdoor apparel, home furnishings, and sporting goods. In 1976 the company was assigned its own ZIP code because of its significant direct mail volume. Led by Chairman Leon A. Gorman and President and CEO Chris McCormick, the private company also operates 10 factory outlets in the United States. In 2001 L.L. Bean posted an estimated $1.2 billion in sales, up more than nine percent from 2000.

Although an increasing amount of sales were made via its Web site in the early 2000s, Lands' End Inc. provides a number of different catalogs featuring its casual and outdoor apparel for men and women. In addition, Lands' End provides specialty clothing for children as well as housewares. The company markets its products abroad and has a physical retail presence in both the United States and the United Kingdom. Supporting Land's End's position as the leader in online apparel sales in the early 2000s was its My Virtual Model technology, which allowed shoppers to enter their measurements and virtually "try on" clothing via the Web. In 2001 Land's End brought in $1.5 billion in sales. David F. Dyer is the company's president, director, and CEO.

J. Crew Inc. markets casual and professional wear for men, women, and children via catalog sales, its Web site, and at physical retails stores in the Unites States and Japan. Chairman and chief designer Emily Cinader Woods heads J. Crew, which reported about $826 million in revenues in 2001. J. Crew had 112 retail stores and 42 outlets in 2001, when it was in the process of opening more than 25 new U.S. stores.

Blair Corporation provides mail-order low- and medium-priced casual and professional clothing for men and women, as well as home furnishing and electronics. A large percentage of the company's customers are older adults. In 2001, Murray K. McComas served as the company's Chairman and John E. Zawacki was its president, CEO, and director. That year, Blair posted sales of approximately $581 million.

Williams-Sonoma Inc. was one of the leading U.S. houseware retailers in the early 2000s. As a leading "threetailer," the company sold products via catalogs, physical store locations, and the Web. In the early 2000s, it operated five different business lines: Williams-Sonoma, Chambers, Hold Everything, Pottery Barn, and Pottery Barn Kids. In 2002, W. Howard Lester was the company's chairman and Dale W. Hilpert was its director and CEO. That year, Williams-Sonoma posted revenues of $2.1 billion.

Industry Projections

Total catalog sales stood at approximately $111 billion in 2000, according to the Direct Marketing Association (DMA). The DMA expects catalog sales to reach $155 billion by 2005. Though catalog revenues grew by 11.5 percent per year between 1995 and 2000, the DMA forecasts the industry's growth rate to cool down to 7.0 percent between 2000 and 2005. Consumer catalog sales climbed to about $68 billion in 2000, while business sales rose to $43 billion. During the last half of the 1990s, the industry's advertising expenses grew at an annual rate of 9.0 percent, totaling almost $14 billion in 2000. The DMA forecast this growth rate would slow down in the first half of the 2000s to 5.6 percent annually, reaching approximately $18 billion in 2005.

Global Presence

The U.S. mail-order industry has remained one of the strongest in the world earning billions of dollars per year and penetrating international markets. Nonetheless, several European companies have not only done well in their respective countries but they also have captured part of the U.S. market. Germany's Otto Versand Gmbh & Co., for example, is the largest mail-order company in the world, selling items via the Web and through approximately 600 different catalogs. In 2001, the company posted sales of $15.6 billion and employed 75,962 people. Otto Versand owns brands popular in the United States such as Crate & Barrel and Spiegel. The company's reach extends to 20 different countries around the globe.

Britain's GUS plc (Great Universal Stores) is another one of the leading mail-order houses in Europe and the world. According to the company, 66 percent of its sales come from its Argos Retail Group, which reaches customers via a variety of channels including the Internet, digital television, in-store, and via catalog. Argos' Kay's, Choice, Great Universal, and Wehkamp catalogs sell more products than any others in Britain. GUS markets its wares throughout Europe and South Africa. In

2001 the company employed 69,708 workers and recorded sales of $8.6 billion.

Mail-order shopping increased by about 11 percent per year in Japan since it was first introduced in the 1970s, according to *Nikkei Weekly*. Although 10 large Japanese companies control about 50 percent of the market, they employ out-dated marketing techniques such as sending out large general catalogs. However, more efficient international companies such as Lands End and Japan KK have begun to flourish using niche-marketing tactics as practiced in the United States. In the mid-1990s, U.S. mail order companies were eager to sell products in Japan, which then had a flourishing economy and a population that was hungry for American products. However, when economic conditions worsened in Japan in 1997, many U.S. firms pulled out. As conditions began to improve in the early 2000s, some catalog retailers began to combine their catalog offerings with Web sites aimed at attracting Japanese customers. Some U.S. firms, such as Land's End, also opened physical locations in Japan to support their mail order operations.

Employment in the Industry

Although the catalog and mail-order industry generally offers fewer employment opportunities in contrast to retail businesses with similar sales volumes and although advances in automation and information systems could reduce job growth as companies eliminate labor-intensive positions, the industry's workforce nonetheless is expected to increase through the mid-2000s. The industry employed about 479,500 workers in 2000 and the DMA predicts that employment will rise to 566,300 by 2002. Even though the industry's employment growth rate is forecast to slow down to 3.4 percent a year, it will remain well ahead of the country's general employment growth rate of 1.3 percent during the same period. According to DMA predictions in the late 1990s, the greatest job opportunities in the mail-order industry will be in the areas of computer programming and information system management as companies seek to integrate and streamline customer, inventory, and financial information.

Sources for Further Study

1999 Economic Impact: U.S. Direct Marketing Today Executive Summary. New York: The Direct Marketing Association, 1999. Available at http://www.the-dma.org.

Boyle, Lois. "Dare to Be Different." *Target Marketing*, June 2001.

The DMA State if the Catalog Industry Report, 2001 Executive Summary. New York: The Direct Marketing Association, 2001. Available at http://www.the-dma.org.

Edelson, Sharon. "Fashion Reevaluates Flickering Fortunes of TV Home Shopping." *WWD*, 8 November 1995.

Fishman, Arnold. "Mail Order Marketplace." *Direct Marketing*, September 1997.

Foch, Dirk J. "Why United States Cataloger Should Enter Europe Now." *Direct Marketing*, June 1997.

Goldner, Paul. "Mail Order Marketing: A World Wide View." *Direct Marketing*, May 1996.

Hoke, Henry R. "Editorial." *Direct Marketing*, June 1996.

Kiener, Sigmund. "The Future of Mail-order." *Direct Marketing*, January 1995.

Kutoba, Coco. "Japanese Buyers Let Their Fingers Shop in U.S. Catalogs." *Journal of Commerce and Commercial*, 22 April 1997.

Mussey, Dagmar. "Otto Expands Family-owned Catalog Empire." *Advertising Age*, 9 September 1996.

"New eMarketer Report Reveals Online Shopping Continues to Grow, Despite Downturn in U.S. Economy." *eMarketer*, 20 September 2001. Available at http://www.emarketer.com.

Sacks, Doug. "Hot Markets for 1998." *Target Marketing*, January 1998.

Vanderwey, Ronald. "Lending to Mail Order Companies." *The Journal of Lending & Credit Risk Management* September 1996.

Yamamoto, Yuri. "Mail-order Companies Home in on Markets." *Nikkei Weekly*, 7 April 1997.

Yorgey, Lisa A. "Far From Over." *Target Marketing*, June 2001.

Communications Equipment

Overview

The telecommunications equipment industry experienced a period of healthy growth in the late 1990s. However, conditions changed in the early 2000s as the economy weakened domestically and internationally and telecommunication service providers scaled back spending on communications equipment and networks. These conditions resulted in excess inventories and significant losses for many leading equipment companies. For example, Lucent Technologies, Inc. lost more than $16 billion in 2001 and was in the process of reducing its workforce by 39,000 employees. Similar cuts were evident at Nortel Networks, Limited, which announced plans to reduce its worldwide employee base from 94,500 to 48,000 workers.

In its *2002 Telecommunications Market Review and Forecast*, the Telecommunications Industry Association (TIA) indicated that in the United States, spending on communications equipment dropped 2.8 percent in 2001, totaling $167 billion. Worldwide, the International Telecommunication Union estimated the value of the equipment sector of the telecommunications industry to be $310 billion in 2001. According to the U.S. Department of Commerce and the TIA, the United States imported $39.7 billion worth of telecommunications equipment from other nations in 2000, but, it was estimated, those imports would drop to $36.1 billion in 2001. On the export side, the United States sold $27.8 billion worth of equipment in 2000 and it was estimated at $25.8 billion worth in 2001.

History of the Industry

The telephone was patented in 1876 in the United States by Alexander Graham Bell. His device consisted of electrical wires that carried sounds. Initial outdoor transmissions used telegraph lines. Some early telephone equipment companies had been manufacturing telegraph equipment and branched out, while the rest were entirely new companies created to satisfy the huge new market. The spread of telephone networks largely replaced the use of telegraph systems, and telegraph equipment has since become a relatively insignificant part of the industry. By 1877, the United States already boasted of telephones in 150,000 homes. In March of 1885, AT&T was founded and went on to become the country's leading telephone manufacturer and telephone service provider.

Prior to the industry's deregulation in the 1980s, AT&T held a monopoly in the telecommunications equipment industry. As a public telecommunications operator, AT&T controlled the U.S. market with the exclusive right to sell telephones and other pieces of telecommunications equipment. Customer communications equipment was considered part of the overall telephone network system and AT&T argued that it had to make sure consumer communications products were compatible with its system or that third-party equipment did not somehow damage the network. Until 1968, AT&T prohibited the use of non-AT&T equipment in the United States. Gradual deregulation of the industry allowed consumers to purchase their own communications equipment and made the U.S. market more competitive.

The wireless segment of the industry largely grew out of technology produced for the defense industry around the middle of the century. For example, Motorola, one of the giants in the industry, began in the car radio business. The company sold Handie-Talkies to the Army in World War II and later installed radios in police cars. Many of the companies in this category have been defense contractors. This technology did not reach the consumer markets until the 1980s and then grew rapidly through the late 1990s. After introducing cellular phones in the early 1980s, AT&T predicted that by 2000, about 900,000 mobile phones would be in use in the United States. By 1993, that prediction had already been exceeded a dozen times.

The telecommunications industry experienced a period of healthy growth in the late 1990s. During that decade, demand increased for products like facsimile machines, modems, pagers, and cellular phones. In addition, U.S. manufacturers saw their exports rise during this period as countries such as Canada and Japan increased their imports from the United States.

Significant Events Affecting the Industry

The most recent developments in research and technology that reshaped the industry have been in data transmission technology rather than voice transmission technology. Much of this can be attributed to the explosion

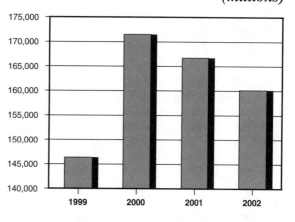

FINANCES:

Telecommunication Equipment and Software Sales, 1999-2002 (millions)

in Internet use, which began in the mid-1990s. Higher speeds and greater bandwidth are being demanded for transmitting computer data and are necessary for the transmission of video images for purposes such as video conferencing. Because of this, industry players began to build networks consisting of fiber optic cable, which allows data to be transmitted at fast speeds over great distances. To take advantage of similar high-speed connectivity on the short end, individual companies and users fueled demand for digital subscriber lines (DSL), high-speed satellite connections, Gigabit Ethernet connections, 10 Gigabit Ethernet connections, and cable modems, which surpass the limitations of traditional dial-up modems.

The terrorist attacks against the United States on September 11, 2001 also had an impact on the industry. In addition to concerns about data security, large numbers of companies and individuals scaled back long distance travel. Accordingly, in November 2001, the TIA indicated that industry segments involving videoconferencing, disaster recovery, network security, backup and network systems, and data storage, would see increased demand.

On the international front, by reducing and eliminating tariffs and duties, trade accords such as the North American Free Trade Agreement (NAFTA) and the General Agreement on Tariffs and Trade (GATT) sought to make foreign markets more accessible to the major telecommunications equipment manufacturers. As demand for basic telecommunications equipment slackens domestically, U.S. manufacturers can increase their revenues by shipping their products to emerging economies of Asia and South America. Furthermore, the World Trade Organization's Telecommunications Agreement of 1997 holds the potential for further expansion because it opens up the industry's major markets around the world to international competition. Although the agreement directly affects telecommunications service providers, manufacturers foresee indirect benefits from it in that increased competition will motivate telephone companies to purchase equipment for the new telephone networks and to upgrade their equipment more often to stay competitive.

Key Competitors

In April of 1996, AT&T spun off Lucent Technologies when it started to focus more on telecommunications services than on telecommunications equipment. Lucent went on to become a worldwide industry leader in the area of wireless, data, and optical networks. By the early 2000s, the company had operations in more than 65 countries. In addition to optoelectronics and communications semiconductors, Lucent's offerings include consulting services in the area of network design. During 2001, however, Lucent announced that it would reduce its workforce by 39,000 employees, 70 percent of which were management. That year, the company reported a $16.2 billion net loss on revenues of $21.3 billion.

Canadian-based Nortel Networks is another leader in the telecommunications equipment industry. The firm was founded in 1895 as Northern Electric and Manufacturing Company. It went on to grow from a manufacturer of emergency call boxes and telephones to a global provider of equipment for optical, enterprise, and wireless networks. Nortel reported a $27.3 billion net loss in 2001, on revenues of $17.5 billion. During 2001, the company announced it would reduce its employee base from 90,000 workers to 48,000.

The Galvin Manufacturing Company, started in 1928, marketed its first commercially successful car radio under the brand name of Motorola, which is a mix of "motor" and "victrola." The company officially changed its name to Motorola, Inc. in 1947, the same year the first Motorola television set was introduced. The Motorola set became so popular that within months of its introduction, the company was the fourth-largest seller in the nation. The company expanded its operations in the 1960s, establishing facilities in Mexico and Japan.

The cellular remote telephone system was developed by AT&T's Bell Laboratories in the early 1970s. Motorola aided in the design and testing of the phones and supplied much of the transmission-switching equipment. In 1989, the company introduced the world's smallest portable telephone. By 1997, it had become the world's second largest producer of analog cellular phones and the third largest producer of digital cellular phones. In 2001, Motorola reported a net loss of $3.9 billion on revenues of $30 billion. Like other industry leaders, the company

significantly scaled back its manufacturing and employee base. Motorola announced that it would eliminate about 33 percent of its employees. It also closed a number of manufacturing facilities and five of its businesses.

Industry Projections

Because of overcapacity, growth was expected to remain slow for communications equipment companies in 2002. Demand for networks was expected to remain low in the wake of the explosive growth that occurred in the late 1990s and early 2000s. However, this was expected to change by 2003 or shortly thereafter. According to the TIA, the U.S. market for communications equipment and software was expected to decrease from $166.7 billion in 2001 to $160.1 billion in 2002. After that, conditions were expected to gradually improve. The TIA estimated that U.S. spending on equipment would increase approximately 7.5 percent in 2003, about 9.0 percent in 2004, and almost 11.0 percent in 2005, when levels would reach approximately $208 billion. Worldwide, the International Telecommunication Union forecast the equipment sector of the telecommunications industry would reach levels of $335 billion by 2002.

The U.S. market for traditional voice communication equipment, including telephones and answering machines, became saturated by the mid-1990s. Following the explosive popularity of the Internet and activities such as electronic mail (e-mail), electronic commerce, and telecommuting, strong growth prospects emerged in areas of data communications, including network upgrades. *Standard & Poor's* reported growth for several key areas within the industry. Consultancy RHK, Inc. estimated that the optical networking segment would grow at an annual compound rate of 15 percent through 2004. In the broadband segment, Telechoice projected strong growth as the number of DSL lines increased from 2.3 million in 2000 to 17.4 million by 2004.

Although the U.S. wireless communications market experienced growth in the late 1990s, this leveled off in 2001 when spending on wireless handsets decreased from 2000 levels. According to Dataquest, Inc., in the wireless segment of the industry, sales of mobile phones increased at a compound annual rate of 60 percent from 1996 through 2000. However, unit sales decreased for the very first time in 2001 by a factor of 3.2 percent. The TIA forecast a compound annual growth rate of 12.8 percent in the wireless market as a whole from 2001 to 2005, when levels were expected to reach $172 billion. Although U.S. consumers slowly chose wireless communications services in the 1980s and early 1990s, they became much more enthusiastic by the middle of the decade. The number of wireless phone subscribers ballooned from 28.1 million in 1995 to 118.3 million in 2001, according to the Cellular Telecommunications & Internet Association. Industry analysts expected healthy growth in this sector through 2005, especially when third generation (3G) wireless phones, which allow data to be transmitted at faster speeds, hit the market. On a worldwide basis, the number of mobile telephone subscribers had grown to approximately 1 billion by 2001, according to the International Telecommunications Union (ITU). The ITU forecast subscriber levels would reach 2 billion by 2005.

Global Presence

By 2002, the global marketplace was opening up for communications equipment providers. The industry's leading firms all had international operations. According to the ITU, based on a 2000 world population of approximately 6 billion, there were 16.2 main lines for every 100 households and 12.14 mobile phones for every 100 people. Most countries had privately-owned telephone companies as opposed to state-owned firms. Competition also was increasing. For example, in markets where traditional "wire line" service was provided by monopolies, private mobile phone providers offered alternative services. In some countries, including Finland, many inhabitants only used wireless phone services. In terms of exports, the top communications equipment markets for U.S. firms in 2001 were Canada, Mexico, Japan, and the United Kingdom. On the import side, the United States purchased the most from Mexico in 2001, followed by Canada, Korea, and China. Data from the U.S. Department of Commerce and the ITA indicated that total 2001 exports amounted to an estimated $25.8 billion, and imports an estimated $36.1 billion.

Employment in the Industry

According to the U.S. Bureau of Labor Statistics (BLS), the industry employed 276,200 workers in 2000, who earned an average hourly wage of $22.16. By 2010, the BLS projected a modest growth of five percent, bringing the industry total to 290,000 workers. Manufacturers continually look for ways to reduce costs and improve productivity through development and implementation of labor-saving technologies plus mergers and acquisitions, all of which allow them to reduce their workforce. Consequently, the number of employees in the industry fell slowly but steadily between 1989 and 1996. In 2001, weak economic conditions and reduced demand from telecommunication service providers resulted in large financial losses and dramatic workforce reductions within the industry.

Sources for Further Study

2002 Telecommunications Market Review and Forecast. Washington, DC: Telecommunications Industry Association, 2002. Available at http://www.tiaonline.org.

Annual Survey of Manufacturers. Washington, DC: U.S. Bureau of the Census, GPO, 1996.

Benjamin, Matthew. "Dialing for Dollars." *U.S. News & World Report*, 14 January 2002.

"Communications Equipment." *Standard & Poor's Industry Surveys*. New York: The McGraw-Hill Companies, December 2001.

Communications Outlook 1997. Paris, France: Organization for Economic Cooperation and Development, 1997.

"Country Data by Region." International Telecommunications Union, Geneva, 2002. Available at http://www.itu.int.

Hill, G. Christian. "The Spoils of War: The Battle for the Wireless Market Promises to Be a Bonanza for Consumers." *The Wall Street Journal*, 11 September 1997.

"Market Survey 3: Telephones." *Retail Business: Market Surveys*, August 1995.

Occupational Employment Statistics. Bureau of Labor Statistics, U.S. Department of Labor, 23 March 2002. Available at http://www.bls.gov/oes/2000/oesi3_366.htm.

Semi-Annual Wireless Industry Survey. Washington: Cellular Telecommunications & Internet Association, 2001. Available at http://www.wow-com.com.

Telecommunications Equipment: Changing Markets and Trade Structures. Paris, France: Organization for Economic Cooperation and Development, 1997.

"The Long Morning After." *Business Week*, 14 January 2002.

U.S. Industry and Trade Outlook 2000. Washington, DC: U.S. Department of Commerce and McGraw-Hill, 2000.

World Telecommunication Development Report 2002. Geneva: International Telecommunications Union, 2002. Available at http://www.itu.int.

World Telecommunications: Equipment and Services. Cleveland, OH: The Freedonia Group Inc., 1993.

"Worldwide Mobile Phone Sales Post Decline in 2001, Study Finds." *CTIA Daily News*, 11 March 2002. Available at http://www.wow-com.com.

Communications Services

Overview

Mid-1990's deregulation in the United States brought about tumultuous change in the communications industry as companies began to diversify and merge, and traditional functional barriers began to erode. Consolidation and diversification continued in the early 2000s. Historically, the main divisions of the communications industry included local telephone service, long distance telephone service, wireless telephone service, cable television, radio broadcasting, and television broadcasting. While broadcast television and radio have remained for the most part in separate hands from the other services, providers across all other service categories have started to branch into one or more new fields since the mid-1990s.

By the early 2000s, communications services that centered on data transmission were beginning to take precedence over voice services. Additionally, the long distance segment of the industry, led by AT&T Corporation, WorldCom, Inc., and Sprint Corporation, was declining. The volume of long-distance calls was decreasing as other communication mediums like chat rooms and e-mail were being used instead of voice communications. Additionally, cut-throat competition resulted in drastically reduced earnings for industry players.

FINANCES:

*Telecom Services
Market Revenue
(million dollars)*

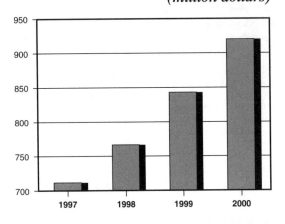

Consequently, many industry leaders were shifting their focus away from long distance and on to other, more profitable sectors.

Part of the competition faced by long distance carriers comes from wireless phone providers, which offer wireless long distance calling as part of their service packages. Unlike long distance, the wireless phone segment of the industry was experiencing explosive growth in the early 2000s. Revenues, which amounted to almost $24 billion in 1996, more than doubled by 2000, reaching $53 billion. Prior to 1995, annual growth rates of 40 to 50 percent were realized when the market was not as mature. From 1996 through 2000, this rate leveled off, averaging about 27 percent. In terms of market share, Verizon, Cingular, AT&T, and Sprint PCS dominated the industry, accounting for almost 77 percent of the market in 2001.

Not surprisingly, AT&T, the United States' historical communications monopoly, has been one of the biggest forces reshaping the industry. Since the dismantling of its monopoly in 1984, AT&T had remained the dominant long distance carrier. But in the wake of technological advances and deregulation in the 1990s, it began to forge a major presence in the cellular phone and wireless communications market as well as local phone service following the passage of the Telecommunications Act of 1996, the cornerstone of telecom deregulation. AT&T launched a consumer Internet service in 1996, and in 1998 acquired Tele-Communications, Inc. (TCI), then the largest U.S. cable service. Cable presented an ideal means for AT&T to disseminate a comprehensive communications package to subscribers: local and long dis-

tance phone service, cable television, and Internet access all simultaneously from the same line.

Other players in the industry didn't sit by idly as AT&T scrambled to become a universal service. Although they continued to provide most of the United States with local phone service, the regional Bells (RBOC) began to offer increasingly diverse services, including wireless communications and Internet access. Additionally, some RBOCs were engaging AT&T and other industry giants in the long distance market. More noticeably, local phone companies began to consolidate and the industry was rocked by a string of mergers. By 2001, RBOC mergers had resulted in four remaining players: BellSouth Corporation; Verizon Communications, Inc., which resulted from the merger of Bell Atlantic Corporation and GTE Corporation; SBC Communications, Inc., which included Southwestern Bell, Pacific Telesis, Cellular One, Southern New England Telecommunications, and Ameritech; and Qwest Communications International, Inc., which acquired U.S. West.

History of the Industry

Telecommunications   The first attempts at an electrical telegraphing system occurred in the mid-eighteenth century in Europe. American Samuel F.B. Morse introduced the first commercially successful telegraph in 1844. "What hath God wrought?" were the first words transmitted on the 37-mile pole line between Baltimore, Maryland, and Washington, D.C.

Alexander Graham Bell is credited with inventing the telephone in 1876, although fellow American Elisha Gray's work closely paralleled Bell's efforts up to that time. The technology was immediately put to use in sophisticated telephone systems by the National Bell Telephone Company (originally the Bell Telephone Company). The public embraced Bell's phone service immediately. By March of 1880, there were over 30,000 U.S. telephone subscribers and 138 telephone exchanges. By 1887, just 10 years after the commercial introduction of the telephone, there were over 150,000 subscribers.

As telephone services proliferated, a demand for long distance services arose. Bell established the American Telephone and Telegraph Company (AT&T) in 1885 as its long distance subsidiary. AT&T became the parent company of the Bell system in 1899. Subscribership ballooned to 3.12 million by 1907, boosted by an overwhelming demand for phone service from isolated rural Americans. Moreover, new management during the 1910s was able to drastically improve the company's performance. AT&T adopted a strategy of expansion, centralized management, and increased research and development.

AT&T began buying up independent operators in the 1910s and 1920s. In 1915, AT&T completed the first telephone line that connected the east and west coasts of the United States. By 1921, AT&T served 64 percent of the 21 million phones installed in the U.S. and owned many of the networks used by its independent competitors. By 1929, the company was generating annual revenues of more than $1 billion dollars. Despite setbacks during the Great Depression, AT&T service continued to expand at a rate of more than 1 million new customers every year during the late 1930s and 1940s. In 1955, AT&T laid the first transatlantic cable, linking its customers to Europe.

AT&T grew quickly during the 1950s and 1960s, meeting surging demand with an influx of new products, services, and technological breakthroughs. By 1966, the company had over 1 million employees and served about 85 percent of the households in the areas in which it operated. Despite pressure by antitrust regulators to cede its market dominance, AT&T continued to grow during the 1960s and 1970s, becoming the largest company in the world. By the early 1970s, it was serving roughly 80 percent of the phone users in the United States and providing 90 percent of all long distance service. However, antitrust suits filed separately by MCI and the Justice Department in 1974 signaled an end to the company's unfettered reign.

In the 1970s, antitrust pressures began to change regulators' attitudes toward AT&T. Many people felt that AT&T and its Bell companies did not have enough incentive to install new technology and improve efficiency. Furthermore, potential industry competitors were pressing for permission to compete with AT&T using proprietary technologies. MCI Communications Corporation, for example, wanted to compete using its microwave long distance technology. Although MCI received permission to offer limited service during the early 1970s, its 1974 suit was the regulatory turning point.

In 1982, after a lengthy court battle, AT&T agreed to divest its operations. The monopoly was broken in 1984, when AT&T was divided into eight "pieces." Under the Modification of Final Judgement (MFJ), AT&T became a regulated long distance carrier, and its 22 Bell Operating Companies (BOCs) were organized into seven regional holding companies: Ameritech, Bell Atlantic, Bell South, NYNEX, Pacific Telesis, Southwestern Bell, and US West. Among other results of industry deregulation, competitors were allowed to enter the long distance service industry.

Television and Radio   Radio was the first broadcasting medium. The first U.S. radio station was KDKA in Pittsburgh, which began operating in 1919. The concept of using radio waves to broadcast information and entertainment spread quickly, and by 1922, 570 licensed stations operated in America. With this emerged the idea of networking, in which stations form affiliations to broadcast programs simultaneously. In 1926, the National Broadcasting Company (NBC) was established with two networks of 24 radio stations under its parent

company RCA. By 1928, Columbia Broadcasting Systems (CBS) had established a network of 16 stations.

The next decades continued with a slow and steady increase in the number of radio stations operating, and by 1945, 95 percent of all homes in America had radio. The end of the 1940s saw an emerging interest in television, however, which began to erode radio's audience.

Television evolved almost directly out of the radio industry, and many of the same companies that had stakes in the radio business were early players in television. Nonetheless, television's presence had a negative impact on the radio industry's expectations for growth and the formats of radio programs. Across America, many radio stations owners sold their stations. Others kept their stations but sold their large studios intended for staged performances. Radio stations changed their format during the 1950s from presenting story and news programs, which were more graphically presented on television, to mostly music. The 1950s also saw the development of smaller and more portable radios that helped sustain audiences.

The 1970s and 1980s saw a change from AM to FM stations, as FM stations started to offer programming similar to AM and had better sound quality. By the mid-1980s, FM radio had taken over much of AM's audiences and held 70 percent of the nation's radio listeners.

Also beginning in the 1970s and flourishing in the 1980s were cable television services, which featured alternative programming to the broadcast networks and, in some places, clearer picture transmission. By the mid-1980s, cable began to take a measurable share of the big three broadcast networks' business. During the 1978/79 season, ABC, CBS, and NBC had a 91 percent share of the prime time television audience, but by 1986/87, that figure had dropped to 75 percent, and it fell further to 61 percent in 1993/1994.

Significant Events Affecting the Industry

The 1996 Telecommunications Act heralded the most sweeping changes to affect the industry since the 1984 divestiture of AT&T. The legislation impacted virtually every corner of the communications industry, including local and long distance phone service, the Internet, and broadcasting. The major provisions of the legislation were to promote healthy competition in the broader industry in order to reduce prices and improve the quality of services. In effect, it ended the formal separation between local phone services, long distance services, and cable system operators, although companies still needed to meet certain criteria in order to participate in all markets. Restrictions on radio station ownership were also eased, and in a separate measure around the same time, the FCC began to allow television networks to engage in program syndication, a business they weren't allowed to enter previously. The wireless industry was relatively unregulated from the start, allowing local and long distance firms to also offer cellular, paging, and personal communications services (PCS), and thus deregulation had minimal impact on that segment.

By the early 2000s, the legislation's effects were still being felt as industry consolidation and diversification continued. While the act made it possible for firms within the industry to branch out and generate revenue in new segments, it also has resulted in smaller market shares and lower profit margins across the board.

Key Competitors

AT&T Corporation AT&T Corporation, originally the American Telephone & Telegraph Company, was the heir to the Bell monopoly founded by Alexander Graham Bell. Historically, AT&T participated in all aspects of the telecommunications industry, including local and long distance service, equipment manufacturing, network management, and phone directory publishing. After the spin-off of the Baby Bells in 1984, AT&T remained the country's largest long distance carrier, a title it never relinquished as of the early 2000s despite encroachments on its market share by competitors like Sprint and WorldCom.

Following a brief stint at computer manufacturing in the early 1990s with its acquisition of NCR, AT&T refocused in the mid-1990s on telecommunications services business. Under the aegis of AT&T Wireless, it acquired McCaw Cellular Communications, the largest U.S. cellular service, in 1994. This purchase gave AT&T a strong position in the rapidly growing wireless communications market. In 1996, it launched its WorldNet Internet access service and spun off NCR and its equipment arm, Lucent Technologies. Under the leadership of a new CEO, AT&T stunned the industry when it announced in 1998 its plans to bring Tele-Communications, Inc. (TCI) into the fold for $48 billion. In October 2000, the company announced a major restructuring plan in which AT&T would be split into four separate, publicly-held companies operating under the AT&T brand name. The initiative was expected to be complete in 2002. By July of 2001, the firm had spun off AT&T Wireless. Early in 2002, plans were in place to sell AT&T Broadband to Comcast as part of the restructuring. In 2001, AT&T generated $52.6 billion in revenues, the largest percentage of which ($28.0 billion) came from its AT&T Business unit, followed by AT&T Consumer ($15.1 billion), and AT&T Broadband ($9.8 billion).

SBC Communications, Inc. SBC Communications, Inc. is a direct result of the mid-1990s deregulation. It was formed when Southwestern Bell, one of the seven RBOCs formed at AT&T's break-up, went on a buying spree to acquire a diverse set of communications businesses. Its highest-profile acquisitions included Pacific Telesis and Ameritech, two fellow Baby Bells serving the West Coast and the Midwest respectively. In addition to being a local service giant, SBC also has holdings through its various subsidiaries in cable television, Internet access, and wireless services. As the nation's number-one provider, SBC leads the way in the area of high-speed (DSL) Internet access. The company's Cingular Wireless subsidiary, a joint venture with BellSouth in which SBC holds a 60 percent interest, is the United States' second-largest cellular phone service after Verizon Wireless. In 2001, the company had revenues of $45.9 billion.

Verizon Communications, Inc. Verizon Communications, Inc. is the result of Bell Atlantic's 2000 merger with GTE Corporation. Prior to that purchase, Bell Atlantic was the active suitor to several of the industry's largest companies. The company explored a merger with TCI as early as 1994, but it never happened. Bell Atlantic merged with fellow Baby Bell NYNEX in 1997. With 2001 revenues of $67 billion, Verizon is the nation's top local phone service provider and the leading global provider of both printed and online telephone directory data. Additionally, the company's Verizon Wireless subsidiary is the top U.S. wireless phone company with more than 29 million subscribers and coverage that reaches 90 percent of the U.S. population.

Industry Projections

Some of the fastest growth will be felt in newer technology segments where data transmission is the focal point. While this applies to fixed wire-line broadband services, some of the strongest potential exists within the wireless segment, where third-generation (3G) wireless will allow for the transmission of data and video to and from a wide range of wireless devices including phones and personal digital assistants. According to Standard & Poor's, most of the U.S. wireless providers were expected to have 3G strategies in place by the end of 2002. In terms of future revenue growth, Standard & Poor's further expects that wireless voice services will play second fiddle to wireless data transmission by 2005. Beyond these devices, satellite TV service also is a strong growth area, which extends beyond programming and involves high-speed wireless Internet services. Within this segment of the communications services industry, consolidation continues to occur, both domestically and abroad.

Global Presence

All of the leading U.S. telecoms and many of the top broadcasting companies have interests in foreign communications ventures. These often take the form of holding stakes in foreign-based services. As an example of the global reach U.S. telecommunication firms have, Verizon's service offerings extend across the globe to approximately 45 different countries. Additionally, the company operates the longest undersea fiber optic cable, known as FLAG. These kinds of activities have been encouraged by a worldwide liberalization of trade in services under new multilateral trade agreements of the 1990s. Telecommunications markets throughout the world were slated to become increasingly open to competition in the first years of the twenty-first century, and Asia and Latin America held the greatest potential for expansion-minded U.S. firms.

In the early 2000s, the wireless segment continued to have a large impact internationally, especially in Europe. In some nations (including Japan and Finland), wireless adoption rates exceeded those for traditional phone service. Because their attention had been devoted mainly to the United States, U.S. wireless providers were slow to branch out abroad. Worldwide, the leading wireless providers include Japan's NTT DoCoMo and UK-based Vodafone, plc.

Employment in the Industry

Workforces in the communications industry were hit hard in the 1980s and early 1990s by companies' implementation of technology that supplanted human jobs and by restructuring initiatives that attempted to make companies more profitable. Nonetheless, the industry's fast sales growth during the 1990s helped turn around the employment situation, and the number of workers actually rose again. In 2000, as reported by the U.S. Bureau of Labor Statistics, the entire telephone communications industry employed 1.13 million workers, a number that was expected to grow by more than 12 percent by 2010. The radio and television broadcasting industry employed 255,300, and cable and other pay television operations employed 215,800 workers. Although the radio and television broadcasting segment was expected to grow by almost 10 percent by 2010, the most explosive growth was forecast in cable and pay TV, which was expected to grow almost 51 percent.

Sources for Further Study

"AT&T to Create Family of Four New Companies; Company to Offer to Exchange AT&T Common Stock for AT&T Wireless Stock." AT&T Corporation, 25 October 2000. Available at http://www.att.com.

"Bell Atlantic Reported Set to Acquire GTE for $52.8 Billion." *New York Times*, 28 July 1998.

"Occupational Employment Statistics." Bureau of Labor Statistics, U.S. Department of Labor, 21 April 2002. Available at http://www.bls.gov.

Standard & Poor's Industry Surveys. New York: Standard & Poor's, 2001.

"Telecommunications Services." *U.S. Industry and Trade Outlook.* New York: McGraw-Hill and U.S. Department of Commerce, 1998.

Thrasher, B. Holt, and Robert McNamara. "How Merger Mania Has Redefined the Communications Landscape." *Telecommunications*, October 1996.

Computers and Office Equipment

Overview

The realm of office equipment has been transformed by computers, first as high-end mainframe systems in the

FINANCES:

Total Value of Shipments of Computers and Office and Accounting Machines, 1997-2000 (billion dollars)

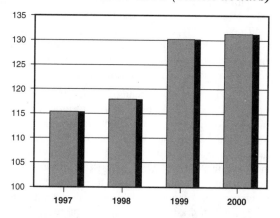

1960s and 1970s and then as desktop workstations and personal computers in the 1980s, 1990s, and 2000s. Computers became essential office tools as they became more affordable and powerful. Equally important to the ascent of computers has been the development of powerful productivity software that simplified and automated common tasks.

While computers have had the highest profile among office equipment, the industry still produces numerous other devices that are required in modern office settings. These range from relatively low-tech tools like postage meters to letter-handling machinery, fax machines, and adding machines. However, one significant type of office machine, the photocopier, is normally considered part of the photographic equipment industry and is thus excluded from this discussion (see the separate entry entitled "Photographic Equipment and Supplies").

In 2000, computers and peripherals accounted for about 95 percent of the U.S. industry's $131 billion in annual sales. Important accessories and peripheral devices include displays, printers, removable storage drives, and multimedia accessories.

History of the Industry

The business machine industry emerged from the Industrial Revolution in the latter part of the nineteenth century. As the need to record and manage business information grew, several products, including the typewriter, were developed to meet demands. Although the typewriter was invented in 1714 by London engineer Henry Mill, the most famous devices were developed in the late nineteenth century. The Remington typewriter, first offered to the public in 1874, was one of the more popular early machines.

The first electromechanical typewriter was invented by Thomas Edison in 1872, although practical application of this device did not occur until the twentieth century. One of the first electric models, the Electromatic, was purchased by International Business Machines in 1933; after World War II, several other companies introduced electric typewriters. During the postwar era, the business machine industry flourished. A booming economy and new technology soon prompted the development of a plethora of labor-saving devices.

Although an early version of the facsimile machine was introduced in 1843 by Scottish inventor Alexander Bain, this device did not have any practical application in the United States until 1925. That year, the American Telephone & Telegraph Company introduced a wire-photo service. The following year, RCA opened the first transatlantic radiophoto circuit for commercial use, which used fax technology. Advances in production technology, which drastically reduced the price of fax machines, made them available to the general public during the late 1970s and 1980s.

While dictation machines also gained widespread public acceptance during the mid-twentieth century, the invention of the integrated circuit in the 1960s brought hand-held recording devices into the professional mainstream. Dictaphones remained the primary means of recording information for doctors, lawyers, and business executives throughout the 1970s and much of the 1980s. The advent of personal computers, notebook computers, and cellular telephone technology adversely affected sales of dictation equipment in the 1980s, and by the early 1990s, dictation machines were largely being replaced with machines featuring alternative technologies.

As increasingly inexpensive computer and cellular technology was rendering dictaphones and typewriters obsolete, many business machine companies struggled to adapt to evolving market demands. Nevertheless, technological advances were opening new markets for other miscellaneous business machines—particularly postal equipment, in demand due to increased postal volume and new postal requirements for addresses.

Meanwhile, computers had first become commercially viable in the early 1950s. The UNIVAC system, developed for the U.S. Bureau of the Census, and a similar system used by the General Electric Company, were two of the first commercially viable computers put into use. By the end of the 1950s, business, government, and scientific communities began to view the computer as a dependable and potentially effective tool for an enormous variety of tasks.

Timesharing systems, pioneered at the Massachusetts Institute of Technology, allowed public and private entities to gain extensive access to large, expensive mainframe computer systems in the 1960s. Timesharing allowed several users at remote locations to simultaneously use a single machine. Users were charged for the amount of time that they were actually connected to the computer by cables or telephone lines. Although timeshare technology was first used primarily for scientific and technical endeavors, business and industry participants soon learned that they, too, could benefit from access to centralized processors.

By the end of the 1960s, the computer industry was poised for rapid growth. Computers in the 1960s were already up to 100 times faster than their counterparts of the 1950s, and computer memory and speed continued to rise quickly. Furthermore, the first minicomputer was installed in 1965, breaking ground for an entirely new segment of the industry. The number of digital computers increased from less than 15 in 1950 to over 40,000 by the late 1960s. Going into the 1970s, though, all sectors of society were beginning to seek the computational power offered by supercomputers and mainframes to handle labor-intensive tasks. In addition, industry leaders were continually striving to expand their market by increasing computer access to end-users, rather than only trained computer professionals.

Development of the microprocessor in 1971 allowed the entire central processor of a computer to be placed on a single silicon chip. This development led to subsequent rapid expansion and transformation of the industry. In addition to the proliferation of supercomputers, mainframes, and midrange systems that took advantage of new chip technology, workstations and PC devices began to emerge. By the early 1980s, over 500,000 general-purpose computers had been installed in North America. Furthermore, the market was growing at an annual rate of about 20 percent.

In the early 1980s, the computer industry consisted of several niches, each dominated by one or two manufacturers that had been the first to successfully exploit an opening in the market. IBM, Sperry, Wang, Unisys, and Digital Equipment Corporation (DEC) were among the many companies that generated immense revenues during the decade. For the most part, these companies succeeded by developing proprietary hardware and operating systems that effectively prohibited customers from switching to a competitor's product.

Manufacturers often enjoyed profit margins of 70 to 90 percent on sales of various mainframe and minicomputer installations. Demand ballooned throughout the decade as business, industry, and the public sector invested billions of dollars to computerize and automate information management, manufacturing, computationally intensive research, and other activities. As many mainframe companies settled into their respective niches, however, the rapid advancement of microprocessor technology caused a market shift that took many industry leaders by surprise.

Many industry participants failed to foresee the dominance of PCs, workstations, and some midrange systems. Within a period of a few years, in fact, technological innovations turned the slow and limited microcomputer of the early 1980s into a relatively low-cost, powerful, and speedy contender. Furthermore, by networking these smaller devices, users were able to develop cost-effective systems that could handle tasks that were previously performed only by mainframes and powerful minicomputers.

Significant Events Affecting the Industry

A development central to the proliferation of PCs was the move away from proprietary technologies and toward open standards. IBM's PC became the leading standard during the 1980s, and many companies began to emulate its standard. This was also made possible by the development of independent software, which ensured that applications and data files were compatible across different PCs.

Major advances and refinements in PC hardware manufacturing from the late 1980s through the early 2000s transformed the average PC from a relatively slow device with limited built-in storage capacity to an extremely powerful tool rivaling the performance formerly only available on larger and much more expensive systems. For example, a typical consumer PC sold in the early 1990s came with 4 megabytes (MB) of RAM, a 50-100 MB hard drive, and had a clock speed of 33 megahertz (MHz). By 1996 an average system likely had 16 or 32 MB of RAM, a 1-2 gigabyte (GB) hard drive, and a clock speed over 100 MHz. By 2002, the respective figures were more typically 256-512 MB, 60-80 GB, and 1.6-1.8 GHz.

As PCs grew faster and more versatile, the market for typewriters and stand-alone word-processing systems quickly eroded. The value of product shipments in the non-computer segment of the office machines industry has steadily declined from $9.9 billion in 1997 to $6.5 billion in 2000. Demand for word-processing machines, in particular, was decimated. From being nearly a $500 million business in the early 1990s, by 1996 sales had fallen to just $175 million, and this trend was expected to continue into the 2000s.

Key Competitors

Dell Computer Corporation was the PC industry's world market leader in 2001, when it posted revenues of $31.2 billion. Dell employs a direct sales model, whereby computers are made to order based on customer specifications. Approximately half of the company's sales are made via the Internet, making it the world leader in that category. In 2002 Dell employed 34,600 workers at: its headquarters in Austin, Texas; its regional headquarters in Europe, Singapore, and Japan; and its manufacturing facilities in Texas, Tennessee, Brazil, Ireland, Malaysia, and China. Although PCs account for about half of Dell's annual sales, approximately 20 percent are attributed to Internet server and storage systems, with the remainder

coming from portable computer sales. According to the Gartner Group, in 2001 Dell surpassed Compaq as the leader in domestic server sales, with a 23.3 percent market share. Dell's name is widely known to consumers, but a large percentage of the company's sales are made to business clients.

In terms of world market share, Compaq Computer Corporation is second behind Dell. The company, which had 2001 revenues of $33.6 billion, introduced its first product, an IBM-compatible PC, as did many other new PC clone manufacturers, in 1982. In time, Compaq, based in Houston, Texas, became the fastest growing publicly held company ever. Compaq has traditionally focused sales through dealers and distributors, but in the face of rising competition from Dell, in 1997 Compaq began expanding its direct sales efforts for the first time.

Compaq produces microcomputers in the desktop, notebook, handheld, and server categories. It expanded its presence in the high-end computer market through its 1998 acquisition of Digital Equipment Corporation (DEC), which was the industry's largest merger to date. In 2002 Compaq was acquired by Hewlett-Packard Company in a deal worth about $20 billion. The merger created a new industry heavyweight with annual revenues exceeding $85 billion.

International Business Machines Corporation (IBM) is no longer the largest maker of PCs, but it still is the world's largest computer company. In 2001 IBM achieved $85.9 billion in sales through a diverse product and service line of PCs, business systems, and service/consulting contracts with other businesses. More than 40 percent of IBM's revenues that year came from its leading Global Services unit, followed by hardware (38.9 percent), and software (15.1 percent). The company, founded in 1910 under the name of Calculating-Tabulating-Recording (CTR), got its start by producing punch-card tabulating machines. IBM grew quickly by stressing large-scale, custom-built systems, and by leasing, rather than selling, its products to most of its customers. Government contracts were largely responsible for the company's rapid growth during the 1940s. It was during this period that IBM developed the Mark I, the first computer capable of retaining a set of rules that could be applied to information that was input at a later time.

By the mid-1960s, IBM owned 65 percent of the U.S. computer market. IBM's mainframe models, the 360 and 370, generated massive profits for the company during the 1970s. Although IBM continued to grow through the mid-1980s, the company began to lose focus, and its hesitation in taking the PC market seriously was only belatedly realized as a miscalculation. Between 1985 and 1992, IBM dismissed 100,000 employees and restructured its operations several times, and by the late 1990s had regained relative stability.

The computer mammoth Hewlett-Packard Company is a major producer of PCs, servers, and printers, as well as a leading computer services firm. The company, which garnered $45.2 billion in revenues during 2001, runs the world's second-largest computer business behind IBM. The vast majority of HP's revenues come from computer-related operations. In late 2001 the company employed 88,000 people in more than 120 different countries. HP was in the process of acquiring Compaq in early 2002, which would dramatically increase the organization's size. However, there was some opposition to the merger, especially among members of the Hewlett family. In early 2002, board member Walter Hewlett filed a lawsuit to prevent the companies from joining.

Pitney Bowes, Inc., headquartered in Stamford, Connecticut, is one of the largest non-computer office machine manufacturers. The company makes mailing systems such as postage meters and letter scales, and also offers a variety of financial and other business services. In 2001, Pitney Bowes recorded $4.1 billion in sales. In December 2001, the company announced that it had spun off its office systems arm, which produced fax and copy machines, as a separate company called Imagistics.

Industry Projections

The market for computers and related equipment will continue to grow at a healthy rate into the 2000s, while demand for general office equipment will continue to stagnate as certain devices from that category increasingly fall into disuse. According to IDC, global sales of PCs fell by about five percent in 2001, but were expected to grow by three percent in 2002 and almost 11 percent in 2003, reaching approximately 139.2 million units. Within the United States, the trend toward low-priced computers, though some manufacturers frown on it because it's not as profitable, is likely to continue. Strong market response in the late 1990s and early 2000s to computers in the $1,000-and-under range is expected to couple with the ongoing improvements in performance to create a continuing supply of affordably priced computers with less-than-cutting-edge features and performance for general users. Also likely to fuel demand for new PCs is Microsoft's new Windows XP operating system, which has higher system requirements than its predecessors.

Global Presence

U.S. companies are significant suppliers of office technology around the world. Giants like IBM and Hewlett-Packard obtain a significant share of their revenues from abroad, where sales are often growing faster. The main competitors to U.S. manufacturers are based in Japan and include formidable diversified industrial companies such as Hitachi, Ltd., Fujitsu, Ltd., and NEC Corporation. The strength of such companies has meant that the United States has a massive trade deficit in computer equipment. Reaching almost $23 billion in 1998, this deficit was projected to exceed $27 billion by 2000. However, these figures don't reflect indirect exports such as when U.S. companies produce computer equipment in

other countries, a practice known as foreign direct investment. When this kind of investment is included in the equation, the U.S. trade deficit appears much smaller.

In the other office machine categories, the international market is much smaller; but surprisingly, demand for some office technologies considered obsolete in the United States, like typewriters, is stronger in other countries. Still, U.S. office machine companies face substantial competition from foreign-based firms for sales abroad.

Employment in the Industry

After a labor shortage during 1999 and 2000, the computer segment of the computer and office equipment industry experienced layoffs in the early 2000s as consumer confidence and overall economic conditions weakened. Analysts expected industry conditions to improve with the economy and as demand for newer equipment increased. Manufacturers employed 361,400 people in 2000, a decrease from 1997 levels of 374,600. Between 1988 and 1997, the industry shed 85,000 workers. Hourly wages in the computer and office equipment industry averaged $25.66 in 2000. Opportunities and pay are greatest for workers with advanced training, such as a computer science background.

Sources for Further Study

"Computer Equipment." *U.S. Industry and Trade Outlook 2000.* New York: McGraw-Hill and U.S. Department of Commerce, 2000.

"Computers and Office and Accounting Machines." *Current Industrial Reports.* Washington, DC: U.S. Department of Commerce, Economics and Statistics Administration, U.S. Census Bureau; September 2001.

"Computers: Hardware." *Standard & Poor's Industry Surveys,* December 2001.

Howard, Bill. "Looking Forward: Technology on the Way." *PC Magazine,* 25 March 1997.

"IDC Raises PC Market Growth Forecast Based on Strength In Consumer Segment." IDC, 13 March 2002. Available at http://www.idc.com.

Kirkpatrick, David. "Why Compaq Envies Dell: The Leading Maker Alters Course." *Fortune,* 17 February 1997.

Liebmann, Lenny. "The Fax of Life." *Communications News,* March 2002.

"Occupational Employment Statistics." Bureau of Labor Statistics, U.S. Department of Labor, 6 April 2002. Available at http://www.bls.gov.

Consumer Electronics and Music Stores

Overview

U.S. electronics and music retailing in the early 2000s was increasingly conducted by a relatively small number of so-called category-killer chains, such as Best Buy and Circuit City, which featured an extensive line of audio and video products, computers and accessories, and musical recordings. More specialized outlets like the music-only chain Sam Goody (owned by Best Buy) and the computer warehouse CompUSA also held notable shares of their respective markets, although non-store retailing options like mail-order clubs and Internet orders also contributed sizable revenue streams in these segments.

In 2000, the industry posted approximately $57 billion in sales, more than 80 percent of which came from radio, TV, and electronics stores. According to the National Association of Recording Merchandisers (NARM), sales of music products totaled $10.5 billion in 2000, slightly below 1999 levels. In *Informationweek*, NARM revealed that music industry sales slipped more than five percent in 2001, as this segment faced competition from the growing number of consumers who chose to download free music off of the Internet or make copies of CDs instead of buying musical recordings in stores.

Technological advancements have introduced many new categories of consumer electronics that scarcely existed a couple decades ago, and have made many existing devices considerably more affordable. As recently as the early 1980s, CD audio recordings made their market debut, and personal computers were largely relegated to hobby electronics shops rather than the centers of mass-merchandising outlets common by the mid-1990s. Other major product introductions that emerged relatively recently have included VCRs and camcorders, a spate of computer peripherals and software titles, cellular phones and pagers, and digital versatile discs (DVD). The development of such new categories has combined with continued demand for updated versions of established technologies like large-screen—and now, high-definition digital—televisions and ever more powerful computers.

History of the Industry

Music Stores   During the 1980s, the new compact disc (CD) format, with its greatly enhanced fidelity, completely revolutionized both the equipment and recordings segments of the industry. While cassette tapes had existed side-by-side with records for over a decade without overtaking the record format, by the early 1990s, companies halted record album production in favor of CDs. The popularity of compact discs showed no signs of abating. The Recording Industry Association of America (RIAA) noted that by 1993 almost half of all U.S. households had CD players.

Because of the greater durability of CDs and the much higher prices (about 50 percent higher than records during the years both were sold), Wherehouse Entertainment and other major retail chains began to move into the used record business, joining small independent music outlets that commonly bought and sold used CDs and tapes. This area had been the last bastion of the independent retail store. "Furious because they don't make any

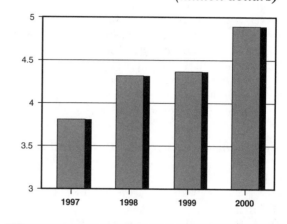

FINANCES:

Prerecorded CD (except software), Tape, and Record Reproducing Value of Shipments 1997-2000 (million dollars)

money off used CDs," commented critic David Browne in *Entertainment Weekly*, "four major distribution companies—CEMA, Uni, Sony, and WEA—stopped underwriting newspaper advertising for those stores that carry them. That move alone was expected to cost the stores hundreds of thousands of dollars in lost revenue."

Consumer Electronics Stores   The commercial sale of personal computers and easy-to-use software developed in the 1980s boosted the retail industry. Retail sales of computers were no longer directed only at large businesses or hobbyists; the target market for computer and software dealers extended to small businesses, schools, and individuals for at-home use.

Overall, however, the sales increases that were once seen in this industry dropped because of market saturation. Approximately 98 percent of American households own at least one color television set, and future sales growth is expected to be seen in replacement and upgrade sets. Similarly, more than 77 percent of all U.S. households that own a television set also own a video cassette recorder; consequently, this product line has been nearing saturation.

While sales have continued to rise slowly, future growth depends upon technological improvements. Long-term growth depended on such promising innovative products as home theater equipment, compact discs, large-screen televisions, and high-quality loudspeakers. Demand for camcorders, televisions, video cassette recorders, and autosound equipment were expected to decline as these technologies reached their saturation points.

There were more than 10,000 radio, television, and consumer electronics stores in the United States in the early 1990s and thousands more music shops. Many of these stores were owned by nationwide chains, such as Tandy Corporation, parent of more than 7,200 Radio Shack stores at that time.

A mini-shakeout of firms took place in the early 1990s as market saturation became more prevalent. Some companies began dropping out of the U.S. electronics market, and some chains were similarly closing their doors. The appliance and electronics chain Highland Superstores Inc., for example, pulled out of the Chicago and Midwestern markets after performing as the area's largest-grossing electronics and appliance retail chain. Competition in many markets continued to pit superstores against each other and led to increased price wars.

Significant Events Affecting the Industry

While some sales categories continued to enjoy impressive annual growth, electronics and music retailers reached the late 1990s a bit weathered from the rampant expansion campaigns of the major firms and the incessant price wars that beat down profits. As a consequence, a number of the industry's largest mass retailers, including Best Buy, Tandy, and Musicland, scaled back some of their construction plans and even closed down less profitable stores. Simultaneously, the music segment faced continued challenges from popular book and music superstores like Borders and Barnes & Noble, which threatened to lure away customers from conventional music chains like Musicland with their wide selection and comfortable atmosphere. The latest entrant into the megaselection fray was Amazon.com, Inc., an Internet-based book retailer that attracted hundreds of millions of dollars in book sales in just two years. In addition to books, by 2002 Amazon.com sold music along with a wide variety of other merchandise.

The ability to download free music from the Internet and burn copies of CDs using personal computers and stand-alone CD burners was having a significant impact on music industry sales. As reported in *Informationweek*, NARM indicated that CD burner ownership rates among music consumers totaled approximately 40 percent by 2002, and that despite efforts of recording companies to copy-protect audio recordings, consumers were still downloading songs at a rate of 3.6 billion per month. While music downloads and copying created challenges for music recording retailers, the same trend had a more positive effect in certain categories of consumer electronics. According to the Consumer Electronics Association (CEA), by the early 2000s portable Internet audio players and CD recorders were increasing in popularity. Additionally, consumers were buying special hard drives for their PCs, called digital music servers, which were used to store music they had downloaded from the Internet (in formats like MP3) or copied from audio CDs.

Key Competitors

Best Buy Co. Inc. is the largest U.S. consumer electronics store, with $19.6 billion in 2002 sales. That year, the Minnesota-based company marketed a broad line of electronics, software, recordings, and home appliances through 480 stores. Although office equipment, including computers, was the company's largest sales segment during the late 1990s, accounting for more than 35 percent of sales, this category was eclipsed by consumer electronics in 2001. Despite a sluggish economy, Best Buy was on solid ground in the early 2000s. Digital products, including DVD players and digital television sets, supported the company's performance. As the leading consumer retailer of computers, Best Buy launched its own store brand of computers, called Matrix, which lessened its dependence on the retail strategies of other leading PC manufacturers. Besides its acquisition of Magnolia Hi-Fi Inc. in December 2000 and Musicland Stores (including Sam Goody, On Cue, Suncoast, and Media Play) in January 2001, the company had plans to open about 60 new Best Buy stores each year into the mid-2000s.

Circuit City Group is Best Buy's largest rival on the national scene. With $9.6 billion in 2002 sales, it trailed Best Buy by a large margin, although it operated many more stores, with 630 that year. Circuit City is less dependent than Best Buy on office equipment for its sales, but that category was increasingly important to the company. In the early 2000s, it stopped selling appliances and increased its focus on electronics and office equipment. Circuit City also owns a chain of car retail superstores called CarMax, which it was planning on spinning off into a separate company in 2002.

A subsidiary of Best Buy, The Musicland Group Inc. is the United States' largest musical recording retailer. It operates primarily under the Sam Goody name, but also runs the Suncoast video chain and the Media Play and On Cue multimedia chains. In 2002, the company's parent was in the process of consolidating all On Cue stores under the Sam Goody brand name.

Although it faced sluggish sales in the early 2000s, CompUSA Inc. still ranked as the top U.S. computer retailer. In 2002 the company operated 220 stores. In 1998 it absorbed one of its leading competitors, the Computer City chain, formerly owned by Tandy, at a $275-million price tag. Two years later, Mexican retailer Grupo Sanborn purchased CompUSA for $800 million. According to *Latin Trade*, the acquisition was noteworthy because it marked the first time an American retail chain fell under the ownership of a Mexican firm. In addition to its retail activities CompUSA also sells directly to organizations, including schools, corporate clients, and the government.

With its ubiquitous chain of retail stores, RadioShack Corp. has struggled to break from its roots as a quirky hobby shop to compete with the electronics category killers of the 1990s and early 2000s. Traditionally its stores carried a line of electronics parts and accessories and a comparatively small assortment of assembled electronic goods, many of which formerly were of its own manufacture. The company was slow to infuse national brands and a wider selection of mainstream electronics into its product mix, causing it to lag behind fast-growing rivals like Circuit City. RadioShack eventually gave up manufacturing its own line of computers and sold off some of its other manufacturing operations. By the late 1990s Tandy had adopted Compaq as RadioShack's exclusive computer brand. As early as the 1970s the company had extended itself to more than 7,300 retail locations, most of which were small, crowded spaces in shopping malls. By 2002 it had scaled back its mushrooming store count, which numbered at 7,100. In 2001 RadioShack recorded sales of $4.8 billion.

Industry Projections

Two of the most important growth categories for the industry in the early 2000s were digital high-definition television (HDTV) and digital versatile discs (DVD). Both of these relatively new technologies were expected to witness fast sales growth through the early-to-mid 2000s. According to the CEA, digital TV products alone were expected to generate more than $8 billion in sales in 2002. By the early 2000s, about 10 percent of U.S. TV stations were broadcasting digital signals, and approximately 60 percent of the nation's homes were capable of receiving digital broadcasts. Many of the leading networks, including ABC, CBS, and PBS, were broadcasting varying amounts of programming in HDTV format.

The RIAA noted several key trends for the music component of the industry. Sales of audiocassettes and vinyl records continued to decrease, as compact discs remained the preferred format for music recordings. Along with the rise of music downloads via the Internet, demand for CD singles also continued to decrease.

Global Presence

The U.S. electronics and music retailing industry is surprisingly absent from foreign markets. While a number of top companies have operations in Canada, and some have made plans to expand elsewhere, most have little or no presence in other countries. This is consistent with a broader pattern in retailing, as relatively few retailers in any category are able to expand in the same way, for example, manufacturers might penetrate foreign markets. The electronics retail segment is even less internationalized than some other kinds of retailing. Part of the problem stems from supplier relations and transportation costs. Most retailers buy in bulk from manufacturers and wholesalers, and distribute their inventory from a system of distribution centers. When entering foreign markets, it may be costly or impossible to distribute merchandise from existing distribution centers. Moreover, retailers' domestic supplier relations may not yield products appropriate for foreign markets. For instance,

there may not be any labeling on the product in the local language of the intended market; in places like the English-speaking parts of Canada, this is not an issue. There are also usually regulatory issues to consider when entering new markets, and some retail practices in the United States may have different legal ramifications elsewhere. For these reasons, retailers that enter foreign markets often need to forge relations with local suppliers— or simply buy out existing retail operations—but the entire process of entering a dissimilar market may be subject to uncertainties and inefficiencies.

Employment in the Industry

Like most retail occupations, employment in the electronics and music store business tends to pay less than manufacturing and professional jobs. In 2000, the industry's average hourly wage was $13.50. That year, there were approximately 487,970 workers in the industry, an increase of more than 16 percent from 1997 levels.

Sources for Further Study

2000 Annual Survey Results. Marlton, NJ: National Association of Recording Merchandisers, 2001. Available at http://www.narm.com.

Annual Benchmark Report for Retail Trade and Food Services: January 1992 Through March 2002. Washington, DC: U.S. Department of Commerce, Economics and Statistics Administration, U.S. Census Bureau, May 2002.

Digital America 2001, the U.S. Consumer Electronics Industry Today. Arlington, VA: Consumer Electronics Association, 2001. Available at http://www.ce.org.

Forest, Stephanie Andersen. "Incredible Universe Lost in Space." *Business Week*, 4 March 1996.

Heun, Christopher T. "Retailers Want A Piece of Online Music Subscriptions." *Informationweek*, 11 March 2002.

"Industry Information." Washington, DC: The Recording Industry Association of America, 9 April 2002. Available at http://www.riaa.com.

Myerson, Allen R. "CompUSA: Revising Computer Retailing." *New York Times*, 29 June 1998.

Recording Industry Association of America. "RIAA Statistics." Washington, DC: 1998. Available at http://www.riaa.org.

"Retail Trade." *U.S. Industry and Trade Outlook*. New York: McGraw-Hill and U.S. Department of Commerce, 1998.

Deep Sea Transportation of Passengers

Overview

The North American passenger cruise industry, as we know it today, was formed around 1970 when approximately 500,000 people took overnight cruises. Since then, the number of passengers has skyrocketed, reaching approximately 7 million people in 2000. According to the International Council of Cruise Lines (ICCL), an industry trade group, passenger counts increased eight percent between 1997 and 1999, and then surged almost 17 percent between 1999 and 2000. Active marketing of package tours by industry participants supported these increases. Estimates from Exton, Pennsylvania-based Business Research & Economic Advisors (BREA) placed North American cruise industry gross revenues at $13.5 billion in 2000. However, the industry also has a significant impact on the overall U.S. economy by generating related business for companies in various industries including airlines, food and beverage, energy, and transportation. BREA estimates placed the industry's overall economic impact at $18 billion in 2000. This figure increased almost 16 percent between 1997 and 1999, and from 1999 to 2000.

The North American cruise industry, which includes the United States and Canada, represents approximately 88 percent of the worldwide cruise industry. More than 50 new ships were built in the 1980s and early 1990s, nearly doubling North American cruise capacity to 106,000 berths. In 1992, cruise ships operated at an average of 77 percent capacity. By 2000, 163 ships served the North American market with an aggregate capacity of 158,434 berths and capacity was on the rise, climbing from levels of 76 percent in 1998 and 75 percent in 1999 to almost 81 percent in 2000.

History of the Industry

Until the early nineteenth century, most oceangoing vessels sailed only when they had a full load of cargo and the weather was favorable. Passengers were secondary. However, in January of 1818, the Black Ball Line in New York began regularly scheduled service between the United States and England. The first ship, the *James Monroe*, left New York Harbor on time, despite a blizzard, and arrived in Liverpool three weeks later. The Black Ball Line proved so successful that other ships began regular service. "Packet ships," as they were known, were the first ships to concern themselves with the comfort of their passengers.

In the 1830s, steamships began to replace packet ships for carrying mail and passengers. The Pacific Mail Steamship Company, an American line founded in 1848, eventually came to dominate passenger service across the Pacific, but English companies dominated transatlantic service. One of these companies was the Cunard Steamship Company, Ltd., founded in 1840 by Samuel Cunard. Cunard was a Canadian who won the contract to deliver mail between England and Halifax, Nova Scotia. He and English partners formed the British and North American Royal Mail Steam Packet Company, which was renamed the Cunard Line in 1878. The first Cunard ship was the *Britannia*, which set sail from Liverpool on July 4, 1840.

In 1852 the *City of Glasgow*, owned by the British Inman Line, became the first ship to provide regular transatlantic passenger service without also having a contract to deliver mail. The *Glasgow* was also the first ship to be fitted with a spar deck covering part of the main deck. The spar deck provided passengers with a sunny recreation area in good weather and protection on the main deck during bad weather.

In 1879 another Inman ship, the *City of Berlin*, became the first passenger ship outfitted with electric lights. The Inman Line was also the first to carry immigrants to the United States on a regular basis in the low-cost "steerage class." Throughout most of the nineteenth century, passengers traveling in steerage slept wherever there was space in the hold and provided their own food or ate out of communal kettles.

An early example of organized recreational activities aboard an oceangoing passenger ship was aboard the *Great Eastern* in 1858. A commercial failure, the *Great Eastern*, owned by the Eastern Navigation Company, was the largest ship of its day. It also was the first ship with enough space for passengers to congregate on deck. On its maiden voyage, passengers organized a marathon and played ninepins. Most on-board recreation would be organized by passengers until after World War I, when deck tennis, shuffleboard, quoits, dancing, and bingo became popular ship-sponsored activities.

By the early 1900s, Germany had begun to dominate transatlantic passenger service with luxury liners that rivaled the most posh European hotels. The *Amerika*, owned by the Hamburg-Amerika Line, was the first ship equipped with an elevator. It also boasted an on-board restaurant operated by the Ritz-Carlton Hotel in London. Even the famed Cunard Line was losing money to the German competition, and American financier J.P. Morgan, who had purchased the White Star Line, was ready to buy the Cunard Line. However, the English government saved Cunard by subsidizing the construction of two new ships, the *RMS Mauretania* and *Lusitania*.

The *Mauretania* and *Lusitania*, launched in 1907, were the first "superliners," the largest and most luxurious passenger ships yet built. Aboard these English superliners, two cruise traditions arose: dressing for dinner and the shipboard romance. Cunard's advertising promised: "Passengers will remember how romantically the glowing phosphorescent waves curled back in the ship's wake falling forever in flakes of diamond and pearl. They will remember how readily the damsel of their choice could be persuaded to a secluded spot in order to observe this poetic phenomenon."

In 1911, the White Star Line surpassed even Cunard for luxury when it launched the *Olympic*. In addition to the amenities that had become standard, the *Olympic* was outfitted with a swimming pool, Turkish baths, and a tennis court. The ill-fated *Titanic*, which sank on its maiden voyage in 1912, was a sister ship to the *Olympic*. White Star never fully recovered financially from the sinking of the *Titanic*. In 1934, the Cunard Line purchased White Star and became Cunard White Star, Ltd.

The *Lusitania* also earned a place in history when it was sunk by a German U-boat in 1915. Although kept secret by the U.S. and British governments for nearly 50 years after the sinking, the *Lusitania* was carrying tons of munitions for the English war effort, in violation of U.S. neutrality laws. Considered unsinkable by many, the *Lusitania* sank in only 21 minutes after being hit by a single torpedo, which detonated the contraband cargo.

The years between 1920 and 1940 were considered the glamour days for transatlantic passenger ships. The rich and famous from Europe and the United States often took long, slow, luxurious, pampered trips at sea, which were captured by the newsreels to be shown to "common folks" in movie theaters. However, the depression of the 1930s almost destroyed the Cunard Line. Again the British government came to the rescue by subsidizing the construction of two more ships, the *Queen Mary* and *Queen Elizabeth*. The *Queen Mary*, launched in 1936, became the new symbol of luxury, surpassing even the *Normandie*, which was destroyed by fire in New York Harbor in 1942. Only 350 of the *Queen Mary*'s 1,100 crew members were needed to operate the ship. The other 750 catered to the needs of 2,100 passengers. The *Queen Elizabeth* was launched in 1940 but was soon converted into a troop carrier during World War II.

After World War II, the glamour of cruises faded. Jet planes replaced ships for those who could afford to fly because planes were able to cross the Atlantic in hours instead of the days it took by ship. By the 1960s, most passenger ships had become drab and dingy. In 1952, the American Line had launched the *United States*, which was the largest passenger ship ever built in the United States and then the fastest oceangoing passenger ship in service. However, low passenger volume forced the ship to be mothballed in 1969. Cunard also sold the *Queen Mary* in 1967, symbolizing the end of an era. The *Queen Elizabeth* was sold in 1968, leaving Cunard with only one ship, the *Queen Elizabeth II*. Cunard repositioned itself as a cruise line in the 1970s.

The modern cruise industry began to take shape in the late 1960s. Faced with declining demand for transatlantic passenger service, especially during the winter when the North Atlantic was stormy and cold, passenger lines began offering vacation cruises to warm-weather locations. Instead of serving as transportation, they were becoming part of the tourist and vacation industry, a trend that would culminate in so-called cruises to nowhere, in which passengers paid fares to simply ride on the ship and participate in its activities without ever docking in a destination port. Princess Cruise Lines, founded in 1965, was one of the pioneers in this emerging industry, leasing a converted ferry from the Canadian Pacific Railway during the winter months to offer cruises from Los Angeles to Mexico. However, many business historians considered Carnival Cruise Lines and its co-founder Ted Arison actually to have invented the modern cruise industry in the mid-1970s.

Significant Events Affecting the Industry

Carnival pioneered the modern notion of a cruise in part by accident. During the energy crisis of the 1970s, Carnival's only ship, the *Mardi Gras*, was forced to sail slowly to save on fuel. To fill the additional time at sea between ports of call, Arison added a disco, comedians, singers, and other live entertainment. He also encouraged less formality, more casual dress, and a festive atmosphere. The crew began to call the *Mardi Gras* the "Fun Ship," and Carnival began advertising that time aboard their ships was as fun and exciting for the passengers as the exotic destinations to which they were sailing.

The "Fun Ship" marketing strategy, adopted as a registered trademark of the Carnival Cruise Lines, was an enormous success and helped to quickly boost passenger counts beyond capacity. Carnival added more ships and soon became the largest cruise line in the world, capturing a quarter of the North American market and carrying twice as many passengers as its nearest competitor.

The cruise industry also received an invaluable boost from *The Love Boat*, a popular TV series that aired on network television for nine seasons beginning in 1977. *The Love Boat*, which featured a ship owned by Los Angeles-based Princess Cruise Lines, revived the golden era link between ocean liners and romance, and made the point that cruises were not only for the rich.

Key Competitors

Founded in 1972 as Carnival Cruise Lines, Inc. and renamed in 1993, the Carnival Corporation is the world's largest cruise operator. In addition to Carnival Cruise Lines, the company owns and operates the Cunard, Holland America, Windstar, Costa Crociere, and Seabourn cruise lines. In 2001, Carnival generated earnings of $926 million on revenues of $4.5 billion. The company employs approximately 33,200 people across all of its businesses, which include a number of regional hotels. The company's fleet included 43 ships in 2001, which it planned to expand by adding 14 new ships by the end of 2005. Carnival suffered bad publicity in 1998 when one of its ships, the *Ecstasy*, caught fire during a cruise. Although no serious injuries resulted, the event renewed calls from U.S. regulators for tighter safety controls on cruise ships, which typically skirt U.S. jurisdiction because they are registered as foreign ships.

Carnival triggered more favorable attention in 1998 when it completed a $500 million buyout of the prestigious Cunard Line, one of the oldest passenger ship companies in the world. The purchase gave Carnival a two-thirds stake in Cunard, which in turn gave it full control over Cunard's management, while Norwegian investors held the remaining third. Founded in 1840 by Samuel Cunard to deliver mail between England and Halifax, Nova Scotia, the Cunard Line included such famous ships as the *Lusitania*, sunk by a German U-boat during World War I, and the *Queen Mary*. Cunard headquarters were moved to New York in 1977 and to Miami in 1997. In the 1990s, Cunard offered cruises to more than 300 ports of call. Cunard also provided the only scheduled passenger service between the United States and Europe. By purchasing Cunard, Carnival obtained the *Queen Elizabeth II* and strengthened its presence in the luxury cruise market. The Cunard business eventually was merged with Carnival's other luxury unit, Seabourn Cruise Line, into a Miami-based division called Cunard Line Limited.

With earnings of $255 million on 2001 revenues of more than $3.1 billion, Royal Caribbean Cruises, Ltd. ranked as the world's second-largest cruise service. In 1997, the company acquired a smaller competitor, Celebrity Cruise Lines, Inc., which added four ships to bring Royal Caribbean's managed fleet to 17. By the early 2000s, the company's growing fleet had increased to 22 ships, and it planned to add an additional six ships by the end of 2004. Along with First Choice Holidays, in the early 2000s Royal Caribbean was part owner of Island Cruises, which mainly served customers in Europe.

The Miami-based cruise line was not without controversy in the 1990s. It was discovered that Royal Caribbean had dumped oil-contaminated water illegally off the coasts of Puerto Rico and Florida during the early 1990s and that the company had tried to hide evidence of the crime from the U.S. Coast Guard. In 1998, it pled guilty to obstruction of justice charges and paid a $9 million fine for the incident.

Formerly a subsidiary of the shipping conglomerate Peninsular and Oriental Steam Navigation Company, P & O Princess Cruises, PLC is the world's third-largest cruise operator. Princess achieved notoriety in the 1970s when one of its ships was used in the *Love Boat* television series, a history that Princess still featured in its marketing two decades later. In 1998, Princess launched what at the time was the world's largest and most expensive cruise ship, the $430 million *Grand Princess*. Two years later, Peninsular and Oriental Steam Navigation Company spun P & O Princess Cruises off as a separate company. By the early 2000s, both Royal Caribbean and Carnival had offered to merge with Princess, which posted 2000 revenues of $2.4 billion. At that time, the company's brands included Princess Cruises, P & O Cruises, P & O Cruises (Australia), Seetours, A'ROSA, AIDA Cruises, Ocean Village, and Swan Hellenic.

Industry Projections

As ships age and as cruise demand continues to swell, the cruise industry is engaged in an ongoing process of new ship building. New ships are generally built in proportion to the anticipated demand for their services, as it isn't profitable to run ships that aren't booked to capacity. While many new ships are built to replace older models and thus may be considered replacement capacity, over time, much new capacity has been added as well. In the late 1990s, the industry entered a period of rapid expansion, adding eight ships in 1997 and 18

between 1997 and 1999. From 2001 to 2005, the industry was slated to launch approximately 49 new ships on the world's oceans, expanding total cruise passenger capacity by more than 92,000 berths. In addition to growth in the overall number of new ships, an emerging trend is the construction of "mega-ships" that have greater capacity than traditional cruise ships.

Global Presence

While the United States and Canada account for an estimated 88 percent of the world's vacation cruise business, cruise ships call at ports throughout the world. By nature, the cruise business is thoroughly international since many cruise destinations entail cross-border travel. Added to this is the long tradition of national registry of ships, which is often done in countries with financial, legal, or employment practices favorable to the shipping industry. Thus the vast majority of cruise ships serving the U.S. market are registered in nations such as Liberia, Panama, or Caribbean countries. Critics charge that this practice allows cruise companies to evade stricter regulations in the national markets they serve.

Employment in the Industry

The leading cruise lines employ tens of thousands of personnel, most of whom work on board the ships. A diverse range of industrial and service occupations are needed to operate a ship. These include the navigation and operations crew, hospitality workers, activity coordinators, and maintenance and cleaning staff. Cruise lines also employ thousands of workers on shore to manage the marketing, booking, and other administrative concerns of the business.

Sources for Further Study

"Cruise Industry Posts 8.6 Percent Gain in 1997." Cruise Lines International Association, New York, 25 June 1998. Available at http://www.cruising.org.

"Cruise Industry Source Book." Cruise Lines International Association, 17 May 2002. Available at http://www.cruising.org.

"Cruise Lines Will Welcome Record Number of Ships in 2002, Taking Travelers On Itineraries Both Near and Far." Cruise Lines International Association, 17 May 2002. Available at http://www.cruising.org.

DuPont, Dale K. "Carnival to Buy Cunard Cruise Line, Owners of QE2." *Miami Herald*, 4 April 1998.

Fields, Gregg. "Cruise Ships Sail Away from U.S. Regulation." *Knight Ridder/Tribune Business News*, 26 July 1998.

Stieghorst, Tom. "Two Passengers File Suit Alleging Carnival Negligence in Cruise Ship Fire." *Knight Ridder/Tribune Business News*, 28 July 1998.

The Contribution of the North American Cruise Industry to the U.S. Economy in 2000. Exton, Pennsylvania: Business Research & Economic Advisors, October 2001. Prepared for the International Council of Cruise Lines. Available at http://www.iccl.org/imi.htm.

Eating and Drinking Places

Overview

The restaurant industry is an important component of the domestic and world economy. According to the National Restaurant Association, the industry was expected to achieve direct sales totaling $408 billion in 2002. However, with sales in related industries like agriculture factored into the equation, restaurants were expected to contribute more than $1 trillion to the nation's economy. Rising U.S. incomes and an increase in the number of single-person and dual-income households have supported demand for restaurants and prepared food. Carryout has remained a strong growth segment of the industry, appealing to people pressed for time who seek a convenient yet economical alternative to cooking at home. Coffee houses continued to expand into the early 2000s because of demand for gourmet coffee and the need for new places to socialize.

Restaurants and restaurant chains watched their sales increase at a moderate pace throughout most of the 1990s and into 2000. However, a slumping economy and the terrorist attacks of September 11 put a significant damper on growth in 2001. Real sales growth within the industry slowed from about three percent from 1998 to 2000, and to less than one percent in 2001, according to the National Restaurant Association.

In the early 2000s, McDonald's held its position as the world's leading fast-food restaurant chain. Among U.S. hamburger chains, the company held approximately 43 percent of the market, ahead of Burger King and Wendy's, which commanded respective market shares of about 19 and 13 percent. McDonald's accelerated expansion in the 1990s eroded its profits. The company's challenges continued in the early 2000s, when it faced a saturated market with more limited expansion opportunities, customer service problems, and a lack of successful new products to entice new customers and ensure repeat visits. Additionally, the company's "Made For You" program was largely unsuccessful, according to some industry analysts. Although Wendy's was third in terms of market share, it was more successful than McDonald's and Burger King in the areas of same-store sales growth and customer service, according to the *Chicago Tribune*. Starbucks Corporation remained the leader of the coffee house segment of the industry.

While the eating and drinking place industry as a whole continued to grow at a steady rate during the late 1990s, the bar and tavern segment (including both alcohol and food receipts) remained flat, and in some years actually fell. According to the National Restaurant Association (NRA), sales at such establishments hovered between $9.0 and $9.5 billion during much of the decade. However, by 2001, sales were projected to reach $12.8 billion and climb to $13.3 billion the following year.

FINANCES:

Food and Drink Sales (billion dollars)

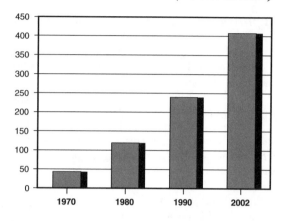

History of the Industry

For many years, the restaurant industry consisted primarily of small, regional diners and cafes. The industry has since grown from family-run restaurants and diners to the chain restaurants of today. Contributing to this growth was the increased number of single-person households, single-parent families, and dual-income families. With less time available for meal preparation, convenience became more important. Since the early 1970s, franchised eating and drinking places have almost tripled their share of the market, from 15 percent of industry volume to about 43 percent in the mid-1990s.

There were a couple of factors contributing to the expansion of eating and drinking places. Many people consider food and beverage houses easy business ventures, manageable by anyone who can cook or prepare a beverage. Therefore, an abundance of new restaurants, cafes, and bars emerge each year. However, half of these ventures fail or change management every five years, according to the U.S. Small Business Administration. Although the industry is still growing, aspiring eating and drinking place owners must recognize industry trends and market demands to stay afloat.

Most growth in the industry, however, is due to the increase in franchised establishments. The popularity of franchising stems from the parent company's ability to expand without as much expense, as start-up costs are usually paid by whomever purchases the franchise. The franchisee—the person or group starting the new branch of a restaurant chain—then pays the franchisor royalties based on sales. For the person buying the franchise, this is an extremely low-risk investment when compared with independent eating and drinking establishments, which do not have an established clientele that can be tapped. However, franchise owners trade flexibility for these advantages. Independent owners can plan their own menus, avoid royalty expenses, and run their businesses as they see fit. Franchisees are restricted by terms of the franchise agreement.

Significant Events Affecting the Industry

With a host of independent and regional dinner house and casual dining restaurants, the veteran operations such as T.G.I. Friday's, Bennigan's, and Applebee's started to recast their images and refocus their restaurants to differentiate themselves from the competition. Friday's began primarily as a singles' bar and evolved into a family-oriented casual dining restaurant that still has strong bar sales. Other such restaurants followed this pattern, attempting to offer something unique and trying to strike a balance between their bar and restaurant facets. Additionally, by the early 2000s, the difference between traditional family dining establishments and casual chains like Friday's was beginning to disappear.

Theme restaurants experienced stagnant sales in the late 1990s, after strong sales in the late 1980s and early 1990s. Although some theme restaurants continued to suffer from the lack of repeat customers, numerous other theme restaurants remained in the works, including a number of Copperfield Magic Underground in New York, Los Angeles, Paris, Tokyo, Sydney, and London, and Michael Jordan and Shaquille O'Neal restaurants, among others.

In the mid-1990s, restaurants and supermarkets introduced prepared foods for carry-out service or what they termed home meal replacements. These allowed customers to enjoy freshly cooked foods conveniently in their own homes without making an occasion out of the meal. This trend worked well with the popularity of VCRs, televisions, computers, and other electronic entertainment devices in homes around the world. It also suited the growing demographics of the country: more single-person and dual-income households that have little time for cooking meals. *Restaurant Business* reported that home meal replacements sales rose to $50 billion in 1997—up 13 percent from 1996—and predicted that sales would climb to $150 to $170 billion by 2005.

Key Competitors

Serving more than 46 million customers a day worldwide, McDonald's ranked as the largest eating and drinking place in the world. The company's brand name, maintained through aggressive advertising, was among the world's most highly recognized along with Coca-Cola and Marlboro. However, in the early 2000s, McDonald's was scaling back the percentage of sales that its franchisees devoted to advertising while competitors like Wendy's were significantly increasing their advertising budgets. McDonald's worldwide sales totaled $14.9 billion in 2001, approximately 25 percent of which

came from the United States. At that time, it operated about 30,000 restaurants in more than 120 different countries and was adding approximately 1,300 restaurants to its chain each year. In addition to its McDonald's restaurants, the company also has ownership stakes in Boston Market, Chipotle, Donatos Pizzeria, and Pret A Manger. According to McDonald's, these "partner brands" allow the organization to offer customers a wider choice of dining experiences.

Darden Restaurants recorded sales of $4.0 billion in 2001. In 1995, General Mills spun off its restaurant holding into Darden Restaurants, which includes four restaurant chains or concepts: Red Lobster, Olive Garden, Bahama Breeze, and Smokey Bones BBQ. Together they constitute the world's largest casual-dining restaurant chain. Red Lobster dominates the United States seafood restaurant sector with 660 units in the United States and Canada. The Olive Garden leads U.S. casual Italian restaurants with 480 eateries throughout North America. Bahama Breeze serves Caribbean cuisine at 24 locations. Darden's growing line of sports bar/barbecue restaurants, Smokey Bones BBQ, had 10 locations in 2001.

Burger King had 2001 sales of $1.5 billion and 11,400 units across the globe. The company is a private subsidiary of Diageo, the result of the merger of Grand Metropolitan Public Limited Company (GrandMet) and Guinness (brewer and alcohol producer and publisher), which was planning to spin off the hamburger chain in the early 2000s. James McLamore and David Edgerton founded Burger King in Miami in 1954, Pillsbury bought it in 1967, and GrandMet acquired it in 1988. Attempting to turn the tide of slower sales, in 2001 the company was in the process of introducing new and enhanced food choices to its menu, which had remained relatively unchanged since the late 1990s. In order to spread the word about these improvements, the company also began new promotional campaigns involving well-known celebrities like blues musician B.B. King.

The leading coffee house in the United States is Starbucks Corporation, based in Seattle, Washington. In 2001, the firm boasted $2.6 billion in sales, employed 54,000 people, and had approximately 5,400 retail locations. The company began in 1971 with one store in Seattle. Three entrepreneurs, Gordon Bowker, Jerry Baldwin, and Zev Siegl, founded the original business. They named it after a character from Herman Melville's classic novel *Moby Dick* who loved coffee, and they developed the now-familiar mermaid logo. Starbucks originally sold bulk tea and specialty coffee beans by the pound, and they did not add a coffee bar to sell drinks until 1984. The coffee bar idea came from Howard Schultz, who was the company's marketing director. Schultz quit the company in 1985, but he raised money from private investors and bought Starbucks from its founders for $3.8 million in 1987. The venture paid off for Schultz, whose personal fortune totaled $100 million in 1997, 75 percent of which came from Starbucks stock.

Industry Projections

During the mid- to late 1990s, the restaurant segment launched new products and services such as salad bars/dinner buffets, specialized menus (such as health food and vegetarian), and home delivery to attract consumers and boost industry growth. The continued rise in single-parent families, single-person households, and dual-income households fueled the growth of the industry worldwide, especially in mature industrialized countries. Restaurants reported that more than 50 percent of their revenues came from carry-out sales.

Although they remained nearly even in the mid-1990s, full-service restaurant sales were outpacing fast-food sales by 2001. That year, full-service sales were projected to reach $140.4 billion, while fast-food sales were projected to reach $111.1 billion. Miscellaneous food services such as cafeterias, caterers, ice cream and frozen yogurt parlors, bars, and commercial food contractors accounted for the remainder of the industry's revenues. According to National Restaurant Association forecasts, full-service sales were expected to reach $146.7 billion in 2002, and fast food sales were expected to reach $115.2 billion.

The coffee house segment of the industry took off in the early 1990s, with national chains such as Starbucks and Caribou Coffee spreading across the country as well as numerous independent cafes and regional chains cropping up in metropolitan areas. By 2000, approximately 5,850 coffee cafes were in operation across the United States, generating an estimated $3.95 billion in sales, according to the Specialty Coffee Association of America (SCAA). This represented an increase from the 5,000 coffee houses operating in 1997. Fueling future demand is America's growing love for coffee. According to *Nation's Restaurant News*, the National Coffee Association reported that 79 percent of the adult population consumed coffee by 2000, an increase from 1996 levels of 72 percent.

In the late 1990s, coffee houses also teamed up with retailers such as J.C. Penney, opening cafes in selected stores. According to the SCAA, the number of retail outlets selling specialty coffee numbered 12,000 in 1999. This number was expected to decline to 10,000 by 2003 and then increase to 12,000 in 2007, 15,000 in 2011, and 18,000 in 2015. In the late 1990s, the SCAA predicted that the industry's growth would crest around the year 2010, and that the number of mergers in the industry would steadily rise between the late 1990s and 2010. The SCAA expected industry consolidation to slow down around the year 2020.

Although the outlook for the bar and tavern portion of the industry was grim in the late 1990s, sales were rising again by the early 2000s and were projected to reach $12.8 billion in 2001 and $13.3 billion by 2002. Nonetheless, many hotel lounges have either been transformed into combination eating/drinking establishments or have been eliminated altogether and replaced by meeting rooms. Although they report that alcohol items have higher profit margins than food items, food was increasingly being emphasized over drinks. The decline in this segment's sales stems from greater consumer health-consciousness, stricter laws defining intoxication by blood-alcohol content, and less public acceptance of drunk driving.

Sports bars emerged in the 1980s and continued to grow in the 1990s and early 2000s. They typically serve lighter fare and have a family-oriented atmosphere, providing an example of industry adaptation to consumer health concerns. Another successful concept that was introduced in the 1990s was the brew pub. Although this is a borderline category since many brew pubs derive more than half of their sales from the food they serve, the brew pub and microbrewed beer generally have helped to revive both a beer industry on the decline and the drinking places industry itself. As of January 1998, there were 1,306 microbreweries, brew pubs, and regional specialty breweries in the United States.

Global Presence

The United States constitutes the world's largest market for restaurants and many of the world's largest restaurant chains started in the United States. The demand for American style food in other countries has presented a growing number of U.S. restaurants with opportunities for international expansion. According to *Restaurants USA*, Technomic, Inc. found that the leading 100 U.S. restaurant chains alone saw their international sales climb 8.5 percent in 1999, reaching $36.5 billion. This increase was almost two percent greater than sales growth in the United States. According to a report by McKinsey and Company, the entire food industry market will continue to expand, reaching $800 billion by the year 2005.

With demand slowing down domestically, U.S. companies have increased their presence across the world. Some of the top U.S. restaurants, such as McDonald's, take in a greater percentage of their overall sales abroad than at home. Nevertheless, chains like McDonald's, Kentucky Fried Chicken, Taco Bell, and Domino's have continued to add new units domestically and overseas. Furthermore, McDonald's led in the European and Japanese restaurant industries as well as the U.S. industry.

One factor that hindered progress for U.S. restaurant chains wishing to enter or expand in Asian markets was that region's economic crisis in the mid to late 1990s. However, by the early 2000s, conditions had improved. Asian countries represent a lucrative market. In the late 1990s, consumers in Japan spent the most per capita on restaurants and prepared food, averaging $1,670 a year. U.S. and French consumers spend about half as much, according to the *Chicago Tribune*. Because many Japanese people live in small apartments far from where they work, eating out is necessary and contributes heavily to the size of the industry. The Japanese restaurant industry changed dramatically after 1969, when it became possible for foreign companies to invest in Japan. As a result, fast food restaurants such as McDonald's and Kentucky Fried Chicken became popular, as did casual dining establishments such as Denny's.

Employment in the Industry

With an employee base exceeding 11.5 million workers, the restaurant industry is the nation's second-largest employer after the U.S. government, according to the National Restaurant Association. Because people over the age of 45 will account for 38 percent of the U.S. population by 2005, the industry has and will continue to experience strong growth since this segment of the population pumps the most money into eating and drinking places. However, with such a high percentage of the population over 45, the eating and drinking place industry faces a labor shortage because the 16 to 24-year-old segment makes up the bulk of its workers. The 16 to 24-year-old segment will remain small through the first part of the next century. U.S. restaurants reported that their applicant pools dwindled over the years and that they had difficulty finding enough employees. To ensure having a quality staff, increasingly, more restaurants instituted training programs for both general employees and managers. By 2002, hiring and retaining employees remained a leading challenge for both full service and fast food restaurants alike.

Sources for Further Study

Casper, Carol. "Bring It on Home." *Restaurant Business*, 15 March 1998.

Dorfman, Michelle. "A Strong Segment Is Brewing." *ID: The Voice of Foodservice Distribution*, October 1996.

"In Japan, Cooking Frenzy Is Boiling Over." *Chicago Tribune*, 15 September 1997.

"Industry at a Glance." National Restaurant Association, 22 April 2002. Available at http://www.restaurant.org.

"Industry Information." Specialty Coffee Association of America, 15 April 2002. Available at http://www.scaa.org.

King, Paul. "Family Dining Chains Launch Redesign to Change Image, Reach New Customers." *Nation's Restaurant News*, 15 January 2001.

LaFrance, Peter. "Sports Bars." *Tavern News*, June 1990.

Oetzel, Donna. "The Global Marketplace: Shopping Your Brand Outside the United States." *Restaurants USA*, June/July 2000.

Papiernik, Richard L. "$1B Growth Plans Dashed by Reality of Rationalization." *Nation's Restaurant News*, 30 March 1998.

———. "Operators Battle to Share $320.4 Billion in Sales." *Nation's Restaurant News*, 6 January 1997.

———. "Outlook 1998: Big Players Vie for $336.4 Billion in Sales." *Nation's Restaurant News*, 5 January 1998.

———. "Tricon Takes $530M Charge to Sell, Shutter 1,400 Units." *Nation's Restaurant News*, 22 December 1997.

Restaurant Industry Forecast, 2002. Washington, DC: National Restaurant Association, 2002. Available at http://www.restaurant.org.

Ruggless, Ron. "Better Latte Than Ever: Coffee Players Perked Up Over Sales." *Nation's Restaurant News*, 12 February 2001.

Sachdev, Ameet. "Wendy's Sizzles As Burger Wars Heat Up." *Chicago Tribune*, 10 March 2002.

Thorn, Bret. "Down, But Not Out: Despite Years of Turmoil Asian Foodservice Looks to Recapture its Former Glory." *Nation's Restaurant News*, 26 November 2001.

Food Products

Overview

Food production encompasses a diverse range of activities and products, and most companies within the food industry focus on just one or a few of the many specialties. Major segments of the industry include: meats; dairy products; canned, dried, and frozen foods; baked goods; candy and confectionery; edible oils and margarine; and beverages.

Because fresh foods like fruits and vegetables require little or no processing before sale to the public, they are often not included in discussions of the food industry. However, a few of the largest fresh fruit and vegetable companies also participate heavily in processed food manufacturing.

In the early 2000s, food manufacturing in the United States was worth more than $434 billion in annual sales, employed some 1.5 million people, and involved tens of thousands of companies. By sales value, meat packing is the United States' largest food segment, accounting for more than a quarter of all manufactured food sales.

While some factors influence food consumption, demand for most foods is fairly stable in the United States and usually rises just slightly ahead of the rate of population growth. In the 1990s, after factoring out inflation, the real growth rate of manufactured food sales hovered around 1 percent each year. Fads or social change, such as a trend toward eating low-fat foods, may influence the relative popularity of certain foods. Likewise, general economic prosperity often leads to somewhat higher per-capita consumption rates. Overall, though, the United States is a mature market for food, meaning that in order to boost sales, manufacturers usually must convince a consumer to purchase one product instead of another.

As a result of these tight market conditions at home, many large manufacturers have sought expansion overseas. They do so either by exporting products made in the United States to foreign countries or by establishing operations in another country and producing locally. U.S. exports of manufactured food totaled an estimated $25 billion in 2000, while imports trailed at about $19 billion. The value of U.S.-company food operations abroad, however, was much greater, at more than $100 billion.

History of the Industry

Food manufacturing's history is as varied as the foods the industry produces. Many of the innovations that led to the modern industry occurred in the second half of the nineteenth century. During this period emerged such common mass-production techniques as canning, meat packing, large-scale baking, and soft drink bottling. Before such technologies were born, comparable foods were purchased from small-scale local producers, made at home, or, in the case of soft drinks, unavailable.

Many of the early forms of food mass production were greeted with mistrust from consumers. Some people, for example, feared that food in tin cans could be spoiled. Similarly, since meat preparation was historically grounded on strict principles of sanitation and immediate use or curing, many consumers hesitated to buy packaged meats.

Advances in refrigeration, both for home and industrial use, thus had a significant impact on the industry. Refrigerated railcars meant that foods prone to spoilage, particularly fresh meats, fruits, and vegetables, could be distributed greater distances from their point of origin. It also prolonged the useful life of these foods, and made consumers more willing to purchase items that weren't produced locally—a necessary step toward establishing national brands—because refrigeration lessened their fears of buying unsafe foods. Moreover, mechanical refrigeration eventually gave rise to completely new genres of manufactured food, such as precooked frozen vegetables and prepared frozen foods.

New forms of packaging represented a second key development in the history of food manufacture. Tin cans and glass bottles were first used in canning in the early nineteenth century, and their use became commonplace by the latter half of the century. Canning significantly increased the useful life of many foods, especially fish, vegetables, and fruits. As glass and metal packaging grew more reliable and easy to produce, a canning industry began to form. The U.S. Civil War (1861-1865) helped spur demand for canned foods, which were used to feed the soldiers. Refinements in bottling late in the nineteenth century made possible the distribution of soft drinks such as Coca-Cola, a beverage sold at first only from soda fountains.

In the twentieth century, numerous enhancements in packaging helped improve the distribution process and the cost efficiency of producing many foods extended the shelf life of processed foods. Most significant among twentieth-century developments was that of plastics in food packaging. Plastics came to be used in everything from simple bread wrappers to structural cartons to highly engineered coatings on metal surfaces and foils. Air and moisture-proof plastic packaging helped protect foods from deterioration or contamination and provided for cheaper, more efficient production.

Significant Events Affecting the Industry

While overall food consumption is fairly stable for a given-sized population over time, the specific kinds of foods preferred by large segments of society may gradually—and, sometimes, very quickly—change. Since the 1960s, the most significant changes in U.S. food consumption have been the rise of health-conscious eating habits and demand for foods that are fast to prepare and eat. Secondary trends have included a shift away from traditional "American" cuisine and toward foods with ethnic or exotic themes; in particular, Mexican and Asian-inspired items.

Healthy eating has been a boon to poultry companies, as U.S. per-capita chicken consumption has nearly doubled since the mid-1970s. Consumers sought chicken because of its lower fat content than most other meats, and consequently, per-capita consumption of beef and pork by the mid-1990s was down from the historic highs of the 1960s and 1970s. Nutritious, low-fat food demand also led to the introduction of numerous product lines directed at health-conscious consumers. In the 1990s and early 2000s, these included the Healthy Choice and SnackWell lines of diverse food offerings from cereals to frozen entrees to yogurt to crackers. Interest in health foods also helped fuel sales of new fruit juices and bottled water in the 1990s and early 2000s.

Demand for convenience has also reshaped the food industry. In the 1980s, many companies rolled out microwave-ready foods to coincide with the popularity of fast-cooked meals, and a number of companies continued to develop easy-to-prepare meal kits into the early 2000s. Convenience has also driven fast sales growth and product-line extensions of ready-to-eat snack foods like tortilla and potato chips.

By the late 1990s, one of the faster growing convenience trends was that of buying freshly cooked, hot entrees from grocery stores or restaurants for in-home consumption, a practice known in the industry as home meal replacement. This represented both an opportunity and a challenge to food manufacturers because at that stage, the food was usually not branded as the manufacturer's product, but as the store's. In order to participate in the emerging market, which could potentially erode sales of their traditional brands, manufacturers needed to market their products as ingredients for store-prepared meals or to establish co-branding deals in which both their products and their brand names were associated with such meals.

Key Competitors

Each segment of the food industry typically has many competitors, and the industry as a whole boasts more than 70 U.S. companies with annual sales above the $1 billion mark. Listed below are a few of the largest and best known.

Philip Morris Companies, Inc. Philip Morris is the United States' largest food maker, principally through its well-known subsidiaries Kraft Foods, Inc., Nabisco, and the Miller Brewing Company. Combined food and beverage sales accounted for 42 percent, or $38.1 billion, of Philip Morris's $89.9 billion in 2001 sales. Tobacco accounted for almost all of the rest. The company, which traces its origins to a London tobacco store in the mid-nineteenth century, began acquiring food businesses in the 1970s to insulate its sales from the maturing and increasingly contentious tobacco business. By the 1980s, it stepped up its pace and bought out two of the largest U.S. food companies, General Foods Corporation and Kraft. The two were later merged. In December 2000 Philip Morris added Nabisco to its formidable list of brands when it purchased Nabisco Holdings Corporation for $19.2 billion. Nabisco's previous owner was tobacco giant RJR Nabisco Holdings Corporation, which acquired the food company in 1985. Originally named the National Biscuit Company, Nabisco was formed by an 1898 merger of two leading bakeries. Among Philip Morris's many food brands are Oscar Mayer, Post, Jell-O, Kool-Aid, Maxwell House, Breyers, Oreo, Ritz, Louis Rich, and Stove Top. These and many other labels place Philip Morris as a major contender among makers of dairy products, lunch meats, coffee, beer, cereal, light beverages, prepared frozen meals (especially pizza), and food condiment and sauce mixes. In 2002, the company had received approval from its board of directors to change its name to the Altria Group. At that time, it employed more than 175,000 workers around the world and held major shares of various food segments in parts of Europe as well.

ConAgra Foods, Inc. Originally known as Nebraska Consolidated Mills, ConAgra's expansion to its present status as a leading diversified food producer began in earnest with its development of the Duncan Hines brand cake mix in the 1950s. The company, which is still based in Omaha, Nebraska, became a multi-faceted food provider in the 1960s and 1970s, establishing a number of poultry processing plants to complement its growing flour mill business. In 1971, the company changed its name to ConAgra and continued its expansion into a variety of manufacturing industries. ConAgra's acquisitions have included United Agri Products (1978), Banquet Frozen Foods Corporation (1980), Armour Food Company (1983), and Beatrice (1990), as well as a number of other businesses. Regarded as the number two U.S. food company, ConAgra offers products under more than 50 brand names (85 percent of sales), including Hunt's, Chef Boyardee, Libby's, Wesson, Armour, and Butterball. It also owns the Healthy Choice label, which it also licenses to other companies for use on their products. ConAgra's product line includes meats, canned goods, oils, and a variety of frozen prepared vegetables, fish, and entrees. The company also has a thriving food ingredients business that sells to other manufacturers. ConAgra's sales for the fiscal year ended May 2001 totaled $27.2 billion, and that year it employed approximately 89,000 people.

The Coca-Cola Company Founded in 1892 (although an early soda fountain version of its product dates back to 1886), the Atlanta-based Coca-Cola Company is the world's largest soft drink maker, claiming an estimated 50 percent of the world market. Its flagship brand is sold in virtually every nation on earth. Coca-Cola distributes its products mostly via independently-owned bottling franchises, usually by geographic region, that purchase their ingredients from Coca-Cola. The company's other soft drink labels include Sprite, Tab, and Diet Coke. It also produces drinks under the Minute Maid, Fruitopia, and Hi-C trademarks. In 2001, the company, which employed a labor force of 38,000, brought in $18.9 billion from all of its operations.

Mars, Inc. Mars possesses one of the largest U.S. candy businesses by marketing the likes of Snickers, Mars, M&M's, and 3 Musketeers candies. It competes head on with Hershey Foods Corporation and Nestle of Switzerland for leadership of the U.S. sweets market. Its Snickers bars were the top-selling U.S. candy in the mid-1990s. The McLean, Virginia-based private company also makes pet food. The company doesn't release its sales figures to the public, but its 2001 sales were estimated at $16.5 billion. That year, the company employed an estimated 30,000 persons.

Industry Projections

In the tight U.S. food market, even the largest of companies must approach the market aggressively in order to maintain their sales volume. ConAgra provides a good example. Though highly diversified across different food segments, ConAgra in the late 1990s obtained the vast majority of its sales from the United States. When prices on commodity items like beef began to slide due to high capacity, ConAgra began to see its net sales lose ground as well. After peaking in 1996, the company's sales declined in 1997. By the late 1990s and early 2000s, net sales were relatively flat. While not all companies faced ConAgra's plight, a number of the leading companies used to more rapid sales growth found themselves in stagnant waters in the early 2000s.

Global Presence

The U.S. industry has a large and expanding presence in foreign markets. In each year since 1989, the value of U.S.-manufactured food exports (which exclude raw agricultural products) has surpassed the value of imports. In 1998, this trade surplus was estimated at $3.26 billion. A much greater source of international revenue, though, comes from U.S. manufacturers' operations in foreign countries, which contribute three to four times as much in annual sales as do exports shipped from the United States. This type of transplant operation is described by economists as "foreign direct investment," and is achieved either by buying stakes in existing foreign companies or by setting up or acquiring manufacturing facilities in which to produce new products. In the mid-

1990s, revenues from U.S. foreign food holdings surpassed $100 billion, and these businesses were among the fastest growing for U.S. manufacturers.

Employment in the Industry

With more than 1.51 million people on its U.S. payroll, the food products industry is one of the country's largest employers. The size of the U.S. workforce crept up gradually between the early and mid-1990s, and despite minor fluctuations was relatively stagnant in the late 1990s and early 2000s. This likely was attributable to large U.S. companies focusing on boosting domestic efficiency and expanding overseas. More than three-quarters of the industry's labor force are production workers or non-management employees. The entire industry's payroll exceeds $42 billion annually, amounting to an average annual compensation of around $28,000 per employee, which is somewhat lower than the average wage for manufacturing employment.

Sources for Further Study

American Meat Institute. *Just the Facts, 1997*. Washington, 1996.

Considine, Douglas M., ed. *Foods and Food Production Encyclopedia*. New York: Van Nostrand Reinhold Company, 1982.

Hui, Y.H., ed. *Encyclopedia of Food Science and Technology*. New York: John Wiley & Sons, 1992.

Nelson, D.C., et al. *ConAgra*. New York: Credit Suisse First Boston Corporation, 2 March 1998.

U.S. Bureau of the Census. *Annual Survey of Manufactures*. Washington, DC, 1998.

U.S. Industry and Trade Outlook. New York: McGraw-Hill and U.S. Department of Commerce, 1998.

Food Stores

Overview

Food retailing in the United States is dominated by supermarkets, which account for the majority of U.S. retail food sales. Among supermarkets, a handful of large multibillion-dollar chains lead the industry. Together, all U.S. food stores had annual sales of more than $442 billion in the early 2000s. In addition to supermarkets, grocery stores, and convenience stores, which together account for 96 percent of sales, the food stores category also includes specialty food stores, fish and seafood markets, fruit and vegetable markets, meat markets, and stores selling confectionaries, nuts, and baked goods. Although they sell some food products, health food stores—which may sell vitamins, nutritional supplements, and foods with other health benefits—are considered to be part of the health and personal care store category, which also includes pharmacies and drug stores.

During the late 1990s and early 2000s, the food retail industry was marked by consolidation, as large supermarket chains acquired smaller competitors in order to survive increasingly stiff competition from the likes of Wal-Mart Stores, Inc. By the early 2000s, Wal-Mart had risen to the top of the industry, establishing itself as the grocery industry's market leader. This environment made it extremely difficult for even the very best independent grocery chains to survive. Thus, a relatively small percent of all U.S. food retail outlets generate the majority of the industry's sales.

Supermarkets are distinguished from grocery stores and other kinds of retailers based on the size and scope of their offerings. A standard measure in the industry is whether a store has an annual sales volume greater than $1 million. Others define supermarkets as having more than a certain amount of square footage. Selection of merchandise is also key, as supermarkets normally stock a full line of groceries that includes dry and canned goods, fresh meats and vegetables, frozen items, and basic nonfood items like paper goods and cleaning supplies. While conventional grocery stores may only stock some of these products, many of the largest supermarkets go further to offer such amenities as deli counters, bakeries, florists, bank branches, and video rental shops. In fact, an important trend that began in the mid to late 1990s and continued into the early 2000s was toward large integrated supermarkets—sometimes called hypermarkets—that featured extensive lines of both food and nonfood merchandise to eliminate shoppers' needs to visit multiple stores.

An important player in the field of large-scale food and nonfood retailing is Wal-Mart Stores, Inc., the nation's leading grocer. By the early 2000s, the company had opened more than 1,000 "supercenters," which, in addition to offering discount general merchandise, include full-line grocery departments. In addition to its line of supercenters, Wal-Mart also was expanding its chain of smaller Neighborhood Market grocery stores in select areas. Wal-Mart's foray into food retailing has created a new competitive environment for supermarkets. Ironically, the retailer's success in capturing a significant share of conventional supermarkets' business (approximately 16 percent in 2002) mirrors the method by which supermarkets eroded the market share of traditional local grocers: offering greater selection than competitors while keeping prices low.

History of the Industry

Characterized by carrying a large variety of different food stuffs, dry goods, and health and beauty products under one roof, supermarkets developed in the early 1930s. The expansion of their stock beyond essential food items was encouraged by rising operating costs, particularly rent and wages, influenced by government regulation and union bargaining. Prior to this, food was sold through local "mom and pop" grocery stores and chain "economy stores." Faced with competition from supermarkets that undercut them by as much as a third or a half, the old style grocery store chains either converted to supermarkets, were bought out, or went out of business.

Supermarkets provided consumers with lower-priced goods during the Depression. Concentrating less on personalized service and more on bare bones cash and carry, supermarkets emphasized the utilitarian aspects of the business and let the customer do the work of selecting and handling goods. With their emphasis on high stock turnover, supermarkets benefited from the new tendency toward bulk buying, supported by the growing use of refrigeration and the proliferation of cars. The growth of automobile traffic also influenced store location, with placement for traffic convenience becoming a primary concern.

From 1930 to 1950, the industry witnessed radical and far-reaching changes in methods of food distribution. Noticeable changes included increased self-service, the wide expansion of lines, and the great increase in the number and size of stores. Consequently, consumers benefited from greater choice and convenience. Through creative marketing techniques and low competitive prices, supermarket chains, both independently affiliated and corporate, had established themselves as the leading outlet for retail food distribution by World War II.

After 1950, increased competition fostered further developments in the retail food business. The large profit margins that stores had been able to realize were undercut as supermarkets found it necessary to increase print and television advertising and initiate such promotional efforts as trading stamps, games, and contests to win business. These efforts succeeded only in pushing up supermarkets' overhead faster than they could increase gross margins. These percentages narrowed consistently throughout the 1950s and 1960s. By 1954, the United States had 288,000 grocery stores, almost 100,000 fewer than in 1948.

By 1965, supermarkets had won a 71 percent share of all retail food sales, with superettes (stores having annual sales between $150,000 and $500,000 a year) accounting for 13 percent and small stores (sales less than $150,000 annually), 16 percent. It had become evident by the 1960s that an integrated chain of self-service supermarkets could offer consumers a better deal due to their economies of scale. It was also clear, however, that cutthroat competition, which forced chains to keep their price margins low, was wiping out some of these economies.

Supermarkets sought ways to cut their costs even further and found inspiration in the new soft goods discount stores that were starting to appear. These businesses applied the same techniques pioneered by supermarkets to create low-price department stores. Supermarket managers subsequently decided to employ the discount idea in their own businesses. This necessitated abandoning their previous promotional schemes and focusing on price-cutting. For consumers, the appeal was immediate, and discount pricing spread throughout the industry.

While the industry was undergoing these transformations, many supermarkets simultaneously endeavored to raise their profit margins by expanding their stock to include more general merchandise. Others bought out existing discount department stores and opened the two kinds of stores side by side or under one roof in strategically located shopping centers. Another development was the trend for supermarkets to ally themselves with discount drug stores.

The net effect of these changes was a gradual decline in the number of general food stores—although the food retailing market saw some increase in the number of specialty stores. The 1972 census recorded 194,000 supermarkets, with sales per establishment more than seven times greater than in 1948. By 1996, the number of grocery stores had fallen to 130,000, but sales had grown upwards of $400 billion.

Significant Events Affecting the Industry

One of the most important developments of the 1990s was the trend among the large supermarket chains toward converting to large-format stores. These stores, some spanning 65,000 square feet or more, focused on providing a more diverse range of products and services than did smaller outlets. Many featured in-store delis, salad bars, and bakeries, and beginning in the late 1990s, they were beginning to offer prepared meals to further allure shoppers with convenience. The so-called home meal replacements, which were either ready-to-heat, store-cooked meals or foods that were kept warm in the store, represented an important growth category for the industry. As U.S. consumers increasingly sought convenience when purchasing foods, grocery stores had been gradually losing their share of consumers' food dollars to restaurants. Innovations like freshly cooked meals in stores were touted as possible weapons against further erosion of food stores' market share.

Related to the preference for large-format stores was Wal-Mart's mid-1990s entry into the food retailing arena. Wal-Mart had long marketed a small line of shelf-stable foods like potato chips and soft drinks, but in the mid to late 1990s, it announced a major new initiative to begin offering in some of its stores an extensive line of foods comparable in breadth to that of any major supermarket. A similar effort was underway at Wal-Mart's faded rival, Kmart Corporation, which was trying to repair its sinking retail empire. Wal-Mart was noted for its aggressive expansion in the general merchandise sector, which propelled it to become the United States' largest company by annual sales by 2002. Towering at four times the annual sales of Kroger, the largest conventional supermarket chain, Wal-Mart's arrival on the food retail scene significantly increased competition within the industry by the early 2000s.

Key Competitors

Although Wal-Mart was the nation's leading grocer by food sales ($80 billion in 2001), the Kroger Company was the United States' largest "pure-play" food store chain in the early 2000s, with 2002 revenues of $50.1 billion. With about 3,600 retail locations across the

United States in 2002, the Ohio-based Kroger Company operated under a variety of brand names. In addition to Kroger stores, the company operates supermarkets under other brand names including Ralph's, Dillon's, Smith's, Pay Less, Baker's, King Soopers, Hilander, Owen's, Fry's Food, QFC, City Market, Jay C, Cala Foods/Bell Markets, Kessel, and Gerbes. In addition, Kroger also operates: multi-department stores called Fry's Marketplace and Fred Meyer; a variety of convenience stores including Tom Thumb, Loaf 'N Jug, Quik Stop, Kwik Shop, and Turkey Hill; and warehouse stores Food 4 Less and Foods Company.

Boise, Idaho-based Albertson's, Inc. was second in the grocery industry behind Kroger. In 1998, the company took center stage in the industry when it announced the purchase of its rival American Stores for $11.7 billion. Albertson's, ranked fourth before the acquisition, was slightly smaller than third-ranked American Stores but in better fiscal shape. By the early 2000s, Albertson's operated 2,400 stores, including both supermarkets and drug stores, under a variety of different brand names including Albertson's, Jewel, Acme Markets, and Osco Drug. The company posted sales of $38.0 billion in 2002, at which time it employed 222,000 workers.

Safeway, Inc. was another leading U.S. food retailer, with 2001 sales of $34.3 billion. The company operates from about 1,770 retail locations and has a strong presence in many regions of the United States. Safeway also wields an extensive line of private-label products, many of which it manufactures itself.

General Nutrition Companies, Inc. operates the United States' largest specialty food retail network through its 5,300 outlets, many of which occupy small storefronts in shopping malls. The company, owned by Dutch firm Royal Numico since 1999, realized $1.4 billion in 2001 sales, up slightly from 2000. The stores feature vitamins and mineral supplements, nutritional and dietary supplements, healthy foods, and fitness merchandise.

Industry Projections

New stores are often the focal point of a growing retail business, and this is no exception in food retailing. Many leading companies, including Kroger, Albertson's, and Wal-Mart, have stated goals for new store openings. However, some of these openings are always offset by closures, because stores seek to maximize profitability of every location. For example, although Albertson's was adding new stores in several cities in Arizona and Nevada, in 2002 the company also announced that it was planning to close 116 under-performing locations in Texas and Tennessee. Thus it's common for a store to close several outlets while building dozens more.

Because net demand for the bulk of the industry's products—groceries—is growing much more slowly than companies would like, they have been forced to compete for customer loyalty. In the early 2000s, food retailers

were expected to continue enticing consumers by adding more in-store amenities and wider selections of merchandise in order to gain and maintain market share. In many ways, this was changing the very face of food retailers, as they began to offer an increasing array of non-traditional products and services to compete with the likes of Wal-Mart. As C.L. King Associates' Gary Giblen said in *Supermarket News*, the blending of distribution channels "will continue as supermarkets try to sell more pharmacy items, drug stores try to sell more food, convenience stores try to sell more fresh merchandise, and Wal-Mart tries to sell more of everything, including food."

Global Presence

The food retailing industry, like many retail segments, is largely confined within U.S. borders. However, a few of the largest players, including Safeway and Kroger, have stores in Canada and Mexico. Perhaps signaling the industry's future direction, Wal-Mart has increased its international presence significantly since the late 1990s. The retailer nearly doubled its lineup of international stores from 314 in 1997 to 601 in 1998. Since then, Wal-Mart continued to grow globally, and by 2002, operated 1,170 stores outside of the United States.

Employment in the Industry

Food retailing employs a massive labor force of more than 3.5 million people, but at $9.61 per hour the industry's average wage lags behind the U.S. average full-time hourly wage. In addition to receiving low pay, female workers in the industry have reportedly suffered from sex discrimination by their employers, as a number of class-action lawsuits were filed against major retailers during the mid-1990s.

Sources for Further Study

"Against a Wal-." *Progressive Grocer*, September 2001.

McNair, Malcolm P. and Eleanor G. May. *The Evolution of Retail Institutions in the United States*. Cambridge, MA: Marketing Science Institute, 1976.

"Occupational Employment Statistics." Bureau of Labor Statistics, U.S. Department of Labor, 24 May 2002. Available at http://www.bls.gov.

Peak, Hugh S. *Supermarket Merchandizing and Management*, New York: Prentice Hall, 1977.

Standard & Poor's Industry Surveys. New York: Standard & Poor's Corporation, 1996.

Supermarket News, weekly.

U.S. Bureau of the Census. *Annual Retail Trade Survey*. Washington, DC: annual.

U.S. Department of Commerce, Economics and Statistics Administration, U.S. Census Bureau. *Annual Benchmark Report for Retail Trade and Food Services: January 1992 Through March 2002*. Washington, May 2002.

"Wal-Mart Is Eating Everybody's Lunch." *Business Week*, 15 April 2002.

Zwiebach, Elliot. "Super Surge; Wal-Mart Supercenters Leap to the Top of the SN Top 75 This Year as Consolidation Puts Pressure on Medium and Small-Sized Retailers and Supermarkets Diversify Their Businesses." *Supermarket News*, 15 January 2001.

General Merchandise Stores

Overview

Merchandise stores are dominated by two retail categories: department stores, which include the likes of Sears, Roebuck and Company and J.C. Penney; and discount mass merchandisers, sometimes called variety stores, such as Wal-Mart Stores, Inc. and Kmart Corporation. While the distinctions have begun to blur as stores diversify, these categories are distinguished from food and grocery stores and from specialized merchandise shops like apparel and electronics stores. Together, all U.S. general merchandise stores sold an estimated $430 billion worth of products in 2001.

History of the Industry

Department Stores   The department store became one of the most durable creations of modern American life. Created in the heart of emerging business districts, department stores gradually became part of the landscape. The first department stores opened as early as 1846 in New York City. Although they primarily catered to the city's elite, early merchants also wanted to make themselves accessible to women of all classes. So instead of keeping their goods behind the counter, they openly displayed merchandise on the floor to encourage browsing.

Stores with elaborate decor and fancy window displays created a new kind of entertainment for the masses. Even if people could not afford to buy the merchandise, they still came to the department store to peer in the windows to see what they might attain someday. The traditional department store sold "soft goods," such as apparel and linens, as well as "hard goods," including furniture, appliances, and housewares.

The now defunct "notions aisle"—the place for button hooks, thread, sewing needles, linens, laces, and silks—was the original foundation of the department store. Notions were first sold by peddlers who traveled by foot through the rural South and Midwest. Eventually they gained a horse and buggy and then graduated to a small store front—the prototype department store.

Another innovation that emerged in the late nineteenth century was the budget floor. Filene's obtained legendary status with its Automatic Bargain Basement, where it sold cashmeres salvaged from a fire at Neiman-Marcus and Schiaparelli and Chanel gowns evacuated from Paris showrooms at the start of World War II.

Credit began in 1911, when Sears Roebuck offered payment plans to farmers for large mail-order purchases. By the 1920s, "layaway" installment plans were common. The introduction of department store charge plates encouraged customer loyalty since that was the only form of consumer credit available at the time.

From the earliest days, merchants catered to women. By 1915, nearly 90 percent of all department store customers were female. Women also began to take the place of men on the selling floor, offering fashion advice and fittings.

Department stores were considered a fantasy land for toy vendors and children alike. Stores became famous for their elaborate Christmas decor. No one knows exactly when Santa Claus began to show up on the scene, but in 1939, Montgomery Ward's started to give away a book featuring a character first called Rollo, then Reginald, and finally Rudolph—a reindeer with a red nose. Rudolph's signature song was recorded by Gene Autry in 1949, and the famous reindeer became a Christmas icon.

Department store managers also influenced other major American holidays. In the past, Thanksgiving was held on the last Thursday in November. In 1939, the holiday fell on the 30th, leaving only 24 days for Christmas shopping. Ohio merchant Fred Lazarus, Jr. led a campaign to move the holiday to the fourth Thursday in November. President Franklin D. Roosevelt complied, and Thanksgiving has remained on that date ever since.

After World War II, department stores began their expansion into the suburbs, following the flight of their customers. By the 1950s, most department stores turned to upscale clients and merchandise, doing away with the low-end, bargain basement sales. This decision opened the way for discount operations like Kmart to enter the market. Customer loyalty quickly dissipated as the arrival of bank credit cards in the 1960s allowed consumers to shop on credit virtually anywhere. In due time, the costs of suburban expansion plus the lack of experience or interest on the part of third or fourth generation family members drove many department store owners to sell their operations.

By the 1980s, many department stores were in fairly poor shape. Although consumer spending was up, the stores found fierce competition from discounters, specialty stores with numerous outlets, and mail order houses, which sent out 14 billion pieces of mail annually. In an attempt to lure back customers, department stores engaged in competitive price-cutting. The result was a frenzied period of leveraged buyouts (LBOs), mergers, and acquisitions. Of the eight companies that composed the Standard & Poor's index at the beginning of 1986, four were acquired or taken private, while a fifth company undertook major restructuring.

As of the mid-1990s, department stores changed their product mix somewhat. "White goods"—appliances such as stoves and refrigerators—were less emphasized to make room for more apparel items. Sears adopted the slogan, "Come see the softer side of Sears," emphasizing that power tools and lawn equipment were not the only items you would see in the store. J.C. Penney upgraded their store merchandising, emphasizing more apparel also.

Discount Stores Although discounted sales have existed since the early 1900s, the discount variety store industry picked up shortly after World War II. During this time, according to *Discount Store News*, entrepreneurs were prompted to open large variety stores due to the increasing demand for consumer goods, including such new products as record players and television sets. In the northeastern part of the country, in particular, large facilities became available to potential variety store owners when several mills were vacated by manufacturers moving their operations to the South. Taking over such facilities for their retail operations, variety store owners found that their proximity to those mills that had remained in operation facilitated the timely restocking of their stores with apparel and domestic items.

By 1962, the industry leaders and a typical store format were well established. Discount department stores were formed by the Dayton Company, which pioneered the Target chain; Kmart stores, an offshoot of S.S. Kresge; the F.W. Woolworth Company's Woolco stores; and Sam Walton's Wal-Mart. These new stores transformed the variety store business into large, low-price, self-service stores, featuring both hard goods and apparel.

Several mergers occurred in the late 1960s and early 1970s, as chains sought to expand quickly through acquisitions. During this time, Kmart became the decided leader with more than 300 stores, which was more than double the number of the next largest chain. While over a dozen discount stores filed for Chapter 11, attributable to economic recession, Kmart and Woolco grew into national companies, while Wal-Mart expanded in the Southeast and Target in the Midwest.

During the 1970s, discount stores began exploring advances in technology, using computers, electronic registers, UPC bar coding systems, POS scanning, and satellite communication systems. Wal-Mart's explosive growth in particular was attributed to its successful implementation of computer technology. The company established highly automated distribution centers, which cut shipping costs and delivery time, and installed an advanced computer system to track inventory and speed up checkout and reordering. As a result, Wal-Mart increased its retail establishments from 18 in 1970 to 270 in 1980.

By the end of the 1980s, Kmart, Target, and Wal-Mart dominated the industry, a pattern that would continue through the late 1990s. At the same time, other chains had filed for bankruptcy, among them Woolco, FedMart, Memco, Twin Fair, Zayre, Zodys, Kings, Ames, and Hills. Regional operators experiencing moderate success included Jamesway, Caldor, and Bradlees in the East; Rose's in the South; Clover in Philadelphia; Fred Meyer

in the Pacific Northwest; Fedco in southern California; and Venture, Meijer, and Value City in the Midwest.

Significant Events Affecting the Industry

In the 1990s, many of the discount stores, especially Wal-Mart, continued to flourish, while the traditional department stores largely stagnated. By the mid-1990s, Wal-Mart had become the world's largest retailer of any kind; and by the early 2000s, it accounted for more than 44 percent of the industry's sales. Target also enjoyed strong growth. However, Kmart was mired in a sales and image slump that forced restructuring. A similar problem existed at Sears, which began a program of divestitures of its peripheral businesses and explored new retail specialty formats. The trend was decidedly toward the discounters, which increasingly offered more diverse product lines, better prices, and maintained a more cost-efficient structure.

Key Competitors

Wal-Mart Stores Inc. has become the industry's runaway success and the primary beneficiary of the business that more stolid retailers like Sears have lost. With sales of $219.8 billion for the fiscal year ending 2002, the company operated 4,440 stores in 10 countries that year, but the overwhelming majority of its business comes from the United States. It is the world's largest retailer and the United States' largest company by revenues, leading the *Fortune* 500 list in 2002. That year, the discounter's workforce of 1.4 million made it the largest U.S. employer. In the mid-1990s, Wal-Mart initiated a push to open large-format combination food and general merchandise stores known as supercenters. By the early 2000s, the company had opened more than 1,000 supercenters and was expanding its chain of smaller Neighborhood Market grocery stores in select areas. These stores proved successful at pulling market share away from conventional grocery stores and, by 2001, Wal-Mart had established itself as the leading grocer in terms of sales. Wal-Mart also operates a chain of membership warehouse clubs that sell discounted merchandise in quantity to members.

Sears, Roebuck and Company had once dominated U.S. merchandise retailing, but it began to fade in the 1980s and 1990s as consumers were increasingly drawn to discount stores and the new category, "killer" formats like Home Depot and Best Buy. In the early and mid-1990s, Sears sold off many of its financial services, including the Discover card, Allstate insurance, and the Dean Witter investment brokerage. A more symbolic change occurred in 1993 when the company ceased production of its annual catalog, which had been a staple of U.S. retailing for nearly a century. In 2001, the company recorded $41.1 billion in sales, a paltry 0.3-percent increase over the previous year. This figure remained far below the $57.3 billion Sears brought in during 1991, when it still owned many non-retail businesses. Sears has tried to recoup sales and market share by investing in specialty stores such as the NTB chain of automotive gear stores. In 2002, the retailer was in the process of buying Land's End.

Target Corporation was another successful mass merchandiser in the early 2000s. Formerly known as Dayton Hudson, the company posted sales of $39.9 billion in fiscal year 2002, an eight percent improvement over the previous year. At that time, Target operated stores under the Mervyn's and Marshall Field's names. However, more than 80 percent of the company's sales came from its namesake Target stores. The retailer is known for selling somewhat more upscale merchandise, such as trendy housewares, making it a popular outlet for wedding gift registry. The company continues an aggressive expansion program to compete with its main rivals Wal-Mart and Kmart, and has introduced its own supercenters, Target Greatland and SuperTarget, which offer food items.

Other industry leaders include Kmart Corp., which had $36.2 billion in sales for the period ending January 2002; J.C. Penney Company, Inc., with $32.0 billion; and Federated Department Stores, Inc., with $15.7 billion.

Industry Projections

In the early 2000s, industry sales were growing at approximately six percent annually. Sales at some leading firms, however, were growing much faster as they added new stores and upgraded existing ones. But as the industry growth trend suggests, much of these retailers' growth would come at the expense of other companies.

Global Presence

Some merchandise retailers have eyed foreign markets with considerable interest, as they expect non-U.S. demand to grow more rapidly than that in the increasingly saturated U.S. market. Wal-Mart in particular has begun to aggressively develop its international business. The retail giant almost doubled the number of international stores it operates from 314 in 1997 to 601 in 1998. Since then, Wal-Mart continued to grow globally, and by 2002 operated 1,167 stores outside of the United States in 10 countries including Mexico, where it operates some 550 stores. It has likewise moved into South America, China, and Europe through both new store openings and acquisitions of local chains.

Employment in the Industry

From 1990 to 1997, employment at general merchandise stores increased 10 percent to 2.97 million people. However, by 2000 this number had decreased slightly to 2.94 million. Most of these positions tend to be low paying. The average non-management wage in 2000 was $9.45 per hour.

Sources for Further Study

"Retail Store Industry." *Value Line Investment Survey*, 21 February 1997.

"Retail Trade." *U.S. Industry and Trade Outlook*. New York: McGraw-Hill and U.S. Department of Commerce, 1998.

"Retailing: General." *Standard & Poor's Industry Surveys*, 1998.

Hotels and Motels

Overview

The hotel and motel industry plays a vital role in the development of trade, commerce, and travel in the United States. In supplying everything from a cheap night's accommodation on the road to meeting and convention spaces and coordination for large corporate events, the remarkably diverse services American hotels provide have made the industry a significant one. The travel industry is a growing sector of the United States economy and ranks as the country's third largest industry behind automobile and food sales. In the early 2000s, the hotel industry's revenues totaled approximately $109 billion per year.

In the United States, there are approximately 4.1 million hotel rooms at roughly 53,500 hotel properties, or about 1 hotel room for every 69 U.S. citizens. Approximately 30 percent of these are at suburban locations, and another 31 percent are on highways. The rest are located in cities (16 percent), resort sites (12 percent), and alongside airport strips (10 percent). In recent years, the room supply has risen significantly in suburban areas, and new construction has focused largely on limited-service facilities—an increasingly popular option for cost-conscious travelers not inclined to frequent more elaborate full-service properties.

Almost 64 percent of the country's hotel rooms are occupied on any given night. According to the American Hotel & Motel Association (AHMA), business travelers make up the largest segment of hotel customers, accounting for about 28 percent of all hotel customers, while conference and meeting attendees account for about 25 percent. The AHMA also found that 25 percent of lodging industry customers are leisure travelers, and another 22 percent are staying in a hotel for personal or family reasons.

History of the Industry

The first American lodging was the colonial inn, which flourished during the late 1700s. Colonial inns and taverns dotted the seaport towns and stagecoach roads. They became popular not only with travelers but with locals as well, who came to use them as public gathering places for town meetings, schools, and even courts of law.

Hotels as we know them were not long in coming as the major cities grew quickly. The very first, the 73-room City Hotel at 115 Broadway in New York City, was completed in 1794, and similar establishments were soon constructed in Philadelphia, Boston, and Baltimore. The early 1800s saw hotel numbers increase dramatically with the westward expansion. With each new hotel, it seemed, some new service was added, which forced other hotels to change or face obsolescence. The City Hotel became so outdated that in just 38 years it was converted into an office building. An industry trend towards luxury accommodations was sparked by the Tremont House in Boston, which was the first to offer such amenities as private guest rooms, locks on doors, a washbowl with free soap, bellboys, French cuisine, and an annunciator that enabled the front desk to communicate with guests in their rooms.

In the twentieth century moderate- and low-priced hotels emerged. First, the Buffalo Statler opened in 1908, and its conveniences included circulating ice water and a free morning newspaper. It's slogan was "A room and a bath for a dollar and a half" and, in making cleanliness and comfort accessible to so many, the Statler, and its imitators, contributed greatly to the middle-class travel bug. By the middle of the century, the early "no-frills" motels were put up quickly and cheaply on large plots by highways. These enterprises appealed to lower-income vacation travelers, salesmen, and middle-management businessmen and competed effectively with hotels in the 1950s. However, the initially significant differences between the two types of lodging in terms of size, start-up costs, operating ratios, and management needs began to diminish in the 1960s as motels franchised, grew in size, and started offering more amenities and services.

Significant Events Affecting the Industry

A number of noticeable trends occurred in the mid- to late 1990s. These included more construction, further automation of labor-intensive tasks, additional emphasis on business-related amenities, involvement by hotel companies in time-sharing projects, and the growing popularity of extended-stay hotels. Construction increased as companies increasingly looked to develop new chains by building new facilities. The automation of labor-intensive functions, such as hotel check-in and checkout should assist in reducing long-term operating costs and increasing customer satisfaction. Through the use of computers, hotel guests can make a reservation with an authorized credit card and upon check-in receive a magnetic key. The key will give the guest access to their room, tally their bar and restaurant bills, and let housekeeping know that they have left their room so it can be cleaned. Business related amenities such as Internet access, voice mail, and fax services appeal especially to business travelers. Involvement by hotel companies in time-sharing projects is a means for companies to leverage their expertise in real estate and financing. Extended-stay facilities offer such amenities as separate living room areas and kitchens.

Key Competitors

Underscoring the phenomenal success of franchising, the top companies in the industry—based on rooms and revenues—are primarily franchise companies. These include Cendant Corp., Six Continents Hotels Inc., and Marriott International Inc.

In 2001 New York-based Cendant (formerly Hospitality Franchise Systems, Inc.) ranked as the world's largest and most successful hotel and real estate agency franchiser. HFS merged with CUC International in the mid-1990s, becoming Cendant Corporation. In 2001 Cendant posted revenues of $8.8 billion. As the parent company of the Days Inn (1,901), Howard Johnson (500), Knights Inn (227), Super 8 (2001), Travelodge (560), Ramada (1,035), Wingate Inns (115), Villager (109), and AmeriHost (92) chains Cendant operates approximately 555,000 rooms, or roughly 13.5 percent of all United States lodging facilities. In addition to its leadership position in the hotel industry, Cendant also operates more than 1,700 Avis car rental businesses and holds the number-two spot among the world's general-use car rental agencies. Additionally, the company was the world's top vacation ownership firm in the early 2000s.

Formerly Bass Hotels & Resorts Inc., Six Continents Hotels Inc. is second among hotel companies. Six Continents Hotels was a part of London-based brewer Bass PLC, until the parent company sold its brewing interests to Interbrew and changed its name to Six Continents PLC. The subsidiary was home to more than 3,200 hotels in more than 100 countries in the early 2000s. Approximately 73 percent of Six Continents' hotels are located in the United States. Among the company's brands are Holiday Inn (1,375), Holiday Inn Express (1,151), Crowne Plaza (155), Inter-Continental Hotels & Resorts (131), Holiday Inn Select (79), Holiday Inn Garden Court (77), Holiday Inn SunSpree Resort (26), Forum Hotels & Resorts (14), and Staybridge Suites by Holiday Inn (22). In 2001, the company's sales reached $2.8 billion and it employed more than 35,500 workers.

In October 1993 Marriott Corp. was divided into two companies: Host Marriott Corporation, which owns real estate and operates airport concessions; and Marriott International, the lodging business. In the early 2000s Marriott International had 1,846 hotels. While other hoteliers have moved into the gaming industry, Maryland-based Marriott has focused on continued segmentation and international expansion. Its product line includes Marriott Hotels, Resorts and Suites and Ritz Carlton (full-service); Courtyard hotels (moderate price); Residence Inn (extended stay); Fairfield Inn (economy segment); as well as Renaissance Hotels and Resorts/Ramada International; TownePlace Suites by Marriott; Spring Hill Suites by Marriott; and Marriott Conference Centers. The firm also operates Marriott Vacation Club International and a food distribution business, among other enterprises. By converting existing properties and developing new hotels, Marriott's international expansion has included the establishment of full-service properties in the Pacific Rim, Europe, Latin America, and the Caribbean.

Industry Projections

The health of the U.S. hotel industry depends largely on the strength and stability of the national economy and on other economies around the world, as the number of travelers—whether traveling for business or pleasure—increases with economic growth and prosperity. After a global recession in the early 1990s, the United States and other countries recovered in the mid-1990s and continued to prosper going into the late 1990s. The U.S. hotel industry followed this pattern by performing poorly in the early part of the decade and recovering in the latter. The economic turnaround, the emergence of new markets, and the balancing of hotel supply and demand all played a decisive role in the industry's success in the mid- to late 1990s.

The U.S. industry experienced a boom in demand in the mid- to late 1990s, posting record sales each year during this period. In 2000, the industry achieved its most profitable year ever. However, by 2001 the U.S. economy weakened and terrorist attacks against the United States that September made conditions even worse as business and leisure travel activity fell. According to *Hotel & Motel Management*, information from Smith Travel Research revealed the industry lost somewhere between $7 billion and $8 billion in room revenue during 2001. This figure was estimated to be much higher when related businesses like food and beverages are factored into the equation. The publication also revealed that more than 400 hotels closed during 2001. In addition, for the most part construction of new hotels ceased. According to some industry analysts, conditions were expected to improve gradually and reach pre-2001 levels sometime in 2004.

A period of industry consolidation also was underway by the mid- to late 1990s. In the first half of 1997 alone, the United States reported mergers and acquisitions worth $4.1 billion, twice as much as reported in the first half of 1996. Marriott International made one of the largest acquisitions, purchasing Renaissance Hotel and its holdings such as Renaissance and Ramada International for $1.0 billion. Extended Stay America also bought Studio Plus hotels for $290 million. In addition, Promus Hotel Corporation acquired Doubletree in 1997. Doubletree had previously bought Red Lion, a chain with a strong presence in the Pacific Northwest. By 2002 industry analysts expected consolidation to continue within the industry as chains struggled financially in the wake of a slack economy and the terrorist attacks of September 11, 2001.

Global Presence

The United States remains the international giant of the hotel industry. It routinely posts the highest amount of international tourism revenue. The United States was the second most popular destination in 1996, behind France, with over 45,000 arrivals. Furthermore, the country's 3.5 million hotel rooms represent around 27 percent of worldwide capacity.

Leading destinations in the United States include Florida, California, and New York. Top American markets for hotel expansion in recent years included Las Vegas, Nevada; Orlando, Florida; New Orleans, Louisiana; and San Antonio, Texas. Hotel developers also have watched the surge in legalized gambling in the United States with great interest, a development that could benefit the hotel industry tremendously. The average room rate stood at $69.66 in 1996, up from $65.81 in 1995. Canadian, Mexican, and Japanese travelers are the leading international travelers to the United States.

Large U.S. hotel chains began seeking new markets in the late 1990s as the domestic market verged on saturation, and this pattern continued in the early 2000s. Companies such as Sheraton relied on their brand names to fuel their international expansions, setting up hotels in large cities and branching out into smaller cities after successfully establishing themselves. Smaller operations opted to place their hotels in strategic locations after careful planning to ensure sufficient demand. In the late 1990s, the top five international emerging hotel markets included Chile, Cuba, India, Poland, and Saudi Arabia, according to *Hotel & Motel Management*.

Employment in the Industry

The hotel industry employed 1.8 million people in 2000. The average wage in the industry was $9.87 per hour, or $20,530 per year. Management occupations averaged $22.52 per hour, or $46,850 per year. North and South America account for about 40 percent of the world's total hotel and motel workers. Marriott International alone employed 140,000 workers in 2001. However, like other service industries in the United States, the hotel industry has been challenged by a glut of open positions. Because of the small number of people in the 16 to 24 year-old age bracket, the United States faces a shortage of hotel employees, since this age bracket usually provides the majority of the entry-level workers to the service industries. According to *Hotel & Motel Management*, PricewaterhouseCoopers indicated that in the last half of 2001 the industry lost 257,000 jobs. This contributed to a sluggish overall annual growth rate of 0.1 percent, considerably lower than rates of more than three percent in 1999 and 2000. However, although many hotels cut staff due to the poor economy in the early 2000s, many were still struggling to recruit the right employees.

Sources for Further Study

"2001 Lodging Industry Profile." American Hotel & Lodging Association, 2001. Available at http://www.ahla.com.

Andorka, Frank H., Jr. "Hot Global Markets." *Hotel & Motel Management*, 11 August 1997.

Benini, Carla. "Travel Suppliers Forced to Merge: Consolidation Might Be Key to Survival, Say Analysts." *Meetings & Conventions*, February 2002.

"Better 2002?" *Travel Agent*, 15 April 2002.

Hanson, Bjorn. "Stock Market Smiled on Industry in 1996." *Hotel & Motel Management*, 13 January 1997.

Higley, Jeff. "Exposing Extended Stay." *Hotel & Motel Management*, 3 November 1997.

————. "Hoteliers Foresee Bumpy Road to Recovery." *Hotel & Motel Management*, 1 April 2002.

Inge, Jon. "Invisible Technology." *Hotel & Motel Management*, 11 August 1997.

"Investors Expect Short-Term Troubles and a Full Recovery in Two Years." *National real Estate Investor*, March 2002.

"Investors Pessimistic About Industry Outlook." *Hotel & Motel Management*, 4 March 2002.

"Job Losses Total 257,000 During Six-Month Period." *Hotel & Motel Management*, 18 February 2002.

Malley, Mike. "Favorable Economy Pushes Travel Spending to Record Levels." *Hotel & Motel Management*, 3 November 1997.

————. "Hotel Values Projected to Decline by 2000." *Hotel & Motel Management*, 3 November 1997.

McDonald, William G., and Scott C. Butera. "Mergers and Acquisitions." *Hotel & Motel Management*, 18 November 1996.

"Occupational Employment Statistics." Bureau of Labor Statistics, U.S. Department of Labor, 30 May 2002. Available at http://www.bls.gov.

Scoviak-Lerner, Mary. "New Markets, Demands Redefine Asia's Hotels." *Hotels*, April 1997.

Shundich, Steven. "A Year to Give and Take." *Hotels*, April 1997.

"Top 50 Hotel Companies." American Hotel & Lodging Association, 2001. Available at http://www.ahla.com.

Tsui, John F. "Emerging Megatrends in Asia." *Lodging Hospitality*, September 1996.

Wilder, Jeff. "Trends Signal Industry's Health." *Hotel & Motel Management*, 1 September 1997.

Household Audio and Video Equipment and Audio Recordings

Overview

In the early 2000s, U.S. manufacturers of household audio and video equipment reported sales of $7.6 billion. This was slightly higher than sales during the 1990s, which averaged about $6.6 billion in the first half of the decade and $7.2 billion in the latter half of the decade. U.S. companies focused largely on producing audio speakers and advanced technology televisions. Virtually all other consumer electronic components sold in the United States were manufactured abroad or manufactured in the United States by foreign-owned companies. Although shipment values of audio and video equipment have increased steadily since 1990, such is not true of TVs, which declined from $5.1 billion in 1995 to approximately $4 billion in the late

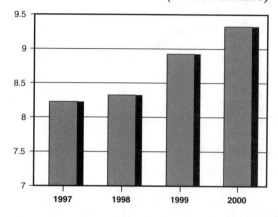

1990s and early 2000s. Driving sales are popular consumer electronic product categories like high-definition television (HDTV) sets, digital versatile disk (DVD) players, home theater systems, and television/VCR combinations.

Approximately 271 companies manufactured household audio and video equipment in the United States in the early 2000s, down from a peak of more than 350 companies in the early 1990s. The decline was due in large part to intense foreign competition, primarily from Japan and South Korea, which forced many U.S. manufacturers to abandon consumer electronics altogether.

Meanwhile, U.S. producers of pre-recorded records, compact disks (CDs), and cassettes posted revenues of $2.9 billion in 2000, up from $2.6 billion in 1999. According to the Recording Industry Association of America (RIAA), in 2000 the industry sold most of its product via record stores (42 percent), other types of stores (41 percent), music clubs (eight percent), and the Internet (three percent). While sales via the Internet have been rising since the late 1990s, sales via music clubs have steadily declined from a 15 percent level in 1994. Though five major companies dominate the audio recording industry, the nature of the music business has always guaranteed a place for the small record company attuned to new forms of popular music.

History of the Industry

The household audio and video equipment industry had its origins in the late nineteenth century. Thomas Edison developed the phonograph using wax cylinders in 1877 and Guglielmo Marconi created a wireless transmission system in 1895 that was used for radio broadcasts. A few years after Thomas Edison invented the phonograph, Emile Berliner developed the disk format of recording. By the beginning of the twentieth century, the disk format replaced the wax cylinder as the phonograph record format. Another important early innovation was Lee DeForest's vacuum tube, developed in 1906, an invention that allowed for the amplification of electronic signals.

The 1920s were important years of research and commercialization for the industry. Developments included the first commercial radio broadcast in 1922, the Western Electric Company's patents for electrical sound recording and the replacement in radios of loudspeakers for headphones in 1924, the introduction of the AC radio in 1926, Philo Farnsworth's television patents, the introduction of automobile radios in 1927, and the first experimental television station permits issued by the government in 1928.

The industry enjoyed rapid growth in the 1920s and 1930s. During that period, more than 100 million radios were sold in the United States. The Federal Communications Commission (FCC) was established in the United States in 1934 to regulate broadcasting. The FCC authorized FM radio and television broadcasting in 1941, but these developments were forestalled by the country's entry into World War II. By the end of World War II, there were nine commercial television stations, 46 commercial FM stations, and 943 AM stations in the United States.

The late 1940s saw the industry return to its pre-war patterns of rapid growth and innovation. In 1947, the first magnetic tape recorders were marketed. Bell Telephone Laboratories demonstrated the first transistor that same year. The transistor marked the birth of solid-state electronic components, commercialized in 1954 with the mass marketing of the first "pocket radio." Home audio hobbyists who put together their own systems revealed that the capacity for fidelity of sound-reproducing equipment far exceeded the fidelity of existing recordings. This led to the introduction of 45 rpm records and 33 rpm long-playing records in 1948. These records were the first mass-produced "hi-fi" recordings. Other important developments in these years included color television broadcasting in 1954, videotape recording for television stations in 1956, and stereophonic audio systems in 1958.

Sales of color televisions surged during the mid-1960s. The first solid-state color television sets were marketed in 1967. By the mid-1970s, solid-state color sets dominated the market. The first color videocassette recorders for household use were marketed in 1975 and sales increased rapidly after the early 1980s. The 1980s saw the introduction and rapid diffusion of digital technologies in household audio and video equipment. The industry developed compact disc and accommodating audio systems, first mass-marketed in 1983, which quickly replaced phonograph systems.

Significant Events Affecting the Industry

The advent of digital music formats has been significant. In the mid to late 1990s, the most significant innovations in audio formats included digital audio tape recorders (DATs), digital compact cassettes (DCCs), and mini-discs (MDs). These formats offered the same sound quality of conventional CDs but also provided buyers with the additional option of recording. In addition to being able to transfer music directly onto recordable CDs (CD-R), by the early 2000s, consumers were buying computer hard drives, also known as digital music servers, for the sole purpose of storing music they had downloaded from the Internet (in formats like MP3) or transferred from their CD collections. Additionally, CD recorders and portable Internet audio players were increasing in popularity.

The digital footprint also made its mark in the video segment, as digital video recorders and video recorders with hard drives (HDD) came onto the scene. Much like VCRs, these devices are capable of recording television programs for viewing at a later time. However, they do so in digital formats and have greater storage capacity than analog cassettes.

U.S. television stations began broadcasting high-definition television (HDTV) shows in 1998. HDTV offers the picture quality of a 35-millimeter photograph combined with the sound quality of a compact disc. In contrast to conventional analog television with its 525 horizontal lines, HDTV has 1,080 horizontal lines, providing much keener images and detail. Led by Dolby Laboratories and Zenith Electronics, the industry developed HDTV standards and manufacturers began selling HDTV sets in 1998. High-definition VCRs followed, along with HDTV direct broadcast satellite dishes. By the early 2000s, about 10 percent of U.S. television stations were broadcasting digital signals. However, approximately 60 percent of the nation's homes were capable of receiving digital broadcasts. Many of the leading networks, including CBS, ABC, and PBS, were broadcasting varying percentages of their programming in HDTV format. Other networks, like Fox, were slower to follow suit. The increase in digital TV (DTV) broadcasts has brought a steep increase in sales of digital TV sets. DTV sales from manufacturers to retailers increased by a factor of about 400 percent from 1999 to 2000, according to the Consumer Electronics Association (CEA).

In the late 1990s, the digital video disk or the digital versatile disk (DVD) emerged as the successor of the CD, CD-ROM, and laser video disk. Pioneering manufacturers Matsushita, Sony, and others hailed it as the next revolutionary consumer electronics product. They anticipated robust sales of the DVD player because they hoped it would eventually replace the VCR. With a 4.7 gigabyte capacity, the DVD can store an entire movie in stereo on a five-inch disk that allows users to instantaneously fast-forward and rewind, just like the audio CD player. Furthermore, manufacturers designed their DVD players to be backwards compatible; that is, to recognize older laser disk formats such as the audio CD and the CD-ROM.

By 2000, DVD Audio (DVD-A) and Super Audio CD (SACD) players were being sold. These devices used DVDs for audio instead of video. They improved upon the sound quality and storage capacity of the standard compact disc introduced in the 1980s in a number of ways. A principal advantage was the ability to offer multi-channel sound. Recordable DVD players also were being marketed by the early 2000s, making DVD an even stronger alternative to the VCR. Additionally, DVD players were being sold along with popular home theater packages, and in combination units that included a TV, VCR, or both. Using industry data, including figures from the Consumers Electronics Association, the DVD Entertainment Group revealed that consumer sales of DVDs reached 16.7 million units in 2001, nearly double the sales rate achieved in 2000. Additionally, the association indicated that about 25 percent of U.S. homes had a DVD player, representing an unprecedented level of market penetration among consumer electronic products.

Key Competitors

The leading makers of household audio and video equipment in the United States have been subsidiaries of foreign-owned companies. Leading the pack in the early 2000s was Matsushita Electric Corporation of America, a subsidiary of Japan's Matsushita Electric Industrial Company, Ltd. The parent company posted 2001 sales of $61.1 billion in 2001. Matsushita has 23 manufacturing sites in the United States and is home to such well-known brands as Panasonic, JVC, Quasar, and Technics. Behind Matsushita was Sony Corporation, which attributed approximately 70 percent of its 2001 revenues ($58.5 billion) to consumer electronic devices like stereo systems, television sets, and VCRs. Netherlands-based Philips Electronic, N.V. posted sales of $28.8 billion in 2001. The company marketed products to U.S. residents through its subsidiary, Philips Electronics North America Corporation.

In the early 2000s, the industry's five leading audio recording producers included world leader Universal Music Group, Sony Music Entertainment, Inc., and BMG Entertainment. Controlling nearly a third of the U.S. Market, Universal owned 15 record labels including Motown and Interscope. The firm posted 2001 sales of $5.8 billion. A subsidiary of consumer electronics powerhouse Sony Corporation, Sony Music Entertainment, Inc. was positioned as the world's second-largest audio recording company. The company owned a number of leading labels including Columbia and Epic. Third-place Warner Music, a division of AOL Time Warner, Inc., remained the only major U.S. audio recording manufacturer in the early 2000s. Warner controlled some of the most profitable labels, including Atlantic, Elektra, Warner Brothers, and Reprise, and had sales of $3.9 billion in 2001.

Industry Projections

According to estimates from the Consumer Electronics Association (CEA), manufacturer-to-dealer sales in the United States hit a record $93.2 billion in 2001. This figure was projected to grow in 2002, setting another industry record at $95.7 billion. Although these figures include more than just household audio and video equipment, they represent the overall strength of the industry. Audio and video equipment account for a significant share of the industry's sales. This was especially true of video, the industry's leading sales category. According to the CEA, DVD players and digital television sales were among key items fueling the growth of home video equipment in the early 2000s. All video categories, with the exception of analog televisions but including VCRs (which were becoming very inexpensive to buy), were achieving growth. Digital TV products alone were expected to generate more than $8 billion in sales in 2002. On the home audio front, the CEA revealed that sales of both components and systems accounted for $3.7 billion in sales in 2000, an increase of more than six percent over 1999 levels. In this category, home theater systems were an important growth driver. Sales of "home-theater-in-a-box" systems, which include all of the necessary components and speakers in one convenient package, achieved growth of more than 130 percent in 2001 and were expected to increase almost 25 percent in 2002, reaching sales of $945 million.

In 2000, the total retail value of the sound recording industry's products fell slightly (almost three percent) along with the number of recording units sold (about nine percent). The total number of audio recordings fell from 1.16 billion in 1999 to 1.07 billion in 2000. According to the Recording Industry Association of America, several key trends were evident in the early 2000s. Among these was the continuing and significant decrease in the number of audiocassettes and vinyl records being sold as the compact disc format continued to represent the preferred format for most recordings. The demand for singles also decreased markedly in the year 2000 by a factor of 50 percent. In response to consumer shopping trends, in the early 2000s, sales via the Internet and non-record stores were on the rise while sales from dedicated record stores and music clubs were declining. The rock music category was the most popular, followed by rap/hip hop, which surpassed country as the second most popular category in 2000.

Global Presence

The United States is the leading importer of home audio and video equipment. The value of imports increased significantly from approximately $20.0 billion in 1997 to about $30 billion in 2000, while exports remained relatively flat. Consequently, the nation's trade deficit increased, growing from $15.5 billion in 1997 to $25.6 billion in 2000. The weakness of the U.S. industry was also reflected in the fact that the top U.S.-based producers in 2001 were subsidiaries of foreign firms. Even Zenith, once the largest U.S.-based producer that was not a subsidiary of a foreign firm, became linked to a foreign company (LG Group of Korea) in the mid-1990s. With its high labor costs, U.S. manufacturers produce very few VCRs, televisions, tape and CD players and radios relative to the Asian giants based in Japan and Korea. Japan was the world's leading producer and exporter of household audio and video equipment in the 1990s and early 2000s. However, since the 1980s, Japan's dominance has been challenged by rapidly expanding production in South Korea, China, Singapore, Hong Kong, Malaysia, and Taiwan.

Worldwide retail audio recording sales totaled $37 billion in 2000, according to the London-based IFPI. In terms of volume, the United States was the leader in compact disc sales, with 943 million units. In second place was Japan (279 million units), followed by Germany (205 million units). The United Kingdom led the way in per capita sales of audio recordings, with each person purchasing about 4.0 recordings per year. Denmark and the United States were close behind, averaging about 3.8 recordings per person. According to the IFPI, local artists account for a growing percentage of worldwide sales in their respective regions, representing almost 70 percent of sales in 2000.

Employment in the Industry

The audio/video equipment industry employed 28,692 workers in 2000, including approximately 19,000 production workers. The sound recording industry, on the other hand, employed 27,053 workers, including 20,424 production workers. Production employees in the audio/video equipment industry earned about $12.36 an hour, while those in the sound recording industry earned $13.74 an hour. The workforce of both industries continued to decrease throughout the 1990s and into the early 2000s with the implementation of new manufacturing technology to automate the production process.

Sources for Further Study

Annual Survey of Manufacturers. Washington, DC: U.S. Department of Commerce, Economics and Statistics Administration, U.S. Census Bureau, February 2002.

Current Industrial Reports. Washington, DC: U.S. Department of Commerce, Economics and Statistics Administration, U.S. Census Bureau, August 2001.

Digital America 2001, the U.S. Consumer Electronics Industry Today. Arlington, VA: Consumer Electronics Association, 2001. Available at http://www.ce.org.

"DVD Software Purchases Increased 2.4 Times to $4.6 Billion, Putting DVD Sales Ahead of VHS for the First Time." Las Vegas: DVD Entertainment Group, 8 January 2001. Available at http://www.recordingmedia.org.

"Industry Information." London: IFPI, 9 April 2002. Available at http://www.ifpi.org.

"Industry Information." Washington, DC: The Recording Industry Association of America, 9 April 2002. Available at http://www.riaa.com.

Remich, Norman C., Jr. "Gunning for Global Gains: World Smarts Coupled with New-Product Initiatives Are Needed to Put a Plus Sign Next to Each Industry Segment for 1998." *Appliance Manufacturer,* January 1998.

———. "3 Record Breakers for 1996." *Appliance Manufacturer,* January 1997.

U.S. Industry and Trade Outlook 1998. Washington, DC: McGraw Hill and Department of Commerce, 1998.

Information Retrieval and Online Services

Overview

As the United States entered the information age and the concept of the "information superhighway" became commonplace, the previously small and obscure online information retrieval industry suddenly emerged as one of the hottest industries. Better known as online information services or simply online services, the core industry generated almost $9.1 billion in revenues in 1997 and was estimated to have revenues of $15.3 billion in 1999. But this was just for the traditional retrieval segment and excluded booming Internet-related business. According to Cahners In-Stat Group, revenues for Internet service providers (ISPs) were expected to total $32.5 billion in 2000, an increase of 37 percent from 1999. Cahners further forecast that revenues for wholesale Internet service, which ISPs resell to consumers, would reach $5.25 billion in 2002. The Internet has completely transformed all sectors of the electronic information industry, leading most traditional information vendors to set up Internet-based operations alongside the companies that specialize in Internet content and services.

The information services industry serves both businesses and consumers. The consumer online services segment of the industry is growing especially rapidly. This is supported by explosive growth in the number of Internet users. In the Unites States alone, more than half of the population, 143 million individuals, was online in early 2002, according to the U.S. Department of Commerce. This represented a 26 percent increase from 2001.

With 34 million subscribers, America Online (AOL) was the largest ISP in 2002. At that time, ISP-Planet reported that AOL served 19.4 percent of the U.S. market. By 2001, ActivMedia Research reported that about 25 percent of information or content-focused Web sites were turning profits, although most earned more from advertising revenues than from other sales. By late 2001, ISPs offering Internet access to businesses operated in an environment of consolidation. At that time, Cahners In-Stat Group indicated that 65 percent of 2001 revenues were attributable to the top ten ISPs, led by WorldCom/UUNet and AT&T.

History of the Industry

The electronic information services industry was born during the post-World War II information explosion. The advent of computers during this period formed the basis for channeling large amounts of data to scientists, engineers, businesses, and government agencies. Government investment in new information technologies in the 1950s and 1960s was supplemented by increased private sector spending on research and higher education. The result was that for the first time, skilled professionals could create, store, and quickly access large amounts of data.

The purpose of the earliest retrieval systems was simply to store and print information, mostly for technical endeavors. As the number and size of the databases grew, however, systems engineers began to focus on searching capabilities that could filter out unneeded data. Eventually, users were able to type commands into a computer that would search and display information containing specific keywords or phrases.

The first computerized bibliographic databases stemmed from the federal government's need for the efficient application of research dollars and the desire to eliminate duplicate analyses. Some of the more popular databases developed in this period included MEDLINE and ERIC. The government also subsidized nonprofit efforts, such as the American Chemical Society's Chemical Abstracts database.

In addition to supporting nonprofit services, government investment in the 1960s initiated many of the private information retrieval services that dominated the market in the 1980s and early 1990s. For instance, DIALOG sprang from a venture between the National Aeronautics and Space Administration (NASA) and Lockheed Corporation called Project RECON. ORBIT Online was developed as a result of System Development Corporation's work with the National Library of Medicine. Industry giant Mead Data Central (now called LEXIS-NEXIS) got its start from seed money provided by U.S. Air Force projects.

The federal government also played a vital role in developing telecommunications networks that made online services possible. Networks that essentially provided affordable access for database online users through local telephone lines stemmed from Department of Defense efforts. The network of all networks, the Internet, also began as a Department of Defense project known as the ARPANET. This network was developed by the department's Advanced Research Projects Agency (ARPA) in an effort to create a decentralized communications network that could be used during wartime. The technology was later passed on to universities, which quickly began to expand the uses of such a network.

As more efficient telecommunications networks arose and computer technology advanced in the late 1960s and 1970s, the market for online information services began to proliferate. Companies and libraries were increasingly relying on technical and legal information to provide a competitive edge in the marketplace or to make their research efforts more efficient. Furthermore,

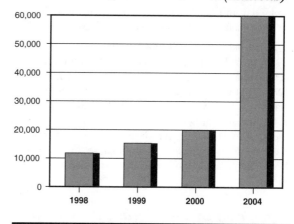

FINANCES:

Information Retrieval Services Estimated Receipts, 1998-2004 (millions)

many users were finding electronic information access to be an important tool for increasing productivity.

As electronic markets began to grow, many publishing houses began to experiment with electronic publishing as a means of delivering their information. H.W. Wilson and Company, for instance, began offering access to Wilson indexes and abstracts online through WILSONLINE. Likewise, McGraw-Hill and other periodical publishers began offering their publications online. One of the greatest commercial uses of electronic information retrieval was for legal publications.

By the end of the 1970s, the emerging information retrieval industry was beginning to establish itself in many sectors of government, academia, and industry. Because of technical limitations, however, retrieval systems remained extremely costly. Furthermore, most systems were complicated and required professional research skills for effective use. As a result, estimated industry revenues were still well under $500 million by 1980.

Technological breakthroughs in personal computer and data storage devices fueled rapid industry growth through the 1980s and early 1990s. At the same time that microcomputers were becoming faster and less expensive, users were becoming accustomed to working with modems, networks, and other communications devices, which allowed large numbers of people to gain access to reservoirs of data. For the first time, information retrieval companies were able to expand their services to the end user, or the person who would actually use the information, rather than professional researchers.

Industry Profiles

As end users increasingly became the market for information providers, companies began to emphasize user-friendly system interfaces that allowed easier data searching and access, such as providing menus instead of requiring the user to memorize arcane commands. Firms were also quick to take advantage of retrieval technologies. For instance, online services were able to make use of faster modem communication speeds, that increased from 1,200 bits per second (bps) in the mid-1980s to more than 56,000 bps by the late 1990s.

The advent of CD-ROM technology in the early 1980s provided a powerful means for the storage and dissemination of information. CD-ROMs could hold up to 650 megabytes of data, a vast amount by that period's standards. By comparison, the magnetic diskettes in use at the time held only 1.44 megabytes or even just 760,000 bytes. As CD-ROM drives became standard hardware, particularly in business or institutional settings, the number of databases and information services offered on CD greatly increased.

Significant Events Affecting the Industry

The commercialization of the Internet, and especially the World Wide Web, in the mid-1990s had a significant impact on the industry. The debut of graphical Web browsers, led by Mosaic and quickly followed by Netscape and Microsoft, made the Web an appealing commercial medium. More importantly, Web browsers began to illustrate the benefits of using a single platform to access numerous sources of information. Traditionally, users needed to install and run a separate interface program on their computer for each database or information service they wished to access. This proprietary software was often idiosyncratic and difficult to use. The Web offered a solution in that only one comparatively user-friendly main program, the browser, needed to be installed on the local computer in order to navigate an infinite number of different services. Thus, information vendors began to test Web-based versions of their services and new Internet-based vendors sprang up rapidly.

Although some traditional information vendors were slow to appreciate the Internet's popularity, by 2002 most were offering online access to their information services as a shift from print to digital resources was taking place. According to *Library Journal*, this shift was especially evident at the nation's academic libraries. In 2001 the publication conducted a survey of academic libraries, which revealed that spending on electronic serials, which totaled 11 percent of library budgets three years before, had grown to 16 percent and was expected to reach 22 percent by 2004.

The Internet's commercial viability also helped create a whole new category of services: that of consumer Internet access providers. While services like America Online and CompuServe had been around for decades, until the Internet emerged they had only managed to attract a small following of business-oriented or technologically savvy users to their closed networks. As they began to open their services so that subscribers could access Web content outside the provider's network, a growing number of independent firms and telecommunications companies began to offer stripped down, Internet-only services that provided little or no custom content but offered full access to the wealth of online information populating the Internet. By the early 2000s, many government agencies, trade associations, newspapers, and magazines offered free searchable databases. These sources complemented the offerings of leading information services, which allowed users to quickly search multiple sources based on many different search criteria.

Key Competitors

A diverse spectrum of companies participate in the electronic information industry. Leading companies fall into one of four main service categories: database information services, Internet access services for consumers, Internet access services for businesses and resellers, and Internet search and navigation services.

The leading online vendors of multiple databases to professional searchers are Dialog Corporation and the LexisNexis Group. Founded by Roger K. Summit in 1972, Dialog Corporation is the world's oldest information retrieval service. The company was known as Knight-Ridder Information, Inc. until 1997, when it was bought out by the British company Market Analysis and Information Database, PLC. The Thomson Corporation, a leading global provider of integrated information solutions, acquired the Information Services Division of Dialog in May of 2000 and incorporated it into its Scientific, Reference & Healthcare group. According to Thomson, which posted 2001 revenues of $7.2 billion, Dialog's commercial online collection of information is the world's largest. In 2002, the company employed more than 1,100 employees. At that time, users were able to search 900 databases containing 6 billion pages of text and 3 million pictures. Dialog's main services included DataStar, DIALOG, and Profound.

The LexisNexis Group is a division of UK-based publishing company Reed Elsevier, which posted 2001 revenues of $6.6 billion. LexisNexis was founded in 1966 as the Data Corporation. In 1968 it was acquired by the Mead Corporation and renamed Mead Data Central. Mead Data Central was sold to Reed Elsevier in 1994. The company's services include Lexis and Nexis. Started in 1973, Lexis offers access to legal databases. Nexis, which began in 1979, is the largest news and business information service. LexisNexis offers its information services electronically via dial-up or the World Wide Web as well as in print and CD-ROM formats. The company's electronic solutions allow users to search more than 3 billion documents.

Known to users as AOL, America Online, Inc. is the world's largest consumer online service, boasting 34 million subscribers in early 2002. In the mid-1990s, it emerged as the most popular U.S. service because it focused its content on serving the interests of a mass audience in contrast to some of the more specialized materials offered on competing services like CompuServe. By 1997, it was able to acquire its long-time rival CompuServe in a complex transaction that preserved the unique identity of the CompuServe service, which had 3 million users by 2002. In January of 2001, AOL merged with Time Warner to form AOL Time Warner, Inc., and America Online, Inc. became a division of the newly formed media and entertainment powerhouse. AOL, Inc. had 2000 revenues of $7.7 billion.

Purchased by the emerging telecommunications colossus WorldCom in 1996, UUNET Technologies, Inc. is the world's largest commercial Internet service provider. UUNET focuses exclusively on providing businesses and online service providers (such as the Microsoft Network) with access to the Internet and its global network backbone. UUNET developed one of the most widely deployed Internet networks in the world. The company's backbone allowed it to offer local access from more than 1,000 locations worldwide at speeds ranging from 28.8 Kbps to 155 Mbps. In February of 1997, WorldCom began a $300 million program to upgrade and expand the existing UUNET backbone bandwidth and dial capacity. By 2002, UUNET had increased the access speed to its backbone from a T-1 level (1.544 Mbps) in 1993 to 10 Gbps. At that time, the company also offered additional services including Web hosting. WorldCom filed for bankruptcy in 2002.

Yahoo! Inc. began as one of the first navigation services on the Internet and remains one of the key access points, known in industry jargon as "portals," to the Internet's content. As opposed to many of its competitors who relied on computer programs, Yahoo used human effort to categorize web pages listed in its search engine, resulting in what some regard as a more valuable structure for storing and retrieving data. In 2002, Yahoo! was still the most widely used search engine on the Internet. The company's 2001 revenues were $717.4 million, which were derived from different forms of advertising, as well as services like auctions and services like Yahoo! Bill Pay and Yahoo! Auctions.

Yahoo! was created in 1994 by David Filo and Jerry Yang, two Stanford University graduate students, and went public in 1996 with one of the first and most successful stock offerings in the Internet services industry. The company acquired HotJobs in late 2001 and launched its Premium Document Search service in January 2002, allowing customers access to more than 70 million full-text documents from more than 7,000 different sources. The latter development put Yahoo! in the same market as traditional information retrieval companies.

Industry Projections

According to figures published by the U.S. Department of Commerce, the information retrieval segment, which again excludes some of the Internet businesses, was growing at an annual rate of approximately 30 percent in the late 1990s. This growth rate was expected to continue through 2004. By 2004, this segment was forecast to exceed $56 billion in annual revenues.

Continued brisk growth is expected for all of the Internet-related services as well. According to IDC, the volume of worldwide Internet traffic is expected to increase 93 times from 2000 to 2005, reaching a level of 943 million users. Another measure of Internet development is advertising revenues. Online advertising revenues, according to published estimates by GartnerG2, were expected to increase from $7.9 billion in 2001 to $11.4 billion in 2002, $14.7 billion in 2003, and $17.2 billion the following year. By 2005, these revenues were expected to be $18.8 billion. As a result, services like Yahoo! that depend heavily on advertiser dollars are likely to achieve proportionate revenue gains in this period. Again according to GartnerG2, of the 2,800 Web sites that sold advertising, a mere 20 of them generated 80 percent of all revenues.

Wireless Internet devices were exploding in popularity in the early 2000s. AOL allowed its subscribers to access a wide variety of information including e-mail, news headlines, stock information, and instant messages via wireless devices like personal digital assistants (PDAs), wireless phones, and the company's AOL Mobile Communicator. Cahners In-Stat Group expected the number of people using business wireless data to grow 32 percent in 2002, reaching 39 million. Furthermore, Ovum predicted that revenues from wireless portals would mushroom to $42 billion by 2005, a significant increase over 2000 revenues of $747 million.

Global Presence

Information is a highly exportable product once language and technology standards barriers are surmounted, and the United States is the world's largest exporter of electronic information services. By nature, Web-based services are accessible from anywhere in the world. Accordingly, services like Yahoo! are widely used by people around the globe. Other kinds of services have an international presence, too. Notably, America Online is a significant provider of online services throughout the world. In March 2002, WebSideStory's StatMarket revealed that AOL served 14 percent of Internet users worldwide. UUNET also has sizable networking operations around the world, particularly in Europe. Its backbone includes direct cable connections across both the Atlantic and Pacific oceans, and employs satellites to reach parts of the world where it lacks cabling.

In the early 2000s, international growth was occurring for Internet service providers, especially in markets like India. Traditional information retrieval companies also had established global customer bases. For example, in 2002, Dialog operated from 32 countries including the

Middle East, South America, and South Africa, and served customers in 103 countries.

Employment in the Industry

Job opportunities abound in the electronic information industry. Conservative estimates suggest the industry's labor force doubled between 1988 and 1997. According to the U.S. Bureau of Labor Statistics' *2002-2003 Career Guide to Industries*, employment in the information retrieval sector had realized significant growth since the late 1980s, resulting in the creation of 196,000 jobs between 1990 and 2000. In 1997, the typical U.S. annual wage for workers in the information retrieval systems industry was $49,582. Between 1990 and 1997, wages in this industry grew at an average rate of 6.2 percent annually.

Sources for Further Study

Albanese, Andrew Richard. "Moving from Books to Bytes." *Library Journal*, 1 September 2001.

Cohen, J., et al. "Internet Navigation." New York: Merrill Lynch Capital Markets, 13 April 1998.

"Computer and Data Processing Services." *Career Guide to Industries 2002-03 Edition*. U.S. Department of Labor, 15 March 2002. Available at http://www.bls.gov/oco/cg/cgs033.htm.

Computer Industry Forecasts. Data Analysis Group, 1997.

"Information Services." *U.S. Industry and Trade Outlook*. New York: McGraw-Hill and U.S. Department of Commerce, 2000.

Tenopir, Carol. "Getting What You Pay For?" *Library Journal*, 1 February 2000.

Tenopir, Carol. "Will Online Vendors Survive?" *Library Journal*, 1 February 1998.

Tenopir, Carol, Gayle Baker, and William Robinson. "Racing at Full Speed." *Library Journal*, 15 May 2001.

Miscellaneous Shopping Goods Stores

Overview

Specialty goods stores faced accelerated competition in the early 2000s from large discount general merchandise stores such as Wal-Mart and Kmart, as well as from office supply giants such as Staples, Office Depot, and OfficeMax. These chains spread their outlets across the country and provided consumers not only with lower prices than small specialty shops but also with greater shopping convenience.

Nonetheless, numerous chain and independent specialty goods stores still operated and thrived in the early 2000s. Specialty stores often have a few competitive advantages over their general merchandise and office supply rivals, namely larger selections of special items and better service. Different sectors in the industry include book stores, jewelry stores, sporting goods stores, toy stores, and sewing and needlework stores.

History of the Industry

Bookstores The first bookstores appeared in the American colonies as early as 1640, with Boston becoming a pre-Revolutionary War center for both bookselling and publishing. By the time Benjamin Harris, who published the first newspaper in the colonies, opened a bookstore in 1686, there were already seven other booksellers in Boston.

Early bookstores were also more like variety stores than bookstores in the modern sense. For example, Andrew Bradford offered his customers merchandise ranging from feathers to pickled sturgeon. Thomas Fleet, a publisher of children's books in Boston, sold slaves from his bookstore. Moreover, colonial bookstores often carried a remarkable variety of books. In 1766, Boston shop owner John Mein published a catalogue listing more than 1,700 titles. Religion and philosophy dominated the early book trade. The widespread availability of books by John Locke and other philosophers who wrote about natural rights helped set the stage for the American Revolution and booksellers were often among the intellectual leaders of the colonies. However, novels were also popular.

Bookstores flourished between 1845 and the beginning of the Civil War. However, bookselling began to change dramatically about the time the war ended. In the late 1860s, most large publishers were operating their own bookstores in competition with independent booksellers. In addition, publishers began offering volume discounts to large drygoods stores that opened up book departments. Volume discounts eventually cut bookstores out of the textbook trade altogether and would remain an issue of contention between publishers and bookstores up until the present time, especially with the development of chain stores in the 1970s.

Drug Stores The drug store industry originated in the mid-1800s, when Americans began using patent remedies to treat illnesses. Some early pharmacists operated out of village apothecaries, where they purchased chemicals in bulk and mixed them on the premises to fill prescriptions. Following the Great Depression, pharmaceutical companies grew rapidly and opened sophisticated research facilities. The number of patents issued for drug products increased from fewer than 100 before 1940 to over 4,000 by the 1950s. Medicines began to be marketed in final-dosage form under a manufacturer's brand name rather than in bulk as generic ingredients. As a result, the number of drug stores increased, while pharmacists adopted a service-oriented role in dispensing prescriptions.

Jewelry Stores Since the beginning of time, jewelry has enriched human life in many ways. Jewelry has been used for gifts, ceremonies, and as a symbol of wealth. Ancient Egyptian kings were mummified with jewelry wrapped in the folds of their burial cloths. Turkish sultans lavished jewelry upon the women in their harems to enhance the women's beauty. Many religions symbolize marriage and other ceremonies with jewelry such as rings, crosses, and rosaries. Until recent history, each piece of jewelry was handcrafted. Now many pieces are mass-produced. Because many people consider jewelry a luxury item, sales are driven by the state of the economy.

The retail fine jewelry industry is divided into two types of enterprise: chain stores and independents, with chain stores predominating. The cyclical nature of the business had ushered in a recessionary era of poor sales in the early 1990s, but the industry had rebounded by mid-decade.

Independent retail jewelers fought a tough battle to maintain their identity in the competitive jewelry business of the 1990s. One such tactic has been the introduction of in-house credit cards, offered by the retailer and his or her bank. As the retail jewelry industry neared the twenty-first century, it faced heavy competition from home shopping channels. Successful jewelers, however, lured customers by adhering to traditional standards of excellence and offering products that could be trusted at reasonable prices.

Toy Stores   With the opening of the first Toys "R" Us in the 1950s, retailing of toys in the United States changed forever. The vast retail chain began as a bicycle shop, was transformed into a juvenile furniture store, and finally became a toy store. Additional Toys "R" Us stores were soon opened. These outlets emphasize deep discounts and wide selections.

Another key factor in the growth of the retail sale of toys was the increase in the use of television advertising. In the late 1950s and early 1960s, television promotions reached into many homes where toy purchasing decisions were made.

Many toy manufacturers helped toy stores sell items by licensing products that were perceived as popular, or "hot toys." The late 1970s and early 1980s also saw the introduction of electronic games and toys. While retailers were enthusiastic about the tendency of buyers to purchase these items year-round, they suffered from a glut of products left on their shelves. These unsold items became so costly for some retailers that losses forced them to close in the late 1980s. This led to the consolidation of stores that occurred in the 1990s.

Sporting Goods Stores   As the fitness industry sparked consumer appeal for exercise equipment, accessories, and athletic wear, trends gradually shifted from sporting goods stores, which were typically sole proprietorships and small "pro shops," to franchises and eventually sporting goods chains. Bicycle shops have even begun billing themselves as "bicycling and fitness" shops and have expanded their product mixes to include exercise bicycles, treadmills, climbers, and weight machines to capitalize on the craze. These types of stores appeal to a growing number of consumers who are exercising in their own home gyms. Although the fitness craze has leveled off,

the demand for other sporting goods such as camping equipment, in-line skates, mountain bikes, and accessories has helped fill the void.

Sewing and Needlework Stores   Many of the businesses in this industry opened in the 1940s and early 1950s as basic fabric outlets. Carrying garment-oriented sewing supplies, these stores catered to the post-World War II mother who sewed a large percentage of her family's clothing. Throughout the 1950s and into the 1960s, businesses in the home sewing industry prospered. Some businesses, such as Fabri-Centers of America, were able to grow from small local enterprises into national chains by acquiring or merging with other fabric retailers. In the late 1960s, however, the home-sewing market began to decline due to the increase of working mothers and affordable "off-the-rack" clothing.

Fortunately for retailers, the decline of home sewing was succeeded by a series of fads in other sewing and needlework segments. Entering the 1970s, the yarn and needlework crafts fared better than garment sewing. These types of crafts took less time and therefore were attractive to time-pressed women.

The industry continued to evolve as different sewing and needlework segments gained and lost popularity. Successive waves of craft trends dictated store inventories. In the late 1980s, for example, quilting became popular, immediately followed by fabric painting. The 1990s saw a revival of cross stitch and embroidery popularity. Though the colors changed year after year, the different crafts required the same raw materials like fabric, yarn, and notions.

Significant Events Affecting the Industry

The retail industry became dominated by large discount general merchandise stores that sold everything from clothes and food to books and household appliances. These stores included Wal-Mart, Target, and Kmart. Because of their large inventories, these stores can sell their products for less than small stores that specialize in one product line such as books, jewelry, or sporting goods. However, these large chains usually cannot provide the kind of personalized customer service available at specialty stores.

Specialty retailers also faced competition from catalog and mail order houses, which provided consumers with the convenience of shopping at home as well as competitive prices. Furthermore, the growth of the Internet allowed merchants to sell their products online, offering the same conveniences as mail order retailers. Some of these operations have experienced remarkable success. For example, Amazon.com, Inc. not only claims to be the largest online bookstore and the world's biggest bookstore (the company literally offered millions of titles at its Web-based store in the early 2000s), it also claims to have "the Earth's biggest selection of products." In addition to books, the Web site's offerings included CDs, DVDs, videos, games, toys, kitchenware, computers, and electronics. With infinite shelf space and no retail rent, overhead can remain low resulting in lower prices to consumers.

Key Competitors

Barnes & Noble, Inc. is the largest bookseller in the United States. In 2001, it operated almost 900 stores, including 590 superstores. The company is credited with introducing the superstore concept (which Borders has embraced) and has also established a significant online presence in an alliance with Bertelsmann. With the acquisition of Marboro Books in 1979, it entered the mail-order and publishing business. Barnes & Noble's subsidiary GameStop is the nation's top seller of video games. The company was first publicly traded in 1993. Sales reached $4.9 billion in 2001, up 11 percent from 2000. In addition to selling books, Barnes & Noble was planning to increase its publishing efforts in the early 2000s.

Once the largest bookstore operator in the United States, Borders Group, Inc. has been second to Barnes & Noble since 1992. Borders Group operates more than 1,200 retail stores, including 385 superstores, across the country. In addition to Borders stores, the company sells books online in partnership with Amazon.com and operates retail locations under the name Waldenbooks. Borders' revenues for 2002 climbed almost four percent to $3.4 billion.

The Sports Authority, Inc. led the sporting goods segment with $1.4 billion in sales in 2001, at which time it operated approximately 200 stores. The Sports Authority was the 1994 brainchild of Kmart. In 1998, Woolworth agreed to purchase the company. Other significant companies in the early 2000s included Gart Sports Company with 2002 sales of $936 million, Big 5 Sporting Goods Corporation with 2001 sales of $623 million, and Sports Chalet with 2001 sales of $215 million.

Although Wal-Mart was the industry's leading toy-seller overall, Toys "R" Us was one of the world's largest toy retailers in the early 2000s, with 2002 sales of $11.0 billion. At that time, the company operated 1,600 discount toy stores in the United States and other countries. K-B Toys also was among the leading American toy retailers, running more than 1,300 toy stores. K-B operates stores domestically and internationally, and also sells toys via the Web. Bain Capital owns K-B, which posted estimated sales of $2 billion in 2001.

Jo-Ann Stores, Inc. led the sewing and needlework segment of the industry. The company operates 960 stores throughout the United States and most of its stores are located in strip malls. Jo-Ann Stores was formerly named Fabri-Centers of America. The firm operates stores under the name Jo-Ann Fabrics and Crafts, as well as Jo-Ann Etc. In 2002, the company's sales rose to $1.6 billion. Hancock Fabrics, Inc. was another one of the country's major sewing and needlework stores in the

early 2000s. In 2002 Hancock boasted of 440 stores all over the country and booked sales of $412 million.

Industry Projections

In the early 2000s, superstores continued to dominate the book store segment, with Barnes & Noble the undisputed leader. In 2001 book sales totaled $25.4 billion, barely increasing from 2000 levels of $25.3 billion, according to a *Publishers Weekly* report. However, this did represent a steady increase over 1997 levels of $21.3 billion. In 2001, book club sales accounted for five percent or $1.3 billion of total book sales. The higher education segment posted $3.5 billion in revenues from textbooks, up seven percent from 2000. In the consumer segment, sales fell about three percent in 2001, reaching $6.4 billion. Sales of both hard cover and paperback adult books fell more than two percent, reaching $2.6 billion and $1.9 billion respectively. Sales of children's paperback books rose almost 18 percent to $888 million, while children's hard cover book sales plunged approximately 23 percent to $929 million. Professional book sales fell almost eight percent to $4.7 billion, due to slack demand, especially in the category of computer books.

The sporting goods segment benefited from the U.S. fitness craze, which led to increased demand for sporting goods and bicycles in the 1990s and early 2000s. By 1996, there were more than 23,000 sporting goods stores and bicycle shops serving the nation. Retail sales of sporting goods more than doubled from $7.5 billion in 1983 to $17.3 billion in 1996. By 2001, manufacturer (wholesale) sales alone totaled approximately $15 billion. According to the National Bicycle Dealers Association, retail sales of bicycles were estimated to exceed $5 billion in the early 2000s. While adults between the ages of 25 and 44 constitute the mainstay of purchasers, industry leaders recognize a need to focus their marketing strategies on the inclusion of both younger as well as older consumer groups.

By the early 2000s, the toy segment had given way to intense competition from discount general merchandise stores, which, according to the Toy Industry Association (TIA), accounted for almost 42 percent of retail sales, followed by toy stores (21 percent). According to TIA, sales volume for the American toy industry in 2000 was $29 billion, a slight decrease from 1999 levels of $30 billion, but up from $27 billion in 1998. Stores ranged from independent shops to national chains that sold toys and hobby supplies exclusively. Leading toys during this period included Hot Wheels Basic Cars, Poo-Chi Robotic Dogs, and Leap Pads. Computer/video games also remained popular during this period.

Although the sewing and needlework segment is dominated by a few large national chains, hundreds of small shops are scattered throughout the country. According to the Hobby Industry Association (HIA), in the early 2000s, needlecraft was the second-most-popular area of the $26 billion U.S. craft and hobby industry, accounting for almost 30 percent of sales. The big chain stores are a dominant industry force, with the top two firms having combined revenues in excess of $2.0 billion. The industry expanded in the mid- to late 1990s as a result of the popularity of arts and crafts and home decorating during this period. However, when discount general merchandise stores became aware of these consumer trends, they quickly expanded their selections of supplies related to sewing needlework, causing heightened competition in the industry. Consequently, stores specializing in sewing and needlework supplies began to consolidate, falling from 2,700 stores in 1991 to 2,000 in 1996. By 2001 discount stores generated 25 percent of overall craft and hobby industry sales, followed by craft chains (19 percent) and fabric and craft chains (12 percent).

Jewelry stores overcame the country's economic recession of the early 1990s with moderate growth in the mid-1990s. As sales picked up at the end of the decade, jewelry stores introduced a number of new products, including many new brands of watches. They also launched an extensive advertising campaign during this period to boost their sales. Sport watches remained one of their leading products. According to *National Jeweler*, this segment of the industry grew more than 40 percent during the decade of the 1990s, and revenues totaled $41 billion in 2000. However, sales fell after mid-2000 and were expected to continue falling into the early 2000s in the wake of a weak economy.

Shops that specialize in gifts and souvenirs were a billion dollar industry by the early 2000s. Gift and souvenir shops began growing in the mid- to late 1990s as U.S. consumers had more money to spend on non-essential merchandise during the country's economic prosperity. Collectible dolls, figurines, and ornaments accounted for a strong share of this segment's sales. In the early 2000s, the industry posted more than $55 billion in sales, according to *Gift & Decorative Accessories*. Home accessories and accents accounted for 30 percent of sales, followed by general gifts like desk accessories and children's gifts (25 percent). Stationary products accounted for another 25 percent of sales. While these segments all were experiencing growth, the seasonal items category remained flat, and sales of collectible items decreased almost seven percent.

Global Presence

Although U.S. toy stores have enjoyed some success abroad, the United States remains the world's largest market for toys. International trade has been a major part of the toy industry and a significant influence on the sporting goods segment as well. By value, the United States imports more than twice the amount of toys than it manufactures, with an average of almost $13 billion in goods imported each year in the late 1990s and early 2000s. China is the leading source of U.S. imports, supplying more than half, followed by Japan and Mexico. Important external markets for U.S. toys and sporting goods include Canada, Japan, the United Kingdom, and Mexico. According to the Toy Industry Association, nearly 45 percent of global retail sales took place in North America in the early 2000s. Many American toy stores have tried to capitalize on the changing face of the world. Toys "R" Us was one of the first U.S. retail stores to open in Japan, where it had established itself as the leading toy retailer by the early 2000s.

Sources for Further Study

"Americas New Bestsellers: How Independent Bookstores Are Shaking Off the Chains." *U.S. News & World Report*, 16 April 1990.

Barbato, Joseph. "Chain Superstores: Good Business for Small Presses?" *Publishers Weekly*, 9 November 1992.

"Consumers In Doubt: In a Time of Uncertainty, How Will the Gift Industry Fare?" *Gift & Decorative Accessories*, December 2001.

Hobby Industry Association. "1996 Nationwide Craft/Hobby Consumer Study," 23 February 1996. Available at http://www.hobby.org/hia/cons.html.

Hobby Industry Association. "2001 Nationwide Craft & Hobby Consumer Usage Study," 6 May 2002. Available at http://www.hobby.org.

"Industry Trends Debated at Leadership Council Meeting." Business Product Industry Association (BPIA) Industry Report, 15 March 1997.

Janowski, Ben. "Mall Stores: How Strong a Future?" *Jewelers' Circular-Keystone*, January 1996.

Lazich, Robert S., ed. *Market Share Reporter*. Detroit, MI: Gale Research, 1997.

Leib, Jeffrey. "Excess Baggage? Major Changes Are Planned for Samsonite, But What Will They Be?" *Denver Post*, 30 September 1996.

Levenson, Maurice. "Fabri-Centers." *The Value Line Investment Survey*, 22 November 1996.

———. "Hancock Fabrics." *The Value Line Investment Survey*, 22 November 1996.

———. "Michaels Stores." *The Value Line Investment Survey*, 22 November 1996.

Meltzer, Stephanie. "A Bear Market For Teddies." *American Demographics*, February 1996.

Milloit, Jim. "BISG Predicts a 5 Percent Gain in Book Sales for 1997." *Publishers Weekly*, 7 July 1997.

Mutter, John and Karen Angel. "Sad Tiding of the New Year: Superstores, Location and Local Economies Drive Some Bookstores out of Business." *Publishers Weekly*, 29 January 1996.

"The Sale of the Year: Great Retail Stocks." *Money*, January 1996.

Specialty Retail Update: Industry Report. New York: Sanford C. Bernstein & Company, Inc., 24 October 1996.

"State of the Jewelry Industry." *National Jeweler*, 1 August 2001.

Taylor, Dennis. "Very Best Not Good Enough." *The Business Journal*, 18 November 1996.

2001-2002 Toy Industry Fact Book. New York: Toy Industry Association Inc, 2001. Available at http://www.toy-tia.org.

Motor Vehicles

Overview

The U.S. automobile industry is among the country's most lucrative in terms of sales volume (sales of new vehicles exceeded $605 billion in 1999), but it's not nearly as profitable as many other industries. The industry is vital to the nation's economy. According to a March 2001 study by the University of Michigan and the Center for Automotive Research, light vehicle production and sales account for almost four percent of the U.S. gross domestic product (GDP). At home the U.S. Big Three—General Motors, Ford, and the Chrysler division of DaimlerChrysler—have endured a saturated market with cyclical demand tied to the health of the general economy. In addition, imported cars and trucks, mainly from Asian companies, continue to wrest market share away from the Big Three. In the latter half of the 1990s, yearly domestic production hovered around 15.0 million cars and light trucks, including sport utility vehicles (SUVs). In 1999, this number reached almost 17.0 million, followed by 17.4 million in 2000. According to some analysts, despite fluctuating levels of demand, this may indicate a higher overall industry sales threshold. Facing poor sales in a weakened economy characterized by decreasing consumer confidence and rising unemployment, the auto industry offered zero percent financing to consumers in 2001 to stimulate demand. While this was a successful tactic in the short term, such offers are not possible over extended periods because they mean significant reductions in interest income for automakers.

History of the Industry

Many people in many nations contributed the ideas, inventions, and innovations required to assemble useful motor vehicles. Roger Bacon, the thirteenth century English philosopher and scientist, prophesied its development. Leonardo de Vinci envisioned plans for its construction. Nicholas Joseph Cugnot constructed the first functioning self-propelled unit; Cugnot's vehicle, built in 1769, had three wheels and was powered with a steam engine.

During the early 1890s, many people in the United States were working separately on producing better "horseless carriages." According to some accounts, two brothers—Charles and Frank Duryea of Springfield, Massachusetts—developed the first successful American gasoline automobile. The Duryea model was based on the German inventor Karl Benz's work as reported in *Scientific American*.

Among the long list of early automotive pioneers, the best remembered is undoubtedly Henry Ford. Ford built his first car, called a "quadricycle," in 1896. He established the Detroit Automobile Company in 1899, but the venture failed. Ford's second company, the Henry Ford Company, founded in 1901, also failed. He finally achieved success with his third organization, the Ford Motor Company, officially founded on June 10, 1903.

Throughout the early decades of the twentieth century, Ford dominated the industry. He achieved nearly legendary status by introducing the automotive industry to the benefits of automated production and by providing an automobile at a price that most people could afford. In 1908, Ford decided to focus his company's efforts on the construction of only one model, the Model T. To help lower costs and speed production, he began moving toward assembly line production.

In 1913, a moving belt was installed in Ford's magneto department. A magneto was a part that provided the electric current required for ignition. After its installation, the moving belt enabled each worker to perform a single task rather than assemble a completed magneto. Production experienced a four-fold increase, and Ford transferred moving assembly lines to other parts of the plant. In its first complete year of assembly line production, the company built 248,000 cars—compared with 78,000 the previous year. In 1915, Ford's annual production reached 500,000 and prices fell. The 1912 Model T sold for $600, the 1914 Model T cost $490, a 1915 touring car cost $440, and the price of the 1925 model dropped to $290. By 1920, an estimated three-fifths of U.S. cars and 50 percent of all the cars in the world were Model Ts.

Although its sales diminished as consumers turned to more modern offerings, the Model T earned its place in history. When Model T production was halted in 1927, an estimated 11 of every 20 cars on American roads were Model Ts. Fifteen million units had been sold. No other single model surpassed Model T sales until the 1960s, when the record went to the Volkswagen Beetle.

Auto sales dropped in 1929—an indication of the coming depression. As the 1930s opened, auto output was down 37 percent. Production in 1931 tumbled 30 percent. The auto industry fell from first place, as measured according to the value of products sold, to fourth in the national economy, and its decline created a ripple effect throughout the nation's entire economic infrastructure. Automakers, however, were among the first to emerge from the Depression years. By 1936, for example, General Motors was close to its pre-Depression profits.

The late 1930s brought technical innovations to the automotive industry. Automatic transmissions became common, increased precision enabled manufacturers to produce better cars, and attention to styling and aerodynamics improved stability and fuel efficiency. Post-Depression era work projects also improved the nation's highway system, and the miles of paved roads more than doubled between 1933 and 1941. The Pennsylvania Turnpike opened in 1940, and although initial estimates projected the toll road would carry 715 vehicles per day, within two weeks, 26,000 vehicles were using the new roadway each day.

American automakers found an eager market in the postwar years. One-half of the nation's 25.8 million registered cars were 10 or more years old and people were ready to purchase new cars. Between 1946 and 1950, 21.4 million new cars were sold. Production in 1949 topped the 5 million mark for the first time since the pre-Depression era. The dominance of car and truck transportation was further assured in 1958 when the National Highway Act was passed. This legislation provided funds for significant construction to improve the nation's highway system.

During the 1950s, the car's appearance assumed greater importance. Car buyers preferred big and powerful vehicles, which resulted in advertising that emphasized engine horsepower. Ornamental tail fins, inspired by aircraft fuselages, were first incorporated into a Cadillac design and came to symbolize cars of the era. Technical developments included power steering, power brakes, and improvements in automatic transmissions—all necessary to help control large cars.

In addition to increased competition from imported cars, the 1960s brought rising criticism of the U.S. auto industry. Ralph Nader's *Unsafe at Any Speed: The Designed-In Dangers of the American Automobile* was published in 1965 and inaugurated a crusade for safer cars. In 1966, Congress passed the National Traffic and Motor Vehicle Safety Act which mandated improvements in passenger safety, driver visibility, and braking. The act also required public announcement of recalls to correct safety defects. During the first 10 years of regulation, 52 million cars and trucks were recalled. Safety was not the only arena for critics; cars were also identified as a source of air pollution. In 1965, Congress passed the Vehicle Air Pollution and Control Act setting mandatory pollution standards. The 1970s opened with another anti-pollution effort—Congress passed the Clean Air Act, which mandated a 90 percent reduction in auto emissions within six years.

Concerns about fuel efficiency dominated the 1970s. In 1973, General Motor's cars averaged less than 12 miles per gallon and other domestic car makers' offerings were only slightly better. Two oil crises during the decade brought the nation increased gas prices, local shortages, a 55-miles-per-hour speed limit, and federally mandated fuel efficiency. The Energy Policy and Conservation Act, passed in 1975, specified that car manufacturers meet a sales-weighted "corporate average fuel economy" (CAFE) standard of 20 miles per gallon by the 1980 model year and 27.5 miles per gallon by the 1985 model year.

During the early 1980s, domestic automakers found themselves unprepared for the sudden surge in the small car market and as a result, they lost substantial ground to imports. A growing sense that the products coming out of Detroit, Michigan were inferior to those of imports further exacerbated the slide of the domestic automotive manufacturers. Chrysler Corporation wavered on the

FINANCES:

U.S. Motor Vehicle Sales and Production, 1996-2000 *(thousands of vehicles)*

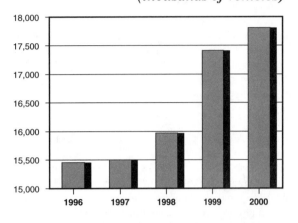

brink of bankruptcy and, under the leadership of Lee Iacocca, secured a federal loan guarantee of $1.5 billion to survive. A resurgence during the middle of the decade failed to provide long term stability. The auto industry achieved record sales of 16.3 million units in 1986, but new light vehicle sales fell in 4 out of the 5 years between 1986 and 1991. In 1990, the Big Three reported combined losses of $1.1 billion, and General Motors was in particularly bad shape. During 1991, U.S. production facilities operated at only 60 to 65 percent of their capacity.

Significant Events Affecting the Industry

The early 1990s recession triggered a period of cost-cutting and efficiency gains for the U.S. auto industry. Through the handiwork of such industry figures as Ignacio Lopez at General Motors, the industry began to place heavy pressure on parts suppliers to cut costs and pass those savings on to the automakers. In some cases, the Big Three gave their parts vendors specific reduction targets; and if these reductions weren't met, suppliers could lose their contracts. Meanwhile, automakers also began to shed some of their own employees, close unprofitable or inefficient plants, and spin off nonessential business units. These moves coincided with trends toward reducing the total number of separate parts suppliers and outsourcing more production tasks to integrated companies that could add more value to the parts and systems they supplied. Despite GM's successes at trimming some of its costs under Lopez, Chrysler and Ford proved to be much more agile at hacking inefficiencies out of their systems. GM continued to be haunted by this deficiency through the end of the decade.

In the early 2000s, business-to-business marketplaces offered further opportunities for the industry to increase efficiency and lower costs. In February 2000, the Big Three announced plans to form a global online exchange for suppliers that eventually was named Covisint.

Key Competitors

The domestic U.S. auto industry was firmly in the control of the Big Three for several decades. However, in the early 2000s, Asian automakers continued to gain an increasing percentage of the U.S. market. For example, according to industry analysts, it appeared likely that Japanese automaker Toyota would replace Daimler-Chrysler's Chrysler division as one of the Big Three by 2005.

General Motors   General Motors is the world's largest auto manufacturer by revenue and by production volume. GM was incorporated in 1908 by William C. Durant. Its first components were Oldsmobile and Buick. The company acquired two more manufacturers in 1909—Oakland and Cadillac—and between 1910 and 1920, Durant obtained more than 30 companies. The unit that would go on to become GM's largest division, Chevrolet, was acquired in 1918. While the megalith company that resulted came to symbolize corporate America, GM never fully surmounted a number of obstacles that increasingly weighed it down in the 1990s. In part because of its sheer size, GM was a bloated and inefficient organization compared to its competitors. In the late 1990s, management at GM publicly agreed with this diagnosis, but the company also engendered the Big Three's worst relationship with its labor union, the United Auto Workers (UAW). Tension between GM and the UAW created recurring showdowns between the company and its workers, often leading to labor strikes. Perhaps the most dramatic—and decidedly the most costly—of these was a 1998 incident involving a stamping plant in Flint, Michigan, that eventually idled virtually all of GM's production activities and cost the company upward of $2 billion in lost sales.

By the early 2000s, GM had improved in several areas including market share, quality, and profitability. Unlike Ford and Chrysler, GM turned a profit in 2001, earning $1.5 billion on annual revenues of $177 billion. The company broke an industry record for truck sales in calendar year 2001, when it also sold more than 1 million sport utility vehicles, an industry first. The company streamlined it workforce from about 608,000 workers in 1998 to 365,000 in 2001, and was making international inroads by acquiring stakes in Asian automakers like Suzuki Motor Corporation and Isuzu Motors, Ltd.

Ford   The Ford Motor Company is the second largest U.S. automaker, with sales of $162.4 billion in 2001. The company was established in 1903 by Henry Ford, considered one of the pioneers of the industry, whose early models bore alphabetic designations. His first offering, the Model A, was introduced in 1903, and the company

introduced the Model C the following year. Looking for a car with mass appeal that could be produced at a low cost, Ford continued making innovations. The Model N was introduced for the 1906/1907 season and boasted speeds up to 45 miles per hour and a fuel economy of 20 miles per gallon. It sold for $600. The Model N was followed by an upgraded Model R and a refined Model S. Arguably the most famous car in automotive history, Ford's Model T was introduced for the 1908/1909 season. Ford's ninth model in six years, the Model T achieved nearly legendary status and dominated the industry for 18 years. During production of the Model T, Ford was credited with introducing in 1913 the world's first moving assembly line, which greatly enhanced productivity for the 1914 model year.

After enjoying a reputation for exceptional management and quality, Ford faced a number of obstacles in the early 2000s. Following a series of accident-related deaths involving the Ford Explorer, Ford initiated a massive $300 million recall of Firestone tires in 2000, followed by a second recall in 2001 that cost the company billions of dollars. In addition to financial losses, Ford was challenged by poor relationships with its dealers and employees. In 2001, William Clay Ford, Jr. replaced Jacques Nasser as the firm's CEO. That year, Ford recorded a $5.5 billion loss on sales of $162.4 billion. In addition to its long-standing vehicle lines like Lincoln and Mercury, Ford operates the car rental company Hertz and has acquired other automakers, including Jaguar in 1990, Volvo in 1999, and Land Rover in 2000.

DaimlerChrysler AG   In 1998 Chrysler Corporation agreed to merge with Germany's Daimler-Benz AG, forming DaimlerChrysler. In 2002 the Chrysler division of DaimlerChrysler still held the third slot among the Big Three U.S. automakers. Chrysler was formed from the remnants of the Maxwell Motor Car Company in 1925 by Walter P. Chrysler. As early as 1929, the company was counted as one of the Big Three. Chrysler experienced high sales during the early 1970s, but events later in the decade pushed the company to the brink of bankruptcy. To help ensure Chrysler's survival, Congress passed the Chrysler Corporation Loan Guarantee Act, which provided the company with $1.5 billion in federal loan guarantees. This money enabled Chrysler to stage a dramatic turnaround in the 1980s, led by sales of its popular minivans. By the 1990s, while it was still a distant third in the U.S. industry, Chrysler was a very lean and efficient company. It was in a period of relative financial health in the late 1990s that Chrysler shocked the industry by announcing its intention to merge with Daimler-Benz.

In 2001 DaimlerChrysler lost $590 million on revenues of $136 billion. The company faced a tough domestic market in the United States. Although it employed 372,500 workers in 2001, DaimlerChrysler was in the process of making significant workforce reductions at its

Chrysler division, which employed more than 104,000 workers.

Industry Projections

One key growth trend in the industry is a marked U.S. consumer preference for light trucks, minivans, and sport utility vehicles. Indeed, in the last years of the twentieth century, analysts expected cars to rapidly lose market share to trucks. In 1997 car sales numbered 8.3 million units and light trucks accounted for 6.9 million units. By 2000 the gap between cars and light trucks had almost vanished. Light truck sales numbered 8.5 million units while car sales totaled 8.8 million units.

Another emerging trend is the popularity of specialty vehicles. One form of specialty vehicle is the hybrid, which incorporates popular features from several different vehicle classifications. For example, the Pontiac Aztec combines features from a sport utility vehicle with a minivan. Nostalgic vehicles also fall into the specialty category. Examples of this vehicle type include Chrysler's PT Cruiser and the Ford Thunderbird. Ford also planned to release the Mercury Marauder in 2003, a throwback to the early 1960s. In general, specialty vehicles command higher prices from automotive enthusiasts despite lower production volumes.

Global Presence

U.S. automakers earn billions from foreign sales, but overall they haven't been as successful exporting their products as their Asian counterparts, which continue to erode the Big Three's domestic market share. According to Standard & Poor's, the industry's trade deficit has grown significantly since the mid-1990s, exceeding $115 billion in 2000. Exports grew less than 25 percent between 1995 and 2000, while imports rose almost 60 percent during the same time period. Since 1995, deficits increased the most among Asian countries like China (288 percent), Korea (331 percent), and Japan (34 percent).

Employment in the Industry

The auto industry is a significant, although declining, employer in the United States. About 1,013,000 workers are employed by manufacturers of motor vehicles and equipment. Of these personnel, approximately 598,000 work in the production sector. The industry's production workers enjoy higher than average wages due in part to the strength of labor unions. In 2000, the average hourly wage for these workers was $17.48 per hour.

Sources for Further Study

"About Covisint." 8 April 2002. Available at http://www.covisint.com/about.

"Autos and Auto Parts." *Standard & Poor's Industry Surveys*, December 2001.

General Motors: The First 75 Years of Transportation Products. Princeton, NJ: General Motors Corporation, 1983.

"Industry Data." *American Automobile Manufacturers Association Web Page.* Washington, 1998. Available at http://www.aama.com.

"Industry Facts." *Alliance of Automobile Manufacturers*, March 2001. Available at http://www.autoalliance.org/ecofacts.htm.

"Industry Report: Automobile Industry." *US Business Reporter*, 6 April 2002. Available at http://www.activemedia-guide.com.

Langworth, Richard M. *The Complete History of Ford Motor Company.* New York: Beekman House, 1987.

"Occupational Employment Statistics." Bureau of Labor Statistics, U.S. Department of Labor, 8 April 2002. Available at http://www.bls.gov/oes/2000/oesi3_371.htm.

Rae, John B. *The American Automobile Industry.* Boston, MA: Twayne Publishers, 1984.

U.S. Industry and Trade Outlook. New York: McGraw-Hill and U.S. Department of Commerce, 2000.

Motorcycles and Bicycles

Overview

U.S. production of bicycles, motorcycles, and parts is worth approximately $3 billion annually. Although far fewer motorcycles are sold each year, they account for about 75 percent of industry sales because they command much higher prices than bicycles.

While bicycles and motorcycles continued to experience broad-based popularity in the early 2000s as forms of recreation and transportation, they faced vastly different market situations. Bicycle manufacturers faced weak sales in the early 2000s. Shipment values, which stood at $1.2 billion in 1997, fell sharply to $774.6 million in 1999 and $589.6 million in 2000. After strong growth earlier in the decade, some of the leading fads in bicycles, notably the preference for mountain bikes, began to recede by 1996. However, according to the National Bicycle Dealers Association (NBDA), as of 2000, mountain bikes remained the most popular category overall. Youth bicycles and comfort bikes (similar to mountain bikes, but with more comfortable features) accounted for 25 and 14 percent of sales respectively. Although U.S. companies manufactured more than half of their bicycles domestically in the mid-1990s, this percentage slipped significantly by the early 2000s as production was shifted to Asia and Mexico where labor costs are much lower. Changes in the bike retail structure aimed at reducing inventories and ordering new merchandise rapidly as it is sold (known as just-in-time inventory) have also cut into manufacturers' sales.

Motorcycle producers, who have established an important and lucrative market among U.S. baby boomers, saw strong demand for their products throughout the 1990s and early 2000s. The decade's consumption levels are estimated to have increased more than 10 percent annually. At market leader Harley-Davidson, business was booming in the 1990s and early 2000s. The motorcycle segment benefits from the deep pockets of its increasingly affluent customers, who as they age are earning and spending more than younger buyers. That the health of motorcycle sales is dependent on one generation of consumers is illustrated by the rising average age of U.S. bikers. From an average age of 34 years in the 1980s, by the early 2000s, the average Harley rider was approximately 46 years old.

History of the Industry

Bicycles   The bicycle originated in France when Paris carriage maker Pierre Michaux fitted cranks to the front wheel of the German-designed draisienne, or hobby horse. By 1867, a bicycle craze was sweeping Europe. According to David A. Hounshell, author of *From the American System to Mass Production: 1800-1932*, the Boston merchant Albert A. Pope deserves credit for introducing the device to America. Pope began importing the British High-Wheel, also known as the "Penny-Farthing," in 1876. By 1878 he was producing his own version at the Weed Sewing Machine plant in Hartford, Connecticut.

The new product tapped a growing demand in America for increased mobility and provided work for the idling American arms industry. Much of the industrial expertise developed for the weapons industry during the Civil War found useful employment in the production of bicycle components. In 1890, 27 bicycle manufacturers produced 40,000 "safety" bicycles, featuring two equal sized wheels.

By 1897 bicycle production increased to 1.2 million annually. Then demand evaporated as the horseless carriage began to make its impact felt. Auto manufacturer Hiram Percy Maxim noted that the bicycle revealed the advantage of quicker personal transportation but failed to answer the challenge. According to Maxim, the bicycle created the demand for the automobile and provided the technology needed to mass produce it.

Bicycles retained a steady but small popularity through the first half of the twentieth century. It was the baby boomer generation that fueled the resurgence of the bicycle starting in the 1950s. The single-speed child's bike gave way to multiple speed versions and, eventually, the popular lightweight ten-speed. Throughout the 1970s, the ten-speed dominated the market with a market share of 56 percent. However, an American innovation, the mountain bike, changed everything. Initially designed for climbing the scrubby hills north of San Francisco, mountain bikes and all-terrain bikes sported fat tires, heavy frames, and multiple gears. By 1991 they boomed in popularity even in areas miles from any mountain and commandeered a 50 percent market share.

Many traditional companies like Schwinn and Murray failed to react quickly enough to the popularity of the mountain bike, leaving the door open for small innovators to carve out a niche and for large foreign firms like Taiwan's Giant Bicycle, Inc. and China's CBC to gain control of trademarks. The showroom models still sport familiar brand names, but many are foreign-made while others use components no longer made in America. Those firms that did react, like Trek and Cannondale, are enjoying great success in the export market, especially in Europe and Japan

Motorcycles   The motorcycle represented a first step from the bicycle to the automobile. The simple expedient of attaching a gasoline-powered engine to a bicycle frame produced a device that was at once exotic and affordable. During the early 1900s, more than 100 companies began manufacturing motorcycles, including Harley-Davidson, Indian, Orient, Excelsior, Cyclone, Henderson, and Marsh. By 1915, they produced models that could exceed 100 mph. The 1915 Cyclone, designed specifically for racing, could reach speeds of 124 mph but had no throttle and no brakes. Harley-Davidson began production of its first model, the Silent Grey Fellow, in 1903, the same year Henry Ford unveiled the Model A. When Ford introduced his mass-produced Model T in 1913 and sold it for $500, most motorcycle manufacturers couldn't compete. After World War I, only Harley-Davidson, Indian, and Excelsior remained. By 1953, only Harley-Davidson remained.

With the OPEC oil embargo of the early 1970s, motorcycles became popular for commuting—but not the Harley. Consumers wanted cheap, reliable, peppy bikes, and those came from Japan. In 1973, sales of motorcycles reached an all-time high of 1.5 million. In 1983, Harley-Davidson sought and received tariff protection from the Reagan administration to help it battle Japanese competition. Even with the 45 percent tariff protection, the company was almost bankrupt by 1985 due to poor quality and inefficient production. By applying Japanese management techniques, Harley-Davidson finally reversed its situation and asked for the tariff to be removed one year before it was due to expire. Meanwhile, Honda miscalculated the heavyweight motorcycle market, concentrating instead on small bikes and high-priced, high-tech super bikes. Honda's market share dropped from 44 percent in 1985 to 32 percent in 1989.

Significant Events Affecting the Industry

Motorcycles in general enjoyed a modest resurgence in the 1980s and 1990s that continued into the early 2000s. This was due in part to market demographics. First-time motorcycle buyers and long absent return buyers more than tripled between 1987 and 1994. Between 1992 and 2001, Harley-Davidson's net sales increased at a compound annual rate of approximately 17 percent per year. Sales of similar bikes from Japanese makers fell 39 percent between 1988 and 1991, but then began to increase again. The market for smaller and faster "sportbikes," which appeal largely to younger riders, was stagnant due to high prices. Sales of off-road motorcycles, also popular among younger riders, experienced growth throughout the 1990s. In the early 2000s, many older riders in this category were buying larger bikes as their levels of disposable income increased.

Meanwhile, there were signs that the popularity of mountain bikes was dwindling by the mid-1990s, as the sales of these bikes decreased in 1996 for the first time in 10 years (from $1.6 billion in 1995 to $1.5 billion in 1996). This was followed by a smaller decrease in sales during 1997, due in part to falling prices. National Bicycle Dealers Association data indicated that as of 2000, mountain bikes accounted for the greatest amount (43 percent) of retail sales in bicycle stores, down from 46 percent in 1999.

But other styles of bicycles continued to enjoy rising demand. Once again, the baby boomer market was seen as fertile, triggering the introduction of expensive "nostalgia" bicycles by the likes of Schwinn. Some automobile manufacturers have begun to produce bicycles under their own logos, hoping to appeal to customers who want to lead an active lifestyle (or at least to project that image). These companies include Mercedes-Benz, Volkswagen, BMW, and Jeep. Bicycles also are being used more frequently by non-recreational riders such as commuters, couriers, and police officers.

Key Competitors

The undisputed leader in the U.S. motorcycle industry is Harley-Davidson of Milwaukee, Wisconsin, which controlled about 44 percent of the North American motorcycle market in 2001, down somewhat from historic highs. The company's sales rose 113 percent between 1988 and 1996. Between 1997 and 2001, net sales climbed more than 90 percent. Sales of Harley bikes totaled a record 234,461 in 2001, giving the company a record $3.4 billion in sales. Although international sales have consistently grown since the early 1990s, domestic shipments of Harley-Davidsons have grown much faster, accounting for a larger percentage of shipments overall. By 2001, the company exported less than 20 percent of its bikes. In 1998 Harley-Davidson acquired Buell Motorcycle Company, which makes sportbikes. Worldwide, Buell accounts for 18 percent of the company's net sales. By the early 2000s, a number of Harley's smaller domestic competitors, like the struggling Indian Motorcycle Corporation and Victory (made by Polaris Industries, Inc.) were competing in the cruiser bike market, hoping to steal market share mainly from Japanese producers such as Honda, Yamaha, and Kawasaki.

Despite the slowdown in sales, during the 1990s the unforeseen popularity of the mountain bike upset the traditional list of leaders within the bicycle manufacturing industry, as mountain bikes captured a large share of the total market. Old industry leaders such as Schwinn did not enter this market soon enough and were overtaken by producers of the new product. In the early 2000s, another development added to the changing face of the industry. American icon Schwinn/GT, which had struggled financially during the 1990s, was acquired at a bank-

ruptcy auction in 2001 by Pacific Cycle, LLC, which traditionally sold most of its bikes (including the Mongoose and Roadmaster brands) through mass retailers like Wal-Mart. That year, Pacific achieved sales of $295 million and employed 480 workers. One of the company's goals was to re-establish relationships with Schwinn/GT's former dealer network, even though it was considering selling Schwinn bikes in retail outlets along with its other brands.

Trek Bicycle Corporation, founded in Waterloo, Wisconsin in 1976, continued to lead the industry in sales of premium bikes sold through specialty shops. In 2001, Trek reported revenues of $375 million and employed 1,500 workers. Cannondale Corporation, with 2001 sales of $147 million and 923 employees, was another leader in Trek's category.

Industry Projections

Modest growth was expected for the bicycle portion of the industry through 2004, due to both economic and demographic factors (including a decline in the number of children in the key 5- to 14-year-old age group). Helping to sustain or increase domestic sales was a U.S. government bill aimed at increasing non-motorized transportation. Approximately $3 billion in funds could be used for building bike paths and other facilities friendly to cyclists. Growth in the motorcycle segment was expected to be somewhat stronger during the same time period. Harley-Davidson and its competitors were ratcheting up production of their popular motorcycles in response to continued strong demand. For example, in 2001, Harley-Davidson invested $290 million to support increased production capabilities. The baby boomer demographic, with increased spending power, continues to fuel a significant amount of growth in the market for large motorcycles.

Global Presence

The motorcycle and bicycle industry has seen the overall value of imports rise significantly since the late 1990s, from $2.1 billion in 1997 to $3.9 billion in 2000. From 1999 to 2000, values increased almost 31 percent. Meanwhile, the value of exports has declined, falling from $976 million in 1997 to $798 million in 2000. In the late 1990s, the majority of motorcycle imports came from Japan, while Japan, Canada, and Germany represented the leading export markets. Large, touring-type motorcycles were a promising product class for international markets. For bicycles, the majority of imports came from Taiwan and China, and the leading export markets were Taiwan, the Netherlands, and Canada.

By the early 2000s, a significant portion of U.S. bicycle manufacturers had shifted domestic production overseas. Bicycles made domestically accounted for more than half of U.S. sales in the mid-1990s. However, by the late 1990s this percentage fell to less than 35 percent. By 1999, the NBDA reported that more than 90 percent of bicycles sold in the United States were imported from other nations. Facing slowing sales at home, bicycle producers looked to international sales as an important part of their growth strategies in the early 2000s. Asia and Europe were seen as strong growth markets for U.S. bicycle manufacturers, although they had to compete with many local producers in those places. Among the greatest opportunities for exports were mountain bikes and BMX bikes.

Employment in the Industry

The industry employs approximately 15,000 workers in the United States, with an annual payroll of about $627 million. These levels make the motorcycle and bicycle business a relatively minor employer in the United States.

Sources for Further Study

Annual Survey of Manufactures. Washington, DC: U.S. Bureau of the Census, annual.

Brown, Don J. "Systemic Change: 1986-1996; Motorcycle Industry." *Dealernews*, January 1997.

Brown, Stuart F. "Gearing Up for the Cruiser Wars." *Fortune*, 3 August 1998.

Duchene, Paul. "Minneapolis-Based Polaris to Fight Harley-Davidson in Motorcycle Market." *Knight-Ridder/Tribune Business News*, 13 May 1998.

Jesitus, John. "On the Road Again; New Top Management Uses a Teamwork Approach to Put Schwinn Back Into the Bicycle-Industry Race." *Industry Week*, 4 November 1996.

Musical Instruments

Overview

At one time, the ability to play a musical instrument was considered an essential part of a person's basic education. During the latter half of the twentieth century, however, electronic equipment such as music recording and playback devices made learning an instrument less of a necessity, allowing people to enjoy music at any time without learning to play it. Nevertheless, many people in the United States still play musical instruments. In the mid-1990s, there were more than 62 million musicians in the country. According to the U.S. Census Bureau musical instrument manufacturers shipped about $1.7 billion worth of product in 2000, following a period of steady growth in the latter part of the 1990s.

As part of the personal consumer durables category, musical instrument purchases depend greatly on consumer confidence. Such purchases are made with disposable personal income. In addition, in times of recession spending for school bands and orchestras, personal music lessons, and high-end instruments is cut. With the country's economic prosperity in the mid- to late 1990s, musical instrument sales shot up well above their levels of the early 1990s. Despite strong performance through

2000, the weak economic conditions and rising unemployment levels that developed during 2001 are likely to have affected the industry. Internationally, the United States continued to play a significant role in the global musical instrument industry as one of the world's leading importers and exporters.

History of the Industry

The musical instrument industry began in earnest during the Renaissance, a period of intense musical activity in Europe that dated from approximately 1450 to 1600. Musical compositions intended for keyboard instruments and consorts—small groups of instruments such as recorders and violins—were created during this time, spurring the manufacture of those instruments. The rise of opera in Italy during the early seventeenth century further boosted the demand for musical instruments.

The Baroque period of the mid-seventeenth century featured the regular use of the ensemble, which became the foundation of the modern orchestra. In the mid-1700s orchestras of the era expanded to include clarinets and trombones. The piano was accepted by composers during this time as well.

The 1830s marked a period of experimentation with musical instruments. Improvements were made to a variety of instruments, including the trumpet, flute, and piano, which continued to grow in popularity. The tuba and saxophone were introduced around this time and became established as legitimate and popular instruments.

By the mid-nineteenth century, instrumental music had become a key aspect of American and European society. Pianos, in particular, were highly valued, and the instrument became a centerpiece of family life in many households. A key factor in the popularity of the piano was the development of the portable grand piano in 1800, an instrument that was the precursor of the upright piano. This innovation provided middle-income citizens with the opportunity to purchase affordable pianos.

Player pianos—mechanically operated pianos that use a perforated paper roll to trigger the piano keys—became popular for a time as well. By 1918 it was estimated that more than 800,000 player pianos were in operation in the eastern United States. By the early 1920s player pianos accounted for more than half of all piano sales in the United States. The emergence of radios and phonographs, however, doomed the player piano market.

As the twentieth century unfolded, mass-production technology was introduced that dramatically increased the number of musical instruments available on the market. Inferior products inevitably appeared as well, but the industry recognized that many customers demanded a certain level of quality in their purchases.

Since the 1950s, which featured the introduction of the television to households around the world, the musical instruments industry depended on the continued vitality of the market despite the emergence of an ever-increasing number of recreational alternatives. The allure of other entertainment options loomed as a continuing concern for industry manufacturers in the mid-1990s. The drop in consumer spending on musical instruments resulted from a number of factors including increased consumer interest in other leisure products and activities. Products such as computer equipment and other audio-visual products began to capture consumer interest in the 1980s. In addition, computer games, movie rentals, and cable television now occupy more consumer recreational time and some industry analysts argue that more of today's consumers prefer spectator, rather than participant, amusements.

Significant Events Affecting the Industry

The electronic revolution had a great effect on the musical instrument industry. Between 1981 and 1986 the price of an acoustic piano doubled because of increasing labor costs. However, electronic keyboard instrument sales jumped 40 percent between 1985 and 1986. In fact, Americans bought twice as many keyboards in 1986 (206 million) as in 1985 and more than four times as many as in 1984. Sales of synthesizers jumped from 220,000 in 1985 to 350,000 in 1986. All that was driven by the increased power and flexibility of computer-assisted music production and a drop in the price of such electronic equipment. Electronic keyboard sales remained strong in the mid-1990s as well.

Computerized music software also revolutionized the musical instrument industry. These programs do everything from teach beginners the basics of music to allow the music savvy to create and record intricate compositions. Coupled with electronic keyboards and other musical instruments, music software gives users added power and capabilities. Although the computer-assisted music industry did not get underway until the 1990s, it promises to be a significant trend in the musical instrument industry's future, since it expands the possibilities of those who already play musical instruments and can encourage others to take up musical instruments.

Key Competitors

At the beginning of the twentieth century, the U.S. musical instrument industry was dominated by a few big names like Baldwin, Steinway, Aeolian, American, Kimball, Wurlitzer, Steger, and Kohler. By the early 2000s, after a century of reorganization, merger, takeover, and bankruptcies, many of these once-famous names had disappeared. And while Baldwin continued to dominate the piano segment, it lost part of its control of the musical instrument industry to Steinway in the mid-1990s.

Baldwin Piano and Organ Co. of Loveland, Ohio survived dropping sales and rising interest rates by getting into the finance business: it bought and sold loan agreements on its pianos and organs. The company was established in 1862 by Dwight Hamilton Baldwin, a retail dealer of pianos and organs in Cincinnati. Its later

FINANCES:

Musical Instrument Manufacturing, Value of Shipments 1997-2000 (million dollars)

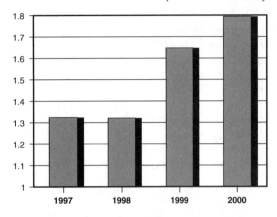

success resulted from the takeover of many small piano manufacturers and the development of a consignment-based dealership contract arrangement. The system, actually begun by the W.W. Kimball Co. of Chicago, put pianos in showrooms across the country without major investments from the dealer and made pianos available to consumers on monthly payment terms. By the late 1930s, innovative marketing and quality products had established Baldwin as the industry leader. By the early 1980s, the piano business was a mere 3 percent of the holding company's $3 billion operations. When parent company Baldwin-United went bankrupt in 1983, it spun off its piano interests in a management-led leveraged buyout. Faced with intense foreign competition, heavy debt and a shrinking customer base, Baldwin struggled to achieve consistent profitability in the 1990s and early 2000s. CEO Karen Hendricks attempted to guide the company to profitable growth in the late 1990s. However, by 2001 Baldwin's sales fell more than 30 percent to $86 million, and the company's loss totaled about $10 million. In 2001 the company filed for bankruptcy protection and was purchased by Gibson Guitar Corp.

Founded before the turn of the twentieth century, for most of its history Selmer Co. concentrated primarily on wind instruments—clarinets, trumpets, and saxophones—as well as violins. Leveraged buyouts in 1988 and 1993 put the company in private hands. In 1994 the company acquired Steinway Musical Properties Inc. for $101.5 million. Steinway had also built a reputation as a maker of quality instruments. Established in 1853 in New York, the firm eschewed price competition, instead cultivating a top-quality image via international endorsements by concert pianists, sponsorship of national concert tours, and with award-winning national advertising campaigns. In 1983 it became Steinway Musical Properties Inc. and in 1985 it spun off the subsidiary, Steinway Inc. of New York. Steinway enjoyed a resurgence in the 1990s and early 2000s, with revenues increasing from $90.0 million in 1993 to $352.6 million in 2001, when the company earned profits of $11.3 million. At that time, it was operating under the name Steinway Musical Instruments Inc.

Leaders of the guitar segment of the industry included Fender Musical Instruments Corp. and Gibson Guitar Corp. Headquartered in Scottsdale, Arizona, privately held Fender, maker of the famed Stratocaster, was acquired by CBS Inc. in 1981 and taken private in 1985. New management revived the company so much that by the mid-1990s, the company boasted almost 50 percent of the guitar market. In addition to its leadership position in the global marketplace, by the early 2000s Fender had established itself as the top U.S. electric guitar manufacturer, posting sales of $275 million in 2001.

Nashville-based Gibson can be traced to the 1870s, when company namesake Orville Gibson opened a mandolin shop in Kalamazoo, Michigan. Best known for its renowned Les Paul model guitars, Gibson also makes banjos, mandolins, drums, synthesizers, and amplifiers. In 2001 this privately held company's revenues were estimated at about $125 million.

Industry Projections

With an economic recovery in the mid- to late 1990s, the U.S. musical instrument industry experienced a period of moderate growth. Revenues from manufacturer shipments totaled $1.8 billion in 2000, up from $1.3 billion in 1997. Guitars are among the best selling musical instruments in the country, with total retail sales of $923 million in 2000, up more than 21 percent over 1999 levels. Additionally, retail sales of guitars rose almost 10 percent in 1999. While guitars, percussion, and other musical instruments accounted for more than 75 percent of manufacturer revenues in 2000, other leading instrument categories included pianos, accounting for more than $188 million of total revenues, and organs accounting for about $87 million. Worsening economic conditions that developed in 2001 will likely impact the industry's output.

In addition to the economy, growth of the school-age segment of the population affects industry demand, since school-age children make up some of the leading customers for musical instruments. While population trends contributed to the prosperity of the industry during the late 1990s, their impact was expected to be minimal through 2004. Children aged five to 17 were only expected to increase by a factor of two percent during this time period.

Global Presence

The United States remained a world leader for musical instrument trade in the early 2000s. U.S. exports, which amounted to an estimated $340 million in 1999, declined about 10 percent in the late 1990s. This was attributed to various international economic factors, including weak Asian economies. The leading global markets for U.S. manufacturers included Japan, the United Kingdom, Canada, Germany, and Mexico, which together represented more than half of exports. Imports, which amounted to an estimated $1 billion in 1999, also declined in the late 1990s, but only slightly. At that time, about one-third of imports came from Japan, followed by other Asian countries like South Korea, Taiwan, and China. Together with Germany, these nations represented more than 70 percent of imports.

Employment in the Industry

Overall, employment within the musical instrument industry has consistently declined since the 1970s. From 1975 to 1985, industry-wide employment fell from 24,500 to 13,200 people. By 2000, the industry retained only 15,279 employees with just 12,217 production workers. However, the average hourly wage for production employees—who constituted more than two-thirds of the workforce—increased from about $3.25 to $13.07 during the 25-year period. Much of the loss of employment resulted from automation, a switch to materials that were easier to work with, and overseas production.

Sources of Further Study

Annual Survey of Manufactures. Washington, DC: U.S. Department of Commerce, Economics and Statistics Administration, U.S. Census Bureau, 2001.

Feibelman, Adam. "The Good Wizard: He Saved Gibson Guitars From Being a Firm That Sold Seconds." *Memphis Business Journal,* 14 October 1996.

Geake, Elisabeth. "And Hello to Playing Music without Keys." *New Scientist,* 14 August 1993.

Gill, Chris. "Gibson's Century of Excellence." *Guitar Player,* September 1994.

Hirokazu, Sayama. "Efforts to Promote Sales Pay off for Musical Instrument Business." *Money,* February 1997.

Matzer, Marla. "Play It Again." *Forbes,* 27 February 1995.

The Music Industry Census. Englewood, NJ: The Music Trades, 2001.

———. "Playing Solo." *Forbes,* 25 March 1996.

Parcel, Ronald. "Music by Proxy: The Invention and Evolution of Mechanical Music." *Impact of Science on Society,* 1987.

Roell, Craig H. *The Piano in America, 1890-1940.* Chapel Hill, NC: University of North Carolina Press, 1989.

U.S. Industry and Trade Outlook. New York: McGraw-Hill and U.S. Department of Commerce, 2000.

Ophthalmic Goods

Overview

Relatively small compared to most industries, the $4.3 billion U.S. optical supplies sector consists of five main product segments: frames for eyeglasses, lenses for eyeglasses, contact lenses, sunglasses, and cleaning solutions and specialty products. When imports are considered, the net U.S. market for optical goods exceeds $6 billion, as a large share of U.S. purchases are of foreign-made goods. Approximately 500 U.S. companies produce optical goods but in terms of sales volume, the industry is dominated by a few large companies. Contact lenses are the largest division by value, worth about half of industry sales excluding solutions.

Of all the industry's segments, sunglasses are by far the most volatile because they are usually considered a convenience rather than a necessity. In addition to economic factors, the weather also has a significant impact on sales. During the 1990s, sunglasses saw two declines in sales: first during the recession in 1992 when sales fell 45 percent, and again in 1997 when sales fell 13 percent. From 1998 to 2000, sales of sunglasses grew moderately, hovering around two percent in 1999 and 2000.

History of the Industry

Until the 1960s, growth in the ophthalmic goods industry had occurred at a steady, predictable rate, largely dictated by the rate of population growth in the United States. During the 1960s, however, an increased demand for optical products elevated industry sales levels to unprecedented highs, prompted by greater availability of eye examinations and the development of contact lenses to be used in place of eyeglasses.

Contact lenses first became a viable alternative in the 1950s, but at that time they were considered by many to be uncomfortable and costly. A typical pair of contacts in the 1950s cost $200, which would equal well over $1,000 in 1998 dollars. Lenses in that period were very large, covering most of the exposed eyeball, and rigid. None were soft or disposable as would become common by the 1990s. As a result, even among the minority of people who purchased contacts, there was a 50 percent attrition rate of going back to glasses.

Despite such drawbacks, the contact segment of the industry grew rapidly through the 1950s and 1960s. The 1960s ushered in a new generation of smaller, thinner contacts that made them much more palatable to consumers; and research was set in motion that would lead to soft lenses, which would come to dominate the market later. Improvements were also made to conventional eyeglasses in the 1960s, including the introduction of plastic and bifocal lenses, although neither achieved significant market share in that period. Overall sales in the 1960s were boosted by federal programs like Medicare and Medicaid, which helped pay for eye exams for the elderly and the poor.

In the 1970s, Bausch & Lomb, one of two leading manufacturers of eyeglasses at the time, introduced the first mass-market soft contact lenses, and their use quickly spread. The next major innovation came from Johnson & Johnson in the late 1980s, when it launched disposable contacts. Disposables became one of the industry's fastest-growing product lines in the 1990s.

Significant Events Affecting the Industry

Pricing of corrective eyewear has been an ongoing concern for government regulators. Since the 1970s, recurring investigations have been conducted by federal and state agencies to determine whether optical products were being priced fairly. In the 1970s, a number of states prohibited the advertising of eyewear prices. A Federal Trade Commission (FTC) investigation found that in states with advertising bans, prices averaged 25 percent higher than in states with no restrictions. By the late 1970s, the FTC moved to end all advertising restrictions in an effort to level out pricing practices. The measure succeeded to some extent, creating a more price-driven market for eyewear.

But pricing issues continued to surface into the 1990s. In 1994, Bausch & Lomb was known to market the same set of contacts under different brands because they were targeted for different lifestyles. The same physical product was marketed as "daily wear," "planned replacement," extended-wear disposables, and one-day disposables. The lenses were priced at $70, $15, $8, and $3 respectively. The only difference was in the marketing: Bausch was trying to attract different groups of consumers who were either value or convenience oriented. Two years later, in a similar practice, the company was accused by regulators in several states of marketing identical products under different labels and charging significantly different prices for some. The investigation resulted in a 1997 settlement of $1.7 million paid by Bausch & Lomb.

The successful development of lightweight, high-quality plastic lenses helped revolutionize the eyeglasses segment, particularly for consumers with stronger prescriptions. In the past, glass lenses tended to be heavy, and if a person's eyesight was worse than average, glass lenses quickly grew thick and were regarded by many as unaesthetic. Plastics, by nature lighter than glass, allowed a typical pair of glasses to be lighter and offered more dramatic reductions in weight and thickness for stronger prescription wearers. Plastic lenses could also be made to better resist breakage than glass and, when treated with coatings, could help reduce the glare associated with traditional glasses. These enhancements helped drive strong sales of the newer technologies, although in large part these sales came at the expense of reductions in demand for older materials.

Key Competitors

Most leading U.S. producers of optical goods are diversified along product and geographic lines, as the traditional eyewear market in the United States grows at a relatively slow pace, even allowing for growth trends such as the rising consumer preference for disposable contacts. In addition, they face significant competitors originating in other countries, notably from Europe.

Bausch & Lomb With 11,600 employees, New York-based Bausch & Lomb, Inc. is the world's top ophthalmic goods company. Founded in 1853 by German immigrant John Jacob Bausch, the company posted sales of $1.7 billion in 2001, of which approximately half was derived from overseas markets. The company was long known for its premium sunglasses, which included the Ray-Ban and Killer Loop brands. However, Bausch & Lomb sold its sunglasses operations so that it could focus more on other businesses areas. The company's line of vision care products includes contact lenses, solutions, ointments, and eye drops sold under trade names like Boston, ReNu, and SofLens66. In addition, Bausch & Lomb markets products for ophthalmic surgery, as well as over-the-counter and prescription drugs for treating eye conditions. Over the course of its history, Bausch & Lomb has made significant contributions to the advancement of optical and ophthalmic technology, including the creation of Ray-Bans (originally developed in 1929 for the U.S. Army Air Corps), the Cinemascope lens, satellite and missile lens technology, and soft contact lenses.

Johnson & Johnson A diversified consumer products company, Johnson & Johnson participates in the ophthalmic goods industry through its subsidiary, Johnson & Johnson Vision Care, Inc., which produces disposable contact lenses, spectacles, and various other products. Its ACUVUE and other brand disposables hold a world-leading market share for that category. With revenues of approximately $33 billion in 2001, the company also produces a wide range of consumer goods such as shampoo, bandages, and dental products.

Allergan Also prominent in the ophthalmic goods industry is Allergan, Inc., a leading producer of intraocular lenses (which are surgically implanted in the eye) and surgical products, lens care items, and pharmaceuticals. Allergan's research and development work is concentrated in five areas: cataracts, contact lens care, glaucoma, neuromuscular disorders, and receptor-selective retinoids. Established in 1950, the company's first product was an antihistamine eye drop called Allergan. The company adopted the name of the eye drop and in 1960 moved into the nascent contact lens market, specializing at first in contact lens solutions and later manufacturing its own lenses. After watching its sales leap from $100 million in 1980 to over $700 million in 1989, the company struggled through a difficult transition period in the early 1990s, and sales fell off from $897 million in 1992 to $857 million in 1993. By 2001, Allergan posted earnings of $225 million on revenues of $1.7 billion. At that time, the company was planning to divest its optical device unit, allowing it to concentrate more on pharmaceuticals.

Sola International U.S.-based Sola International, Inc. is a major producer of plastic lenses, commanding a market share of 25 percent of the world's plastic lenses. Sola is known for its Spectralite brand of lightweight polycarbonate lenses, but it manufactures glass lenses as well. In 2001 the company posted earnings of approximately $67 million on revenues of $545 million and employed more than 7,000 workers.

Oakley With 2001 sales of $429 million, Oakley, Inc. is best known for its popular athletic sunglasses, although it also has launched a line of athletic shoes, apparel, watches, and other accessories. The publicly traded company's main product line is premium sunglasses, some of which cost more than $350. In 2001, Oakley employed 1,685 workers.

Industry Projections

About half of the U.S. population requires some vision correction, but as much as 90 percent of those over age 45 need corrective eyewear. These demographics bode well for the industry in a country with a large number of baby boomers growing older and a rising share of the population living longer. The demand for corrective eyewear overall will continue to follow slow, steady growth into the 2000s. Although some proponents of various surgeries to permanently correct vision problems have predicted their services will eventually eliminate the need for corrective products, as of the early 2000s, optical goods had lost no significant market share to such operations.

Global Presence

U.S. companies rank among some of the world's largest optical goods producers, and many obtain significant shares of their annual sales from abroad, but they face mounting competition from overseas competitors. Production of low-cost frames, and sometimes lenses, is increasingly more cost efficient in places like Asia, where lower wages translate into cost savings for producers. U.S. imports of low-tech eyewear typically dwarf exports. For example, in trade of plastic frames and mountings, in 1997 the value of U.S. imports was nearly four times that of exports; and in trade of other frames and mountings, U.S. exports were just a tenth of imports. The United States also has trade deficits in sunglasses and plastic lenses. However, in the trade of contact lenses, which require greater technical sophistication to produce, U.S. exports totaled almost three times the value of imports. Overall, the value of industry imports totaled about $1.9 billion in 2000, compared to exports of $929 million. On average, both imports and exports grew at an annual rate of seven percent between 1997 and 2000.

Employment in the Industry

The U.S. optical goods industry employs approximately 26,000 people, of whom about 69 percent are in non-management positions. The industry's annual domestic payroll is worth more than $861 million and represents slightly more than 20 percent of annual revenues. On average, production workers at optical goods businesses earn less than the average manufacturing wage. Employment within the industry was expected to grow modestly through 2010, by approximately two percent.

Sources for Further Study

"Bausch & Lomb to Pay $1.7 Million to End Investigation." *New York Times*, 20 August 1997.

Clark, Jane Bennett. "Bausch & Lomb: Pulling the Wool Over Its Customer's Eyes?" *Kiplinger's Personal Finance Magazine*, March 1994.

"Kids' Sports Lines May Jump Start Sunglasses." *Drug Store News*, 26 March 2001.

Miller, M.R. "Optics." New York: Merrill Lynch Capital Markets, 1 December 1997.

"Occupational Employment Statistics." Bureau of Labor Statistics, U.S. Department of Labor, 23 April 2002. Available at http://www.bls.gov.

U.S. Department of Commerce, Economics and Statistics Administration, U.S. Census Bureau. *Annual Survey of Manufacturers*. Washington, 2002.

Paper Mills

Overview

With output of 87 million metric tons as of the late 1990s, the United States is the world's largest manufacturer of paper and paperboard. It produces a significantly greater amount of paper and paperboard than Japan, its nearest rival, and consistently supplies about one third of total world production. While the $59 billion U.S. paper industry remains generally healthy, foreign competition has increased as new regions—notably Asia and Latin America—have developed strong paper industries. At the same time, the paper industry has suffered periodic fluctuation in prices, and consequently in sales, mainly due to varying production capacities and shifts in demand. In the early 2000s, the paper industry was suffering from the negative impact of an overvalued U.S. dollar. This caused a decrease in domestic market share, as well as weak international demand for U.S. paper products. In turn, a large number of paper mill closings took place, along with corresponding workforce reductions. Although rates of domestic paper consumption rose from 1997 to 2000, the majority of that demand was being met by imports from foreign competitors.

Domestic U.S. paper and paperboard mills—of which there are approximately 500—historically have produced more than 90 percent of the paper consumed in the United States. Most of these mills are integrated producers of paper and pulp, the raw ingredient in paper. Pulp that is consumed internally at the mill is known as captive pulp, while pulp sold on the open market is termed market pulp. Many of the same integrated mills may also make paperboard, also known as cardboard, although statistically paper and paperboard production are often tallied separately.

History of the Industry

American papermaking began just over 300 years ago in Philadelphia. In September of 1690, an entrepreneur named William Bradford, a recent English immigrant, built the first American paper mill on the shore of Wissahickon Creek in Philadelphia. At the time, paper manufacturing had not yet become an important part of the colonial economy. The small amount of paper consumed in the colonies was produced in Holland and France. However, economic growth in the colonies soon created a booming market for paper. Bradford and other papermakers were soon ready to produce products for this market. Bradford built his mill with the assistance of William Rittenhouse, an immigrant from Holland, and other financial backers. The mill produced about 20 pounds of pulp, paper, and board a day. While at the time there was some mechanization of papermaking, it was largely a handmade process.

After 1690, the population of the American colonies grew quickly and so did the number of U.S. paper mills. By the time of the American Revolution—in which printed materials played a key role—there were more than 45 mills producing about 300 tons of paper per year. This production was used by more than 50 printers throughout the new nation.

At the beginning of the 1800s, an event occurred that would revolutionize the paper industry throughout the world. A Frenchman, Louis-Nicolas Robert, invented a machine to produce paper. Eventually, the machine patents were purchased by two English papermakers, the brothers Henry and Sealy Fourdrinier. After modification, the Fourdrinier machine began to catch on in England, and it later was produced in the United States as well. The name Fourdrinier is still used today to describe certain paper machines. The development of the paper machine changed what had been a lengthy and time-consuming handmade art into a manufacturing process.

The other event that forever changed papermaking occurred in the middle of the nineteenth century. After 1851, the preferred fiber source for papermaking began to change from old rags to wood pulp. This event, along with the invention of the paper machine, in effect created the modern paper industry. The size and speed of paper machines increased rapidly between 1850 and 1916. Paper use was booming by 1889, when the annual U.S. production of paper reached 1 million tons. This figure doubled in the next 10 years.

At the end of World War I, the United States began a period of rapid economic growth and the paper industry grew along with the general economy. Several new associations, including the Paper Industry Management Association and the Technical Association of the Pulp and Paper Industry, were founded and developed during this time. Paper containers and packaging, a growing use of corrugated medium and linerboard to make shipping boxes, and a host of new products, such as tissues and sanitary napkins, all emerged as major trends in the post-war era. It was during this time that Canadian mills became dominant in newsprint manufacture, producing the majority of American newsprint. It is only recently that U.S. manufacturers have produced the majority of newsprint consumed in the United States.

It was also during this period that the Pacific Northwest became a major pulp producer. The southern United States, however, saw the greatest growth. Prior to this time, it was difficult to use southern pine to make paper because of its high resin content. However, new processes were developed using southern pine to make bleached and unbleached kraft paper. Southern pine was ideal for this type of paper because its long fibers produced very strong paper and board. Kraft production in the South shot up from just 258 tons per day (TPD) in 1919 to 9,128 tons a day in 1940. By the end of World War II, this total was up to about 13,000 (TPD).

The growth of southern paperboard mills—and other board mills around the country—was greatly enhanced by a 1914 Federal Trade Commission decision that legalized the use of corrugated medium packaging in shipping. Prior to that, wooden boxes were used for shipping goods around the country. Military development of paper packaging materials during World War I helped provide new technology and methods for producing superior paper packaging. Southern newsprint production also began during this time, due in large part to the talents of Charles H. Herty. Methods developed by Herty and his relentless promotion of southern papermaking helped create today's paper industry in the South.

While the Great Depression of the 1930s severely hurt other industries, it did not affect the pulp and paper industry as much since paper was being used in new ways throughout the economy. It was around 1930 that machine-coated paper was first manufactured in the United States.

During World War II, the paper industry worked closely with the federal government to make sure that adequate supplies of paper were available both for domestic use and for the armed forces. Paper was one of the main materials used for shipping and storing military supplies. Recycling of paper reached a peak during the war years as well, with paper drives being common in many big cities.

After World War II, the paper industry continued growing. New pulping strategies and tree planting allowed the paper industry to develop the fiber sources it needed to meet the expanding demand. Prior to this time, paper companies tended to cut down trees and not replant. It was during this time that southern pine first began to be used to make white printing paper.

During the late 1940s, all areas of the paper industry were growing fast, but some new areas, such as milk cartons and drinking cups, saw exponential growth.

Many of the growth trends were centered around the use of disposable paper products, a trend that had started in World War II.

In the 1950s and 1960s, paper machines grew wider and faster, which helped multiply the supply of paper and board. By 1970, however, the paper industry faced sustained challenges to its environmental practices. New clean air and water rules from federal and state governments in the early 1970s forced the industry to install expensive new treatment systems. Many other capital projects were put on hold and then frozen when the economy entered a severe recession in the early 1980s. However, in the mid to late 1980s, the paper industry initiated what has been called its greatest modernization ever. These capital-intensive projects included mill-wide automation, technological innovations, mill modernization, environmental upgrades, and a push for total quality. The U.S. paper industry began competing more effectively in global markets during this time as well.

Significant Events Affecting the Industry

Concerns about environmental damage caused by paper production and use, articulated in the form of government regulations, have led to substantial changes in the paper business. Environmental compliance was a daunting—and expensive—challenge for the paper industry in the 1990s and early 2000s. There is sustained opposition from environmental groups and increased government regulation in nearly all steps of production. For example, the lumber industry in the Pacific Northwest has been drastically reduced in scale. Due to successful court challenges by environmental groups under the Endangered Species Act, tree harvests in the early to mid-1990s dropped to one-sixth of harvesting levels in the mid-1980s. Despite the release of some lands for harvesting and permits for salvage logging issued in 1995, harvesting was still greatly reduced in the mid-1990s.

Pulp and paper mills in the Northwest dependent on lumber operations for raw material have had to look to new sources—even overseas—for wood chips. Many northwestern U.S. mills have converted partially or completely to the use of recycled paper. Also, the pulping and bleaching of wood fiber was the focus of proposals for stringent and costly new federal regulation in the mid-1990s. By the early 2000s, many paper producers were proactively working with government agencies on matters of environmental policy. Additionally, they devoted considerable amounts of resources toward environmental improvements.

While paper recycling represented a major environmental challenge in the early 1990s, the industry's quick response to recycle more paper has convinced many of its critics both in the public and government that the industry is serious about recycling. The U.S. paper industry reached an overall recycling rate of 40 percent in 1993, which increased to about 46 percent in 2000, and is estimated to reach 48 percent in 2001.

Recycling of certain grades, such as newsprint and old corrugated containers, has traditionally been high, while recycling rates for other grades, such as printing and writing papers, are growing rapidly. For example, over 59 percent of all newsprint used in the United States was recovered in 1994, up from just 29 percent in 1980. In linerboard, almost all capacity increases in the early 1990s came from new recycled linerboard mills; and by 1994, over 62 percent of old corrugated containers—known as OCC in the business—was being recovered, up from 47.9 percent in 1986.

Recycling rates for printing and writing paper, while lower than other grades, have also increased dramatically, thanks in part to aggressive state and federal legislation in the early 1990s that sought to increase recycling rates in all grades. In 1993, President Clinton signed an executive order mandating higher levels of recycled fiber in paper purchased by the federal government. In 1994, the recovery rate from printing and writing paper stood at 34.1 percent, up from just 22.9 percent in 1986.

While highly touted as an environmental "silver bullet," recycling itself has some environmental liabilities. Most recycling mills generate a major waste stream and consume large amounts of purchased energy. With recycled newsprint, for example, only 85 percent of incoming newsprint is usable as fiber. The rest is unusable sludge that must be cleaned out of the process and then burned or placed in landfills. In some recycled grades, sludge can be up to 50 percent of the incoming waste paper. Considering that some mills make up to 2,500 tons per day of paper, sludge can pose a major disposal problem. Also, since recycling mills can't burn bark or spent pulping chemicals to generate their own electricity, as is done in conventional integrated mills, they must purchase large amounts of power from local utilities.

Key Competitors

Founded in 1898 by the merger of 18 northeastern pulp and paper companies, International Paper Company (IP), located in Stamford, Connecticut, is the world's largest paper company. In 2001, IP had total sales of $26.4 billion, approximately three-quarters of which was from pulp, paper, and converted products sales. That year, the company employed more than 100,000 workers in approximately 50 different countries. Operating via a number of different business divisions, IP is one of the largest producers of printing and writing papers, kraft paper and packaging, containerboard and corrugated boxes, and folding boxboard. Additionally, the company claims to be the nation's largest private landowner, holding claim to more than 10 million acres of forestland.

Atlanta-based Georgia-Pacific Group (G-P) has major interests in building products, pulp and paper, and paper chemicals, although it has spun off its forest management holdings into a separate entity called The Timber Company. In November 2000, G-P acquired Fort James Corporation and became the world's top producer of tissue products. In 2001, G-P had total sales of $25 billion, of which $8.5 billion came from paper-related sales. In that year, it employed 75,000 people and operated in more than 600 locations. G-P produces containerboard and packaging, communications papers, market pulp, and packaging products. In 2000 it had the capacity to produce 2.8 million tons of communication paper (16 percent of total U.S. capacity) and 2.4 million tons of market pulp (9 percent of total U.S. capacity).

Irving, Texas-based Kimberly-Clark Corporation (K-C) is a leading global manufacturer of products for personal, business, and industrial uses. In 2001, K-C employed 64,000 workers and had total sales of $14.5 billion, a large percentage of which came from pulp, paper, and converted product sales. K-C is best known for its Kleenex, Huggies, Scott, and Kotex brand consumer products. In December 1995, it completed a stock-for-stock merger with Scott Paper Company, a global producer of sanitary tissue products. The $9.4-billion merger made K-C the largest tissue manufacturer in the world. Following the merger, K-C operated manufacturing operations in 42 countries, with products available in more than 150 countries. According to the company, each year about 25 percent of the world's population uses its products.

Industry Projections

The paper industry's cyclical nature influences all projections of its growth. During the early 2000s, it was emerging from a weakened economy along with other industry sectors. As global competition became more of a factor, worldwide demand for U.S. paper products was initially forecast to increase in the early 2000s. However, the overvalued U.S. dollar and a growing trade deficit presented serious challenges for the nation's producers at home and abroad. Growth in Asia likely will lead to a decline in the United States' share of worldwide production. According to the U.S. Department of Commerce, this was expected to decline slightly, from 29 percent in 2000 to 27 percent by 2004. As the world continues to shift from a paper-based society to a digital one, some have painted a bleak picture for the paper industry's future. Despite this trend, the overall market for certain categories of paper products appears to be strong.

Global Presence

While U.S. companies collectively form the largest national paper industry, there are many major paper companies based outside the United States. Important paper-producing countries include Japan, China, Germany, Finland, Sweden, and Canada. In addition, aggressive new paper operations have emerged in places like South America and Southeast Asia, which are increasingly influencing the international dynamics of the paper business. According to *Pulp & Paper*, in early 2000, Europe, Asia, and Latin America together accounted for nearly 70 percent of paperboard and paper consumption worldwide, while the remainder was attributed to North America.

Employment in the Industry

The U.S. paper industry employs more than 123,600 people, and the broader paper, pulp, and converted product industry employs more than 551,500 workers. Employment in the broader group declined from 574,274 in 1997 to 551,560 in 2000. The same downward trend applies to employment at paper mills. According to the American Forest & Paper Association, from 1997 to 2002, seventy-two paper mills closed their doors, resulting in a workforce reduction of about 32,000 people.

Sources for Further Study

Annual Survey of Manufacturers. Washington, DC: U.S. Department of Commerce, Economics and Statistics Administration, U.S. Census Bureau, February 2002.

"Overvalued Dollar Threatens U.S. Paper Industry." Washington: American Forest & Paper Association, 11 March 2002. Available at http://www.afandpa.org.

"Paper and Allied Products." *U.S. Industry and Trade Outlook*. New York: McGraw-Hill and U.S. Department of Commerce, 2000.

Paper, Paperboard, Pulp Capacity and Fiber Consumption. Washington, DC: American Forest & Paper Association, 1996.

"Recycling Levels Remain High Despite Drop in Consumption, AF&PA Says." Washington: American Forest & Paper Association, 12 March 2002. Available at http://www.afandpa.org.

Routson, Joyce, et al. "North American Industry Outlook Bright Over Next Two Years." *Pulp & Paper*, January 2000.

Smook, Gary A. *Handbook of Pulp & Paper Terminology: A Guide to Industrial and Technological Usage*. Bellingham, WA: Angus Wilde Publications, 1990.

Thesaurus of Pulp and Paper Terminology. Atlanta, GA: Institute of Paper Science and Technology, 1991.

Wright, Helena. *300 Years of American Papermaking*. Washington, DC: Smithsonian Institution, 1991.

Personnel Supply

Overview

During the 1990s and into the early 2000s, the personnel industry achieved rapid growth in the United States, reaching approximately $56 billion in annual revenues by 2001. Much of this growth came as companies increasingly sought to downsize their full-time workforces and to outsource specialized or peripheral work tasks. They turned to "temp" firms, which provided a ready pool of personnel, sometimes known as "contingency workers," who were able to work either for very short periods, sometimes just days, to fill in during a crunch time, or for longer periods spanning many months if the company had longer-term needs. An estimated 90 percent of all mid to large-sized U.S. companies hire temporary workers at some point.

Traditionally associated with general clerical and light industrial work, the personnel supply industry has evolved to embrace some highly specialized fields. While the major firms all still offer staff to perform general office duties, most have branched out into the more profitable specialized personnel services. In the early 2000s, leading agencies' temp pools included such professionals as lawyers, accountants, engineers, and nurses. Numerous smaller agencies serve the niche markets as well, and many firms focus exclusively on a particular market need. For example, offering computer programmers on a temporary basis. As of the late 1990s, there were an estimated 7,000 personnel supply companies of all types in the United States.

In early 2001, approximately 21 percent of all temporary and contract employees were administrative or clerical workers. Operators, fabricators, and laborers accounted for 17 percent, followed by those in the precision production, craft, and repair sector (12 percent). However, those in professional specialties and executive, administrative, sales or managerial roles together accounted for a full 31 percent of all temporary and contract workers. Between 1999 and 2001, U.S. Bureau of Labor Statistics figures showed declines in the number of manufacturing and administrative workers and a rise in the number of workers in sales, management, and technical roles.

In addition to providing temporary workers, personnel supply firms may also offer consulting services and human resources management services to their clients.

History of the Industry

The modern personnel supply industry didn't begin in earnest until after World War II, when small firms began to market short-term clerical help to companies that either didn't need a permanent employee to perform certain tasks or had short-term vacancies in their staffs due to vacation or illness. These firms found a vast untapped market for their services, and several grew quickly to become national, and later, international, leaders. Among the important personnel services to emerge in the early years were Kelly Services, Inc. of Detroit—better known in the 1950s and 1960s as "Kelly Girl" because its help pool was then almost exclusively female office workers—and Manpower, Inc. of Milwaukee.

Temporary agencies enjoyed quick growth in the 1970s and 1980s, with industry sales growing by more than 20 percent in some years. This growth coincided with the rising rate at which women entered the workforce, and the industry continued to employ a disproportionately high number of women in its ranks. Over the course of the 1970s, the industry's employment more than doubled, and by 1985 it had grown by another 60 percent. Even more dramatically, between 1985 and 1997, the industry's employment ranks nearly tripled, reaching 2.6 million by 1997, and annual revenues more than tripled from $15 to $47 billion.

Significant Events Affecting the Industry

While firms like Kelly began to develop non-clerical services as early as the 1960s, only gradually did a large market evolve for more specialized labor on a temporary basis. In the early 1990s, conventional clerical and light industrial work still accounted for half of the industry's sales. This changed quickly, however, as the U.S. business community began to embrace temporary staffing as a means to cut labor costs and improve efficiency well beyond simply having a "temp" come in to do data entry and filing. Corporate leaders realized they could reduce their overhead expenses—the business costs that aren't directly related to manufacturing a product or delivering a service—by relying on other firms to fulfill some of their recruitment and staffing functions. The flip side to the growing practice of downsizing at large companies was the rise in outsourcing tasks to more specialized contractors, and increasingly, personnel services were among the contractors.

This climate made for explosive growth in the U.S. personnel industry, with annual sales more than tripling during the 1990s. By 2000 the industry's annual sales increased to $63.6 billion, and then fell in 2001 to $56.2 billion in the wake of an economic recession.

The 1990s and early 2000s also marked an era of growing consolidation in the industry. The rate of mergers and acquisitions, both within the United States and around the globe, accelerated briskly as large firms bought out many smaller niche firms in order to broaden the scope of their services. In the period from 1994 to 1997 alone, estimates suggest that more than 900 mergers or acquisitions took place in the U.S. industry.

Key Competitors

Switzerland-based Adecco SA is the world's largest personnel service. The company's Adecco Staffing Division places more than 700,000 workers each day throughout the world in such industries as hotels, hospitals, and banks. The company's Ajilon Staffing and Managed Services Unit concentrates on professional staffing, providing workers in the legal, financial, and information technology sectors. Adecco's Lee Hecht Harrison career services division provides a variety of services including outplacement, career coaching, and leadership development. In addition, the company operates executive search firm Alexandre TIC and IdealJob, an e-human resources service that operates in several European markets. Adecco also is home to Olsten Staffing Services, which has provided staffing services in the United States for more than 50 years. In 2001 Adecco posted revenues of $16.4 billion.

Milwaukee-based Manpower, Inc. is the world's second-largest personnel service in terms of the number of employees it places. Manpower provides approximately 2 million workers to 400,000 clients worldwide, including almost all *Fortune* 500 firms. In 2001 its sales reached $10.5 billion, a slight decline from the previous year. Founded in 1948, Manpower staffs businesses in 61 countries through 3,900 franchises and corporate-owned branches. More than 80 percent of Manpower's revenues come from outside the United States. Geographically, France is the company's top market, accounting for about 36 percent of sales, followed by the United States (19 percent). Manpower also has a substantial presence in the United Kingdom and other European countries.

Founded in 1946, Kelly Services, Inc. offers a diverse staff of professionals and technical workers in addition to its well-known clerical labor pool. In 2001 the Troy, Michigan-based company placed approximately 700,000 workers through its 2,300 branch offices around the world. Among the professionals in its specialty ranks are accountants, attorneys, engineers, and scientists. With $4.3 billion in 2001 sales, almost 75 percent of Kelly's sales that year came from the United States. It also has services in Canada, France, Australia, New Zealand, Russia, and elsewhere in Europe.

Formerly Interim Services, Inc., Fort Lauderdale, Florida-based Spherion Corporation offers businesses around the world some 370,000 personnel. In 2001 the company posted revenues of $2.7 billion and operated more than 900 offices worldwide. In addition to U.S. locations, Spherion operated in Canada, Europe, Asia, and Australia. The company, which originated in Chicago as a train-cargo staffing service, was growing its outsourcing division in the early 2000s.

Industry Projections

The U.S. personnel industry experienced strong growth during the 1990s and early 2000s, and this was expected to continue well into the mid and late 2000s. According to the American Staffing Association, based on data from the Employment Policy Foundation, the demand for labor in the United States was expected to outpace supply by 2006. After 2006 this variance was expected to widen continually into and beyond 2010. It likely will become more difficult for staffing companies to find the right temporary workers as time progresses because jobs requiring higher levels of education and skill are expected to increase, while manual labor and production jobs are expected to decline. According to the U.S. Bureau of Labor Statistics, personnel supply services will lead the way in creating new U.S. jobs through 2010. From 2000 to 2010, the industry is expected to grow a whopping 49.2 percent, creating 1.9 million new jobs.

Because most firms use temporary staff when they don't wish to make a long-term commitment, it follows that when the economy sours, employers first cut back on their use of temps. This makes the personnel supply industry highly sensitive to economic cycles, and thus general economic conditions hold considerable sway over the industry's future performance. However, the personnel industry can also benefit from economic downturns: after a period of cutbacks, many companies use temporary staff as a transition measure before their business is again growing quickly enough to support hiring permanent staff.

Global Presence

The personnel industry is highly internationalized, and most leading companies have significant international operations. Particularly in Europe, some of the world's largest personnel firms generate most of their business in markets outside their home country.

The United States is among the world's largest national markets for personnel supply. However, the industry has enjoyed exceptional growth in other places, especially in Europe. As a matter of fact, in terms of staffing penetration levels, the United States (2.40 percent) lags behind European countries like France (2.50 percent), the United Kingdom (3.20 percent), and the Netherlands (4.50 percent). These figures from the American Staffing Association are based on research conducted by McKinsey & Company, which estimates that penetration levels in the Netherlands could rise as high as 6.2 percent by 2010.

Employment in the Industry

In 2000 an estimated 2.7 percent of the entire U.S. labor force of 3.9 million people were engaged in temporary employment. Not surprisingly, since it's an industry centered around employment, it is one of the nation's largest industries in terms of employee count.

In addition to using temporary staff to simply fill in for a period, many employers contract with personnel services as a way to screen potential permanent employees while keeping their in-house recruitment expenses down. This arrangement enables the employer to test an employee on the job before offering a permanent position. This practice may result from either an explicit agreement with a personnel firm to find a suitable permanent employee or it may arise informally when an employer is pleased with a temp worker's performance. Many temporary agencies have policies to regulate the migration of workers from temporary status on their payrolls to permanent status on client payrolls, but in general they don't prohibit crossover. In fact, some encourage it, and the transition is usually easy.

Most of the world's large agencies perform one or more stages of screening to ensure they hire employees who will meet their clients' expectations. The minimal screening usually involves completion of a conventional job application form to collect such data as work history and educational background, followed by some form of personal interview with the applicant. Most firms also administer a variety of tests, some general and some job-specific, to better ascertain applicants' skills. Examples of such tests include general math and reading quizzes, typing tests, computer software proficiency exams, and job-specific questionnaires. The largest companies have developed custom software for evaluating candidates' ap-

titudes. When applicants lack the necessary skills, some agencies offer training services. In addition, once a worker has been placed in a position, most temp services perform some form of follow-up with the employer to determine whether it was a successful match.

Concerns have arisen over the social implications of having a large segment of the workforce employed on a temporary basis. While it serves as an efficient mechanism for quickly moving labor where it's needed, critics argue that the arrangement can short-change workers by depriving them of stability and, in some cases, the same level of compensation they would enjoy as permanent employees. Health insurance and other benefits are a particular issue, because not all temporary workers—even when they work full time—are given insurance, paid vacation time, or other benefits. This is mostly true of smaller temp agencies, however, and many of the leading firms do offer full benefits.

Sources for Further Study

Berchem, Steven P. "Poised for Growth." *Staffing Success*, May/June 2002.

Hipple, Steven. "Earnings and Benefits of Contingent and Non-contingent Workers." *Monthly Labor Review*, October 1996.

Litfin, M.A. *Specialty Staffing Industry*. Chicago: William Blair & Company, L.L.C., 1998.

Martinez, Tomas. *The Human Marketplace*. New Brunswick, NJ: Transaction Books, 1976.

"Occupational Employment Statistics." Bureau of Labor Statistics: U.S. Department of Labor, 5 June 2002. Available at http://www.bls.gov.

"Where Have All the Workers Gone?" *Managing Office Technology*, June 1996.

Petroleum Refining

Overview

While oil companies remain some of the largest companies—and in a few cases the most profitable—in the world, the industry has faced a number of challenges in recent years, including low prices in the late 1990s (due to a large supply and slack demand), and costly environmental restrictions to curtail the industry's harmful effects on the earth's natural resources. Amidst these conditions a rising level of consolidation marked the industry, as companies joined forces in an increasingly challenging business climate. For example, British Petroleum acquired Amoco Corp. in 1998, followed by Atlantic Richfield Co. (ARCO). In 1999 Mobil and Exxon joined in what, at the time, was the largest merger on record, forming Exxon Mobil Corp. Finally, in 2001 Chevron acquired Texaco, forming ChevronTexaco.

After consistently low prices into the late 1990s, when crude oil prices reached $11.97 per barrel in 1998 and $17.51 in 1999, prices rose more than 57 percent to

$27.52 in 2000. That year, North American refineries collectively produced an average of 14.3 million barrels of refined petroleum products each day. This level was expected to remain flat in 2001. From 1990 to 1997 U.S. production grew by about 10 percent, while capacity rose by just two-tenths of a percent. This improvement indicates the industry's renewed emphasis on cost efficiency, as it's usually less profitable to operate a refinery below capacity. U.S. refinery production in 1997 stood at 93 percent of the industry's installed capacity of 15.705 million barrels per day, up from an 84-percent utilization rate in 1990. After rising to almost 96 percent in 1998, utilization rates remained steady at approximately 93 percent in the late 1990s and early 2000s, when estimated capacity had increased to 16.52 million barrels per day. In 2000, North American countries supplied almost one-fifth of the world's oil, ahead of European countries, which supplied about nine percent.

It's not so much volume growth as depressed prices that have adversely impacted the industry. In 1990 wholesale prices of gasoline, by far refineries' largest end product, averaged 78.6 cents per gallon. After falling as low as 59.9 cents in 1994, by 1997 prices had rebounded to 70.0 cents per gallon. But when inflation is factored out, 70.0 cents in 1997 would equal just 57.8 cents in 1990 dollars, amounting to a real decrease in gasoline prices of more than 26 percent over the eight years. After 1997, wholesale gasoline prices (including inflation) fell sharply again in 1998, reaching 52.6 cents per gallon. However, by 1999 and 2000 prices were rising, reaching levels of 64.5 cents and 87.9 cents, respectively.

The industry is dominated by a handful of huge oil conglomerates, sometimes known as the "majors," that are involved in crude oil production as well as refining, distribution, and retail sale of petroleum products. Below them is a second tier of independent refiners, some of which are quite large in their own right. The leading U.S. oil companies include Exxon Mobil Corp. and Chevron-Texaco.

History of the Industry

The use of semi-refined fossil fuels dates back several millennia before the common era. From ancient Mesopotamia, 6,000-year-old inscriptions include descriptions of oil and asphalt use as waterproofing materials. Egyptians embalmed their dead in asphalt, and Romans wrote by the light of oil lamps and drove chariots with wheels lubricated by crudely refined greases.

The invention of the kerosene lamp by Dr. Abraham Gesner of Pittsburgh prompted the formation of the Pennsylvania Rock Oil Company in 1854. During this time Americans sought alternative lamp fuels in response to a shortage of whale oil. Dr. Gesner extracted his "improved illuminating oil" from coal, but his methodology proved invaluable to petroleum refining's founding father, Benjamin Silliman, Jr., who wrote a treatise on the chemistry of petroleum in 1855 and then promptly figured out how to distill it. Steam was introduced into the distillation process in 1858. In 1860 the first semi-continuous refining system, operating in a battery of stills, was patented by D.S. Stombs and Julius Brace of Virginia. Luther Atwood cracked petroleum later that year, and Jean Lenoir then produced a three horsepower motor, which ran on benzene. The first full-fledged refinery began production in 1861 near Titusville, Pennsylvania, adjacent to the site where Edwin Drake and W.A. Smith had discovered the first producing oil field in the country at Oil Creek. The refinery churned out little except kerosene; contemporaneous demand for lubricating oils and greases wasn't high enough to keep anyone in business, and petroleum as a transport fuel was still several decades away.

Julius Hock's invention of the noncompression petroleum engine in Vienna in 1869 perhaps marked the beginning of the modern refining process, as engine fuel would become the primary vehicle for petroleum markets worldwide. "Horseless carriages"—powered by burning hay, steam, or electricity until Frank and Charles Duryea built the first gasoline-powered automobile in 1892—eventually became the channel through which refined petroleum captured public attention. The internal combustion engine, invented early in the twentieth century, and then Henry Ford's production of the Model T, suddenly brought petroleum to a pinnacle of economic significance.

In the early part of the twentieth century new technology was developed in petroleum-driven locomotion; automobiles, airplanes, and military vehicles proliferated as petroleum exploration and refining outpaced itself annually. Intense demand for petroleum products during World War I led to production facilities that would continue to produce innovations even after the war; solutions to agricultural, industrial, and transportation problems came with each new piece of understanding about the capabilities of a barrel of crude. Even food supply was drastically affected, as gasoline powered tractors enabled farmers to increase their productivity, and asphalt surfaces on highways allowed diesel-powered trucks to speed goods to market.

World War II also prompted an upsurge in refining capacity, yielding subsequent massive peacetime productivity. American consumers during the 1950s demanded large, stylish automobiles, warm houses, and air travel. For nearly three decades, Americans found uses for more refined petroleum. The "more is more" credo became refining's byline; a constant, steadily increasing demand for new products was met by the constant, steadily increasing supply of new crude oil supplies. Unfettered by environmental controls or financial limits, refiners expanded and enjoyed a long, golden age of prosperity.

Then, in 1973, a political crisis in the Middle East spurred a severe recession and highlighted the extent to which the United States had become dependent of foreign oil supplies. Furthermore, the fall of the shah of Iran in 1979 precipitated a series of supply interruptions and price increases. Overcompensating for the shortages brought on by Iran's domestic turbulence, refiners misjudged the oil demand for the early 1980s. While worldwide refining capacity increased tenfold between 1938 and 1981, "more is more" no longer held true, and in the 1980s refiners faced a loose market with substantial excesses in place.

Refiners entered the 1990s burdened by unpredictable supply and demand factors and the potential business consequences of the burgeoning environmental movement. Such issues as recycling, the hole in the ozone layer, and water pollution became an increasingly more importantt part of the U.S. legislativ agenda. Consequently, the business strategy of refiners shifted to finding cleaner-burning, more efficient fuels for smaller cars, as well as finding more environmentally friendly ways in which those fuels could be created.

Significant Events Affecting the Industry

One legislative package designed to address environmental pollution has had a significant impact on the industry. The Clean Air Act Amendments of 1990 required that the United States' 39 smoggiest cities substitute oxygenated gasoline for winter use beginning in November 1992. By 1995, the country's nine smoggiest cities—Baltimore, Chicago, Hartford, Houston, Los Angeles, Milwaukee, New York, Philadelphia, and San Diego—were to have implemented its Phase I specifications. Phase I stipulated that oxygenates (MTBE) be substituted for aromatics (which don't burn completely) in octane enhancers, essentially prescribing complete reformulation of automotive gasoline.

This new gasoline was required to have a minimum oxygen content of 2 percent by weight, a maximum of 1 percent benzene by volume, a maximum aromatics content of 25 percent, and no heavy metals. It could not cause an increase in nitrogen oxide emissions and must create less tailpipe emissions of volatile organic compounds and toxic air pollutants (relative to a baseline of 1990 summertime gasoline). The cost to refiners of implementing substitutions and reformulations prescribed in Phase I was estimated to run $3 to $5 billion.

Furthermore, the California Air Resources Board (CARB) instituted standards exceeding those of the Clean Air Act, requiring them to be met by 1996. Some analysts predicted the CARB standards would eventually replace Clean Air standards nationwide.

Costs of compliance prompted a spate of refinery closures in the early 1990s, including five smaller company sites in 1992, representing a total of 145,000 b/cd capacity lost. More streamlining was required of major companies, particularly Chevron. Chevron drastically scaled back operations at its Port Arthur, Texas, refinery (140,000 b/cd lost) and cut its Richmond, California, refinery capacity by 40,000 b/cd.

By the early 2000s, environmental concerns had developed over the use of MTBE (which is a possible carcinogen, according to the U.S. Environmental Protection Agency). One way that MTBE posed an environment threat was the contamination of groundwater supplies. The government was exploring alternatives to using MTBE, including the use of ethanol. Additionally, many states passed legislation restricting or banning its use in the near future. Meanwhile, several oil companies claimed that they were capable of meeting environmental standards without using government-mandated substitutes like MTBE. One consequence of different regions using different formulations of gasoline in order to meet environmental requirements is that the dynamics of supply and demand become more complicated. If the government requires a rapid change to MTBE alternatives, it is possible that smaller oil companies will be forced out of business. This could lead to a smaller supply of gasoline, and thus higher prices.

Key Competitors

The largest integrated oil company in the world (and thus the United States) by sales revenue is Exxon Mobil Corp. The massive oil conglomerate also holds the distinction of being the United States' second-largest corporation in terms of annual sales, behind Wal-Mart Stores. In 2001 it weighed in with $191.6 billion in sales. That year it posted a healthy profit of $15.3 billion, an eight-percent margin. Exxon Mobil, which employs 97,900 workers throughout the world, was formed through the 1999 merger of Exxon and The Mobil Corp. Mobil was formed in 1934 with the merger of Standard Oil Company of New Jersey and Anglo-American Oil Company Ltd. Exxon struggled to shake the fallout resulting from the *Exxon Valdez* disaster and other public relations debacles early in the 1990s. In the *Valdez* incident, an Exxon shipping vessel ran aground and caused a 11 million-gallon oil spill in Prince William Sound, Alaska, on March 24, 1989. The disaster caused significant environmental and economic harm to the region. The company also suffered from negative attention surrounding an early 1990s marketing campaign involving a tiger, which was criticized for being insensitive to animal rights.

Posting $104.4 billion in 2001 sales, of which $3.3 billion was net profit, ChevronTexaco Corp. gleans most of its revenue from petroleum operations. The San Francisco-based conglomerate originated from the 1911 break-up of the Standard Oil trust as Standard Oil Company (California), better known to some as Socal. In 1984 the company was renamed Chevron to correspond with its retail brand. In addition to its oil drilling, piping, and refining operations, Chevron operates more than 25,000 retail service stations bearing its name.

Industry Projections

According to data from DRI-WEFA reported in *Standard & Poor's*, from 2000 to 2005 crude oil prices are expected to fall about five percent each year and then grow at annual rates of approximately four percent. Contributing to these gains will be refined production originating from new crude oil reserves, which companies are constantly seeking to expand their businesses. In the early 2000s, major new exploration projects were underway at Exxon Mobil in the Gulf of Mexico, Asia, western Africa, and the Caspian Sea.

Global Presence

The major U.S. oil companies have operations spread throughout the world, and most own exploration and drilling properties on several continents. They also obtain significant shares of their annual sales from foreign markets, some of which are considered much more attractive than the United States because their demand for petroleum products is growing much more rapidly. Exxon Mobil, for example, only pulls in 39 percent of its net earnings from the United States.

Employment in the Industry

U.S. refinery employment has been edging downward for decades. In 2000 it stood at 80,690 people, which was down from 93,000 persons in 1998 and 120,000 in the late 1980s. Production workers in the industry earned an average of $21.63 per hour in 2000.

Sources for Further Study

Anderson, Robert O. *Fundamentals of the Petroleum Industry.* Norman: University of Oklahoma Press, n.d.

British Petroleum Company. *BP Statistical Review of World Energy 1998.* London, 1998. Available at http://www.bp.com.

Rosenberger, Gary. "Merger Trend Called Irreversible." *Journal of Commerce and Commercial,* 1 May 1996.

Standard & Poor's Industry Surveys. New York: Standard & Poor's Corporation, semiannual.

"Occupational Employment Statistics." Bureau of Labor Statistics, U.S. Department of Labor, 2 June 2002. Available at http://www.bls.gov.

"Oil & Gas: Production & Marketing Industry Survey." *Standard & Poor's Industry Surveys.* New York: The McGraw-Hill Companies. December 2001.

U.S. Energy Information Administration. "Annual Energy Review." Washington, 2000. Available at http://www.eia.doe.gov.

———. "Monthly Petroleum Product Sales Report." Washington, 1998. Available at http://www.eia.doe.gov.

Pharmaceuticals

Overview

The United States is the world's largest producer and consumer of pharmaceutical preparations. Prescription drug sales alone reached approximately $165 billion in 2001, according to Washington-based Pharmaceutical Research and Manufacturers Association (PhRMA). That

FINANCES:
Pharmaceutical and Medicine Manufacturing, 1997-2000 (million dollars)

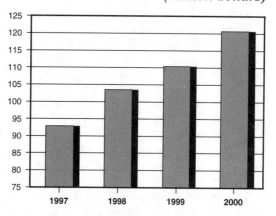

year, the largest prescription categories within the retail market were central nervous system drugs (21 percent), cardiovascular drugs (18 percent), and drugs involving the gastrointestinal system and metabolism (15 percent). In 2002 Connecticut-based IMS Health Inc. revealed that more than 3 billion prescriptions are dispensed in the United States, with more than 75 percent of sales occurring in chain stores and independent locations.

The country's relatively open market also made it the leader in research and development (R&D). In its *Annual Report, 2001-2002* PhRMA explained that research-based pharmaceutical companies devote more to R&D (about 17 percent of sales) than companies in any other industry including electrical/electronics (8.4 percent) and computer software/services (7.8 percent). Since 1980, when spending totaled $2 billion, the industry has seen healthy annual increases in this area. However, PhRMA estimated that an especially sharp increase in R&D spending would occur in 2001, as totals rose from $26.4 billion in 2000 to $30.5 billion.

While short-term patent protection offers some potential for profits, major pharmaceutical producers often face tight competition on price. When a drug loses its patent, another producer, usually a low-cost, off-brand competitor, can offer an equivalent product, and the price of the drug can be quickly cut in half. The commodity nature of off-patent, or generic, drugs offers slim profit margins and sometimes forces name-brand manufacturers to eventually abandon making the compounds they originate, while low-end manufacturers continue to churn them out. As a result, new research is at the core of the pharmaceutical industry's health.

History of the Industry

Prior to the late nineteenth century, the U.S. pharmaceutical industry barely resembled its current structure. Simple chemical compounds such as iodine chlorate, along with plant extracts such as quinine, constituted the prime ingredients of available remedies. However, these drugs lacked specific scientific formulas. Thus a doctor's order for a medication might not yield the product intended. To offset this problem, doctors often dispensed medicines in addition to prescribing them. But they did not have a monopoly on medical advice or drug selection for patients. Given the uneven quality of medical care before the twentieth century, patients often chose to dose themselves with "patent" medicines or to describe symptoms to the druggist, who would offer his own remedy for purchase. Some traditional treatments, like digitalis, remain part of the pharmacological arsenal.

The War of 1812 and the Civil War stimulated an increase in domestic pharmaceutical manufacturing capacity. Both events temporarily disrupted the supply of fine chemicals (those with a purity level high enough for human consumption) from Europe with which pharmacists and doctors produced the few chemical medicaments that they knew. Advances in the isolation and creation of new chemical substances, such as the 1840 discovery of the medicinal applications for nitrous oxide (laughing gas) by an American dentist, Horace Wells, stimulated demand for more fine chemical capacity. During the Civil War, American firms like Squibb were able to establish themselves profitably by providing advanced machinery and quality products to the Union Army.

As the century progressed, other companies turned to the production of "ethical" drugs for physicians and hospitals. These drugs had clearly labeled and pharmacologically reliable contents (and were thus termed "ethical"). They were intended to supply drugs of standardized quality. Brand name ethicals were also promoted as alternatives to the wide variety of other proprietaries, mainly bottled "patent" medicines. These extremely popular elixirs claimed great therapeutic value while the contents—often only colored water, alcohol, and opiates—were generally ineffectual and occasionally dangerous. The reliability of the new ethical suppliers, on the other hand, induced doctors to begin requesting branded pharmaceuticals in prescriptions by the end of the century.

Following scientific breakthroughs in understanding the causes and potential treatments for many of the diseases that had long been the scourge of mankind, demand for these reliable drugs and vaccines soon increased. The germ theory of disease, based upon the research of bacteriologists like Pasteur, revolutionized medicine and drug therapy in the 20 years immediately before and after World War I.

Between the two world wars, U.S. firms copied the research orientation and patenting habits of German counterparts. Merck and Squibb opened direct ties with academic research institutions, financing research fellowships, laboratories, and institutes in the natural sciences. Drug companies hired academic research leaders to head or staff in-house labs. Firms developed some interest in basic research, but the major concern was using expanded research and development area capabilities to create new drug products for the expanding market.

World War II and the U.S. postwar economic dominance secured the foundation for phenomenal growth in the pharmaceutical industry. The desire to find new drugs, especially antibiotics, led companies to sometimes absurd extremes. Pfizer requested that people send samples of dirt from all corners of the world on the chance that some might contain new molds from which to extract antibiotics. In fact, a Pfizer employee did find a profitable new treatment, terramycin, in a sample of dirt outside a company plant in Indiana. This and other "broad-spectrum" antibiotics, those effective for a wide range of illnesses, provided revolutionary therapeutic regimens for physicians after the 1940s. Other breakthrough medications in the 1950s included Jonas Salk's polio vaccine, and tranquilizers and amphetamines, like Librium and Dexedrine, which promised to significantly aid patients suffering from mental illness.

In the early 1960s, a European sleeping pill called Thalidomide was found to cause severe birth defects when taken during pregnancy. Because the drug was widely used in Europe and would likely have gained approval under U.S. policy, the federal government responded to the resulting uproar by passing the Kefauver-Harris Amendments of 1962. These amendments to the Food, Drug and Cosmetic Act of 1938 required pharmaceutical companies to prove both safety and efficacy before a drug entered the marketplace. Formal procedures for new drug applications (NDAs) to the FDA and for the clinical investigation of potential therapies were established. All adverse drug reactions in clinical studies would have to be fully reported, and human clinical subjects had to be informed of the dangers of involvement in trials before giving consent. Additionally, the new act required that drugs must follow specific production guidelines, called Good Manufacturing Practices (GMP). Manufacturing plants became subject to both registration and inspection procedures. Finally, advertising for prescription drugs was placed under Food and Drug Administration (FDA) supervision, while over-the-counter (OTC) drug advertising continued under Federal Trade Commission (FTC) oversight.

The immediate effect of the new law was to drastically slow the rate at which pharmaceutical manufacturers introduced new drugs to the market. According to the Pharmaceutical Manufacturers Association (PMA), drug introductions fell from 45 to 24 annually between 1961 and 1962 alone. In the 1970s, they stayed below 20 in most years, and fared little better over the next two decades until changes were initiated in the mid-1990s.

However, larger research budgets needed to comply with the new requirements yielding a whole crop of profitable new drug therapies in the 1980s, including drugs for hypertension (Merck's Vasotec), cholesterol treatment (Lopid from Warner-Lambert and Mevacor from Merck), and blood-clot dissolvers for heart-attack victims (Genentech's TPA). Meanwhile, Ortho Pharmaceutical's (owned by Johnson & Johnson) anti-acne Retin-A, and Upjohn's baldness treatment Rogaine, created new markets for cosmetic drugs. Even standbys like aspirin enjoyed increased sales as a result of studies that showed its potential to avert some heart attacks.

Lavish research budgets soon helped to breed what critics charged were unjustifiably high prices in prescription drugs, with companies allegedly spending more money on advertising, brand support, and lobbying efforts than they did on research and development. Some analysts felt that price was determining costs rather than the other way around. The prices of drugs were less related to cost inputs, they claimed, than to companies' needs to maintain corporate structures. Drug companies insisted that the prices were needed to recoup the vast research costs of all the compounds that never made it to the market, which were a necessary part of releasing the comparatively few successful drugs. Meanwhile, the soaring costs of health care in general in the 1980s and early 1990s added fuel to demands for drug price control policies similar to those in Europe or Japan. Medications sold in Europe and the United States were reported to have price differentials exceeding 50 percent.

Significant Events Affecting the Industry

In the mid-1990s, reforms at the U.S. Food and Drug Administration resulted in a reduction in the average approval time for new drugs. By the late 1990s the average drug typically took 15 years to bring to market, factoring in all initial testing through final regulatory approval. Final approval, on average, consumed between one and two years of this period. After a decade of hovering between 20 and 30 new approvals per year, in 1996 the FDA pushed through approvals on a striking 53 new drugs. However, from 1997 to 2000 a number of drugs had to be recalled or restricted. Facing criticism over hasty approvals, the agency slowed the number of drugs it approved each year and began to lengthen approval times.

The terrorist attacks against the United States on September 11, 2001 brought a heightened focus on bioterrorism. Following the attacks, a number of Americans contracted the disease Anthrax after coming into contact with bacteria sent via U.S. Mail. Concerns also emerged over Smallpox, a deadly disease that had been largely eliminated years earlier, but which existed in laboratories in several countries including Russia and North Korea. The expensive antibiotic Cipro, manufactured by Bayer AG, is one of the primary drugs used to treat Anthrax infections. Following the attacks, a need emerged to stockpile large quantities of Cipro, as well as smallpox vaccines. This led to controversy concerning the potential suspension of pharmaceutical company patents, because of the need to make large amounts of desperately needed drugs at lower prices during times of crisis. Although such intervention was not necessary in the United States because Bayer agreed to provide Cipro to the federal government at a reduced price, the Canadian government did temporarily revoke Bayer's patent. In general, scenarios like the attacks of September 11 could change the dynamics of the industry by placing increased restrictions on domestic drug makers.

Key Competitors

With $47.7 billion in total 2001 revenues, of which about $21.3 billion came from pharmaceutical production, Merck & Co. Inc. is a world pharmaceutical industry leader. Merck initiated the 1990s trend toward purchasing drug distributors with its 1993 acquisition of Medco Containment Services Inc. for $6.6 billion. By 2001 the company's Merck-Medco pharmacy benefits management arm accounted for $26.4 billion in annual sales. The subsidiary had evolved into the leader in its category, managing upwards of 530 million prescriptions each year for 65 million people in the United States. In 2002, Merck announced that it would seek to spin the subsidiary off as a separate publicly traded firm. Merck's leading products include two cholesterol drugs, Mevacor and Zocor, as well as respiratory drug Singulair, and ulcer drug Pepcid.

Another one the world's leading drug makers is New York-based Pfizer Inc. With 2001 revenues of $32.3 billion, Pfizer manufactures a number of leading prescription drugs including Lipitor, Zithromax, Celebrex, Viagra, and Zyrtec. Accordingly, in 2001 a large percentage of the company's sales ($25.5 billion) came from its human pharmaceutical business, which experienced healthy growth rates of 12 percent in 2000 and 13 percent in 2001. In 2000 Pfizer merged with Warner-Lambert, a former competitor with a strong tradition in the area of research and development. Pfizer's Warner-Lambert Consumer Group manufactures leading over-the-counter pharmaceuticals like Benadryl, Listerine, Visine, and BenGay.

A 1998 merger brought two diversified U.S. pharmaceutical/biotechnology interests together, American Home Products Corporation and Monsanto Company. In March of 2002, the new company adopted the name Wyeth, based on one of its earliest prescription businesses founded in 1860. Through its Wyeth Consumer Healthcare subsidiary, Wyeth manufactures well-known OTC drugs such as Advil, Anacin, Anbesol, Caltrate, Preparation H, and Robitussin. The company's Wyeth Pharmaceuticals division markets a profitable line of estrogen tablets called Premarin, which generated more than $2 billion in 2001. The firm's other two divisions are Wyeth Research and Fort Dodge Animal Health. In 2001, the company had revenues of $14.1 billion, and spent almost $2 billion on research and development in areas like biotechnology products, vaccines, and various other drugs. It marketed its preparations in more than

140 different countries and employed more than 52,000 workers.

Other major U.S. drug companies include Abbott Laboratories, Bristol-Myers Squibb Co., Eli Lilly & Co., and Johnson & Johnson.

Industry Projections

In the early 2000s, the United States was expected to retain its leading position within the industry. According to IMS projections, from 2000 to 2005 U.S. sales should increase annually at a compound rate of approximately 12 percent. Comparatively, corresponding growth rates will hover around 11 percent in Canada, 10 percent in Spain, nine percent in Australia, and eight percent in the United Kingdom. Additionally, IMS projects that within 10 key international markets, the United States will have a market share of more than 60 percent by 2005, followed by Japan with about 15 percent, and Germany with more than 5 percent. The booming elderly segment of the population will fuel increasing levels of demand for pharmaceuticals well into the first quarter of the twenty-first century.

Global Presence

Of the world's 10 leading pharmaceutical companies, more than half are headquartered in the United States and the rest are based in Europe. Consolidation continues to take place throughout the industry on a global basis. Together, the leading 10 firms control almost half of the market, which is significantly higher than in past years. In addition to selling their products domestically, the major U.S. pharmaceutical companies also market their pharmaceuticals internationally. Among the leading European pharmaceutical firms are Novartis AG of Switzerland; GlaxoSmithKline plc and AstraZeneca of the United Kingdom; and Aventis, based in Schiltigheim, France. Although foreign markets like those of Europe and Japan often have greater controls on prices, many also present fewer regulatory hurdles to pass before introducing a new drug. Thus, many U.S. drugmakers issue new products abroad before they're able to do so in the United States.

Employment in the Industry

The pharmaceutical industry employs more than 315,000 people in the United States. According to the U.S. Department of Labor's Bureau of Labor Statistics, this number was expected to grow almost 24 percent between 2000 and 2010, eventually reaching 390,000 workers. The average annual salary within the industry exceeds $42,000 annually, or $20.41 per hour which is substantially higher than the average annual salary in many industries. This is true because a high share of the industry's workforce holds advanced and highly specialized training, including a large number of workers with doctoral degrees. While such highly trained workers usually face few difficulties finding jobs, pressures to contain costs have caused a number of leading companies to trim their workforces at home and abroad. As a result, net employment in the drug industry has dropped since the early 1990s, brought about in part through merger and acquisition activities.

Sources for Further Study

Annual Report 2001-2002. Washington: Pharmaceutical Research and Manufacturers of America, July 2001.

"Healthcare: Pharmaceuticals." *Standard & Poor's Industry Surveys,* December 2001.

Occupational Employment Statistics. Bureau of Labor Statistics, U.S. Department of Labor, 30 March 2002. Available at http://www.bls.gov/oes/2000/oesi3_283.htm.

"Pharmaceuticals." *Hoover's Online,* 28 March 2002. Available at http://www.hoovers.com.

Pharmaceutical Research and Manufacturers. "New Drug Approvals in 1997." Washington, January 1998.

"Pharmaceutical Results Improve Helped By New Product Launches." *Chemical Market Reporter,* 27 January 1997.

Serwer, Andrew E. "Layoffs Tail Off-But Only For Some." *Fortune,* 20 March 1995.

Taggart, James. *The World Pharmaceutical Industry.* London: Routledge, 1991.

Tighe, S.C., et al. *Merck & Co.* New York: Merrill Lynch, 12 November 1997.

U.S. Industry and Trade Outlook. New York: McGraw-Hill and U.S. Department of Commerce, 1998.

U.S. Pharmaceutical Industry Year in Review 2000. Connecticut: IMS Health Inc., 2002.

Photographic Equipment and Supplies

Overview

The $22 billion U.S. photography industry manufactures a host of photographic technologies and supplies. Included in the industry's product line are still and motion cameras (but not video cameras), film, photographic papers and chemicals, and a variety of photography-based technologies like photocopiers and scanners. Important new product introductions in the latter half of the 1990s included digital cameras, which rely on the magnetic storage of images rather than light-sensitive film, and the Advanced Photo System (APS) format of cameras and film, which streamlined the picture-taking process for amateurs and offered more predictable results than conventional 35mm cameras and film.

However, the U.S. industry faces continued challenges from foreign manufacturers, especially those in Asian countries. Although imports historically have outpaced exports by a large margin, the value of imports was steadily decreasing in the early 2000s while the value of exports was increasing.

History of the Industry

Although photographic equipment and supplies first became available to consumers in the 1880s, it wasn't until the 1950s that the industry's sales grew rapidly toward modern proportions. Several developments during the mid-twentieth century spurred the industry's growth: a significant increase in consumers' disposable incomes; the emergence of photocopying and microfilming products as lucrative segments of the industry; and the development of still cameras that were very easy to operate.

Several key technological advances enabled the photographic market to flourish. These innovations were spearheaded by Eastman Kodak Company, the predominant force in the industry. Perhaps the most significant early contribution was George Eastman's adaptation during the 1870s of the dry-plate process in his cameras. The dry-plate process was much simpler and cleaner than the wet-process, which had been the leading process in the United States until that time. This marked an important step toward making photographic equipment available to all consumers. Eastman followed his innovation in the 1890s with the introduction of roll film, which he was the first to market.

In a bid to capture the nation's interest in photography, manufacturers of this era labored to improve the performance of cameras and the quality of film. A giant leap toward this goal was made in 1900 when Kodak introduced the first model of its popular, inexpensive, and easy-to-use Brownie line of cameras. Retailing at $1, the first Brownie signaled the beginning of affordable cameras with mass-market appeal. Having achieved its first appreciable market penetration with the Brownie, Kodak began to develop products aimed at diversifying the applications of photographic equipment. The first 8-mm picture system designed for the amateur photographer entered the market in 1932, followed by the advent of color film three years later.

Additional offerings to spark interest in amateur photography emerged before the onset of World War II, but in the immediate postwar years these were overshadowed when Edwin H. Land, founder of Polaroid Corporation, developed a process to instantly develop film. This 1947 breakthrough gave birth to a whole new genre of cameras and film, closely associated with the Polaroid name, that eliminated the need to take film in for development.

By this time photographic equipment had become very reliable and consumers had grown accustomed to taking pictures. As these two trends dovetailed in the midst of the postwar prosperity, sales of photographic equipment more than doubled during the 1950s. From a market of just $500 million in 1950, the industry's annual sales had topped $1.2 billion by 1960. This prodigious growth was partly due to the rising disposable incomes that U.S. consumers enjoyed; but it was also encouraged by demographic trends such as the period's high birth rate, which supplied ample opportunities for

picture taking as parents sought to record their children's upbringing on film. In fact, in 1960 newborn babies and young children were the object of 55 percent of the 2.2 billion photos taken that year.

Kodak held a virtual monopoly on the industry from the turn of the century through the 1950s, perennially controlling about 90 percent of the film market and a similar share of the camera market. In the early 1950s the federal government began to intervene, filing an antitrust suit against Kodak that eventually resulted in a 1954 settlement decree. Part of Kodak's dominance before the settlement stemmed from its practice of charging a development fee with every roll of film it sold. By including a built-in processing fee, Kodak in effect cornered the film processing market and thus discouraged other manufacturers from competing—the dearth of independent processing facilities inhibited film sales by other companies. The 1954 decree ended this practice when Kodak agreed to sell film without charging for processing and to license other processing companies to develop its film. While Kodak retained a firm grip on most parts of the industry, the changes allowed smaller companies to coexist with Kodak's dominance more easily.

Just as competition between film manufacturers intensified, competitors began to secure a foothold in the fledgling photocopier market, which also promised to be a lucrative enterprise. Although total photocopying sales didn't exceed $100 million until 1958, sales increased rapidly when such a product was marketed for office use. Until that point photocopiers were very large and had largely been relegated to specialized facilities rather than being located near the end users. As new technology yielded smaller and more user-friendly photocopiers, a market for copiers in office settings quickly sprang up. While Kodak and a number of other firms introduced early models using a variety of processing techniques, Xerox Corporation's xerographic process proved the most commercially successful. Xerography involved electrostatic dry copying that replaced the chemicals required by other systems, allowing a cleaner process that could be run on plain paper rather than the specialized papers other processes required. Xerographic photocopiers quickly became Xerox's main business during the 1950s, and a number of competitors followed suit. By the mid-1960s the booming photocopier market was worth $500 million in its own right and included over a hundred competitors, some of which still produced the older, wet-type process copiers.

The 1960s saw another introduction by Kodak intended to further popularize amateur photography through ease of use. Kodak's Instamatic, released in 1963 and foreshadowing similar endeavors that would continue through the 1990s, featured an integrated film cartridge and camera system that eliminated the need to thread film manually. This and other features made the inexpensive Instamatic a popular and reliable tool for taking simple snapshots. The model's marketing was particularly successful, as Kodak had concealed its development until the point of release, when it took the industry by surprise. Within its first two years, approximately 7.5 million units were sold, and a corresponding surge was experienced in film sales. In fact, according to figures gathered by Kodak at the time, the Instamatic's convenience led to higher film consumption rates among the camera's users. Kodak reported that consumers with ordinary cameras used an average of four rolls of film per year, but those who owned Instamatics splurged for an average of eight rolls each year.

At the same time the consumer and general office uses of photographic equipment were burgeoning, important new industrial applications were being pioneered as well. High-speed camera equipment was used on production lines as a quality control measure to identify product inconsistencies. Similar high-tech uses of photography were found in military and space exploration applications, such that by 1964 industrial uses accounted for nearly half of the industry's $1.4 billion in annual sales.

Microfilm and micropublishing proved to be an important growth market during the 1970s. In that period there were fewer options for storing large amounts of information, and microfilm and microfiche grew as popular media for archiving documents such as newspapers, periodicals, and corporate and government documents. In the early 1970s microfilm equipment sales were rising at an annual clip of 18 percent, and the microfilm segment soon became a $500 million component of the broader photographic equipment industry.

By the 1980s there were signs that the U.S. market was maturing, and many of the leading companies were forced to restructure their businesses in order to remain profitable as demand for conventional products slackened. One major development was the debut of video camcorders in the consumer market. While many tended to be high-end devices, sales of video cameras and video tape—which encode images as data on magnetic tape instead of on light-sensitive film—began to sap some of the market for film-based photographic equipment. Some leading manufacturers of video cameras also had ties to the conventional photography industry, but for the most part these devices functioned as part of the home audio and video equipment industry. The rise of camcorders was a direct offshoot of the popularity of VCRs, which were rapidly penetrating the home entertainment market at the time.

Significant Events Affecting the Industry

Digital cameras—those that record still images using semiconductor sensors and save the information as binary data—were launched as an important new consumer technology in the mid-1990s, buoyed in large part by the widespread use of personal computers and the Internet. An earlier related technology on the processing side of the business was that of photo collections on CD-ROMs, which can hold images from several rolls of film

and usually come with a browsing program for computers. Digital cameras enabled images to be captured on computer disks or memory sticks, which could then be loaded directly into image-processing software and manipulated. These photos could also be readily published on web pages. Although resolution and performance of the entry-level models was still far beneath the quality of conventional 35-mm film technology, the speed and convenience of these cameras attracted 500,000 unit sales in 1995, considered the first year of digital cameras' commercial viability in the consumer market, and 1.2 million unit sales the following year. By 2001, monthly unit sales alone exceeded 250,000. As digital cameras increased in popularity, household penetration levels climbed from about four percent in 1999 to more than nine percent in 2000, according to the Photo Marketing Association (PMA).

Convenience was also the predominant factor driving sales of disposable cameras, sometimes called single-use cameras. These low-tech devices essentially are a roll of film built into an inexpensive camera body made of cardboard and light plastics. They include simple versions of all the basic elements of a standard camera: a winding mechanism and frame counter, a viewfinder, a lens, and sometimes a battery and flash unit. But these inexpensive cameras, which typically cost little more than a conventional roll of film, can only be used to expose the film that comes in them. Their convenience made them one of the fastest-growing segments of the photography industry into the early 2000s.

Another major new product initiative of the 1990s was the introduction of Advanced Photo System (APS) cameras and film. The APS standard came about through a collaboration between five of the global industry's top manufacturers—Canon, Fuji, Kodak, Minolta, and Nikon—with Kodak being the lone representative from the United States. A successor to the convenience formats of the past, which included Kodak's Instamatic and disk cameras, APS involves a proprietary camera and film cartridge system that is easy to load and operate. The highly automated cameras advance and rewind the film for the users, who only have to insert and remove the cartridge. More importantly, APS self-adjusts for lighting conditions, records images for three different printing options, and has a magnetic strip for recording digital information about each frame. Unveiled in 1996, U.S. retailers initially reported mixed interest in the product. One early drawback was that processing labs required expensive special technology in order to accommodate APS film, and thus not all photo-finishing services could accept it. According to figures from the PMA, by early 2002 APS cameras accounted for approximately 11 percent of the market, in terms of unit sales.

Key Competitors

Eastman Kodak Company has been at the forefront of the U.S. photographic equipment industry for more than a century. Incorporated in 1889, its founder George Eastman had been active in the business for over a decade before establishing the company. Despite its predominance in the U.S. industry, Kodak faced mounting troubles in the 1980s and 1990s as its domestic market share was eroded by foreign competition and its products failed to keep pace with buyers' changing expectations. One of Kodak's sore spots was in the photocopier business, into which it poured significant sums of money toward developing a digital color copier. But overall, its copiers lagged technologically behind those of its competitors, and Kodak finally divested itself of its copier unit in 1996. While Kodak still supplies the vast majority of the United States' film and photographic paper, executives at the company charged that the import market of Japan—home to most of its rivals—was unfairly closed to its products. Kodak's allegations led to ongoing trade disputes in the 1990s. In 2001, Kodak acquired Ofoto Inc. in order to bolster its strength in the area of online imaging products and services. Additionally, the company also acquired the imaging services business of Bell & Howell Co. With $13.2 billion in 2001, Kodak's worldwide sales equal more than half of the U.S. industry's annual sales.

Industry Projections

The industry will continue to find its best growth markets outside the United States in the early 2000s, but imports will continue to represent a very large share of domestic photographic equipment and supplies purchases, maintaining the wide U.S. trade deficit for the category. Through 2004, according to U.S. Department of Commerce figures, industry shipments will rise at a compound average rate of less than one percent. The shift from analog to digital photography will continue in the early 2000s. According to PMA, in 2002 25 percent of professional photo labs and 30 percent of retail photo stores were expected to buy digital processing equipment. This largely was in response to the growing popularity of digital photography amongst both amateur and professional audiences. The PMA also indicated that from March 2001 to March 2002, overall unit sales of analog cameras decreased 31 percent while digital camera unit sales increased 28 percent. During the same time period, unit sales of single-use cameras increased 10 percent, indicating the popularity of these convenient and affordable cameras with consumers.

Global Presence

Kodak's dispute with Japan aside, the company has a very strong international business. It manufactures products in a number of countries including Asia, Australia, Europe, and North and South America. In 2001, non-U.S. sales made up approximately 51 percent of Kodak's total revenues. As of that year, Kodak was expanding in emerging markets like Asia, where it operated some 14,000 Kodak Express stores. Some of these stores were in China, where Kodak has purchased a number of established film companies to capitalize on that nation's flourishing economic growth. Kodak also has expanded into India, where it has more than 4,000 retail locations. However, the company faces formidable challenges in many places from its nemesis, Fuji Photo Film, and leading Japanese camera makers like Canon, Minolta, and Nikon.

Employment in the Industry

Employment in the photographic equipment industry receded quickly during the 1990s in response to growing pressures on corporate profitability caused by stagnant domestic sales. From nearly 110,000 workers in 1988, the industry's payroll dropped to just 84,400 people in 1997. By 2000 this number had decreased to 68,450. On average, though, industry wages have remained fairly strong, reaching $21.71 per hour in 2000.

Sources for Further Study

1996-97 PMA Industry Trends Report. Photo Marketing Association International, 1997.

"All the Film in China." *U.S. News & World Report,* 6 July 1998.

Heller, Laura. "Digital Adoption Grows, but Use is Still Limited." *DSN Retailing Today,* 20 August 2001.

"New PMA Report Looks At Changing Equipment Needs. Photo Marketing Association International, 1 May 2002. Available at http://www.pmai.org.

"Occupational Employment Statistics." Bureau of Labor Statistics: U.S. Department of Labor, 26 May 2002. Available at http://www.bls.gov.

"Photographic Equipment and Supplies." *U.S. Industry and Trade Outlook.* New York: McGraw-Hill and U.S. Department of Commerce, 1998.

"Photographic Equipment and Supplies." *U.S. Industry and Trade Outlook.* New York: McGraw-Hill and U.S. Department of Commerce, 2000.

"PMA Processing Survey. Highlights and Overview Through March 2002." Photo Marketing Association International, 20 May 2002. Available at http://www.pmai.org.

Seymour, Jim. "Digital Cameras: Reality vs. Hype." *PC Magazine,* 21 April 1998.

U.S. Department of Commerce, Economics and Statistics Administration, U.S. Census Bureau. *Annual Survey of Manufacturers.* Washington, 2002.

Plastics Products

Overview

The plastics industry produces an extraordinarily diverse range of finished goods and components made from plastics. While this industry category excludes the manufacture of plastic sheets, bottles, and pipes, it encompasses such diverse products as air mattresses, plastic kitchen and bath accessories, plastic windows and doors, plastic hardware, and apparel and accessories fabricated from plastics. These products combined account for more than half of all finished plastics goods sales in the United States.

By value, the most important specific categories within the industry are plastics used in transportation equipment (mainly automobiles), packaging, and construction. Together these three areas are worth more than $31 billion annually, or 47 percent of industry sales. The broad category of consumer and institutional products that includes kitchen goods, waste baskets, storage bins, and many other items, commands another 21 percent of industry sales.

Manufacturers of finished plastic goods and components often obtain their resins, which come as pellets or other crude shapes, from chemical and plastic resin producers, although some manufacture their own resins. Plastics product manufacturers then apply any number of processes to the raw materials in order to produce finished goods.

Many different kinds of resins may be used in plastics manufacturing depending on the structural requirements of the end product. The two main classes of plastics are thermosets and thermoplastics. Thermosets, which account for only 10 percent of the materials used in this industry's products, harden by chemical reaction and can't be melted and reshaped once they are created. Thermosets are used in applications like epoxies, an ingredient in flooring, coatings, and adhesives. Thermoplastics account for the vast majority of industry products and include materials like acrylics, polyethylene, and polyvinyl chloride (PVC), which yield such products as construction materials, machine parts, packaging, and automotive parts.

There are at least 12 major processing techniques used to form plastic goods, but three of the most important are extrusion, blow molding, and injection molding. Others include calendering, film casting, rotational molding, laminating, and casting.

Extrusion entails melting and compressing plastic granules in a tube. A screw conveyor inside the tube then forces the plastic through a nozzle at the end of the tube. The physical characteristics of the plastics can be altered by applying heat or cold to the barrel, adjusting the screw pressure, or using different types and sizes of screws. Extrusion is used to make pipe, sheeting, film, and other various forms.

Blow molding takes the extrusion process one step further. In blow-molding, the extruded plastic is forced into a bottle-shaped mold, to which compressed air is applied to inflate the plastic and press it against the cold surface of the mold.

In a similar process, injection molding entails extruding plastic directly into a two-piece mold, where it hardens into a solid form. When the shape has cooled enough to hold its form, the mold can be opened and the shape removed. Depending on the product's specifica-

tions, the molds may be made of simple, low-cost soft alloys like aluminum or more expensive and durable materials for high-precision molding.

History of the Industry

Keratin, a natural plastic, was used in the United States to make lantern windows and other simple items as early as 1740. Gutta percha, or gum elastic, was first used during the mid-1850s to make billiard balls and ocean cable insulation. Manufacturers borrowed forming and processing techniques from Malayan natives (in present-day Malaysia), who first discovered use of natural plastics. Shellac plastics, developed by Samuel Speck, also emerged during the mid-nineteenth century and were used to create goods such as checkers, buttons, and insulators.

Following the invention of the first synthetic plastics in the late 1870s, plastics products sales began to accelerate. American Dr. Leo Baekland introduced the first moldable plastic, Bakelite, in 1909. This invention prompted a flurry of new molding techniques and resins, the materials from which plastics are made, in the following decades. Additional refinements and new uses for plastics during the 1960s and 1970s made them commonplace in U.S. manufacturing. In many cases they were cheaper and more versatile than the materials they replaced.

Significant Events Affecting the Industry

Environmental concerns about plastics became an increasingly important issue during the 1990s as consumer demand and government regulations called for controls on various forms of pollution plastics can cause. In addition to taking up space in landfills, some plastics also leech harmful chemicals into the ground, and the manufacturing process can release harmful substances into the environment as well. As a result, some manufacturers have sought ways to lessen the environmental impact of their products. They have made plastics easier to recycle and, in some cases, have changed materials or processes used in order to reduce the threat of pollution. The broader U.S. plastics industry spent an estimated $1 billion between 1990 and 1998 to improve the recycling rates of plastics. In the early 2000s, the industry continued to work toward this goal. At that time, approximately 2000 firms were involved in the recycling of plastics at the consumer and industrial levels.

Key Competitors

The plastics industry is highly fragmented, and many of its participants serve as component contractors to other manufacturers rather than producing finished products for sale to end users. In the late 1990s, according to U.S. Census Bureau figures, there were more than 7,500 separate plastics facilities in the United States, and the 50 largest firms accounted for about 23 percent of shipment values. Most industry firms specialize in just a few lines of plastics products.

Tupperware The Tupperware Corporation, until 1996 part of Premark International, is a major international manufacturer and direct marketer of household plastic goods. Traditionally, the firm's storage bins, kitchenware, and containers have been sold primarily via "Tupperware parties," in which the salesperson performs in-home demonstration and marketing of the product line. By the early 2000s, showcases in shopping malls, the Internet, and infomercials were among other channels Tupperware was using to sell its products. In 2000 the company acquired BeautiControl Inc., a direct seller of beauty products. The company's flagship brand is noted for its lifetime product guarantee. In 2001 Tupperware earned about 20 percent of its $1.1 billion in sales from the United States. The remainder came from all parts of the globe, especially Europe and Asia. As in the late 1990s, the company struggled in certain Asian markets like Korea due to volatile economic conditions.

Newell Rubbermaid Inc. While some of its household products are direct competitors to those of Tupperware, Newell Rubbermaid Inc. has a much more diverse product line, which as its name suggests, includes products made of rubber and other materials that aren't considered part of the plastic industry. Also unlike Tupperware, Rubbermaid distributes its wares through conventional retail channels like supermarkets and general merchandise stores. In 1999, Rubbermaid was purchased by Newell Inc. and the organization was re-named Newell Rubbermaid Inc. In addition to Rubbermaid brand products, the firm also is home to well-known brands like Sharpie markers; Paper Mate pens; Little Tikes and Graco/Century toys; and Levolor blinds. The company's Wooster, Ohio-based Rubbermaid Home Products division accounted for about 26 percent of its $6.9 billion 2001 revenues. Although domestic sales represented approximately three-quarters of the company's revenues in the late 1990s and early 2000s, international sales were growing at a faster rate.

Industry Projections

Because plastics products are used in so many different applications, the future performance of the industry's various segments hinges on many economic variables. In the transportation sector, the trend toward lighter-weight materials in vehicles, along with stable production levels in the late 1990s and early 2000s, has meant healthy demand for plastic components. Similarly, the relatively strong U.S. construction market of the mid-1990s and early 2000s helped generate sales in that segment. In areas like consumer goods, sales in some product categories is relatively flat—growing at the rate of inflation at best—although broad-based economic growth tends to boost sales as consumers have greater disposable income to spend.

Global Presence

Most of the U.S. industry's largest firms have some international presence, although as the examples of Rubbermaid and Tupperware illustrate, the amount of company sales outside the United States may vary greatly. Since the United States is considered a mature market for many of the industry's products, international diversification has been important to some plastics products manufacturers.

The globalization of the plastics products industry is coincided by the emergence of significant resins production outside the United States. Producers in countries such as China, Saudi Arabia, and Malaysia are rapidly building up their capacities to produce plastic resins. While this trend doesn't necessarily affect finished product manufacturers, increasingly a rift is forming between the pricing of well-established, low-tech plastics and highly engineered plastics. Low-tech plastics are being produced increasingly by developing countries at significant cost savings compared to U.S. producers, driving prices downward in a commodity-like environment. Meanwhile, since they can't compete as well on low-cost goods, U.S. firms are concentrating more on high-tech plastics that can demand a higher price and thus greater profits. The key effect of these trends on U.S. plastic product makers is that they face volatile pricing for their raw materials and, ultimately, some may begin to purchase increasing shares of their raw materials from foreign suppliers. The value of industry imports and exports were both growing at a healthy pace in the late 1990s and early 2000s, averaging 11 percent and 13 percent, respectively, between 1997 and 2000.

Employment in the Industry

The plastics industry is a major employer in the United States, with a labor force of approximately 555,600, according to U.S. Census Bureau statistics. These workers have a net payroll of about $16 billion annually. Almost 80 percent of the industry's workforce is made up of production workers, as opposed to management and administrative personnel. This percentage suggests a leaner management and administrative structure in the plastics industry compared to the average manufacturing industry. Production workers earn hourly wages that are lower than the average for other kinds of manufacturing work.

Sources for Further Study

1997 Economic Census. Washington, DC: U.S. Department of Commerce, Economics and Statistics Administration, U.S. Census Bureau, May 2001.

Annual Survey of Manufactures. Washington, DC: U.S. Department of Commerce, Economics and Statistics Administration, U.S. Census Bureau, February 2002.

"Plastics and Rubber." *U.S. Industry and Trade Outlook.* New York: McGraw-Hill and U.S. Department of Commerce, 1998.

"Recycling Facts from the American Plastics Council." *Plastics Resource.* American Plastics Council, 2002. Available at http://www.plasticsresource.com.

"Recycling Rate Study." *Plastics Resource.* American Plastics Council, 1998. Available at http://www.plastics.org.

Prepackaged Software

Overview

The booming U.S. software industry took in an estimated $195 billion in sales during 2001, accounting for about half of the world's software production. Led by the powerful Microsoft Corporation, the U.S. industry consists of many of the world's largest software vendors, and sales abroad, including those from foreign-based holdings, represent a major revenue stream for the industry. Compared to the explosive growth the industry experienced in the late 1990s, by 2001 the weakening economy led to declining earnings and employment levels. Leading industry developments in the early 2000s included the continued focus on the Internet as a computing platform, as well as the final outcome of Microsoft's ongoing legal battles. Although it appeared that the software giant would soon clear antitrust hurdles by settling with the federal government, the outcome could affect the way the company does business. Additionally, by 2002 scores of private antitrust lawsuits also had been waged against Microsoft, including one filed by competitor Sun Microsystems.

History of the Industry

The prepackaged software industry has its origins in a 1969 U.S. Justice Department settlement that forced IBM to sell software for its mainframe computers separately from the hardware. IBM had included basic software with the computer and additional programming was generally done in-house. With this decision, individual entrepreneurs were finally able to compete with IBM. Small software companies sprang up, usually to offer a single program or utility. Most mainframe software was licensed rather than sold, however.

For the most part, the rise of the prepackaged software industry was a direct result of the appetite for software for personal computers. PCs got off the ground in the late 1970s as computer enthusiasts bought machines by Apple Computer, Inc., Tandy Corporation, Atari, and Commodore. Software publishers such as Microsoft formed to write programming languages for them, and soon these languages were being sold to the public through retail outlets. By the end of 1979, Microsoft had already sold 1 million copies of its version of the BASIC programming language. Primitive spreadsheets and other applications began to appear as well, all of them created by small, relatively unknown companies. At this stage, prepackaged software was something of a cottage industry, with programs often written by individuals at home in their spare time. Because software program creation requires virtually no equipment, people who wrote software programs risked only their own time, and stood to gain $200,000 to $1 million if the program proved suc-

cessful, as perhaps 1 percent were, as *Forbes* noted in 1983. These small companies were encouraged by hardware manufacturers, particularly Apple, because desirable software helped sell hardware. Visicalc, the first spreadsheet for microcomputers, was introduced in 1979. Its popularity sold many Apple computers and raised the public awareness level of PCs in general. The Apple Fortran programming language was introduced in March 1980 and led to the creation of additional software, particularly in the areas of technical and educational applications.

In 1981 IBM introduced its version of the personal computer and chose Microsoft's DOS as its standard operating system. Other hardware manufacturers, with the notable exception of Apple, began making their hardware compatible with the IBM system, providing standardization for the industry. This development meant that the compatible computers all used MS-DOS and software that ran on one manufacturer's equipment would run on all with minimal modification.

More than 21,000 PC software packages were available by 1983. Packaged software had garnered about $2.7 billion worth of retail sales a year as early as 1981, and the industry grew at a rate of nearly 50 percent a year. Given this record of tremendous growth, the prepackaged software industry and PCs began to attract a great deal of attention from the press and investors, and a number of successful software firms soon went public. Over $180 million in venture capital was raised by about 90 software firms in 1983, and 20 firms went public.

With sales of software for PCs growing far faster than any other segment, companies that had formerly focused exclusively on software for mainframe computers bought PC software firms, and firms that had specialized in PC systems software began to sell applications software as well. As competition rapidly intensified in the still-fragmented market, prices fell wherever similar programs existed, while the cost of marketing new software rose dramatically; it thus became much harder to launch new companies on a shoestring. *Business Week* noted in 1984 that "as prices fall, the opportunity for a newcomer to jump in and grab quick and easy profits will all but disappear." The magazine noted that VisiCorp introduced Visicalc with a $500 budget in 1978, but by 1984 had spent more than $10 million developing its Visi On computing environment.

As corporations invested in personal computers at the expense of mainframe systems, methods for linking computers to share information became increasingly important. Packaged software could only be used when the computers all had the same operating system, however, and businesses often wanted to link computers that used different operating systems. This forced software companies to make heavy use of consultants and, sometimes, to custom-design solutions. Networking forced software firms accustomed to mass production of software to pay increasing attention to service. As market growth for PC software slowed to 15 percent by 1990, down from 40 percent in 1988, network applications, which run on network servers and facilitate sharing of storage space and resources such as network printers, also provided a new and lucrative niche for software publishers.

One of the most frequent complaints about early software concerned the difficulty many users experienced in running the programs. Making software easier to use became an important goal. In 1984 Apple introduced its Macintosh computer, which employed a graphic user interface (GUI), a new type of operating system that used images rather than text-based commands to control the computer and its software. Apple also issued rules for companies writing Macintosh software to ensure that all software intended for use on Apple systems would look and behave similarly and utilize many of the same commands. Macintosh proponents asserted that this made the software easier to use. As PC software became easier to use, vendors of mainframe software were forced to make their software more user friendly as well.

Despite its premium price, the Macintosh sold well, convincing many software companies that the graphic interface would do well in the far-larger IBM market as well. Microsoft, which had become the leading publisher of Macintosh software, convinced many software and hardware companies that IBM had too much power over computer standards. It persuaded them to accept its graphic interface, called Windows, as the graphic standard for IBM PCs. As software firms wrote applications for Windows, some of the standardization of the Macintosh system appeared in the PC environment.

Windows was initially released in late 1985. Early versions were slow and cumbersome and didn't sell well. Microsoft worked to upgrade Windows, but it and IBM also began work on an operating system to replace the aging DOS. Called OS/2, the new operating system was supposed to be a more powerful graphic interface than Windows. Initial reviews and sales of OS/2 were disappointing, and a rift soon grew between Microsoft and IBM, as Microsoft wanted to move ahead with Windows while IBM backed OS/2. Finally the disagreement over operating systems led to an open break between Microsoft and IBM.

In April 1990, Microsoft released Windows 3, which brought DOS-based computers closer to the graphic standards and ease of use of Apple's Macintosh computers. Consumers responded and purchased millions of copies for use both at home and in the office. Microsoft's sales increased by 55 percent in 1990, reaching a total of $1.48 billion. The wide acceptance of Windows continued through the mid-1990s—and did so at the expense of Apple and IBM. After the release of Microsoft's next major overhaul version, Windows 95, in summer 1995, sales of OS/2 continued to plummet and IBM formally announced that it would no longer attempt to compete with Microsoft in the PC operating system market. Apple's Macintosh was relegated largely to niche markets of

FINANCES:

Software Revenues, 1999-2002 (billion dollars)

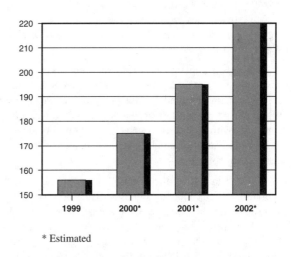

* Estimated

graphic artists, desktop publishers, and schools. By 1997, Microsoft remained the only serious player in this arena.

While low-cost software had always been available for PCs, in the early and mid-1990s there was a pronounced trend toward making the top-of-the-line products more affordable. As prices of PCs fell, the $500 or more price tags for single applications were hard for some potential buyers to swallow. At the same time, competition among software vendors mounted as software market growth slowed. Several of the leading companies, including Microsoft, Lotus, and Novell, introduced suite packages that bundled a number of their most popular products and served as a coherent unit.

In the late 1980s, as workstations and PCs became more comparable in power, an operating system called Unix assumed increasing importance. Unix, originally designed in the 1960s by AT&T for telecommunications use, had gradually become the standard for high-powered scientific and technical computers working on networks. As workstation computers made by Sun Microsystems and Silicon Graphics became popular during the 1980s, Unix slowly entered the mainstream of business and academic computing. Among Unix's strengths was the ability to run several programs simultaneously and process large amounts of data more speedily that systems like Windows could. As a result, some PC software companies began to write programs for Unix, while Sun began to produce PCs that used Unix. Sun also sold a Unix operating system for PCs called Solaris.

Yet Unix remained a fragmented OS because so many companies created competing versions of it. In 1991, AT&T created Unix Systems Laboratories (USL) to manage the Unix operating system, and sold portions of it to various companies, including Novell and hardware companies such as Sun, Motorola, and NEC. In 1992 Novell bought USL from AT&T for $360 million in stock to take control of the Unix operating system. Novell quickly moved to widen the appeal of Unix, trying to standardize its competing versions and link its NetWare networking software.

Microsoft's major entry into the networking business came with its 1993 release of Windows NT, an operating system designed for use on computer networks. While at first it wasn't clear that NT would be a serious contender with programs like NetWare, it quickly gained market share and, eventually, would become the leading networking software.

Driven in part by the fear of Microsoft and its NT operating system, a half-dozen major Unix companies finally agreed in 1993 on a standardization scheme designed to allow Unix applications to look and function the same way on different computers. These companies—IBM, Hewlett-Packard, Sun Microsystems, Santa Cruz Operation, USL, and Univel—signed what was in effect a "peace pact." The alliance released specifications for the Unix interface and other key elements of the operating system, while allowing companies to pursue their own variations. In the months leading up to the release of Microsoft's Windows NT, many of these companies released new versions of Unix.

In the late 1990s the software industry was reacting to the rollout of Microsoft's Windows 98 operating system. While the differences in the new system weren't as dramatic as those unveiled three years earlier when it launched Windows 95, the new package spurred a modest wave of applications upgrades as software vendors sought to optimize their products for the new environment. At that time, Microsoft authored an estimated 80 percent of all U.S. operating systems in use.

Significant Events Affecting the Industry

The mid-1990s popularity of the Internet gave rise to several new categories of software, as well as another Microsoft-related saga. In 1994 the newly formed Netscape Communications Corporation introduced a graphical browser for the then-obscure World Wide Web. Netscape's only competitor at the time was a university-authored program called Mosaic that one of Netscape's engineers helped design. Netscape quickly became popular, in large part through free distribution, and amassed a commanding share in the browser market. Demand for other Internet-related programs likewise swelled, as businesses and private individuals sought tools to access e-mail, news groups, and even to author web pages. Both Microsoft and Netscape soon introduced more integrated

products that enabled users to perform a variety of Internet tasks without needing separate applications.

Stemming partially from its competition with Netscape, whose market share plummeted as Microsoft aggressively pushed the Internet Explorer browser, Microsoft fell under increasing scrutiny of U.S. anti-trust regulators. It wasn't the first time the operating system giant had been accused of uncompetitive behavior, but by the late 1990s the Justice Department appeared adamant that Microsoft change its practices and took the company to court. In June of 2000, U.S. District Judge Thomas Penfield Jackson ruled that Microsoft had violated antitrust laws and should be broken up into two companies. By the following June, that ruling had been reversed by the U.S. Appeals Court. Shortly thereafter, Microsoft appealed to the U.S. Supreme Court regarding the antitrust findings, but the case was returned to the appeals court. The ultimate outcome could change the way Microsoft operates, and therefore the dynamics of the larger software industry.

Beyond Web browsers, the increasing use of the Internet by businesses and consumers has led to other developments within the software industry. One major development is the use of hosted software solutions. In this scenario, programs are hosted by a third party "application service provider" (ASP) and accessed remotely for a fee by end-users as needed, as opposed to being installed locally on a user's hard drive. This arrangement is an attractive alternative for individuals and companies that don't wish to incur the expense and human resources required to purchase, install, maintain, and upgrade the applications they need to use. Although the initial adoption of hosted applications was slower than many industry analysts first expected, they represent a major shift in the way a wide variety of software applications are used and paid for.

Key Competitors

Microsoft Corporation, based in Redmond, Washington, was founded in 1975 by Bill Gates and Paul Allen; Gates has since emerged as one of the most visible businessmen in the United States. Microsoft currently stands as the dominant force in prepackaged software. Its first big contract came in 1981, when IBM chose it to supply the operating system of its first PC. As IBM's PC became accepted as the industry standard, so did Microsoft's operating system. The firm quickly began offering application packages as well, and became a major player in the Macintosh market after its release in 1984. Its Windows graphical interface, which emulated the Macintosh interface, became another standard in the IBM-compatible market. By the early 2000s, Microsoft had launched home and professional editions of Windows XP, the latest version of its popular operating system. It also had ventured into the gaming market with its Xbox video game system. In 2001 the company posted $25.3 billion in revenue and had 47,600 employees.

Despite Microsoft's greater visibility, International Business Machines Corp. (IBM) remains a major U.S. packaged software developer. In 2001, the company's software sales totaled $12.9 billion, and overall revenues amounted to $85.8 billion. In 1995 it purchased the Lotus Development Corporation to bolster its position in client/server and applications software. With the purchase, it not only received the one-time market leading Lotus 1-2-3 spreadsheet, but also Lotus Notes, a leading e-mail/e-business software application. Despite the fact that 2001 was a difficult year for many software companies, IBM was able to devote almost $6 billion to research and development and allot approximately $1 billion for strategic acquisitions.

Based in Palo Alto, California, Sun Microsystems Inc. is a leading manufacturer of network computing systems and Unix-based servers and workstations, with total 2001 revenues of $18.3 billion. Since it was founded in 1982 with four employees, the company has achieved explosive growth. By 2002 Sun had offices in 170 countries and employed approximately 43,700 people. Sun revolutionized Internet software by developing the Java programming language, which was used by more than 2.5 million programmers by the early 2000s. Java was designed to enable compact and platform-independent programs ideal for use with the Internet. It provided a much wider range of functions to developers than most existing Internet-related languages.

Industry Projections

While annual sales growth has slowed considerably from the period when the industry's revenue was doubling or tripling each year, in the early 2000s the industry continued to register sales growth in the 10 to 13 percent range. According to International Data Corporation, the U.S. software market was expected to achieve revenues of $220 billion by 2002. Through 2005, especially strong growth was expected in the area of Internet security software. According to Standard & Poor's, IDC forecast revenues in that sector to mushroom from more than $5 billion in 2000 to more than $14 billion by 2005. Additionally, IDC forecast healthy growth in the worldwide ASP market, with spending approaching the $20 billion mark by 2006.

Global Presence

U.S. software industry sales tower above those of international competitors. Through sales of software produced within its borders, the United States directly controls about 45 percent of the world's $195 billion software market, and U.S. firms with foreign operations bring in each year tens of billions of dollars not included in that figure.

Employment in the Industry

The software industry offers expansive job opportunities and attractive wages to people with key skills.

Employment in the industry nearly tripled between 1988 and 1998, rising from 86,400 workers to an estimated 259,000. By 2001 the number of industry employees exceeded 335,000. In the late 1990s the industry faced a shortage of skilled workers to populate its mushrooming new job vacancies. However, because of the weakening economy, many companies reduced their workforces in the early 2000s. This was expected to change when the economy regained strength and workers with specialized IT backgrounds once again became scarce.

Sources for Further Study

"ASP and Application Management Services Markets to Both Reach the $20 Billion Mark by 2006, IDC Reveals." International Data Corp., 27 March 2002. Available at http://www.idc.com.

"Computers: Software." *Standard & Poor's Industry Surveys,* December 2001.

"Computer Software and Networking." *U.S. Industry and Trade Outlook.* New York: McGraw-Hill and U.S. Department of Commerce, 1998.

Cortese, Amy. "Group Therapy: Why IBM Paid All That Loot for Lotus." *Business Week,* 26 June 1995.

Garber, Lee. "Employment in 1998: Focus on Y2K and the Internet." *Computer,* January 1998.

Gillmor, Dan. "Antitrust Suits Dent Microsoft Cash, Not Its Monopoly." *Chicago Tribune*, 24 March 2001.

Hof, Robert D. "Commentary: Java Can Be a Contender—If Sun Lets It." *Business Week*, 6 April 1998.

Trends Report 2001—Trends Shaping the Digital Economy. Washington, DC: The Software & Information Industry Association, 3 October 2001. Available at http://www.siia.net.

Printing and Publishing

Overview

Leading sectors of the $243 billion U.S. printing and publishing industry include book publishing, newspaper publishing, periodical publishing, and commercial printing. The largest of these by sales volume is commercial printing, which accounts for more than 30 percent of all industry sales. Newspaper publishing is second, contributing about 20 percent. Smaller segments of the industry include typesetting and platemaking services, and publishing of greeting cards, forms, catalogs, and directories. Few companies are active in more than a couple of these segments.

Printing Commercial printing refers to vendors that operate printing presses and related technologies to produce printed materials for outside clients, as opposed to an integrated firm that prints its own publications. The bulk of commercial printing in the United States—about 56 percent by dollar value—is completed using the lithographic process. "Lithography" describes the printing process in which ink is transferred from a plate with a level surface that has been chemically treated to make some areas ink-receptive and others ink-repellent. The term "offset lithography" was coined to describe the process by which an image or text is transferred from a lithographic plate onto a rubber blanket cylinder and then pressed from the cylinder onto paper or other substrates. Lithography produces high-quality printing jobs and is widely used for printing advertisements, books, and magazines. Advertising is the single largest market for lithographic printing, supplying more than one-third of all lithographic printing business. Moreover, among all forms of commercial printing advertising accounts for a full 60 percent of sales.

The second leading printing process is gravure, which is a form of intaglio printing. The word "intaglio" comes from an Italian word meaning "to engrave"; the word "gravure" is taken from the French and has the same meaning. Intaglio printing methods were developed by carving or engraving an image in stone or metal. In contemporary commercial gravure printing, a reversed image is cut into a thick metal plate wrapped around a cylinder. Ink, applied to the plate and wiped off the surface with a blade, remains in the incised image cells so that when paper is placed against the plate it absorbs the ink and produces a crisp copy of the image.

The contemporary gravure printing process has generally been used for very long press runs on projects requiring superior color accuracy and clarity on thin papers. Gravure is preferred in runs over 300,000 copies, like printing weekly or monthly magazines or mass-distributed catalogs. Gravure's primary advantage over other forms of printing is its ability to produce millions of impressions without suffering any image deterioration. Gravure can also print a superior image on light papers better than other printing methods can, since gravure lays down wet ink over dry. Other commercial printing methods lay wet ink over wet ink, which causes the image to degrade more quickly. Gravure's disadvantages include generally higher costs and increased press set-up time. Because it is a fairly specialized process, gravure accounts for about 4 percent of commercial printing sales.

Many other forms of printing exist. Some common processes include screen printing, flexography, letterpress, digital printing, embossing, engraving, debossing, and thermography. In addition, within the industry there's a niche of book printers who print books exclusively, usually using the lithographic process.

Publishing In terms of revenues, publishing is dominated by newspapers, which constituted a $51.5 billion business in the early 2000s. The magazine and book segments are the next largest, accounting for $39.8 billion and $25.2 billion, respectively. The three main publishing segments are usually subject to completely different market conditions, although naturally all tend to correlate to some degree with general economic health. U.S. newspapers in particular have faced difficult market conditions over the past few decades. For most, circulation

figures are down, and some have been forced out of business or into joint operating agreements with competitors. Newspapers are much more directly dependent on advertising dollars than subscription fees, but circulation size is a key determinant for ad prices and the attractiveness of a given newspaper as an advertising vehicle. Periodicals operate under a similar dependence on advertisers, but for the most part they haven't struggled like newspapers. However, although periodicals enjoyed sales growth in the latter part of the 1990s (at four times that experienced by newspapers), advertising revenues declined in 2000. This situation continued to challenge the industry in 2001 as the economy weakened and terrorist attacks against the United States made conditions much worse in the last quarter of the year. As reported in *Mediaweek,* figures from the Publishers Information Bureau revealed that magazine revenues declined almost five percent in 2001. Meanwhile, book publishing, which has proven the most robust of the publishing sectors, involves a completely different set of economics, as third-party advertising isn't present in most books. Book publishers are more affected by factors like school and library funding and consumers' disposable income.

History of the Industry

Printing History The lithographic process was developed by the German inventor Aloys Senefelder, who discovered that by treating limestone with gum arabic, nitric acid, and a mixture of soap and tallow he could make parts of the stone repel printing ink and parts of it repel water. In 1798, he perfected his process for use in printing.

The twentieth century brought innovations to increase press speeds and improve image resolution. Ira W. Rubel and Caspar Hermann, both of New Jersey, developed thin metal plates in 1904. Their success enabled the development of rotary lithography, a procedure in which the plate was mounted on a cylinder. By the late 1980s, advances in offset rotary press technology had produced presses capable of making 30,000 impressions per hour, printing on both sides of the paper, and receiving paper in sheets or from large rolls called "webs."

The gravure printing process developed from copperplate engraving techniques employed during the fifteenth century. Early plates were flat and had to be hand engraved. The development of engraved cylinders to replace flat plates led to rotary gravure, called "rotogravure." Rotary gravure presses operate by squeezing paper between the image cylinder and a second cylinder called an impression cylinder. Rotary technology enabled the development of presses with increased printing speeds. A process by which rotary gravure presses were able to print on both sides of the paper was patented in 1860 by Auguste Godchaux, a publisher located in Paris. A photographic etching technique developed in 1878 by a Czech painter helped simplify platemaking procedures.

Gravure printing was further refined in 1908 when two German textile printers, Ernst Rolffs and Eduard Mertens, developed the "doctor blade." Gravure printing techniques relied on creating height differences between the image and non-image areas of the plate. An image was formed by making small recessed ink cells. The doctor blade assured the removal of excess ink from the surface level and enhanced the quality of reproductions. One of the most popular items reliant on gravure technology was the Sunday newspaper magazine section.

Publishing History   Some of the world's earliest newspapers included the *Acta Diurna* of the Roman empire and the Chinese gazettes of the first century A.D. The first modern newspapers appeared in Europe in the sixteenth century.

A formative event in U.S. history involved the issue of freedom of the press. Editor John Peter Zenger was brought to trial in 1735 on charges of seditious libel for printing articles that were critical of colonial governor Sir William Cosby. In his successful defense of Zenger, Alexander Hamilton invoked the Magna Carta and stressed that opposition to the establishment was a basic civil liberty, thus creating the foundation on which the American press was built.

An overriding objective for American newspapers was to reach as many readers as possible. One early manifestation of this aim could be seen in the *New York Tribune,* founded by Horace Greeley in 1841. Priced at one penny, the paper was written by Greeley and other advocates of social change in a style that was described as simple but not condescending. It boasted a tremendous readership throughout the country, which led to enthusiastic support from its advertisers. The populist instincts that Greeley embodied eventually evolved into "yellow journalism," a term originally referring to the practices of many of the New York daily newspapers during the late nineteenth century. Joseph Pulitzer, editor of the *New York World,* and William Randolph Hearst, editor of the *New York Journal* strove to increase circulation through a variety of aggressive tactics, such as reporting sensational stories, setting headlines in large type, making extensive use of pictures, and issuing Sunday supplements with color comics.

In the early twentieth century, newspapers began to contend with the rise of new media that was capable of quickly bringing more information into American homes. The formation of the Radio Corporation of America (RCA) in 1919 represented the first of these challenges. In 1929, advertising revenues at newspapers were still far ahead of those of radio, but the newer medium was quickly growing. The Depression, which left the newspaper industry with barely more than half of its advertising income, had little effect on radio advertising, which doubled in the years from 1929 to 1933. A second news forum arose in the 1930s—the newsreel, which was shown between features at movie theaters.

The 1950s brought another challenge for print journalism: television captured the leisure time of many Americans. As it quickly became the medium of choice, television siphoned advertising dollars away from newspapers. Network television news became more readily identified with news of major events. The 24-hour Cable News Network (CNN) debuted in 1980, and its phenomenal growth contributed to the sense that newspapers were becoming an outmoded form of transmitting breaking stories. By 1995, the average adult spent approximately 1,580 hours per year watching television—30 hours per week. During the same time period, newspapers across the country were battling circulation losses. As a result, the number of daily newspapers dropped from 1,745 in 1980 to 1,533 in 1995.

Throughout its history, the periodical industry followed a course similar to that of newspapers, only it was not hit as hard by circulation declines. While it did face scarcer advertising dollars once television was mainstream, many periodical publishers were more flexible than newspapers to adapt to changing demographics and reader interests. Thus, waves of new specialty magazines were introduced to more than account for any declining sales on established ones. Newspapers, in contrast, traditionally had a more utilitarian approach as factual publications and were less apt to modify their content or launch spin-offs in the way that magazines could.

On the book publishing side, the U.S. book publishing industry grew rapidly after the Civil War, as the country moved from an agrarian to an industrial society. Rising rates of formal education and technological developments helped spur the market for printed materials. Several publishing houses became prominent in the fight against censorship in the early twentieth century. One celebrated case occurred in the 1930s when Bennett Cerf, one of the founders of Random House, intentionally notified U.S. Customs about the arrival of James Joyce's allegedly obscene novel *Ulysses* from Paris. Cerf wanted Customs to confiscate the book so that he could fight the censorship in court. Publishing houses that supported freedom of speech often attracted the top literary and editorial talent.

Paperback books first appeared in the United States in the 1770s, but they did not gain a wide audience until Simon & Schuster introduced its line of Pocket Books in 1939. These early softcover editions sold for $.25 each and met with great success—more than 25 million copies were shipped overseas during World War II. Public acceptance of paperbacks increased the overall market for books and made it necessary for publishers to adopt high-volume, low-cost production methods.

As the U.S. population grew and became more educated, book publishing boomed. This rapid growth culminated in a period of consolidation in the 1960s. Many publishing houses either acquired one another or joined forces with communications conglomerates that held interests in newspapers, magazines, television, and motion pictures. By the early 1970s, the industry was dominated by about 15 giant companies. The consolidation of power continued into the late 1990s, when a handful of publishers mostly of foreign origin controlled the majority of U.S. book publishing.

Significant Events Affecting the Industry

The advent of user-friendly, powerful computers had an enormous impact on most parts of the industry. In some cases, sophisticated and easy-to-use software and relatively low-cost, high-quality printers have eliminated the need for the services of typesetters, giving rise to what is popularly known as desktop publishing. Computer technologies have also improved the printing process in various ways—including saving steps in the platemaking process—and have dramatically improved the productivity of some publishing functions. By the early 2000s, the use of digital technology within the printing industry continued to increase, changing not only production processes but also the number of workers and the kinds of skills required for employment.

Key Competitors

R.R. Donnelley & Sons is the largest U.S. commercial printer, with $5.3 billion in 2001 sales. It is active in many types of printing, including books, phone directories, and software manuals. Quebecor Inc.'s Quebecor World, a Canadian-headquartered firm, is among the world's largest commercial printers, and it has substantial operations in the United States. In 2001, the parent company's revenues totaled $7.3 billion, most of which (86 percent) came from its printing operations.

In the early 2000s, the leading U.S. newspaper was the *Wall Street Journal,* with circulation of 1.76 million. Other leading papers included *USA Today* (1.69 million), the *New York Times* (1.10 million), the *Los Angeles Times* (1.03 million), and the *Washington Post* (762,009).

Among the top U.S. periodicals were *People Weekly* with total 2001 revenues of $668.9 million, *Sports Illustrated* ($521.1 million), *TV Guide* ($493.9 million), *Time* ($459.4 million), *Businessweek* ($307.3 million), *Better Homes & Gardens* ($303.8 million), and The Reader's Digest Association's flagship title *Reader's Digest* ($301.7 million).

Time Inc., a subsidiary of AOL Time Warner Inc., publishes *People Weekly, Sports Illustrated,* and *Time.* However, through its AOL Time Warner Book Group division, the company also is one of the United States' largest book publishers, along with Viacom's Simon & Schuster Inc.

Industry Projections

Each segment of the industry is likely to experience differing sales performance in the early 2000s. According to the Association of American Publishers Inc., U.S. book sales reached $25.4 billion in 2001, barely in-

creasing over the previous year ($25.3 billion). From 1992 to 2001, sales in this segment were growing at a compound annual rate of 4.6 percent. Improvement within the periodicals segment will depend largely on the overall economy, including corporate advertising revenues and consumer spending. While printing sales were rising in the early 2000s, climbing from $94.7 billion in 1999 to $97.8 billion in 2000, growth in the newspaper segment will likely follow existing downward trends. According to the Newspaper Association of America, the number of daily newspapers and total daily circulation decreased throughout the 1990s and into the early 2000s.

Global Presence

Many of the leading trade book publishers serving the U.S. market are held by British and German firms. Notably Random House, which has the largest domestic and international trade market share, was bought in 1998 by Bertelsmann AG of Germany, a diversified media company. Bertelsmann already owned Bantam Doubleday Dell, another top-five publishing house.

Employment in the Industry

The printing and publishing industry is a noteworthy employer in the United States. In 2000, the industry employed 1.54 million workers, down slightly from 1.56 million in 1997 but still above levels during the early 1990s, when job losses caused employment to fall to 1.51 million. In 2000 the industry's average hourly wage was $17.01.

Sources for Further Study

"Book Sales Total $25 Billion in 2001." Association of American Publishers Inc., 1 March 2002. Available at http://www.publishers.org.

"Editor & Publisher Interactive." New York: The Editor & Publisher Co., 1997. Available at http://mediainfo.elpress.com.

"The FOLIO 30." *Folio: the Magazine for Magazine Management,* 15 September 2001.

Granatstein, Lisa. "Boom or Bust: ABC Fas-Fax Shows Swings on Stands." *Mediaweek,* 18 February 2002.

"Industry Information." Newspaper Association of America, 23 May 2002. Available at http://www.naa.org.

"Magazines in 2001: From Bad to Worse." *Mediaweek,* 14 January 2002.

"Occupational Employment Statistics." Bureau of Labor Statistics, U.S. Department of Labor, 23 May 2002. Available at http://www.bls.gov.

Pogrebin, Robin. "Magazines Multiplying As Their Focuses Narrow." *New York Times,* 2 January 1997.

"Printing, Publishing, and Electronic Media." *U.S. Industry and Trade Outlook.* New York: McGraw-Hill and U.S. Department of Commerce, 1998.

"Top 300 Magazines by Gross Revenues." *Ad Age Dataplace.* Advertising Age, 1998. Available at hht://www.adage.com.

U.S. Department of Commerce, Economics and Statistics Administration, U.S. Census Bureau. *Annual Survey of Manufacturers.* Washington, 2002.

Soaps, Detergents, Cosmetics, and Toiletries

Overview

Makers of cleaning products, cosmetics, and toiletries participated in a combined U.S. market worth more than $55 billion in the early 2000s. By segment, cosmetics and personal toiletries, which include such items as cologne, perfume, shampoo, and shaving preparations, accounted for about 49 percent of industry sales. Soaps and detergents, including bar soap and laundry detergent, was the second-largest segment, contributing around 27 percent of annual revenues. The remaining 24 percent of sales was dispersed among many household and industrial cleaning products. Some of these include household kitchen and bathroom cleaners, dusting and polishing compounds, and surfactants.

Most companies in the industry specialize within one or several lines of toiletries, cosmetics, or cleaning goods, and while some are diversified, few have products in all segments.

History of the Industry

The various specialties within the industry evolved at different rates and in different periods, but many of the industry's most basic products have historical antecedents dating back thousands of years.

Soaps, Detergents, and Surfactants   Different accounts place soap's invention between 2500 B.C. and 300 B.C. The word "soap" may have been derived from Mt. Sapo, near Rome, a place where burnt offerings were made to the gods. People discovered that the fat and ash residue from the offerings had cleaning properties.

By definition, soap is a cleansing product created through the chemical process of combining a fat or natural oil with an alkali (such as wood ashes or lye) under controlled conditions. Soap-producing factories developed in France and Italy, where olive oil was plentiful and used as the main ingredient, throughout the sixteenth, seventeenth, and eighteenth centuries. In the nineteenth century, palm oil began to replace olive oil in formulations. By the turn of the twentieth century, many people still made soap by boiling fats and lye to produce solid cakes.

In the United States, the soapmaking industry marks 1837 as an important year. In that year, William Procter and James Gamble established a candle and soapmaking business. Their company, Procter & Gamble, went on to become one of the foremost soap and detergent makers in the country. Procter and Gamble's famous Ivory soap bar was first introduced in 1882. Lever Brothers, another

major soap and detergent company, offered Lifebuoy and Sunlight soap bars in 1895.

Procter & Gamble introduced Oxydol, a flaked laundry soap, in 1924. Oxydol was followed in 1933 by Dreft, the nation's first synthetic household detergent. Instead of soap, Dreft's formula was based on alcohol sulfates. Alcohol sulfates were the first type of surfactants to make a significant impact in the formulation of cleaning products.

The term "surfactant" comes from shortening the phrase "surface active agent." A surfactant is a type of chemical capable of changing the surface properties of a liquid. As a result of their chemical nature, surfactants help water wet the surface to be cleaned more quickly and thoroughly than use of water alone. When water and mechanical action combine to remove soils from a surface, surfactants also help keep the soil suspended in the liquid so that it does not redeposit on the item being cleaned. Surfactants are basic ingredients in most products intended for use in washing clothes and dishes.

The first synthetic detergents based on sodium dodecylbenzene sulfonate were developed in 1939. They were followed by detergents based on alkylbenzene sulfonate (ABS), which provided better cleaning and more suds than traditional soaps at lower prices. ABS grew in popularity and its use expanded with the introduction of front-loading drum washing machines.

Cosmetics and Toiletries   The use of cosmetics, fragrances, and personal care products can be traced to prehistoric times. The Neanderthals, who lived approximately from 250,000 years to 35,000 years ago, painted their faces with reds, browns, and yellows derived from clay, mud, and arsenic. Bones were used to curl hair. Makeup, tattoos, and adornments conveyed necessary social information. The ancients also used fragrances. Some believed that a flower's aroma contained the presence of a deity, while others burned incense during religious rites. Different fragrances often had symbolic meanings and ceremonial oils were used for anointing.

During the reign of the Pharaohs, Egyptian aristocrats wore cones of solidified perfume that would melt under warm temperatures to mask odors. A mineral called hematite was applied as rouge, and faces were painted with white lead. Black kohl encircled eyes. Egyptians curled their hair with sticks or straightened their hair with iron bands and weights. Aloe vera was known as an anti-irritant.

Greek women also painted their faces white and put red circles on their cheeks. Galen, an ancient Greek physician, invented cold cream. The Romans used oil-based perfumes on their bodies, in their baths and fountains, and applied them to their weapons. In the ninth century, Arabs developed alcohol-based perfumes. Crusaders of the thirteenth century brought fragrances back to Europe from Asia.

The perfumes developed during the sixteenth century were powders or gelatinous pastes. They could be applied to scented fans or carried in jewelry with fragrance compartments. The ability to create new fragrances by blending ingredients was developed during the seventeenth century in France. A person who developed new perfume scents by blending ingredients was called a "nose." Some of the compounding establishments developed in France during the eighteenth and nineteenth centuries were still operating at the close of the twentieth century. America's first cologne water, Caswell-Massey's Number Six, was a blend of 27 ingredients and was said to have been a favorite of George Washington.

Natural perfumes were made from a variety of ingredients containing aroma. These included: essential oils, which were found in flowers, roots, fruits, rinds, or barks depending on the type of plant; resinoids, which were gums or resins that were purified with a solvent; and absolutes, which were aromas extracted with solvents existing in viscous liquid form. Natural perfumes were expensive, primarily because of the labor involved in gathering ingredients. For example, *Smithsonian* magazine reported that a pound of jasmine flowers contained approximately 5,000 blooms, and one pound of the flowers yielded only 1/800th of a pound of jasmine absolute.

Chemical formulations developed during the nineteenth century began to replace expensive natural ingredients and make perfumes more widely available. Early synthetic fragrances included vanilla and violet. In the United States, Francis Despard Dodge developed citronellol and citronellal with various floral scents.

The nineteenth century also brought changes in facial makeup. Ceruse, a cosmetic that had been widely used in Europe since the time of the second century, was replaced by a powder made from zinc oxide. Ceruse, made from white lead, was discovered to be toxic. It was blamed for causing physical problems such as facial tremors, muscle paralysis, and even death.

Antiperspirants and deodorants were developed during the 1890s. Aluminum chloride, the original active ingredient, frequently caused skin irritation and damage to clothes. These difficulties were overcome during the 1940s when aluminum chlorohydrate was developed. Although additives were subsequently produced to improve antiperspirant activity, aluminum chlorohydrate remained the primary ingredient in antiperspirants for the remainder of the twentieth century.

Cosmetics played a role during World War II. Leg makeup was developed in response to shortages of stockings. In Germany, women sacrificed lipstick, but U.S. officials judged it vital and necessary. Following the war, biological ingredients began to receive attention. Human placental products were first used in cosmetics during the 1940s. Cosmetic makers claimed that they stimulated tissue growth and removed wrinkles. The FDA ruled that such claims were medical in nature, and as a result classified these products as drugs and declared them ineffective. Placental products later reappeared in cosmetics but were listed only as a source of protein. Other biological ingredients (derived primarily from cows) included amniotic liquid, collagen (a protein substance), and cerebrosides (fatty substances with carbohydrates produced at the deepest layer of skin).

Fashion trends continued to bring new innovations. Artificial skin tanning aids were developed during the late 1950s. False eyelashes became popular during the 1960s. The 1960s also saw the introduction of "natural" products based on botanical ingredients such as carrot juice and watermelon extract. During the 1970s, the growing environmental movement brought challenges to the cosmetic and fragrance industry. The use of some popular ingredients was banned following the enactment of endangered species protection legislation. Some examples of banned ingredients included musk (from Himalayan deer, Ethiopian civet, and certain types of beaver) and ambergris (taken from sperm whales).

Concerns about contaminated makeup emerged during the late 1980s. An FDA report in 1989 found that over five percent of samples collected from counters in department stores were contaminated with molds, fungi, and pathogenic organisms. Such contamination was supposed to be controlled by preservatives in the cosmetics. Preservatives, however, proved ineffective against the microorganisms responsible for causing product contamination when they lacked stability or when a particular product was kept longer than the shelf life of its preservative system.

Significant Events Affecting the Industry

One of the most recent significant events for the soap and detergent market was the value-pricing trend. The early 1990s saw a move in this market away from premium pricing for name brands as customers became more value conscious. Although exceptions existed, many soaps and detergents were seen as undifferentiated commodity items. In 1992, reduced value pricing was being used by approximately 40 percent of detergent manufacturers. Typically, a value-priced product cost $1 or more less than a premium-priced product. By the early 2000s, leading discount stores like Wal-Mart were selling an increasing amount of their own store-branded soap and detergent products, offering consumers additional opportunities to save money.

A similar trend brought the increased popularity of "value added," multi-purpose products. These included items such as detergent with bleach or fabric softener and three-in-one personal cleansing bars. Moisturizing, deodorant, and anti-bacterial-multi-benefit synthetic detergent (also called syndet) bars and soap/syndet combination bars became popular following the introduction of Lever 2000 in 1990. Analysts expected multi-benefit bars to capture 10 to 20 percent of the soap market by the mid-1990s.

In addition to value, consumers in the early 2000s were pressed for time. As the pace of work and home life became more stressful and hectic, soap and toiletries that emphasized relaxation, but which could still be used quickly, constituted a strong category within the industry. Among these products were aromatherapy products like scented body washes, as well as other liquid and gel soaps. These were replacing bar soaps, which were declining in popularity.

For the perfume, cosmetic, and toiletry segment recent challenges including regulatory changes, product safety concerns, calls for scientific data to document product claims, increasing environmentalism, and pressure from the growing animal rights movement heavily affected the industry. Congress began investigating possible revisions to the traditional "drug" and "cosmetic" definitions established under the Food, Drug and Cosmetic Act. A report titled *Classification and Regulation of Cosmetics and Drugs: A Legal Overview and Alternatives for Legislative Change* included provisions for a third category of "cosmeceuticals" to include products like sunscreens that fell in the gap between traditional drugs and cosmetics. Some industry analysts welcomed legislative changes to clarify product distinctions but doubted whether manufacturers would accept proposals that would require safety and efficacy testing to substantiate label claims.

Key Competitors

The world's largest consumer products company, Procter & Gamble has more than 250 well-known brands, including Pantene, Cover Girl, Max Factor, Camay, Ivory, Olay, Old Spice, Head & Shoulders, Pert Plus, Zest, Cascade, Cheer, Dash, Dawn, Dreft, Safeguard, Mr. Clean, and Tide. These product lines give Procter & Gamble significant shares of the bar soap, shampoo, cosmetic, and laundry detergent markets, although it also markets toiletries and many products outside the scope of this industry, with such staple food brands as Pringles, Folgers, and Puritan Oil. In 2001, Procter & Gamble's Fabric and Home Care unit, which includes dish soaps and laundry detergents, generated almost 30 percent of the company's $39.2 billion in revenues. The company's Beauty Care division, which includes cosmetics, shampoos, and bath soaps, brought in about 18 percent of revenues.

Colgate-Palmolive is another major player in the industry. Its $9.4 billion business as of 2001 is built upon such brands as Ajax, Murphy Oil Soap, Mennen, Speed Stick, and Irish Spring, in addition to the two leading brands that form its name: Colgate is a top toothpaste brand and Palmolive is a major line of dish detergents. The New York-based company is dependent on foreign markets for a striking 70 percent of its sales. About 25 percent of sales come from North America, 26 percent come from Latin America, 20 percent from Europe, and 16 percent from Asia/Africa.

Unilever is the industry's largest company by annual sales, which totaled $46.7 billion in 2001, although more than half of its revenue comes from food products. The company has two headquarters: Unilever PLC is headquartered in London, United Kingdom and Unilever NV is based in Rotterdam, The Netherlands. The conglomerate also has U.S.-based holdings and is an important contender in the U.S. market. Although most of its revenue comes from Europe (39 percent), 27 percent of the firm's earnings come from North America, where it possesses a sizable percent of detergent market, behind Procter & Gamble. In addition to its soap and detergent business, Unilever is also a major producer of edible oils, dairy products, and prepared foods. Among Unilever's brands are Dove, Lever 2000, Lux, Snuggle, ThermaSilk, and Pond's.

Other key participants in the industry include L'Oréal S.A., with $12.2 billion in 2001 sales; Reckitt Benckiser plc, with $4.8 billion; S.C. Johnson & Son, with approximately $4.5 billion; The Clorox Company, with $3.9 billion; The Dial Corporation, with $1.7 billion; Revlon Inc., with $1.3 billion; and Church & Dwight Co. Inc., with $1.1 billion.

Industry Projections

The industry's performance varies widely by product segment, but overall U.S. industry growth was stagnant at the dawn of the twenty–first century. Shipment values within the industry barely increased from 1997 to 2000, from $55.1 billion to $55.8 billion. Within the soaps and detergents segment, values declined from $17.8 billion in 1997 to $15.1 billion in 2000. Meanwhile, the value of cosmetics and personal toiletries shipments increased from $24.2 billion to $27.1 billion during the same time period. Because the U.S. market was saturated, companies were seeking growth through international markets.

Global Presence

Many of the industry's top companies derive a significant share of their revenue from international sales, and a number of the world's largest cleaning product and toiletry firms—including Unilever and L'Oréal—are based outside the United States. These companies have come to face relatively tight, slow-growing markets in saturated markets like that of the United States. To fuel sales growth, they've looked instead to emerging markets in such places as eastern Europe, Asia, and Latin America, where product penetration and national brand names tend to be weaker.

According to *Global Cosmetic Industry*, the Americas claimed the greatest percentage of the $22.8 billion world market for personal hygiene products in 2000 ($7.7 billion), followed by Asia/Pacific ($7.4 billion), and Western Europe ($6.5 billion). The Americas also comprised the greatest share of the $19.7 billion worldwide cosmetics market in 2000 ($7.7 billion), followed by

Western Europe ($6.1 billion), and Asia/Pacific ($5.5 billion). Data from Euromonitor, listed in *Chemical Market Reporter*, ranked the world's leading cosmetic companies in the early 2000s. Leading the list was L'Oréal, with almost 17 percent of the market; Estee Lauder Cos. Inc., with nearly 11 percent of the market; Procter & Gamble Co., with about nine percent of the market; and Revlon, with seven percent.

Employment in the Industry

Overall, the industry employs some 120,000 personnel in the United States, more than half of whom work for toiletry and cosmetic manufacturers. The annual industry payroll exceeds $4.5 billion, and the average annual salary exceeds $36,000 per worker. Modest growth was expected during the first decade of the 2000s, with employment levels expected to grow about six percent between 2000 and 2010.

Sources for Further Study

Annual Survey of Manufactures. Washington, DC: U.S. Department of Commerce, Economics and Statistics Administration, U.S. Census Bureau, 2001.

"Chemicals and Allied Products." *U.S. Industry and Trade Outlook*. New York: McGraw-Hill and U.S. Department of Commerce, 1998.

Gerry, Roberta. "Cleaning Up the Body and Spirit: Soap Market is Bubbling with New Body Washes Gaining Significant Market Share." *Chemical Market Reporter*, 22 January 1996.

Sauer, Pamela. "A Makeover of Global Proportions." *Chemical Market Reporter*, 3 December 2001.

"Occupational Employment Statistics." Bureau of Labor Statistics, U.S. Department of Labor, 23 April 2002. Available at http://www.bls.gov.

"State of the Industry 2001." *Global Cosmetic Industry*, June 2001.

Tobacco

Overview

The $80 billion U.S. tobacco industry is among the most powerful and controversial in the country's history. In the early 2000s, three companies generated all but 15 percent of domestic sales. Among these firms were Philip Morris Companies Inc. and R.J. Reynolds Tobacco Holdings Inc. The former company also operates Miller Brewing Co. and Kraft Foods. The tobacco industry remains a formidable and profitable economic force. However, the health risks associated with tobacco consumption have made it a beleaguered one in many ways. Beginning in the mid-1990s and continuing into the early 2000s, the industry faced a barrage of legal attacks in courts and legislatures as private citizens and government agencies challenged industry practices and sought financial compensation. Such compensation was intended both to pay for tangible damages attributed to tobacco use (mainly healthcare costs) and to penalize the industry for what some regarded as unethical or illegal behavior. Alleged abuses by tobacco companies include marketing tobacco to minors and manipulating cigarette composition to encourage addiction.

Cigarettes account for almost 95 percent of U.S. tobacco sales and an estimated 90 percent of world sales. Chewing tobacco is the second most popular end use, but accounts for just 5 percent of annual U.S. sales. And cigars, although they enjoyed renewed popularity in the 1990s, lure only about 1 percent of industry sales. Processed tobacco (an intermediate form of tobacco that is generally unavailable on the open market) rounds out the remaining 9 percent of the nation's tobacco production.

History of the Industry

The origins of tobacco in the United States date back to before the formation of the nation itself, but the use of tobacco to produce cigarettes in any widespread fashion didn't occur until the dawn of the twentieth century. Other uses for tobacco precluded the popularity of cigarettes, as Americans in the early nineteenth century enjoyed plug and twist tobacco, then smoking tobacco, and finally cigars, all of which overshadowed cigarette production in terms of volume for most of the century. Even in the mid-nineteenth century, the use of tobacco had its detractors, and cigarette smokers, many of whom were women, suffered from a somewhat ignoble image.

Cigarette production reached 500 million in 1880 and eclipsed the 1-billion mark five years later. By the 1880s there were five principal manufacturers of cigarettes: Washington Duke Sons & Co., Allen & Ginter, Kinney Tobacco Co., William S. Kimball & Co., and Goodwin & Co. Together these companies produced 2.18 billion cigarettes annually by the end of the decade, 91.7 percent of the national output of 2.41 billion. These companies, referred to as the "Tobacco Trust," essentially controlled the cigarette market, a trait that would characterize the industry throughout much of its existence.

In 1890 the five leaders merged to form the American Tobacco Co. Over the next 20 years, American Tobacco acquired an interest in roughly 250 companies. This cigarette giant broadened to become a tobacco giant, securing commanding leads in every product branch of the tobacco industry with the exception of cigars.

If the five leading manufacturers in the 1880s justly earned the moniker "Tobacco Trust" when operating as separate companies, then their union certainly deserved the same label. The U.S. Supreme Court came to this realization in May of 1911, when it found the American Tobacco Co. in violation of the Sherman Antitrust Act. The court forced the powerful tobacco company to be divided into 16 independent corporations.

The break-up of American Tobacco didn't affect the cigarette industry as greatly as the cigar industry, primarily because cigarettes still did not represent a major branch of the tobacco industry. The cigarette industry was burgeoning, however, and stood on the brink of catapulting past all other branches of the tobacco industry. The first step toward this end came six years after the restructuring of the industry, when the United States entered World War I and cigarettes were issued to soldiers in the U.S. Army and Navy.

Once the habit of smoking cigarettes had extended to women, thereby doubling the potential customer base of the industry, sales began to mushroom and the cigarette branch of the industry at last overtook all other branches. In this period many of the widely popular brands—Chesterfield, Lucky Strike, Old Gold, Camel, Raleigh, and Marlboro—emerged. Between 1910 and 1930, the production of cigarettes skyrocketed from 8.6 to 125.2 billion. Despite the break-up of American Tobacco, only four manufacturers, commonly referred to as the "Big Four," held any appreciable share of the market. Indeed, these manufacturers—the restructured American Tobacco Co., R.J. Reynolds Tobacco Co., P. Lorillard Co., and Liggett & Meyers Tobacco Co.—held more than 95 percent of the market.

The next two decades of business brought continued success to the industry's four largest manufacturers and witnessed the rise of an additional member to the industry's elite, Philip Morris & Company Ltd., Inc. Philip Morris introduced its soon-to-be-mainstay Marlboro brand in 1925, which reached an annual production total of approximately 500 million cigarettes. But the industry's leading brands during these years, Camel and Lucky Strike, each sold 25 billion cigarettes a year, by far outpacing Philip Morris's production. Nonetheless, Philip Morris was able to climb the industry's ranking list through strong relationships with cigarette jobbers in its distribution network and through savvy management. By the end of the 1940s, after Philip Morris had already unseated Lorillard to occupy the industry's fourth place position, the top five companies generated combined sales of $357.3 million.

In 1964 the U.S. Surgeon General issued a landmark report linking smoking with lung cancer and heart disease. A year later, the U.S. Congress promulgated the Cigarette Advertising and Labeling Act, which stipulated that health warnings be placed on each cigarette package. In 1971 cigarette advertisements on radio and television were banned. Although these announcements and restrictions didn't cause the industry to collapse, the rate of smoking in the United States began to spiral downward.

During the 1980s, discount cigarettes began to enter the market with increasing frequency. This enabled smaller cigarette manufacturers to thrive for a short time, until the industry's preeminent leaders dropped their prices and set about capturing the low-end market. Cigarette taxation doubled in 1983 and continued to rise, particularly during the late 1980s, increasing the popularity of lower-priced cigarettes. Consequently, cigarette man-

FINANCES:

Cigarettes/U.S. Per Capita Consumption, 1997-2000 (units)

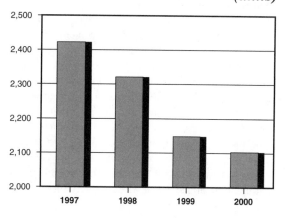

ufacturers diversified their operations with unprecedented fervor, while casting an eye to international business opportunities.

Significant Events Affecting the Industry

A trailblazing California smoking ban, the strictest in the country, went into effect in 1998. It originated in 1995 when smoking in most public places, including restaurants and public buildings, was prohibited as a protection for nonsmokers against second-hand exposure. The legislation was later expanded to include bars and casinos beginning in 1998. While no other state in the late 1990s had yet followed California's example, the legislation was likely to dampen cigarette and cigar sales in one of the country's largest markets.

By far the most important development for the tobacco industry has been its ongoing legal struggles on various fronts. Because tobacco-related illnesses are estimated to cause 400,000 deaths in the United States each year, tobacco foes have attempted to both reduce smoking and recoup medical costs by attacking tobacco companies. These initiatives first gained momentum in 1992 when the U.S. Supreme Court held that tobacco firms could be liable for harm caused by their products. This decision reversed lower court rulings to the contrary. As a result, a flurry of liability litigation was brought against tobacco companies by individuals, organized groups such as flight attendants, insurance companies, and states.

Individual tobacco companies settled some of the class-action and state lawsuits, but the majority of the state-sponsored litigation came to be bundled in a set of negotiations between the tobacco firms and a group of state attorneys general. In 1997 these talks produced a $369-billion settlement agreement between the two sides. The agreement called for federal legislation that would require tobacco companies to pay the states that sum over a period of years and, in return, exempt tobacco companies from certain types of further litigation. The deal also specified marketing restrictions and obligations to inform the public of smoking's risks and to curb underage smoking. Industry critics believed the agreement didn't penalize tobacco companies hard enough. Meanwhile, industry proponents countered that such harsh penalties would bankrupt the industry, cause job losses, and hurt the economy. A sharply divided Congress appeared more sympathetic to the industry, and an important 1998 attempt to legislate terms similar to the agreement failed. The terms of both the original agreement and the defeated legislation suggested that while potentially weakened by anti-smoking movements, the industry would emerge from its political and social battles largely unscathed.

Key Competitors

The U.S. tobacco industry is controlled by a handful of major producers. The two largest, Philip Morris and R.J. Reynolds, have commanded nearly three-quarters of the U.S. cigarette market throughout the 1990s. Meanwhile, U.S. Tobacco Co. held the leading share of the chewing tobacco market.

Philip Morris   Maker of the well-known Marlboro and Virginia Slims brands, among many others, Philip Morris was founded in the United States as a holding of a British company. It became an autonomous U.S. company in 1919. The company grew from being a relatively insignificant player in an industry dominated by a few big companies to become the world's largest tobacco company by the 1980s, propelled in part by the infamous Marlboro Man advertising campaign it began in 1955. Since the 1970s, international expansion also figured prominently in Philip Morris's rise to the top. In the process, the company also acquired a massive non-tobacco empire consisting of such U.S. food and beverage mainstays as Kraft, General Foods, and the Miller Brewing Company. By the late 1990s, Philip Morris brands accounted for half of the U.S. cigarette market and 14 percent of the world market. By market segment, in 1997 Philip Morris held a 58-percent share of the U.S. premium cigarette market and a 26-percent share of the discount market. Shipping more than a trillion cigarettes worldwide each year, Philip Morris earned about $40 billion from its U.S. and international tobacco sales in 1997. That year, the parent company brought in sales of more than $72 billion from all product lines and posted a vigorous 16-percent profit margin (within the tobacco segment its margin was closer to 20 percent). The company's 1997 employee roster numbered at 152,000 worldwide.

R.J. Reynolds   R.J. Reynolds Company, the tobacco arm of the RJR Nabisco Holdings Corp., claims second rank in the U.S. tobacco industry. R.J. Reynolds had long been the world's largest tobacco firm until Philip Morris eclipsed its position in the early 1980s (Philip Morris had already overtaken Reynolds in the U.S. market a few years earlier). R.J. Reynolds has nonetheless remained a formidable competitor with such brands as Camel, Winston, and Salem cigarettes, although negative publicity forced it to withdraw its popular Joe Camel marketing campaign in 1997. At the same time it attempted to revive sales of Winston, its leading brand, with a new campaign entitled "No Bull," an attempt to highlight that the product contained no additives. Like Philip Morris, R.J. Reynolds pursued diversification in the 1980s by purchasing a major food company—in this case, Nabisco Brands, Inc. In the late 1990s R.J. Reynolds held an estimated 25 percent of the U.S. cigarette market, and the company's tobacco line generated 1997 sales of $8.3 billion globally. Its tobacco business employed about 26,400 of the parent company's 80,400 workers. In 1997 RJR Nabisco had revenues of $17 billion, of which about 17 percent was profit.

U.S. Tobacco   Though it's much smaller than the leading cigarette companies, the United States Tobacco Company is the world's largest producer of chewing tobacco, with such leading brands as Copenhagen and Skoal, and also is a top U.S. manufacturer of cigars. First incorporated in 1911, the company is owned by the public holding company UST Inc. Tobacco sales (excluding cigars) made up 84 percent of the firm's $1.4 billion in 1997 sales. A full 32 percent of sales that year were operating profits.

Industry Projections

In the early the 2000s, tobacco makers will continue to find some of their most lucrative opportunities outside the United States. According to estimates from Standard & Poor's, the international market for American-style cigarettes increased steadily throughout the 1990s, at a compound rate of about three percent annually, and accounted for more than one-third of sales internationally by 2000. The industry's continued health at home hinges on the outcomes of its numerous legal battles, which, if not resolved on terms favorable to the industry, could severely curtail domestic profits.

Global Presence

While the United States is one of the world's biggest tobacco markets, other countries also offer strong prospects for the tobacco industry. Tobacco sales are rising faster in many international markets than they are in the United States, and in some cases there are fewer social and regulatory hurdles facing tobacco companies abroad. At Philip Morris, for instance, non-U.S. tobacco sales during 1997 were almost twice as large as the company's revenue from its home turf. Worldwide tobacco sales exceed $275 billion each year.

China is both the world's largest producer and consumer of tobacco products, averaging twice the annual production of the United States, the world's second-largest player. China's tobacco industry functions as a monopoly, a common practice in Asia, under the control of the China National Tobacco Company. Thailand, South Korea, and Japan have historically had national tobacco monopolies as well, although the Japanese government began to privatize its industry in the mid-1990s. Government-run tobacco businesses also exist in certain European countries, notably France, Italy, and Spain, but the trend there is also toward greater privatization. Prominent European tobacco companies include British American Tobacco PLC (United Kingdom) and Reemtsma (Germany).

Employment in the Industry

As in most U.S. manufacturing industries, employment in tobacco production has declined since the 1980s, according to figures compiled by the U.S. Bureau of Labor Statistics. From about 56,000 workers as recently as 1988, industry employment ranks dropped to about 41,000 people by 1998. Production workers (as opposed to management and administrative employees) make up about three-quarters of the tobacco labor force. In 1997 the industry's production employees earned an average of $19.20 per hour, higher than the average for U.S. manufacturing positions in general. On average, the tobacco manufacturing work week in 1997 totaled about 39 hours.

Sources for Further Study

"100% Smoke-Free Ordinances." American Nonsmokers Rights Foundation, 13 March 2002. Available at http://www.no-smoke.org.

"Alcoholic Beverages and Tobacco." *Standard & Poor's Industry Surveys*, December 2001.

"The Anti-Tobacco Troops Smell Blood." *Business Week*, 1 April 1996.

"Decision Against PMI (Philip Morris Companies Inc.) Tops List of 2001 Jury Awards." *Tobacco Retailer*, February 2002.

Flanigan, William G. "Cigar Madness." *Forbes*, 21 April 1997.

Occupational Employment Statistics. Bureau of Labor Statistics, U.S. Department of Labor, 23 March 2002. Available at http://www.bls.gov/oes/2000/oesi2_21.htm.

Reynolds, Patrick, and Tom Shachtman. *The Gilded Leaf: Triumph, Tragedy, and Tobacco.* Boston: Little, Brown and Company, 1989.

"Tobacco." *Hoover's Online*, 13 March 2002. Available at http://www.hoovers.com.

"The Tobacco Deal: Smoke and Mirrors?" *Business Week*, 25 August 1997.

"Trends in Tobacco Use." American Lung Association, Epidemiology and Statistics Unit, February 2001. Available at http://www.lungusa.org.

Toys and Sporting Goods

Overview

In the United States, toys and sporting goods manufacturing was worth an average of $15.0 billion each year in the late 1990s and early 2000s. At the same time, an additional $16.5 billion worth of industry products—mostly toys—was imported from other countries, whereas only $3.0 billion of U.S. production was exported. These figures indicate a net demand for toys and sporting goods in the United States in excess of $28.0 billion.

Sporting goods account for more than 70 percent of industry shipments by value, and the sporting goods sector as a whole has enjoyed faster sales growth than have domestically produced toys. Meanwhile, toys accounted for almost 80 percent of industry imports, which increased at a steady pace in the early 2000s.

History of the Industry

Toys   The first U.S. toy manufacturer was established in the 1830s. Tower Toy Company produced doll furniture, toy tools, and toy boats. In 1860 Milton Bradley Co. established a publishing and lithography business, but as financial problems plagued the company, Bradley diversified by inventing and publishing The Checkered Game of Life, which was the precursor of The Game of Life. The Civil War slowed the toy industry somewhat, although toy guns were popular, as were Milton Bradley's portable editions of chess, checkers, and dominoes.

In 1883, 16-year-old George S. Parker started his own game company. When his brothers joined him, the company became Parker Brothers & Company Inc. It became the publisher of many games that remained popular into the twenty-first century, including the perennial number one-selling board game, Monopoly, as well as Sorry!, Risk, and Clue.

Around the turn of the century, the so-called golden age of toys brought walking and talking dolls, toy pianos, friction motorized vehicles, steam-powered toys, the Erector Set, the Flexible Flyer sled, Lionel toy trains, and Crayola crayons. In 1906 the Teddy bear craze began with the stuffed animals named for Teddy Roosevelt (because he had refused to shoot a trapped bear cub during a hunting trip). Between 1900 and 1910, American toy production doubled. During the next decade, it grew 500 percent, largely because World War I had halted the import of European toys. In 1923 Hasbro Inc. brought out its classic real estate game, Monopoly, and Milton Bradley introduced Easy Money—games that allowed players to imagine being rich by making deals with play dollars. In 1930 Herman G. Fisher and Irving R. Price established the very successful Fisher-Price, Inc., which in the 1990s was the biggest name in infant and preschool toys and merchandise.

World War II slowed the toy industry's growth because of labor and material shortages, but the postwar years brought prosperity to the entire country, and the toy industry reaped the benefits as well. Following World War II, the toy world was revolutionized with the introduction of plastic.

In 1955 an advertising move by Mattel, Inc. changed the way toys and games were marketed and also launched the promotional toy business. The American Broadcasting Company (ABC) television network approached Mattel about weekly national advertising on its new show, Walt Disney Co.'s "The Mickey Mouse Club," which started in November as the Christmas shopping season opened. To the surprise of many, Mattel took a big financial risk and paid half a million dollars to become a sponsor. Before this bold move, most advertising money was spent on catalogs and trade ads during the Christmas season and an occasional local TV ad to promote the most promising items. With this advertising agreement between Mattel and ABC, Mattel's famous slogan was born—"You can tell it's Mattel, it's swell"—and the power of weekly advertising to kids was launched. The product Mattel had advertised, the Burp Gun, sold out, and the promotional toy business had been established.

It was in the late 1950s that Mattel introduced the Barbie Doll, created by company co-founder Ruth Handler who named the doll after her teenage daughter. Barbie sales skyrocketed after the doll was introduced, surpassing the 350,000 mark in the first year alone and contributing significant sums to the company's revenues for decades. The doll evolved with the times and transcended the toy market. According to the *Chicago Tribune*, "Under pressure from feminists, Barbie evolved from fashion model to career woman, including doctor, astronaut, police officer, paramedic, athlete, veterinarian and teacher. Over the years, the toy inspired Barbie clubs, conventions, magazines and Web sites." After the introduction of Barbie, Handler named other dolls in the product line after her relatives including Ken, after her son, as well as grandchildren Cheryl, Todd, and Stacie. In 2002 Handler died at the age of 85, but her doll lives on as one of the most successful toys in history.

Promotional toys were products advertised on television directly to the consumers—the kids. Television became the number one advertising force in the toy industry. With the line between advertising and entertainment blurred in the late 1980s and early 1990s, entire shows became based on the exploits of a line of characters invented or promoted by a toy company. In 1969 Mattel underwrote a program based on its very successful Hot Wheels line. When a competitor complained, the Federal Communications Commission (FCC) banned it, calling it a "program-length commercial." In 1983 the FCC ruled that the marketplace should determine programming. This change of policy cleared the way for toy-based programming. By the 1986-1987 season, more than 40 toy-based programs were on the air.

Sporting Goods Albert G. Spalding, the man often misidentified as the inventor of baseball, was actually one of the pioneers of the sporting goods industry. After pitching his team, the Boston Red Stockings, to victory in three consecutive National Professional Association pennant races in the early 1870s, Spalding helped found the National League in 1876. In 1878 he opened a sporting goods store with his brother in Chicago. The company expanded from 2 to 14 stores within two years and soon afterwards began selling products it manufactured directly to other retail dealers. Spalding is given much of the credit for introducing gloves to baseball; after developing a sore arm from pitching, he switched to first base in 1877 and started wearing highly visible black gloves. (Cynics have suggested, however, that Spalding's interest in wearing gloves was not unrelated to his desire to sell them.)

Spalding also figures prominently in the history of basketball. James Naismith, the inventor of the game, commissioned him to create the world's first basketball in 1892. In 2002 Spalding balls were still the official ball of the National Basketball Association (NBA).

Another important sporting goods company with a colorful history is Wilson. The firm was originally known as the Ashland Manufacturing Company and was a subsidiary of a meat-packing firm. It sold violin strings, surgical sutures, and strings for tennis products, all by-products of animal gut. In 1914 the company was forced into receivership and was taken over by New York bankers. They picked Thomas Wilson to manage the company, partly because of his name—President Woodrow Wilson was then at the height of his popularity, and the owners hoped to capitalize on the association in the consumer's mind. The new firm became Wilson & Company. The firm soon expanded into tennis rackets, hunting and camping equipment, and fishing tackle. With a full line of sporting equipment, it continued to be one of the top manufacturers in the 1990s.

A more modern, but already legendary, figure in the history of sports equipment is Scott Olson. Olson was a 19-year-old goaltender with a minor-league hockey team in 1980 when he found a pair of roller skates on which the wheels were arranged in a single row. While the skates felt slow and clumsy, they gave him the sense of skating on ice that traditional roller skates did not. Olson contacted the manufacturer, who had stopped making the line, and bought up the back stock. He put the blades on good skate boots and began selling them out of his house. In 1983 he quit pro hockey, bought up the existing patents, and started the company that would eventually become Rollerblade. While Olson was forced out of the business in 1985, he continued to design and develop new products, including a lightweight golf bag with wheels and a built-in pull handle.

Significant Events Affecting the Industry

The gradual ascent of video games into daily life created an important new category of toys. In 1972 Nolan

Bushnell and a friend invested $250 each to found Atari Corp. and produce Pong, a simple video table tennis game. It became a coin-operated hit in bars and arcades, and in 1975 Bushnell began marketing a home version to compete with Odyssey, a video game system being produced by Magnavox Co. Atari was sold to Warner Communications Inc. in 1976. Mattel followed with Intellivision in late 1979, and Coleco Industries Inc. brought out ColecoVision in 1983.

Soon, the industry was licensing the most popular arcade games for home video systems. Video games were bringing in hundreds of millions of dollars. Many new companies formed just to manufacture and sell cartridges for Atari and other game systems, thus taking valuable profits from the systems' developers. Large and small toy companies rushed to produce their own video systems. In a few short years, however, the video game and cartridge fad ran out of steam. Warner lost $539 million on its consumer electronics segment in 1983, and it ended up burying truckloads of game cartridges. Warner, Mattel, and Coleco sold their video game businesses during the next two years.

Nintendo Co., Ltd., a Japanese electronics company, learned from the mistakes of its predecessors. In the late 1980s, Nintendo was generating sales of more than $1 billion in the United States alone. It was making this money at the expense of other traditional toys and games, taking market share from industry leaders Hasbro Inc. and Mattel. Nintendo controlled licensing and sales of all game cartridges so that it would not meet the same fate as Atari.

Sega Enterprises Co., Ltd., another Japanese company, challenged Nintendo in the United States during the early 1990s. In 1991 Sega introduced its Genesis system, and Nintendo responded with Super Nintendo. The battle continued throughout the 1990s with Sega launching a major market offensive with its high-performance, CD-based Saturn game system. During this period, a number of other companies entered the fray—most notably a U.S. company, 3DO Co., and the Japanese electronic giant Sony Corp. While Sony's PlayStation managed to establish itself in the market, 3DO's game player eventually fell by the wayside, largely as a result of being priced too high for the average consumer. In 1996 Nintendo struck back with the 64-bit Nintendo 64. Boasting high-resolution 3D graphics, Nintendo 64 delivered processing power exceeding that of many personal computers, and its eagerly awaited introduction led to long waiting lists, high-priced black marketing, and even theft. By the early 2000s, Nintendo was marketing its latest system, the powerful Nintendo GAMECUBE, which incorporated a 485 MHz processor and 40 megabytes of system memory. Sony's latest product, PlayStation 2, operated on a 294.912 MHz processor and 32 megabytes of memory.

Key Competitors

In the latter half of the 1990s, Mattel Inc. reigned as the world's largest toy maker, reaching $4.8 billion in sales in 2001. After Mattel built a strong alliance with Walt Disney Co., Mattel's president called its Disney-related products "the second cornerstone of our company"—its primary "cornerstone" was Barbie and Barbie-related products. Mattel also made an exclusive licensing agreement to produce toys based on Hanna-Barbera characters, such as Flintstones, Scooby Doo, Jetsons, and Yogi Bear, as well as Harry Potter and Barney. Other principal Mattel brands include Fisher-Price, Hot Wheels, and Cabbage Patch Kids. Convinced that children everywhere like the same toys, the company has traditionally made little effort to modify its products for different markets. Instead, it attempts to design products with universal appeal and market them globally; this policy is succeeding since the company sells its toys in more than 150 countries with about half of its revenues coming from outside the United States.

Hasbro Inc., a small company in the early 1980s, became the largest U.S. toy manufacturer in 1985 by eschewing the video market and benefiting from widely popular products such as G.I. Joe, Transformers, and My Little Pony. In 1984, Hasbro bought the Milton Bradley company, the fourth largest company in the toy industry. With Milton Bradley came the rights to The Game of Life, Twister, and other solid-selling games. By 1988 Milton Bradley accounted for 20 percent of Hasbro's sales. Hasbro also acquired Coleco and Tonka just as each was headed for bankruptcy. Tonka had owned Kenner Products and Parker Brothers, so the acquisition of Tonka also brought a second most-famous game company into the Hasbro empire. Hasbro decided to leave the two separate divisions with their own identities. In the 1990s, Hasbro's position as the leading U.S. toymaker was eclipsed by Mattel. Nevertheless, Hasbro finished a strong second with 2001 sales of $2.9 billion.

The sporting goods operations of Amer Group Plc of Finland encompass Wilson Sporting Goods Co., Atomic Austria GmbH, and Suunto Oy. Wilson is a leading producer of golf, racquet, and team sports equipment; the Atomic Group produces skiing equipment and in-line skates (under the Oxygen brand); and Suunto makes sports instruments. In February 1997, Amer completed the sale of its MacGregor Golf division. Amer's Wilson, based in Chicago, was founded in 1914 and is one of the oldest names in American sporting goods. In 2001 Amer's sporting goods operations generated an estimated $885 million. The rest of the company's $974 million in total sales came from cigarettes—Amer is Finland's largest cigarette company.

Spalding Sports Worldwide Inc. is one of the most famous names in sporting equipment. The company makes a complete line of golf and team sports equipment. Founded in the 1870s by Boston Red Stockings pitcher Albert Goodwill Spalding, the company grew from a small sporting goods store to a global manufacturer of sporting goods. The company claims a long list of firsts, including first Major League baseball (1876); first American-made football (1887); first official basketball (1894); and first American-made golf club (1894). In 2000 Spalding posted earnings of $20 million on sales of $409 million.

Industry Projections

Within the toy industry, the overall value of manufacturer shipments was declining in the late 1990s and early 2000s. Shipment values fell from $4.8 billion in 1997 to $3.9 billion in 2000. As the domestic market for toys becomes saturated, companies are looking to international markets for growth opportunities. The Toy Industry Association indicated that an increasing percentage of toy manufacturers' revenues will come from international markets throughout the 2000s.

During the 1990s, the sporting goods industry enjoyed a 4 percent annual growth rate. However, in 2001 the industry was affected by weak economic conditions, as well as the terrorist attacks against the United States that occurred in September. Because of this, industry sales declined for the first time in 10 years, dipping almost three percent. However, conditions were expected to improve in 2002.

Global Presence

International trade has been a major part of the toy industry and a significant influence on the sporting goods segment as well. By value, the United States imports more than twice the amount of toys that it manufactures, with an average of almost $13 billion in goods imported each year in the late 1990s and early 2000s. China is the leading source of U.S. imports—supplying more than half—followed by Japan and Mexico. Important external markets for U.S. toys and sporting goods include Canada, Japan, the United Kingdom, and Mexico. According to the Toy Industry Association, nearly 45 percent of global retail sales took place in North America in the early 2000s.

Employment in the Industry

The toys and sporting goods business is a moderate-sized employer in the United States, with approximately 97,089 employees in 2000. Aggregate employment in the industry rose during the early 1990s. After peaking in 1995 at 117,600, the industry experienced modest declines. Production workers in the industry earned an average of just $10.30 per hour, which is lower than a typical U.S. manufacturing wage.

Sources for Further Study

2001-2002 Toy Industry Fact Book. New York: Toy Industry Association Inc, 2001. Available at http://www.toy-tia.org.

Annual Survey of Manufactures. Washington, DC: U.S. Department of Commerce, Economics and Statistics Administration, U.S. Census Bureau. February 2002.

Levy, Richard, and Ronald O. Weingartner. *Inside Santa's Workshop.* New York: Henry Holt and Company, 1990.

"Recreational Equipment." *U.S. Industry and Trade Outlook.* New York: McGraw-Hill and U.S. Department of Commerce, 1998.

Riddle, John. "State of the Industry Report." Sporting Goods Manufacturers Association, August 1998. Available at http://www.sportlink.com.

Stern, Sydney Ladensohn, and Ted Schoenhaus. *Toyland, The High-Stakes Game of the Toy Industry.* Chicago: Contemporary Books, 1990.

"U.S. Sporting Goods Market Outlook for 2002." Sporting Goods Manufacturers Association, 11 April 2002. Available at http://www.sgma.com.

Woo, Elaine. "Marketing Genius Created Cultural Icon in Barbie." *Chicago Tribune,* 28 April 2002.

U.S. Postal Service

Overview

The U.S. Postal Service (USPS) is the world's largest mail delivery service. Run as a self-funded independent agency of the U.S. government, the USPS processes approximately 680 million pieces of mail each day for a total of 207 billion annually. In fact, it handles an estimated 50 percent of the world's mail. With annual revenues of $65.8 billion in 2001, the USPS would rank as the country's twelfth-largest corporation by revenues, and its nearly 797,800 employees make it one of the largest civilian employers in the United States, behind Wal-Mart.

Although tight fiscal management in the 1990s helped to make the organization increasingly profitable after years of indebtedness, by the early 2000s, the organization was losing money and was saddled with more than $11 billion in debt. In 2001 the U.S. Postal Service's net loss was $1.7 billion. At that time, it faced a number of challenges including a weakening economy and rising operational costs. Some of these costs were associated with mail-related terrorist acts, such as the Anthrax scares that plagued the nation in 2001 and pipe bombs placed in rural midwestern mailboxes in mid-2002. The USPS also was trying to do more with less. For example, the agency was adding about 1.7 million additional addresses to its delivery base each year while reducing its workforce by approximately 30,000 employees.

History of the Industry

The U.S. Postal Service has a long and rich history that began in the early days of the colonial period. This historical period gave birth to the first American post office. Following repeated failures to develop a postal system in colonial North America in the seventeenth century, the British government delegated this critical responsibility to Thomas Neal in 1692. Neal's mail service was a dismal failure, and by 1707, the British government acquired the rights to the mail system. Although this new system was more successful than Neal's and broke even in the 1720s, it did not produce a profit until 1761. This newfound profitability was partly due to the management skills of Benjamin Franklin, who became co-deputy postmaster general in 1753, and partly due to a reciprocal agreement between the colonies and England.

Ironically, the successful postal service improved England's control over the American colonies at a time when the relationship between the two was deteriorating. The high postal rates were considered a prime example of "taxation without representation," and some Americans started to send mail via "alternative" mail distribution sources, such as postmen not associated with the British mail system who delivered mail for far less than what the colonial post office charged.

In 1774 Maryland newspaper publisher William Goddard initiated an independent postal system called the "Constitutional Post," which eliminated the need for alternative postmen. The system became more formal in 1775 when the Second Continental Congress made Benjamin Franklin the first postmaster general. In 1782, the Confederate Congress wrote an innovative, first-ever postal law allowing the Post Office a monopoly in the carrying and delivering of mail, establishing the office of postmaster general (PMG), setting postal rates, and carefully detailing the operating regulations of the postal service.

The U.S. Constitution's ratification in 1789 gave Congress the right to establish a post office, which it did that year on a temporary basis, but no comprehensive legislation had been passed to establish a permanent postal service within the new government's structure. Such a measure came in 1792, when Congress enacted a law to establish a new U.S. Post Office. Still, this new law was more an addendum to an earlier ordinance from 1782 under the Articles of Confederation than radical new legislation. The primary contribution was the establishment of the principles of the nation's postal policy, which stipulated that the Post Office was to be self-supporting (using any profits to expand the postal service), and that Congress (not the PMG) was to approve post offices and post roads. Therefore, Congress would completely control the post office and its growth, although the president would nominate the PMG. Moreover, the PMG was given the responsibility of managing the postal service, which included providing an annual budget to Congress that estimated the needs of the department.

In response to complaints by both rural and urban customers concerning high postal rates in 1851, Congress reduced the rates and stated that this would in no way reduce the postal service, even if postal deficits resulted from this action. Therefore, a customer service policy as opposed to a "self-supporting" policy drove the Post Office. This new policy eliminated distance as a factor in determining the price of a letter and led to greater use of

the mail service through the modernization of the postal system, although it also produced annual postal deficits.

The Post Office continued to expand its service and influence throughout the nineteenth century. In 1829, under Andrew Jackson the postmaster general became a member of the president's cabinet, although organizationally it didn't become part of the executive branch for another 50 years. Other developments included initiation of mandatory prepayment of postage and the use of stamps in the 1850s; institution of a registered letter service in 1855 and a city free delivery system in 1863; development of the first railroad post office in 1864, which revolutionized postal service by allowing employees to sort mail as they traveled on trains; introduction of mail delivery to farm homes in 1896 and parcel service to rural areas in 1913; use of automobiles to deliver the mail, replacing horses, in the early 1900s; and initiation of the first regular airmail service between Washington and New York in 1918.

The Postal Reorganization Act of 1970, which created the current structure of the U.S. Postal Service, was the most detailed and radical reorganization in two centuries. The postal department was removed from the president's cabinet and Congress was no longer able to set both postal employee wages and postal rates. The "new" Postal Service was able to run more like a business enterprise. For example, it could hire its own personnel. Other changes resulting from the act included: establishment of a board of governors to oversee operations and select the postmaster general, who would also be considered the organization's chief executive officer; creation of the independent Postal Rate Commission to provide advice to the board of governors on postal rates and classifications; establishment of provisions for an independent personnel system and direct collective bargaining between postal management and unions; authorization of a general "public service" subsidy in an amount equal to 10 percent ($920 million) of the fiscal 1971 appropriations to the Post Office Department through the year 1979, declining by 1 percent per year through 1984, by which time the Postal Service was expected to be self sufficient; provision of a plan for gradually phasing out the preferential rates for various categories of mail, an attempt to ensure no class of service was subsidized by another; and authorization to modernize the postal system through borrowing money and issuing public bonds up to $10 billion.

Significant Events Affecting the Industry

Despite these efforts to make the Postal Service a more efficient organization, in the early 1990s its expenses continued to surpass revenues in some years and the organization was roundly criticized for being inefficient. Ironically, the USPS consistently operated on postal rates that were substantially lower than those in other major countries. While this comparison served as a rallying point for calls within the USPS to raise stamp prices, these attempts met with considerable opposition from the U.S. public. Against such opposition, rates for first-class stamps were boosted three times between 1990 and 1999, in contrast to four rate hikes during the 1980s. The net rate increase during the 1980s was ten cents or about 67 percent, while in the 1990s, including the increase of one cent in 1999, it was eight cents or 32 percent. Overall, U.S. postal rate hikes in the 1990s lagged behind the general rate of inflation, making the relative cost of mailing cheaper over the course of the decade. In January of 2001, the USPS raised its overall rates almost five percent. First-class stamps increased by a penny to a cost of 34 cents. An overall rate increase of almost eight percent followed in June 2002. At that time, the price of a first-class stamp climbed to 37 cents.

In the early 1990s, debt and declining business mail volume along with persistent public dissatisfaction forced the USPS to restructure and focus more on customer service. It hired independent companies to track its customer service and in 1992 brought in an aggressive new postmaster general, Marvin T. Runyon. Runyon was credited for turning the USPS around and making it a profitable enterprise. Borrowing principles common to private sector business, Runyon trimmed the ranks of management within the USPS to arrive at a more efficient decision-making structure. He also reduced the overall non-production workforce by 30,000 through early retirement packages and other incentives rather than resorting to lay-offs. From running budget deficits as high as $2 billion in the early 1990s, changes under Runyon helped turn the organization around so that by the mid-1990s, aided by a key rate increase, the USPS was able to post profits in excess of $1 billion.

In 1998, Runyon ended his successful six-year tenure as postmaster general. His successor was William J. Henderson, a career postal official who had most recently served as Runyon's chief operating officer. By the early 2000s, John E. Potter was serving as the agency's postmaster general and CEO. Although the USPS continued to trim its expenses and reduce the size of its workforce, the negative effects of a weak economy, concerns about terrorism and safety, and declining mail volumes resulted in large financial losses. However, despite these difficulties, the agency continued to deliver to a growing number of addresses and achieve high customer satisfaction levels.

Following the terrorist attacks against the United States on September 11, 2001, the USPS was forced to respond to the circulation of mail tainted with deadly anthrax bacteria, which resulted in a number of deaths across the country. One security measure implemented by the agency was the use of electron-beam irradiation in certain locations to sanitize mail. This was in addition to other measures such as purchasing almost 5 million facemasks and 90 million pairs of rubber gloves to safeguard postal workers. The large supply of gloves was sufficient to supply each employee with as many as five pairs per day. In addition, 145 million postcards were sent to U.S. residents explaining what to do if they re-

ceived suspicious items in the mail. Following the anthrax scare, the USPS was challenged again when Luke Helder, a 21-year-old college student from Wisconsin, planted 18 pipe bombs in the mail boxes of rural Americans in five states including Colorado, Illinois, Iowa, Nebraska, and Texas. Although no one was killed, the bombs caused injuries to several residents and postal workers. Over the course of five days, the agency devoted 150 postal inspectors to the case before it was finally resolved.

Key Competitors

The U.S. Postal Service faces competition not only from specific services such as United Parcel Service and Federal Express but also from advances in technology that make conventional letter mailing inconvenient or unnecessary. The growing use of faxes and private overnight delivery services in the early 1990s contributed to a loss of business mail volume. While demand gradually rebounded, beginning in the mid-1990s the Postal Service faced renewed competition from e-mail, which is much quicker and sometimes more versatile than conventional mail, and often may be sent with no added cost other than the price of Internet service access. Responding to this threat, the USPS developed a number of e-services for specialized needs. The agency's NetPost service provided customers with a new way to send either first class or standard (A) mail. Essentially, customers created a document to mail on their computer using one of several leading word processing or design software applications, including Microsoft Word. Next, they sent the document electronically to the USPS with their mailing list. Working with one of several approved print-and-mail services, the USPS then facilitated the rest of the process for the customer. Other services included USPS eBillPay, which allowed customers to pay their bills online, and USPS Send Money, which enabled people to send funds to other individuals, including those participating in online auctions.

Industry Projections

Postal volume in the United States expanded at uneven rates during the 1990s, including declines early in the decade and healthy growth late in the decade. From an average volume increase of 1.5 percent in 1995 and 1996, postal volume surged by 4.1 percent in 1997. After growing 2.4 percent in 1999 and 3.1 percent in 2000, volume fell 0.2 percent in 2001 and was expected to fall in 2001 by about 6 billion pieces, resulting in a projected net loss of $1.5 billion.

In April 2002 Postmaster General Jack Potter introduced the USPS Transformation Plan. A blueprint for the agency's future, the plan was developed to ensure its survival in a changing world. It "outlines strategies USPS can follow under current law, examines moderate legislative reform in key areas such as pricing flexibility, and presents long-term options to maintain universal service." Additionally, the plan proposes different possible business models under which the agency could operate including a government agency model, a private corporate model, and a commercial government enterprise model.

Global Presence

The U.S. Postal Service is the world's largest postal organization. However, about 97 percent of revenues come from domestic operations. The United States also continues to operate one of the lowest-cost postal services among major industrial countries. Compared to the United States' $.37 for regular first-class stamps in 2002, consumers in Japan paid $.65 and those in Italy paid $.55.

Employment in the Industry

The U.S. Postal Service maintains the second-largest civilian workforce in the United States. With approximately 776,000 career workers and another 115,100 part time and contingency workers, the Postal Service's payroll continued to grow during the latter part of the 1990s as it hired more workers to keep up with growing mail volumes. However, the agency was scaling back its workforce in the early 2000s, at which time operating expenses included $51.4 billion for compensation and benefits. For more than a decade, the USPS was plagued by periodic episodes of violence, often involving fatal shootings, at its facilities by current and former employees. These high-profile incidents caused management to take steps to avert such catastrophes in the future.

Sources for Further Study

Bates, Steve. "Postal Service Tackles Competition." *Nation's Business*, April 1997.

Kurlantzick, Joshua. "Life in the Slow Lane: Money and Market Share Are Two Things the USPS is Losing Its Grip On. Ready to Step In?" *Entrepreneur*, March 2002.

McAllister, Bill. "In Computer Age, Postal Service Needs More Checks in the Mail." *Washington Post*, 30 June 1997.

"Postal Service Projects $1.5 Billion Year-End Deficit; Tackles Transformation Challenges At May 28 Ratemaking Summit." United States Postal Service, 7 May 2002. Available at http://www.usps.gov.

"PMG Unveils USPS Transformation Plan Today at the National Press Club." United States Postal Service, 5 April 2002. Available at http://www.usps.gov.

Pugh, Tony. "U.S. Postal Service Struggles to Overcome History of Waste, Fraud, Mismanagement." Knight-Ridder/Tribune News Service, 20 December 2001.

"Security of the Mail." United States Postal Service, 29 October 2001. Available at http://www.usps.gov.

United States Postal Service Annual Report. Washington, DC: United States Postal Service, 1997. Available at http://www.usps .gov.

United States Postal Service Annual Report. Washington, DC: United States Postal Service, 2001. Available at http://www .usps.gov.

United States Postal Service. *History of the United States Postal Service*. Washington, DC: United States Postal Service, 1993. Available at http://www.usps.gov.

Video Tape Rental

Overview

As the price of videocassette recorders (VCRs) plummeted and the cost of cinema admission rose, the demand for video rental increased in late 1980s and continued rising into the early 2000s. By 2001, rental revenues slightly eclipsed box office earnings. In 2002 movie admission for new releases started at about $7 for general admission, whereas video rental fees averaged only $3 at major video rental outlets and even less at in-store video departments at leading supermarkets and discount stores.

When the industry began, video rental outlets, including video-only stores and chain grocery stores' video rental departments, could reap modest profits simply by stocking the leading new releases and some all-time favorites. In the late 1990s, however, the market grew much more competitive with a glut of shops and slower industry growth. Consequently, those companies that could not change with the times wound up exiting the video rental scene. The most significant companies to quit the business included retail and grocery chains that did not want to invest additional effort and money into expanding and promoting their video rental services. Besides the increasing internal competition, the industry also faced external competition from cable movie channels, which began to offer an abundance of newly released movies to cut into the video rental market. Furthermore, new satellite services providing direct-to-home, on-demand movies also made an effort to convert video rental customers to a more convenient, although more expensive, way of watching movies at home.

Nonetheless, the industry remained highly profitable. According to the Video Software Dealers Association (VSDA), the industry witnessed modest revenue increases in 2001 with sales of about $8.4 billion. Approximately 83 percent of sales were from VHS rentals, while the remaining were attributed to digital video disc (DVD) rentals. The latter category achieved explosive growth in 2001, climbing 164 percent over the previous year's levels. This was largely due to the rapidly falling price of DVD players. With growing DVD adoption rates, most leading rental chains were increasing inventories of DVDs in the early 2000s. At that time, more supermarket chains were finding it difficult to compete with leading chains like Blockbuster, on-demand movies from cable and satellite providers, and a retail operations environment that was increasingly more complex. While this caused a growing number of supermarkets to close their video rental operations, some continued to add rental service.

History of the Industry

The videocassette recorder (VCR) appeared in 1975, planting the seeds of the video rental industry. New entertainment services also emerged around this time, including cable television, which complemented the VCR by allowing users to tape television movies and shows. Shortly after the introduction of the VCR, movie studios released videocassettes of classic movies to add to their revenues. The advent of the VCR/video cassette combination presented consumers with more entertainment options. No longer did they have to rely on the schedules of movie theaters or premium cable channels to see movies. Instead, they could see them any time they wanted by purchasing movies on videocassette or sell-through videos. However, sell-through videos (those purchased outright, not rented) carry a financial burden in that few consumers can afford to pay $10 to $25 every time they want to see a movie.

Video rental shops emerged to serve the market of people who wanted the convenience of home video without the expense of sell-through videocassettes. Video rental caught on quickly because, after an initial $150 to $500 investment for a VCR, people could rent a cassette for a lower price than they could go to the theater. Video rental especially filled the family entertainment niche where families paid $20 to $30 for a movie in contrast to a $3 expenditure to rent a video. By 1985, the industry posted revenues of $3.5 billion, and by 1990 revenues were $9.8 billion, according to the VSDA.

Significant Events Affecting the Industry

With the emergence of competitive alternatives to video rentals and sales, video rental stores have been seeking ways of maintaining and increasing their customer base. Supermarkets have tried to offer "grub and movie" specials to keeping their video departments thriving, according to Dan Alaimo in *Supermarket News*. Stores have provided promotions giving customers movie rental discounts with the purchase of deli items and prepared entrees. By 2001, national franchises like Figaro's Italian Pizza Inc. were operating within video stores in an effort to capitalize on the pizza-movie connection. Video stores also rely on different promotional strategies. For example, in late 2000 Blockbuster began selling DIRECTV equipment in some of its U.S. stores. The following year, Blockbuster went a step further when it partnered with DIRECTV to co-brand the satellite provider's movie service, thereby entering the pay-per-view market. The retailer also relied on partnerships with companies like Coca-Cola, as well as various sweepstakes and promotions. In 2002 Blockbuster planned to test a new subscription service that allowed customers to have up to three titles out at any given time without incurring a late fee.

In order to track industry performance and consumer habits, the VSDA introduced VidTrac in January 1996. The point-of-sale service collects data from a large sample of video rental operations throughout the country. More than 12,000 stores participate in VidTrac with many of the most successful rental chains among them. With VidTrac, VSDA is able to offer rich and accurate statistics and projections for the video rental community.

Other modes of entertainment also continued to compete with the video rental industry. Alternative forms of in-home entertainment such as digital television, pay-per-view, and direct-broadcast satellite remained a challenging force for video stores in the early 2000s. Although these alternatives provide some advantages over video rental—namely, higher resolution for digital television and some greater conveniences such as not having to return videos for pay-per-view and direct broadcast movies—they also cost more. By the early 2000s, video-on-demand services allowed subscribers to rent movies in digital formats for 24-hour periods and take advantage of the ability to pause, fast-forward and rewind in a manner similar to VCRs. Selections of on-demand movies included new releases, as well as a limited but growing selection of older titles.

Video rental stores embraced a new laser disc format for recording and playback in the early 2000s: the Digital Video Disc (DVD). DVDs can store between 4.5 and 17 gigabytes of data, which translates to between 135 and 540 minutes of playing time. Besides offering more disk space and better audio and video qualities, DVDs also have interactive capabilities, allowing users to witness multiple angle shots of a single scene, to read sets of multiple subtitles, and to move to favorite parts of movies by the press of a button. Additionally, unlike videotape releases, selections often include various special features such as the ability to view movies in full- or wide-screen, as well as bonus material including theatrical trailers, documentaries, and movie versions with actor/director commentary. According to the DVD Entertainment Group, based on industry data from the Consumer Electronics Association and other sources, consumer sales of DVDs reached 16.7 million units in 2001. This total was almost double the sales rate achieved in 2000. Boding well for video and DVD rental stores, the association revealed that approximately 25 percent of U.S. homes had a DVD player. Although they were still expensive, DVD players with the ability to record also were being marketed by the early 2000s, making DVD players more appealing to consumers.

Key Competitors

Blockbuster Inc. led the video rental industry in the early 2000s. Headquartered in Dallas, Texas, Blockbuster, in 2002, had nearly 8,000 stores dispersed throughout the Americas, Asia, Europe, and Australia, making it the world industry leader. More than 50 percent of the company's locations were in the United States. As of 2002, Viacom Inc. owned most of Blockbuster, which lost $240 million on 2001 revenues of $5.2 billion. Blockbuster has faced problems of slumping growth and inconsistent leadership, though the company's performance improved in the late 1990s. With growing sales and an estimated 40-percent stake of the DVD rental market in 2002, the company was in a strong position to benefit from the increasingly popular rental format.

Based in Wilsonville, Oregon, Hollywood Entertainment Corp. grew quickly in the mid-1990s to become the second largest national video rental chain. With a series of acquisitions and expansions, Hollywood has marched across the country to secure its hold on the number two video chain position. In 2001 Hollywood Entertainment operated 1,800 Hollywood Video superstores— a dramatic increase over its 25 stores in 1994. Hollywood has successfully competed with small video stores as well as with in-store departments for selection. Part of the company's strategy includes providing an upbeat atmosphere complete with neon lights and many television monitors playing movies. Hollywood Entertainment experienced financial difficulties in the late 1990s, partially because of an unsuccessful e-commerce operation called Reel.com. However, by 2002 the company had improved its financial situation and was preparing to expand by opening up some 250 stores by 2003. Headed by founder Mark J. Wattles, Hollywood Entertainment posted sales of $1.4 billion in 2001, up 6.4 percent from 2000.

Movie Gallery Inc. (and its subsidiary Video Update Inc.) rounds out the number-three slot, behind Hollywood and Blockbuster. In 2001, Movie Gallery operated approximately 1,400 stores, some of which were franchised, in the United States and Canada. Focusing on small suburban towns, Movie Gallery brought in $369 million in 2001, an increase of almost 16 percent over 2000 levels. The company's earnings, which amounted to $14 million, mushroomed almost 51 percent during the same time period.

Industry Projections

The Video Software Dealers Association reports that about 27,000 video rental outlets operated in 1996, down from 31,000 in 1990, which the VSDA attributes to consolidation and the rise of the video megashops. By the early 2000s, consolidation continued to occur within the industry, and many smaller independent video rental operations had been acquired by larger chains or had closed their doors due to stiff competition. By 2002 the top three video chains alone accounted for approximately 7,250 stores in the United States. According to Alexander & Associates, consumer spending on home video rental increased steadily in the early 2000s, reaching $12.4 billion in 2000 and $12.9 billion in 2001, after hovering around $11.0 billion for most of the 1990s. While these annual figures are somewhat higher than those of the VSDA, they illustrate the growing value of the rental market.

U.S. video rental operations have achieved great success because of high VCR penetration levels (approximately 94 percent of all U.S. households have a VCR). In addition, with the explosion in DVD player sales that was taking place in the early 2000s, rental firms were in a strong position to profit from this segment into the early years of the decade. In 2001 Blockbuster announced that it would scale back its VHS inventory by approximately 25 percent to make room for more DVDs, which were expected to account for a growing percentage of all titles into the early 2000s. By 2006 there is a strong possibility that DVDs will account for the lion's share of all movie rentals. Video-on-demand services were expected to take some market share away from rental chains in the short-term. However, because of technological limitations like the need for significantly higher broadband connections, these services were not expected to have a major impact on industry sales for some time.

Global Presence

The United States leads the world in video rentals and sales. With the majority of the movies domestically produced and with approximately 94 percent VCR penetration, the home video industry thrives in the United States. However, Australia, Canada, and Japan also have strong VCR bases, which makes their home video markets strong and key target areas of U.S. video store chains and U.S. video cassette distributors.

U.S. movie studios did well abroad in the mid-1990s in terms of video rentals and sell-throughs. In 1996, they posted revenues of more than $3.4 billion from video rental and sales, according to Don Groves in *Variety*. International customers showed heightened interest in video rentals and purchases after ebbing in 1995. In addition, VCR penetration has increased throughout the world and video piracy has decreased. Peter Dean reported in *Billboard,* for example, that VCR penetration hit 64 percent in the European Union, while video piracy dropped by as much as 28 percent in the United Kingdom.

Employment in the Industry

The number of employees in the industry rose from 54,000 in 1983 to 167,800 in 2000. By 2010 the Bureau of Labor Statistics predicts the industry's workforce will reach 172,800. Typically, positions at video stores pay minimum wage for general full-time and part-time employees. Managerial positions, on the other hand, can pay a few dollars an hour over minimum wage.

Sources for Further Study

Alaimo, Dan. "Keeping Pace in the Race: The Competition in Home Video Is Tough, But Supermarkets Are Still Doing Well." *Supermarket News*, 13 April 1998.

———. "Harris Teeter Looks to Heat Up Video with HMR Tie-in." *Supermarket News*, 9 June 1997.

———. "Kroger Lifting Curtain on more Video Rental 'Stores'." *Supermarket News*, 20 November 1995.

———. "Rental Bloom: Seeding the Department with New Releases" *Supermarket News*, 14 April 1997.

———. "Rental Properties: Supplies Say Chains in Video Rental for the Long Haul Need to Apply More Sophisticated Approaches to Inventory." *Supermarket News*, 20 January 1997.

Chezzi, Derek. "The Death of the VCR: From DVDs to Video On Demand, New Digital Offerings are Squeezing Out Tape." *Maclean's*, 15 April 2002.

Dean, Peter. "The U.K. and Europe." *Billboard*, 11 January 1997.

Desjardins, Doug. "Video Chains Experience Fast-Forward Growth." *DSN Retailing Today*, 17 September 2001.

Digital America 2001, the U.S. Consumer Electronics Industry Today. Arlington, VA: Consumer Electronics Association, 2001. Available at http://www.ce.org.

"DVDs Fueled 2001 Video Rental Growth." *United Press International*, 7 January 2002.

"Fourth Quarter 2001 Banner Finish for Home Video Industry." Alexander & Associates, 7 January 2002. Available at http://www.alexassoc.com.

Geistman, Bob. "Time to Take Stock of New Technologies." *Supermarket News,* 22 April 1996.

Groves, Don. "O'seas Video Takeout Makes Comeback Bid." *Variety*, 3 March 1997.

Hamstra, Mark. "Hanging By a Thread; More and More Supermarkets Seem to be Abandoning Video Rental, But Some See Encouraging Signs Ahead for the Category." *Supermarket News*, 7 January 2002.

———. "More Supermarkets Eliminate Video Rental." *Supermarket News*, 12 November 2001.

Lenius, Pat Natschke. *Supermarket News*, 3 February 1997.

McClellan, Stephen. "Viacom Hit by Lackluster Blockbuster." *Broadcasting and Cable*, 28 April 1997.

McMurray, Scott. "Time to Hit the Fast-forward Button." *U.S. News & World Report*, 26 August 1996.

Video Software Dealer Association. "A White Paper on the Future of the Home Video Industry." Video Software Dealer Association, 1998. Available at http://206.71.226.123/whitepaper/WHITPAPR.HTM.

Directory of Specialized Business Web Sites

A Guide for Internet Researching

The Internet as an Investment Tool

The Internet is a formidable tool for researching business data because information on public companies is extensive and updated frequently. Web services providing this information are numerous and represent a broad spectrum of industries. Virtually all of the Web guides and search engines prominently display a business/investment category. Generally, the stock exchanges around the world maintain their Internet presence. Other businesses offering investment services on the Internet include stock brokerage companies, investor associations, professional business organizations/consultants, and magazine and newspaper publications. Many public companies maintain a Web site to advertise their products and services, as well as to provide financial data to potential investors. The Internet's comprehensive view of the global financial community allows investors the opportunity to secure information as never before possible.

Cautious Use of the Internet

The cautious investor who evaluates sources of information and scrutinizes financial reports may find important facts to assist in stock selection. Recognizing the pros and the cons of the Internet is key to utilizing the information in picking investment stocks. The Internet is the only mass media information source that allows someone to author, edit, and publish material for an interactive worldwide audience and maintain it on an easily accessible Web site for an infinite time period. Radio, television, and book and magazine publishing all have screening processes, which can lessen the chance of in-

accuracies, misinformation, and fraud. Information found on the Internet requires no proof of authenticity; the phrase "Let the buyer beware" certainly is appropriate when using the Internet to select business data from Web sites. For example, an attractive Web site providing business information may be a carefully calculated presentation designed to hype a stock that, if all the facts were known, may not be a prudent investment.

Evaluating Internet Web Sites

Internet users seeking business, company, and investment data must develop critical evaluation skills for each Web site encountered. Great stock tips that are tantalizingly offered to the amateur investor need to be substantiated with authoritative data. The Security and Exchange Commission (SEC) and various investor associations are active in monitoring fraud on the Internet, but it is a difficult task given the hundreds of thousands of Web sites. The SEC's Web site offering advice on Internet investment fraud is **http://sec.gov/consumer/cyberfr.htm**. The Investor Guide also maintains a site at **http://investerguide.com/Fraud.htm**. To be critical of Web sites, remember the "6 A's" of evaluating electronic sites:

Accessibility: Have you seen the site's name at another site? Generally, links to Web sites with valuable information are found on many of the Web guides and business sites. The access factor may be revealing in determining the strength and validity of a Web site.

Accuracy: Is the data consistent with what you know about the company? Does the data included on the Web site provide investors with a complete, objective picture of the company?

Appearance: Just because the site looks good, does it necessarily mean it is good? Not always. On the other hand, some Web sites may look very bad, which could indicate bad information. Some warning signs may include typing and spelling errors, incomplete sentences, and pronouncements promising results that seem difficult or impossible to deliver.

Arrangement: Are the financial tables and data arranged so information can be located easily? The Web site's organization is key to efficient use. If the site is not user friendly, that is, the information is limited and difficult to find for companies, the Web master should be contacted with specific suggestions and criticism.

Authenticity: Is the information properly footnoted (the source is indicated)? Does the information appear to be derived from respected commercial database companies?

Authorship: Does the site clearly indicate who is authoring the information? If so, does the name of the person or institution add to your confidence that the information is true and relevant?

Selected Business Web Sites

Search Engines and Search Guides

About.com/Investing for Beginners
http://about.com
> Student investors may find the various workshops, glossaries, and "how to" articles very helpful. Links to a variety of financial sites are also included. The novice should look at this site carefully.

Excite Business Information
http://money.excite.com/jsp/ps/mymoney.jsp?PG=home?SEC=qkclk
> Excite maintains an attractive investment site with links to SEC filings, conference calls, a market screener, and a sign in opportunity for investor's personal portfolios.

Lycos Business Information
http://my.finance.lycos.com
> This site provides stock quotes, stock news, mutual funds, IPOs, portfolio tracking, news by industry, and other services similar to Yahoo. The active message boards are available for information and perhaps misinformation. Registration is recommended to use the site optimally, and an e-mail address is required.

Yahoo Business Information
http://quote.yahoo.com
> This site provides a comprehensive collection of investment data for the student researcher, including business news, U.S. stock news, news by industry, Associated Press reports, Standard and Poor's Business Wire, mutual funds, and SEC filings. Students may create and track their portfolio after registering, which requires an e-mail address. Individual stock quotes and stock information are easily accessed. For individual stocks, Yahoo reports on company news, SEC announcements, insider transactions, analysts' research recommendations, and company stock charts, and it also contains a message center for individual investors. The free investment information offered on Yahoo is difficult to find anywhere else on the Web.

Investor Services Web Sites

Annual Report Gallery

http://www.reportgallery.com
> This site provides annual reports and links to the Web pages of many publicly traded companies.

Bloomberg.com
http://www.bloomberg.com
> This is a convenient site to use because so much information is available free without prior registration. Of course, the personal portfolio portion of the site requires registration, and the registration allows for more in-depth use of the material. This site is ideal for garnering information quickly and without the red tape required of many financial sites.

Clearstation Investment Web Site
http://www.clearstation.com
> This site offers free membership for a wide variety of stock services, including portfolio tracking, stock quotes, and information on specific companies. It does not recommend or take responsibility for stocks mentioned on its site, but many stock names are noted as possible investment choices. Further investigation of investment ideas must be done before the purchase of these stocks.

Investor Guide
http://investorguide.com
> Investor Guide claims to be the "only investing site you need," and it does have well-designed sections. For the beginning investor, the links to "learning about investments," "advice from the pros," "advice on taking advice," and "overall strategy" warrant attention.

Money Central.Com
http://moneycentral.msn.com
> This is an extensive Web site because it combines the multifaceted business news of CNBC with useful management tools such as portfolios, news alerts delivered via e-mail, essential investment questions and answers, and many other financial topics.

Thomas Register
http://www.thomasregister.com
> If a brand name or company name cannot be found, this site may have the answer. It includes some 155,000 companies; 124,000 brand names; 60,000 service headings; and 5,500 supplier catalogs.

U.S. Government SEC Web Site
http://www.freeedgar.gov
> Excellent source for company information required by government regulations, such as insider trading and financial disclosure statements.

Media Web Sites Presenting Business News

Barron's
http://barrons.com
> Free access to *Barron's* comprehensive stock listings and a calendar of 2002 economic events. Otherwise, this widely read financial weekly maintains a Web site on a subscription basis.

Britain's Financial Times
http://news.ft.com/home/us
> This is an outstanding site for financial news presented from a British/European perspective. Registration and an e-mail address are required, but once signed on, the daily coverage of business news is complete and exhaustive.

Business Week
http://www.businessweek.com/index.html

The investment data available on this site includes stock quotes, stock groups, lists of market movers, free newsletters, forum and message boards, and other useful business data such as currency and interest rate trends. Personal portfolios may be created, but an e-mail address is required.

CBS Market Watch

http://cbs.marketwatch.com

News on companies is extensive. With proper signup, free services are offered for custom portfolios, e-newsletters, alerts, and message boards.

Chicago Tribune

http://chicagotribune.com/business

The "Business" portion of the *Tribune's* Web site provides quotes, market movers, and a number of other special features, such as the CEO Wealthmeter. Alerts and access to portions of the *Chicago Tribune* are available with registration. Investors may take advantage of a portfolio service, which provides daily news alerts and quotes.

CNN Financial News

http://www.money.cnn.com

Provides news and stock information, as well as access to many articles and ideas from *Money Magazine*.

Ecola 24-Hour Newsstand

http://www.newsdirectory.com

A comprehensive collection of links to all media home pages is provided, including newspapers, magazines, and electronic titles. The lengthy and diverse listings of publication homepage links allow them to be found easily and quickly.

Fortune Magazine

http://www.fortune.com

This is chiefly a subscription Web site. Some useful articles from *Forbes* magazine on investing make a stop at this site worth the visit. This site also provides free stock quotes.

Investor's Business Daily/Investors Web site

http://investors.com

Sponsored by the respected financial newspaper, *IBD*, the site is free, although registration is required. A highlight of this site is the stock market course, which is found by using the "Learning Center" link.

Kiplinger

http://Kiplinger.com

This site has useful information and articles, but it is by subscription only.

New York Times

http://www.nytimes.com

The excellent coverage of business news makes this site a must. One may register at no charge and gain additional access, including the use of the stock portfolio.

USA Today

http://www.usatoday.com/money/mfront.htm

This newspaper site includes the financial news, quotes, and important data from currency, commodity, and stock markets. Using this site, the investor may create and edit up to six portfolios, with up to 10 securities each, through the "Bloomberg Market Scoreboard."

U.S. News/Business

http://www.usnews.com/usnews/nycu/nycuhome.htm

The personal finance page provides useful questions and answers to intriguing queries like "how long does it take to be a millionaire."

Web Sites of World Stock Markets

American Stock Exchange

http://amex.com

The AMEX provides information only on American Stock Exchange company listings.

NASDAQ Stock Exchange

http://www.nasdaq.com

This site includes quotes and information on all stocks on the NYSE, AMEX, and NASDAQ exchanges. News, profiles on companies, portfolio tracking, and investor resources are linked. Investor resources include helpful sections on "an introduction to investing," "investment options," and "setting goals and objectives."

New York Stock Exchange

http://nyse.com

In its "Education" section, this exchange site includes such appropriate articles as "Market Cycles: What Drives Stock Prices," "The Educated Investor," and "Putting your Money to Work." Other features include information on the NYSE specifically.

Stock Exchanges Worldwide

http://www.tdd.it/s/news/stocks_Exchanges?Exchanges.html

This site provides a comprehensive listing of stock exchanges around the world arranged alphabetically by location.

Web Sites of Stock Brokerage Companies

Yahoo Brokerage List

http://www.yahoo.com/Business_and_Economy/Finance_and_Investment

Lists of brokerage companies are maintained by all the major search engines. The Yahoo list includes full-service and discount brokers. Virtually all of these sites require guest registration and provide only basic news about the market. If one is a customer of the brokerage firm, data and research reports are much more available through a password.

Robert Kirsch, Librarian

Lake Forest High School

Lake Forest, Illinois

Glossary

401(k) plan: A tax-deferred investment and savings plan that acts as a personal pension fund for employees. (The name refers to the relevant section in the tax code.) This plan lets you defer taxes on a portion of your salary until you retire. Taxes on investment gains are deferred until you withdraw money from the plan. You can begin withdrawing from a tax-deferred investment account without penalty at age 59-1/2. Unlike pensions, 401(k) accounts are portable in that you can "roll over" the account—take it with you—and continue building it at your next place of employment with no penalty.

A

account: A device for representing the amount for any line in the balance sheet or income statement. An account is any device for accumulating additions and subtractions relating to a single asset, liability, or owner's equity item, including revenues and expenses.

acquisition: Gaining control of a corporation by stock purchase or exchange, either hostile or friendly. *See* corporate takeover *or* hostile takeover.

advertising: Description or presentation of a product, idea, or organization, in order to induce individuals to buy, support, or approve of it.

advertising, online: Driving traffic to Web sites, brand building, and brand sponsorship, often through banner ads.

affiliates: A company in which another company has a minority interest. Or more generally, a company that is related to another company in some way.

alliance: The joining together of two or more companies for the purpose of developing a unique product or service utilizing a combination of the companies' expertise. The alliance exists only for the purpose of the unique product or service, and the individual companies retain the rights to their own products. Similar to a joint venture.

amortization: The gradual elimination of a liability, such as a mortgage, in regular payments over a specified period of time. Such payments must be sufficient to cover both principal and interest.

annual bonus: A premium amount paid over normal annual wages or salary, usually paid for meritorious performance over the course of one year.

annual percentage rate (APR): An interest rate reflecting the cost of a mortgage as a yearly rate. The rate is generally higher than the advertised rate on the mortgage because it takes into account credit costs.

annual report: A yearly record of a publicly held company's financial condition that includes a description of the firm's operations, its balance sheet, and income statement.

antitrust: The federal laws forbidding businesses from monopolizing a market or restraining free trade.

asset: Any item of economic value owned by an individual or corporation, especially that which could be converted to cash. Opposite of liability.

audit: Systematic inspection of accounting records involving analyses, tests, and confirmations.

B

bankruptcy: Occurs when a company's liabilities exceed its assets and the firm or one of its creditors has filed a legal petition that the bankruptcy court has accepted under the bankruptcy law. *See* chapter 11.

banner ads: Ads appearing on Web sites to build brand awareness, sell something, and drive traffic to other Internet sites.

base salary: Compensation earned by managers, administrators, and professionals in a firm for a one-year period; excludes any other bonus payments or stock options.

bear market: A prolonged period of falling prices, usually by 20 percent or more, accompanied by widespread pessimism. Opposite of bull market.

board of directors: Individuals elected by a corporation's shareholders to oversee the management of the corporation.

boycott: The refusal of an individual or organized group to purchase products or services from a company because of a conflict in beliefs or values.

brand: Identifying symbols, words, or marks that distinguish a product or company from its competitors. *See* logo.

budget: An itemized forecast of a company's income and expenses expected for some period in the future.

bull market: A prolonged period of rising prices, usually by 20 percent or more. Opposite of bear market.

business-to-business e-commerce: Commerce conducted through industry-sponsored marketplaces and private exchanges set up by large companies for suppliers and customers.

business-to-consumer e-commerce: Commerce conducted by strictly online retailers, traditional retailers with an online presence, or portals where goods and services from several retailers are offered to consumers.

buyout: The purchase of controlling interest in one corporation by another corporation in order to take over assets and/or operations.

C

capital: Cash or goods used to generate income. Also, the net worth of a business, i.e. the amount by which its assets exceed its liabilities.

cash flow: A measure of a company's financial health. Equals cash receipts minus cash payments over a given period of time, or equivalently, net profit plus amounts charged off for depreciation, depletion, and amortization.

chairman: The highest-ranking officer in a corporation's board of directors. Presides over corporate meetings. Sometimes, but not necessarily, has executive authority over a firm.

chapter 11: The part of the U.S. Bankruptcy Code describing how a company or creditor can file for court protection. In the case of a corporation, reorganization occurs under the existing management. *See* bankruptcy.

charge against earnings: To treat as a loss or expense an amount originally recorded as an asset. Use of this term implies that the charge is not in accord with original expectations.

chief executive officer (CEO): The leading executive officer of a corporation charged with the principal responsibility of the organization and accountable only to the owners, directors, and/or stockholders.

chief financial officer (CFO): The primary executive officer responsible for the financial management of a corporation.

chief operating officer (COO): Person who has full operational responsibilities for the day-to-day activities of an organization.

class-action lawsuit: A lawsuit brought by one party on behalf of a group of individuals all having the same grievance.

commodity: A physical substance, such as food, grains, or metals that are interchangeable with other products of the same type and that investors buy or sell.

common stock: Securities representing equity ownership in a corporation, providing voting rights and entitling the holder to a share of the company's success through dividends and/or capital appreciation. In the event of liquidation, common stock holders have rights to a company's assets only after bondholders, other debt holders, and preferred stock holders have been satisfied.

compensation: The total monetary value an employee receives.

competition: When two or more companies with similar products and/or services try to secure the business of consumers by offering the best terms, such as price.

consumer: The ultimate user of a product or service.

cooperative: A type of common property ownership, such as when the residents of a multi-unit housing complex own shares in the corporation that owns the property, rather than owning their own units.

core market: A group of consumers that represent the majority of a company's marketing efforts and sales revenues. Also, the part of a market that is the company's primary business focus.

corporate credit ratings: A grade assigned to a company that an investor utilizes to determine the attractiveness of its stock.

corporate culture: Refers to the shared values, attitudes, standards, codes, and behaviors that characterize members of an organization and define its nature as a socioeconomic unit.

corporate takeover: A takeover that is supported by the management of the target company. *See* acquisition *or* hostile takeover.

corporation: The most common form of a business organization, and one that is chartered by a state and given many legal rights as an entity separate from its owners. Characterized by the limited liability of its owners, the issuance of shares of easily transferable stock, and existence as a going concern.

currency: Any form of money that is in public circulation.

D

demand: The desire and ability by individuals to purchase economic goods or services at the market price; along with supply, one of the two key determinants of price. *See* supply.

demographics: Socioeconomic groups characterized by age, income, gender, education, occupation, etc., that comprise a market niche.

depreciation: The allocation of the cost of an asset over a period of time for accounting and tax purposes. Also, a decline in the value of a property due to general wear and tear or obsolescence.

depression: A period when business activity drops significantly. High unemployment rates and deflation often accompany a depression.

deregulation: The removal of government controls from an industry or sector to allow for a free and efficient marketplace.

direct sales: The selling of a company's products directly to the customer without relying on wholesalers or retailers.

discrimination: Applying special treatment (generally unfavorable) to an individual solely on the basis of the person's ethnicity, age, religion, or sex.

dissolved: The end of the legal existence of a corporation by shareholder vote, acquisition, or order of a state attorney general.

distribution: The payment of a dividend or capital gain. Also, a company's allocation of income and expenses among its various accounts.

diversification: A portfolio strategy designed to reduce exposure to risk by combining a variety of investments such as stocks, bonds, and real estate, which are unlikely to all move in the same direction.

diversity: Refers to the way in which people differ from one another such as those that involve cultural or identity groups based on ethnicity, national origin, race, and religion.

divest: To sell off.

divestiture: Disposition or sale of an asset by a company.

dividend: Earnings and profits of a corporation appropriated for distribution among shareholders, usually paid quarterly.

division: A more or less self-contained business unit that is part of a larger family of business units under common control.

domain name: Identifies an Internal Protocol(IP) address, or series of addresses, on the Internet. Each site on the Internet is assigned a series of 11 or 12 numbers, known as an IP address. Addresses are translated via a Domain Name System (DNS) server into domain names, which simply are the names assigned to the numbers.

domestic rights: The entitlement of a company to the products/services it sells within its own country; a company does not necessarily have the rights to its products worldwide due to competition from existing businesses in other regions. *See* foreign rights.

dot-com: A colloquial term born of the suffix appended to Uniform Resource Locators (URLs), as in www.companyname.com; it can also be used to refer to Internet-based businesses.

Dow Jones Industrial Average A collection of 30 stocks that trade on the New York Stock Exchange, it is a gauge of how shares in the largest U.S. companies are performing.

downsizing: Reducing the total number of employees at a company through terminations or retirements.

E

earnings: Revenues minus cost of sales, operating expenses, and taxes over a given period of time. Often the single most important determinant of a stock's price. Also called income.

earnings per share (EPS): Total earnings divided by the number of shares outstanding.

e-business service provider: A company that helps other companies use e-business technologies to improve operations, such as the design of a Web site.

e-mail: Electronic messages sent over a network.

emerging market: A market to which a previously untapped potential for U.S. exports or investment might be anticipated.

employees: Person or persons hired to work for a business.

endorsement: A signature used to legally transfer a negotiable instrument.

enterprise: A business or venture.

entrepreneur: An individual who starts his/her own business.

equal opportunity: Refers to the equality of access to jobs, promotions, and other opportunities in corporations, associations, and nonprofit organizations.

e-tailing: Electronic retailing, or the practice of selling goods and services over an electronic medium like the Internet.

export: To ship a product outside a country or region. Opposite of import.

F

fiscal year: An accounting period of 365 days (366 in leap years), but not necessarily starting on January 1.

foreign rights: The entitlement of a company to the products/services it sells in other countries and regions of the world, usually including rights within its own country. Often times, foreign rights are separate from domestic rights. *See* domestic rights.

franchising: A form of business organization in which a firm that already has a successful product or service (the franchisor) enters into a continuing contractual relationship with other businesses (franchisees) operating under the franchisor's trade name and usually with the franchisor's guidance in exchange for a fee.

G

glass ceiling: An imaginary barrier to career advancement. Reference implies that an employee can see to the top through a glass ceiling but cannot penetrate the barrier due to some type of discrimination. Usually applies to women and minorities.

grant: Funding for a non-profit organization, usually for a specific project.

gross profit margin: The amount of revenues from sales after deducting cost of goods sold that is available for operating expenses.

H

holding company: A company that owns enough voting stock in another firm to control management and operations by influencing or electing its board of directors.

holdings: The stock and/or assets owned by a holding company that represents ownership or controlling interest of another company.

hostile takeover: A takeover that goes against the wishes of the target company's management and board of directors. *See* corporate takeover *or* acquisition.

I

import: To have a product shipped into a country or region. Opposite of export.

income: For corporations, same as earnings. For individuals, money earned through employment and investments.

incorporate: The process by which a business receives a state charter allowing it to become a corporation.

information technology: The processing and management of data in computer systems, including hardware and software.

initial public offering (IPO): A company's first sale of stock to the public. Securities offered in an IPO are often, but not always, those of young, small companies seeking outside equity capital and a public market for their stock. Investors purchasing stock in IPOs generally must be prepared to accept very large risks for the possibility of large gains.

international market: When products and services are directed toward consumers in more than one country.

Internet: An online network linking millions of computers throughout the world for things like research, communication, and commerce transactions.

internship: A temporary job assignment taken by a student with a company in a relevant field to their studies. Traditionally, the assignment is not compensated with wages but with college credit or is done for experience only.

inventory: A company's merchandise, raw materials, and finished and unfinished products that have not yet been sold.

investment: An item of value purchased for income or capital appreciation.

investor: One who makes investments.

J

joint ownership: Situation in which two or more people share ownership of property, securities, or rights.

joint venture: An agreement between firms to work together on a project for mutual benefit. Similar to an alliance.

junk bond: A bond from a company with a questionable credit rating. Junk bonds give investors higher yields than bonds from financially stable companies.

L

labor: Work of any type; includes organized laborers, such as a union, working for the management of a corporation. *See* management.

layoff: The elimination of jobs, often without regard to employee performance, usually when a company is experiencing financial difficulties.

leveraged buy-out: A transaction used to take a public company private, usually financed through bank loans, bonds, and other debt funds. Investors can participate through either the purchase of the debt (participation in the bank loan or purchasing the bond) or the purchase of equity.

liability: Financial obligation, debt, claim, or potential loss. Opposite of an asset.

licensing: The granting of permission to use intellectual property rights, such as brand or trade names or characters, under defined conditions. Once the rights are granted, it is referred to as a licensing agreement.

liquidation: To convert to cash. Also, to sell all of a company's assets, pay outstanding debts, and distribute the remainder to shareholders and then go out of business.

logo: A company emblem or device. *See* brand.

M

majority interest: Ownership of more than 50 percent of a company's voting stock; or a significant fraction, even less than 50 percent, if the remaining ownership is sufficiently spread out.

managed assets: A collection of stocks, bonds, and/or mutual funds owned by an individual or company, but controlled by a professional financial planner for the purpose of financial gain.

management: The collective body of those who plan, organize, staff, lead, and control any enterprise or interest.

manufacture: The organized action of making of goods and services for sale.

market: The number of potential customers that have in common one or more easily identifiable characteristic that affect their wants.

market analysis: Research to predict what a market will do.

market capitalization: The total dollar value of all outstanding shares within a corporation.

market share: The percentage of sales a company captures for a particular product line and in a specific market niche.

market value: A stock's last reported sale price.

marketing: A process that brings ideas, goods, or services to the market through planning, pricing, coordinating, promoting, selling, and distribution.

marketing strategy: The specific philosophy and marketing techniques employed to maximize impact on a market niche.

merchandising: The purchasing, distribution, and reselling of goods at the retail level.

merger: The combining of two or more corporations, either through a pooling of interests, where the accounts are combined; a purchase, where the amount paid over and above the acquired company's book value is carried on the books of the purchaser as good will; or a consolidation, where a new company is formed to acquire the net assets of the combining companies.

merit pay: A form of compensation paid to an employee, above their normal wages, in recognition of an outstanding performance.

mission statement: The definitive scope of the overall business and its objectives in a concise narrative format.

monopoly: A situation where at least one-third of a local or national market is controlled by a single company or group of people.

mutual fund: An investment trust in which investors may contribute funds in exchange for a position in the trust. The total of these contributed funds are, in turn, invested in various securities, such as stocks, bonds, guaranteed investment contracts, Treasury bills, and other vehicles.

N

North American Free Trade Agreement (NAFTA): An agreement between Canada, Mexico, and the United States that resolves to increase the development and expansion of world trade with the goal of creating an expanded and secure market for the goods and services produced in their territories.

net earnings: Gross sales minus taxes, interest, depreciation, and other expenses.

net income: Gross income less all operating expenses, taxes, and losses, except interest and financial charges on borrowed capital.

net loss: The amount by which total expenses exceed total revenues for a given period of time.

net revenues: Gross revenues less all costs of doing business and income taxes.

net sales: A firm's gross sales minus returns and allowances, freight, and cash discounts allowed.

network: An extended group of people with similar interests or concerns who interact and remain in informal contact for mutual assistance or support.

non-profit: An incorporated organization that works for educational or charitable purposes, and its shareholders and trustees do not benefit financially.

O

operating expenses: Costs associated with sales and administrative functions as distinct from those associated with production.

operating income: The amount of revenue remaining after the cost of goods sold and selling, general, and administrative costs have been subtracted from sales revenue.

operating margin: Operating income divided by revenues.

operating profit: Income before deductions minus expenses.

operating subsidiary: A company for which a majority of the voting stock is owned by a holding company.

operating units: Working or functioning divisions within a corporation.

overhead: The ongoing administrative expenses (rent, insurance, and maintenance) of a business, also called burden.

over-the-counter market: A decentralized market where dealers are linked through computers and phone lines. The market is for companies not listed on any stock exchange.

P

parent company: A company that owns the majority stock and fully controls another company.

partnership: A relationship of two or more individuals for the express purpose of conducting a business enterprise on a for-profit basis.

patent: A title by which the government grants the exclusive right to make use of an invention for a fixed time period. In America, a patent takes about 18 months to secure.

patent infringement: Violation of another's exclusive rights to the production or sale of a product.

payroll: The financial record of employees' salaries, wages, bonuses, net pay, and deductions for a given accounting period.

pension plan: A fund that is established for the payment of retirement benefits.

preferred stock: A security that shows ownership in a corporation and gives the shareholder a claim, before the claim by common stock holders, on earnings and usually on assets in the case of liquidation. Most preferred stock does not carry voting rights and pays a fixed dividend.

president: The highest ranking officer in a corporation after the chairman of the board, unless the title chief executive officer is used, in which case the president can outrank the chairman. The president is appointed by the board of directors and usually reports directly to the board.

price/earnings (P/E): Shows the "multiple" of earnings at which a stock sells. Determined by dividing current price by current earnings per share. Earnings per share for the P/E ratio is determined by dividing earnings for the past 12 months by the number of common shares outstanding.

private label: A retail establishment's proprietary brand of product.

privately held company: A company whose shares are not traded on the open market.

proceeds: Money resulting from the sale of goods or services.

product line: A set of related products sold by a single company.

production cost: Expenses incurred by production. Includes both fixed and variable costs of production.

profit: Money earned in excess of the cost of producing and selling goods.

profit margin: Indicator of profitability, determined by dividing net income by revenue for the same 12-month period. Result is shown as a percentage.

profit sharing: An arrangement in which an employer shares its profits with its employees. The compensation can be stocks, bonds, or cash, and can be immediate or deferred until retirement.

publicly owned company: A company with securities issued through an initial public offering (IPO), which are traded on the open market.

R

recession: A downturn in a country's economy, as measured by a decline in gross national product for two consecutive quarters.

reorganize: To change a company's operations and procedures in an effort to improve business and efficiency.

restructuring: To reorganize a company's operations and debts to stay in business.

retail: The business of selling products and services to the public as the ultimate consumer.

revenues: The total sum of money that returns from the sale of goods or services.

rights: A privilege given to stockholders to subscribe to a new issue of securities, generally below market price.

royalties: A duty paid by a manufacturer to the owner of a patent or a copyright at a certain rate for each article manufactured.

S

sales: Income received in exchange for goods and services recorded for a given accounting period.

securities: Stocks and bonds.

shareholder: Someone who holds shares of stock in a corporation.

shares: Certificates representing units of ownership in a corporation, mutual fund, or limited partnership.

short-term debt: A loan repayable within 2 to 3 months.

slogan: A phrase or saying that attempts to define the main benefit or cause of an organization or its products.

spin-off: The act of creating an independent company from an existing part of the company by selling new shares of the spin-off.

spokesperson: An advocate who represents an organization and its purpose.

stock: An instrument that signifies an ownership position, or equity, in a corporation and represents a claim on its proportionate share in the corporation's assets and profits.

stock options: The right given to a buyer to purchase or sell stock at a fixed price on or before a given date.

stockholder: Someone who holds shares of stock in a corporation.

sub-franchise: An organization in which a firm with a successful product or service (the franchisor) enters into a continuing contractual relationship with another business (franchisees), that in turn enters into a contractual relationship with another business (sub-franchisee). Both the franchisee and sub-franchisee operate under the franchisor's trade name and guidance in exchange for a fee.

subsidiary: A company that is completely controlled by another company.

subsidies: A grant from the government to a private company to assist the establishment or support of an enterprise deemed advantageous to the public.

supply: The total amount of a good or service available for purchase; along with demand, it is one of the two key determinants of price. *See* demand.

sweatshop: A shop or factory where employees work long hours for poor pay.

T

targeted marketing: The specific market niche a product or service is directed towards. *See* marketing.

tariff: A tax imposed on a commodity when it is imported into a country.

test marketing: The launching of a new product in a limited area and in such a manner designed to limit risk. *See* marketing.

trademark: A symbol, logo, or design that legally identifies a business or its product. *See* logo.

trading volume: The number of shares, bonds, or contracts that change hands during a specified period of time.

U

union: An organization of employees formed to bargain with the employer.

universal product code (UPC): Refers to a machine-scannable bar code used to identify products, inventory, and many other purposes.

URLs: Uniform Resource Locators, or strings of letters, numbers, and special characters that constitute the addresses of documents, files, electronic mailboxes, images, and other resources in cyberspace.

U.S. Securities and Exchange Commission: Responsible for administering federal securities laws written to provide protection for investors.

V

venture: An entrepreneurial activity in which capital is exposed to the risk of loss for the possibility of reaping a profit reward.

vice president: A corporate officer, subordinate to the president, often having responsibility over a functional department.

W

wholesale trade: The purchase of goods or services in bulk by businesses or persons who may add something to those goods or services, or use them in production, and then sell them to others, rather than to the ultimate consumers.

World Wide Web: One of several utilities, including e-mail, File Transfer Protocol (FTP), Internet Relay Chat (IRC), Telnet, and Usenet, that form the Internet; often just referred to as the Web.

Master Index

Master Index

DWI (Driving while intoxicated)
    Anheuser-Busch and, 1:97–99
    Miller Brewing and, 2:893
Dyer, David F., 3:843
Dyes, BASF Aktiengesellschaft and,
    1:141–142
Dynamic random access semiconductors
    (DRAMS), 3:348

E

E! Entertainment Television, 2:1410
E.A. Pierce and Company, 2:881
Eagle Managed Care Corporation,
    2:1107
Eagle Snacks, 1:506–507
Earl, Robert, 1:631, 1049–1051
Earthlink Network Inc., 2:1224–1228
Earthquake (movie), 2:1353
Eastbay Company, 1:483
Eastern Airlines, 1:382, 963
Eastern Navigation Company, 2:1471,
    3:858
Eastman, George, 1:427–428, 430,
    1519, 1521, 3:909, 911
Eastman Kodak Company, **1:425–434,**
    1:426*f, 1:427, 428,* 2:1518–1521,
    3:909–911
    America Online and, 1:45
    DreamWorks and, 1:409
    Fuji Photo Film and, 1:516–518
    Panavision, Inc.and, 3:569
    Polaroid and, 2:1054, 1056
Eaton, Robert J., 1:293, 3:191–192
eBay, Inc., **3:226–231,** 227*f,* 587
Eberhard, Ernest, 3:249
EBONY, 3:409–412
E-books, 3:41
EC Company, Ace Hardware
    Corporation and, 1:24
Eckerd Corporation, 1:726, 728–729
Eckerd Drugstores, 1:729
Eckert, Robert, 2:993
Eco-Challenge, **3:232–236**
E-commerce
    Amazon.com, 3:883–884
    Apple Computer Inc., 3:59
    Barnes & Noble, 3:884
    Dell Computer, 1:376–377, 379,
        3:194–195, 853
    eBay, Inc, 3:226–231, 227*f*
    E*TRADE, 3:263–267, 264*f*
    Expedia, 3:268–271
    FAO Schwarz, 1:463
    Fleetwood Enterprises, 3:286
    FMR Corporation, 3:291–293
    FUBU "For Us, By Us," 3:308, 311
    groceries, 3:29
    Hollywood Entertainment
        Corporation, 3:368
    Hyundai, 3:375, 378
    IBM, 3:383
    iVilliage, 3:398–402
    Jenny Craig, 3:406–407

Knight Ridder, 3:433–436
Lands' End, 3:843
mail-order businesses, 2:1456, 1458,
    3:841, 842
Martha Stewart Living Omnimedia,
    3:474
music CDs, 3:856, 877
Oracle, 3:549–550
Orbitz, 3:831
PETsMART, 3:572, 573
priceline.com, Inc.., 3:586–591, 587*f*
Publix Super Markets, Inc, 3:595
Ronco Inventions, LLC, 3:615–616
Skechers U.S.A., Inc, 3:647
Snap-On Inc., 3:653
specialty stores and, 3:883
Target Corp., 3:690
Topps Company and, 3:706
toys, 3:884
Travelocity.com Inc, 3:710, 712
TY, Inc., 3:714, 716
Unilever, 3:722
U.S. Postal Service, 3:932
USA Networks, 2:1368–1372
Verizon Communications, Inc.,
    3:763, 764
Weight Watchers and, 3:781
See also Amazon.com
Ecstasy (ship), 2:1472, 3:859
Eddie Bauer, Inc., **1:435–439,**
    1220–1222, 1454, 1455, 3:839,
    840–841
Edgerton, David, 1:233–235, 1475,
    3:862
Edge-Server, 2:1366
Edison, Thomas Alva, 1:538, 541, 1465,
    1487, 3:322, 326, 852, 876
EDS. *See* Electronic Data Systems
Educational products
    American Greetings and, 1:72
    Intel Corporation, 3:392
    Josten's, Inc, 3:414–417, 415*f*
    Lucasfilm Ltd., 3:461, 465, 466
    Oracle Corporation, 3:551
Educational television, 3:1–6, *3:3, 2f*
eGames, Inc., **3:237–241**
E.I. du Pont de Nemours and Co.,
    1:415–419, 416*f*
Einstein/Noah Bagels, 2:1475
Eisner, Michael, 2:1408
El Torito, 1:702
Electric Boat. *See* General Dynamics
    Corporation
Electric power generation. *See* Power
    generation
Electric vehicles, from Toyota Motor,
    2:1299–1300
Electrical equipment, 2:1292–1296,
    1434–1437
Electrolux Group, 1:499–502
Electronic commerce. *See* E-commerce
Electronic Data Systems (EDS),
    1:551–552, 3:10, **242–247,** 331
Electronic information services. *See*
    Online information services

Electronic keyboards, 2:1503–1504
Electronic mail. *See* E-mail
Electronic publishing, 2:1203–1207,
    1490, 3:879
Electronics industry
    Delphi, 3:199–203
    General Motors, 3:333
    Hewlett-Packard, 3:346–353, *3:347*
    Hitachi, 1:680–684
    Intel, 1:721–725, 3:389–393
    Lockheed Martin, 3:447
    Lucent Technologies, 1:823–826
    Matsushita, 2:852–856
    Motorola, 3:499–505, *3:502*
    Philips, 2:1030–1033
    Qualcomm, Inc., 3:597–601, 598*f*
    RadioShack Corp., 3:602–607, 603*f*
    Siemens AG, 3:632–638, *3:633*
    Texas Instruments, 2:1264–1269
    U.S. Robotics, 2:1362–1367
    See also Appliance industry;
        Consumer electronics
Elektra, 2:1320
Eli Lilly and Company, 2:1518,
    3:248–253, 3:249*f, 3:250*
Elizabeth Glaser Pediatric AIDS
    Foundation, 3:716, 717
Eller Media Co., 3:158
Elliot, Sam, 3:729
Ellis, J. L., 3:699
Ellis, Reuben, 2:1027
Ellison, Lawrence J., 3:546–547, 548,
    550, 551
Elsenham Quality Foods Ltd., 1:737
Elton John AIDS Foundation,
    3:775–776
Eltra Corporation, Converse and, 1:359,
    361
EM, 3:410
E-mail, 1:669, 3:492
    United States Postal Service, 3:741
    Yahoo! Inc., 3:815–820, 816*f*
Emerson, Edward O., 3:678
Emhart Corporation, 1:191
EMI Group, 2:1384–1387
EMI-Capitol Entertainment, 2:1051
Empire Brushes, 2:1130
Empire Pencil Corporation, 1:645
Employee leasing services. *See*
    Personnel supply
Employee ownership, of Birkenstock
    Footprint Sandals, 1:185, 187
Employee pensions. *See* Pensions
Employee training, Applebee's
    International and, 1:110
Enchanted Hill. *See* La Cuesta
    Encantada
Endangered Species Act, 2:1509, 1532,
    3:898, 922
Endorsements, 2:1094–1096
    Acclaim Entertainment, 1:18–20
    adidas-Salomon AG, 1:29
    Boston Market, 3:111
    Converse, 1:358–362
    FUBU "For Us, By Us," 3:309–311

Pharmaceutical Manufacturers
Association (PMA), 2:1517,
3:906
Pharmaceutical Research and
Manufacturers (PhRMA), 3:905
Pharmacies. *See* Drugstores
Pharmacy Direct Network, 2:1399
Philip Morris Companies, Inc.,
1:777–780, 891, **1023–1029,**
1024*f*, 1478, 1533–1536,
3:865–866, 924–926
Philips, Anton, 2:1031
Philips, Gerard, 2:1031–1032
Philips Electronics North America
Corporation, **2:1030–1034,** 3:877
Philips Electronics NV, 1:825, 1354,
1488, 3:877
Phoenix Pictures, 2:1200
Phoenix Suns, America West Airlines
and, 1:48
Photo Marketing Association (PMA),
3:910, 911
Photocopiers, 2:1428–1433, 1519–1520,
3:909, 911
Photographic equipment and supplies,
1:250, **1518–1521,** 1519*f*, 3:636,
908–911
See also specific companies
Photographic film, 2:1518, 3:908, 910
Eastman Kodak, 1:425–433
Fuji Photo Film, 1:515–518
Poloroid, 2:1053–1057
PhRMA (Pharmaceutical Research and
Manufacturers), 3:905
Physical fitness industry. *See* Fitness
industry
Piacentini, Diego, 3:38
Pianos, 2:1502–1504, 3:892–894
Picard, Adolphe, 1:260
Pick-A-Deli, 2:1314
Picture Pipeline, LLC, 3:568
Piech, Ferdinand, 2:1395
Piedmont Airlines, 2:1359
Pier 1 Imports, Inc., **2:1035–1039,**
1036*f, 1037*
Pierce, Don, 1:113–114
Piet, William, 2:1424
Pillar, Russell I., 2:1082
Pillsbury Company, 1:234–235
PinPoint, 1:759
Pioneer North America, Inc.,
2:1040–1043
Pipelines, 1:592, 596
Piracy (crime), Adobe Systems and,
1:35–36
Pischetreider, Bernd, 1:199
Pitney Bowes Inc., 2:1467, 3:854
Pittman, Bob, 1:44
Pizza Hut, Inc., 1:806–807, **1044–1047,**
1474
Pizza restaurants
Domino's, 1:392–396, 1476
Little Caesar Enterprises, 1:804–808
Pizza Hut, 1:806–807, 1044–1047,
1474

PLA (Polylactic acid), 3:135
Plane Crazy, 2:1410, 1411
Planet Hollywood International, Inc.,
2:1048–1052, 1049*f*
Planet Music, 2:1494
PlanetAll, 1:828
Plank Road Brewery, 2:891
Plastics industry, **2:1521–1523,** 1522*f,*
3:911–914
Amoco, 1:92
BASF Aktiengesellschaft, 1:141–143
Dow Chemical Company,
3:213–218, 214*f*
eyeglasses and, 2:1505, 3:895
food packaging, 2:1477, 3:865
Tupperware, 2:1312–1317
Platemaking, 3:918–919
See also Printing industry
Platt, Lew, 1:670, 3:349
Player pianos, 2:1502, 1504, 3:892
Playland (Rye, N.Y.), 2:1451, 3:836
Playskool, 1:643, 647, 896
PlayStation, 2:1213, 1538, 3:929
Playtex, 2:1159, 1160
PMA (Pharmaceutical Manufacturers
Association), 2:1517
PMA (Photo Marketing Association),
3:910, 911
PMG (Postmaster general), 2:1540,
3:931
PNB, 2:1364, 1365
Pocket Books, 2:1204, 1205, 1529,
3:919
Poerink, John, 1:165
Pokemon, 3:2–4, 703, 704
Polaris Industries Inc., 2:1501,
3:582–585, 583*f*, 891
Polaroid Corporation, 1:428–429, 724,
1053–1058, 1054*f*, 1519, 3:909
Polfus, Lester (Les Paul), 1:579
Pollution
aircraft design and, 2:1449, 3:834
automobile industry and, 2:1498,
3:887
petroleum industry and, 2:1514,
3:904
Royal Caribbean Cruises, 3:860
See also Environment
Polo Ralph Lauren Corporation,
2:1059–1062, 1392
Polyesters, from Amoco, 1:92
PolyGram, 2:1172, 1174–1176, 1199,
1488–1489
Polygram Records, **3:749–754**
Polylactic acid (PLA), 3:135
Polymers, Bayer, 3:98
Polystyrene, 1:141–143
Pontiac Aztec, 3:889
Pony Express, 2:1347, 3:738, 740
Poo-Chi Robotic Dogs, 3:884
Popcorn, Faith, 1:195
Pope, Albert A., 2:1500, 3:890
Popeil, Ronald, 3:615, 616
Popular Club Plan, 1:731–732, 1457
Porizkova, Paulina, 1:447

Porsche, Ferdinand, 2:1393
Porsche, Volkswagen and, 2:1393
Portable Internet audio players, 3:856
Portals (Internet). *See* Internet, portals
Portege, 2:1295
Porter, William, 3:264, 266
Posner, Victor, 1:113–114
Post, C.W., 1:751, 778
Post cereal, 1:779–780
Postage stamps, 3:742
Postal equipment, 2:1465, 1467, 3:852,
854
Postal Life, 3:741
Postal Rate Commission, 2:1540, 3:931
Postal Reorganization Act,
2:1540–1541, 3:741, 931
Postal Service, U.S. *See* United States
Postal Service
Post-it Notes, 1:1–6
Postmaster general (PMG), 2:1540,
3:931
PostScript, 1:32, 34–35
Postum Cereal Company, 1:778
Potato chips, 1:504–508
Potter, John E., 3:932
Pottery, 3:809–814, 810*f*
Pottery Barn, 2:1457, 3:810–813, 843
Poultry industry
growth in, 2:1477–1478, 3:865
Tyson Foods, 2:1328–1333
Power generation
Caterpillar, 1:263, 265
Duke Energy Company, 3:219–225,
219*f, 3:222*
Enron, 3:254–258
Honeywell International, 3:372, 374
Pacific Gas & Electric, 3:559–563,
560*f*
Siemens AG, 3:632, 635, 636
See also Natural gas industry;
Utilities
Powerstreet, 3:292
Powers-Weightmann-Rosengarten,
2:875
Prada, Estee Lauder and, 1:448
Precor, 2:1314
Premark International, Inc., 2:1314,
1522, 3:913
Premier Parks, Inc., **2:1063–1067,**
1064*f*, 1451–1452, 3:837
Prentice Hall, 2:1203–1206, 1376
Prepackaged software. *See* Computer
software
Prepared foods, 2:1477, 3:865
See also Food industry and trade;
Food processing industry; Home
meal replacements
Prep-Rite, 2:1197
Prescriptions (drug). *See* Pharmaceutical
industry
Preserves (fruit). *See* Jam
Presidio Trust, 3:464–465
Press. *See* Magazine publishing;
Newspaper publishing
Preston, Andrew, 1:286

U

Master Index